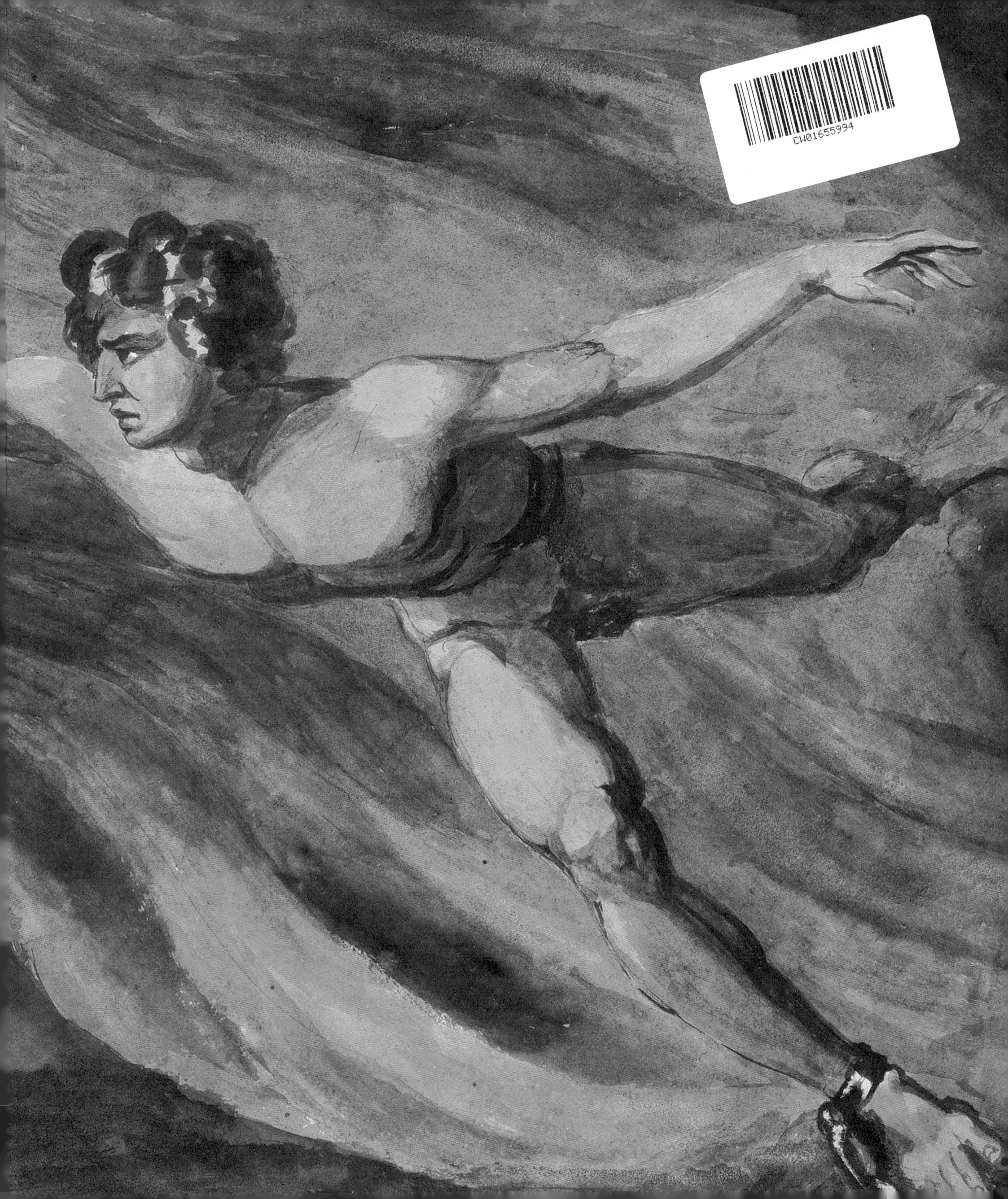

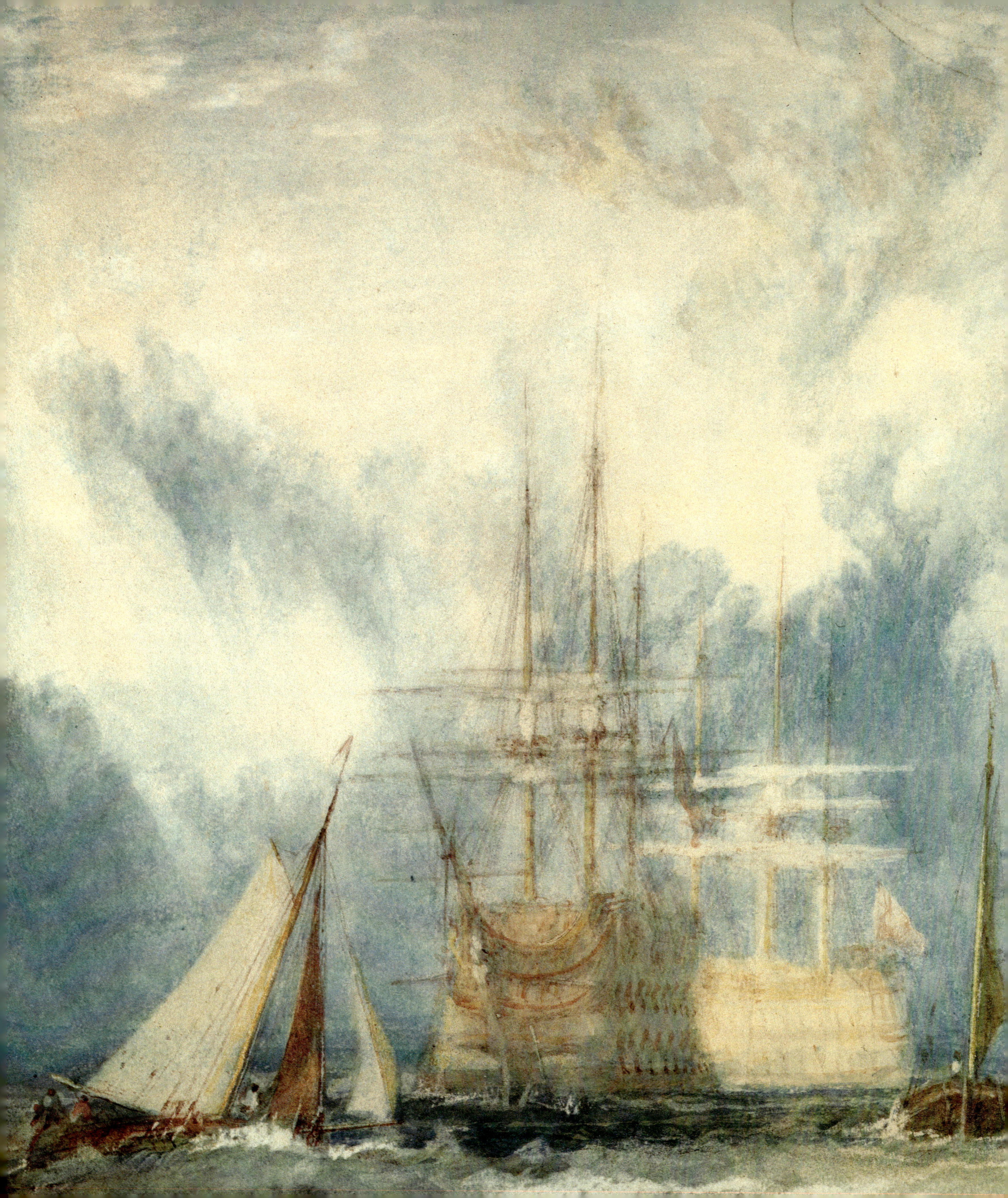

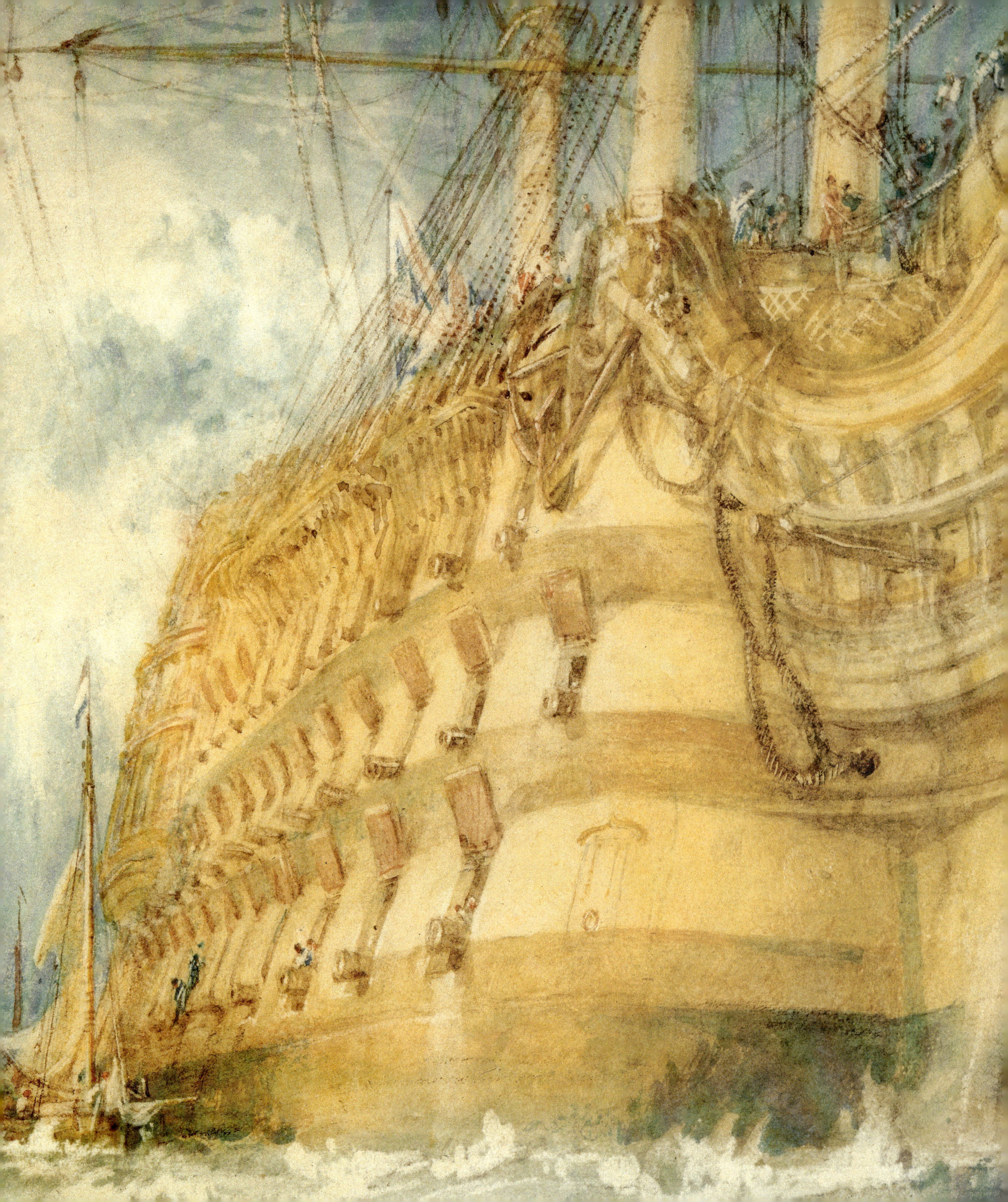

Dedicated to the life and work of Evelyn Joll

This catalogue has been generously supported by the Paul Mellon Centre for Studies in British Art.

CONTRIBUTORS
Evelyn Joll
Caroline Bacon
James McGregor
John Christian

PHOTOGRAPHERS
Nick Nicholson
John Roan
David Stubbs

PHOTOGRAPHIC AND COPYRIGHT COORDINATOR
Jennie Clarke

DESIGNER
Isambard Thomas

COPY EDITORS
Graham Parlett
Caroline Bacon
James McGregor
Michela Rausa

Printed in Italy by E.B.S.

Published by the Trustees of the Cecil Higgins Art Gallery,
Castle Lane, Bedford, MK40 3RP

ISBN 0-9512657-2-5

ILLUSTRATIONS
FRONT JACKET: Edward Burne-Jones, *Cupid & Psyche* (detail)
BACK JACKET: Eric Gill, *Nude*, (detail) © courtesy of the artist's estate/Bridgeman Art Library
TITLE PAGE: J.M.W. Turner, *A First Rate Taking in Stores* (detail)
ENDPAPERS: William Blake, *Good and Evil Angels struggling for the Possession of the Child* (detail)

Introduction

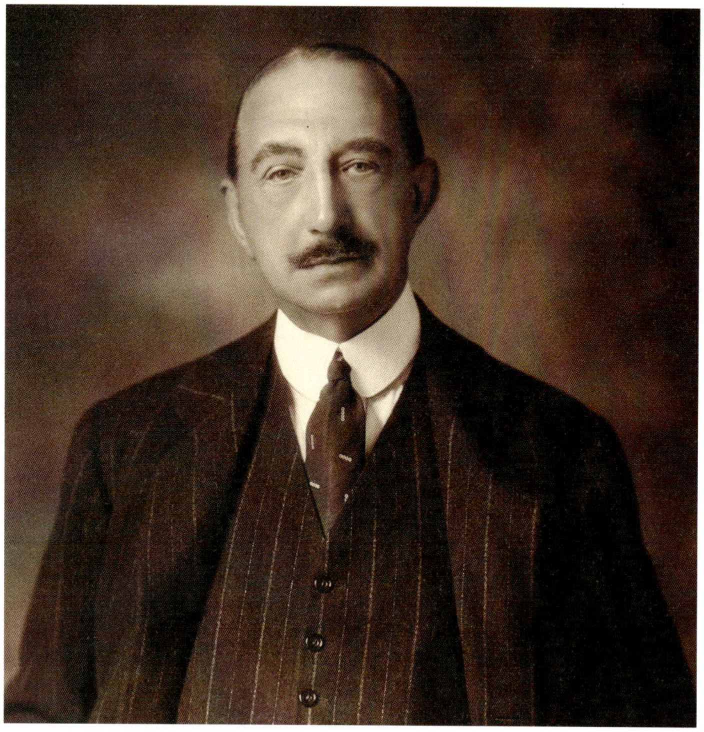

The Cecil Higgins Museum, as it was formerly known, opened its doors to the public on 25th July 1949. It had been created by the philanthropic brewer, Cecil Higgins (1856–1941) ***fig. 1*** , to house his collection of ceramics, glass and objets d'art 'for the benefit, interest and education of the inhabitants of, and visitors to, Bedford'[1]. As a shrewd businessman he realised that public museums were vulnerable, and to protect his collection he left a very complex will, which stipulated how the museum was to be organised. He also left a considerable trust fund, to be used for museum purposes, but principally for acquiring works of art (which included Decorative and Applied). While the collection of ceramics and glass was of the finest quality (each had been selected by James Kiddell of Sotheby's), the collection lacked any notable paintings, save a few 18th century oils and a small collection of miniatures. The Art Gallery Board made the important decision to collect English watercolours in 1951. By the terms of Cecil Higgins' will, all acquisitions have to be approved by a 'recognised artistic authority such as … the Victoria and Albert Museum'[2] and in 1951, the then Director of the V&A, Sir Leigh Ashton, nominated Graham Reynolds, then Deputy Keeper of the Department of Engraving, Illustration, Designing and Painting, to approve all watercolours and drawings for acquisition. Graham Reynolds remained an advisor until 1955 when he was succeeded by two leading authorities in their respective fields who were to shape and expand the collection significantly: Edward Croft-Murray (1907–80) of the British Museum and Ronald Alley (1926–99) of the Tate Gallery, from 1957.

The period between 1952 and 1964 were the most productive in terms of collecting watercolours. Over 500 were acquired in twelve years. The Gallery was able to achieve this by the availability of watercolours from private collections in the post-war years and the generosity of Cecil Higgins' Trust Fund. Edward Croft-Murray and Ronald Alley brought their knowledge, vision and taste to the growing collection. Their collecting was divided – Croft-Murray to works made pre-1850 and Alley to post-1850. The Gallery owes a great deal to their dedication and skill, for they were to develop one of the finest post-war collections outside London. That the collection is strong in the greatest painters of every generation is one thing, but that it is also representative of artists who were once popular and influential in their own day and less so at the time of acquisition, is due to their expert scholarship.

Over the past fifty years many talented Trustees and Board members have devoted their time and knowledge for the benefit of the collection and to ensure the continuing quality of the Gallery. This catalogue is also a fitting tribute to my predecessors, the former Curators of the Gallery, Maurice Palmer, Alister Campbell, Margaret Greenshields, Halina Graham, Amanda Beresford and all their assistants, who have each contributed their knowledge and skill to the collection.

1 Codicil to Cecil Higgins will Clause 5(1) (c)

2 ibid. (e)

Evelyn Joll (1925–2001) began his long association with the Gallery in 1951 while a director at Thomas Agnew & Sons Ltd. He was responsible for the Gallery acquiring one of the most famous works in the collection, *A First Rate taking in Stores* by J.M.W.Turner, of 1818. The watercolour had remained within the Fawkes family since its completion, but its provenance was further heightened by the fact that it is one of the only works by Turner that has been observed and documented while it was painted. Evelyn secured its acquisition for the Gallery and it was to be the jewel of the collection. In 1998, the Gallery was able to acquire its companion, *A Loss of an East Indiaman*, due to the generous support of the Heritage Lottery Fund, the National Art Collections Fund and the V&A/M.G.C. Purchase Grant Fund. As Evelyn's association with the Gallery and its watercolours, which he knew intimately and could recall their history without prompt, had stretched back fifty years, he was the obvious choice to catalogue the collection, which was long over-due.

While the majority of the collection has been purchased, sometimes through the generosity of the V&A/M.G.C. Purchase Grant Fund, the National Art Collections Fund and the National Lottery Heritage Fund, a few works have been given to the Gallery by a number of public-spirited individuals, most notably, Elisabeth and Barbara Kitson, daughters of the great Cotman authority and collector, Sydney Kitson. From 1972 to 1999 they gave 31 watercolours and drawings by artists such as John Sell Cotman, Peter De Wint, William Russell Flint, Charles Gascoyne, Edward Lear, John Nash, Thomas Rowlandson, Philip Wilson Steer, Francis Towne and John Varley.

Although the collection is representative of artists and art movements of the period, there are some omissions, and there are numerous viewpoints on that issue. One watercolour that has eluded the Gallery on three separate occasions is J.M.W. Turner's *Bedford Bridge*, from the *England and Wales* series. Each time the Gallery has simply been outbid, as prices for well-documented watercolours are outside the Gallery's grasp.

The Cecil Higgins Art Gallery has not been without its controversy, and not all acquisitions suit everyone's tastes. When Alan Davie's *First Movement in Pink,* 1957, was acquired in 1959, it was accused of heralding a 'new age of barbarism'[3]. Mistakes have also been made. A number of works have been re-attributed since they entered the collection (see entry on Thomas Barker of Bath), but one stands out as the most infamous. In 1965, the Gallery acquired 'an early sketch by Samuel Palmer'. Hindsight is a wonderful gift, but in 1965 no one had heard of Tom Keating (1917–84). It is, as far as is known, the only deliberate forgery in the collection, and as such, very popular.

3 Daily Express, 19 October 1959

The catalogue has been arranged in alphabetical order, and each artist's work has been listed chronologically to provide a comprehensive reference to works available in the Cecil Higgins Trustees' collection. The local authority, Bedford Borough Council, also owns a small but notable collection of works by established artists – at the time of acquisition they were not deemed suitable for the main collection. The Borough's collection has not been included within this catalogue, but details are available from the Gallery and the website (www.cecilhigginsartgallery.org). The main purpose of the publication of the watercolour collection is to advertise that such a collection exists at all in Bedford. While many of the works have featured in international exhibitions, to which the Gallery has always been a generous lender, few people know of its depth and quality. As the works catalogued are on paper or similar, they are not on permanent display. However, the Gallery will always make any part of the collection available for viewing, with prior notice, whether for research or pleasure.

The publication of this catalogue has been dedicated to the memory and work of Evelyn Joll, who very sadly died before he was able to see the finished catalogue. All those who ever had the pleasure and fortune to work alongside him, will appreciate what a joy it was for the Gallery to be associated with him on such a vast undertaking. Despite his illness, he approached the task with excellent humour, patience and professionalism. While he was able to cover the majority of the collection, the Gallery and John Christian have completed some entries, hopefully in a manner he would have approved of. I am indebted to James McGregor, Keeper of Fine and Decorative Arts, who has assisted in the preparation of this catalogue, to John Christian for contributing his expertise on Burne-Jones and to Isambard Thomas who has enhanced the beauty of a great collection.

The publication of this catalogue has been made possible by a generous grant from the Paul Mellon Foundation.

Caroline Bacon, CURATOR, January 2002

Evelyn Joll [1925–2001]

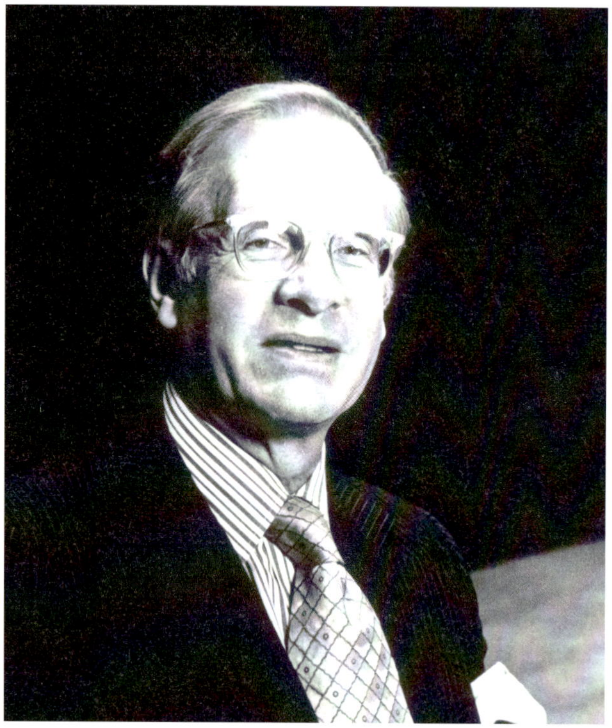

Evelyn Joll will be remembered as the greatest authority in our time on the life and work of J.M.W. Turner. To the very end of a wonderfully happy and successful life he was working on the painter whose vision, imagination, tenacity, eccentricity and superb technique had fascinated him for 50 years.

As 'the senior figure of Turner studies', in the words of the President of the Royal Academy, Philip King, he had played a leading role in organising the unforgettable display *Turner: The Great Watercolours*, which attracted more than 180,000 visitors to the Royal Academy last winter. His special skill, as with the academy's earlier exhibition *Turner 1775–1851* (1974), was as a scholarly facilitator: he not only had an extraordinary visual memory for pictures, their history and their location, but was persuasive, when necessary, in eliciting their loan for exhibition.

With two old friends and colleagues, Martin Butlin and Luke Hermann, he collaborated on the 440-page *The Oxford Companion to J.M.W. Turner*, published in January [2001]: an invaluable, richly detailed and most professionally arranged guide to every aspect of the painter's life and work and to the world in which he lived so long. And in the last six months of his life, when seriously ill with cancer, Joll effectively completed the catalogue of the watercolours in the Cecil Higgins Museum, in Bedford. The collection, started by a far-sighted brewer philanthropist who died in 1941, and subsequently added to since (notably through the offices of Agnew's the art dealers with which Joll was associated for 43 years), includes important examples by Turner.

Evelyn Joll was born in London in 1925. As a child he had to overcome one great sadness. His mother died when he was four years old; but a rich compensation awaited him in the idyllic family life that he later created. His father, Cecil Joll, was a senior surgeon at the London Cancer and Royal Free Hospitals. Evelyn spent much of his boyhood with friends of the family in the Pytchley country.

From the Dragon School he went to Eton. He spoke always with affection, and with a remarkable power of recall, of both schools. He was a good cricketer who bowled A.P. Herbert first ball in a match at the Dragon and got into the XXII at Eton. A bout of rheumatic fever probably denied him his XI.

In 1943 he joined the 60th Rifles, a regiment which has always had more that its fair share of charming, intelligent and unconventional officers. Three years later he went up to Magdalen College, Oxford, where he read History under A.J.P. Taylor. In 1949 he married Pamela Kingzett, a great-great-granddaughter of the art dealer Thomas Agnew, and was taken on by the family firm of Thomas Agnew and Sons. Founded in 1817, Agnew's has occupied the same London premises, in Old Bond Street, since 1876.

Colin Agnew, Pam's uncle and an affectionate and cultivated man, was a partner; and he took Joll and his brother-in-law Dick Kingzett under his wing. Joll and Kingzett, who seemed inseparable, brought warmth and a sense of fun into the august, rather awe-inspiring firm of which they became directors in 1955. Joll succeeded Sir Geoffrey Agnew, Pam's second cousin, as chairman in 1982, coping with great wisdom and subtlety with the problems of a steeply rising market, and retired in 1992.

To his old friends Joll, with his critical intelligence, his contempt for any kind of pomposity, his lack of materialism and his unquenchable and most original, sometimes rather iconoclastic, sense of humour, seemed miscast as a dealer, but he was much respected in the trade and those who had the good fortune to work with him loved him. They admired him for his quick, efficient way of conducting business and — the essential quality in a colleague — his unfailing good-humour and high spirits. He was a trusted seller of pictures who never forced a picture on a client and was only concerned that the client should get the best, and the best service, that his illustrious firm could provide. He was especially liked by his friends in the United States.

In 1951 Agnew's put on an exhibition of works by Turner, a painter with whom the firm had been particularly associated since before his death, and Joll wrote the catalogue. This was his initiation into the world he soon made his own. It gave him great pleasure to be closely involved, after his retirement, in the Turner exhibition held in Canberra and Melbourne in 1996, the most important exhibition of the artist ever mounted in the southern hemisphere.

In 1977 he had produced, with Martin Butlin, the magisterial catalogue *The Paintings of J.M.W. Turner*. It was the first in the great series of *catalogues raisonnés* of the work of British painters undertaken by Yale University Press. The authors' complete success in their stated objective ('to collate all the information at present available about Turner's oil paintings') won them the 1978 Mitchell Prize for Art History.

Pam Joll's name appears as one of those to whom the *Oxford Companion* is dedicated. For more than 50 years she and Evelyn enjoyed a marriage of unsurpassed happiness, a joy and wonder to their friends. They never exchanged a cross word. They loved books and good writing. They had many happy trips abroad together, and Evelyn was miserable, totally unhinged, when he had to be away from her. He adored his children and grandchildren.

Evelyn Joll's tremendous, robust, sense of enjoyment, his warmth, his love of his friends, made him an enchanting companion. He loved old jokes and the old nicknames that he and his friends had devised. Most of all he loved his home on the Isle of Wight, revelling in the sailing, playing every sort of conventional or unconventional game — and watching birds (he had been a very good ornithologist since his days at Eton).

He kept up his cricket until he was nearly 60. He looked every inch a cricketer in his faded Rambler cap, a left-hander with an enviable sense of timing and a very strong throw from extra cover. He had first suggested in 1959 that we should have a game against our village and this became a red-letter day in July. Twenty-five years later, before the last game, he announced his retirement (the fixture, the planning of it and recapitulation later, would have been inconceivable without him) and marked it with an effortless 50.

I was Evelyn Joll's friend for more than 50 years. The last of our regular lunches together took place just before *The Great Watercolours* closed. He was wretchedly ill. We left our favourite Italian restaurant and walked down Albemarle Street, Joll in old country clothes and a cap. We didn't properly say goodbye. I said I was nipping into Rymans for something. 'I'm going' he said, 'to have a last look at Turner'.

Oliver Millar 2001

Acknowledgements

The Cecil Higgins Art Gallery wishes to thank the following who in many ways helped in the preparation and publication of this catalogue:

Alison Adnitt; Thos. Agnew & Sons Ltd; Annely Juda Fine Art; Robin Baring; Peter Black; Patti Bratby; Sir Alan Bowness; David Boswell; The staff of The British Library; Anita Brookner; Reg Butler; David Case; The staff of Cecil Higgins Art Gallery, past and present; John Christian; Jennie Clarke; Michael Croker; Alan Davie; Robin Deacon; Lucy Ducat-Hamersley; Nigel Duck; Judy Egerton; Helen Elletson; Dr Mark Evans; Alison Faden; William Feaver; Lucian Freud; Rhiannan Gooding; David Gowers; Hilary Guest; Vivien Hamilton; Janeen Haythornwaite; Nina Herman; John Hitchens; Sarah Hobrough; James Holloway; Christopher Hull; The Independent Newspaper; The Joll Family; Hugh Jolly; Tim Jupp and E.B.S.; Esther Kirk; Cecily Langdale; Lowell Libson; Rupert Maas; Paul Martin; Sandra Martin; Leonard McComb; Clare McGread; Beth McIntyre; Neil McGregor; Paul Mellon Centre for Studies in British Art; Oliver Millar; Julie Milne; The staff of the National Art Library, Nick Nicholson; V&A; Dr Graham Parlett; Geoffrey Parton; Marc Pascale; Tom Phillips; Godfrey Pilkington; Kenneth Pople; Mickie Rausa; Diana Rawstron; Alan Reynolds; Bridget Riley; John Roan; Hugh Robertson; Martin Royalton-Kisch; Eric Shanes; Richard Shone; John Sibley; Peter Smith; David Stubbs; Ann Sumner; Tate Gallery; Edward P Taylor; Isambard Thomas; Estate of Henry Tonks; Jessica Wallwork; Christopher Webster, Sam Whitbread and Andrew Wyld.

Contributors

EVELYN JOLL [EJ] was the leading authority on the life and work of J.M.W. Turner and a director of Thos. Agnew & Sons Ltd.

JOHN CHRISTIAN [JC] is the leading scholar on Burne-Jones. He is the author of numerous essays, articles and publications devoted to the artist's work. He is also a consultant at Christie's, London.

CAROLINE BACON [CB] has been the Curator of the Cecil Higgins Art Gallery since 1998. She joined the Gallery in 1992 as the Assistant Curator. Previously she worked at the V&A and BBC.

JAMES McGREGOR [JM] has been the Keeper of Fine and Decorative Arts at the Cecil Higgins Art Gallery since 1998. Previously he worked at the V&A and as a fine art lecturer.

Abbreviations

A.R.A.	Associate of the Royal Academy
A.R.S.A.	Associate of the Royal Scottish Academy
B.B.C.	British Broadcasting Corporation
Bt.	Baronet
C.A.S.	Contemporary Art Society
cat.	Catalogue
C.B.E.	Commander of the Order of the British Empire
C.H.	Companion of Honour
D.B.E.	Dame of the British Empire
exhib.	Exhibition
F.R.I.B.A.	Fellow of the Royal Institute of British Architects
F.S.A.	Fellow of the Society of Antiquaries
I.W.M.	Imperial War Museum
K.C.V.O.	Knight Commander of the Royal Victorian Order
M.B.E.	Member of the Order of the British Empire
M.C.	Military Cross
N.E.A.C.	New English Art Club
no.	Number
N.P.G.	National Portrait Gallery, London
N.W.S.	New Watercolour Society
O.B.E.	Officer of the Order of the British Empire
O.M.	Order of Merit
O.S.B.	Order of St. Benedict
O.W.S.	Old Watercolour Society
P.R.A.	President of the Royal Academy
P.P.R.A.	Past President of the Royal Academy
R.A.	Royal Academy, Royal Academician
R.A.F.	Royal Air Force
R.C.A.	Royal College of Art
R.H.A.	Royal Hibernian Academy
R.I.B.A.	Royal Institute of British Architects
R.N.V.R.	Royal Naval Volunteer Reserve
R.W.S.	Royal Watercolour Society
V&A	Victoria and Albert Museum

Catalogue

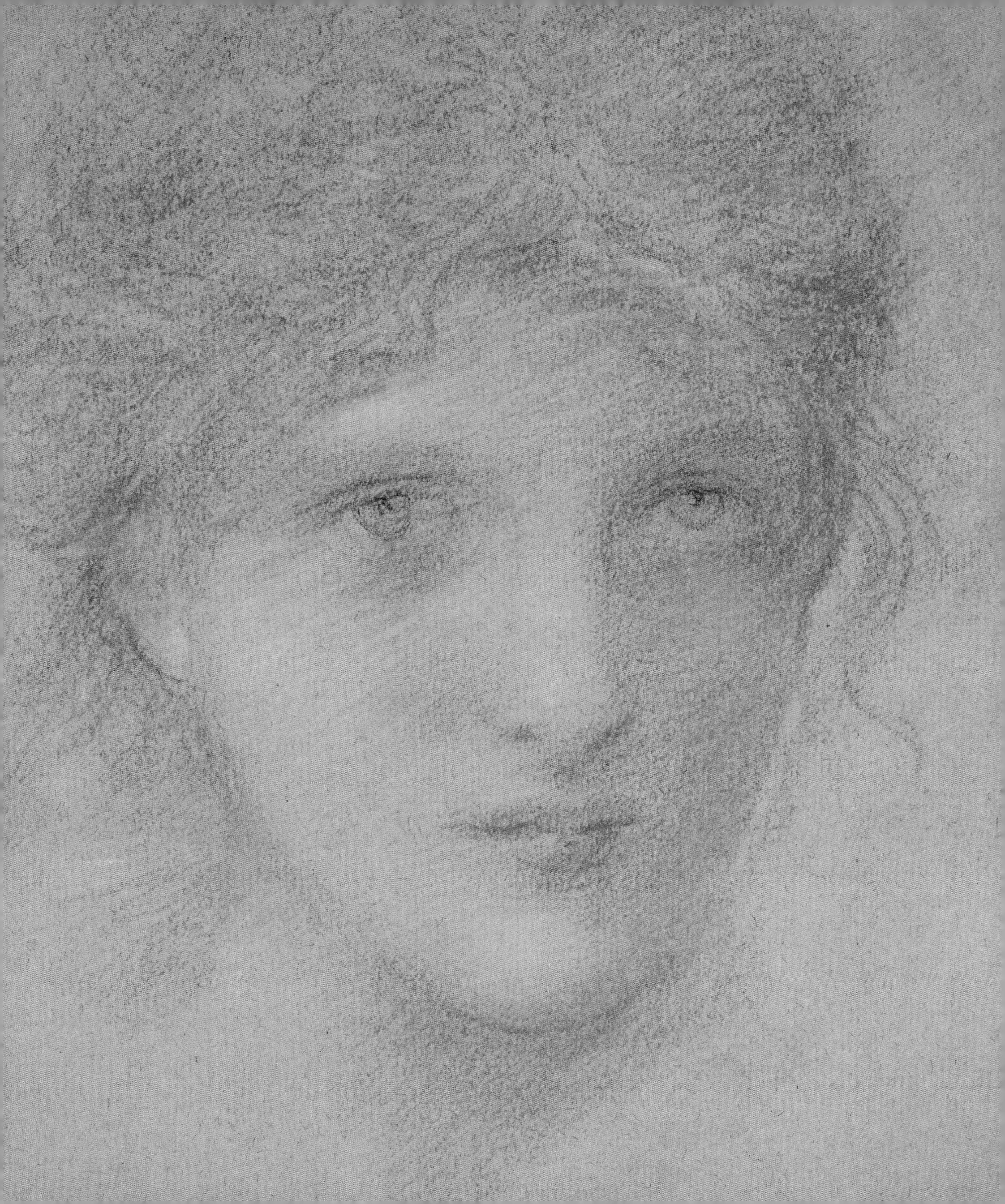

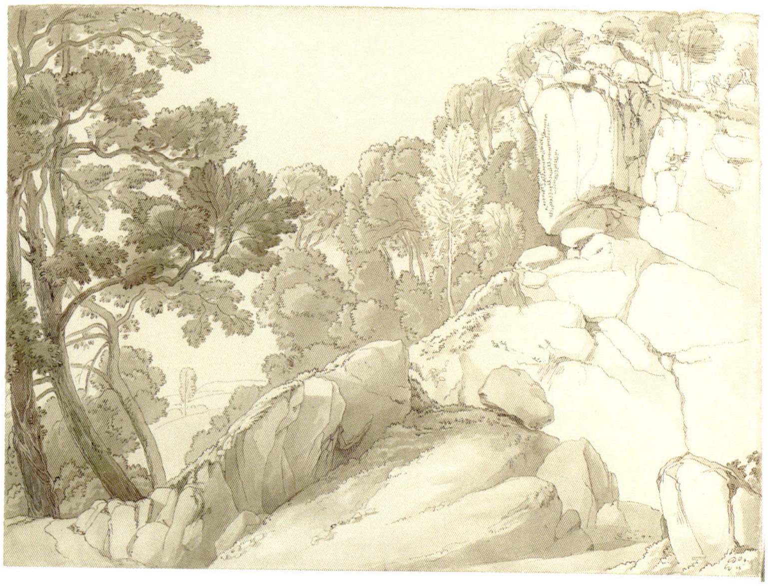

John White ABBOTT
[1763–1851]
Chudleigh, Devonshire, 1809

pen and wash on paper, 27.3 × 38.2 cm
inscribed on reverse: *Chudleigh July 27 1809*
P.55

PROVENANCE: Purchased from J. Leger & Son, January 1952.
EXHIBITIONS: *English Watercolours from the Hickman Bacon and other collections*, Bedford, Cecil Higgins Art Gallery, 1952, no.1; *The English Tradition: an exhibition of watercolours from two private collections*, Bedford, Cecil Higgins Art Gallery, 1972, no.1.

Chudleigh is about nine miles south-west of Exeter, where White Abbott was born. He remained a Devon man all his life although he did go on one sketching tour to Scotland and the north of England in 1791. He also practised as an apothecary and surgeon. He exhibited oils at the R.A. between 1793 and 1805 and on later occasions. Some of these won contemporary praise but he never sold a picture or exhibited a watercolour.

This drawing shows the influence of his master, Francis TOWNE, who had settled in Exeter in 1807. His work is sometimes almost indistinguishable from Towne's although lacking the latter's grandeur and rich colour. Abbott's watercolours are nearly always outlined in pen. He was at his best painting woodlands and trees, taking pains to suggest the individual features of different species rather than using a generalized formula as many contemporary amateurs did.

EJ

Prof. Norman ADAMS, R.A.
[b. 1927]
Ribblesdale, 1956

watercolour and ink on paper, 19 × 28.1 cm
inscribed: *N.A. 56 Ribblesdale*
P.220

PROVENANCE: The artist; purchased by Roland Browse and Delbanco, purchased by Gallery, April 1958.

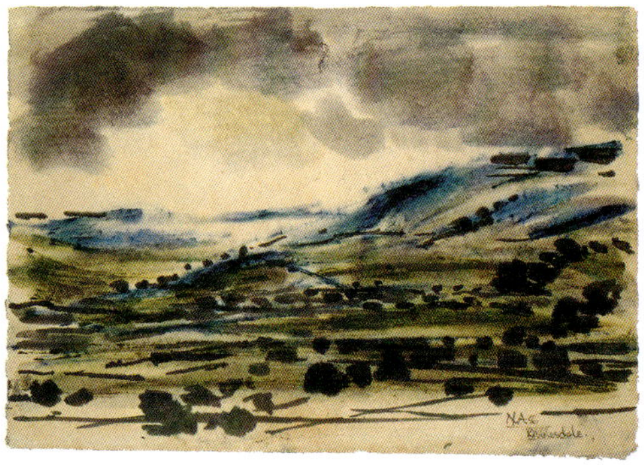

Born in London, Adams studied at Harrow School of Art and R.C.A. from 1948–51. During the war he was a conscientious objector and was imprisoned in Wormwood Scrubs for contempt of court. He moved to Horton-in-Ribblesdale, North Yorkshire in 1956 and from that date Ribblesdale became the main source of his subject matter and inspiration. In 1962 he was appointed Head of Painting at Manchester College of Art and Design. Adams was created an A.R.A. in 1967, R.A. in 1972 and R.W.S. in 1987. In 1981 he was appointed Professor of Fine Art at the University of Newcastle upon Tyne. During 1986 he was elected Keeper of the R.A. Known principally for his landscape paintings, Adams has been quoted as saying 'Subject matter has always been most important. I cannot start painting until I am driven by an almost moralist idea'.

EJ/CB

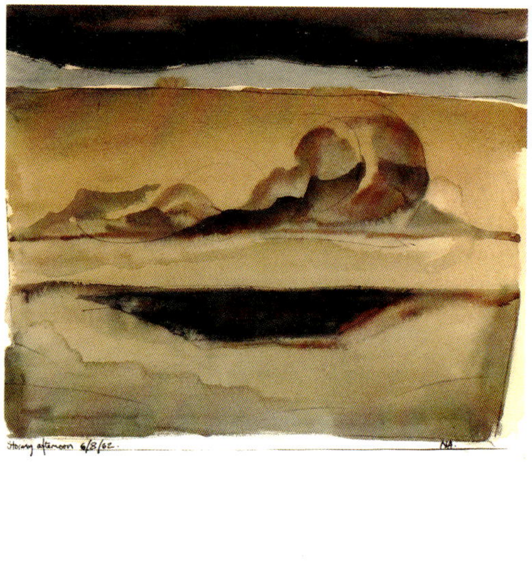

Prof. Norman ADAMS, R.A.
[b. 1927]
Stormy Afternoon, 1962

watercolour and inks on paper, 19.7 × 24.5 cm
inscribed: *N.A. Stormy afternoon 6/8/62*
P.441

PROVENANCE: The artist; purchased by Roland Browse and Delbanco, purchased by Gallery, January 1963.

This picture, made in front of the subject, contains the kind of rapid notation and use of wet-on-wet ideal for capturing the fleeting effects of weather. Everything, in fact, the medium of watercolour is best able to convey.

In 1962, Adams began living full-time at Ribblesdale. Many ideas for his paintings have been conceived whilst 'under the influence of music'.

EJ/CB

Jankel ADLER

[1895–1949]

Portrait of Mr. Murray, 1942

ink on paper, 51 × 43.8 cm
inscribed: *Adler Portrait drawing of Mr.Murray of Kirkudbright by Jankel Adler 1942*

P.374
PROVENANCE: Purchased from the Reid Gallery, October 1960.
EXHIBITIONS: *British Drawings 1939–49*, Edinburgh, Scottish National Gallery of Modern Art, 1969, no cat.; *The English Tradition: an exhibition of watercolours from two private collections*, Bedford, Cecil Higgins Art Gallery, 1972, no.2.

Adler was born in Poland and studied art in Düsseldorf before being conscripted into the Russian army in the 1914–18 war. He went to Germany after the war where he lectured at the Akademie der Kunst, Düsseldorf, until his work was declared 'degenerate' by the Nazis. He moved to France where he worked with S. W. Hayter (1901–88) at the Atelier 17. When he enlisted in the Polish Free Army during the Second World War, he was sent to Scotland (where he drew this portrait) before settling in London. His images have been described as being 'expressive of a melancholy acceptance of fate', of which the sitter here is a striking example.

Kircudbright is in Dumfriesshire but the local library has no trace of Mr Murray.

EJ/CB

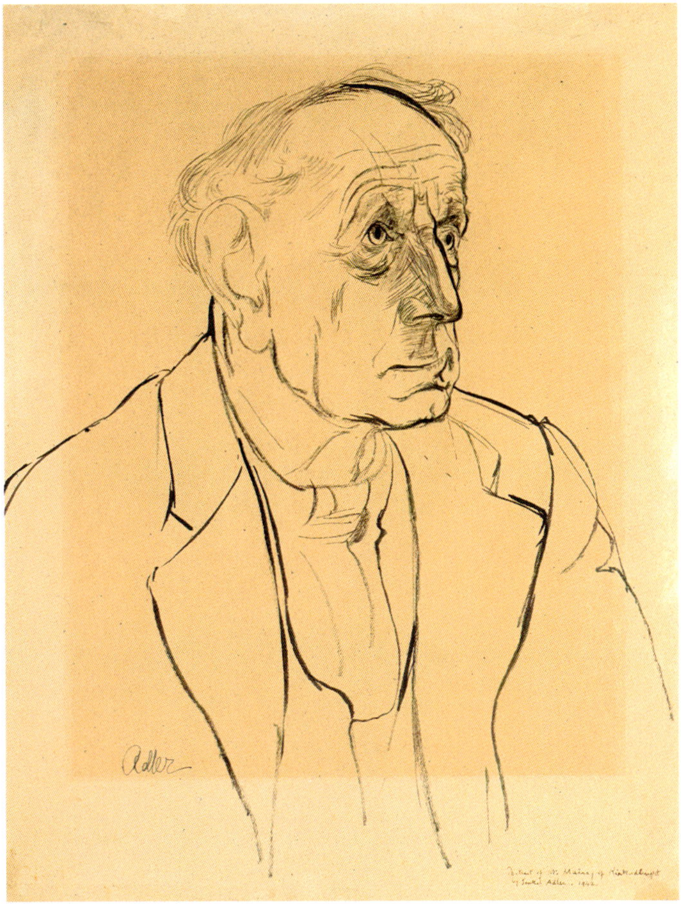

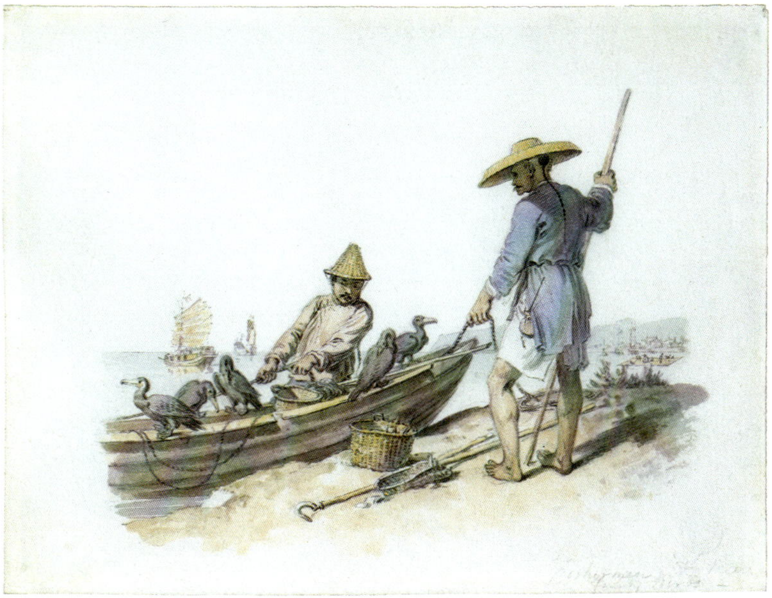

William ALEXANDER

[1767–1816]

Chinese Fishermen with Cormorants

watercolour over black lead on paper, 16.3 × 21.6 cm
inscribed: *Fishermen with birds*

P.315
PROVENANCE: Earl of Derby; Thos. Agnew & Sons Ltd, purchased by Gallery, January 1960.

This picture depicts the traditional way of catching fish in China. As can be seen in the watercolour, the cormorants are attached to the boat by long strings. They are then put into the water and hauled back when they have a full catch, which they are trained to then surrender to their owners.

Alexander's boat, the *Hindostan*, reached the mouth of the Canton River on 7 December 1793, when the crew first heard the news of 'the execution of the King of France and that the trial of Tom Paine & c. had excited some fermentations in London'.

EJ/CB

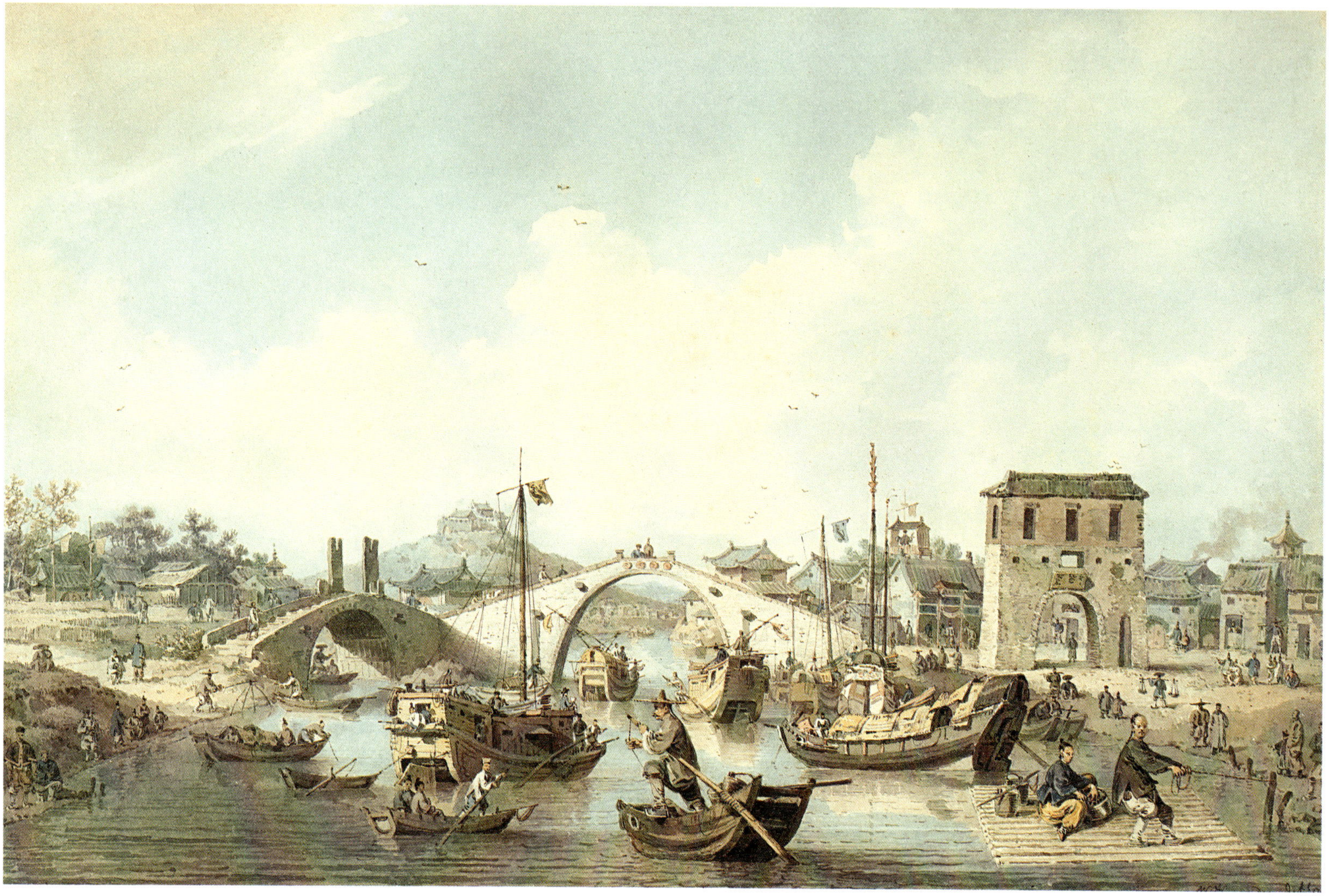

William ALEXANDER
[1767–1816]
Boats on the River at Suchow, China, 1795

watercolour and pencil on paper, 27.9 × 43.7 cm
inscribed: *W.Alexander deli 1795*

P.438
PROVENANCE: Sir Osbert Sitwell, Bart., C.H.; F.R. Meatyard; purchased by Gallery, December 1962.
EXHIBITIONS: *English Watercolours from The Cecil Higgins Art Gallery Bedford*, Reading, Reading Art Gallery, 1965, no.1; *Watercolours from Bedford,* Norwich, Norwich Castle Museum, 1965, no.2; *Canaletto & England*, Birmingham, Birmingham City Museum & Art Gallery, 1993–4, no.99, p.162.
REFERENCES: Engraved by Byrne in Sir G. Staunton, *An Authentic Account of an Embassy from the King of Great Britain to the Emperor of China*, 1797, pl.40.

Alexander, the son of a Maidstone coachmaker, went to London to study landscape drawing under Julius Caesar Ibbetson (1759–1817) and PARS. Following a recommendation from Ibbetson, Alexander went to China in 1792 as an artist attached to the embassy of Lord Macartney (1737–1806). The purpose of the visit was to protect British trade and protest against conditions of East India Company merchants in Canton. He returned in 1794 with many drawings, some of the first authentic views of China, continuing to produce more on his return to England. This drawing was among those chosen to illustrate an account of the embassy by Sir George Staunton (1781–1859) which was published in 1797. He made very good use of the voyage and published the *Costume of China* based on his observations.

In 1808 Alexander was appointed Keeper of Prints and Drawings at the British Museum, which now houses many examples of his work, including another version of this subject, signed and dated 1796.

EJ/CB

Helen ALLINGHAM, R.W.S

[1848–1926]

A Garden in October, Aldworth, 1891

watercolour on paper, 33 × 44.5 cm
inscribed: *H.Allingham*

P.338
PROVENANCE: Mr F. Pennington; J. Leger & Son; purchased by Gallery, April 1960.
REFERENCES: M.B. Huish, *The Happy England of Helen Allingham*, 1985, p.177 and pl.47.

The garden at Aldworth near Haslemere in Surrey was that of the Allinghams' friend Alfred, Lord Tennyson (1809–92). This watercolour was painted while it was raining in the kitchen garden, a favourite view of Tennyson's. After watching her paint, Tennyson remarked 'I should like to do that. It does not look very difficult'.

Helen Paterson married the Irish poet William Allingham (1824–89) in 1874 and at once joined the literary circle of Thomas Carlyle (1795–1881), RUSKIN, ROSSETTI and Tennyson. Her watercolours were strongly influenced by those of Birket FOSTER and Fred WALKER. She was among the first women to be admitted to full membership of the R.W.S. in 1890 and her diploma drawing, *Feeding the Fowls, Pinner* (repr. Hardie, vol.III, pl.134) is entirely characteristic of her customary subject matter. She is reputed to have used only nine colours, five of them yellows. Her friends would remark that she painted very quickly, to which she would reply 'Perhaps I make a quick beginning, but I take a long time to finish'.

EJ/CB

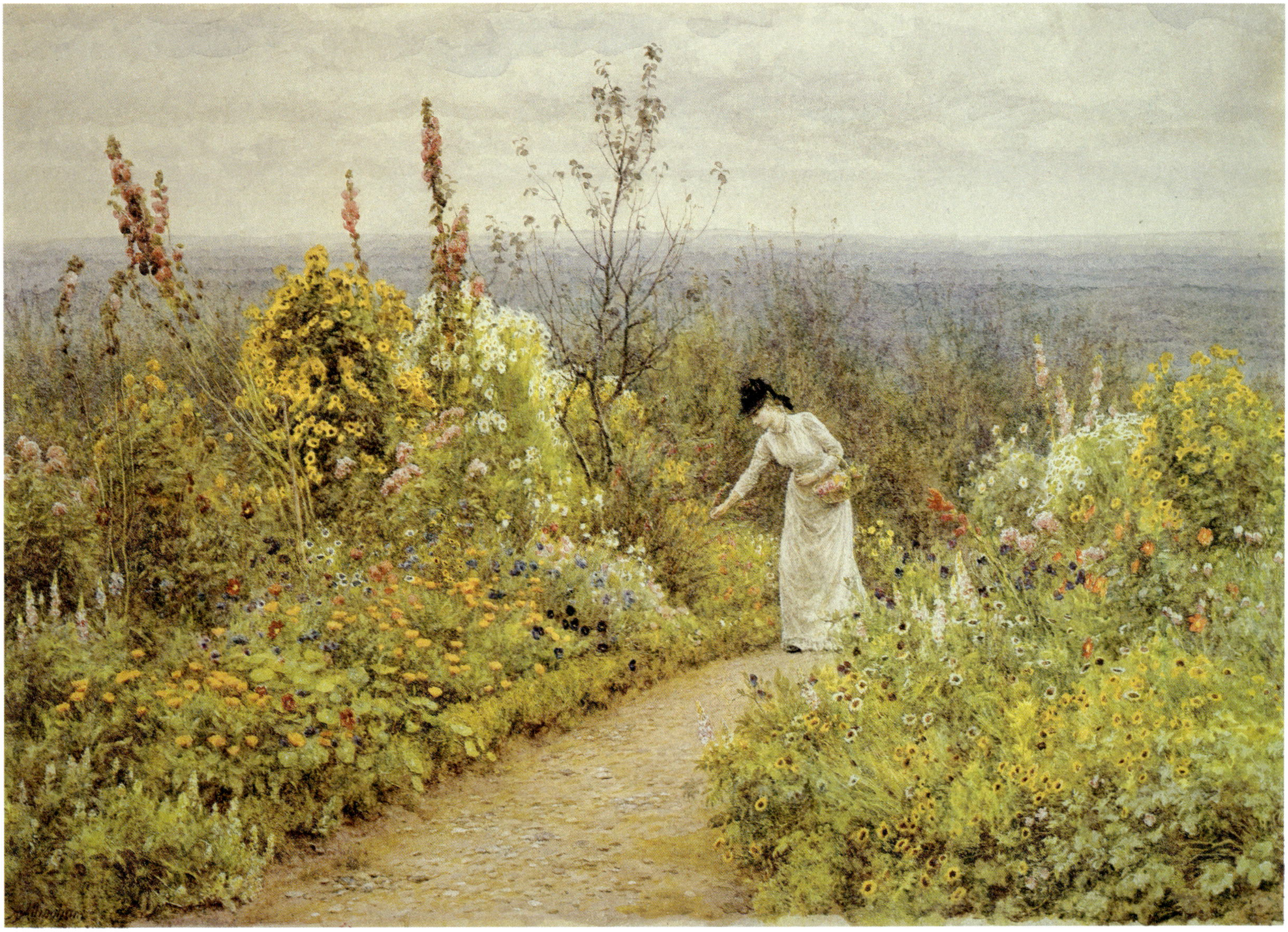

Sir Lawrence ALMA-TADEMA, O.M., R.A., R.W.S.

[1836–1912]

The Street Altar, 1883

watercolour on paper, 34.7 × 17.3 cm
inscribed: *L Alma- Tadema Nov LXXXIII opus CCLVI*

P.637

PROVENANCE: James Reid; Andrew T. Reid; Handley-Read Collection; Fine Art Society, lot 2 June 1974; purchased by Gallery with assistance from V&A/M.G.C. Purchase Grant Fund, June 1974.
EXHIBITIONS: Royal Society of Painters in water-colour, London, no.247, 1884; *Victorian and Edwardian Decorative Art*, London, RA, 1972, no.D130, p.77; *Sir Lawrence Alma-Tadema*, Amsterdam, Van Gogh Museum and Liverpool, Walker Art Gallery, 1997, no.61.
REFERENCES: *Academy Sketches*, 1884, p.114, illus.; Becker & E. Prettejohn (eds.), *Sir Lawrence Alma-Tadema*, 1996, no.61, p.223.

Alma-Tadema was born in Holland and trained in Belgium. His success was due to the dealer Ernest Gambart (1814–1902) promoting his Roman paintings, which in 1865 he brought to London. Alma-Tadema settled there in 1870. His historical subjects, if sometimes rather banal, were accurate in every detail and painted with enormous technical skill, his rendering of marble being especially famed. He was a great showman and a major figure in the English art establishment, so much so that his biographer, Vern Swanson, claimed that his name was as familiar to his generation as Picasso is to ours.

EJ

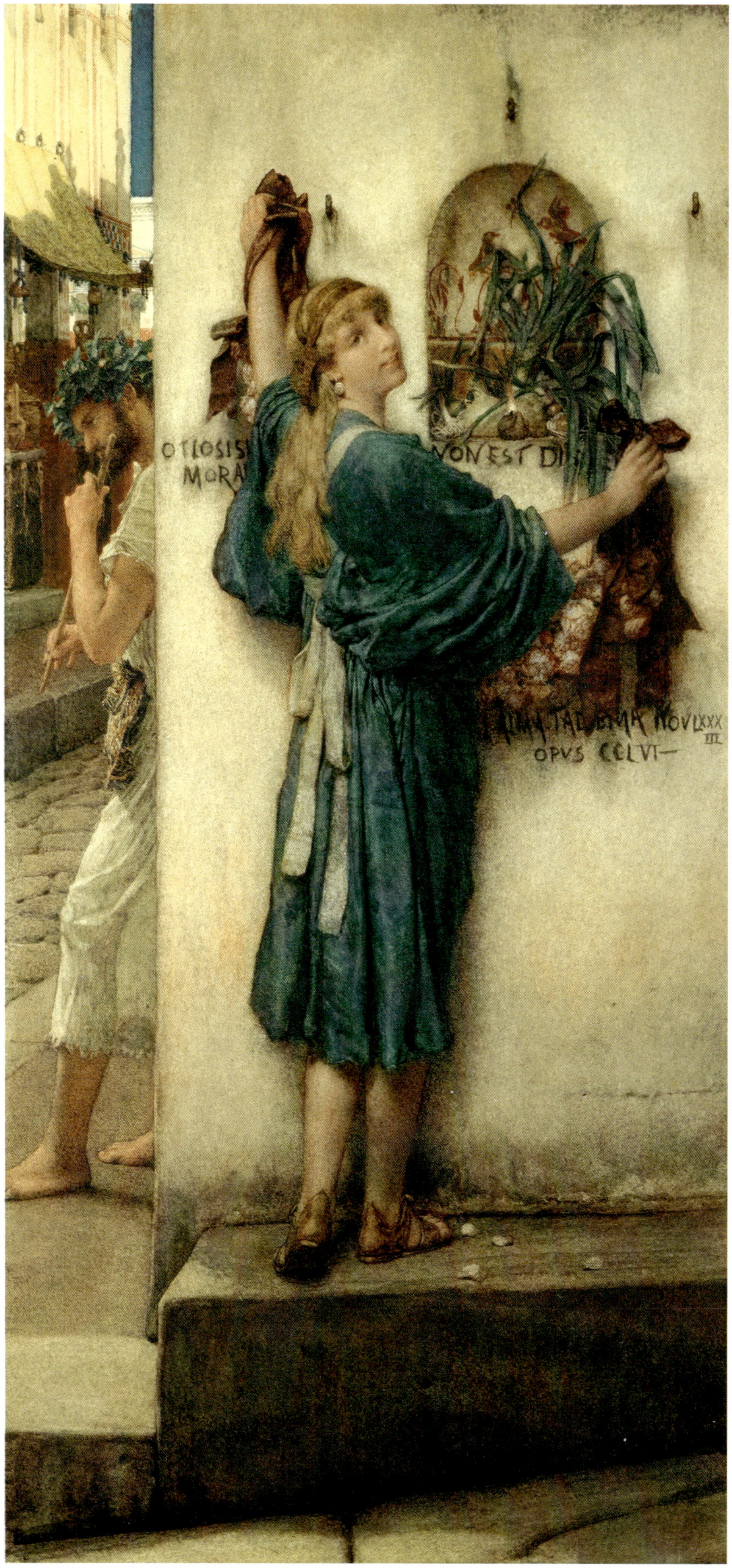

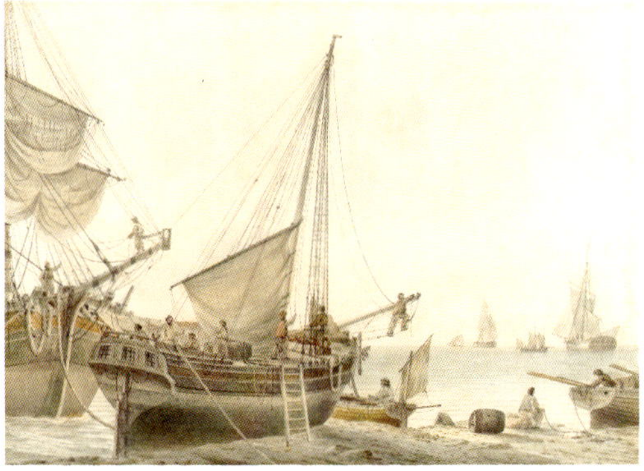

Samuel ATKINS

[fl. 1787–1808]

Shore Scene with boats

watercolour and pen and ink on paper,
34.3 × 47.5 cm
inscribed: *Atkins*

P.362

PROVENANCE: J. Pearce Higgins; Spink & Son Ltd; purchased by Gallery, October 1960.
EXHIBITIONS: *Watercolours from Bedford*, Norwich, Castle Museum, 1965, no.3.

Atkins was a marine artist whose drawings are fairly rare. His work is perhaps at its most attractive on a small scale.

He first exhibited at the R.A. in 1787 and showed eighteen pictures between then and 1808. In 1788 he advertised as a tutor giving drawing lessons from an address off the Strand, London. From 1796–1804 he was in the West Indies.

His signature can often be found on a floating spar within his paintings.

EJ

Frank AUERBACH

[b. 1931]

Two preparatory drawings for the painting

Primrose Hill – Autumn 1970, 1970

oil pastel on paper, 22.5 × 30.3 cm
inscribed on reverse: *12/29 Marlborough 5*

P.615

pencil with patches of bodycolour on paper, 22.5 × 30 cm
inscribed on reverse: *12/29 Marlborough 4*

P.615A

PROVENANCE: The artist; Marlborough Fine Art, purchased by Gallery, January 1971.
EXHIBITIONS: *Frank Auerbach*, London, Marlborough Fine Art, January 1971, no.40.

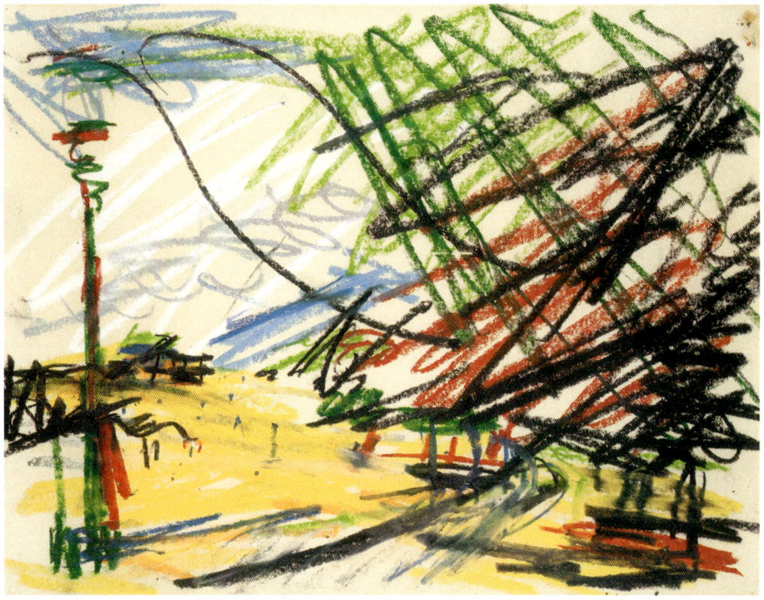

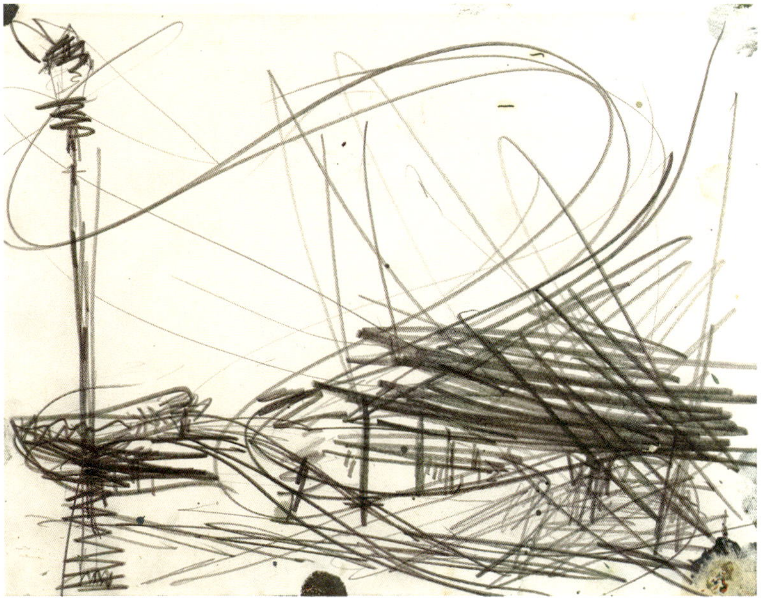

Born in Berlin, Auerbach was sent to London in 1939 to escape Nazism; his parents, who remained in Germany, died in concentration camps. He attended art classes at the Borough Polytechnic under BOMBERG (together with KOSSOFF), and also studied at St Martin's School of Art (1948–52) and the R.C.A. (1952–5).

Auerbach's approach to making pictures involves drawing in front of the subject and then working from these drawings back in the studio. He has said 'for a painter the problem is to go as long as possible with one work and drive it to its most comprehensive and economical conclusion'.

Auerbach has a strong work ethic, working ten hours a day, seven days a week. He has lived and worked in the same North London studio since 1954.

EJ/CB

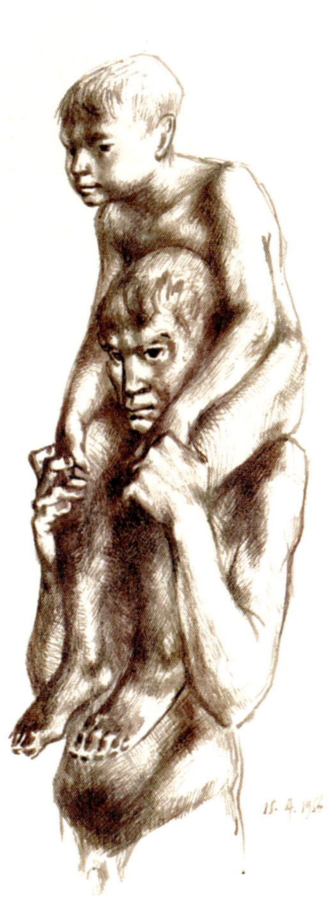

Michael AYRTON

[1921–75]

Study for Bather with a Child III, 1956

sepia wash on paper, 43.8 × 29.2 cm
inscribed: *Michael Ayrton 15.4.56*

P.262
PROVENANCE: The artist, purchased by Leicester Gallery, purchased by Gallery, October 1958.

A study for a bronze maquette which was exhibited, together with another sepia study, at the Bruton Gallery, Bruton, Somerset (*Michael Ayrton: work of the 1950s, sculpture, paintings and drawings*, 1974, 8,55). The other study is dated *3.1.56* and shows the whole of the bather's figure viewed directly from the front.

Born in London, Ayrton was the son of Gerald Gould (1885–1936), the writer, and the Labour politician Barbara Ayrton. He adopted his mother's name at the time of his father's death, so that he would appear at the top of exhibition lists. In Paris he shared a studio with John MINTON during 1938–9, both studying under Eugene Berman (1899–1972). During the Second World War, he and Minton were given leave from the R.A.F. to design sets and costumes for a production of *Macbeth* by John Gielgud (1904–2000). He was an all-rounder: painter, sculptor, illustrator, theatre designer, broadcaster, author and art critic.

EJ/CB

Thomas BARKER of Bath

[1769–1847]

Figures in a Wooded Clearing, late 1780s or 1790s

black and brown chalk and wash on paper, 38.6 × 30.4 cm
on reverse: a pencil sketch of horse-drawn cart by trees
An old label on the reverse of the picture gave the title as *The Old Oak*.

P.70
PROVENANCE: Thos. Agnew & Sons, Ltd, from whom purchased by Gallery, January 1952
EXHIBITIONS: *English Watercolours from the Hickman Bacon and other Collections*, Bedford, Cecil Higgins Art Gallery, 1952, no.40.
REFERENCES: J. Hayes, *The Drawings of Thomas Gainsborough*, 1970, pp.79, 323.

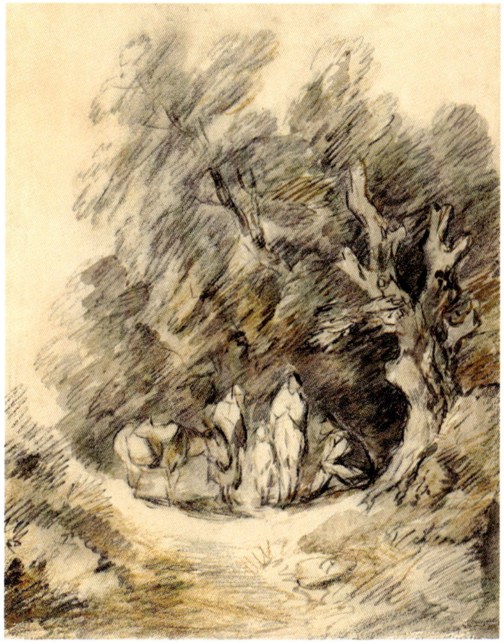

Although this painting was purchased as a GAINSBOROUGH, Dr Hayes has convincingly reattributed this drawing to Barker, known as "Barker of Bath", who moved from Wales to Bath in 1782. There his industry, facility and skilful imitations were soon cause for comment and complaint. *The Morning Herald* of 11 June 1789 described him as 'an execrable *Imposter* at the brush' who imposed on the public by 'pictures and Drawings in this Master's [Gainsborough's] stile [*sic*]'. Thomas Barker made a reasonable living producing works in Gainsborough's fashionable style and frequently exhibited at the R.A. from 1791 to 1847.

Hayes dates this group of drawings to either the very late 1780s or the 1790s. The Cecil Higgins' example belongs to a small number which share identical treatment of foliage and figures, and Hayes illustrates a *Landscape*, clearly by the same hand, in the Ulster Museum and Art Gallery, Belfast as plate 396. He lists almost 200 other examples in public collections world-wide which he considers wrongly attributed to Gainsborough.

EJ/CB

Francis BARLOW

[1626–1702]

A Hen with Chicks in a Landscape, c.1658

pen and brown ink with grey wash on paper, 12.4 × 17.5 cm

P.207
PROVENANCE: H.M. Calman; P&D Colnaghi Ltd, from whom purchased by Gallery, April 1958.
EXHIBITIONS: *17th Century Farming,* Elstow, Moot Hall, 1962; *Watercolours from The Cecil Higgins Art Gallery Bedford,* London, Thos. Agnew & Sons Ltd, 1962, no.3; *Watercolours from Bedford,* Norwich, Castle Museum, 1962, no.4.
REFERENCES: P. Atterbury, *The History of Porcelain,* 1982, p.129.

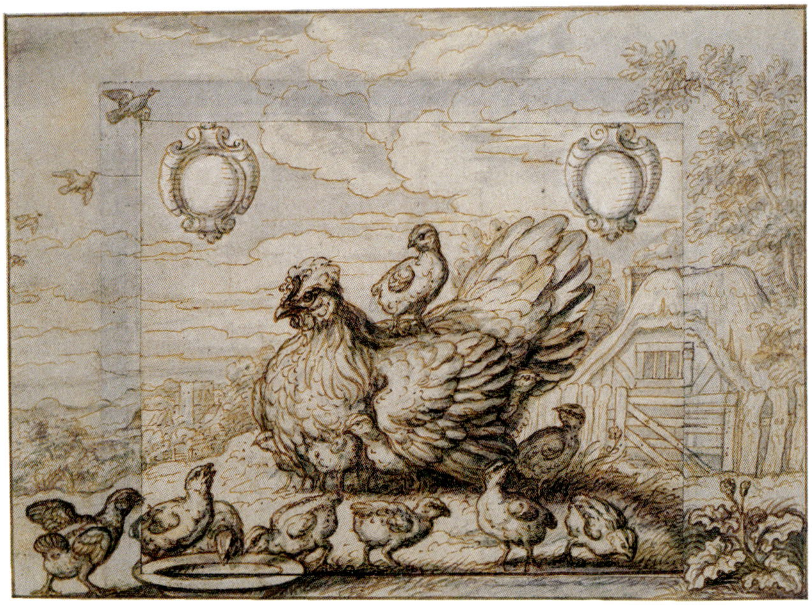

The central group was used in an etching by Wenceslas Hollar (1607–77), in the series *Multae et Diversae Avium Species Multivarius, Formis et Pernaturalibus Figuris per Franciscum Barlovium*, printed and sold by John Overton (1670–1713) at the White Horse without Newgate, in 1658, with new editions in 1671, pl.XIV.

Barlow was described by John Evelyn (1620–1706) as *the famous painter of Fowle* [*sic*], *Beasts and Birds* and this is a fine example of his work in this genre. He is best known today for his illustrations to *Aesop's Fables* and other books. Although he had influential patrons he died in poverty.

EJ

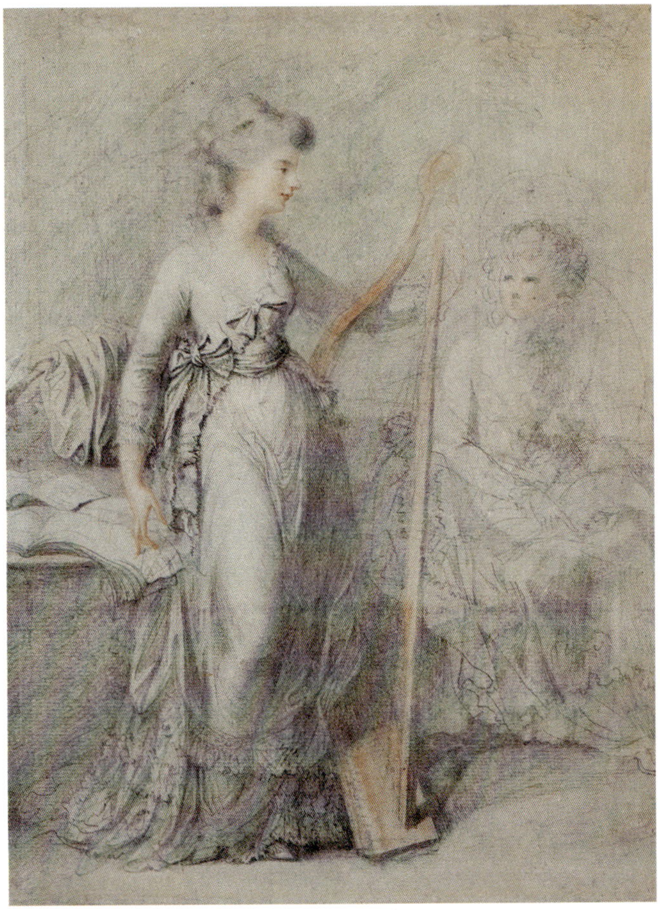

Francesco BARTOLOZZI, R.A.

[1727–1815]

Georgiana, Duchess of Devonshire

pencil and red chalk on paper, 27.5 × 20.2 cm

P.277
PROVENANCE: Given by the Duchess of Devonshire to Richard Brinsley Sheridan; given by Lady Stacey to Walter Sichel; Leicester Galleries, from whom purchased by Gallery, January 1959.
EXHIBITIONS: *The English Tradition: an exhibition of watercolours from two private collections,* Bedford, Cecil Higgins Art Gallery, 1972, no.3.
REFERENCES: W. Sichel, *Sheridan: From new and original material,* 2 vols., London, 1909, illus. facing p.464.

The sitter (1757–1806), eldest daughter of the first Earl Spencer, married the fifth Duke of Devonshire (1748–1811) in 1774. He was described by Sichel as 'that marital iceberg'. She was a charismatic figure, at once a rake and a recluse but also a model mother. Horace Walpole (1717–97) wrote: 'She effaces all others without beauty'. She canvassed for Charles Fox (1749–1806), her hero, in the Westminster election of 1784. The woman seated in the background is her closest friend, Lady Elizabeth Foster (1757–1824).

Bartolozzi trained in Venice as an engraver but, on arrival in England in 1764, soon adapted to the new stipple method with which his name is always linked. His many pupils executed numerous plates that bore his name. He was elected a founder member of the R.A. in 1768, which enraged other engravers who had been excluded. His drawings appear only rarely.

The artist John DOWNMAN produced portraits of Georgiana and Elizabeth, which were later engraved by Bartolozzi in 1788.

EJ/CB

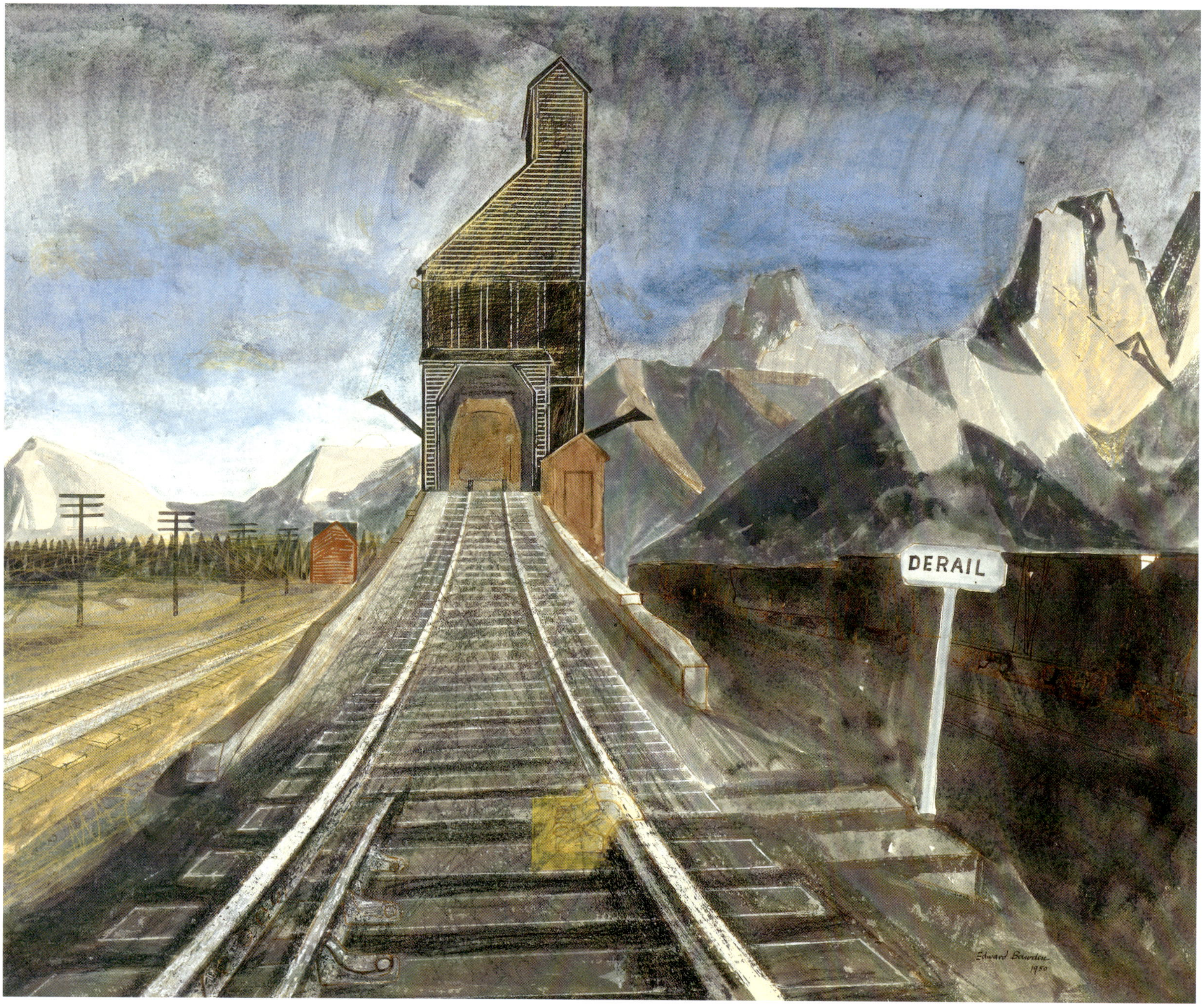
DERAIL
Edward Bawden
1950

Edward BAWDEN, C.B.E., R.A.
[1903–89]
To Winnipeg, 1950

watercolour, bodycolour, crayon, ink and cobbler's wax on paper, 56.6 × 71.1 cm
inscribed: *Edward Bawden 1950*

P.270
PROVENANCE: Sold by the artist to the Zwemmer Gallery from whom purchased by Gallery, October 1958.
EXHIBITIONS: *Water-colour Drawings of the Canadian Rockies*, London, Leicester Galleries, 1951, no. 18.
REFERENCES: F. Spalding, *British Art Since 1900*, 1986, p.73; J. Howes, *Edward Bawden: A Retrospective Survey*, 1988, p.59, no.122.

Bawden spent some months teaching in Canada during the summers of 1949 and 1950. This was painted in the small mining town of Canmore about fourteen miles from Banff. He worked entirely on the spot and, due to a rail strike, was able to sit on the line itself. The line to Winnipeg is shown on the left. The Zwemmer Gallery changed Bawden's title to *Railroad to the Rockies*, but Bawden corrected this in a conversation with the Curator in June 1983, saying he would never dream of using the American word 'railroad'. Bawden also proposed 'mixed media' to describe this drawing as it contains heel ball (cobbler's wax), which he did not have in his log cabin in Canmore and so must have put on in London later.

EJ

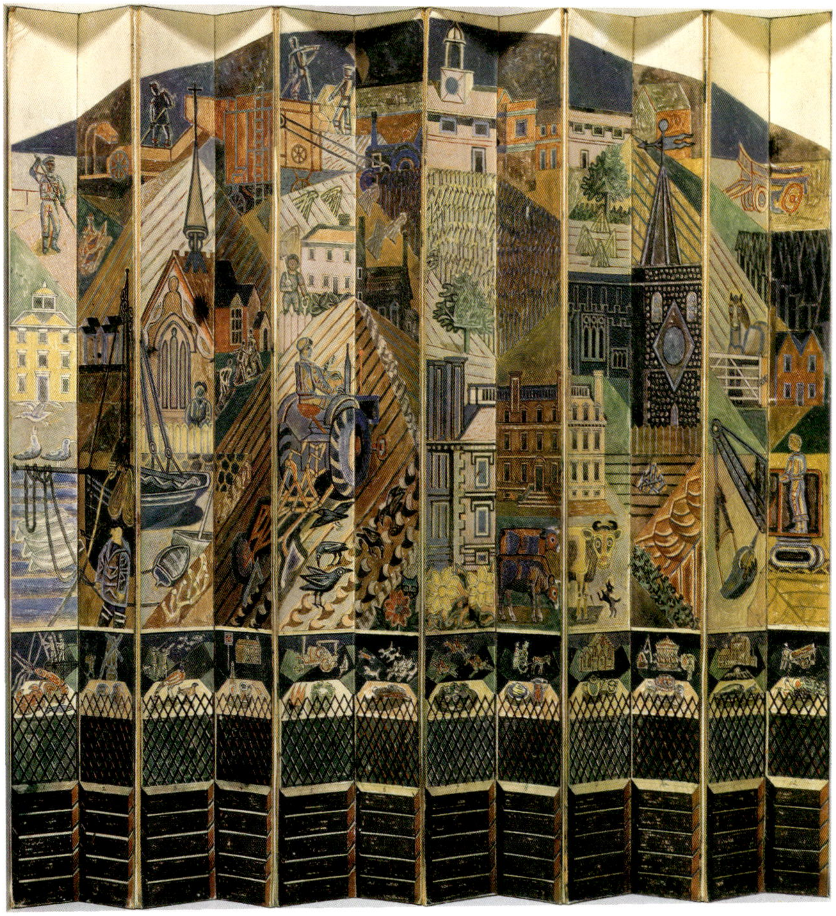

Edward BAWDEN, C.B.E., R.A.
[1903–89]
Study for Mural of **Country Life, 1951**

watercolour on folded card, 51.7 × 48.4 cm
inscribed on reverse: *Study for the Festival of Britain Mural in the Royal College of Art's Lion and the Unicorn Pavilion*

P.755
PROVENANCE: Given to Gallery by artist 1989.
EXHIBITIONS: *A Tonic to the Nation*, London, V&A, 1976–7 no cat. no.
REFERENCES: M. Banham & B. Hillier (eds.), *A Tonic to the Nation: The Festival of Britain*, 1976, pp.98 & 101; D.P. Bliss, *Edward Bawden*, 1980, pp.153–4.

Painted in 1951 for the Festival of Britain's 'Lion and Unicorn Pavilion', the mural told the story of the British character and traditions. The whole end of the building, measuring thirty-six feet high by forty-five feet wide, was filled with Bawden's mural painted on seventy-one plywood panels. At the end of the exhibition this was one of four works which the Arts Council decided should be kept in public ownership. They were then placed in long-term storage in a Ministry of Works building, which has since been demolished, leaving no record of what became of the mural.

EJ

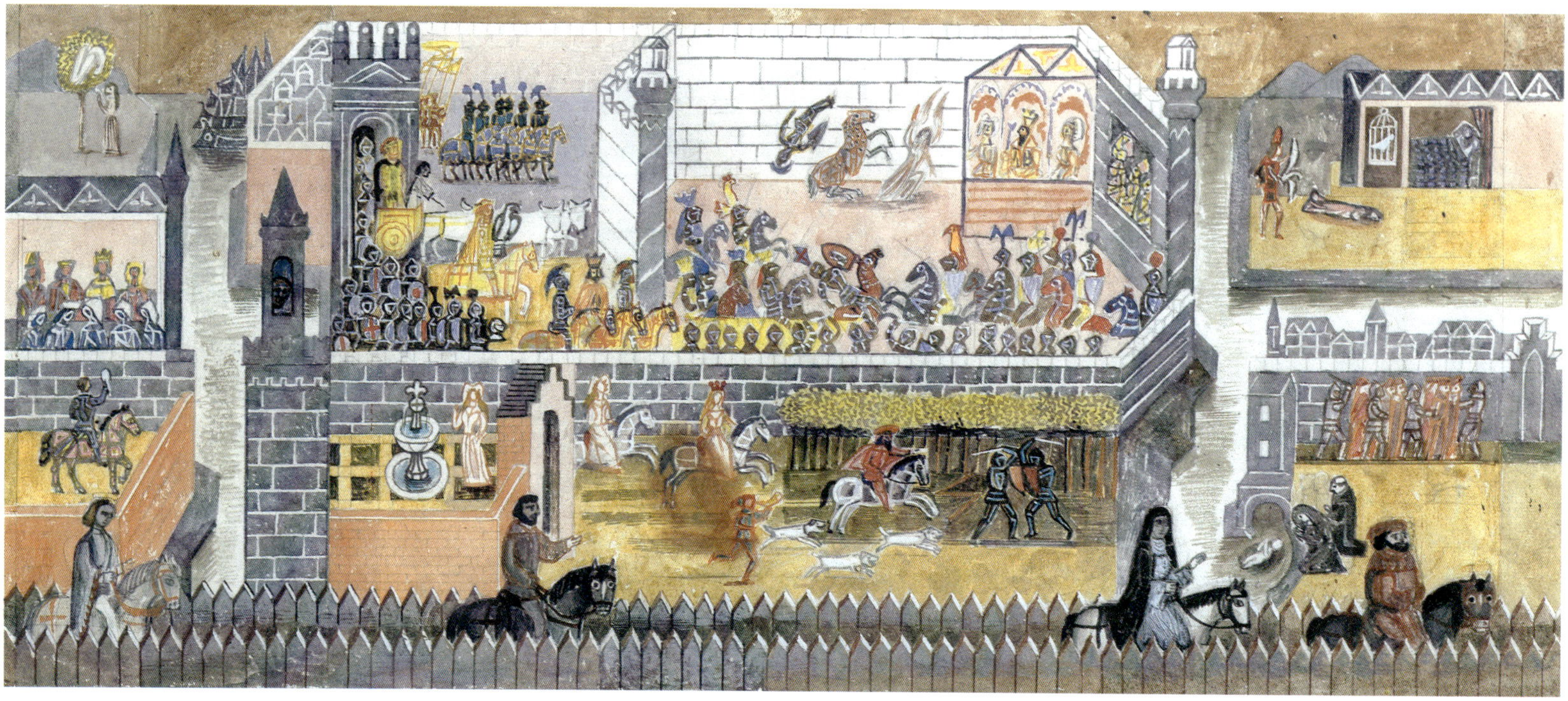

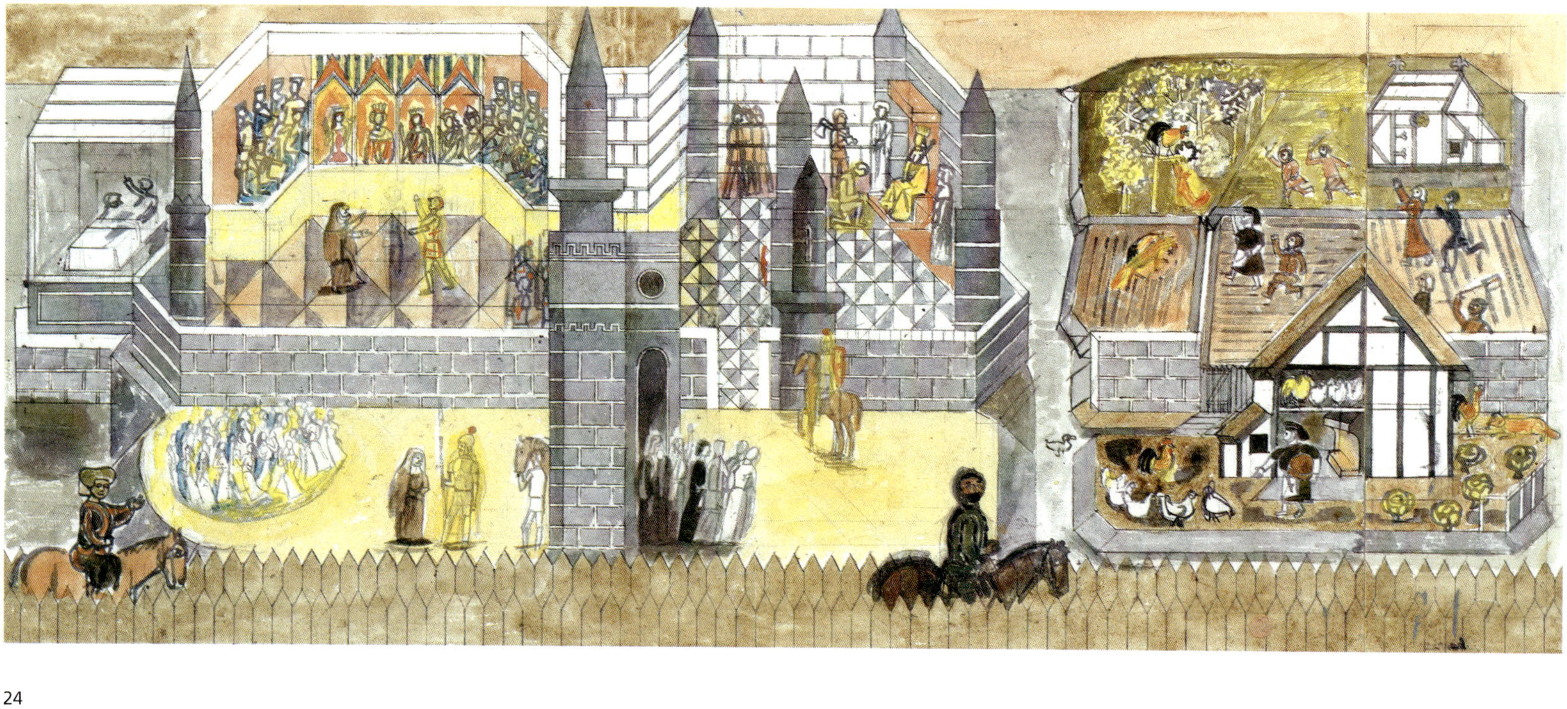

Edward BAWDEN, C.B.E., R.A.
[1903–89]
Sketch for mural of Chaucer's **Canterbury Tales, 1958**

pencil, watercolour and bodycolour on paper, 32.4 × 71.8 cm
inscribed: *Edward Bawden*
on reverse: *Morley College/Final Sketch 91 Cecil Higgins List* – refers to master list of items given by the artist in 1981.

P.740
PROVENANCE: Given to Gallery by artist with the Bawden archive, October 1981.
REFERENCES: D.P. Bliss, *Edward Bawden*, 1980, pp.150–1, 158 & 159; J. Howes, *Edward Bawden: A Retrospective Survey*, 1988, p.81, no.167.

This and P.741 were painted as studies for the murals for the restaurant of Morley College, London, to replace an earlier set by Bawden and RAVILIOUS destroyed by bombing in 1940.

On the left is the squire and his Tale of Cambuscan, King of Tartary; in the centre is the Knight and his Tale of Palamon and Arcite, and on the right are the Prioress and the Manciple (a steward) and their Tales, which are super-imposed.

EJ

Edward BAWDEN, C.B.E., R.A.
[1903–89]
Sketch for mural of Chaucer's **Canterbury Tales, 1958**

pencil, watercolour and bodycolour on paper, 32 × 76.7 cm
inscribed: *Edward Bawden*
on reverse: *Mural/Morley College/5 90 Cecil Higgins List* for explanation see P.740.

P.741
PROVENANCE: Given to Gallery by artist with the Bawden archive, October 1981.
REFERENCES: D.P. Bliss, *Edward Bawden*, 1980, pp.150–1; J. Howes, *Edward Bawden: A Retrospective Survey*, 1988, p.81, no.167.

On the left is the Wife of Bath. Her Tale, about a knight at King Arthur's court who, to save his life, has to discover what most women desire (which is to dominate their husbands), occupies two-thirds of the picture. On the right is the Nun's Priest and his Tale of Chanticleer and the Fox. Both were altered considerably in the final mural itself.

Both these studies for murals show Bawden's great skill in marshalling complex material so that the stories he is illustrating are presented very clearly.

EJ

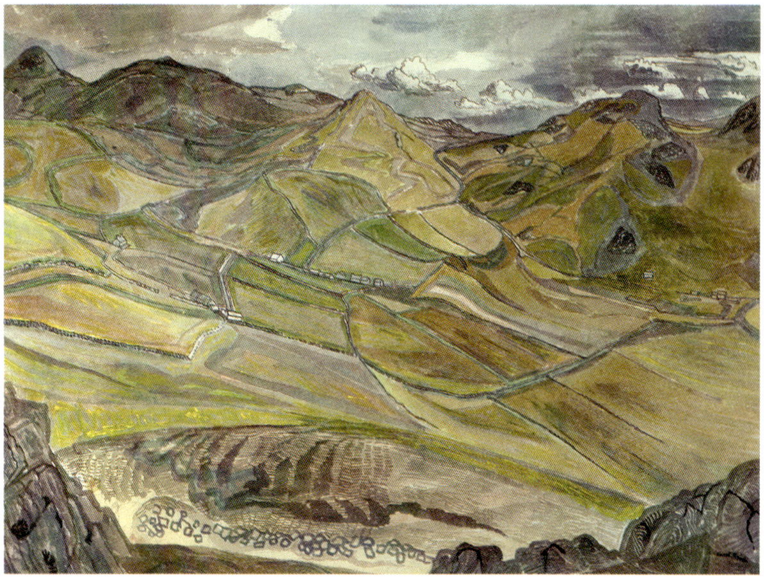

Edward BAWDEN, C.B.E., R.A.
[1903–89]
Horn Head V, Donegal, Eire, 1968

watercolour on paper, 54 × 74 cm
inscribed: *Edward Bawden*

P.587
PROVENANCE: Fine Art Society, from whom purchased by *Gallery, December 1968.*
EXHIBITIONS: *Edward Bawden, C.B.E. R.A., Recent works,* London, Fine Art Society, 1968, no.15.
REFERENCES: J. Howes, *Edward Bawden: A Retrospective Survey*, 1988, p.99, no.209.

Bawden went with his wife, Charlotte, and a friend, Emily Davis, to Ireland in the summer of 1968 to prepare work for his forthcoming exhibition at the Fine Art Society, London. Bawden recalled his visit:

> I was attracted to Horn Head by its spectacular scenery. I was working at full pressure for the Fine Art exhibition, starting one watercolour in the morning and completing it on the next morning, and working on another watercolour in the afternoons. The summer was exceptionally dry, and I sat on one of the rocks painting this watercolour.

This is one of seven pictures he painted while in Ireland. Bawden was a watercolourist, especially of landscapes, a printmaker, an illustrator and designer of posters, ceramics, furniture and theatre décor. He studied under Paul NASH at the R.C.A., where his contemporaries were Eric RAVILIOUS and Douglas Percy Bliss (1900–84). He was a member of the 7 & 5 Society, 1932–4 and settled at Great Bardfield, Essex in 1935. Bawden was appointed an Official War Artist from 1940–4. He was awarded the C.B.E. in 1946, elected A.R.A. in 1947 and R.A. in 1956. In 1951 he was appointed as a trustee of the Tate Gallery.

In 1989, Bawden donated the contents of his studio to the Gallery, which included examples of his work from 1922 to 1989.

EJ/CB

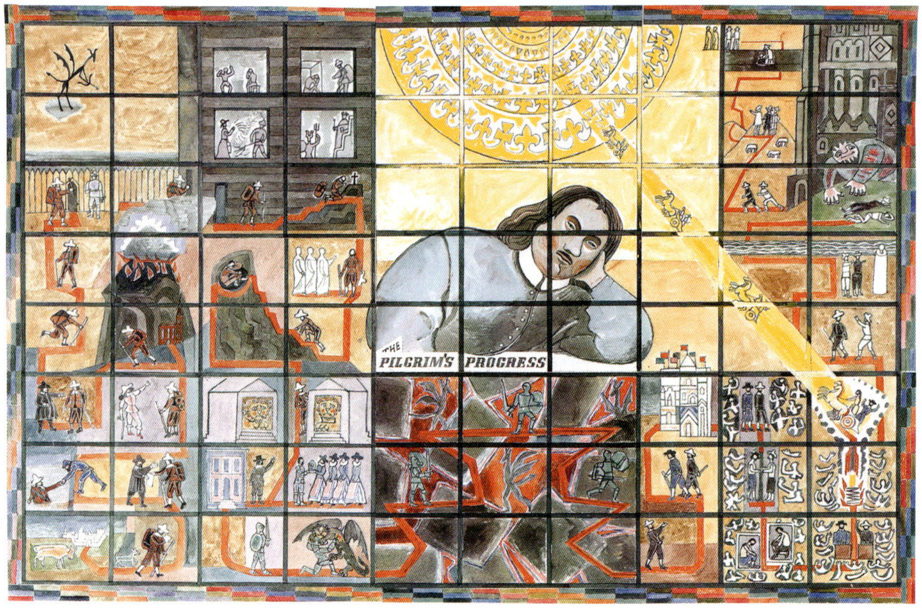

Edward BAWDEN, C.B.E., R.A.

[1903–89]

Tapestry cartoon for Bunyan's Dream from **The Pilgrim's Progress, 1977**

watercolour and bodycolour on paper, 56.5 × 89.2 cm
signed: *Edward Bawden*

P.692
PROVENANCE: Commissioned by the Gallery, 1977.
EXHIBITIONS: *Edward Bawden: The Art of Design*, London, V&A and Canterbury, Herbert Read Gallery, 1989, no.27.
REFERENCES: J. Howes, *Edward Bawden: A Retrospective Survey*, 1988, p.105, no.224.

This was a commission by the Trustees of the Cecil Higgins Art Gallery, from the artist, for a tapestry to be worked by local needlewomen to commemorate both the tercentenary of *The Pilgrim's Progress* by John Bunyan and the Queen's Silver Jubilee.

Bunyan (1628–88) was born at Elstow, near Bedford. In November 1660 he was arrested for preaching without a licence and spent the next twelve years in Bedford Gaol where he wrote part of *The Pilgrim's Progress*, finishing the first part during another spell in gaol in 1676. This was published in 1678 and part two in 1684.

The book, an allegory, takes the form of a dream, by the author, of the pilgrimage of Christian and, in part two, of his wife Christiana. The work is remarkable for the simplicity and beauty of its language and its humour. It has been translated into well over 100 languages. There is a museum devoted to the life and times of John Bunyan in Bedford.

EJ

Aubrey BEARDSLEY

[1872–98]

Frontispiece for **Venus and Tannhäuser, 1895**

pen and ink on paper, 21.9 × 17.8 cm
inscribed: *Venus*

P.225
PROVENANCE: Messrs. H. Henry & Co. Ltd; John Lane Esq.; Herbert Charles Pollitt (1871–1942); purchased by Gallery from Matthiesen Ltd, December 1957.
EXHIBITIONS: *Paris Exposition, 1900*, no.20; *Aubrey Beardsley*, London, V&A and Manchester, Manchester City Art Gallery, Bradford, Bradford Art Gallery, Southampton, Southampton University, 1966, no. 441; *Aubrey Beardsley*, New York, The Gallery of Modern Art, 1967, no.180; *The English Tradition, an exhibition of watercolours from two private collections*, Bedford, Cecil Higgins Art Gallery, 1972, no.4; *Het Symbolisme in Europa*, Rotterdam, Baden-Baden & Paris, 1976, no.4; *Aubrey Beardsley:An Exhibition for Japan*, Kawasaki Museum, Wakayama Art Gallery, Hokkaido Museum and Gunma Museum, 1998, no.135.
REFERENCES: A. Vallance, *A Book of Fifty Drawings by Aubrey Beardsley*, 1897, p.209; A.E. Gallatin, *Aubrey Beardsley's drawings: A Catalogue*, 1903, p.34; L. Smithers, *A Second book of Fifty Drawings by Aubrey Beardsley*, 1899, p.179; H. MacFall, *Aubrey Beardsley: The Man and His Work*, 1928, pp.72,74–7; H. Wölfflin, *Principles of Art History: The Problem of the Development of Style in Later Art*, 1932, p.159; R. Walker, *The Best of Beardsley*, 1948, p.44; W. Sypher, *Rococo to Cubism in Art and Literature*, 1960, p.27; B. Reade, *Collection of the Greatest Works of Aubrey Beardsley*, 1966, p.9; C. Brinitzer, *Immer Arger mit den Frauen*, 1973, p.188; I. Fletcher, *Aubrey Beardsley*, 1987, p.251; L. Zatlin, *Aubrey Beardsley and Victorian Sexual Politics*, 1990, illus. p.108; A. Reid, *Beardsley*, 1991, p.78; C. Snodgrass, *Aubrey Beardsley: Dandy of the Grotesque*, 1995, p.149.

This beautiful drawing, executed in 1895, was made as a frontispiece to Beardsley's unfinished erotic novel *Venus and Tannhäuser* (a version of the medieval legend of Venus, goddess of love, and the knight Tannhäuser) which was later published as *Under the Hill* in *The Savoy*, nos.1 & 2, 1896.

Critics have seen this drawing as exemplifying the new order and classicism that Beardsley introduced into his art after his dismissal from *The Yellow Book*. Yet the seemingly idealised and placid Venus, set against the profuse and sprawling foliage behind her, creates a tension between them which is one of the drawing's strengths.

Although largely self-taught, Beardsley achieved a mastery of black and white line drawing unequalled in its balance of space and telling detail. His vision, as much as Wilde's writings, has shaped our image of the decadence of the 1890s. Beardsley died of tuberculosis aged only twenty-five.

EJ

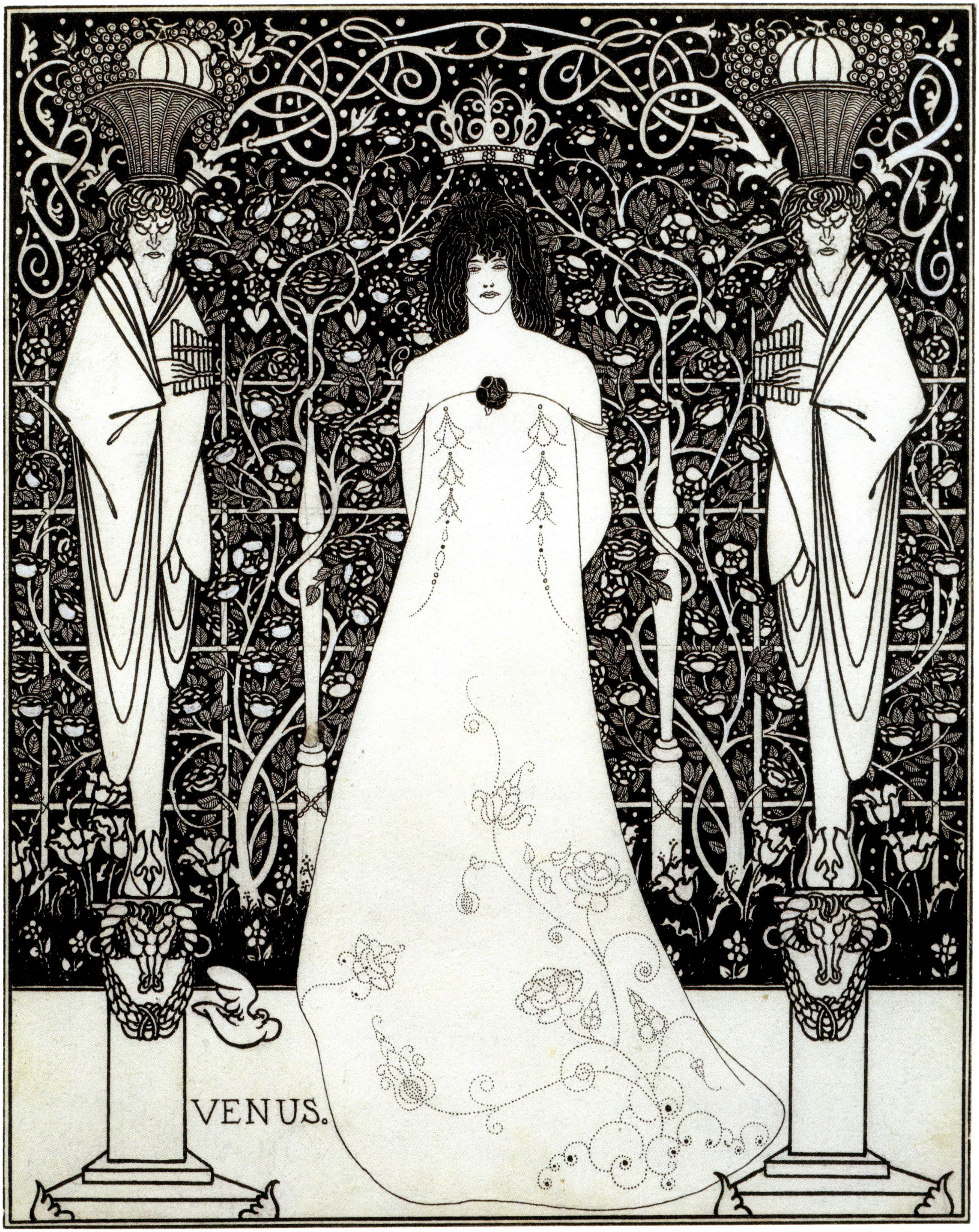
VENUS.

Sir Max BEERBOHM

[1872–1956]

Mr. Mortimer Menpes, closeted with Mr. Raymond Blaithwayt in whose benefit he evaluates an Almond Blossom, 1908

watercolour and pencil on paper, 33.1 × 26.7 cm
inscribed: *Max 1908* and title as above

P.145
PROVENANCE: The Leicester Galleries; from whom purchased by Gallery, December 1957.
EXHIBITIONS: *Beerbohm Memorial Exhibition*, London, Leicester Galleries, 1957, no.168; *The English Tradition, an exhibition of watercolours from two private collections*, Bedford, Cecil Higgins Art Gallery, 1972, no.5.
REFERENCES: R. Hart-Davis, *A Catalogue of the Caricatures of Max Beerbohm*, 1972, p.100, no.1027.

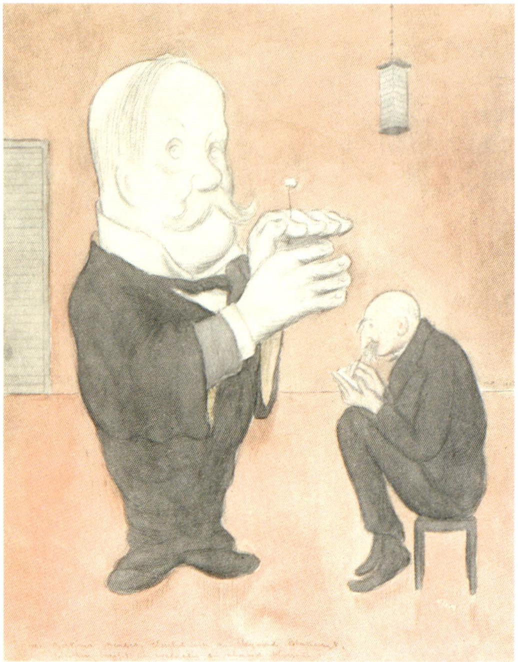

Mortimer Menpes (1859–1938) was an Australian artist and one-time follower and associate of WHISTLER. He later gave up painting in favour of market gardening in Pangbourne. Raymond Blaithwayt (1855–1935) was a journalist who appears by himself in two other Beerbohm cartoons (Hart-Davis, nos. 152/3).

Writer and caricaturist, Beerbohm's urbane wit captures the stylishness and spirit of the 1890s and the Edwardian era. He contributed to *The Yellow Book* and was dubbed the 'incomparable Max' by Bernard Shaw (1856–1950). Knighted in 1939 he had already been living for many years in Rapallo, Italy, where he died.

EJ/CB

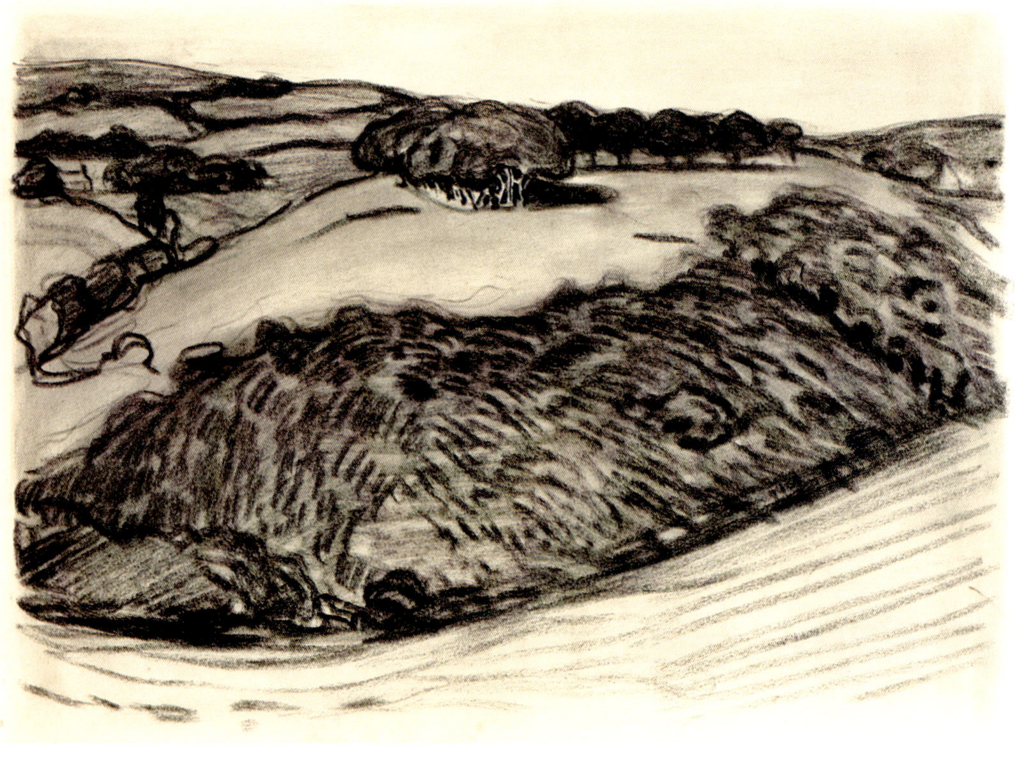

Robert Polhill BEVAN

[1865–1925]

The Big Covert, c.1912–15

charcoal on paper, 25 × 35.2 cm
inscribed: monogram *RPB* studio stamp

P.290
PROVENANCE: P&D Colnaghi Ltd; from whom purchased by Gallery, April 1959.
EXHIBITIONS: *An Exhibition of Drawings and Lithographs by Robert Bevan*, London, P&D Colnaghi Ltd, 1959, no.9; *The Camden Town Group*, Bedford, Cecil Higgins Art Gallery, 1969, no.6.

Possibly a scene on Exmoor or in the Blackdown Hills, on the borders of Somerset and Devon. Bevan spent every summer but two in the Blackdown Hills, from 1912 to 1925. He stayed with the retired Argentinian rancher Harold Bertram Harrison, who had built a studio onto his property to give artists an opportunity to paint there.

EJ

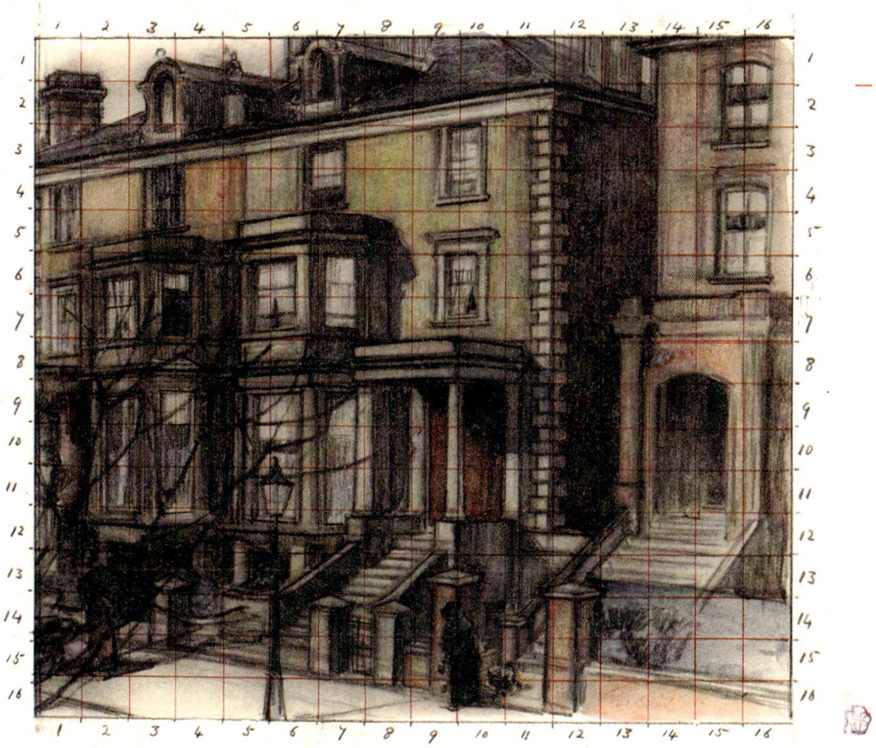

Robert Polhill BEVAN

[1865–1925]

Adamson Road, Hampstead, c.1915

pastel, wash and ink on paper, 25.1 × 28.8 cm
inscribed: monogram *RPB* studio stamp

P.289
PROVENANCE: The artist; sold to P&D Colnaghi Ltd; purchased by Gallery, April 1959.
EXHIBITIONS: *The Camden Town Group*, Bedford, Cecil Higgins Art Gallery, 1969, no.5.
REFERENCES: J. Rimmer, *Robert Bevan, Swiss Cottage and the Urban Landscape*, Leicester, De Montfort University, 1993.

In 1900 Bevan moved to 14 Adamson Road in Hampstead. This drawing was made from the front room of his house as a study for the oil painting, *Houses in Sunlight*. The drawing is squared for transfer to canvas and was used for the oil.

Bevan was a painter of horses, market scenes and landscapes. He studied at the Westminster School of Art and in Paris. In 1894 he met Paul Gauguin (1848–1903) in Brittany, whose influence appears in some early paintings. He joined SICKERT's circle in Fitzroy Street in 1908 and was a founder member of the Camden Town Group, 1911, of the London Group, 1913 and of the Cumberland Market Group, 1915. His best pictures are the *Cab Yard* series of c.1910 executed from drawings in a Neo-Impressionist manner.

EJ/CB

Peter BLAKE, R.A.

[b. 1932]

Mabel Stark, an 80 year-old Lion Tamer, 1963

bodycolour, pencil and coloured pencils on paper, 27.3 × 20.3 cm
inscribed: *Peter Blake Nov.1963*
on reverse: *Mabel Stark. 80 year old Animal Tamer at Jungle-land. Los Angeles Nov 1963*

P.486
PROVENANCE: Robert Fraser Gallery; purchased by Gallery, January 1965.
EXHIBITIONS: *Peter Blake*, Bristol, Bristol Art Gallery, 1969, no.94; *Peter Blake*, London, Tate Gallery, 1983, no.222.
REFERENCES: Sunday Times Colour Magazine, 15 November 1964.

Mabel Stark kept the Circus World Zoo in Los Angeles, where animals that had starred in films were exhibited. Although Blake met her, this drawing was made from a postcard.

Peter Blake's early pictures showed boys and girls with their comics, badges and other symbols (see also his *Self-Portrait with Badges* of 1961 in the collection of Tate Britain). Then he moved on to film stars and pop singers becoming a 'POP' artist before the label was coined. Many of his pictures derive from photographs and are worked on over long periods. They contain a strong element of fantasy yet remain compellingly convincing.

EJ

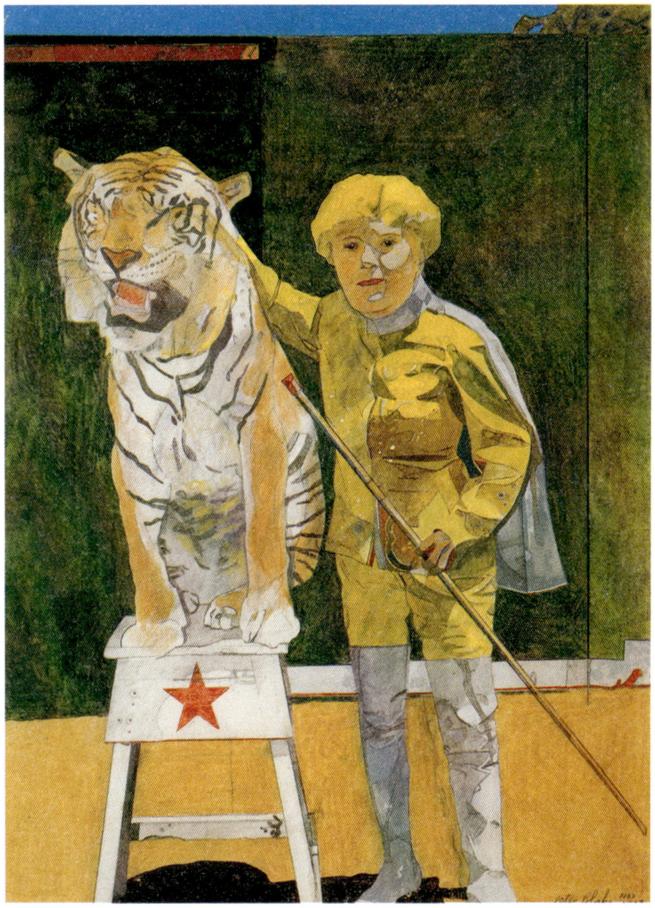

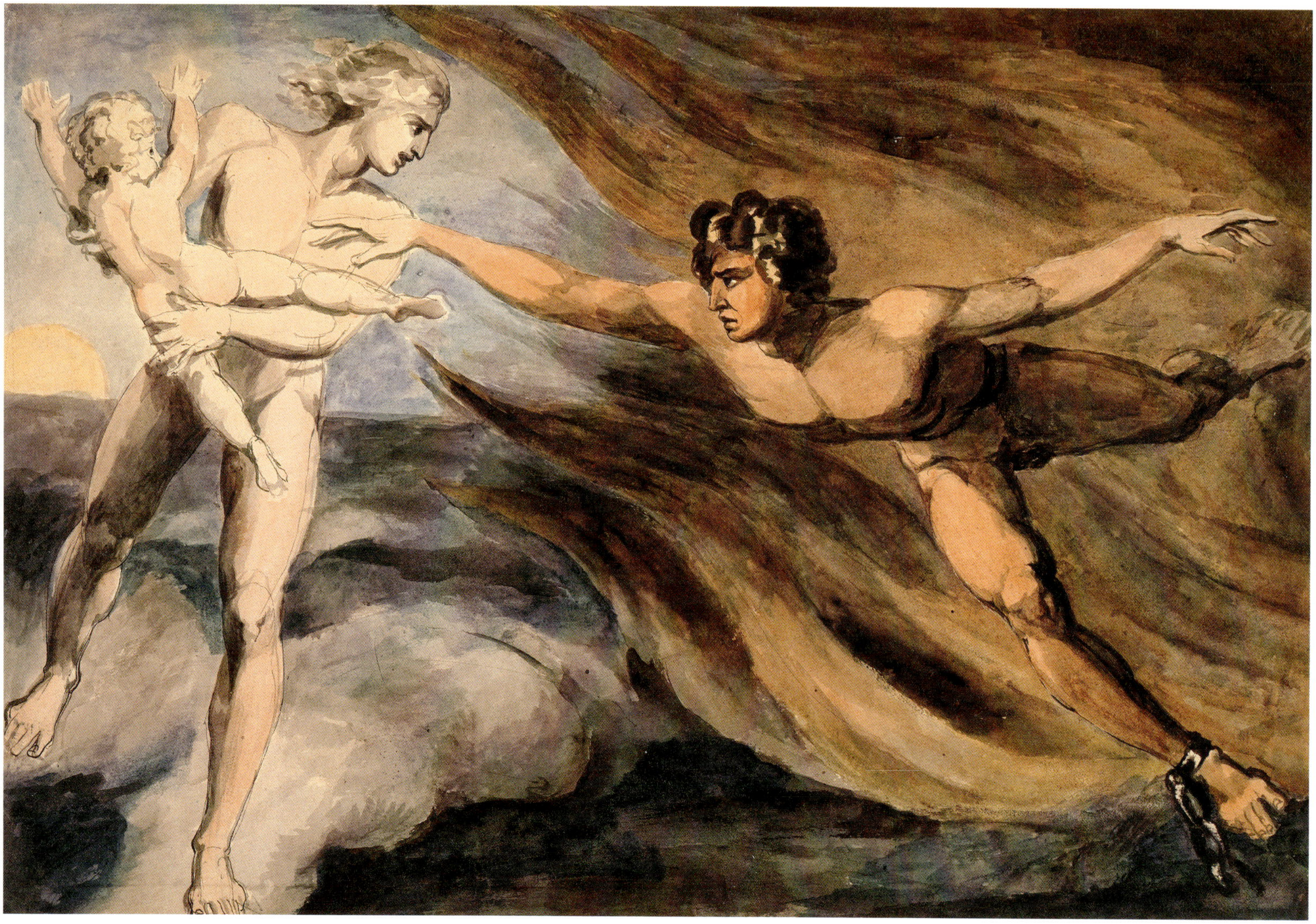

William BLAKE

[1757–1827]

The Good and Evil Angels Struggling for Possession of a Child, c.1793–4

pen and watercolour on paper, 29.5 × 44.2 cm
inscribed on reverse: *£5–5*

P.272

PROVENANCE: Mrs. Blake; sold to C.A. Tulk or brother-in-law Sigismund Stolterforth; by descent to Mrs. Gladys Nottidge; Sotheby's 10 December 1958, lot 95, bought by P&D Colnaghi Ltd, for the Gallery.

EXHIBITIONS: *William Blake and his Circle*, London, British Museum, 1958, no.5; *Watercolours and Drawings from The Cecil Higgins Art Gallery Bedford,* London, Thos. Agnew & Sons Ltd, 1962, no.28; *The English Tradition*, Bedford, Cecil Higgins Art Gallery, 1972, no.6; *William Wordsworth and the Age of English Romanticism*, Chicago, Chicago Historical Society, 1988, no.47; *Innocence and Experience: images of children in British Art from 1600 to the present*, Manchester, Manchester City Art Gallery, 1992, no.53.

REFERENCES: M. Butlin, 'The Bicentenary of William Blake', *Burlington Magazine,* vol.C, 1958, pp.41–2, ill. p.45 fig. 3; A. Blunt, *The Art of William Blake*, 1959, p.42, 61 & 62, pl. 32a; M. Butlin ,'Blakes Vala, or the Four Zoas and a new Water-colour in the Tate Gallery', *Burlington Magazine*, vol. CVI, 1964, pp.381–382; J. Beer, *Blake's Humanism*, 1968, pp. 192, 256, ill. 30b; G.E. Bentley, *Blake Records*, 1969, pp.353–4; D. Bindman, *Blake as an Artist*, 1977, p.69; M. Butlin, *The Paintings and Drawings of William Blake*, 1981, vol. I, p.130, no.257; vol. II, pl.197; R. Lester, *The Paintings of William Blake,* 1986, no.8.

This is a slightly later development of the design on plate IV of *The Marriage of Heaven and Hell*, dated 1790 on one copy but almost certainly not completed until 1793. The watercolour was the basis for the large colour print of 1795 which is in reverse, and must have been painted between these two dates.

A complex stylistic and iconographic link with the watercolour of *Los and Orc* (Butlin no.225) makes it possible to identify the tethered figure as Orc and the figure holding the child as Los. The figure of the child and its relationship to the 'Good' Angel, and indeed the general composition, are close to Blake's engraving after Stothard for one of the illustrations to Joseph Ritson's *Select Collection of English Songs*, 1793, I, p.170.

EJ

William BLAKE

[1757–1827]

David Pardoning Absalom, c.1800–03

pen and watercolour over black lead on paper, 41.3 × 42.2 cm
inscribed: *WB inv II Samuel. XIV c.33 v.*
in Blake's hand: *And Joab brought Absalom to the King and the King kissed Absalom*

P.114

PROVENANCE: Thomas Butts; Thomas Butts, jun.; Capt. F.J. Butts, Sotheby's, 24 June 1903, lot 9; bought by Hamlett; sold by his widow; Carfax Gallery; W. Graham Robertson; Christies 22 July 1949, lot 15; Leger Galleries; purchased by Gallery, January 1957.

EXHIBITIONS: *The Works of William Blake*, London, Burlington Fine Arts Club, 1876, no.62; *Works by William Blake*, London, Carfax Gallery, 1904, no.39; *Frescoes, Prints and Drawings by William Blake*, London, Carfax Gallery, 1906, no.68; *Watercolours from The Cecil Higgins Art Gallery Bedford*, London, Thos. Agnew & Sons Ltd, 1962, no.26.

REFERENCES: W.M. Rossetti, *Annotated Catalogue of Blake's Pictures and Drawings,* in vol. II of Gilchrist's biography, 1863, p.225, no.126; 1880, p.132, no.47; K. Preston, *The Blake Collection of W. Graham Robertson by the Collector,* 1952, p.132, no.47; G. Keynes, *William Blake's Illustrations to the Bible,* 1957, p.18, no.61 repr.; A. Blunt, *The Art of William Blake,* 1959, p.71; M.D. Paley, *William Blake,* 1978, pl.74; M. Butlin, *The Paintings and Drawings of William Blake,* 1981, vol. I, p.346, no.459; vol. II, pl.540; T. Wright, *The Life of William Blake*, vol. II, pl.62; L. Herrmann, *Nineteenth Century British Painting,* 2000, pp.71–2, fig.52.

Absalom, King David's favourite son, spent several years in exile for the murder of his half-brother before being restored to favour through the intercession of Joab, his father's most highly regarded general.

Blake was the most imaginative and singular of all major British artists and was, moreover, as gifted a poet as a painter. He was, however, first trained as an engraver and apprenticed to James Basire (1730–1802) in 1772–9, but his reputation is due to the visionary quality (he frequently saw angels) of his illuminated books and watercolours and upon his experimental printmaking.

His originality springs – in David Bindman's words – 'from his religious attitudes, in his conception of the true artist as a prophet in the Old Testament tradition, granted the obligation to show mankind the way to redemption'. He met with little success until 1818 when LINNELL commissioned watercolours from him to illustrate the book of Job. Linnell was joined by VARLEY, Samuel PALMER, Edward Calvert (1803–83) and George Richmond (1809–96), in admiration of Blake, which cheered his last years.

EJ

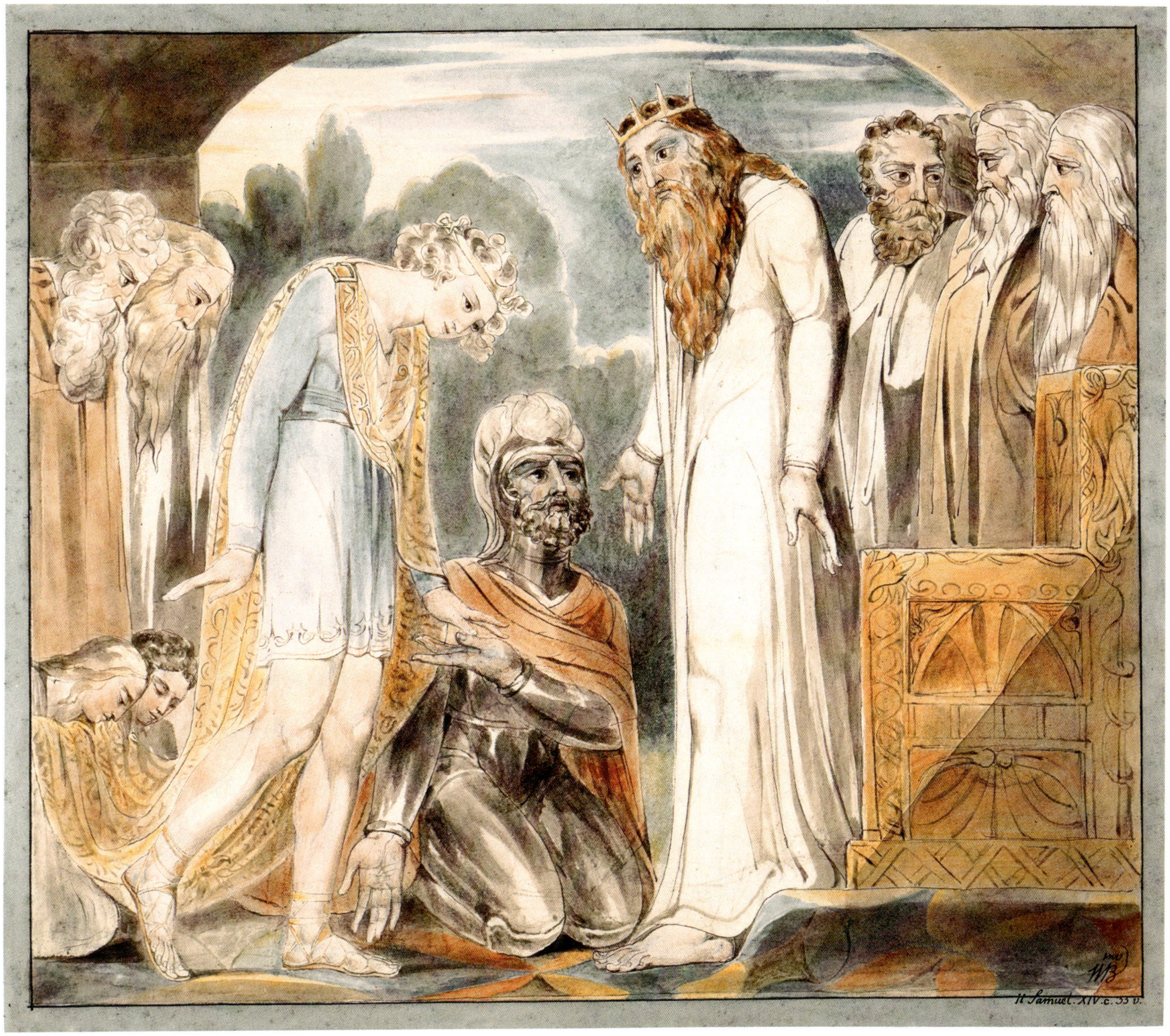

Martin BLOCH

[1883–1954]

Portrait of the artist's wife, Charlotte, c.1921

pen, ink and watercolour on paper, 25 × 20 cm

P.665

PROVENANCE: The artist; Mrs. Bloch; given to Gallery, December 1975.
EXHIBITIONS: *Martin Bloch Retrospective*, London, Crane Kalman Gallery, 1974.

Bloch was an Anglo-German Expressionist painter, born in Silesia. He studied under Heinrich Wölfflin (1864–1945) in Munich and Lovis Corinth (1858–1925) in Berlin.

Exhibiting with the Expressionists in Germany, 1920–33, he was labelled as a 'degenerate' artist by the Nazis and was one of the first refugees to arrive from Germany settling in England in 1939. He painted mainly in London, Dorset and Wales (from 1939) and became a naturalized British subject in 1947.

Josef HERMAN told a former Curator, in January 1992, that he had offered Bloch the use of his studio after Bloch's was bombed in the war and that Bloch was extremely difficult to work with.

Charlotte Bloch was first married to a theatre manager and had her own box. She was a great beauty and felt that, in marrying Bloch, she had gone down socially. Her attempts to improve his social graces and awareness were apparently unsuccessful.

EJ/CB

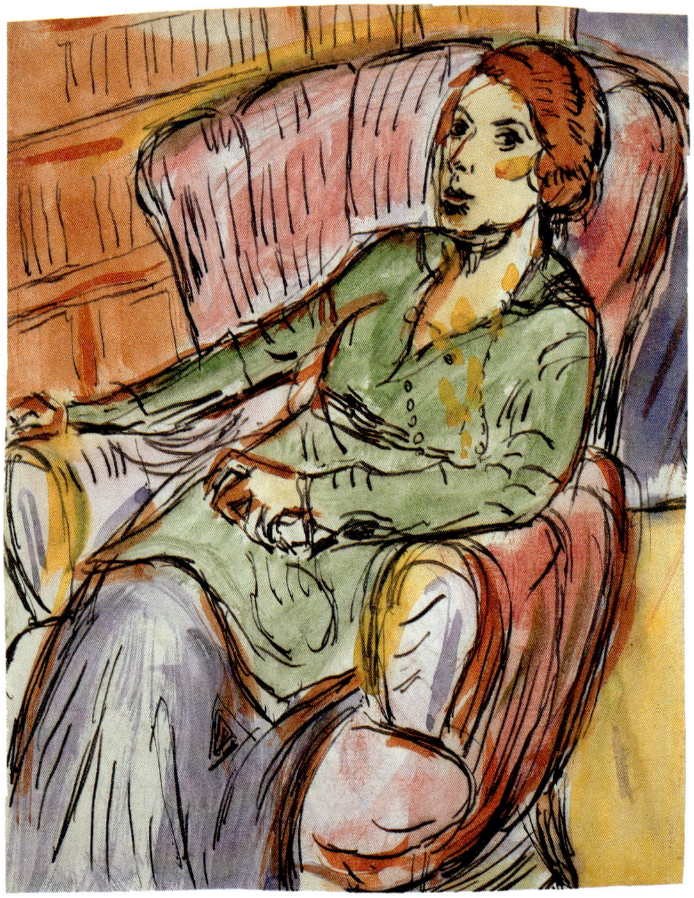

David BOMBERG

[1890–1957]

Cubist study for **The Dancer.** Cover for John Rodker's Poems, **1913–14**

watercolour and charcoal on paper, 37.7 × 27.5 cm
inscribed: *David Bomberg*
on reverse: *Cubist period Painting probably for 'The Dances' cover John Rodker poems 1914 authenticated by David Bomberg*
similar charcoal sketch of a dancer

P.561

PROVENANCE: Purchased from Marlborough Fine Art, March 1967.
EXHIBITIONS: *Vorticism and its Allies*, London, Hayward Gallery, 1974, no.366; *Abstraction: Towards a New Art. Painting 1910–20*, London, Tate Gallery, 1980, no.402; *Futurismo & Futurismi*, Venice, Palazzo Grassi, 1986, cat. P.295; *Art in Performance – Performance in Art*, Nottingham, Castle Museum, 1987, no.3; *David Bomberg*, London, Tate Gallery, 1988, no. 49; *Herbert Read*, Leeds, City Art Galleries, 1994, no.27; *Blast: Vortizismus – Die erste Avantgarde in England 1914–1918*, Hannover, Sprengel Museum & Munich, Haus der Kunst, 1996–7, no.17, p.146.
REFERENCES: B. Read & D. Thistlewood (eds.), *Herbert Read: A British Vision of World Art*, 1993, p.169; *Blast: Vortizismus – Die Erste Avantgarde In England 1914–18*, 1996, p.146.

The poet John Rodker (1884–1955) spent the First World War in hiding as a conscientious objector. His interest in dance stems from his relationship with the dancer Sonia Cohen, with whom he had lived and had a child.

Bomberg was also a friend of Sonia Cohen, who danced outdoors on the south coast cliff-tops with Margaret Morris (1891–1980). His prolonged sequence of exhilarating *Dancer* watercolours seems to have originated in their friendship. In 1915 Alice Mayes (1880–1973), also a dancer, came to live with Bomberg and later became his first wife. Writing on his approach to drawing Bomberg said: 'The most satisfactory definition of Drawing I have found is the one that defines Drawing as the representation of form – Not the representation of appearances of form, but more the representation of all our feelings about a form'.

In July 1914 Bomberg staged a one-man show at the Chenil Gallery, Chelsea, London, with a militant foreword in which he championed *Pure Form*. In 1915 he exhibited at the *Vorticist Exhibition*. However, when his work dating from 1914 was included in the Tate Gallery's exhibition *Wyndham Lewis and the Vorticists* of 1956, Bomberg was outraged by the misrepresentation of his work of this period.

EJ/CB

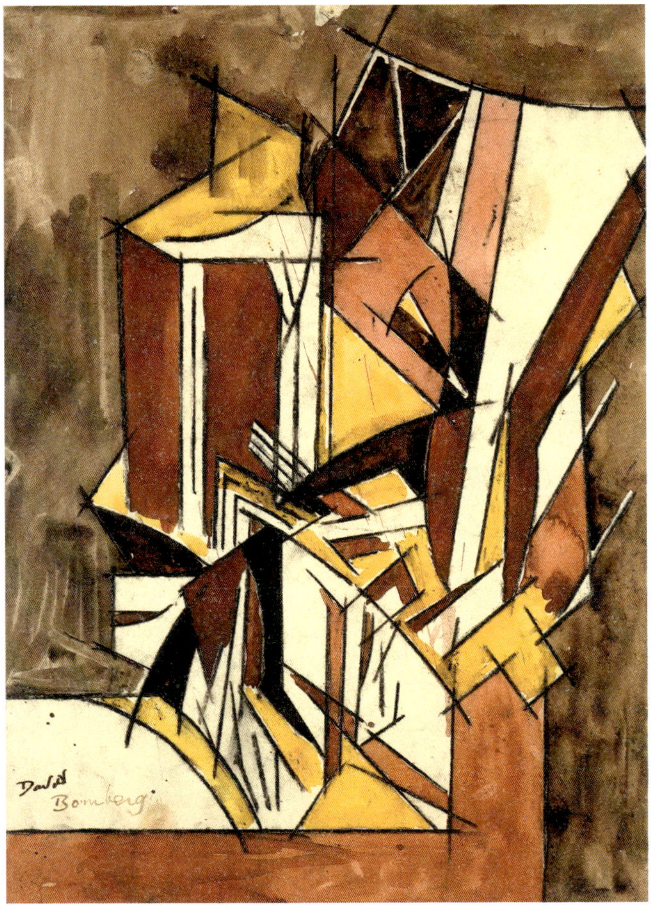

David BOMBERG

[1890–1957]

Across the Valley, Ronda, 1954

charcoal on paper, 46.6 × 61.9 cm
inscribed: *Bomberg 54*

P.560
PROVENANCE: Mrs Bomberg (artist's widow); purchased from Marlborough Fine Art, March 1967.
EXHIBITIONS: *David Bomberg*, London, Tate Gallery, 1988, no. 184; *Figurative Painting of London*, Mexico, Museo de Arte Moderno & Museo de Monterrey, 2000, no.4.

Ronda, some 40 miles west of Malaga, is one of the most dramatically situated towns in Spain, spanning a deep gorge over the river Guadalgorce. It inspired some of Bomberg's finest landscapes.

Bomberg, born in Birmingham, was the son of a leather craftsman from Poland. He was initially apprenticed to a lithographer, but a chance meeting with John Singer SARGENT in the Sculpture gallery at the V&A inspired him to study at the Westminster School of Art under SICKERT in 1908–10 and at the Slade, 1911–13. He travelled widely – particularly to Spain in 1912, 1934–5 and 1954–6 when he made this drawing.

Considered as among the very finest British painters of his time, Bomberg, unable to show or sell his work, was driven by poverty to teach from 1944 onwards. At the Borough Polytechnic he proved to be an inspiring and influential teacher, AUERBACH and KOSSOFF being two of his students. In 1954 he and his wife Lillian moved to Spain with a view to founding an art school in the Ronda region but this proved unsuccessful. Lillian collapsed under the strain and Bomberg returned to Britain, where he died a year later. Bomberg wrote: 'Drawing flows from beginning to end with one sustained impulse…The approach is through feeling and touch and less by sight…Drawing…reveals the unknown things. Style is ephemeral – Form is eternal'.

EJ/CB

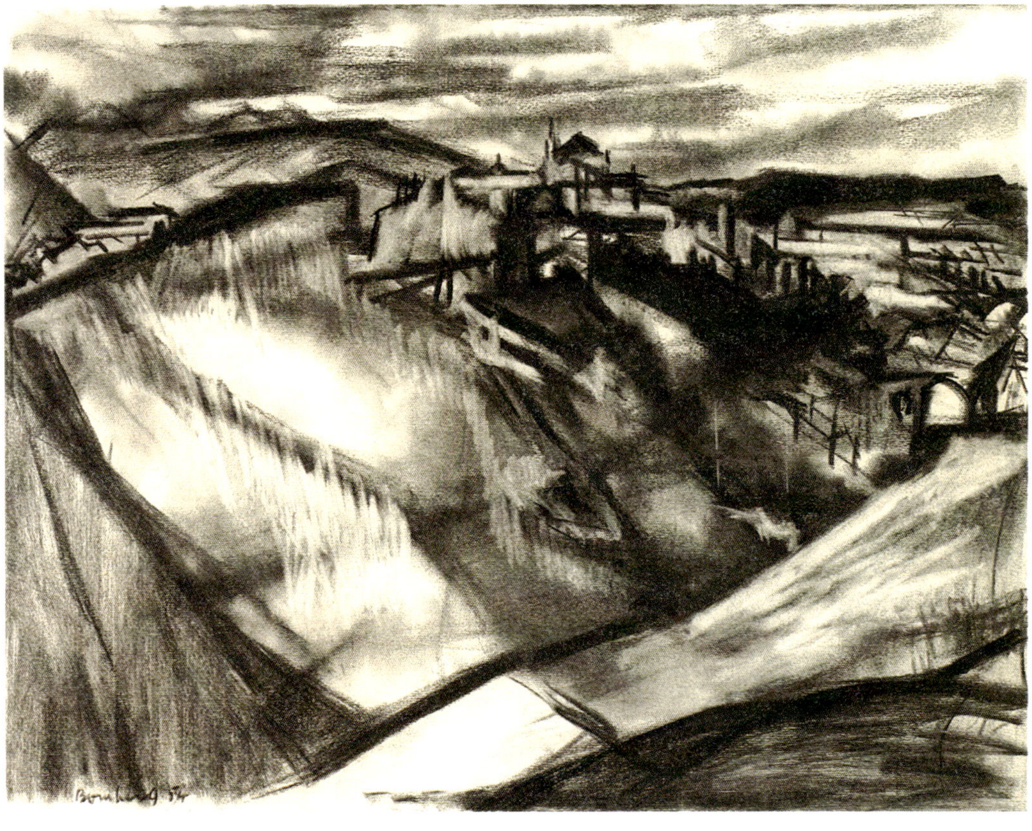

Richard Parkes BONINGTON

[1802–28]

Pile Drivers, Rouen, 1821–2

black lead on grey wove paper, 35.8 × 26.4 cm
inscribed: *R.P.B.*

P.415
PROVENANCE: Sutton Palmer; Dr John Percy (Lugt 1504); Dr John Percy; Christie's 22 April 1890, lot 102 as *Harbour Scene;* Kidson; O'Byrne; Christie's 3 April 1962, lot 50, purchased by Gallery.
EXHIBITIONS: *Watercolours and Drawings from the Cecil Higgins Art Gallery Bedford,* London, Thos. Agnew & Sons Ltd, 1962, no.23; *R. P. Bonington,* Nottingham, Castle Museum and Art Gallery, 1965, no.48; *Bonington,* Cherbourg, Musée des Beaux-Arts, 1966, no.20; *Richard Parkes Bonington 'On the Pleasure of Painting',* New Haven, Yale Center for British Art, Paris, Petit Palais, 1992, no.11.
REFERENCES: M. Cormack, *Bonington,* 1989, p.34, pl.19, P. Noon, *Richard Parkes Bonington 'On the Pleasure of Painting',* 1991, p.95.

This was sketched at Rouen in 1821, a preliminary study for the slightly later and considerably larger watercolour in the Fitzwilliam Museum, Cambridge, commissioned by a 'Miss C.' for two hundred francs. There is also a watercolour version of the same size in the British Museum.

A critic in the *New Monthly Magazine* (1 August 1829), reviewing Bonington's studio sale, praised the rough sketches of pile-driving etc. where 'it appears as though he had arrested the figures in their progress and transferred then to his paper, there is so much life and reality about them'.

EJ

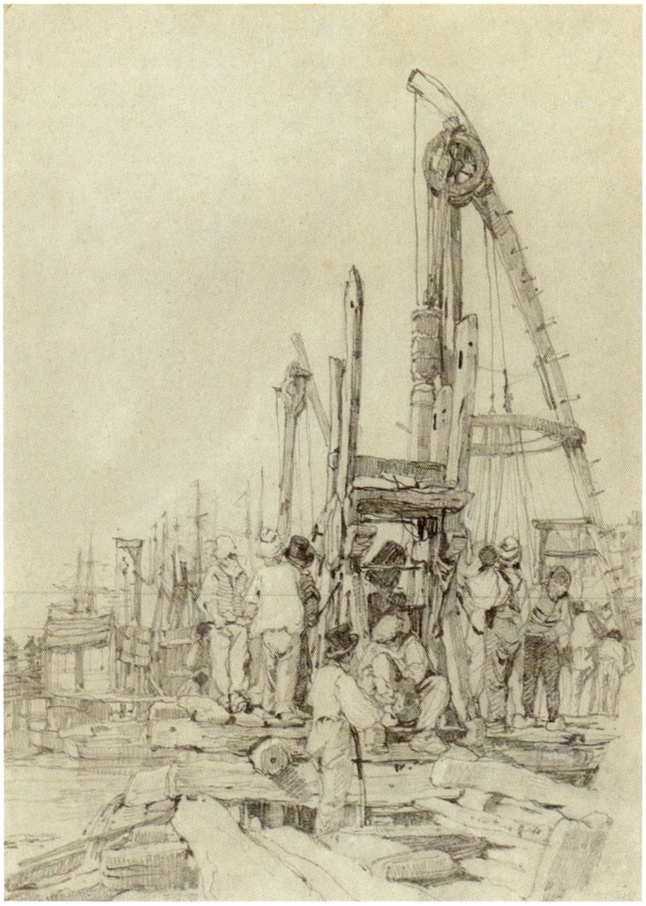

Richard Parkes BONINGTON

[1802–28]

Palace of the Tuileries, Paris

watercolour on paper, 25.5 × 19 cm

P.569
PROVENANCE: Thos. Agnew & Sons Ltd.; William Yates; his sale Sotheby's 19 October 1967, lot no.27, bought by Thos. Agnew & Sons Ltd for the Gallery.
EXHIBITIONS: *Loan exhibition of watercolour drawings by deceased British Artists,* Manchester, Whitworth Art Gallery, 1912, no.159; *Bonington,* Nottingham, Nottingham Castle Museum, 1965, no.225.

Patrick Noon has suggested that this watercolour might be a copy by Thomas Shotter BOYS of a lost Bonington watercolour. There is a watercolour of this scene by Boys, now in the Fitzwilliam Museum, Cambridge; this was among the twenty-five plates lithographed in Boys' *Picturesque Architecture in Paris, Ghent, Antwerp and Rouen*, 1839.

After Bonington's death, his father had copies of his son's work made and sold them. The art of the nineteenth century copyist was frequently employed, not as an attempt to produce a deliberate fake, but as a means to recreate a faithful reproduction.

EJ/CB

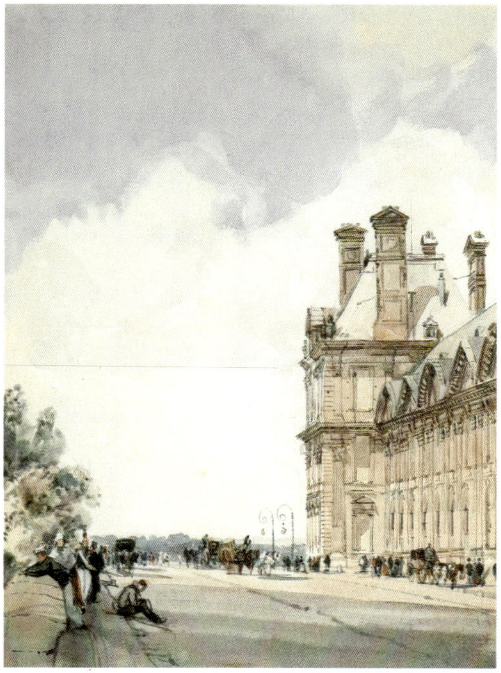

Richard Parkes BONINGTON

[1802–28]

L'Institut, Paris, 1828

pencil, chalk and bodycolour on grey paper, 35.1 × 26.7 cm

P.582
PROVENANCE: Bonington sale 1829, lot 51, as *View of the Ecole des Arts, Paris, in pencil and chalk, very spirited,* bought Colnaghi; E. Martin; Fine Art Society, 1968, from whom purchased by Gallery with a Treasury Grant, May 1968.
EXHIBITIONS: *Richard Parkes Bonington 'On the Pleasure of Painting',* New Haven, Yale Center for British Art and Paris, Petit Palais, 1991–2, no.161.
REFERENCES: P. Noon, *Richard Parkes Bonington: 'On the Pleasure of Painting',* 1991, p.300–1, no.161.

Painted in the last few months of his life when suffering from tuberculosis, Bonington probably drew this while sitting in a carriage.

Considered to be one of his finest topographical drawings, this is borne out by the comparatively high price it fetched in 1829 (£26). It was evidently the study from which the pendant watercolour was made, now in the British Museum (Salting Bequest). An anomaly of both compositions is the absence of the Pont des Arts, the first iron bridge to be built over the Seine, which had been virtually completed by 1818. Bonington must have considered it compositionally disruptive.

Bonington spent much of his short life in France as his family moved in 1817–8 to Calais, where the boy studied with FRANCIA and later in Paris with Baron Gros (1771–1835). There he also became friends with Eugène Delacroix (1798–1863), who influenced his costume pictures. Delacroix wrote in 1856 that Bonington had ' a sense of mastery, sureness of touch going hand in hand with clear ideas'. Bonington's brilliant watercolours attracted a host of admirers and imitators in both France and England.

EJ

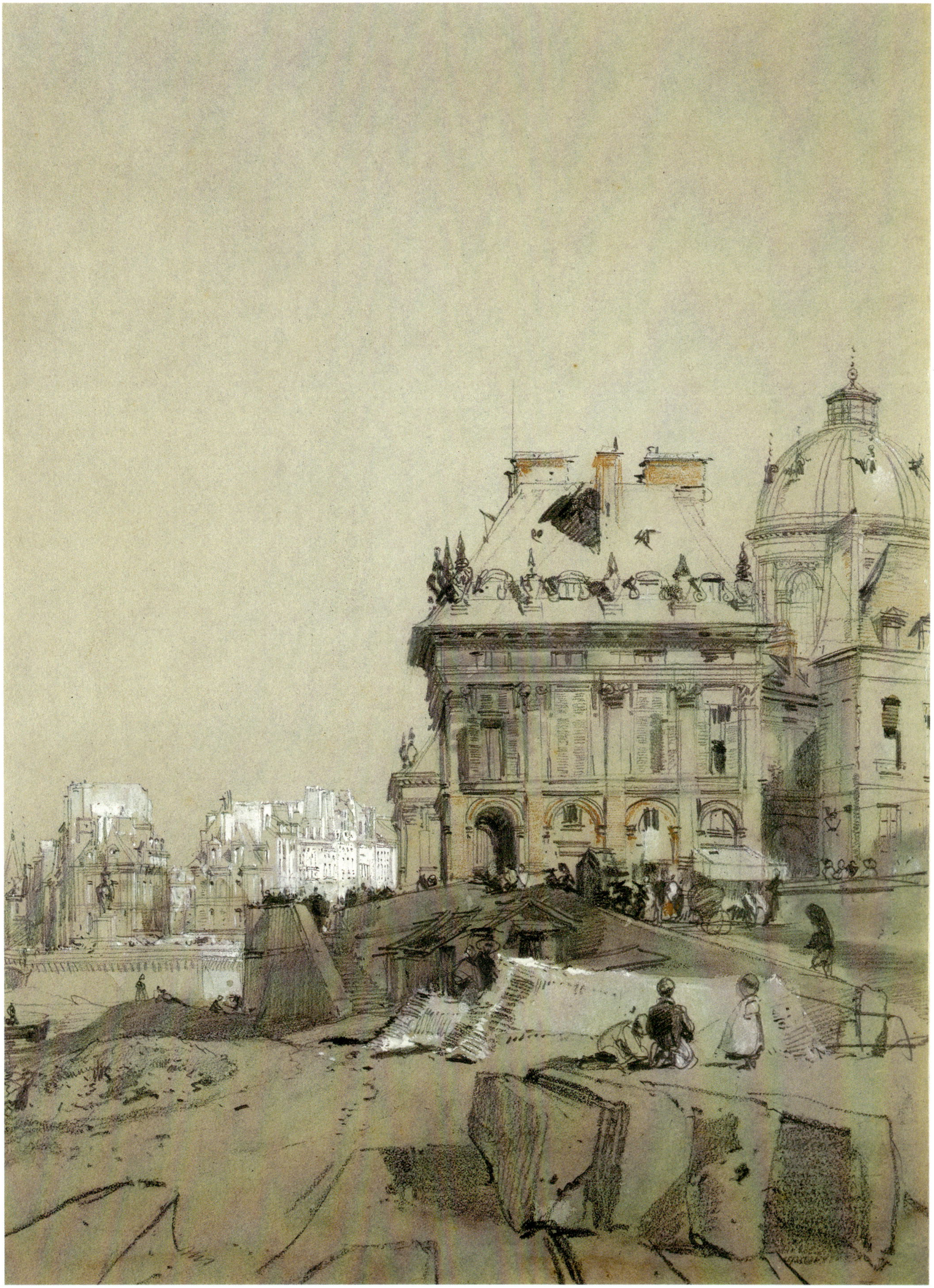

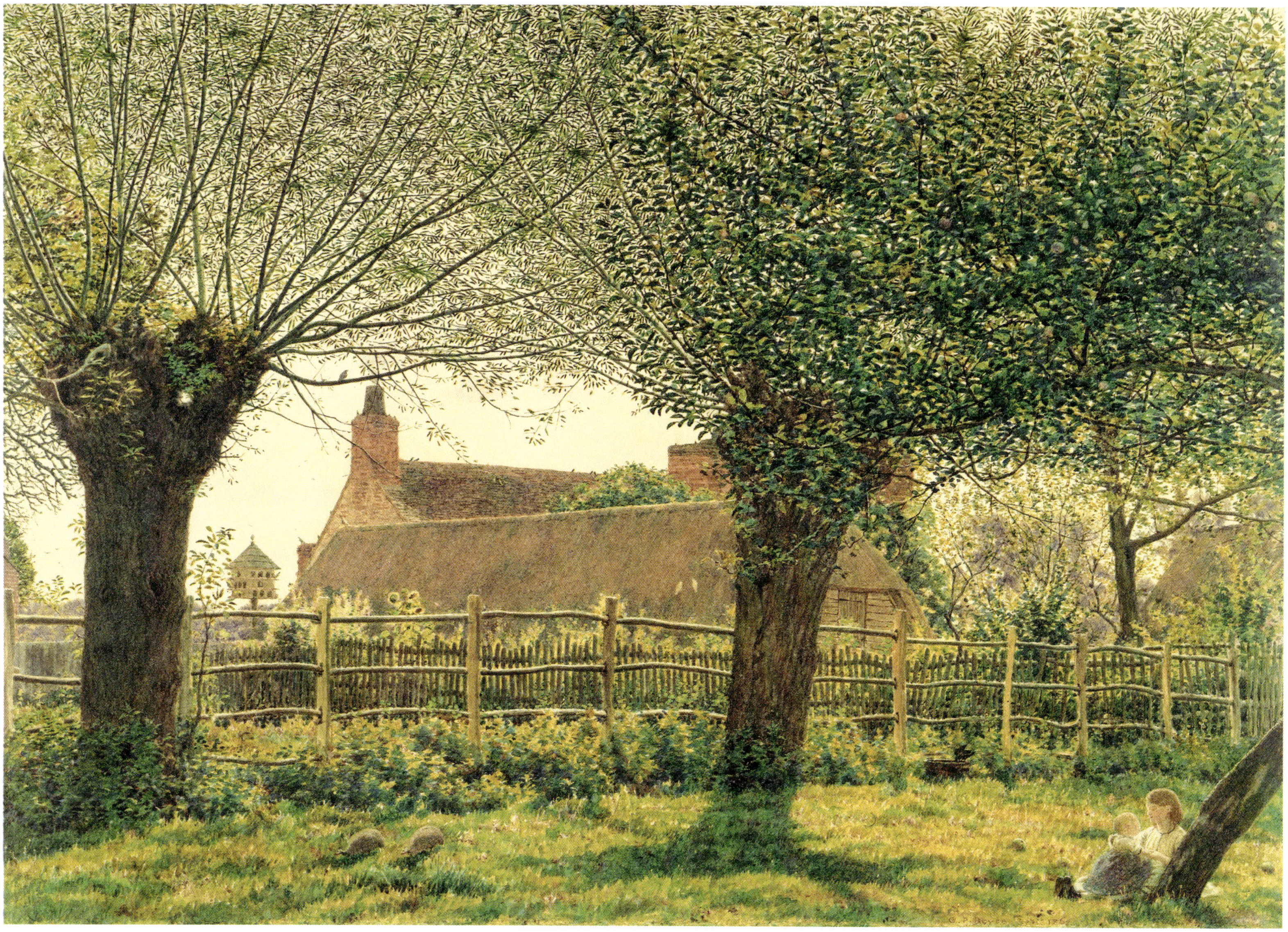

George Price BOYCE
[1826–97]
At Binsey, near Oxford, 1862

watercolour and ink on paper, 31.1 × 53.7 cm
inscribed: *G.P.Boyce Sep.1862*

P.188
PROVENANCE: Bought from the artist by J. Stewart Hodgson 1863; Robert Frank; Marquess of Sligo; P&D Colnaghi, from whom purchased by Gallery, April 1958.
EXHIBITIONS: *Paris Universal Exhibition*, 1867, no.8; *O.W.C.S. Summer Exhibition*, 1864, no.106; *George Price Boyce*, London, Tate Gallery, 1987, no.35; *Victorian Painting*, Munich, Neue Pinakothek Museum and Madrid, The Prado, 1993, no.57.
REFERENCES: A. Staley, *The Pre-Raphaelite Landscape*, 1973, p.109, pl.55b; G. Grigson, *Britain Observed*, 1975, p.138, pl.99; G. Reynolds, *English Watercolours*, 1988, pl.110; J. Treuherz, *Victorian Paintings*, 1993, pp.91–2, pl.61.

Boyce studied architecture on the Continent. A fortuitous meeting with David COX at Bettws-y-Coed in 1849 encouraged him to take up landscape painting.

From 1851 to 1875 Boyce kept a diary (extracts published in O.W.S. Club Vol.XIX, 1941) which gives us intimate pictures of RUSKIN, MILLAIS, Holman HUNT, William Morris (1834–96), Algernon Swinburne (1837–1909), WHISTLER and, above all, ROSSETTI. The meticulous style of Boyce's painting was clearly influenced by the Pre-Raphaelites.

The Tate exhibition catalogue by Christopher Newall and Judy Egerton quotes Staley's opinion that this is a very good example of 'the sense of intimacy' which Boyce gives his subjects by restricting the space he allows them.

EJ/CB

Thomas Shotter BOYS
[1803–74]
The Old Hôtel de Ville, St.Omer, 1832

watercolour and bodycolour on paper, 26.7 × 34.9 cm
inscribed: *Thos. Boys 1832*

P.56
PROVENANCE: Thos. Agnew & Sons Ltd; purchased by Gallery, January 1953.
EXHIBITIONS: *Watercolours and Drawings from the Cecil Higgins Art Gallery Bedford*, London, Thos. Agnew & Sons Ltd., 1962, no.32; *English Watercolours from The Cecil Higgins Art Gallery Bedford*, Reading, Reading Museum and Art Gallery, 1965, no.2.
REFERENCES: A. Bury, ' The Cecil Higgins Museum, Bedford: A Preliminary Survey' *Old Water-colour Society's Club*, vol. XXXVI, 1961, pp.31–40.

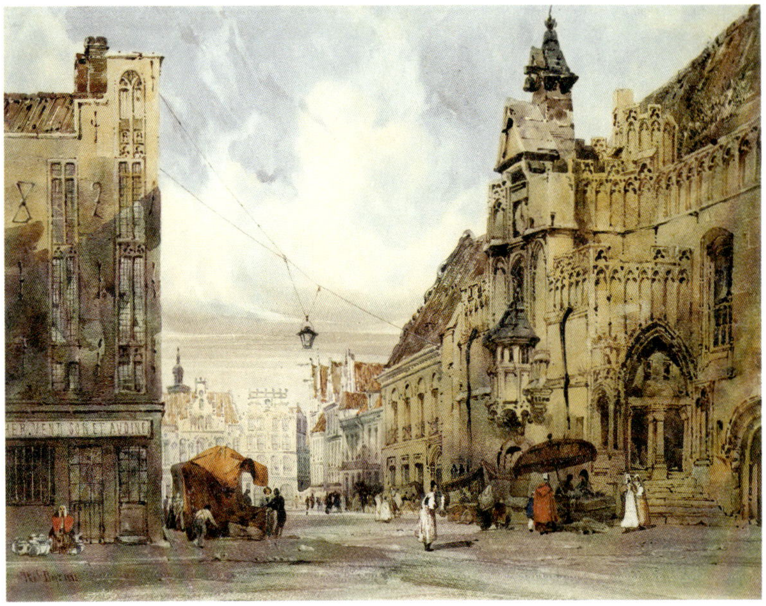

Another version is in the Birmingham City Art Gallery while yet another, but with composition in reverse, was sold from the Newall collection at Christie's 13 December 1979 (lot 8) and later exhibited at Agnew's *117th Annual Watercolour Exhibition*, 1990, (no.66). Finally, a view taken from the other direction, also painted in 1832, is in the Laing Art Gallery, Newcastle upon Tyne.

EJ

Thomas Shotter BOYS
[1803–74]
St.Laurent, Rouen, 1832

watercolour and bodycolour on paper, 31.7 × 25.1 cm
inscribed: *T. Boys 1832*
on reverse: *St Laurent, Rouen*

P.489
PROVENANCE: Alex A. Haworth, Blackburn; Richard Haworth; Sotheby's 10 March 1965, lot.68, purchased by Gallery.
REFERENCES: Lithographed with alterations in *Picturesque Architecture in Paris, Antwerp and Rouen*, 1839, pl. 9.

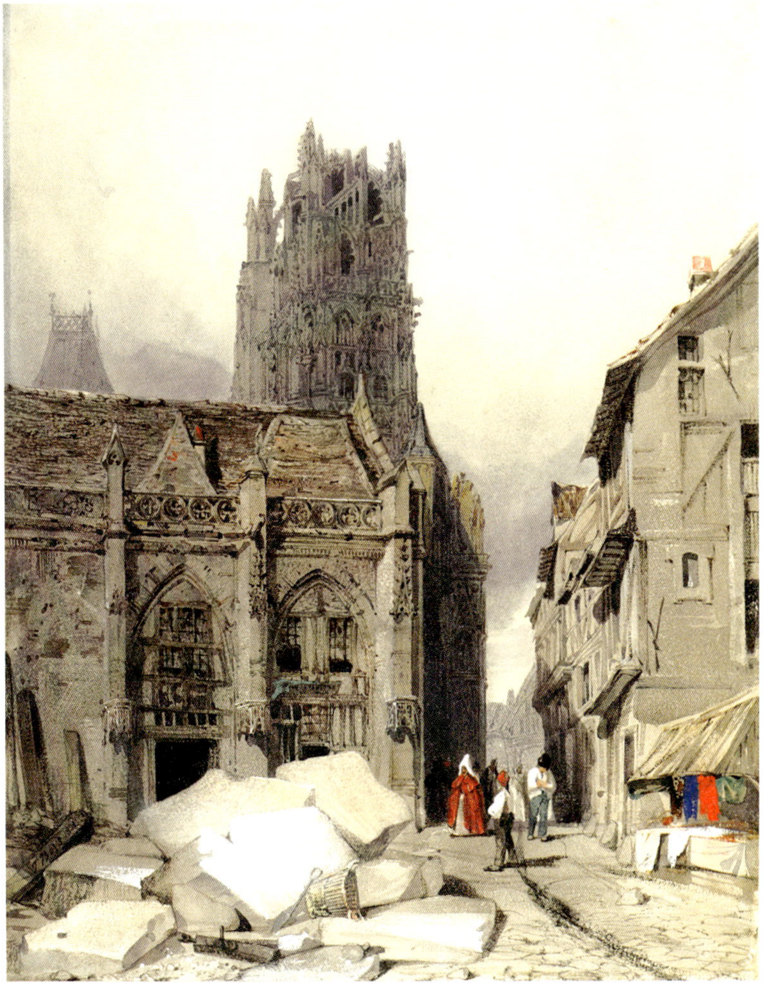

With some alterations, this was lithographed as plate IX in Boys' *Picturesque Architecture in Paris, Ghent, Antwerp and Rouen*, 1839, with twenty-six superb colour-plates. A writer in the *Quarterly Review* expressed surprise that '26 prints, equal in effect to watercolour paintings, could be bought for so small a sum as eight guineas'.

Only two months younger than BONINGTON, the two became friends in Paris in the mid-1820s. Boys' finest watercolours, of which this is a prime example, were painted 1830–5 and reveal his debt to Bonington's example. They were followed by the highly successful series of twenty coloured lithographs, *Original Views of London As It Is*, published in 1842, but his later works never equalled those of the decade 1830–40.

EJ

Hercules Brabazon BRABAZON
[1821–1906]
Constantinople ?

watercolour and bodycolour over black lead on paper,
13.3 × 16.5 cm
inscribed: *H.B.B.*
on reverse: *Constantinople ?*

P.137
PROVENANCE: Leger Galleries, from whom purchased by Gallery, November 1957.

Although Brabazon was the subject of a number of studies after he died, notably by D.S. MacColl and C.L. Hind, his work fell from favour until quite recently. Born in Paris, he was named Hercules Brabazon Sharpe. He gained a degree in Maths from Trinity College, Cambridge, but, against his father's wishes, travelled to Rome to study art and music. The first time he exhibited in public he was seventy.

Described as the 'ultra-impressionist', Brabazon was able to devote his life to his art due to an inheritance.

EJ/CB

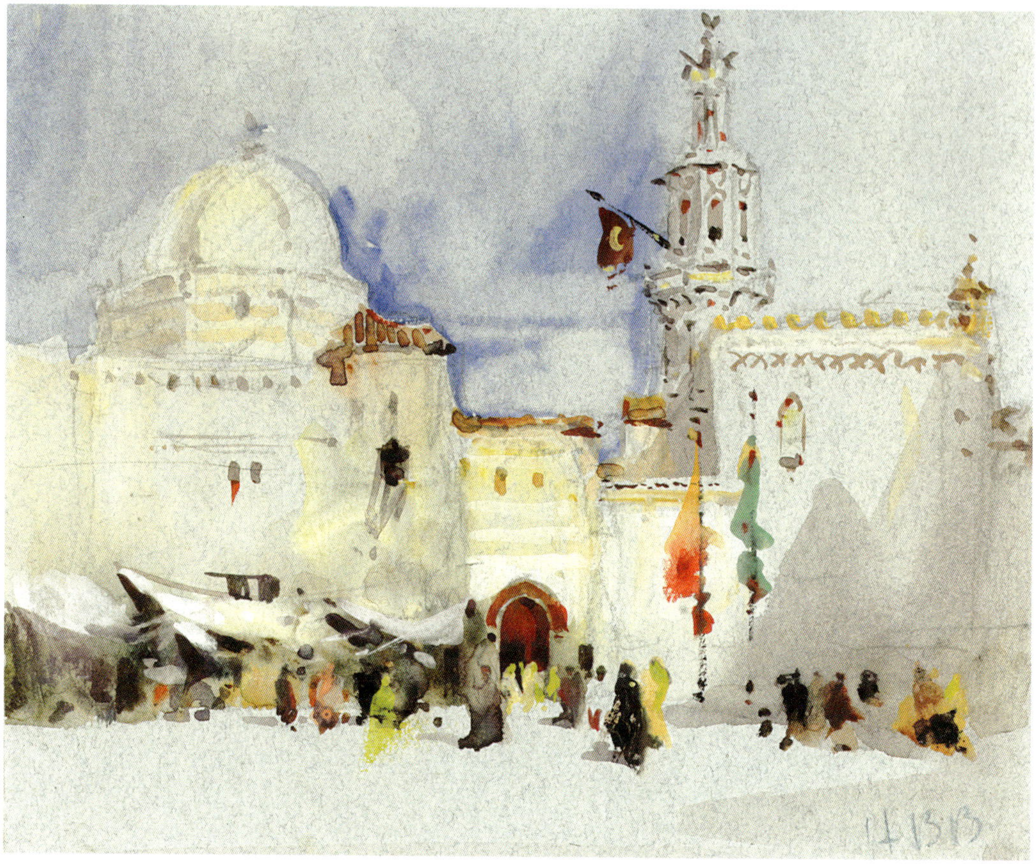

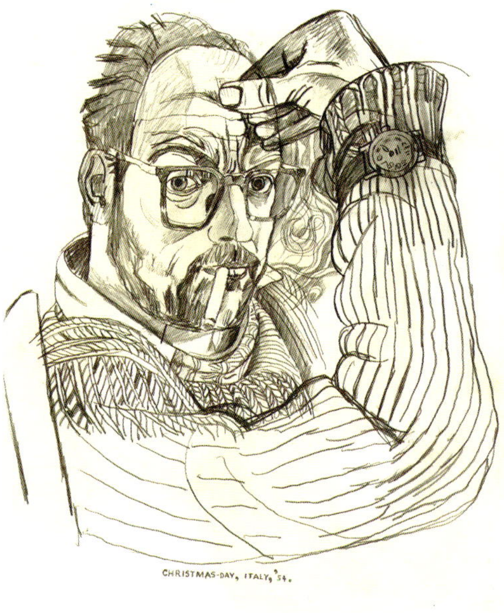

John BRATBY, R.A.
[1928–92]
Self-Portrait I, 1954

pencil on paper, 32 × 23.1 cm
inscribed: *Christmas-Day, Italy, '54.*

P.241
PROVENANCE: Beaux Arts Gallery, from whom purchased by Gallery, July 1958.
EXHIBITIONS: *Watercolours and Drawings from the Cecil Higgins Art Gallery, Bedford,* London, Thos. Agnew & Sons Ltd., 1962, no.95.

In a letter to the Gallery in 1986, Bratby commented that this was drawn in Rome while he was on a scholarship from the R.C.A. The drawing was done at the British School in Rome while Bratby was recovering from the effects of jaundice.

A painter of still-life, figure and landscape compositions. He studied at the R.C.A.from 1951–4. In 1953 he married the painter Jean Cooke who often appears in his pictures. He was included in the British Pavilion at the Venice Biennale 1956. Bratby also designed sets for the film of Joyce Cary's (1888–1957) novel *The Horse's Mouth* 1957–8. He was elected A.R.A in 1959.

Ronald Alley considered Bratby a leading figure in the post-war realist 'kitchen-sink' school, together with John Osborne (1929–94) and Kingsley Amis (1922–95), and noted that this uncompromising self-portrait reflects something of the mood of the period. The artist Carel Weight considered him the most talented student he ever taught.

EJ/CB

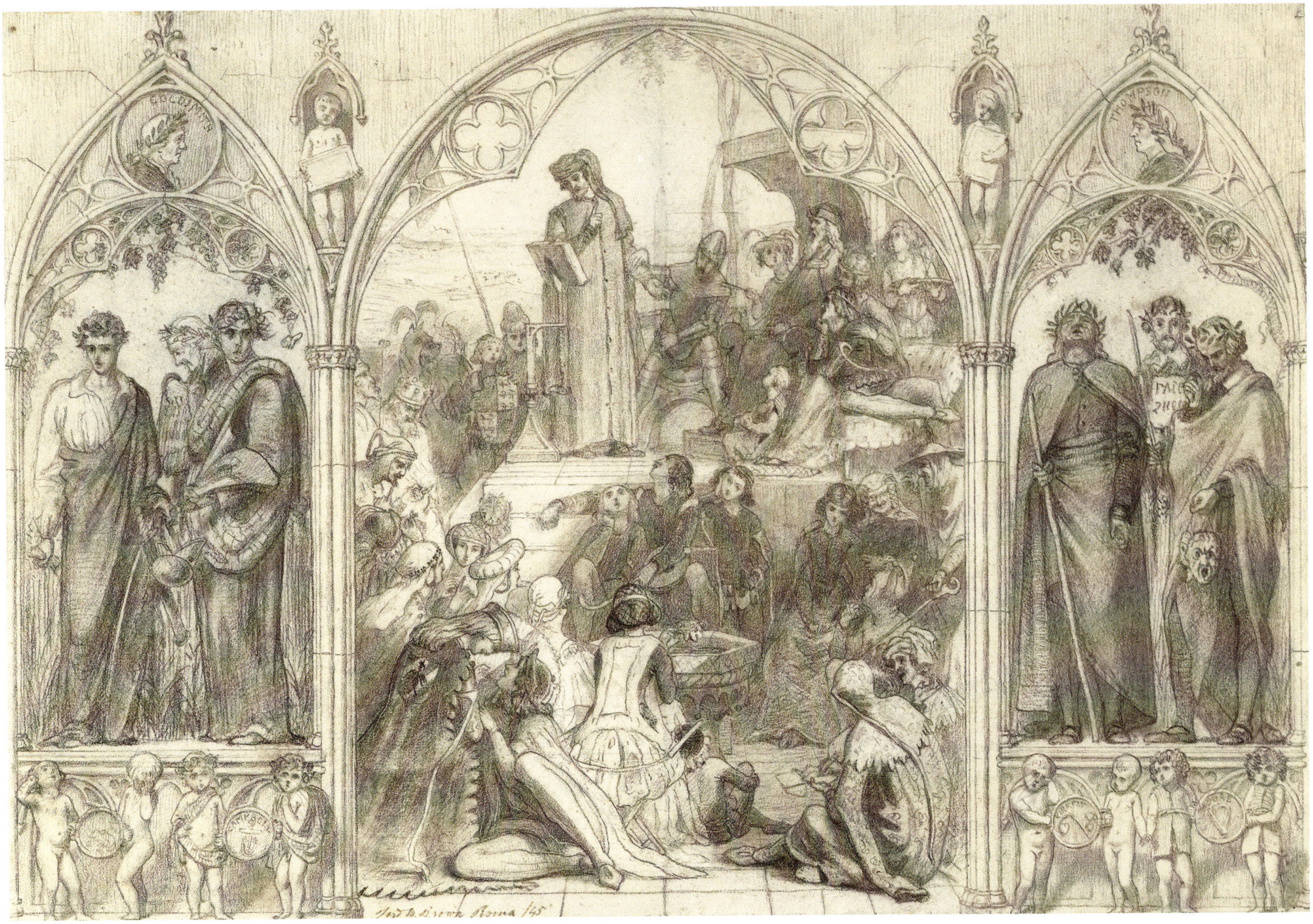

Ford Madox BROWN

[1821–93]

The Seeds and Fruits of English Poetry (Chaucer reading his poem at the Court of Edward III), 1845

chalk on paper, 34 × 50.3 cm
inscribed: *Ford M Brown Roma 45'*

P.131

PROVENANCE: Perhaps the study intended for J.E.Millais ?; sold by artist to D.T.White, dealer, June 1855; his sale Christie's 21 April 1868, lot 611; bought by Tooth; Harold Rathbone (before 1911); sold to Lord Leverhulme 17 Feb 1919; his sale Knight, Frank and Rutley 16 June 1926, lot 204; anon. sale Christie's 23 October 1953, lot 131; bought by Brown; The Leicester Galleries, from whom purchased by Gallery, November 1957.
EXHIBITIONS: *Loan Exhibition of works by Ford Madox Brown and the Pre Raphaelites*, Manchester, 1911, no.118 as *Chaucer at the Court of Edward III*; London, Tate Gallery, 1913, no.60; Bath, Victoria Art Gallery, 1913; *Ford Madox Brown*, Liverpool, Walker Art Gallery, Southampton, Southampton City Art Gallery, 1964, no.50; Manchester & Birmingham, 1965.
REFERENCES: W.M. Rossetti (ed.), *Pre-Raphaelite Diaries and Letters*, London, 1900, pp.65, 169, 185; R. Watkinson, *Pre-Raphaelite art and design*, London, 1970; T. Newman & R. Watkinson, *Ford Madox Brown and the Pre-Raphaelite Circle*, 1991, pp.25–6, 29–31, 33–4, pl.40; Diary 4 March, 27 June 1855 (Ashmolean Museum); invoice 17 Feb 1919 (Lady Lever Art Gallery).

A preliminary drawing for an oil sketch of comparable size in the Ashmolean Museum, Oxford. The same composition was used for other versions in the Art Gallery of New South Wales, Sydney, and the Tate Gallery.

Geoffrey Chaucer (c.1343–1400), is shown reading his poems at the Court of Edward III (d.1377). The figures, wearing laurel wreaths, in the two wings of the triptych are, on the left, Milton, Spenser and Shakespeare with the head of Goldsmith above and, on the right, Byron, Pope and Burns with the head of Thomson above.

The idea for this subject grew naturally from those being considered for the Houses of Parliament decorations which depicted the splendours of English literature and history. The architectural framework and tracery are characteristic of the Gothic Revival, while the figures in the wings echo the Italian altarpieces that the artist saw on his way to Rome. However, Madox Brown decided to abandon the wings when he came to paint the large version.

This is perhaps the chalk drawing made at Rome after a pencil design for the central panel he had brought from England. Madox Brown noted, (4 March 1855), that he took the chalk drawing out of his book of sketches and sent it to be mounted and framed. White, the dealer, bought it on 27 June and the artist noted that he had given it to MILLAIS 'three years ago and (he forgetting it) I have now sold it for £8'.

EJ

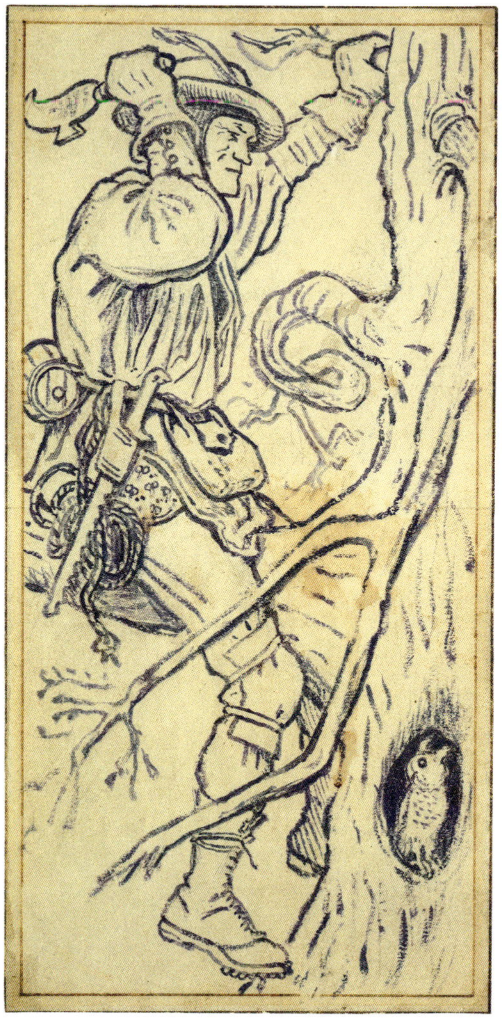

Ford Madox BROWN
[1821–93]
The Woodcutter – study for March, 1862

watercolour and chalk on paper, 24.8 × 12.1 cm

P.189
PROVENANCE: Dr Wilde, Holland, relation of artist; P&D.Colnaghi Ltd, from whom purchased by Gallery, April 1958.
EXHIBITIONS: *Morris & Co. Tiles*, Walthamstow, London, William Morris Gallery, 1996/7, no.cat.
REFERENCES: T. Newman & R. Watkinson, *Ford Madox Brown and the Pre-Raphaelite Circle,* 1991, pl.101; S. Wildman, *Morris & Company in Cambridge*, Cambridge, Fitzwilliam Museum, 1980, pp.27–8.

The Woodcutter or *Cutting Down Trees* was a study for *March*, one of the tiles for the fireplace at Queen's College, Cambridge, by Morris, Marshall, Faulkner & Co. The fireplace depicted months of the year through representative labours. Other artists commissioned included BURNE-JONES(*Warming – February)*, William Morris (*Flower-bearer – April)* and ROSSETTI *(Reaping – July).*

JM

Ford Madox BROWN
[1821–93]
The Death of Sir Tristram – Sketch for Stained Glass, c.1863

watercolour and pencil on paper, 10.8 × 9.5 cm
inscribed: *MFB*
on reverse in pencil: *Death of Sir Tristram by Ford Madox Brown in swap for study near the Pyramids of Ghizah by the latter given by him to G P Boyce April 13 1865*

P.298
PROVENANCE: Given by artist to G.P.Boyce 1865; Boyce Sale Christie's 2 July 1897, lot 128; Hoeue; Edward Marsh; Thos. Agnew & Sons Ltd, from whom purchased by Gallery, July 1959.
EXHIBITIONS: *Spring Exhibition*, London, Whitechapel Art Gallery, 1904, no.500; *Watercolours and Drawings from The Cecil Higgins Art Gallery, Bedford*, London, Thos. Agnew & Sons Ltd, 1962, no.36; *Matthew Arnold Centenary,* Grasmere, Wordsworth Trust, 1988.
REFERENCES: F.M. Hueffer, *Ford Madox Brown: a record of his life and work*, London, 1896, p.440; Walker Art Gallery, *Ford Madox Brown*, 1964, p.28, no.47; Birmingham City Art Gallery & Museum, *Catalogue of Paintings,* 1960, p.21, *no.2616.;* D. Robinson & S. Wildman, *Morris & Company in Cambridge,* 1980, pp.71–72, no.93; A.C. Sewter, *The Stained Glass of William Morris and his circle – A Catalogue,* 1975, pp.26–7.

This illustrates the story of Tristram and Iseult from *Morte D'Arthur* by Sir Thomas Malory (d.1471). Sir Tristram, nephew of King Mark of Cornwall, was dispatched to Ireland to bring Iseult the Fair back as his uncle's bride. Before they sailed Iseult's mother, Queen Isaud, brewed a love potion which she gave to Brangwain, Iseult's attendant, with instructions that the pair were to drink it on their wedding night. Brangwain carelessly left the flask in the cabin and, being thirsty, Tristram and Iseult drank it and immediately fell in love. Iseult married Mark but continued to love Tristram. When he and Iseult were seen together by Mark, Tristram was banished from Cornwall and came to Camelot where King Arthur made him a Knight of the Round Table.

Later Tristram marries another woman, also named Iseult. When dying of a poisoned wound he sent for Iseult the Fair to cure him. She set sail at once but his wife, in her jealousy, lied saying that there was no sign of her ship and Tristram died. When Iseult the Fair arrived and found him dead she too died and they were buried in one grave. King Mark, furiously jealous, is seen behind the lovers although he does not appear there in the story.

Brown was born in Calais and studied in Antwerp and Paris. He came to England where he entered – unsuccessfully – the competitions to decorate the Palace of Westminster. In 1845 he went to Rome and made contact with the Nazarenes, which increased his interest in medievalism (see *The Seeds and Fruits of English Poetry* in the Gallery's collection).

Back in England he became friends with ROSSETTI and would have joined the Pre-Raphaelite Brotherhood if Holman HUNT had not objected to his 'germanic' style. Later he became more interested in realism which led to his masterpieces, *Work* and *The Last of England* and to some remarkable *plein-air* landscapes. Madox Brown was a prickly man who was at odds with the artistic establishment, which led him to abandon exhibiting at the R.A. after 1853.

This watercolour appears as a stained glass window commissioned by Walter Dunlop for Harden Grange, near Bingley, from Morris & Co. The stained glass is inscribed with the following caption: 'How Sir Tristram and King Mark were made one again by King Arthur's means and how nevertheless King Mark slew Sir Tristram by treachery as he sat harping to La Belle Isoude and Isoude died the third day after.'

EJ

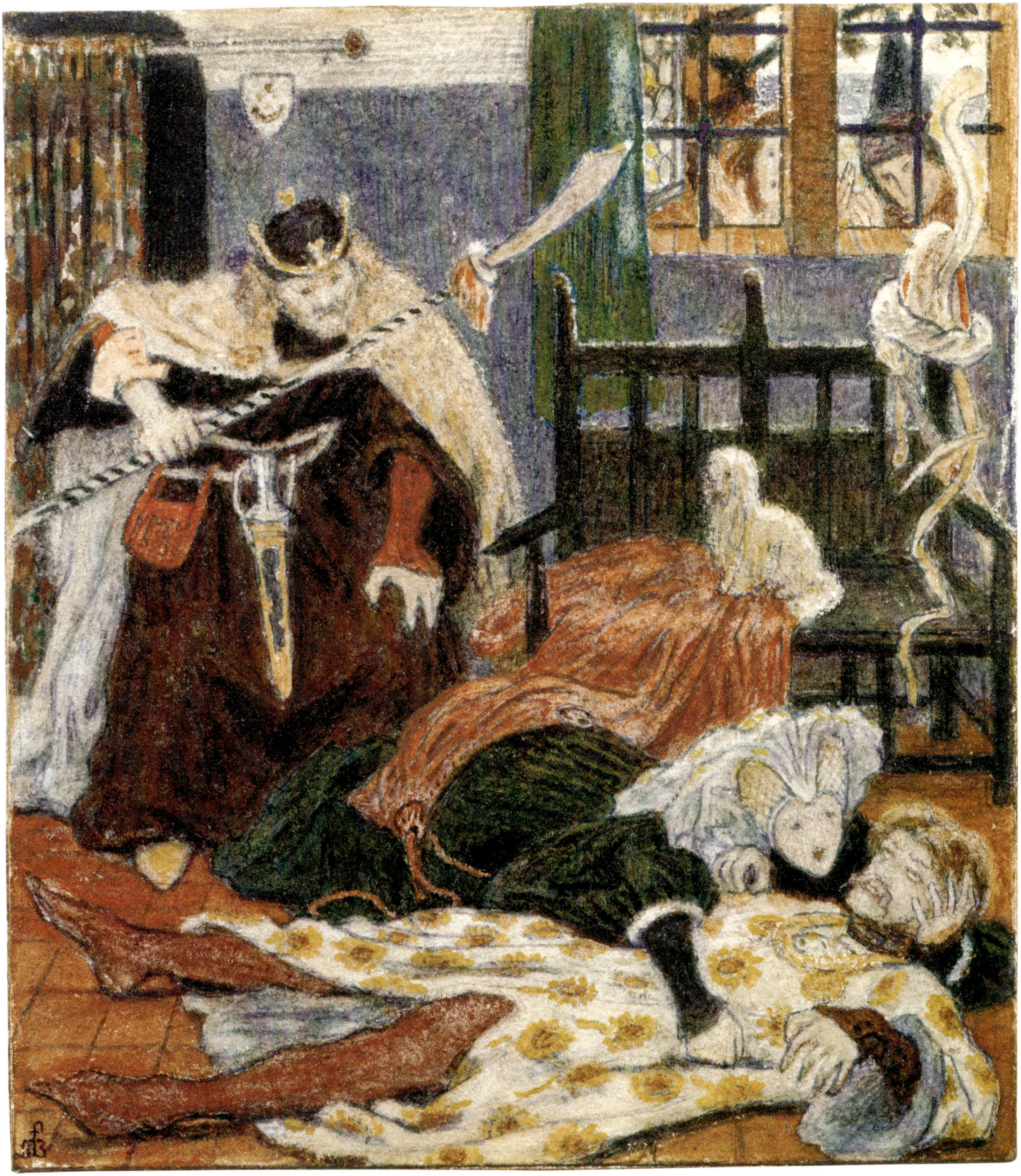

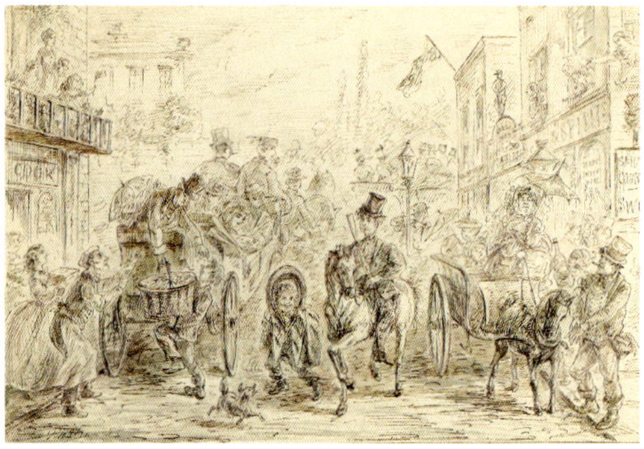

Hablot Knight BROWNE ('Phiz')
[1815–82]
The Derby Morn

pen, ink and wash on paper, 71.1 × 25.4 cm
inscribed: *Phiz The Derby Morn*

P.500
PROVENANCE: Fine Art Society, from whom purchased by Gallery, June 1965.
EXHIBITIONS: *British Illustration*, London, Fine Art Society, 1965, no.57.

Browne, who signed his drawings 'PHIZ' as here, was early apprenticed to the engraver William Finden (1787–1852) before attending St. Martin's Lane School. Following the death of Robert Seymour (1798–1836), Browne succeeded him as Dickens' illustrator of *Pickwick Papers* in 1836 and continued as far as 1857 with *Little Dorrit*. He became paralyzed in 1867 and moved to Brighton in 1880, where he died.

Browne's draughtsmanship followed the Regency tradition, verging on caricature as here with these raffish types off to a day at the races, with some touches of humorous observation added, such as 'Smut Court' inscribed on the wall on the right.

EJ

Sir Edward Coley BURNE-JONES, A.R.A.
[1833–98]
Childe Roland, 1861

pen and ink and wash on paper, 43 × 24 cm
inscribed: *EBJ 1861 CHILDE.ROLAND.TO.THE.DARK.TOWER.CAME*

P.727
PROVENANCE: Commissioned by John Ruskin; F.S. Ellis; Arthur West; purchased through Christie's by Gallery with assistance from the V&A/M.G.C. Purchase Grant Fund and National Art Collections Fund, September 1983.
EXHIBITIONS: *Burne-Jones*, London, Hayward Gallery, Southampton, Southampton Art Gallery, & Birmingham, City Museum & Art Gallery, 1975–6, no.22; *From Monet to Freud*, London, Sotheby's, 1989, no.1; *John Ruskin & the Victorian Eye*, Phoenix, Phoenix Art Gallery, & Indianapolis, Indianapolis Museum of Art, 1993, no.14; *Knights, Chivalry, Romance, Legend*, Newcastle upon Tyne, Laing Art Gallery, 1995–6, no catalogue; *Edward Burne-Jones: Victorian Artist-Dreamer*, New York, The Metropolitan Museum of Art, & Birmingham, Birmingham Museum & Art Gallery only, 1998–9, no.14.
REFERENCES: Burne-Jones's autograph work-record, under 1861 (Fitzwilliam Museum, Cambridge); F.S. Ellis, *Memories of Men, Places and Things*, n.d., pp.7–8, no.6; M. Bell, *Sir Edward Burne-Jones: A Record and Review*, 1898,pp.28, 129; F.de Lisle, *Burne-Jones*, 1904, pp.57, 188; G. Burne-Jones, *Memorials of Edward Burne-Jones*, 1904,vol. I, p.225; Old Water-Colour Society's Club, 'Extracts from G.P. Boyce's Diaries', *19th Annual Volume*, 1941, p.39; M. Harrison and B. Waters, *Burne-Jones*, 1973, pp.58,61; V. Surtees (ed.), *The Diaries of George Price Boyce*, 1980, pp.32, 93, note 5; O. Wilson (ed.), *My Dearest Dora: Letters to Dora Livesey…from John Ruskin*, 1984, pp.88–9; J. Christian, 'Burne-Jones's "Childe Roland"', *National Art Collections Fund Review*, 1984, pp.122–4; C. Wood, *Burne-Jones*, 1998, p.41, illus.

Childe Roland is the last and one of the largest of the pen-and-ink drawings that Burne-Jones made at the outset of his career, that is to say between 1856, when he left Oxford and started to work under the guidance of D.G. ROSSETTI, and 1861, when watercolour took over as his primary medium of expression. Meticulously finished and replete with romantic feeling for the Middle Ages, these drawings form a close parallel both to Rossetti's contemporary watercolours with 'chivalric Froissartian themes', and with William Morris's first volume of poetry, *The Defence of Guenevere* (1858). Technically they owe much to the engravings of Albrecht Dürer. Indeed Rossetti described them in 1857 as 'marvels of finish and imaginative detail, unequalled by anything unless perhaps Albert Dürer's finest works'.

Childe Roland illustrates the well-known poem by Robert Browning (1812–89) 'Childe Roland to the Dark Tower Came', published in *Men and Women* in 1855. Taking its title from words spoken by Edgar when feigning madness in *King Lear* (Act III, Scene 4), the poem describes a young knight's journey through a nightmarish landscape to reach a mysterious Dark Tower. He succeeds where many before him have failed, and the poem ends with the 'dauntless' hero putting a 'slug-horn' to his lips and blowing a challenge. This is the subject of Burne-Jones's drawing.

At this period Browning still suffered from public neglect, his work being considered difficult, but despite, or perhaps because of this he was passionately admired by Rossetti, Burne-Jones and their circle. Rossetti introduced Burne-Jones to Browning in July 1856. Browning, Burne-Jones wrote the following year, was 'the deepest and intensest of all poets', and they met again in Italy in 1859, Burne-Jones probably benefiting from Browning's knowledge of Italian pictures. Nonetheless, the relationship between the drawing and its literary source is complex. While the mood of Browning's poem is deeply introspective, Burne-Jones adopts a heraldic, decorative approach, even introducing a gravity-defying scroll inscribed with the title. Equally, he replaces the poem's terrifyingly barren landscape with nothing less than a riot of sunflowers. In her *Memorials*, Lady Burne-Jones described how carefully he studied these in preparation for the drawing. In fact *Childe Roland* is one of the earliest examples of the sunflower motif which was to play such a prominent part in the Aesthetic Movement.

This was one of the first works by Burne-Jones to be acquired by RUSKIN, who played a decisive part in the artist's early development. Ruskin lent the drawing to Winnington Hall, the girls' school in Cheshire in which he took such an interest in the 1860s, but when Miss Bell, the headmistress, went bankrupt in 1873, he was unable to reclaim it, and it was probably sold to raise funds. Later it belonged to F.S. Ellis, who published works by William Morris (1834–96) and ROSSETTI. Ellis remembered buying it at Sotheby's about 1878 'for something between twenty and thirty pounds'.

JC

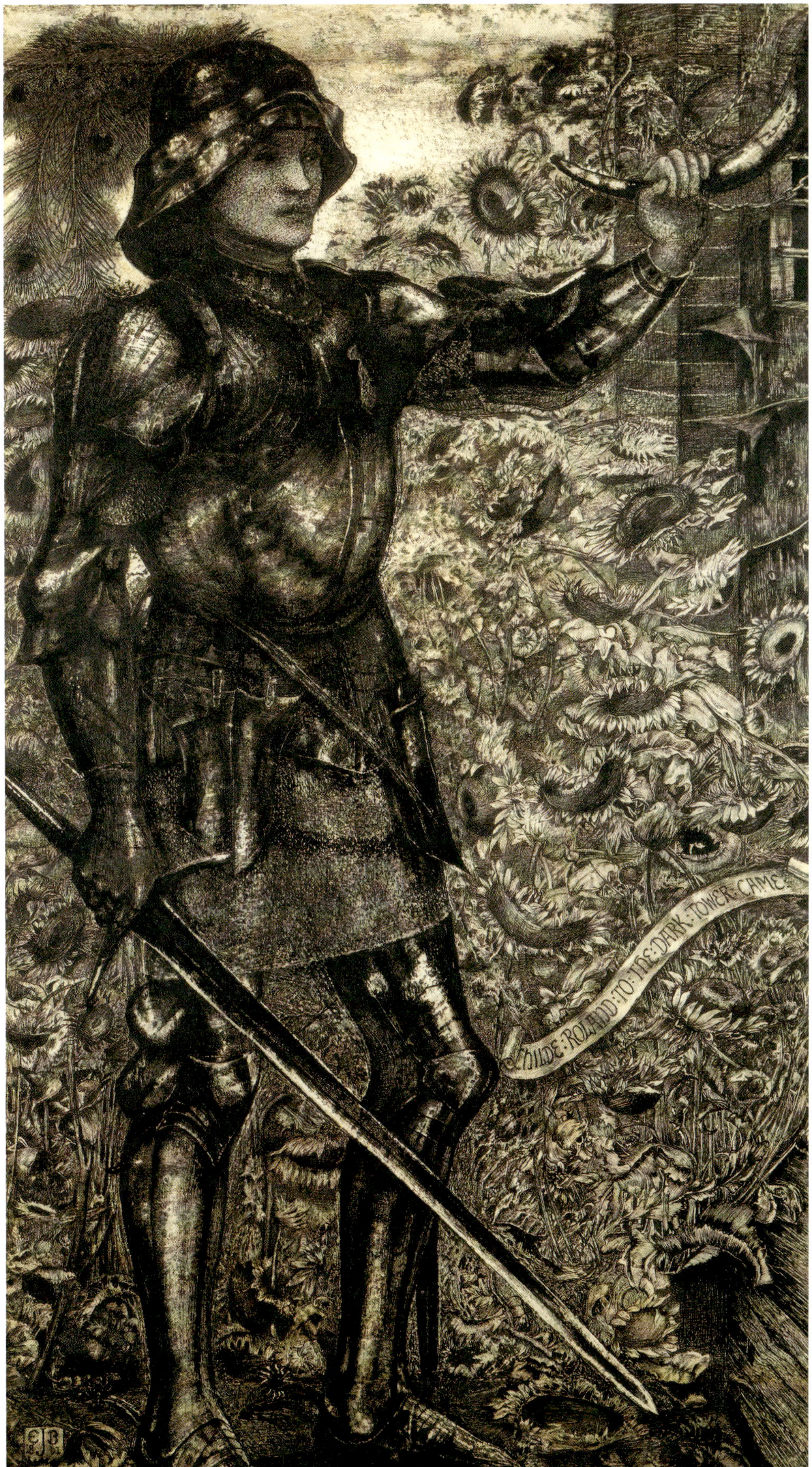
CHILDE : ROLAND : TO : THE : DARK : TOWER : CAME

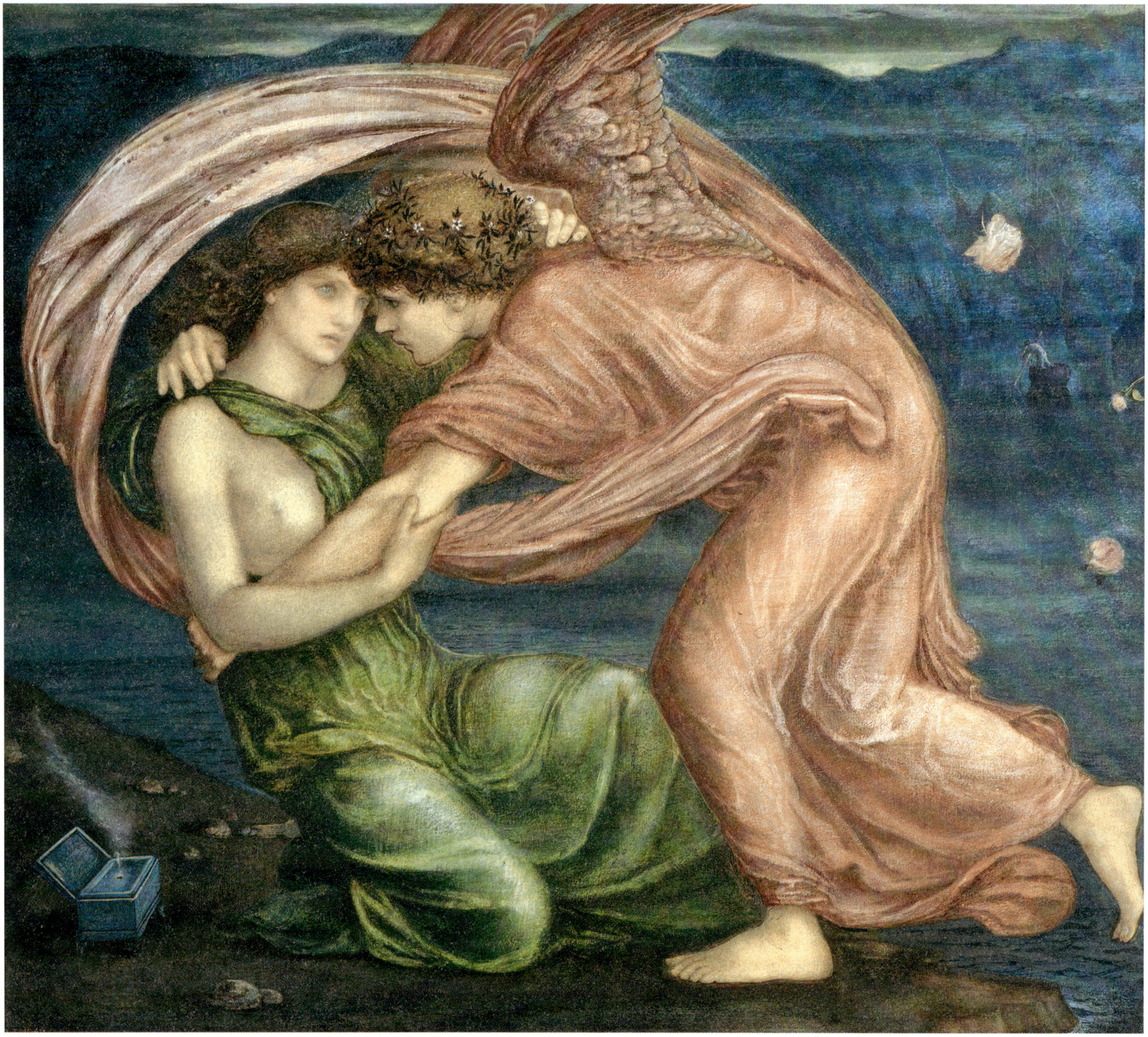

Sir Edward Coley BURNE-JONES, A.R.A.
[1833–98]
Cupid delivering Psyche, 1867

watercolour, bodycolour, chalk and oil pastel on paper, 52.1 × 61 cm
inscribed: *E.B.J. 1867*

P.296
PROVENANCE: Sir Philip Burne-Jones (1861–1926), the artist's son; William R. Moss, Lancashire, by 1887; The Leicester Galleries; Roland, Browse and Delbanco, from whom purchased by Gallery, July 1959.
EXHIBITIONS: *Royal Jubilee Exhibition*, Manchester, 1887, Fine Art Section, no.1347; *Southport Centenary Exhibition*, Southport, 1892; *Dei ed Eroi: Tradizione Classica e interpretazione del mito nella cultura figurativa fra 1800–1900*, Rome, Palazzo delle Esposizioni, 1996, no.40; *Edward Burne-Jones: Victorian Artist-Dreamer*, New York, The Metropolitan Museum of Art, & Birmingham, Birmingham Museums & Art Gallery only, 1998–99, no.39.
REFERENCE: *Burne-Jones*, Arts Council exhib., 1975–6, cat.p.43, under no.99.

The composition is based on one of the designs that Burne-Jones made in 1865 for 'The Story of Cupid and Psyche' in William Morris's *Earthly Paradise*. Morris originally intended the book to be lavishly illustrated with woodcuts, and Burne-Jones executed hundreds of designs for this purpose over several years. Although the project was eventually abandoned for technical reasons, the book being published without illustrations in 1868–70, the designs provided him with a bank of compositional ideas for paintings on which he was to draw until the very end of his life.

This is particularly true of the illustrations to 'Cupid and Psyche', which were begun first and carried further than those for any of the other poems; forty-seven finished designs survive (Ashmolean Museum, Oxford). The present painting illustrates one of the closing scenes in the narrative. Psyche, having lost Cupid through her own disobedience, is subjected by Venus, her enemy, to a series of daunting tasks. The last is to take a casket to Proserpine in Hades. Psyche accomplishes this mission, but when Proserpine returns the casket to her, she foolishly opens it, hoping that the beauty it contains will be hers. Overcome by the fumes which emerge, she falls into a death-like trance. However, Cupid is alerted to her peril and rushes to her rescue:

And kneeling down he whispered in her ear,
'Rise, Psyche, and be mine for evermore,
For evil is long tarrying on this shore'.
Then when she heard him, straightway she arose,
And from her fell the burden of her woes.

Re-united with her lover, Psyche enters the portals of Olympus, and is granted immortality by the gods.

The primary version is a watercolour exhibited at the Old Water-Colour Society in 1867 (London Borough of Hammersmith Public Libraries, on loan to Leighton House, Kensington), and there is an unfinished oil version of about the same date (Sheffield Art Gallery). The composition also occurs in one of the mural paintings based on the Cupid and Psyche designs that Burne-Jones, assisted by Walter CRANE, carried out for the dining room at George Howard's London House, 1 Palace Green, in 1872–81 (now in Birmingham Museum and Art Gallery).

JC

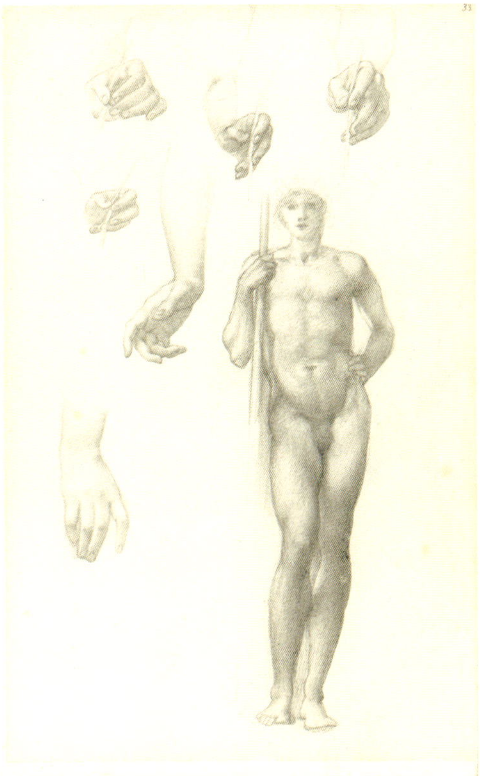

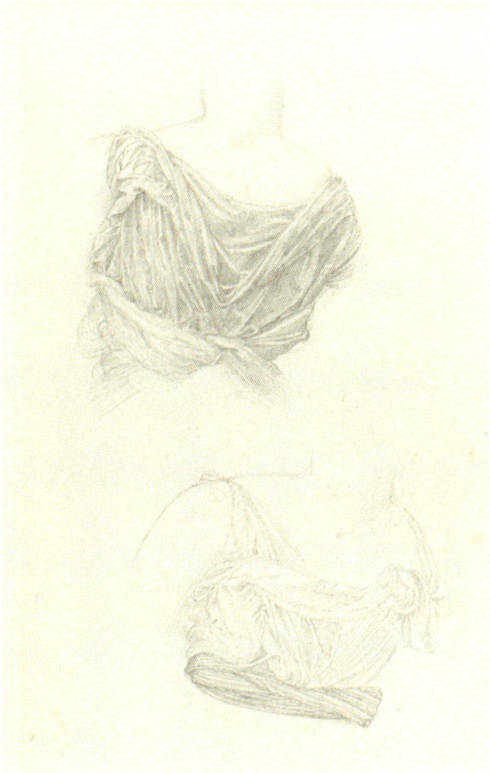

Sir Edward Coley BURNE-JONES, A.R.A.
[1833–98]
Study for St George, c.1873

pencil on paper, 27.1 × 18 cm
on reverse: studies of drapery

P.238B
PROVENANCE: Lady Lewis; The Leicester Galleries, from whom purchased by Gallery, July 1958.
EXHIBITIONS: *Drawings and Studies by Sir Edward Burne-Jones, Bart.*, London, Burlington Fine Arts Club, 1899, part of a sketchbook listed in catalogue, p.43, no.4; *Knights, Chivalry, Romance, Legend*, Newcastle upon Tyne, Laing Art Gallery, 1995–6, no catalogue.

This study from the nude is for an oil painting of St George (Wadsworth Atheneum, Hartford, Conn., USA) that Burne-Jones executed in 1873 and showed at the famous opening exhibition at the Grosvenor Gallery in 1877 (see S. Wildman and J. Christian, *Edward Burne-Jones: Victorian Artist-Dreamer,* 1998, pp.214–5, no.85). The painting was based on a design for stained glass commissioned for the Hall at Peterhouse, Cambridge, in 1871. There are also later oil versions.

The studies of hands are for a different figure. The four showing a left hand writing with a quill pen may be connected with one of the figures of the Evangelists which Burne-Jones designed in 1872–4 for stained glass in the Chapel at Jesus College, Cambridge, although none of these is depicted as left-handed.

The two studies of a bodice on the verso can also be dated to c.1873. They might have been made for one of the figures in *The Mirror of Venus* (Gulbenkian Collection, Lisbon) or the large oil version of *Laus Veneris* (Laing Art Gallery, Newcastle upon Tyne). Both begun that year, the pictures were exhibited at the Grosvenor Gallery respectively in 1877 and 1878.

JC

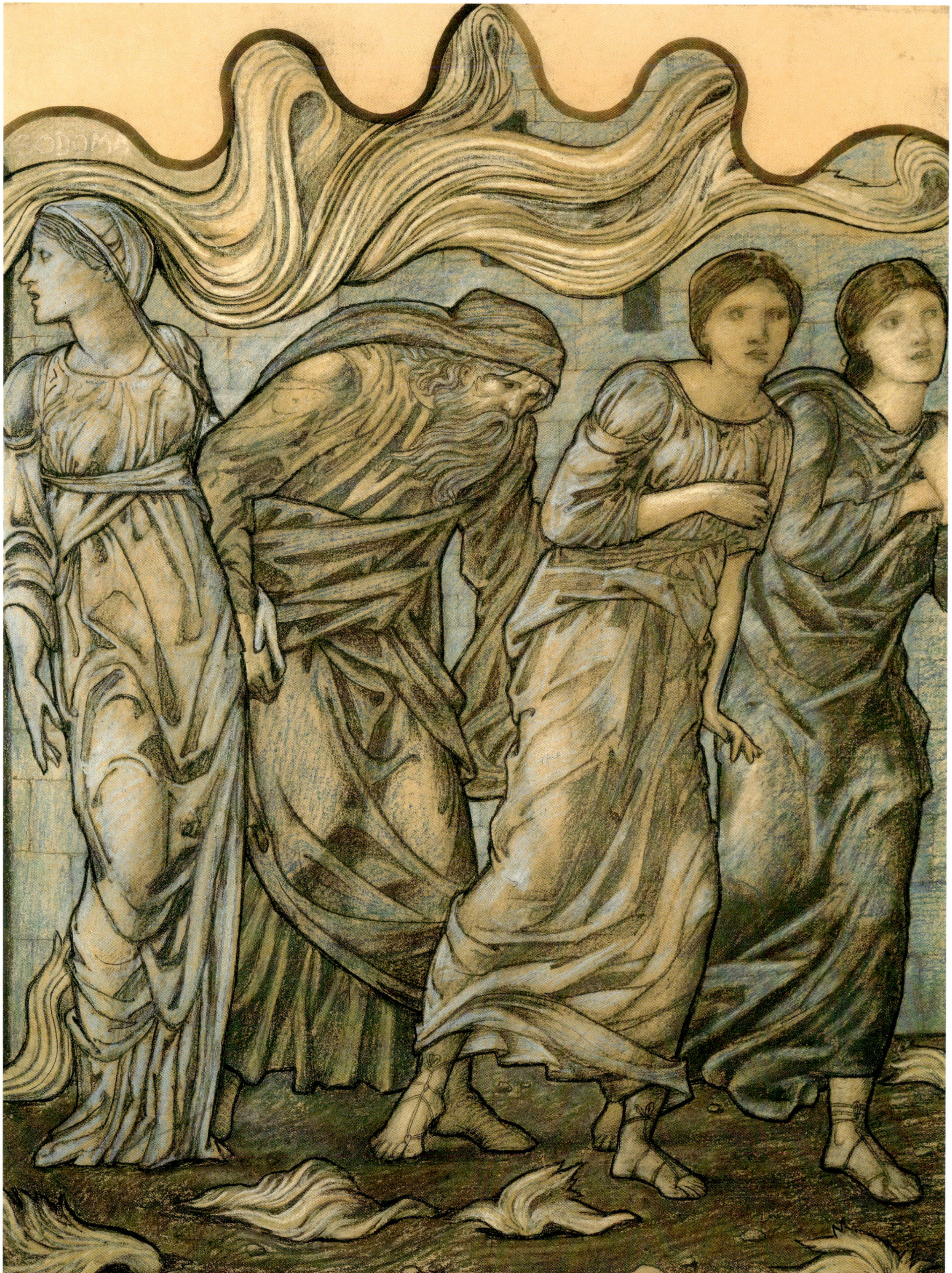
SODOMA

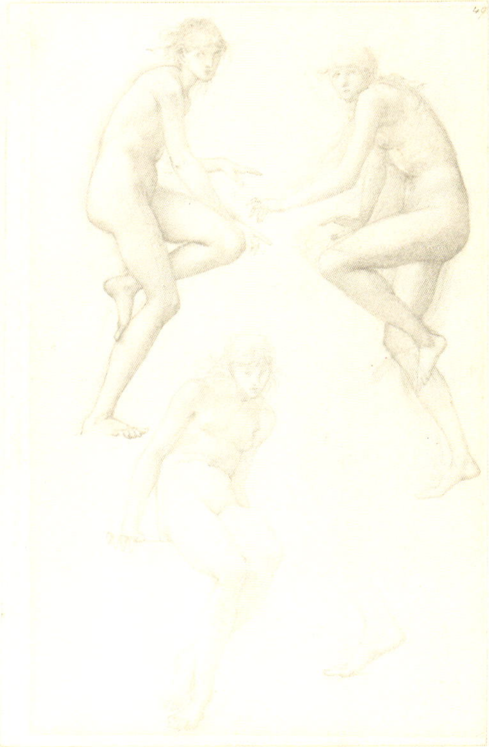

Sir Edward Coley BURNE-JONES, A.R.A.
[1833–98]
Studies of figures for **Cupid's Hunting Ground, 1870s**

pencil on paper, 27.1 × 18 cm
inscribed: *no.49*

P.238A
PROVENANCE: Lady Lewis; The Leicester Galleries, from whom purchased by Gallery, July 1958.
EXHIBITIONS: *Drawings and Studies by Sir Edward Burne-Jones, Bart.*, London, Burlington Fine Arts Club, 1899, part of a sketchbook listed in catalogue, p.43, no.4.

The composition known as *Cupid's Hunting Ground* (or *Cupid's Hunting Fields*; Burne-Jones himself used both forms) shows the blindfold god of love shooting arrows at a group of lightly-clad female victims, three of whom are represented by these studies. As so often with Burne-Jones, the idea went through many variations over a long period of time. It began life as part of a larger design in which Cupid shoots his arrows while his mother, Venus, passes in her chariot. This extended subject was conceived in 1861, when it occurs both as a design for a set of tiles to be carried out by the Morris firm (see M. Harrison and B. Waters, *Burne-Jones*, 1973, p.52, fig.59) and on a tapestry in the background of *Laus Veneris* (private collection), a watercolour painted the same year. The motif is repeated in the well-known large oil version of this watercolour (Laing Art Gallery, Newcastle upon Tyne), begun in 1873, but the two themes it incorporates were then divided and treated in separate compositions.

Cupid's Hunting Ground itself exists in at least four versions, all decorative in character. The primary version is a monochrome oil painting executed in 1880 and shown at the Grosvenor Gallery two years later. It was bought by Constantine Alexander Ionides, who left it to the V&A with the rest of his collection in 1901. A second version was also carried out in 1880. Commissioned by Hugh Lupus Grosvenor, first Duke of Westminster, it took the form of a painted and gilt gesso relief. A third version (Art Institute of Chicago) was painted in watercolour and gold paint in 1885. Finally, there is a small drawing in bodycolour and gold paint on a dark blue ground (Christie's, London, 7 April 1998, lot 166). This belonged to Aglaia Coronio, the younger sister of Constantine Ionides, and, like her brother's version and the present drawing, was included in the memorial exhibition of Burne-Jones's drawings held at the Burlington Fine Arts Club in 1899.

JC

Sir Edward Coley BURNE-JONES, A.R.A.
[1833–98]
Cartoon for stained glass window: **Lot and his Daughters, 1874**

watercolour, bodycolour and chalk on paper, 76.2 × 59.4 cm
inscribed: *SODOMA*

P.431
PROVENANCE: John Nicholson Gallery, USA; J.S. Maas & Co. Ltd, from whom purchased by Gallery, October 1962.
EXHIBITIONS: *Jubilee Exhibition*, Bradford, Bradford Art Gallery, 1930, no.467; *The Pre-Raphaelites and their Contemporaries*, London, J.S. Maas & Co. Ltd, 1962, no.23; *The English Tradition*, Bedford, Cecil Higgins Art Gallery, 1972, no.9.
REFERENCES: Burne-Jones's autograph account book, entry for May-June 1874 (Fitzwilliam Museum, Cambridge); M. Harrison & B. Waters, *Burne-Jones*, 1973, p.112, fig.162, as *Destruction of Sodom;* A.C. Sewter, *The Stained Glass of William Morris and his Circle*, 1974–5, vol.2, p.219.

Lot and his family flee the burning city of Sodom; his wife turns back to look at the stricken city and is transformed into a pillar of salt.

The cartoon was drawn in the summer of 1874 for a large west window in the Cathedral at Calcutta, although the design was not in fact included in the finished work. Executed by Morris & Co., the window was a memorial to the recently assassinated Viceroy, Lord Mayo (1822–72).

JC

Sir Edward Coley BURNE-JONES, A.R.A.
[1833–98]
William Burges in Bed, c.1881

pencil on paper, 12.5 × 11.9 cm
inscribed: *E.B.J. The Late Wm.Burges*

P.723
PROVENANCE: Mrs Henry Holiday; by descent to Alfred Holiday; his sale Christie's, 16 October 1981, lot 42, from whom purchased by Gallery with the assistance of a grant from the V&A/M.G.C. Purchase Grant Fund.

'Billy' Burges (1827–81), the eccentric architect and designer, was a long-standing friend of both Burne-Jones and Henry Holiday (1839–1927), who commissioned the drawing for his wife. Both Burges and Burne-Jones shared the same Victorian humour. Burges would include visual puns within his furniture, while Burne-Jones was famous for his caricatures of friends and family, leading Graham Robertson (1866–1948) to describe him as having 'the impish eyes of Puck beneath the cowl of a monk'.

The acquisition of this caricature is particularly apt for the Gallery, which also owns William Burges's bed in which he died on 20 April 1881, (the bed-head was painted by Henry Holiday). It is no exaggeration that Burges wore his glasses in bed, for Edmund Gosse (1849–1928) in a letter to Austin Dobson (1840–1921) said: 'He was much blinder than any near-sighted man ... (he) mistook a peacock seen *en face* for a man!'. He was also given the epithet of *ugly Burges*, as he was rather stout and short in stature.

CB

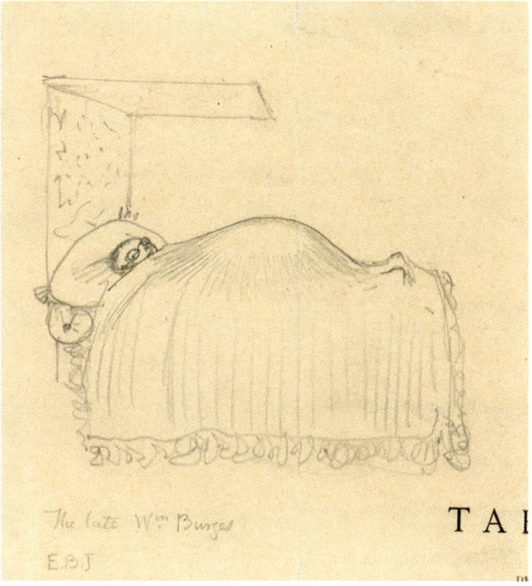

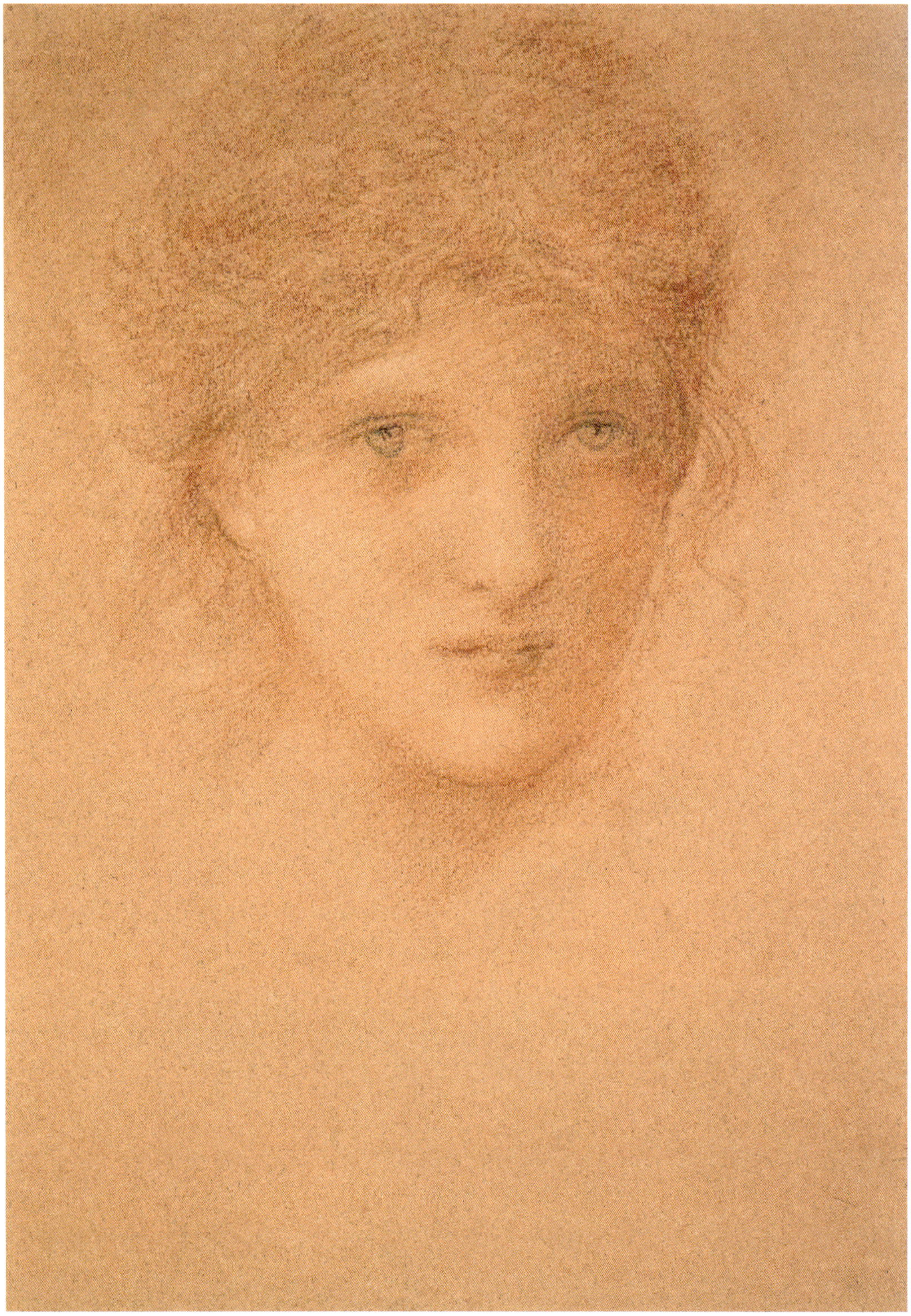

Sir Edward Coley BURNE-JONES, A.R.A.
[1833–98]
Girl's Head, late 1880s–early 1890s

red, black and white chalk on terracotta paper, 39.3 × 27.6 cm

P.240
PROVENANCE: Thos. Agnew & Sons Ltd; 1st Lord Leverhulme; Lady Lever Art Gallery, Port Sunlight; Christie's, 6 June 1958, part of lot 23, with P.239, purchased by Gallery.
EXHIBITIONS: *Drawings and Studies by Sir Edward Burne-Jones, Bart.*, Berlin, 1898; *The English Tradition*, Bedford, Cecil Higgins Art Gallery, 1972, no.11; *Burne-Jones*, London, Hayward Gallery, Southampton, Southampton Art Gallery, & Birmingham, City Museum & Art Gallery, 1975–6, no.322; *The Last Romantics,* London, Barbican Art Gallery, 1989, no.11.
REFERENCE: R.R. Tatlock, *A Record of the Collection in the Lady Lever Art Gallery, Port Sunlight,* vol.1, 1928, p.123, no.718.

This attractive drawing exemplifies the wistful, enigmatic expression that Burne-Jones loved to give his models. The technique is one he often used at this period. Lady Burne-Jones quotes him writing on the subject of red chalk to the artist E. R. Hughes, who also favoured the medium for his drawings:

The ancient red is a far more crimson and rosy tint than the dusty brown sticks they give us now, and I have understood always that the ancient red is exhausted and that we have fallen on evil days and can get no more of it, and...I am always asking about it of every colourman I meet, in vain...I am waiting till I can find one stick of the tint Correggio used (*Memorials of Edward Burne-Jones*, 1904, vol.2, p.322)

As so often with Burne-Jones at this date, the drawing seems to have been conceived as an independent study, unrelated to a picture. Given his tendency to impose his own visual ideal on his models, it is unlikely that the sitter will ever be identified.

Like P.239, the drawing was in the vast collection formed by William Hesketh Lever, first Viscount Leverhulme, the wealthy manufacturer of Sunlight Soap. The drawings were given by him to the Lady Lever Art Gallery, Port Sunlight, which he built after the First World War for the benefit of his workforce and in memory of his wife; but they were among many items which were sold by the Trustees at Christie's in 1958, at a time when Victorian art was out of fashion.

JC

Sir Edward Coley BURNE-JONES, A.R.A.

[1833–98]

Study for The Car of Love, 1895

pencil on paper, 50.2 × 35.2 cm
inscribed: *EB-J for the CAR OF LOVE no. XVI 1895*

P.239

PROVENANCE: 1st Lord Leverhulme; Lady Lever Art Gallery, Port Sunlight; Christie's, 6 June 1958, part of lot 23, with P.240, purchased by Gallery.
EXHIBITIONS: *Drawings and Studies by Sir Edward Burne-Jones, Bart.*, Berlin, 1898, no. 74; *Drawings and Studies by Sir Edward Burne-Jones, Bart.*, London, Burlington Fine Arts Club, 1899 (label on picture); *The English Tradition*, Bedford, Cecil Higgins Art Gallery, 1972, no.12; *Burne-Jones*, London, Hayward Gallery, Southampton, Southampton Art Gallery, & Birmingham, City Museum & Art Gallery, 1975–6, not in catalogue; *The Last Romantics*, London, Barbican Art Gallery, 1989, no.12.
REFERENCES: *The Studio*, vol.XXXI, 1904, p.313, illus.; R.R. Tatlock, *A Record of the Collection in the Lady Lever Art Gallery, Port Sunlight*, vol.1, 1928, p.125; no.3878; K. Preston (ed.), *Letters from Graham Robertson*, 1953, p.487.

The Car of Love (also known as *The Chariot of Love* or *Love's Wayfaring*) shows Cupid standing on a chariot which is pulled down a narrow street by a team of male and female lovers. Some smile or laugh happily, others find the god's sway oppressive. Burne-Jones conceived the idea in 1871 at the height of his most Italianate phase. It is based on one of the 'Triumphs' of Petrarch, and had often been illustrated by early Renaissance artists. Some of these treatments were undoubtedly known to Burne-Jones. As he observed, it 'isn't a new subject. It has been done before, but not as I like' (G. Burne-Jones, *Memorials of Edward Burne-Jones,* 1904, vol. 2, p.266).

In his work-record for 1872 Burne-Jones wrote that 'the Chariot of Love – to be painted life-size' was one of 'four subjects which above all others I desire to paint'. A version in the Auckland City Art Gallery, New Zealand, seems to be a large chalk drawing made at this time but re-touched in the early 1890s, when he began the subject again on a canvas so enormous (17ft. × 8ft. 11½in.) that it required a two-storey scaffold to paint and took up almost an entire end wall of the garden studio at his house in Fulham. When Burne-Jones died in June 1898 the picture was still little more than sketched in monochrome, although even in this state it is one of his most impressive works (see M. Harrison & B. Waters, *Burne-Jones*, 1973, p.159, fig.237). His widow presented it to the V&A in 1909.

The present drawing is dated 1895 and was probably executed that summer, when Burne-Jones's work-record specifically mentions the picture as in progress. The name of the model is not known, but she appears in a number of Burne-Jones's late head studies, and is particularly associated with *The Car of Love*. The artist's young friend Graham Robertson (1866–1948) recalled 'several studies of heads for the "Car of Love" picture. He [Burne-Jones] had got a new model, a curious type quite away from his usual face. She had very small eyes which gave her a rather sly expression, and she evidently interested him (pictorially) very much'.

JC

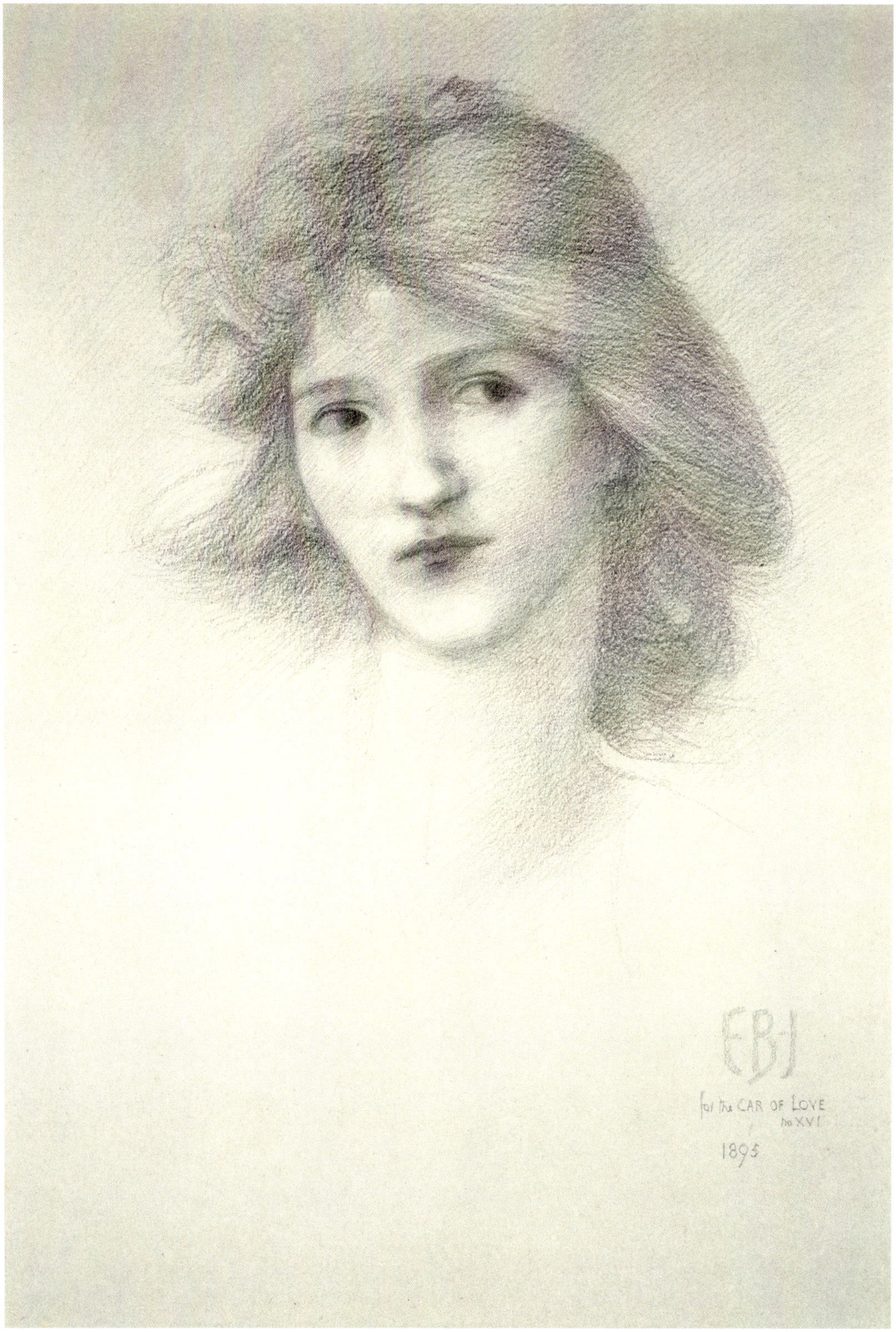

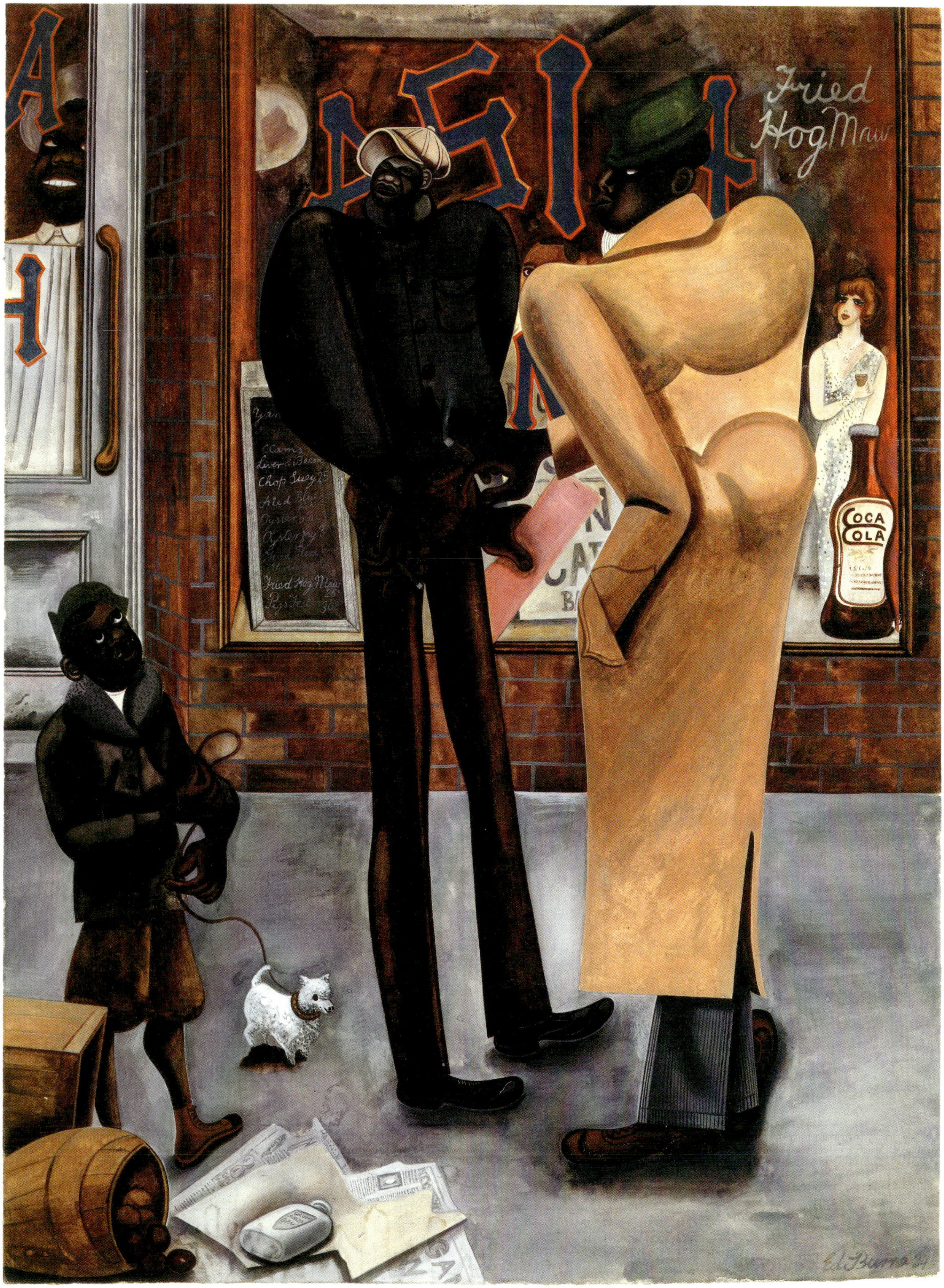
Fried
Hog Maw
COCA
COLA

Edward BURRA, A.R.A.

[1905–76]

Harlem, 1934

watercolour and bodycolour on paper, 55.3 × 41.9 cm
inscribed: *Ed.Burra '34*

P.133

PROVENANCE: Leicester Galleries, from whom purchased by Gallery, November 1957.
EXHIBITIONS: *Watercolours and Drawings from The Cecil Higgins Art Gallery Bedford*, London, Thos. Agnew & Sons Ltd, 1962, no.88; *Narrative Painting in Britain in the 20th Century*, London, Camden Arts Centre, 1970; *Cityscape*, Arts Council, Bradford, Bradford Art Gallery & London, R.A., 1977/78, no.32; *Unit 1*, Portsmouth, Portsmouth City Museum, 1978, no.E.B.4; *Edward Burra*, London, Hayward Gallery, 1985, no.81; *Rhapsodies in Black: Art of the Harlem Renaissance*, London, Hayward Gallery, Bristol, The Arnolfini & Coventry, Mead Gallery only, 1997, no.7.; *Edward Burra*, London, Olympia, 2001, no.26.
REFERENCES: A. Jenkins, *The Thirties*, 1976, p.206; R. Alley, *Modern British Painting – Tate Gallery*, vol.1, 1964, p.85; A. Causey, *Edward Burra*, 1985, no.109, unpaginated; H. Grubert, 'Cecil Higgins and his Collection', *Apollo*, Vol. CXVIII, No. 260, October, 1983, p.301; Sir J. Graham, 'A new Gainsborough watercolour and the Watercolour collection of the Cecil Higgins Art Gallery, Bedford', *Watercolours, Drawings and Prints,* vol.5, no.4, winter 1990, p.33, fig.4.

Burra lived in Harlem, New York, during 1933. This is one of a number of drawings of the neighbourhood he painted on his return to Britain in 1934. The figures depicted provided Burra with the opportunity to emphasize the fashions of New York City of the 1930s. By the thirties Harlem had become a vibrant centre for popular music such as jazz and blues. An even larger gouache of Harlem was bought by the Tate Gallery in 1939 (NO5004).

Born in London, Burra spent most of his life in Rye, Sussex. He studied art at the Chelsea Polytechnic School of Art and the R.C.A. When he travelled to Paris, Burra was inspired by the nightlife of the red-light districts and continued to paint these scenes from his imagination for several years.

EJ/CB

Edward BURRA, A.R.A.

[1905–76]

Rye Landscape with Figure, 1947

watercolour and pencil on paper, 88.3 × 110.2 cm

P.588

PROVENANCE: Alex Reid & Lefevre Ltd., from whom purchased by Gallery, January 1969.
EXHIBITIONS: *Narrative Painting in Britain in the 20th Century*, London, Camden Arts Centre, 1970; *Edward Burra*, London, Tate Gallery, 1973, no.80; *Edward Burra*, London, Hayward Gallery, 1985, no.104; *Burra in Rye*, Rye, Rye Art Gallery, 1989, no.25; *Edward Burra*, London, Olympia, 2001, no.8.
REFERENCES: M. Jacobs and M. Warner, *The Phaidon Companion to Art and Artists in the British Isles*, 1980, S.E.27; A.Causey, *Edward Burra*, 1985, no.180, unpaginated; E. Mullins, *A Love Affair with Nature*, 1985, p.149; A.Causey, *Edward Burra*, exhib. cat., 1985, p.123, no.104, repr. p.125.

Painted on four sheets of paper. Owing to ill health Burra often painted in bed on small pieces of paper which he afterwards joined together. The scene is a composite of two different views of Rye in Sussex, one towards Winchelsea and the other eastwards to the gravel pits. The figure was based on Dick Mills, Keeper at Springfield, the Burra home.

Burra lived in Rye, which he referred to derisively as the *Tinkerbell Town*. In 1929 he went to France with Jean Cocteau (1889–1963). In the early 1930s his satirical and forceful work recalled that of George Grosz (1893–1959). Later he concentrated more on landscape and everyday objects but his sharp, somewhat exaggerated figurative style changed little.

EJ/CB

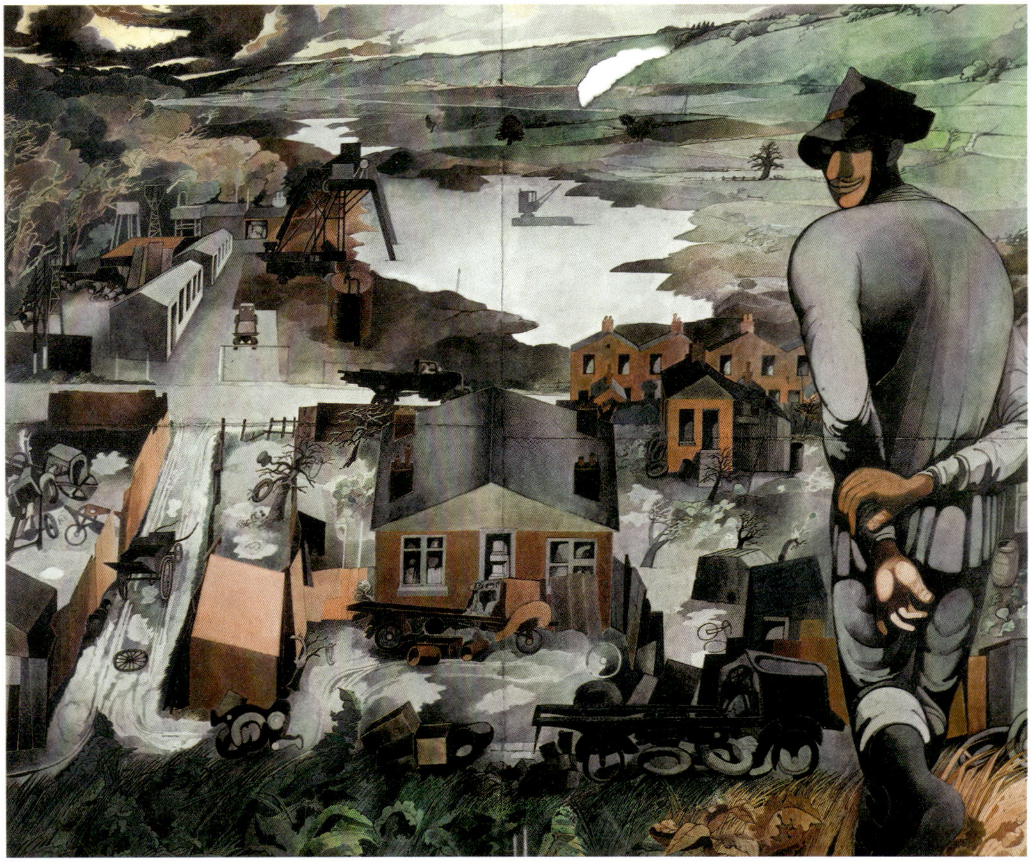

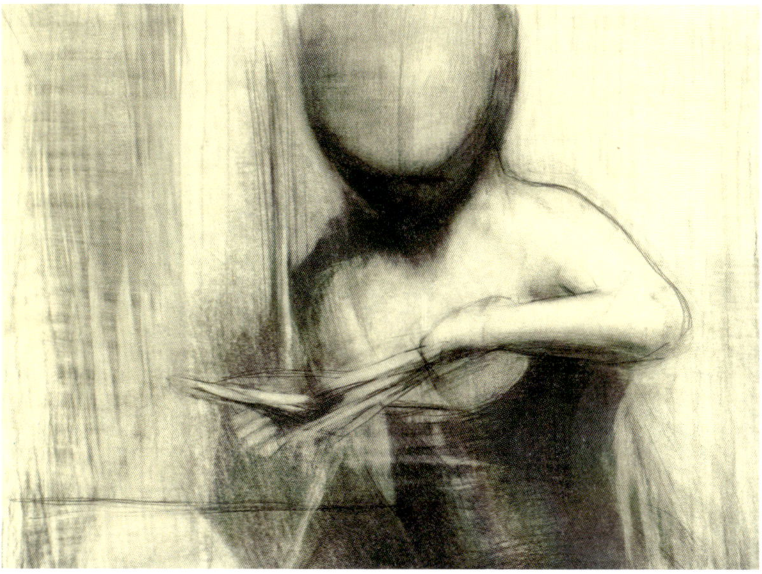

Reginald BUTLER

[1913–81]

The Manipulator, 1960

pencil and chalk on paper, 45.3 × 62.7 cm
inscribed: *Butler '60*

P.358
PROVENANCE: Hanover Gallery, from whom purchased by Gallery, July 1960.
EXHIBITIONS: *Primitives to Picasso*, London, R.A., 1962, no.418; *Watercolours and Drawings from The Cecil Higgins Art Gallery Bedford*, London, Thos. Agnew & Sons Ltd, 1962, no.116; *Watercolours from Bedford*, Norwich, Castle Museum, 1965, no. 5.

Butler trained as an architect, then worked as a blacksmith from 1941–5 before taking up sculpture and becoming an assistant to Henry MOORE in 1947. In 1952 he won a competition for a monument to the Unknown Political Prisoner. His original maquette (now destroyed) was enlarged into a working model, although the monument, intended to be over 300 feet high, was never made. Later he turned to naturalistically modelled sculptures of girls which dominated his work thereafter, their poses becoming more overtly erotic.

EJ

Randolph CALDECOTT

[1846–86]

Five Illustrations to **The Strange Adventures of a Dog-cart, c.1885**

watercolour, bodycolour and ink on paper,
P.161: 11.2 × 16.5 cm
P.162: 7.4 × 15.4 cm
P.163: 8.4 × 12.4 cm
P.164: 11.4 × 5.4 cm
P.501: 10.2 × 15.9 cm

P.161–164, 501
PROVENANCE: (P.501) Fine Art Society , from whom purchased by Gallery, June 1965; (P.161–4) P&D Colnaghi Ltd, from whom purchased by Gallery, January 1958.
REFERENCES: A. Locker (preface), *The Complete Collection of Randolph Caldecott's contributions to the 'Graphic'*, 1888, pp.273–290; R. Engen, *Randolph Caldecott, Lord of the Nursery*, 1976, p.100.

These five drawings were illustrated in the *Graphic*, summer, 1885. They told the story of *D* and *F*, and their misfortunes during a tour in their dog-cart. Three further drawings from the series were exhibited at the Chris Beetles Gallery in 1999.

Caldecott began life as a bank clerk in Manchester but, encouraged by the success of his sketches published in local papers, he came to London in 1872. He made his name with his illustrations to Washington Irving's (1783–1859) *Old Christmas* (1875) and *Bracebridge Hall* (1876). He was above all a caricaturist but his caricatures are always poetical and romantic, delicately coloured and drawn with great economy of line. He later achieved considerable success by his coloured illustrations to children's books, especially *The House that Jack Built* and *John Gilpin*, both issued in 1878.

EJ

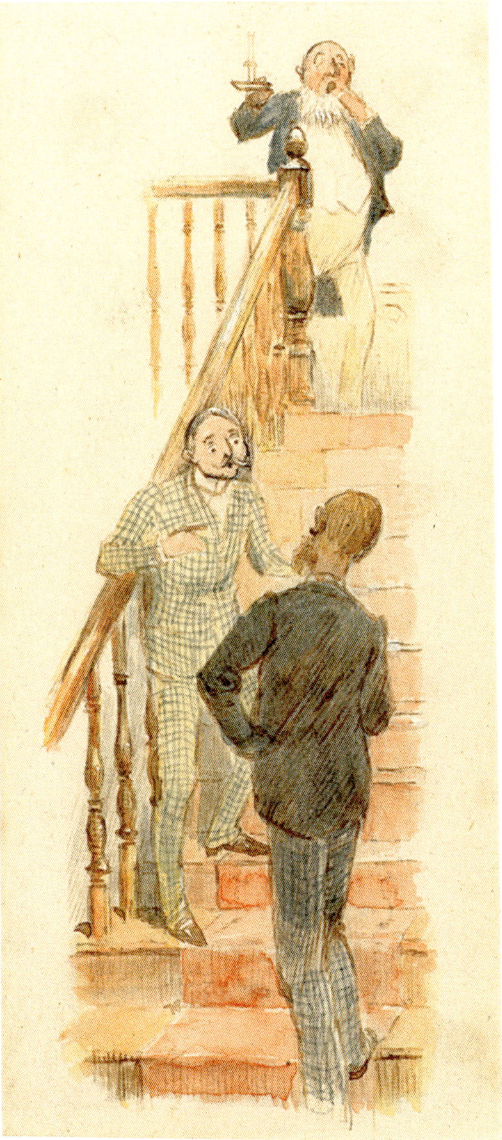

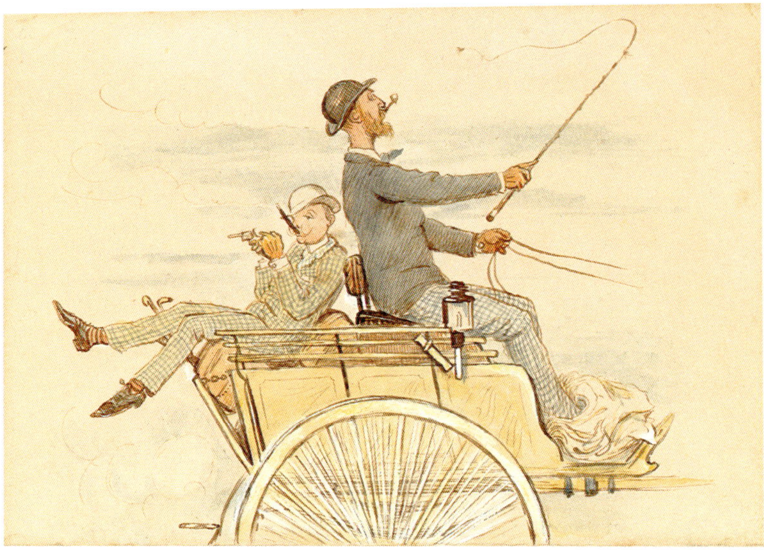

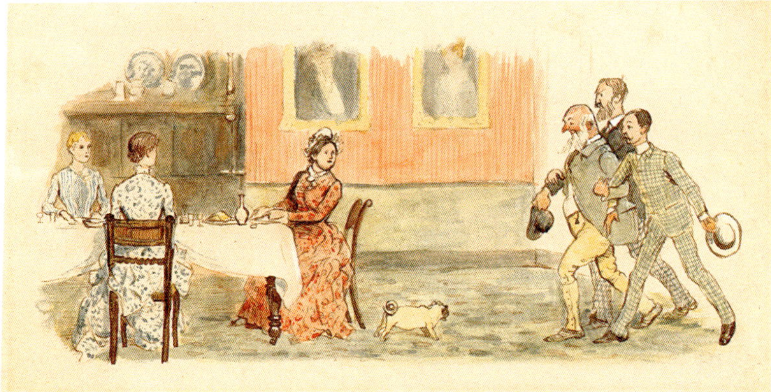

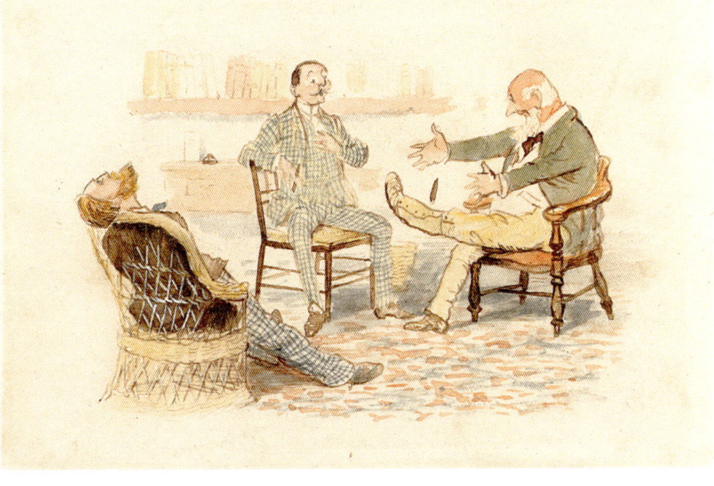

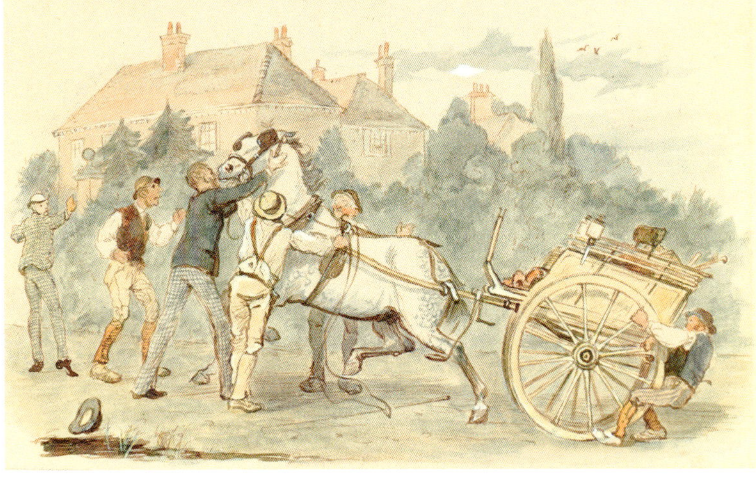

William CALLOW, R.W.S.
[1812–1908]
Le Château de Montélimar, 1836

watercolour and bodycolour on grey paper, 13.3 × 23.1 cm
inscribed: *CW Château de Montélimort [sic] Aout 2.36*

P.350
PROVENANCE: K.M. Gardiner; P&D Colnaghi Ltd, from whom purchased by Gallery, July 1960.
EXHIBITIONS: *Watercolours and Drawings from The Cecil Higgins Art Gallery, Bedford*, London, Thos. Agnew & Sons Ltd, 1962, no.55.
REFERENCES: J. Reynolds, *William Callow R.W.S.*, 1980, pp.62–3, 171, ill.14.

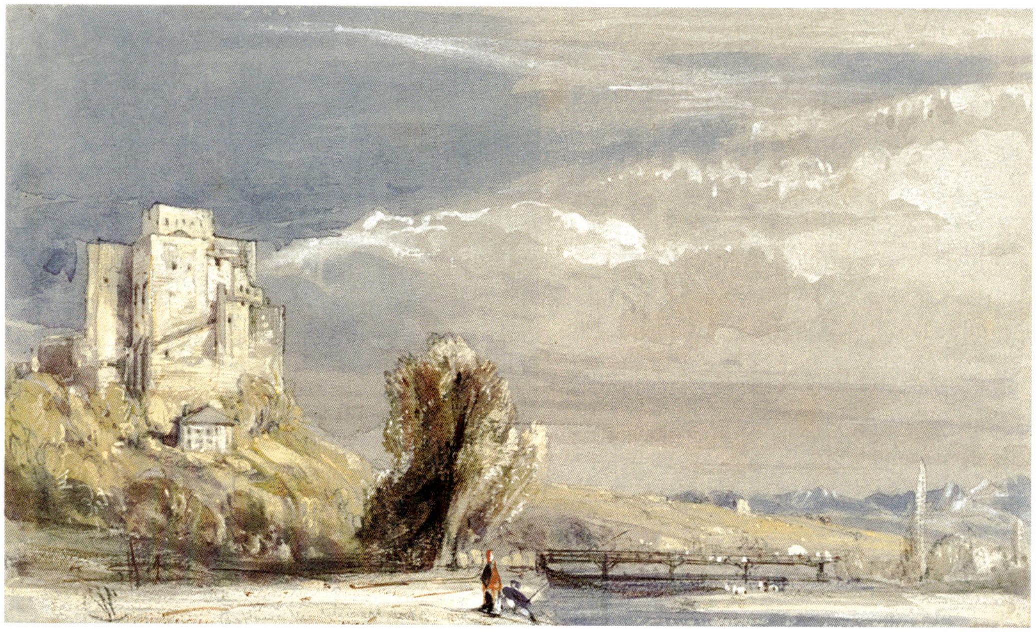

In his diary of 2 August 1836, Callow describes how, while walking towards Montélimar ' I was over taken by a patache, the worst description of a coach ever invented, and I was to my sorrow tempted by an offer to take me to Montélimar for ten sous. I was almost suffocated by the heat, and every bone in my body was nearly dislocated by the jolting'.

Perhaps it was this experience that caused Callow to suggest, by his punning inscription on the reverse, that he was almost dead on arrival at Montélimar, which is on the Rhône about 50 miles north of Avignon.

EJ

William CALLOW, R.W.S.
[1812–1908]
Near Huddersfield, 1862

watercolour over pencil on paper, 20.3 × 50.2 cm
inscribed: *Wm. Callow Near Huddersfield 1862*

P.57
PROVENANCE: Gilbert Davis; P&D Colnaghi Ltd, from whom purchased by Gallery, February 1953.
EXHIBITIONS: Royal Society of Painters in Water-colours, *Summer Exhibition*, London, 1908, no.233.
REFERENCE: J. Reynolds, *William Callow R.W.S.,* 1980, p.155, 171, 228, illus.77.

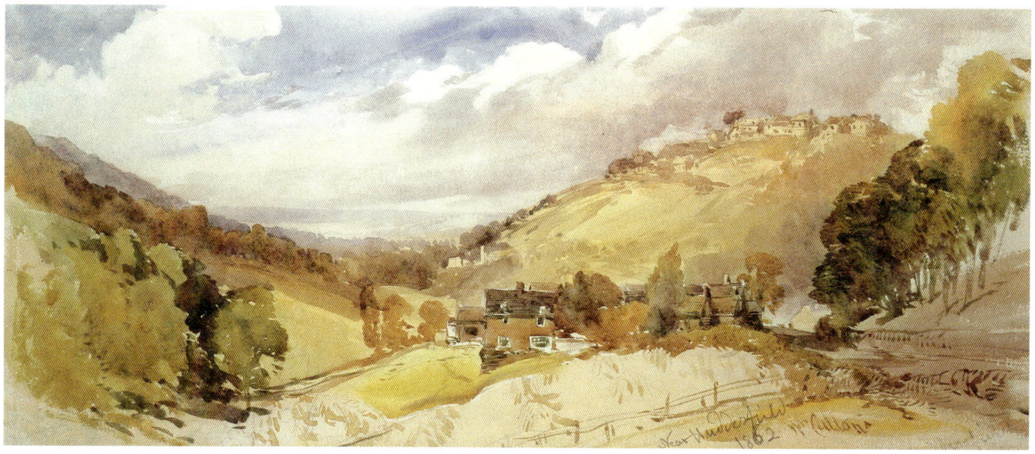

This work, despite having been painted in 1862, was first exhibited after Callow's death in 1908. In earlier days, Callow would not have thought this suitable for display. However, the watercolour was selected by his wife, who appeared to show more business acumen than Callow himself.

CB

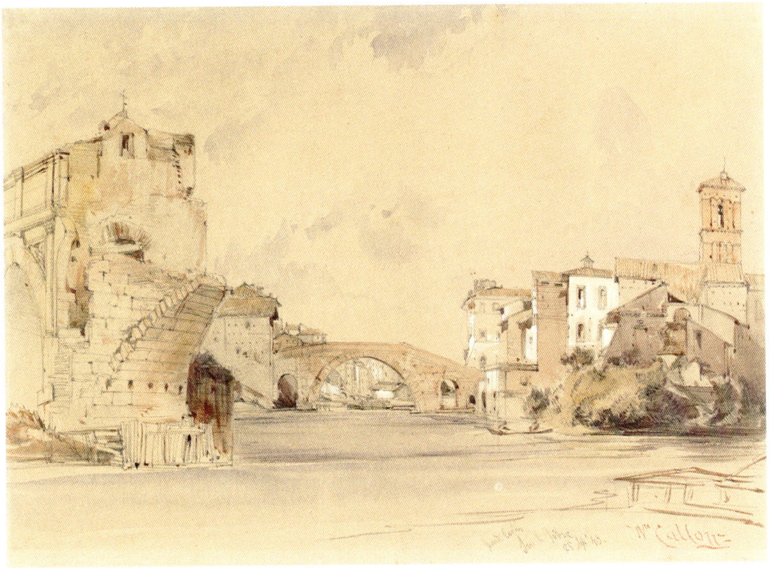

William CALLOW, R.W.S.

[1812–1908]

Ponte Cestio, Rome, 1840

watercolour, bodycolour and pencil on buff paper,
26 × 36.6 cm
inscribed: *Wm.Callow Ponte Cestio sur Le Tibre, 25 Sept'40*

P.318
PROVENANCE: Walker's Galleries; Sotheby's; P&D Colnaghi Ltd, from whom purchased by Gallery, January 1960.
EXHIBITIONS: *William Callow's Sketches,* London, Walker's Galleries, 1927, no.30 as *The Old Bridge, Verona.*
REFERENCES: J. Reynolds, *William Callow R.W.S.,* 1980, pp.171, 247, illus. 28, as *Ponte Cartro.*

The Ponte Cestio (originally the Pons Cestius) was built in the first century B.C. but largely rebuilt 1887–90. The view is taken looking upstream towards the bridge with the Ponte Rotto ('broken bridge') in the foreground. A similar view by David ROBERTS is also in the Gallery's collection (P.256).

EJ

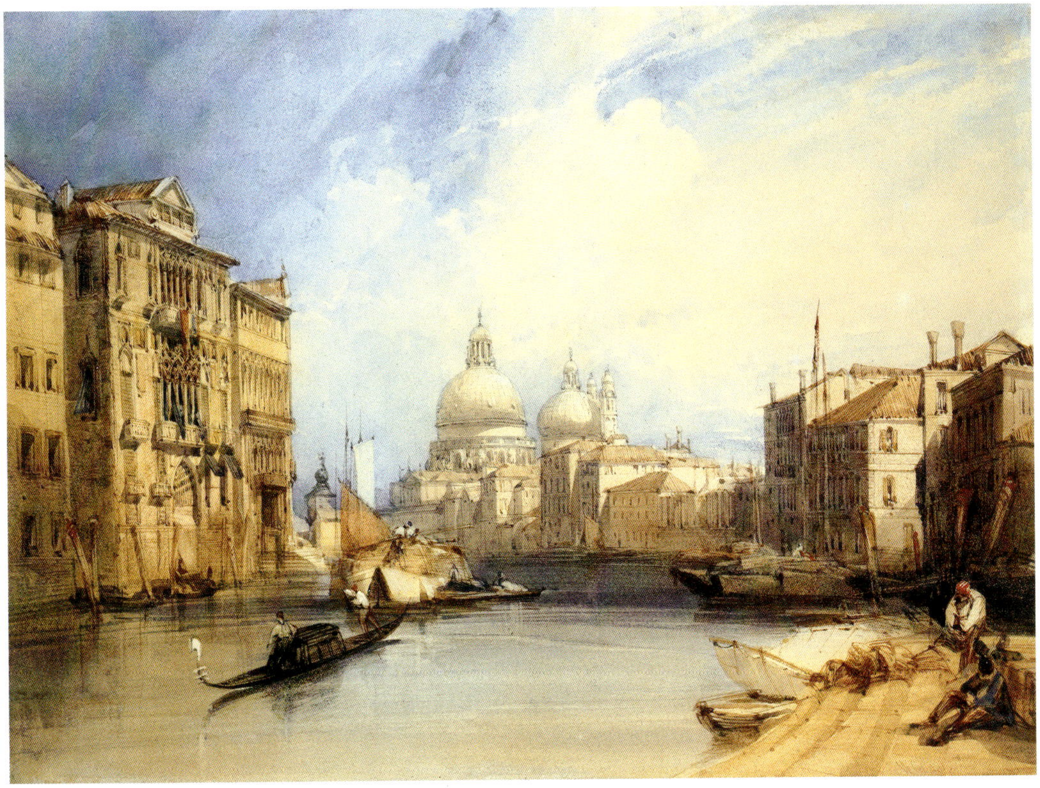

William CALLOW, R.W.S.

[1812–1908]

The Grand Canal, Venice, 1879

watercolour, bodycolour and pen and ink on paper,
23.2 × 32.1 cm
inscribed: *W.Callow 79*

P.610
PROVENANCE: Mrs M. Noel; Christie's sale, 20 October 1970, lot 72, Thos. Agnew & Sons Ltd, on behalf of Gallery.
EXHIBITIONS: *British Watercolours: A Golden Age 1750–1850,* Louisville, Kentucky, J.B. Speed Art Museum, 1977, no.91.
REFERENCES: J. Reynolds, *William Callow,* 1980, p.171; S. Somerville, *British Watercolours: A Golden Age 1750–1850,* 1977, p.118, repr.p.119, no.91.

This view, showing the cupolas of Santa Maria della Salute in the middle distance, has a strong claim to being the most frequently painted in European art.

Callow was the longest-lived and one of the most prolific of all watercolourists. He trained under Theodore Fielding (1781–1851), Copley FIELDING's elder brother. Callow moved to Paris in 1829 where he soon became friends with T.S. BOYS, whose studio he took over in 1834 and whose watercolours had a marked influence on his. During his stay in Paris, Callow became the tutor of the children of Louis Philippe (1773–1850). Callow was a great traveller and, before the introduction of railways, covered much of Europe on foot.

EJ

Thomas CARWITHAM
[fl.1713–33]
Illustration to Ovid's **Metamorphoses, Book 2, c.1723**

pen and ink on paper, 28.1 × 19 cm
inscribed: *Met.lib.2*

P.445
PROVENANCE: Maas Gallery, from whom purchased by Gallery, March 1963.
EXHIBITIONS: *Spring Exhibition,* London, Maas Gallery , 1963, no.7.
REFERENCES: I. Williams, *Early English Watercolours,* 1952, p.14.

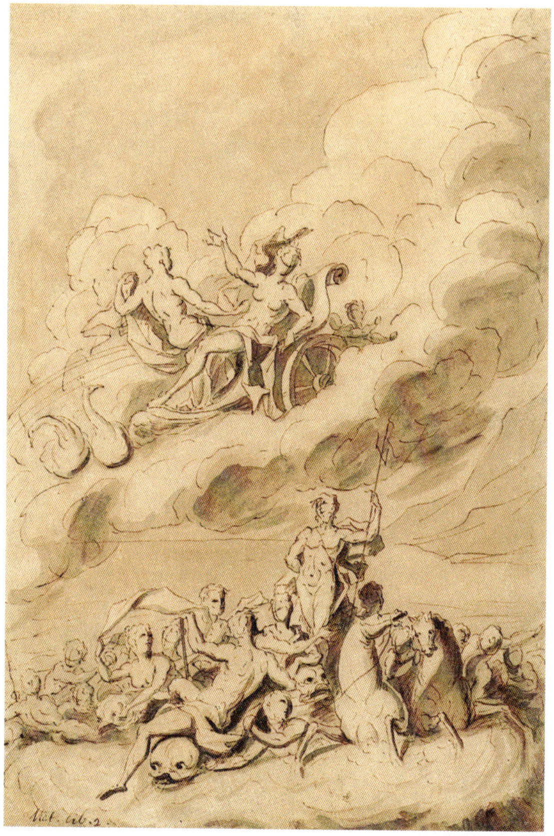

This drawing illustrates the end of the story of Callisto, one of Diana's nymphs who, seduced by Jupiter, bore a son, Arcas. Juno was so enraged by this that she changed Callisto into a bear. Years later, when Arcas was out hunting, he came across the bear. He was about to kill her with his javelin when Jupiter stayed his hand and swept them both into the sky as the constellation – the Great Bear and the Little Bear.

Juno, in fury when 'that concubine shone among the stars', descended to the sea-gods and made the promise to debar the stars 'from your green deeps...nor let that prostitute your waters' pure integrity pollute'. This they agreed to do, and so Juno departed heavenwards with her light chariot and her peacock team.

Almost nothing is known of Carwitham except that he was an architectural draughtsman and painter who lived at Twickenham. In 1723, he wrote *The Description and Use of an Architectonic Sector*. Iolo Williams describes him as an *imitator* of THORNHILL's and illustrates another ambitious composition for Ovid's *Metamorphoses* (*Early English Watercolours*, 1952, pl.24) which was then in his own collection but is now in the British Museum.

EJ

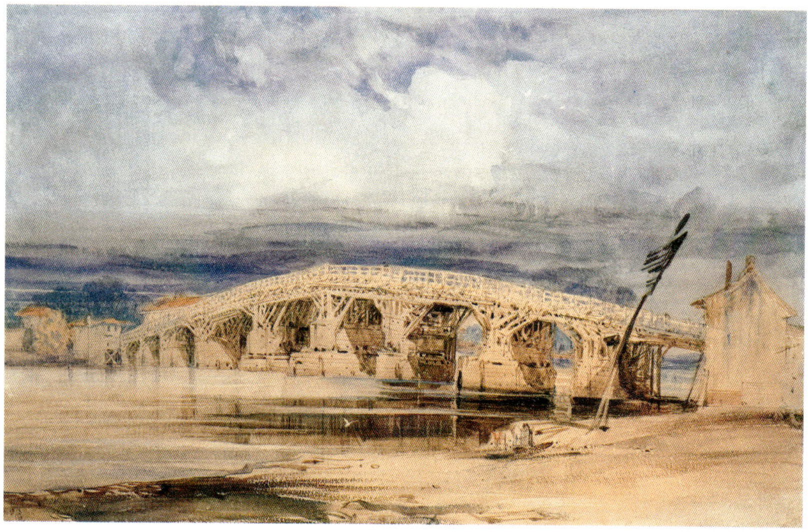

George CATTERMOLE, R.W.S.
[1800–68]
A Bridge, c.1840

watercolour with pencil with scratching out on buff paper, 29.2 × 47 cm
inscribed: with monogram *GC*

P.708
PROVENANCE: Sotheby's, London, sale 22 November 1979, lot 163 as *Putney Bridge,* from whom purchased by Thos. Agnew & Sons Ltd, on behalf of Gallery with the assistance of a grant from the V&A/M.G.C. Purchase Grant Fund.
REFERENCES: H. Grubert, 'Cattermole's Bridge', *Country Life*, 24 April 1980.

Previously catalogued as *Putney Bridge*, which is incorrect; all attempts to identify the bridge have so far failed. The second bridge to be built across the Thames (c.1778–c.1865) at Hampton Court seems the most likely candidate but this has not been established beyond doubt.

This is a welcome departure from his usual subjects for Cattermole, who concentrated on historical – especially medieval scenes. William Thackeray (1811–63) wrote: 'Monks, cavaliers, battles, banditti, knightly halls and awful enchanted forests...are the subjects in which he chiefly delights'. Cattermole was also a close friend of Charles Dickens (1812–70), whose *Barnaby Rudge* and *Old Curiosity Shop* he illustrated.

In 1839 he declined a knighthood from Queen Victoria for the large *Diet of Spires, 1529*, a subject the Queen had proposed.

EJ

George CHINNERY
[1774–1852]
Street in Macao

pen, ink and watercolour over black lead on paper, 17.8 × 26.5 cm

P.384
PROVENANCE: E. Martin; Thos. Agnew & Sons Ltd, from whom purchased by Gallery, January 1961.
EXHIBITIONS: *Watercolours and Drawings from The Cecil Higgins Art Gallery Bedford*, London, Thos. Agnew & Sons Ltd, 1962, no.51.
REFERENCES: *Illustrated London News*, 28 January, 1961, p.147, illus.

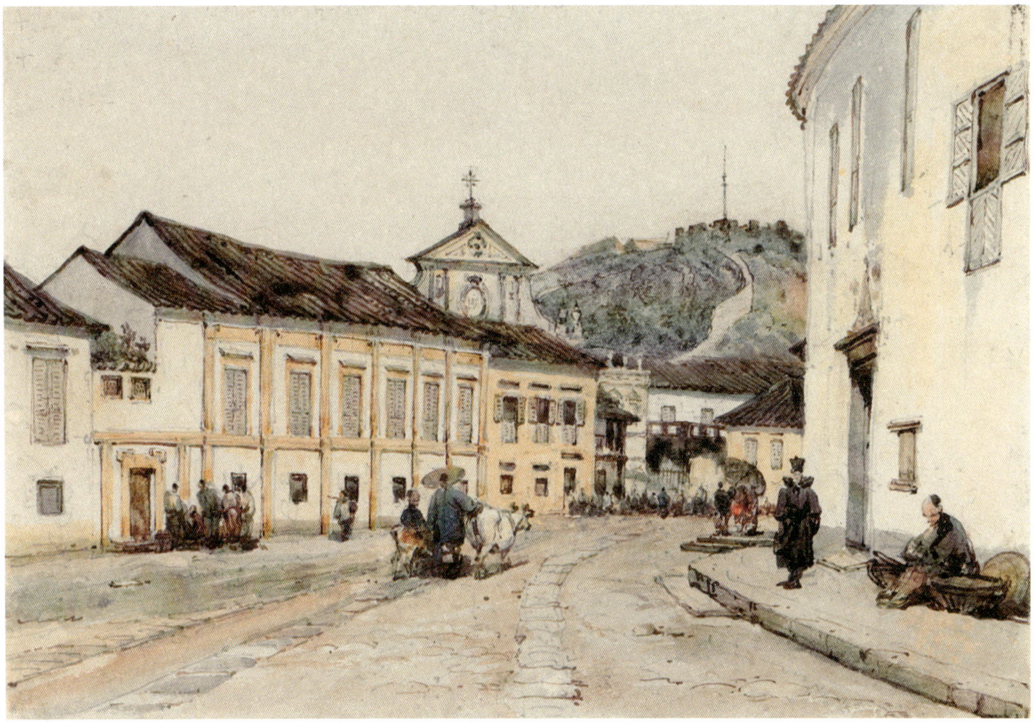

After a few years in Dublin where he painted portraits, Chinnery went to India in 1802, probably to escape from his wife, of whom he later said: 'Mrs Chinnery's appearance cannot be exaggerated. She was an ugly woman thirty years ago. What in the name of the Graces can she be now?' He stayed in India, working in Madras and Calcutta until 1825 when, in order to get rid of his debts, he moved to China, remaining there for the rest of his life. He is buried in Macao.

His watercolours are usually small, rich in colour and with lively pen drawing. Like James WARD, he often annotated his rough sketches in shorthand.

EJ

George CHINNERY
[1774–1852]
Chow

watercolour on paper, 13.2 × 21.6 cm

P.385
PROVENANCE: E. Martin; Thos. Agnew & Sons Ltd., from whom purchased by Gallery, January 1961

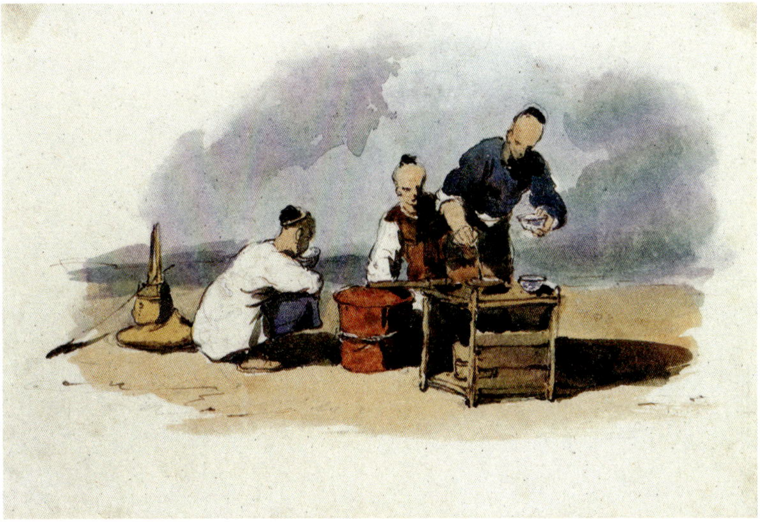

Chinnery spent the last twenty-five years of his life living in Macao. He was unable to travel while in China, as the government restricted the movement of visitors. However, he would set off at dawn each morning to draw scenes of everyday life, such as street-cooking, as depicted here.

He taught two Chinese pupils, Lamqua and Sunqua, to paint in the European manner. However, they undercut Chinnery's prices while he was still alive and produced fake 'Chinnerys' after his death.

CB

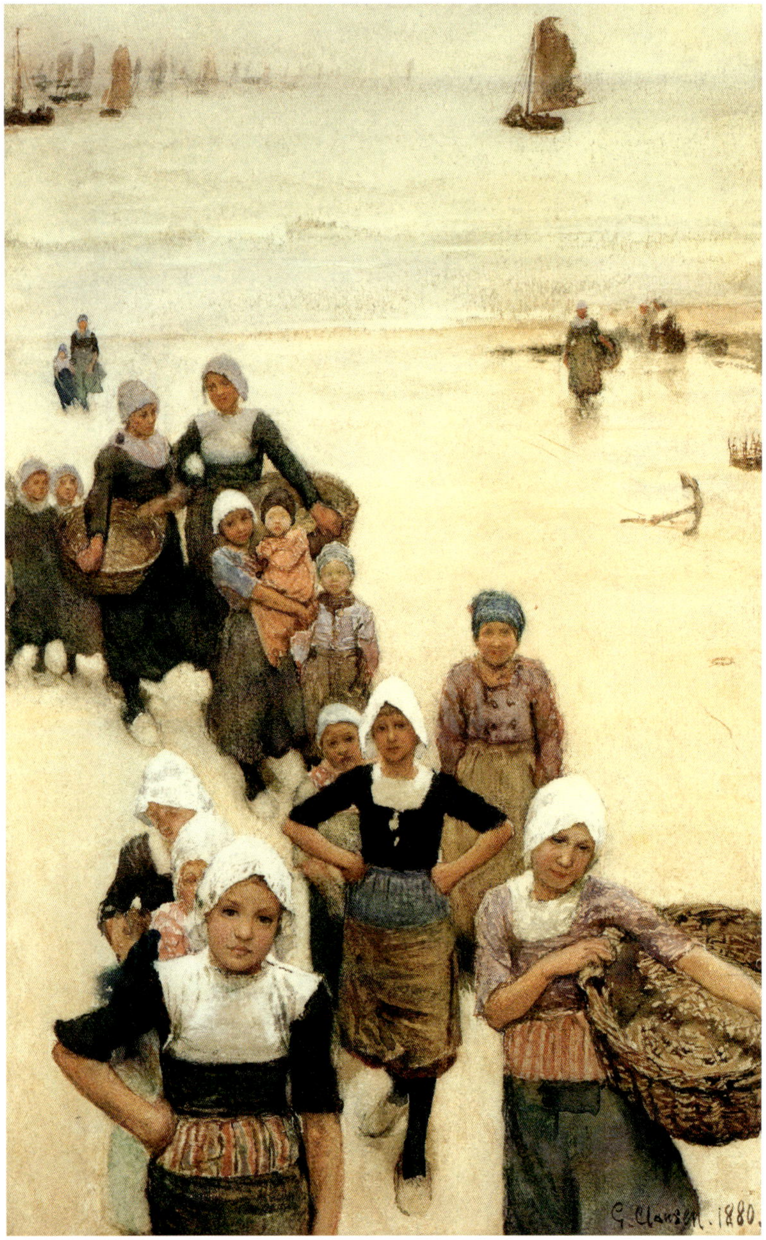

Sir George CLAUSEN, R.A., R.W.S.

[1852–1944]

Fisher Girls on Beach, 1880

watercolour and bodycolour on paper, 41.8 × 26.8 cm
inscribed: *G. Clausen 1880*

P.242

PROVENANCE: Piccadilly Gallery, from whom purchased by Gallery, July 1958.
EXHIBITIONS: *Sir George Clausen R.A.*, Bradford, Cartwright Hall, London, R.A., Bristol, Bristol City Art Gallery & Newcastle upon Tyne, Laing Art Gallery, 1980, no.6.
REFERENCES: K. McConkey, *Sir George Clausen R.A.*, exhib. cat., 1980, pp.19–21, illus. p.20.

Fisher girls on beaches were a popular Victorian subject matter. Clausen visited Holland and Belgium in 1875 and subsequently exhibited a number of Dutch subjects in London until 1883. A sketch of this painting is in the Royal Academy collection.

Clausen, the son of a Danish decorative artist, initially trained as an architect before studying art at the South Kensington Schools and in Paris. He was a founder member of the N.E.A.C. but never broke away from the R.A and can best be classified as a 'progressive Academician'.

EJ/CB

Sir George CLAUSEN, R.A., R.W.S.

[1852–1944]

A Shepherd with a Lamb, 1883

watercolour on paper, 41.1 × 31.2 cm
inscribed: *G.Clausen 1883*

P.151

PROVENANCE: Sharpley Bainbridge, Hatfield House, Lincoln; P&D Colnaghi Ltd., from whom purchased by Gallery, January 1958.
EXHIBITIONS: London, *Institute of Painters in Watercolour 65th exhibition*, 1883, no.417, illus. 23; *Autumn Exhibition of Modern Pictures*, Liverpool, Walker Art Gallery, 1884, no.964; *Autumn Exhibition*, Manchester, Corporation of Manchester Art Gallery, 1910, no.73; Manchester, Manchester Art Gallery, 1919; *Watercolours from Bedford*, Norwich, Castle Museum, 1965, no.6; *George Clausen R.A.*, Bradford, Cartwright Hall, London, R.A., Bristol, Bristol City Art Gallery & Newcastle upon Tyne, Laing Art Gallery, 1980, no.34, p.39, illus.
REFERENCES: 'Art Notes', *The Magazine of Art*, vol. 6, 1884, p.429, p.xxix; *The Magazine of Art*, vol. 18, 1895, p.403; A. Bury, 'The Cecil Higgins Museum, Bedford: A Preliminary Survey', *The Old Water-colour Society's Club*, 1961, vol.XXXVI, pp.31–40, pl. xiv; K. McConkey, *George Clausen*, exhib. cat., 1980, pp.39–40.

In the 1880s Clausen specialized in painting realistic scenes of rural life. His sketchbooks of the period show this shepherd, who worked at Childwick Green near St. Albans, where the artist had moved in 1881. Clausen's sketchbooks also contain drawings of the shepherd carrying hurdles to build the sheep pen, so perhaps Clausen intended to paint finished pictures of both these clearly related subjects.

When this painting was exhibited at the Institute of Painters in Watercolour in 1883, a critic writing in *The Magazine of Art* of 1884 wrote 'Mr. Clausen, we are glad to see, has returned to Millet'. Clausen was indeed much influenced by the French Realist painters, in particular Jules Bastien-Lepage (1848–84). He described painting scenes from real life as a 'liberation'.

EJ/CB

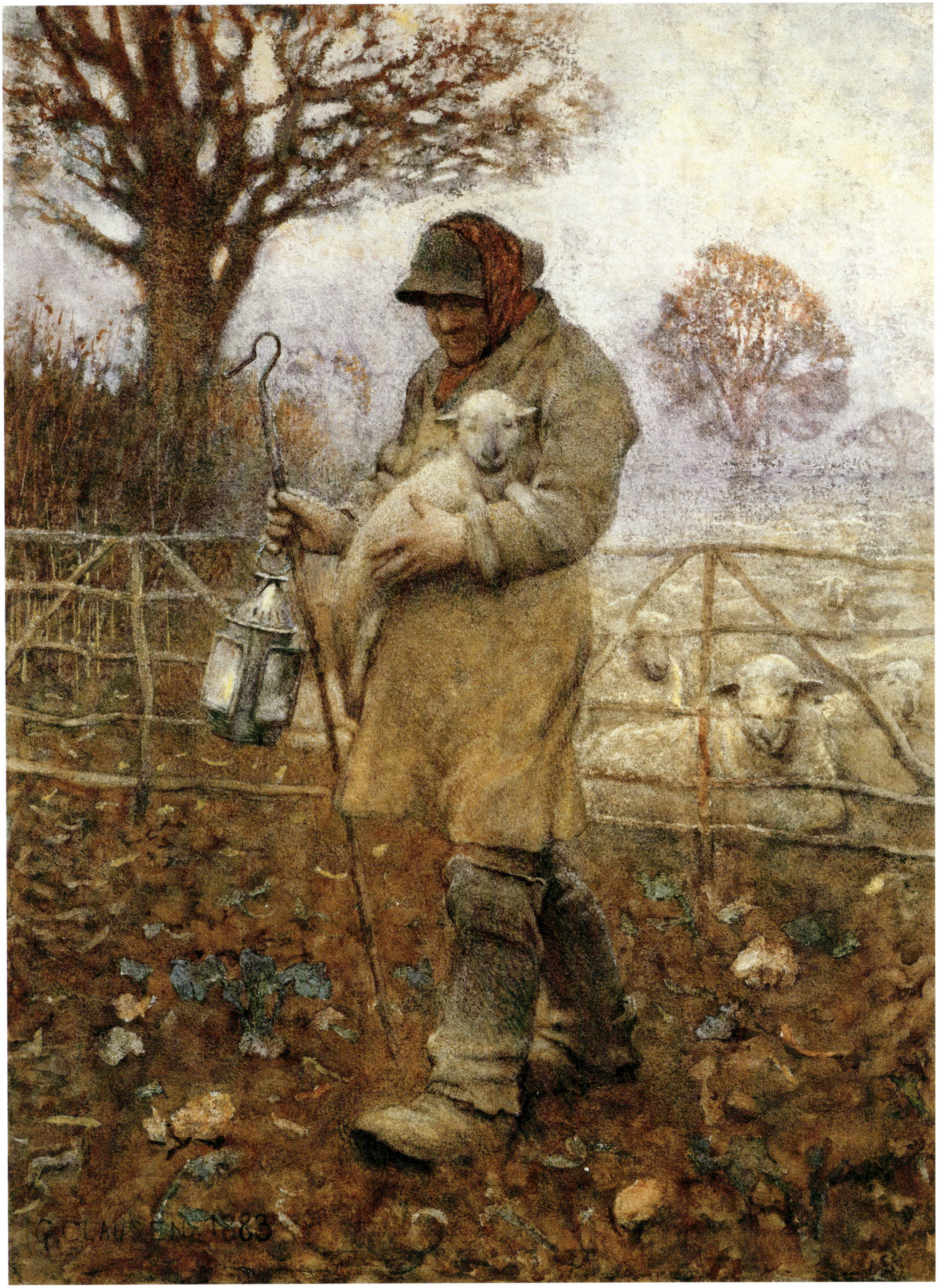
G. CLAUSEN 1883

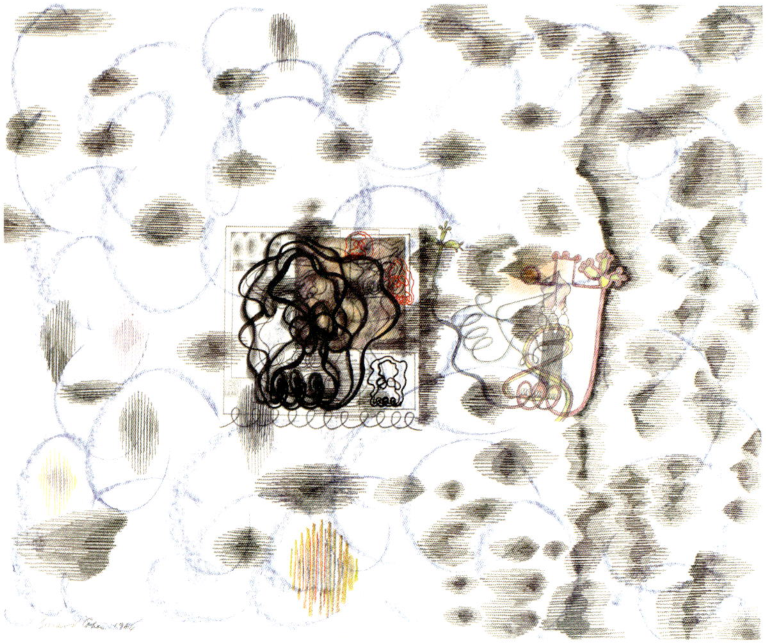

Bernard COHEN

[b. 1933]

Untitled Drawing, 1964

pen, ink and crayon on paper, 43.8 × 54.6 cm
inscribed: *Bernard Cohen 1964*

P.485
PROVENANCE: The artist; Kasmin Ltd, from whom purchased by Gallery, January 1965.

Referring to his work, Bernard Cohen was quoted in *Art Review*, November 1994, as saying: 'I don't have natural 'models' to work from, so I don't draw from a one-eyed, fixed position view of the world. I don't want to communicate theories, messages or ideas. I draw and paint because I love the activity and know that my art is the best part of me …'

Cohen is an abstract painter and younger brother of Harold Cohen. He studied at St. Martin's School of Art and then at the Slade 1951–4. He contributed to the 'Situation' exhibitions of 1960 and 1961 at the Royal Society of British Artists (where pictures had to measure not less than 30 sq. feet). From 1980–87 Cohen was the Head of Painting at the Wimbledon School of Art; in 1988 he was appointed Professor and Director of the Slade.

EJ

Sir William COLDSTREAM

[1908–87]

Ruins of the Temple Malatestiano, Rimini, 1945

pencil on paper, 17.5 × 25.4 cm

P.360
PROVENANCE: Victor Pasmore, from whom purchased by Gallery, July 1960.

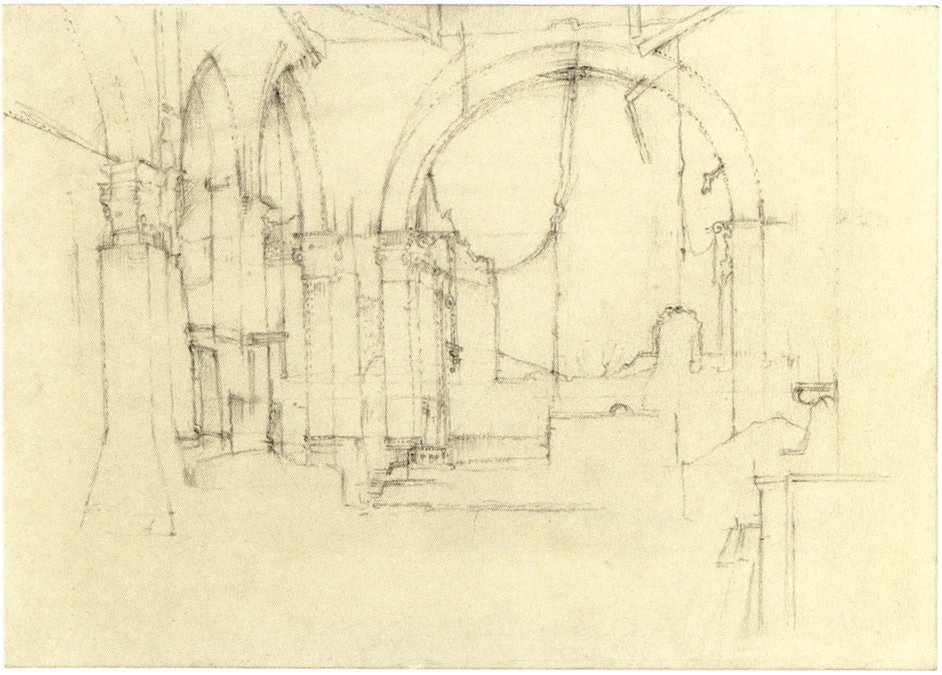

Drawn in 1945 when Coldstream was an Official War Artist in Italy, after the Tempio had suffered bomb damage.

Painter and teacher, Coldstream studied at the Slade, later meeting W.H. Auden (1907–73), PASMORE and SICKERT. During the economic slump of the 1930s Auden persuaded him to turn to painting portraits, which brought him considerable success. In an attempt to exclude subjective responses to both his subject and his painting, Coldstream devised a system of measuring using horizontal and vertical marks. He kept his sitters awake by encouraging them to tell him stories about themselves, saying 'Much better to sit for a painter than go to a psychiatrist'.

Co-founder, with Pasmore and Claude Rogers (1907–79), of the Euston Road School in 1937. He taught at Camberwell, 1945–8 and was Slade Professor of Fine Art, 1949–75. He was a trustee of both the National and Tate Galleries; a director of the Royal Opera House and a chairman of the British Film Institute. As author of the first and second Coldstream Reports in 1960 and 1970, he was said to have reshaped art education. He was knighted in 1956.

EJ/CB

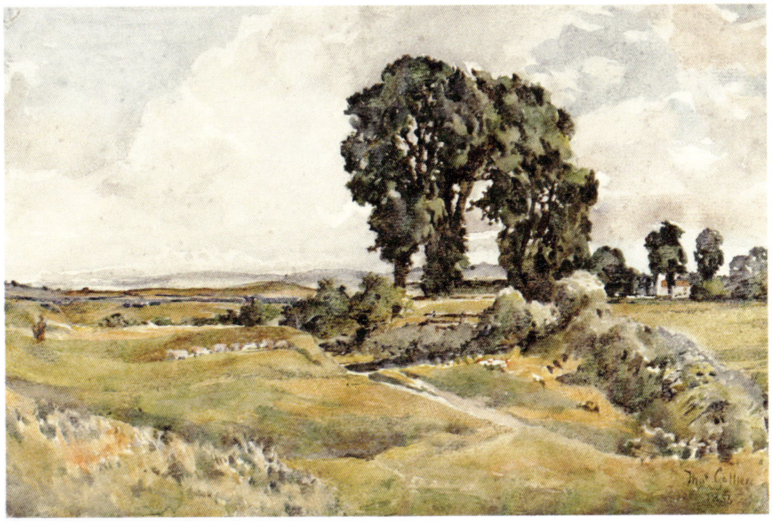

Thomas COLLIER

[1840–91]

A Landscape with Cattle, 1855

watercolour and bodycolour on paper, 17.5 × 26.7 cm
inscribed: Thos. Collier 1855

P.149
PROVENANCE: P&D Colnaghi Ltd, from whom purchased by Gallery, January 1958.

A largely self-taught artist of independent means but with indifferent health, Collier is considered by Martin HARDIE to be 'one of the supreme water-colour painters of England'. Hardie credits him with 'bringing back the open air into the art of water-colour' after the Pre-Raphaelites and their followers favoured instead high polish and jewel-like finish. Although his range was limited, he preferred to work outdoors with fluid brushstrokes in the manner of COX and DE WINT.

EJ

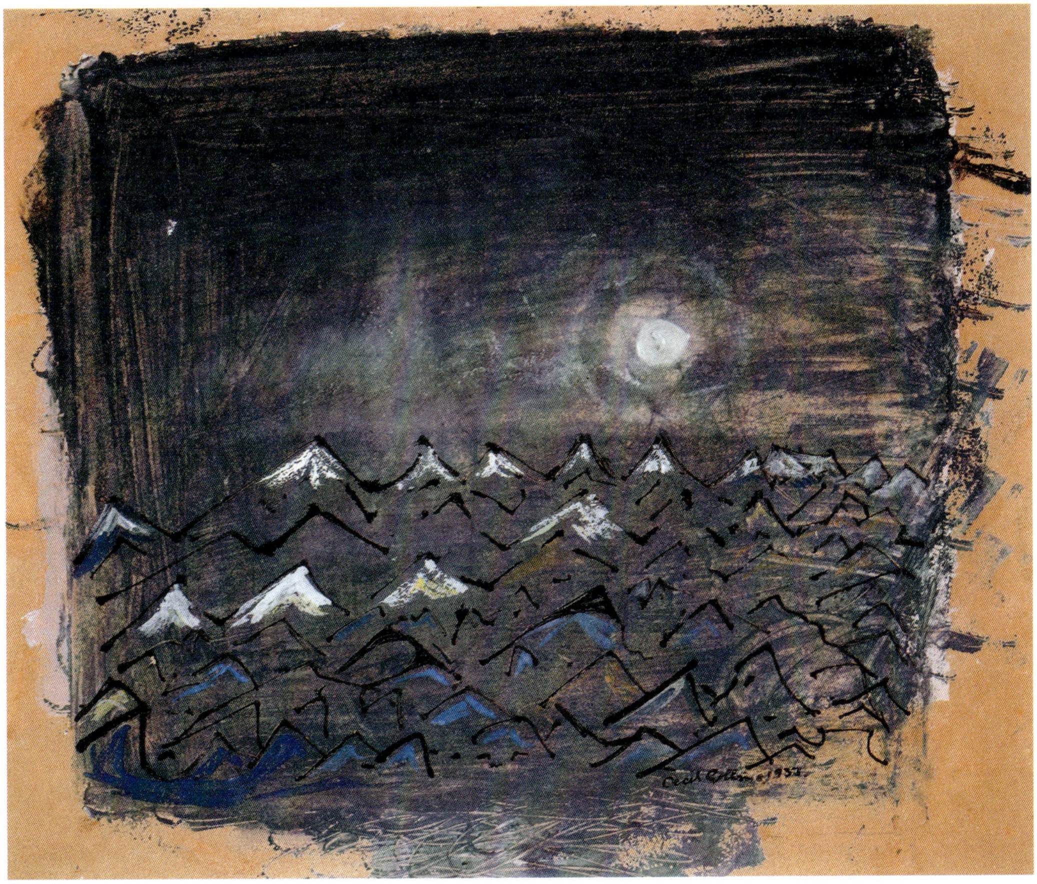

Cecil COLLINS, R.A.

[1908–89]

The Rising Moon, 1937

bodycolour and ink on pink paper, 25.5 × 26.5 cm
inscribed: *Cecil Collins 1937*
on reverse: *The Rising Moon September October 1937 Devonshire*

P.554
PROVENANCE: Crane Kalman Gallery, from whom purchased by Gallery, April 1967.

Collins was an artist in the visionary tradition of William BLAKE. Painter of mystical works, also an illustrator and tapestry designer. His early works were much influenced by Surrealism, Paul Klee (1879–1940), Pablo Picasso (1881–1973) and Max Ernst (1891–1976). He trained at the Plymouth School of Art and later won a scholarship to the R.C.A., 1927–31. He exhibited in the International Surrealist exhibition of 1936 and in the same year moved to Totnes in Devon, near Dartington Hall, where he later taught. One of his major commissions included the altar front for the Chapel of St. Clement in Chichester Cathedral in 1973.

EJ

Charles COLLINS

[*c.* 1680–1744]

The Common Buzzard (Buteo buteo), 1739

watercolour and bodycolour on paper, 54 × 38 cm
inscribed: *Chas. Collins. G:ool 1739*
on reverse: *Common Buzzard or Dunkite from Mr More*

P.343
PROVENANCE: Sotheby's, 16 February 1960, lot no. 313; from whom purchased by Gallery, February 1960.
EXHIBITIONS: *Watercolours and Drawings from The Cecil Higgins Art Gallery Bedford*, London, Thos. Agnew & Sons Ltd, 1962, no.4; *English Watercolours from The Cecil Higgins Art Gallery, Bedford*, Reading, Reading Art Gallery, 1965, no.3.
REFERENCES: C. Jackson, *Bird Painting: the 18th Century*, 1994, p.50.

The Common Buzzard was made for *British Zoology*, Folio ed.1761–6, p.66, written by Thomas Pennant (1726–98).

Collins' bird portraits are remarkable for their accuracy of plumage and colour. They are often shown in a way that depicts their habits: a tern swooping, a ruff displaying in breeding plumage and so on. Here, although Collins shows the buzzard, so majestic in flight, on the ground, he has imparted a predatory gleam to its eye.

EJ

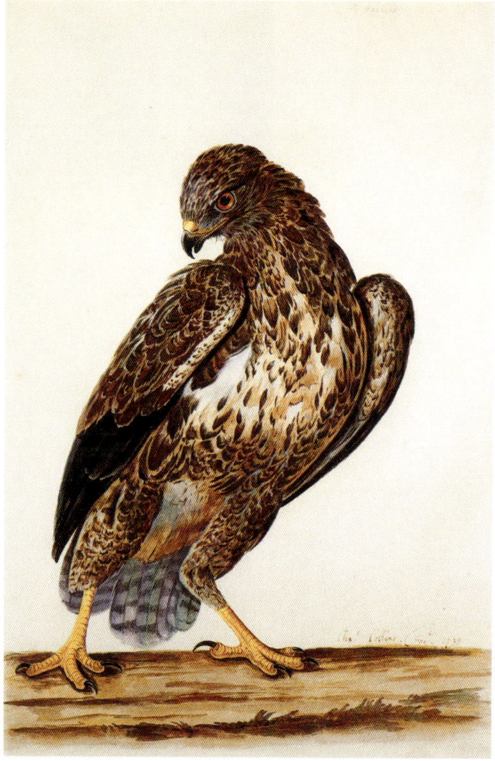

Charles Edward CONDER

[1868–1909]

A Masque for 'The Yellow Book', 1897

pen and ink on paper, 21.9 × 13.5 cm
inscribed: *CONDER*
on reverse: *a Masque see the 'Yellow Book' XIII April 1897*

P.168
PROVENANCE: P&D Colnaghi Ltd, from whom purchased by Gallery, January 1958.

A masque is defined as a form of amateur histrionic entertainment, popular at Court in the 16th and 17th centuries, consisting of dancing and acting in dumb show, where performers are masked.

The Yellow Book (1894–7) was a handsome but short-lived publication, devoted to literature and art, which immediately became notorious due to an essay in its first issue by Max BEERBOHM: *A Defence of Cosmetics*. Besides Conder, other artists represented were BEARDSLEY, SICKERT and STEER while Edmund Gosse (1849–1928), Arnold Bennett (1867–1931) and Henry James (1843–1916) were among the authors it published.

EJ

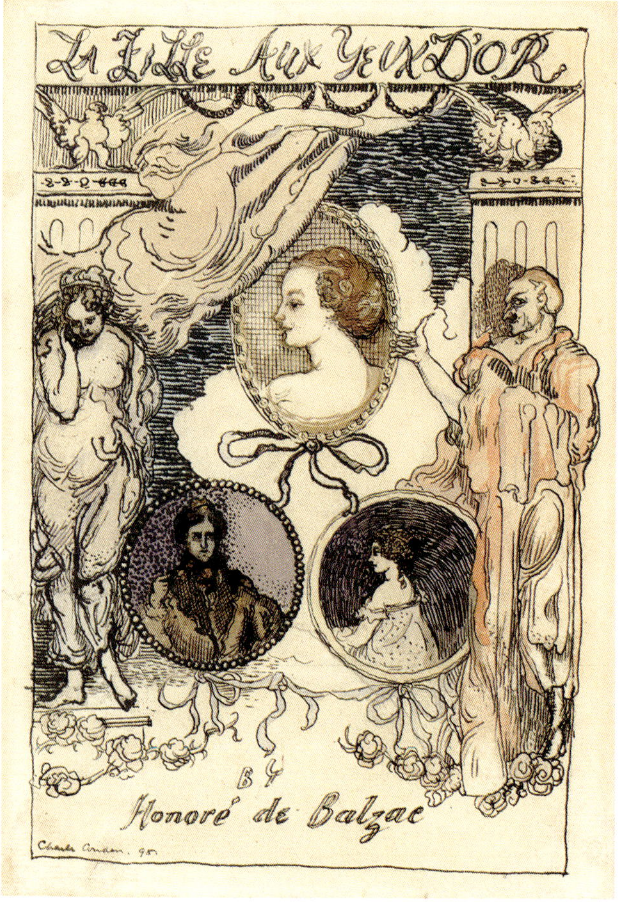

Charles Edward CONDER

[1868–1909]

Frontispiece for **La Fille aux Yeux d'Or** by Honoré de Balzac, **1895**

pen, ink and watercolour on paper, 20.5 × 13.5 cm
inscribed: *Charles Conder '95*

P.167
PROVENANCE: Elkin, Matthews Ltd; P&D Colnaghi Ltd, from whom purchased by Gallery, January 1958.
REFERENCES: V.S. Pritchetts, *Life of Balzac*, 1973, p.150.

La Fille aux Yeux d'Or (The Girl with the Golden Eyes), which was published in 1835, is said to have been inspired by Eugène Delacroix's (1798–1863)*The Girl with the Perroquet*.

This story concerns a young man named Henri de Marsya, who falls in love on seeing 'The Girl with the Golden Eyes', a ravishingly beautiful Spaniard named Paquita Valdes. He determines to possess her but she is closely guarded. Eventually she arranges an assignation to which Henri is led blindfold. During the climax of their love-making, Paquita calls out 'Mariquita', the name of her lesbian lover. Furious, Henri decides to kill her but when he returns later to do so, he finds her already dying, stabbed many times by Mariquita for betraying her with Henri.

As a final twist, when Henri and Mariquita face each other over Paquita's body, they realize that they resemble each other so closely that they must be related and discover that they both have the same father, Lord Dudley.

A wood-engraving of the drawing was reproduced in the August 1896 edition of *The Savoy* magazine. This work relates to a set of six woodcut illustrations made after Conder drawings for M. Ernest Dowson's translation (Vol. XIII, April 1897, p.285).

EJ/CB

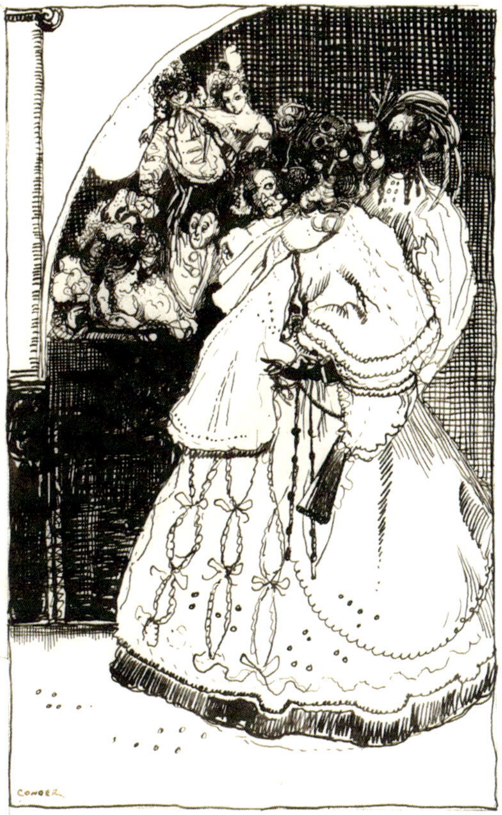

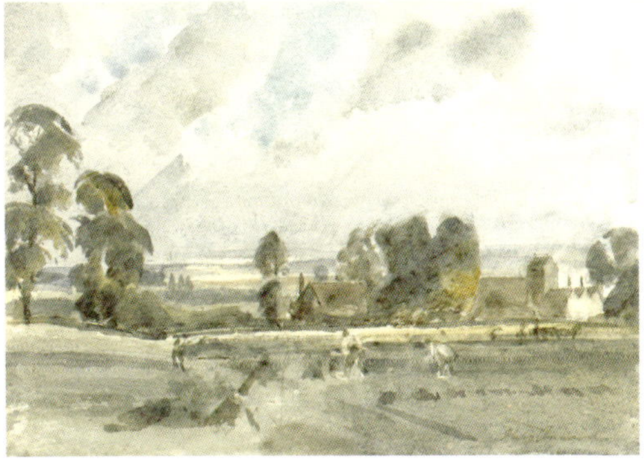

Philip CONNARD, R.A.
[1875–1958]
Shorne, Kent

watercolour on paper, 19.7 × 27.6 cm
inscribed: *Philip Connard*

P.177
PROVENANCE: Christie's 5 November 1954, lot 46 as *Kentish Village;* Thos. Agnew & Sons Ltd, from whom purchased by Gallery, December 1957.

The Kentish village of Shorne lies between Gravesend and Rochester.

Connard won a scholarship to the R.C.A. and later worked in Paris. He exhibited at the N.E.A.C. from 1906, made an A.R.A. in 1918 and R.A. in 1925. He was appointed the Keeper of the Academy Schools in 1945–9. Connard was appointed as an Official War Artist during the First World War in 1916. He also painted the murals for Queen Mary's Dolls' House, Windsor, 1924 and for the liner *Queen Mary*, 1935.

EJ

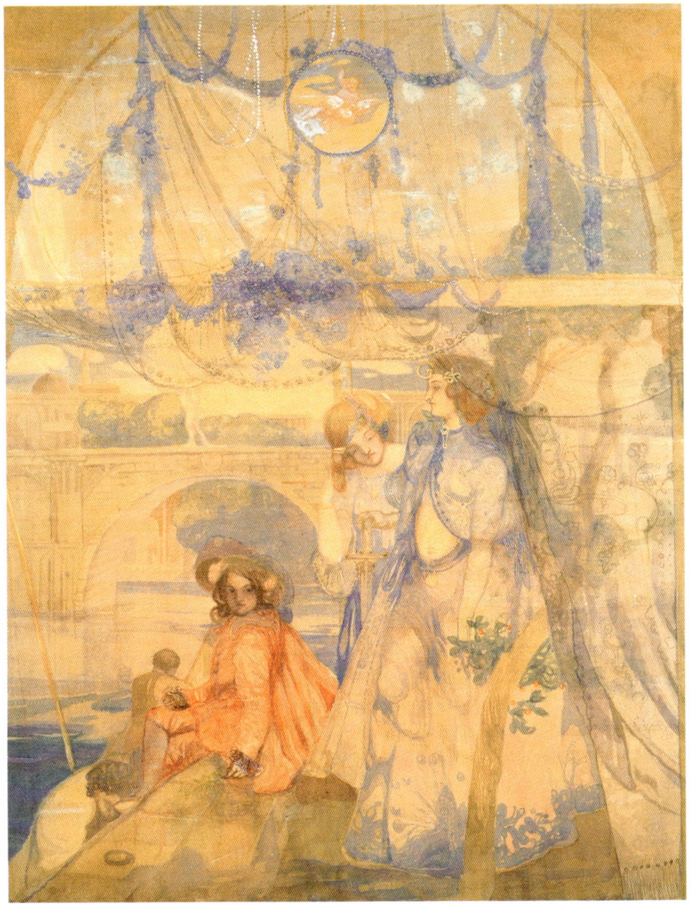

Charles Edward CONDER
[1868–1909]
Design for a Decorative Panel, 1897

watercolour on silk, 58.5 × 45.7 cm
inscribed: *CONDER 1897*

P.418
PROVENANCE: John Bergeman; Maas Gallery, from whom purchased by Gallery, April 1962.

A painter of Arcadian fantasies, landscapes and fans, Conder was also an etcher and lithographer. He made a speciality of painting on silk, which he did with great deftness and delicacy.

Although born in London, Conder spent his earliest years in India. He went to New South Wales to work as a government surveyor, but chose to paint instead. Returning to Europe in 1890, firstly to Paris, where he studied at the Académie Julian and shared a studio with William ROTHENSTEIN. He settled in London in 1902, exhibiting with the N.E.A.C. and, later, with the Society of Twelve, 1904–6.

EJ/CB

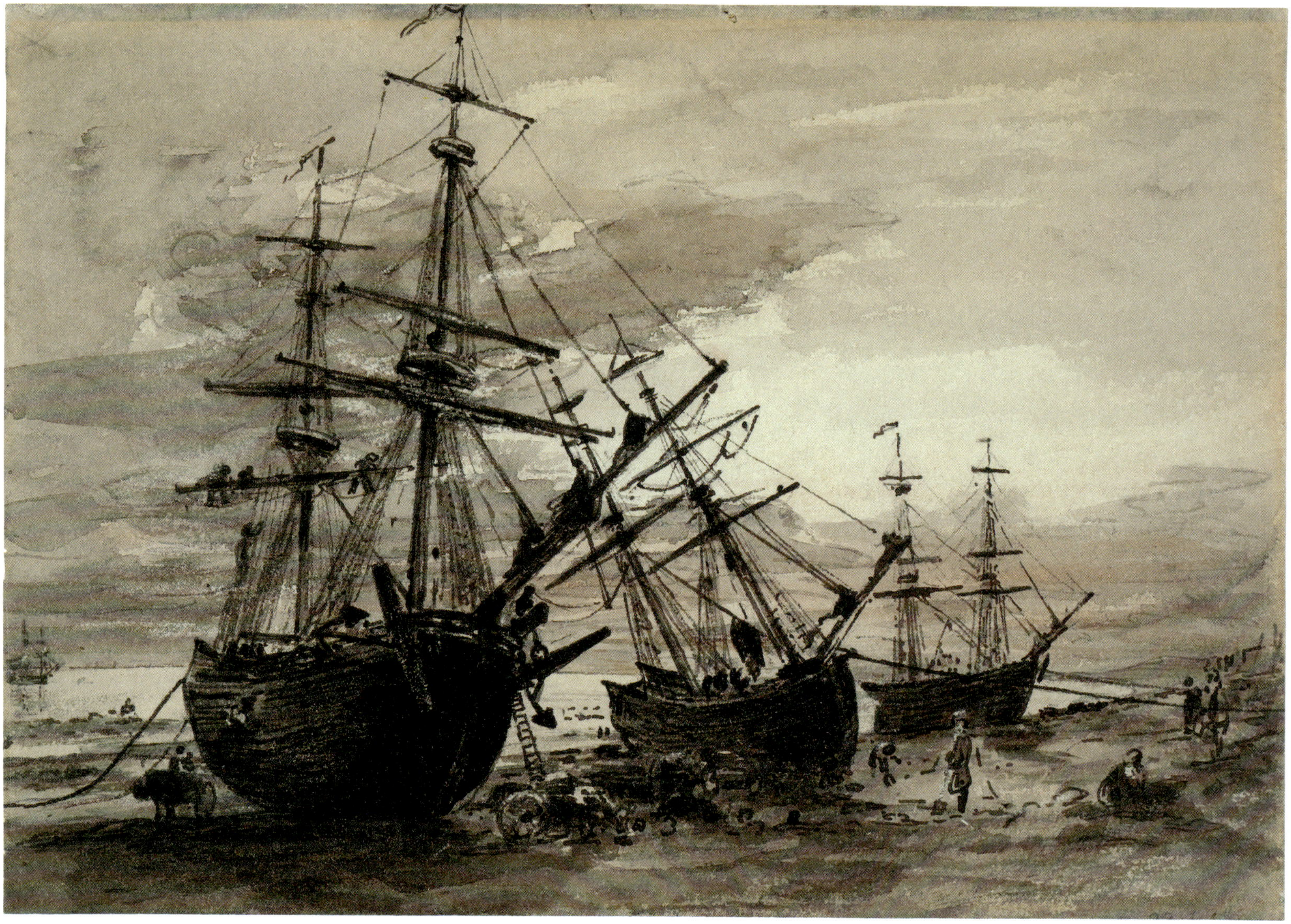

John CONSTABLE, R.A.

[1776–1837]

Coal Brigs on Brighton Beach, 1824

pencil, pen and ink and wash on paper, 17.5 × 25.5 cm

P.119

PROVENANCE: Spink & Son Ltd, from whom purchased by Gallery, May 1957.
EXHIBITIONS: *Watercolours and Drawings from The Cecil Higgins Art Gallery Bedford*, London, Thos. Agnew & Sons Ltd, 1962, no.54; *A Loan Exhibition of Drawings & Watercolours by East Anglian Artists of 18th & 19th centuries,* London, P&D Colnaghi Ltd., 1970, no.14; *British Watercolours– A Golden Age 1750–1850,* Kentucky, J.B. Speed Museum, 1977, no.52; *Masters of the Sea,* New Haven, Yale Center for British Art & Greenwich, National Maritime Museum, 1987, no.81; *The Art Treasures of England: The Regional Collections,* London, R.A., 1998, no.223.
REFERENCES: H. Day, *John Constable Drawings,* 1975, p.147, pl.149; G. Reynolds, *The Later Paintings and Drawings of John Constable,* 2 vols., 1984, I, p.144, no.24.47, illus. pl. 518; M. Rosenthal, *Constable,* 1987, p.151; I. Fleming-Williams, *Constable and his Drawings,* 1990, p.212, n.5.

Drawn in 1824 when Constable took his wife, Maria, to Brighton for her health; she was suffering from tuberculosis and died in 1828. He disliked the crowds and the bustle; writing in a letter of 29 August 1824 he describes it thus: 'Brighton is the receptacle of the fashion and off-scouring of London. The magnificence of the sea…is drowned in the din and tumult of stage coaches, gigs, flys etc., and the beach is only Piccadilly or worse by the seaside'. However, he made a number of drawings of the life on the beach including several of colliers. Reynolds suggests this drawing is one of thirty by Constable from 1824, twelve of which were to be engraved in Britain and published in Paris by his dealer John Arrowsmith. However, the project was not undertaken. This drawing was probably started on the beach and worked up later with the addition of pen and ink to provide greater contrasts. The high contrast depicted in this sunset would have been ideal for a printer to transcribe.

Coal had been an important part of the family business and Constable's father had owned a brig called the *Telegraph*.

Constable was born at East Bergholt in Suffolk, in 1776. While his parents wished him to be 'worldly', they were able to provide financial support from the family business, so that he might pursue his artistic ambitions. Despite this, his proposal of marriage to Maria Bicknell was opposed by her grandfather, the Reverend Dr Durand Rhudde who was Rector of East Bergholt, due to Constable's refusal to abandon painting and take a profitable profession. They eventually married in 1816. He was elected A.R.A. in 1819 and R.A. in 1829.

EJ/CB

John CONSTABLE, R.A.

[1776–1837]

Fir Trees at Hampstead, c.1833

black lead on paper, 73.4 × 49.3 cm

P.276

PROVENANCE: Gilbert Davis; P&D Colnaghi Ltd, from whom purchased by Gallery, January 1959.

EXHIBITIONS: London, R.A., 1834, no.548 ?; *Old Master Drawings*, London, R.A., 1953, no.481; *J. Constable 1776–1837*, Manchester, Manchester Art Gallery 1956, no.93; *Primitives to Picasso*, London, R.A., 1962, no.385; *Watercolours and Drawings from The Cecil Higgins Art Gallery Bedford*, London, Thos. Agnew & Sons Ltd, 1962, no.31; *English Watercolours from the Cecil Higgins Art Gallery, Bedford*, Reading, Reading Art Gallery, 1965, no.4; *Watercolours from Bedford*, Norwich, Castle Museum, no.7; *Bicentenary Exhibition*, London, R.A., 1968/9, no.205; *Constable Paintings, Watercolours and Drawings*, London, Tate Gallery, 1976, no.306; *Constable*, London, Tate Gallery, 1991, no.332.

REFERENCES: C. Rhyne, 'Fresh Light on John Constable', *Apollo*, LXXXVII, 1968, p.230, n.11; R. Whitlock, *Historic Forests of England* , 1979; G. Reynolds, *The Later Paintings and Drawings of John Constable*, 2 vols., 1984, I, p.257, no.34.3, illus. p.914.

Constable drew this study of trees over four sheets of paper. It was possibly exhibited at the R.A. in 1834, no.548, as *Study of trees made in the grounds of Charles Holford, Esq., at Hampstead*, which is known to have been a pencil drawing of a similar size. If this were shown at the Academy in 1834, it must have been drawn sometime in 1833, perhaps July, when Constable made a stylistically similar study of trees at West End Fields.

Constable had known Charles Holford and his wife since 1824 and Holford appears to have been one of the organisers of some lectures that Constable gave to the Hampstead Literary and Scientific Society.

From 1819 to 1826, the Constables rented a house at Hampstead every summer, bar one, and moved to Well Walk in 1827. Hampstead had become a popular residence for writers and artists in the early 19th century as a rural neighbourhood in close proximity to London. During the early years at Hampstead, Constable made a number of tree studies on the Heath.

EJ/CB

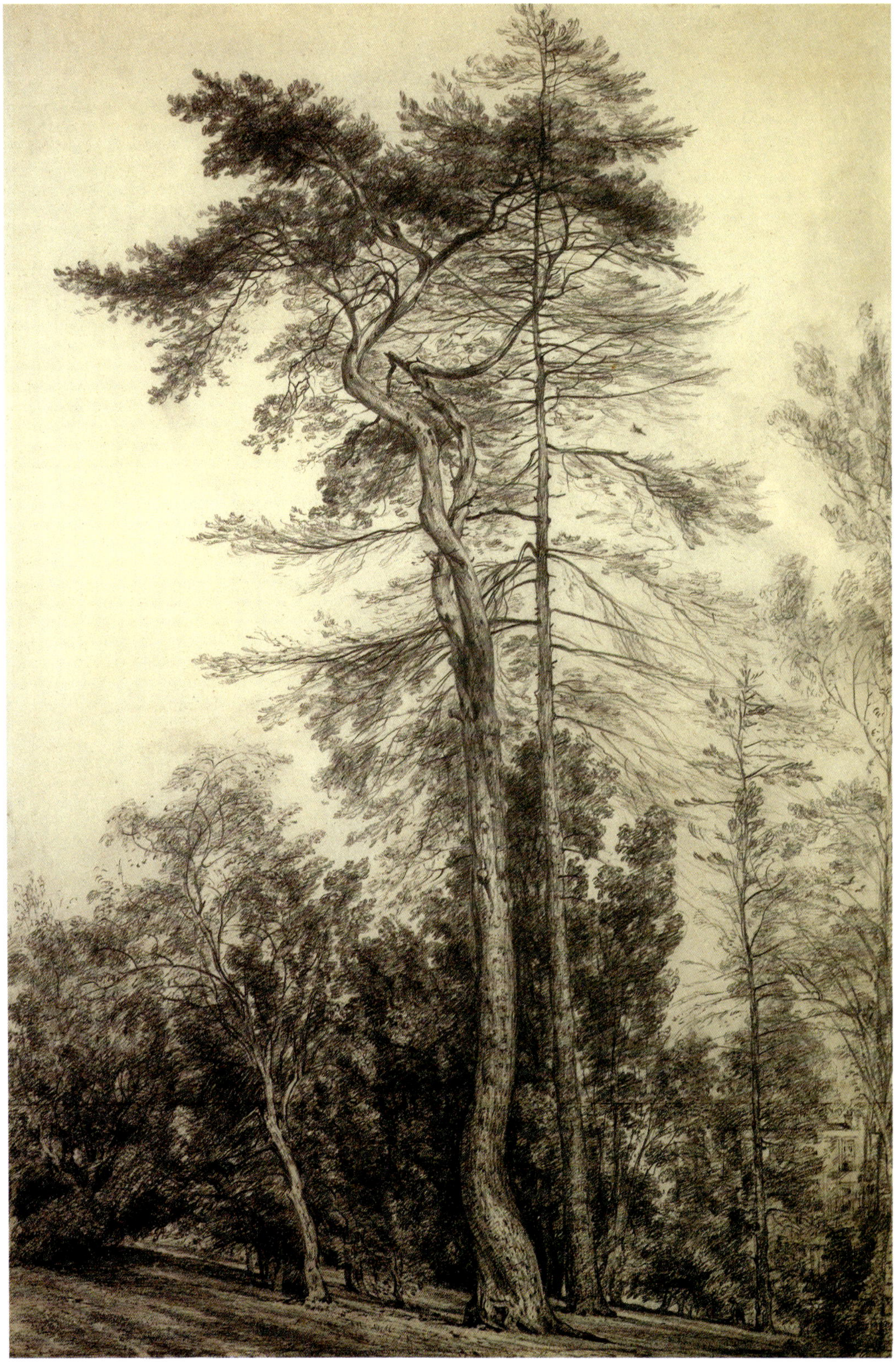

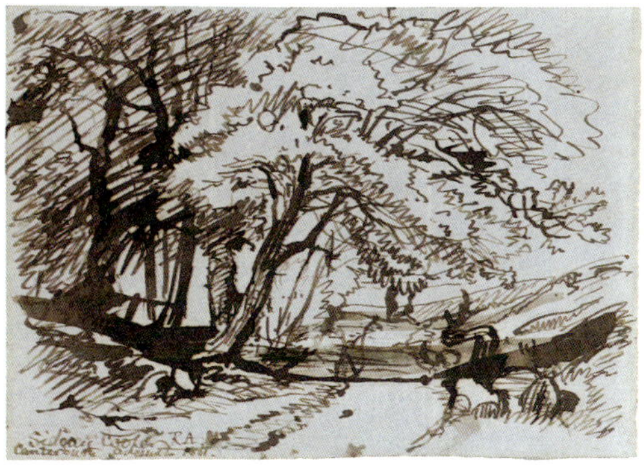

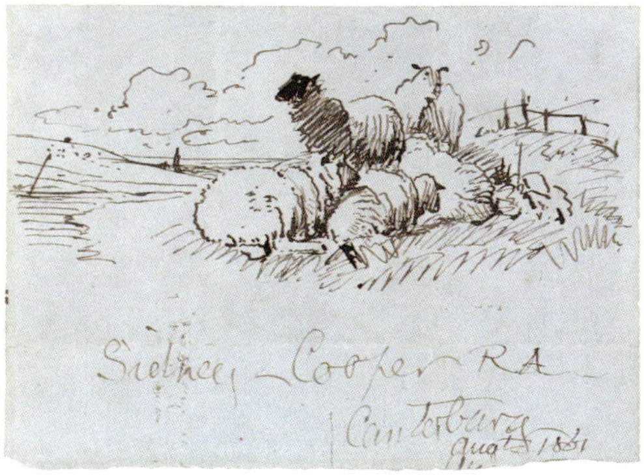

Thomas Sidney COOPER, R.A.
[1803–1902]
Landscape at Canterbury, and Sheep in a Landscape, 1861

pen and brown ink on blue paper, 13.9 × 20.3 cm
inscribed: *Sidney Cooper RA Canterbury August 1861*
P.58

pen and brown ink on blue paper, 14.3 × 20.3 cm
inscribed: *Sidney Cooper RA Canterbury August 1861*
P.59

PROVENANCE: Cecil Higgins (1856–1941); transferred to the Gallery collection 1949.

Cooper, born in Canterbury, was determined to enter the R.A. and so was barred from membership of any watercolour society. In 1827 he went to Brussels and spent four years there studying under Eugène Verboeckhoven (1798–1881), the famous Flemish animal painter. On his return to London, Cooper's name became so synonymous with paintings of cattle and sheep that he was nicknamed 'Cow Cooper'.

EJ

Richard COSWAY, R.A.
[1742–1821]
Charles, 4th Earl of Harrington with his dog Peter, c.1800–5

black chalk, tinted in watercolour on paper, 23.2 × 14.1 cm
inscribed: monogram *CR* Dog collar *Petersham*

P.607
PROVENANCE: Christie's 29 April 1970 via P&D Colnaghi Ltd, from whom purchased by Gallery, May 1970.
EXHIBITIONS: *Summer Exhibition*, London, P&D Colnaghi Ltd, 1970; *The English Tradition: an exhibition of watercolours from two private collections*, Bedford, Cecil Higgins Art Gallery, 1972, no.27; *Richard & Maria Cosway: Regency Artists of Taste & Fashion*, Edinburgh, Scottish National Portrait Gallery and London, National Portrait Gallery, 1995/6, no.153.
REFERENCES: A. Riberio, *The Art of Dress Fashion in England & France 1750–1820*, 1995, p.242; S. Lloyd, *Richard & Maria Cosway : Regency Artists of Taste and Fashion*, 1995, p.126.

Trained at Shipley's School, together with TOWNE and PARS, and at the R.A. schools. Cosway was elected R.A. in 1771 and later became principal painter to the Prince of Wales. He painted some fine portraits in oils but he excelled particularly as a miniaturist. He also had a reputation as a connoisseur, being often consulted by collectors, including the sitter.

Lord Harrington (1780–1851), better known by his earlier title of Lord Petersham, was well known in London society. He was also an eccentric: never going out of doors until 6 p.m., mixing his own snuff and making his own boot blacking.

EJ

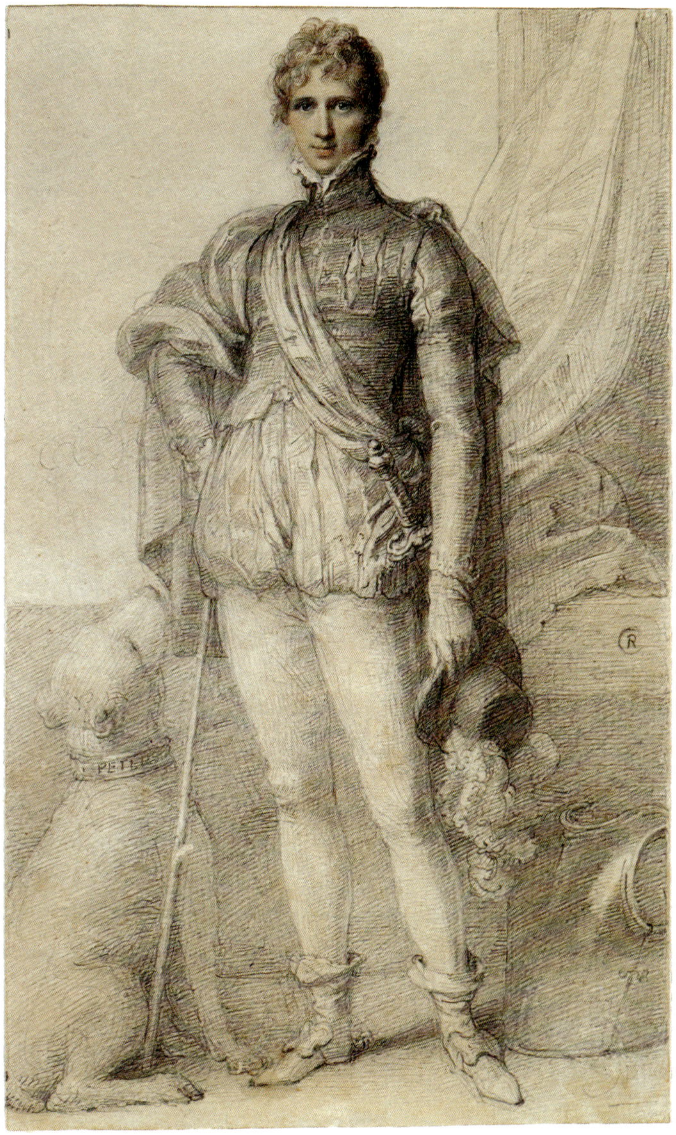

John Sell COTMAN
[1782–1842]
Cain and Abel (formerly known as *Abraham & Isaac*), c.1800–3

sepia wash over black lead and heightened with white on paper, 33.1 × 23 cm

P.627
PROVENANCE: Mrs Arthur Clifton, who consigned it to Thos. Agnew & Sons Ltd, for sale in 1941; returned to her unsold in March 1950; Christie's 6 November 1973, lot 47, purchased by the Gallery with assistance of V&A/M.G.C. Purchase Grant Fund.
EXHIBITIONS: *72nd Annual Watercolour Exhibition*, London, Thos. Agnew & Sons Ltd, 1947, no.70 as *Abraham & Isaac; John Sell Cotman*, London, V&A, Manchester, Whitworth Art Gallery & Bristol, Bristol City Art Gallery, 1982–3, no.53.
REFERENCES: *Country Life*, 8 March 1941, p.xxvi illus; *The Antique Collector*, Jan.-Feb. 1945, p.33.

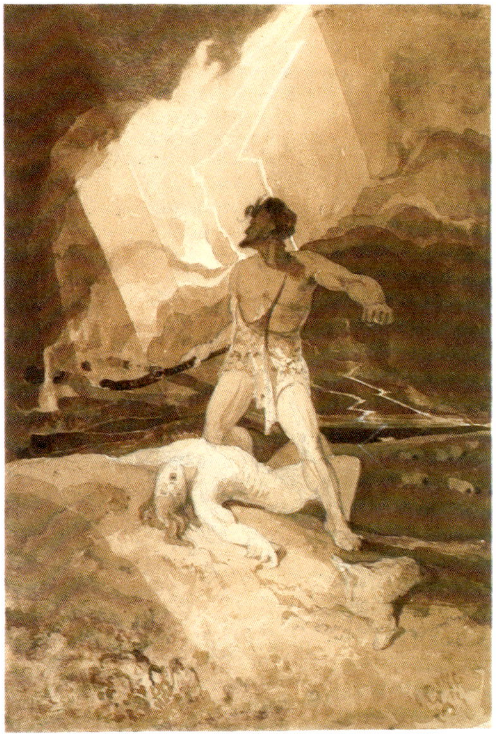

In 1799, a number of artists who included GIRTIN, Sandby MUNN, VARLEY and FRANCIA formed a drawing society and dubbed themselves *The Brothers*. They would meet at each other's houses and set a subject every night from contemporary Romantic poetry, Shakespeare, Milton or, as depicted here, the Bible. The rules were strict: 'At ten o'clock all drawings shall cease, when simple fare shall be produced with Ale and Porter'– and fines would be levied on absent members. Cotman is known to have become associated with the society from 1800.

CB

John Sell COTMAN
[1782–1842]
Chepstow Castle and Bridge, 1801

watercolour and black lead on paper, 16.2 × 26.7 cm

P.728
PROVENANCE: Robert Bateman; by descent to Mrs Gilbert; by descent to Barbara Stratham, from whom purchased by Gallery with assistance from V&A/M.G.C. Purchase Grant Fund, June 1985.
EXHIBITIONS: *Loan Exhibition of Water Colour Drawings by Deceased British Artists also of a collection of Paintings and Drawings by J.S. Cotman*, Manchester, Whitworth Institute, 1912, no. 250; *Watercolour drawings by J.R. Cozens and J.S. Cotman*, Manchester, Whitworth Art Gallery, 1937, no. 6, lent by Mrs R. Bateman.

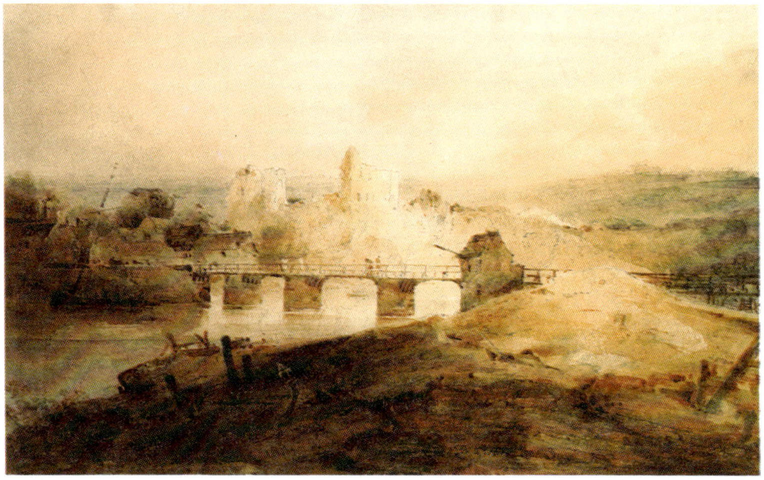

In 1800 Cotman set off for Wales on what has been well described as an 'obligatory' tour for any self-respecting watercolourist in search of the Picturesque and the 'Sublime'. In this he was following in the footsteps of many predecessors including Paul SANDBY and ROOKER.

In early July he left Bristol, crossed the Severn and went to Chepstow where he made several drawings of the castle and bridge.

In this example, Cotman outlines dramatically the two towers of the castle by obscuring its lower part in the mist rising from the Severn beyond the bridge.

EJ

John Sell COTMAN
[1782–1842]
A View of Dolgelly, 1802

black lead and wash on paper, 26.5 × 39.3 cm

P.612
PROVENANCE: Christie's 17 November 1970, lot 8, as by John Varley, Thos. Agnew & Sons Ltd, from whom purchased by Gallery.
EXHIBITIONS: *John Sell Cotman*, London, V&A, Manchester, Whitworth Art Gallery & Bristol, Bristol City Art Gallery, 1982–3, no.8.
REFERENCES: M. Rajnai and M. Allthorpe-Guyton, *Early Drawings by John Sell Cotman in Norwich Castle Museum*, 1979, p.44.

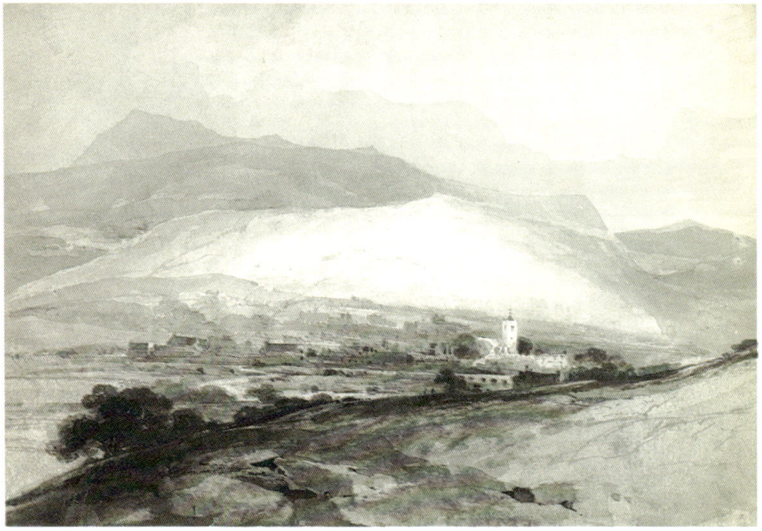

This view is taken from the north-east. Cotman must have passed through here on his way from Aberystwyth to Harlech between the 18 and 30 July 1800. Kitson suggests that Cotman and MUNN also stayed at Dolgelly from the 19 to 23 July 1802 as there are drawings dated by Munn to support this.

EJ

John Sell COTMAN

[1782–1842]

The Old College House, Conway, 1802

watercolour on paper, 27.8 × 19cm
inscribed on reverse: *J.S.Cotman 1802*

P.613
PROVENANCE: Christie's 17 November 1970 lot 9, from whom purchased by Gallery.
EXHIBITIONS: *John Sell Cotman*, London, V&A, Manchester, Whitworth Art Gallery & Bristol, Bristol City Art Gallery, 1982–3, no.7.
REFERENCES: J.S. Cotman, *Etchings of Ancient Building in various parts of the British Isles*, vol. I, 1811.

Cotman may have visited Conway towards the end of his tour of Wales in 1800, probably in mid– or late August. Cotman returned to the subject again during his first Norwich period 1807–8 and also in 1824, when he showed a watercolour of this title with the Norwich Society, no.154.

A watercolour of the same building, but from a different viewpoint, by William ALEXANDER, is in the Yale Center for British Art, New Haven.

EJ

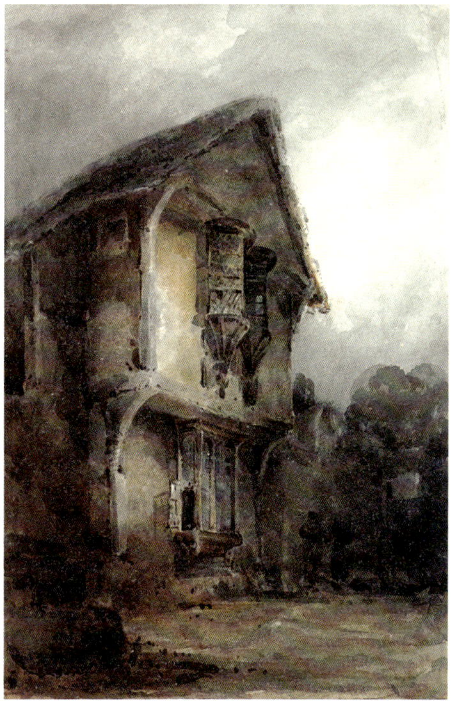

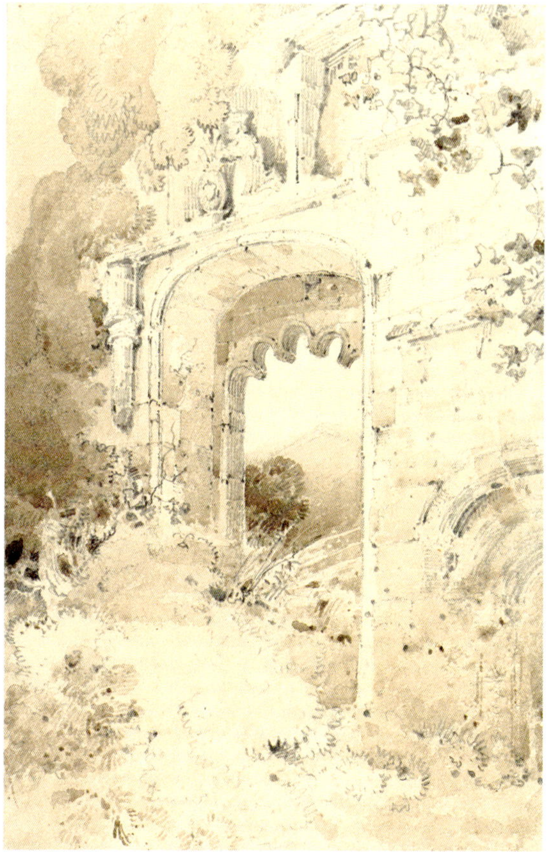

John Sell COTMAN

[1782–1842]

Mountain-Bordered Lake, c.1802–3

brush drawing in sepia wash on paper, 21.6 × 30 cm
on reverse: pencil sketch of harbour

P.125
PROVENANCE: Sir Frank Brangwyn R.A.; bequeathed to Gallery, June 1957.
EXHIBITIONS: *John Sell Cotman*, Bedford, Cecil Higgins Art Gallery, 1961, no.11, as *Mountain Scene with Lake*.

Drawn c.1802–3 and, to judge from the surface, Cotman was caught in a shower while drawing it.

EJ

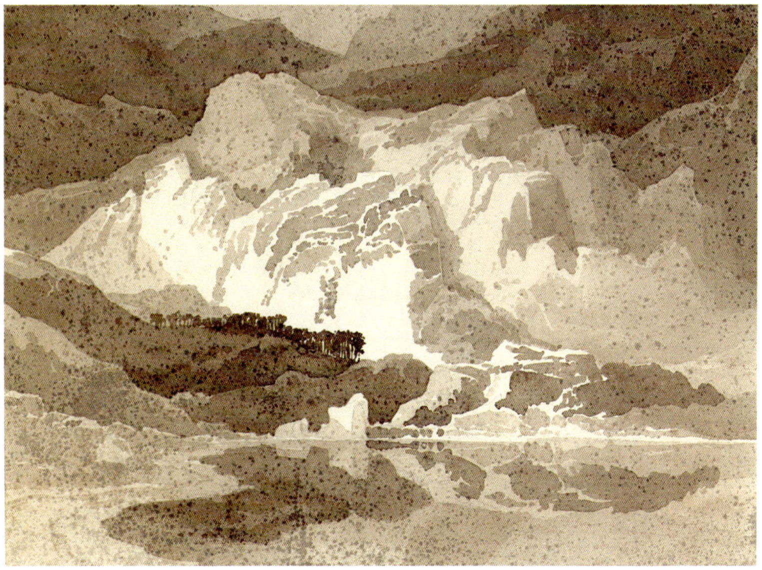

John Sell COTMAN

[1782–1842]

The Doorway to the Abbot's Hall, Rievaulx Abbey, 1803

sepia wash and black lead on paper, 32.5 × 21.1 cm
inscribed on reverse of a previous mount: *'Pt of Rivaux* [sic] *Abbey, Yorkshire'*.

P.700
PROVENANCE: Squire's Gallery 1936; L.G. Duke; Sydney Kitson 1937 (843); by descent Elisabeth and Alice Barbara Kitson, given to Gallery, May 1973.
EXHIBITIONS: *The English Tradition: an exhibition of watercolours from two private collections* Bedford, Cecil Higgins Art Gallery, 1972, no.22; *John Sell Cotman*, London, V&A, Manchester, Whitworth Art Gallery & Bristol, Bristol City Art Gallery, 1982–3, no.17; *Cotmania & Mr.Kitson*, Leeds, Leeds City Art Gallery, 1992, no.11.
REFERENCES: D. Boswell & C. Miller, *Cotmania & Mr Kitson*, 1992, p.44, no.11.

In his last letter to his brother Robert, 25 May 1937, Kitson wrote: 'about a month ago I acquired a lovely Cotman sepia (c.1803–4) of a part of Rievaulx Abbey: very Japanesy'. In fact this was almost certainly painted in 1803 when *Doorway of the Refectory at Rievaulx* is dated.

Cotman and MUNN visited Helmsley and Rievaulx from the 8 to the 17 July while he was staying with the Cholmeley family at Brandsby Hall. Cotman returned to Rievaulx on the 7 August to work and stayed for two more days. He produced a number of drawings of the famous Cistercian abbey during this period. Cotman was not in the vicinity again until July 1805, which is too late stylistically for this drawing.

This drawing was purchased by Milling of Squire's Gallery in a furniture shop for two shillings and later sold on to L.G. Duke for £18. Occasionally, Kitson swapped works in his own collection with other collectors'; this work was exchanged with Duke for a study of a barn by John Crome. Its acquisition was a compensation for the *Doorway of the Refectory*, (now Tate Collection T08248), which, when on sale at Christie's, Kitson and Oppé agreed to toss for, and Oppé won.

According to Dr Alec Cotman this was etched in 1811.

EJ

John Sell COTMAN

[1782–1842]

Rokeby Woods, c.1805

black lead and watercolour on paper, 43.6 × 33.5 cm

P.593

PROVENANCE: Lewis Fry; Thos. Agnew & Sons Ltd, from whom purchased by Gallery with assistance from V&A/M.G.C. Purchase Grant Fund, June 1969.
EXHIBITIONS: *Walking the Landscape: Cotman & Turner in Teesdale*, Barnard Castle, Bowes Museum, 1996, no cat.
REFERENCES: S. Kitson, *Cotman*, 1937, pp.84–5, pl.34, p.54; M. Hardie, *Watercolour Painting in Britain*, 1967, pp.77–8.

In 1805 Cotman stayed for the month of August at Greta Bridge, near Barnard Castle, first at Rokeby Park, home of the Morritt family, and then at an inn. The drawings that resulted from what is known as his 'Greta Bridge' period show a change from his earlier picturesque style and are generally considered as his masterpieces. Unfortunately, however, some of them have suffered exposure to strong light, as is the case here. The extent of the fading can be gauged by the strips of paint round the edge of the drawing; these must have been covered by the mount in the past and still retain their original colour in sharp and sad contrast to the rest of the composition.

Despite this, Cotman's mastery at rendering the play of sunlight filtering through the trees is still clearly apparent.

Rokeby was to inspire Sir Walter Scott (1771–1832), who wrote the eponymous poem in 1809, and J.M.W.TURNER (see entry for Turner's *Rokeby*).

EJ

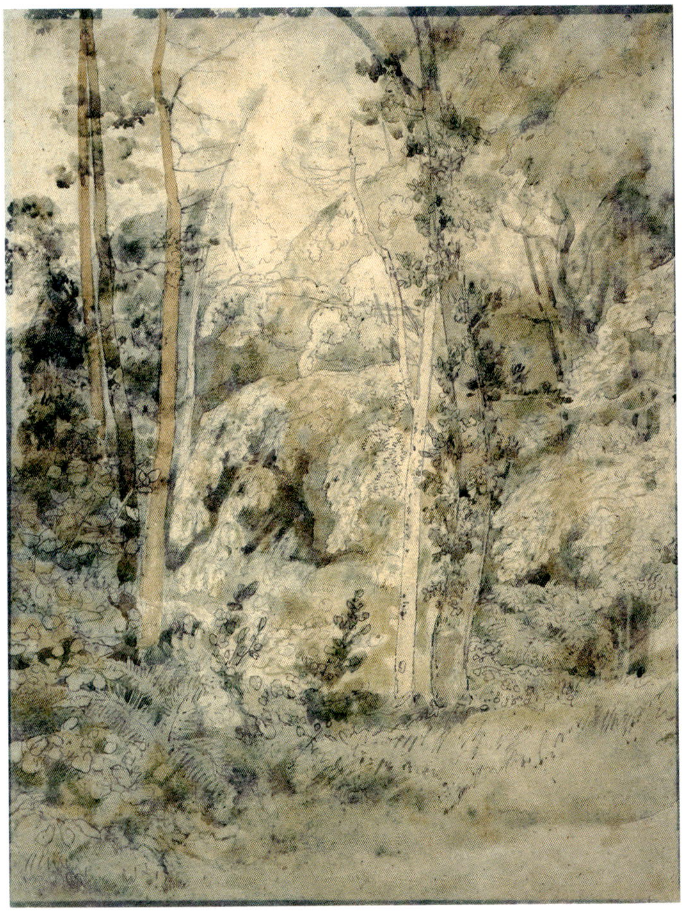

John Sell COTMAN

[1782–1842]

The Interior of the Nave, Norwich Cathedral, c.1807

watercolour and black lead on paper, 33.1 × 22.1 cm

P.695

PROVENANCE: Acquired from the artist by Rev. James Bulwer, then by descent; Walker's Galleries Ltd.; 1926 bought by Sydney Kitson; Elisabeth and Alice Barbara Kitson, given to Gallery, May 1973.
EXHIBITIONS: *John Sell Cotman (The Bulwer Collection)*, London, Walker's Galleries Ltd., 1926, no.8; Oxford, Oxford Art Club, 1928, catalogue not traced; *Twee Eeuwem Engelse Kunst*, Amsterdam, Stedelijk Museum, 1936, no.181; *Watercolour Drawings by J.R.Cozens and J.S.Cotman*, Manchester, Whitworth Art Gallery, 1937, no.32; *The English Tradition: an exhibition of watercolours from two private collections*, Bedford, Cecil Higgins Art Gallery, 1972, no.18; *John Sell Cotman*, London, V&A, Manchester, Whitworth Art Gallery and Bristol, Bristol City Art Gallery, 1982–3, no.62
REFERENCES: S. Kitson, *The Life of John Sell Cotman*, 1937, p.107, pl.43; M. Pidgley, *John Sell Cotman's Patrons and The Romantic Subject Pictures in the 1820s and 1830s*, 1975, p.79, no.252; L. Herrmann, *Nineteenth Century British Painting*, 2000, p.51. fig.36.

This is one of a series of about ten drawings Cotman made of the interior of Norwich Cathedral.

Painted c.1807, this shows the pillars on the northern side immediately west of the organ screen, seen from the centre of the nave. The tomb is that of Sir James Hobart, now almost hidden by pews.

The 1982–3 catalogue (see above) comments: 'Nothing shows more clearly Cotman's artistic power at this time than the way this rather ungainly corner of the Cathedral became the vehicle for one of the most poetic interior pieces he ever did'.

EJ

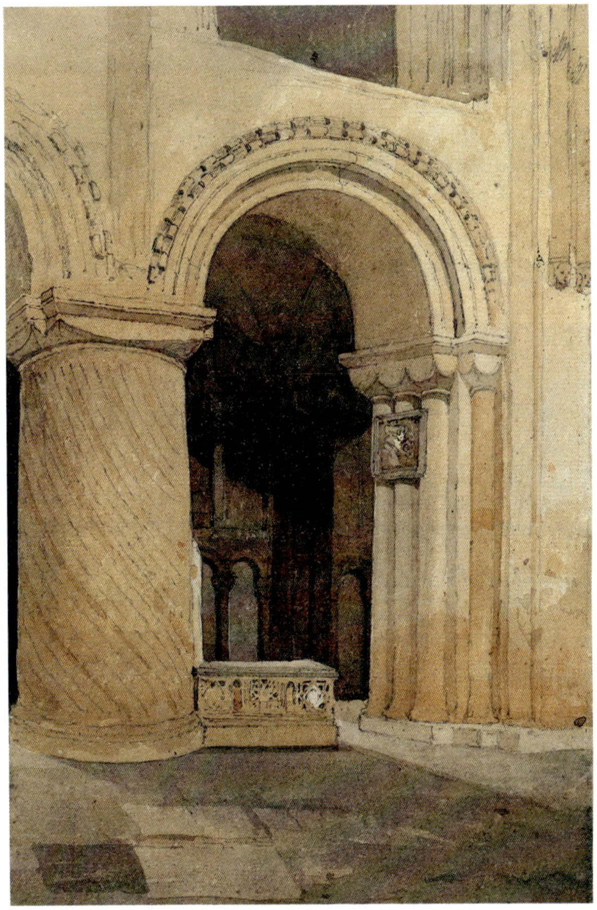

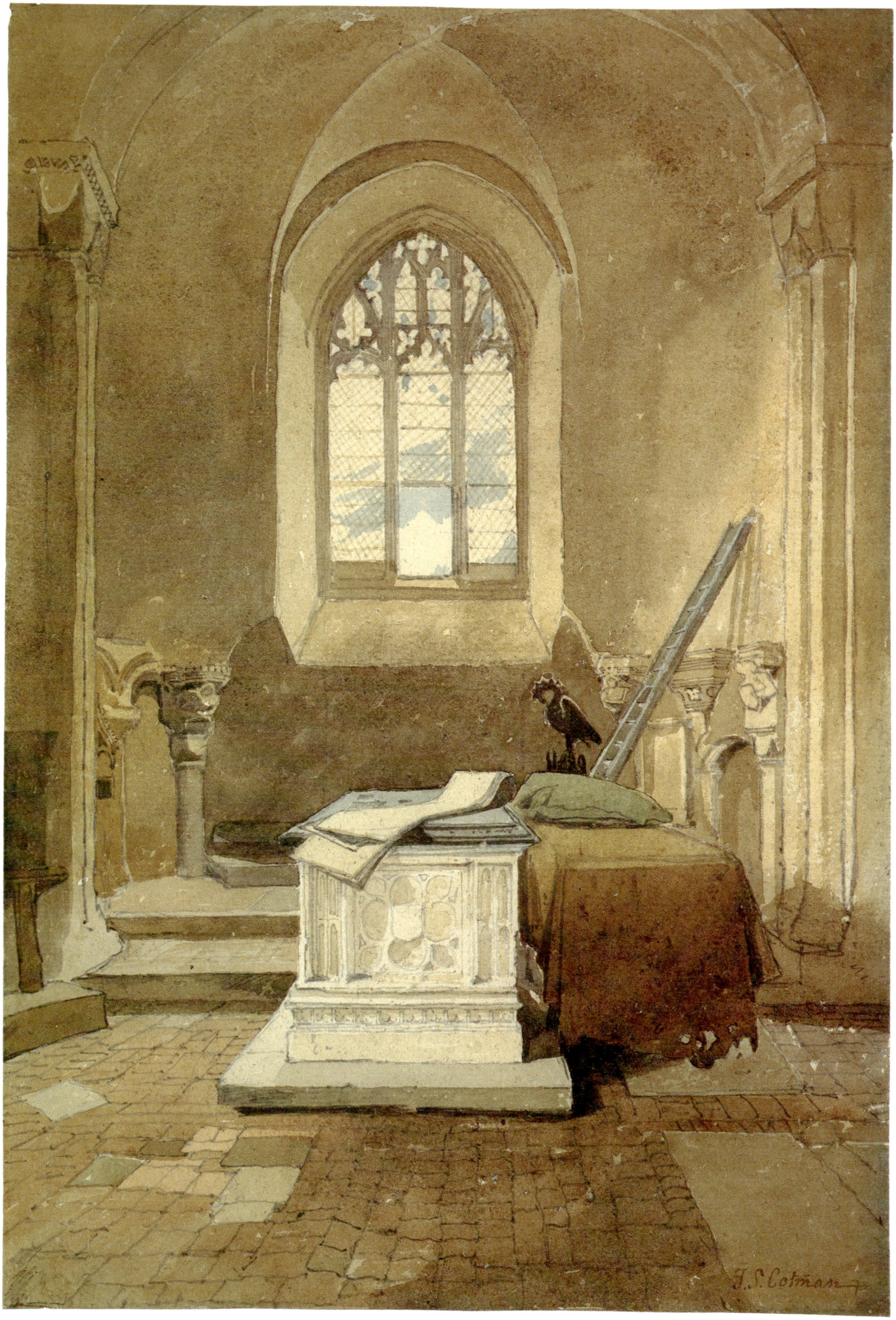
J. S. Cotman

John Sell COTMAN

[1782–1842]

In the Jesus Chapel, Norwich Cathedral, c.1807

watercolour and black lead on paper, 38.5 × 26.9 cm
inscribed: *J.S. Cotman*

P.698

PROVENANCE: Rev. James Bulwer, acquired from the artist; Walker's Galleries Ltd ; Sydney Kitson; Elisabeth and Alice Barbara Kitson, given to Gallery, May 1973.
EXHIBITIONS: Norwich Art Circle's 9th Exhibition. *Drawings by the late John Sell Cotman*, Norwich, Arts Circle, 1888, no.58; *Exhibition of Drawings in Water Colour and in Black and White by John Sell Cotman*, London, Burlington Fine Arts Club, 1888, no.28; *John Sell Cotman (The Bulwer Collection)*, London, Walker's Galleries Ltd, 1926 no.6; *Exposition Retrospective de Peinture Anglaise*, Brussels, Musée Moderne, 1929, no.148; *The English Tradition: an exhibition of watercolours from two private collections*, Bedford, Cecil Higgins Art Gallery, 1972, no.16; *John Sell Cotman*, London, V&A, Manchester, Whitworth Art Gallery & Bristol, Bristol City Art Gallery, 1982–3, no.65; *Cotmania and Mr. Kitson*, Leeds, Leeds City Art Gallery, 1993, no.22.
REFERENCES: S. Kitson, *The Life of John Sell Cotman*, 1937, p.107.

One of ten drawings by Cotman of Norwich Cathedral. Dated c.1807–8 in the 1982–2 exhibition catalogue, the view is taken looking east, whereas a watercolour now in Sydney (probably D.Y. Cameron Collection in 1937) shows the Chapel looking west. The tomb in the centre is a monument to the Windham family – since removed to the nave (see P.695). Kitson notes that the Cathedral's medieval pelican lantern, visible next to a ladder, may mean that the Chapel was at that time used as a sort of lumber room.

EJ

John Sell COTMAN

[1782–1842]

Draining Mill in Lincolnshire, c.1807–8

watercolour and black lead on paper, 28.5 × 22.1 cm
inscribed on reverse: *The Four Windmills*

P.696

PROVENANCE: Sydney Kitson; Elisabeth and Alice Barbara Kitson; given to Gallery, May 1973.
EXHIBITIONS: *Watercolours by Turner and other Masters of the English School*, *London*, The Cotswold Gallery, 1924, no.10 as *The Four Windmills*; *The English Tradition: an exhibition of watercolours from two private collections*, Bedford, Cecil Higgins Art Gallery, 1972, no.14.
REFERENCES: *The Times*, 20 March 1924; S. Kitson, *Life of John Sell Cotman*, 1937, p.73.

In August 1804 Cotman made a leisurely journey from Norwich to Yorkshire, visiting, among other places on the way, Croyland Abbey in Lincolnshire, which he admired enormously. From Croyland he made a short trip afield and drew a draining mill with three further mills receding into the distance. He made much use of the sketch: a large version of 1804 is in the V&A, and this drawing, probably drawn c.1807–8 (Dr Miklos Rajnai prefers c.1809), belonged to Sydney Kitson. A third version of the composition, made perhaps in the late 1820s, is in the Bacon collection.

EJ

John Sell COTMAN

[1782–1842]

Still Life with Cast of Dog, c.1809

watercolour and black lead on paper, 32.9 × 23.7 cm
on reverse: A River Scene, drawn c.1810–16, black lead 17.7 × 27.7 cm

P.703

PROVENANCE: Sydney Kitson; Elisabeth and Alice Barbara Kitson, given to the Gallery, May 1973.
EXHIBITIONS: *The English Tradition: an exhibition of watercolours from two private collections,* Bedford, Cecil Higgins Art Gallery, 1972, no.25.

The dog depicted in the painting is a cast of a Roman statue known as The Dog of Alcibiades.

Cotman is known to have collected items intended for use in still-lifes.

EJ

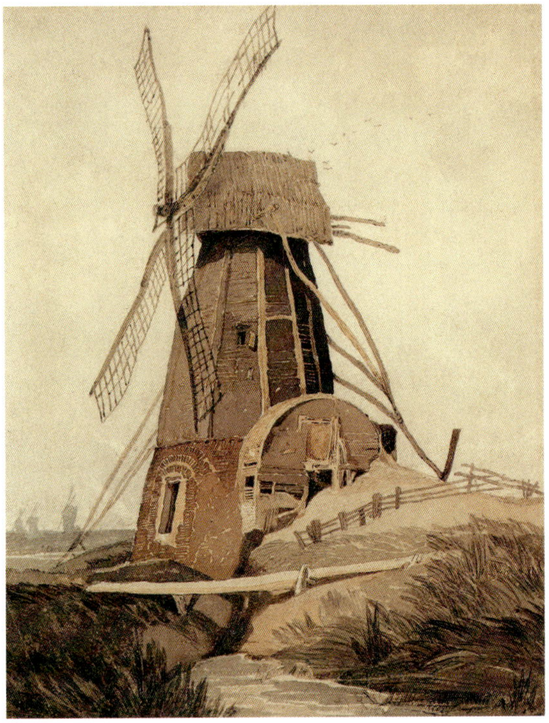

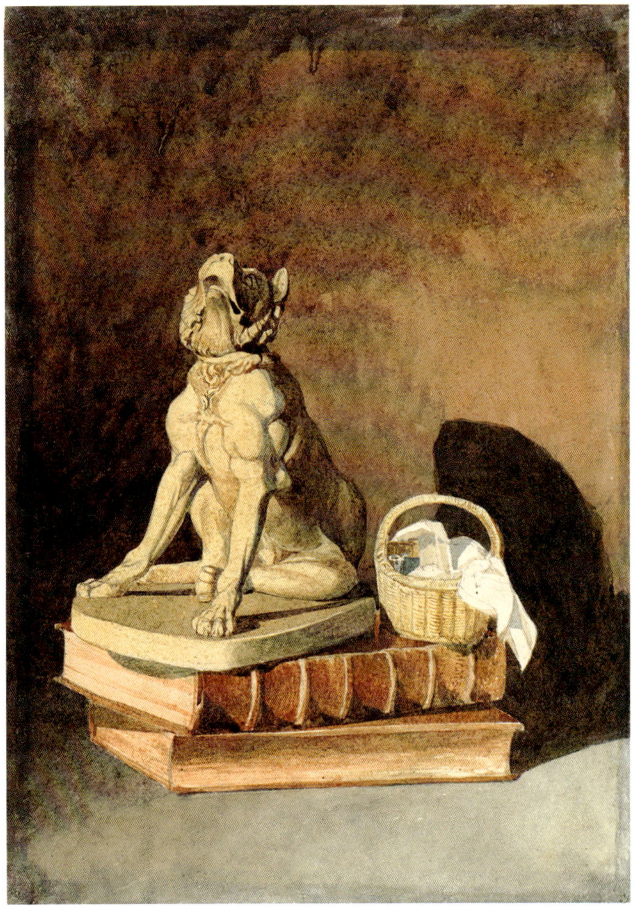

John Sell COTMAN
[1782–1842]
Windmills on the Coast, 1812–13

watercolour, bodycolour and black lead on paper, 18.5 × 27 cm
inscribed: *Cotman*

P.791
PROVENANCE: Sydney Kitson; Elisabeth and Alice Barbara Kitson, given by Alice Barbara Kitson to the Gallery, October 1992.

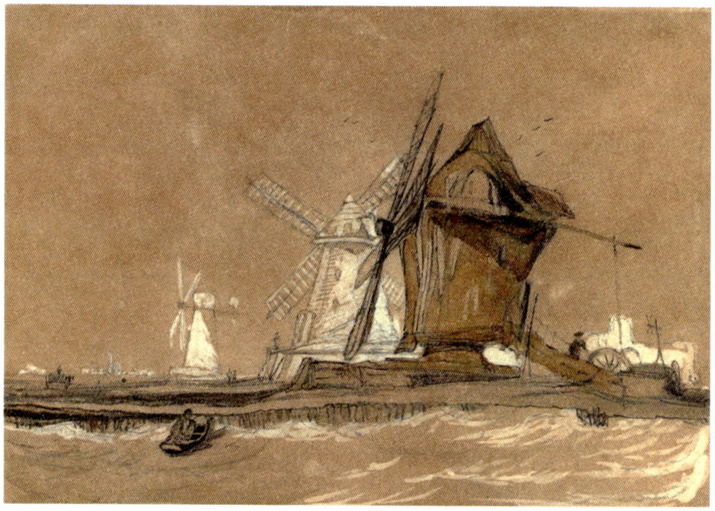

The location is so far unidentified but is presumably on the Norfolk coast. A fine drawing in which one can almost hear the slap of the waves as they beat against the shore at high tide and in a strong wind. Cotman skilfully leads the eye into the distance by contrasting angles and colours of the windmills' sails.

The paper used has not been sealed and as a consequence the bodycolour has seeped through the paper giving the appearance of flat colour.

EJ/CB

John Sell COTMAN
[1782–1842]
Church at Hunstanton, Norfolk, 1815

black lead on paper, 24.1 × 19 cm
inscribed: *East End of Hunstanton Ch. Norfk. J.S.Cotman 1815*

P.175
PROVENANCE: Acquired from the artist by Rev. James Bulwer; then by descent ; Walker Galleries Ltd; Humphrey Whitbread, from whom purchased by Gallery, January 1958.
EXHIBITIONS: *J.S.Cotman (The Bulwer Collection)*, London, Walker Galleries Ltd., 1926, no.60.

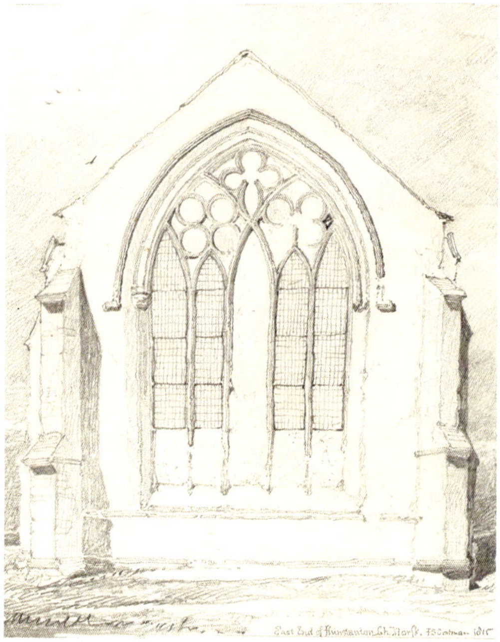

Between 1814 and 1819 Cotman concentrated on local subjects for his publications of prints. This view was etched for *A series of Etchings Illustrative of the Architectural Antiquities of Norfolk*, published in 1818. However, in 1814 he underwent an eye operation and employed apprentices to complete the etchings.

CB

John Sell COTMAN
[1782–1842]
La Tour du Château D'Arques, 1818

black lead and wash on paper, 25.5 × 20 cm
inscribed: *J.S.Cotman 18 La Tour la plus remarquable des fortifications du Château d'Arques prise exterieurement*

P.451
PROVENANCE: Property of a Lady; Sotheby's, 20 November 1963, lot 1, purchased by Gallery.
EXHIBITIONS: Norwich Society of Artists, 1824; *English Watercolours from the Cecil Higgins Art Gallery, Bedford*, Reading, Reading Art Gallery, 1965, no.5.

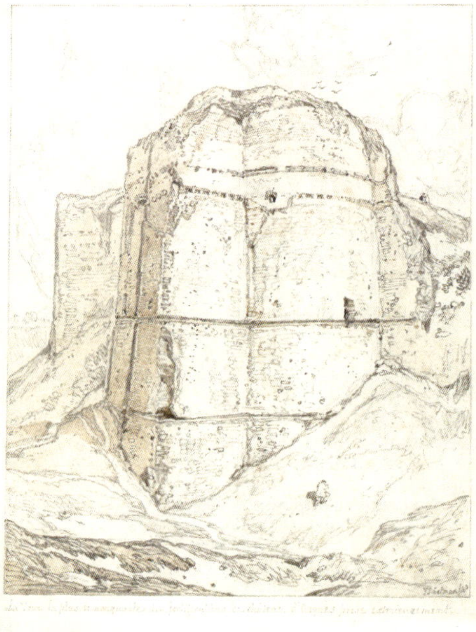

In 1817, Cotman's patron, Mr Dawson Turner, suggested that Cotman visit Normandy to find fresh subjects, which he did in 1817, 1819 and 1820. The sketches he produced formed the basis of *Architectural Antiquities of Normandy*, published in 1822.

Château d'Arques is about five miles south-east of Dieppe on a commanding height above the river Varenne and close to the Forêt d'Arques. It was a favourite subject with artists and was sketched a dozen times by Turner in 1827. Cotman's tower is at the south end of the Château and this dates from his second tour of Normandy. Cotman has cleverly suggested the size and solidity of the tower by contrasting it with the scale of the man toiling up the slope below it.

EJ/CB

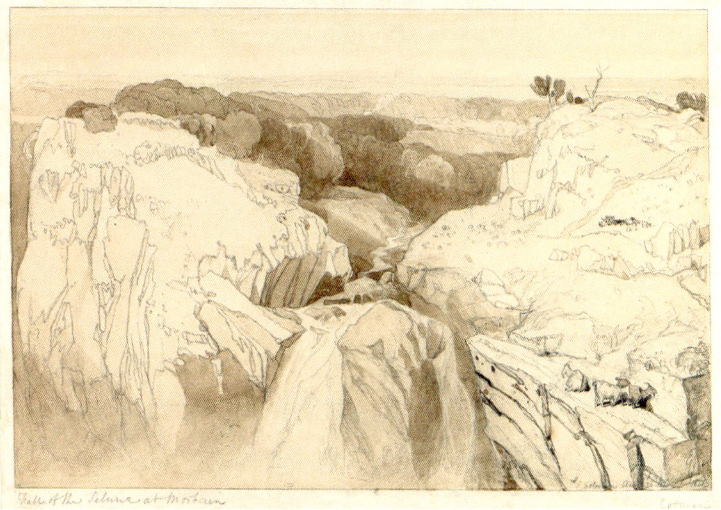

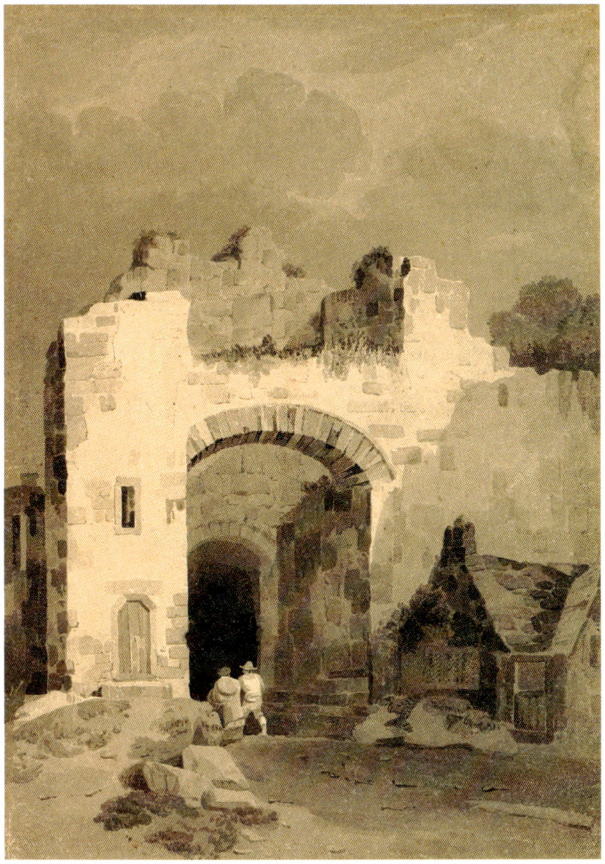

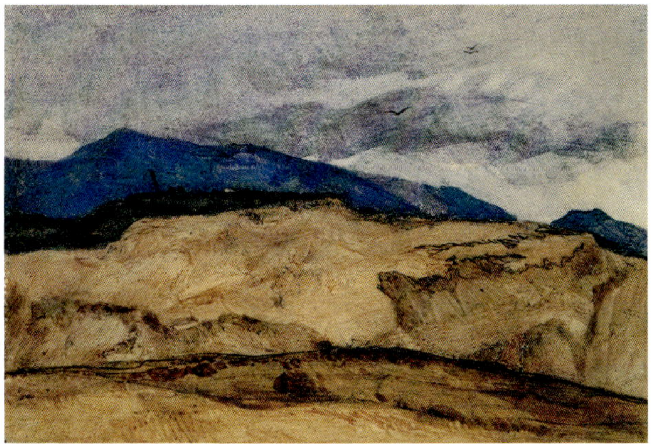

John Sell COTMAN
[1782–1842]
Falls of The Sélune at Mortain, Normandy, 1820–1

sepia wash and black lead on paper, 24.8 × 35.9 cm
inscribed: *J.S.Cotman Aug.st 26. 1820–1821 The Falls of the Salune at Mortain*

P.701
PROVENANCE: Cotman Sale 1842; whereabouts unknown; Sydney Kitson; Elisabeth and Alice Barbara Kitson, given to Gallery, May 1973.
EXHIBITIONS: *British Art c.1000–1860*, London, R.A., 1934, no.1186; *Watercolour Drawings by J.R.Cozens and J.S.Cotman*, Manchester, Whitworth Art Gallery, 1937, no.2, *The English Tradition: an exhibition of watercolours from two private collections*, Bedford, Cecil Higgins Art Gallery, 1972, no.15.
REFERENCES: H. Isherwood Kay (ed.), 'Cotman's Letters from Normandy' 1820, *Walpole Society*, vol.xv, 1926–7, p.116; S. Kitson, *The Life of John Sell Cotman*, 1937, p.225, pl.101, for finished watercolour of sketch; D. Boswell, 'Art & Architecture for Leeds: Sydney and Robert Kitsons' quest for Cotman' in *Cotmania & Mr Kitson*, Leeds, 1992, p.15.

Cotman made three tours in Normandy in 1817, 1818 and 1820. These led to some of his finest watercolours and drawings – and particularly those in sepia – which he continued to produce throughout the 1820s.

This detailed and exceptionally fine sketch served as the basis for a more finished sepia and deeper-toned version, illustrated as pl.101 in Kitson's book. As it bears the same date it would seem that Cotman may have begun it that same evening in his lodgings and then put in the finishing touches the following year. Two letters from Cotman, dated 26 August and 2 September, written to Dawson Turner and his wife respectively, record his lyrical enthusiasm for the landscape around Mortain.

EJ

John Sell COTMAN
[1782–1842]
Figures by a Ruined Gatehouse, c.1820–23

sepia on paper, 42.2 × 30.5 cm

P.174
PROVENANCE: John Manning Gallery, from whom purchased by Gallery, November 1957.
EXHIBITIONS: *John Sell Cotman*, Bedford, Cecil Higgins Art Gallery, 1961, no.43.

Cotman developed a distinctive drawing style, in which he flattened surfaces and pattern. He advised his son 'Draw sternly and true, leave out, but add nothing'.

CB

John Sell COTMAN
[1782–1842]
Mountain Landscape, c.1832–40

watercolour, paste and black lead on paper, 15.9 × 23.7 cm

P.694
PROVENANCE: Sutton Palmer; Christie's 11 December 1933, lot 176; Sydney Kitson; Elisabeth and Alice Barbara Kitson; given to Gallery, May 1973.
EXHIBITIONS: *The English Tradition: an exhibition of watercolours from two private collections*, Bedford, Cecil Higgins Art Gallery, 1972, no.20.

One of the most original artists of his time, Cotman was born in Norwich but had moved to London by 1799 where he became part of Dr MONRO's 'Academy'. There he met GIRTIN, a formative influence on his development. He spent much of the 1810s concentrating on etching, while from 1822–33 he relied mainly on teaching. In 1834 he was appointed Professor of Drawing at King's College, London, owing to the influence of his friend J.M.W.TURNER, where he taught, among others, Dante Gabriel ROSSETTI and his brother William, who remembered Cotman as 'an alert, forceful-looking man, of modest stature, with a fine well-moulded face, which testified to an impulsive nature, somewhat worn and worried'.

Although unsuccessful commercially, Cotman is now recognized as among the very finest of watercolour artists with an innate sense of structure. His style, in its patterning of areas of flat colour, contrasting sharply in tone, has an almost oriental look about it.

His two sons were also artists: Miles Edmund (1810–58) acted as his father's pupil and assistant for much of his life while John Joseph (1814–78) was more independent, his work marked by strong contrasts of bright colours.

EJ/CB

John Sell COTMAN
[1782–1842]
The Interior of a Manor House, 1833

watercolour, bodycolour and pencil on paper, 31.2 × 46.3 cm
inscribed: *Cotman 1833*

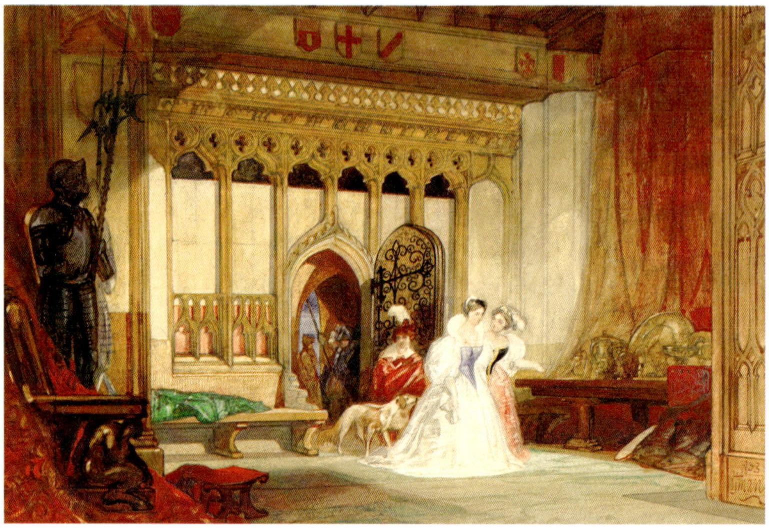

P.488
PROVENANCE: Appleby Brothers, from whom purchased by Gallery, May 1965.
EXHIBITIONS: Norfolk and Suffolk Institution Exhibition, Norwich, 1833; *The English Tradition: an exhibition of watercolours from two private collections,* Bedford, Cecil Higgins Art Gallery, 1972, no.17; *Knights, Chivalry Romance, Legend,* Newcastle upon Tyne, Laing Art Gallery, 1995–6, no cat.

The drawing has been cut and enlarged by Cotman, whose signature is on the additional part. In 1826, Cotman wrote to Dawson Turner complaining about lack of money. Dawson Turner replied on 22 June 1826:

Your present income from teaching you state to be about £200 a year and you have £40 in the bank…there may be much cause for regret…The times are wretchedly bad. They are unfavourable to everything; but particularly to the luxuries of life, with retrenchment naturally first begins … You have lived long enough to learn that your present style will not succeed, and you have talent enough to adopt another.

As a result of this letter, Cotman attempted to find new markets for his work and in the 1830s he began a series of historical subjects. Until 1834, Cotman owned a large collection of costume prints and armour, which provided him with essential reference material for his historical pictures, such as this one.

CB

John Sell COTMAN
[1782–1842]
Knight on Horseback, 1835

watercolour and black lead with gum arabic on cut-out cardboard, 40.9 × 24.7 cm at widest point
inscribed: *Hannah the Fairest PURR on cat's collar*

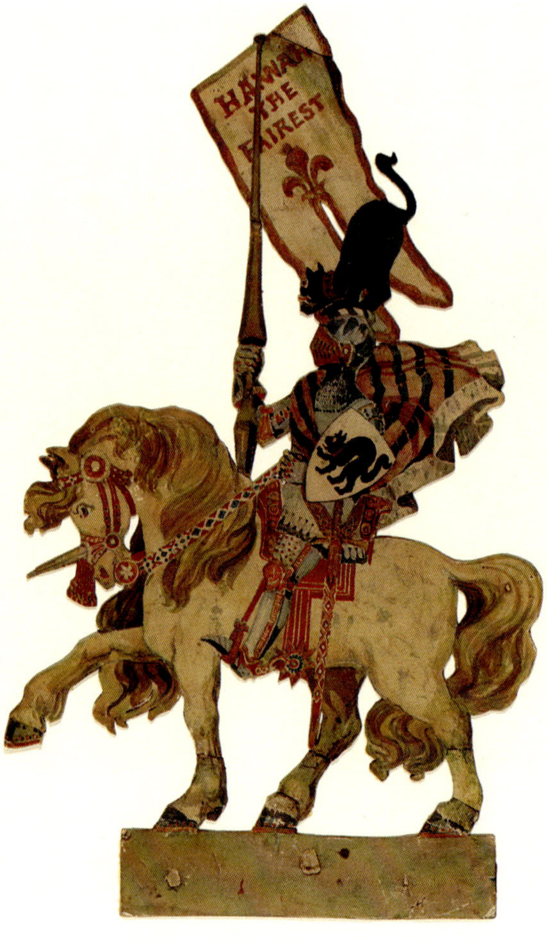

P.697
PROVENANCE: Hannah Maw; Prof. Francis Derwent Wood R.A.; Christie's with A Spanish Arquebusier P.704; Thos. Agnew & Sons Ltd; Sydney Kitson; Elisabeth and Alice Barbara Kitson, given to Gallery, May 1973.
EXHIBITIONS: *Exhibition of works by John Sell Cotman and some related painters of the Norwich School*, London, Tate Gallery, 1922, no.226; *The English Tradition: an exhibition of watercolours from two private collections,* Bedford, Cecil Higgins Art Gallery, 1972, no.19; *John Sell Cotman 1782–1842,* London, V&A, Manchester, Whitworth Art Gallery & Bristol, Bristol City Art Gallery, 1982–3, no.104; *Knights, Chivalry, Romance, Legend*, Newcastle upon Tyne, Laing Art Gallery, 1995, no cat.
REFERENCES: A.P. Oppé, 'The Watercolour Drawings of John Sell Cotman', *The Studio,* 1923, p.xiv; S. Kitson, *The Life of John Sell Cotman*, 1937, p.348. pl.137; B. Llewellyn, 'A Troubled Genius', *The Antique Dealer and Collector's Guide*, September 1982, p.65.

Painted in 1835 for the daughter of John Hornby Maw (fl.1825–48), a maker of surgical instruments, amateur artist and active patron of Cotman, COX, DE WINT and TURNER.

The occasion was Hannah's fifth birthday, which was celebrated on 12 February with a grand dinner party. In a memoir Hannah, later Mrs Wood, wrote:

At this were present the Cotmans, the D.Coxs, Wm.Hunt, the De Wints and many others besides relations-and (crowning glory) the great J.M.W.Turner himself, who did me the honour to take me on his knee and cut a pencil for me out of my new paints-box, that I might draw him a house–remarking "dash it the child draws crows better than I do !"– And Cotman brought me two beautiful artistic cardboard toys of his own making, still preserved – a knight errant on his war-horse and a Cromwellian Arquebusier.

Although only 'a playful experiment in the nursery', this is in line with Cotman's interest at this period in historical subjects and costume pieces. The cat on the shield may refer to the black cat that the superstitious Cotman kept for luck.

EJ/CB

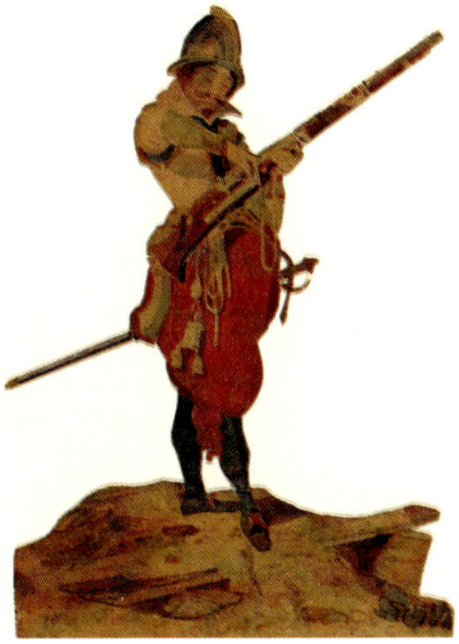

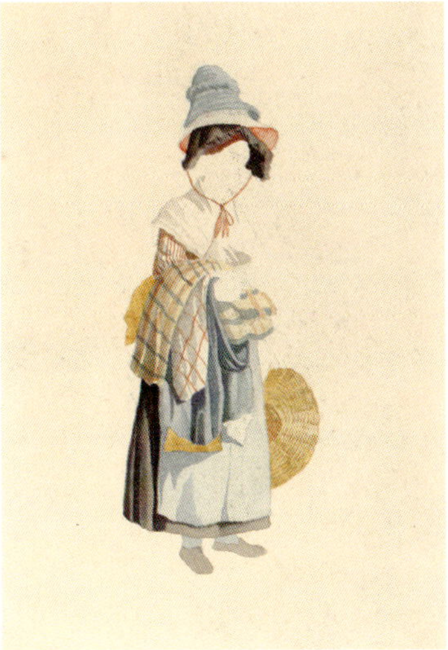

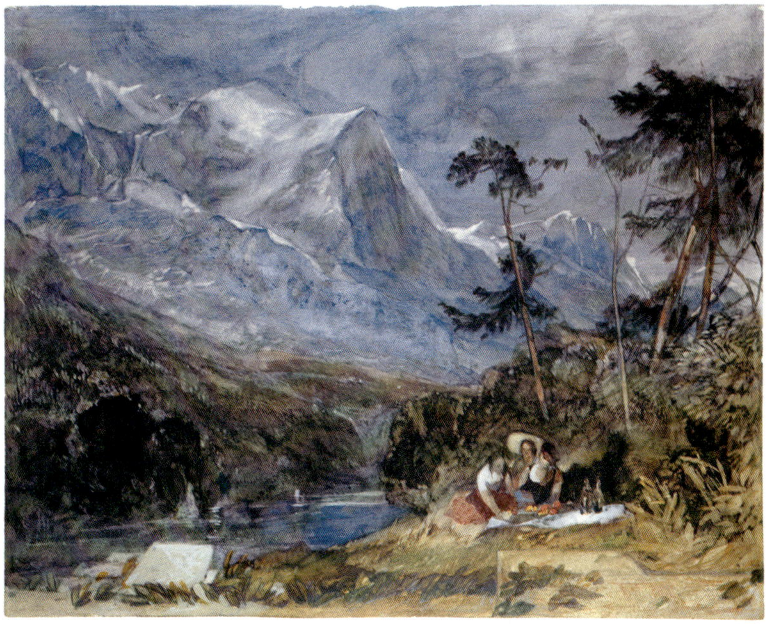

John Sell COTMAN
[1782–1842]
A Spanish Arquebusier, 1835

watercolour and black lead on cut-out cardboard, 26.3 × 19 cm
inscribed: *Cotman*

P.704
PROVENANCE: Hannah Maw; Prof. Francis Derwent Wood R.A.; Sydney Kitson; Elisabeth and Alice Barbara Kitson, given to Gallery, May 1973.
EXHIBITIONS: *Exhibition of works by John Sell Cotman and some related painters of the Norwich School*, London, National Gallery, Millbank (Tate Gallery), 1922, no.225; *The English Tradition: an exhibition of watercolours from two private collections*, Bedford, Cecil Higgins Art Gallery, 1972, no.24.
REFERENCES: S. Kitson, *The Life of John Sell Cotman*, 1937, p.348.

Like *Knight on Horseback* (P.697), this was painted for Hannah (Ann Mary) Maw, daughter of John Hornby Maw (fl.1825–48), for her fifth birthday in 1835 and then cut out. The figure is after *Maniement d'armes d'arquebusier, mouquetz et piques* by Jacob de Gheyn (1565 – 1629) 1608 in Amsterdam. As noted in the entry for P.697, this dates from the period that coincided with Cotman's interest in costume pieces and historical subjects.

EJ

John Sell COTMAN
[1782–1842]
Old Woman with Hats, mid 1830's

watercolour and black lead on paper, 37.5 × 27.8 cm
inscribed: *J.S.Cotman*
on reverse: pencil sketch of thatched church 19.8 × 27.8 cm

P.702
PROVENANCE: Sydney Kitson; Elisabeth and Alice Barbara Kitson, given to Gallery, May 1973.
EXHIBITIONS: *The English Tradition: an exhibition of watercolours from two private collections*, Bedford, Cecil Higgins Art Gallery, 1972, no.21.

Not easy to date but it probably belongs to the mid 1830s, when Cotman drew somewhat similar subjects for Hannah Maw on her fifth birthday (see nos. P.697 and P.704).

EJ

John Sell COTMAN
[1782–1842]
Mountain Scene with Figures in the foreground, c.1839

watercolour with black lead, ink and paste on paper, 35 × 44.2 cm

P.361
PROVENANCE: John Manning Gallery, from whom purchased by Gallery, July 1960.
EXHIBITIONS: *John Sell Cotman*, Bedford, Cecil Higgins Art Gallery, 1961, no.60; *Watercolours and Drawings from The Cecil Higgins Art Gallery Bedford*, London, Thos. Agnew & Sons Ltd, 1962, no.44.

In the last decade of his life, Cotman began experimenting with paste as a medium. The exact formula is unknown but is believed to be made from rotting flour paste. It provided Cotman with a base for strong, vibrant colours, which became characteristic of his later work.

A suggested date of c.1839 in the Gallery's files seems to be challenged in the catalogue of the exhibition *John Sell Cotman 1782–1842*, Arts Council, 1982, in the entry for *The Entrance of the Valley of Lauterbrunnen, from Interlaken*, 1831 (Private Collection), perhaps based on a sketch by Joseph Geldart, Cotman's pupil and the first owner of the drawing.

The catalogue states: 'A rather similar composition, both in conception and execution, is at Bedford'. Certainly the figures picnicking in the foreground of both drawings seem closely related and the scene may well depict Switzerland, but the still stronger colour and use of paste here argue for a later date in the 1830s than 1831.

EJ/CB

Pupil of JOHN SELL COTMAN
Garden House on the River Yare

black lead and wash on paper, 29.7 × 22.4 cm
inscribed on reverse: *J.S.Cotman*

P.699
PROVENANCE: Sydney Kitson; Elisabeth and Alice Barbara Kitson, given to Gallery, May 1973.

According to Barbara Kitson (letter of 8 August 1992 in the Gallery's historical file), this was the first drawing that her father, Sydney Kitson, bought attributed to Cotman. It was only years later that he came to believe it to be a copy, by a pupil, of the drawing which Cotman made on his return from Wales to Norwich in the late summer of 1800. That drawing signed 'Cotman' and dated 1800, is mentioned in S. Kitson *The Life of John Sell Cotman*, 1937, p.22.

EJ

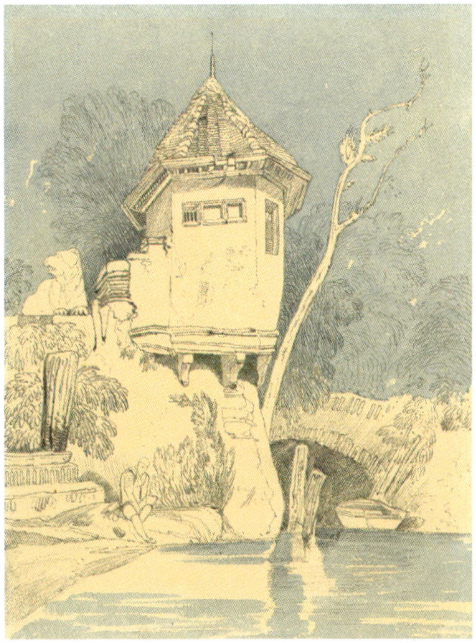

David COX, R.W.S.
[1783–1859]
Shrimpers at Boulogne, 1832

watercolour with scratching out on paper, 20 × 29.3 cm
inscribed: *David Cox 1832*
inscribed on reverse: *Between Boulogne & Calais D. Cox*

P.257
PROVENANCE: Sotheby's 16 April 1958 lot 1; Thos. Agnew & Sons Ltd, from whom purchased by Gallery, October 1958.
EXHIBITIONS: *Watercolours and Drawings from The Cecil Higgins Art Gallery Bedford*, London, Thos. Agnew & Sons Ltd, 1962, no.47; *English Watercolours from The Cecil Higgins Art Gallery Bedford*, Reading, Reading Art Gallery, 1965, no.8.

This coast scene, with its long vista of drying sand as the tide goes out, may reflect the influence of shore scenes by BONINGTON, who had died in 1828. Cox would have been familiar with his work following the artist's studio sale in 1829.

In 1829 Cox paid his first visit to Paris calling on FRANCIA, Bonington's teacher, in Calais and then sketching at Boulogne, which he may have revisited on his final trip to France in 1832.

EJ

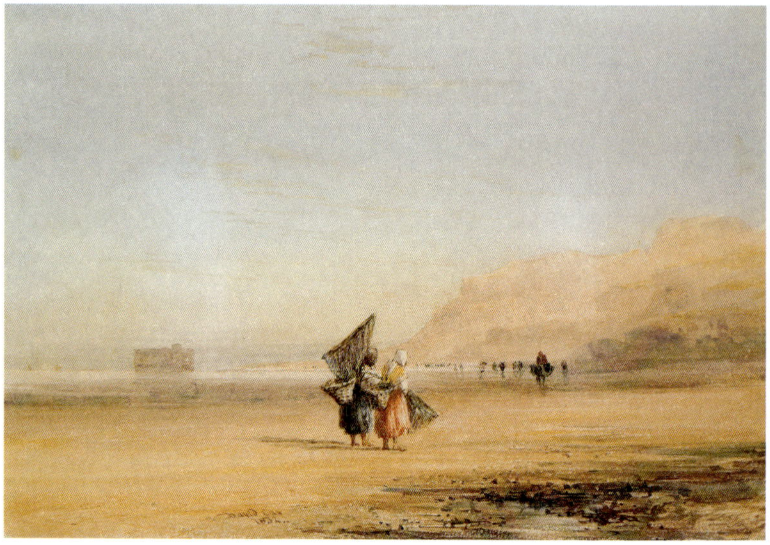

David COX, R.W.S.
[1783–1859]
Bolton Abbey, mid-1840s

watercolour over black chalk on paper, 36.8 × 51.4 cm
on reverse: *pencil sketch of landscape*

P.61
PROVENANCE: Walter Turner; the Wilmott Family until 1937 (Mr Wilmott was a partner in the firm of Wilmott & Roberts, Birmingham, and Mr William Roberts was a friend of David Cox); Gilbert Davis; P&D Colnaghi Ltd, from whom purchased by Gallery, May 1953.
EXHIBITIONS: *Watercolours from the Gilbert Davis Collection*, Arts Council, 1949, no.47; *English Watercolours from The Cecil Higgins Art Gallery Bedford*, Reading, Reading Art Gallery, 1965, no. 7.

Bolton Abbey, originally Bolton Priory, an Augustinian Foundation dating from the early 12th century, fell into ruin after 1540. Its spectacular setting, on a double bend of the river Wharfe about seven miles north-west of Ilkley in Yorkshire, ensured that it became a favourite subject with artists. Cox certainly painted it frequently, as did DE WINT and, before them, both GIRTIN and TURNER.

This drawing is probably datable to the mid-1840s when Cox's broadening and loosening of touch mark his best work. Here Cox depicts the old abbey becoming gradually obscured by the encroaching foliage and vegetation.

EJ

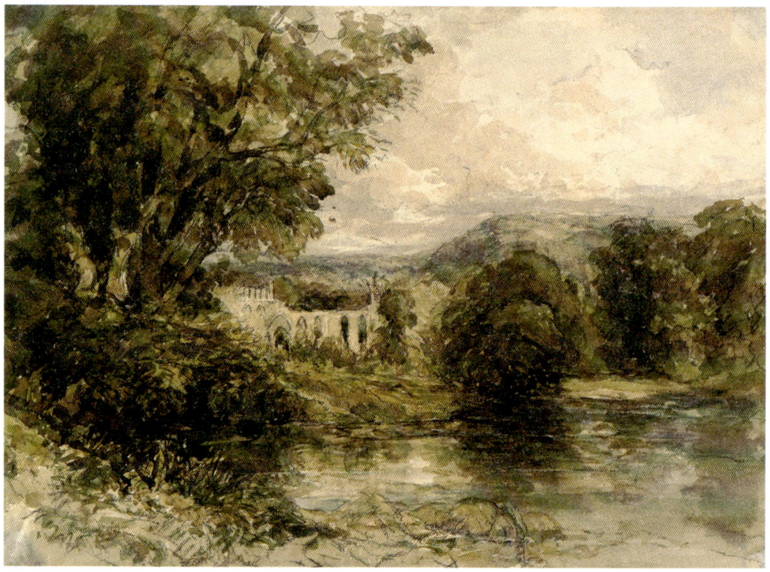

David COX, R.W.S.
[1783–1859]
Mountain Landscape with Sheep, 1850

watercolour on paper, 45.7 × 67.9 cm
on reverse: watercolour landscape

P.60
PROVENANCE: Lt-Colonel James B. Gaskell; Holbrook Gaskell; Colonel Allen; Squire Gallery, Baker Street, London, from whom purchased by Gallery, March 1952.
EXHIBITIONS: *David Cox*, Birmingham, Birmingham Art Gallery, 1890, no.175, as *Welsh Lane; English watercolours from the Hickman Bacon and other collections*, Bedford, Cecil Higgins Art Gallery, 1952, no.19; *English Watercolours from The Cecil Higgins Art Gallery Bedford,* Reading, Reading Museum and Art Gallery, 1965, no.6.

In 1841 Cox returned to Birmingham. For the rest of his career his favourite sketching ground became the area round Bettws-y-Coed, which he visited almost every year from 1844 to 1856. This scene has not been identified but surely depicts a typically damp day in the Welsh mountains, their peaks still hidden in the clouds. Naturally there are also some sheep, for no artist included sheep so often in his oils and watercolours as Cox did.

EJ

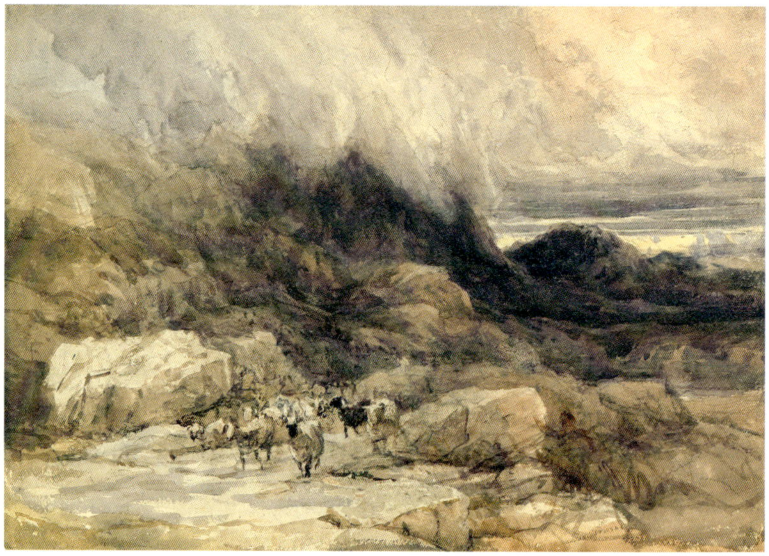

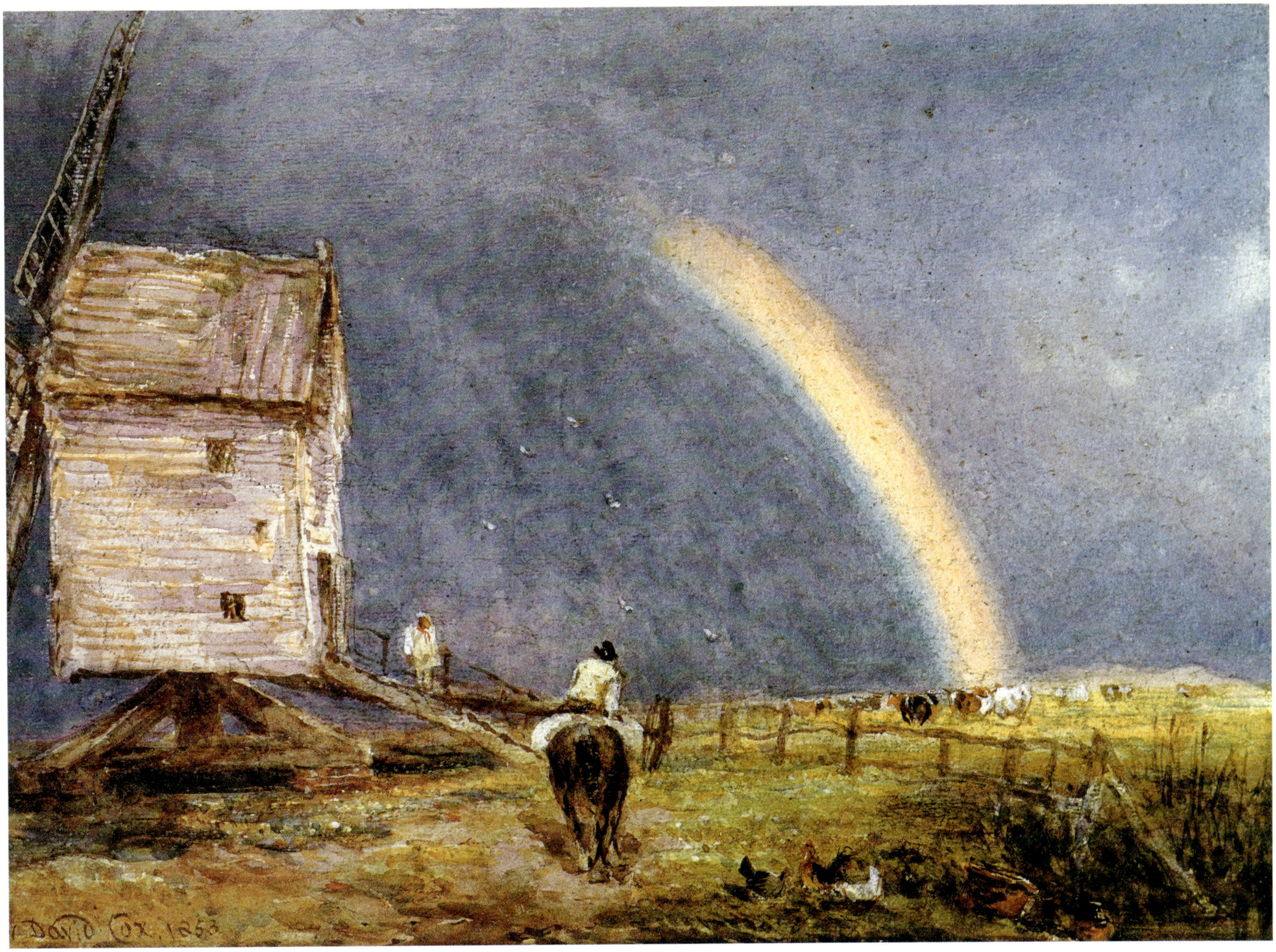

David COX, R.W.S.
[1783–1859]
The Mill, 1853

watercolour heightened with white on textured paper, 26.6 × 36.8 cm
inscribed: *David Cox 1853*

P.281

PROVENANCE: C.W.Dyson Perrins; sold by executors; Sotheby's 22 April 1959, lot 48; P&D Colnaghi Ltd purchased on behalf of Gallery, April 1959.
EXHIBITIONS: *D.H.Lawrence & the Visual Arts*, Nottingham, Castle Museum, 1985, no.17; *The Art of Seeing: John Ruskin and the Victorian Eye*, Arizona, Phoenix Art Gallery and Indianapolis, Indianapolis Museum of Art, 1993, fig.89, p.125.
REFERENCES: J. Egerton, *English Watercolour Painting*, 1979, pp.12–13, pl.40; G. Bauer, *David Cox 1783–1859: Précurseur des Impressionistes?*, 2000, p.102

A typical late, breezy drawing painted on the rough absorbent paper that Cox favoured as it enabled him to paint quickly and freely with a loaded brush. In a letter to his son dated 15 March 1850 Cox wrote: 'My drawing upon the Scotch paper is so rough I fear I shall bring down all against me, but the paper has plagued me so I am very nervous'. Cox's contemporaries complained of a 'careless haste' in his painting style and a sketchiness of finish. The textured paper would also contain dark flecks. In landscapes these could be hidden, but skies posed a problem; Cox's response was 'Oh, I just put wings to them, and then they fly away as birds'.

Cox was born near Birmingham, the son of a blacksmith. At fifteen he was apprenticed to a miniature painter named Fielder (Cox discovered his hanged body). He worked as a scene painter at the Birmingham Theatre Royal, while studying at night with Joseph Barber (c.1757–1811). By 1808 he was taking watercolour lessons from John VARLEY. In his early career he earned his living as a drawing-master. He retired to Harborne in Birmingham in 1841. During 1853, Cox had a slight stroke which permanently damaged his eyesight.

CB

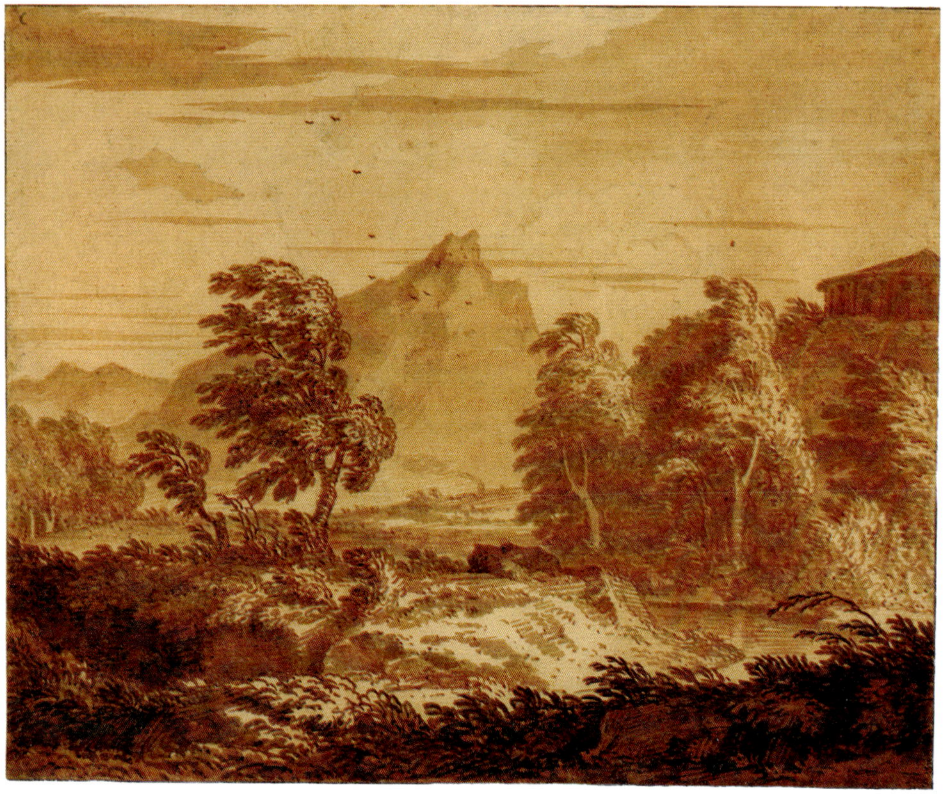

Alexander COZENS

[1717–86]

A Mountainous Landscape, c.1785

brush drawing in brown wash on varnished paper,
16.8 × 20.7 cm

P.62

PROVENANCE: Herbert Horne; Sir Edward Marsh; Thos. Agnew & Sons Ltd, from whom purchased by Gallery, April 1952.
EXHIBITIONS: *The Drawings in the Collection of Herbert Horne*, London, Burlington Fine Arts Club, 1916, no.26; *Alexander Cozens*, London, Tate Gallery, 1946, no.28, pl.5; *English Watercolours from the Hickman Bacon and other collections*, Bedford, Cecil Higgins Art Gallery, 1952, no.23; *Watercolours and Drawings from The Cecil Higgins Art Gallery Bedford*, London, Thos. Agnew & Sons Ltd, 1962, no.6.

In 1746, Alexander Cozens travelled to Rome to study drawing, painting and etching, one of the earliest British artists to do so. Luke Hermann highlights the many similarities with the work of Claude Lorrain, and asserts that Cozens must have been influenced by Lorrain's approach to landscape painting. From 1778 to c.1784, Cozens was the drawing master to two of George III's sons, William and Edward, and other pupils included William Beckford (1759–1844) and Sir George Beaumont (1753–1827).

EJ

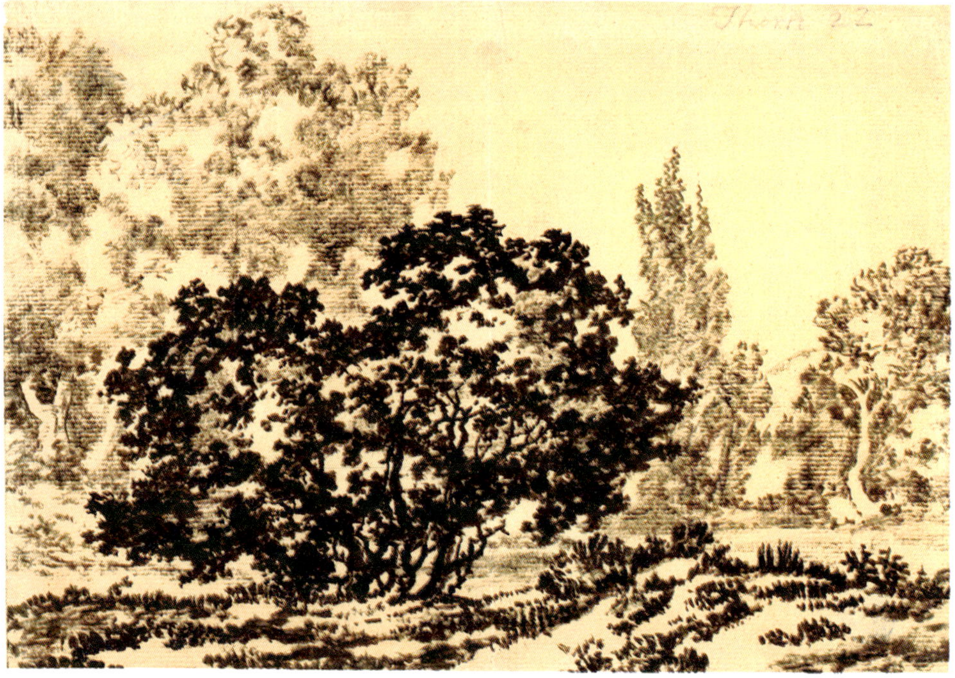

Alexander COZENS

[1717–86]

Woodland Scene with Thorn-tree, c.1785

brown ink on paper, 15.2 × 22 cm
inscribed: *Thorn 22*

P.446

PROVENANCE: H.N. Squire; Maas Gallery, from whom purchased by Gallery, March 1963.
EXHIBITIONS: *Spring Exhibition*, London, Maas Gallery, 1963, no.24.

In about 1785, Cozens published his treatise on a method of composing the ideal landscape entitled *A New Method of Assisting the Invention in Drawing Original Compositions of Landscapes*. Within the introduction he states: 'I am persuaded, that some instantaneous method of bringing forth the conception of an ideal subject fully to the view (through the crudest manner) would promote original composition in painting; and that the want of some such method has retarded the progress of it more than impotence of execution'. The treatise clarified the accidental 'blot' paintings, which Cozens had invented as a method to release the creativity within his students. They were made with a soft brush and ink made to his own recipe; he would apply random blots and then create the ideal landscape from the result, either by enhancing the composition or transferring it to another piece of paper. He painted almost entirely in monochrome, which provided even greater contrasts and enhanced the Romantic landscape.

CB

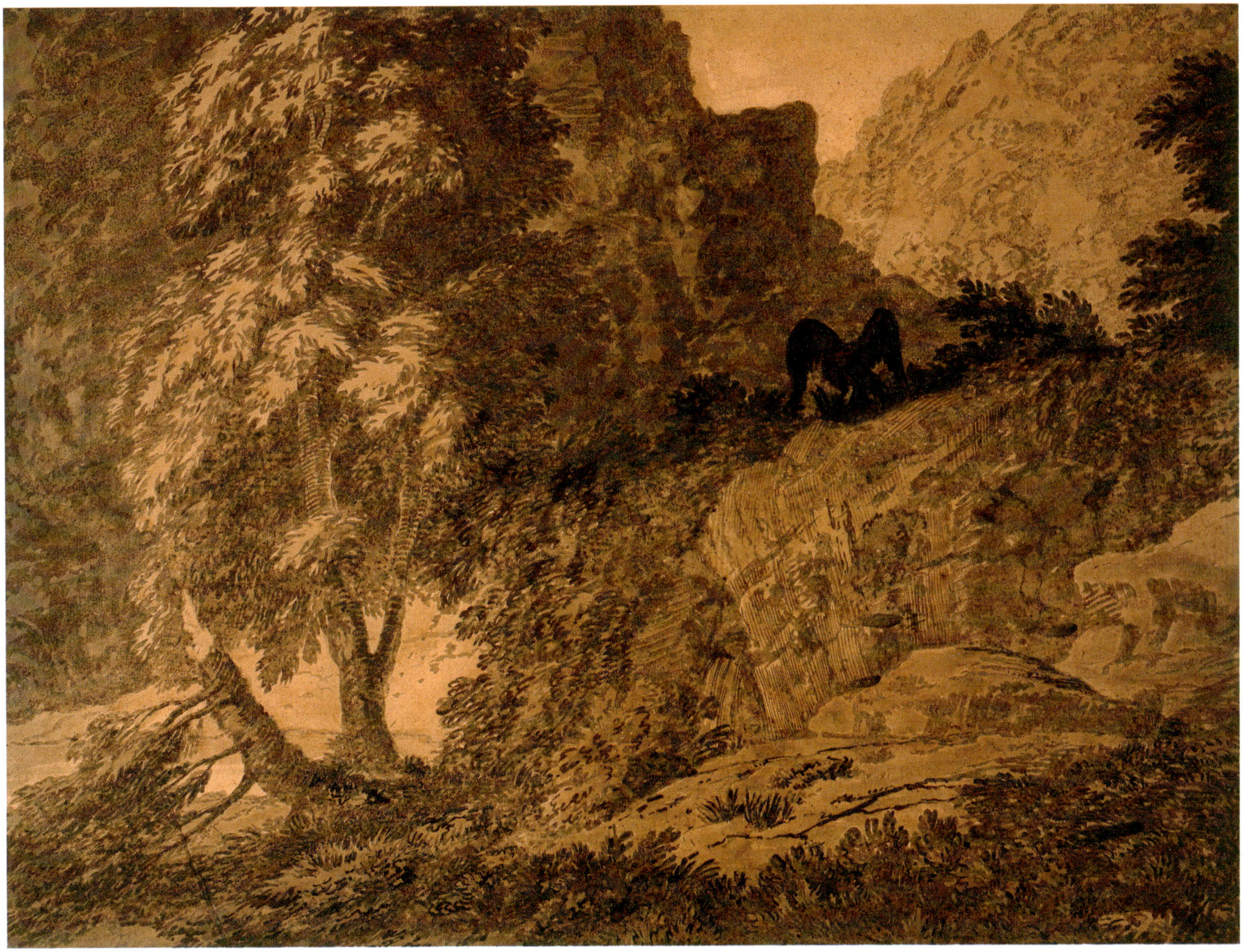

Alexander COZENS
[1717–86]
A Rocky Wooded Landscape with an Eagle and its Prey, c.1785

sepia wash on paper, 46 × 62.2 cm
inscribed: *Alexr Cozens*

P.584
PROVENANCE: Christie's 31 March 1787; Thomas Sunderland; Miss Joan Sunderland; Randall Davies, 1931; Mrs Walter Sedgwick; Sotheby's 27 June 1968 lot 70; Thos. Agnew & Sons Ltd, from whom purchased by Gallery, July 1968.
EXHIBITIONS: *Alexander Cozens*, London, Tate Gallery, 1946, no.46 as *The Eagles Nest.*

An unusually 'Sublime' subject for Cozens which surely owes something to the rocky landscapes of Salvator Rosa. It is noteworthy that the first owner was a fellow watercolourist, Thomas Sunderland (1744–1823).

Although born in Russia, Cozens was not the son of Peter the Great as was once believed. He was educated and trained as an artist in London. He became a drawing master and a popular tutor among the aristocracy and gentry, forming a close relationship with William Beckford (1759–1844). His best-known work was a treatise, which proposed the use of random 'blots', developing an idea of Leonardo da Vinci (see P.446 for details). This led to Beckford describing him as 'almost as full of systems as the Universe'.

His landscapes, usually in monochrome wash, are essays in this type of abstraction which, as Andrew Wilton has written, 'often attain an otherwordly poetry which must have influenced his son, John Robert'.

EJ

John Robert COZENS

[1752–97]

In the Canton of Unterwalden, c.1776–8

pen, ink with washes of grey and watercolour, 22.5 × 34.6 cm
inscribed on reverse: *Vale of Grindelwald from the Northwest*

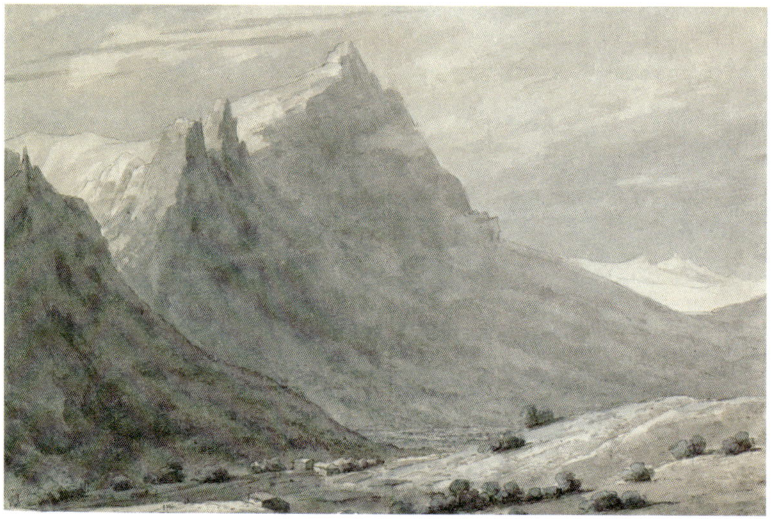

P.116
PROVENANCE: Mr Somerset Beaumont; by descent Miss Mary Welland; Thos. Agnew & Sons Ltd, from whom purchased by Gallery, March 1957.
EXHIBITIONS: *84th Annual Watercolour Exhibition*, London, Thos. Agnew & Sons Ltd, 1957, no.30.
REFERENCES: C.F. Bell & T. Girtin, 'J.R. Cozens', *Walpole Society Journal*, XXIII, 1934–5, no.29 (111); D. Farr and W. Bradford, *Flemish, Dutch and British Drawings from the Courtauld Collections*, 1986, p.194. no.85.

This stems from Cozens' first visit to the Continent, 1776–8. He travelled through Switzerland and Italy with his patron Richard Payne Knight (1750–1824), the connoisseur, arbiter of taste and trustee of the British Museum (he voted against acquiring the Elgin Marbles).

Three other versions exist: in the National Gallery of Ireland, Dublin, the Courtauld Gallery, Somerset House, London, and the Leeds City Art Gallery (Lupton Bequest). T. Girtin attempted to reconstruct Cozens' first journey through the Swiss Alps but encountered difficulties in tracing the artist's route in the Unterwalden district.

EJ

John Robert COZENS

[1752–97]

The Coast between Vietri and Salerno, 1782

watercolour and black lead on paper, 25.7 × 37.1 cm

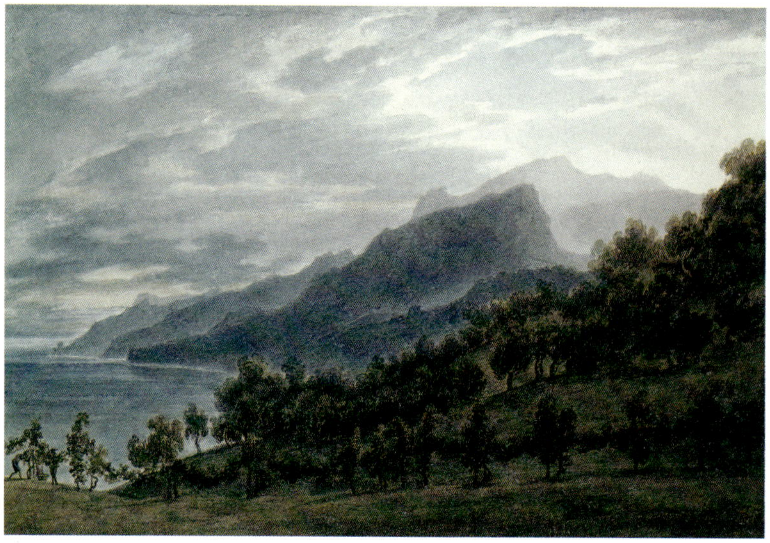

P.63
PROVENANCE: William Beckford; Beckford Sale 1805, lot 90, Anon. Buyer; Victor Rienaecker no.99; E.A. Morrison to 1952; Spink & Son Ltd., from whom purchased by Gallery, October 1952.
EXHIBITIONS: *English watercolours from the Hickman Bacon and other collections*, Bedford, Cecil Higgins Art Gallery, 1952, no.29; *English Watercolours 1750–1820*, Norwich, Norwich Castle Museum, 1955, no.19; *Watercolours and Drawings from The Cecil Higgins Art Gallery Bedford*, London, Thos. Agnew & Sons Ltd, 1962, no.17; *English Watercolours from The Cecil Higgins Art Gallery Bedford*, Reading, Reading Art Gallery, 1965, no.9; *Watercolours by John Robert Cozens*, Manchester, Whitworth Art Gallery and London, V&A, 1971, no.56; *British Watercolours: A Golden Age 1750–1850*, J.B. Speed Museum, Louisville, Kentucky, 1977, no.12.
REFERENCES: C.F. Bell & T. Girtin, 'The Sketches and Drawings of John Robert Cozens', *Illustrated Walpole Society*, vol.XXIII pl. XXIB, no.269, drg.1; *Beckford Sketchbook* vol. III p.10 for sketch dated 22 Sept. 1782; K. Sloan, *Alexander & John Robert Cozens: The Poetry of Landscape*, 1986, p.148, no.163; A. Ambrose, *Discovering English Watercolours*, 1987,p.39, pl.11.

Based on a study in the Hamilton Sketch Books (now in the British Museum) inscribed *The Coast of Vietri – from Salerno* and *Illumined vapour on the upper part of the highest mountain – evening* and dated *September 22nd* (1782).

Other versions are in the Ashmolean Museum, Oxford, and the Huntington Art Gallery, San Marino, California.

In 1782 Cozens accompanied the young millionaire, William Beckford (1759–1844), to the Continent as his draughtsman. The Beckford sale in 1805 contained ninety-four of Cozens' drawings; this one was described in the catalogue as 'executed with uncommon spirit; very fine'.

A note on the back of the frame reads:

Similar (but with important differences) to a larger drawing in the possession of Professor Barnard the original study from nature for which, dated September 22nd, 1782, is in the Beckford Sketch Books, vol.III p.10. Professor Barnard's drawing is illustrated in the Burlington Fine Arts Cat. 1923, pl.25. Two drawings at the V&A Museum are from sketches done a few days later and are probably views further along the coast near the Tower.

EJ

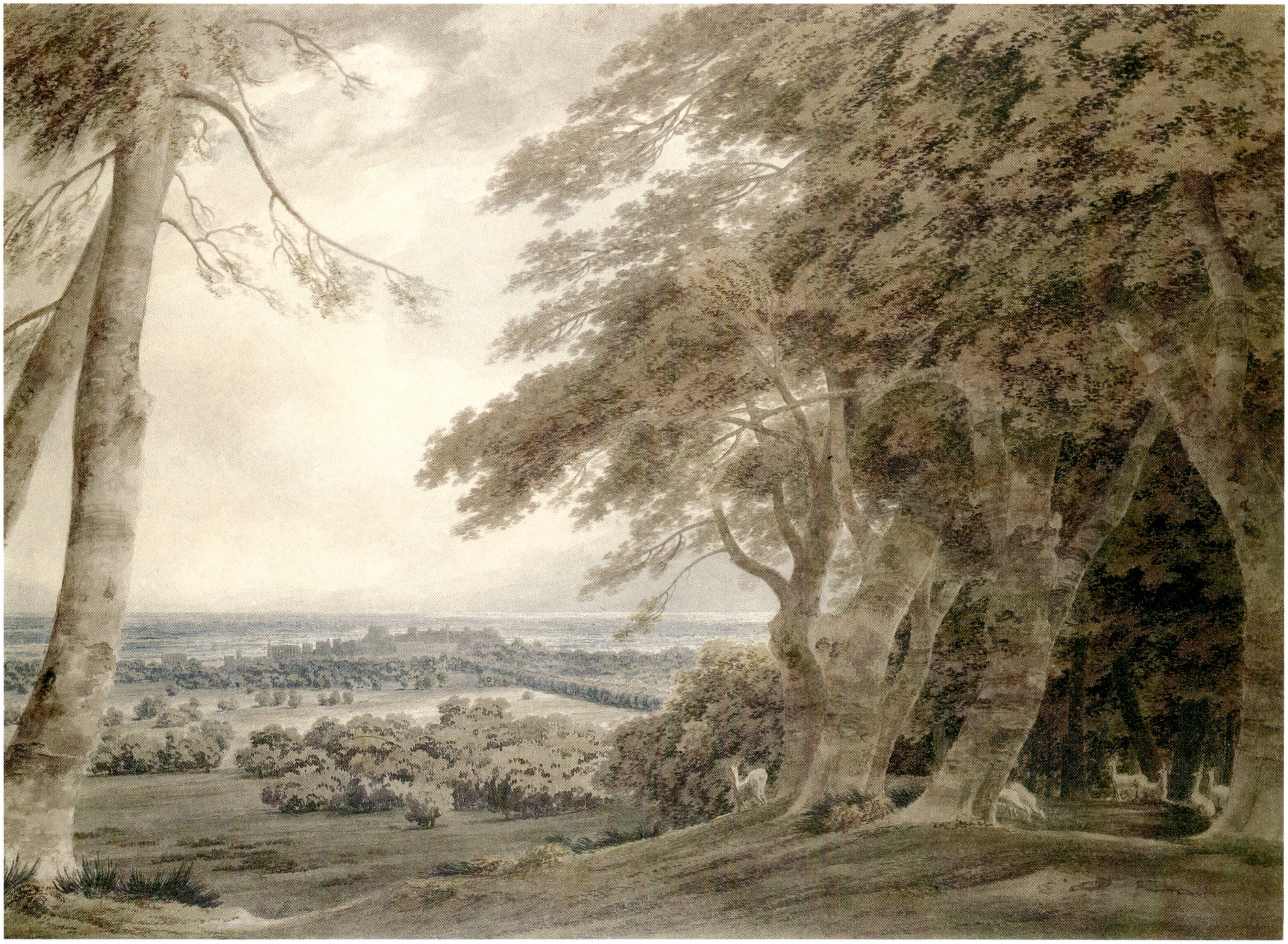

John Robert COZENS

[1752–97]

Distant View of Windsor Castle from the South West, after 1787

watercolour on paper, 49.2 × 69.5 cm

P.295

PROVENANCE: William Smith F.S.A.; bequeathed to his brother George; by descent to Mrs A.D. Cowan, from whom bought by Thos. Agnew & Sons Ltd., purchased by Gallery, July 1959.

EXHIBITIONS: *Primitives to Picasso*, London, R.A., 1962, no.366; *Watercolours and Drawings from The Cecil Higgins Art Gallery, Bedford,* London, Thos. Agnew & Sons Ltd, 1962, no.63; *English Watercolours and Drawings from The Cecil Higgins Art Gallery, Bedford,* Reading, Reading Museum and Art Gallery, 1965, no.10; *Watercolours from Bedford,* Norwich, Norwich Castle Museum, 1965, no.8; *Watercolours by John Robert Cozens,* Manchester, Whitworth Art Gallery & London, V&A, 1971, no.98; *The English Tradition: an exhibition of watercolours from two private collections,* Bedford, Cecil Higgins Art Gallery, 1972, no.29; *British Watercolours: A Golden Age 1750–1850,* Louisville, Kentucky, J.B. Speed Art Museum, 1977, no.16.

REFERENCES: C.F. Bell, *Some Additions and Notes to the Twenty-third Volume of the Walpole Society,* 1947, p.12, no.447; A.P. Oppé, *Alexander and John Robert Cozens,* 1952, pl.45; A. Bury, 'Cecil Higgins Art Gallery: Illustrated Guide', *Old Water-colour Society's Club,* 1961, vol.XXXVI, pp.31–2, pl. X; L. Herrmann, *British Landscape Painting*, 1970; K. Sloan, *Alexander and John Robert Cozens: Poetry of Landscape*, 1986, p.160.

Cozens' drawings of English subjects are dated to the last decade of his life. They are generally considered to lack the poetry of his finest Italian views perhaps due to failing health. This is certainly the finest of his English drawings and Oppé considers that it still bears 'something of character' of the Italian drawings while Francis Hawcroft praises the 'nobility in the composition' (1971 exhib. cat., p.10).

Son of Alexander, John Robert was born in London. Despite his father's many theories on the practice of art, J. R. did not paint solely from his imagination. From 1793, he suffered from mental illness and spent his final years in the care of Dr Thomas MONRO. The doctor acquired a number of his works, which Monro made available for a number of young artists to copy at his 'Academy', including GIRTIN and TURNER. John CONSTABLE considered John Robert Cozens to be 'the greatest genius that ever touched landscape', describing his work as 'all poetry'.

EJ/CB

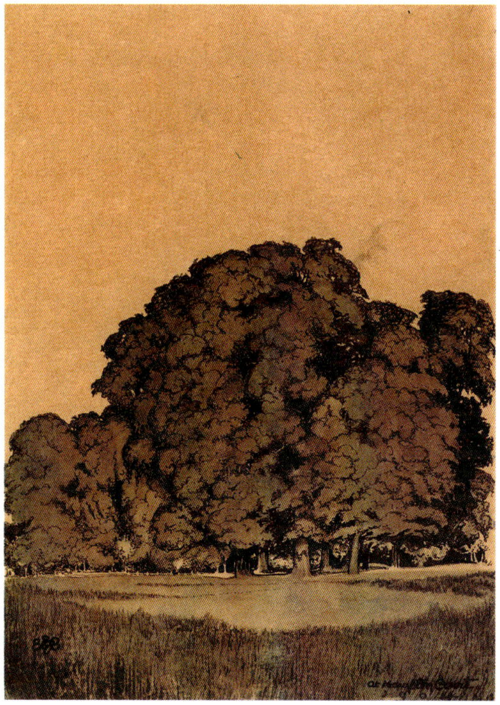

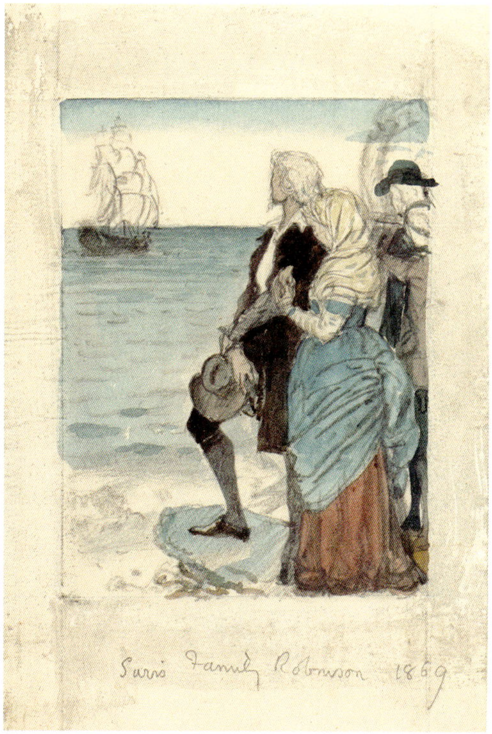

Edward Gordon CRAIG

[1872–1966]

Study of Trees at Hampton Court, 1904

pen, ink and wash on buff paper, 27.3 × 19.7 cm
inscribed: *EGC At Hampton Court 1904*

P.264
PROVENANCE: Leicester Galleries, from whom purchased by Gallery, October 1958.

Craig, son of the actress Ellen Terry (1847–1928) and the architect E.W.Godwin (1833–86), was a theatrical designer and wood-engraver who was self-taught. He produced over 500 engravings and exhibited widely in Europe. A man of influence in the world of theatre, he was the author of several books on the subject.

His drawings are rare and little known. They were presumably done to please himself by way of relaxation.

EJ/CB

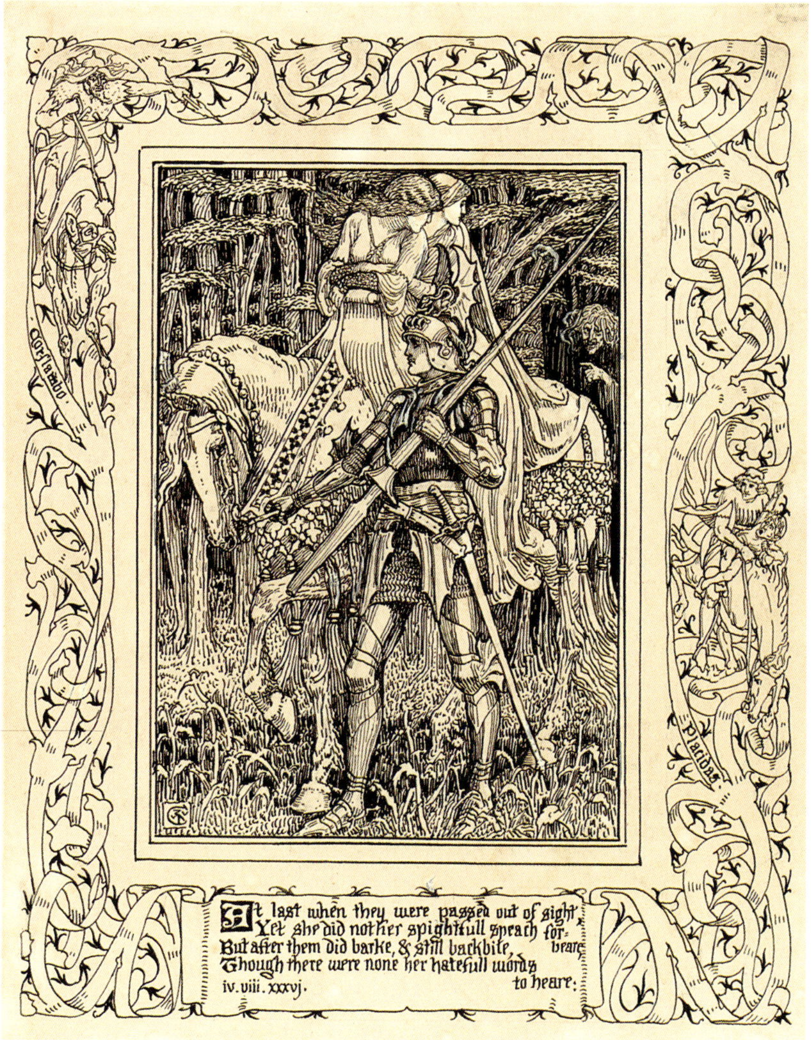

Walter CRANE, R.W.S.
[1845–1915]
Waving Farewell, 1869

watercolour and pencil on paper, 13.3 × 10.2 cm
inscribed: *Swiss Family Robinson 1869*

P.190
PROVENANCE: Elkin, Matthews Ltd; P&D Colnaghi Ltd, from whom purchased by Gallery, April 1958.

The Swiss Family Robinson, the story of a family wrecked on a desert island, was written by a Swiss pastor, Johann David Wyss (1743–1818) and published in 1812–13. The first English translation followed a year later.

This is an early sketch dating from the time that Crane was illustrating a series of sixpenny toy-books for which he was limited to the use of red, blue and black. In appearance it could hardly present a greater contrast to the Gallery's other illustration by Crane (P.165).

EJ

Walter CRANE, R.W.S.
[1845–1915]
Illustration to Spenser's Faerie Queene, c.1897

pen and ink on paper, 24.3 × 19.5 cm
inscribed: with monogram
At last when they were passed out of sight
Yet she did not her spightfull speach for
beare
But after them did barke, & still backbite,
Though there were none her hateful words
to heare
iv.viii.xxxvi.

P.165
PROVENANCE: Elkin Matthews Ltd; P&D Colnaghi, from whom purchased by Gallery, January 1958.
EXHIBITIONS: *Knights, Chivalry, Romance, Legend*, Newcastle upon Tyne, Laing Art Gallery 1995, no cat.
REFERENCES: E. Spenser with illustrations by W. Crane, *The Faerie Queene*, 1897, volume IV.

Published in 1897, by George Allen, Walter Crane produced a series of black and white drawings to accompany the six volumes.

Edmund Spenser (?1552–99) began his masterpiece, *The Faerie Queene*, in 1579; the first three books were published in 1590 and Books IV-VI in 1596. This drawing illustrates the lines from Book IV given above. Prince Arthur, the hero of the poem, is seeking the Faerie Queene with whom he has fallen in love in a vision. He comes upon Aemilia (lover of the Squire of Low Degree) and Amoret (loved by Scudamour); they are in a wretched state so he puts them up on his horse and takes them to a cottage nearby. This is owned by an old hag, Slander, who insults them and when they depart in the morning, pursues them with vile words – as she is seen doing here.

Crane was an engraver, designer, painter and, above all, an illustrator. His pre-eminence in this field, together with Randolph CALDECOTT and Kate Greenaway (1846–1901), owed much to the enterprise and artistic skill of Edmund Evans, who published much of their best work.

Many of Crane's watercolour designs for book illustrations and several of his landscape studies are now in the V&A.

EJ

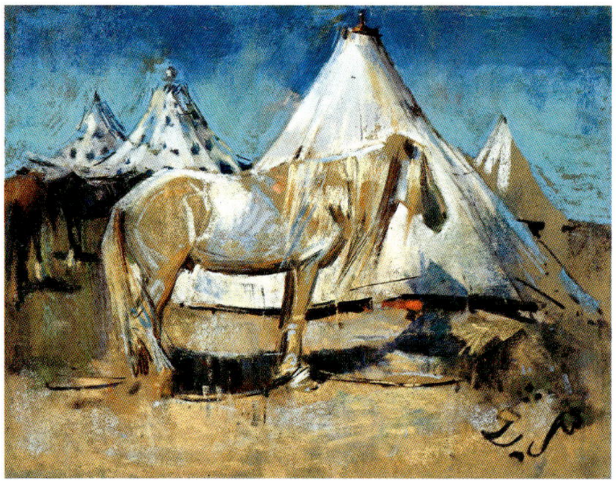

Joseph CRAWHALL
[1861–1913]
Horses and Tents, 1888

pastel on paper, 23.4 × 31.8 cm

P.434
PROVENANCE: Fine Art Society, from whom purchased by Gallery, October 1962.
REFERENCES: A. Bury, *Joseph Crawhall, the Man & Artist,* 1958, pl.49, as *At Tangier.*

Crawhall visited Tangier on numerous occasions between 1884 and 1893 and painted many subjects there, but horses were among his favourite. He may have been drawn there for his health as he suffered from lung problems. His father wrote in 1888: 'Joe's been quite laid up in Tangier with dysentery – he's not too strong I fancy he hasn't a constitution to play with these varied climates – however, he's doing good work'. Crawhall managed to live there for six shillings a day, which provided him with two horses, a man, a maid servant, and board and lodging.

CB

Joseph CRAWHALL
[1861–1913]
A Study of Goldfish

watercolour on paper, 16.5 × 24.8 cm

P.427
PROVENANCE: Mrs H.M. Crawhall Hallowes to 1962; Spink & Son Ltd, from whom purchased by Gallery, July 1962.

Painter in watercolour, mainly of birds and animals, he was much influenced by Chinese and Japanese art. Crawhall studied at the Glasgow School which flourished in the late 19th century. He made frequent visits to Tangier and Spain 1884–93, later living in Yorkshire where he bred horses from 1898. Crawhall destroyed many works that he was dissatisfied with.

EJ

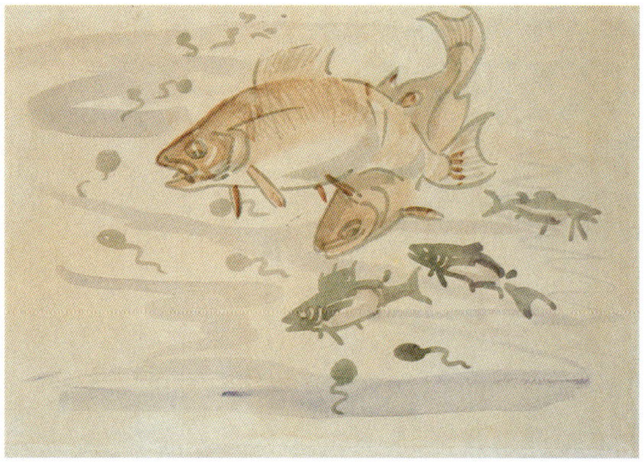

John CRAXTON, R.A.

[born 1922]

Still Life with Water Pot, 1946

Conté crayon on brown paper, 33.4 × 48.6 cm
inscribed: *To Lucian from John Craxton 5.7.46*

P.574

PROVENANCE: Lucian Freud; sold to Crane Kalman Gallery, from whom purchased by Gallery, January 1968.
EXHIBITIONS: *British Drawings 1939–49*, Edinburgh, Scottish National Gallery of Modern Art, 1969, no cat.

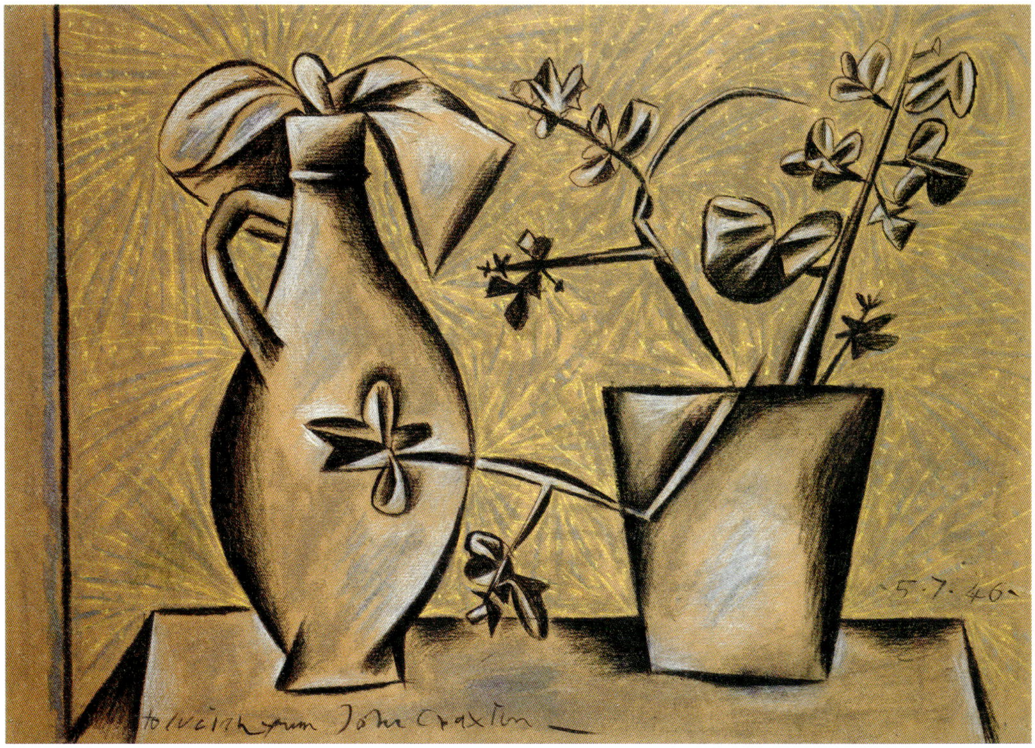

Christopher Hull kindly showed the photograph to John Craxton in December 1999, who added 'with water pot' to the title and recalled giving the drawing to Lucian FREUD when they were working together on the island of Paros, in 1946.

Craxton studied at the Central School and Goldsmiths' College from 1942. A painter and designer of theatrical décor, he designed the décor for Ravel's *Daphnis and Chloe*, first performed by the Sadler's Wells Ballet in 1951. Craxton lived and worked for many years in Greece. Now probably equally known as both a designer and an easel painter.

EJ

Joshua CRISTALL, R.W.S.

[1768–1847]

Fishermen with Boats at Hastings, 1807

pencil and pen and ink on paper, 8.9 × 14.7 cm
inscribed: *at Hastings. J.Cristall 1807*
on reverse: figure drawings in pencil

P.691

PROVENANCE: Given to Gallery by Mr Fearnside, Bedford, 1977.

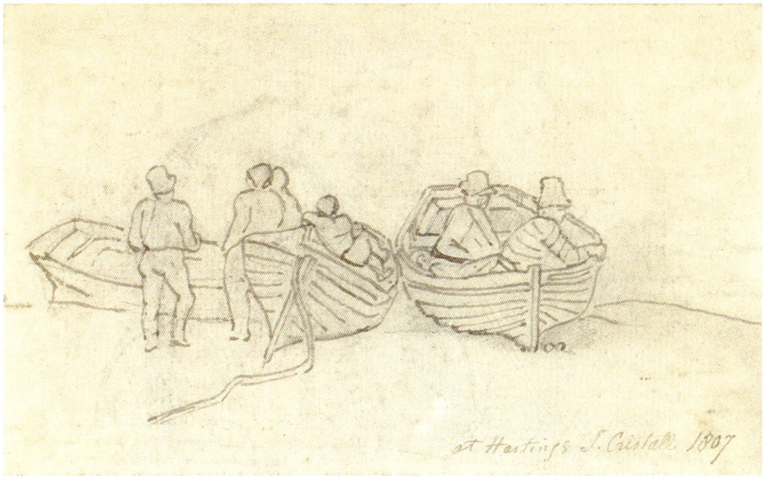

Cristall was a late starter entering the R.A. schools when about twenty-eight. His early work is akin to that of George Barret (1732–84), depicting classical figures in landscape, which may have influenced COTMAN's early style. His studies at Hastings in 1807, such as this one, led to his large *The Fishmarket on the Beach, Hastings*, probably exhibited in 1808 (V&A). His cottage maids, if a trifle sentimental, are observed from life and not studio properties.

But his work was not much prized as the 617 lots, many of them comprising several items, in his posthumous sale in 1848, fetched only £185–13s, with a top price of £5–10s.

EJ

Richard DADD
[1817–86]
A Hermit, 1853

watercolour on paper, 35.7 × 25.7 cm
inscribed: *Sketch of a Hermit by Richard Dadd Bethlem Hospital 1853*

P.397
PROVENANCE: S.E. Lucas; Christie's sale 17 March 1961, lot 25; Maas Gallery, from whom purchased by Gallery, July 1961.
EXHIBITIONS: *Pre-Raphaelites and Contemporaries*, London, Maas Gallery, 1961, no.25; *Watercolours from Bedford*, Norwich, Castle Museum, 1965, no.9 as *Hermit in his Cell*; *The Late Richard Dadd*, London, Tate Gallery, 1974, no.110.
REFERENCES: P. Allderidge, *Richard Dadd*, 1974, p.57, pl.50; D. Greysmith, *Richard Dadd: the Rock and Castle of Seclusion*, 1973, pp.82 & 174,p.47; P. Allderidge, *The Late Richard Dadd*, 1974, p.86, no.110; P. Allderidge, *Richard Dadd*, 1993, pp.24 & 65, pl.19.

After murdering his father on 28 August 1843 in the grounds of Cobham Park, Kent, Dadd escaped to France, where he was soon arrested and brought back to England. The following year he was certified insane and was admitted to the state criminal lunatic asylum at Bethlem Hospital, St. George's Fields, Southwark. In 1864 he was transferred to the newly built Broadmoor Hospital in Berkshire where he died of consumption in January 1886.

EJ

Richard DADD
[1817–86]
Hunting Scene, 1855

watercolour on paper, 30.8 × 16.6 cm
inscribed: *Richard Dadd. Bethlehem* [sic] *Hospital, London. September 27th 1855*

P.129
PROVENANCE: Irving Gallery; The Leicester Galleries, from whom purchased by Gallery, November 1957.
EXHIBITIONS: *Watercolours and Drawings from The Cecil Higgins Art Gallery Bedford*, London, Thos. Agnew & Sons Ltd, 1962, no.42; *The Late Richard Dadd*, London, Tate Gallery, 1974, no.152.
REFERENCES: D. Greysmith, *Richard Dadd: The Rock and Castle of Seclusion*, 1973, pp.87 & 178, pl.80 as *The Flight into Egypt*; P. Allderidge, *The Late Richard Dadd*, 1974, p.106, no.152; P. Allderidge, *Richard Dadd*, 1993, pp.36 & 67, pl.37.

In both Bethlem and Broadmoor Hospitals Dadd continued to paint 'Fairy' pictures, as well as scenes based on his Middle Eastern journey in 1842, until three years before his death. Many of these are of haunting intensity combined with exquisite detail and the most delicate colours. Formerly called *The Flight*, this was correctly re-titled at the time of the Tate exhibition. The Tate catalogue suggests it has been cut down from Dadd's more usual size of c. 14 × 10 in. It also comments on the highly artificial counterbalancing of the horses' heads and points out that, as in other crowded scenes, there is a loss of spatial definition in the over-complicated surface design.

EJ

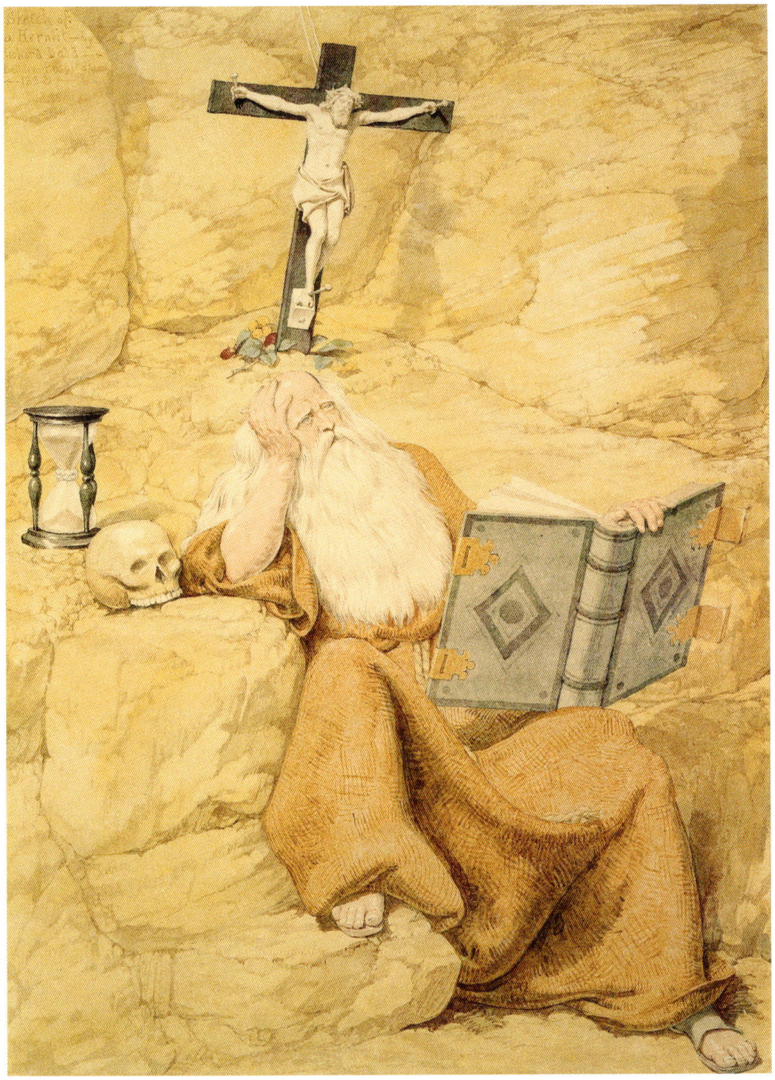

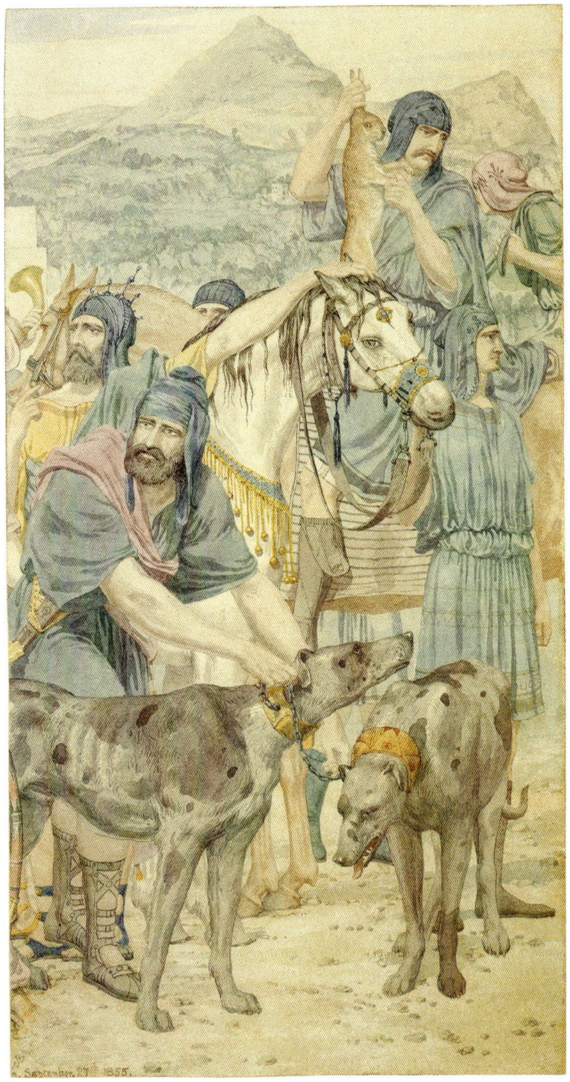

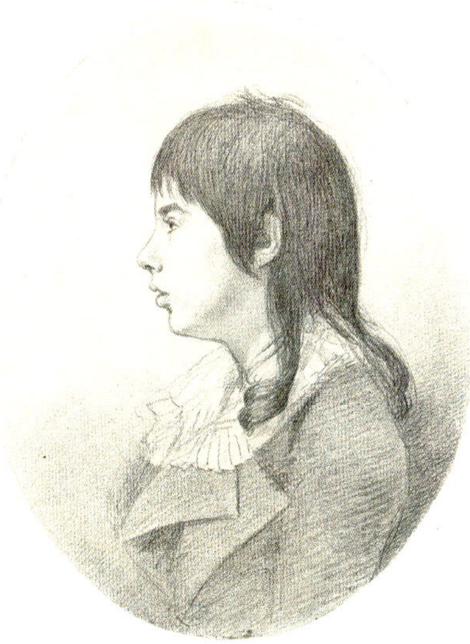

George DANCE, R.A.
[1741–1825]
Portrait of a Boy in Profile, c.1790s

pencil on oval paper, 20 × 16 cm

P.414
PROVENANCE: P&D Colnaghi Ltd., from whom purchased by Gallery, November 1961.

Dance specialized in these profile portraits; among the very many that he produced were a number of his fellow artists including HEARNE, TURNER and Francis WHEATLEY (1747–1801).

He seems to have been considered a sound judge of pictures as Farington asked his opinion of Sir George Beaumont's (1753–1827) oil sketches. He recorded Dance's reply in his *Diary* (6 January 1808), which was to the effect that 'it was the sort of thing that ten thousand persons might do if disposed to adopt the practice'.

EJ

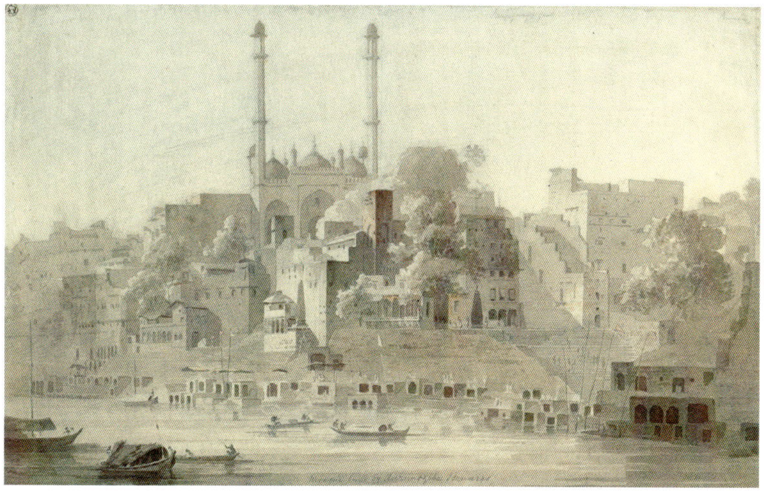

William DANIELL, R.A.
[1769–1837]
The Mosque built by Aurungzebe at Benares, 1789–90

sepia wash over black lead on paper, 33.1 × 54.3 cm
inscribed: *W.Daniell Mosque built by Aurungzebe Benares*

P.64
PROVENANCE: Gilbert Davis; P&D Colnaghi Ltd., from whom purchased by Gallery, February 1953.

Since Indian Independence, Benares has been called Varanasi.

William Daniell, aged only fifteen, accompanied his uncle Thomas (1749–1840) first to China and then to India. They reached Calcutta in 1786 and made the first of their long tours throughout India 1788–91. The main result of their travels was *Oriental Scenery*, published in parts, 1795–1808. It contained 144 plates in colour and cost subscribers £210. Although Thomas is accorded foremost place as draughtsman, William was by then a highly proficient engraver in aquatint.

EJ

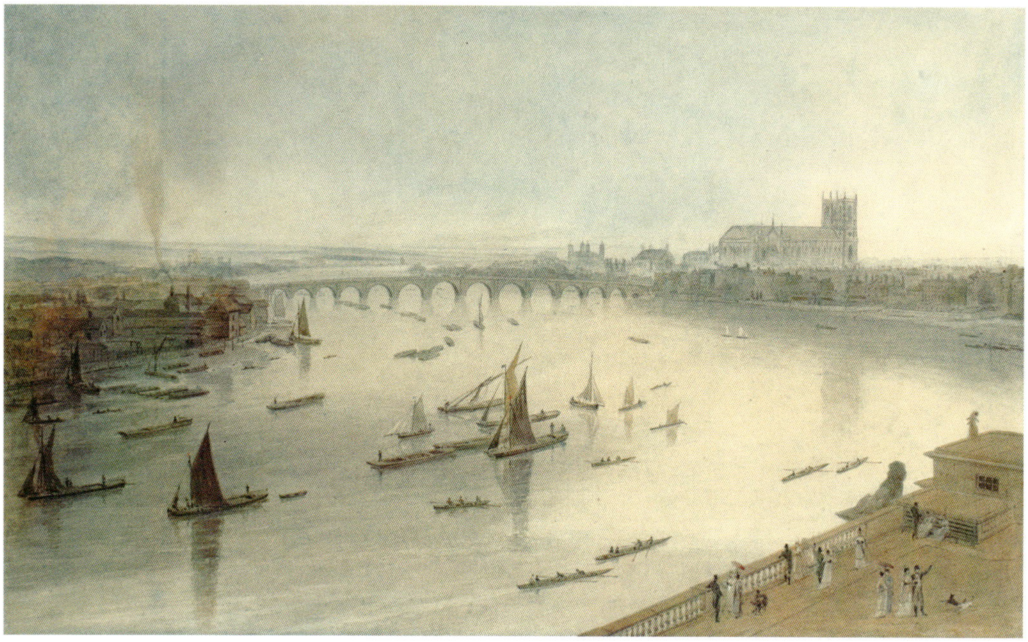

William DANIELL, R.A.
[1769–1837]
Westminster Bridge from the Terrace of Somerset House, c.1804

watercolour on paper, 36 × 64.9 cm

P.183
PROVENANCE: Mrs Rose Wood (the artists' daughter) until her death in 1914 at 102; Ellen Murray; Sabin Galleries, from whom purchased by Gallery, April 1958.
EXHIBITIONS: London, R.A., 1804, no.494; *English Watercolours from The Cecil Higgins Art Gallery Bedford*, Reading, Reading Museum and Art Gallery, 1965, no.11.
REFERENCES: W. Daniell, *Six Views of London*, 1805, pl.vi.

Although after his return from India, William's oil paintings gained him election to A.R.A. in 1807 and R.A. in 1822, his main source of income came from his watercolours and his aquatint engravings. In particular his *Voyage round Great Britain*, with 308 colour plates, published in eight volumes from 1814 to 1825, stamped him as one of the country's best topographical artists. He had a real eye for composition and was an accomplished architectural draughtsman. He was also among the first to emulate TURNER in wiping out lights in his watercolours.

This watercolour was engraved in 1805 by the artist for his *Six Views of London*, pl.vi., published by Daniell on 1 January 1805.

EJ

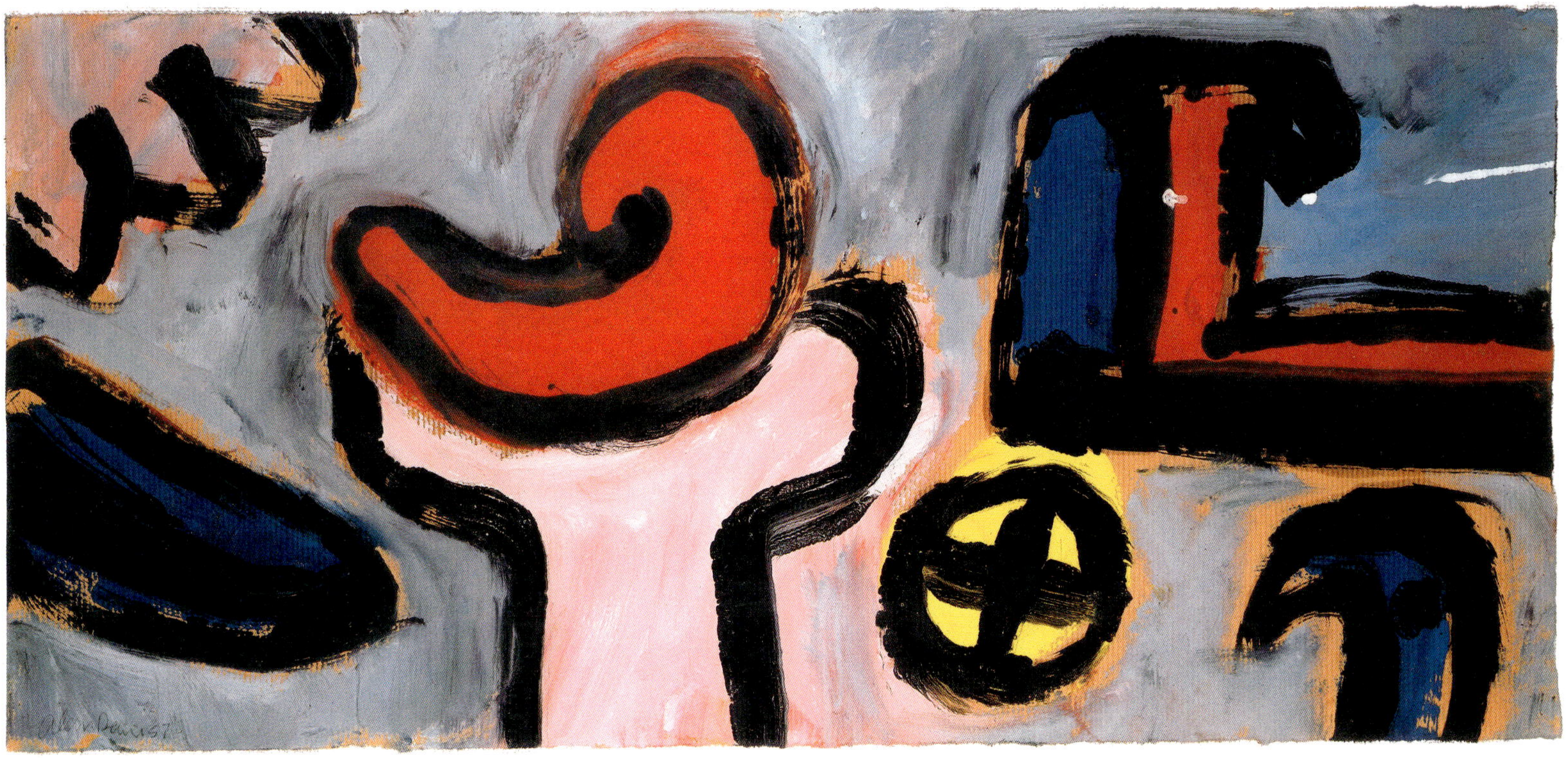

Alan DAVIE
[b. 1920]
First Movement in Pink, 1957

oil on paper, 27.3 × 59.9 cm
inscribed: *Alan Davie '57*

P.313
PROVENANCE: Gimpel Fils, from whom purchased by Gallery, October 1959.

The acquisition of this painting caused great controversy at the Gallery. Sir Albert RICHARDSON, then a Board member, was quoted as saying ' It's not even a painting. It's a diagram composed of one straight line, a circle, and two hieroglyphics which look like a map of the Underground Transport's Circle Line….We are entering an age of barbarism' (*Daily Express* 19 October 1959).

The artist gave an account of this painting to the Gallery in 1983:

It is one of a long number of oils on paper that were painted very directly in a "trance-like" state without preconceived idea which often liberated a deeper source of knowledge and intuition which is beyond immediate consciousness... Music and painting are the same. The spirit is the same, except, of course, there is no realism in music. Music gives sound waves whereas painting gives light waves but the effect it has on the mind is the same. When Sir Albert Richardson said that 'we are entering in a new age of barbarism', in a way he was right.

Born in Grangemouth, Scotland, Davie entered Edinburgh College of Art where he won the Andrew Grant scholarship. During the Second World War he served with the Royal Artillery, while continuing to paint and play modern jazz. On leaving the military, Davie was able to take up the travel scholarship awarded him in 1941. His extensive travels through Europe offered the opportunity to study a variety of artists from Klee to Pollock. During the period 1949 to 1954 Davie not only painted, but also made a living as a goldsmith and jeweller. In 1953 he began teaching in the Jewellery department of the Central School of Arts and Crafts.

Davie's distinctive and arresting paintings combine bold colours with idiosyncratic symbols and Zen Buddhism.

CB

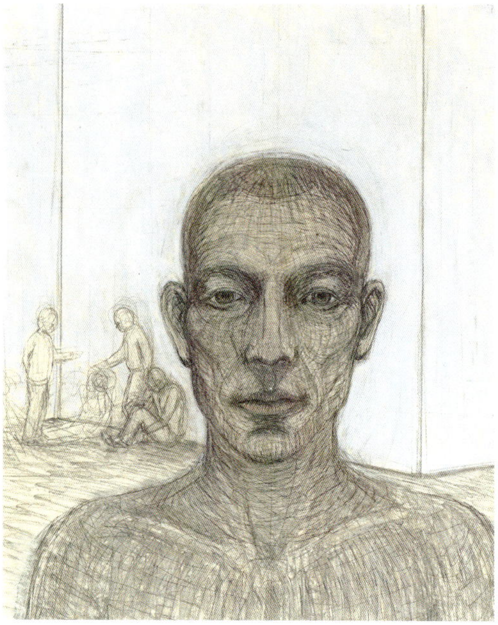

John DAVIES
[born 1946]
Head (Figures in background), 1979–80

pastel and pencil on paper, 50.2 × 41.3 cm

P.726
PROVENANCE: The Artist; Marlborough Fine Art; Belle Shenkman, purchased for the Contemporary Art Society, given to Gallery, January 1983.
REFERENCES: Contemporary Art Society, *The Contemporary Art Society 1910–1985,* 1986, p.34.

Mixed media artist but primarily a sculptor, Davies trained at Manchester, Hull and the Slade schools of art. His first exhibition at the Whitechapel Art Gallery in 1972, with life-size figures wearing real clothes, caused quite a sensation. His figurative art focuses on the human figure and head and conveys a strong feeling of isolation. Davies has written: 'All I hope is that there is something of the human circus – life's circus here'.

EJ

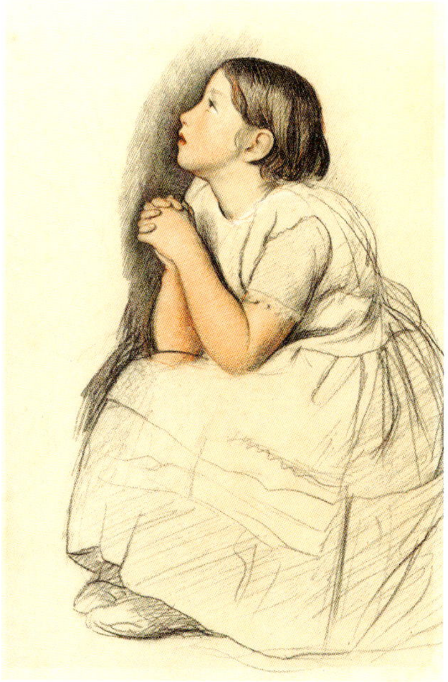

Edward Thompson DAVIS of Worcester
[1833–67]
Seated Girl

pastel on paper, 36.7 × 24.3 cm

P.425
PROVENANCE: V. Hutchins; J.S. Maas & Co. Ltd., from whom purchased by Gallery, July 1962.
EXHIBITIONS: *The English Tradition: an exhibition of watercolours from two private collections,* Bedford, Cecil Higgins Art Gallery, 1972, no.31.

William MULREADY seems to be the influence most readily discernible in Davis's work but he soon established his own highly individual style.

EJ

Edward Thompson DAVIS of Worcester
[1833–67]
Lands End, 1856

watercolour and bodycolour and ink on paper, 20.6 × 31 cm
inscribed: *Lands End 1856*

P.424
PROVENANCE: V. Hutchins; J.S. Maas & Co. Ltd., from whom purchased by Gallery, July 1962.

Davis was born in Worcester and studied at the School of Design there, winning several prizes. He seems to have endured neglect, poverty and ill-health, finally going abroad for his health in 1866 but dying in Rome the following year.

His work was virtually unknown until three albums of his drawings appeared at Colnaghi's, in 1951, when they were eagerly bought by discerning collectors. Foremost among these was Brinsley Ford who bought sixty-two drawings for £48; this he later described as 'The most remarkable acquisition I have made, taking the price into account'. The Walpole Society, in two volumes, catalogued Sir Brinsley's collection in 1998 with more details about Davis's subject matter and a number of illustrations.

This comes from the first album, which contained 169 drawings, 158 in watercolour, ranging between 1853 and1856 and including views in Scotland, Wales and other sites in Cornwall.

EJ

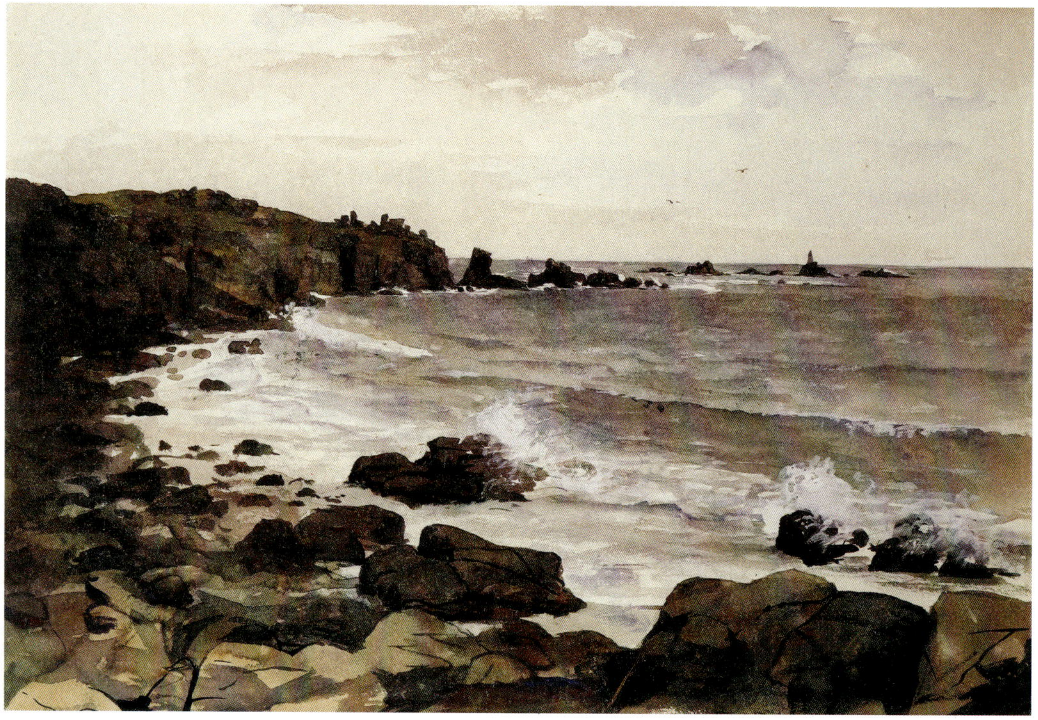

Edward DAYES

[1763–1804]

Magdalen College, Oxford. View from the Cherwell looking N.W., 1791–92

watercolour and pen and ink on paper, 33.1 × 46.7 cm

P.66

PROVENANCE: Fine Art Society, from whom purchased by Gallery, May 1953.
EXHIBITIONS: *Watercolours and Drawings from The Cecil Higgins Art Gallery Bedford,* London, Thos. Agnew & Sons Ltd, 1962, no.8; *English Watercolours from The Cecil Higgins Art Gallery Bedford,* Reading, Reading Art Gallery, 1965, no.12; *Watercolours from Bedford,* Norwich, Castle Museum, 1965, no.10.
REFERENCES: W. & J. Walker, *Copper Plate Magazine,* February 1792; M. Hardie, *Water-colour painting in Britain: I The Eighteenth Century,* vol.1, 1966, p.180; A. Barlow, 'Messing about on the River', *Country Life,* 1977, 7 April, pp.860–2.

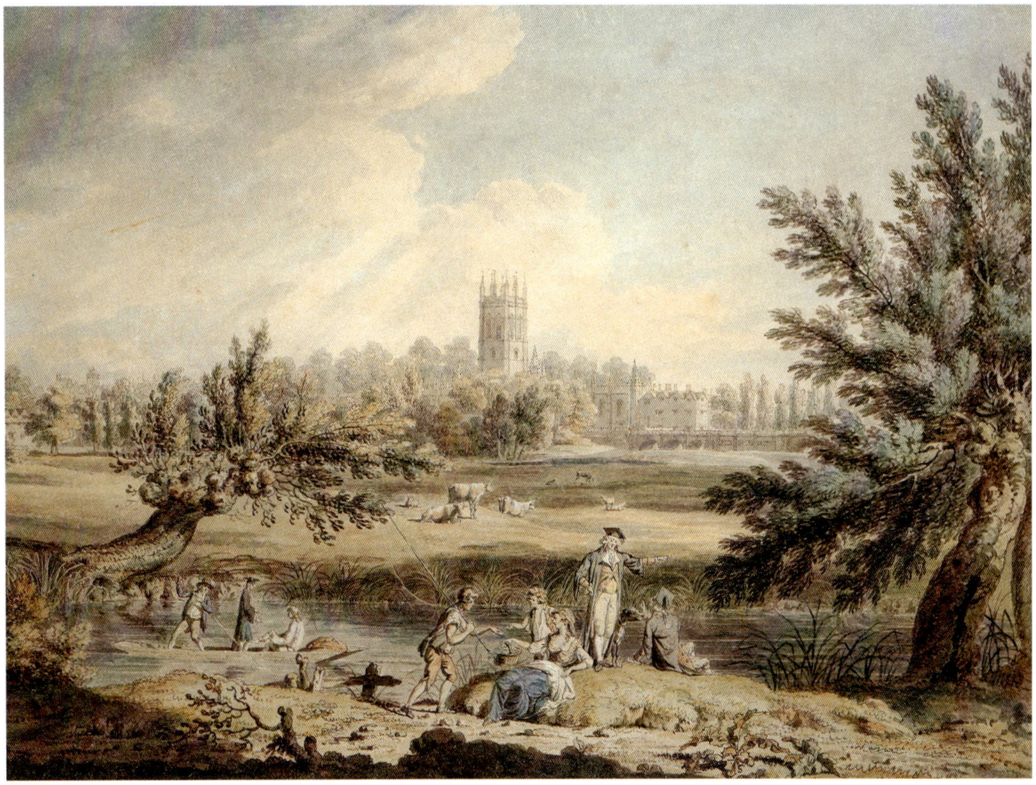

The original title was *Oxford from the Meadows*. It was engraved by W. & J. Walker for *The Copper Plate Magazine*, February 1792 and published in monthly parts, at 1 shilling or 1s.6d., from 1792 to 1802.

Dayes is described by Martin HARDIE as 'the outstanding member of the group of topographers at the close of the 18th century', and of course he is well known as the teacher of GIRTIN. In his *Anecdotes of Painters* of 1808, Edwards described him as 'neither amiable or happy' (p.285). Dayes committed suicide in 1804.

An article in *Country Life*, 7 April 1977, comments that although this watercolour suggests that punting had already been adopted as a relaxation, it was to be at least another fifty years before punts began to be built specially for this purpose.

EJ

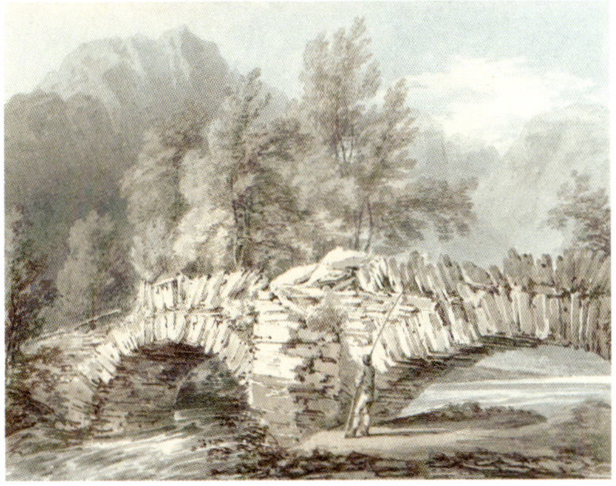

Edward DAYES

[1763–1804]

Rosthwaite Bridge, Cumberland

washes of grey and blue over black lead on paper, 22.1 × 28.5 cm

P.124

PROVENANCE: Major R.C. Sloane Stanley; Woolley & Wallis; P&D Colnaghi Ltd, from whom purchased by Gallery, November 1955.

Martin HARDIE notes that Dayes' 'tree drawing is characteristic, the foliage at the edges spreading out into shapes resembling bunches of bananas or fingers spread open' (*Water-colour Painting in Britain*, vol.1, 1966, p.181)

EJ

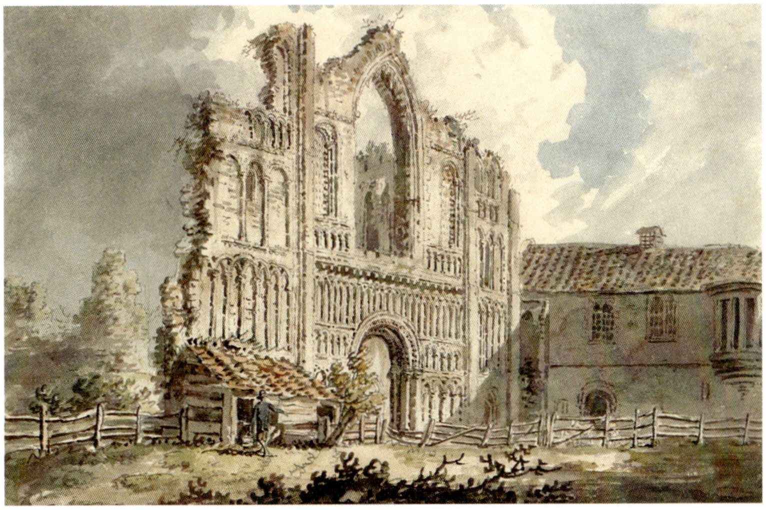

Edward DAYES

[1763–1804]

Castle Acre Priory, Norfolk

watercolour on paper, 13.9 × 22.2 cm
inscribed on reverse: *Castle Acre Priory*

P.65

PROVENANCE: Squire Gallery, from whom purchased by Gallery, May 1952.
EXHIBITIONS: *English Water-colours from the Hickman Bacon and other collections,* Bedford, Cecil Higgins Art Gallery, 1952, no.32.

Castle Acre Priory is about five miles north of Swaffham and just west of the main road to Fakenham and the coast. It is exactly the kind of picturesque and romantic ruin to appeal to an 18th century topographer such as Dayes.

EJ

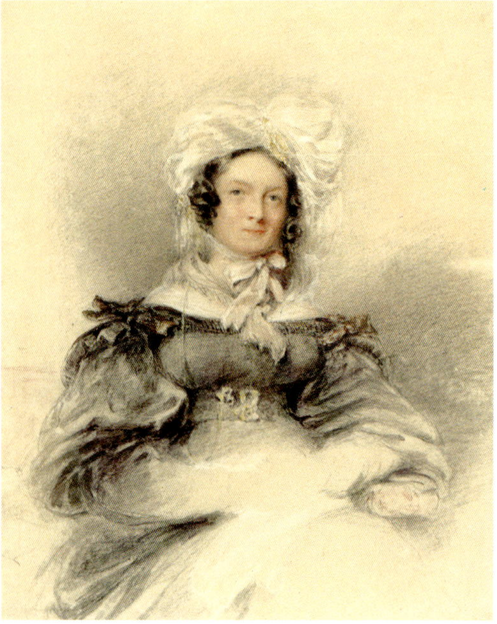

Stephen Poyntz DENNING
[1795–1864]
Portrait of a Lady, late 1830s

black crayon, watercolour and bodycolour on paper, 30.2 × 24.2 cm

P.843
PROVENANCE: Lt. Colonel A.M. Scott; presented to the National Art Collections Fund; given by the N.A.C.F. to Gallery, December 1975.

Originally attributed to Henry EDRIDGE.The sitter is unknown but the portrait can be dated on the evidence of her dress to the late 1830s.

Little is known about Denning, who began life as a beggar boy, but, at the age of twenty-six, was appointed Curator of the Dulwich Picture Gallery where he remained for the rest of his life. A portrait and miniature painter, he exhibited at the R.A. from 1814 to 1852 and painted Queen Victoria prior to her accession to the throne in 1823. His delightful portrait group in watercolour of *The Children of Elhanan Bicknell*, exhibited R.A. 1842, is in the V&A.

EJ

Peter DE WINT
[1784–1849]
Winchester Gateway, c.1810–15

watercolour with scratching out on paper, 35.5 × 38.6 cm
inscribed on reverse: *Winchester*

P.706
PROVENANCE: Sydney Kitson; Elisabeth and Alice Barbara Kitson, given to Gallery, May 1973.
EXHIBITIONS: *The English Tradition: an exhibition of watercolours from two private collections,* Bedford, Cecil Higgins Art Gallery, 1972, no.34; *The Great Age of British Watercolours 1750–1880,* London, R.A., and Washington D.C., National Gallery, 1993, no.110, pl.82.
REFERENCES: H. Smith, *Peter de Wint,* 1982, p.163; The International Writers Center, *The Dual Muse-The Writer as Artist – The Artist as Writer,* 1999, p.28.

This drawing has similarities with *The Devil's Hole, Lincoln* (private collection), usually dated to c.1810, in going from a foreground in shadow through an archway to glimpse a distant view bathed in sunlight, thus providing the composition with a sense of recession.

EJ

Peter DE WINT
[1784–1849]
Gledstone House, Yorkshire, c.1838

watercolour on paper, 54.4 × 63.9 cm

P.380
PROVENANCE: R. A. Roundall; Mrs B.M. Roundell; P&D Colnaghi Ltd, from whom purchased by Gallery, August 1960.
EXHIBITIONS: *Old Water-Colour Society Exhibition*, Pall Mall Galleries, London, 1838, no.6; *Primitives to Picasso,* London, R.A., 1962, no.384; *Peter De Wint,* Reading, Reading Museum & Art Gallery, 1966, no.22.
REFERENCES: 'Another Export Saved', *Museums Journal,* September 1960, pp.150–1; R. Mailland, *Dictionnaire de l'Art et des Artistes,* 1965.

Gledstone House, near Skipton in West Yorkshire, was built in c.1770 to a design created by Carr of York. R.A. Roundell, a descendant of the first owner of the house, was one of de Wint's most promising pupils. The house was demolished in the 1920s.

When this watercolour came onto the market in 1960 it seemed likely that it would go abroad, but fortunately the Gallery stepped in to buy it. What appears to be a preparatory version of the subject is in the Toledo Museum of Art, Ohio.

EJ

Peter DE WINT
[1784–1849]
Gloucester Cathedral, with Ruins of Saint Catherine's Church, c.1840

watercolour with scratched out highlights on paper, 28.2 × 46.2 cm
inscribed on reverse: *Gloucester with ruins of St Catherine's Church*

P.67
PROVENANCE: Studio Sale 24 May 1850, no.317; Christie's; J. & W. Vokins (Ellison Collection); Thos. Agnew & Sons Ltd. 1908; Christie's 1 May 1908, lot 139; Hetherington Collection (John Muir); sold to Reginald Smith 1909; Mrs R. Smith, her sale Sotheby's 24 January 1951, lot 78; Thos. Agnew & Sons Ltd., from whom purchased by Gallery, December 1951.
EXHIBITIONS: *79th Annual Watercolour Exhibition*, London, Thos. Agnew & Sons Ltd, 1952, no.36; *English Watercolours from the Hickman Bacon and other collections*, Bedford, Cecil Higgins Art Gallery, 1952, no.37; *Watercolours and Drawings from The Cecil Higgins Art Gallery Bedford*, London, Thos. Agnew & Sons Ltd, 1962, no.60; *Peter De Wint,* Reading, Reading Art Gallery, 1966, no.33; *Peter De Wint Bicentenary Exhibition*, Hanley, Stoke-on-Trent Museum and Art Gallery, Newcastle upon Tyne, Laing Art Gallery, Kingston upon Hull, Ferens Art Gallery and London, Bankside Gallery, 1984–5, no.91.
REFERENCES: H. Smith, *Peter De Wint,* 1982, pp. 147 & 163, pl.58.

Gloucester was a favourite subject of de Wint's, second only to Lincoln, which inspired him to produce some of his very finest watercolours – as is certainly the case here.

De Wint was born at Hanley, Stoke-on-Trent. He moved to London in 1802 and was apprenticed to John Raphael Smith (1752–1812), an engraver and portrait painter. He bought his freedom from Smith by promising to supply eighteen oil paintings over a two-year period. Subsequently he took drawing lessons from VARLEY and studied at the R.A. Schools.

EJ/CB

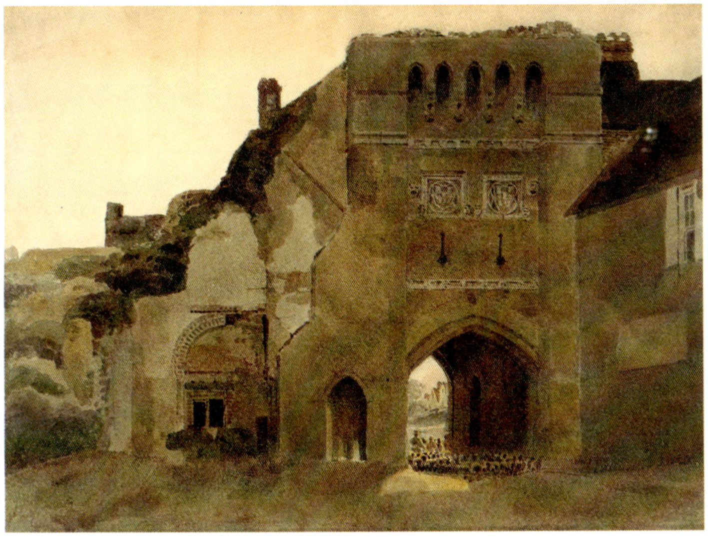

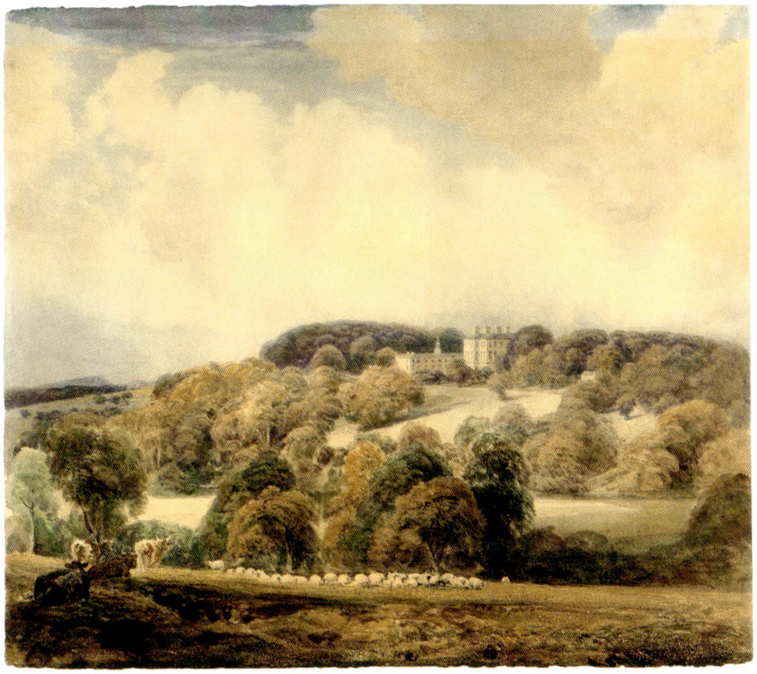

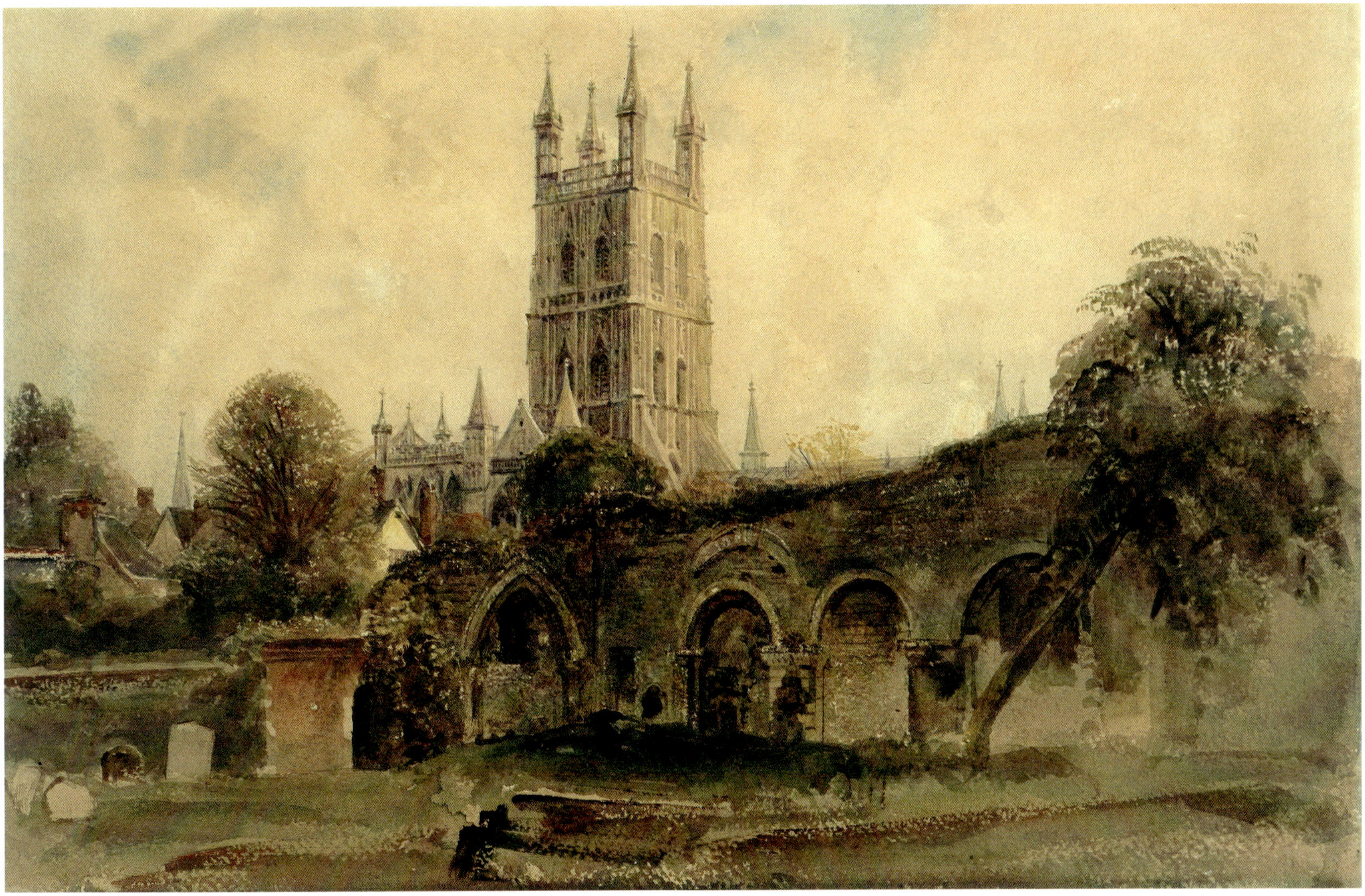

Peter DE WINT
[1784–1849]
The Peak District

watercolour with scratching out on paper, 36.7 × 53.6 cm

P.68
PROVENANCE: Thos. Agnew & Sons Ltd, from whom purchased by Gallery, March 1952.
REFERENCES: H. Smith, *Peter de Wint*, 1982, p.164.

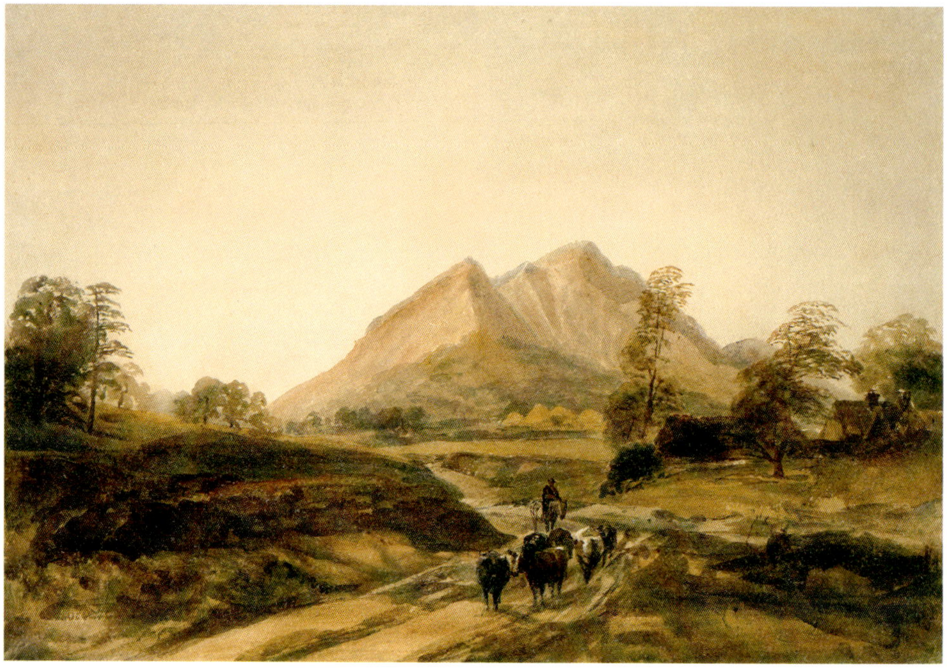

On his move to London in 1802, de Wint met William Hilton whose sister, Harriet, he married. In 1806 he began to frequent Dr MONRO's house where he must have seen works by GIRTIN which influenced his early style.

He had an orderly and successful career exhibiting prolifically, travelling widely in Britain (he only went abroad once – to Normandy in 1812) and had many pupils. His favourite form of composition was a wide but shallow panoramic view, which enabled him to sweep across the whole watercolour horizontally with a loaded brush with extraordinary freedom. This produced the effect of a sketch even in works clearly considered as finished but which is extremely attractive and unlike any of his contemporaries.

EJ

Peter DE WINT
[1784–1849]
Park Landscape

black chalk heightened with white on grey paper, 25.4 × 72.4 cm

P.366
PROVENANCE: Spink & Son Ltd, from whom purchased by Gallery, October 1960.
EXHIBITIONS: *The English Tradition: an exhibition of watercolours from two private collections*, Bedford, Cecil Higgins Art Gallery, 1972, no.32.

This is de Wint's favourite landscape format, as mentioned earlier, in this case drawn on two pages of a sketchbook.

The scene is as yet unidentified but may be in the neighbourhood of Lowther Castle in Cumbria, owned by the Earl of Lonsdale (1757–1844), who was a regular patron of de Wint's.

EJ

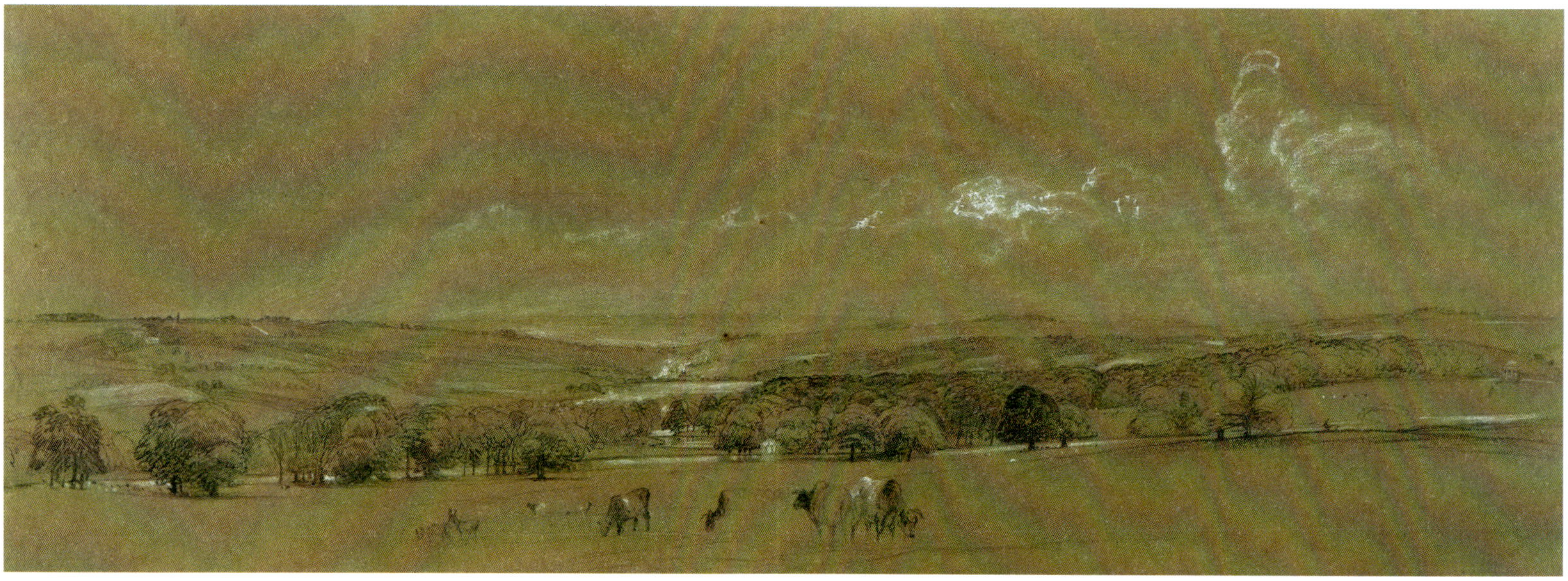

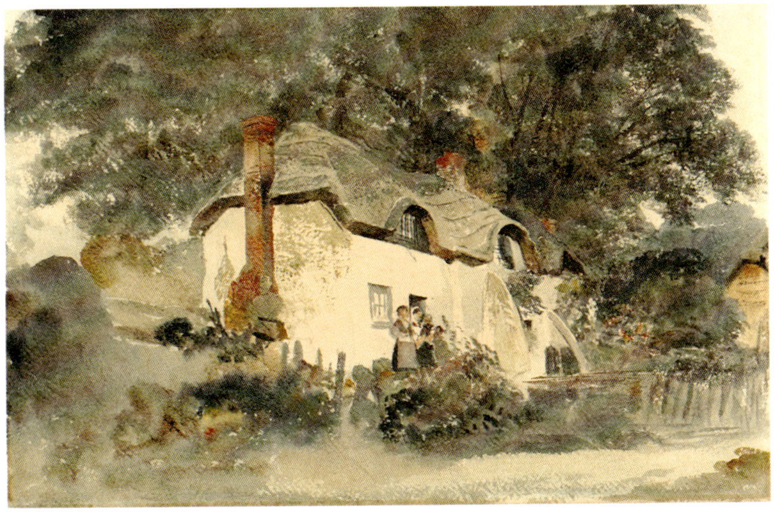

Peter DE WINT
[1784–1849]
Thatched Cottage at Minehead

watercolour with scratching out on paper, 29.6 × 39.6 cm
inscribed on reverse: *Minehead, Somersetshire*

P.381
PROVENANCE: W.G. Boulton, Stoke-on-Trent, from whom purchased by Gallery, October 1960.
REFERENCES: H. Smith, *Peter de Wint*, 1982, p.163, as *Unfinished Sketch*.

Although it is true that this has not been finished, it seems doubtful that he intended to work on it further, for one feels that this rapidly executed watercolour succeeds in depicting exactly what attracted him to the subject.

EJ

FRANK DOBSON, C.B.E., R.A.
[1888–1963]
Service 29, 1918

chalk and wash, squared in red on paper, 48.6 × 40.3 cm
inscribed: *F.Dobson '18*

P.342
PROVENANCE: O. Raymond Drey Esq.; Leicester Galleries, from whom purchased by Gallery, April 1960.
EXHIBITIONS: *Wyndham Lewis & Vorticism*, London, Tate Gallery, 1956, no.163; *Watercolours from Bedford*, Norwich Castle Museum, 1965, no.11; *Frank Dobson Memorial Exhibition*, London, Arts Council Gallery, Bradford, City Art Gallery, Coventry, Herbert Art Gallery, Gateshead, Shipley Art Gallery & Portsmouth, Cumberland House Museum, 1966, no.89; *Frank Dobson*, Cambridge, Kettle's Yard Gallery only, 1981, no.6.

This drawing has been squared for an oil painting.

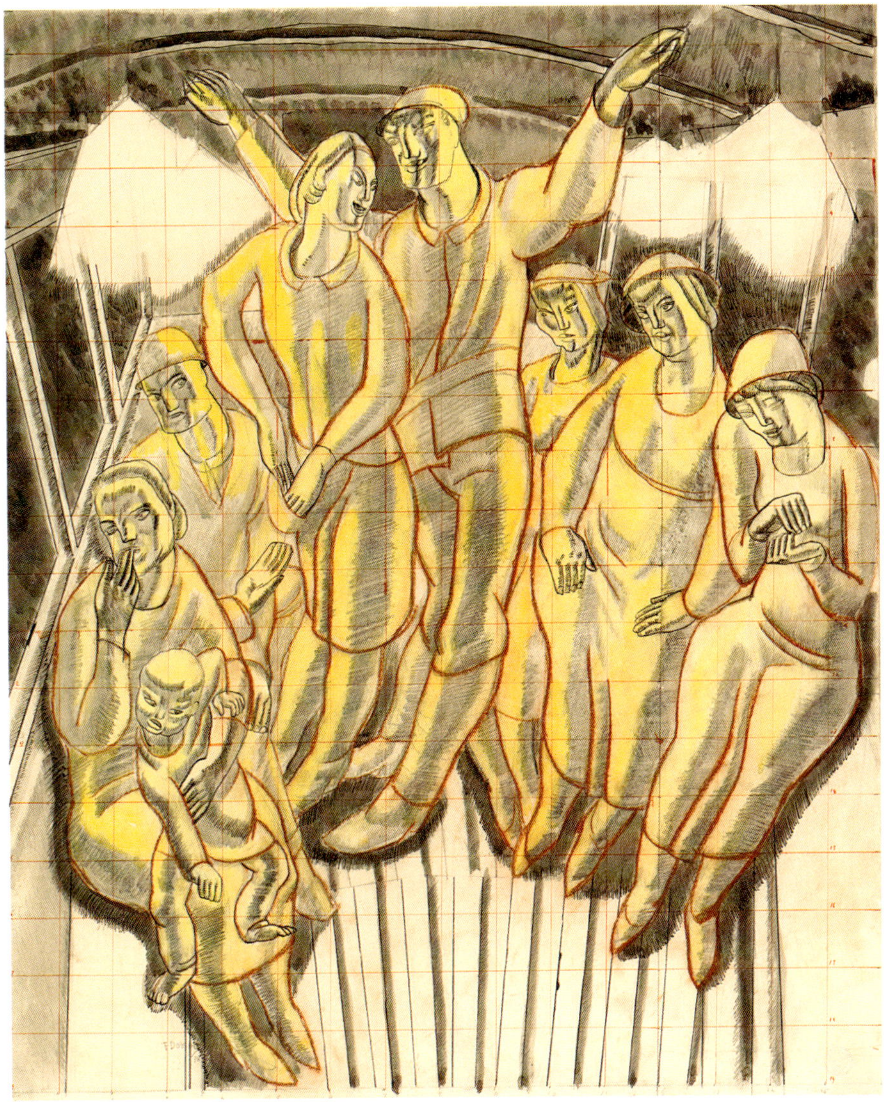

Thanks to help from the London Transport Museum in Covent Garden, this has been identified as a B-type bus, the first mass-produced, open-top, double-deck London bus, introduced in 1910 and finally withdrawn in 1926. Photographs in the museum's archive show the same slatted floorboards, ribbed roof and lighting as in Dobson's drawing.

Route (or 'service') 29 ran daily between Victoria Station and Southgate, via Trafalgar Square, Camden Town and Finsbury Circus.

Dobson was a sculptor of figurative subjects and a decorative painter. His early carved figures were praised by Roger Fry (1866–1934) and he was a member of the avant-garde Group X. He was also a member of the London Group from 1922 and its President from 1923–7. Appointed Professor of Sculpture at the R.C.A. from 1946 to 1953; he was awarded the C.B.E. in 1947 and elected R.A. in 1953. His later sculptures, often in terracotta, have a classicizing spirit that is reminiscent of Aristide Maillol (1861–1944).

EJ

John DOWNMAN, A.R.A.
[1750–1824]
Portrait of a Lady, 1785

watercolour and chalk on paper, 23 × 19cm
inscribed: *J.Downman 1785*

P.722
PROVENANCE: Mr H. Gregory, Harrogate, from whom purchased by Gallery with a grant from the V&A/M.G.C. Purchase Grant Fund, March 1981.

A typical and attractive example of the small, oval portrait drawings with charming colour that were Downman's speciality and brought him many sitters.

Born in Wrexham, Downman left Wales in 1768 to study in London, firstly with Benjamin WEST and then at the R.A. Schools a year later. In 1774 he travelled to France and Italy, returning in 1775. He retired in 1819 and returned to live in Wales.

EJ/CB

John DOWNMAN, A.R.A.
[1750–1824]
Mrs.Wolfe, 1803

black chalk and stump tinted with watercolour on paper, 30.3 × 23.9 cm
inscribed: *Mrs Wolfe of Sherwood Lodge Batersea* [sic] *1803 Lady of Jens Wolfe Esq. Danish Consul With colour notes*

P.233
PROVENANCE: Commander Daintry; Mrs Maitland; Captain P.L. Neville R.N; Thos. Agnew & Sons Ltd, from whom purchased by Gallery, September 1958.
EXHIBITIONS: *English Watercolours from The Cecil Higgins Art Gallery Bedford,* Reading, Reading Museum and Art Gallery, 1965, no.13.

The sitter is Mrs Jens Wolfe (1771–1829). Born Isabella Anne, third daughter of Norton Hutchinson of Woodhall Park, Hertfordshire, she married Jens Wolfe, Danish Consul in London, in 1792, separating in 1810. She was Sir Thomas Lawrence's (1769–1830) closest and dearest woman friend. It was said that her death hastened that of his, six months later. His celebrated portrait of her (ex. R.A. 1815) in the pose of the Erythraean Sibyl in the Sistine Chapel, is now in the Art Institute of Chicago.

EJ/CB

John DOWNMAN, A.R.A.
[1750–1824]
Mrs.Croad, The Determined Widow, 1806

black chalk and stump tinted with watercolour on paper, 31 × 23.6 cm
inscribed: *The determined widow Mrs Croad 1806 a whole-length Group with her only daughter*

P.269
PROVENANCE: Commander Daintry; Mrs Maitland; Capt. P.L. Neville R.N.; Thos. Agnew & Sons Ltd, from whom purchased by Gallery, October 1958.
EXHIBITIONS: *Primitives to Picasso,* London, R.A., 1962, no.386; *English Watercolours from The Cecil Higgins Art Gallery Bedford,* Reading, Reading Museum and Art Gallery, 1965, no.14; *Art Treasures of England, London,* R.A., 1998, no.217.

This is number twenty-nine from an album of drawings, which was broken up and sold separately. An erased and barely legible pencil note on the drawing itself reads *Mrs Croad with her only daughter*.

Mrs Ann Chappell (1771–1837) married John Croad, a prosperous Plymouth builder, in 1798, and was widowed fourteen months later. She earned her sobriquet by the resolution to continue with her husband's business after his death.

Another version is in the Huntington Art Gallery, San Marino, California.

CB

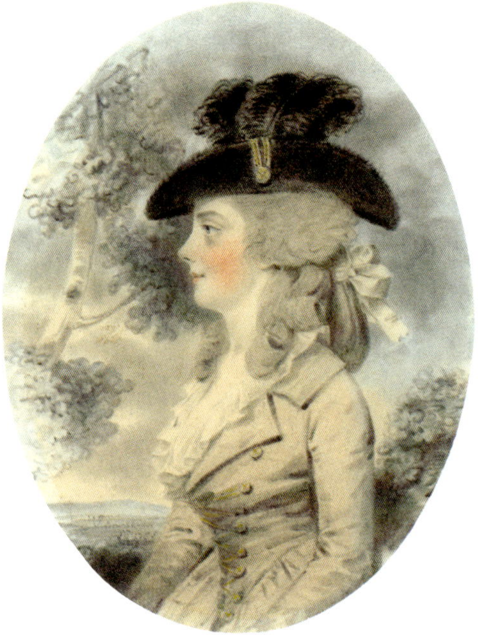

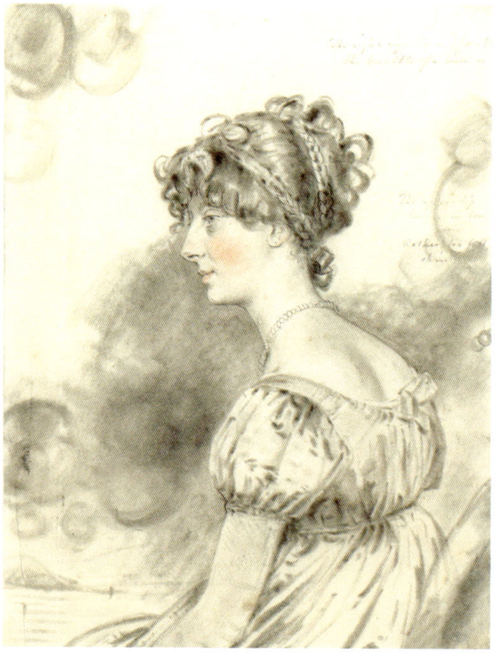

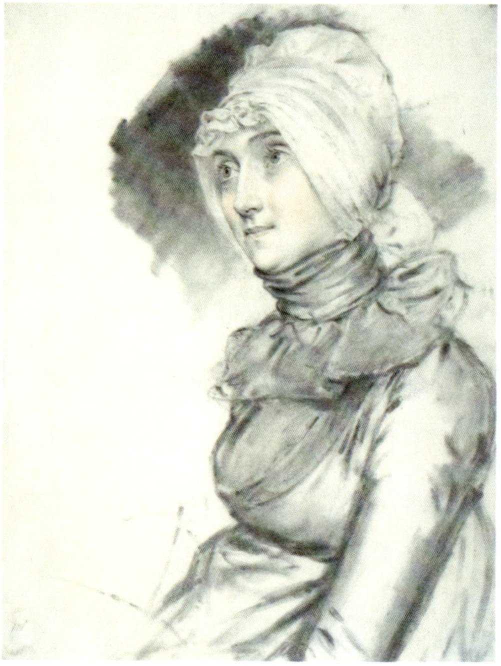

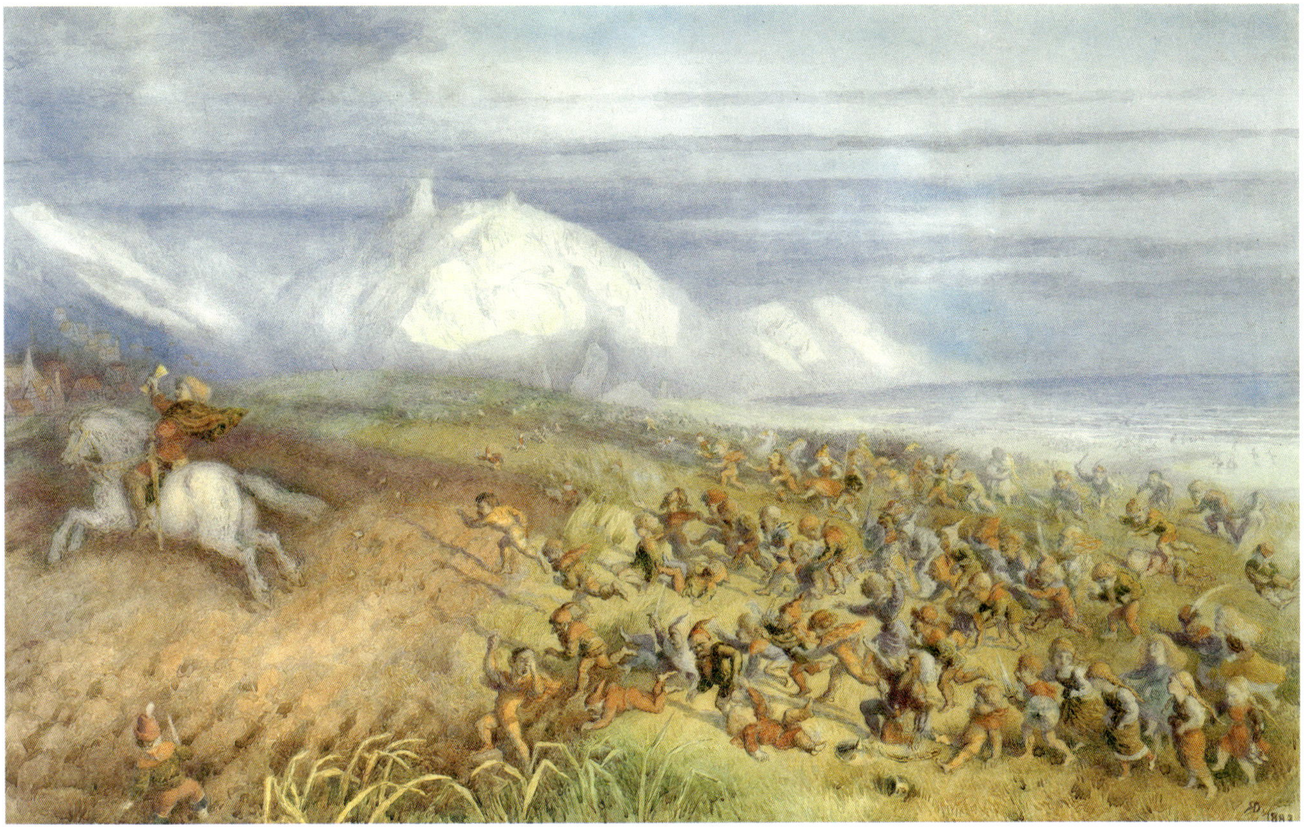

Richard DOYLE
[1824–83]
The Altar Cup of Aagerup, 1883

watercolour on paper, 41.2 × 63.9 cm
inscribed: monogram *RD 1883*

P.398
PROVENANCE: J.S. Maas & Co. Ltd., from whom purchased by Gallery, July 1961.
EXHIBITIONS: *Richard Doyle and his Family,* London, V&A, 1983–4, no. 151.

One of Doyle's last completed works, it returns to a subject he had painted earlier taken from Thomas Keightley's *The Fairy Mythology*, 1828.

The old Danish story describes what befalls a farmer's servant in the village of Aagerup in Zealand who spends Christmas Eve with the trolls. At day-break he mounts his horse to ride home when he is invited to drink a stirrup-cup. Suspicious, he tosses the drink over his shoulder and it immediately singes the hair on the horse's rump. He gallops off, the trolls in pursuit, vowing to give the cup, still in his hand, to the church as an altar cup, if he escapes, which he does.

As an illustrator of fairy tales, Doyle was especially attracted to those involving strange creatures and, above all, dragons. But he was also fascinated by witches and trolls, which appear in many of his illustrations.

EJ

Richard DOYLE
[1824–83]
Riding Through the Air

pen, ink and watercolour on paper, 20.2 × 61.2 cm

P.540
PROVENANCE: Anthony d'Offay Gallery; Fine Art Society, from whom purchased by Gallery, October 1966.
EXHIBITIONS: *Richard Doyle and his Family,* London, V&A, 1983–4, no. 131.

Son of the caricaturist, John Doyle (1797–1868), Richard was employed by *Punch* from 1843 to 1850, resigning when asked to draw anti-Catholic caricatures. After leaving the periodical he devoted his career to illustrating books and painting imaginary watercolours such as this work. His nephew was the writer Sir Arthur Conan Doyle (1859–1930).

CB

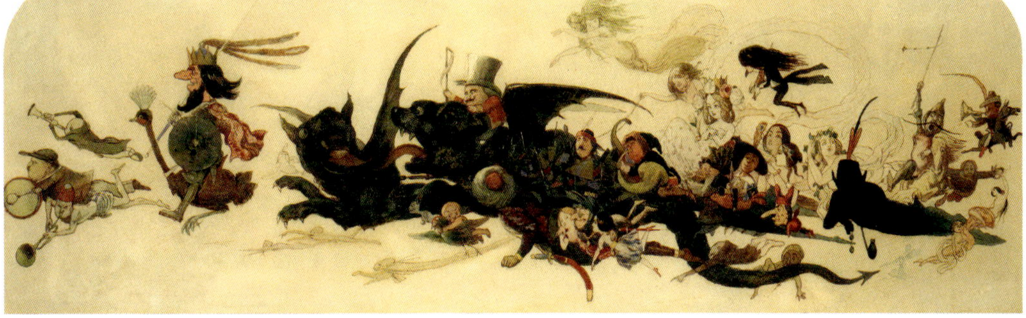

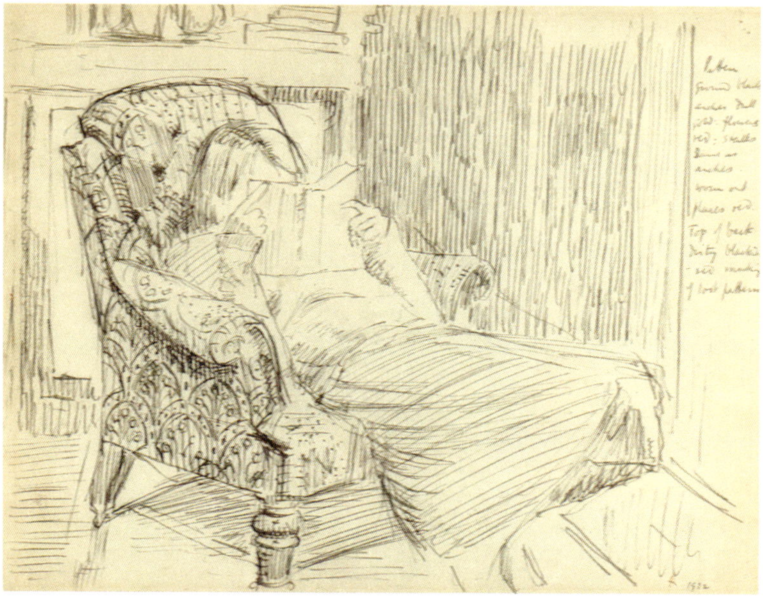

Malcolm DRUMMOND

[1880–1945]

Study of a Girl Reading, 1922

pen and ink on paper, 22.6 × 30 cm
inscribed: *1922 Pattern/ground black/arches dull gold: flowers red: stalks same as arches. Worn out places red. Top of back/dirty blackish red marking of lost pattern.*

P.595
PROVENANCE: Margaret Triquet Drummond, artist's widow; Thos. Agnew & Sons Ltd, from whom purchased by Gallery, May 1969.
EXHIBITIONS: *The Camden Town Group*, Bedford, Cecil Higgins Art Gallery, 1969, no.7.

Study for the oil *Two Girls Reading*, 1922, which was sold at Bonham's 27 November 1997, lot 76.

Drummond studied at the Slade from 1903–7 and later under SICKERT. He exhibited with the Camden Town Group and later with the London Group from 1914–32. He went blind three years before his death.

EJ/CB

Edmund DULAC

[1882–1953]

Illustration to **The Tempest, act II, scene I,** 1908

watercolour and pencil on paper, 34.7 × 25.5 cm
inscribed: *Edmund Dulac 08 The Tempest No.24 Act II Sc I*
Antonio: "Here lies your brother and no better than the earth he lies upon"

P.340
PROVENANCE: G.M. Hutchinson; J. Leger & Son, from whom purchased by Gallery, April 1960.
EXHIBITIONS: *Exhibition of Water-colour Drawings illustrating Shakespeare's Comedy 'The Tempest' By Edmund Dulac*, London, Leicester Gallery, 1908, no.39; *The English Tradition: an exhibition of watercolours from two private collections*, Bedford, Cecil Higgins Art Gallery, 1972, no.36; *Paintings by Edwardian Artists*, Sheffield, Graves Art Gallery, 1952, no.46; *The Last Romantics: The Romantic Tradition in British Art – Burne-Jones to Stanley Spencer*, London, Barbican Art Gallery, 1989, no.358.
REFERENCES: W. Shakespeare, *The Tempest*, 1908.

This illustrates act II, scene I, on Prospero's island where Alonso, King of Naples, and his crew have been shipwrecked. Ariel has put all the party to sleep save Antonio (who has usurped Prospero's dukedom of Milan), and Sebastian, Alonso's brother. Antonio encourages Sebastian, with the words quoted above, to murder the sleeping Alonso and take his kingdom, but Arial wakens Gonzalo, an honest counsellor, in time to foil the plot.

This is among forty illustrations to *The Tempest* by Dulac, published in 1908 by Hodder & Stoughton in a series of Shakespeare's plays, each illustrated by a different artist.

Dulac, following Arthur RACKHAM, was a pioneer in the process of three-colour printing, which transformed book illustration.

EJ

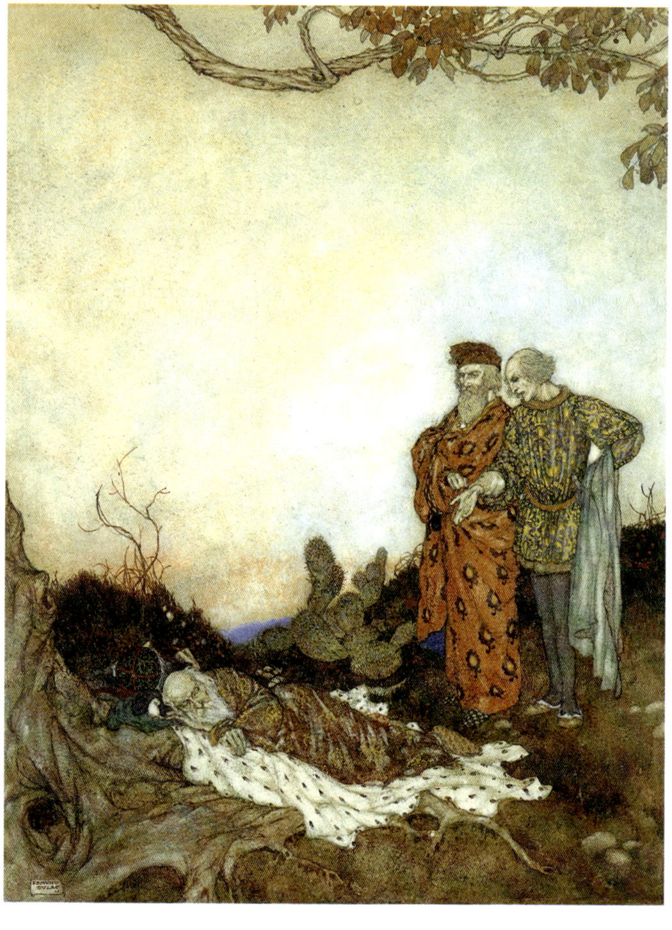

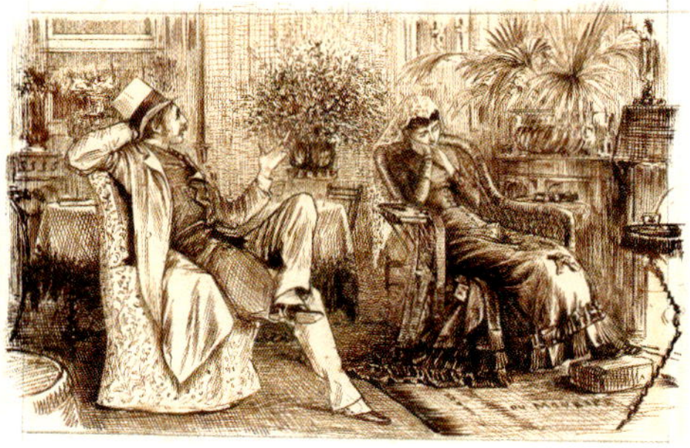

George DU MAURIER

[1834–96]

A Hard Case, c.1878

pen and ink on paper, 13.6 × 22.2 cm
inscribed: *Du Maurier*

P.136
PROVENANCE: Leger Galleries, from whom purchased by Gallery, November 1957.
EXHIBITIONS: *Irish International Exhibition*, Dublin, Herbert Park, Ball's Bridge, 1907.
REFERENCES: *Punch Magazine*, 1 June 1878, p.246; *Society Pictures drawn by George Du Maurier selected from Punch*, vol.1, 1891, p.84.

Reproduced in *Punch,* 1 June 1878, p.246, with the printed text as it appears on the following inscription:

"A HARD CASE"
(Enter young husband, who throws himself into a chair and exclaims):
"What! Toothache again, Maria ! I do call that hard upon a fellow ! Why you had toothache when I left this morning! …and here I have been at Epsom all day with the jolliest lot a fellow ever got together on one day, and won a pot o' money, and had no-end of a jolly time, and I did think I should find something cheerful & jolly to greet a fellow when I got home ! and there you are, Toothache again – I do call it hard upon a fellow…precious hard".

CB

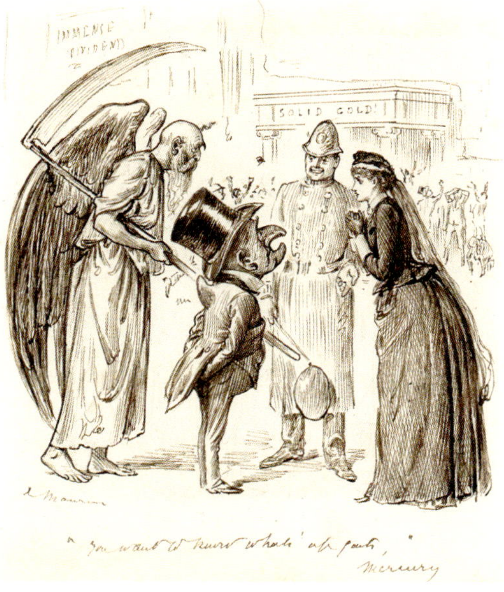

George DU MAURIER

[1834–96]

Illustration for **Mercury 'You want to know what's up Punch'**, c.1890

pen and ink on paper, 19.1 × 25.5 cm
inscribed: *du Maurier*
"You want to know what's up punch" Mercury

P.405
PROVENANCE: P&D Colnaghi Ltd, from whom purchased by Gallery, January 1962.
REFERENCES: *Punch Christmas Number,* 1890, not paginated.

Reproduced in *Punch Christmas Number 1890*, not paginated. One of the illustrations to a humorous, semi-satirical story *Punch among the Planets*. Mr Punch visits each planet in turn; this is from the section entitled '*Visit to Mercury*'. Part of the text runs :

There was a profusion of advertisement-boards, these, in many instances, entirely covering the whole façade of the building, with large-lettered announcements of the nature of the trade or business conducted within. An eager and excited crowd thronging the pavements, and hustling each other, without any apparent purpose or aim, was pushing in all directions.

" I wonder what all this is about", observed Mr. Punch; "suppose we ask a Policeman". They noticed a being attired in every respect like the familiar guardians of the peace on Earth, except that he carried a harmless and gaily-decked bladder in place of the more serviceable bâton, and beckoned to him. "You want to know what's up, Gents ?" he commenced, diving their purpose instinctively. "It's the Half-Quarterly Meeting of the Solid Gold Extract of Brick-Dust Company…." (shortly afterwards, they are approached by a young widow).

CB

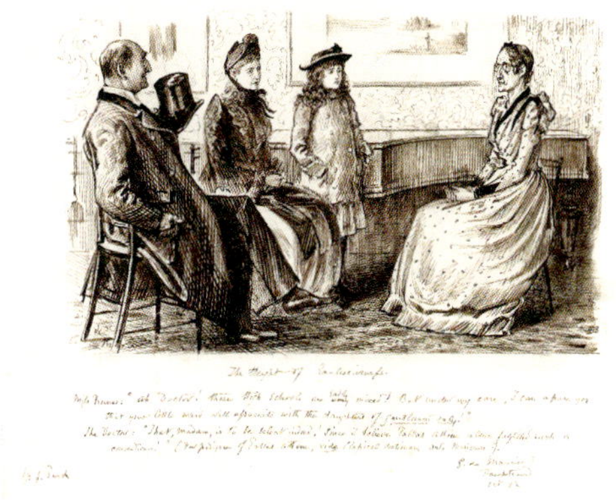

George DU MAURIER

[1834–96]

The Height of Exclusiveness, 1892

pen and ink on paper, 15.2 × 24.5 cm
inscribed: *G. du Maurier. Hampstead Oct.'92 ? p. Punch*
Miss Prunes: "Oh Doctor ! these High Schools are sadly mixed ! But under my care, I can assure you that your little ward will associate with the daughters of gentlemen only !".
The Doctor: " That, Madam, is to be select indeed! Since I believe that Pallas Athene alone fulfilled such a condition !.
(For pedigree of Pallas Athene, vide Classical Dictionary, art Minerva.

P.406
PROVENANCE: P&D Colnaghi Ltd, from whom purchased by Gallery, January 1962.
REFERENCES: *Punch*, 22 October 1892, p.186.

Born in Paris, du Maurier studied art there in 1856–7 where he met WHISTLER and E.J.POYNTER. The loss of an eye prevented him from becoming a painter and so he decided to concentrate on black and white work, which had become popular in the early 1860s. He became a fine figure draughtsman and an outstanding social satirist, contributing regularly to *Punch* from 1864, when he succeeded John Leech (1817–64) as the chief caricaturist of fashion and high life. He also wrote three novels of which *Trilby* (1894) is the best-known. His daughter was the writer Daphne du Maurier (1907–89).

EJ/CB

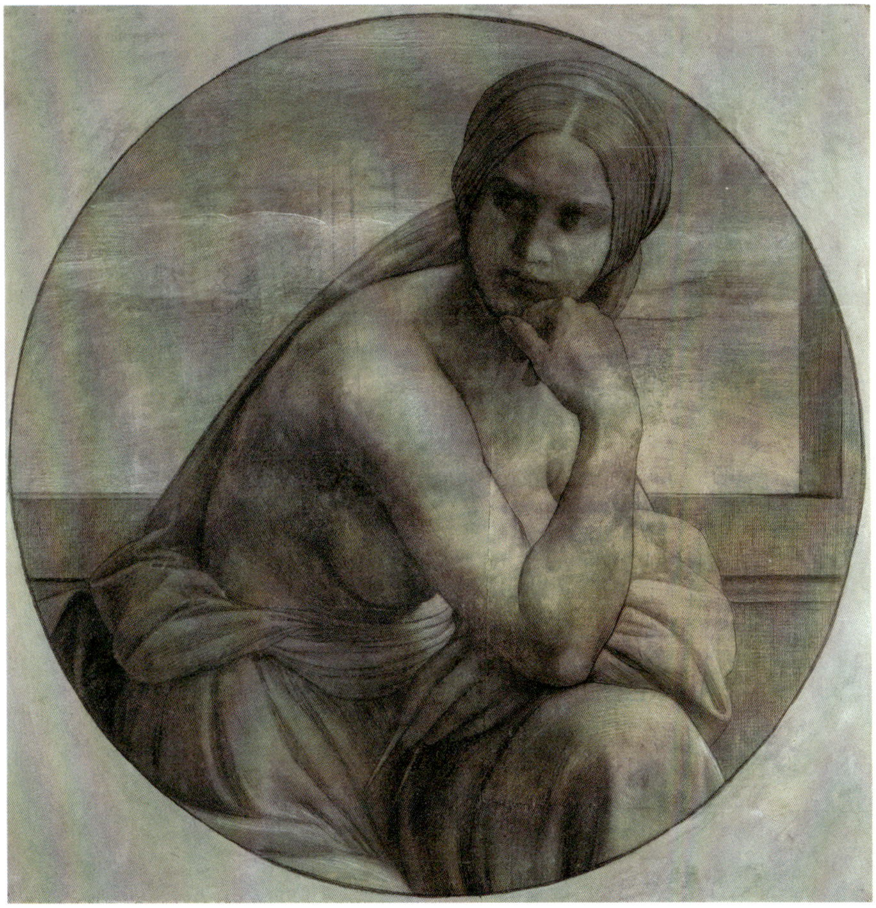

Joan EARDLEY
[1921–63]
Ragwort No.II, c.1960

watercolour, bodycolour and ink on paper, 51 × 38.6 cm

P.465
PROVENANCE: Roland, Browse and Delbanco, from whom purchased by Gallery, October 1964.
EXHIBITIONS: *Joan Eardley*, London, Roland, Browse and Delbanco, 1964, no.26.

This scene was painted in the village of Catterline on the north-east coast of Scotland.

Painter of figures, landscapes and seascapes, Eardley trained at the Glasgow School of Art and at Hospitalfield House, Arbroath. In 1948 she was awarded a travelling scholarship to France and Italy. She began to teach at Glasgow School of Art in 1949, taking her painting subjects from the Glasgow tenements, often concentrating on children. In 1956 she moved to Catterline, where she painted landscapes and seascapes, during this period she divided her time between Catterline and Glasgow.

EJ/CB

William DYCE, R.A.
[1806–64]
A Sibyl, study for fresco, c.1852

black and white chalk with grey wash on paper, 91.2 × 87.5 cm

P.422
PROVENANCE: J.S. Maas & Co. Ltd, from whom purchased by Gallery, July 1962.
EXHIBITIONS: *Annual Exhibition*, London, R.A., 1852, no.954 as *Study for fresco*; *Centenary Exhibition of the work of William Dyce RA*, Aberdeen, Aberdeen Art Gallery and London, Thos. Agnew & Sons Ltd, 1964, no.53.
REFERENCES: *Art Journal*, 1860, p.296; M. Pointon, *William Dyce 1806–64*, 1979, p.125, no.206, pl. 128.

Although exhibited as a *Study for a Fresco*, it does not appear to have been executed in that medium.

Born in Aberdeen, Dyce came to London to study art. Two visits to Rome in 1825 and 1827–30 inspired him with a love of early Italian art and brought him into contact with the Nazarenes. In 1830 he settled in Edinburgh as a portrait painter but, at Sir Charles Eastlake's (1793–1865) suggestion, he was brought to London in 1836 as director of the new Government Schools of Design. His work in the Palace of Westminster, which occupied him until his death, kept him from his chosen career as a religious painter. He was an early supporter of the Pre-Raphaelites.

EJ

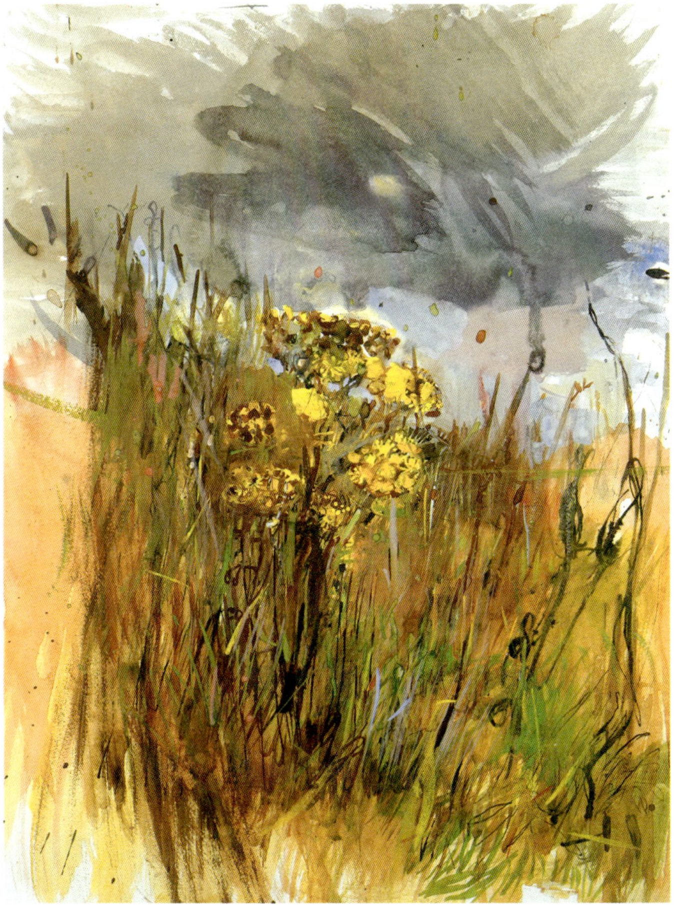

Henry EDRIDGE, A.R.A.
[1769–1821]
John and Charlotte, children of General Vere Poulett of Addington, Bucks., 1801

grey wash over black lead on paper, 32.3 × 23.8 cm
inscribed : *Edridge 1801*

P.399
PROVENANCE: Lucy, Lady Nugent (sister of the sitters); Lucy, wife of Sir Francis Boileau; Villers David; P&D Colnaghi Ltd, from whom purchased by Gallery, August 1961.
EXHIBITIONS: London, R.A., 1801, no.366; *Drawings by Old Masters*, London, R. A., 1953, no.458; *Watercolours and Drawings from The Cecil Higgins Art Gallery Bedford*, London, Thos. Agnew & Sons Ltd, 1962, no.21; *Art on the line: The Royal Academy at Somerset House*, London 2001–2.
REFERENCES: S. Houfe, 'Henry Edridge 1769–1821: A Neo-Classical Portraitist', *The Antique Collector*, August 1972, pp.211–216, fig.3; S. Fenwick and G. Smith, *The Business of Watercolour*: A Guide to the Archives of the Royal Watercolour Society, 1998, pl.15, p.17; A. Buck, *Clothes and the Child: A Handbook of Children's Dress in England 1500–1900*, 1996, p.200.

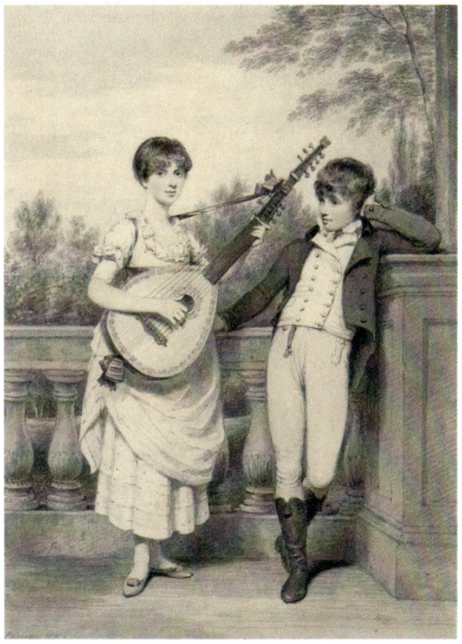

Edridge specialized in this type of charming portrait drawing and there are many examples in the V&A and the Royal Collection. Although he had exhibited at the R.A. since 1786, the Academy was prejudiced against watercolourists and he was not elected an Associate until the year before he died.

EJ

Henry EDRIDGE, A.R.A.
[1769–1821]
Wormley Church, Hertfordshire, Early 1800s

watercolour over black lead on paper, 23.2 × 33.2 cm

P.532
PROVENANCE: Gilbert Davis; P&D Colnaghi Ltd, from whom purchased by Gallery, May 1966.

Edridge served his apprenticeship under William Pether (1738–1821), an engraver and landscape painter who also instructed DAYES. Edridge always had an affection for landscapes partly no doubt as a change from his portrait commissions. He got to know Dr MONRO and went sketching both with GIRTIN and HEARNE from 1810–15. In 1817 he visited France and began to exhibit foreign views at the R.A. His drawing of architecture is considered superior to that of PROUT's by Martin HARDIE, although there is not one mention of him in *Modern Painters*, in which RUSKIN praises Prout highly.

EJ

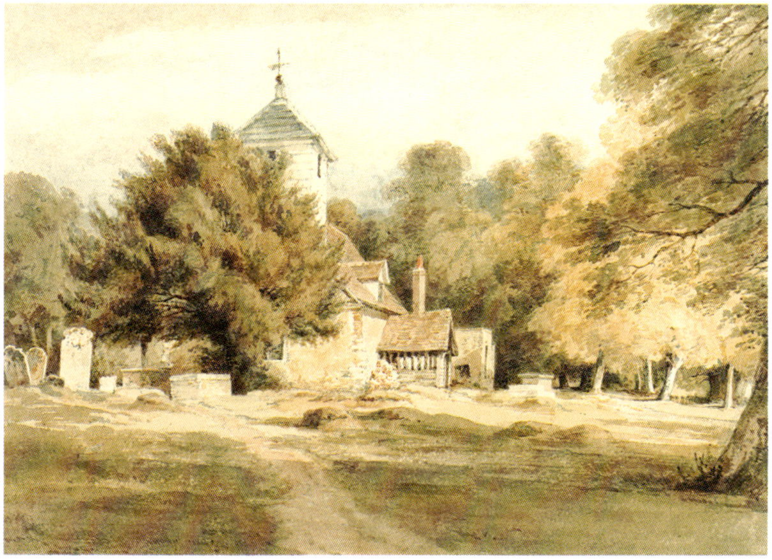

George EDWARDS
[1694–1773]
The Lesser Ash-coloured Seagull, 1733

watercolour and ink on paper, 27.2 × 22 cm
inscribed: *The Lesser Ash-coloured Sea Gull 34 Geo. Edwards 1733 Larus cinereus minor Willuy P.a. 343*

P.299
PROVENANCE: Earnshaw; P&D Colnaghi Ltd, from whom purchased by Gallery October 1959.
EXHIBITIONS: *English Watercolours from The Cecil Higgins Art Gallery, Bedford*, Reading, Reading Museum and Art Gallery, 1965, no.15.

The latter part of the inscription refers to the books by Francis Willoughby (1635–72) and John Ray (1627–1705) *Ornithologiae Libri Tres*, 1676 (English translation 1678). The names used by Edwards, 'Lesser Ash-coloured Seagull' and 'Larus Cinereus Minor', refer to what is now known as the Common Gull (Larus Canus), which is no longer one of the two most common West European gulls.

Edwards carried on BARLOW'S and Cradock's practice of painting birds into the first half of the 18th century. Many of his drawings are in bodycolour and show the birds in their natural surroundings.

In 1733 he was appointed librarian of the Royal College of Physicians and later became a fellow of the Royal Society. *The Natural History of Birds*, published in four volumes 1743–51, was his chief work and contained a great many species never illustrated before.

EJ

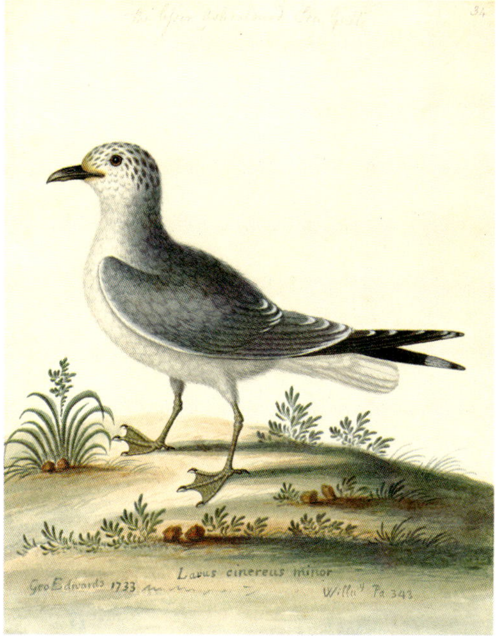

Sir Jacob Kramer EPSTEIN
[1880–1959]
Draped Nude, c.1930

pencil on paper, 48.4 × 34.5 cm
inscribed: *Epstein*

P.356
PROVENANCE: Roland, Browse and Delbanco, from whom purchased by Gallery, July 1960.
EXHIBITIONS: *The English Tradition: an exhibition of watercolours from two private collections*, Bedford, Cecil Higgins Art Gallery, 1972, no.35.

The sitter is Sunita, an Indian model, favoured by both Epstein and Matthew SMITH. She lived in the Epstein household for a short period.

Born in New York of Russian and Polish parents, Epstein studied at the École des Beaux Arts in Paris, 1902–4, before settling in London in 1905. He soon became a major figure in British sculpture although his career was marked by a number of public scandals beginning with his tomb of Oscar Wilde (1854–1900) in Paris in 1911, which was labelled 'indecent'. By contrast, his modelled busts were in great demand from the 1920s and these portraits show an unrivalled immediacy and vivacity. He was knighted in 1954, and completed *St.Michael* for Coventry Cathedral just before his death.

EJ/CB

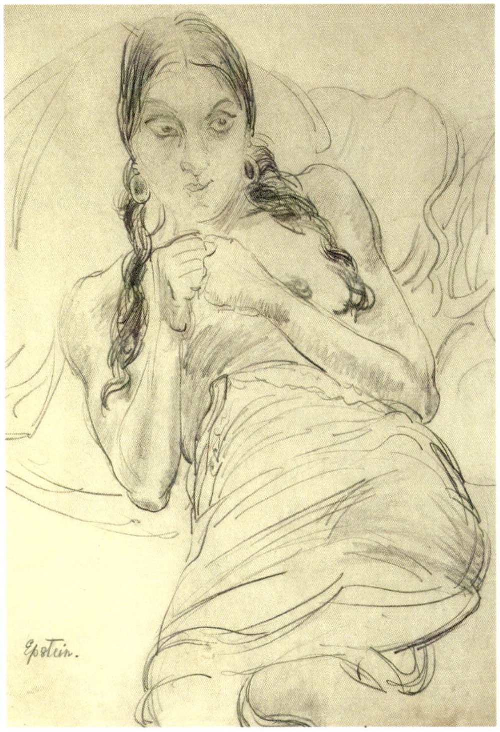

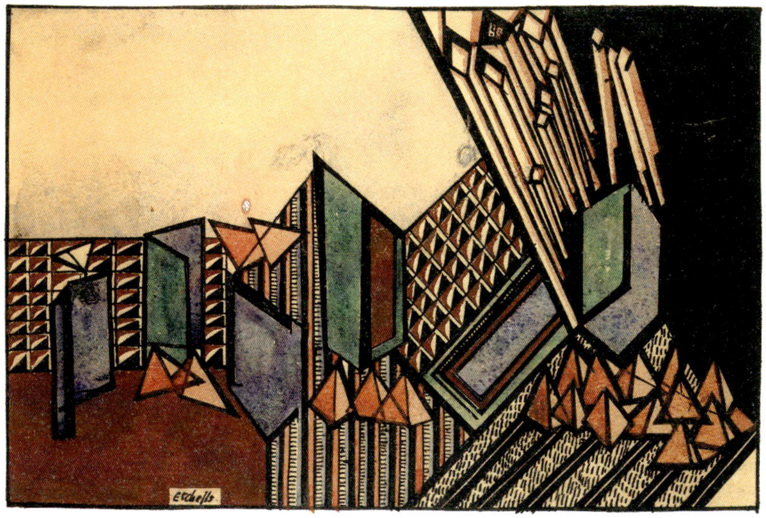

Frederick ETCHELLS
[1886–1973]
Progression, 1914–15

pen and inks on paper, 14.3 × 22.3 cm
inscribed: *Etchells*

P.312
PROVENANCE: Quinn Collection; Quinn sale 1927 lot 292A; Mayor Gallery, from whom purchased by Gallery, October 1959.
EXHIBITIONS: *Vorticist Exhibition*, New York, 1917, no.49; *Abstract Art in England 1913–1915*, London, d'Offay Couper Gallery, 1969, no.25; *Vorticism and its allies*, London, Hayward Gallery, 1975, no.375; *British Art 1910–1916*, Norwich, University of East Anglia, 1976; *Pound's Artists: Ezra Pound and the Visual Arts in London, Paris and Italy*, Cambridge, Kettles Yard Gallery and London, Tate Gallery, 1985,no.12; *Futurismo & Futurismi*, Venice, Palazzo Grassi, 1986,p. 301 illus.; *Blast*, Hannover, Sprengal Museum and Munich, Haus der Kunst, 1996–7, no.63.
REFERENCES: Wyndham Lewis (ed.) *BLAST: Review of the Great English Vortex*, Journal II, 1915, p.53; A. Nicolai, *Blast*, 1996, p.146.

Etchells, whose wife, Jesse, was also a painter, was initially part of the Bloomsbury circle (where Clive Bell (1881–1964) thought him 'dull and uncouth'). In 1914, however, he joined Wyndham LEWIS and the Vorticists where his pictures, often of urban subjects, became increasingly abstract. After the 1914–18 war he gave up painting and became an architect.

EJ

Merlyn EVANS
[1910–73]
Wharfside Construction, 1953

charcoal with pencil and wash on paper, 47 × 52 cm
inscribed: *Evans 28th Oct*

P.709
PROVENANCE: The New Art Centre; Anthony Diamond; presented by the Contemporary Art Society to Gallery, February 1980.
EXHIBITIONS: *Works on Paper*, Arts Council Tour, 1977–8, no.27.

This drawing relates to an oil of the same title in the Art Galleries and Museums of Glasgow.

Evans was born in Cardiff, studying at the Glasgow School of Art and the R.C.A. 1931–3, and later in Paris, Berlin, Italy and Copenhagen. His contacts in Paris with, among others, Piet Mondrian (1872–1944) and Wassily Kandinsky (1866–1944) confirmed his commitment to abstraction, manifest in his work while a student. His paintings, which often link mechanical and natural forms, are essentially Celtic and romantic in spirit. He designed a mural for Southampton General Hospital in 1961. Evans said of his work 'By temperament and preference, I have been from an early age of seventeen, an abstract painter'.

EJ/CB

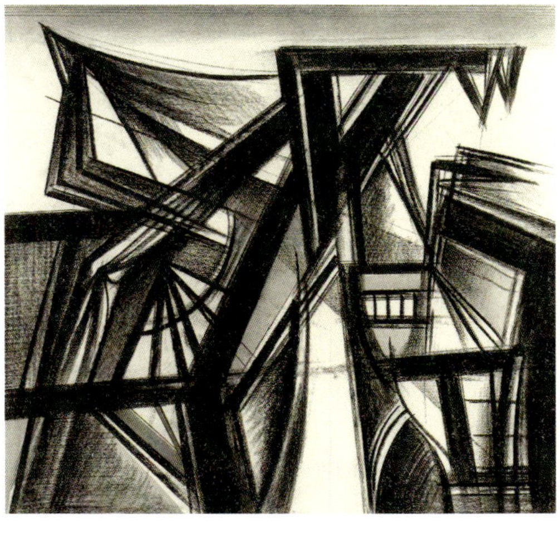

Anthony Vandyke Copley FIELDING

[1787–1855]

Landscape with Buildings

watercolour on paper, 18.4 × 25.5 cm

P.586

PROVENANCE: R.W. Reford, Montreal; Christie's 19 November 1968, lot 14; Thos. Agnew & Sons Ltd, from whom purchased by Gallery, November 1968.

Fielding was named after not one but two artists: Van Dyck (1599–1641) and his father's friend John Singleton Copley (1738–1815). He was surely the most prolific exhibitor of watercolours in the 19th century, amassing a total of 1,748 works at the Old Water-Colour Society, apart from those he showed at the R.A. and the British Institution.

Although it is difficult to date, this is certainly an early drawing, when young Fielding travelled widely in Wales and the north of England, and his exhibits up to 1816 reflected this. His wife's health necessitated a move from London, where he had learned much from VARLEY, to the coast near Sandgate in Kent. There the sea became a fresh theme which, on occasion, he painted with considerable verve. Later a move to Brighton caused the South Downs to become his favourite subject. RUSKIN, an admirer who had some lessons from Fielding, said of him: 'Had he painted five instead of five hundred, he might have been one of our greatest artists'.

EJ

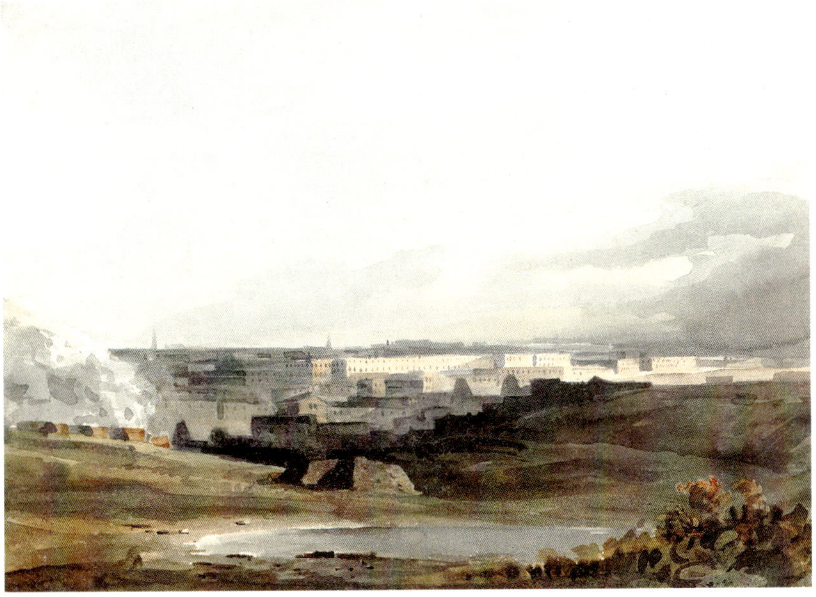

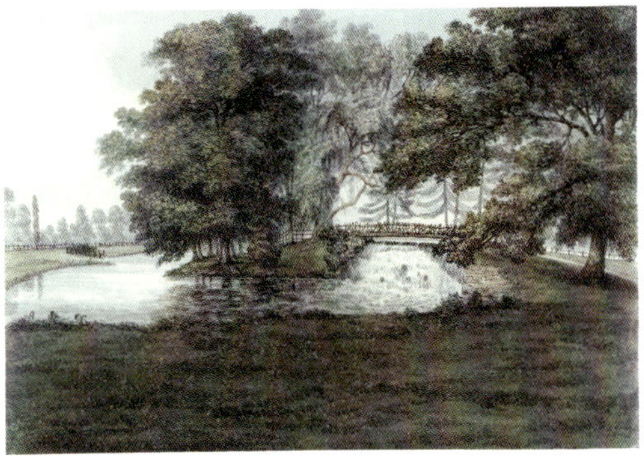

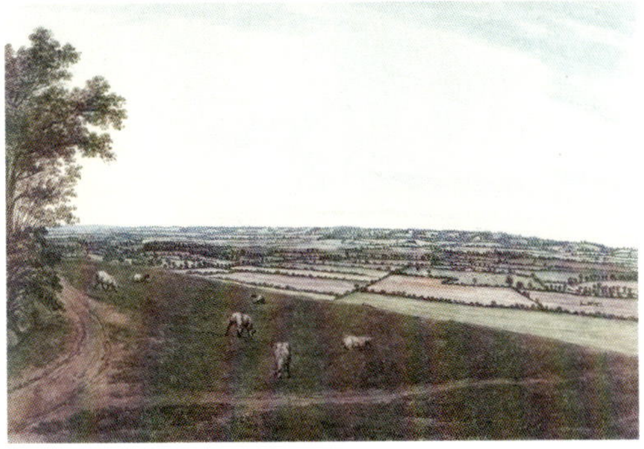

Thomas FISHER

[1782–1836]

Cascade in Chicksands Park, Bedfordshire, c.1820

watercolour and ink over pencil on paper, 29.9 × 44.5 cm
inscribed: *Cascade in Chicksands Park, Bedfordshire*

P.714

PROVENANCE: Sir Gregory Page-Turner, Battlesden House, Beds.; Battlesden sale 1824 cat.no.2503; Emily Page-Turner; purchased from her executors 1885; then by descent; Sotheby's sale 12 June 1980 lot 26; Thos. Agnew & Sons Ltd; from whom purchased by Gallery, June 1980, with a grant from the V&A/M.G.C. Purchase Grant Fund.

A preparatory pen and ink drawing (FB127) now belongs to the Gallery, one of a collection of drawings by Fisher given by Mr T.W. Bagshawe to the Corporation of Bedford.

The gardens of Chicksands Priory were improved under the auspices of Sir George Osborn (1742–1818), who had employed James Wyatt (1746–1813) to alter the house c.1800. Chicksands Park now forms part of the Defence Intelligence and Security Centre.

EJ/CB

Thomas FISHER

[1782–1836]

View from Hunger-Hill, Near Marston Park, Bedfordshire, c.1820

watercolour and ink over pencil on paper, 30 × 44.5 cm
inscribed: *View from Hunger-Hill, near Marston Park, Bedfordshire Houghton-park House in ruins Ampthill park Warren-house near Lidlington*

P.715

PROVENANCE: Sir Gregory Page-Turner, Battlesden House, Beds; Battlesden sale 1824 cat.no.2503; Emily Page-Turner; purchased from her executors 1885; then by descent; Sotheby's sale 12 June 1980 lot 27; Thos.Agnew & Sons Ltd; from whom purchased by Gallery, June 1980, with a grant from the V&A/M.G.C.Purchase Grant Fund.

Thomas Fisher was born in Rochester but worked from 1786 to 1834 at India House, from 1816 as Searcher of Records. He soon showed skill as a draughtsman and exhibited at the R.A. in the early 1800s. He seems to have decided to record Bedfordshire's monuments because no one had done so until then. Most of his studies of the county took place between 1812 and 1822 (this drawing is watermarked *J.Whatman 1819*).

The fullest account of Fisher's work in the county, 'A Bedfordshire Topographer', appeared in *Bedfordshire Magazine*, volume V, pp.135–9 by Margaret Greenshields, a former curator of the Gallery. As one might expect from an artist whose main interests were antiquarian, his watercolours were accurate records of the scenes depicted but lacking in atmosphere.

EJ

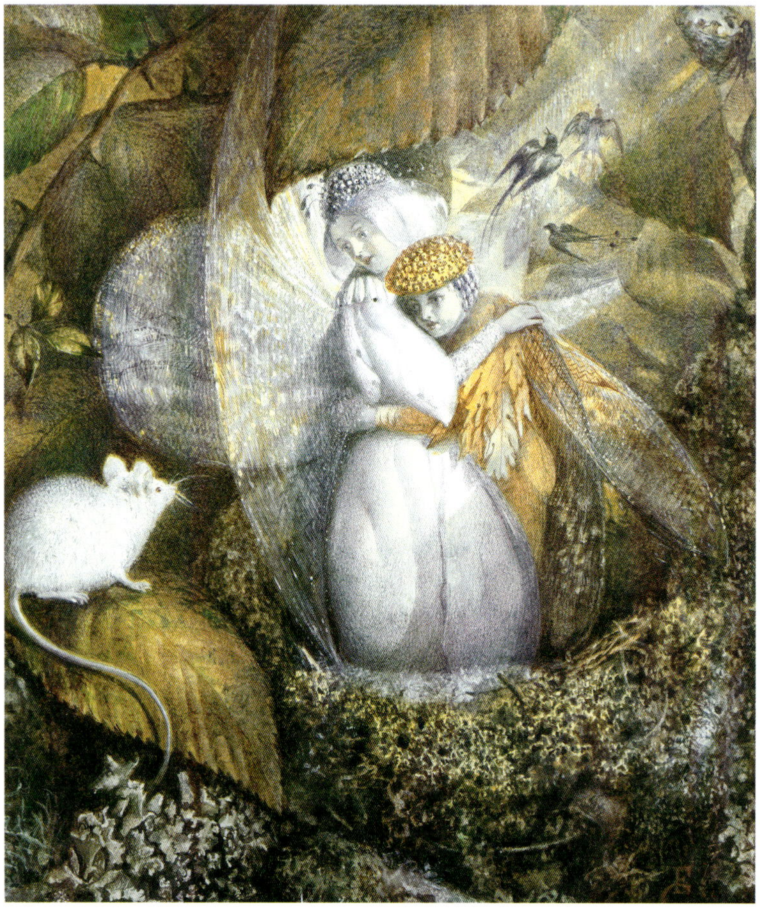

John Anster FITZGERALD

[1823–1906]

Fairy Lovers in a Bird's nest watching a white mouse, c.1860

watercolour and bodycolour on paper, 19.9 × 16.7 cm
inscribed: monogram *FG*

P.423

PROVENANCE: J.S. Maas & Co Ltd, from whom purchased by Gallery July 1962 as *A Fairy Scene* by Frederick Goodall RA.
EXHIBITIONS: *Watercolours From Bedford*, Norwich, Castle Museum, 1965, no.17 as *Fairy Scene* by Goodall; *Fairies*, Brighton, Brighton Art Gallery and Museums, 1980, no.D48 as *Fairy Scene*; *Victorian Fairy Painting*, London, R.A., Iowa, University of Iowa Museum of Art and Toronto, Art Gallery of Ontario, 1998, no.48.
REFERENCES: J.S. Maas, *Victorian Painters*, 1969, p.160, as *Fairy Scene*; B. Phillpotts, *Fairy Paintings*, 1978, pl.17 as *Fairy Scene*; J. Martineau (ed.), *Victorian Fairy Painting*, 1997, p.125, cat.no.48.

Originally attributed to Frederick Goodall, R.A. (1822–1904), who occasionally painted similar subjects, though with less whimsy.

Fitzgerald was a painter of fairy scenes and dreams (people asleep surrounded by goblins); all his works are of his imagination. His paintings are rare and little is known of his life. He was the son of the poet William Thomas Fitzgerald and had little or no formal art training. By the 1850s he was contributing to *The Illustrated London News* as an illustrator. He belonged to the Maddox St Sketching Club and exhibited at the R.A., 1845–1902, his final exhibit there being *Alice in Wonderland*.

EJ

John FLAXMAN, R.A.

[1775–1826]

Two Volumes of Drawings, c.1804–11

pencil, ink and wash on paper, various sizes

P.711 & P.712

PROVENANCE: J. P. Heseltine; Sotheby's 29 May 1935, lot 310; Alex Finberg; Edward Croft-Murray, given to Gallery, February 1980, to commemorate Croft-Murray's twenty-five years of service on the Gallery Board.

Two volumes of 104 drawings, ranging in subject from classical, mythology and portraits to fantasy, as well as various drawings of memorials and statues. Volume I includes a portrait of G. Denman, dated 1804.

Flaxman was one of the most influential exponents of the Neo-Classical style. During 1775–87 he worked for Josiah Wedgwood (1730–95) in Stoke-on-Trent, after which he worked in Rome until 1794. Principally known for his sculpture and reliefs (he was Professor of Sculpture at the R.A.), his delicate drawings show the epitome of the Classical ideal.

CB

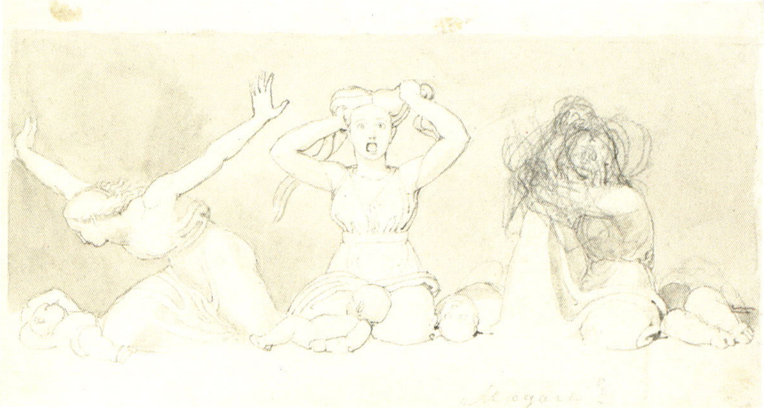

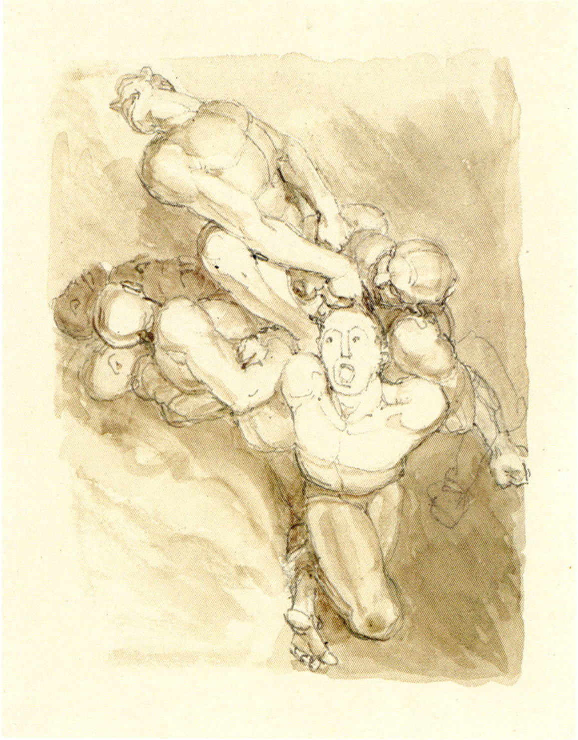

John FLAXMAN, R.A.
[1775–1826]
Design for the Tablet to Nathaniel Marchant, R.A. in Stoke Poges Church, 1816

pencil and wash on paper, 18 × 13 cm
inscribed: *Marchant*
inscribed on reverse: *N.Marchant Esq*

P.620
PROVENANCE: J.P. Heseltine; Sotheby's 29 May 1935, lot 310; Alex Finberg; Edward Croft-Murray, C.B.E. F.S.A. (acquisitions advisor to the Gallery); given to Gallery, March 1971.

Nathaniel Marchant (1739–1816) is chiefly remembered as an engraver of cameos and gems but he also sculpted a few busts. He was held in high esteem, becoming gem-sculptor to the Prince of Wales, engraver to King George III and chief engraver of stamps. He exhibited at the Society of Artists 1765–74 and at the R.A. 1781–1811. He was elected A.R.A. in 1791 and R.A. in 1809.

He is buried at Stoke Poges, where the tablet to his memory was carved by his executor John Flaxman. His choice of Stoke Poges was due to his friendship 'with Mr. John Penn, the owner of the adjoining Mansion House'.

This delicate but very slight drawing hardly gives a fair impression of Flaxman's skills as a draughtsman.

EJ

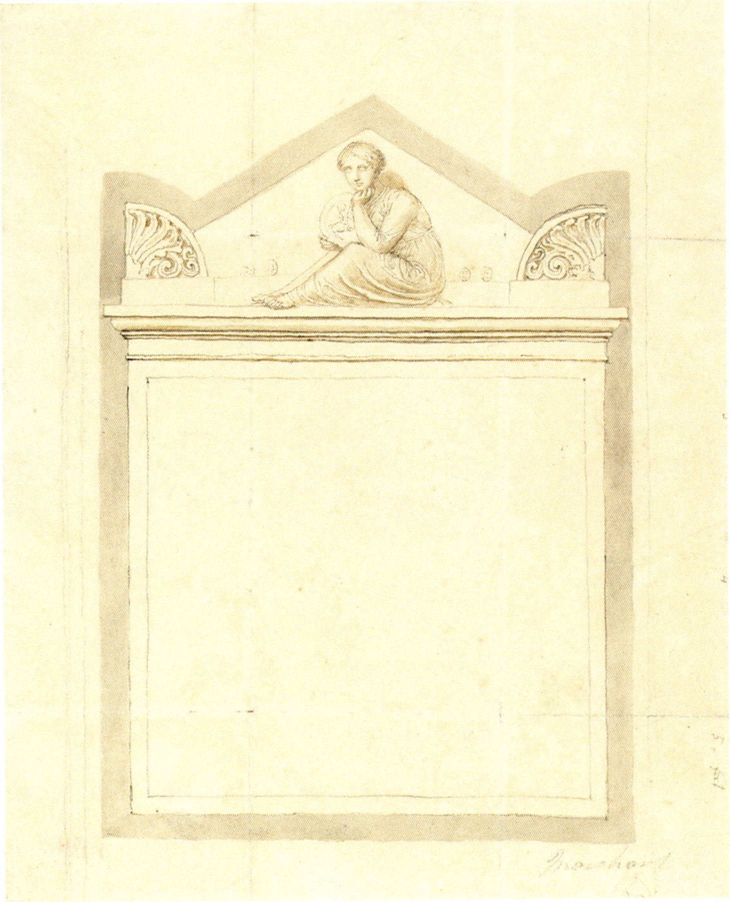

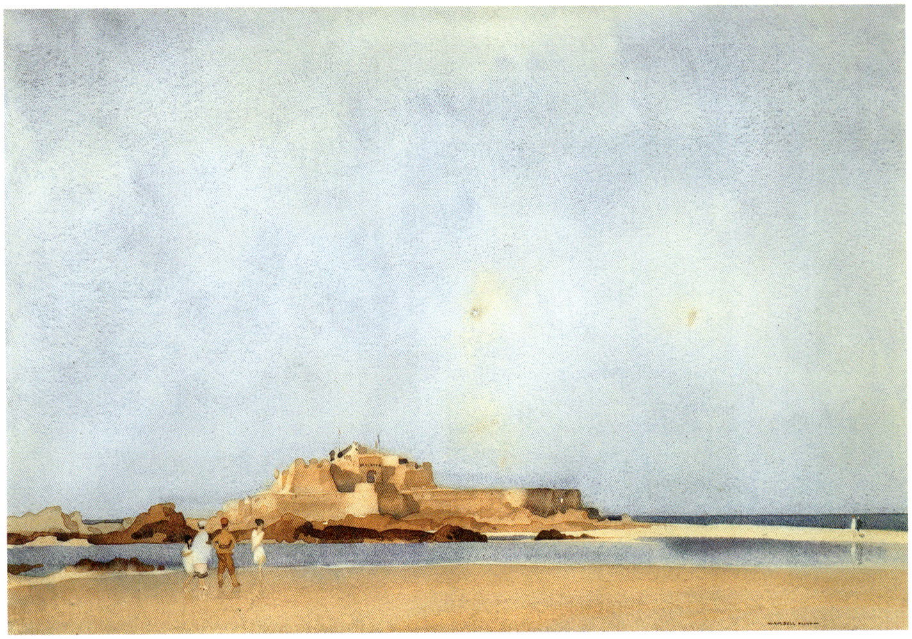

Sir William Russell FLINT, R.A., R.W.S.
[1880–1969]
The Beach at St. Malo, c.1930–40

watercolour on paper, 33 × 48.9 cm
inscibed: *W Russell Flint*

P.792
PROVENANCE: Mrs Sydney Kitson; Elisabeth & Alice Barbara Kitson, given to Gallery, October 1992.

Between the wars Flint spent many summers with his family at St. Malo, France.

Given to the Gallery by Barbara and Elisabeth Kitson, in 1993. At that time Barbara Kitson told the Curator that their father, Sydney Kitson, the expert on John Sell COTMAN, frequently bought pictures. As compensation his wife chose to buy this Russell Flint.

Born in Edinburgh, the son of a commercial artist, Flint was apprenticed to lithographers. On moving to London, he worked as a medical illustrator before joining the *Illustrated London News*. His work has become so synonymous with nudes that his landscapes are often disregarded.

EJ/CB

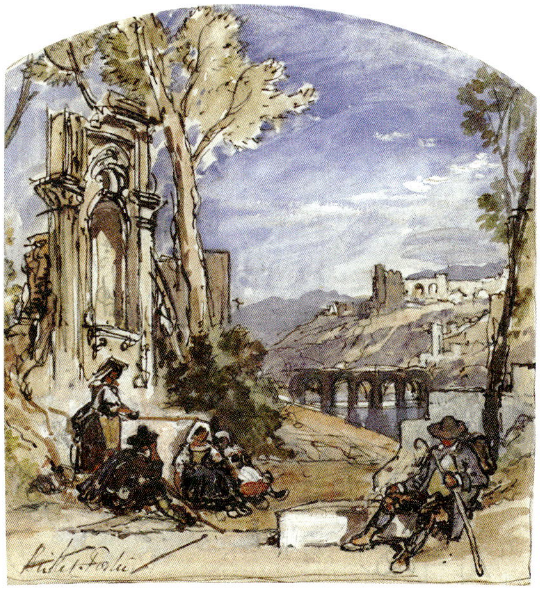

Myles Birket FOSTER, R.W.S.

[1825–99]

Illustration to **The Traveller** by Oliver Goldsmith, c.1856

pen, watercolour, bodycolour and pencil on paper with arched top, 9.5 × 8.9 cm
inscribed: *Birket Foster*
on reverse: similar illustration in pen and ink

P.160
PROVENANCE: P&D Colnaghi Ltd, from whom purchased by Gallery, January 1958.
EXHIBITIONS: *Birket Foster*, Reading, Reading Museum and Art Gallery, 1985, no.32.
REFERENCES: J. Reynolds, *Birket Foster*, 1984, p.207.

Oliver Goldsmith (1728–74) first published *The Traveller* or *A Prospect of Society*, dedicated to his brother the Rev. Henry Goldsmith, in December 1764. Consisting of 438 lines, it won immediate and lasting acclaim, Dr Johnson declaring it 'the best poem since the death of Pope'. It ran to many editions, some early ones being illustrated by Samuel Wale R.A. (d.1786) and Richard WESTALL. In 1856 Macaulay defined its message as concluding 'that our happiness depends little on political institutions, and much on the temper and regulation of our own minds'.

This drawing was made for an edition published in 1856, the period when Foster was known as an illustrator of books of poetry and before he had established himself as a watercolourist of the pretty rustic scenes that are now chiefly associated with his name.

EJ

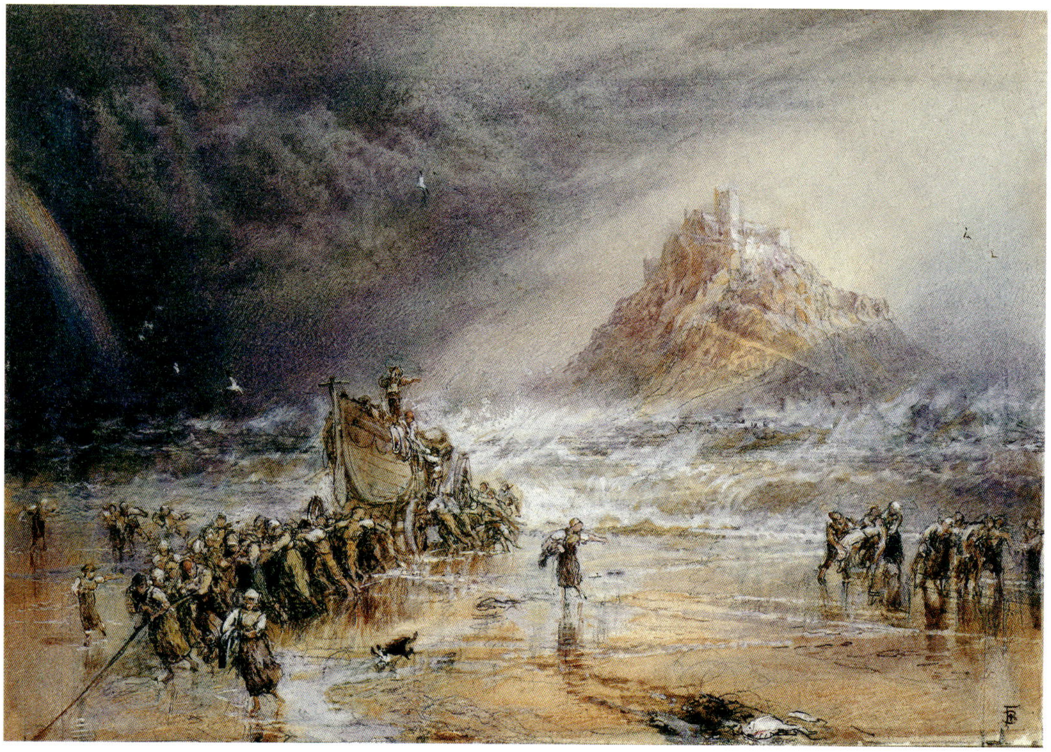

Myles Birket FOSTER, R.W.S.

[1825–99]

Return of the Lifeboat with St. Michael's Mount in the distance, c.1874

watercolour, bodycolour and pencil, heightened with white on paper, 19.8 × 28.5 cm
inscribed: *monogram BF*

P.417
PROVENANCE: P&D Colnaghi Ltd, from whom purchased by Gallery, April 1962.
EXHIBITIONS: *Royal Society of Painters in Water-colours*, London, 1874, no.226; *Watercolours and Drawings from The Cecil Higgins Art Gallery Bedford*, London, Thos. Agnew & Sons Ltd, 1962, no.58.
REFERENCES: J. Reynolds, *Birket Foster*, 1984, pp.133, 196 & 207, no.80.

Born in North Shields, Foster was brought to London at the age of five. In 1846 he was employed painting landscape and rustic subjects for the *Illustrated London News*. He soon attracted patrons, and much of his work mirrors the taste and sentiment of the time. While his pictures are often 'overloaded with pretty conceits' and tend towards the sugary, he had amazing technical skill, a sure sense of composition and a fine command of colour.

EJ

François Louis Thomas FRANCIA
[1772–1839]
St Benet's Abbey, Norfolk, 1802

watercolour on paper, 28.5 × 41.1 cm
inscribed: *L.Francia 1802*

P.382
PROVENANCE: Mark Fletcher; Sotheby's 30 November 1960, lot 43; Thos. Agnew & Sons Ltd, from whom purchased by Gallery, November 1960.
EXHIBITIONS: *Watercolours from Bedford*, Norwich, Castle Museum, 1965, no.12; *Bonington and his followers and Samuel Prout*, London, V&A, 1985; *Louis Francia 1772–1839*, Calais, Musée des Beaux Arts, 1988–9, no.11.
REFERENCES: Engraved by J. Greig in *Excursions in the County of Norfolk*, 1818, vol.1; C. Shaw Smith, *From Francia to Delacroix: the English influence on French Romantic Landscape painting*, Thesis, University of North Carolina, 1982, vol.1, pp.22 & 53, n.77; M. Pointon, *The Bonington Circle: English Watercolours and Anglo-French Landscape 1790–1855*, 1985, pp.13–14; M. Pointon, *Bonington, Francia and Wyld*, 1985, fig.46; A. Wilton & A. Lyles, *The Great Age of British Watercolours 1750–1880*, 1993, p.223, fig.47.

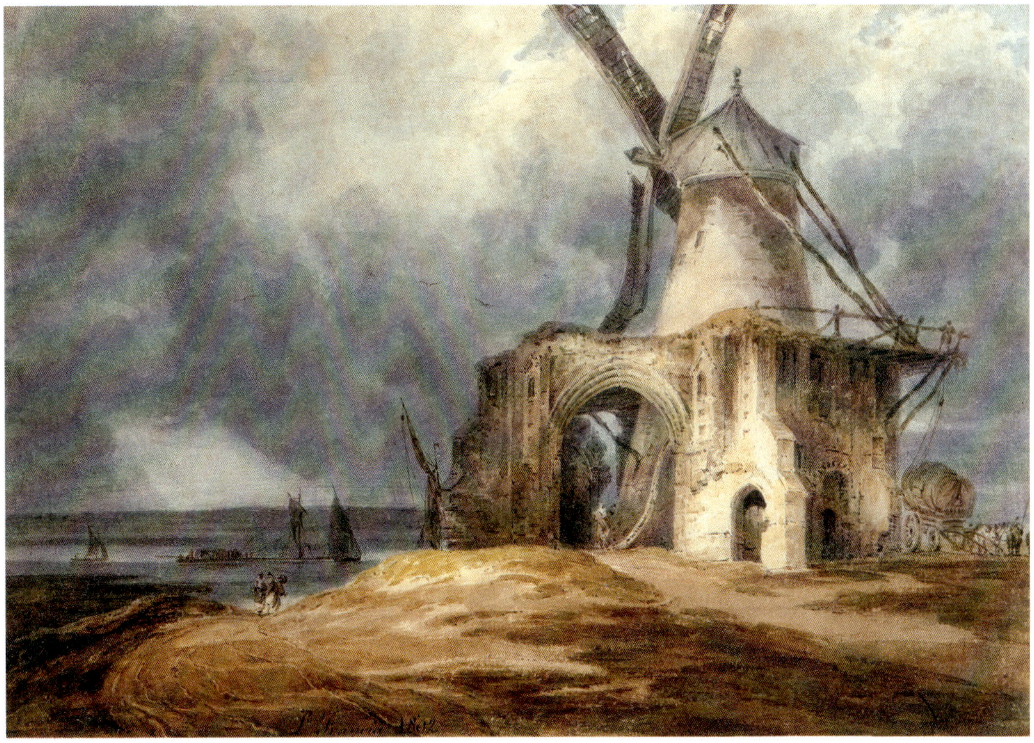

Francia made a tour of Norfolk from July to October 1802. He chose a popular subject with East Anglian artists as essentially the same view was engraved by COTMAN and published in 1813. Francia's drawing clearly shows the influence of GIRTIN.

Francia was born in Calais but was brought to London as a boy. He showed eighty-five exhibits at the R.A. between 1795 and 1821. He attended Dr MONRO's 'Academy', along with Girtin and TURNER and copied landscapes by Canaletto (1697–1768), GAINSBOROUGH and J.R.COZENS. J.P. Neale (1780–1847), a topographical draughtsman who knew Francia, described him as 'a conceited French refugee who used to amuse the party with his blundering absurdities'. In 1817 he returned to Calais where he gave lessons to BONINGTON. Francia's nephew, Alexandre Thomas, was also a painter and their work is sometimes confused, as occurred with the Gallery's *Calais* (P.69).

EJ/CB

François Louis Thomas FRANCIA [1772–1839] or **Alexandre Thomas FRANCIA** [1815 or 1820–84]
Fort Rouge at Calais

watercolour and bodycolour on paper, 19.6 × 31.3 cm
inscribed: *Francia*

P.69
PROVENANCE: Gilbert Davis; P&D Colnaghi Ltd, from whom purchased by Gallery, February 1953.
EXHIBITIONS: *Watercolours by F.L.T.Francia*, London, The Fine Art Society, 1948, no.4; *Gilbert Davis Watercolours*, Arts Council, 1949, no.31 as *Boulogne* by F.L. Francia.

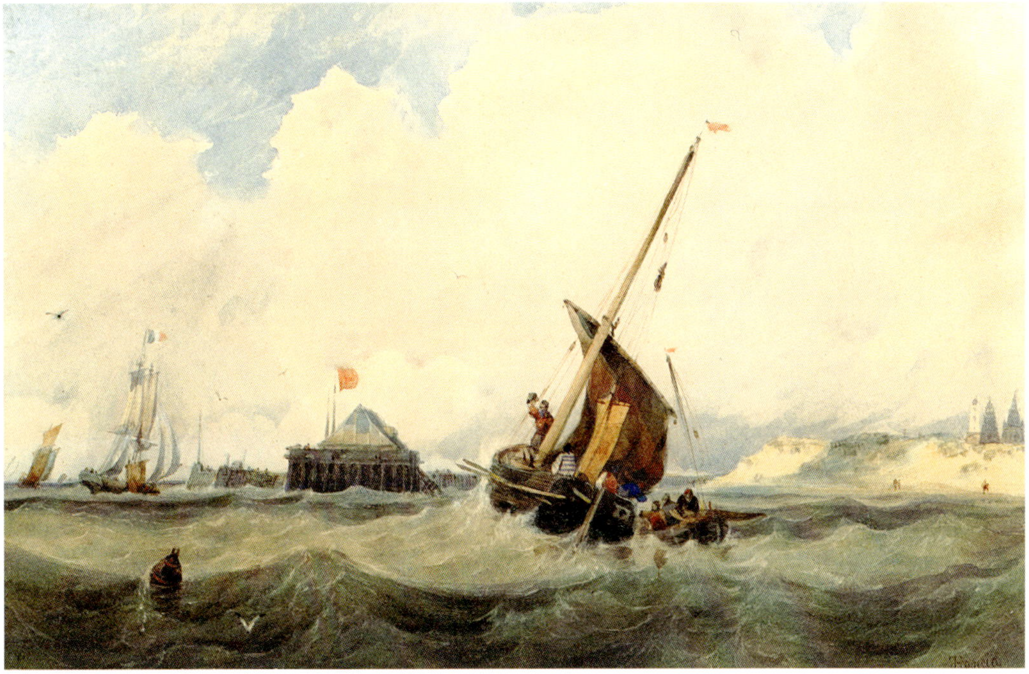

The attribution has been disputed: in 1988 when a exhibition was being planned in Calais, the Gallery received a letter from Patrick Noon who suggested that Francia's nephew and pupil, Alexandre Thomas Francia, had painted this watercolour; it was not therefore chosen for the exhibition.

EJ

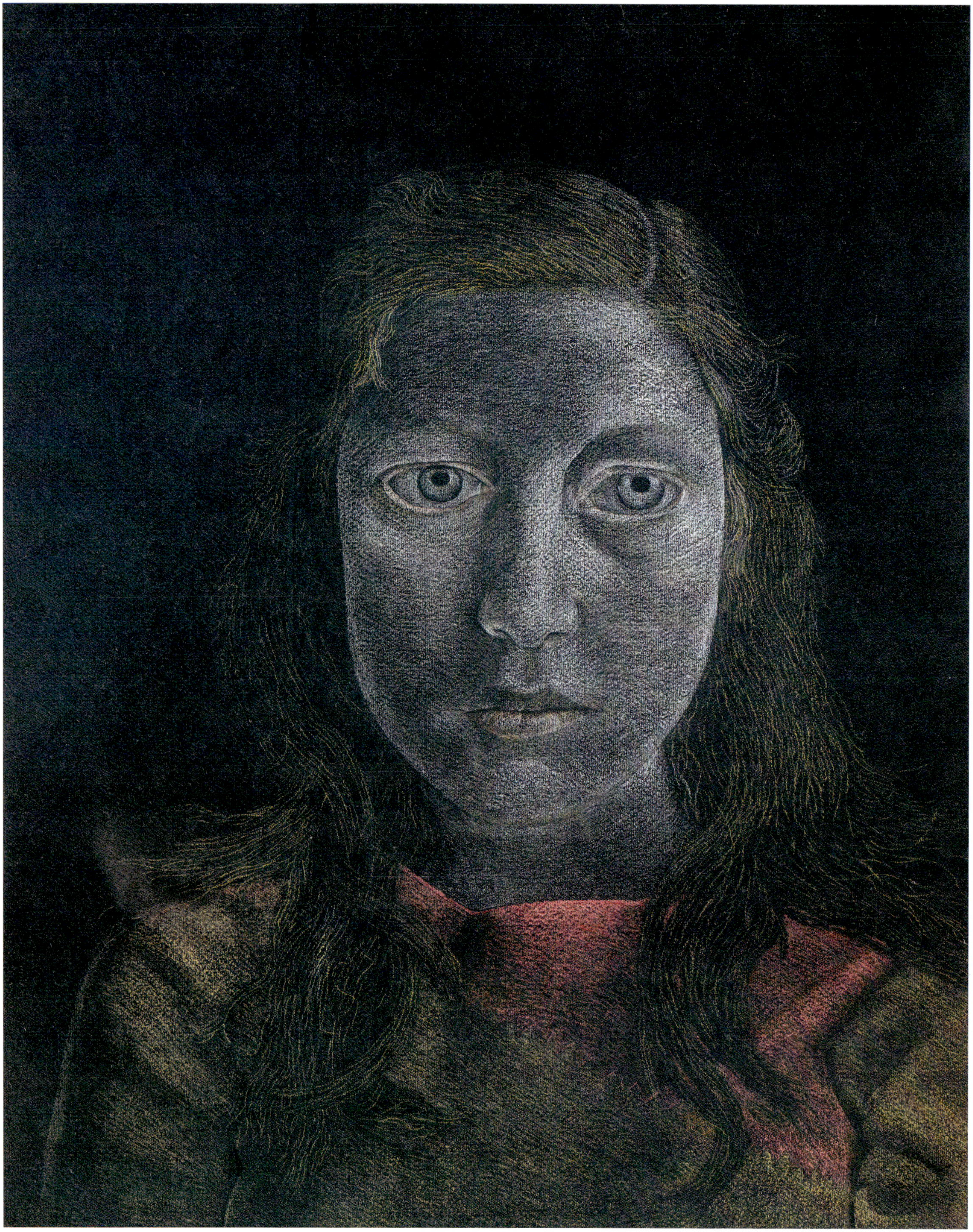

Lucian FREUD, C.B.E.

[b.1922]

Head of a girl with red hair, c.1948

pastel on black paper, 40.5 × 32.8 cm

P.186

PROVENANCE: Erica Bronsen ? – see entry; Hanover Gallery, from whom purchased by Gallery, April 1958.

EXHIBITIONS: *Portrait Paintings and Drawings*, Rye, Rye Art Gallery, 1967; *Change of Scene XVII – Lucian Freud*, Frankfurt, Museum of Modern Art, 2000–01.

William Feaver, the leading authority on Freud, thinks this could be one of two sitters: Joan Landor, the wife of architect Ron Landor, was lodging with the Freuds at 28 Clifton Hill, NW8, when this drawing was made. Feaver believes the most likely candidate, however, is the Freuds' nanny, an Irish girl. Freud's first wife, Kitty, engaged her on the premiss that because she had a child she might therefore be good with children. In fact, she went off to be an usherette at a cinema in Kilburn leaving the child behind. Feaver believes it was of this drawing that Freud said: 'I tried something of her, pastel on black paper, tried and failed'. Erica Bronsen later sold this picture.

The style is typical of Freud's early concern for linear description rather than the heavy use of paint for which he is now better known. Throughout his career, Freud has produced a number of intimate and intense portraits that have concentrated on the eyes and face of the sitter, most notably, Francis Bacon, Caroline Blackwood, the artist's mother and more recently, the Queen. Freud has said of his work 'I hoped that if I concentrated enough, the intensity of scrutiny alone would force life into the pictures'.

Freud was born in Berlin the son of the architect Ernst Freud and grandson of Sigmund Freud. He came to England in 1932 and first studied at the Central School. In 1939 he enrolled at the East Anglian School of Drawing and Painting under the direction of Cedric Morris (he is said to have burnt the school down after smoking at night with David Carr).

EJ/CB

Lucian FREUD, C.B.E.

[b.1922]

Botanical Gardens (Landscape with Scillonian Pine), 1945

conté pencil, coloured chalks, pen and ink on paper, 45.7 × 47.6 cm

P.575

PROVENANCE: Purchased from Crane Kalman Gallery, January 1968.

EXHIBITIONS: *Lucian Freud*, London, Hayward Gallery, 1974, no.31, p.44; *Lucian Freud– Works on Paper*, Oxford, Ashmolean Museum, 1988, no.24.

Freud and John CRAXTON were discovered stowed away on a ship bound for France and were diverted to the Scilly Islands where this picture was probably drawn.

Freud was born in Berlin the grandson of Sigmund Freud (1856–1939). He came to England in 1932 and studied at the Central School in 1939 and Goldsmith's College in 1942. His combination of meticulous accuracy and disquieting intensity in his early work caused him to be dubbed 'The Ingres of Existentialism' by Herbert Read (1893–1968). By the end of the 1950s this tight graphic style gave way to a looser, more painterly technique. The bulk of his work comprises of portraits and nudes, but his output also includes landscapes and flower pictures.

EJ/CB

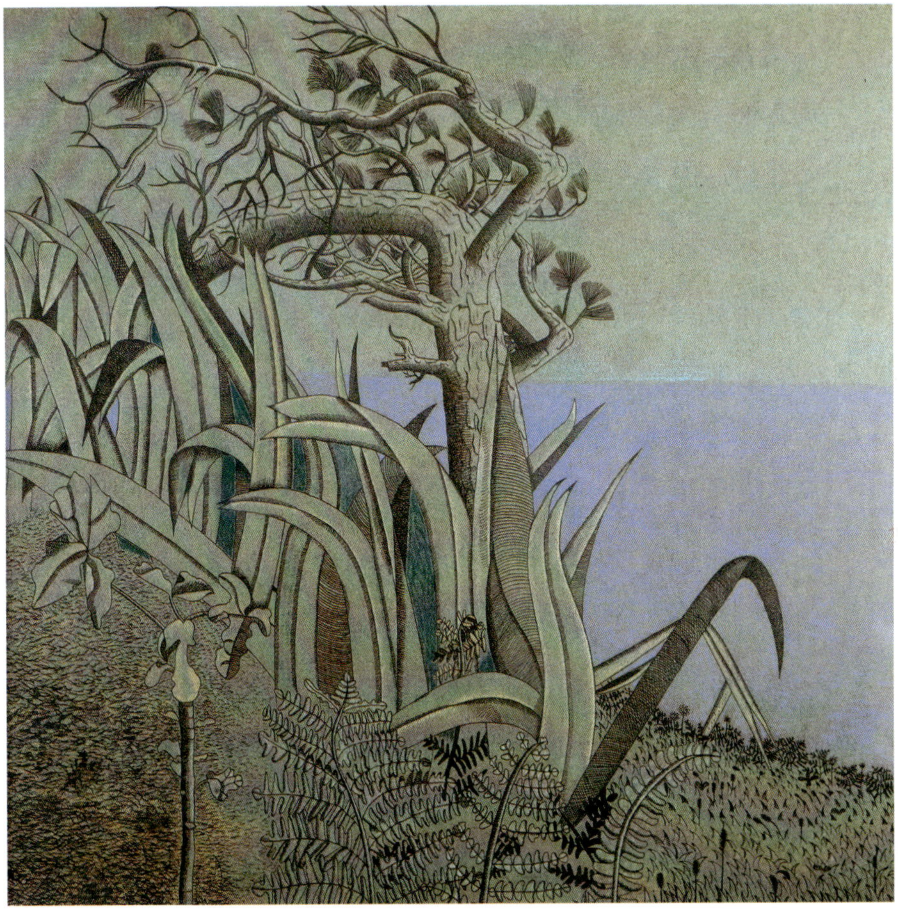

Dame Elisabeth FRINK, A.R.A.

[1930–93]

Horse and Fallen Rider, 1950

ink and wash heightened with white on paper, 55 × 38.9 cm
inscribed: *Frink 50*

P.435

PROVENANCE: Mr Terence Rowe; J.S. Maas & Co.Ltd., from whom purchased by Gallery, October 1962.

EXHIBITIONS: *Watercolours from Bedford*, Norwich, Castle Museum 1965, no.13; *Animals in Art: A Celebration of animals through eyes of artists*, London, Sotheby's, Brighton, Brighton Art Gallery and Museums and Preston, Harris Museum and Art Gallery, 1997.

Drawn when the artist was still a student at Chelsea Art School, it recalls paintings of *The Conversion of St.Paul* by much earlier artists such as Caravaggio's in S.Maria del Popolo, Rome. Frink had exhibited a number of drawings of this type at Heffer's bookshop in Cambridge, c.1948.

Primarily a sculptor, but also a draughtsman and printer, Frink's main subjects were man, dog and horse. The appeal of her work lies in its directness. She received many public commissions including *Wild Boar* for Harlow New Town, *Blind Beggar and Dog* for Bethnal Green and *Walking Madonna* for Salisbury Cathedral. She was created a D.B.E. in 1982.

EJ/CB

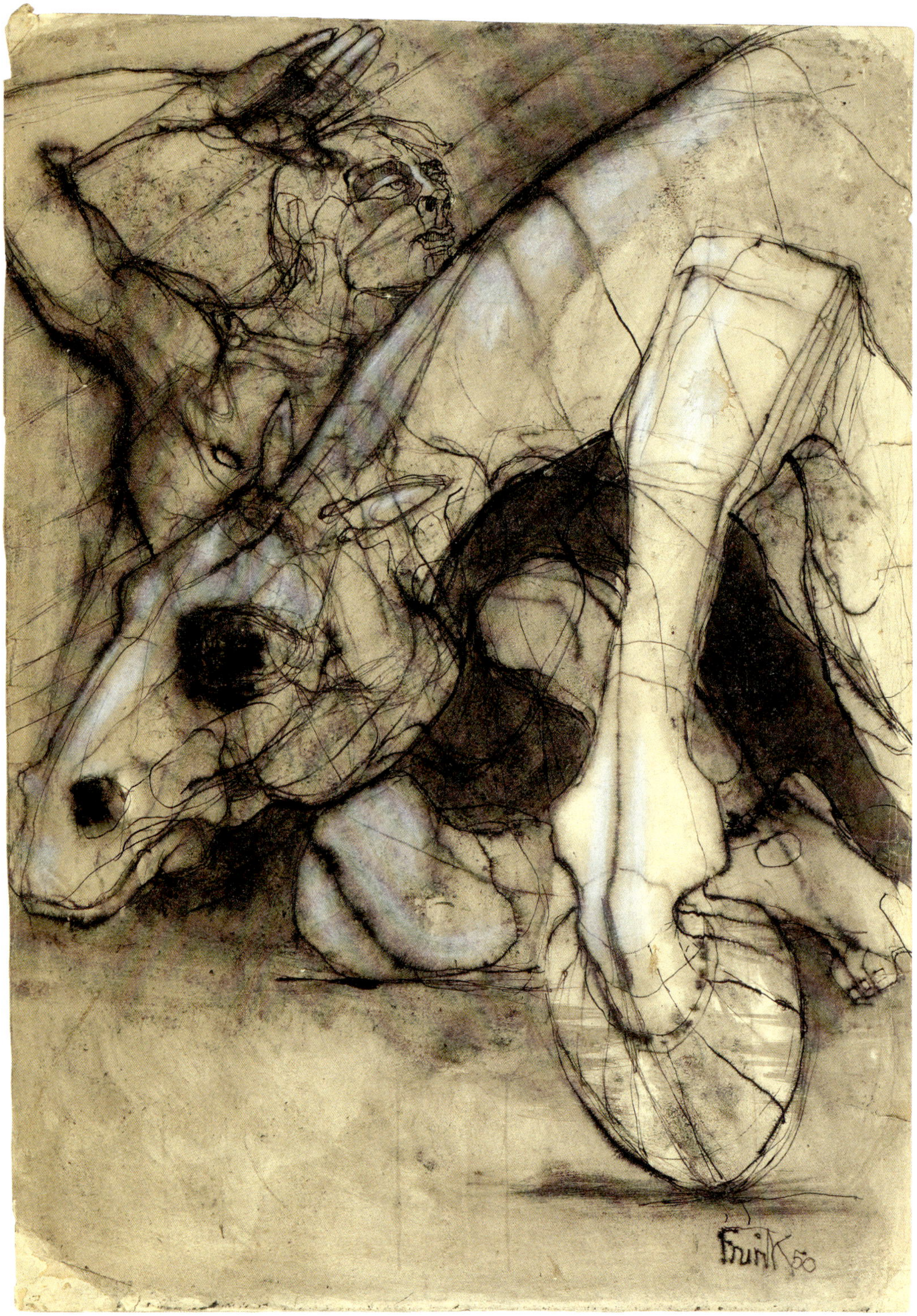

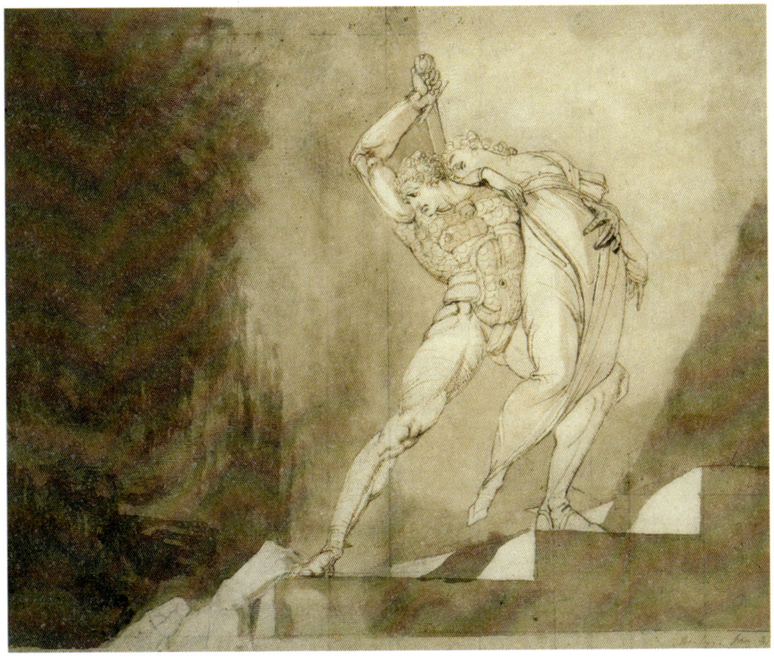

Henry FUSELI, R.A.
[1741–1825]
A Warrior rescuing a Lady, 1781

pen and brown ink with brown-grey wash on paper, 30.4 × 37 cm
inscribed: *Monday Jan 81*
on reverse: *In these deep To be or not to be that is the question whether tis better in the mind to suffer*
Figure drawing in black lead

P.364
PROVENANCE: Miss J.B. Shaw; P&D Colnaghi Ltd, from whom purchased by Gallery, October 1960.
EXHIBITIONS: *Watercolours and Drawings from the Cecil Higgins Art Gallery, Bedford*, London, Thos. Agnew & Sons Ltd, 1962, no.53; *English Watercolours from The Cecil Higgins Art Gallery Bedford*, Reading, Reading Museum and Art Gallery, 1965, no.16.

On the reverse are two, unfinished figure studies and quotations from *Hamlet*, written in mirror writing. These it would seem were written on the obverse and then deliberately painted out so that they are only visible on the reverse.
In 1989 Bert Winther of New York University sent the Gallery an article of his which advanced strong arguments that Fuseli had taken his subject from a *History of Denmark* by Saxo Grammaticus (c.1150–1220). Book VII relates how Prince Ottar rescued Princess Sigrid by killing a giant who had abducted her. The quotation from *Hamlet* is relevant here since Saxo's account of the legend of Prince Amleth is the ultimate source of Shakespeare's tragedy.

Born Fussli as he was Swiss by birth, Fuseli began life as a Zwinglian minister but this did not last and, during a visit to London, he was encouraged by Reynolds to become a painter. After eight years in Rome he returned to London. He quickly established himself in the R.A., was Professor of Painting 1799–1805, and again from 1810, and Keeper from 1804.

Although his pictures are imaginative in subject matter and dramatic in expression, his painterly technique was limited; however, he was a masterly draughtsman and his innumerable drawings have an intensity that makes them especially compelling.

EJ

Henry FUSELI, R.A.
[1741–1825]
Achilles' Victory over Memnon, 1813

pencil and watercolour on paper, 31.6 × 21.5 cm
inscribed: *Fuseli K July 28 13*
ΨΥΧΟΣΤΑΣΙΑ (PSUCHOSTASIA)

P.363
PROVENANCE: P&D Colnaghi Ltd, from whom purchased by Gallery, October 1960.

Memnon, king of the Ethiopians, brought ten thousand men to assisit Priam in the Trojan war. There he killed Antilochus, the son of Nestor, who then challenged Memnon to fight. Memnon refused on account of Nestor's great age. Instead he fought the mightiest warrior of all the Greeks, Achilles, who slew him.

A statue was erected in Memnon's honour which uttered a melodious sound every day at sunrise. Tennyson alludes to this statue in the forty-third verse of *The Palace of Art* thus:

> And from her lips, as morn from Memnon
> Drew
> Rivers of Melodies

In April 1961 Dr Gert Schiff of the Swiss Institute for Art Research and the leading authority on Fuseli, wrote to the Gallery to say that another version of this composition belonged to Mrs Murray-Crane in New York. He also pointed out that the Greek word *psuchostasia* ('Ecstasy of the Soul') is the title of a tragedy by Aeschylus about Achilles and Memnon. However, the *Lexicon of Classical Greek* defines *psuchostasia* as 'weighing of souls'. In Aeschylus' play, of which only fragments are extant, Thetis and Eos (the mothers of Achilles and Memnon) weighed their sons' souls against one another, and that of Memnon was found lighter.

EJ

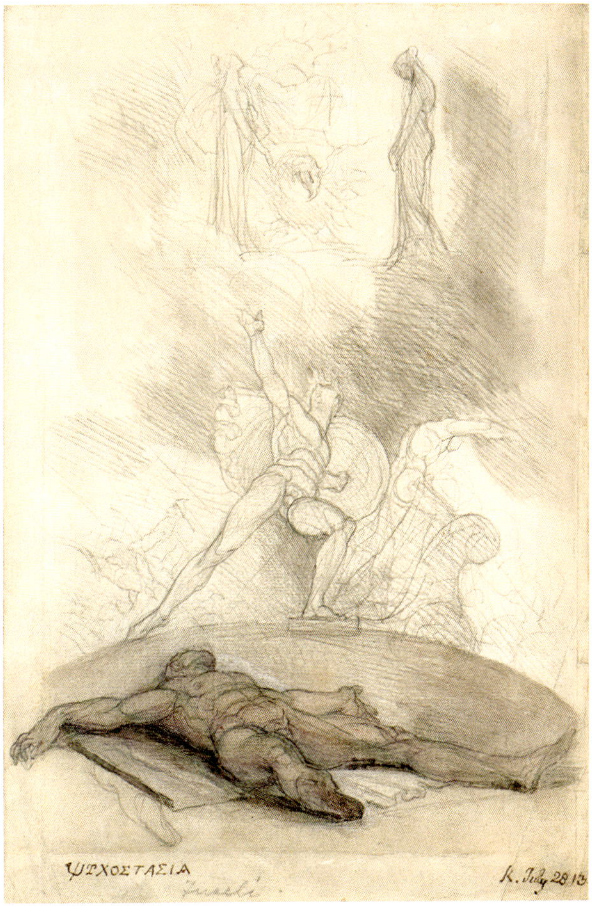

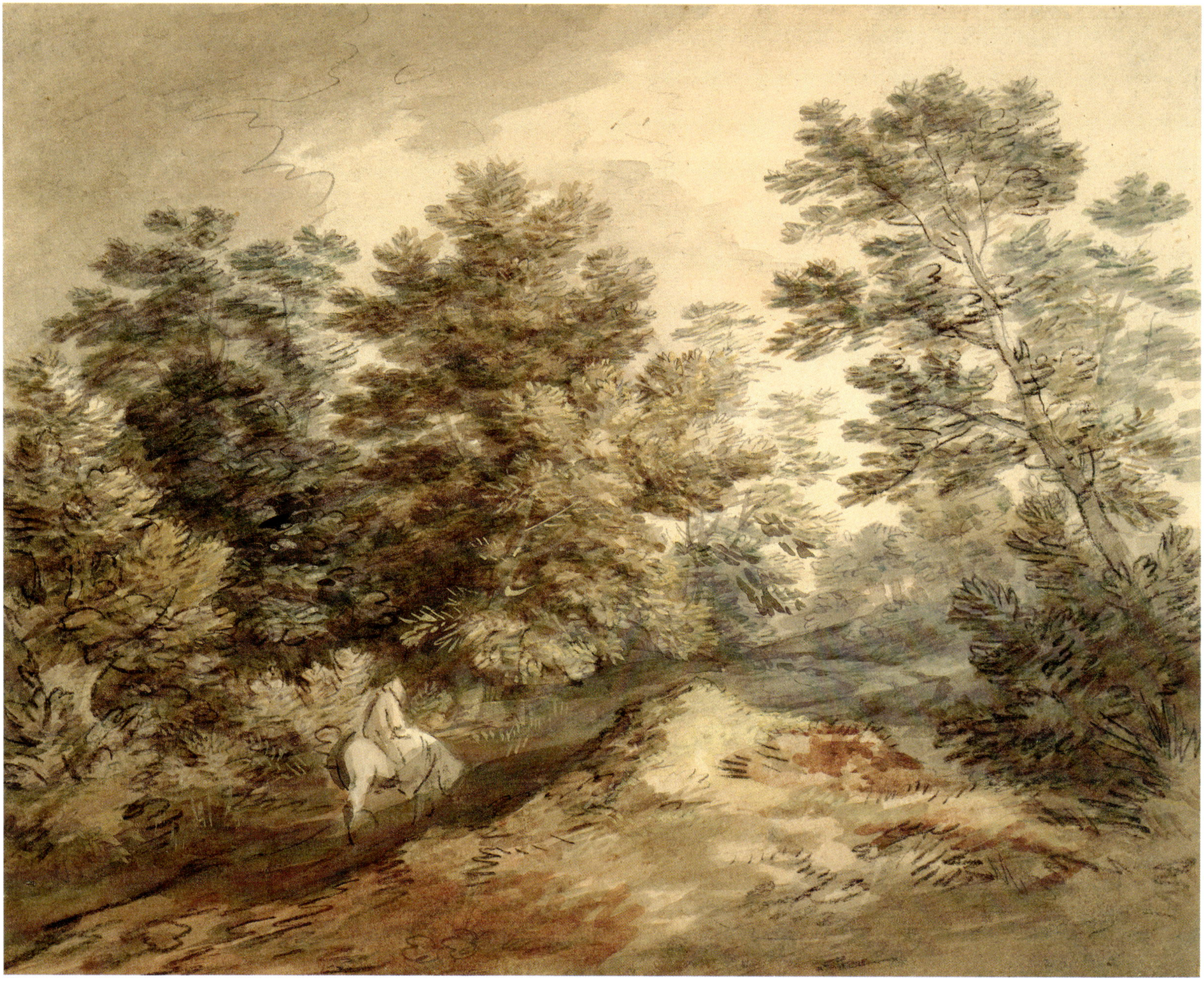

Thomas GAINSBOROUGH, R.A.

[1727–88]

A Wooded Landscape with a Horseman, c.1765–70

watercolour, bodycolour, black chalk and black lead on paper, 23.9 × 30 cm
inscribed on reverse: *purshased* [sic] *at Bath at the Sale of Gainsborough's drawings soon after his Death by S.Wollaston Esre. For £3–12*
beneath in pencil, largely illegible inscription: *....bought at the sale of S.Wollaston's effects by ...*

P.756

PROVENANCE: S. Wollaston; whereabouts unknown; 1880–1894 purchased by Henry Robertson; Miss Pauline Robertson; 1973 bequeathed to Mrs W.L.A. Griffin; James R. Griffin, from whom purchased by Gallery, November 1989, with assistance from the V&A/M.G.C. Purchase Grant Fund, the National Art Collections Fund (Woodroffe Fund) and the Esmée Fairbairn Memorial Trust.

REFERENCES: Sir J. Graham, 'A new Gainsborough watercolour and the Watercolour collection of the Cecil Higgins Art Gallery, Bedford', *Watercolours, Drawings and Prints*, winter, vol. 5, 1990, pp.31–3, fig.1; *National Art Collections Fund Review*, 1990, p.169.

No 'S. Wollaston' appears in Bath directories from 1788–1800, although W. Wollaston, an old friend of Gainsborough's, died there in 1797. He, Henry Robertson and Gainsborough all had connections with Ipswich. This drawing was discovered after the publication of John Hayes' catalogue of Gainsborough's Drawings (1970) and his Addendum to it (1983). Dr Hayes dates the drawing to the late 1760s and considers it closely comparable to the *Wooded Landscape with Figures and Farmhouse* (collection Bois Penrose, Pennsylvania, Hayes no.309, pl.106).

In April 1985, a Mrs Griffin took some paintings by Henry Robertson (1848–1930), which had been left to her by a cousin, the artists' daughter, to be examined by her art teacher. When these were sorted out, the Gainsborough came to light and was placed on loan at the Gallery.

On 4 June 1768, Gainsborough wrote from Bath to his friend William Jackson: 'I'm sick of Portraits and wish very much to take my viol-da gamba and walk off to some sweet village, where I can paint landskips [*sic*] and enjoy the fag-end of life in quietness and ease'.

EJ/CB

Thomas GAINSBOROUGH, R.A.
[1727–88]
Mountain Landscape with Figures and Sheep, c.1783

black and white chalks and stump on brown paper, 25.6 × 35 cm

P.71
PROVENANCE: The Rev. H. Burgess; Sir George Clausen, his sale Sotheby's 2 June 1943, lot 92, Thos. Agnew & Sons Ltd; Sir William Worsley 1944; Thos. Agnew & Sons Ltd; Howard Bliss, Esq.1949; Leicester Galleries; G. Churchill; Spink & Son, Ltd, from whom purchased by Gallery, January 1952.
EXHIBITIONS: *71st Annual Watercolour Exhibition*, London, Thos. Agnew & Sons Ltd, 1944, no.58; *From Gainsborough to Hitchens*, London, Leicester Galleries, 1950, no.15; *English Water-Colours from the Hickman Bacon and other collections*, Bedford, Cecil Higgins Art Gallery, 1952, no.41; *Landscapes by Thomas Gainsborough*, Nottingham, Nottingham University Art Gallery, 1962, no.56; *Watercolours and Drawings by East Anglian artists of the 18th & 19th centuries*, London, P&D Colnaghi Ltd, 1970, no.74, pl.xx.
REFERENCES: Sir G. Clausen, *Aims and Ideals in Art*, 1906, illus. p.160; M. Woodall, *Gainsborough's Landscape Drawings*, 1939, no. 28, pl.81and pp.67–8, 71; ibid., Thomas Gainsborough. *His Life and Work*, 1949, p.98; J. Hayes, *The Drawings of Thomas Gainsborough*, 1970, no.564, pp.15, 39, 239, pl.183.

Formerly known as Welsh Pass.

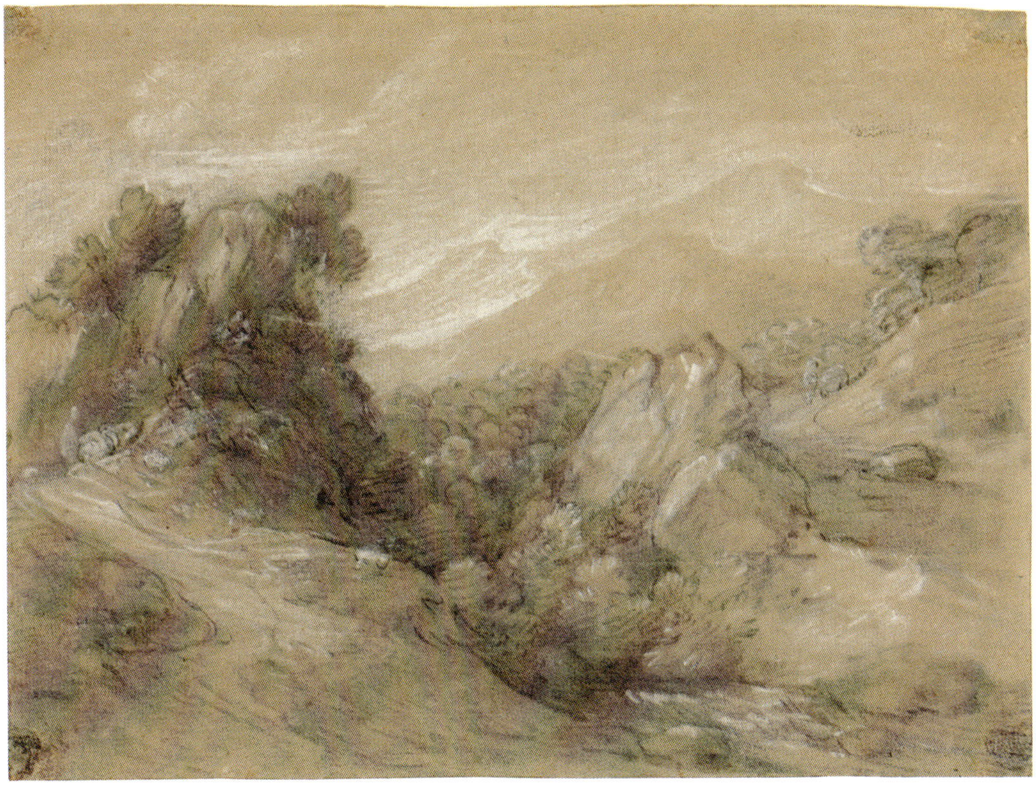

A study for an oil in the Duke of Sutherland's collection, exhibited at the R.A. in May 1783, now in the National Gallery of Scotland.

The oil differs only in the inclusion of a village in the middle distance, and the shepherd is shown reclining instead of standing. There is also a large oil sketch in the Museum of Art, Cleveland, Ohio.

EJ/CB

Thomas GAINSBOROUGH, R.A.
[1727–88]
Wooded Landscape with Country House, mid-1780s

black chalk and stump, heightened with white on paper, 25.4 × 36.5 cm

P.228
PROVENANCE: Gilbert Davies; anon sale, Sotheby's 19 March 1958, lot no.18, as *The White House, Hampstead,* P&D Colnaghi Ltd on behalf of Gallery, March 1958.
REFERENCES: J. Hayes, *The Drawings of Thomas Gainsborough*, 1970, p.258, no.652.

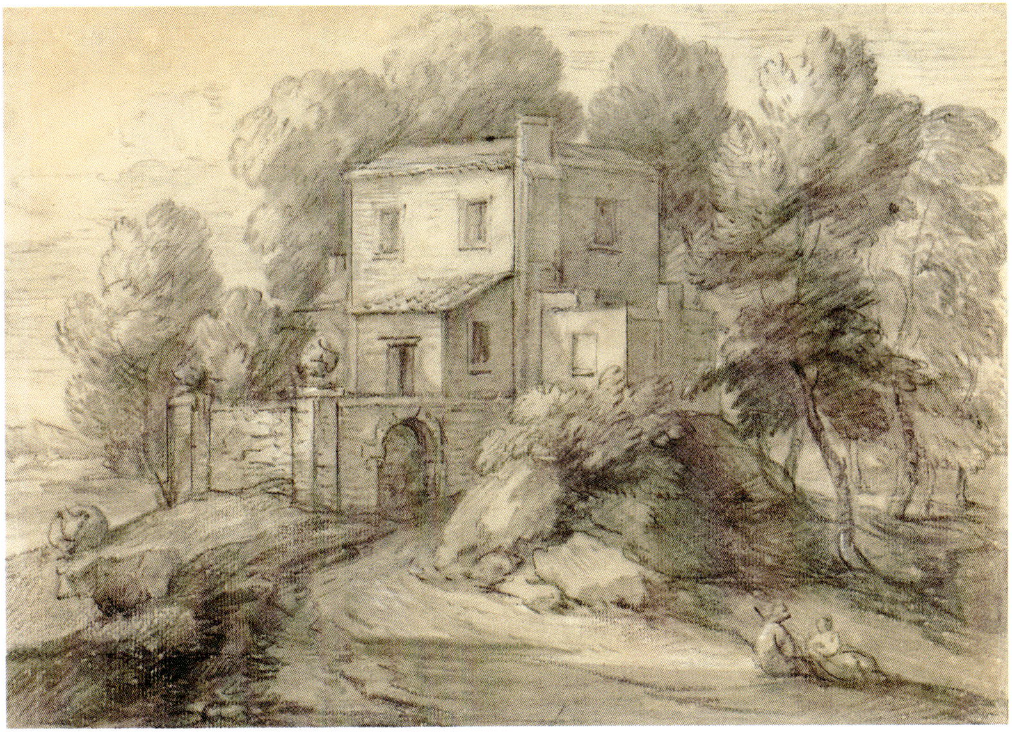

Hayes evidently rejects the identification in Sotheby's catalogue of the scene as Hampstead but does not discuss this in his entry.

Another version of the drawing, titled *Landscape with Country House*, was sold at the Albany Gallery, Duke Street, London, in 1969.

EJ/CB

Thomas GAINSBOROUGH, R.A.

[1727–88]

A Woodland landscape with Packhorses descending to a Pool, late 1780s

black and white chalks with grey wash on paper, 32.7 × 46.2 cm
on reverse: sketch in wash

P.314
PROVENANCE: J.P. Heseltine Collection; Sir Henry Oppenheimer; P&D Colnaghi Ltd; Mrs Robert Opton, New Hampshire; Vose Galleries, Boston; Thos. Agnew & Sons Ltd, from whom purchased by Gallery, January 1960.
EXHIBITIONS: *82nd Annual Exhibition of Water-Colour Drawings*, London, Thos. Agnew & Sons Ltd, 1960, no.54 as *The Pool; Landscapes by Thomas Gainsborough*, Nottingham, University of Nottingham, 1962, no.65 as *Rocky Landscape with Horses at a Watering Place; English Watercolours from the Cecil Higgins Art Gallery Bedford*, Reading, Reading Museum and Art Gallery, 1965, no.18 as *Rocky Landscape with Horses; Thomas Gainsborough*, Ferrara, Palazzo dei Diamanti, 1998, no.80, pp.222–3.
REFERENCES: J. Hayes, *Catalgoue Raisonné of Gainsborough's Drawings*, 1970, no.759, p.282.

Born in Sudbury, Suffolk, Gainsborough's precocious artistic talent led to him being sent to London at the age of thirteen. Apprenticed first to the French engraver and painter Hubert-François Gravelot (1699–1773) in 1740, he then worked under Francis Hayman (1708–76), whose informal portrait style was to be influential. Establishing himself as a portrait painter in Ipswich, Bath and eventually London, landscape painting remained his real passion. His landscapes are not exact topographical scenes but 'picturesque' interpretations. He would make imaginary compositions in his studio, using cork or coal for the foreground and set up distant woods of broccoli and use slivers of looking glass for water.

CB

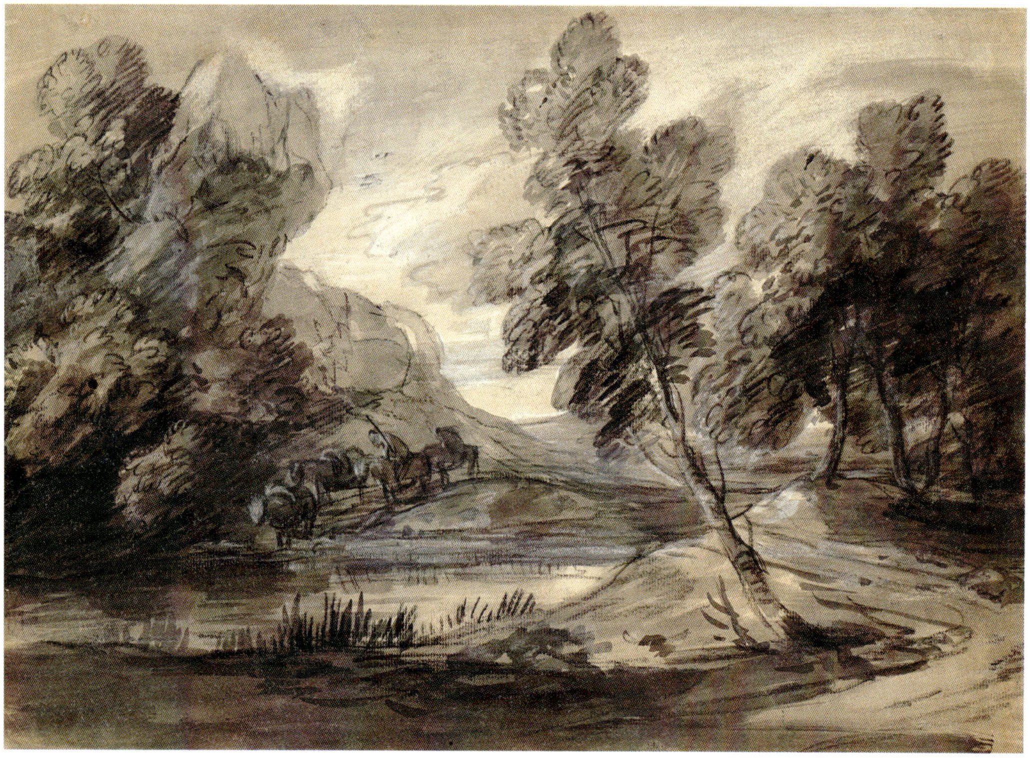

Thomas GAINSBOROUGH, R.A.

[1727–88]

Study for Diana and Actaeon, 1784–5

black chalk and wash, heightened with white on paper, 27.5 × 35.4 cm

P.118
PROVENANCE: Sir Thomas Lawrence P.R.A. ?; C.R. Rudolph, Esq.; Spink & Son Ltd, from whom purchased by Gallery, May 1957.
EXHIBITIONS: *European Masters of the Eighteenth Century*, London, R.A., 1954/5, no.548; *Primitives to Picasso*, London, R.A., 1962, no.356; *Watercolours and Drawings from the Cecil Higgins Art Gallery Bedford*, London, Thos. Agnew & Sons Ltd, 1962, no.16; *English Watercolours from the Cecil Higgins Art Gallery Bedford*, Reading, Reading Museum and Art Gallery, 1965, no.17; *A Loan Exhibition of Drawings and Watercolours by East Anglian Artists of the 18th and 19th Centuries*, London, P & D Colnaghi Ltd, 1970, no.75; *Gainsborough*, Paris, Grand Palais, 1981, no.106; *Gainsborough Drawings*, Washington, National Gallery of Art, Fort Worth, Kimbell Art Museum and New Haven, Yale Center for British Art, 1983, no.67, pp.152–4; *Thomas Gainsborough*, Ferrara, Palazzo dei Diamanti, 1998, no.87, pp.236–7.
REFERENCES: K.E. Maison, *Master Studies*, 1961; J. Hayes, *Catalogue Raisonné of Gainsborough Drawings*, 1961, pp.537–9, pl.160c; F.W. Hawcroft, *English Drawings*, 1965; G. Rainbird, *Art Treasures of Great Britain*, 1968; O. Millar, *The Later Georgian Pictures in the Collection of Her Majesty the Queen*, 1969, vol.I, p.43, illus. fig.13; J. Hayes, *The Drawings of Thomas Gainsborough*, 1970, no.812, pp.19, 40, 45, 51, 62 and 296, pl.345; J. Hayes, *Gainsborough*, 1975, p.225; F. Malins, *Drawing Ideas of the Masters*, 1981, p.71; J. Hayes & L. Stainton, *Gainsborough Drawings*, 1983, p.67, repr.; M. Rosenthal, 'Gainsborough's Diana and Actaeon', J. Barrell (ed.), *Painting and the Politics of Culture*, 1992, pp.172–74; M. Rosenthal, *The Art of Thomas Gainsborough*, 1999, no.278, p.270.

The subject is taken from Book III of Ovid's *Metamorphoses*. Actaeon, a famous huntsman, silhouetted here between the trees, comes upon Diana and her attendants bathing. Diana turns him into a stag, whereupon he is devoured by his own dogs.

This is the third and final study for the unfinished canvas (158.1 × 188 cm) of the subject in the Royal Collection. The first (Hayes no.810) belongs to the Marchioness of Anglesey and the second (Hayes no.811) to the Huntington Art Gallery, San Marino, California.

Hayes notes that this version is the most restrained in treatment; neither the figures nor the trees suggest agitation, while the compositional relationship between Actaeon and Diana is less dramatic than in the Huntington version.

EJ

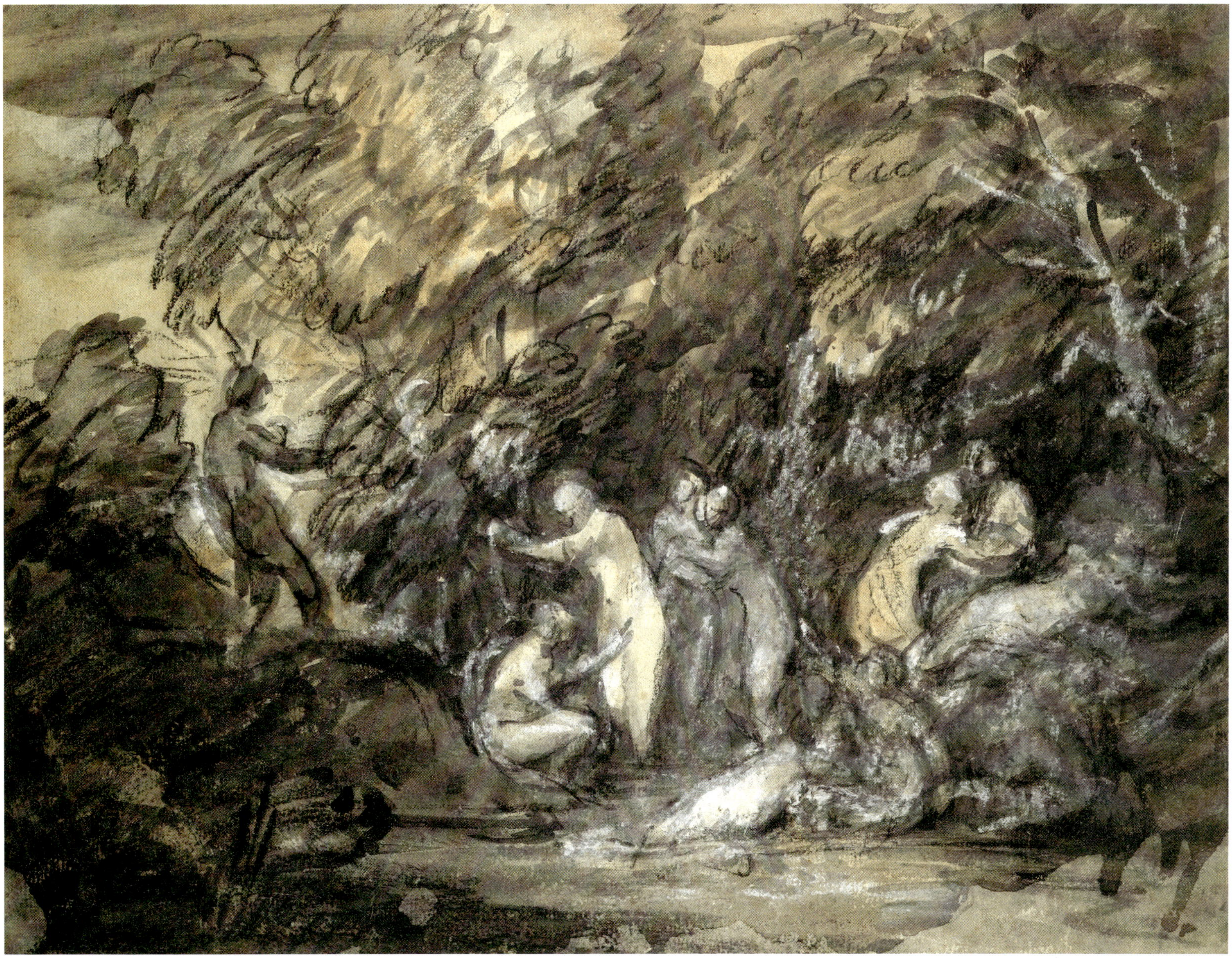

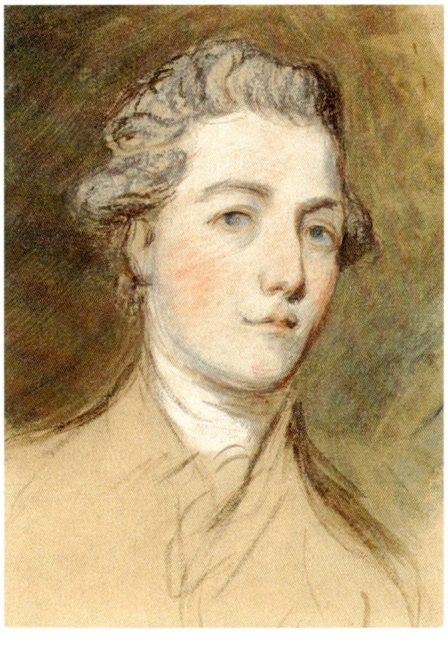

Daniel GARDNER

[1750–1805]

Head of a Young Man, 1770s

brush drawing in watercolour heightened in white on buff paper, 19 × 14 cm

P.491

PROVENANCE: C.R. Rudolph; P&D Colnaghi Ltd, from whom purchased by Gallery, May 1965.

Gardner became a fashionable portrait painter in pastels and gouache in the 1770s, specializing in small whole-lengths. He worked as an assistant in Reynolds' studio for a short time and many of his poses are borrowed from his master, although with a stronger decorative element. Pastel never achieved the same popularity in Britain as it did in France in the 18th century, but Gardner was one of its most popular and successful practitioners.

EJ

Charles GASCOYNE
[1891–1917]
A Cypress Avenue at the Ville D'Este, Cernobbio, c.1906

watercolour and bodycolour on paper, 37.6 × 26.2 cm

P.793
PROVENANCE: Sydney Kitson; Elisabeth and Alice Barbara Kitson; given to the Gallery by Alice Barbara Kitson, October 1992.

Born in Nottingham, Gascoyne was an Owen Jones student at R.I.B.A, where he was awarded a travel scholarship in 1906. Gascoyne joined Sydney Kitson's (1871–1937) architectural practice in 1912 producing architectural perspective drawings. He soon became a close friend of the family (Kitson's daughters referred to him as 'Uncle Gaslight') but had not been made a partner by the outbreak of the war in 1914 when he volunteered and was commissioned as a Captain in the Sherwood Foresters. He was stationed on the Western Front, where he was injured and captured. In 1917 he was imprisoned in Germany, where he died, aged twenty-six.

CB

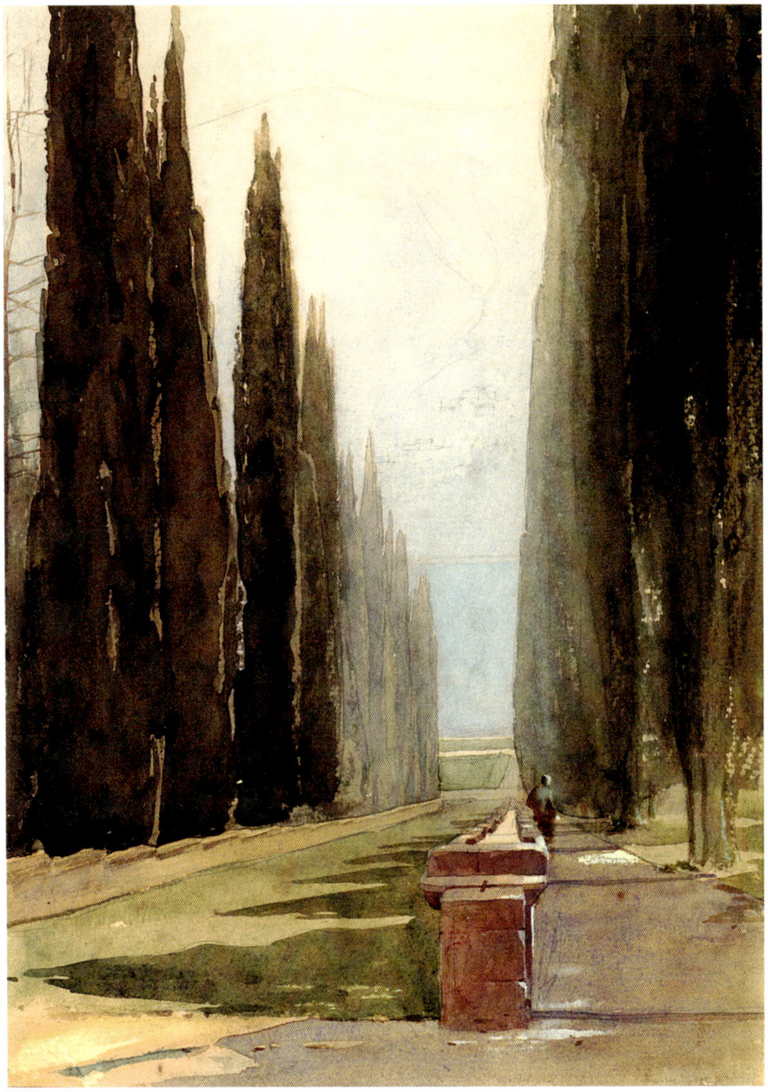

Charles GASCOYNE
[1891–1917]
A Dutch Church Interior, c.1906

watercolour and pencil on paper, 46 × 33 cm

P.796
PROVENANCE: Sydney Kitson; Elisabeth and Alice Barbara Kitson, given by Alice Barbara Kitson to Gallery, October 1992.

Probably painted on a travel scholarship to the Netherlands in 1906.

Gascoyne often painted rather sombre watercolours of buildings designed by Kitson's architectural practice. His premature death meant he did not have an opportunity to fulfill the early promise represented by this accomplished architectural watercolour.

CB

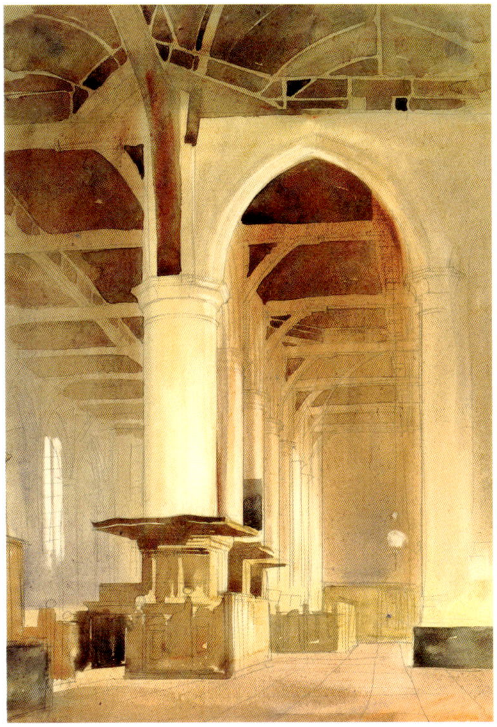

Charles GASCOYNE
[1891–1917]
Country Lane at Sunset, 1910–14

watercolour and bodycolour on paper, 27.1 × 38 cm

P.794
PROVENANCE: Sydney Kitson; Elisabeth and Alice Barbara Kitson, given by Alice Barbara Kitson to Gallery, October 1992.

The scene has not been identified, but it may well have been painted on one of Gascoyne's many painting holidays with the Kitson family.

CB

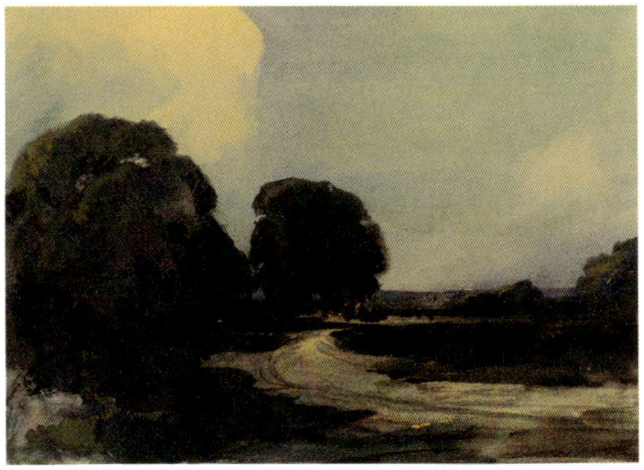

Charles GASCOYNE
[1891–1917]
Portrait of Sydney Kitson, 1913
pencil, bodycolour and ink on paper, 34.6 × 25 cm

P.925
PROVENANCE: Sydney Kitson; Elisabeth and Alice Barbara Kitson, bequeathed by Alice Barbara Kitson, May 1999.
EXHIBITIONS: *Cotmania & Mr Kitson*, Leeds, Leeds City Art Galleries, 1992, no cat. no.
REFERENCES: D. Boswell & C. Miller, *Cotmania & Mr Kitson*, 1992, p.3

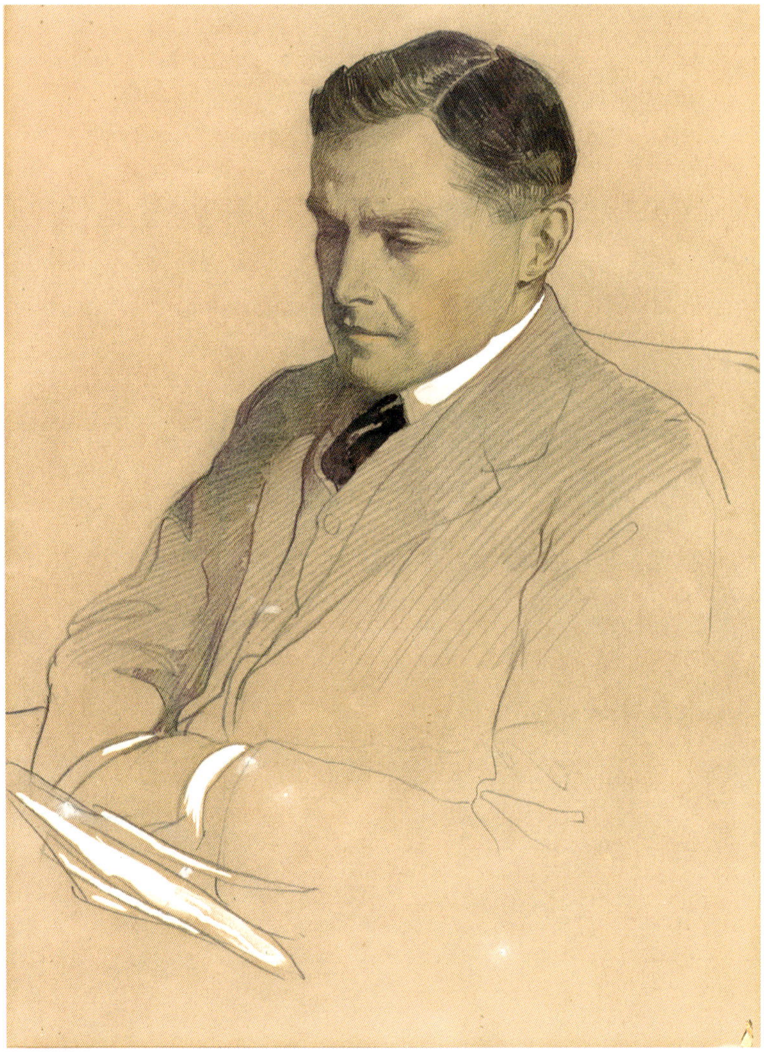

Sydney Kitson (1871–1937) was born at Roundhay, Leeds. After Charterhouse and Trinity College, Cambridge, he trained as an architect, joining Francis Bedford as a partner in 1897. Together they designed houses and public buildings, many of which still survive, in and around Leeds. After Bedford's death in 1904 Sydney took on James Parish as his partner and the practice flourished.

Meanwhile Sydney and his nephew Robert Kitson (1873–1947), a painter, had become founding members of the Leeds Art Collections Fund. Robert recommended that its resources should forthwith be switched from oil paintings to English watercolours.

During the 1914–18 war Sydney joined the Yorkshire Hussars but remained mainly in England. However, a young member of his firm, Charles GASCOYNE, was killed in 1917 aged twenty-six. An amateur watercolourist, a number of his landscapes, together with this portrait, were later given to the Gallery by Sydney's daughter, Barbara.

In 1922 an exhibition of COTMAN's work at the Tate Gallery led to the acquisition of three works by Leeds. Suffering from tuberculosis, Sydney suffered a number of haemorrhages causing him to reduce his architectural commitments. While convalescing in 1923 he was given a copy of Paul Oppé's *Studio* volume on Cotman, which led to what his daughters termed their father's *Cotmania*. This sustained him for the rest of his life, culminating in his definitive life of the artist and his work (and remains so sixty-four years later), published shortly before his death in 1937.

Prior to this, the dispersal of part of the Bulwer Collection of Cotmans at Walker's Gallery in 1926, gave Sydney and Robert the opportunity to buy some of Cotman's paintings.

Thanks to the generosity of Elisabeth and Alice Barbara Kitson, Sydney's daughters, eleven of his Cotmans were given to the Cecil Higgins Art Gallery in 1972, while a twelfth, *Windmills on the Coast*, was bequeathed by Alice Barbara in 1992.

EJ

Charles GASCOYNE
[1891–1917]
Harlech Castle, c.1913
watercolour, bodycolour and pencil on paper, 30.9 × 45.4 cm

P. 795
PROVENANCE: Sydney Kitson; Elisabeth and Alice Barbara Kitson; given to Gallery by Alice Barbara Kitson, October 1992.

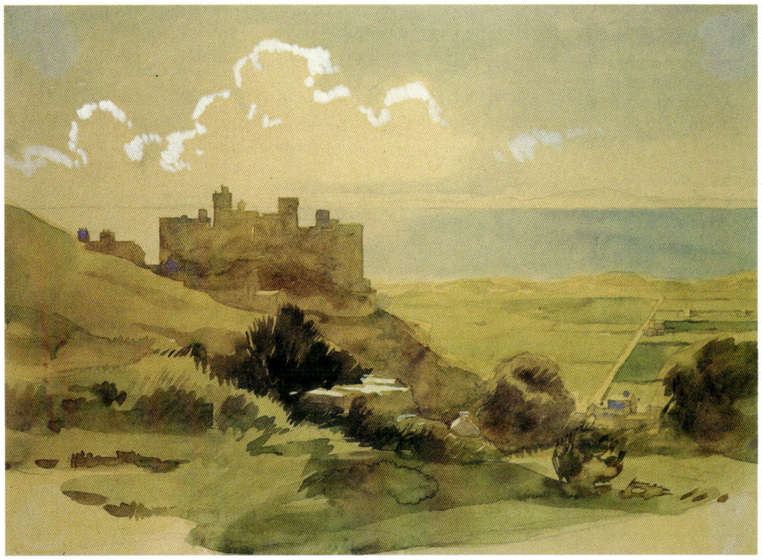

Painted while on holiday with the Kitson family, when staying at Llys Bach, Harlech, in a cottage designed by Sydney for his sister. Gascoyne would often use the cottage as a base to tour around Wales in the footsteps of Cotman, no doubt encouraged by Sydney Kitson (1871–1937).

CB

Henri GAUDIER-BRZESKA
[1891–1915]
Mrs. Alfred Wolmark, 1912

pencil on paper, 34.5 × 24.4 cm
inscribed: *Mrs Wolmark, Brzeska drawing 1912*

P.178
PROVENANCE: Wolmark Collection; Lord's Art Gallery, from whom purchased by Gallery, December 1957.
EXHIBITIONS: *Portrait Paintings and Drawings*, Rye, Rye Art Gallery, 1967; *The English Tradition: an exhibition of watercolours from two private collections*, Bedford, Cecil Higgins Art Gallery, 1972, no.39.
REFERENCES: R. Cole, *Gaudier-Brzeska: Artist and Myth*, 1995, p.65.

The sitter was the wife of Alfred Wolmark (1877–1961), a painter, designer of pottery and stained glass who was a friend of the artist. He encouraged the young artist and often sat for him. Gaudier-Brzeska returned the compliment.

This simplified, linear drawing is typical of Gaudier-Brzeska's style. It dates from the same year as a painting of Mrs Wolmark exhibited at the Leicester Galleries in 1958.

EJ/CB

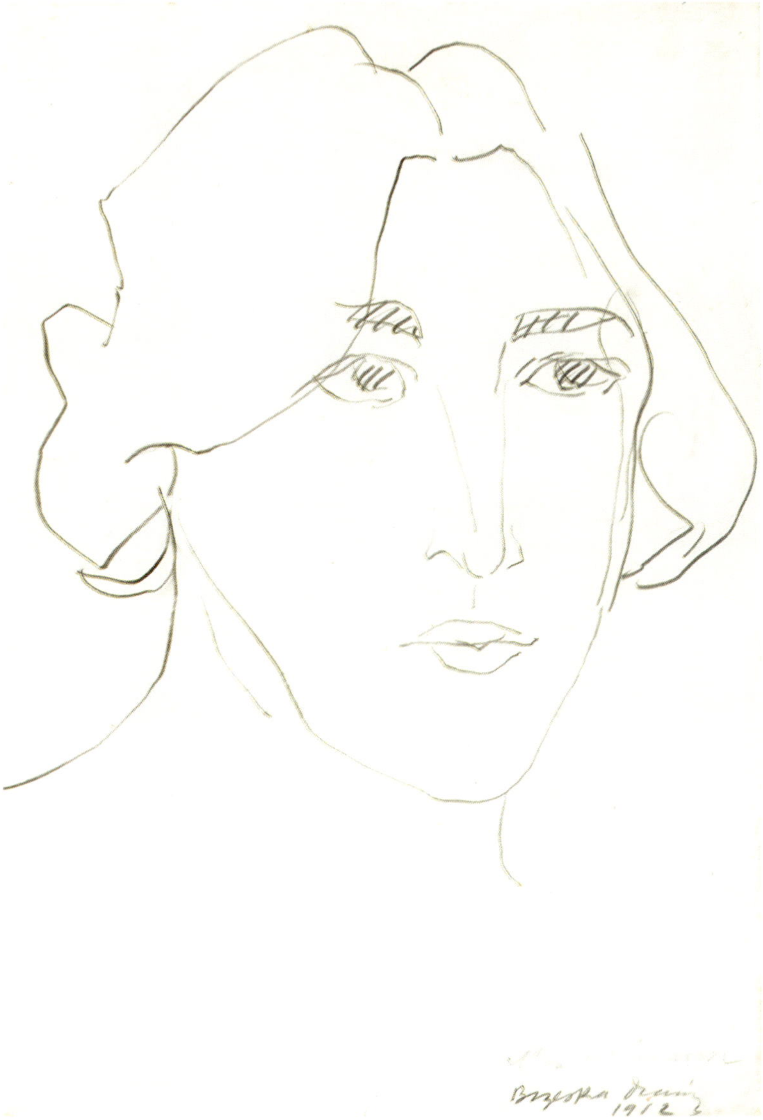

Henri GAUDIER-BRZESKA
[1891–1915]
Stag at Arundel, 1913

pen and ink on brown paper, 21.2 × 34 cm
inscribed: *to Mrs Kibblewhite H Gaudierbrzeska*

P.280
PROVENANCE: Francis Brett Young; Lord's Gallery, from whom purchased by Gallery, January 1959.
EXHIBITIONS: *Watercolours and Drawings from The Cecil Higgins Art Gallery, Bedford*, London, Thos. Agnew & Sons Ltd, 1962, no.65.
REFERENCES: H.S. Ede, *A Life of Gaudier-Brzeska*, 1930, pl .xxxv; H.S. Ede, *Savage Messiah*, 1931, pp.146–7; R. Cole, *Gaudier-Brzeska: Artist and Myth*, 1995, p.75.

The artist and Sophie Brzeska visited Arundel Park for a day in September 1913. Ede made a direct reference to the day: 'It was one of the happiest days they had ever had…they walked on the hillside…one big stag was calling deeply…he looked magnificent with his great antlers sweeping the air' (*Savage Messiah*, p.146).

Mrs Kibblewhite is not otherwise recorded but Henri freely gave away drawings to anyone who admired them.

Henri was born in France, later spending two years, 1907–9, in England studying business methods. He eventually left France for England in 1911 with Sophie Brzeska, a Polish woman twenty years his senior whom he had met in a library and whose name he adopted. He worked in London in the circle of EPSTEIN and the future Vorticists. Without formal training he made some innovative carvings inspired by primitive art as well as more conventional figurative and animal subjects.

He joined the French Army and was killed in the trenches in June 1915. His achievement has been overshadowed by his colourful life, as featured in Ken Russell's film *Savage Messiah*.

EJ/CB

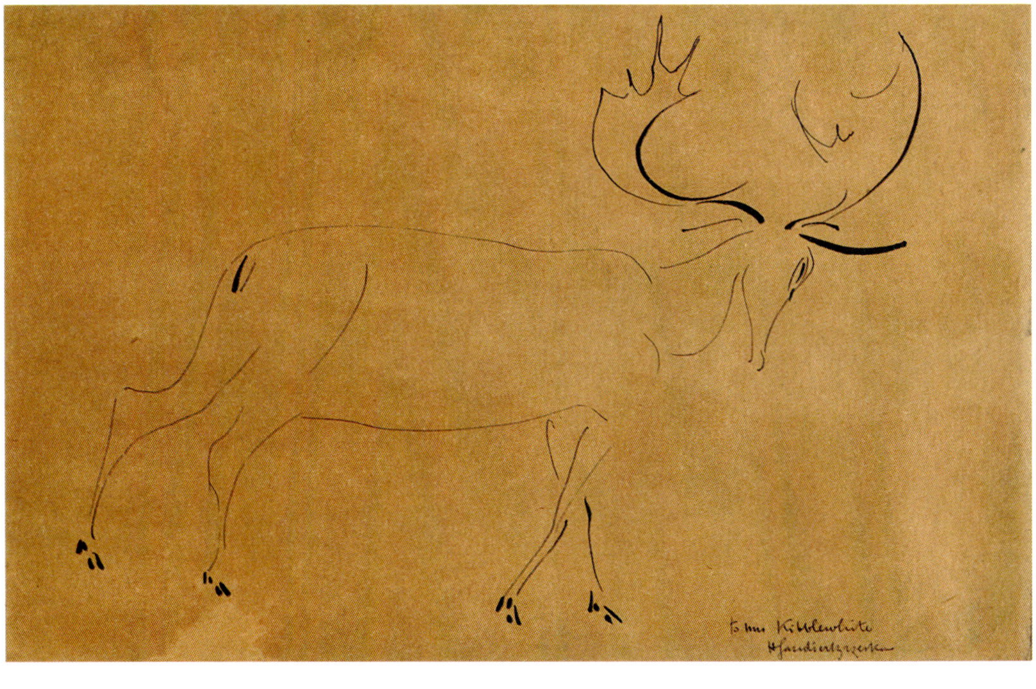

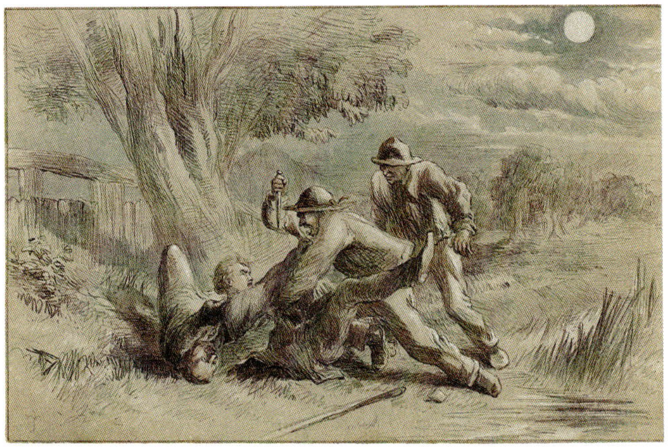

Sir John GILBERT, R.A.

[1817–97]

Three Assassins attacking a Young Man by Moonlight, c.1857

pencil and watercolour on grey paper, 12 × 18.2 cm
inscribed: copy of Millais's monogram

P.407
PROVENANCE: P&D Colnaghi Ltd, from whom purchased by Gallery as a Millais, January 1962.
REFERENCES: Illustration to 'Harding the Money-spinner', *The London Journal*, 21–8 March 1857, no.631, vol.xxv.

This drawing was reproduced in *The London Journal*, 21–28 March 1857 illustrating an episode of *Harding the Money-spinner*, a story by Miles Gerald Keon which was serialised in that periodical.

The Gallery's four drawings by Gilbert were previously thought to be by Sir John MILLAIS (1829–95). The monogram is neither that of Millais nor of Gilbert.

Original illustrations by Gilbert are by no means common as most of them were drawn on woodblocks (no one drew more of these) and lost after they were engraved. Gilbert's work appeared in the first number of *The Illustrated London News* in 1823. He remained a regular contributor until late in life, by which time he had contributed the staggering total of 30,000 illustrations to the paper. His work was very highly prized by the Victorians, who considered him the equal of Gustave Doré (1832–83).

EJ

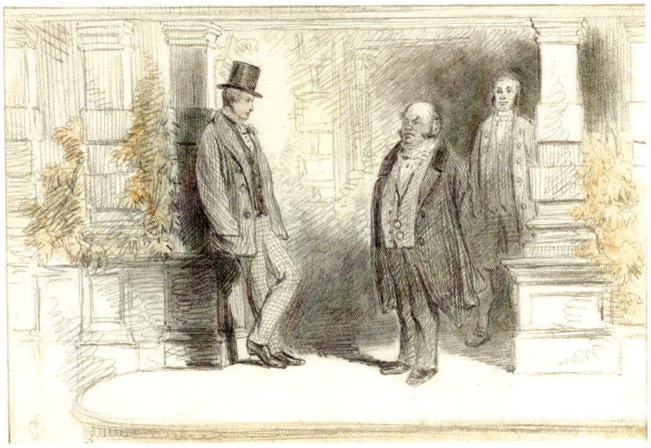

Sir John GILBERT, R.A.

[1817–97]

Scene in a Portico: young man and portly gentleman, 1860s

pencil and watercolour on paper, 12.9 × 19.3 cm
inscribed: copy of Millais's monogram

P.410
PROVENANCE: P&D Colnaghi Ltd, from whom purchased by Gallery, January 1962.

Again the story illustrated here has yet to be traced. The third figure in the background appears to be wearing some kind of livery and is thus presumably a servant.

EJ

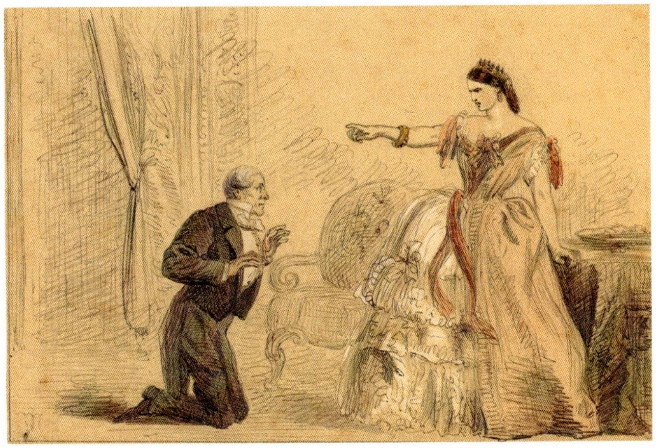

Sir John GILBERT, R.A.

[1817–97]

Angry Lady with kneeling Gentleman, 1860s

pencil and watercolour on paper, 12.1 × 18.4 cm
inscribed: copy of Millais's monogram

P.408
PROVENANCE: P&D Colnaghi Ltd, from whom purchased by Gallery, January 1962.

The story for this illustration has not been traced. Gilbert was born and lived all his life in Blackheath, London. The son of an estate agent, he initially followed in his father's footsteps. In 1836 he abandoned estate agency to study painting with George Lance.

CB

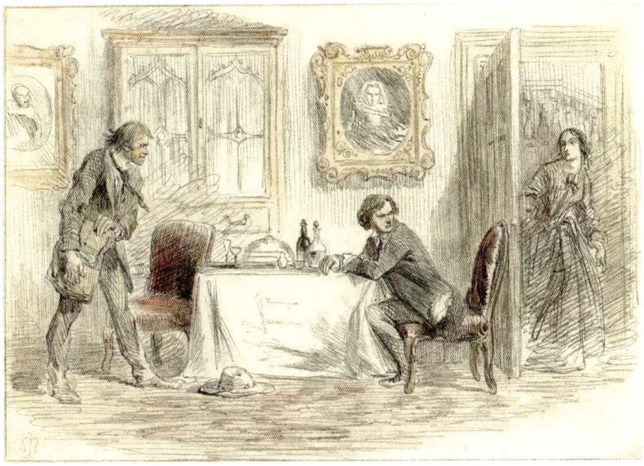

Sir John GILBERT, R.A.

[1817–97]

Woman interrupting threatening interview between a Gentleman and a Ruffian

pencil and watercolour on paper, 13.6 × 19.3 cm
inscribed: copy of Millais's monogram
on reverse: pencil sketch of figure

P.409
PROVENANCE: P&D Colnaghi Ltd, from whom purchased by Gallery, January 1962.

As the story illustrated here has not yet been traced, it is not known if the ruffian is demanding money or has incriminating evidence of some kind in his satchel.

EJ

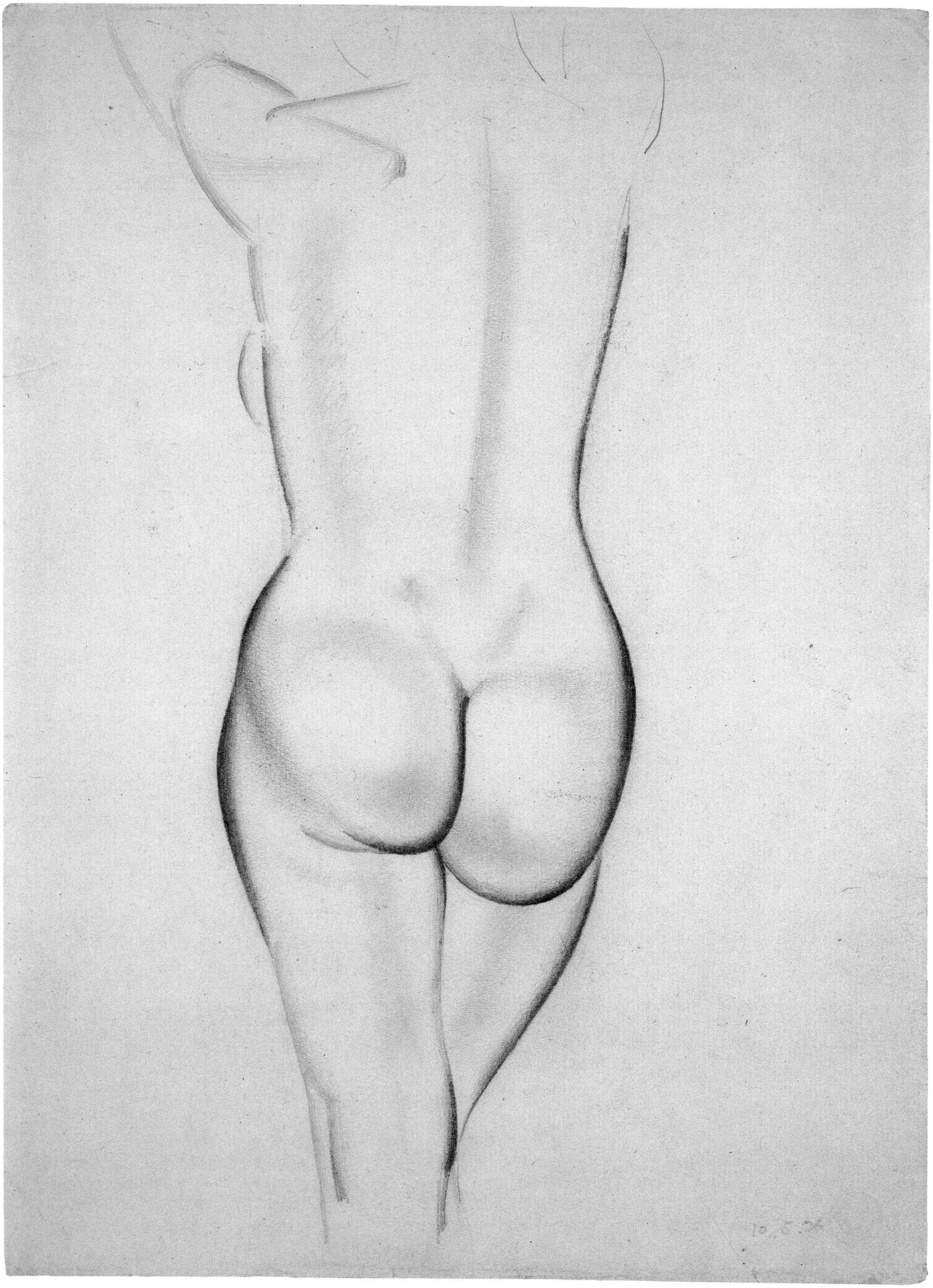

Eric GILL, A.R.A.

[1882–1940]

Nude, 1926

pencil on paper, 29.5 × 22 cm
inscribed: *10.5.26*

P.243
PROVENANCE: Leicester Galleries, from whom purchased by Gallery, July 1958.
REFERENCES: E. Gill & Sir. J. Rothenstein (introd.), *First Nudes by Eric Gill*, 1954, first plate.

One of a number from a portfolio of pencil drawings. This drawing was used for the first plate of *First Nudes* by Eric Gill, which was published in 1954. The sketch book contained the first life-drawings done by Gill, which he began in Paris in May 1926. He preferred to use non-professional models stating: 'what is wrong with your friends and relations'. Of his work with life models Gill said 'It is what is in your head that matters most and not what the model has in his or her body'.

A stone carver, wood and line engraver, designer of alphabets and writer, Gill studied letter-design under Edward Johnston (1872–1944) and began figure sculpture in 1910. He became a Roman Catholic in 1913 and moved to Wales in 1924 where he did much of his best work for the Golden Cockerel Press. A controversial figure due to his sexual improprieties, he is nonetheless regarded as one of the greatest craftsmen of the 20th Century.

Gill's principal public works include *Stations of the Cross* for Westminster Cathedral and *Prospero and Ariel* for Broadcasting House.

EJ/CB

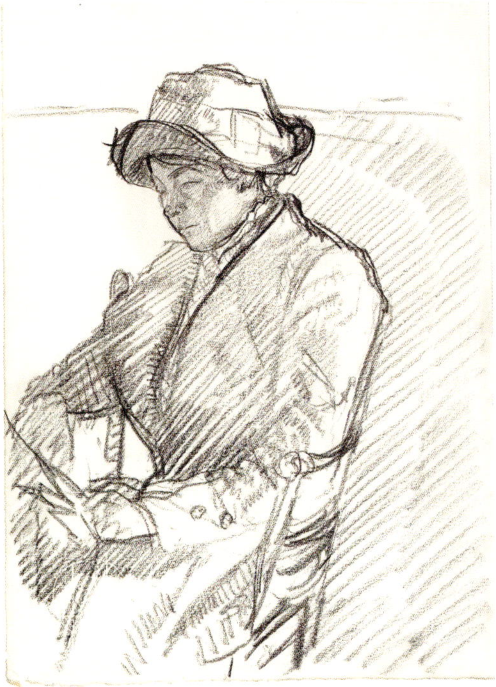

Harold GILMAN

[1876–1919]

A Seated Woman, c.1914

chalk on paper, 34.9 × 26.2 cm

P.279
PROVENANCE: Arthur Crossland of Heaton Manor, Bradford, Yorkshire; his sale Christie's 3 February 1956, lot 48; Thos. Agnew & Sons Ltd, from whom purchased by Gallery, January 1959.
EXHIBITIONS: *The Arthur Crossland Collection*, Newcastle upon Tyne, Laing Art Gallery, 1939, no.71; *The Camden Town Group*, Bedford, Cecil Higgins Art Gallery, 1969, no.14.
REFERENCES: A. Causey & R. Thomson, *Harold Gilman*, 1981, exhib. cat., pp. 67 & 71.

This drawing relates to the oil *Girl with a Teacup*, painted in 1914, now in a private collection.

The sitter seems to be unaware that she is being drawn; the result is an informal but at the same time penetrating study. Gilman, Spencer GORE and SICKERT were the leading members of the Camden Town Group, founded in 1911, which introduced French Post-Impressionism into England.

EJ/CB

Harold GILMAN

[1876–1919]

House at Halifax, Nova Scotia, 1918

pen and ink on paper, 41.8 × 54 cm
inscribed: *H. Gilman*

P.172
PROVENANCE: Mrs Sylvia Gilman, the artist's widow; Lefevre Gallery, from whom purchased by Gallery, January 1958.
EXHIBITIONS: *Camden Town Group Exhibition*, Southampton, Southampton Art Gallery, 1951, no.40; *Harold Gilman*, London, Tate Gallery, 1954, no.59, pl.6; Arts Council, *Drawings of the Camden Town Group*, 1961, no.31; *Watercolours and Drawings from The Cecil Higgins Art Gallery, Bedford*, London, Thos. Agnew & Sons Ltd, 1962, no.69, illus. pl.vii; *Watercolours from Bedford*, Norwich, Castle Museum, 1965, no.14; *Harold Gilman, An English Post-Impressionist*, Colchester, The Minories, Oxford, Ashmolean Museum, and Sheffield, Graves Art Gallery, 1969, no.60; *The Camden Town Group*, Bedford, Cecil Higgins Art Gallery, 1969, no.13.
REFERENCES: A. Causey & R. Thomson, *Harold Gilman*, 1981, exhib. cat., p.90.

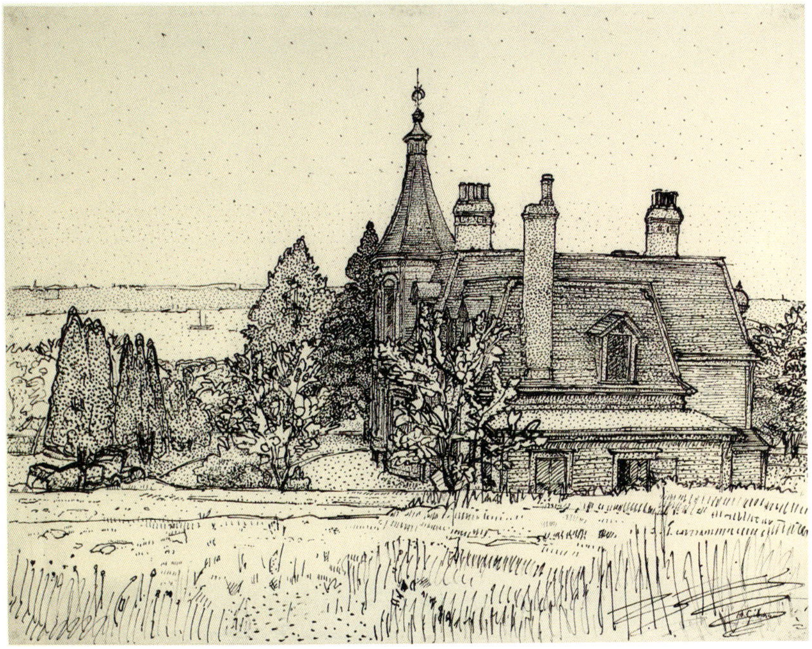

Drawn in 1918 on the artist's visit to Canada, where he was commissioned to paint Halifax Harbour for Canadian War Records. It is a fine example of Gilman's use of a pointillist technique to indicate the house and surrounding trees.

Born in Somerset, Gilman studied painting at the Hastings Art School, later transferring to the Slade, where he met Spencer GORE. In 1906 he became a member of the Fitzroy group which included SICKERT, Gore, and GINNER; in 1911 he was a founding member of the Camden Town Group. Gilman died in the Spanish 'flu epidemic of 1919. Afterwards Wyndham LEWIS wrote: ' I consider his death a flat contradiction to every feeling that one had about his destiny'.

EJ/CB

Sawrey GILPIN, R.A.
[1733–1807]
A Lion with Cubs in a Cave

pen and ink, with washes of grey and brown over black lead on paper, 31.6 × 26.6 cm
inscribed: *S.Gilpin*

P.301
PROVENANCE: E. Williams; P&D Colnaghi Ltd, from whom purchased by Gallery, October 1959.

Gilpin's drawings are usually in pencil or pen (sometimes both) but less commonly, as here, in wash or watercolour. He was an animal painter, pupil of Samuel Scott (?1702–72), who often collaborated with George Barret I R.A. (1728 or 1732–84) by introducing animals into Barret's landscapes. He also did this on one occasion when Turner exhibited at the R.A. in 1811: *Windsor Park, with horses by the late Sawrey Gilpin, Esq., R.A.*

He was the brother of William Gilpin (1724–1804), a leading figure in the Picturesque movement, and the father of William Sawrey Gilpin (1762–1843), the first president of the Old Water-Colour Society which was founded in 1804.

EJ

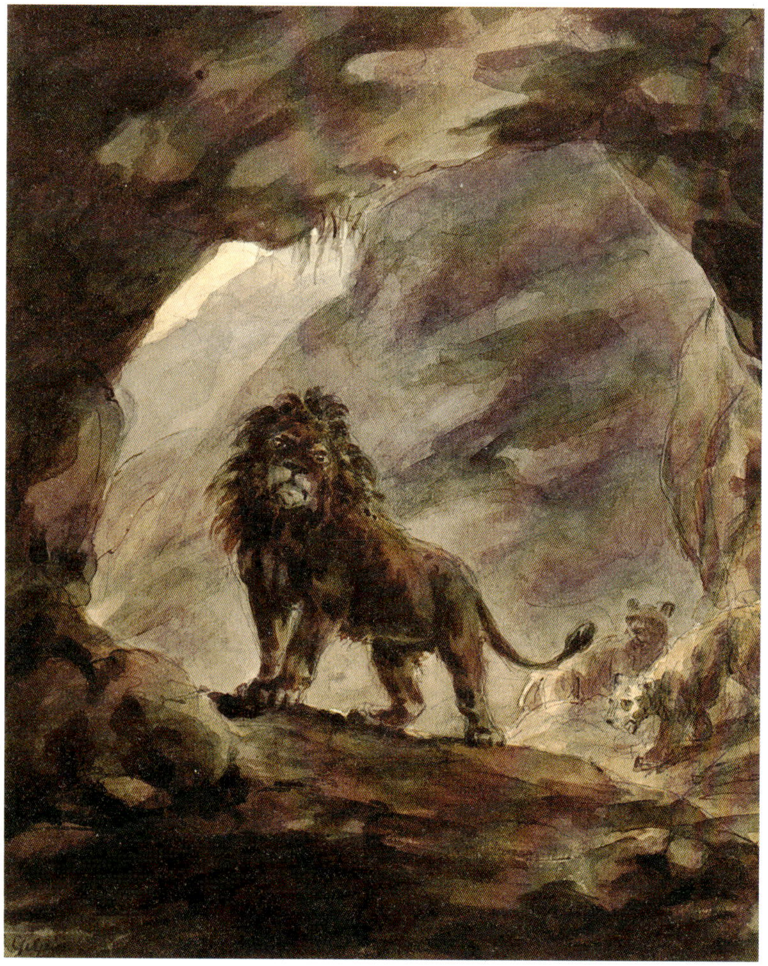

Charles GINNER, C.B.E., A.R.A., R.W.S.
[1878–1952]
A London Back-garden, early 1920s

watercolour and pen and ink on paper, 40.6 × 25.1cm
inscribed: *C.GINNER*

P.191
PROVENANCE: Leicester Galleries, from whom purchased by Gallery, April 1958.
EXHIBITIONS: *Watercolours from Bedford*, Norwich, Castle Museum, 1965, no.15; *The Camden Town Group*, Bedford, Cecil Higgins Art Gallery, 1969, no.17.
REFERENCES: R. Phillips, *Painter's Progress*, 1983, p.120.

Ginner was born in France and worked in an architect's office in Paris until 1904 when he overcame parental opposition to study art at the École des Beaux Arts. In 1908 he was encouraged by SICKERT to settle in England joining the Fitzroy Group in 1910 and the Camden Town Group in 1911 as a founder member. Van Gogh was the most powerful influence on his work throughout his life. He was also a close friend of Harold GILMAN, with whom he shared an exhibition at the Goupil Gallery in 1914.

His oil painting technique is easily recognizable: small touches of thick paint which fill the whole surface of the canvas and, at a distance, resemble tapestry. He was an Official War Artist in 1914–18, joined the N.E.A.C. in 1920 and was elected A.R.A. in 1942. His penchant for tackling unfashionable architectural subjects like the Albert Memorial (Southampton Art Gallery), earned him the epithet of 'a Betjeman of the brush'.

EJ

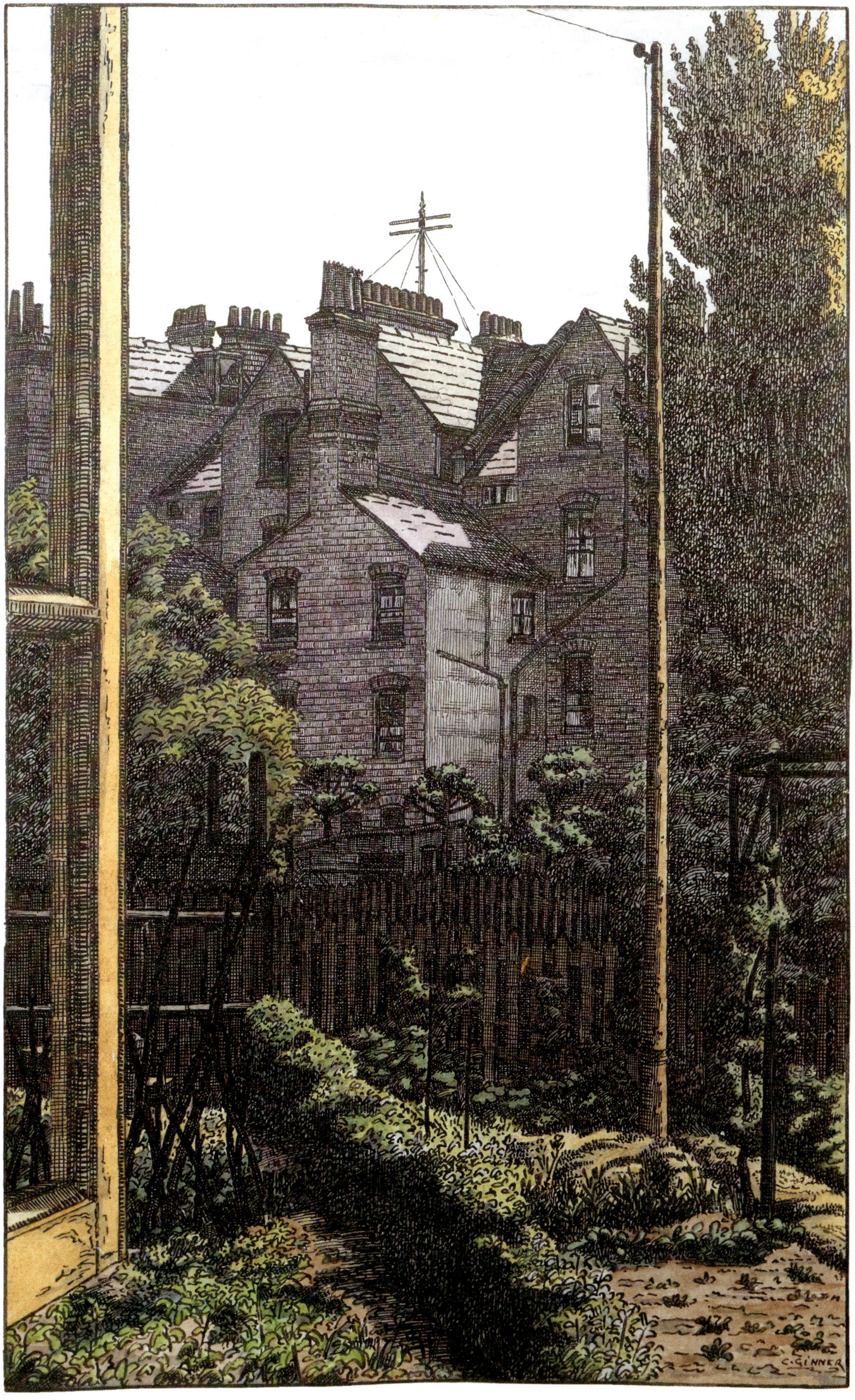
C. GINNER

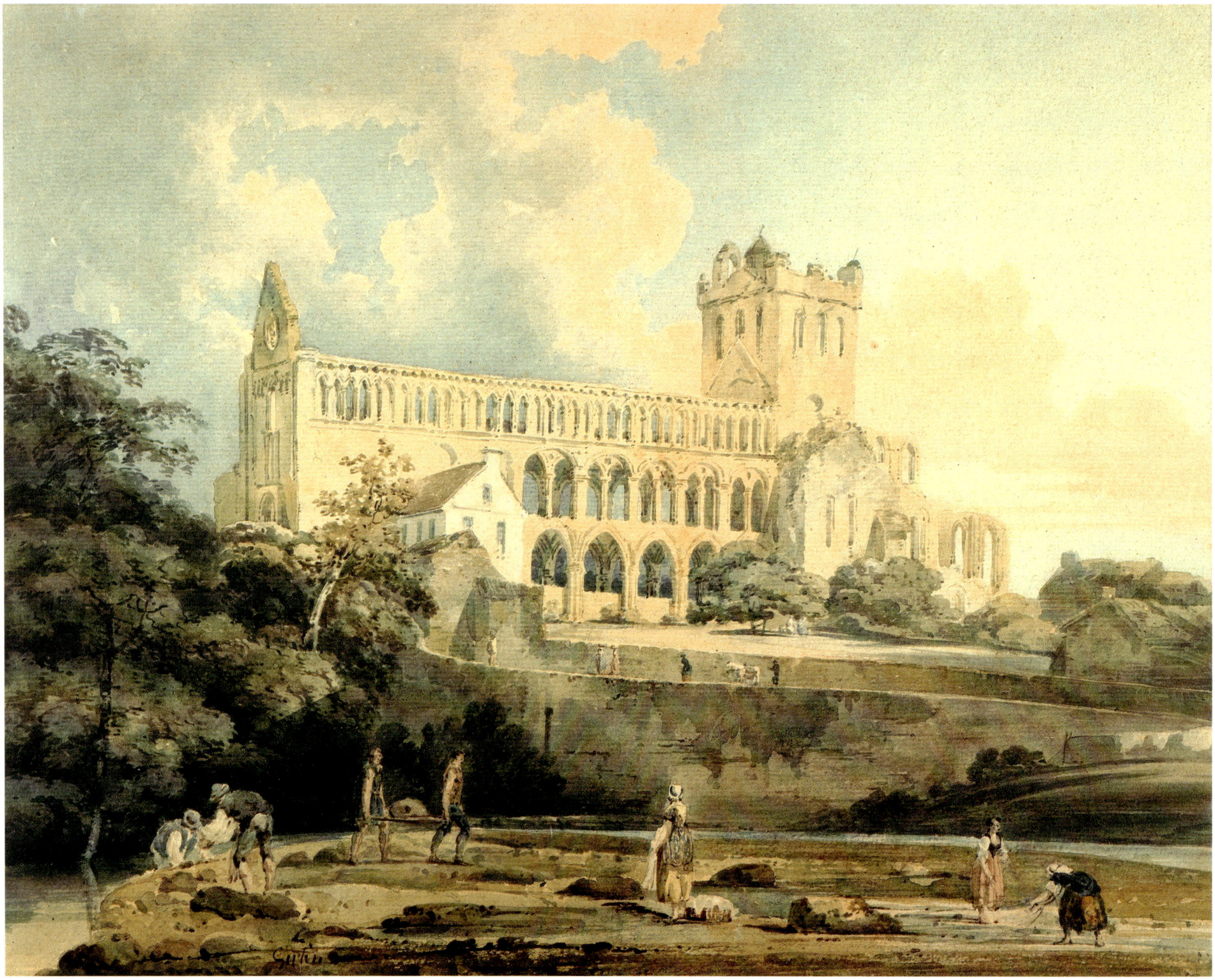

Thomas GIRTIN
[1775–1802]
Jedburgh Abbey from the river, c.1798–9

watercolour on paper, 41.9 × 54.6 cm
inscribed: *Girtin*

P.72
PROVENANCE: Bluett and Rayer families, Holcombe Court, Devon, then by descent; Major Rayer; Rev. G.W. Jenkins; 'Auction in country'; Sir George Davies; Thos. Agnew & Sons Ltd, from whom purchased by Gallery, February 1952.
EXHIBITIONS: *79th Annual Watercolour Exhibition*, London, Thos. Agnew & Sons Ltd, 1952, no.53; *English watercolours from the Hickman Bacon and other collections*, Bedford, Cecil Higgins Art Gallery, 1952, no.46; *Loan Exhibition of Watercolours by Thomas Girtin*, London, Thos. Agnew & Sons Ltd, 1953, no.55; *Watercolours and Drawings from The Cecil Higgins Art Gallery, Bedford*, London, Thos. Agnew & Sons Ltd., 1962, no.59; *English Watercolours from The Cecil Higgins Art Gallery Bedford*, Reading, Reading Museum and Art Gallery, 1965, no.19; *Wordsworth Bicentenary Exhibition*, Kendal, Abbot Hall Art Gallery and Southampton, Southampton Art Gallery, 1970, no.48; *Watercolours by Thomas Girtin*, Manchester, Whitworth Art Gallery and London, V&A, 1975, no.47.
REFERENCES: T. Girtin and D. Loshak, *The Art of Thomas Girtin*, 1954, p.173, no.286; A. Bury, 'The Cecil Higgins Museum, Bedford: A Preliminary Survey', *Old Water-colour Society's Club Volume*, 1961, pl.xiii; F. Hawcroft, *Watercolours by Thomas Girtin*, p.42, no.47.

Girtin painted the village and abbey of Jedburgh in Roxburghshire over a number of years. The earliest view of the abbey was taken from a drawing by James Moore in 1793 and later engraved in the *Copper Plate Magazine*, pl.cxlii, published in 1797. A sketch of the village dated 11 October 1796 is the only precisely dated study by Girtin. The National Gallery of Scotland now owns the finest view of the village, dated 1800 (G & L no.355), while other watercolours of the abbey are in the British Museum (1796–7) and the National Gallery of Ireland (1798, G & L nos. 187, 253).

An exact contemporary of TURNER, Girtin was born in Southwark, the son of a brushmaker. In 1789 he was apprenticed to Edward DAYES, a topographical watercolourist. His friendship with Turner began at a young age, and they would study at Dr MONRO's 'Academy' where according to Joseph Farrington R.A. (1747–1821) 'Girtin drew in outlines and Turner washed in the effects'. In 1796, free from his apprenticeship, Girtin began his tour of Yorkshire, Northumberland and the Scottish borders. He died prematurely young at twenty-seven, causing Turner to utter his famous observation: 'If poor Tom Girtin had lived, I should have starved'.

EJ/CB

Thomas GIRTIN
[1775–1802]
The Palace of the Louvre, 1801–2

watercolour on paper, 37.4 × 31 cm

P.273
PROVENANCE: Sotheby's 12 December 1958, lot 43b, purchased by Gallery, December 1958.
EXHIBITIONS: *Primitives to Picasso*, London, R.A., 1962, no.376; *Watercolours and Drawings from The Cecil Higgins Art Gallery, Bedford*, London, Thos. Agnew & Sons Ltd, 1962, no.18; *English Watercolours from The Cecil Higgins Art Gallery, Bedford*, Reading, Reading Museum and Art Gallery, 1965, no.20; *Watercolours from Bedford*, Norwich, Castle Museum, no.16, as *The Palace of Louvre with workmen by a ruined house in the foreground.*

Also known in the past as The Pavilion de Maison at the Tuilleries and as View of the Tuileries with workman by a ruined house in the foreground.

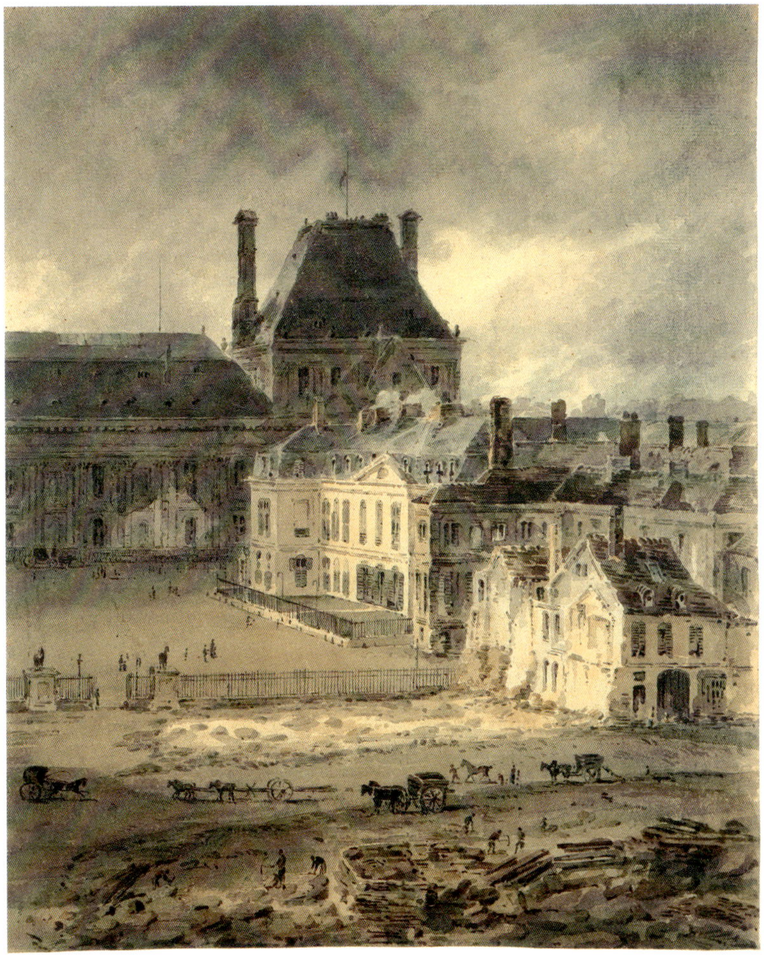

This drawing seems to have been unknown before its appearance at Sotheby's, which was after Girtin's and Loshak's catalogue of Girtin's work was published in 1954. An almost identical watercolour was sold at Spink's in 1982, dated 1801. On the reverse of Spink's picture is the inscription, in Girtin's hand: *Part of the Tuilleries the Palace where Buonaparte resides the house of Lucien Buonaparte and the ruins of the house blown up by the infernal machine.*

Girtin visited Paris in 1801, following the armistice with France, leaving his eight months' pregnant wife in Islington (though he was spotted in London two days after his supposed departure, saying his farewells to his mistress). While there he produced his *Twenty Views* of the city and its environs, soft-ground etchings which rank amongst his finest works. These were published posthumously in 1803. Girtin was forced to sketch from a hackney carriage, in case of arrest as an English spy. The playwright Thomas Holcroft (1745–1809) met him in Paris and remarked: 'His facility was great, and I was surprised at the dispatch with which he made his drawings'.

EJ/CB

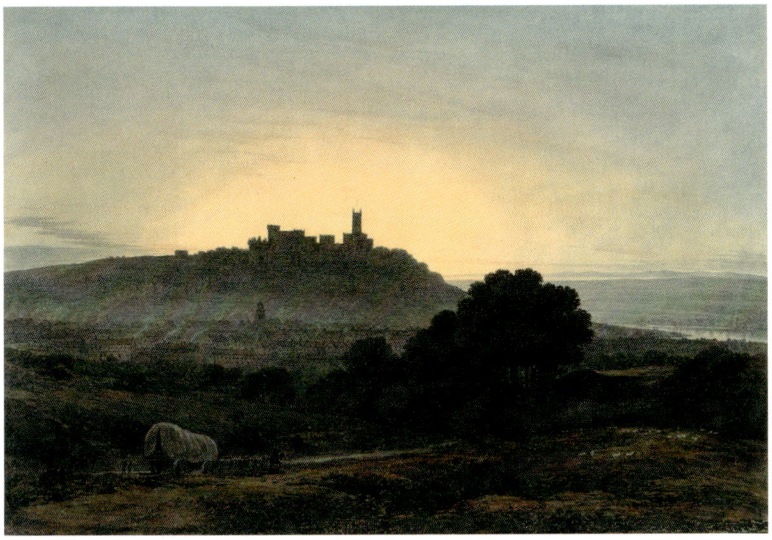

John GLOVER
[1767–1849]
Lancaster, 1820s

watercolour with gum arabic on paper, 27.2 × 41.2 cm

P.365
PROVENANCE: Miss S Lockerhampson; P&D Colnaghi Ltd, from whom purchased by Gallery, October 1960.
EXHIBITIONS: *Watercolours and Drawings from The Cecil Higgins Art Gallery, Bedford*, London, Thos. Agnew & Sons Ltd, 1962, no.30; *English Watercolours from The Cecil Higgins Art Gallery, Bedford*, Reading, Reading Museum and Art Gallery, 1965, no.21.

Glover, who had lessons with William Payne (fl. c.1776–1830) and one from 'Warwick' SMITH, set up as a drawing master in Lichfield in 1794. He remained there until 1805 when he moved to London encouraged by the success of the Water-Colour Society's first exhibition. He then travelled widely both in Britain and on the Continent.

His watercolours, which are seldom signed, contain distinctly painted foliage. He used a 'split brush' with twisted hairs in two or more small points, which enabled him to produce the parallel touches, which are his hallmark.

Glover, sometimes, but misleadingly, known as 'the English Claude', has chosen to show Lancaster at its most commanding in this exceptional example. He knew the town well, often passing through it on his way to and from the Lake District, his preferred sketching ground, Ullswater, being a particular favourite. He owned a farm near there in the 1820s before emigrating to Australia in 1831 and then settling in Tasmania the following year.

EJ

Albert GOODWIN, R.W.S.
[1845–1932]
On the South Downs, 1879

watercolour, bodycolour, ink and scratching out on paper, 33.8 × 50.5 cm
inscribed: *A. Goodwin 79*

P.543
PROVENANCE: Maas Gallery, from whom purchased by Gallery, November 1966.
EXHIBITIONS: *Early English watercolours*, London, Maas Gallery, 1966, no.52.

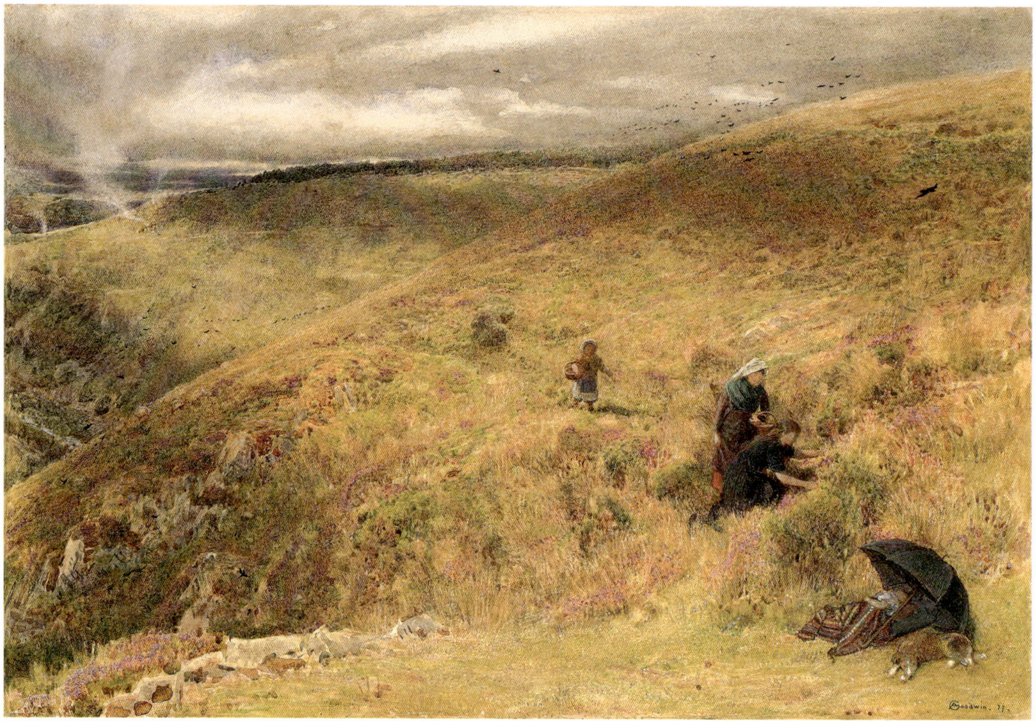

Martin HARDIE says that Goodwin 'never found the medium of watercolour tractable or submissive; he was always building, unbuilding and rebuilding'. Here, however, he has successfully captured the impression of a wide expanse of landscape; the sense of recession being achieved by means of the diagonal of the brow of the hill stretching from lower left to top right, and also by the subtle gradation of tone and colour between foreground and horizon.

EJ

Albert GOODWIN, R.W.S.
[1845–1932]
Eton, 1907

watercolour and bodycolour on paper, 25.4 × 37.6 cm
inscribed: *Eton Albert Goodwin*

P.306
PROVENANCE: Christie's; P&D Colnaghi Ltd, from whom purchased by Gallery, October 1959.

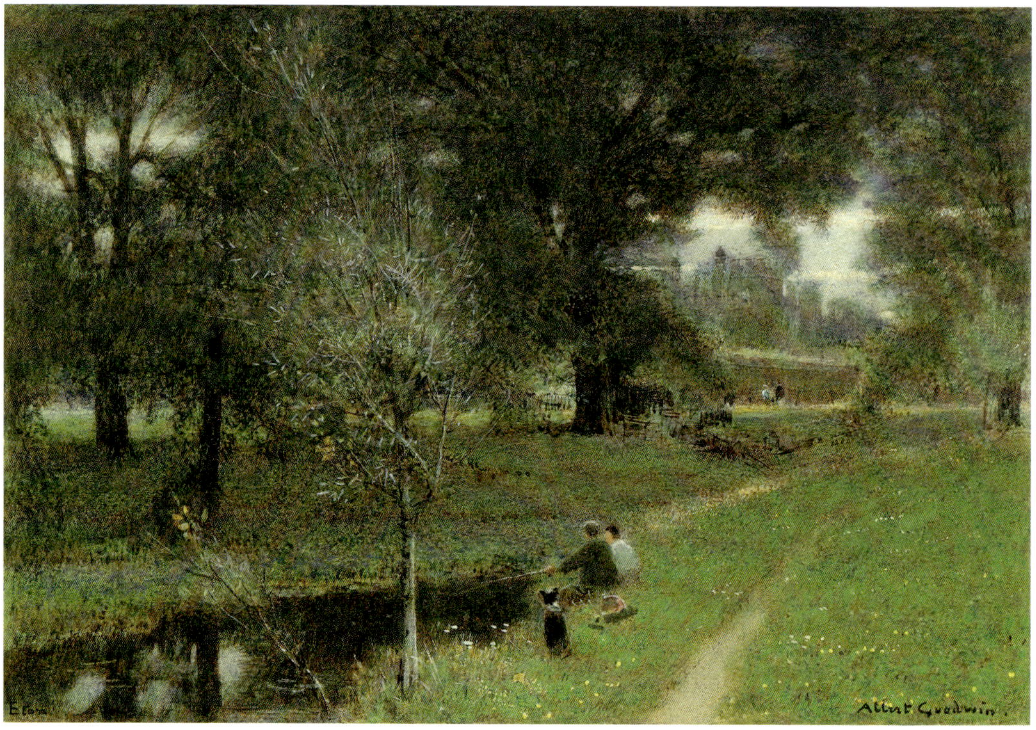

Almost certainly painted in 1907 when Goodwin is known to have worked at Eton. The view, which reveals some artistic licence, is best described as 'Eton College buildings from the Playing Fields'; it includes the pinnacles at the east end of College Chapel and the north-east corner tower of the Cloisters where the Headmaster lives.

An ardent admirer of TURNER, Goodwin also first exhibited at the R.A. as a boy of fifteen. He was taught by Arthur HUGHES and Ford Madox BROWN, and was supported by John RUSKIN with whom he toured Italy in 1872. Although he began in oils, later his work was almost entirely confined to watercolours and especially so after he was elected R.W.S. in 1881.

Sometimes unduly laboured, he is nonetheless adept at conveying the effects of misty dawn as well as those of twilight and sunset. He was one of the first artists to use a pen-line in combination with watercolour washes, employing this effectively and unobtrusively. He was extremely prolific.

EJ/CB

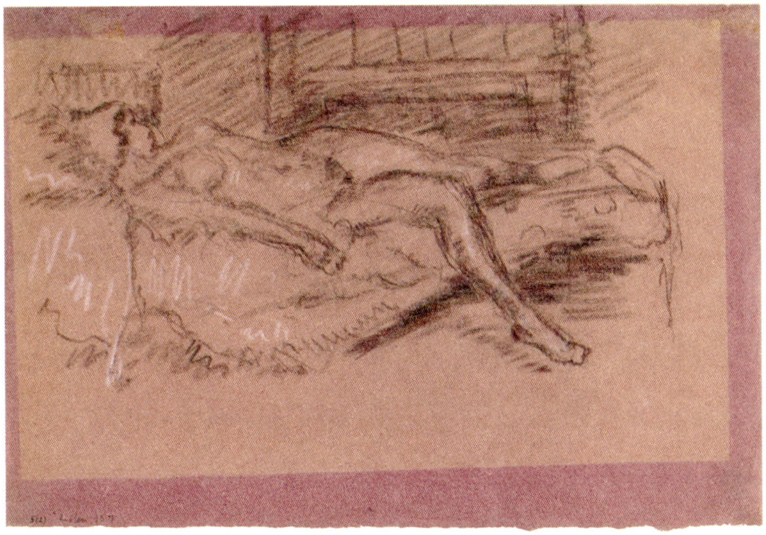

Spencer GORE
[1878–1914]
Reclining Nude, c.1908

charcoal and chalk on purple paper, 25.1 × 37.7 cm

P.416
PROVENANCE: Redfern Gallery, from whom purchased by Gallery, February 1962.
EXHIBITIONS: *Watercolours and Drawings from The Cecil Higgins Art Gallery, Bedford*, London, Thos. Agnew & Sons Ltd, 1962, no.70; *Watercolours from Bedford*, Norwich, Castle Museum, 1965, no.18; *The Camden Town Group*, Bedford, Cecil Higgins Art Gallery, 1969, no.20.

SICKERT and Gore both sketched this model at the same time. The paper has faded due to exposure to light; the original colour can be seen around the edge.

A painter of landscapes, music-hall scenes and interiors with figures. Gore trained at the Slade School, 1896–9, at the same time as his friend GILMAN. In 1904 he met Sickert in Dieppe and later became associated with the Fitzroy Street Group, which included Sickert, Lucien PISSARRO and GINNER. From 1907–10 his paintings were influenced by Pointillism, later his style became more versatile. He was the first President of the Camden Town Group in 1911 and a member of the London Group from 1913.

Inspired by Gauguin, he began to apply strong colours to the landscapes he painted at Letchworth in Hertfordshire and elsewhere. His last works are strongly structured but also quieter in effect suggesting a new influence from Cézanne. Gore died prematurely from pneumonia brought on by getting wet while painting in Richmond Park.

EJ

Duncan GRANT
[1885–1978]
Study for The Coffee Pot, c.1918

charcoal over pencil on paper, 52.5 × 34.8 cm
inscribed: *D Grant 1921*

P.287
PROVENANCE: The artist, from whom purchased by Gallery, April 1959.
EXHIBITIONS: *Duncan Grant*, London, Tate Gallery, 1959, no.96, pl. 3; *The Camden Town Group*, Bedford, Cecil Higgins Art Gallery, 1969, no.22; *The Art of Bloomsbury*, London, Tate Gallery, San Marino, The Huntington and New Haven, Yale Center for British Art, 2000, no.180.
REFERENCES: R. Shone, *The Art of Bloomsbury*, 1999, p.264, p.180.

Although dated 1921, Richard Shone dates this to c.1918. Grant dated the drawing prior to his exhibition at the Tate Gallery in 1959. Shone believes it was drawn at Charleston, Sussex. It is a study for *The Coffee Pot* c.1918, oil on canvas, in the Metropolitan Museum, New York, for which Grant made a number of studies.

Grant studied in Paris under Jacques-Emile Blanche (1862–1942) in 1906 before joining the Bloomsbury Group through his cousin Lytton Strachey (1880–1932). Influenced by the Fauves and Cézanne, his work was highly esteemed by Roger Fry (1866–1934). As was not uncommon within the Bloomsbury group, he shared relationships with other members of both sexes.

EJ/CB

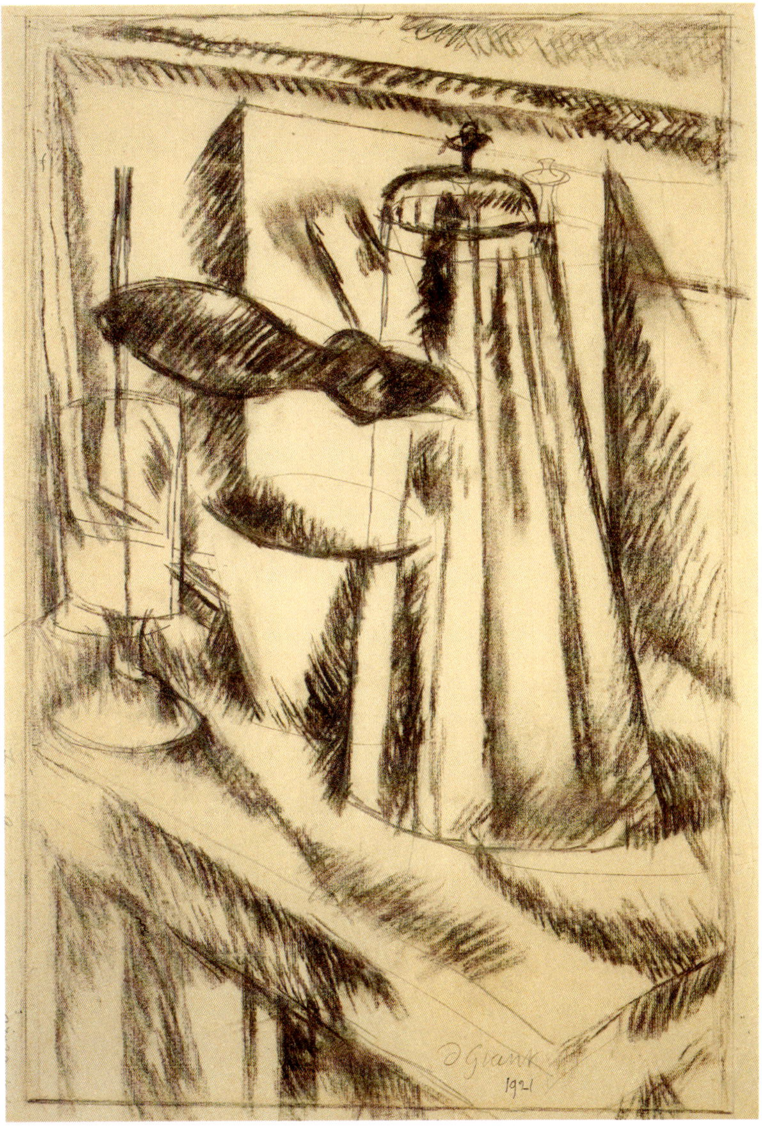

Paul GRAY
[1842–1866]
Illustration to **Quid Femina Possit** by George Stott, c.1865

pen and ink on paper, 15.6 × 11.1 cm
monogram: unidentified

P.159
PROVENANCE: P&D Colnaghi Ltd, from whom purchased by Gallery, January 1958.
REFERENCES: *Once a Week*, 1865, vol. xii, p.491; H.S. Reitlinger, *From Hogarth to Keene*, 1938, pl. xxxix as *The Lost Hat*.

Previously attributed to MILLAIS as *Gentleman retrieving a Lady's Hat from a River Bank*. In 1977 Malcolm Warner supplied the correct title and author. The illustration appeared in *Once a Week* in 1865, vol. xii, p.491.

Gray was born in Dublin; he taught drawing at Tullabeg School and worked for the Dublin printseller Dillon. From 1863 he worked in London getting his first commissions from *Punch* magazine. By 1865 he was quite successful but was then struck down by consumption and died the next year. His pastoral studies are amongst the most fetching of this period.

EJ/CB

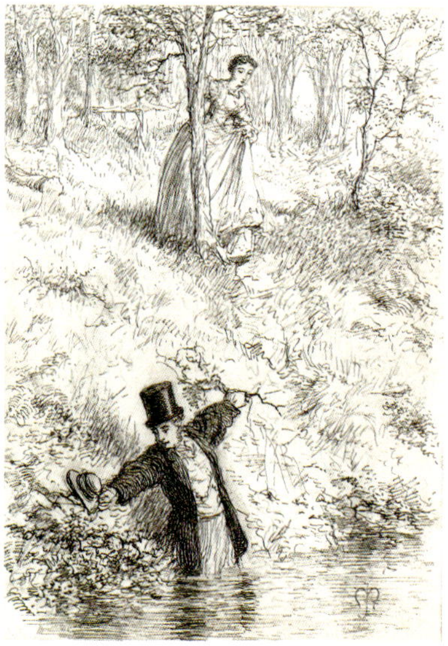

Walter GREAVES
[1846–1930]
Thomas Carlyle, 1872

chalk on grey washed paper, 35.5 × 24.4 cm
inscribed: *Walter Greaves 1872*

P.307
PROVENANCE: Elkin Mathews; P&D Colnaghi Ltd, from whom purchased by Gallery, October 1959.
EXHIBITIONS: *Watercolours and Drawings from The Cecil Higgins Art Gallery, Bedford*, London, Thos. Agnew & Sons Ltd, 1962, no.72.

Greaves was a pupil of WHISTLER, whose celebrated portrait of Carlyle is in the Glasgow Art Gallery and dates from the same period.

Carlyle (1795–1881) has been described as exerting a greater influence on British literature and the ethical, religious and political beliefs of his time, than any of his contemporaries of the 19th century.

EJ

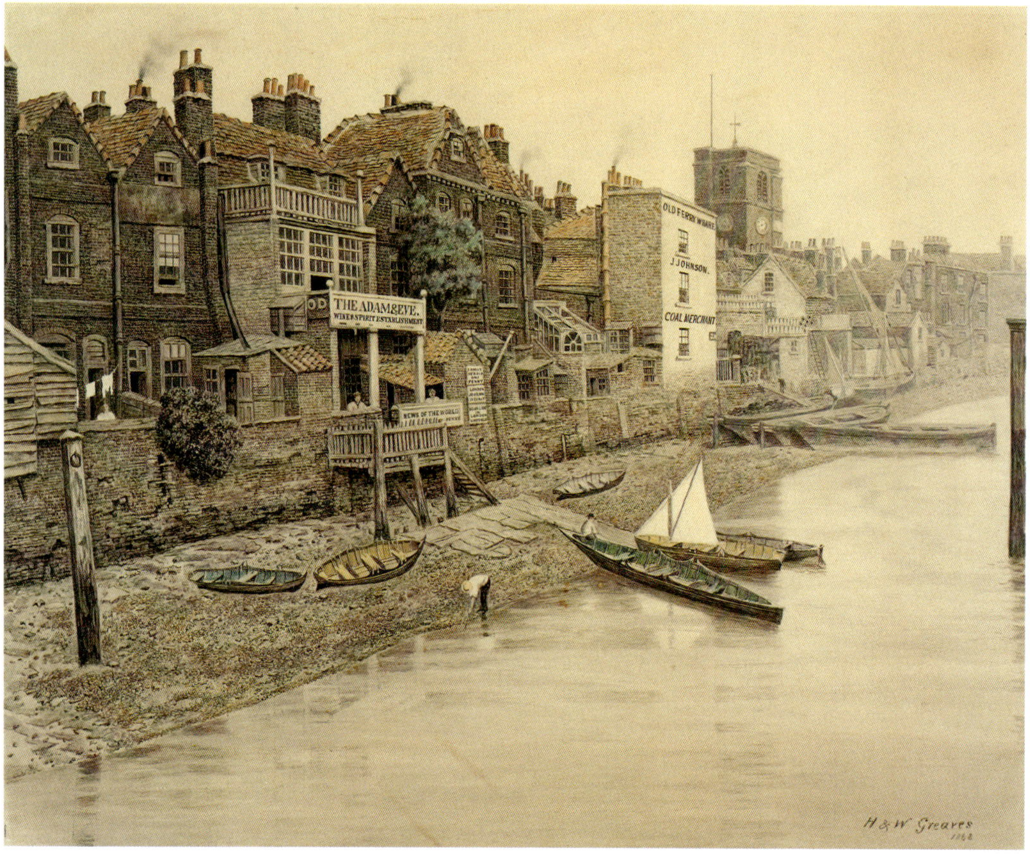

Walter GREAVES [1846–1930]
and **Henry GREAVES** [1850–1900]
A Thames View, showing "The Adam and Eve", 1868

watercolour on paper, 48.1 × 60.8 cm
inscribed: *H&W Greaves 1868*

P.403
PROVENANCE: J.Leger & Son, from whom purchased by Gallery, January 1962.
EXHIBITIONS: *Old and Modern Masters*, London, The Leger Galleries, 1961, no cat.; *Watercolours from Bedford*, Norwich, Castle Museum, 1965, no.19.

The Chelsea waterfront, as depicted here, was demolished during the re-development of the Chelsea Embankment by Sir Joseph Bazalgette (1819–91) from 1871.

The Greaves brothers produced many versions of this scene on the River Thames, including *Chelsea Regatta*, which is in the Manchester City Art Gallery.

In 1911, after WHISTLER's death, a Walter Greaves exhibition was held at the Goupil Gallery and initially enjoyed great success. The accusation that Greaves had signed paintings by Whistler destroyed his reputation.

CB

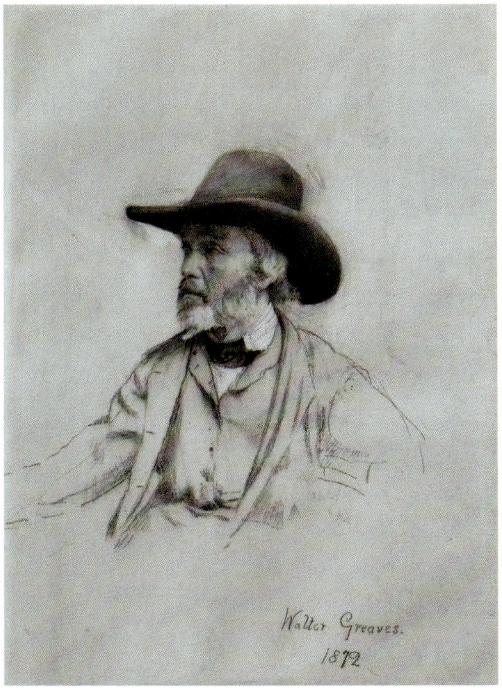

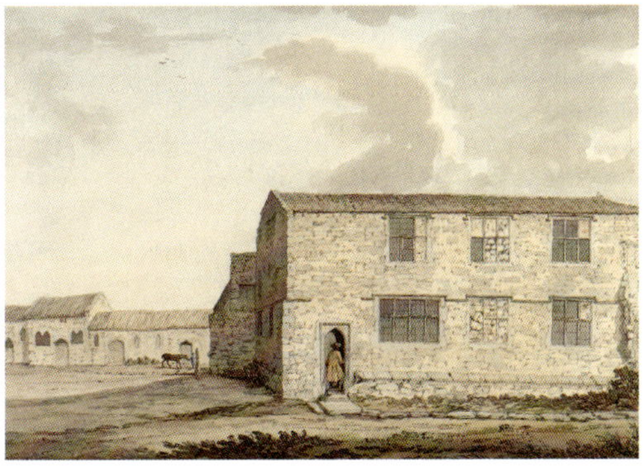

Samuel Hieronymous GRIMM

[1733–94]

Woodthorpe Hall, Derbyshire, 1780

pen and ink with watercolour on paper, 36.3 × 52.9 cm
inscribed: *Grimm fecit 1780*

P.73
PROVENANCE: Cornelius Heathcote Rodes, Barlborough Hall, nr. Chesterfield; Mrs Locker Lampson; Gilbert Davis; P&D Colnaghi Ltd, from whom purchased by Gallery, February 1953.
EXHIBITIONS: *English Watercolours from The Cecil Higgins Art Gallery, Bedford,* Reading, Reading Museum and Art Gallery, 1965, no.22.

A characteristic topographical record of a local house made for Grimm's patron, Cornelius Heathcote Rodes (1755–1825), of Barlborough Hall, Derbyshire.

Although born in the Swiss Alps, Grimm settled in England in 1768, and became a typical topographer painting old houses, ruined abbeys and village streets. In 1776 he was engaged by Gilbert White to make drawings of Selborne at two guineas per week. He exhibited at the R.A. 1769–84 , the Society of Artists, and the Free Society.

Grimm continued the tradition of the 'stained drawing' in England, and his work is always accurate and sometimes embellished by lively figures.

EJ

Anthony GROSS, C.B.E.,R.A.

[1905–84]

Fishing on the Serpentine, c.1947

pen, ink and watercolour on paper, 36.4 × 54.8 cm
inscribed: *Anthony Gross*
inscribed on reverse: *Fine Sport on the Serpentine*

P.139
PROVENANCE: Zwemmer Gallery, from whom purchased by Gallery, November 1957.
EXHIBITIONS: *Watercolours from Bedford,* Norwich, Castle Museum, 1965, no.20.

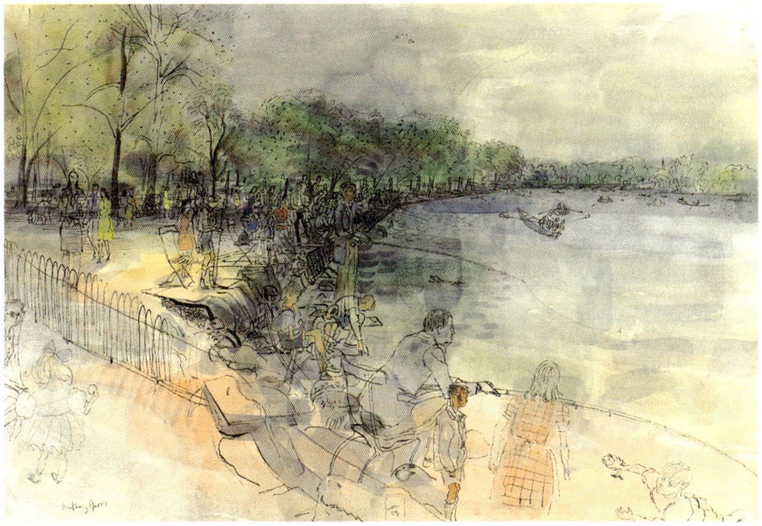

A painter and printmaker, Gross is probably best known for his scenes of contemporary life. He was also an illustrator and creator of animated cartoons. His work is characteristically full of invention and wit. An Official War Artist in the Middle East, India and Europe, he subsequently spent summers in the Dordogne. His etchings, with their hyperactive figures and abundant vegetation, reflect Continental influences, primarily that of James Ensor (1860–1949).

In 1971 John Read made a BBC film, *A Printmaker's Workshop*, focussing on the work of Gross.

EJ

William HAMILTON, R.A.
[1751–1801]
Nymphs and Shepherds dancing in a ruined Temple

watercolour over black lead on paper, 56.7 × 73.5 cm
inscribed: *Willm Hamilton*
stamped: *JMW Turner bequest stamp*

P.182
PROVENANCE: J.M.W. Turner R.A.; Leicester Galleries, from whom purchased by Gallery, April 1958.

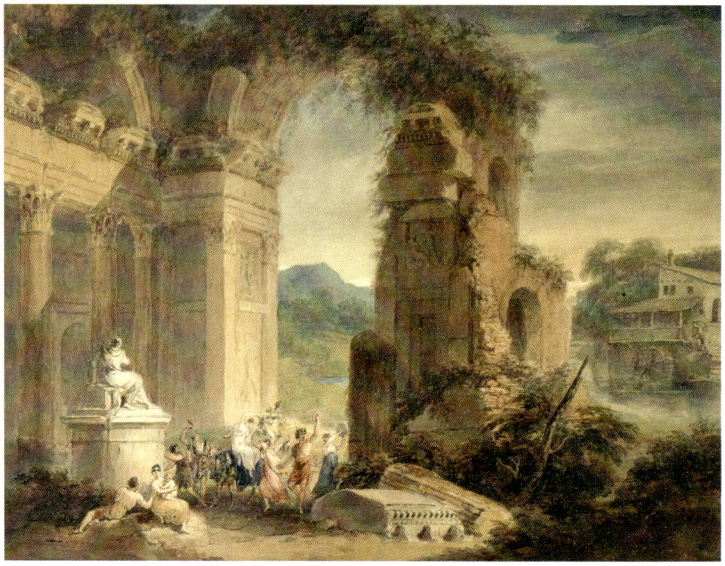

As a young man Hamilton, with the assistance of Robert Adam (1728–92), visited Italy where he studied under ZUCCHI. On his return to England he entered the R.A. schools. He exhibited at the R.A. from 1774, was elected A.R.A. in 1784 and R.A. in 1789. His watercolours of mythological and rustic scenes are elegant and prettily coloured but his drawings of children, made for stipple engraving, verge on sentimentality.

In the British Museum there is an illustration by Hamilton to *As You Like It* which also belonged to TURNER. It must therefore have been still in Turner's studio when he died in 1851 but was later sold because it was not by Turner himself.

EJ

Martin HARDIE, C.B.E., R.W.S.
[1875–1952]
Helmsley Castle, 1946

watercolour over pencil on paper, 38.6 × 28.7 cm
inscribed: *Martin Hardie*
inscribed on reverse: *Helmsley Castle Martin Hardie June 1946*

P.622
PROVENANCE: The artist; given to the Gallery by the artist's sons Captain Maurice Hardie R.N. and Dr Frank Hardie, in memory of their father, August 1972.

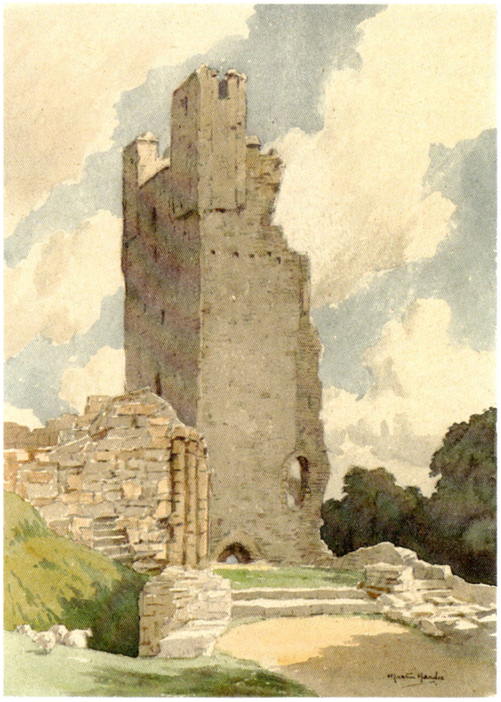

Helmsley is about twenty-five miles north of York. Although he is not a major watercolourist, this is a striking image, and Hardie's great familiarity with the medium enabled him to employ it with considerable facility.

Hardie worked in the V&A from c.1898 to 1935, initially in the library, and later became the Keeper of the Engraving, Illustration, Design and Painting department. His *magnum opus* in three volumes, *Water-colour Painting in Britain*, although finished before he died, was not published until 1966–8. It remains the most comprehensive and knowledgeable survey of the subject. The Ashmolean Museum, Oxford, has almost all his prints and twenty-five of his sketchbooks.

EJ/CB

Dorothy Webster HAWKSLEY
[1884–1970]
Refugees, c.1945

watercolour and bodycolour on paper, 42.4 × 60.8 cm
inscribed: *D.W. Hawksley*

P.328
PROVENANCE: The artist via the Art Exhibitions Bureau, from whom purchased by Gallery, January 1960.
EXHIBITIONS: *Summer Exhibition*, London, R.A., 1945, no.921; *Contemporary British Book Illustrators*, London , Art Exhibitions Bureau & Bedford, Cecil Higgins Art Gallery, 1959, catalogue not traced.

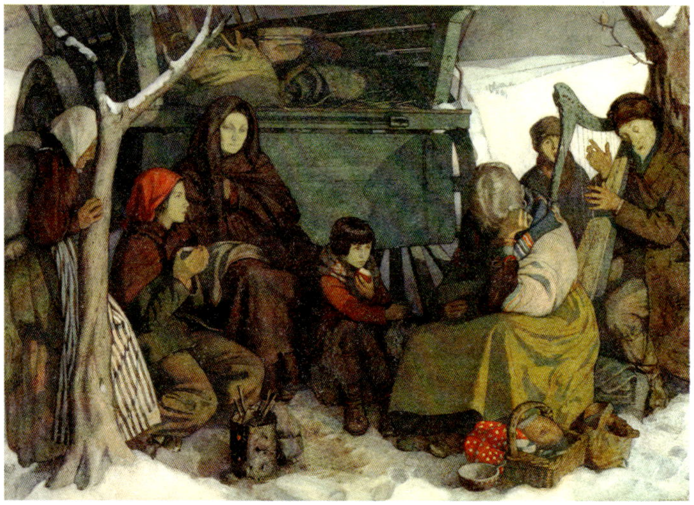

The scene depicted here shows the aftermath of the Second World War and the displacement of people.

Dorothy Hawksley began her training at the St. John's Wood School of Art, later moving to the R.A. Schools, where her teachers were CLAUSEN and Sir Frank Dicksee P.R.A. (1853–1928). While at the R.A. she won the Landseer Scholarship and the Silver Medal. She exhibited at the R.A., Royal Institute and at the Paris Salon of 1931, where she was awarded a silver medal. A painter mainly in watercolour and tempera, Hawksley was known for her portraits and illustrations.

CB

Thomas HEARNE

[1744–1817]

Joseph Andrews, Fanny Goodwill and Parson Adams outside an Inn, c.1777

watercolour and pencil on oval paper, 28 × 33 cm
inscribed: *T Hearne*

P.75
PROVENANCE: Randolph Greenway, Esq.; Frank Jenkins; Sotheby's Sale 7 April 1954, lot 26; Leggatt Bros., from whom purchased by Gallery, April 1954.
EXHIBITIONS: *Society of Artists*, 1777, no.208; *English Watercolours from The Cecil Higgins Art Gallery, Bedford*, Reading, Reading Museum & Art Gallery, 1965, no.23; *Thomas Hearne*, Bolton, Bolton Museum & Art Gallery, 1985, no.38.
REFERENCES: Engraved by W. Ellis with minor changes, published 1781; A. Buck, *Dress in 18th Century England*, 1979, p.128, no.64; D. Morris, *Thomas Hearne & His Landscape*, 1989, pp.52–54, illus. p.55.

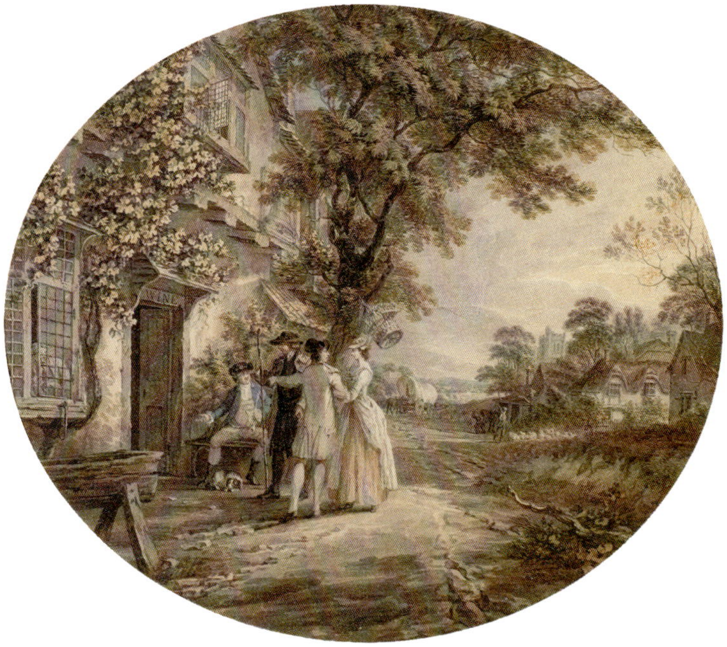

This illustrates an episode from book II, chapter XVI of *Joseph Andrews* (1742) by Henry Fielding (1707–54). Joseph and his sweetheart Fanny have fallen in with Parson Adams and they are making their way back to Somerset together. Robbed of their money, they arrive at an inn where they encounter the local squire sitting outside. In the course of conversation, the squire seems to take a great liking to the travellers, offering them hospitality in his house, his carriage at their disposal and so on. The credulous parson can hardly believe their luck. The squire returns home but then sends absurd excuses for reneging on his promises, which leaves the travellers with a bill to pay. Fortunately the landlord knows the squire's deceptions of old and agrees to score the bill until they can repay him.

EJ

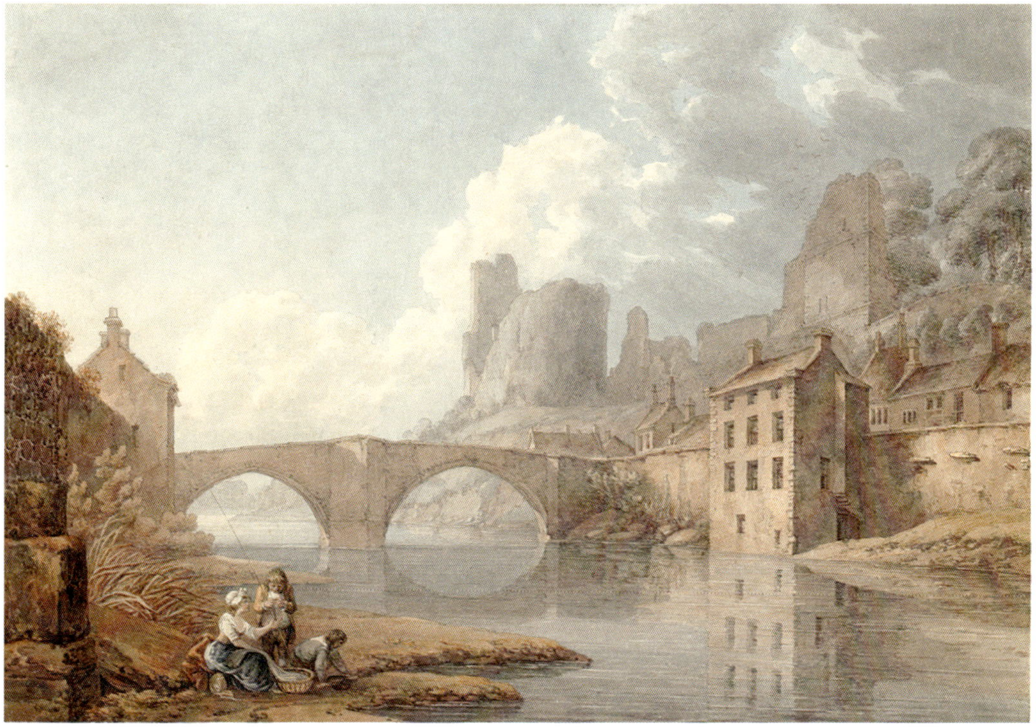

Thomas HEARNE

[1744–1817]

Barnard Castle, 1788

watercolour on paper, 26.9 × 39.5 cm
inscribed: *Hearne*

P.74
PROVENANCE: Squire Gallery, from whom purchased by Gallery, November 1952.
EXHIBITIONS: *The Picturesque Tour in Northumberland & Durham c.1720–1820*, Newcastle upon Tyne, Laing Art Gallery, 1982, no.101, p.77; *Walking the Landscape with Cotman and Turner in Teesdale*, Barnard Castle, Bowes Museum, 1996, p.3, illus.

Hearne began his career as an apprentice to the engraver William Woollett (1735–85), subsequently going to the Leeward Islands as draughtsman to the Governor. Afterwards Hearne travelled widely in Britain making topographical drawings to be engraved. He was a close friend of Sir George Beaumont (1753–1827), and Dr MONRO considered him 'superior to everyone in drawing'. He owned a large collection of Hearne's works which doubtless influenced both GIRTIN and TURNER when they worked for Monro as young men from 1794–7. Two other versions exist: one in the Rochdale Art Gallery and the other in the Bowes Museum, Barnard Castle.

EJ

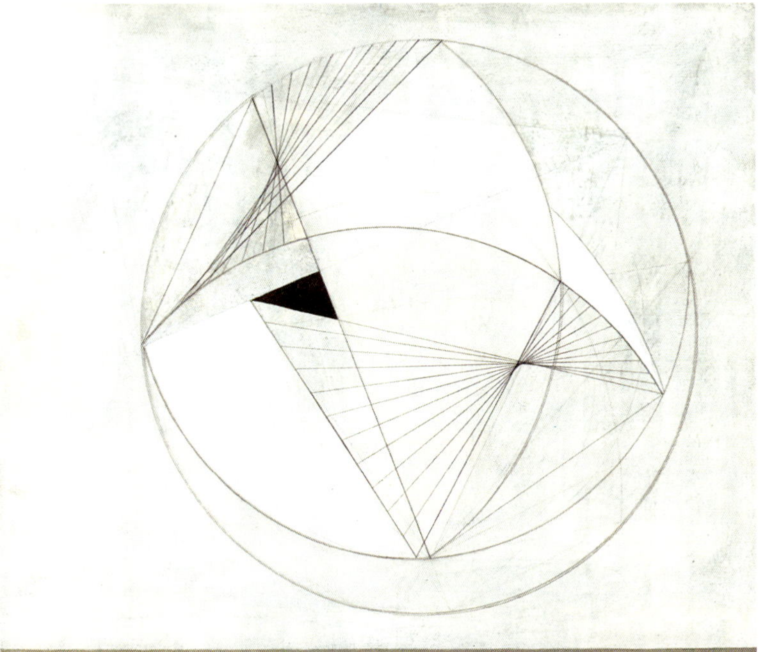

Dame Barbara HEPWORTH
[1903–75]
Two Forms, 1941

bodycolour and pencil on paper, 50.5 × 35.3 cm
inscribed: *Barbara Hepworth 1941*

P.428
PROVENANCE: Piccadilly Gallery, from whom purchased by Gallery, July 1962.
EXHIBITIONS: *Watercolours and Drawings from The Cecil Higgins Art Gallery, Bedford*, London, Thos. Agnew & Sons Ltd, 1962, no.96, pl.xi; *Watercolours from Bedford*, Norwich, Castle Museum, 1965, no.21; *Barbara Hepworth*, Japan, Hakone Sculpture Museum and National Museum of Modern Art, Kyoto, 1970–1, no.40.

When war broke out in 1939 Hepworth moved to Cornwall with Ben NICHOLSON and their triplets and did not sculpt again until 1943. During these years she continued to draw, and this example shows her experimenting with something she was soon to introduce into her sculpture: the use of strings to explore the tension or space within a sculpture.

EJ

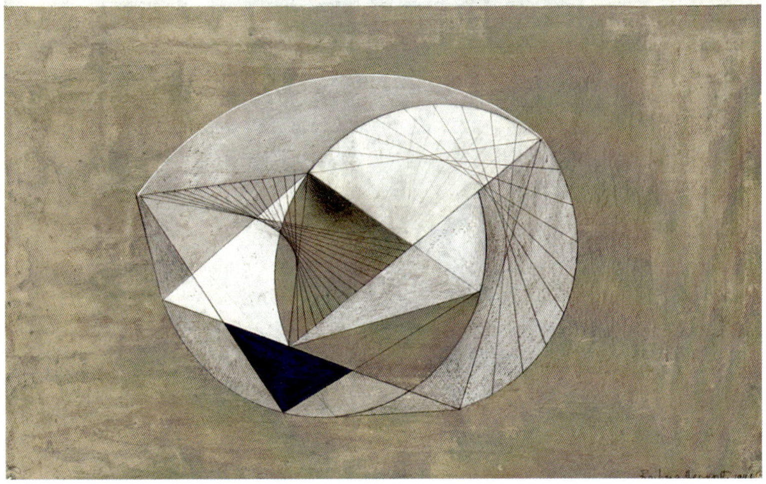

Dame Barbara HEPWORTH
[1903–75]
Quartet "Arthroplasty", 1948

oil and pencil on board, 59.6 × 50 cm
inscribed: *Barbara Hepworth 1948*
inscribed on backboard: *Quartet (arthoplasty)*[sic] *1949* [sic]
Oil & pencil

P.245
PROVENANCE: Gimpel Fils, from whom purchased by Gallery, July 1958.
EXHIBITIONS: Durlacher Bros, New York, 1949; *Watercolours and Drawings from The Cecil Higgins Art Gallery, Bedford*, London, Thos. Agnew & Sons Ltd, 1962, no.114; *Watercolours from Bedford*, Norwich, Castle Museum, 1965, no.22; *The English Tradition: an exhibition of watercolours from two private collections*, Bedford, Cecil Higgins Art Gallery, 1972, no.41; *Barbara Hepworth Hospital Drawings*, St. Ives, Barbara Hepworth Museum, 1993, no cat.

One of a series of remarkable surgical drawings made at a hospital in 1948. In her autobiography Hepworth wrote:

> In 1947 it was suggested to me that I might be interested in watching an operation in a hospital. At first I was very scared but then I found there was such beauty in the coordinated human endeavour in the operating theatre that the whole composition-human in appearance-became abstract in shape. I became completely absorbed by two things: first the extraordinary beauty of purpose between human beings all dedicated to saving life; and secondly by the way this special grace (grace of mind and body) induced a spontaneous space composition, an articulated and animated kind of abstract sculpture very close to what I had been seeking in my own work.

Arthroplasty is an operation to relieve diseased joints, often caused by osteo-arthritis or ankylosis, which means fixation or stiffness of a joint produced by intra-articular lesions.

Hepworth studied at Leeds College of Art and the R.C.A. She married the sculptor John Skeaping and met Henry MOORE and Ben NICHOLSON, who was later to become her second husband and by whom she had triplets.

In 1933 she moved into an abstract phase and, like Moore, introduced the hole into her carved sculpture. Settling in Cornwall before the war, her finest works have harmonious elegance quite unlike the aged and weathered aspects of nature that were characteristics of Moore's work. She was created D.B.E. in 1958. After her tragic death in a fire, her studio at St. Ives was opened as a museum.

EJ/CB

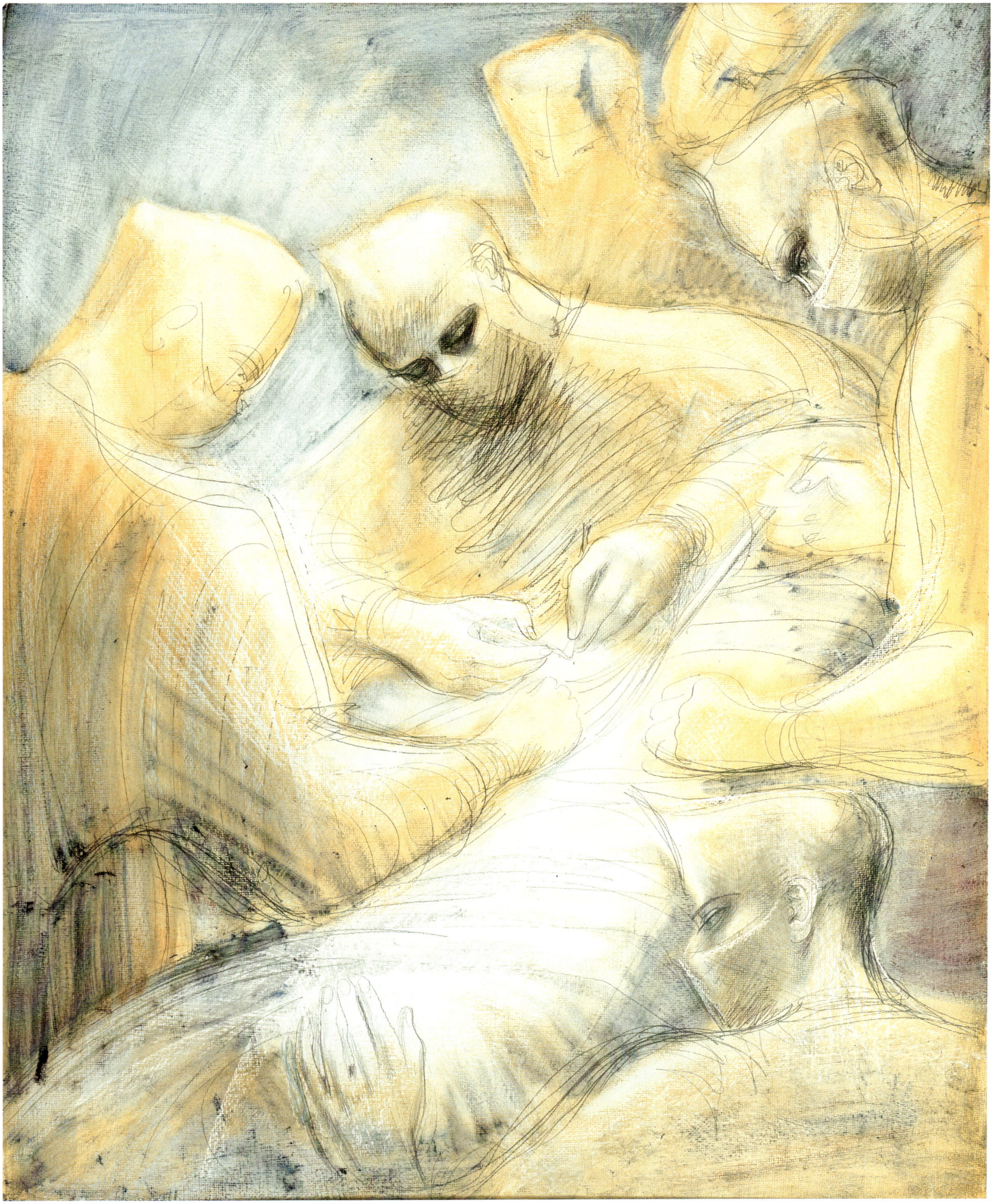

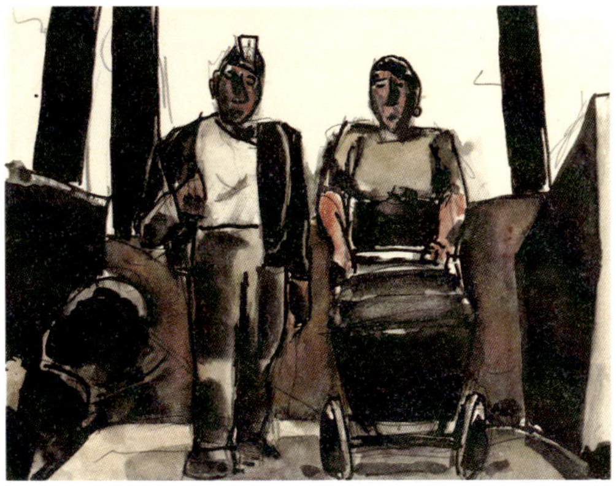

Josef HERMAN, O.B.E., R.A.
[1911–2000]
Family Outing, c.1956

pen, watercolour and pencil on paper, 17.2 × 22.3 cm

P.140
PROVENANCE: Roland, Browse and Delbanco, from whom purchased by Gallery, November 1957.
EXHIBITIONS: *Watercolours and Drawings from the Cecil Higgins Art Gallery, Bedford*, London, Thos. Agnew & Sons Ltd., 1962, no.108; *Watercolours from Bedford*, Norwich, Castle Museum, 1965, no.23.

In a letter of 1989 from the artist to the Gallery, Herman said:

I left Wales in 1955, but still continued working on many themes relating to my years in Ystradgynlais. The family outing was one of several 'studies' for an oil painting…My way of working is still so today: I make pencil notes on the spot and later in the studio I translate some of them into pen and wash drawings, or paintings.

Born in Warsaw, Poland, Herman came to Britain as a refugee in 1940, living in Glasgow, where he met his old friend from Warsaw, Jankel ADLER. In 1944 he settled in a mining village in South Wales, where he remained for eleven years.

CB

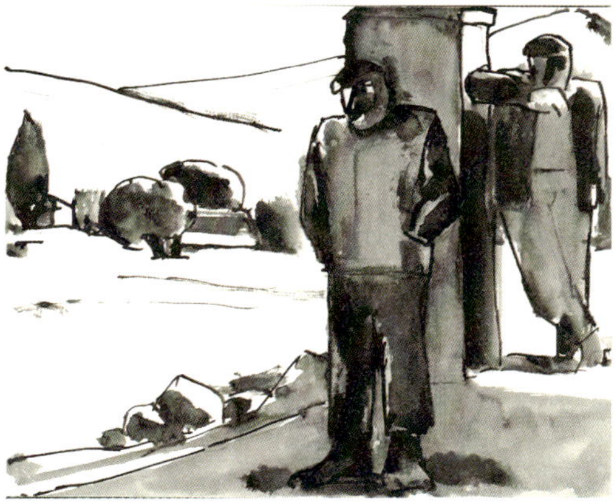

Josef HERMAN, O.B.E., R.A.
[1911–2000]
Landscape with two figures, c.1956

ink, wash and pencil on paper, 17 × 19.9 cm

P.395
PROVENANCE: Piccadilly Gallery, from whom purchased by Gallery, January 1961.

In a letter to the Gallery in 1989, the artist said: 'The landscape with two figures relates to some of my drawings belonging to my travels, but again I cannot tell you whether I made it after a pencil note from Provence or Spain'.

He never gave any of his works titles and believed this one, thought up by his dealers Roland, Browse and Delbanco, would prove quite unsaleable.

EJ/CB

Patrick HERON, C.B.E.
[1920–99]
Black and White – Pink Lines: March 1962, 1962

bodycolour on paper, 38.6 × 57.5 cm

P.442
PROVENANCE: Waddington Galleries, from whom purchased by Gallery, January 1963.
EXHIBITIONS: *Watercolours from Bedford*, Norwich, Castle Museum, 1965, no.24.
REFERENCES: A. Ambrose, *Discovering English Watercolours*, 1987, p.91.

This influential painter and art critic studied at the Slade School in 1937–9. He published *Changing Forms of Art*, 1955 and moved to Zennor near St Ives in 1956, the year he turned to abstract art under the influence of American abstract painting.

He has written of his work: 'I have always been obsessed with *space in colour* …and believe that all pictorial spatial features that depend mainly on *colour* display an ambiguity in that they both advance *and* recede at the same time'.

EJ

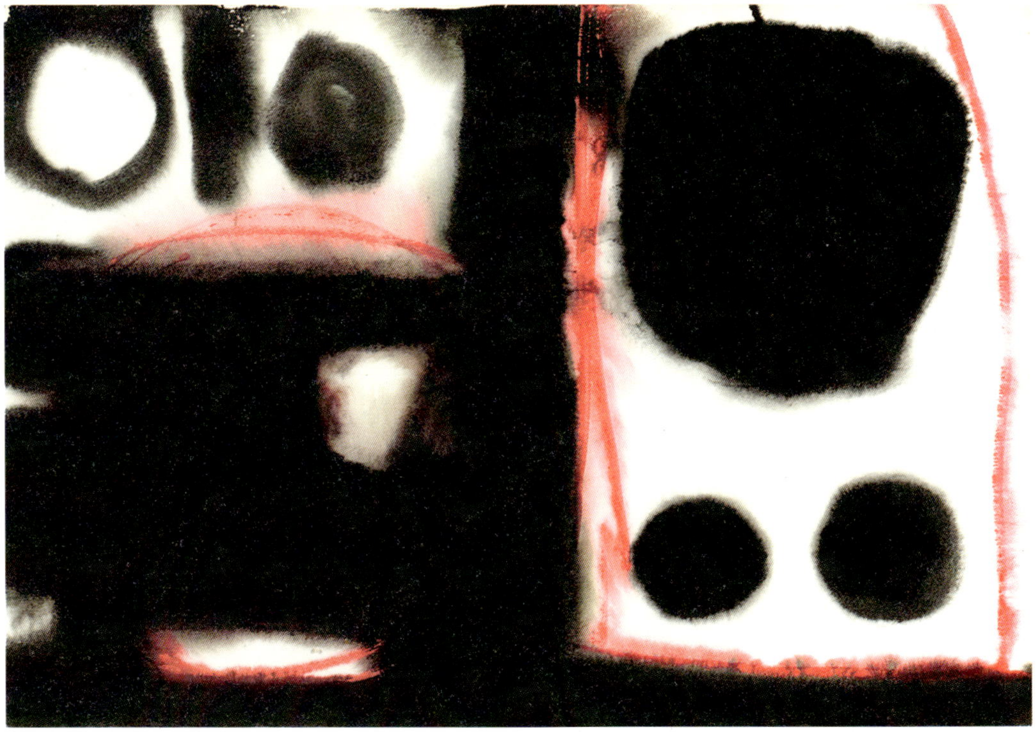

Roger HILTON
[1911–75]
Untitled, 1974

bodycolour and chalks on paper, 43 × 34.5 cm
inscribed: *RH '74 XI*

P.739
PROVENANCE: Waddington Galleries; bought by David Brown for the Contemporary Art Society, given to Gallery by C.A.S., May 1986.
EXHIBITIONS: *Roger Hilton,* London, Waddington Galleries, 1983, no no.; *Contemporary Art for Museums,* Guildford, Sutton Place, 1985, no.15.

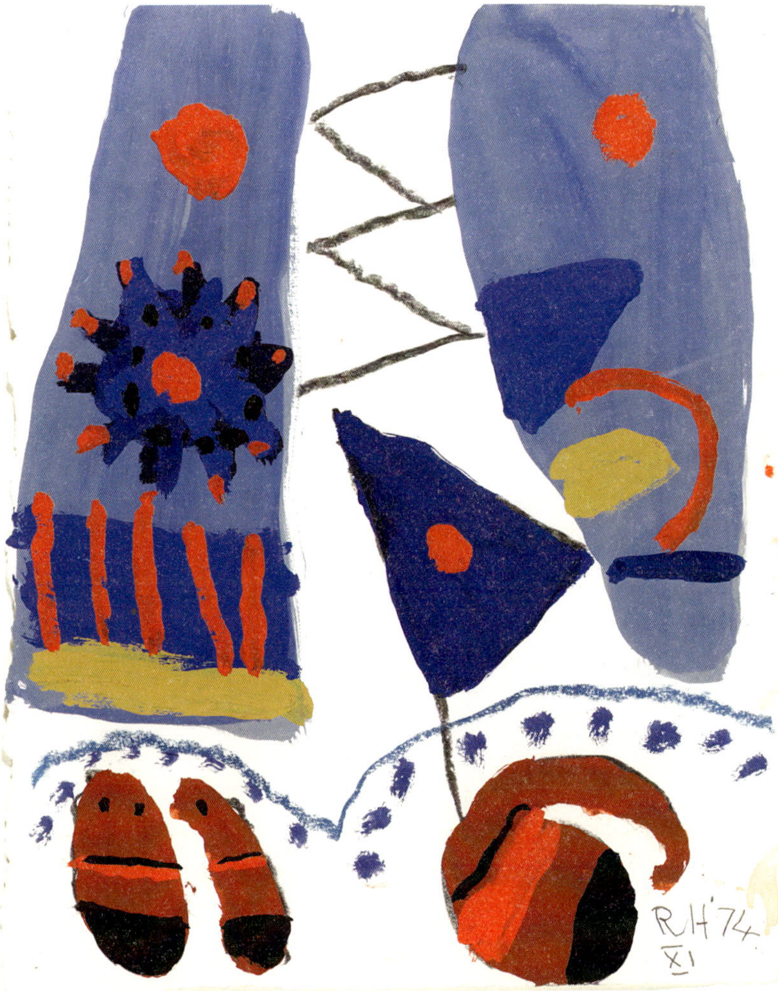

This drawing belongs to the last two and a half years of his life when he was confined to bed and able to work only in gouache (bodycolour). In later years he said: 'Now I have got to the stage where I think to hell with it. Doesn't matter whether you figurate or abstract'.[*sic*]. Nonetheless these final drawings reveal his enduring sensitivity in handling paint and an undiminished zest for life.

Hilton studied at the Slade School in 1929–31 and 1935–6, where his draughtsmanship was praised by TONKS. He enlisted into the Commandos in 1940, was captured during the Dieppe Raid and spent 1942–5 as a prisoner of war. He turned to abstraction around 1950, and started to visit St.Ives from 1956, where the sea and seascapes provided limitless inspiration. He moved to St. Just in Cornwall in 1965, where he remained until his death.

EJ/CB

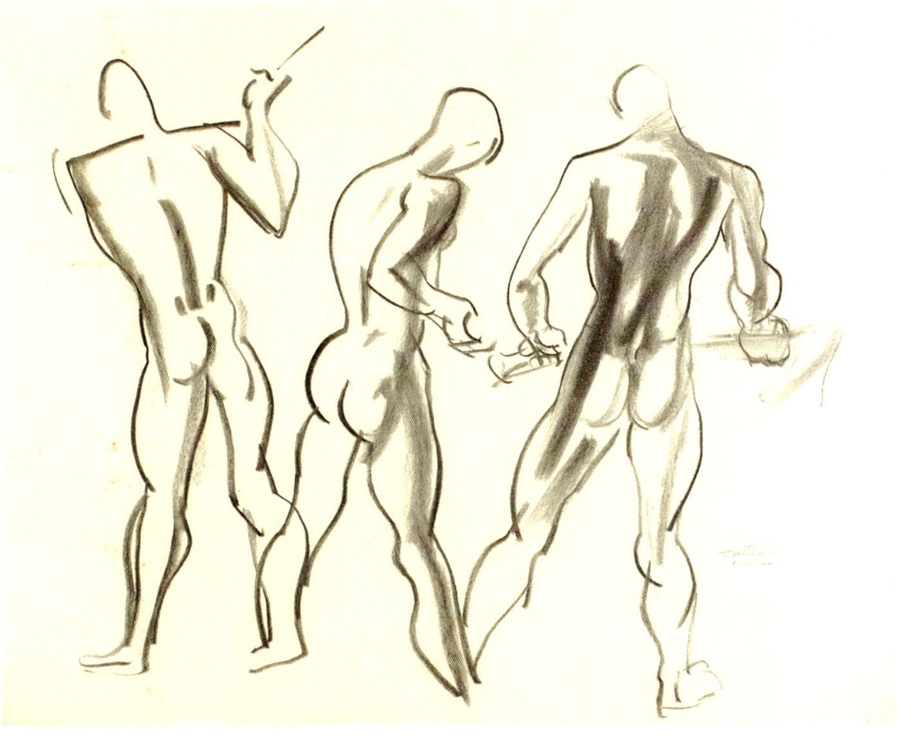

Ivon HITCHENS, C.B.E.
[1893–1979]
Three Studies of Man with Axe, study for a Mural at Sussex University, 1960

charcoal on paper, 44.1 × 56.6 cm
inscribed: *I Hitchens 8.2.60*

P.551
PROVENANCE: Waddington Galleries, from whom purchased by Gallery, April 1967.
EXHIBITIONS: *Ivon Hitchens Centenary Exhibition,* Chichester, Pallant House, 1993, no.46a.
REFERENCES: J.R. Taylor, *Ivon Hitchens-Figure Subjects,* 1993, exhib. cat., p.12, incorrectly stated as *study for Cecil Sharp House mural.*

A painter mainly of landscapes, but also of flowers, nudes and mural decorations, Hitchens studied at the R.A. Schools, where SARGENT and ORPEN influenced him. He exhibited with the 7 and 5 Society, 1921–35, and was influenced by Surrealism in the 1930s. Hitchens moved from London to Lavington Common, Sussex, in 1940. The man with the axe is almost certainly 'Ted', a woodman in Sussex.

Hitchens developed a wide landscape but fairly shallow format from 1936, reminiscent in shape of de Wint's watercolours, and many of his most appealing pictures are painted on this scale, with fluid brushwork and richly bold colouring.

EJ

Frances HODGKINS
[1869–1947]
Flowers and Still Life, early 1930s

watercolour, pencil and bodycolour on paper, 63.2 × 38.1 cm
inscribed: *Frances Hodgkins*

P.144
PROVENANCE: Leicester Galleries, from whom purchased by Gallery, December 1957.

Hodgkins was born in Dunedin, New Zealand, and studied there before coming to Europe in 1901. She travelled widely and then settled in Paris in 1908, where she gained a reputation as a *plein-air* watercolourist. Later, still-life occupied her as much as landscape, as in this characteristically colourful and somewhat crowded composition. She spent her last years in England.

EJ

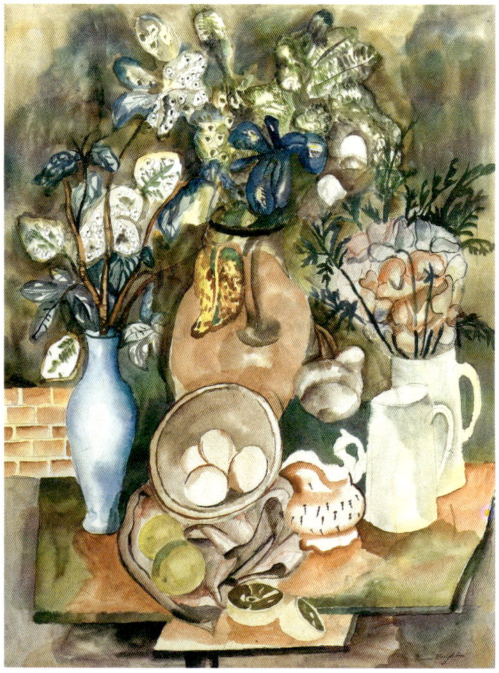

Frances HODGKINS
[1869–1947]
Mushrooms, 1941

bodycolour and pencil on paper, 38.5 × 49.9 cm
inscribed: *Frances Hodgkins 1941*

P.322
PROVENANCE: Leicester Galleries, from whom purchased by Gallery, January 1960.
EXHIBITIONS: *New Year Exhibition*, London, Leicester Galleries, 1960, no.23; *Frances Hodgkins 1869–1947*, New Zealand, Dunedin Public Art Gallery, Robert McDougall Art Gallery, National Art Gallery, Auckland City Art Gallery and London, Commonwealth Institute Gallery, 1969, no.92; *Watercolours from Bedford*, Norwich, Castle Museum, 1965, no.25.
REFERENCES: L. Bensemann & B. Brooke (eds.), 'Frances Hodgkins', *Ascent: A Journal of the Arts in New Zealand*, 1969, p.70, illus.

Painted when Hodgkins was living at Corfe in Dorset. During her time in Paris, Hodgkins opened her own watercolour school, which was intended for women artists. Upon the outbreak of the First World War, she moved to St. Ives, Cornwall, which had traditionally attracted artists due to the clarity of light. In the period following the war, Hodgkins would travel around Britain giving sketching classes. After touring Europe, Hodgkins finally settled in Dorset during the 1930s.

EJ/CB

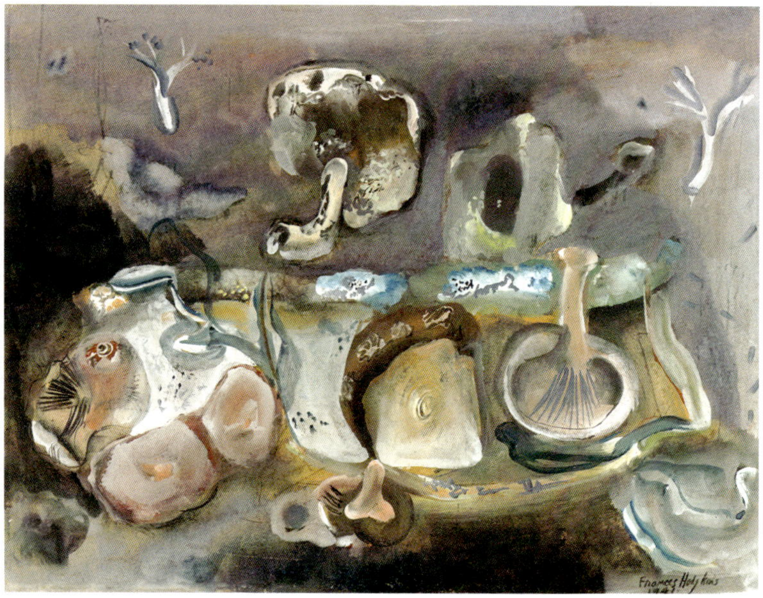

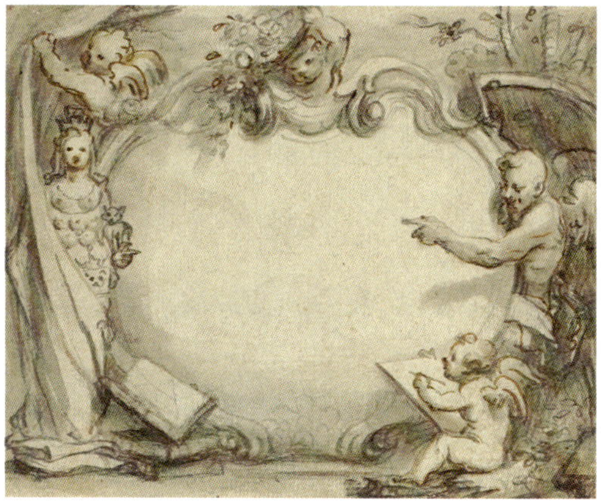

William HOGARTH
[1697–1764]
Design for a Trade Card, 1720s

pen and ink with grey wash over black lead on paper, 13.3 × 16.1 cm
inscribed on old mount: *Hogarth*

P.503
PROVENANCE: Sir Bruce Ingram, O.B.E.; P&D Colnaghi Ltd, from whom purchased by Gallery, July 1965.
EXHIBITIONS: *English Drawings and Watercolours*, London, P&D Colnaghi Ltd, 1965, no.11.
REFERENCES: A.P. Oppé, *The Drawings of William Hogarth*, 1948, p.32.

The figure of Nature on the left appears in Hogarth's *Study of the Arms for the Foundling Hospital* (1747), and in *Boys peeping at Nature* (1731), at the Royal Library. An 18th century inscription on the old mount may have been written by Horace Walpole (1717–97).

Although Hogarth was the outstanding British artist of the first half of the 18th century, he began on the lowest rung of the artistic ladder as an apprentice to a silver-engraver in 1713 before setting up as an independent engraver in 1720. He scarcely painted in watercolour at all.

EJ/CB

James HOLLAND
[1799–1870]
Edward the Confessor's Chapel, Westminster Abbey, 1834

pencil and watercolour on paper, 26.3 × 17.5 cm
inscribed: *J.Holland 1834*

P.349
PROVENANCE: W.G. Walford; P&D Colnaghi Ltd, from whom purchased by Gallery, July 1960.
EXHIBITIONS: *James Holland Bi-Centennial Exhibition*, Stoke-on-Trent, The Potteries Museum and Art Gallery, 1999, no cat.

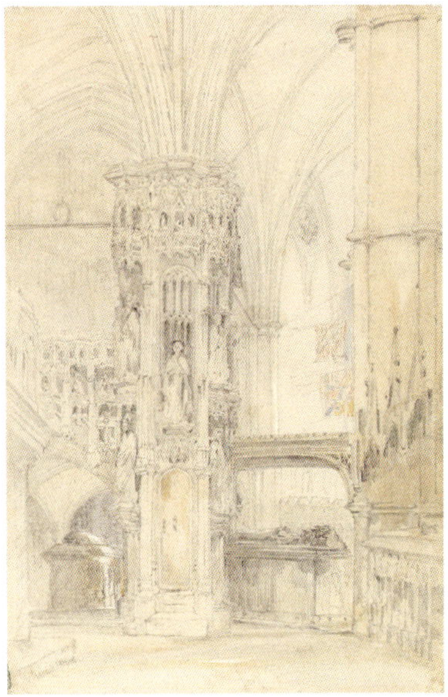

This drawing was formerly thought to depict Canterbury Cathedral. This is a watercolour sketch for either the oil painting *Part of St.Edward's Chapel with the tombs of Edward III and his Queen Phillippa*, exhibited at the Society of British Artists in 1835, or for another version, also an oil, exhibited at the British Institution in 1835 entitled *St.Edward's Chapel, Westminster Abbey.*

Rebuilt by Edward the Confessor c.1050–65, Westminster Abbey is the earliest example of the Norman Style in England. The Confessor's shrine was commissioned by Henry III before he began the new abbey in 1241.

EJ/CB

James HOLLAND
[1799–1870]
Mountainous Landscape with Rocky stream, 1855

watercolour, black chalk and pen and ink heightened with white on paper, 36.4 × 52.5 cm
inscribed: *H Sept.18 '55*

P.76
PROVENANCE: J. Wenniker; P&D Colnaghi Ltd, from whom purchased by Gallery, September 1952.
EXHIBITIONS: *English water-colours from the Hickman Bacon and other collections*, Bedford, Cecil Higgins Art Gallery, 1952, no.48; *English Watercolours from The Cecil Higgins Art Gallery, Bedford*, Reading, Reading Museum and Art Gallery, 1965, no.24.

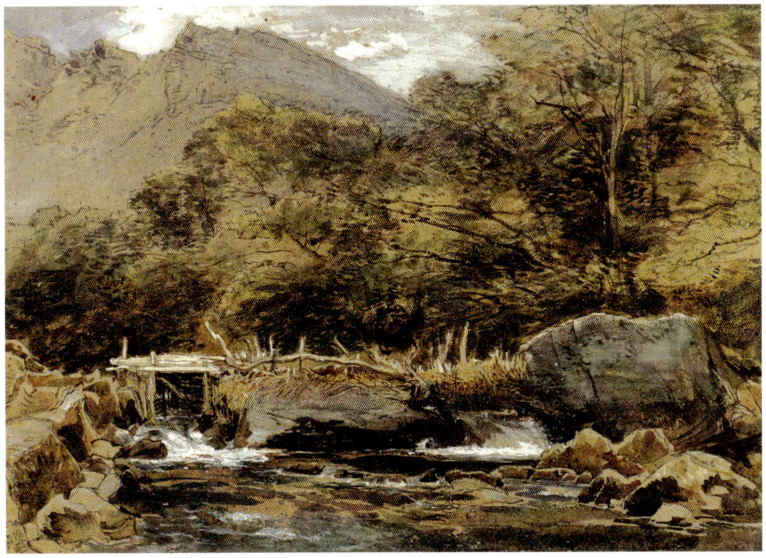

Probably painted in Wales.

Martin HARDIE considers that Holland's oils together with 'the dire influences of Victorian prosperity' had an adverse effect on his watercolours in the latter part of his career. But he was still capable of fine work when he came across a subject that appealed to him, as this fast flowing stream running towards distant mountains clearly did. While the result recalls the work of David COX, Holland's line here is loose in an entirely convincing manner.

EJ

James HOLLAND
[1799–1870]
Venice, 1857

watercolour with black lead heightened with white on paper, 36.7 × 52 cm
inscribed: *Venice Sept. 30th '57 N.W*

P.258
PROVENANCE: Property of a Lady; Christie's Sale, 16 May 1958, lot 4; Thos. Agnew & Sons Ltd, from whom purchased by Gallery, October 1958.
EXHIBITIONS: *Watercolours and Drawings from The Cecil Higgins Art Gallery, Bedford*, London, Thos. Agnew & Sons Ltd, 1962, no.29.

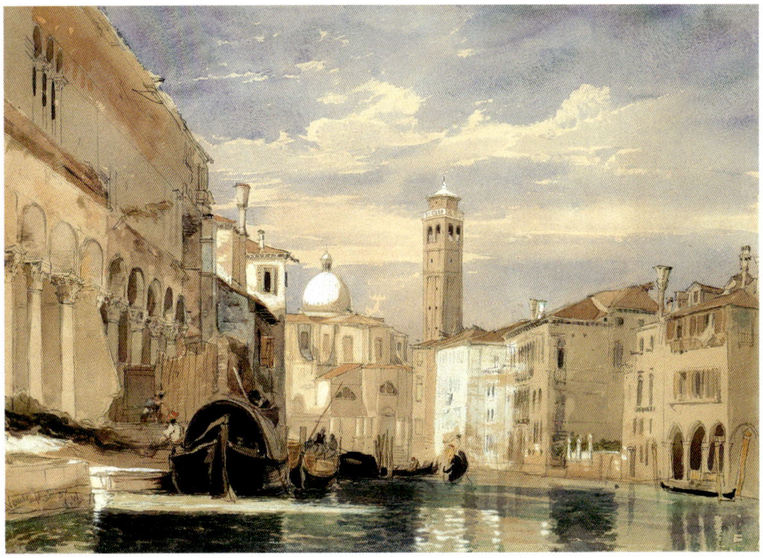

Born in Stoke-on-Trent, Holland began as a ceramic flower painter supplementing his meagre income by giving drawing lessons. His watercolours of 1830–40 show the influence of BONINGTON and he then also began painting in oils. In 1835 he paid his first visit to Venice, continuing to exhibit Venetian subjects regularly for many years thereafter. In 1837 he went to Portugal, a trip which produced some of his most brilliant watercolours. Holland's work was also often at its best in Venice especially until about 1850. Afterwards, although this is fortunately an exception, his colours became too lurid and crude. RUSKIN, who had thought his earlier work as 'near perfection as watercolour can be carried', later wrote that he 'produced worse pictures every year'.

EJ

Arthur Boyd HOUGHTON

[1836–75]

Caught in the Act, 1858–60

watercolour, bodycolour and pencil on paper, 12.9 × 18.2 cm
inscribed: *A.Houghton*

P.170

PROVENANCE: Sydney Morse; P&D Colnaghi Ltd, from whom purchased by Gallery, January 1958.
REFERENCES: P. Hogarth, *Arthur Boyd Houghton,* 1981, p.14.

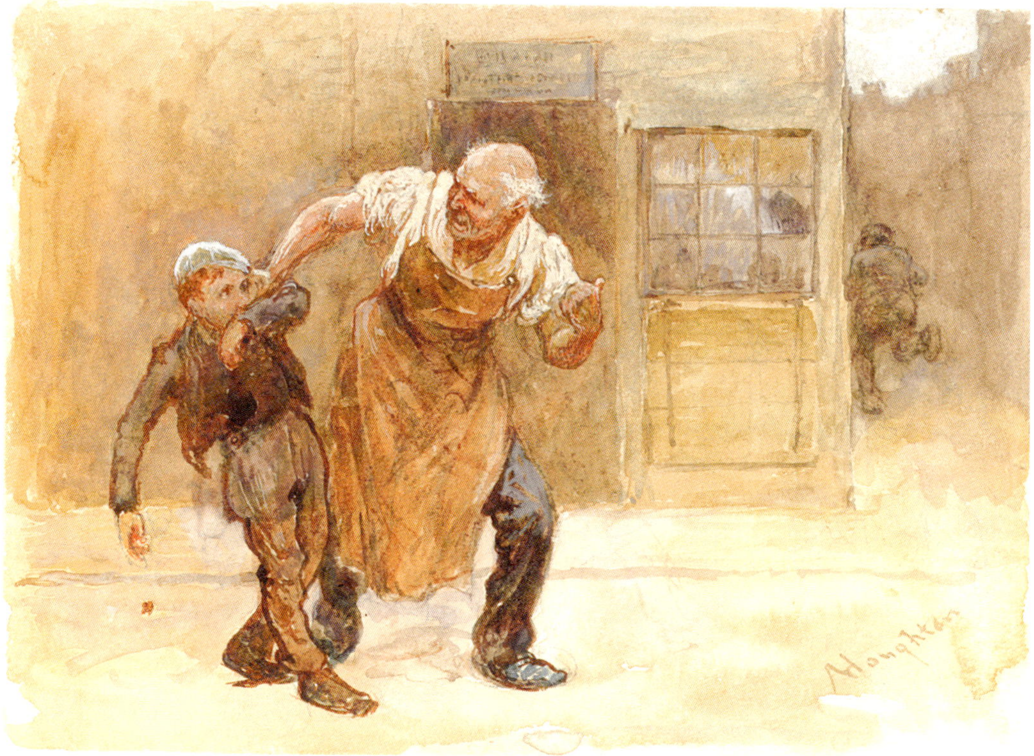

Hogarth, Houghton's biographer, concludes that this was probably a 'Langham' project. The Artists' Society or 'The Langham' offered such facilities as models, lectures, a library and the hire of historical costumes. Students would be set a weekly subject, which they had to complete within two hours.

A book illustrator and painter of contemporary genre, Houghton entered the R.A. Schools in 1854 and soon became known for his brilliant illustrations to Dalziel's *Arabian Nights*, 1866.

The founding of *The Graphic* in 1869 led to him being sent to the U.S.A for several months to draw the Americans and their way of life, resulting in what has been described as the finest pictorial journalism of the whole period. Houghton died of alcoholism in 1875.

EJ/CB

Arthur Boyd HOUGHTON

[1836–75]

'Helga and Hildebrand' drawing for **Ballad Stories of the Affections, 1866**

pencil and bodycolour on wood, 12.6 × 10.1 cm
inscribed : *A*

P.244

PROVENANCE: Dalziel Collection; Georgina Maud Davis; Leicester Galleries, from whom purchased by Gallery, July 1958.
EXHIBITIONS: *Arthur Boyd Houghton*, London, V&A, 1975, no.173.
REFERENCES: E.J. Sullivan, 'Arthur Boyd Houghton – II; An Artist's Artist', *Print Collector's Quarterly,* X, 1923, pp.125–48, p.137; P. Hogarth, *Arthur Boyd Houghton,* 1981, p.39.

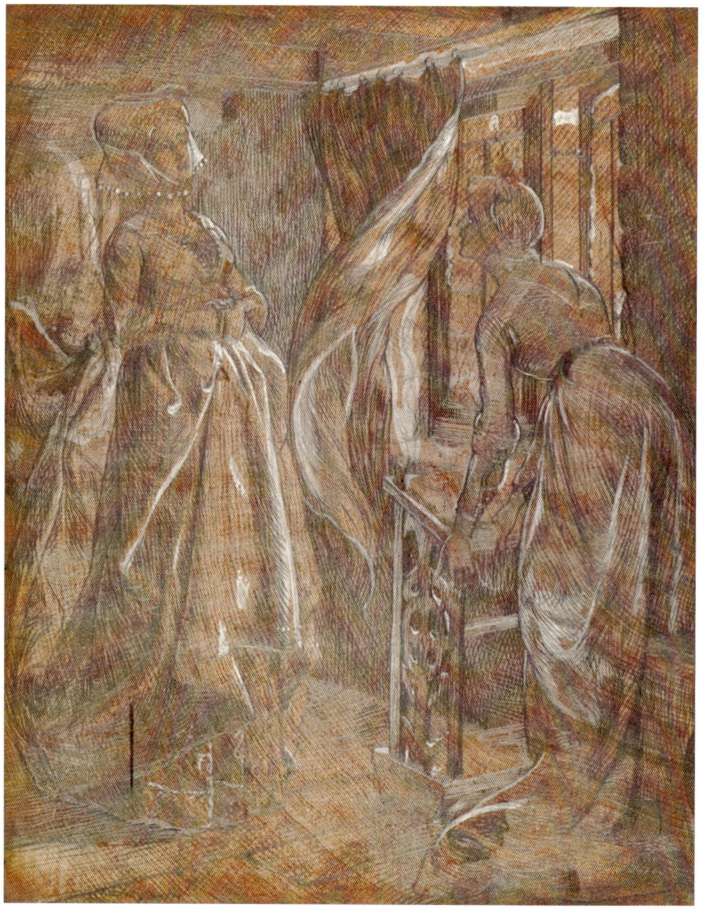

An original illustration, intended for engraving, for the book, *Ballad Stories of the Affections* by Robert Buchanan (1841–1901), p.17, published in 1866.

This example belonged to the Dalziel Brothers. They were able to preserve this original drawing by photographing it onto another block for engraving.

CB

Arthur HUGHES

[1832–1915]

The Four-Wheeler, and A Gentleman to the rescue, c.1868

pen and ink on paper, 8 × 5.8 and 8.3 × 6 cm
inscribed: *AH monogram*

P.192 & 193
PROVENANCE: Henry Scipio Reitlinger; Reitlinger Sale, Sotheby's 26 May 1954, lot 493; P&D Colnaghi Ltd, from whom purchased by Gallery, April 1958.
EXHIBITIONS: *Victorian Life Centenary*, London, Leicester Galleries, 1937, no.8; *English Paintings & Drawings of the XIX Century*, London, P&D Colnaghi Ltd, 1938, nos. 38 & 39.
REFERENCES: H.S. Reitlinger, *From Hogarth to Keene*, 1938, pp.54 & 61; L. Roberts, *Arthur Hughes: His Life & Works*, 1997, p.253, nos. B18.40 & B18.56.

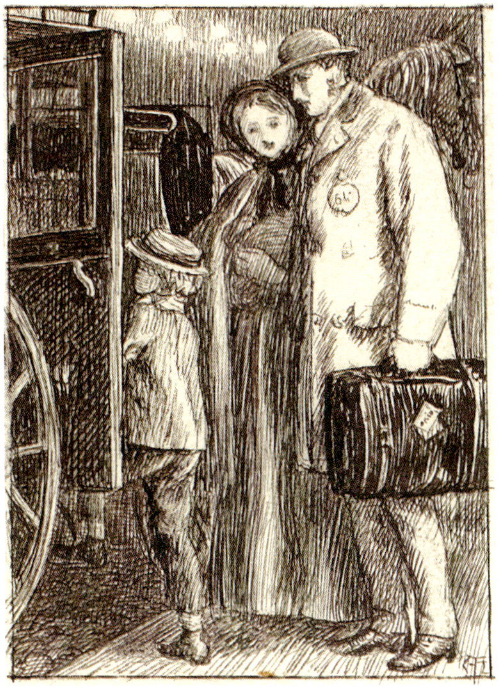

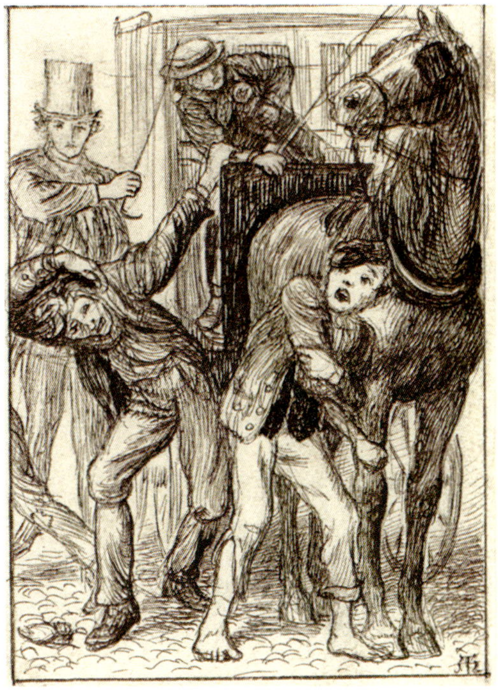

These are two of the seventy-seven illustrations by Hughes for 'At the Back of the North Wind' by George MacDonald (1824–1905) in *Good Words for the Young*, 1868–70. No.40 illustrates p.152 and no.56, p.380.

Hughes was a subject-painter closely associated with the Pre-Raphaelites; *Home from the Sea, The Long Engagement* and *April Love*, which RUSKIN thought 'exquisite in every way', are his best-known works. But Hughes was also much in demand as an illustrator: many novels including Allinghams's *Music Master*, children's books and periodicals all benefited from his skills in this field.

EJ

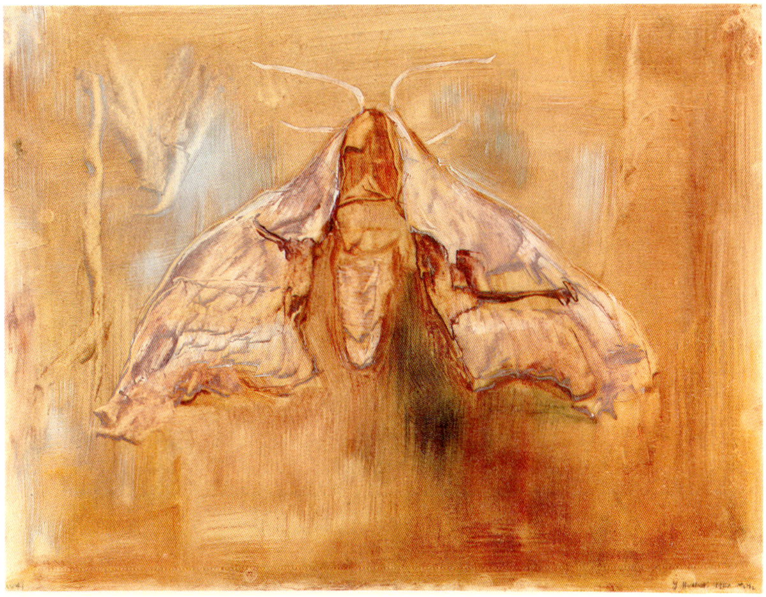

Thelma HULBERT

[1913–95]

Moth, 1960

oil, watercolour and bodycolour on paper, 37.4 × 50 cm
inscribed: *T Hulbert 1960 Moth*

P.490
PROVENANCE: Redfern Gallery Ltd, from whom purchased by Gallery, May 1965.

Born in Bath, Hulbert studied painting and design at the Bath School of Art 1927–33, before moving to London in the early 1930s. During the late 1930s she studied at the Euston Road School, where she became the Group's Secretary. After the war, she taught art at both the Camden School for Girls and the Central School of Arts and Crafts. In 1984 she moved to Honiton, Devon, where she remained until her death. A museum has since been opened in her former home, Elmfield House, Honiton.

EJ/CB

William Henry HUNT, o.w.s.
[1790–1864]
Village Scene with Timbered Houses, 1815–20

pen and brown ink with watercolour on paper, 27.1 × 33 cm

P.77
PROVENANCE: Gilbert Davis; P&D Colnaghi Ltd, from whom purchased by Gallery, February 1953.
EXHIBITIONS: *English Watercolours from The Cecil Higgins Art Gallery, Bedford*, Reading, Reading Museum and Art Gallery, 1965, no.25.
REFERENCES: J. Witt, *William Henry Hunt*, 1982, p.144, no.6.

Witt dates this 1815–20 and suggests the scene is *A Bushey neighbourhood*.

EJ

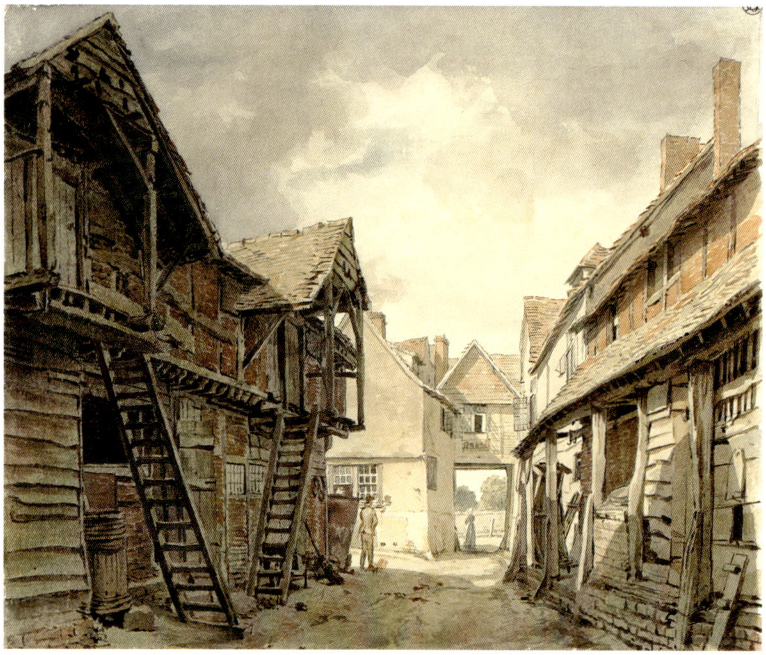

William Henry HUNT, o.w.s.
[1790–1864]
The Water Mill, Bushey, Herts., 1815–20

pen and ink with watercolour over black lead on paper, 33.5 × 42.7 cm

P.108
PROVENANCE: Major Rt. Hon. Sloane Stanley; Messrs. Woolley & Wallis; P&D Colnaghi Ltd, from whom purchased by Gallery, November 1955.
EXHIBITIONS: *English Watercolours from The Cecil Higgins Art Gallery, Bedford,* Reading, Reading Museum and Art Gallery, November 1955.
REFERENCES: J. Witt, *William Henry Hunt,* 1982, no.8, pl.17; G. Longman, *Bushey Then & Now,* 1968, no.4, pl.3; V.H. Wotton, *The Misbourne Miscellany,* 1990, p.22.

Born in London, William Hunt suffered from malformation of the bones and according to his uncle 'nervy little Billy Hunt was always a cripple, and as he was fit for nothing, they made an artist of him'. He was apprenticed to John VARLEY for seven years, and also studied at the R.A. Schools and at Dr MONRO's 'Academy'. It was due to the support of Dr Thomas Monro that Hunt spent the summers of 1815 to 1820 in Bushey, Hertfordshire, staying at Monro's country house.

CB

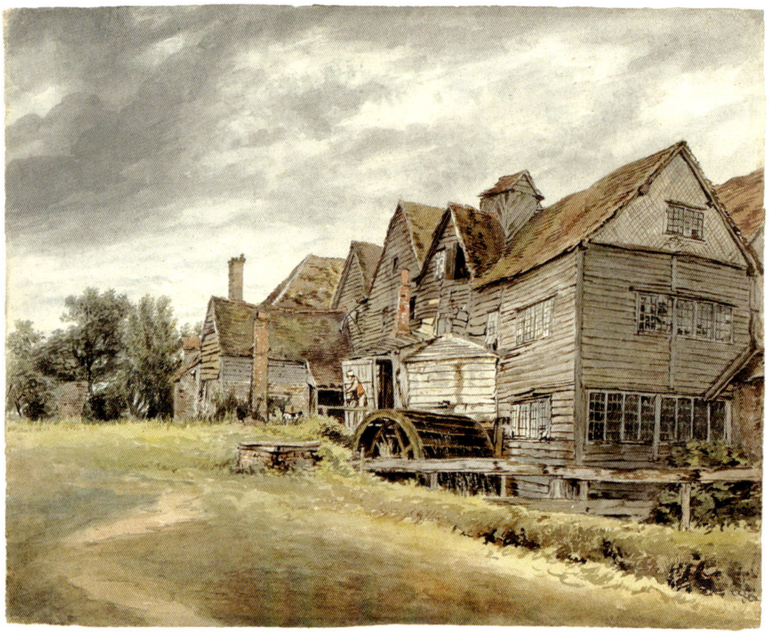

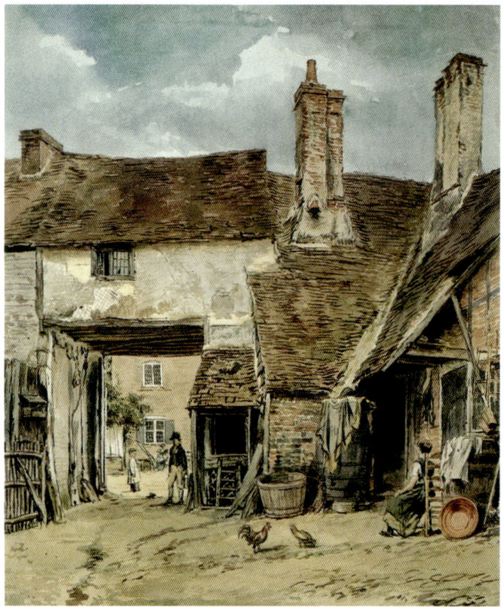

William Henry HUNT, o.w.s.
[1790–1864]
Old Bell Yard, Bushey, 1815–20
reed pen, ink and watercolour on paper, 39.5 × 33 cm

P.109
PROVENANCE: Major Rt. Hon. Sloane Stanley; Messrs. Woolley & Wallis; P&D Colnaghi Ltd, from whom purchased by Gallery, November 1955.
EXHIBITIONS: *The Great Age of British Watercolours: 1750–1850,* London, R.A. and Washington, National Gallery of Art, 1993, no.178, p.306, pl.81.
REFERENCES: G. Longman, *Bushey Then & Now,* 1968, pl.4; J. Witt, *William Henry Hunt,* 1982,p.144,no.7.

Drawn c.1815 probably when staying with his patron Dr MONRO, who paid Hunt 7s 6d a day for the drawings he produced. Some of Hunt's best work was done around Bushey where, because he was physically disabled, he was 'trundled on a sort of barrow with a hood over it, drawn by a man or a donkey'.

EJ

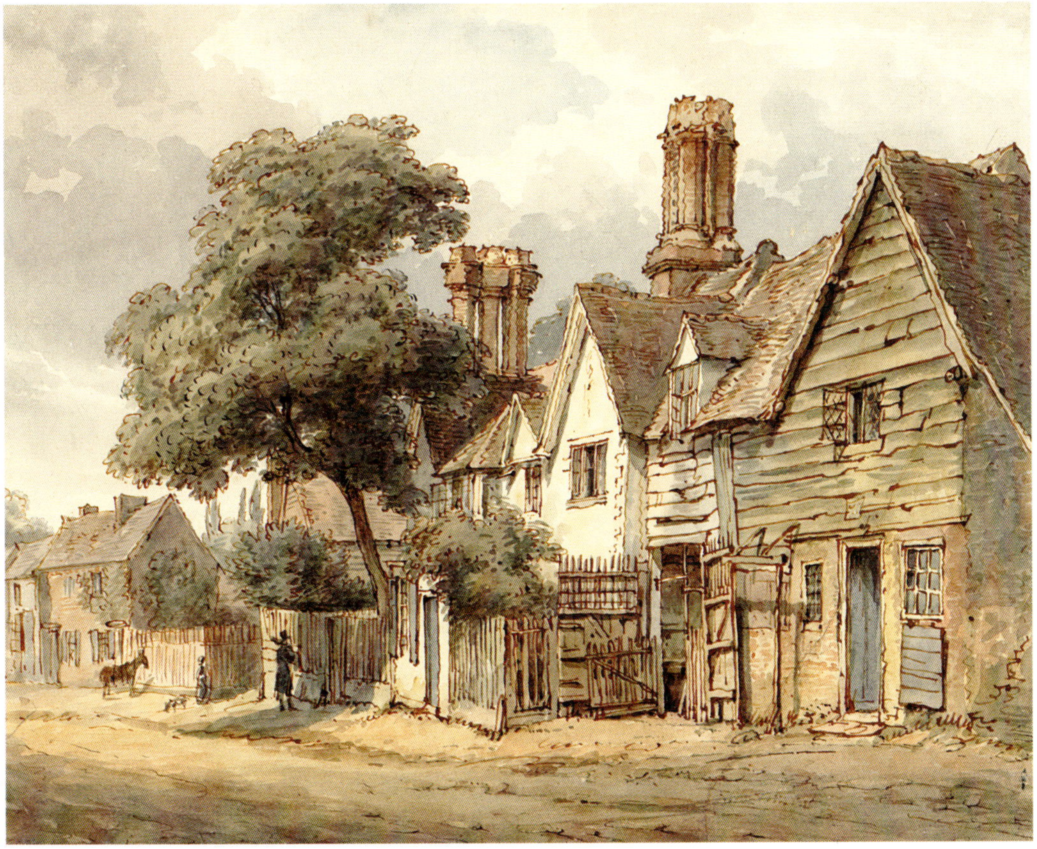

William Henry HUNT, o.w.s.
[1790–1864]
Bushey High Street, 1815–20

reed pen, ink and watercolour on paper, 28.8 × 36.7 cm

P.110
PROVENANCE: Major Rt. Hon. Sloane Stanley; Messrs. Woolley and Wallis; P&D Colnaghi Ltd., from whom purchased by Gallery, November 1955.
REFERENCES: G. Longman, *Bushey Then & Now,* 1968, pl.2; J. Witt, *William Henry Hunt,* 1982, p.144, no.9.

Witt dates this to 1815–20 and compares it to the back view of the same cottages (no.241 in his catalogue) now in the Yale Center for British Art, New Haven.

EJ

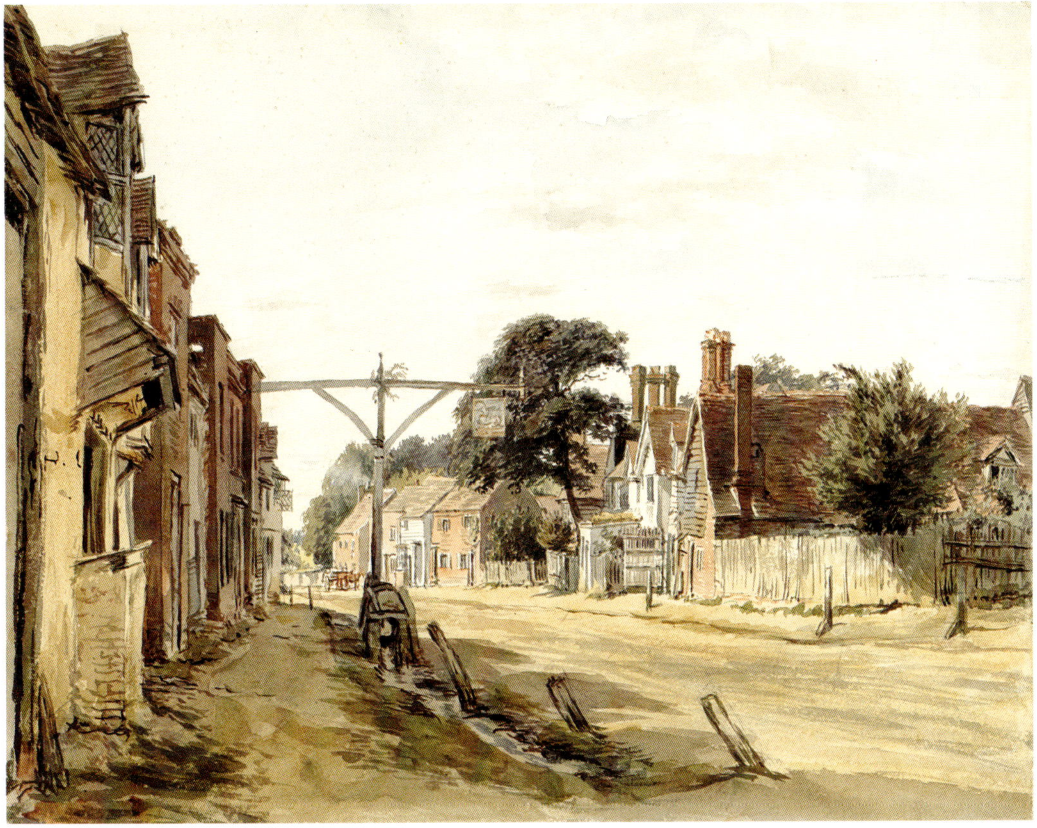

William Henry HUNT, o.w.s.
[1790–1864]
The White Hart Inn, Bushey High Street, 1815–20

reed pen, ink and watercolour on paper, 32.8 × 42.4 cm

P.111
PROVENANCE: Major Rt. Hon. Sloane Stanley, Messrs. Woolley and Wallis; P&D Colnaghi Ltd, from whom purchased by Gallery, November 1955.
EXHIBITIONS: *Watercolours and Drawings from The Cecil Higgins Art Gallery, Bedford*, London, Thos. Agnew & Sons Ltd, 1962, no.48; *William Henry Hunt 1790–1864,* Wolverhampton, Central Art Gallery, Preston, Harris Museum and Art Gallery and Hastings, Hastings Museum and Art Gallery, 1981, no.30, p.19.
REFERENCES: J. Witt, *William Henry Hunt 1970–1864,* 1982, p.145, no.10; G. Longman, *Bushey Then & Now,* 1968, pl.1.

Witt dates this drawing 1815–20. The 1981 exhibition catalogue suggests that this gives 'an early hint of Hunt's later exploration of light effects', possibly due to his seeing GAINSBOROUGH's *Show-box* at Dr MONRO's. (The *Show-box* was a light box that enabled Gainsborough to view transparent paintings by artificial light.)

EJ

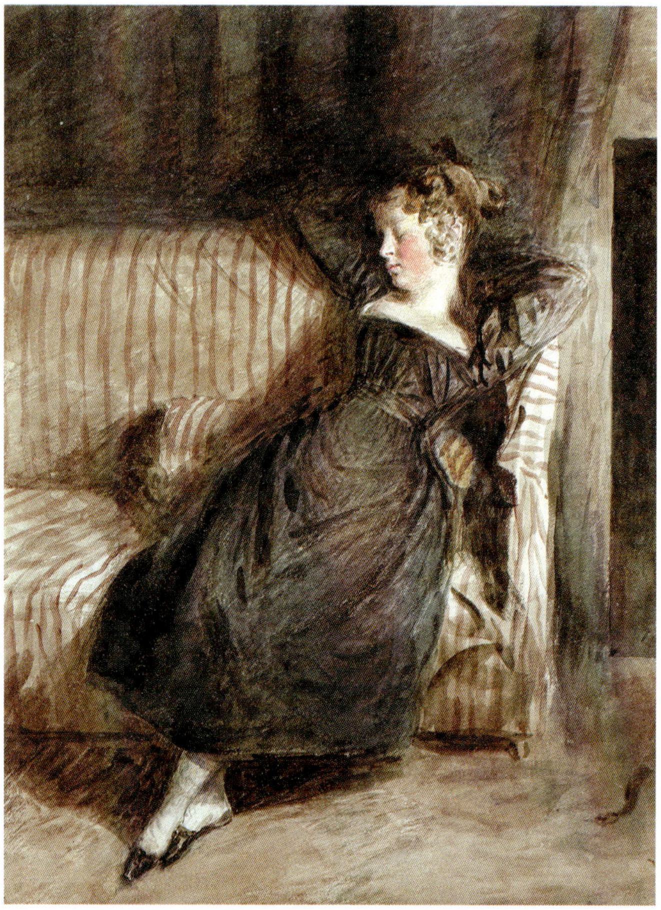

William Henry HUNT, o.w.s.
[1790–1864]
Young Girl asleep on a Couch, c.1830

watercolour and pencil heightened with white on paper, 35.4 × 26.5 cm

P.194
PROVENANCE: J. Bryson; P&D Colnaghi Ltd, from whom purchased by Gallery, April 1958.
EXHIBITIONS: *English Watercolours from The Cecil Higgins Art Gallery, Bedford,* Reading, Reading Museum and Art Gallery, 1965, no.27.
REFERENCES: A. Bury, 'The Cecil Higgins Museum, Bedford: A Preliminary Study', *Old Watercolour Society's Club, 1961,* vol.xxxvi, pl.xiv; J. Witt, *William Henry Hunt,* 1982, p.168, no.266, pl.41.

Witt suggests a date of c.1830, which seems likely both on stylistic grounds and from the sitter's dress. Adrian Bury suggests that the girl may well be Hunt's daughter.

EJ

William Henry HUNT, o.w.s.
[1790–1864]
Mrs. Gurney Hoare, early 1830s

pencil, watercolour and bodycolour with scratching out on paper, 31.3 × 22.9 cm
inscribed: *W Hunt* *Mrs Gurney Hoare* (not Hunt's hand)

P.320
PROVENANCE: P&D Colnaghi Ltd., from whom purchased by Gallery, January 1960.
EXHIBITIONS: *Watercolours and Drawings from The Cecil Higgins Art Gallery, Bedford,* London, Thos. Agnew & Sons Ltd, 1962, no.38; *English Watercolours from The Cecil Higgins Art Gallery, Bedford,* Reading, Reading Museum and Art Gallery, 1965, no.28.
REFERENCES: J. Witt, *William Henry Hunt,* 1982, p.168, no.265.

The sitter was born Caroline Barclay; her family were brewers (now Courage's). In 1837 she married John Gurney Hoare (1810–76), a banker. Her elaborate hairstyle and the very full upper sleeves of her dress are typical of the 1830s, indicating that Witt's date of 1825–30 is rather too early.

EJ

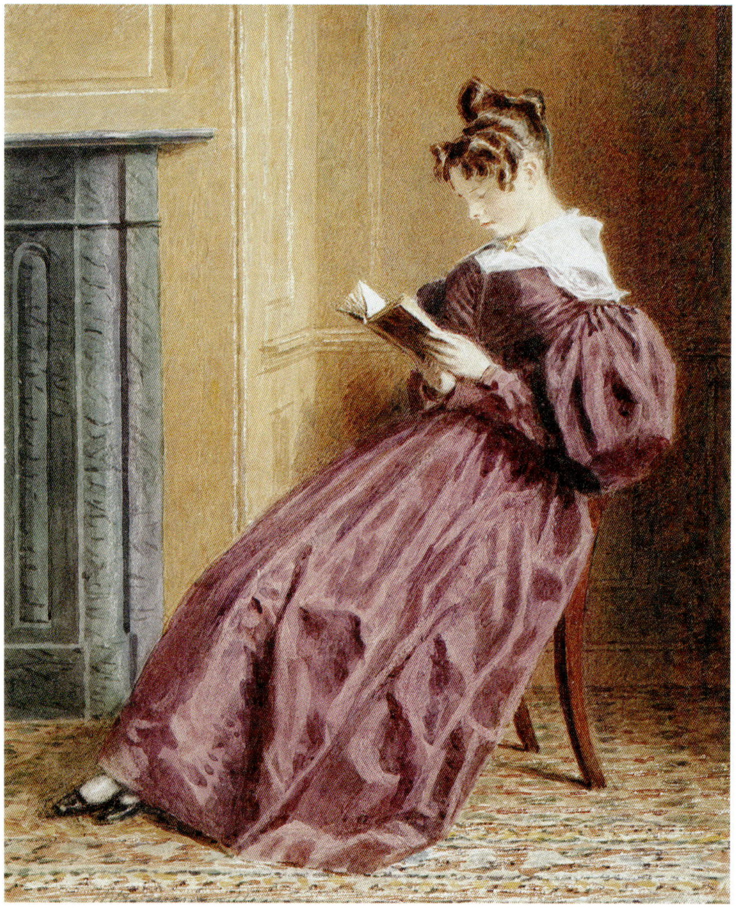

William Henry HUNT, o.w.s.
[1790–1864]
The Maid and the Magpie, 1834

watercolour heightened with white on paper, 44.1 × 56.9 cm
inscribed on reverse: *George A Musgrave, Esq F.R.G.S. 45 Holland Park, W*
William Hunt *Exposed to the*
Date 1838 *light for 48 years*
Interior of cottage at Shillington now the Property of Horace Musgrave, Esq
Painted for George Musgrave, Esq. Deceased of Shillington Manor, Beds.
Shillington Beds. Cottage – David Coppers daughter pairing apples
School benches – cut straw ends of plaittings. Drawn by William Hunt for my father in 1838

P.609
PROVENANCE: George Musgrave, for whom painted; Horace Musgrave; C. Fairfax Murray; Property of a Gentleman; Sotheby's sale 18 June 1970, lot 171, Thos. Agnew & Sons Ltd, from whom purchased by Gallery, June 1970.
EXHIBITIONS: *Old Watercolour Society,* 1834, no.20; *Winter Exhibition,* London, R.A., 1908, no.214; *William Henry Hunt 1790–1864,* Wolverhampton, Central Art Gallery, Preston, Harris Museum and Art Gallery and Hastings, Museum and Art Gallery, 1981, no.115; *Art Treasures of England: The Regional Collections,* 1998, no.219.
REFERENCES: J. Witt, *William Henry Hunt,* 1982, p.168, no.267, pl.75; *Painter's Progress,* 1983, p.216.

Ostensibly a genre subject, this is in fact a reference to a popular melodrama of the same title by Isaac Pocock, first produced at Covent Garden in 1815. It concerns a poor serving girl saved from conviction for stealing a spoon by the discovery of a magpie as the culprit. Rossini's opera *The Thieving Magpie* (1817) is based on a French version of the same story.

Shillington is not far from Bedford; Shillington Manor belonged to the drawing's first owner, George Musgrave, while his son, Horace, came to own the cottage shown here. Despite the later inscription quoted above, Lindsay Stainton, in the 1998 exhibition catalogue, confirms Witt's view that this is certainly the drawing exhibited in 1834 and that 1838 is therefore incorrect. She draws attention to the beautiful play of light on the girl's face as she turns her head.

EJ

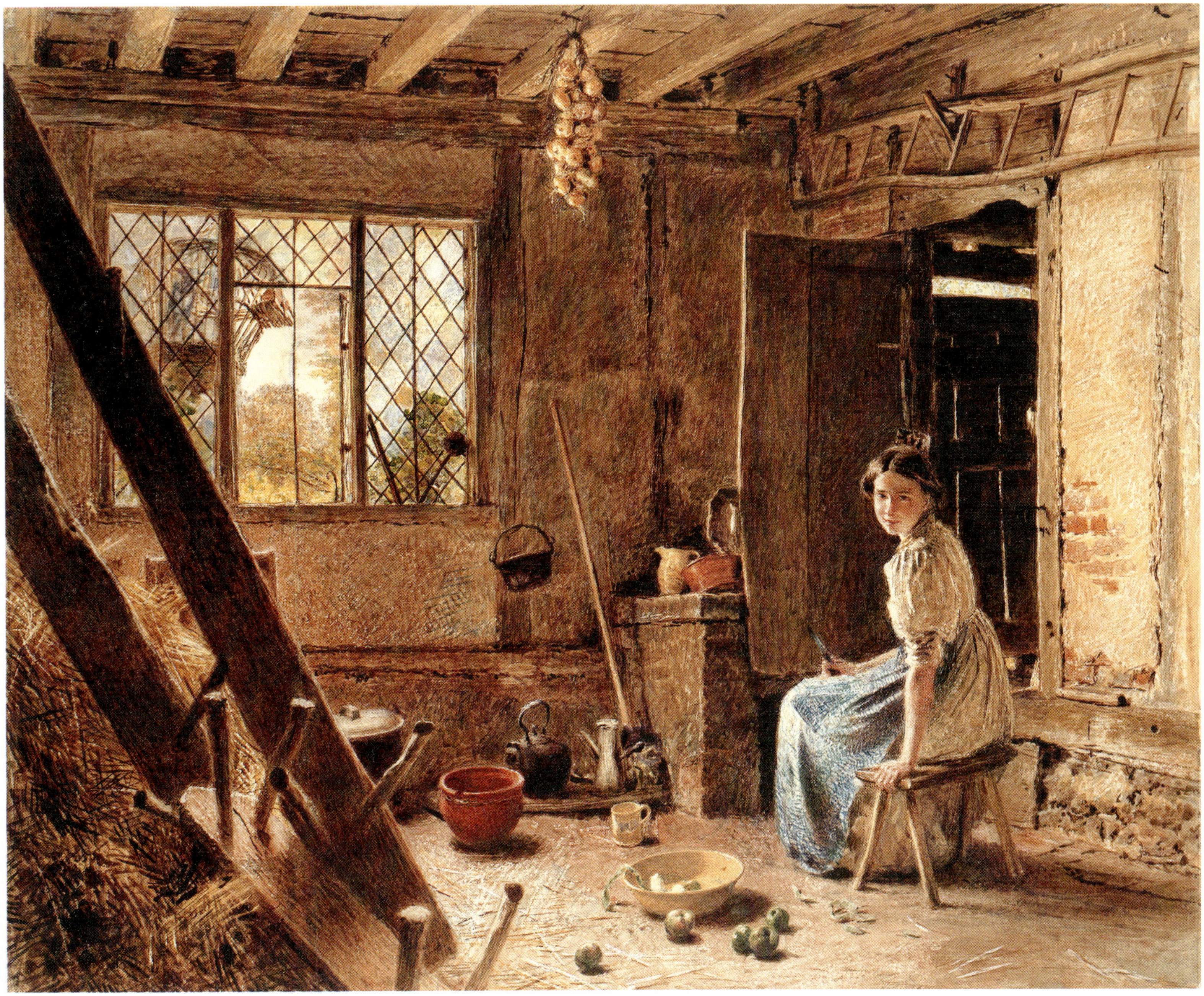

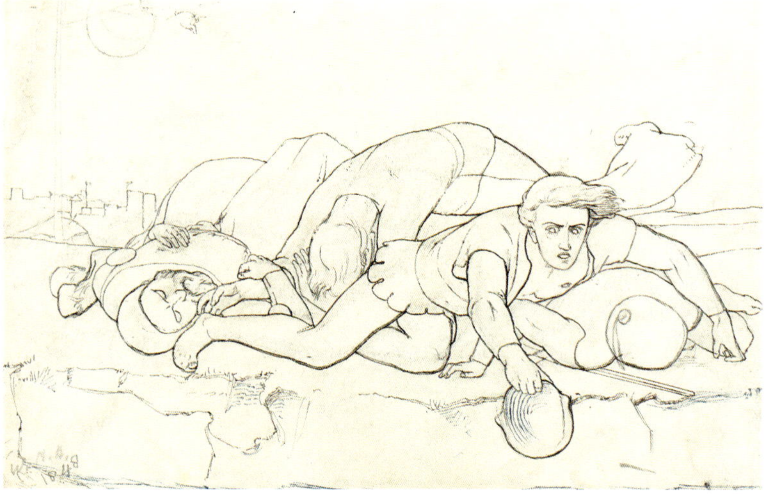

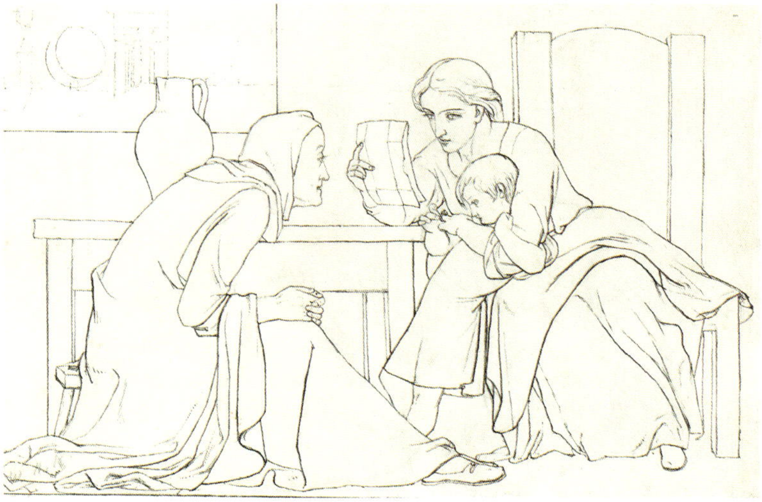

William Holman HUNT, O.M.

[1827–1910]

Peace and War illustrations to a poem by Leigh Hunt, 1848

pen and ink on paper, 13.2 × 21.5 cm
inscribed probably at a later date: *WHH Peace 1848*
on reverse: *Figure sketches in pencil*

P.135

PROVENANCE: The artist; by descent to Hilary Holman Hunt; anon. sale Christie's, 3 August 1945, lot no.132 (with a third drawing illustrating Keats' *Hyperion*); bought by Walker; Leger Gallery from whom purchased by Gallery, November 1957.
EXHIBITIONS: *Paintings and Drawings of the 1860's Period*, London, Tate Gallery, 1923, no.314 with manuscript opinions of Rossetti and Millais; *Victorian Romantics*, London, Leicester Galleries, 1949, no.50; *William Holman Hunt*, Liverpool, Walker Art Gallery and London, V&A, 1969, nos. 96 & 97.
REFERENCES: William Holman Hunt, *Pre-Raphaelitism and the Pre-Raphaelite Brotherhood*, 2 vols., 1st edition 1905, II, pp.81 illus. 82; 2nd edition 1913, II, pp.56 illus., 58; R. Watkinson, *Pre-Raphaelites and Design*, 1969, pl.28.

According to Hunt these were designed for the Cyclographic Club in 1848. The club would set subjects for members to draw and later criticize. Of this work D.G. ROSSETTI said:

The Subject new and impressive being taken moreover from a glorious poem which deserves illustration. In the first sketch I agree with Mr Deverill that the old woman too much resembles the German 'StoryTeller', although with him I doubt not that the coincidence is accidental.
I think too that this figure is rather too angular in lines and that the leg is too much forward for the position, something more over should be seen of the left arm. I like the second sketch equally, although it is evidently executed more in haste and is therefore deficient in certain details which can be easily supplied.

John Everett MILLAIS added: 'This sketch is very beautiful in sentiment and careful in composition if the legs of the boy were continued downwards they would reach the bottom of the drawing – No.2 – quite as good in its style'.

They illustrate the poem *Captain Sword and Captain Pen* by Leigh Hunt (1784–1859), first published in 1835 and dedicated to Lord Brougham (1778–1868). More precisely they illustrate the second and third stanzas of Part IV of the poem: 'On what took place on the field of Battle the Night after Victory'. Despite Captain Sword's triumph of arms, the husband of one of the women in *Peace* is slain and finally Captain Sword 'rusted apart', leaving Captain Pen 'To make a world of swordless men'.

EJ/CB

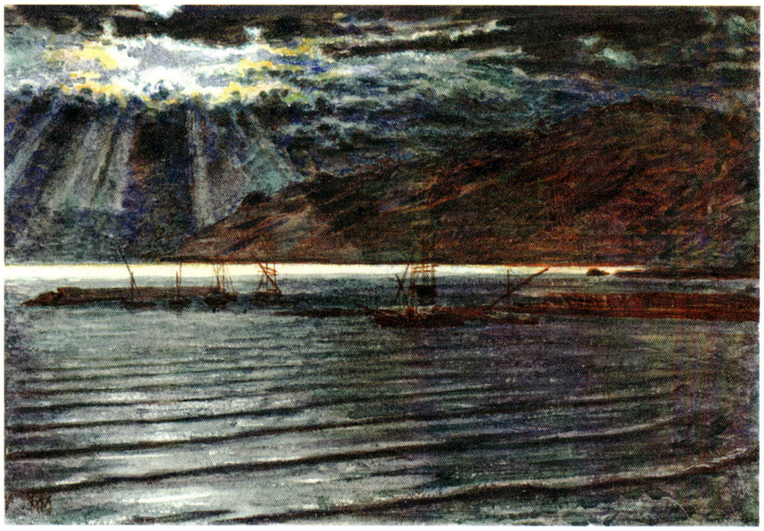

William Holman HUNT, O.M.

[1827–1910]

Fishing-Boats by Moonlight, c.1869

watercolour, bodycolour and pencil on paper, 10.1 × 15.2 cm
inscribed with monogram

P.351

PROVENANCE: C.W. Dyson Perrins; Sotheby's, 22 April 1959, lot 56; Thos. Agnew & Sons Ltd. from whom purchased by Gallery, July 1960.
EXHIBITIONS: *Watercolours and Drawings from The Cecil Higgins Art Gallery, Bedford*, London, Thos. Agnew & Sons Ltd, 1962, no.43; *William Holman Hunt*, Liverpool, Walker Art Gallery and London, V&A, 1969, no.218; *The Great Age of British Watercolours 1750–1880*, London, R.A. and Washington D.C., National Gallery of Art, 1993, no.185.
REFERENCES: Letter from Hunt to E.R. Dibdin, Curator of the Walker Art Gallery, 4 January 1907, which possibly identifies this drawing with a watercolour, *The Haven of Rest*, which depicts shipping in a harbour on a moonlit stormy night but the measurements do not tally; R. Watkinson, *Pre-Rahaelites and Design*, 1969, pl.30; A. Wilton & A. Lyles, *The Great Age of British Watercolours 1750–1880*, 1993, p.306, pl.271, where dated c.1869.

Holman Hunt's output in watercolour was tiny compared with his work in oil. Between 1869 and 1903 he exhibited thirty-nine works at the R.W.S., which Martin HARDIE considers 'comprise the greater part of his water-colour work'.

A leading member of the Pre-Raphaelite Brotherhood, Hunt's pictures *The Light of the World* and *The Scapegoat* must be as well known as any Victorian paintings. His watercolours differ from those of the other Pre-Raphaelite artists in only very rarely using body-colour (but see above); instead he worked in transparent colours on brilliant white paper, which produced an effect of radiant illumination and vivid sunlight.

EJ

Rudolph IHLEE
[1883–1968]
The Quarrel, c.1906–10

pen, ink and chalk on blue paper, 20 × 24.7 cm
inscribed: *R. Ihlee*

P.263
PROVENANCE: Leicester Galleries, from whom purchased by Gallery, October 1958.
EXHIBITIONS: *Ihlee Retrospective,* Peterborough, St. Peter's College Hall, Arts Council, 1951; *Artists of Fame and Promise,* London, Leicester Galleries, 1958, no.17.

Following an apprenticeship as an engineer, Ihlee attended the Slade School of Art between 1906–10 when this was drawn. He proved a brilliant student, winning many prizes, among some outstanding contemporaries such as Mark Gertler (1892–1939), NEVINSON, Derwent Lees (1885–1931), INNES and WADSWORTH. After two one-man shows at the Carfax Gallery 1912–14, he worked as an engineering draughtsman in Peterborough during the First World War.

Between the wars he exhibited mainly in France, having settled in Collioure in 1922, a decision that affected his subsequent career adversely although he was the least ambitious of men. After the fall of France, in 1940, he returned to England and worked in a factory in Leicester during the war. He later settled in West Deeping, Lincolnshire.

EJ/CB

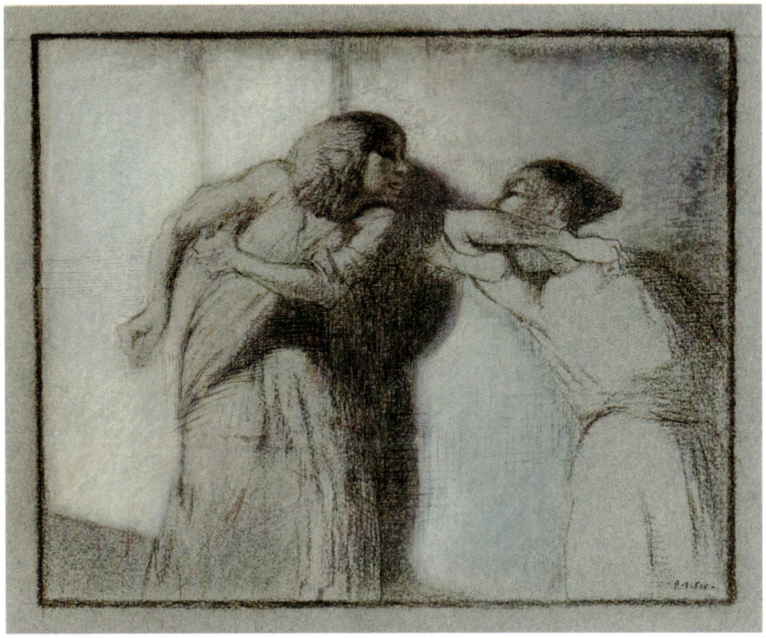

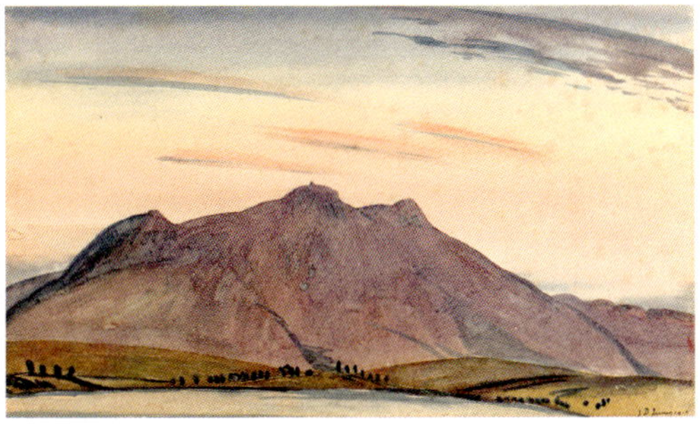

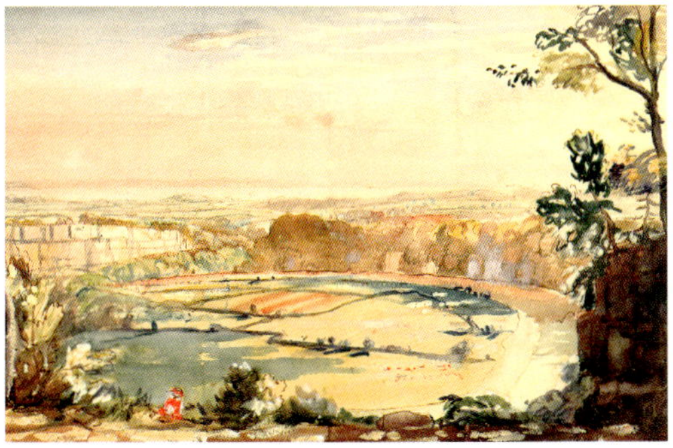

James Dickson INNES
[1887–1914]
The Valley of the Wye, 1907

watercolour, bodycolour and pen on paper, 31 × 49.1 cm

P.326
PROVENANCE: Lady Margaret Montagu-Pollock; Thos. Agnew & Sons Ltd, from whom purchased by Gallery, January 1960.
EXHIBITIONS: *J. D. Innes,* Sheffield, Graves Art Gallery only, 1961, no.63; *The Camden Town Group,* Bedford, Cecil Higgins Art Gallery, 1969, no.26; *J. D. Innes,* Southampton, Southampton Art Gallery, Cardiff, National Museum of Wales and London, Fine Art Society only, 1977–8, no.15.
REFERENCES: C. Hampton, *Some of the Sources for the Art of J.D. Innes,* BA Thesis, Cambridge University, 1970, no.205.

Innes attended the Slade School from 1906–8, where he was taught by Wilson STEER. In 1907 he spent the summer vacation at Chepstow, visible in the distance of this painting, on the Wye.

At the Slade he met Derwent Lees (1885–1931) and formed a close working relationship with him; they later often painted together at Collioure in southern France. He also became friends with Augustus JOHN, through his connection with the Camden Town Group. After he contracted tuberculosis he travelled and painted in Spain, France, Ireland as well as Wales, finally, but unsuccessfully, seeking to recuperate in Morocco and Tenerife. A portrait of Innes by Randolph SCHWABE, a fellow student, is in the Gallery's collection (P.541).

EJ

James Dickson INNES
[1887–1914]
Arenig, 1912

watercolour on paper, 20.9 × 35.4 cm
inscribed: *J D Innes 1912*

P.246
PROVENANCE: Leicester Galleries, from whom purchased by Gallery, July 1958.
EXHIBITIONS: *J.D. Innes,* London, Leicester Galleries, 1952, no.9; *J. D. Innes,* Sheffield, Graves Art Gallery only, 1961, no.64; *Watercolours and Drawings from The Cecil Higgins Art Gallery Bedford,* London, Thos. Agnew & Sons Ltd, 1962, no.66; *The Camden Town Group,* Bedford, Cecil Higgins Art Gallery, 1969, no.25; *J. D. Innes,* Southampton, Southampton Art Gallery, Cardiff, Glynn Vivian Gallery and London, Fine Art Society only, 1977–8, no.94.
REFERENCES: C. Hampton, *Some of the Sources for the Art of J. D. Innes,* BA Thesis, Cambridge University, 1970, no.143

Painted in 1912 when Innes, although already mortally ill with tuberculosis, was at the height of his powers. He was particularly attracted to the Arenig valley near Bala in Snowdonia and even more to the mountain itself, 853 metres above sea level. He painted it repeatedly both in oil and watercolour; indeed one might say that it obsessed him to almost the same extent that Mont Sainte-Victoire obsessed Cézanne. It was certainly the subject, as this example shows, of some of his finest watercolours.

EJ

Bill JACKLIN, R.A.

[b.1943]

Man with a Bib, 1980

watercolour on paper, 77.5 × 55.9 cm
inscribed: *Man with a bib! Jacklin 25.9.80*

P. 928
PROVENANCE: Marlborough Gallery; Gift of Dasha Shenkman, in memory of her mother Belle Shenkman. Presented by the Contemporary Art Society, 2000.
EXHIBITION: *Heads*, London, Anne Berthoud Gallery, 1982.

This moving drawing depicts Jacklin's father in hospital. During his father's illness, Jacklin made a number of drawings of him just prior to his death in the early 1960s. However, it was only with the passing of time that Jacklin felt able to tackle the subject again through a number of works during the early 1980s.

Born in Hampstead, London, Jacklin attended the R.C.A. from 1964 to 1967. His early work was abstract in nature, but he became concerned with the effects of light and movement in figurative works from the mid-1970s. Since 1985 Jacklin has lived and worked in New York, where he concentrates on the urban landscape. As a consequence, John Russell Taylor has described him as 'New York's definitive painter'.

CB with thanks to David Case

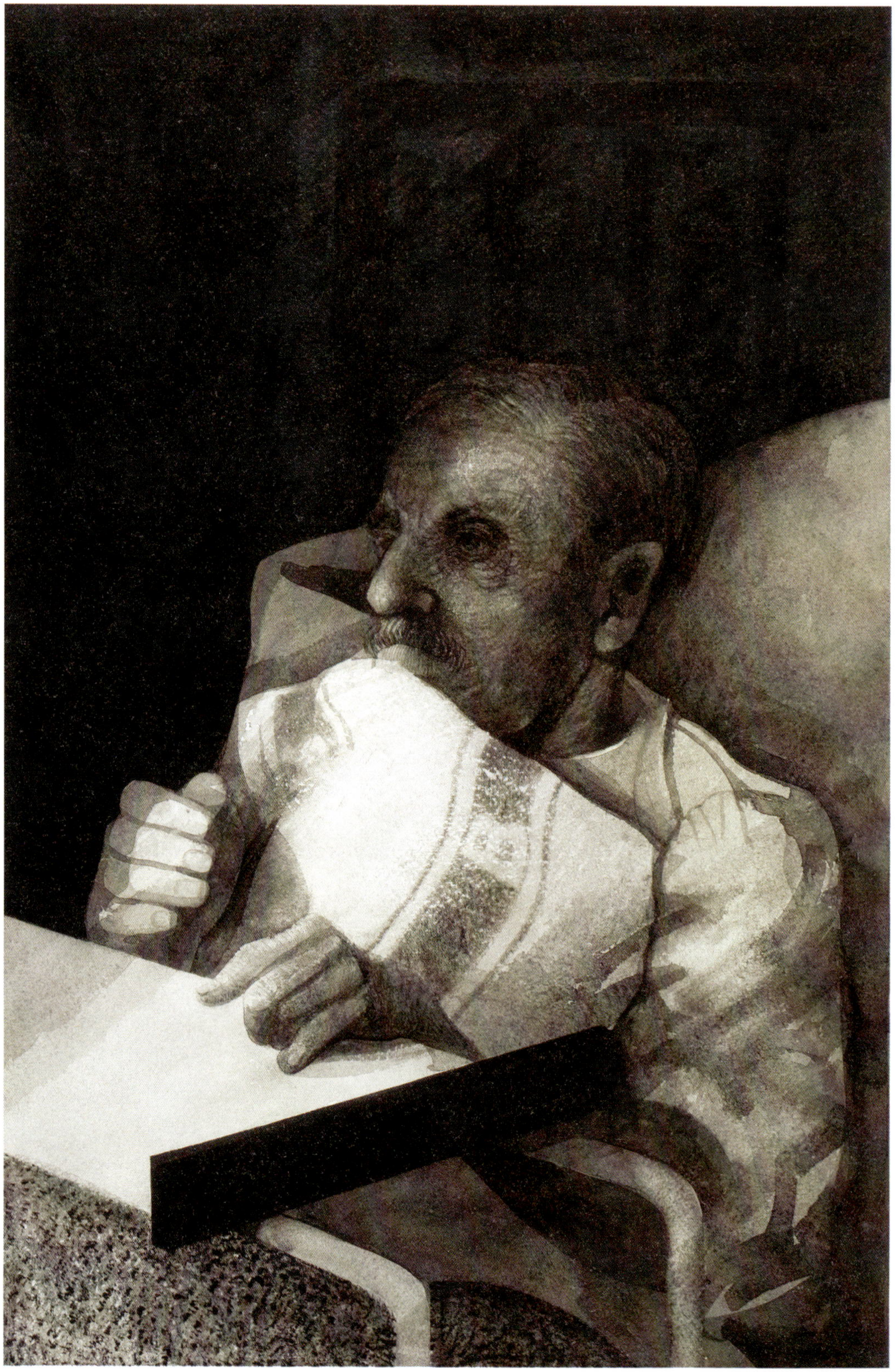

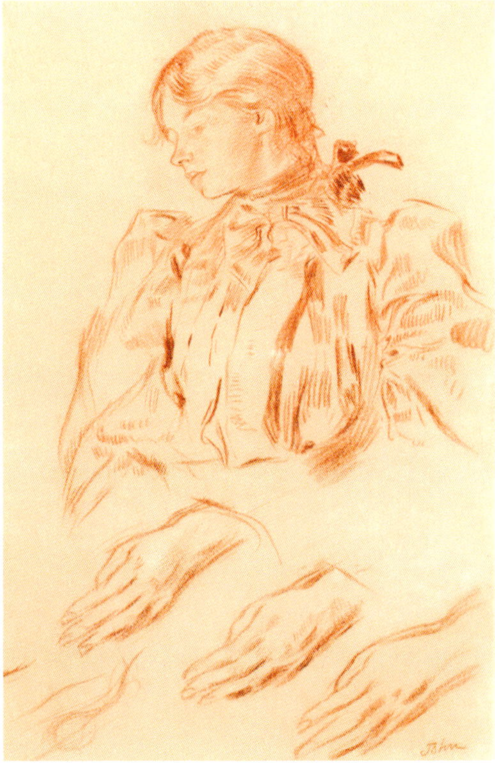

Augustus JOHN, O.M., R.A.
[1878–1961]
Portrait of Ursula Tyrwhitt and Studies of hands, c.1897

red chalk on paper, 29.9 × 19.9 cm
inscribed: *John*

P.426
PROVENANCE: Sir M.F. Montagu Pollock, Bart; executors of Lady Montagu Pollock for whom sold by Agnew's to R.J. Bailey, January 1960; Spink & Sons Ltd, from whom purchased by Gallery, July 1962.
EXHIBITIONS: *87th Annual Watercolour Exhibition*, London, Thos. Agnew & Sons Ltd, 1960, no.166; *Watercolours and Drawings from The Cecil Higgins Art Gallery, Bedford*, London, Thos. Agnew & Sons Ltd, 1962, no.71; *The Camden Town Group*, Bedford, Cecil Higgins Art Gallery, 1969, no.27.

Bought merely as *Portrait of a Girl*, the sitter has been identified by Cecily Langdale. Ursula Tyrwhitt (1878–1966) was a fellow student at the Slade School of Art, then at its zenith, with Augustus and Gwen JOHN. She appears as the centre figure in the magnificent drawing by Augustus of *Ida Nettleship, Gwen John and Ursula Tyrwhitt* in the Yale Center for British Art, New Haven, also dated c.1897.

Ursula Tyrwhitt was the lifelong friend and confidante of Gwen and one of her most regular correspondents. She was the first owner of Gwen's *Dorelia in a Black Dress* of 1903–4, now in the Tate Gallery (5910).

EJ

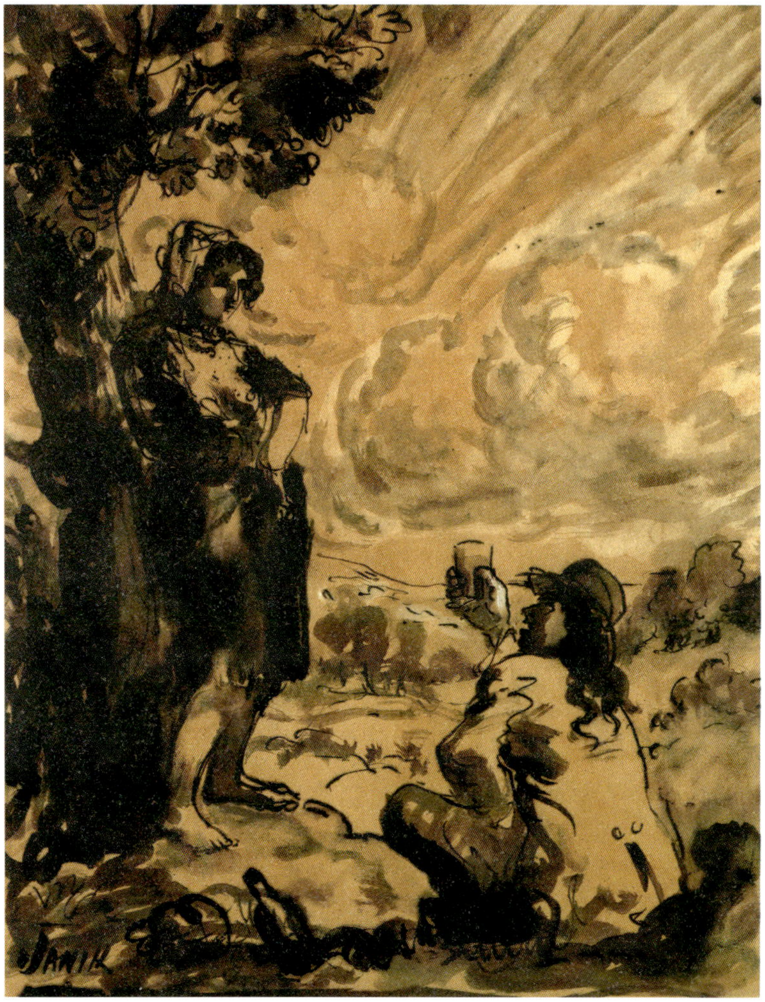

Augustus JOHN, O.M., R.A.
[1878–1961]
Illustration to Omar Khayyam, 1901

ink and wash heightened with white on paper, 38.5 × 30.4 cm
inscribed: *JANIK*

P.394
PROVENANCE: Sir Michael Sadler; Arthur Tooth & Sons Ltd, from whom purchased by Gallery, January 1961.
EXHIBITIONS: *Watercolours from Bedford*, Norwich, Castle Museum, 1965, no.26; *The Camden Town Group*, Bedford, Cecil Higgins Art Gallery, 1969, no.30; *Augustus John – Studies for Composition*, Cardiff, National Museum of Wales and New Haven, Yale Center for British Art, 1978, no.21; *Themes and Variations: The Drawings of Augustus John 1901–1931*, Cardiff, National Museum of Wales, 1996, no.2.
REFERENCES: J. Rothenstein, *Augustus John*, 1944, p.8, no.86; M. Holroyd, M. Evans & R. John, *Themes and Variations*, 1996, p.30.

After John left the Slade in 1901 he taught at Liverpool for a year. There he met and became a close friend of John Sampson, the university's librarian. Sampson, a linguist and philologist, introduced him to gypsies and taught him their Romany language. This accounts for the signature here, which is the Romany version of John.

John Sampson produced a Romany translation of the *Rubaiyat* by the Persian astronomer-poet Omar Khayyam (c.1050–c.1123) for which this drawing is a study for the frontispiece. Two other preliminary drawings exist: one in which the man is not offering a toast and there is no landscape; the other also lacks the landscape and there is no glass. The Gallery's version is probably therefore the final study and brilliantly conveys the pleasures of the fleeting moment, a constant theme of the original poem.

EJ

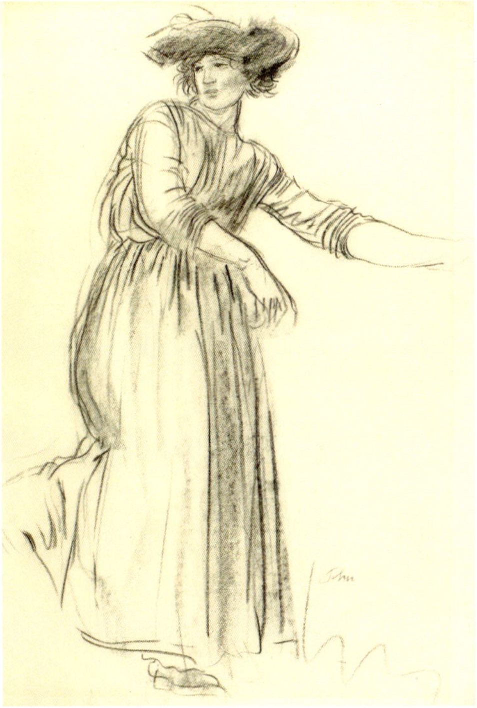

Augustus JOHN, O.M., R.A.
[1878–1961]
Ida, c.1900–7

chalk on paper, 60.8 × 40.5 cm,
inscribed: *John*

P.392
PROVENANCE: Arthur Tooth & Sons Ltd, from whom purchased by Gallery, January 1961.
EXHIBITIONS: *The English Tradition: an exhibition of watercolours from two private collections*, Bedford, Cecil Higgins Art Gallery, 1972, no.45.

The sitter, Ida Nettleship, a fellow student at the Slade School of Art, was John's first wife. They were married in 1901 but she died in Paris in March 1907 following the birth of their fifth son, Henry.

John was the most notable painter in Britain in the generation after SICKERT. He trained at the Slade, and then went to Paris where he was influenced by Puvis de Chavannes (1824–98) and Post-Impressionism. His frankness and characterizations as a portrait painter assured his fame. A larger-than-life character, the bohemian lifestyle he adopted in the late 1920s eclipsed his artistic achievements and precipitated a decline in his reputation.

EJ

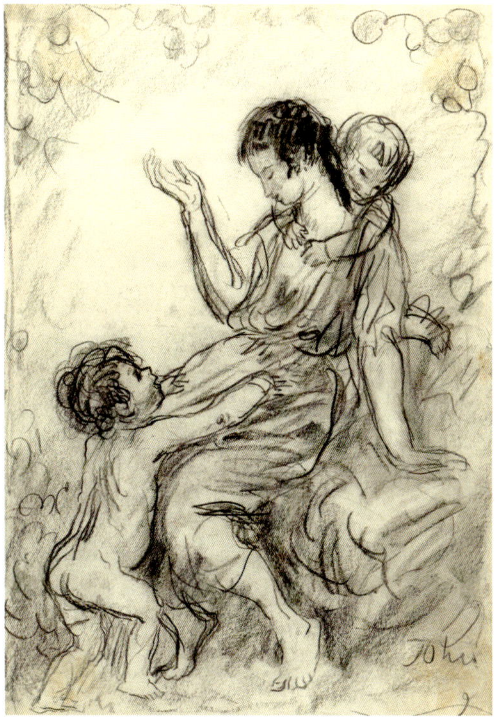

Augustus JOHN, O.M., R.A.
[1878–1961]
Dorelia and her Children, c.1903–4

charcoal on paper, 35.4 × 25.3 cm
inscribed: *John*

P.372
PROVENANCE: Redfern Gallery, from whom purchased by Gallery, October 1960.
EXHIBITIONS: *The English Tradition: an exhibition of watercolours from two private collections,* Bedford, Cecil Higgins Art Gallery, 1972, no.46.

A photograph of an almost identical drawing (untraced) is in the Augustus John archive, National Museums and Galleries of Wales, Cardiff. A chalk drawing of c.1904 depicting two women and two children, which the artist presented to the British Museum in 1906, also appears to be connected.

EJ

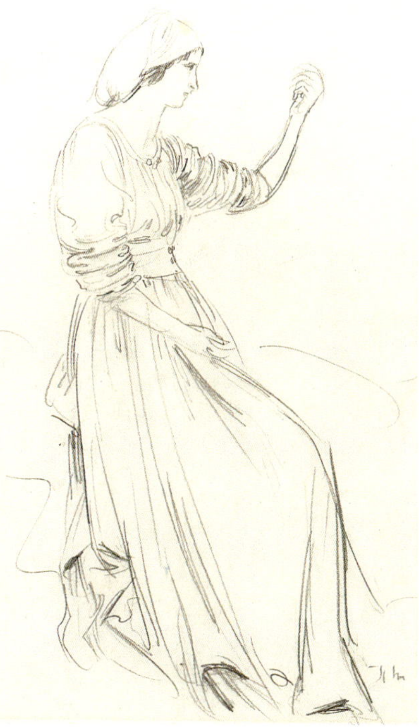

Augustus JOHN, O.M., R.A.
[1878–1961]
Dorelia with hand upraised, c.1904–6

pencil on paper, 32.8 × 20.3 cm
inscribed: *John*

P.78
PROVENANCE: Arthur Tooth & Sons, from whom purchased by Gallery, August 1952.
EXHIBITIONS: *Watercolours and Drawings from The Cecil Higgins Art Gallery, Bedford*, London, Thos. Agnew & Sons Ltd, 1962, no.68; *The Camden Town Group*, Bedford, Cecil Higgins Art Gallery, 1969, no.28.

Dorelia, born Dorothy McNeill (1881–1969), was always known as Dorelia or Dodo. She and John first met in 1903 and he soon fell passionately in love with her, painting and drawing her obsessively for almost sixty years. She soon joined John and Ida in a *ménage à trois* and bore John two sons and two daughters. She was with John when he died, surviving him until July 1969.

EJ

Augustus JOHN, O.M., R.A.
[1878–1961]
The Artist's Son (Robin John ?), c.1915–20
pencil and pastel on blue paper, 20.3 × 27.2 cm

P.179
PROVENANCE: Mrs Arthur Clifton; Thos. Agnew & Sons Ltd, from whom purchased by Gallery, January 1958.
EXHIBITIONS: *Portrait Paintings and Drawings*, Rye, Rye Art Gallery, 1967, cat. untraced.

Robin John (1904–88) was Ida's third son. As he grew up he was the quietest of John's nine children. In a letter John complained: 'He hardly utters a word and radiates *hostility*'. He grew up to be rather a loner, mainly living abroad and very rarely returning to Britain.

CB

Augustus JOHN, O.M., R.A.
[1878–1961]
Seated Nude, 1930s

pencil and pastel on paper, 50.5 × 35.4 cm
inscribed: *John*

P.393
PROVENANCE: Arthur Tooth & Sons Ltd,, from whom purchased by Gallery, January 1961.
EXHIBITIONS: *The Camden Town Group*, Bedford, Cecil Higgins Art Gallery, 1969, no.29.

Probably drawn in the 1930s, though the numerous late nude studies are not easy to date precisely. There are many such studies in the John archive at Cardiff.

EJ

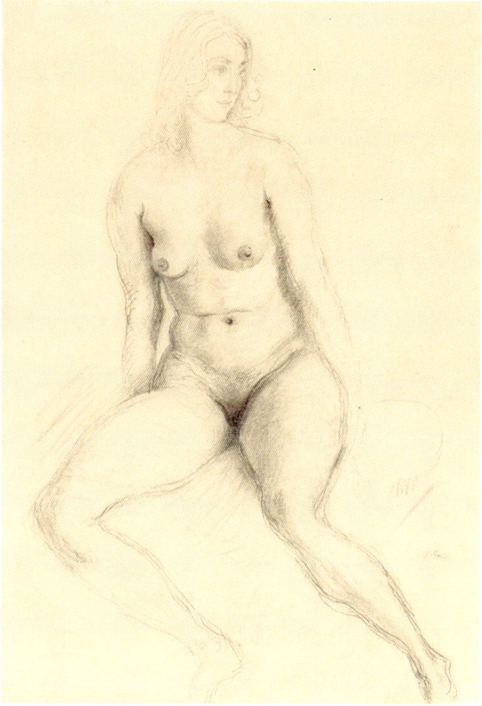

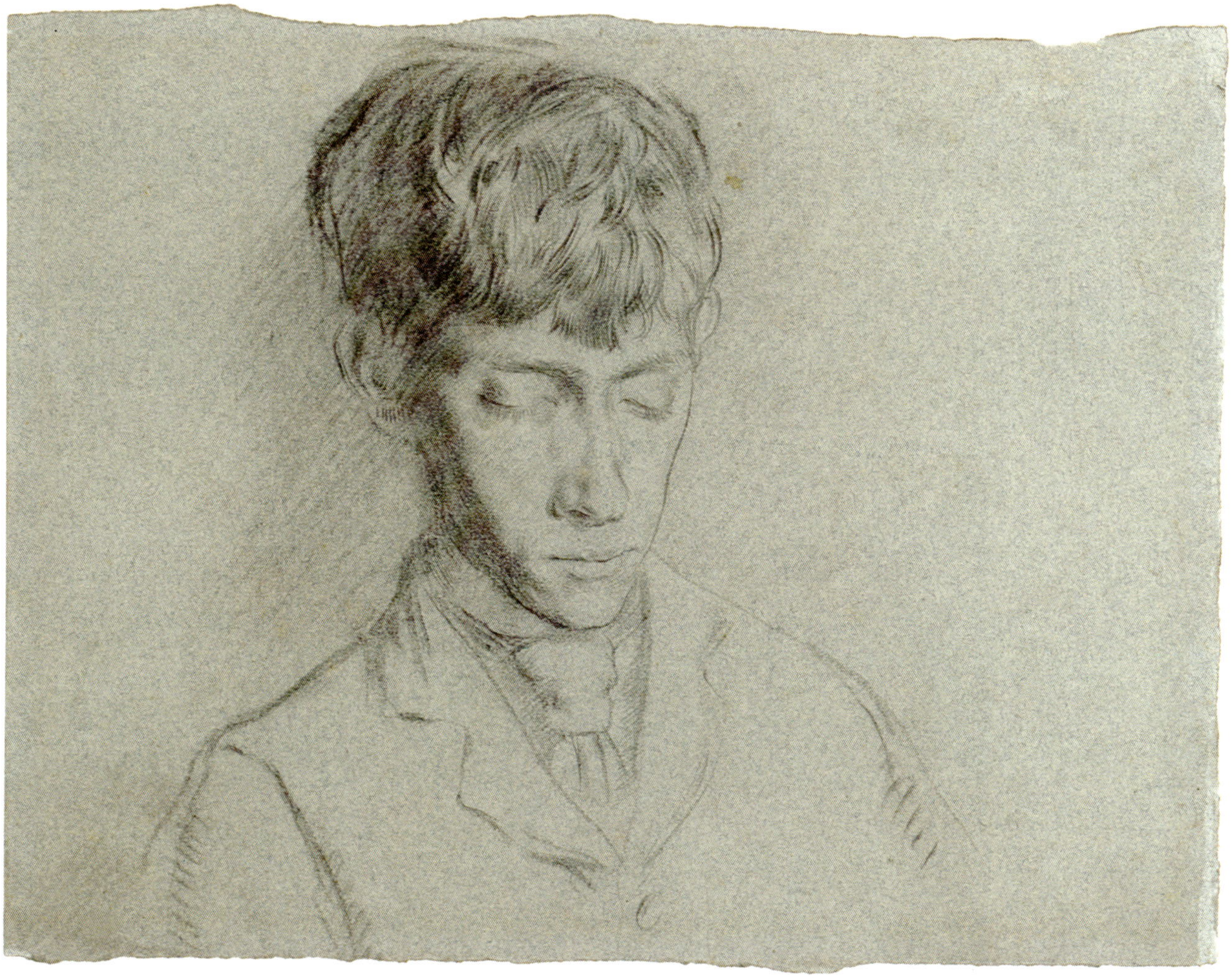

Gwen JOHN
[1876–1939]
Winifred John in a Flowered Hat, 1895–8

charcoal on paper, 31.9 × 23.8 cm

P.354
PROVENANCE: The artist's estate; Edwin John, the artist's and the sitter's nephew; Wilton Gallery, from whom purchased by Gallery, July 1960.
EXHIBITIONS: *Gwen John Memorial Exhibition*, London, Matthiesen Gallery, 1946, no.60; *Gwen John*, London, Arts Council, 1946, no.58 as *Winifred John Looking Down*; *The English Tradition*, Bedford, Cecil Higgins Art Gallery, 1972, no.49; *Gwen John & Lucie Rie*, London, Olympia, 2000, no.46.

Winifred John (1879–1967), the artist's sister, was a violinist who emigrated to America in 1905. This drawing can be dated 1895–8 during Gwen's years at the Slade School and shows what an assured draughtsman she had already become.

EJ

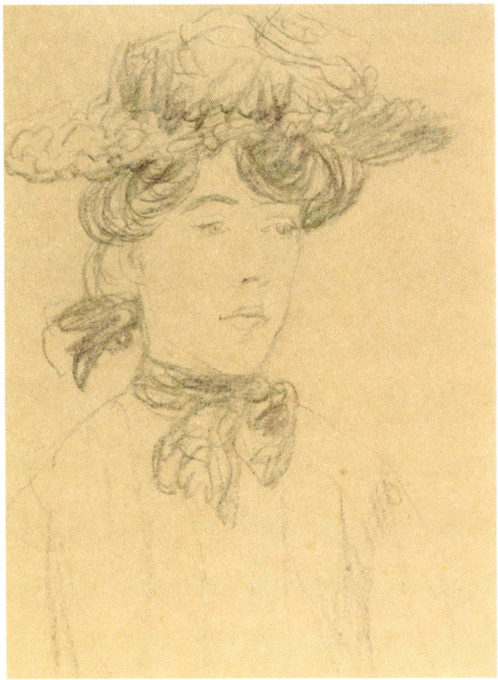

Gwen JOHN
[1876–1939]
Study of a Cat, c.1904–8

watercolour, bodycolour and pencil on buff paper, 10.6 × 15 cm
inscribed/stamped: *Gwen John*
E.J. 350

P.404
PROVENANCE: Matthiesen Ltd, from whom purchased by Gallery, January 1962.
EXHIBITIONS: *Watercolours and Drawings from The Cecil Higgins Art Gallery, Bedford*, London, Thos. Agnew & Sons Ltd, 1962, no.92; *Gwen John*, London, Hayward Gallery, Sheffield, Graves Art Gallery and Cardiff, National Museum of Wales, 1968, no.119; *The English Tradition: an exhibition of watercolours from two private collections*, Bedford, Cecil Higgins Art Gallery, 1972, no.48; *Animals in Art*, London, Sotheby's, Brighton, Brighton Museums & Art Gallery and Preston Harris Museum & Art Gallery, 1997, no cat. no.; *Gwen John & Lucie Rie*, London, Olympia, 2000, no.47.

Gwen John was devoted to this tortoise-shell cat, the subject of most of her cat drawings. She acquired her in 1904, while living at 19 boulevard Edgar Quinet and named her after that address, despite the fact that she was female. Edgar Quinet disappeared twice, the second time in 1908, permanently. A poem, 'Au Chat', that Gwen John wrote about Edgar Quinet was found among Rodin's papers after his death.

CB

Gwen JOHN
[1876–1939]
A Young Woman with High Cheekbones, late 1910s

grey wash on brown paper, 27.7 × 23 cm
stamped: *Gwen John's estate stamp*
inscribed on reverse: *EJ 70*

P.224
PROVENANCE: The artist's estate until 1957 (EJ 70); Matthiesen Ltd, from whom purchased by Gallery, December 1957.
EXHIBITIONS: *Gwen John Memorial Exhibition*, London, Matthiesen Gallery, 1946, no.90; *Gwen John 1876–1939*, London, Arts Council, 1946, no.18; *Gwen John: An Interior Life*, London, Barbican Art Gallery, 1985, no.94; *Gwen John & Lucie Rie*, London, Olympia, 2000, no.43.
REFERENCES: C. Langdale, *Gwen John*, 1987, p.211, no.264, pl.104.

The unidentified model is probably one of the Breton peasant children who posed for Gwen John during her stays in Finistere and Pleneuf.

EJ

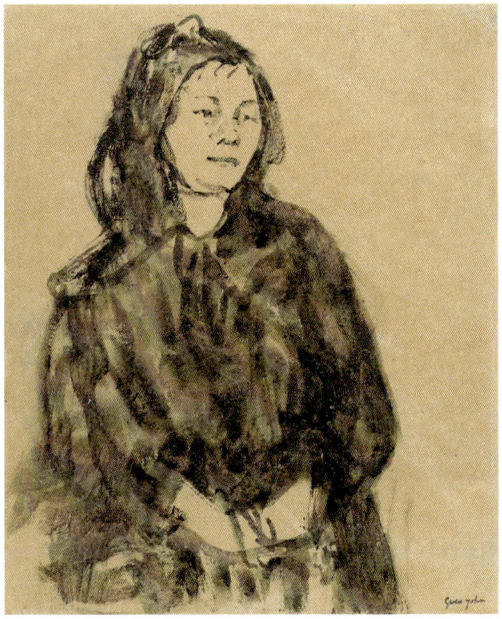

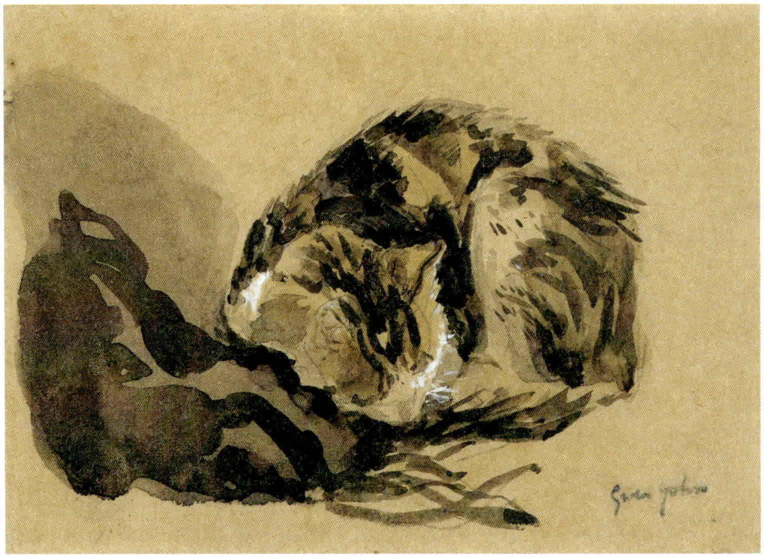

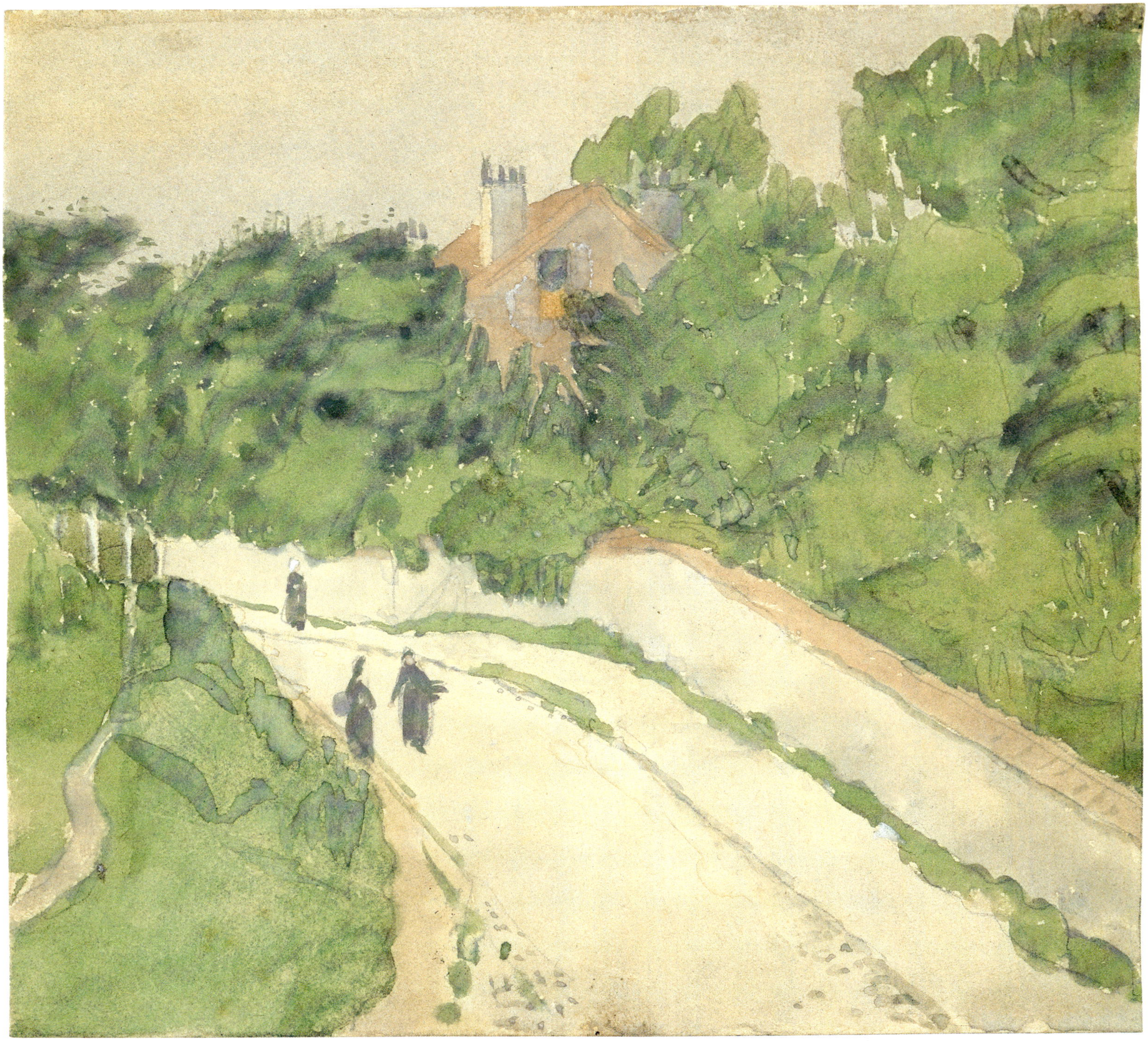

Gwen JOHN

[1876–1939]

Rue Terre Neuve, Meudon, probably late 1910s to early 1920s

bodycolour and pencil on paper, 17 × 19 cm
inscribed: Gwen John studio stamp

P.371

PROVENANCE: Gilbert Davis; Dr C. B. M. Warren; Spink & Son Ltd, from whom purchased by Gallery, October 1960, as *Figures in a lane with a house and trees in the background.*
EXHIBITIONS: *Gwen John*, London, Hayward Gallery, Sheffield, Graves Art Gallery and Cardiff, National Museum of Wales, 1968, no.130, illus.p.42 as *Figures in a lane with houses and trees; Gwen John & Lucie Rie*, London, Olympia, 2000, no.45.

In 1898 Gwen John left the Slade and went to study at WHISTLER's 'Academy' in Paris. She remained in Paris for most of her life and included amongst her friends Rainer Maria Rilke (1872–1926) and Auguste Rodin (1840–1917), with whom she had a passionate affair while modelling for him. In 1911 she moved to the top floor flat at 29 rue Terre Neuve, at Meudon, on the outskirts of Paris, and converted to Catholicism. There she painted mainly small-scale portraits, still-lifes and landscapes, such as this view from her window, with narrow tonal ranges of matt greys and pinks.

Although a complete contrast as an artist to her brother, Augustus, her reputation stands today at least as high as his. Indeed Augustus himself observed: 'One day I shall be remembered as the brother of Gwen John'. Her work is reticent and austere but reveals an exquisite sensibility that ensures that her vision will endure.

EJ/CB

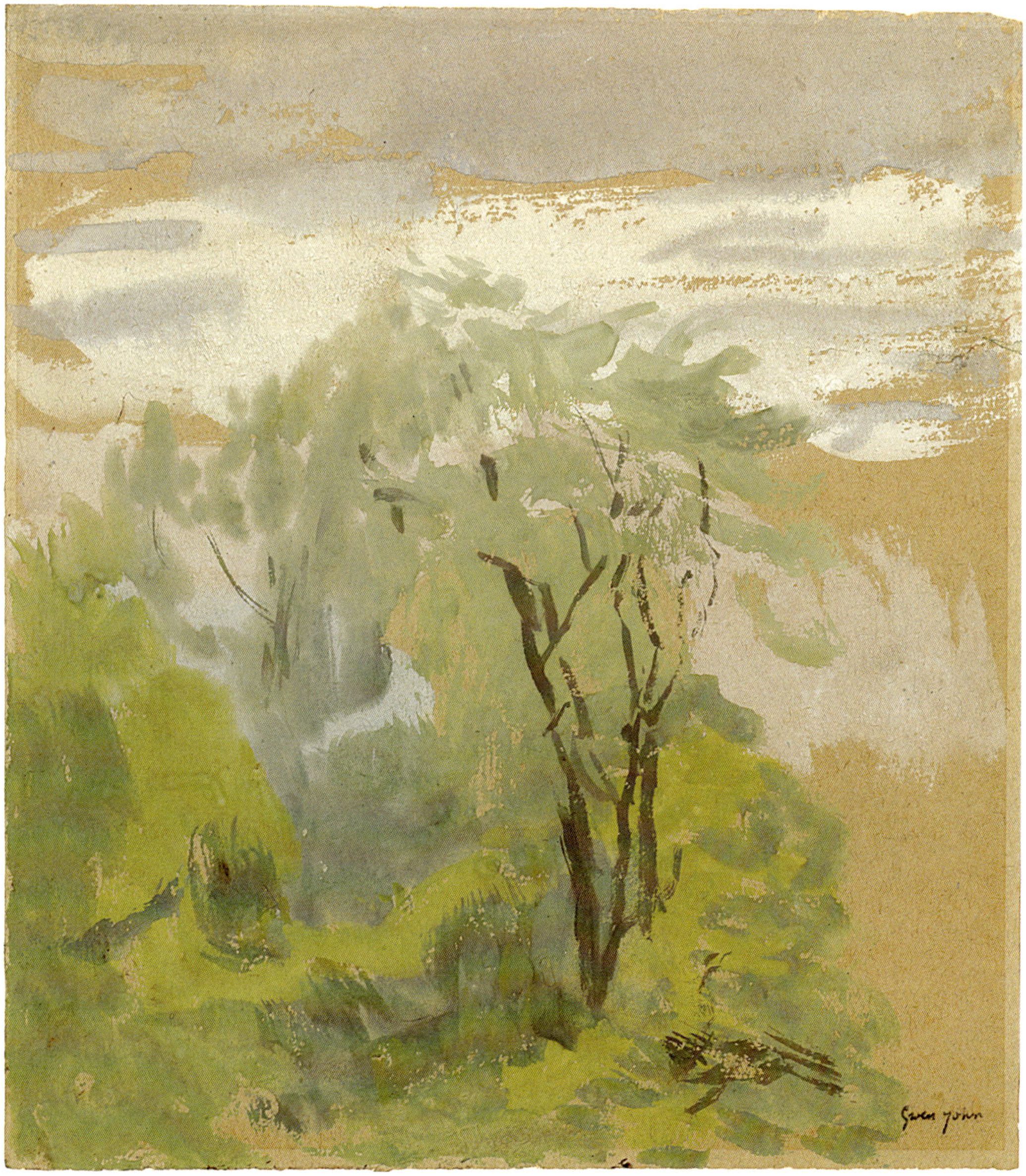

Gwen JOHN
[1876–1939]
Landscape with Trees, c.1920s

bodycolour on buff paper, 24.4 × 22.3 cm
inscribed/stamped: *Gwen John*

P.370
PROVENANCE: Matthiesen Gallery, from whom purchased by Gallery, October 1960.
EXHIBITIONS: *Gwen John Memorial Exhibition*, London, Matthiesen Gallery, 1946, no.209 as *Tree Tops against a Clouded Sky; Gwen John & Lucie Rie*, London, Olympia, 2000, no.44.

Otherwise known as *Tree Tops against a Clouded Sky,* this gouache was probably painted from her top-floor studio window at Meudon, France. The composition has been achieved with rapid and loose brushstrokes to suggest the movement of branches on a breezy day.

CB

Formerly attributed to **Gwen JOHN**
[1876–1939]
Seated Nude, c.1895–98 ?

pencil on paper, 19 × 19.5 cm
on reverse: profile of a woman

P.324
PROVENANCE: Leicester Galleries, from whom purchased by Gallery, January 1960.
EXHIBITIONS: *Gwen John & Lucie Rie*, London, Olympia, 2000, no.42 as a Gwen John.

Originally believed to be an early Slade School drawing, Cecily Langdale is certain that it is not by Gwen John, but by an unidentified 'Sladeian hand'.

EJ

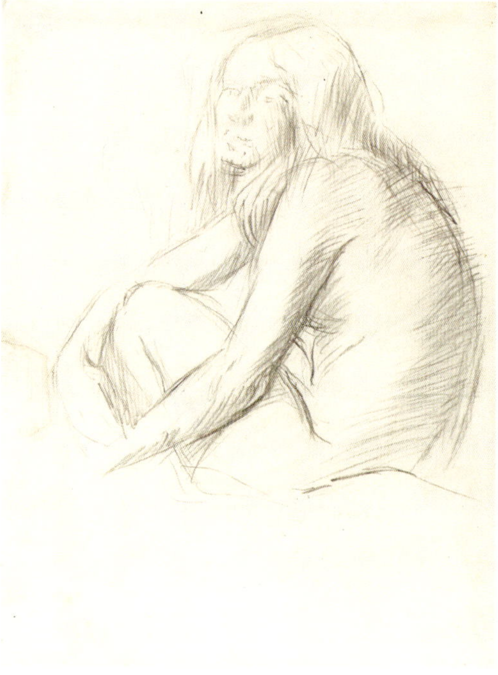

David JONES, C.H., C.B.E.

[1895–1974]

Piggott's Farm (Eric Gill's House), c.1931

watercolour on paper, 31.9 × 47.5 cm

P.419

PROVENANCE: Leicester Galleries, from whom purchased by Gallery, May 1962.

EXHIBITIONS: *Watercolours from Bedford,* Norwich, Castle Museum, 1965, no.27; *English Landscape in the 20th Century,* London, Camden Arts Centre, 1969.

REFERENCES: J. Miles and D. Shiel, *David Jones – the Maker Unmade,* 1995, p.168 as *Pigotts Garden no.5.*

Piggott's (or Pigot's) Farm, at Speen in Buckinghamshire, was the home of Eric GILL, his family and his apprentices, from 1928 until his death in 1940. Jones was engaged to Gill's second daughter, Petra in 1924, but it was broken off three years later.

Son of a printer, Jones was a painter and draughtsman, engraver and writer. Working mainly in watercolour he painted landscapes, still-lifes, animals, literary and imaginative subjects. He served in France as a private 1915–8 and then studied under Walter Bayes (1869–1956) at the Westminster School of Art. Jones converted to Catholicism and joined Gill's community at Ditchling, Sussex from 1922–4, following him to Wales in 1925–7. In the 1930s he exhibited with the 7 and 5 Society with Paul NASH and Ben NICHOLSON.

His pale tonality is often compared to BLAKE, whose visionary tradition he carried on into the 20th century.

EJ

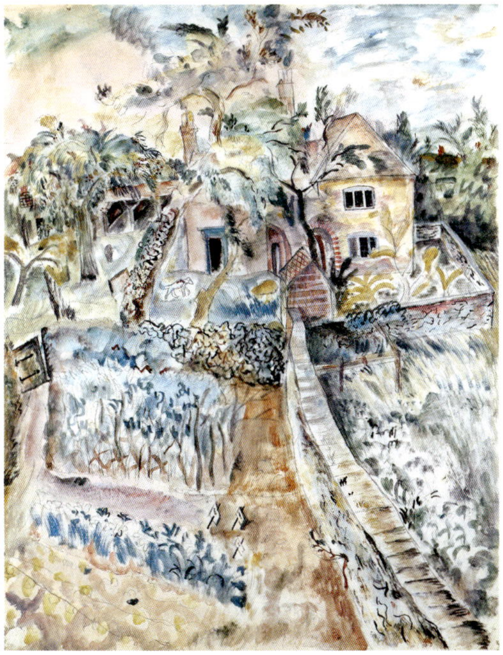

David JONES, C.H., C.B.E.

[1895–1974]

Cumberland Landscape, 1946

watercolour on paper, 49.9 × 28.8 cm
inscribed: *David Jones 1946*

P.211

PROVENANCE: Mrs Lynette Rhys née Roberts; Zwemmer Gallery from whom purchased by Gallery, April 1958.

EXHIBITIONS: *David Jones,* Aberystwyth, National Library of Wales, Cardiff, National Museum of Wales, Swansea, Glynn Vivian Art Gallery, Edinburgh, Royal Scottish Academy and London, Tate Gallery, 1954, no.57 as *The Legions Ridge from Cockley Moor; David Jones,* Edinburgh, Scottish National Gallery of Modern Art, 1969; *English Landscape in the 20th Century,* London, Camden Arts Centre, 1969; *David Jones: A Map of the Artist's Mind,* Cardiff, National Museum of Wales only, 1996, no.35.

This is one of several paintings done in Cumberland at the home of his friend Helen Sutherland, in which Jones returns to pure landscape motifs. Merlin James has suggested, in the 1995 exhibition catalogue, that these Cumberland landscapes were 'not unlike the views by Courbet or Derain that hung on his hostess's walls'.

CB

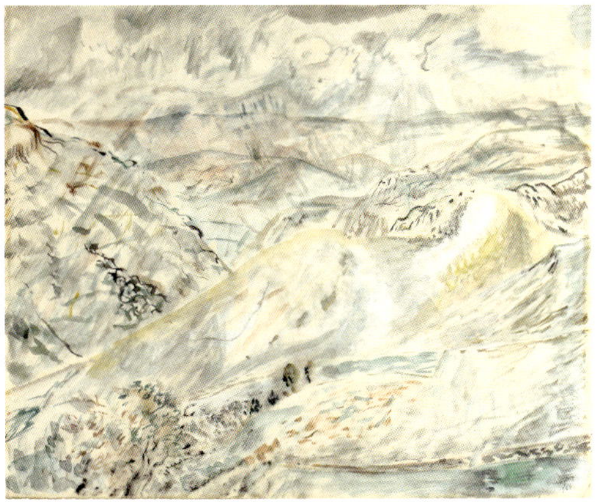

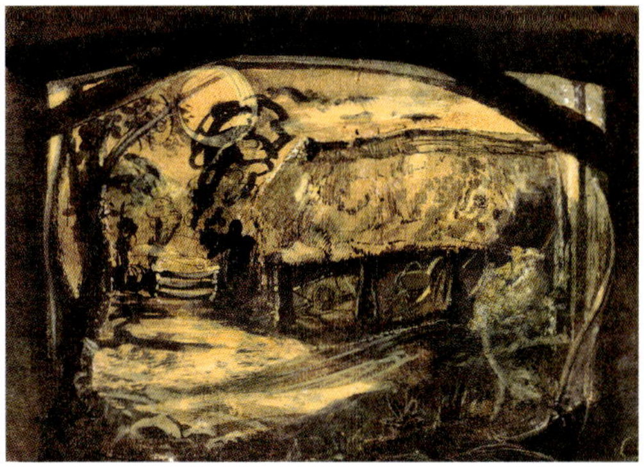

Tom KEATING

[1917–84]

A Barn at Shoreham, c.1965

sepia mixed with gum, heightened with bodycolour on paper, 25.9 × 37.3 cm

P.502

PROVENANCE: Jane Kelly, the artist's former pupil and agent, who sold it together with another drawing, at Bonham's for £30 where it was bought by Paul Branson, a country dealer, who, believing that he had discovered a Samuel Palmer, took it to Colnaghi's and sold them a half-share in the drawing; purchased by the Gallery from P&D Colnaghi Ltd, July 1965, as a Samuel Palmer.

EXHIBITIONS: *English Watercolours and Drawings,* London, P&D Colnaghi Ltd., 1965, no.21; *Seeing is Deceiving,* Manchester, Whitworth Art Gallery, 1984; *Don't Trust the Label,* Hull, Ferens Art Gallery, Nottingham, University Art Gallery, York, City Art Gallery and Exeter, Royal Albert Memorial Museum, 1986–7, no.12b; *FAKE?,* London, British Museum, 1990, no.259.

REFERENCES: *Burlington Magazine,* vol. CVII, 1965, p.438, repr. p.439; J. Sellars, *Samuel Palmer,* 1974, pp.85–7 as *Barn at Shoreham,* 1833–4 by Palmer; G. Norman(ed.), *The Tom Keating Catalogue,* 1977, p.26; T. Keating, *The Fake's Progress,* 1977, pp.172–3; A. Beckett, *Fakes: Forgery and the Art World,* 1995, pp.67–8 .

This, a deliberate forgery, was probably the first 'Samuel Palmer' to be foisted on the market. In Keating's ghosted autobiography, *The Fake's Progress*, Keating describes making a large number of drawings in the style of Palmer following an accident he suffered on 7 January 1965. If this was one of them, it must have been sold *very* soon afterwards by Jane Kelly at Bonham's, in time for it to be included in Colnaghi's exhibition in June of that year. The review of the exhibition in the *Burlington Magazine* describes it as 'newly discovered' and observes that it 'immediately brings to mind the name of Graham Sutherland'.

Geraldine Norman's exposure of the forged Palmers, which she first published in two articles in *The Times* (16 July and 10 August 1976), created a sensation in the art world and generated enormous and unwelcome publicity for the Gallery. However, Colnaghi's refunded the purchase price, and the watercolour, because of its colourful history, is of great interest to Gallery visitors.

EJ

Charles Samuel KEENE

[1823–91]

Man Smoking a Pipe 1860s

pen and ink on paper, 13 × 7.8 cm
signed: *C.K.* Studio Stamp of Henry Keene, the artist's brother

P.155
PROVENANCE: Henry Keene; Purchased from P&D Colnaghi Ltd, January 1958.

A splendid example of Keene's draughtmanship showing his skill with shading and sureness of line. Keene has been described as the 'English Daumier', and WHISTLER went on to pronounce that he was 'the greatest English artist since Hogarth'.

EJ

Charles Samuel KEENE

[1823–91]

Two Jovial Men conversing, 1860s

pen and ink on paper, 17.5 × 10.9 cm
signed: *C.K.*

P.156
PROVENANCE: Purchased from P&D Colnaghi Ltd, January 1958.
EXHIBITIONS: *Watercolours and Drawings from The Cecil Higgins Art Gallery, Bedford*, London, Thos. Agnew & Sons Ltd, 1962, no.37.

An unidentified illustration, probably for *Punch* magazine. TENNIEL's impression of Keene at *Punch* meetings was quoted in Layard's *The Life and Letters of Charles Keene*, 1892, p.76 'He spoke very little and was apt to throw cold water on projects under discussion. If specially appealed to for his opinion, he would, as likely as not, pass upon them a short and comprehensive criticism, such as "D…d bad", and relapse, with a twinkle in his eye, into smoke and silence'.

CB

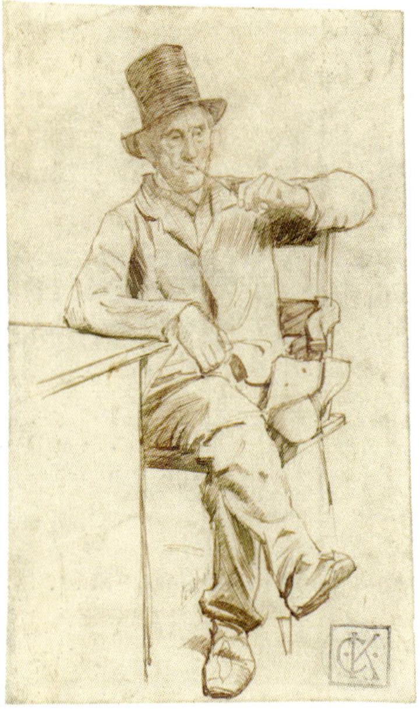

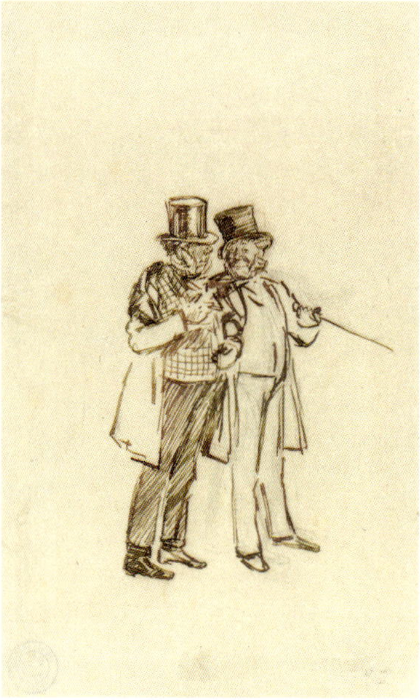

Charles Samuel KEENE

[1823–91]

A Vested Interest (Drawing for *Punch* magazine), 1888

pen and brown ink, heightened with white on paper,
12.7 × 19.7 cm
signed: *C.K.*

P.130
PROVENANCE: Purchased from the Leicester Galleries, November 1957.
REFERENCES: *Punch's Almanac* 1889, not paginated.

Reproduced in *Punch's Almanac* for 1889 (not paginated). The *Almanac* is dated 6 December 1888. The text ran as follows:

A VESTED INTEREST
Bystander (to excited Scot, whose Friend has been run over).
"Not a near Relative, I hope Sir"
Scot. "Na-but-he has on a pair o'ma breeks".

Perhaps the most brilliant of all the 19th century artists who worked for *Punch*, Keene was brought up in Suffolk. Keene was articled first to a solicitor and then to the wood-engraver Charles Whymper, leaving him in 1852 to set up on his own in the Strand. In that year he began to work for *Punch*, a connection that lasted for the rest of his life. His subjects were drawn from a different social stratum than du Maurier's and he relied on his friends for amusing situations.

EJ

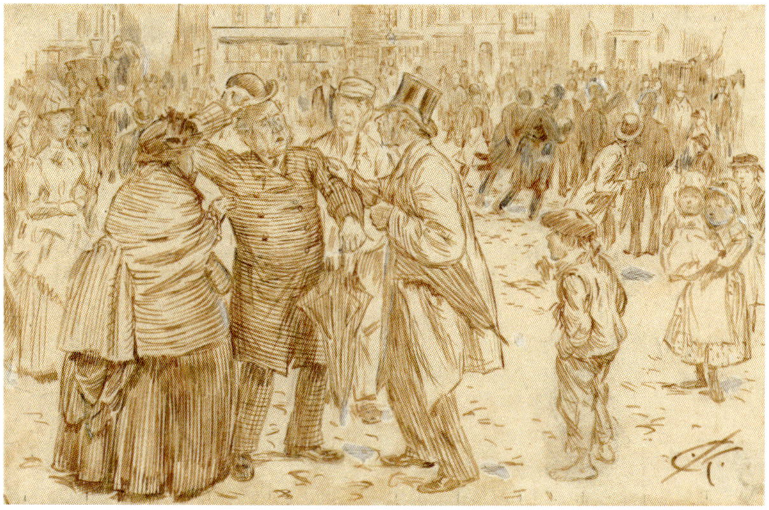

Charles Samuel KEENE
[1823–91]
The Interior of a Railway Carriage (Drawing for *Punch* magazine), 1888

pen and ink heightened with white on paper, 19.2 × 12.6cm
signed: *C.K.* bottom right corner

P.158
PROVENANCE: Purchased from P&D Colnaghi Ltd, January 1958.
REFERENCES: *Punch*, 11 February 1888, p.70.

A drawing for *Number One* (the man and woman in a railway carriage), was reproduced in *Punch* 11 February 1888, p.70. The text ran as follows:

NUMBER ONE
Bridegroom (on their way to Paris), "You're sure you're quite warm and comfortable, love?"
Bride , "Oh yes, dear – quite"
Bridegroom , "I don't like to see you sitting with your back to the engine, darling. You don't feel any draught ?"
Bride, "Oh, not the slightest !"
Bridegroom (who does!), "Then, sweetest, would you mind changing places !!!"

EJ

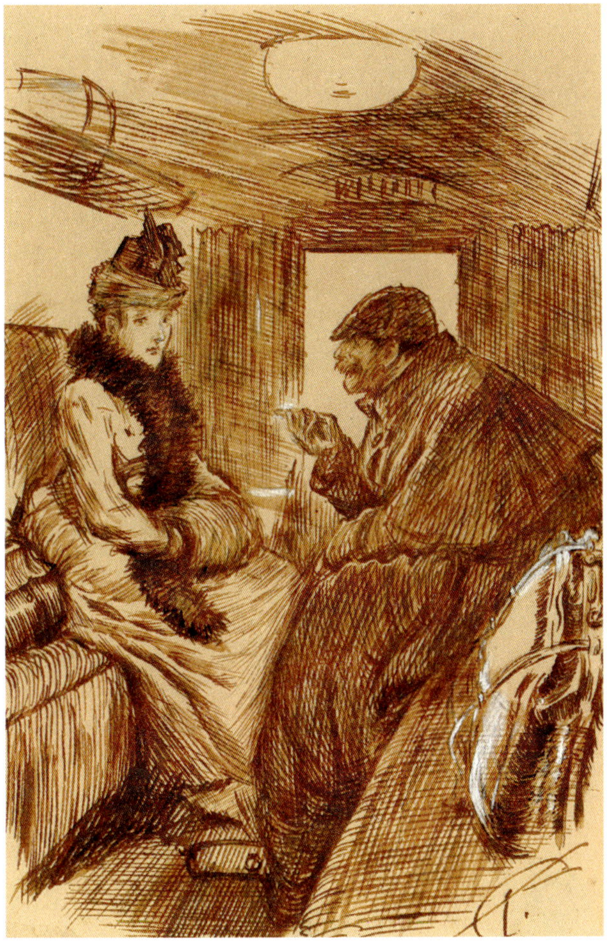

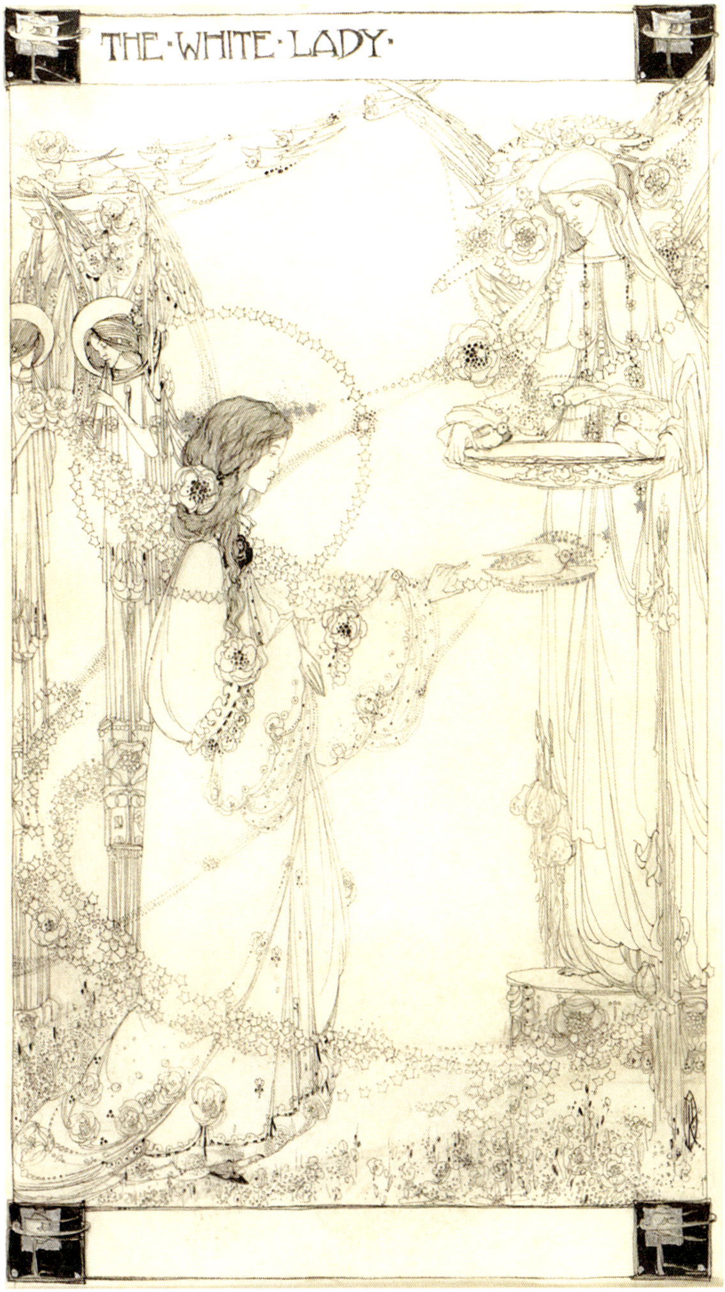

Jessie Marion KING
[1875–1949]
The White Lady, c.1903

pen and ink, heightened with silver on vellum, 24.6 × 14.2 cm
inscribed: *The White Lady*
signed with monogram

P.573
PROVENANCE: Purchased from the Fine Art Society, December 1967.
EXHIBITIONS: *Some British Illustrators*, London, Fine Art Society, 1967, no.178; *The Last Romantics – The Romantic Tradition in British Art – Burne-Jones to Stanley Spencer*, London, Barbican Art Gallery, 1989, no.532.

Jessie King (Mrs E.A.Taylor) was born in Scotland and studied at the Glasgow School of Art. She revealed a precocious talent for illustration, her subjects being mainly romantic or exotic. Her work appeared regularly in *The Studio* and she also worked for the Bodley Head illustrating two books for William Morris (1834–96). She also wrote books as well as illustrating them, dividing her time between Scotland and Paris.

EJ

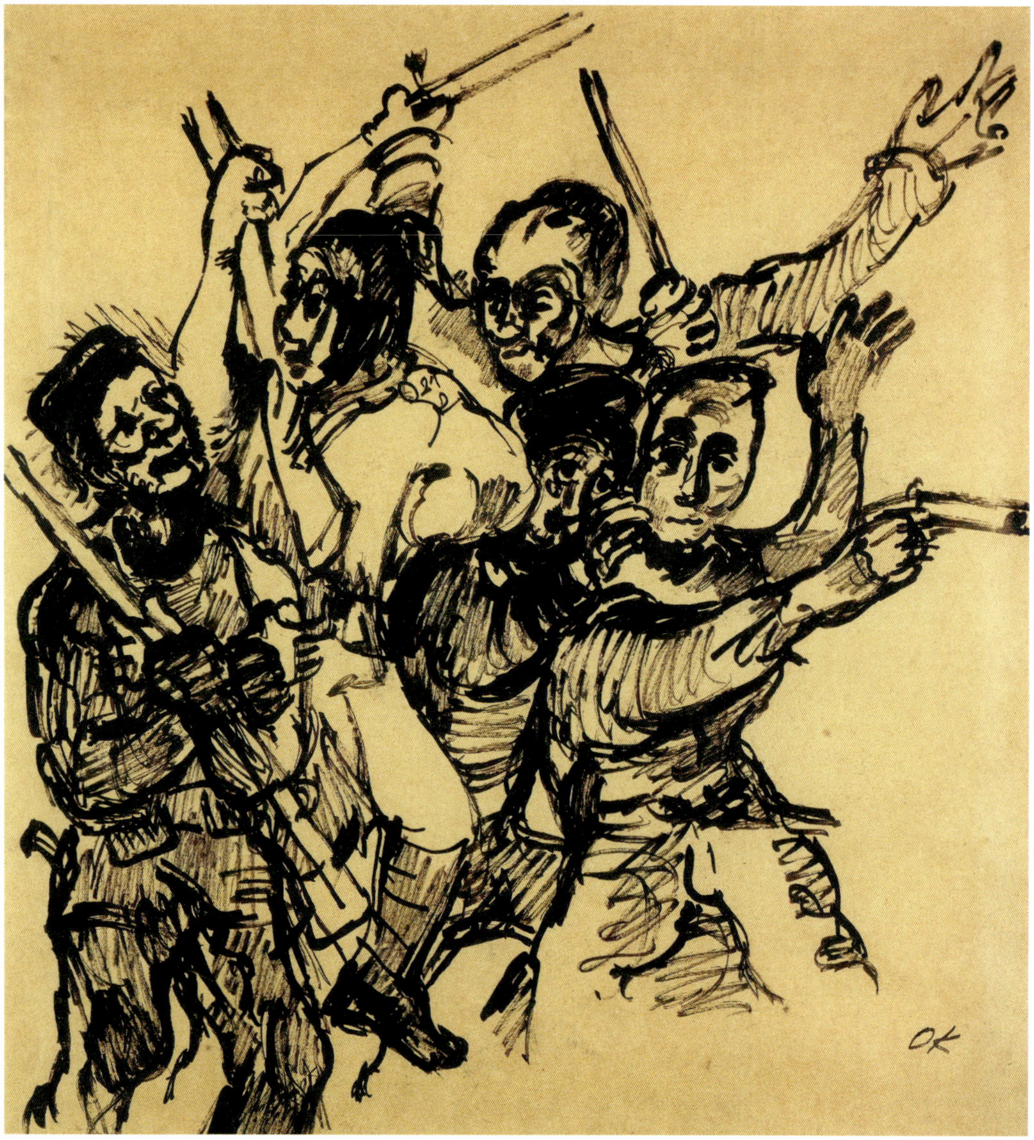

Oskar KOKOSCHKA, C.B.E.
[1886–1980]
The Battle, 1916

brush and ink on buff paper, 33.1 × 31 cm
inscribed: *O.K.*
inscribed on reverse: *No.17 Oskar Kokoschka: Kampf*

P.379
PROVENANCE: Hjalmar Gabrielson, Göteborg; Marlborough Fine Art, from whom purchased by Gallery, October 1960.
EXHIBITIONS: *Oskar Kokoschka,* London, Tate Gallery and Zürich, Kunsthaus, 1986, no.161; *A Bitter Truth – The Avant-Garde and the Great War,* London, Barbican Art Gallery only, 1994.
REFERENCES: R. Cork, *A Bitter Truth – Avant-Garde Art and the Great War,* 1994, pp.118, 120, pl.151.

Kokoschka fought in the Great War, where he was badly wounded on the Russian Front. An injury to the inner ear permanently impaired his sense of balance. In August 1916 he was caught by a grenade explosion in no-man's-land and, shell-shocked, was sent to a Viennese hospital. This drawing may have been executed there.

CB

Oskar KOKOSCHKA, C.B.E.
[1886–1980]
A Lobster, 1946

watercolour on paper, 40.5 × 59.6 cm
inscribed: *o. kokoschka 1946*

P.383

PROVENANCE: Purchased from Marlborough Fine Art, London, January 1961.
EXHIBITIONS: *Oskar Kokoschka in England and Scotland,* London, Marlborough Fine Art, 1960, no.58; *Primitives to Picasso,* London, R.A., 1962, no.430; *Watercolours and Drawings from The Cecil Higgins Art Gallery, Bedford,* London, Thos. Agnew & Sons Ltd, 1962, no.94, pl.x; *Watercolours from Bedford,* Norwich, Norwich Castle Museum, 1965, no.28.
REFERENCES: H.M. Wingler, *Introduction to Kokoschka,* 1958, p.93, repr.

Kokoschka was born at Poshlarn, Lower Austria. He studied at the Vienna School of Applied Arts 1905–9, where he was influenced by Vincent Van Gogh (1853–90) and Gustav Klimt (1862–1918). After the First World War, he taught at the Dresden Academy between 1920–4. He then travelled widely, living in Vienna 1931–4 and in Prague 1934–8 before arriving in England 1938. He became a British citizen in 1947. From 1954 he settled in Villeneuve on Lake Geneva. A smaller, coloured pencil version of the same subject exists in a private collection.

EJ/CB

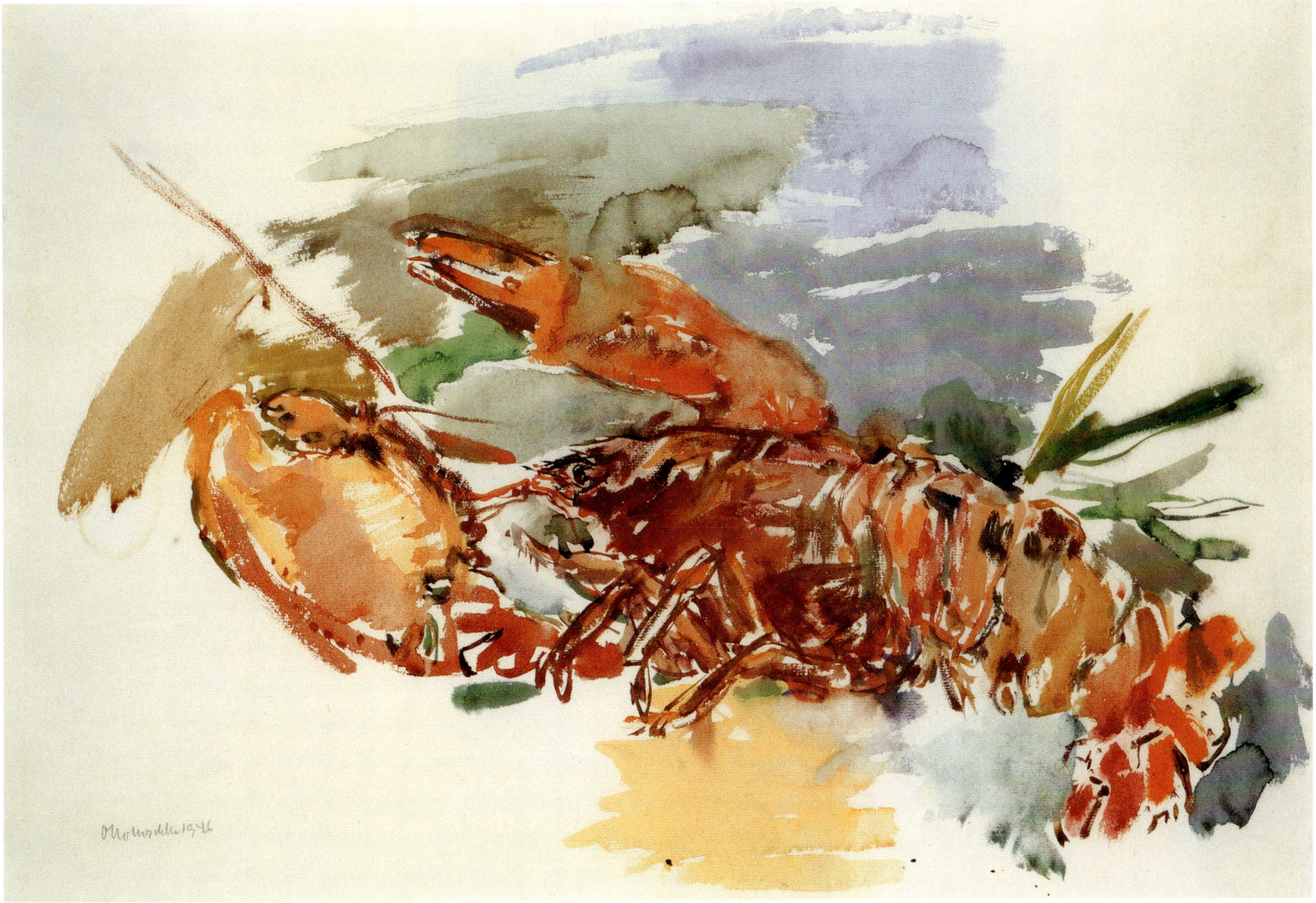

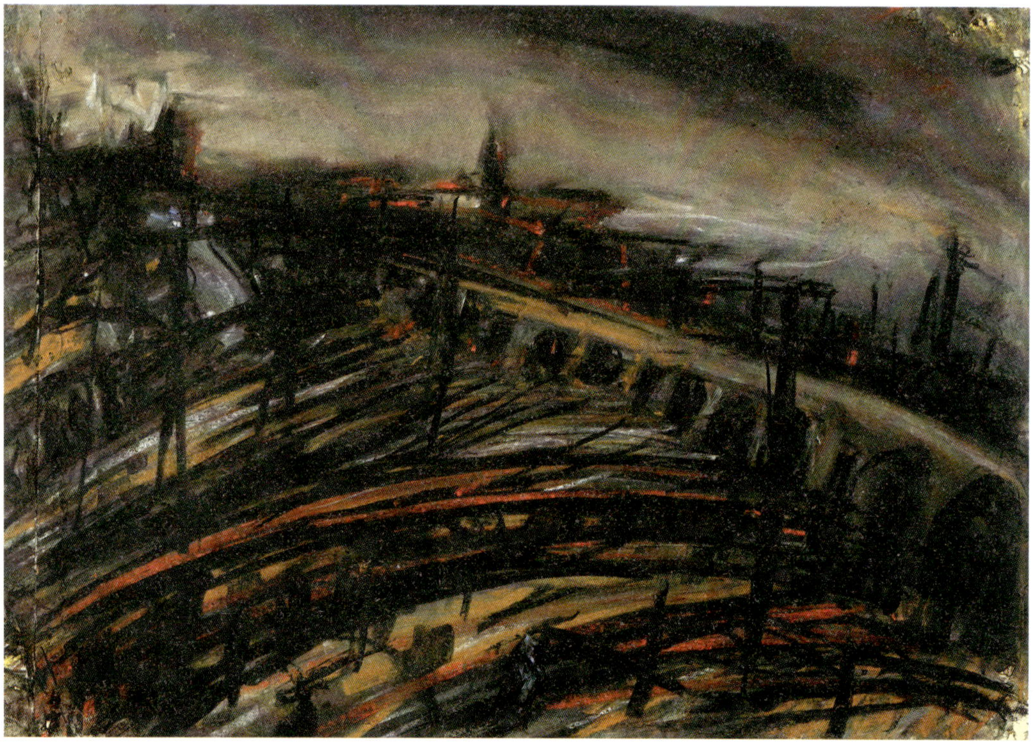

Leon KOSSOFF
[b. 1926]
York Way Railway Bridge from Caledonian Road, 1966

coloured chalk and gouache on paper, 55.9 × 80 cm

P.576
PROVENANCE: Purchased from Marlborough Fine Art, January 1968.

Kossoff's parents were Russian-Jewish immigrants who settled in North-East London. He studied at the St Martin's School of Art, and in the evenings between 1950–2 attended BOMBERG's classes at the Borough Polytechnic (together with Frank AUERBACH). From 1953–6 he studied at the R.C.A.

Kossoff said in 1974: 'Ever since the age of 12 I have drawn and painted London… The strange ever-changing light, the endless streets and the shuddering feel of the sprawling city linger in my mind like a faintly glimmering memory of a long forgotten perhaps never experienced childhood'.

During painting, Kossoff regularly scrapes off his thickly layered impasto paint into what he calls a *grey mass* on the studio floor, destroying one picture to make way for another. He works in the studio from drawings made in front of his subject.

EJ/CB

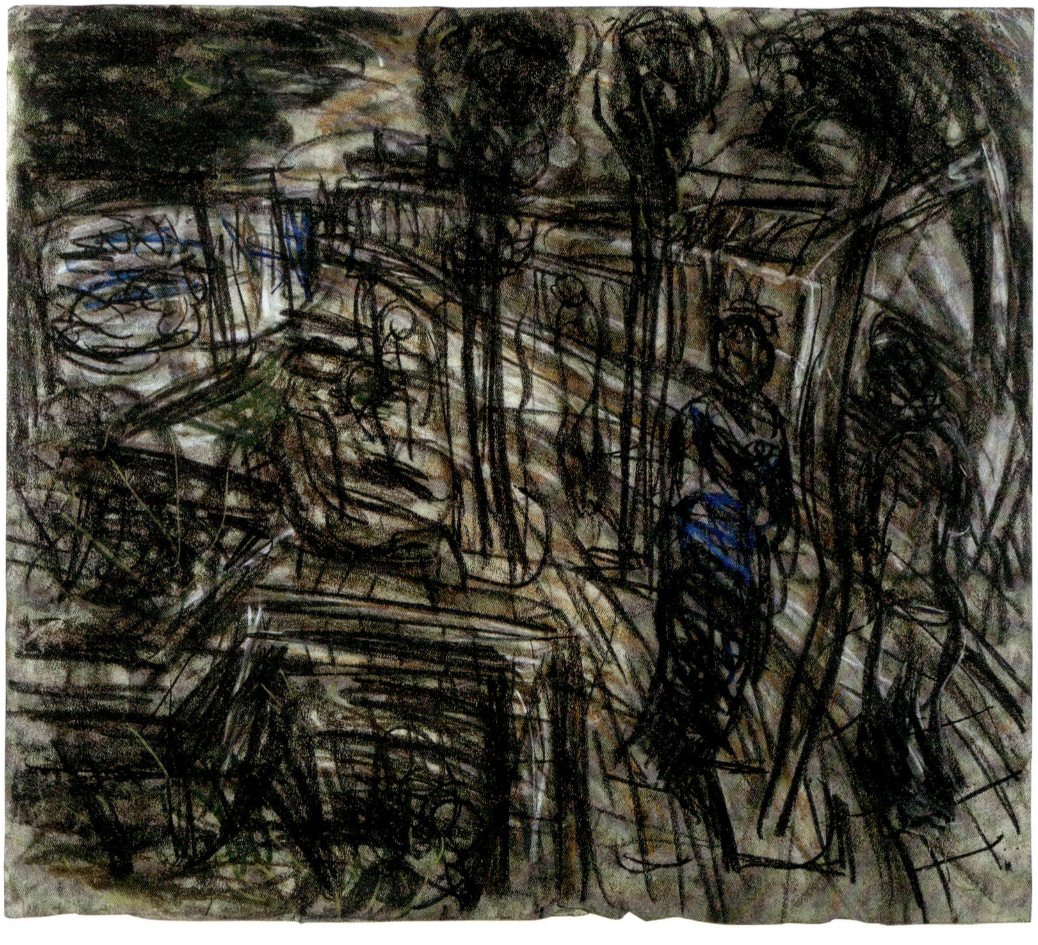

Leon KOSSOFF
[b. 1926]
A Street in Willesden, 1984

pastel on paper, 66.8 × 78.2 cm

P.754
PROVENANCE: Sold by artist to the Anthony d'Offay Gallery; Caryl Hubbard for the Contemporary Art Society, given to Gallery by the C.A.S., December 1988.

Willesden, London, has provided Kossoff with many subjects as have other suburbs such as Kilburn and Dalston. Frances Spalding considers that his portrayal of their 'shuddering sprawl, energy and sense of decay' is unsurpassed.

EJ

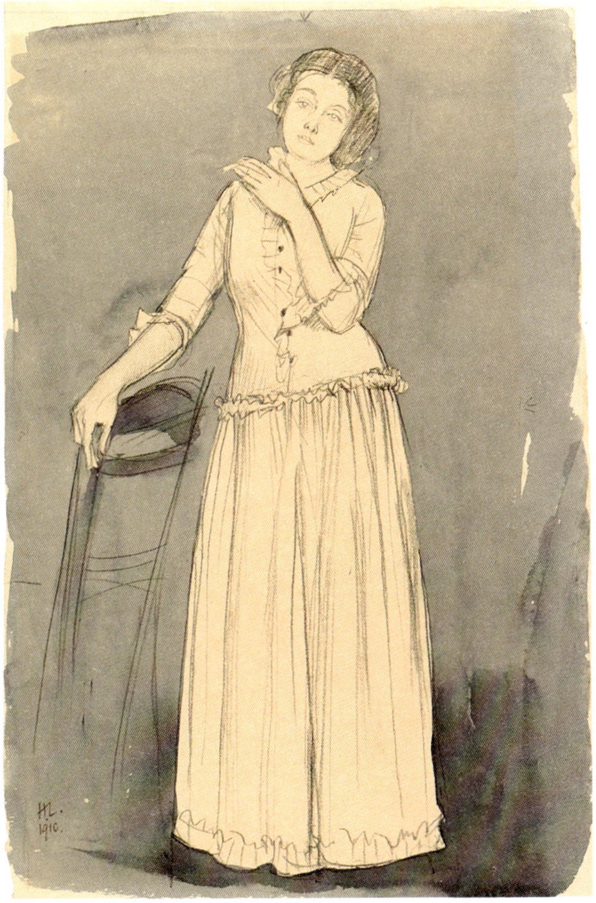

Henry LAMB, R.A., M.C.
[1883–1960]
Figure of a Girl Standing, 1910

black chalk and grey wash on paper, 37.2 × 25.6 cm
inscribed: *HL 1910*

P.499
PROVENANCE: Sir Henry Rushbury, R.A.; M. D'Aguilar; Maas Gallery, from whom purchased by Gallery, June 1965.
EXHIBITIONS: *Pre-Raphaelites to Post-Impressionism*, London, Maas Gallery, 1965, no.58 as *Girl standing by a chair*; *The Camden Town Group*, Bedford, Cecil Higgins Art Gallery, 1969, no.32.

Painted a year earlier than P.265, perhaps also in Brittany. The girl appears to be looking at – or listening to – someone, her head slightly tilted and with a quizzical expression, while disregarding the cigarette burning away between her fingertips.

EJ

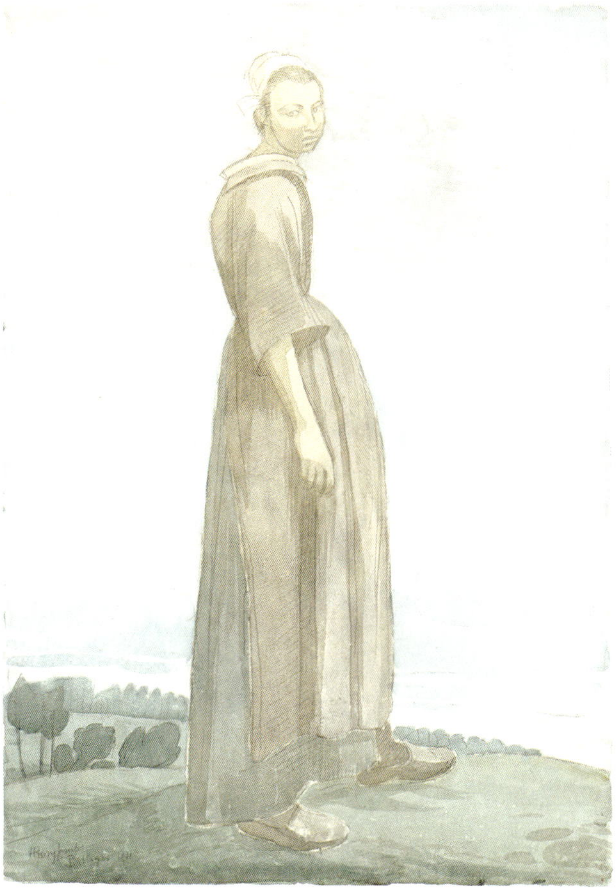

Henry LAMB, R.A., M.C.
[1883–1960]
A Breton Peasant Woman, 1911

watercolour and pencil on paper, 35.6 × 25.6 cm
signed: *Henry Lamb Bretagne 1911*

P.265
PROVENANCE: Purchased from Leicester Galleries, October 1958.
EXHIBITIONS: *Watercolours and Drawings from The Cecil Higgins Art Gallery, Bedford*, London, Thos. Agnew & Sons Ltd, 1962, no.76; *The Camden Town Group*, Bedford, Cecil Higgins Art Gallery, 1969, no.33.

Lamb was born in Adelaide, Australia, but then brought up in Manchester. He trained as a doctor until 1916 before studying art in Chelsea and then in Paris, under J.E. Blanche (1862–1942). He spent the summers of 1910 and 1911 in Brittany, the latter being the date also of *Death of a Peasant* (Tate Gallery NO5630).

A member of the Camden Town Group, he was also associated with the Bloomsbury Group. He was a Trustee of both the National Portrait Gallery and the Tate Gallery, which also owns *Lytton Strachey* (TOO118), his most celebrated portrait.

EJ

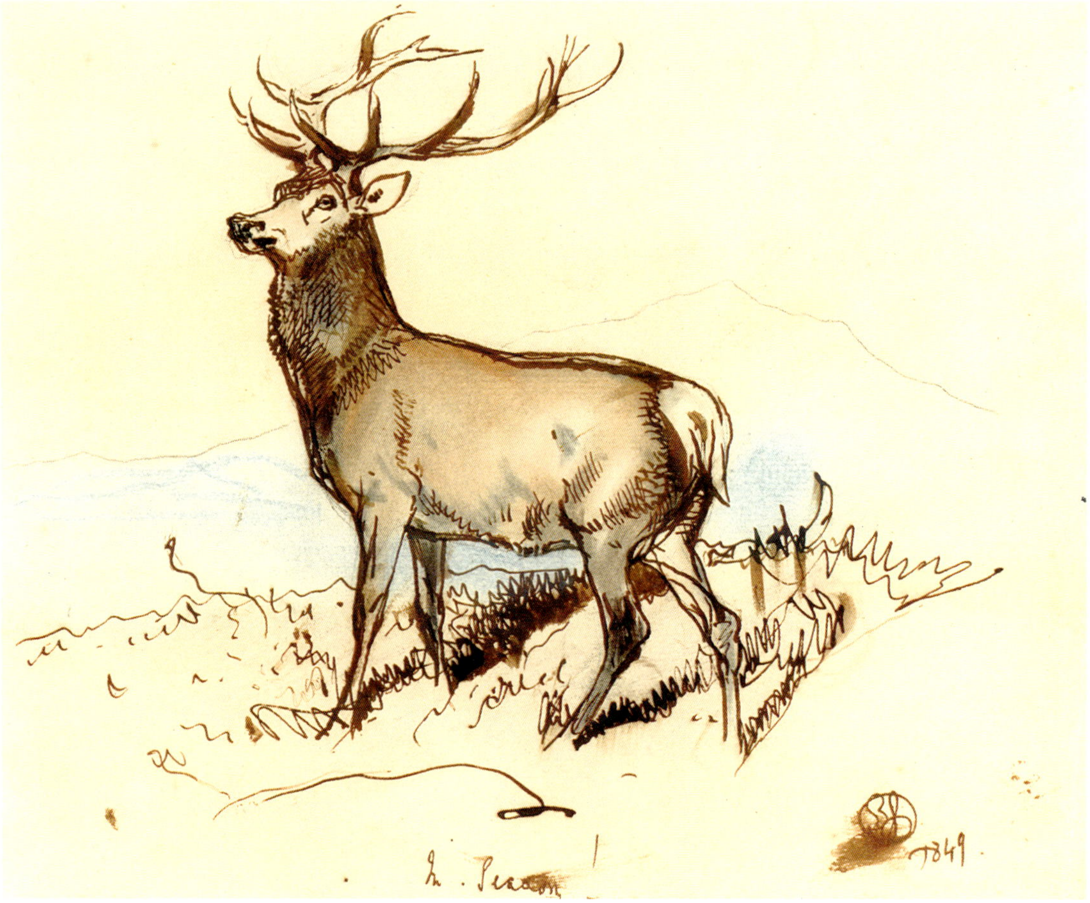

Sir Edwin LANDSEER, R.A.
[1802–73]
In Season, 1849

brown ink, watercolour, chalk and pencil on paper,
21.1 × 26.9 cm
inscribed: *In Season ! 1849*

P.552
PROVENANCE: Purchased from the Fine Art Society, April 1967.
EXHIBITIONS: *47th Exhibition of Early English Watercolours*, London, Fine Art Society, 1967, no.144; *The English Tradition*, Bedford, Cecil Higgins Art Gallery, 1972, no.51.

The most famous and successful of all British animal painters, Landseer became a great friend of Queen Victoria. His pictures are characterised by their brilliant, fluent technique (although Martin HARDIE considers that J.F. LEWIS excelled him as a draughtsman of animals) and by his tendency to endow his animals with human sentiments and expressions. Pictures such as *Dignity and Impudence* (Tate Gallery) reveal a humorous streak, but as he grew increasingly morbid with age, his later works emphasize the savage side of nature.

This watercolour precedes the oil painting, *The Monarch of the Glen*, by two years.

EJ/CB

Sir Edwin LANDSEER, R.A.
[1802–73]
A Dog Chained up outside its kennel

pencil and wash on paper, 13.2 × 15.5 cm

P.304
PROVENANCE: Mrs Hoare; P&D Colnaghi Ltd, from whom purchased by Gallery, October 1959.

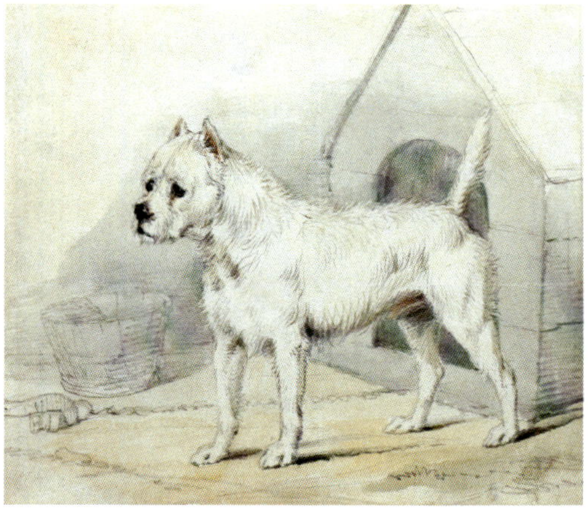

A study in which Landseer skilfully conveys the alertness and latent pugnacity of the dog, which looks ready to attack any intruder who approaches too close.

Son of the engraver John Landseer, Edwin studied with Benjamin Hayden (1786–1846). He displayed a precocious talent, first exhibiting at the Royal Academy aged only thirteen. FUSELI prophetically called him 'my little dog boy'. He was elected A.R.A. at twenty-four, the youngest statutory age for the Academy, and R.A. in 1831. He was knighted in 1850. His anthropomorphic animal subjects proved popular in mid-Victorian Britain, and attracted Royal patronage.

As a sculptor, he is best known for the lions, which he modelled in 1867, for the base of Nelson's column in Trafalgar Square, London.

EJ/CB

Peter LANYON
[1918 –64]
Sennen, 1958

bodycolour on paper, 75.5 × 55.5 cm
inscribed: *Lanyon Sennen 58*

P.247
PROVENANCE: Purchased from Gimpel Fils, 1958.
EXHIBITIONS: *Primitives to Picasso*, London, R.A., 1962, no.433; *Peter Lanyon Paintings, drawings and constructions 1937–1964*, Manchester, Whitworth Art Gallery, Glasgow, Art Gallery & Museum Kelvingrove, Cambridge, Kettle's Yard, 1978, no.67, as *Sennen*.
REFERENCES: A. Causey, *Peter Lanyon Paintings, drawings and constructions*, Manchester, 1978, p.38, no.67, as Sennen, illus. no.32.

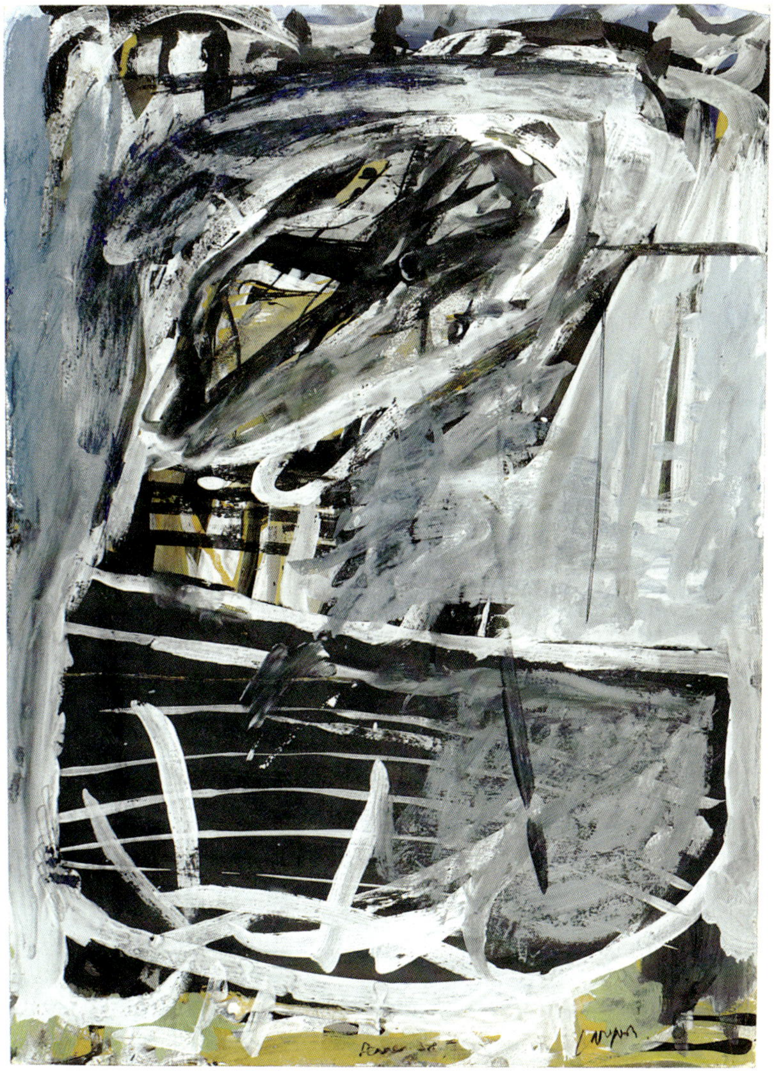

Born in St Ives, Lanyon was the only Cornishman of the St. Ives School. He studied at the Penzance School of Art and the Euston Road School. In 1939 he met Ben NICHOLSON, Naum Gabo (1890–1977) and Barbara HEPWORTH, who influenced his work.

From 1950 his work was largely abstract with clear allusions to Cornish landscape. Spatial relationships were often resolved with the help of constructions. Later, his paint handling became looser with more references to weather and sky, elements reinforced when he took up gliding. He died as a result of a gliding accident. In 1959 he wrote, 'Since 1945 my journey has been along this strip and wherever I have been in the world it is these few miles which I have inhabited'.

EJ/CB

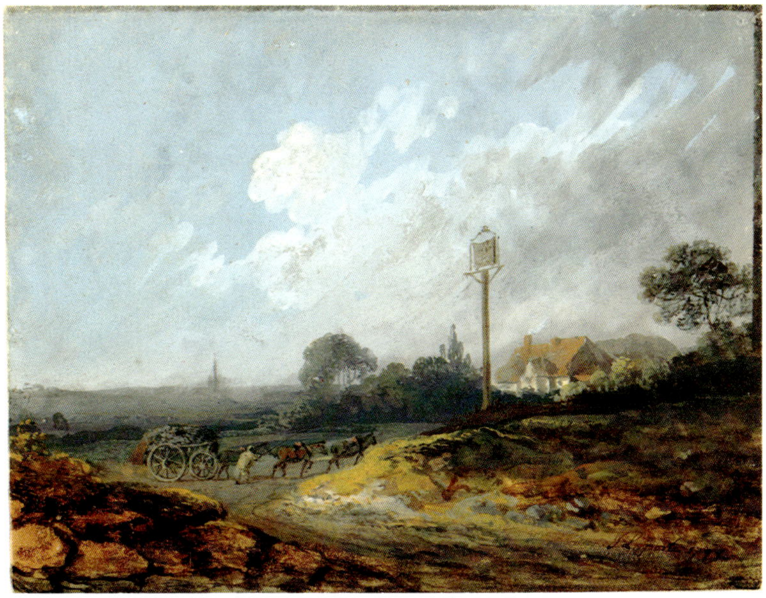

John LAPORTE
[1761–1839]
Knockholt, Near Sevenoaks, Kent, 1799

bodycolour on paper, 16.5 × 21.8 cm
inscribed: *J Laporte 1799*
on reverse *Knockholt near Seven Oakes* [sic] *Kent*
Sir Bruce Ingram's collector's mark

P.463
PROVENANCE: Sir Bruce Ingram; Sotheby's 20 October 1964, lot 78, purchased by Gallery.

Laporte was a topographical artist, much of whose most accomplished work was in bodycolour. He also produced, in collaboration with W.F. Wells, a series of soft-ground etchings after GAINSBOROUGH. Like SANDBY, who was a strong influence, he sometimes painted in watercolour over a soft-ground etching.

He gave lessons to Dr MONRO who bought £500 or £600 worth of drawings from him.

EJ

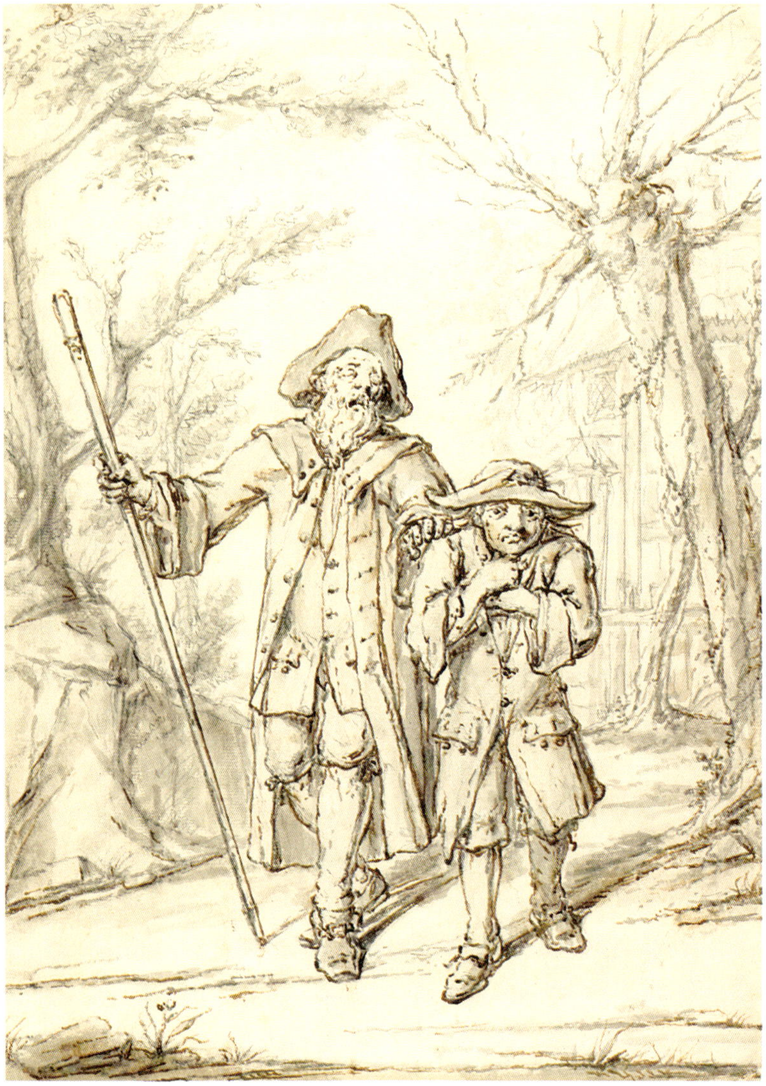

Cecil LAWSON

[1851–82]

Stormy Landscape, 1881

watercolour and ink on paper, 30.7 × 41.2 cm
inscribed: *Cecil Lawson 1881*

P.195
PROVENANCE: Leicester Galleries, from whom purchased by Gallery, April 1958.

Lawson, Scottish by birth, was largely self-taught as an artist. His success with oils, coupled with his short life, left him little time for watercolours, which are so rare that he has suffered undeserved neglect as a watercolourist. Martin HARDIE considers that such existing drawings show 'that he would have undoubtedly won a very prominent place in the history of British art if he had lived longer'.

EJ

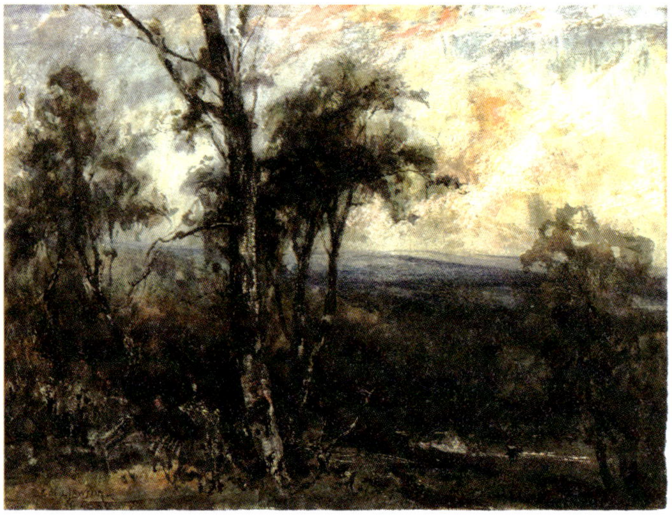

Marcellus LAROON

[1679–1772]

The Winter of Life, c.1730

black lead, pen and brown ink, grey wash on paper,
42.7 × 31.4 cm
inscribed on reverse: *The Winter of Life 53P61*

P.664
PROVENANCE: Christie's sale 7 June 1975, lot.72, purchased by Gallery with a grant from the V&A/M.G.C. Purchase Grant Fund.

Perhaps an illustration to a fable or to the Four Seasons. Laroon was an amateur artist and a soldier who retired from the army in 1730. His idiosyncratic style, which has been described as resembling 'stained tapestry', is applied to subjects which contain elements of both the peasant genre scenes of David Teniers the younger (1610–90) and the Rococo *fête galante*, stemming from Antoine Watteau (1684–1721).

EJ

Edward LEAR
[1812–88]
Parrot: 'Microglossus aterrimus', c.1830

watercolour and ink on paper, 18.7 × 11.5 cm
inscribed: *E Lear Microglossus Aterrimus. Plate 16*

P.402
PROVENANCE: Thos. Agnew & Sons Ltd, from whom purchased by Gallery, January 1962.
REFERENCES: Illustrated as plate 16 in vol. XVIII of Sir William Jardine's *Naturalists Library,* published 1843.

Between 1828 and 1830 Lear began to earn his living by drawing birds. He decided to concentrate on parrots and planned an ambitious book *Illustration of the family of Psittacidae, or Parrots* in fourteen folios. Although he worked hard throughout 1831, the costs of production were high and the twelfth folio, published in April 1832, was the last to appear. However, the work was highly praised and no doubt led to the commission from Lord Stanley (1799–1869) later that year, to draw the animals in his menagerie at Knowsley.

EJ

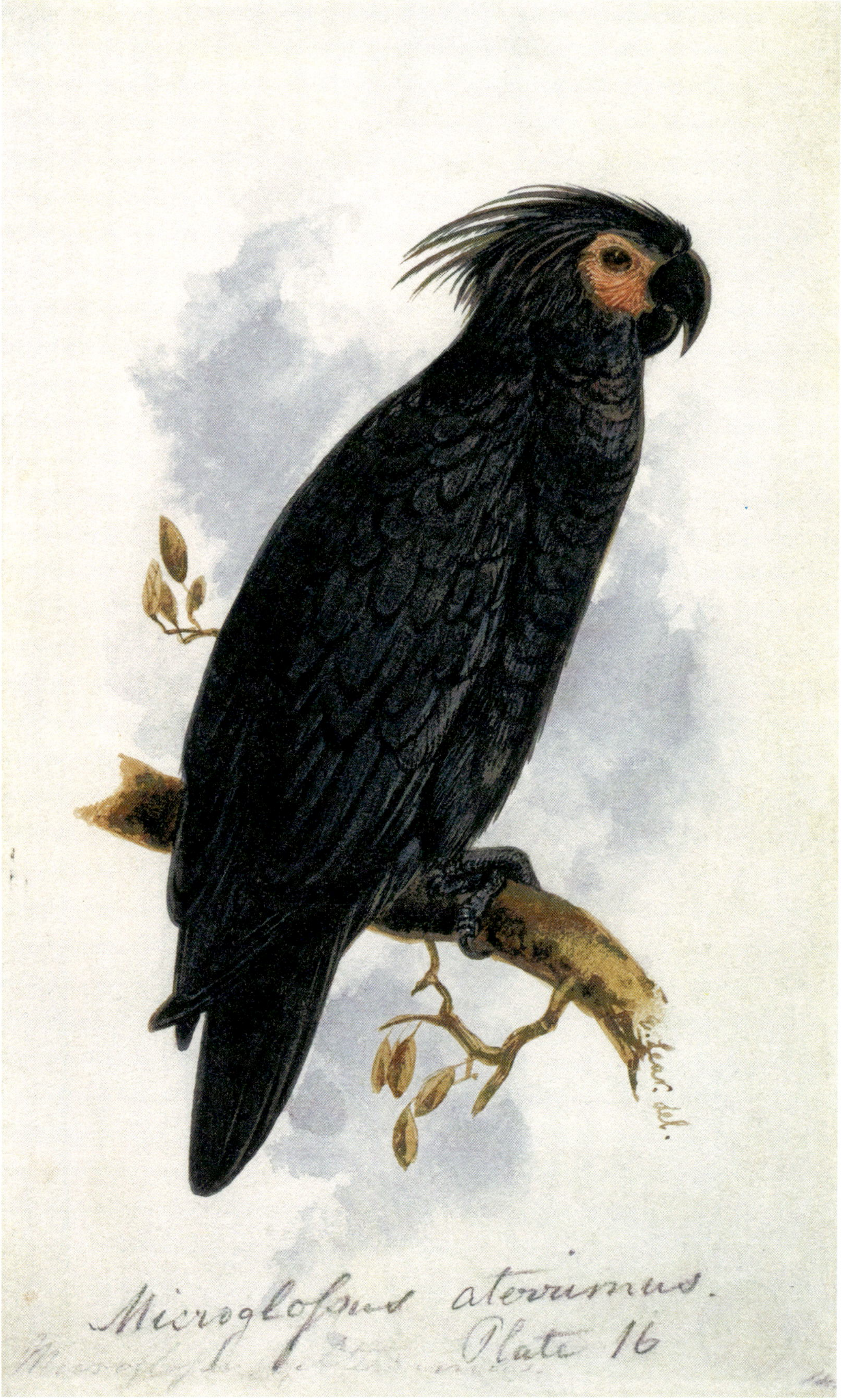

Edward LEAR
[1812–88]
Study of Shells, 1834

watercolour on paper, 15.6 × 23.8 cm
inscribed: *E Lear December 1834*

P.568
PROVENANCE: Appleby Bros. Ltd, from whom purchased by Gallery, October 1967.
EXHIBITIONS: *Summer Exhibition*, London, Appleby Bros. Ltd, 1967.

Drawn during the period that Lear was working for Lord Derby at Knowsley. During the same period he was also drawing for Gould on *The Birds of Europe*, so much close work straining his never very strong eyesight.

EJ

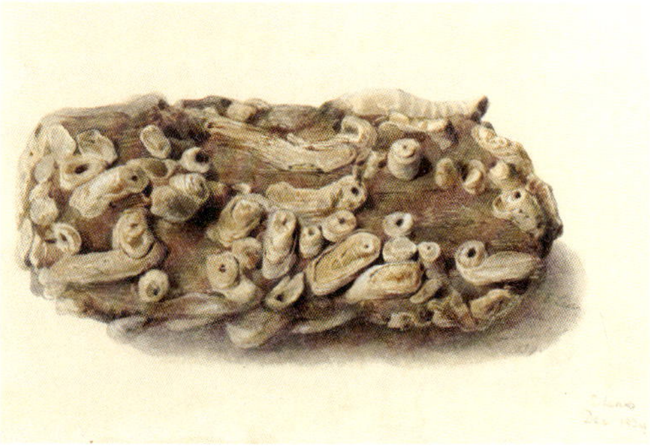

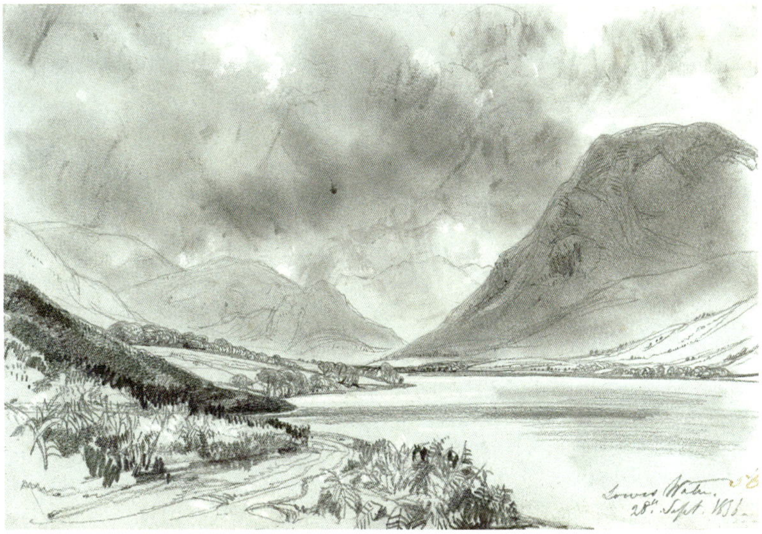

Edward LEAR

[1812–88]

Lowes Water, 1836

pencil and wash heightened with white on tinted paper, 17.8 × 25.9 cm
inscribed: *Lowes Water 28th Sept.1836*

P.319
PROVENANCE: H. V. Day; P&D Colnaghi Ltd., from whom purchased by Gallery, January 1960.
EXHIBITIONS: *English Watercolours from The Cecil Higgins Art Gallery, Bedford*, Reading, Reading Museum and Art Gallery, 1965, no.31.

Lowes Water is a small lake about five miles south of Cockermouth in Cumbria. In the summer of 1836 Lear spent ten weeks in the Lake District. This experience led him to concentrate on landscape painting.

EJ

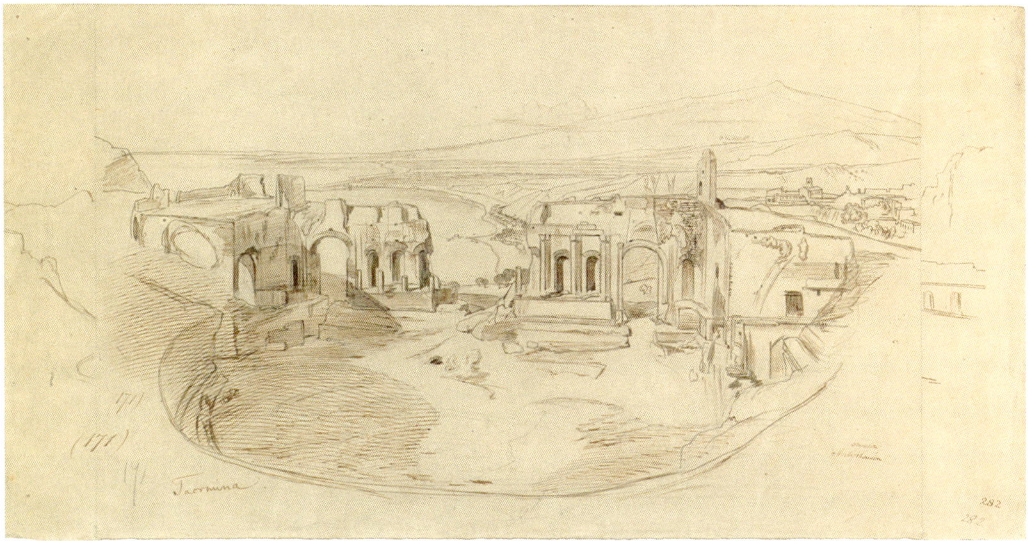

Edward LEAR

[1812–88]

The Amphitheatre, Taormina, Sicily, 1842 or 1847

pen and ink on paper, 25.3 × 50.7 cm
inscribed: *Taormina no.171* with colour notes

P.127
PROVENANCE: Pierre E. Verbeke, from whom purchased by Gallery, June 1957.

Lear first visited Sicily in the spring of 1842, returning there again with his friend John Proby in May 1847, when they climbed Mount Etna not far from Taormina.

EJ

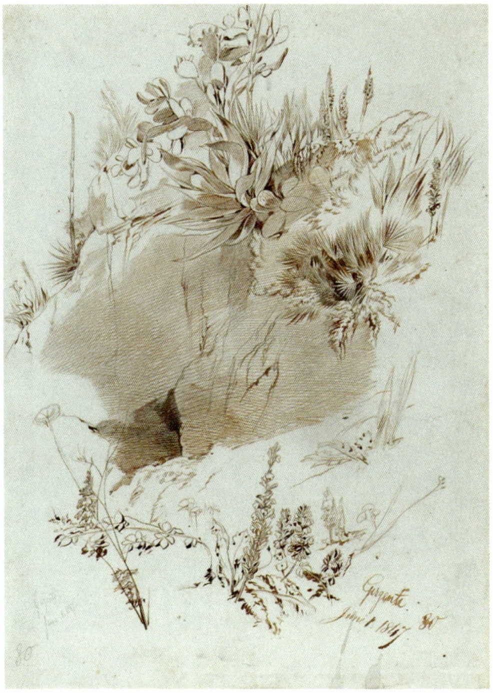

Edward LEAR

[1812–88]

Botanical Study, 1847

pen and ink on paper, 34.6 × 25.7 cm
inscribed: *Girgenti June 1 1847 no.80*

P.126
PROVENANCE: Pierre E. Verbeke, from whom purchased by Gallery, June 1957.

On 11 May 1847 Lear arrived at Palermo, where he was joined by a new friend, John Proby (son of Lord Carysfort). They found Sicily 'hot, dirty and poor' and the bread full of aniseed. They travelled around the island visiting Segesta, Agrigentum and then Girgenti before arriving in Syracuse on 8 June.

EJ

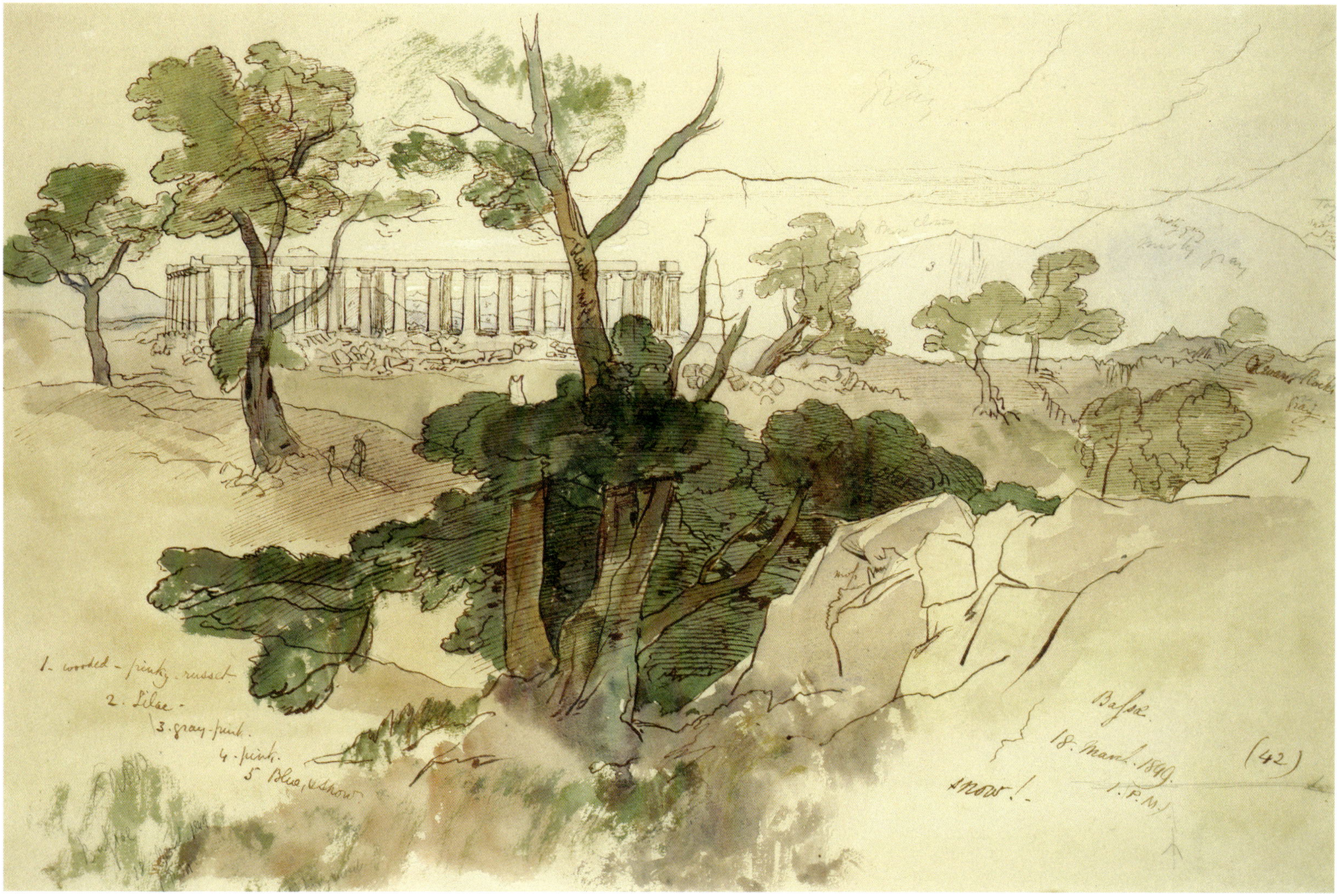

Edward LEAR

[1812–88]

The Temple at Bassae, 1849

pen, ink and watercolour on paper, 32.3 × 50.5 cm
inscribed: *Bassae 18 March 1849 1pm (42) SNOW!*
with colour notes

P.797
PROVENANCE: Elisabeth and Alice Barbara Kitson, given by Alice Barbara Kitson to Gallery, October 1992.

Lear and his close friend Franklin Lushington arrived in Greece in March 1849. They travelled south walking and sketching, reaching the Temple of Apollo on 18 March. Lear later painted a large oil of the subject which was bought by subscribers and presented to the Fitzwilliam Museum, Cambridge, in 1859.

EJ

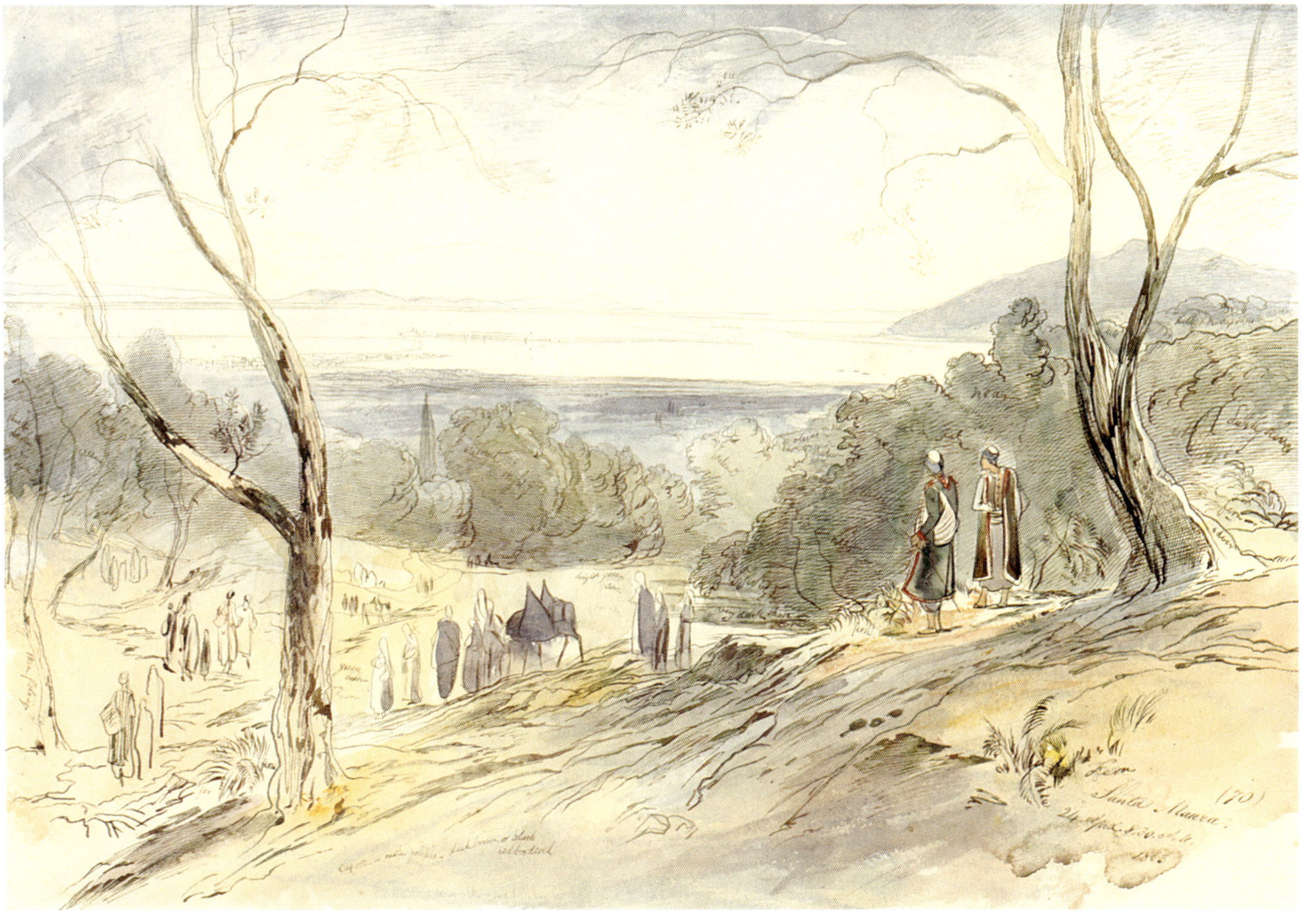
Santa Maura
(70)

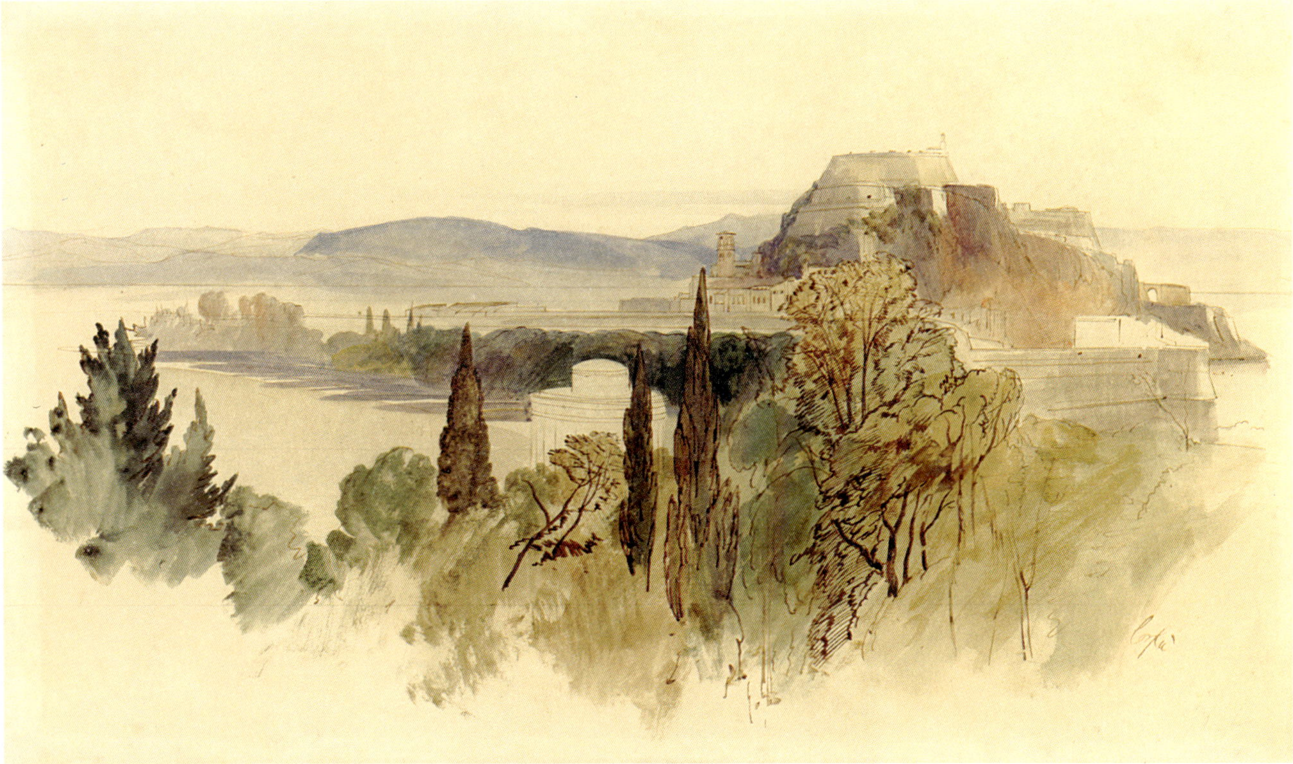

Edward LEAR

[1812–88]

Santa Maura in the Ionian Islands, 1863

pen, ink and watercolour on paper, 35 × 52.2 cm
inscribed: *(70) Santa Maura 24 April 8.30 AM 1863*
with various colour notes

P.79
PROVENANCE: Part of a collection given by artist to Lord Aberdare, a former Governor of the Ionian Islands, as a wedding present; by descent in the Aberdare family until 1951; Adams Bros., New Bond Street, from whom purchased by Gallery, January 1952.
EXHIBITIONS: *English water-colours from the Hickman Bacon and other collections,* Bedford, Cecil Higgins Art Gallery, 1952, no.49; *Watercolours and Drawings from The Cecil Higgins Art Gallery, Bedford*, London, Thos. Agnew & Sons Ltd, 1962, no.57; *English Watercolours from The Cecil Higgins Art Gallery, Bedford,* Reading, Reading Museum and Art Gallery, 1965, no.29.

At the end of March 1863 Lear decided to make a tour of the Ionian Islands before they ceased to be under British rule – for in 1862 the Cabinet decided they must be returned to Greece. He left Corfu and was away for two months, walking and drawing on each island (see Vivien Noakes, *Edward Lear, The Life of a Wanderer*, 1968, p.196).

The author of *The Book of Nonsense,* Lear was the twentieth of twenty-one children of a stockbroker in Holloway. In 1831 he was employed as a draughtsman at the Zoological Gardens and later worked for Lord Derby at Knowsley. In 1836 he decided he wanted to concentrate on landscape and for the rest of his life did so, travelling to Greece, Turkey, Egypt, Italy, Malta, Syria, Nice and San Remo, where he settled and died.

He was enormously prolific, many sketches not only being dated, but also having the exact time they were painted, and also embellished with colour notes spelt phonetically e.g rox for rocks.

EJ

Edward LEAR

[1812–88]

Corfu

watercolour and brown ink on paper, 25 × 43 cm
inscribed: *Corfu*

P.292
PROVENANCE: Sotheby's sale 22 April 1959, lot 29, from whom purchased by Gallery.
EXHIBITIONS: *English Watercolours from The Cecil Higgins Art Gallery, Bedford,* Reading, Reading Museum and Art Gallery, 1965, no.30.

Lear first visited Corfu in April 1848, at the invitation of a new acquaintance, Sir George Ferguson Bowen, President of the University of Corfu. The island was then still under British rule. Lear returned there several times, describing it in 1864 as 'the loveliest place in the world'.

EJ

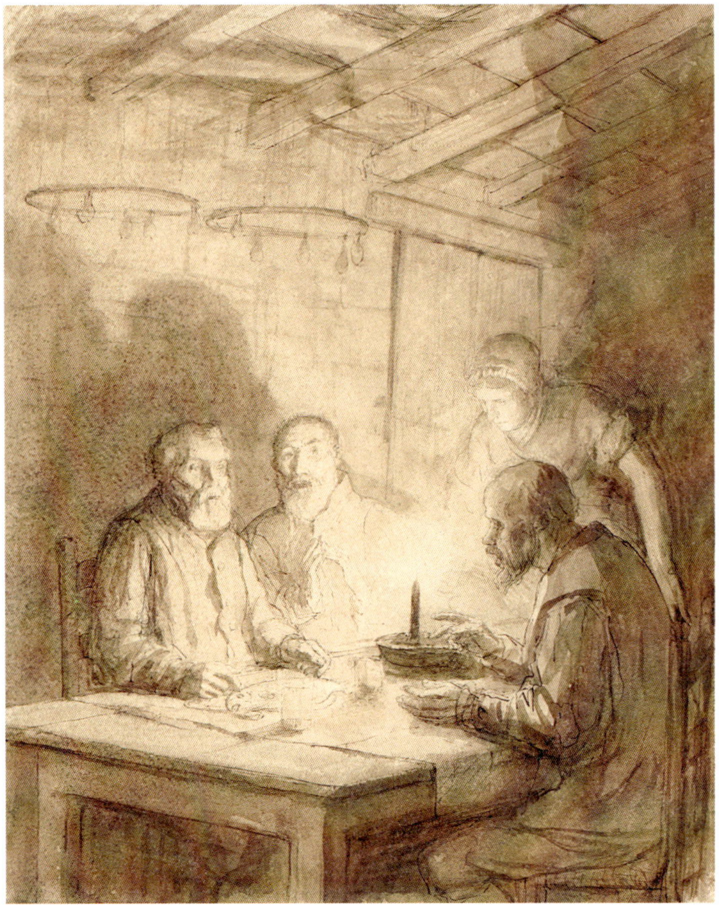

Alphonse LEGROS

[1837–1911]

Le Souper chez Misère, 1870s

pen and wash on paper, 37.3 × 30.4 cm

P.352
PROVENANCE: Purchased from the Reid Gallery, July 1960.

Presumably *Misère* is used here to mean extreme poverty as these old men appear to have precious little to eat and nothing to drink for their supper. The subject was inspired by the French Realist movement epitomised by the work of Gustave Courbet (1819–77), who had influenced Legros.

Legros was born in Dijon into a very poor family and received almost no education. In 1851 he went to Paris to work with Cambon in the theatre before entering the École de Lecocq de Boisboudran. A friend of Édouard Manet (1832–83) and Edgar Degas (1834–1917), he first showed at the Salon in 1857. Although his exhibits there won him some '*succès d'estime*', they never won him a medal. Disillusioned with Paris, he accepted an invitation to join his friend WHISTLER in London, where he received immediate acclaim.

In Paris he had begun some etchings which he expanded in London to a series of 258 prints. He had considerable influence on the teaching of drawing in England where he had numerous pupils. He died in Watford.

EJ

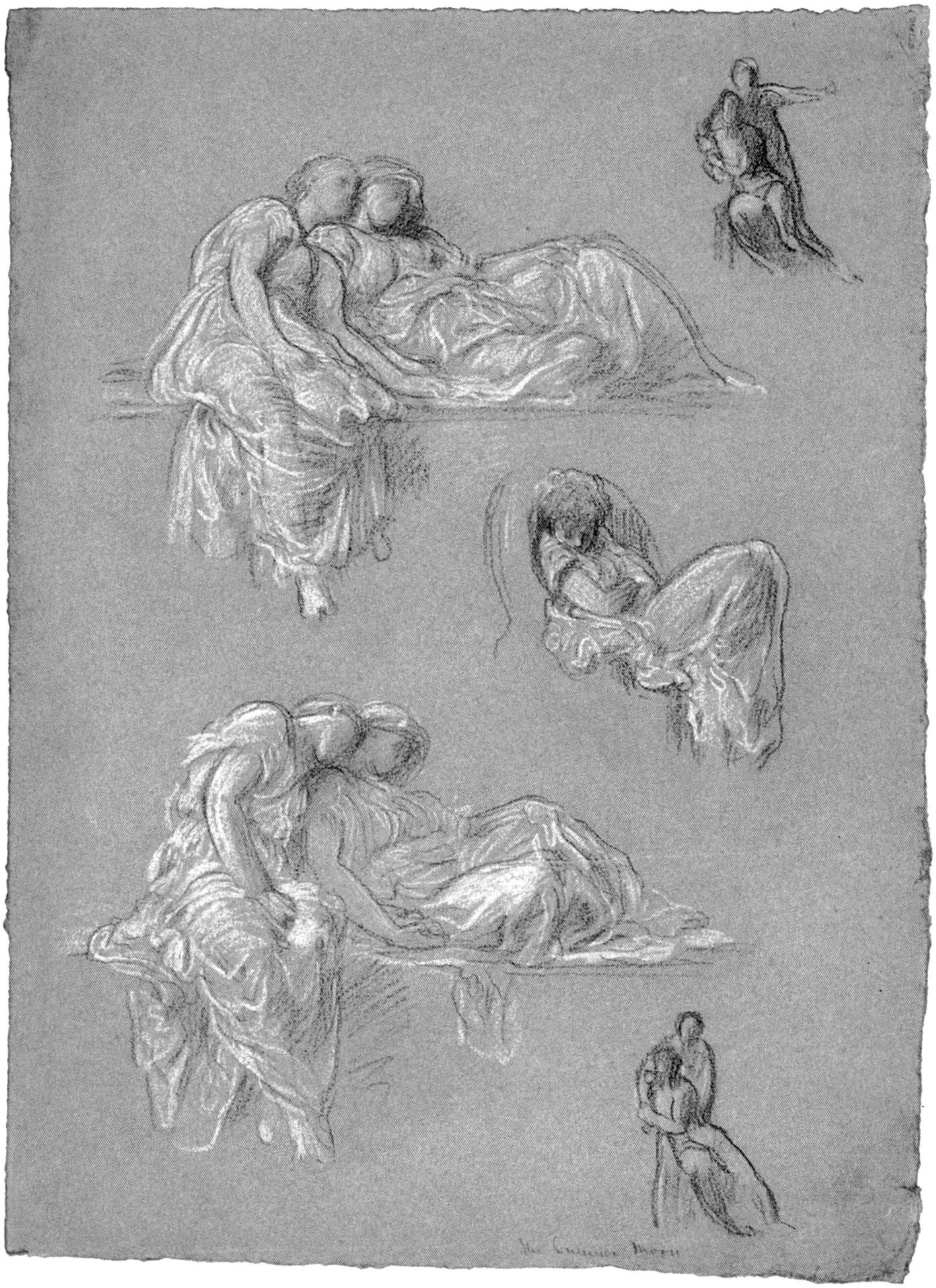

Frederic, Lord LEIGHTON, P.R.A., R.W.S.

[1830–96]

Studies for **Summer Moon, c.1872**

chalk on blue paper, 31.9 × 24 cm
inscribed: *The Summer Moon*
inscribed on reverse: *Mr Knowles* (illegible) *Leyton* [sic]

P.184

PROVENANCE: James Knowles, Esq., Trafford Bank House, Manchester; A. Morrison, Esq.; The Wilton Gallery, from whom purchased by Gallery, April 1958.

REFERENCES: *Drawings and Studies in Pencil, Chalk and Other mediums by The Late Lord Leighton*, published by Fine Art Society and MacMillan & Co., 1898; L. Zatlin, *Aubrey Beardsley and Victorian Sexual Politics*, 1990, p.131.

Studies for the picture exhibited at the R.A. in 1872 (202) now in a private collection, India (see Leonee and Richard Ormond, *Lord Leighton*, 1975, p.129, pl.18).

Acknowledged leader of the Victorian classical school of painters and lion of cultured London society, Leighton occupied a position between the Grosvenor Gallery aesthetes and the R.A., of which he was President from 1878. He painted historical and biblical themes until, in the mid-1860s, he turned to the Greek classical subjects, which dominated the rest of his work.

His house and studio in Holland Park, which he built 1864–6, is now a museum devoted to his life and work. In 1896 he became the only artist ever to receive a barony.

EJ

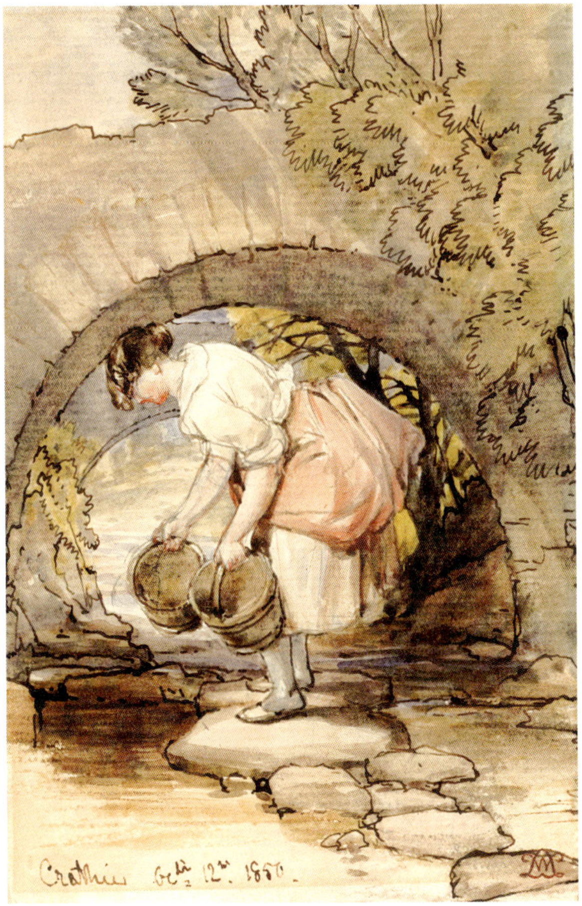

William Leighton LEITCH
[1804–83]
A Girl drawing Water from a Stream, 1850

pen and watercolour on paper, 15.8 × 10.1 cm
inscribed: *Crathie Oct.12th 1850* monogram *WLL*

P.169
PROVENANCE: Alpine Club Galleries; P&D Colnaghi Ltd, from whom purchased by Gallery, January 1958.

Born in Glasgow, Leitch became a scene-painter at the Theatre Royal there in 1824. On arrival in London he succeeded George Chambers (1803–40) as scene-painter at the Pavilion Theatre and also worked with George Clarkson Stanfield (1828–78) and David ROBERTS. After five years in Italy he returned to London and exhibited at the R.A. 1833–61. He taught Queen Victoria watercolour painting which led to WHISTLER remarking, on catching Leitch's name: 'Leitch ? Didn't he teach the Queen to paint ? Or did she teach him ?'.

EJ

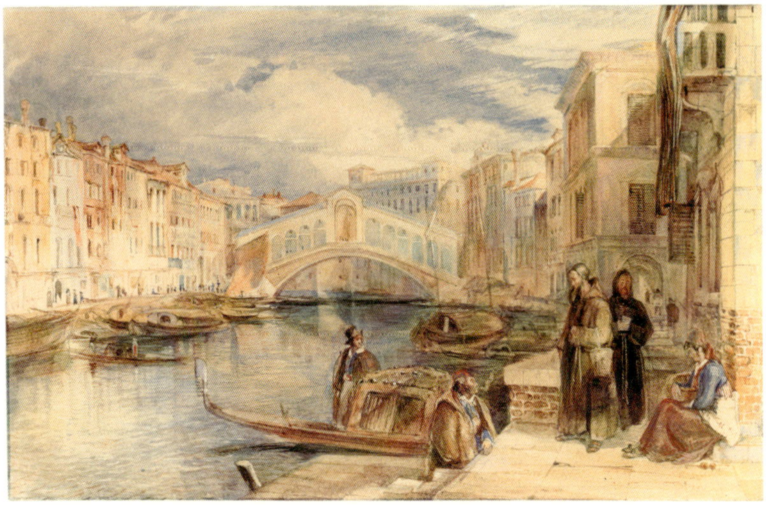

John Frederick LEWIS, R.A.
[1805–76]
The Rialto Bridge, Venice, 1827

watercolour, bodycolour and gum arabic on paper, 21.5 × 34.4 cm
inscribed: *JF Lewis*

P.283
PROVENANCE: Dyson Perrins, Sotheby's 2 April 1959, lot 20, from whom purchased by Gallery.
EXHIBITIONS: *Old Water-colour Society*, London, 1830, no.245; *English Watercolours from The Cecil Higgins Art Gallery, Bedford*, Reading, Reading Museum and Art Gallery, 1965, no.33.
REFERENCES: M. Lewis, *John Frederick Lewis*, 1978, p.76, no.300.

The Rialto Bridge has been a very popular subject with artists over the centuries. Lewis emphasizes the importance of the Rialto by placing it firmly in the centre of the composition with the two sides of the Grand Canal leading the eye diagonally towards it.

Painted in 1827 when Lewis, having just been elected an associate of the O.W.C.S., travelled through Switzerland to Venice.

EJ

John Frederick LEWIS, R.A.
[1805–76]
The Market, Toledo, Spain, 1832–4

watercolour, pastel and bodycolour on paper, 24.5 × 36 cm

P.147
PROVENANCE: P&D Colnaghi Ltd., from whom purchased by Gallery, January 1958.
REFERENCES: M. Lewis, *John Frederick Lewis*, 1978, p.73, no.258.

Painted 1832–4, the years in which Lewis was in Spain and Morocco, where he produced some of his most attractive and freely-painted watercolours.

EJ

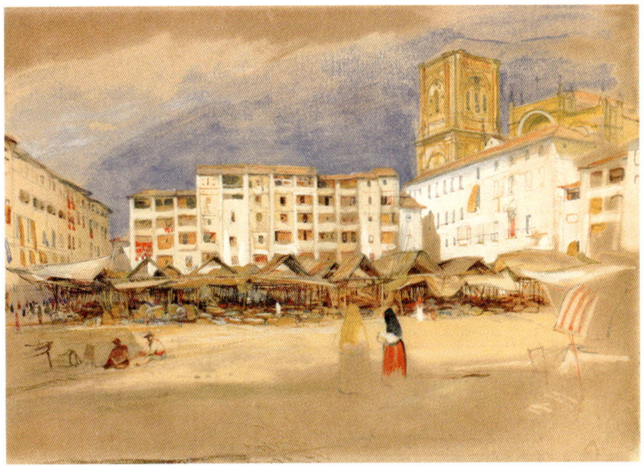

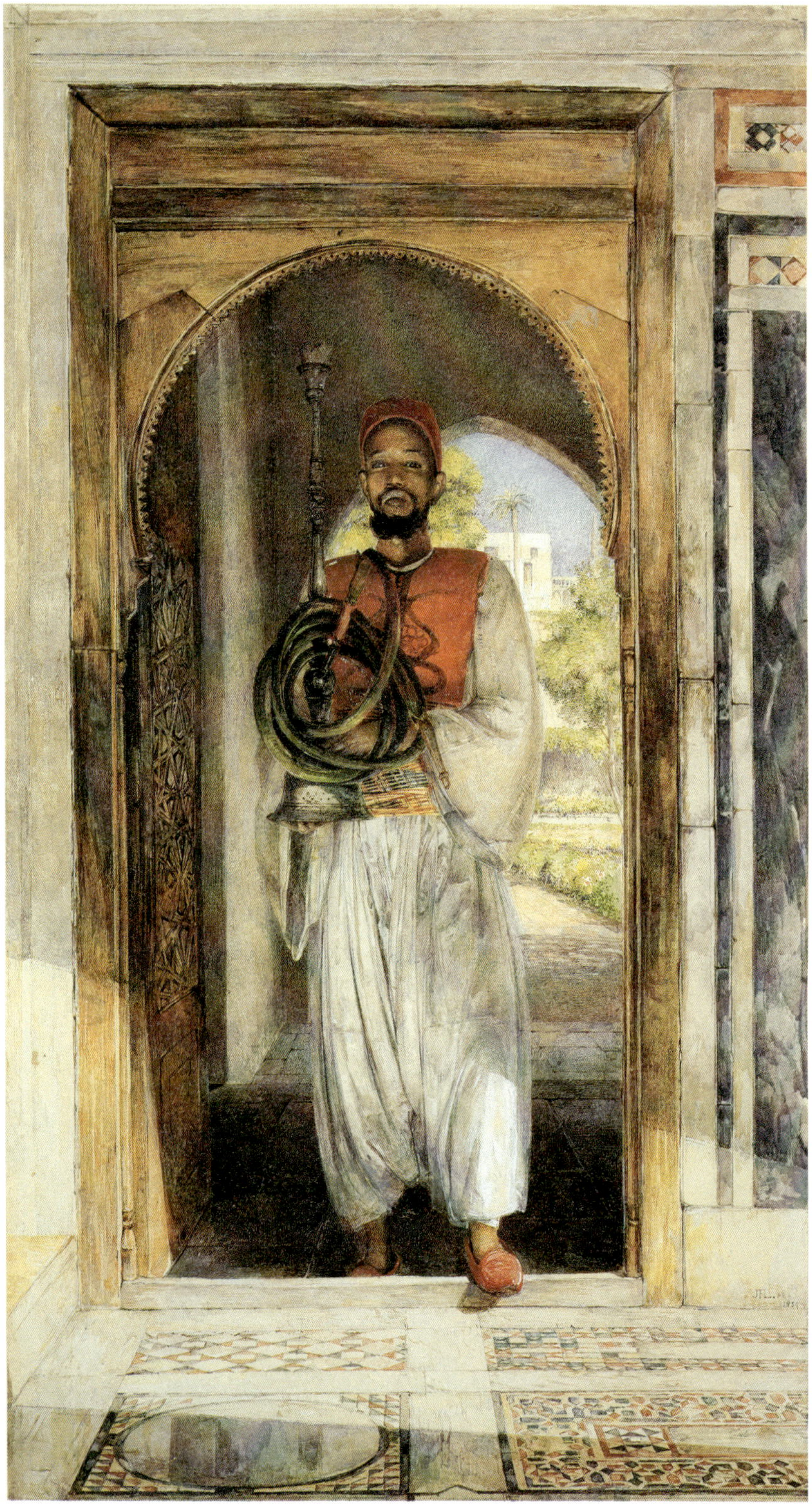

John Frederick LEWIS, R.A.
[1805–76]
The Pipe-Bearer, 1859

watercolour, pencil and body colour on paper, 38.3 × 21.3 cm
inscribed: *JFL ARA 1859*

P.305

PROVENANCE: Humphrey Roberts; Gilbert Davies; Sotheby's 19 March 1958, lot no.54; P&D Colnaghi Ltd, from whom purchased by Gallery, October 1959.
EXHIBITIONS: London, R.A., 1862, no.812 as *Egyptian Servant; Winter Exhibition*, London, R.A., 1906, no.52; *Water-colours from the Gilbert Davies Collection, London*, Arts Council, 1949, no.70; *Watercolours and Drawings from The Cecil Higgins Art Gallery, Bedford*, London, Thos. Agnew & Sons Ltd, 1962, no.46; *English Watercolours from The Cecil Higgins Art Gallery, Bedford*, Reading, Reading Museum and Art Gallery, 1965, no.34; *The English Tradition: an exhibition of watercolours from two private collections*, Bedford, Cecil Higgins Art Gallery, 1972, no.52; *The Great Age of British Watercolours 1750–1880*, London, R.A. and Washington D.C., National Gallery of Art, 1993, no.201.
REFERENCES: M. Lewis, *John Frederick Lewis*, 1978, p.94, no.578; A. Wilton & A. Lyles, *The Great Age of British Watercolours 1750–1880*, 1993, p.306, pl.313; J. Welton, *Looking at Pictures*, 1994, p.25.

This kind of Egyptian figure-study became very popular among Victorian collectors who admired the high finish and meticulous detail typical of Lewis's work at this date. Despite the accuracy of detail, it was painted in Surrey, eight years after leaving Cairo.

Like the Pre-Raphaelites, Lewis adopted the technique of painting watercolour on a white ground to reinforce the intensity of colour.

EJ/CB

John Frederick LEWIS, R.A.
[1805–76]
The Bazaar, Cairo, 1872

watercolour and bodycolour on paper, 57.3 × 43 cm
inscribed: *JF Lewis RA 1872*

P.282

PROVENANCE: J. Dyson Perrins; Sotheby's 22 April 1959, lot 58, from whom purchased by Gallery.
EXHIBITIONS: *Universal Exposition*, Paris, 1878, no.91 as *Street Scene in Cairo; English Watercolours from The Cecil Higgins Art Gallery, Bedford*, Reading, Reading Museum and Art Gallery. 1965, no.32; *The English Tradition: an exhibition of watercolours from two private collections*, Bedford, Cecil Higgins Art Gallery, 1972, no.53.
REFERENCES: M. Lewis, *John Frederick Lewis*, 1978, p.97, no.608; M. Lewis, *The Lewis Family: Art & Travel*, 1992, p.37.

A version in oil was sold at Sotheby's, London in 1980 (9 April 1980, lot.28). The scene depicts the Bezestein Bazaar of El Khan Khalil, one of the most important markets in Cairo, which dates back to the 14th century.

Lewis left England in 1837 eventually settling in Cairo in 1841. According to his friend, Lord Elphinstone, he lived in the 'most Ottoman quarter', where he remained for ten years. While in Cairo, Lewis adopted local customs and style of dress. The writer Thackery referred to his existence thus: 'like a languid Lotus-eater – a dreamy, hazy, lazy, tobaccofied Life'. Despite references to the Egyptian tradition of pipe-smoking and a 'languid' life, Lewis produced numerous sketches of Cairo life, and, concerned about authenticity, amassed an extraordinary collection of Egyptian costumes and accessories. This material enabled Lewis to continue with Egyptian subjects even on his return to England in 1851, where this picture was painted.

Son of the painter and engraver Frederick Christian Lewis (1779–1856), John Frederick was initially encouraged to take up engraving. However, his early friendship with fellow animal-lover LANDSEER prompted Lewis to become an animal-painter. He was employed, briefly, to Sir Thomas Lawrence, but soon abandoned animal-painting in favour of travelling. On his return to Britain, Lewis settled in Walton-on-Thames, where he continued to paint Egyptian scenes until his death.

CB

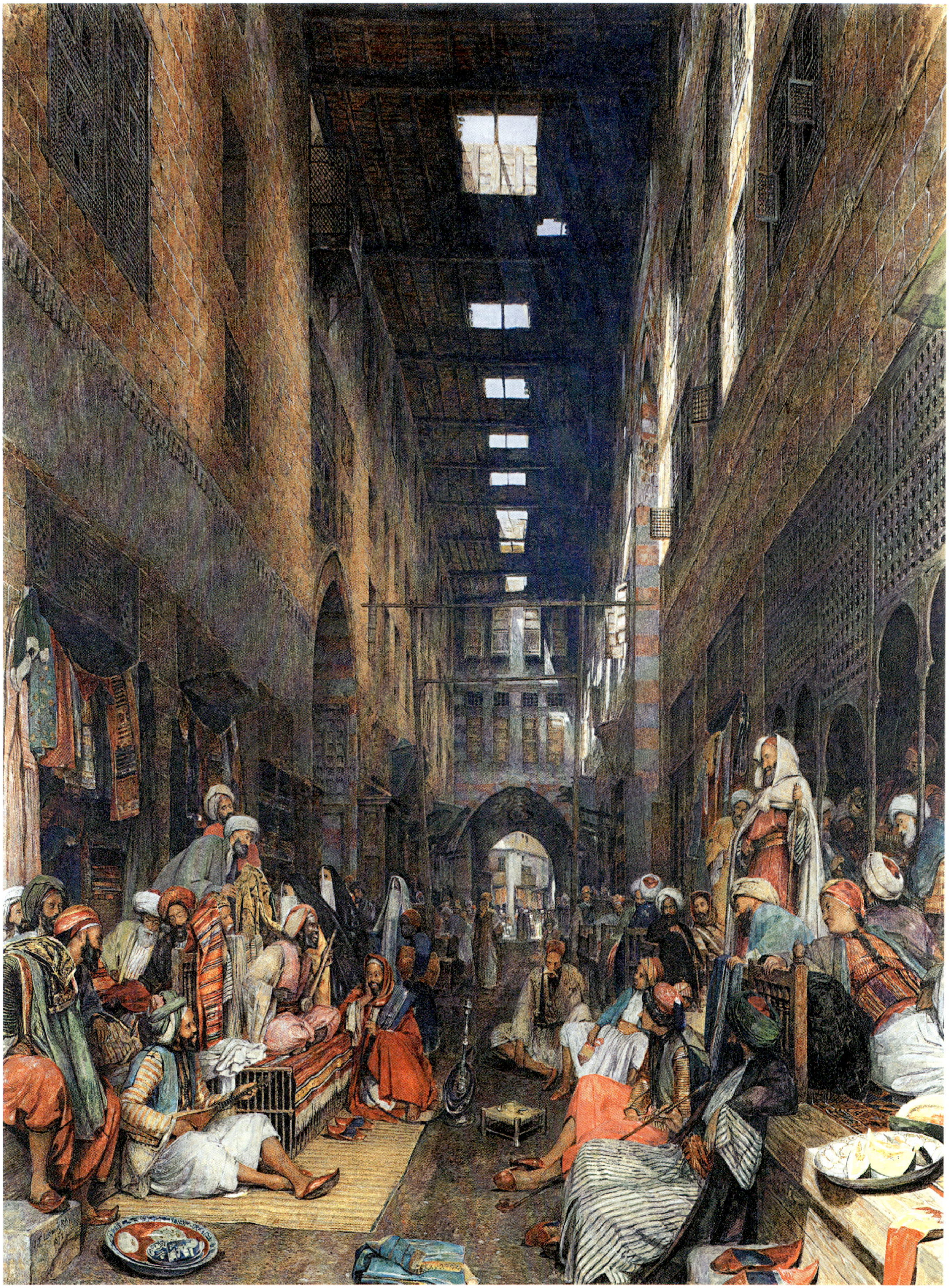

Percy Wyndham LEWIS
[1882–1957]
The Centauress I, 1912

pen and ink and wash on paper, 31.1 × 37 cm
inscribed: *Wyndham Lewis 1912*

P.138
PROVENANCE: John Quinn, purchased from the artist; American Art Association, New York, 10 February 1927, no.175B; Richard Wyndham; Mayor Gallery; Charles Handley-Read; Zwemmer Gallery, from whom purchased by Gallery, November 1957.
EXHIBITIONS: *Vorticist Exhibition*, New York, 1917, no.4 as *Centauride; Wyndham Lewis Retrospective*, London, Redfern Gallery, 1949, no.20; *Wyndham Lewis*, London, Tate Gallery, 1956, no.27; *Wyndham Lewis & Vorticism*, Arts Council of Great Britain, 1956, no.11; *Watercolours from Bedford*, Norwich, Norwich Castle Museum, 1965, no.30; *The Camden Town Group*, Bedford, Cecil Higgins Art Gallery, 1969, no.35; *Vorticism and its Allies*, London, Hayward Gallery, 1974, no.13; *Wyndham Lewis*, Manchester, Manchester City Art Gallery, 1980, no.10; *Vorticism*, Hannover, Sprengel Museum and Munich, Haus der Kunst, 1996–7, no.100.
REFERENCES: C. Handley-Read, *The Art of Wyndham Lewis*, 1951, pp.22, 36, 52, 84–5, pl.5; W. Michel, *Wyndham Lewis: Paintings & Drawings*, 1971, no.41; R. Cork, *Vorticism & Abstract Art in the First Machine Age*, 1976, p.29; J. Farrington, *Wyndham Lewis*, 1980, pp.51–2, no.10; T. Kush, *Wyndham Lewis's Pictorial Integer*, 1981, pp.31, 46–7, pl.3; S. Cooney, *Blast 3*, 1984, p.233, pl.2; A. Nicoli, *Blast*, 1996, p.112; Sir J. Graham, 'A new Gainsborough watercolour and the Watercolour collection of the Cecil Higgins Art Gallery, Bedford', *Watercolours, Drawings and Prints*, winter 1990, vol.5 no.4, pp.31–3, fig.5.

The Manchester exhibition catalogue comments thus: 'A fragile mythological creature confronted by the harsh and threatening forms of the modern industrial world. The forms are awkward and unresolved, but nevertheless the design has considerable power'.

An exhibition catalogue at the d'Offay Gallery in 1984 claimed that Lewis had created the concept of a centauress but this is refuted by *The Flight of the Centaurs and the Lapithae* by Piero di Cosimo (c.1462–after 1515) in the National Gallery which includes centauresses. The word itself is certainly recorded in print by 1754 at the latest.

During the period preceding the First World War, Wyndham Lewis published *BLAST*, which attempted to challenge the old order. In the 1949 Redfern Retrospective catalogue, he wrote: 'In the year or two prior to World War I, I attempted totally to eliminate from my work all reference to nature…it is enough to say that you will not find any work of mine later in date so "abstract" as that…'

Wyndham Lewis's avant-garde approach is symbolized here by the classical centauress whose path has been blocked by the abstract, jagged screen.

EJ/CB

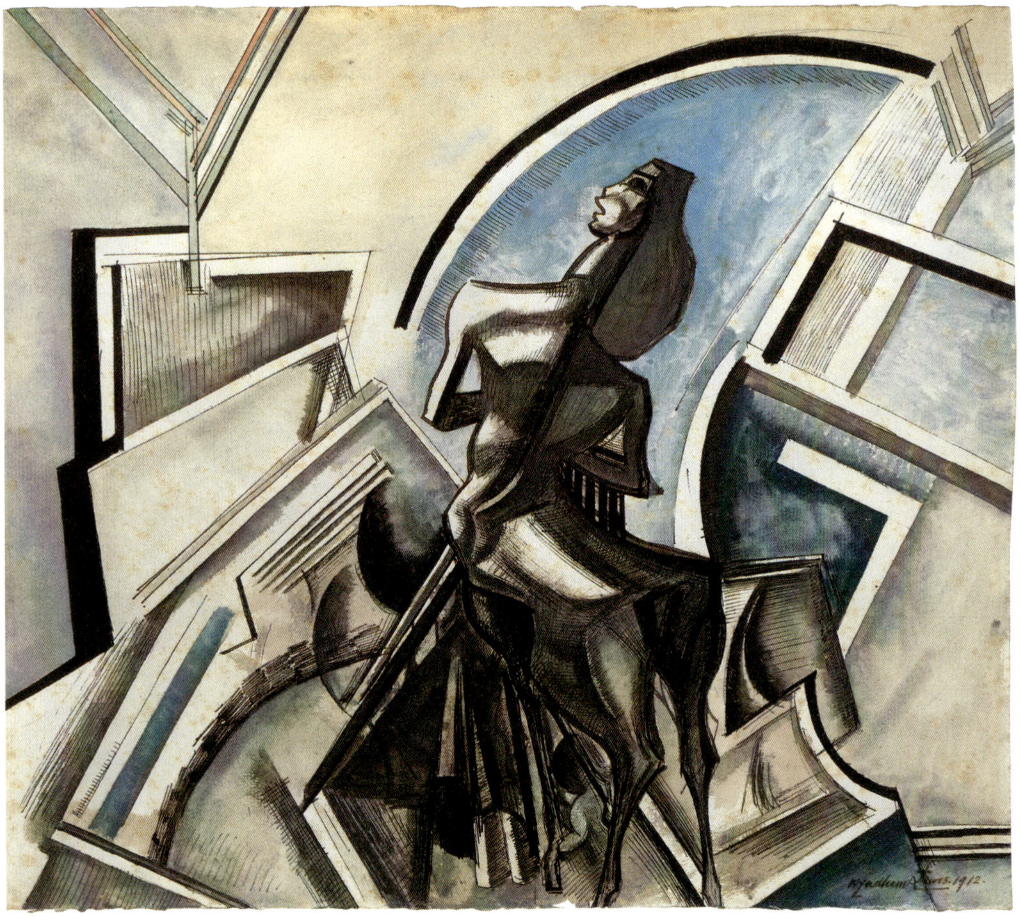

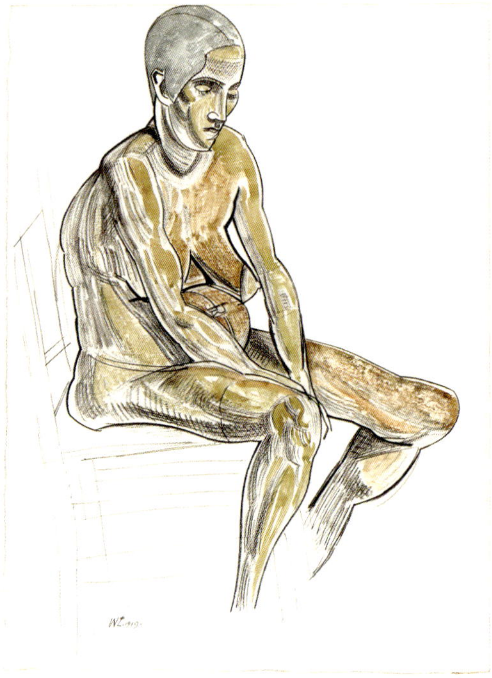

Percy Wyndham LEWIS
[1882–1957]
Seated Nude, 1919

pen and ink and watercolour on paper, 38 × 28.5 cm
inscribed: *WL 1919*
inscribed on reverse: *hudson chair*

P.325
PROVENANCE: Lord's Gallery, from whom purchased by Gallery, January 1960.

This drawing is one of a number Lewis made in 1919, using the same model. Another version is in the Manchester City Art Gallery (1925.575).

CB

Percy Wyndham LEWIS
[1882–1957]
Dame Edith Sitwell, c.1921

watercolour and pencil on paper, 40.4 × 27.8 cm

P.420
PROVENANCE: Brook Street Gallery, from whom purchased by Gallery, May 1962.
EXHIBITIONS: *Watercolours and Drawings from The Cecil Higgins Art Gallery, Bedford*, London, Thos. Agnew & Sons Ltd., 1962, no.83, pl.IX; *Watercolours from Bedford*, Norwich, Norwich Castle Museum, 1965, no.29; *The Camden Town Group*, Bedford, Cecil Higgins Art Gallery, 1969, no.36; *Wyndham Lewis*, Manchester, Manchester City Art Gallery, 1980, no.89.
REFERENCES: W. Michel, *Wyndham Lewis: paintings and drawings*, 1971, no.488.

Edith Sitwell (1887–1964), together with her brothers Osbert (1892–1969) and Sacheverell (1897–1988), made a lively contribution to the English artistic scene in the 1920s. Edith was a major and prolific poet and writer who dressed and behaved eccentrically. She met Lewis towards the end of the 1914–18 war and he was a frequent visitor to her flat. After Lewis satirized the Sitwells in *The Apes of God* their friendship soured and Lewis later wrote: 'I do not think I would be exaggerating if I described myself as Miss Edith Sitwell's favourite enemy'.

Lewis painted and drew her several times; this drawing of c.1912 is both subtle and the least formal and is considered by the family to be the best likeness, her 'anteater's nose', as Lytton Strachey (1880–1932) described it, being partly masked by a tactfully placed shadow. About Lewis's celebrated portrait of her in the Tate Gallery (begun in 1923, but not completed until about 1935), she afterwards wrote that she had sat for it 'every day except Sundays for ten months. But in the end his manner became so threatening that I ceased to pose for him…'.

EJ

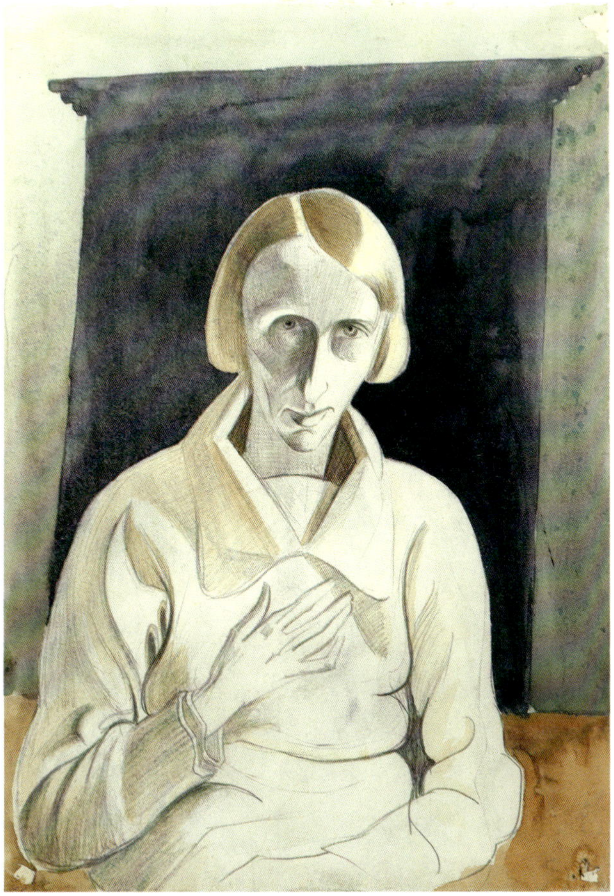

Percy Wyndham LEWIS
[1882–1957]
Sir Stafford Cripps, c.1934

pen and ink and watercolour on paper, 35.5 × 25.1 cm
inscribed: *Wyndham Lewis*
inscribed on reverse: *Sir Stafford Cripps*

P.146
PROVENANCE: Arthur Crossland; Leicester Galleries, from whom purchased by Gallery, December 1957.
EXHIBITIONS: *Portrait Painting and Drawings*, Rye, Rye Art Gallery, 1967; *Wyndham Lewis*, Manchester, Manchester City Art Gallery, 1980, no.127; *In Close-Up: Stafford Cripps*, London, N.P.G., 1984–5, no cat.; *Wyndham Lewis:* Art & War, London, I.W.M., 1992, no.59.
REFERENCES: W. Michel, *Wyndham Lewis: paintings and drawings*, 1971, no.842; P. Edwards, *Wyndham Lewis: Art & War*, 1992, p.138, pl.59; repr. *The London Mercury*, October 1934, p.530, opp. Sir Oswald Moseley with caption 'Two Dictators'.

Sir Stafford Cripps (1889–1952) was a lawyer and Labour politician of strong Socialist principles. His appearance of implacable austerity is clearly emphasized in this drawing. Cripps became Chancellor of the Exchequer from 1940–5.

Painter, draughtsman, novelist, critic, political theorist and pamphleteer, Lewis studied at the Slade School 1898–1901 before travelling on the Continent, 1902–9. He was a member of the Camden Town Group, 1911, and of the London Group from 1913. He worked briefly in the Omega Workshops before breaking away in 1914 to found the Vorticist Group, where he edited its paper *Blast*. He wrote his first novel *Tarr* in 1924. He spent the Second World War in Canada and the United States.

EJ

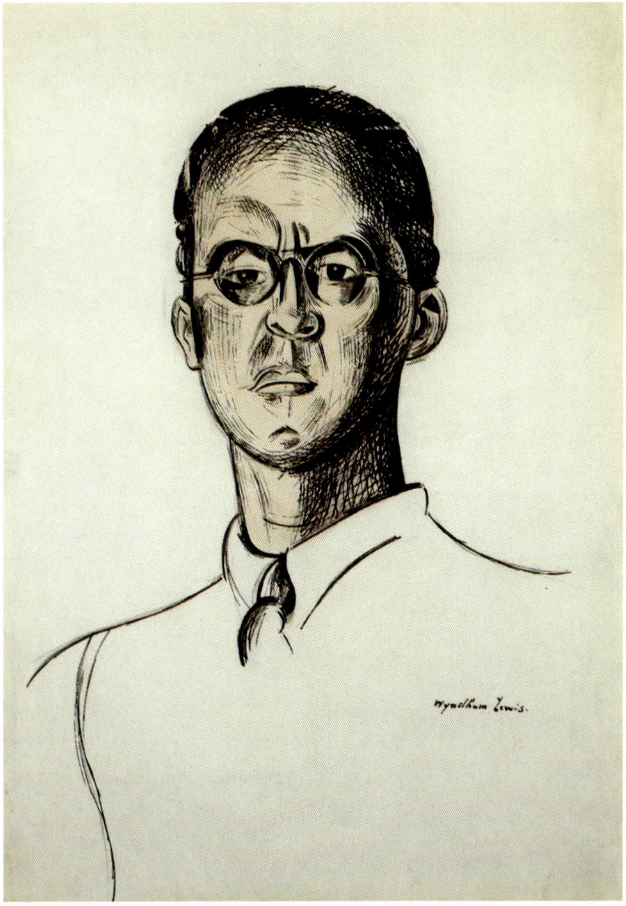

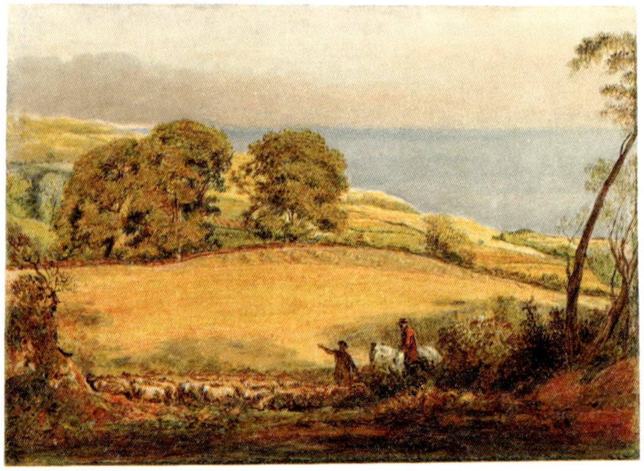

John LINNELL
[1792–1882]
Changing Pasture

watercolour heightened with bodycolour over black lead on paper, 22.9 × 32.3 cm

P.229
PROVENANCE: Gilbert Davies; Sotheby's sale 19 March1958, lot no.55 (Property of a Gentleman), purchased by Gallery.
EXHIBITIONS: *Samuel Palmer & John Linnell*, Reigate, Town Hall, 1963, no.80; *The English Tradition: an exhibition of watercolours from two private collections*, Bedford, Cecil Higgins Art Gallery, 1972, no.54.

Linnell is best known today for his connection with Samuel PALMER. He introduced Palmer to BLAKE and Palmer married Linnell's daughter. Clearly an ambitious man, John CONSTABLE recalled the time he tried to solicit votes for election to the R.A.: 'he spoke long to Landseer in Regent Street with his hat off all the (while)– I should not have wanted any other reason not to vote for him'.

After a year as one of John VARLEY's pupils, Linnell entered the Academy Schools in 1805 where he was encouraged by Dr MONRO. His best watercolours – usually moderate in size as here and often of scenes on the outskirts of London – were done early in his career. He then made his reputation in oils and resorted only occasionally to watercolour in later life.

EJ/CB

Lawrence Stephen LOWRY, R.A.
[1887–1976]
Church Street, Kirkham, 1925

pencil on paper, 25.7 × 36.4 cm
inscribed: *L.S.Lowry 1925*
inscribed on reverse: *Kirkham. The Drawing from which Mr.Denham's picture was done*

P.171
PROVENANCE: Alex Reid & Lefevre Ltd., from whom purchased by Gallery, January 1958.
EXHIBITIONS: *L.S. Lowry 1887–1976*, London, R.A., 1976, no.61 as *Pendlebury*; *Lowry Centenary Exhibition*, Salford, Salford Art Gallery, 1987, no.H.732, p.99.
REFERENCES: M. Leber & J. Sandling (eds.), *L.S. Lowry*, 1987, Catalogue of work in public collections, no.3, repr.

This drawing was formerly entitled *Pendlebury*. Kirkham is about eight miles west of Preston in Lancashire.

Lowry was a painter mainly of industrial landscapes in Manchester and Salford. He studied under Adolphe Valette (1876–1942), a disciple of Degas, but did not have a one-man exhibition until 1939. He was elected A.R.A. in 1955, and R.A. in 1962. His pictures of life in the north of England are often peopled, as here, with 'Chaplinesque figures', as Tim Hyman has so aptly described them.

EJ

Lawrence Stephen LOWRY, R.A.
[1887–1976]
Industrial Landscape, 1934

chalk and pencil on paper, 27.6 × 40.2 cm
inscribed: *LS Lowry 1934*

P.487
PROVENANCE: Piccadilly Gallery, from whom purchased by Gallery, January 1965.
EXHIBITIONS: *L.S. Lowry*. London, R.A., 1976,pp.62–4, no.108; *Lowry Centenary Exhibition*, Salford, City of Salford Art Gallery, 1987, H.732.
REFERENCES: M. Leber & J. Sandling (eds.), *L.S .Lowry, 1987*, p.99, no.4, repr.

A characteristic Lowry subject which conveys a bleak, but compellingly authentic impression of the industrial north of England.

When Lowry's pictures began to fetch handsome prices he started to collect Pre-Raphaelite and other Victorian works.

There is a museum devoted to the works of Lowry at Salford Quays in Manchester.

EJ

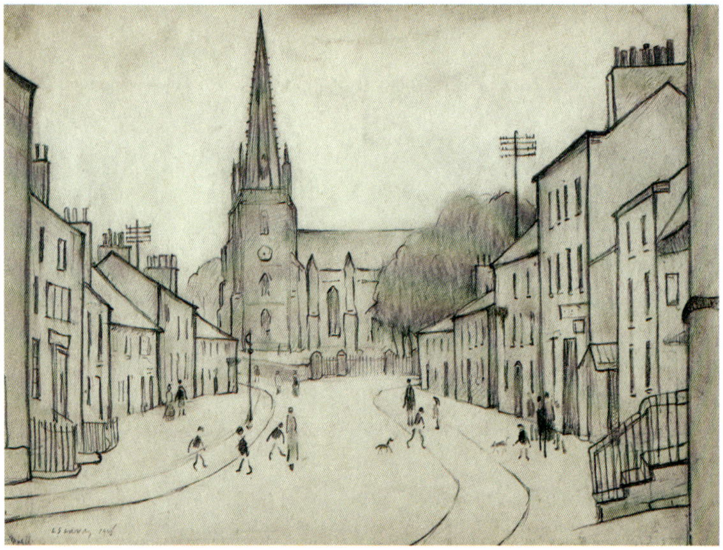

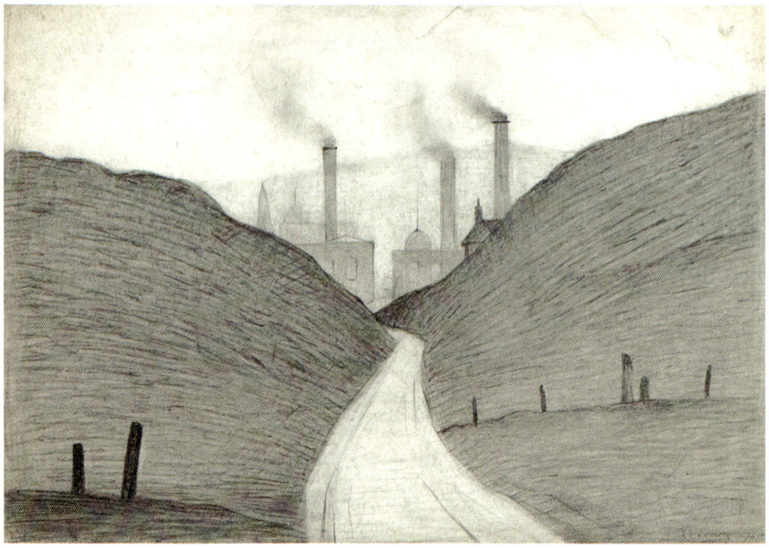

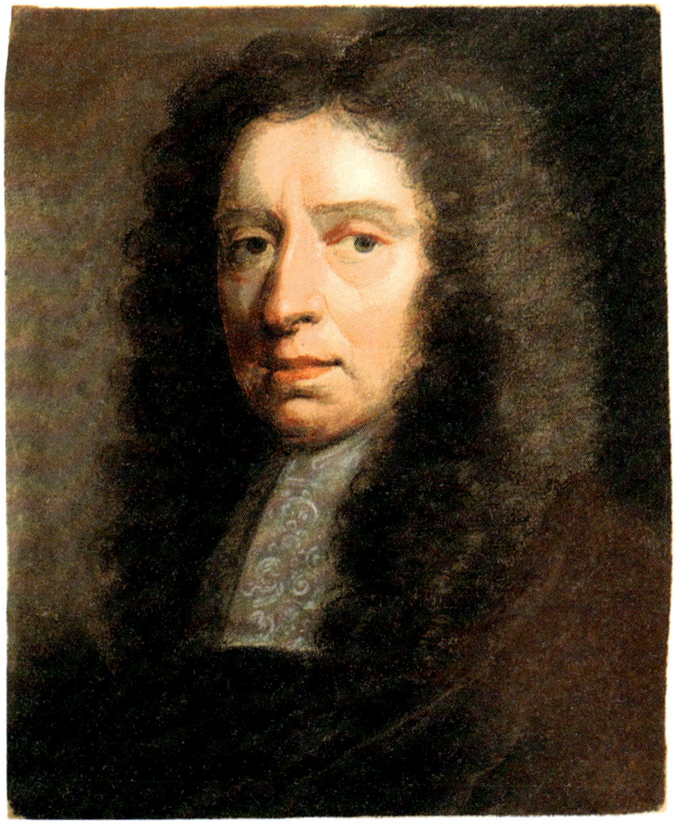

Edward LUTTEREL
[c.1650–c.1724]
Portrait of Samuel Luke (?)

pastel on paper, 20.6 × 17.4 cm

P.464
PROVENANCE: Mrs. Penderick Graham; P&D Colnaghi; L.G. Duke; P&D Colnaghi; Sir Bruce Ingram Collection; Sotheby's 20 October 1964, lot no.81, purchased by P&D Colnaghi, on behalf of Gallery, by Lord Luke of Pavenham (no relation to the sitter) and presented to Gallery, 1964.

Sir Samuel Luke (d.1670), a Parliamentarian and M.P. for Bedford, was knighted in 1624. Although present at Edgehill in 1642 and Chalgrove Field in 1643 where he distinguished himself, he took no part in public affairs during the Commonwealth and Protectorate. Because of his small stature he became the butt of royalist satire and was the supposed original of Samuel Butler's *Sir Hudibras*.

Luttrell (or Lutterell) was born in Dublin but came early to England. He returned to portraiture in crayons and studied under Ashfield, but he also invented a technique of pastel on a roughened copper base. His early portraits tend to be clumsy but he developed a style parallel to Sir Godfrey Kneller's (?1649-1723). He was one of the first practitioners of mezzotint in England.

EJ

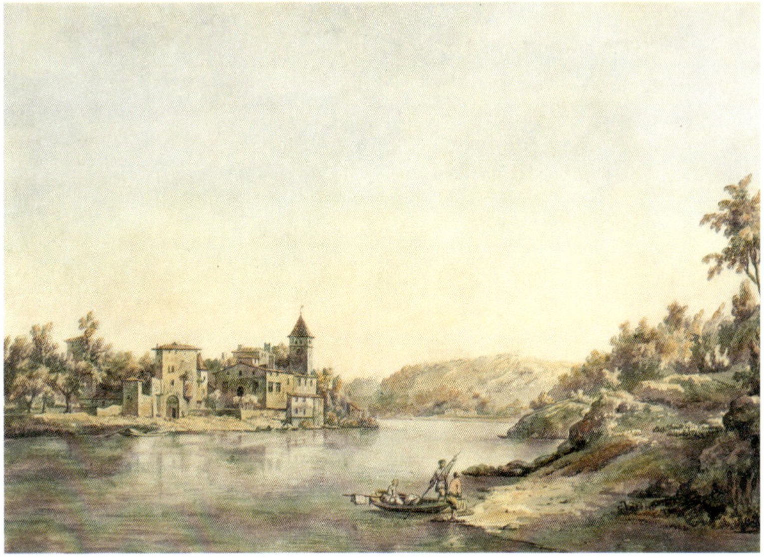

William MARLOW
[1740–1813]
River Landscape with Figures and a Boat in the Foreground

pen and ink with watercolour on paper, 37.1 × 53.2 cm
inscribed: *W. Marlow*

P.226
PROVENANCE: Earl of Chichester, from whom purchased by Gallery, March 1958.

The scene has not so far been identified although it is probably somewhere in France, perhaps on the Meuse where Marlow often painted Château Huy.

EJ

William MARLOW
[1740–1813]
River Landscape with Tower and Fishermen in a Boat

pen and ink with watercolour on paper, 37.1 × 54 cm

P.227
PROVENANCE: Earl of Chichester, from whom purchased by Gallery, March 1958.

This scene has not been identified, although it may be a composite landscape based on some on-the-spot drawings.

CB

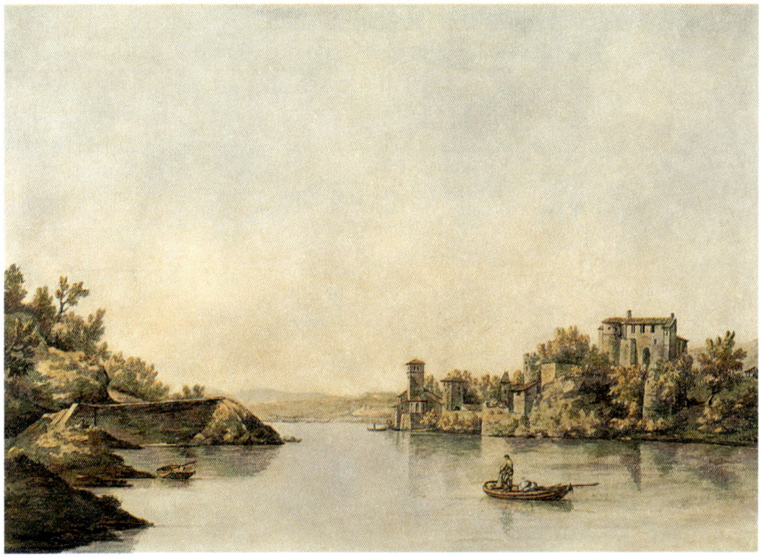

William MARLOW
[1740–1813]
Tivoli

pen and ink and watercolour on paper, 34 × 28.6 cm
inscribed: *W.M*

P.294
PROVENANCE: P&D Colnaghi Ltd, from whom purchased by Gallery, July 1959.

Marlow, a pupil of Samuel Scott from 1756 to 1761, worked in France and Italy from 1765 to 1768 finding subjects for many of his later oils and watercolours.

In 1788 he settled in Twickenham and much of his most characteristic work features the Thames nearby. He was first and foremost a topographer but also with a strong sense of the picturesque and a liking for rich colours. Marlow painted Tivoli frequently both in oils and watercolour.

EJ

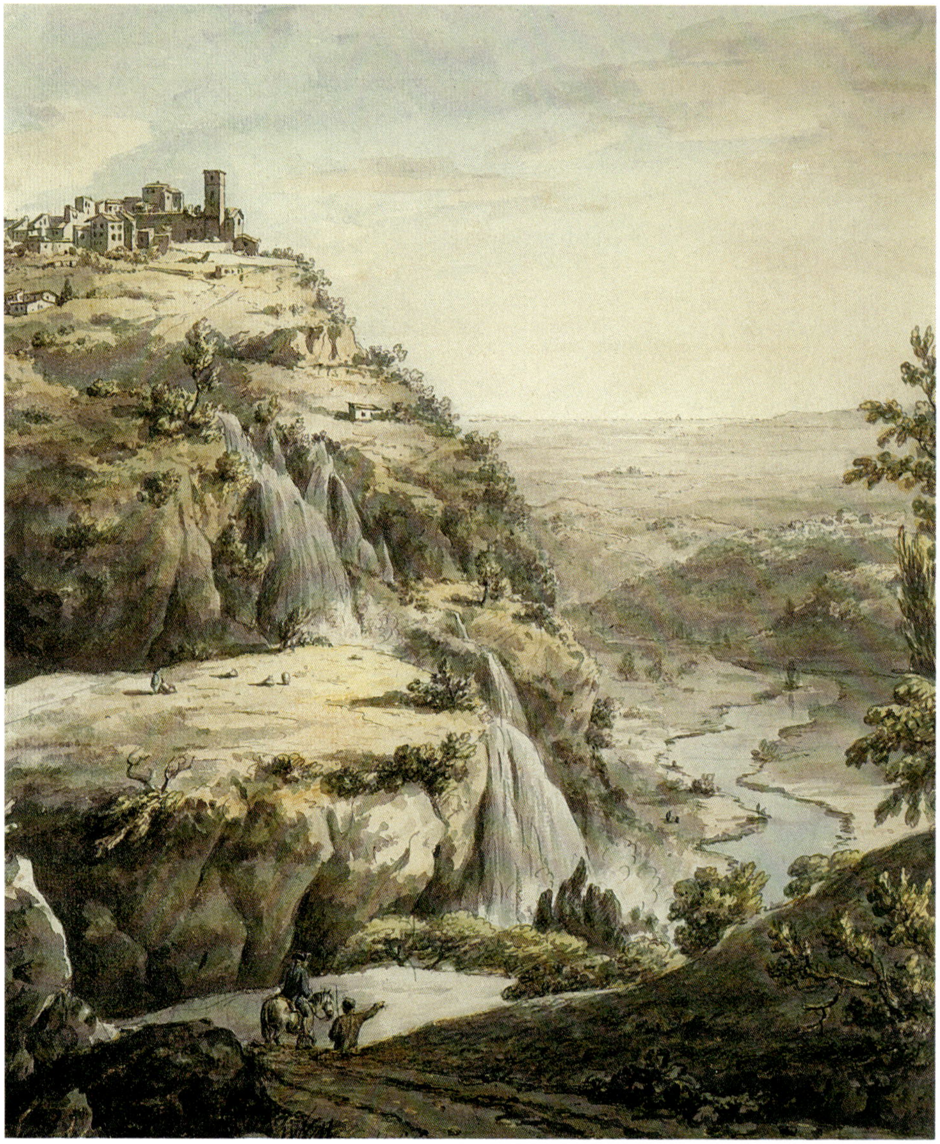

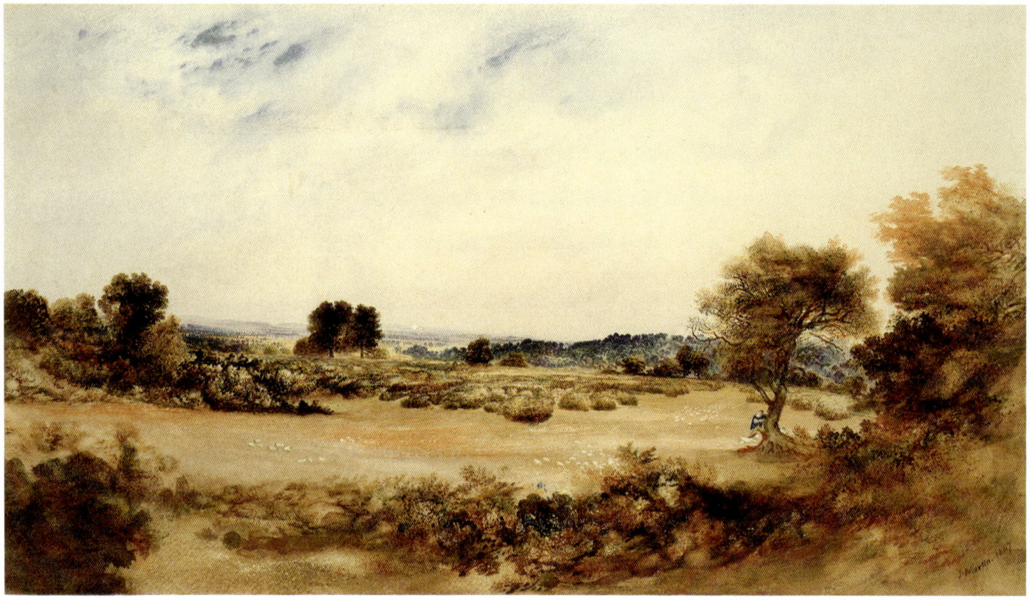

John MARTIN
[1789–1854]
Landscape with Two Figures Beneath a Tree, 1847

watercolour heightened with white on paper, 30.1 × 54 cm
inscribed: *J.Martin 1847*

P.600
PROVENANCE: Joseph Lovegrove F.S.A., Christie's lot no.22, 31 March 1883; Christie's (anon sale) lot no.163, 17 June 1969, from whom purchased by Thos. Agnew & Sons Ltd for Gallery.
EXHIBITIONS: *The English Tradition: an exhibition of watercolours from two private collections*, Bedford, Cecil Higgins Art Gallery, 1972, no.58.

Martin is chiefly known for his large oils of historical, religious and apocalyptic subjects, revealing a wild imagination and a taste for the sensational. But he also painted straightforward landscape watercolours, many in and around Richmond Park, the probable subject for this view.

EJ

Phil MAY

[1864–1903]

A Woman in Black , 1897

pen and ink on paper, 20.9 × 13 cm
inscribed: *Phil May 97*

P.157
PROVENANCE: P&D Colnaghi Ltd, from whom purchased by Gallery, January 1958.

May was born in Leeds where he became an assistant scene painter at the theatre, spending 1885–8 in Sydney before studying art in Paris. As a black and white artist, caricaturist and illustrator he had an instant success after joining Punch in 1895, vividly portraying the same subjects – street urchins, costers, cabbies and drunks – as had the recently deceased Charles KEENE.

May's economy of line and simplified language of strokes made him the most important black and white artist of the 1890s in the British tradition. He was also extremely prolific, producing an immense volume of work both for magazines and books.

He lived a bohemian life, squandered his money and died of liver cirrhosis and tuberculosis aged only thirty-nine.

EJ

Phil MAY

[1864–1903]

The Dumas Craze, 1899

pen and ink on paper, paper size 24.2 × 18.5 cm
inscribed: *Phil May 99*
THE DUMAS CRAZE – "LET EM ALL COME"

P.308
PROVENANCE: P&D Colnaghi Ltd, from whom purchased by Gallery, October 1959.

With inscription as follows: *Brown (who with his friends Jones and Robinson, is in town for a week and is "going it"). "Now, Mr.Costumier, we are going to this 'ere ball, and we want you to make us hup as the Three Musketeers !"*

This drawing was made for *Punch* and is illustrated in the anthology *Mr Punch in Bohemia*. The issue in which it originally appeared has not yet been traced.

These three characters are to masquerade as *The Three Musketeers*, an historical romance by Alexandre Dumas (1802–70), published 1844–5, which recounts the exploits of d'Artagnan, who joined Louis XIII's musketeers and shared the fortunes of three of them, Athos, Porthos, and Aramis. 'The Dumas Craze' was indeed all the rage at this date so that May's drawing was highly topical and easily appreciated by the readership of *Punch*.

EJ/JM

Phil MAY

[1864–1903]

Collection of Black and White China, 1901

pen and ink on paper, 24.7 × 17.7 cm
inscribed: *Phil May 1901*
"Punch's" Holiday Book Collection of "Black -and-White" China ! and with captions to each individual sketch.

P.309
PROVENANCE: P&D Colnaghi Ltd, from whom purchased by Gallery, October 1959.

The title is presumably also a joke, alluding not only to May's own role as a black and white artist but as a contrast to the blue and white china that was then so much sought after as part of the *Japonisme* and Aesthetic Movement then in vogue.

During the late nineteenth century, Punch often depicted racial stereotypes and reinforced British xenophobia. This was frequently aimed at the Chinese immigrant population who were subjected to racial jibes bordering on hysteria.

EJ/CB

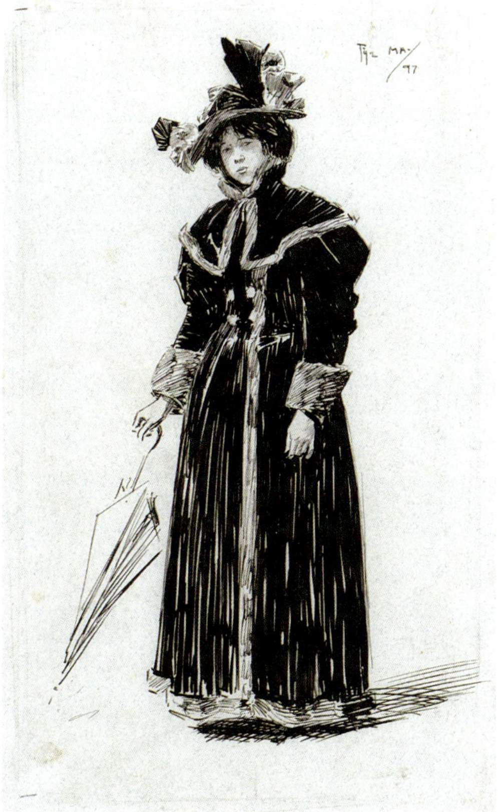

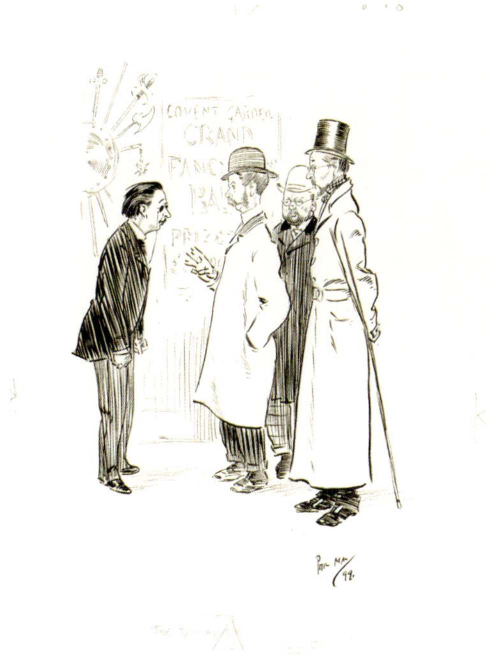

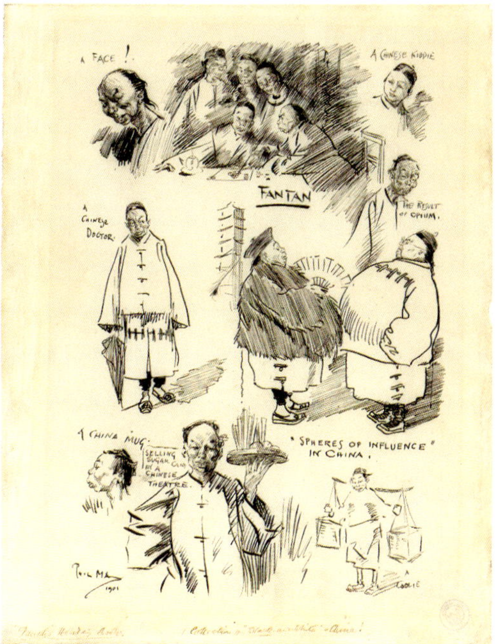

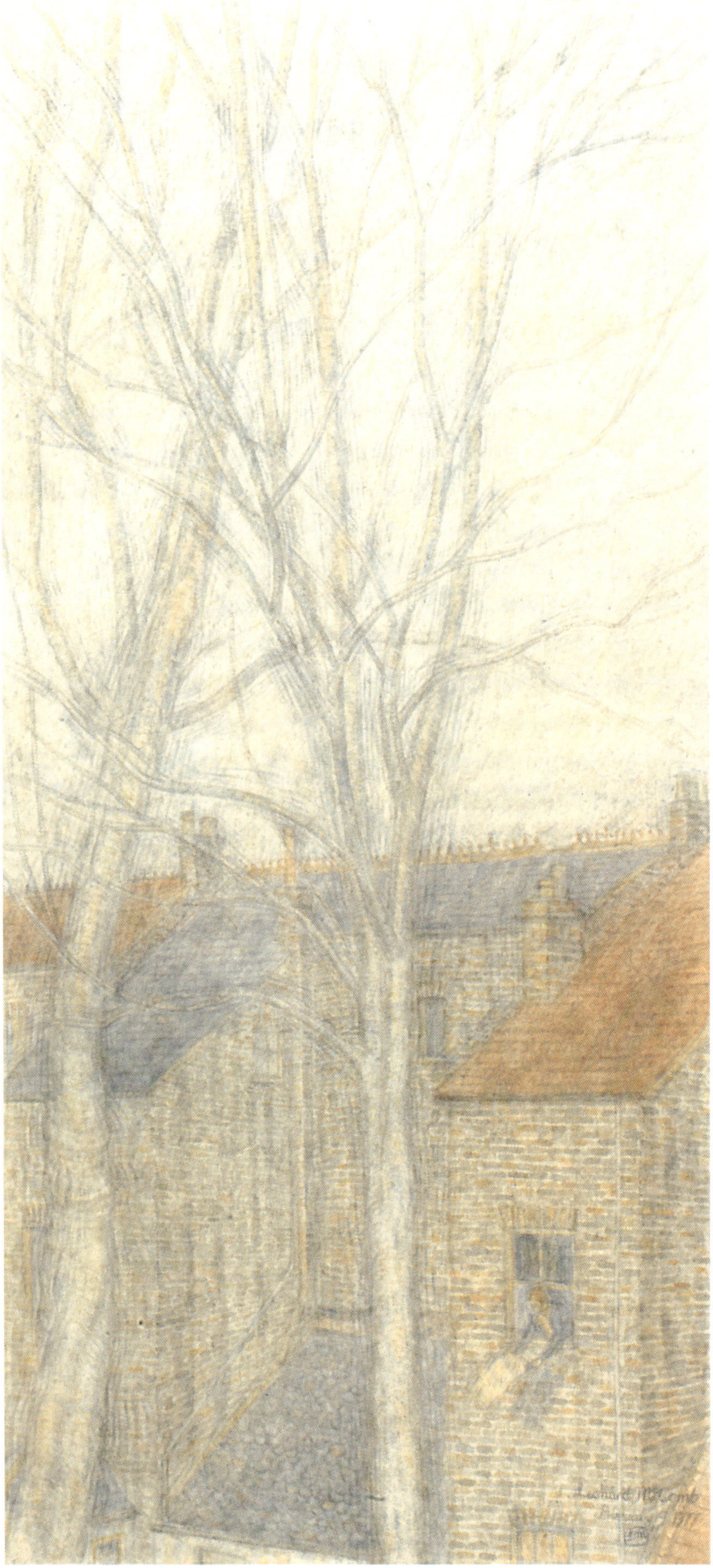

Leonard McCOMB, R.A.

[b. 1930]

Back Garden in South London, 1977

watercolour on paper, 79 × 37 cm
inscribed: *Leonard McComb February 19 1977* and *Leonard McComb*

P.827
PROVENANCE: Purchased from the artist with assistance from V&A/M.G.C. Purchase Grant Fund, April 1994.

McComb also designed and completed the picture frame for this work. The subject is a view from the top floor of the artist's house in Brixton.

Although best known as a painter, McComb originally trained as a sculptor, first at Manchester School of Art 1954–6 and then at the Slade 1956–9. An influential teacher, McComb has taught at amongst others, the Slade and Goldsmiths College. In recent years he has been Keeper of the R.A. Schools. He was elected R.A. in 1990.

Writing in Art Review, 1993, Giles Auty refers to his 'Unfailing enthusiasm and love of beauty' and goes on to say: 'His paintings celebrate the world in all its complex glory, and are rooted in a subtle blend of observation and intuition'.

CB

Ambrose McEVOY, A.R.A.

[1878–1927]

Lady Gwendoline Churchill, 1917

watercolour on paper, 56 × 38.5 cm

P.196
PROVENANCE: Sir Joseph Duveen?, Mrs A. Douglas; Leicester Galleries from whom purchased by Gallery, April 1958.
EXHIBITIONS: London, National Portrait Society, 1917, no.215?; *Winter Exhibition*, London, R.A., 1928, no.399; *North East Coast Exhibition*, Newcastle upon Tyne, Palace of Art, 1929, no.49; *20th Century British Painting*, London, National Gallery, 1940, no.38 ? lent by Mrs Douglas; *Watercolours and Drawings from The Cecil Higgins Art Gallery, Bedford*, London, Thos. Agnew & Sons Ltd, 1962, no.112; *Watercolours from Bedford*, Norwich, Castle Museum, 1965, no.31.
REFERENCES: 'Wigs', *The Work of Ambrose McEvoy*, 1923, p.66, illus. p.29; R. Gleadowe, 'Ambrose McEvoy A.R.A.', *Old Watercolour Society's Club*, vol.7, 1929–30, pp.55–64, pl.xxviii.

Lady Gwendoline Bertie (1885–1941), daughter of the Earl of Abingdon, married John Churchill, Winston Churchill's younger brother, in 1908. This charming if slightly fey portrait was painted in 1917, about the time that the Tate Gallery catalogue says of McEvoy: 'Gained success as a portrait painter, mainly of women and often in watercolour c.1915'.

McEvoy had previously been encouraged by WHISTLER to enter the Slade School, where he met Augustus JOHN in 1893. Later he worked with SICKERT in Dieppe painting landscapes and interiors with figures.

EJ

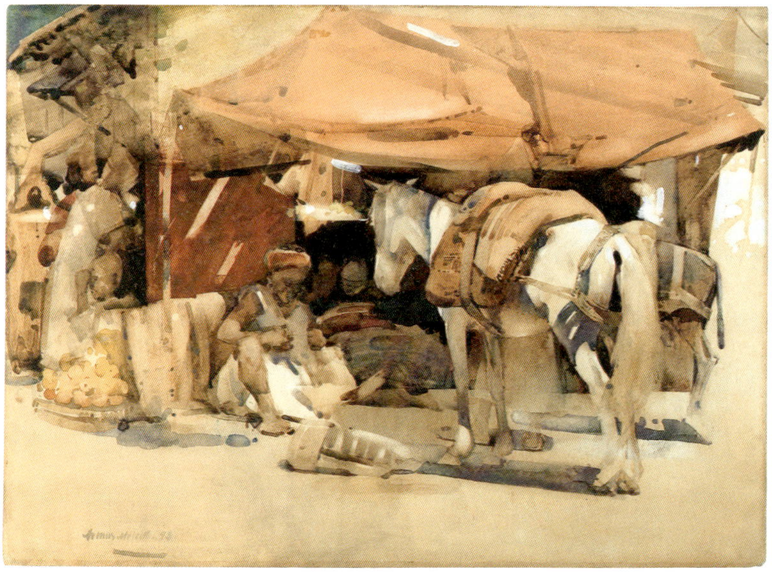

Arthur MELVILLE, A.R.S.A., R.W.S.
[1855–1904]
The Saddler's Shop, Tangier, 1893

watercolour heightened with white on paper, 60.7 × 86.1 cm
inscribed: *Arthur Melville 93*

P.578
PROVENANCE: Mrs Arthur Melville; Fine Art Society, from whom purchased by Gallery, January 1968.
EXHIBITIONS: *Arthur Melville R.W.S., A.R.S.A.*, Newcastle, Laing Art Gallery, 1906, no.41; Glasgow, Royal Glasgow Institute of the Fine Arts, 1907, no.102; Nottingham, 1907, no.62; *Muhammadan Art and Life in Turkey, Persia, Egypt, Morocco and India,* London, Whitechapel Art Gallery, 1908, no.138; *Arthur Melville A.R.S.A., R.S.W., R.W.S. (1855–1904),* Dundee, Dundee Museums & Art Galleries, 1978, no.44.
REFERENCES: A.E. Mackay, *Arthur Melville, Scottish Impressionist*, 1951, p.143, no.279, pl.32.

Melville began painting over-elaborated oils but, after studying in Paris in 1878, he turned to watercolour and soon set off for Egypt in search of romantic colour. He travelled widely: Spain, Morocco and Baghdad were his favourite subjects and he conveys brilliantly their heat, glitter and clamour. He was in Spain and Tangier in the spring of 1893 and in the late summer joined Joseph CRAWHALL at Brig O'Turk.

He invented his own technique, painting in pure watercolour on specially prepared paper soaked in diluted Chinese White until impregnated with white. BRABAZON and Brangwyn were among those influenced by Melville.

EJ/JM

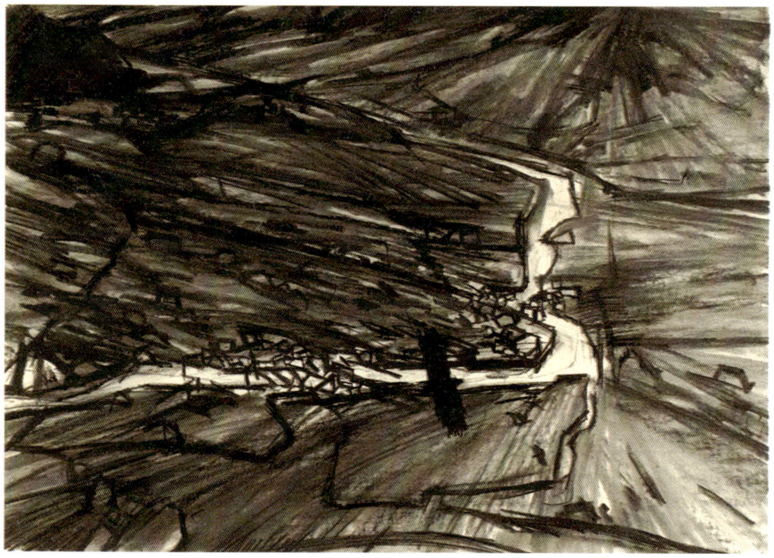

Edward MIDDLEDITCH, M.C., R.A.
[1923–87]
River Bed, Grazalem, c.1960

black chalk on paper, 35.1 × 93.3 cm

P.439
PROVENANCE: Beaux Arts Gallery, from whom purchased by Gallery, December 1962.
EXHIBITIONS: *Edward Middleditch,* London, Beaux Arts Gallery, 1962, no.27.

Middleditch visited Spain in 1956, 1957 and 1960. Like BOMBERG he was much influenced by the scenery of South-West Spain. Grazelema (to give the proper spelling) is a small town seventeen miles west of Ronda. In contrasting his paintings and drawings Middleditch said, 'a good drawing has a degree of finality and authority about it which a painting cannot have'.

Commissioned in the Middlesex Regiment in 1944, Middleditch served in the Normandy campaign of 1944–5, where he was wounded and awarded the Military Cross. In 1948, he attended evening classes at the Regent Street Polytechnic and studied at the R.C.A. from 1949–52, where he was referred to as '[Ruskin] Spear's protégé'. He was supported by the Beaux Arts Gallery which championed figurative painting, although Middleditch could never be described as a follower of the socialist-realist style, which was emerging in the 1950s. He occupied various teaching posts including the Head of Norwich School of Art from 1964 and Keeper of the R.A. Schools in 1984.

CB

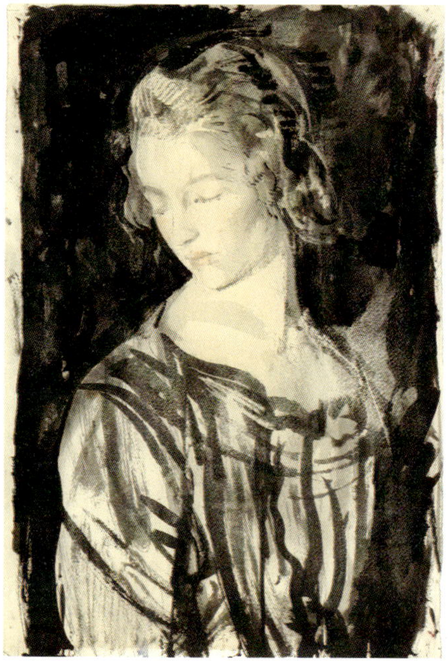

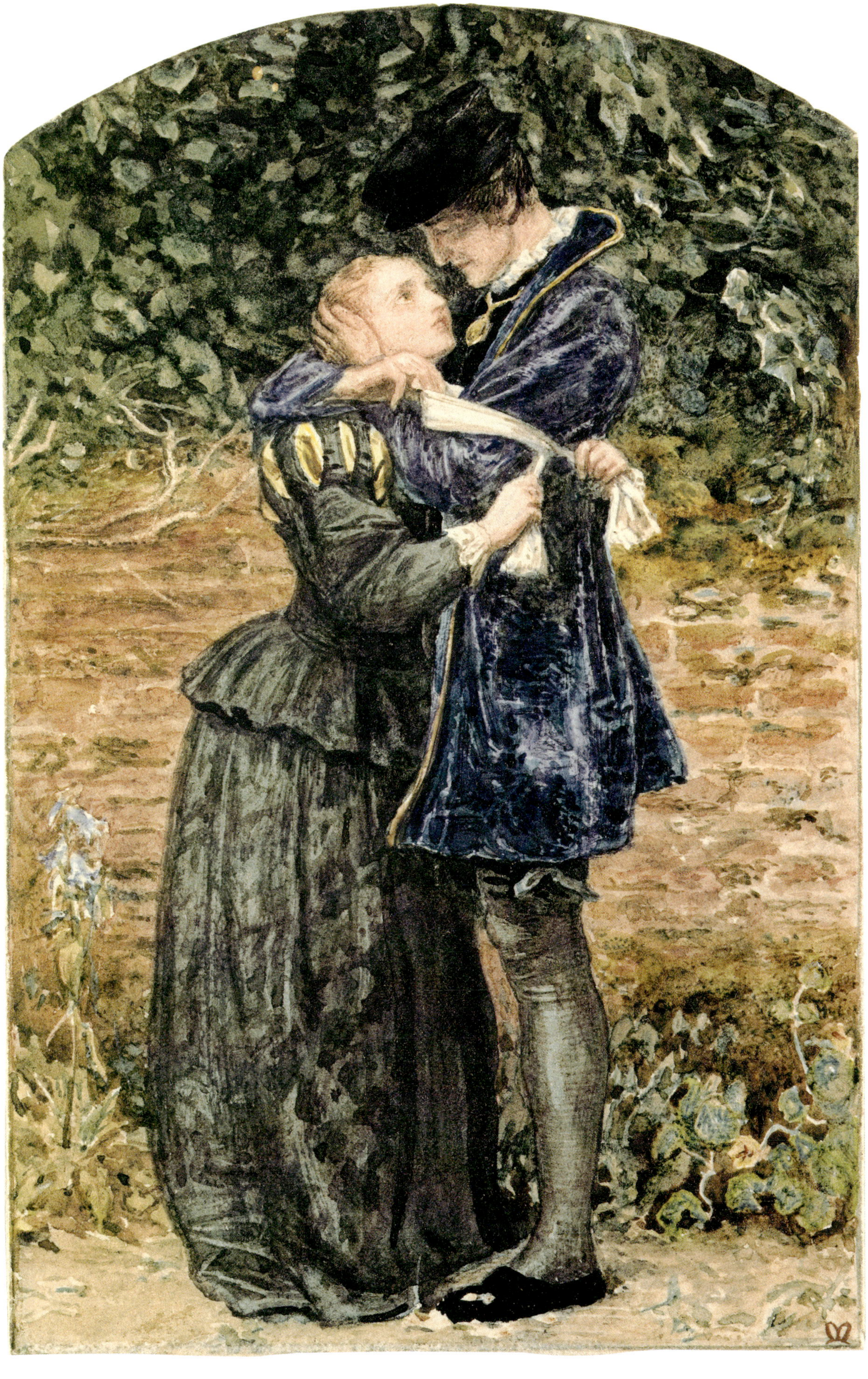

Sir John Everett MILLAIS, Bt., P.R.A.
[1829–96]
The Huguenot, c.1852

watercolour and pen and ink on paper, 13.3 × 8.7 cm
inscribed: monogram

P.260
PROVENANCE: Charles Langton of Liverpool (probably); Mrs M. Hull; Thos. Agnew & Sons Ltd, from whom purchased by Gallery, October 1958.
EXHIBITIONS: *Watercolours and Drawings from The Cecil Higgins Art Gallery Bedford*, London, Thos. Agnew & Sons Ltd, 1962, no.40.

A replica of the whole composition of one of Millais' most famous and popular pictures, exhibited at the R.A. in 1852 together with this quotation:

When the clock of the Palais de Justice shall sound upon the great bell, at day-break, (on St Bartholomew's day) then each good Catholic must bind a strip of white linen round his arm, and place a fair white cross in his cap.
The Order of the Duke of Guise.

The Massacre of St Bartholomew took place on the morning of 24 August 1572.

Here, a young Catholic woman, during a stolen meeting, is entreating her Protestant lover to wear the white linen sash, but he is gently resisting and refusing to save his skin by denying his faith. At his feet nasturtiums grow, a token of sorrow, while ivy, the emblem of constancy, clings to the wall behind the lovers.

The model for the Huguenot was a friend of Millais' family, General Arthur Lemprière, while a professional model, Miss Ryan, posed for the young woman; Mrs George Hodgkinson, wife of Millais' half-brother, also posed for this figure.

The oil was warmly praised in *The Times*, 14 May, 1852 although the figure of the lover, *a thorough Calvinist*, was criticised because, 'his right leg has disappeared altogether, which gives him the appearance of what ornithologists call a "wader".

A leading member of the Pre-Raphaelite Brotherhood, Millais later pursued a brilliantly successful career as an academic and society painter. He claimed to be the highest paid artist in history, was the first painter to be created a baronet and was also elected President of the R.A. a few months before he died.

EJ

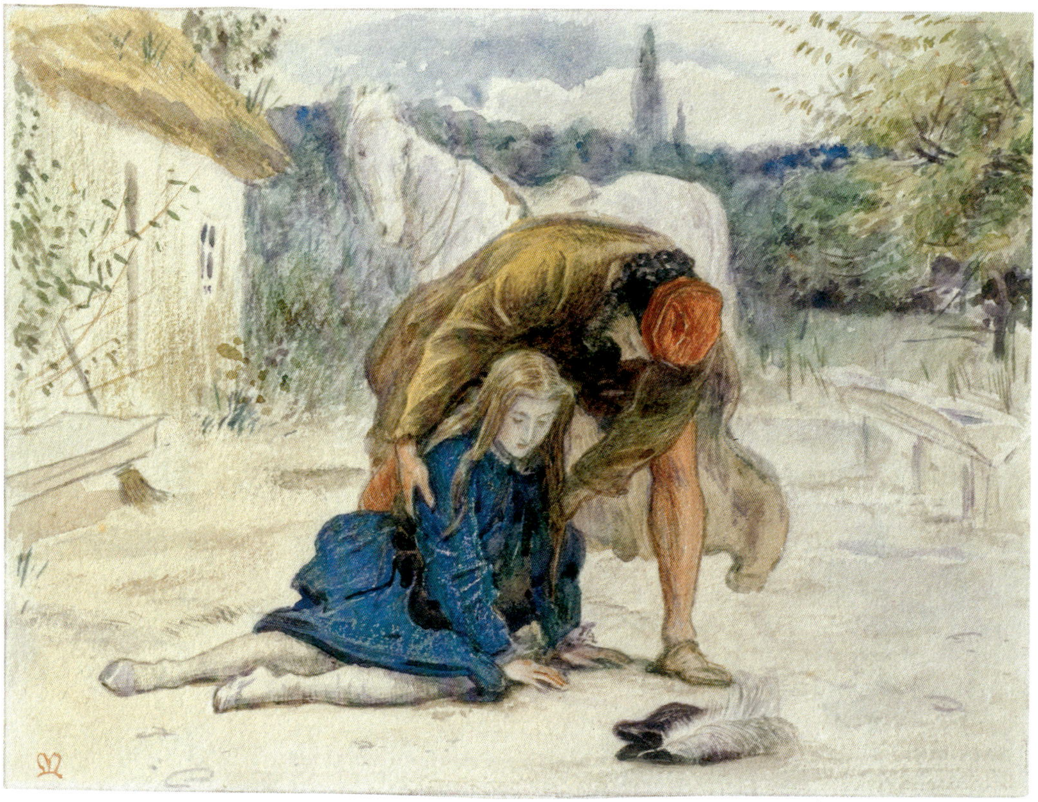

Sir John Everett MILLAIS, Bt., P.R.A.
[1829–96]
After an illustration to the poem **Maid Avoraine** by R. Williams Buchanan, c.1861–2

watercolour on paper, 10.7 × 14.5 cm
inscribed: monogram

P.166
PROVENANCE: P&D Colnaghi Ltd, from whom purchased by Gallery, January 1958.
EXHIBITIONS: *Watercolours and Drawings from The Cecil Higgins Art Gallery, Bedford,* London, Thos. Agnew & Sons Ltd, 1962, no.45, as Illustration for Dalziel's Edition of Wood Engravings for *The Arabian Nights*.

The illustration to the poem *Maid Avoraine* by R. Williams Buchanan (1841–1901) appeared in *Once a Week* in July 1862 (Vol. VII, p.98), so Millais' drawing can be dated 1861–2. He may have made a second version as well.

The poem recounts the story of Sir Gawain and the 'country-bred' Maid Avoraine. Sir Gawain forsakes the Court to seek a more peaceful life but on meeting Avoraine doubts her love for him now 'Stript of my sword and coat of gold'. Sir Gawain puts her love to the test, asking that she should run at his side, dressed as a page as he rides 'O'er wood and field and flood' for two days. The maid agrees and on the second day Buchanan recounts,

When at the cottage door they stopt
Down at his feet the maiden dropt,
Worn with the weary race;
But Gawain leapt to earth in bliss,
And caught her to him with a kiss
That burned the tearful face,-
Saying aloud, "At last 'tis plain
Thou lovest me well, Maid Avoraine.

Sir Gawain now has the proof he needs that she does truly love him, but, unfortunately for him, she spurns his renewed love for her by casting 'away thy worth/ In pity for my lowly birth'. Sir Gawain in his anger returns to Court leaving Avoraine whose 'hope be dead'.

EJ/JM

John MINTON
[1917–57]
The Foundry, c.1939–41

pen and ink and watercolour on paper, 27.3 × 21.7 cm
inscribed: *Vertical Distillation. Casting with a ladle into Cylinders. 99.99 Zinc.*

P.341
PROVENANCE: Crane Kalman Gallery, from whom purchased by Gallery, April 1960.

Minton was one of the central figures in the Neo-Romantic movement of the 1940s, sharing a studio with Robert Colquhoun and Robert MacBryde from 1943–6 and with Keith VAUGHAN 1946–52. In addition to his painting he also undertook fabric and wallpaper designs and also several large murals including *Harbour* for the Festival of Britain, 1951, in the Dome of Discovery.

This was an unusual subject for Minton, who normally painted portraits or landscapes. Ronald Alley suggested that it may have been painted during the Second World War. He had registered as a conscientious objector in 1940 but had withdrawn this by 1941 when he enlisted in the Pioneer Corps.

He taught at three schools successively: Camberwell, the Central and the R.C.A. from 1943–56. He committed suicide in January 1957.

EJ/JM

John MINTON
[1917–57]
Birds of Omen, 1945

drawn with a sharp metal rod on carbon paper, paper size 38.6 × 56 cm
inscribed: *John Minton 1945*

P.546
PROVENANCE: G. Delbanco; Roland, Browse and Delbanco, from whom purchased by Gallery, January 1967.

Minton made illustrations for a number of magazines, such as *Vogue*, *Circus* and *The Radio Times* and books including *The Wanderer*, 1947.

This must be an illustration although the source is so far unidentified. Perhaps 'Birds of Ill Omen' would be a more accurate title to judge by the figure on the waggon, whose limbs are so contorted that it must indicate that he is dead.

EJ/JM

John MINTON
[1917–57]
Cargésé, Corsica, 1947

pen and ink with some brushwork on paper, 39.3 × 28.2 cm
inscribed: *John Minton 1947*
inscribed on reverse: *Relates to* (indicipherable) *29th Aug* (crossed out) *and 48*

P.286
PROVENANCE: Piccadilly Gallery, from whom purchased by Gallery, February 1959.
REFERENCES: A. Ross, *Time was away. a notebook in Corsica*. London, 1948, p.147.

Minton visited Corsica with Alan Ross in the summer of 1947 and the drawings that resulted are amongst his best work.

The visit was for a commission by the publisher John Lehmann for the book, *Time was Away: a notebook in Corsica*. Minton made a series of black and white and colour illustrations for this book, with the typography and design by Keith VAUGHAN. Lehmann recalls the visit in his autobiography, *The Ample Proposition*, vol III, 1966.

EJ/JM

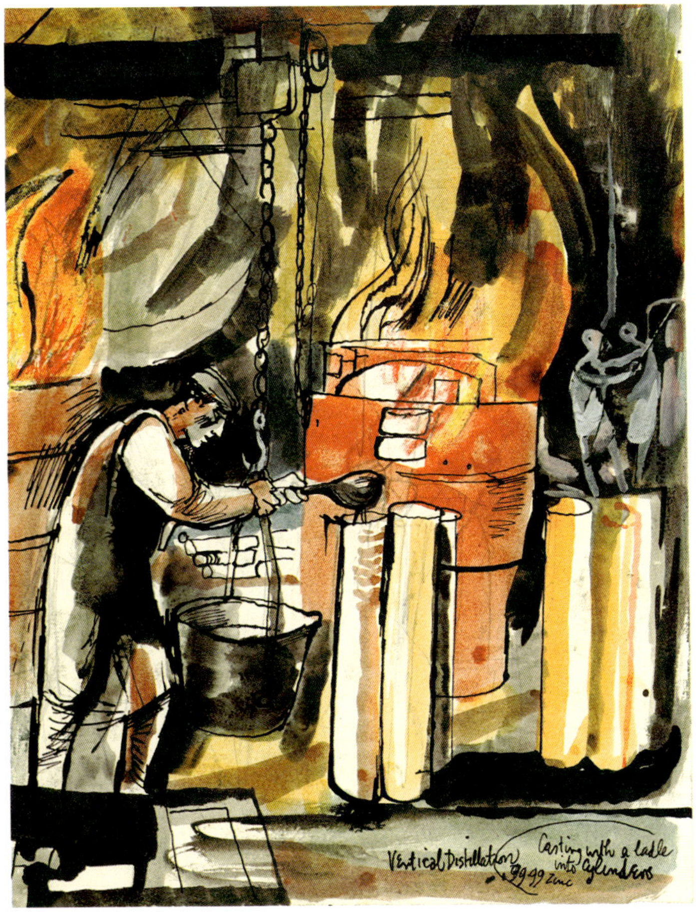

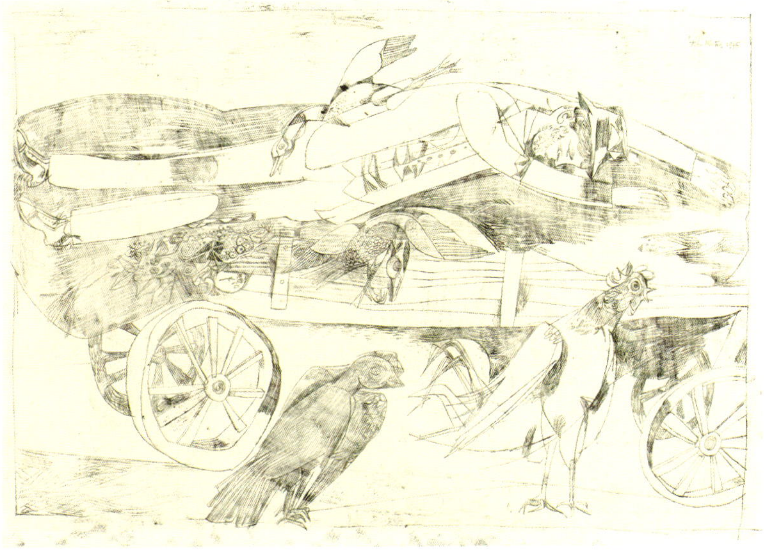

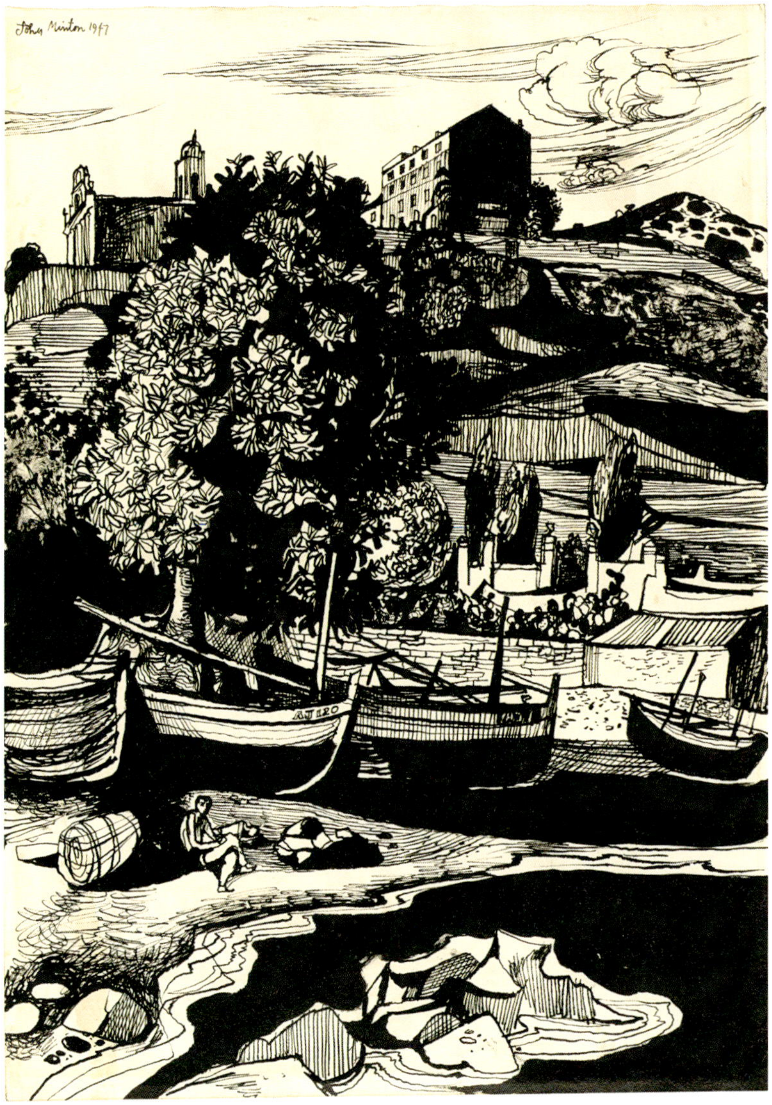

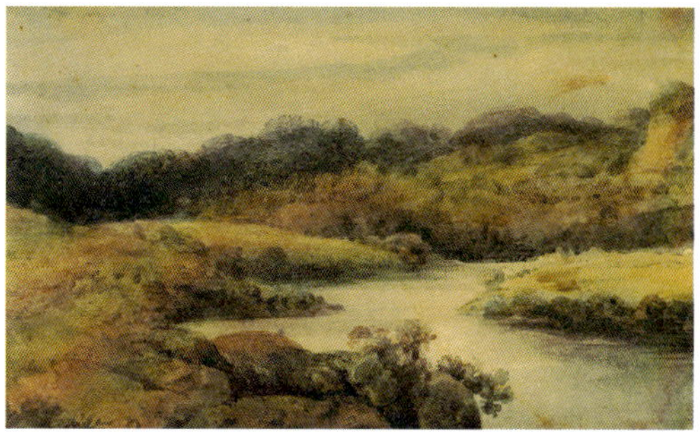

Dr Thomas MONRO
[1759–1833]
Landscape with River and Trees

watercolour on paper, 12.3 × 20.9 cm

P.148
PROVENANCE: Sir Guy Williams (whose wife was a direct descendant of Dr Thomas Monro); P&D Colnaghi Ltd, from whom purchased by Gallery, January 1958.

Although influenced by GAINSBOROUGH'S landscape drawings, Monro was an artist of only minor talent. However, he was an outstanding figure in the development of British watercolour: J.R. COZENS was his patient and Monro owned a large number of his drawings. It was these, together with works by 'Warwick' SMITH, HEARNE and ROOKER that GIRTIN and TURNER used to copy in the evenings at the doctor's house in Adelphi Terrace. Later, many others destined to become major watercolourists, including COTMAN, both the VARLEYS and DE WINT, also worked at the 'Monro Academy'. His encouragement and patronage of many of these young artists provided vital help at the outset of their careers.

EJ

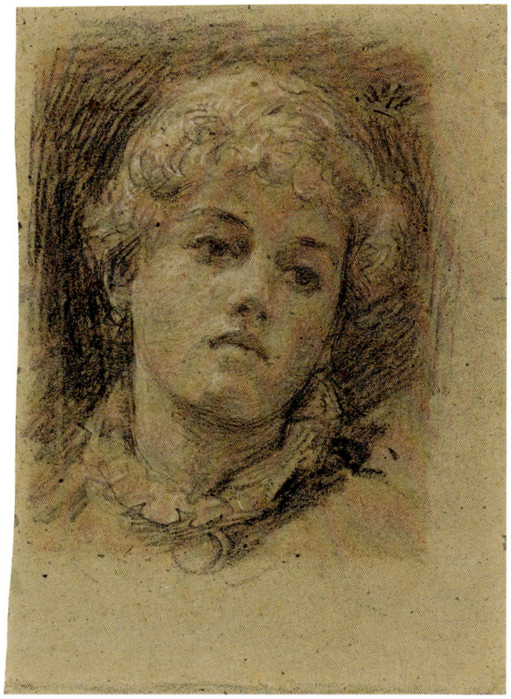

Albert Joseph MOORE
[1841–93]
Head of a Girl

crayon and chalk on buff paper, 26 × 19.3 cm

P.185
PROVENANCE: Graham Robertson; Wilton Gallery, from whom purchased by Gallery, April 1958.
EXHIBITIONS: *Watercolours from Bedford*, Norwich, Castle Museum, 1965, no.33.

Moore was ten years younger than his brother Henry (1831–95), the successful marine painter. This girl's somewhat soulful expression perhaps owes something to the example of ROSSETTI whose watercolour, *Golden Water* in the Fitzwilliam Museum, Cambridge, was responsible, in Martin HARDIE'S opinion, 'for much that is cheap and undignified in Albert Moore and other later men'.

EJ

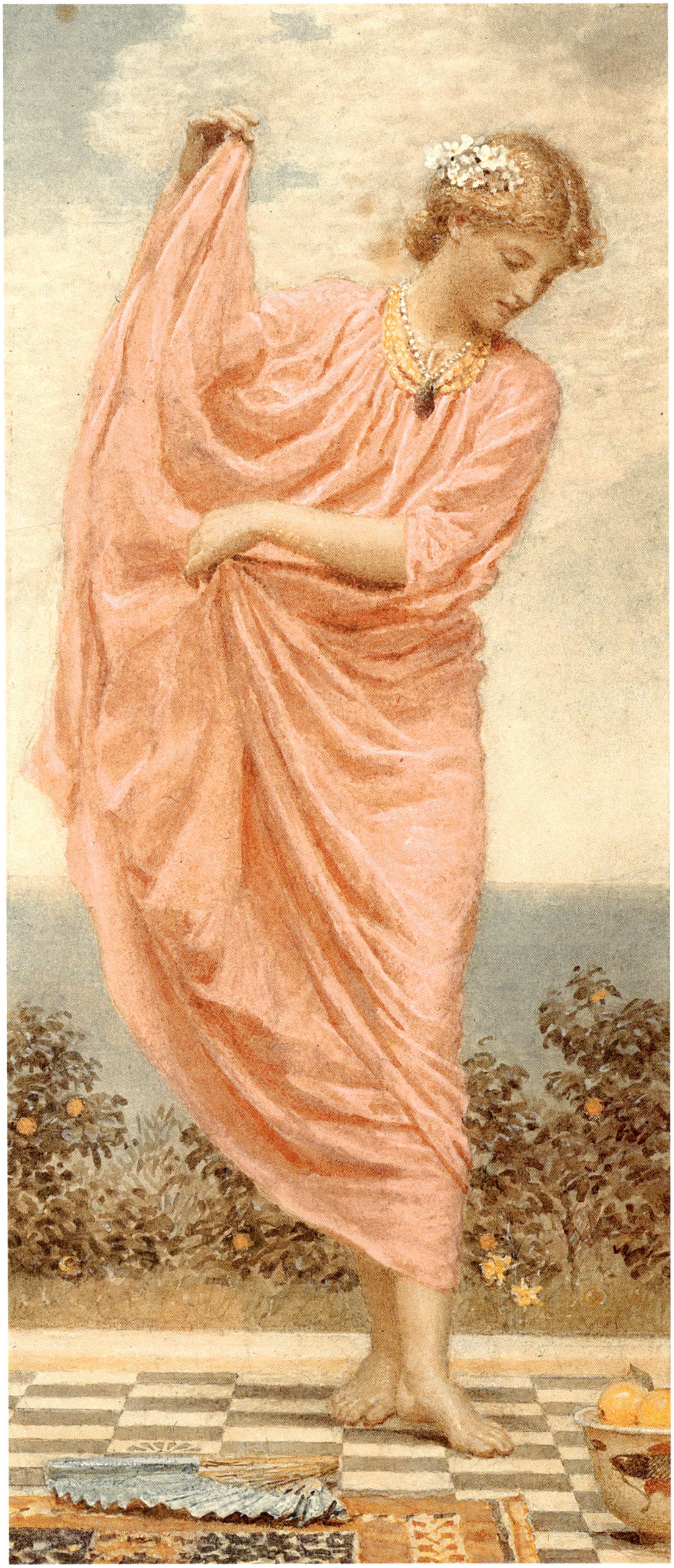

Albert Joseph MOORE

[1841–93]

Oranges, c.1885

watercolour and pencil heightened with white on paper, 37.3 × 17 cm

P.594

PROVENANCE: James Barrow by 1886; with Thos. Agnew & Sons Ltd before 1906; Maas Gallery, from whom purchased by Gallery, May 1969 with the assistance of the V&A/M.G.C. Purchase Grant Fund.
EXHIBITIONS: Royal Society of Painters in Watercolours, summer 1885, no.286; *Grand Loan Exhibition of Pictures*, Liverpool, Walker Art Gallery, 1886, no.849, lent by James Barrow; *Victorian Exhibition*, London, Maas Gallery, 1968, no.81.
REFERENCES: A.L. Baldry, *Albert Moore*, London, 1894, pp.58,84,105, repr. facing p.86; ibid., 'Albert Moore', *Old Watercolour Society's Club*, vol.VIII, 1930–1, p.47, pl.13.

Probably painted just before it was first exhibited; Moore had been elected an associate of the R.W.S. the previous year. It was characteristic of Moore to name the drawings after a comparatively minor element, or in the case of *Oranges* the title also alludes to the overall colour scheme. *Oranges* is atypical of his work in that it shows a figure in motion; most of Moore's figures are static.

Moore's early works were strongly influenced by the Pre-Raphaelites, but from 1864 his study of sculpture formed his mature style: single Grecian figures, or groups of figures carefully posed in an elaborate design often incorporating flowers. Indeed in his early career he found it difficult to work without the stimulus of flowers in his studio. His paintings were worked up from careful studies and drawings of the figures, first nude and then draped; in this he used a similar working practice to Lord LEIGHTON.

WHISTLER greatly admired his work, and for a period in the 1860s introduced classical elements into figure groups. It has also been suggested that Whistler took his idea for the Butterfly monogram from Moore's incorporation of the Greek anthemion in his work.

Swinburne described one of Moore's paintings thus: 'such a painting has no reason for being except its beauty, its melody of colour and "symphony of form"'. Moore's style reflected the concerns of the Aesthetic Movement: draped female figures with an air of detached reverie bathed in a sultry Mediterranean light.

EJ/JM

Henry MOORE, O.M., C.H.
[1898–1986]
Designs for Sculpture, 1935

chalk, charcoal and wash on paper, 37.7 × 27.5 cm
inscribed: *Moore 35*

P.248
PROVENANCE: Roland, Browse and Delbanco, from whom purchased by Gallery, 1958.
EXHIBITIONS: *Watercolours from Bedford,* Norwich, Castle Museum, 1965, no.34.
REFERENCES: A. Garrould (ed.), *Henry Moore Complete Drawings 1930–39,* 1998, vol.2, repr. p.157, no.AG35.61, HMF.1152.

The reclining figure, first introduced in 1929 is one of the most constant themes in Moore's work, reflecting his lifelong interest in the human figure. As he stated: '[it] is what interests me most deeply'.

JM

Henry MOORE, O.M., C.H.
[1898–1986]
Studies for Sculpture, 1939

chalk with pen and ink and watercolour on paper, 27.8 × 18.3 cm
inscribed: *Moore 39*

P.268
PROVENANCE: Ewan Phillips, from whom purchased by Gallery, October 1958.
REFERENCES: A. Garrould (ed.), *Henry Moore Complete Drawings 1930–39,* vol.2, p.221, AG.39.12, HMF.1453.

In the late 1930s Moore made a series of reclining figures in lead. His drawings at this time combine his interest with bone (and sometimes rock formations) with an evocation of the human figure.

JM

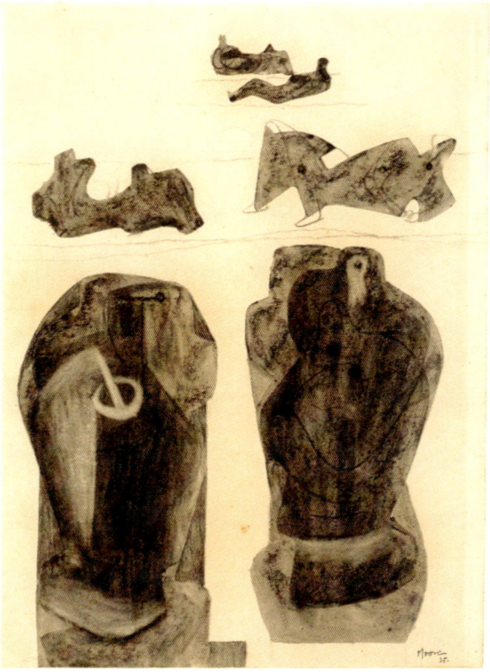

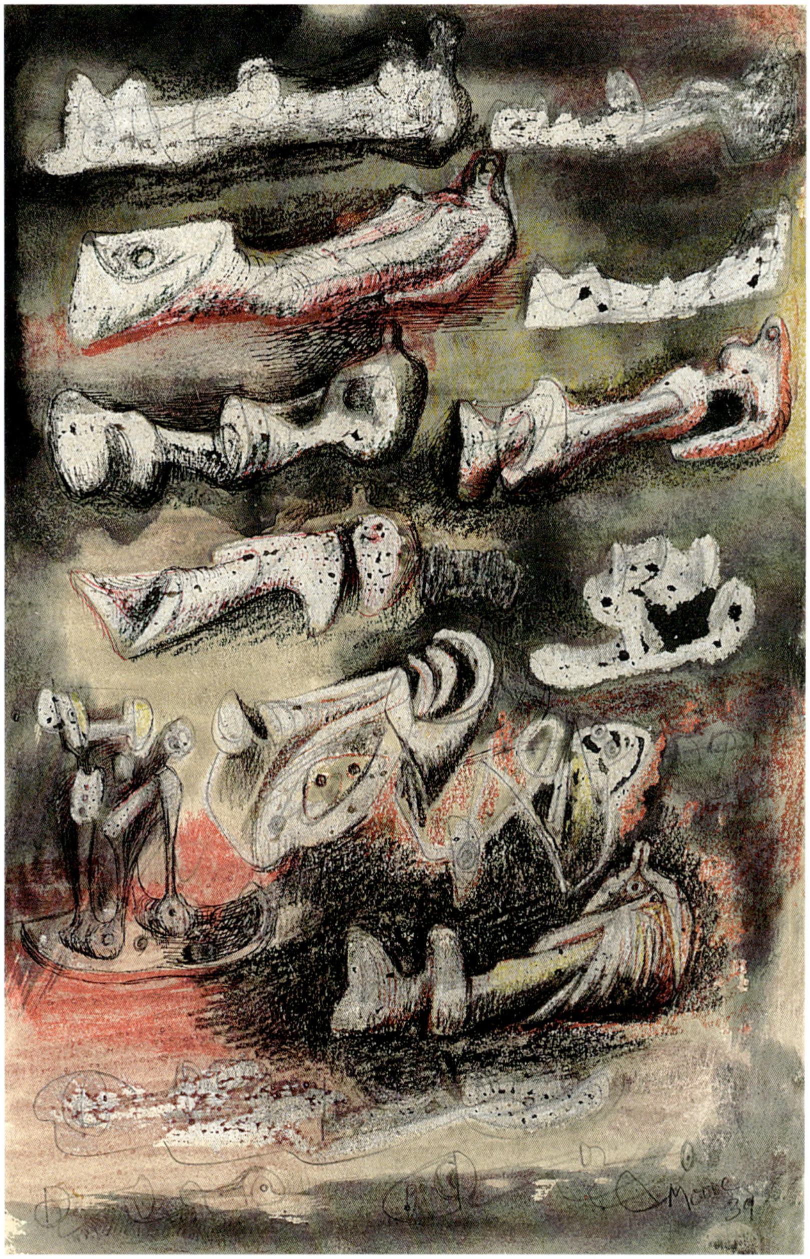

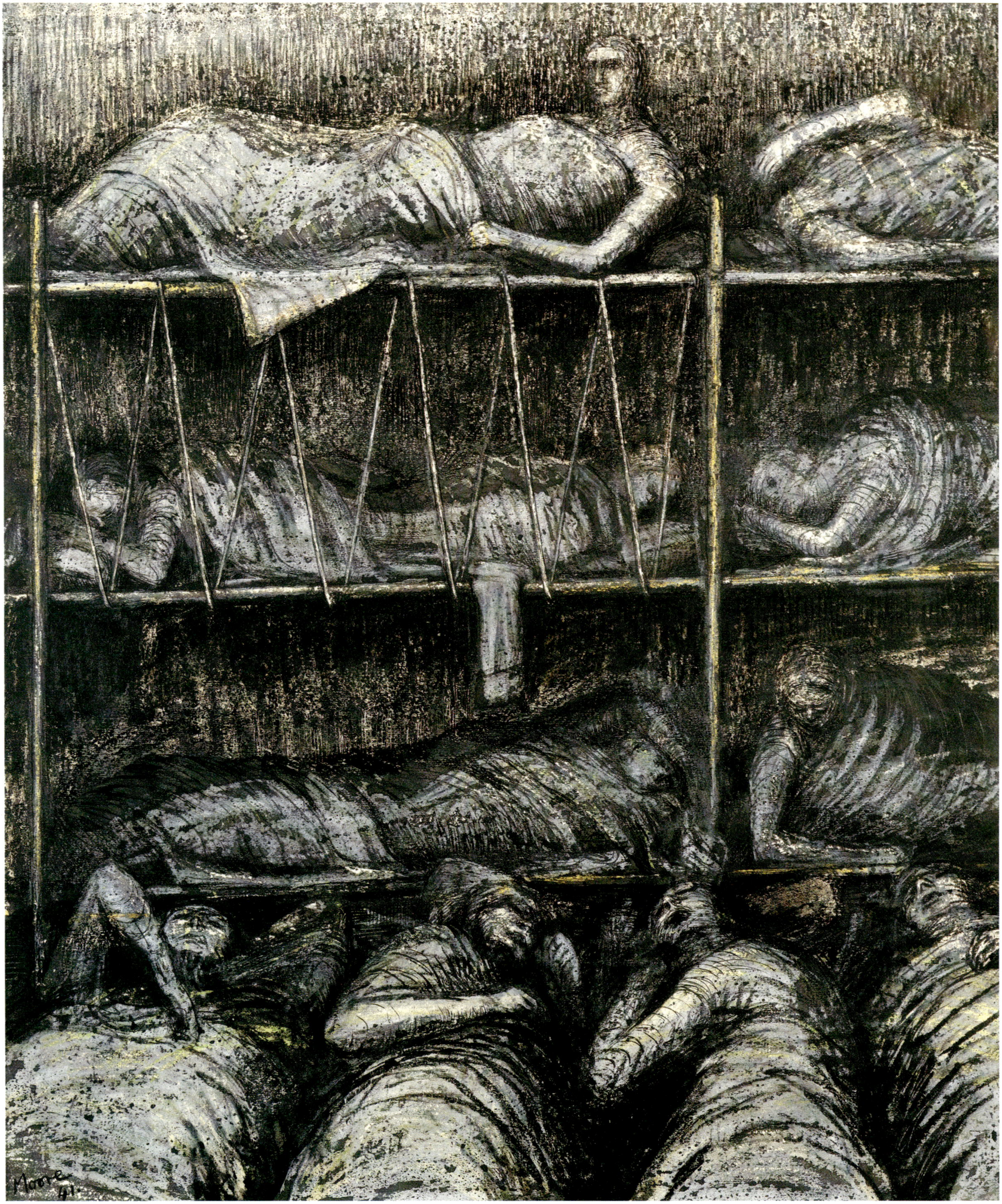
Moore
41

Henry MOORE, O.M., C.H.
[1898–1986]
Shelter Scene: Bunks and Sleepers, 1941

pen and ink with wash and crayon on paper, 48.2 × 43 cm
inscribed: *Moore 41*

P.533
PROVENANCE: Mr and Mrs Harold Weinstein ?; Redfern Gallery, from whom purchased by Gallery, July 1966.
EXHIBITIONS: *Treasures of Chicago Collectors,* Chicago, Art Institute of Chicago, 1963, lent by Mr & Mrs Harold Weinstein ?; *Henry Moore Shelter Drawings,* Stuttgart, Staatsgalerie, 1967, no.110; *Henry Moore Retrospective,* London, Tate Gallery, 1968, no.200; *Henry Moore War Drawings,* London, I.W.M., 1976; *Henry Moore: The Shelter Drawings,* London, British Museum, 1989–9.
REFERENCES: A. Garrould (ed.), *Henry Moore Complete Drawings 1940–49,* 2001, vol.3, p.90, repr. p.91, no.AG41.45, HMF.1790.

When war was declared in 1939, Moore was living and working at his cottage at Kingston near Dover. In 1940 the Moores returned to London, relocating to a studio vacated by Barbara HEPWORTH and Ben NICHOLSON who had moved to Cornwall.

It was possibly the night of 11 September that Moore first became fully aware of the role of the Underground stations as a haven for Londoners. He had been advised to stay below ground for his own safety and said of the scene, 'I saw hundreds of Henry Moore Reclining Figures stretched along the platforms, even the train tunnels seemed to be like holes in my sculpture'. Moore responded rapidly to this new stimulus creating his first shelter drawing, *Women and Children in the Tube*, 1940, (I.W.M.) a few days later.

Moore described his creative process as being 'from the memory of actuality'. He did not wish to intrude on family groups. If a certain group held his attention he would walk past a number of times fixing the idea firmly in his mind, or, alternatively, would make notes on an envelope or scrap of paper. After returning home, Moore would spend several days drawing in sketchbooks while the ideas were still fresh in his mind. Some of these would then be made up into large more finished pictures, using a variety of media, thus giving the surface an extraordinary richness; he described his mixed media method as being 'the scratch and spit technique'.

His shelter drawings received immediate critical and public acclaim, with the War Artists' Advisory Committee organizing exhibitions at the National Gallery. Moore commented on the profound influence that this period had on his later career: 'Without the War which directed one's direction to life itself, I think I would have been a far less sensitive and responsible person – if I had ignored all that and went on working just as before. The war brought out and encouraged the humanist side in one's work'.

JM

Henry MOORE, O.M., C.H.
[1898–1986]
Penelope and her Suitors. The Odyssey, 1944

chalk and wash and ink on paper, 45.3 × 30 cm
inscribed: *Moore 44*

P.377
PROVENANCE: Martin Secker and Warburg, London; Marlborough Fine Art, from whom purchased by Gallery, 1960.
EXHIBITIONS: *New Sculpture and Drawings by Henry Moore,* London, Leicester Galleries, 1946, no.27; *Henry Moore: The Shelter Drawings,* London, British Museum, 1989.
REFERENCES: A. Garrould (ed.), *Henry Moore Complete Drawings 1940–49,* 2001, vol.3, repr. p.221, no.AG44.40, HMF.2298.

These were among the illustrations that Henry Moore made for the publication of Edward Sackville-West's *The Rescue*, 1945, a melodrama for broadcasting, based on Homer's *Odyssey*.

Penelope, wife of Odysseus, was parted from him during the Trojan war but when he failed to return after the war, she was beset by a number of suitors. They told her that her husband would never return and urged her to give herself to one of them. She received their advances coldly but was almost a prisoner in their hands. For ten long years she temporized with them until, after twenty years' absence, Odysseus finally returned and, with his son Telemachus and other companions, delivered Penelope from her suitors by slaying them all.

EJ

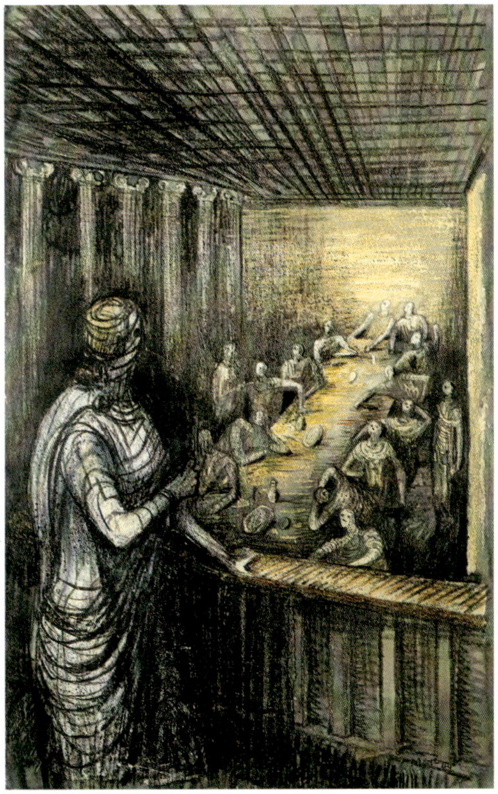

Henry MOORE, O.M., C.H.
[1898–1986]
Death of the Suitors. The Odyssey, 1944

pen and ink with chalk and watercolour on paper, 45.6 × 30 cm
inscribed: *Moore 44*

P.378
PROVENANCE: Marlborough Fine Art, from whom purchased by Gallery, 1960.
EXHIBITIONS: *New Sculpture and Drawings by Henry Moore,* London, Leicester Galleries, 1946, no.23; *Henry Moore Sculpture and Drawings 1923–1948,* Wakefield, Wakefield City Art Gallery, Manchester, Manchester City Art Gallery, 1949, no.120; *Henry Moore: The Shelter Drawings,* London, British Museum, 1989.
REFERENCES: E. Sackville-West, *The Rescue,* London, 1945, repr. facing p.90; E. Bond, *Bond Plays: Four,* London, 1991, repr. front cover; A. Garrould (ed.), *Henry Moore Complete Drawings 1940–49,* 2001, vol.3, p.223, repr. p.222, no.AG44.47, HMF.2305.

This was one of the illustrations that Henry Moore made for the publication of Edward Sackville-West's *The Rescue*, 1945, a melodrama for broadcasting, based on Homer's *Odyssey*. The play was first broadcast in November 1943 with incidental music by Benjamin Britten.

EJ

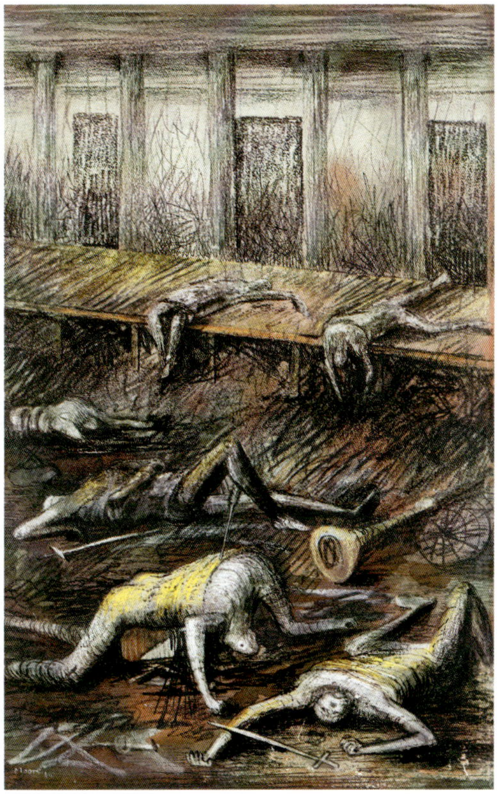

Henry MOORE, O.M., C.H.
[1898–1986]
Studies for Sculpture, 1948

pen and ink and watercolour on board, 29.1 × 23.8 cm
inscribed: *Moore 48*
Two women winding wool

P.450
PROVENANCE: Redfern Gallery, from whom purchased by Gallery, May 1963.
REFERENCES: A. Garrould (ed.), *Henry Moore Complete Drawings 1940–49*, 2001, vol.3, p.270, repr. p.271 no.AG47–49.54, HMF.2442.

One of a series of domestic activities from this period including knitting and sewing. The Mother and Child was one of the themes Moore was concerned with for the commission of a *Family Group*, 1948–49, at Barclay School, Stevenage, a theme realised earlier in *Mother and Child*, 1943–4, Church of St Matthew, Northampton.

JM

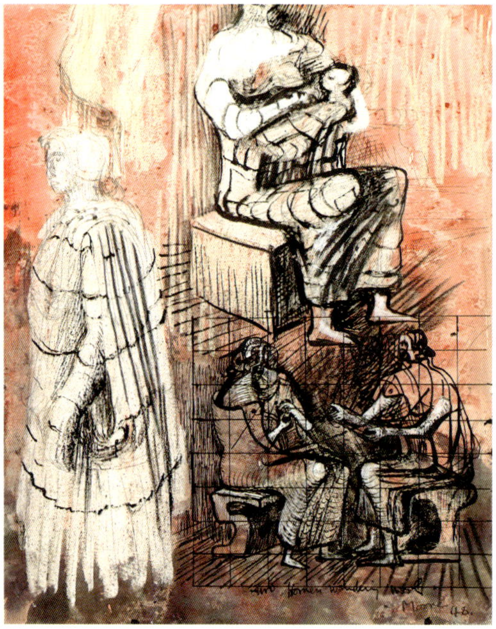

William James MULLER
[1812–45]
Karnac, Egypt, c.1843–44

watercolour, bodycolour and graphite on paper, 44.4 × 31.5 cm
inscribed: *W. Muller*
Karnac, Egypt

P.344
PROVENANCE: John Manning Fine Art, from whom purchased by Gallery, April 1960.
EXHIBITIONS: *The English Tradition: an exhibition of watercolours from two private collections*, Bedford, Cecil Higgins Art Gallery, 1972, no.61.

The site has been identified as the north or south aisle of the great Hypostyle Hall of the Temple of Amun at Karnak. Since Muller's time the temple has been extensively excavated so that the floor level is now much lower and the pillars correspondingly much taller.

Muller was a Bristolian, the son of a German refugee who fled from Danzig in the Napoleonic wars, and was apprenticed to J.B. Pyne there. He was a prodigious worker whose watercolours were painted very rapidly and never corrected or retouched afterwards.

He travelled widely on the continent and, from 1843–44, he joined Sir Charles Fellows on his expedition to Lycia, which must be when this watercolour was painted.

EJ

George MORLAND
[1763–1804]
Study of Rustics, a Cart and Wheelbarrow, 1791

black lead on paper, 43.1 × 54.3 cm
inscribed: *G. Morland 1791*

P.628
PROVENANCE: Spink & Son Ltd, from whom purchased by Gallery, April 1974.

Morland was the son of the painter Henry Morland (1730–97) under whom he trained from 1771–84. His scenes of middle and lower class rural life were popularized in mezzotint by his brother-in-law William Ward (1761–1826), reflecting the contemporary taste for portrayals of a picturesque and contented English peasantry.

Morland was mainly an oil painter with a precocious talent, first exhibiting at the R.A. when only ten. Most of his life, however, was given over to drunkenness, debts and unremitting work to pay these off. He composed his own epitaph: 'Here lies a drunken dog'.

His drawings are generally in black and red chalk, pencil and coloured chalk, or pencil alone. He drew animals very well and his landscapes with trees can capture an almost Dutch precision. However, the quality of his drawing is very variable and copies abound.

EJ/JM

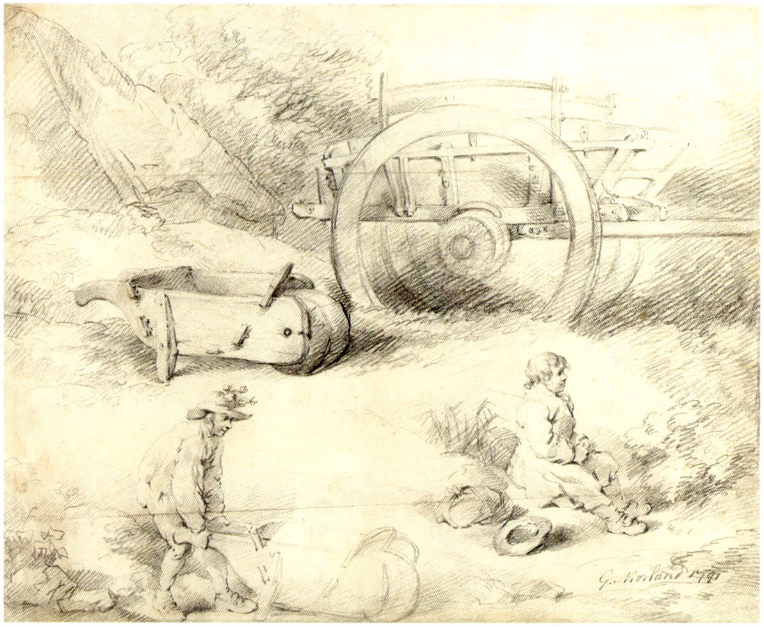

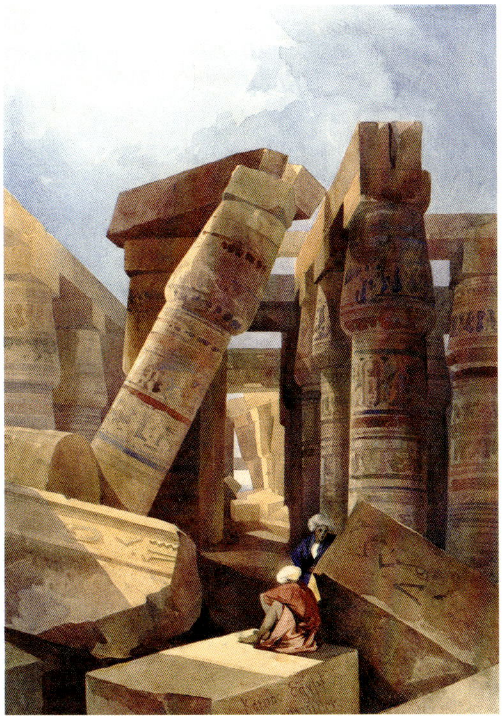

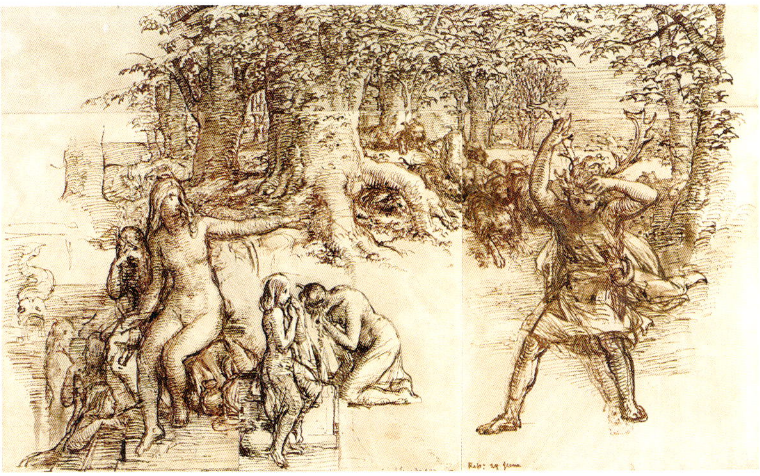

William MULREADY, R.A.
[1786–1863]
Diana and Actaeon, c.1853

pen and brown ink on paper, 16.5 × 27.8 cm
inscribed: *comp. June Wed.25; Rep:29 June.*

P.611
PROVENANCE: Artist's sale, 28 April 1864, lot 412; Thos. Agnew & Sons Ltd (32 gns); J.P. Heseltine (L.1508); E.L. Paget no.319; purchased by Gallery from Christie's sale, lot 62 (Property of a Lady), 20 October 1970.
EXHIBITIONS: *Winter Exhibition,* London, Burlington Fine Arts Club, 1938–9, no.102.
REFERENCES: K. Heleniak, *William Mulready,* 1980, p.220, no.169, pl.152, and p.258, no.22.

This drawing, dating from c.1853, captures the dramatic moment when Actaeon, who has come upon Diana bathing naked, is punished for his intrusion by being turned into a stag – antlers are already visibly sprouting from his head.

Mulready was born in Ireland, the son of a leather breeches maker. The family moved to London when he was about five, where he spent the rest of his life. He showed an early aptitude for drawing and with his father's encouragement entered the R.A. Schools at fifteen. As a pupil of John VARLEY he came in contact with LINNELL and W.H. HUNT.

He is best known for his genre paintings, originally influenced by WILKIE, but he later developed an individual style distinguished for its precision of draughtsmanship.

EJ/JM

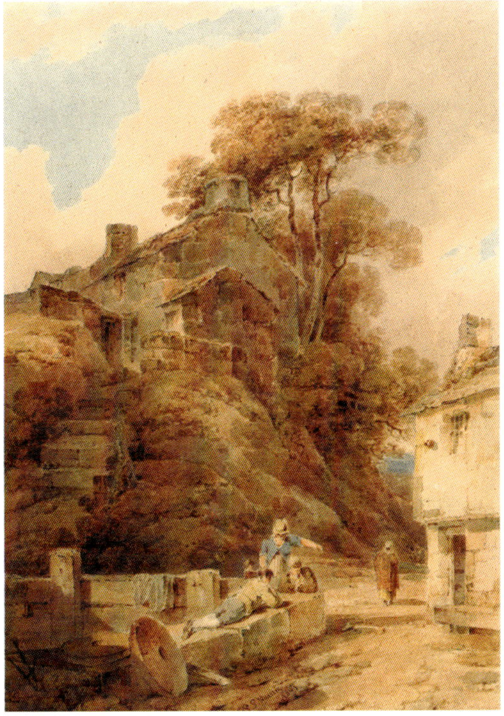

Paul Sandby MUNN
[1773–1845]
Hilly Landscape with Cottages and Figures, 1807

watercolour on paper, 35 × 24.7 cm
inscribed: *P. S. Munn 1807*

P.80
PROVENANCE: H.M. Orange ?; P&D Colnaghi Ltd, from whom purchased by Gallery, September 1952.
EXHIBITIONS: *English Watercolours from the Hickman Bacon and other Collections,* Bedford, Cecil Higgins Art Gallery, 1952, no.52.

Munn was named after his father's friend, Paul SANDBY, who was both the boy's godfather and first teacher. In 1799 he became a member of the Sketching Club founded by GIRTIN and later became a close friend of COTMAN, with whom he went on several sketching tours. Despite these contacts, Munn's watercolours remained, in Martin HARDIE'S opinion, no more than 'sound and pedestrian'.

EJ

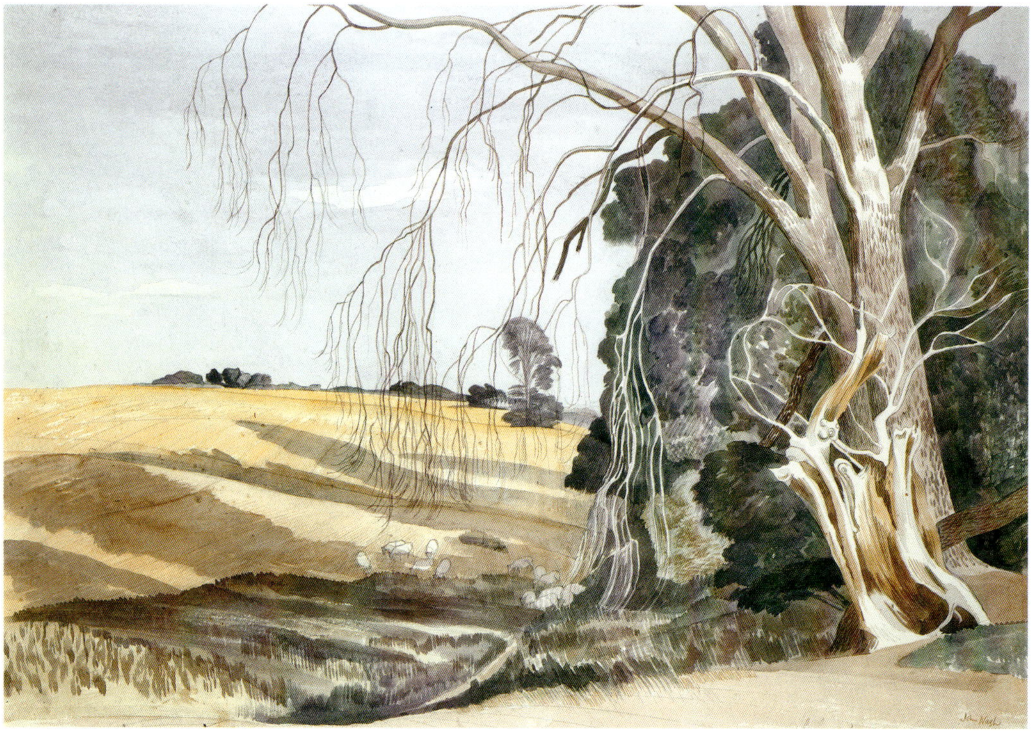

John NASH, C.B.E.
[1893–1977]
Berkshire Landscape

watercolour on paper, 38.8 × 55.8 cm
inscribed: *John Nash*

P.212
PROVENANCE: Redfern Gallery, from whom purchased by Gallery, April 1958.
EXHIBITIONS: *Watercolours from Bedford*, Norwich, Castle Museum, 1965, no.36.

John Nash, four years younger than his more famous brother Paul, who encouraged him, was entirely self-taught as an artist. His subject was the English countryside where he lived and which he painted as a countryman. He began to paint in oils in 1914, then joined the Artists Rifles and later became an Official War Artist, which he was again from 1940–44. He taught at the Ruskin School 1922–7 and at the R.C.A. 1934–40 and 1945–57. He was also a prolific book illustrator with a speciality in botanical works including Gilbert White's *The Natural History of Selborne*, 1951. He is better known as a watercolourist than an oil painter; his dedicated and reticent watercolours of pastoral scenes are perhaps still under-appreciated.

EJ

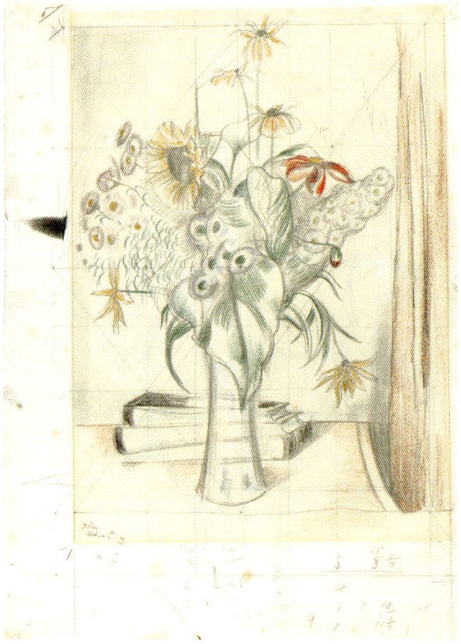

John NASH, C.B.E.
[1893–1977]
A Vase of Flowers

pencil and watercolour on paper squared in pencil, 42 × 31.5 cm
inscribed: *John Nash*
on reverse: pencil sketch of a view through a window

P.798
PROVENANCE: Elisabeth and Alice Barbara Kitson; given to Gallery by Alice Barbara Kitson, October 1992.

Nash was famous for his meticulous flower drawings and botanical studies (see P.212).

JM

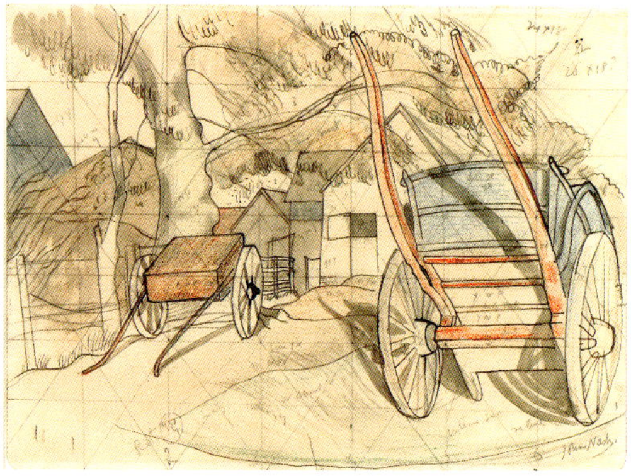

John NASH, C.B.E.
[1893–1977]
Study of Two Farm Carts

coloured pencil and ink squared in pencil on paper, 20.5 × 27.8 cm
inscribed: *John Nash* and with measurements and colour notations

P.799.
PROVENANCE: Elisabeth and Alice Barbara Kitson; given to Gallery by Alice Barbara Kitson, October 1992.

Perhaps a study for a larger painting as yet untraced. John Nash was without formal training as an artist but began painting shortly before the First World War, exhibiting with the London Group. He served on the Western Front in the First World War, his best known work of this time being *Over the Top, Ist Artists Rifles at Marcoing* (I.W.M.).

His better known work was concerned with the English landscape, mostly in watercolour. He was also renowned for his woodcuts and botanical illustrations.

JM

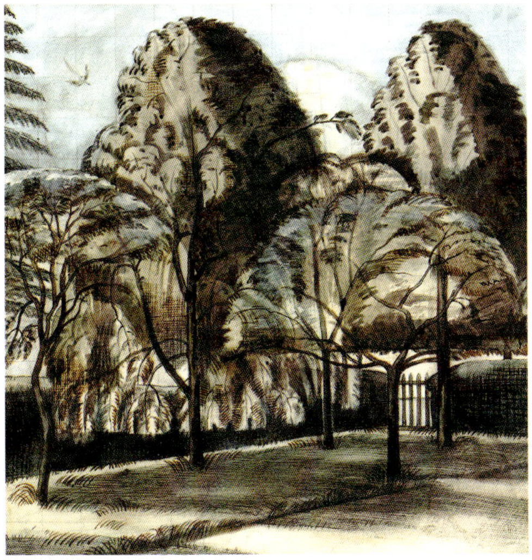

Paul NASH
[1889–1946]
The Garden, c.1914

pen and ink and watercolour squared in pencil on paper, 38.5 × 36.8 cm

P.440
PROVENANCE: Leicester Galleries, from whom purchased by Gallery, January 1963.
EXHIBITIONS: *Exhibition of Works by 19th & 20th Century Artists*, London, Leicester Galleries, 1963, no.19; *Watercolours from Bedford*, Norwich, Castle Museum, 1965, no.37.
REFERENCES: *Illustrated London News*, 2 February 1963, vol. 242, p.155.

In one of his poems Nash expressed his feeling for trees as subject matter for much of his work at this time:

O dreaming trees sunk in a swoon of sleep
What have ye seen in those mysterious places?
What images? What faces?
What unknown pageant thro' these hollows moves
At night? What blood fights have ye seen?
What scenes of life and death? What haunted loves?

(extract from a poem written for Mercia Oakley, c.1909).

JM

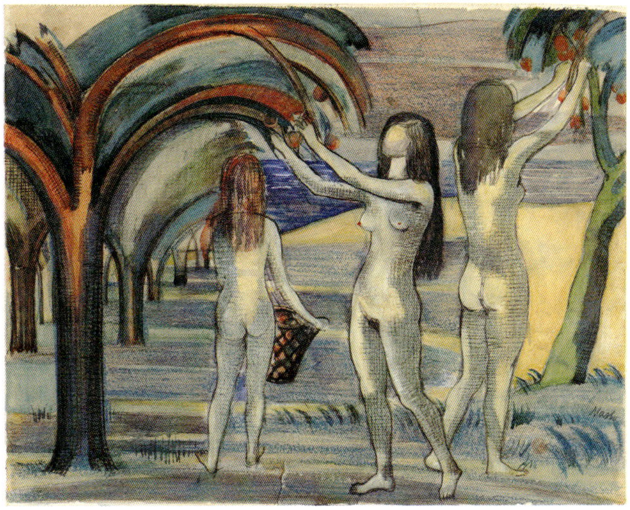

Paul NASH
[1889–1946]
The Fruit Pickers, c.1916

watercolour and chalk on paper, 26.7 × 34 cm
inscribed: *Nash*

P.267
PROVENANCE: Ewan Phillips, from whom purchased by Gallery, October 1958.

Nash and his fiancée, Margaret Theodosia Odeh, stayed with the playwright Gordon Bottomley and his wife at Silverdale near Carnforth, Lancashire, in July 1914. Another watercolour of this period (*The Orchard*, c. 1914), depicts the orchard from a distance, incorporating the fruit baskets, but excluding the figures. A further watercolour *Nymph in a Landscape*, 1916, also bears strong similarities in the handling of the foliage and includes the figure of a nymph walking through the trees.

JM

Paul NASH
[1889–1946]
Dymchurch, Kent, 1922

ink and watercolour on paper, 20.4 × 32.8 cm
inscribed: *Paul Nash 1922*

P.132
PROVENANCE: Leicester Galleries, from whom purchased by Gallery, November 1957.
EXHIBITIONS: *Watercolours and Drawings from The Cecil Higgins Art Gallery Bedford*, London, Thos. Agnew & Sons Ltd, 1962, no.87.

Dymchurch, on the Kent Coast, became a central theme in much of Nash's work after the First World War. He had suffered a nervous breakdown in 1921, and through his paintings of the beach and extensive sea wall he came to recognize something of his own emotional state. He was to reject it as a subject matter in 1925 declaring, 'I shall never work there any more' and moving to Iden in Sussex.

JM

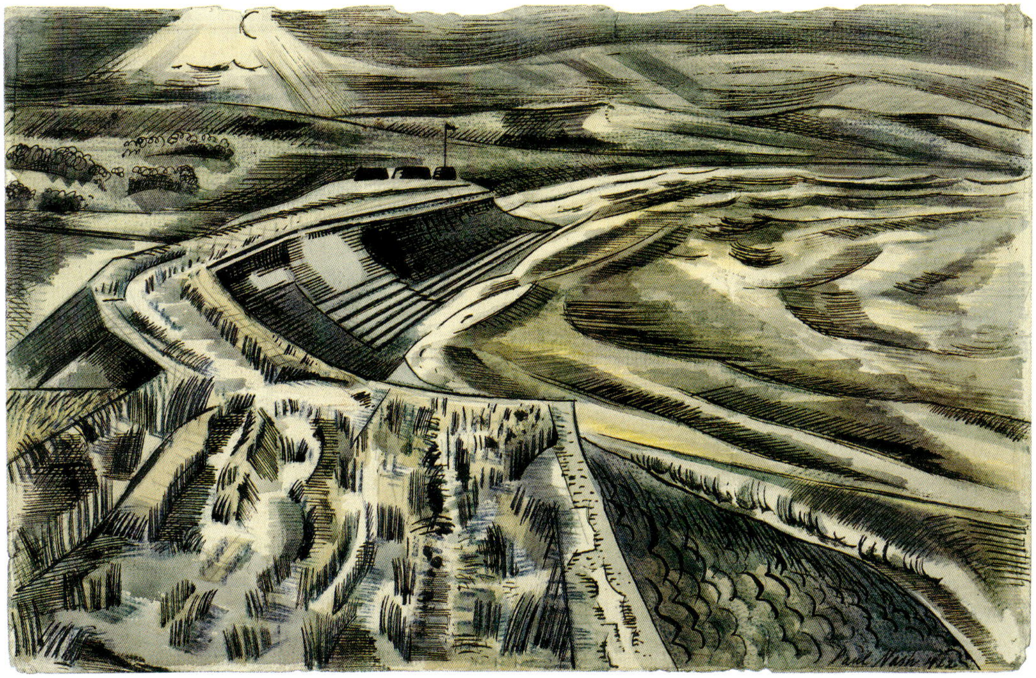

Paul NASH
[1889–1946]
Ballard Landscape , c.1934–5

watercolour and graphite on paper, 17.8 × 25.6 cm
inscribed: *Paul Nash*

P.197
PROVENANCE: Redfern Gallery, from whom purchased by Gallery, April 1958.

Nash stayed at Whitecliff Farm, Swanage from October 1934 to February 1945. It was a period of stylistic change when Nash was looking 'to find my way between the claim of "Abstractions" and pure interpretation', (letter to Anthony Bertram, April 1934).

JM

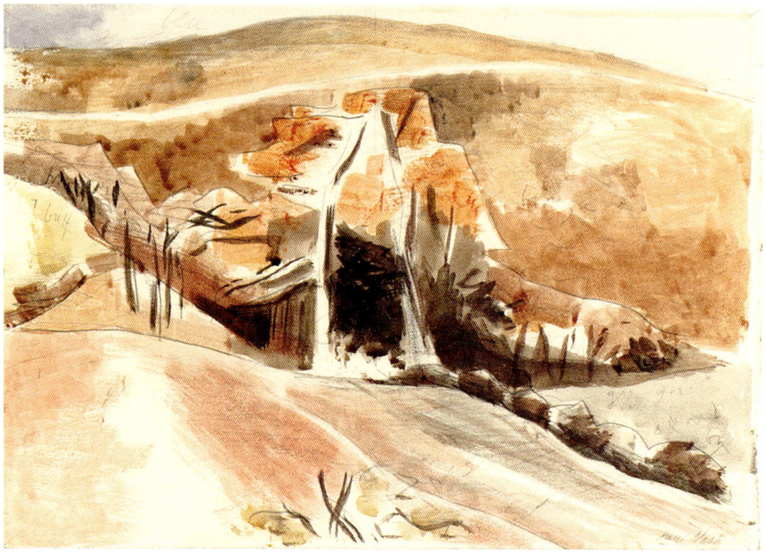

Paul NASH
[1889–1946]
Gloucestershire Valley, c.1943

watercolour and chalk on paper, 40.3 × 58.1 cm
inscribed: *Paul Nash*
on reverse: *Gloucestershire Valley 3502/1*

P.198
PROVENANCE: Arthur Tooth & Sons Ltd, from whom purchased by Gallery, April 1958.
EXHIBITIONS: *Watercolours and Drawings from The Cecil Higgins Art Gallery, Bedford*, London, Thos. Agnew & Sons Ltd, 1962, no.113.

Nash trained at the Slade, first exhibiting at the Carfax Gallery in 1912, encouraged by Roger Fry (1866–1934) and William ROTHENSTEIN. After being invalided from the trenches in 1917 he became an Official War Artist, producing some powerfully moving works which emphasized the desolation of the scene in Flanders.

His most experimental period was the late 1920s and early 1930s when he painted semi-abstract pictures based on late decorative Cubism, but he never abandoned nature. His later landscapes display an intense visionary character.

EJ

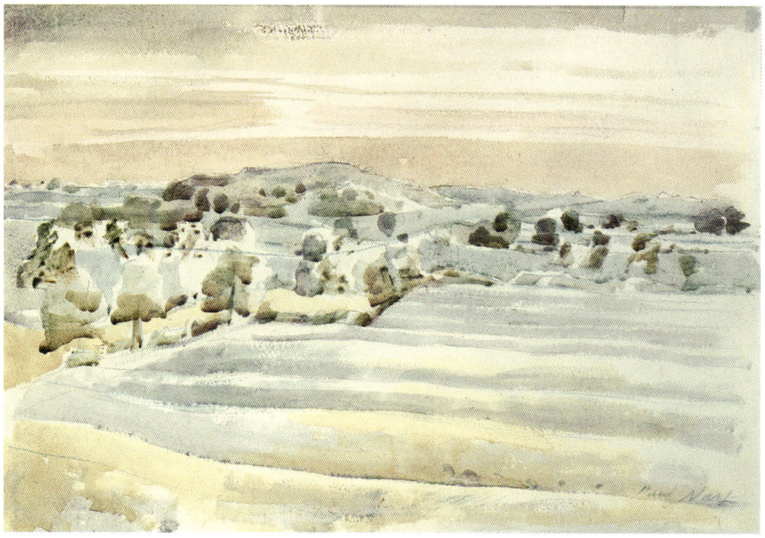

Paul NASH
[1889–1946]
Snow Scene, c.1943

watercolour and pencil on paper, 31.2 × 23.6 cm
inscribed: *Paul Nash*

P.81
PROVENANCE: Redfern Gallery ?; Sir Michael Culme-Seymour ?; Mayor Gallery, from whom purchased by Gallery, November, 1953.
REFERENCES: A. Rutherston (ed.), introduction by A. Bertram, *Paul Nash*, p.23, illus. no.17.

In his late works the watercolours achieve a vibrancy of colour belied by the limited palette. Nash became less concerned with the geography of a particular landscape, with the foreground often not recorded and the trees becoming groups of localized colour.

JM

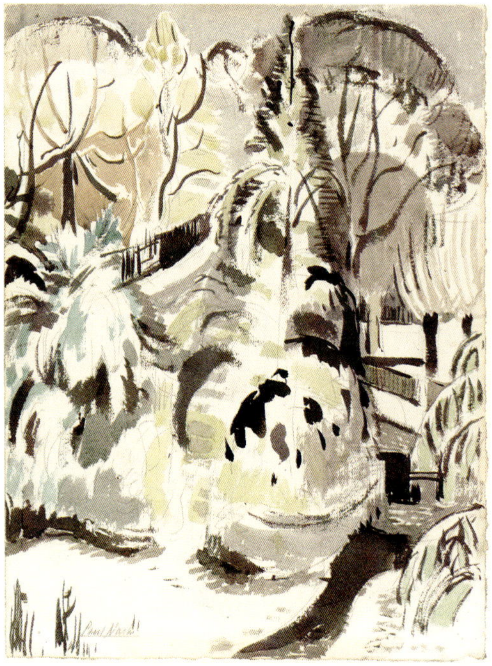

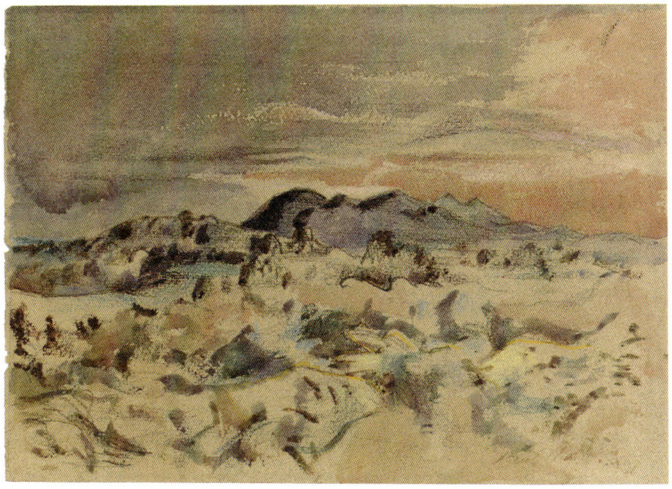

Paul NASH

[1889–1946]

Landscape of the Malvern Distance, c.1944

watercolour and chalk on buff paper, 19.8 × 28.1 cm
inscribed: *Paul Nash*

P.507
PROVENANCE: Roland, Browse and Delbanco, from whom purchased by Gallery, October 1965.

This is a late work by Nash most probably painted when he stayed at the Rising Sun Hotel at Cleeve near Cheltenham in October 1944, where he was able to paint the view across the Severn Valley towards the Malverns from inside the hotel. The Nashes returned to Cleeve again in the same year, staying for Christmas and New Year.

JM

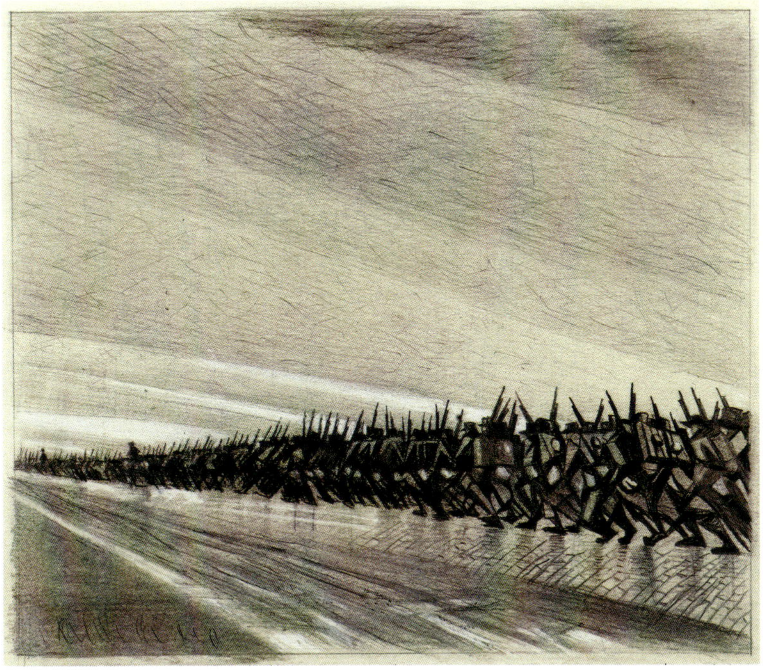

Christopher Richard Wynne NEVINSON, A.R.A.

[1889–1946]

Study for Column on the March, c.1914

black chalk over pencil on paper, 19.1 × 22.5 cm

P.293
PROVENANCE: Leicester Galleries, from whom purchased by Gallery, April, 1959.
EXHIBITIONS: *Watercolours and Drawings from The Cecil Higgins Art Gallery, Bedford*, London, Thos. Agnew & Sons Ltd, 1962, no.78; *C.R.W. Nevinson, 1889–1946. Retrospective Exhibition of Paintings Drawings and Prints*, Cambridge, Kettle's Yard, 1988, no.9.

This haunting image suggests the waste of lives in the 1914–18 war just as forcibly as scenes of explicit carnage. It is a study for the oil, dated 1915, which belonged in 1962 to Laurence Cadbury of Birmingham. Another study in gouache belongs to the I.W.M. Nevinson studied at the Slade and then in Paris where he shared a studio with Amedeo Modigliani (1884–1920). He was a founder member of the London Group, 1913 and closely associated with the Futurist Movement.

After war service in the Royal Army Medical Corps, he was invalided out and became a war artist in 1917. After the war he returned to urban subjects – his preferred motifs.

EJ

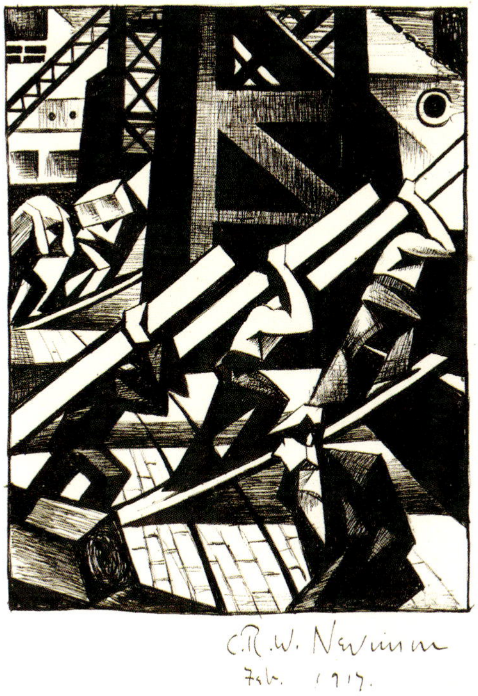

Christopher Richard Wynne NEVINSON, A.R.A.

[1889–1946]

Loading Timbers at Southampton Docks, 1917

pen and ink on paper, 27 × 19.2 cm
inscribed: *C.R.W Nevinson, Feb.1917*

P.261
PROVENANCE: Leicester Galleries, from whom purchased by Gallery, October 1958.
EXHIBITIONS: *C.R.W. Nevinson, 1889–1946. Retrospective Exhibition of Paintings, Drawings and Prints*, Cambridge, Kettle's Yard, 1988, no.23.
REFERENCES: *C.R.W. Nevinson, 1889–1946. Retrospective Exhibition of Paintings, Drawings and Prints*, 1988, p.15, repr. p.16.

Probably a preparatory drawing for the 1917 lithograph *Loading the Ship*, illustrated in a press cutting of October 1922 as *The Endless Chain*. Nevinson also made a drypoint of this subject, *Southampton*, 1916. In an article on Nevinson in *The Artist*, August 1943, pp.133–5, F.G. Mortimer wrote: 'His novel style suited the novelty of his themes. He won a huge following and many disciples until he took landscape as a subject and naturalism as a style, at which the disciples raved against him'.

EJ

Ben NICHOLSON, O.M.
[1894–1982]
Gouache 1940, 1940

bodycolour on paper, 40.2 × 44.6 cm
inscribed on reverse: *when exhibiting please see that the frame is an immaculate white, 18gns, Top Ben Nicholson 1940*

P.375
PROVENANCE: Gimpel Fils, from whom purchased by Gallery, April 1958.
EXHIBITIONS: *Watercolours and Drawings from The Cecil Higgins Art Gallery, Bedford*, London, Thos. Agnew & Sons Ltd, 1962, no.107; *Watercolours from Bedford*, Norwich, Castle Museum, 1965, no.38.

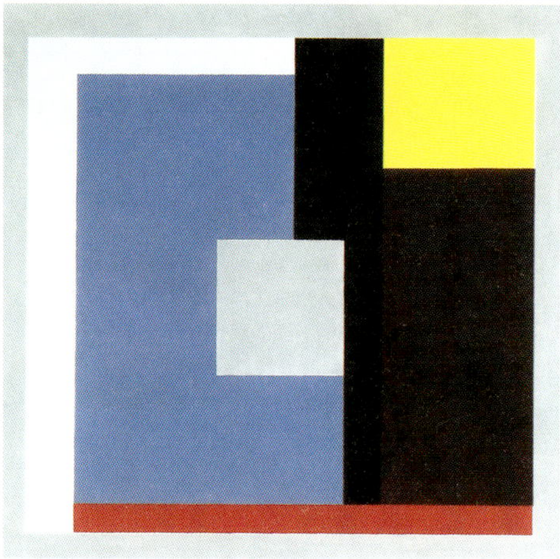

Ben was born the son of the painter William NICHOLSON and Mabel, sister of James PRYDE. As a child he suffered asthma, which interrupted his schooling, and although not encouraged by his father he enrolled at the Slade in 1910, supported by his mother: 'she backed me up completely (quite as completely as father never backed one up)'. Whilst there he met a lifelong friend in Paul NASH, stating he was 'much more serious than I was – I was in the painting world trying to get out and he was out and trying to get in'. He appears to have disliked the curriculum under Henry TONKS and later claimed that in his year at the Slade he spent most of his time playing billiards at the Gower Hotel: 'The red ivory ball and the two white, one with a spot and one without, and the clink of their relationship became an "experience" far more related to art than anything they taught at the Slade'.

Ben made numerous trips abroad, including America in 1917. However his father had little enthusiasm for his paintings at this time, describing them as having 'a certain depressing distinction', but still considering them to be the work 'of an untrained eye'.

Through visits to Paris in the 1930s, he met Joan Miró (1893–1983), Piet Mondrian (1872–1944), and, encouraged by his second wife Barbara HEPWORTH, his work saw a move away from still life as subject matter into depictions of discs and armatures with biomorphic origins. By December 1933 he was investigating the construction of low reliefs often made from very thin board or cardboard.

The war years were spent in St Ives (his Hampstead studio being occupied by Henry MOORE). The landscape provided a new stimulus for Nicholson, the colour in his work reflecting the subdued palette of Cornwall. He said of his work at this time: 'I like the actual shadows cast in the reliefs among the illusions of shadows but I like them cast from the same angle as those that I've experienced by sun and moonlight. I don't want a disembodied idea but one with grass roots!'

JM

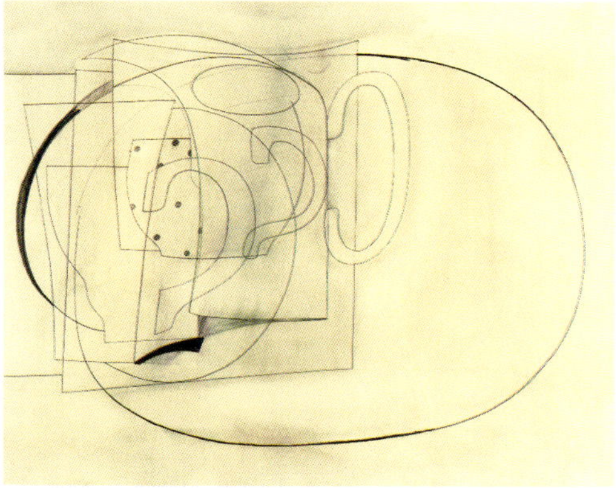

Ben NICHOLSON, O.M.
[1894–1982]
March 26.54, (Birds and Spots), 1954

pencil and wash on paper, 40.5 × 53.3 cm
on reverse: *Mch 26 (?) 54. BN*

P.213
PROVENANCE: Gimpel Fils, from whom purchased by Gallery, April 1958.
REFERENCES: B. Nicholson, *Ben Nicholson:* volume 2 work since 1947, with an introduction by Herbert Read, 1956, illus. no.79.

In his essay on Nicholson in *Modern English Painters*, Sir John Rothenstein states his view that 'it is upon his most intransigently abstract works that Nicholson's reputation will finally depend'. He also stresses Piet Mondrian's influence on Nicholson and, in particular, his dictum that 'the straight line is a stronger and more profound expression than the curve'.

EJ

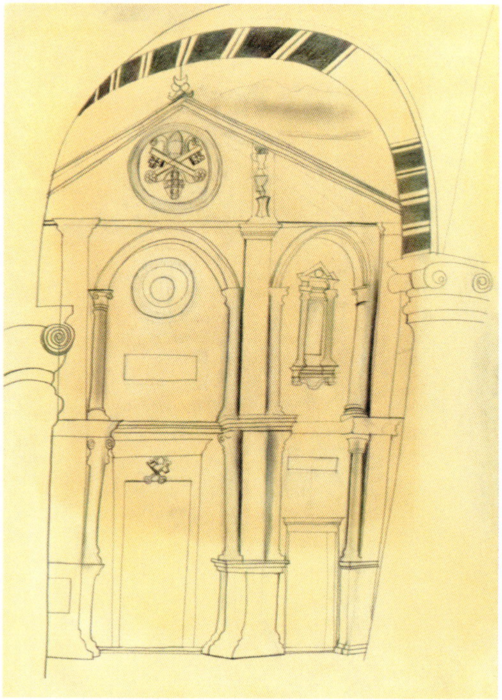

Ben NICHOLSON, O.M.
[1894–1982]
Oct.1955. (Cattedrale, Pienza), 1955

pencil and oil wash on paper, 53.5 × 38.2 cm
on reverse: *Oct 5 Cattedrale, Pienza*

P.214
PROVENANCE: Gimpel Fils, from whom purchased by Gallery, April 1958.
EXHIBITIONS: *Primitives to Picasso*, London, R.A., 1962, no.417; *Watercolours and Drawings from The Cecil Higgins Art Gallery, Bedford*, London, Thos. Agnew & Sons Ltd, 1962, no.102; *Watercolours from Bedford*, Norwich, Castle Museum, 1965, no.39; *St Ives 1939–64*, London, Tate Gallery, 1985, no.141; *Ben Nicholson*, London, Tate Gallery, 1993–4, no.102.
REFERENCES: B. Nicholson, *Ben Nicholson: volume 2 work since 1947*, with an introduction by Herbert Read, 1956, illus. no.109; *St Ives 1939–64, Twenty five years of Painting, Sculpture and Pottery*, 1985, repr. p.193; J. Lewison, *Ben Nicholson*, 1993, p.229, repr. p.178.

In 1955 Ben Nicholson went to Rome and then on to a number of other cities including Siena, Assisi and Spoleto.

Pienza is about thirty miles south-east of Siena on the way to Orvieto. When Aeneas Sylvius Piccolomini, who was born in Pienza, became Pope as Pius II in 1458, he remembered his birthplace and had it rebuilt by Bernardo Rossellino between 1459 and 1462. The resulting Piazza Pio II, which contains both the Cathedral and the Palazzo Piccolomini, is one of the finest in Tuscany.

EJ

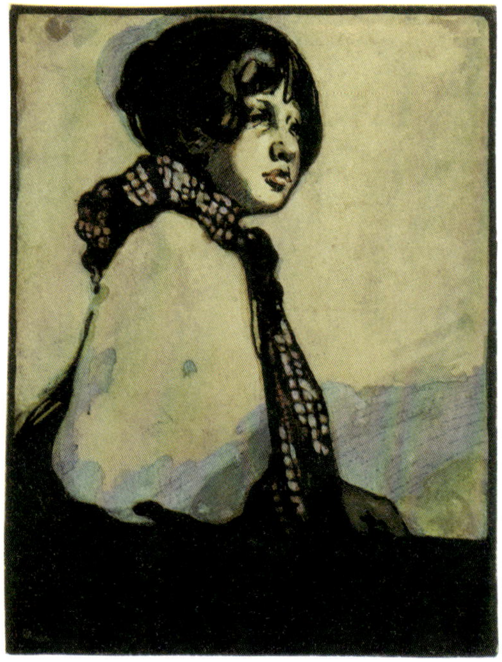

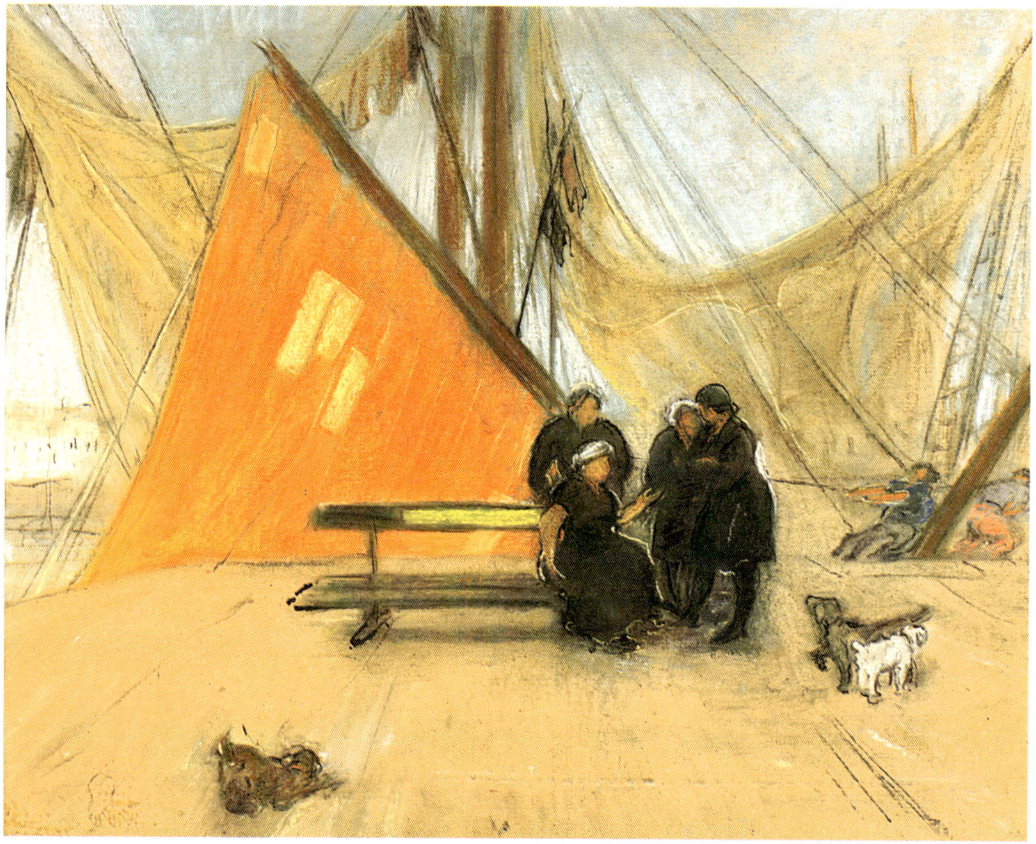

Sir William NICHOLSON
[1872–1949]
A Girl – half length, 1898

ink and watercolour on paper, 10.8 × 8.5 cm
inscribed on original mount: *William Nicholson 1898*

P.199
PROVENANCE: Ralph Edwards; P&D Colnaghi Ltd, from whom purchased by Gallery, April 1958.

Drawn in the same year that Nicholson's two series of woodcuts were published by Heinemann (see P.553). The contrasting areas of light and dark here reflect the artist's preoccupation with woodcuts at this date.

EJ

Sir William NICHOLSON
[1872–1949]
Women on the quay at La Rochelle (also known as Women on quay, Dieppe), c.1938

pastel on paper, 43.7 ? 56.1 cm
on reverse: *View of La Rochelle Harbour*

P.553
PROVENANCE: Sir John Hay; Fine Art Society, from whom purchased by Gallery, April 1967.
REFERENCES: A. Nicholson (ed.), *William Nicholson painter,* 1996, illus. p.262, repr. as *The Women, Quayside, La Rochelle*, sketch on reverse repr. as *View of La Rochelle Harbour.*

In the past occasionally but incorrectly titled *Dieppe Quayside*; the identification of the sketch on the reverse has led to the change of title.

Nicholson was born in Newark-on-Trent the son of a well-to-do industrialist. Wishing to become an artist from an early age, he persuaded his parents to allow him to study at Herkomer's in London; this was followed at the age of eighteen by study at the Académie Julian in Paris. Nicholson had met Mabel Pryde whilst in London, and with their marriage he went into partnership with her brother James PRYDE to form the *Beggerstaff Brothers*, designing bold posters in the manner of Toulouse-Lautrec. Subsequently Nicholson went on to design several series of woodcuts including *The Alphabet* and *London Types*, both in 1898.

From 1906 he became more established as a portrait painter (partly through financial necessity brought on by the birth of his fourth child in 1904). For his formal portraits he used the studio of William ORPEN, who painted the Nicholsons, *A Bloomsbury Family*, 1908 (Scottish National Gallery of Modern Art). It was in 1904 that he designed the costumes for J.M. Barrie's *Peter Pan* at the Duke of York Theatre. His costumes were frighteningly authentic, especially the pirate costumes, which led to reports of some children being terrified on the opening night.

Moving to Rottingdean in Sussex, Nicholson pursued landscape and still-lifes for his subject matter. After the tragic deaths of Mabel from pneumonia and his son Tony (killed in France), Nicholson remarried in 1919, to Edie, widow of Colonel Jack Stuart Wortley, who had died on active service in France. The marriage brought some sense of financial security, and he no longer had to accept portrait commissions. But it also brought a cooling of relations with his son Ben, who married Winifred Roberts and moved away from the family circle.

Nicholson was knighted in 1936, commenting that he 'didn't feel like a knight'.

He visited La Rochelle twice in 1938. In a letter to his son Ben and his second wife Barbara HEPWORTH he said of this time: 'Wester winds and sun are here, their joys tempered by funerals of sailormen who were lost in the bitter gales two months ago. The big fishing boats with blue, rust-red, pure white, fleshcolour and brown-paper-coloured patched sails, flying their "drapeau" at half mast, these many days'. (A. Nicholson (ed.), *William Nicholson painter*, 1996, p.262).

EJ/JM

Sir Sidney NOLAN, O.M., C.B.E.
[1917–92]
Rain Forest, 1959

oil on paper, 30.4 x 24.6 cm
inscribed: *Nolan*

P.376
PROVENANCE: Purchased from the artist, October 1960.
EXHIBITIONS: *Primitives to Picasso*, London, R.A., 1962, no.413; *Watercolours and Drawings from The Cecil Higgins Art Gallery, Bedford,* London, Thos. Agnew & Sons Ltd, 1962, no.90; *Watercolours from Bedford,* Norwich, Castle Museum, 1965, no.40.

Nolan was born in a suburb of Melbourne, the son of a tram driver of Irish descent. His early training was at the Art School of the National Gallery, Melbourne. The first exhibited works were abstract but in 1941–42 he turned to representational painting. It was at this time that he also designed the décor and costumes for Serge Lifar's experimental ballet *Icarus*.

Nolan's importance as an Australian artist was in his ability to paint the feel of his native landscape, blending direct observation with visionary imagination into what he described as a 'composite impression'. His most famous works are the two series about the outlaw Ned Kelly (1946 and 1951). After 1953 he worked outside Australia mainly in England, his work finding a new direction away from the Australian landscape, including subject matter as diverse as the Gallipoli campaign of 1915–16, Shakespeare's Sonnets and his travels in Greece, Africa and Antarctica. Sidney Nolan was knighted in 1981 and awarded the O.M. in 1983.

EJ/JM

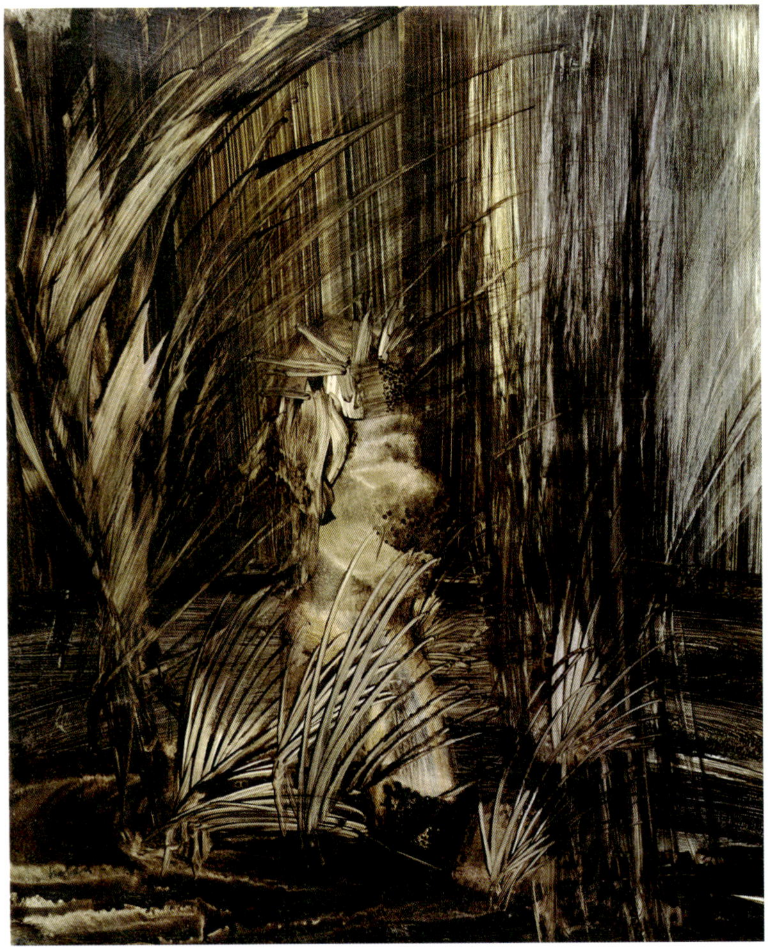

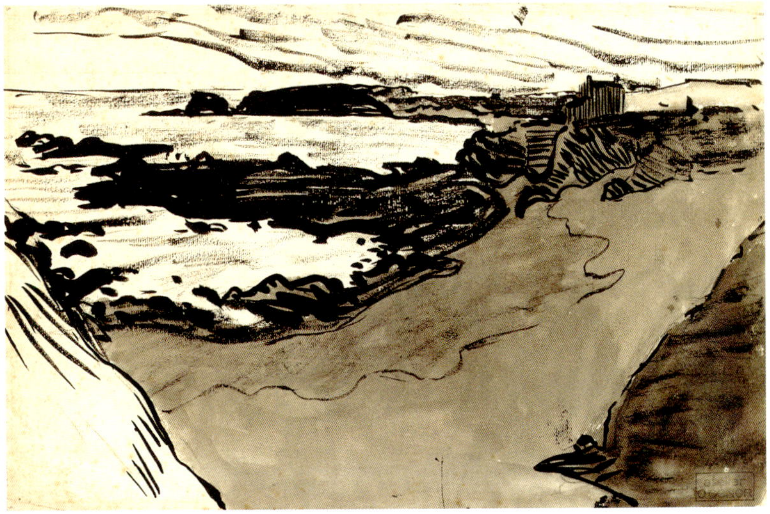

Roderic O'CONOR
[1860–1940]
Brittany Coast, c.1893

ink and wash and some chalk on paper, 30.8 × 47.5 cm
stamped: *atelier O'CONOR*

P.218
PROVENANCE: Hôtel Drouot, Paris, Sale O'Conor, 7 February 1956; Roland, Browse and Delbanco, from whom purchased by Gallery, April 1958.
EXHIBITIONS: *Roderic O'Conor,* Pont-Aven, Musée de Pont-Aven, 1984, no.66; *Roderic O'Conor,* Belfast, Ulster Museum, Dublin, National Gallery of Ireland, Manchester, Whitworth Art Gallery, 1985–86, no.125.
REFERENCES: J. Benington, *Roderic O'Conor: A Biography with a catalogue of his work,* 1992, p.229, illus. no.337; A. Crookshank & the Knight of Glin, *The Watercolours of Ireland*, 1994, p.263, illus. no.371 as *Côtes Bretagne*.

O'Conor was born at Milton in County Roscommon, Ireland, the second eldest in a family of six. The O'Conor family was of some note in this area of Ireland with a lineage that could be traced back several hundred years.

After initial study at the Metropolitan School of Art in Dublin, he transferred to the Hibernian Academy of Art in 1881–82 (collecting four prizes for his work). Owing to the success of his studies his tutors recommended that he go to Europe to further his career, initially at the Académie Royale des Beaux-Arts d'Anvers in Antwerp and then in Paris, under the portrait painter Carolus-Duran, (1837–1917).

O'Conor was certainly in Pont-Aven from 1892, although he was probably there earlier as his paintings exhibited at the Salon des Indépendents of that year had Breton titles. Initially painting elderly Breton peasants, O'Conor had by 1893 developed an interest in the Breton landscape as a subject, painting in a style noticeably influenced by Van Gogh. The end of 1893 was significant for O'Conor as, with the death of his father he inherited the family estate and achieved financial security through ground rents from his tenant farmers.

Returning to Paris, O'Conor lived in Montparnasse. The young Clive Bell described him and his circle as having 'played as influential a part in my life as any of my Cambridge contemporaries'. The meeting place for artists was the Chat Blanc restaurant, amongst whose occasional visitors were Aleister Crowley and Somerset Maugham, whom Crowley described as having 'suffered terribly under the lash of universal contempt…The man he most hated was Roderic O'Conor'.

JM

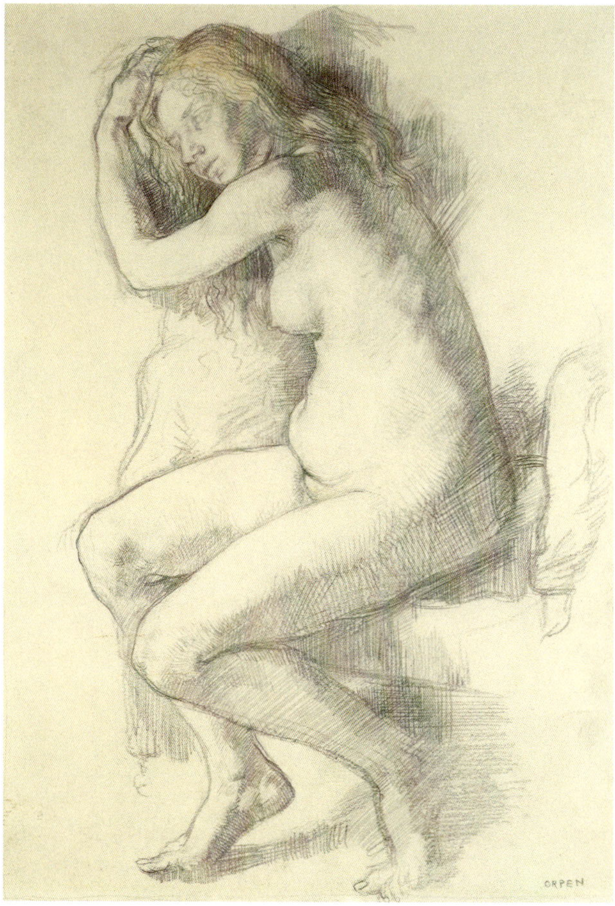

Sir William ORPEN, R.A.

[1878–1931]

Head of a Young Man (Charles Hazlewood Shannon ?) , 1904

charcoal on paper, 24 × 18.5 cm
inscribed: *William Orpen '04*

P.411
PROVENANCE: P&D Colnaghi Ltd, from whom purchased by Gallery, February 1962.

It has been suggested that the sitter in this fine portrait is Charles Hazlewood Shannon, R.A. (1863–1937), lithographer, painter and lifelong companion of Charles RICKETTS.

Orpen and Shannon were certainly acquainted by 1904, and in 1906 Orpen took a studio in South Bolton Gardens next door to Ricketts and Shannon.

EJ

Sir William ORPEN, R.A.

[1878–1931]

Portrait of a Girl

pencil on paper, 28.1 × 20.6 cm
inscribed on reverse: *W.ORPEN*

P.331
PROVENANCE: Professor Isaacs, from whom purchased by Gallery, January 1960.
EXHIBITIONS: *Watercolours and Drawings from The Cecil Higgins Art Gallery, Bedford*, London, Thos. Agnew & Sons Ltd, 1962, no.67.
NOTES: Sheet taken from a sketchbook.

It has been suggested that this portrays Mary, Orpen's eldest daughter, born in 1902. Known in the family as Bunny, she appears as a child in a number of Orpen's paintings and drawings.

EJ

Sir William ORPEN, R.A.

[1878–1931]

Nude Woman, c.1899–1900

pencil and watercolour on paper, 32.5 × 27 cm
inscribed: *ORPEN*
collector's mark: *H.S. Reitlinger*

P.152
PROVENANCE: H.S. Reitlinger; Sotheby's, lot 20; P&D Colnaghi Ltd, from whom purchased by Gallery, January 1958.

Alison Smith of the Tate Gallery suggests that the model is Emily Scobel and the date 1899–1900, when Orpen painted *The Mirror* (Tate Gallery) and *The English Nude* (City of Mildura Art Center, Australia), both of which feature Emily, to whom Orpen was briefly engaged. (See Bruce Arnold, *Orpen: Mirror to an Age*, 1981, pp.75–80.) Similar studies are in the Ashmolean Museum, Oxford, and the Barber Institute, University of Birmingham.

Orpen was born in Ireland and studied at the Metropolitan School of Art, Dublin, before going to the Slade from 1897–9 where his brilliance rivalled that of Augustus JOHN, winning the Slade prize for *Play Scene with Hamlet*. He debuted at the N.E.A.C. with a portrait of John in 1900.

From 1917–19 he was an Official War Artist, attending the Peace Conference in Paris as official painter. He was known mainly for his portraits and portrait groups and in the 1920s was referred to as 'England's most popular painter'. Orpen was knighted in 1918 and elected R.A. in 1919.

EJ/JM

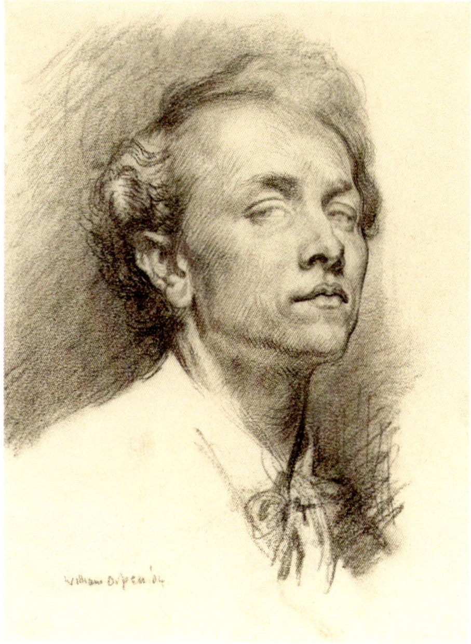

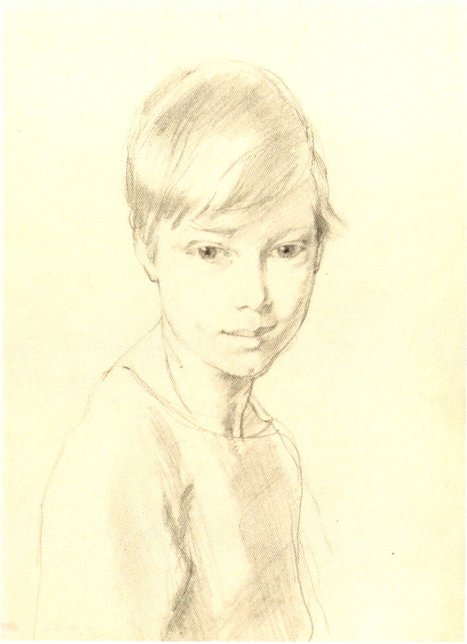

Samuel PALMER

[1805–81]

Harvest in the Vineyard, 1859

watercolour and bodycolour on paper, 19.9 × 42.7 cm

P.117

PROVENANCE: Walter Turner, Solihull near Birmingham; sale Sotheby's 2 June 1948 (no.159) bought Thos. Agnew & Sons Ltd; sold to J.M. Finn February 1953; later returned by him and then sold to the Leger Galleries January 1957, from whom purchased by Gallery, March 1957.

EXHIBITIONS: *Old Watercolour Society,* London, 1859, no.241; *80th Annual Watercolour Exhibition,* London, Thos. Agnew & Sons Ltd, 1953, no.44; *Works by Samuel Palmer,* Sheffield, Graves Art Gallery, 1961, no.75; *Watercolours and Drawings from The Cecil Higgins Art Gallery, Bedford,* London, Thos. Agnew & Sons Ltd, 1962, no.33; *An Exhibition of the Paintings of Samuel Palmer and John Linnell,* Reigate, Reigate Town Hall, 1963, no.55; *English Watercolours from The Cecil Higgins Art Gallery, Bedford,* Reading, Reading Art Gallery, 1965, no.36; *Watercolours from Bedford,* Norwich, Castle Museum, 1965, no.42; *The English Tradition: an exhibition of watercolours from two private collections,* Bedford, Cecil Higgins Art Gallery, 1972, no.63.

REFERENCES: R. Lister, *Catalogue Raisonné of the works of Samuel Palmer,* 1988, p.187, no.573, repr. as *Harvesting the Vineyard or Returning from the Vintage.*

Lister, who gives this drawing an alternative title of *Returning from the Vintage*, suggests that it is no doubt based on scenes Palmer witnessed during his Italian tour of 1837–9 and describes it as one 'of happy abandon'. Although not exhibited until 1859, Lister notes some stylistic affinities here with works of the immediate post-Shoreham period (1828–35).

Palmer married Hannah Linnell in 1837 and for their 'wedding trip' as Palmer described it, the couple visited Italy, a trip beset from the outset with financial difficulties; it was later described by his son as 'humiliating and penurious'.

Palmer had hoped that through George Richmond's influence he might find buyers for his work in Rome but he met with little success. Palmer considered Richmond to blame but he also lacked in social judgement; his clothing, for example, being described as 'appalling'.

It was, however, a period in their lives when they enjoyed a degree of happiness and freedom, away from Palmer's over-bearing father-in-law, John LINNELL.

EJ/JM

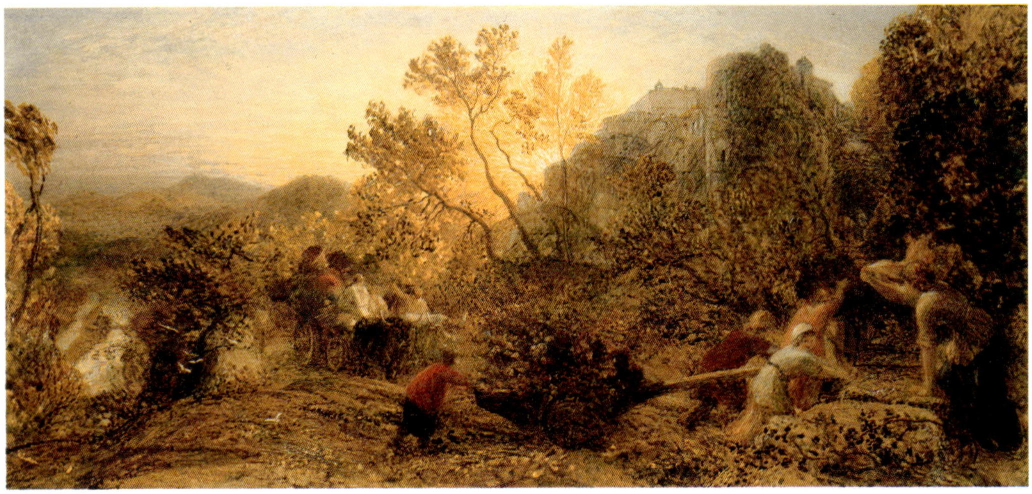

Samuel PALMER

[1805–81]

The Bellman from *Il Penseroso,* 1881

watercolour and bodycolour with gum arabic and pencil on paper; image size 17.2 × 23.9 cm; sheet size 22.5 × 31.7 cm inscribed: *S.PALMER*

P.436

PROVENANCE: J. Douglas Fletcher; Miss Augusta Smith; Sir Alexander Napier; Eardley Knollys, his sale Sotheby's 14 November 1962, lot 54 purchased by Thos. Agnew and Sons Ltd on behalf of Gallery, November 1962.

EXHIBITIONS: *Royal Society Painters in Watercolours,* London, 1882, no.61; *Old Masters,* London, R.A., 1893, no.125; *Works of Samuel Palmer,* New York, Durlacher Bros, 1949, no.42; *Works by Samuel Palmer,* Sheffield, Graves Art Gallery, 1961, no.68; *Watercolours from Bedford,* Norwich, Castle Museum, 1965, no.41; *English Watercolours from The Cecil Higgins Art Gallery,* Reading, Reading Art Gallery, 1965, no.37; *The English Tradition: An exhibition of watercolours from two private collections,* Bedford, Cecil Higgins Art Gallery, 1972, no.62; *Illustrations to Virgil & Milton,* London, V&A, 1978–79, no.XXI(c); *Viktorianische Malerei von Turner bis Whistler,* Munich, Neue Pinakothek, 1993 and Madrid, Prado, no.18.

REFERENCES: A.H. Palmer, *The life and letters of Samuel Palmer,* 1892, p.166; ed. R. Lister, *The Letters of Samuel Palmer,* 1974, p.691; *Vision Recaptured: The Complete Etchings and the Paintings for Milton and for Virgil,* 1978, pp.70–2, pl.18; R.Lister, *Samuel Palmer: His Life and Art,* 1987, pp.186, 215–24; R. Lister, *Catalogue Raisonné of the works of Samuel Palmer,* 1988, pp.223–4, no.M19.

NOTES: In upper margin: *Midd. dist wood is thick gamboge over* [illegible] *finish with sepia* [illegible] *Sepia / A to be the same width as B or a very little less – Midd dist wood is thick gamboge over* [? bistre]

In right margin: *Place on plate /* [illegible] */ ? /* [illegible] */ Arch a / little more / to right of / church tower /* [scribble] */ 19 ? x 6 ?* [written vertically] / [sketch of a cow] */ This the cow /* [illegible] */ light* [illegible] / [sketch of ox] */ The ox behind it / dark – though against hedge /* [sketch of ox].

In left margin: *1* [double underscore] *5/42-/15 18/4/22/60x40/*
2400
1200 [sketch marked A and B] *4 ? by 6 5/8/ x8 /*
3600
49
74
196
343
3626

In lower left margin: *Base line here—-/*[vertical arrow].

In lower right margin: [sketch marked triangle] *Lonely tower* [illegible] / *Bellman 9 / Remember the nearest ox to be light the next behind the* [illegible].

Lister dates this 'before 1881' and attempts to transcribe a long and often illegible inscription (see notes). This leads him to conclude that this is probably a study for the large watercolour of 1881 now at Chatsworth (Lister M.20) and also for the etching (Lister E11).

When M.20 was exhibited at the R.A. in 1893 the frame bore a label on the back citing 11.83–4 from 'Il Penseroso' by Milton,

'And the bellman's drowsy charm
To bless the doors from Nightly harm;'

This work bears strong similarities to Palmer's Shoreham period (1828–35), a fact indicated by Palmer who, writing to P.G. Hamerton about the etching of the same subject, said: 'It is a breaking out of village-fever long after contact – a dream of that genuine village where I mused away some of my best years.'

EJ/JM

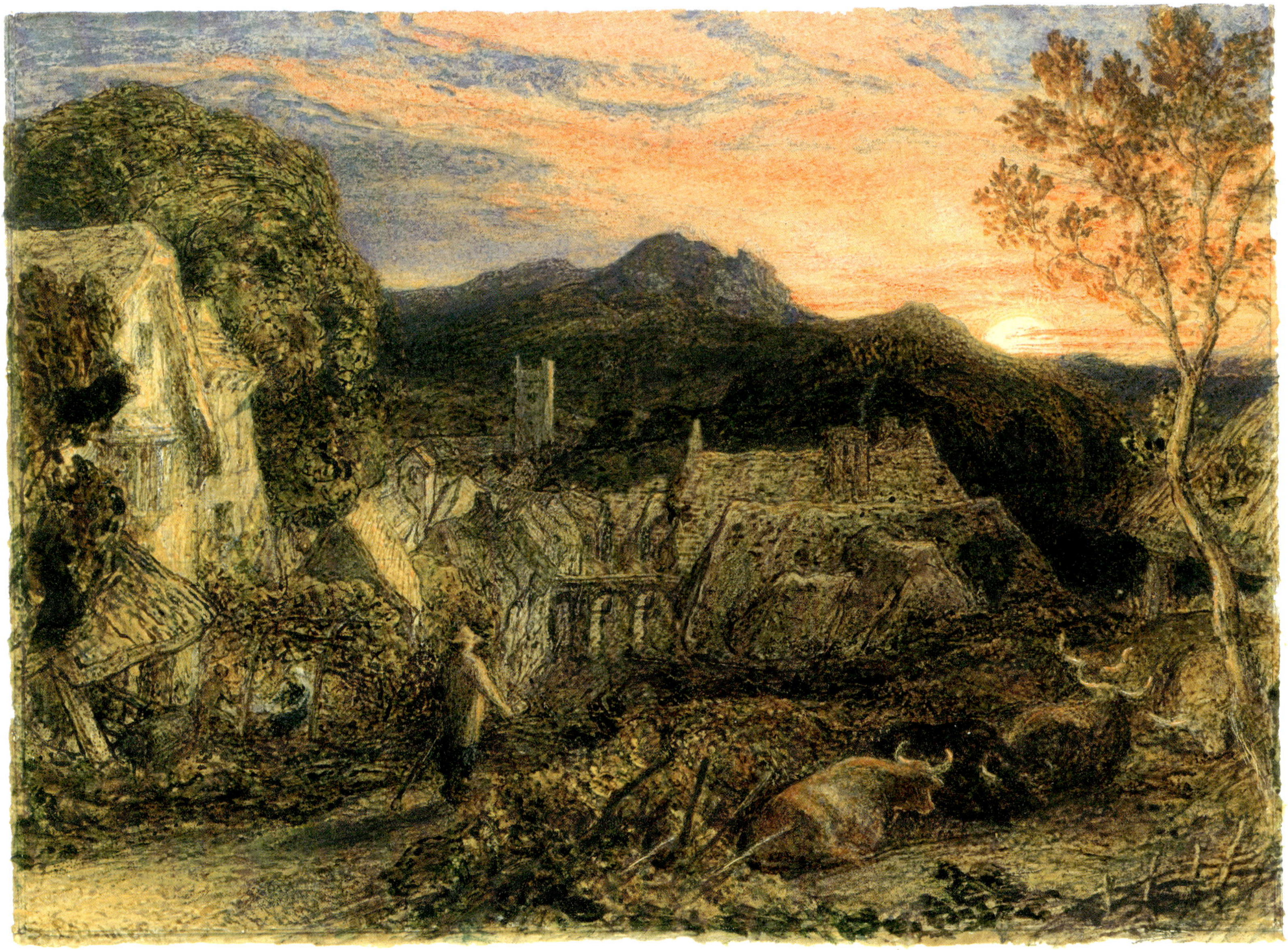

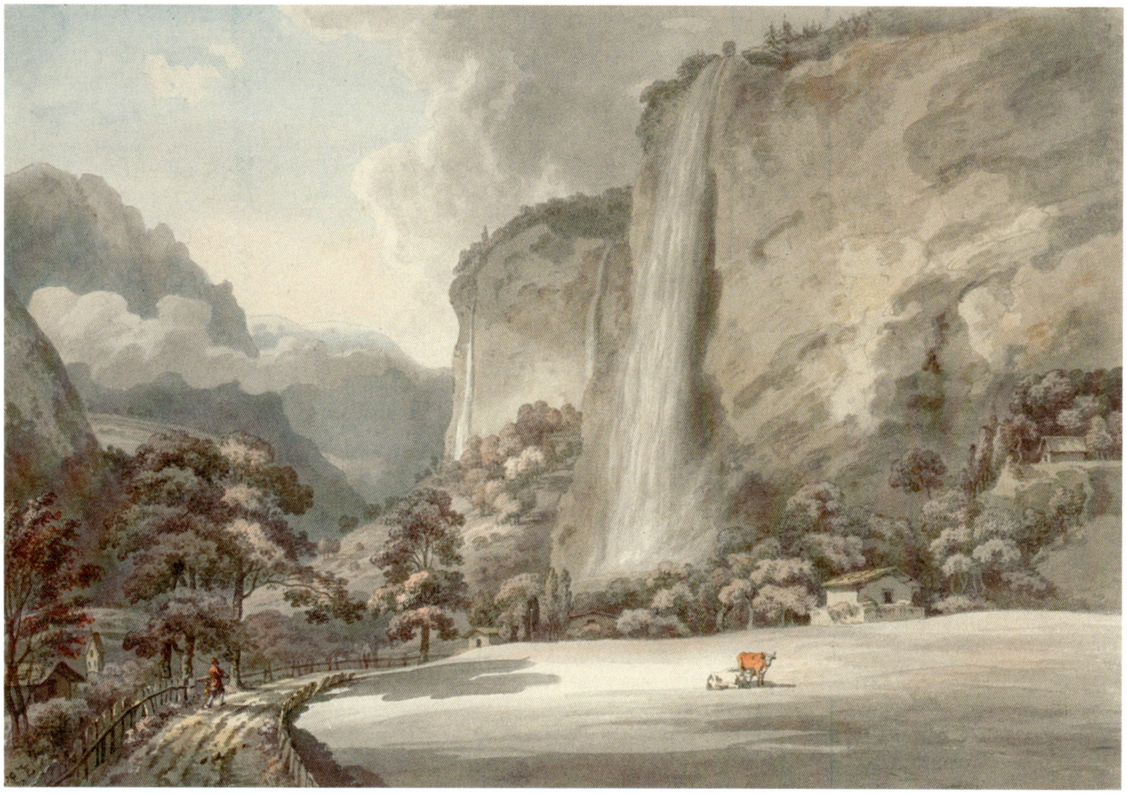

William PARS, A.R.A.
[1742–82]
The Staubbach Falls, Lauterbrunnen, 1775

watercolour on paper, 33.4 × 49.2 cm
inscribed: *W.P. 1775*

P.562
PROVENANCE: George Goyder; Thos. Agnew & Sons Ltd, from whom purchased by Gallery, July 1967.
EXHIBITIONS: *The English Tradition:an exhibition of watercolours from two private collections*, Bedford, Cecil Higgins Art Gallery, 1972, no.65.

Waterfalls were popular subjects with watercolourists in the late 18th and early 19th centuries for their relation to the 'Sublime'. TURNER painted much the same view in 1809. Pars probably painted this watercolour from a sketch made when he accompanied Lord Palmerston c.1770 through Switzerland and the Tyrol to Rome.

Pars is still an underrated artist who, had he lived longer, might have become one of the very greats. As it is, his influence on both TOWNE and J.R. COZENS cannot be denied.

In 1764 he joined the newly-formed Dilettanti Society which sent an expedition to Asia Minor and Greece with Pars as its recording artist. Ten years later the Society decided to pay for an artist to complete his studies in Rome and chose Pars as its first recipient. His watercolours of and around Rome constitute his finest work: they are characterized by great spaciousness and delicate pen work. Towne admired them enormously.

Unfortunately, in order to make a drawing at Tivoli, Pars stood under a waterfall and, in so doing, caught 'an aguish complaint' from which he died a few days later.

EJ

William PARS, A.R.A.
[1742–82]
The Colosseum seen from an Adjoining Street

watercolour and graphite on paper, 33 × 44.4 cm

P.389
PROVENANCE: P&D Colnaghi Ltd, from whom purchased by Gallery, January 1961.

Many of Pars' views of Rome were executed for Lord Palmerston (see entry for P.562). This drawing was formerly attributed to Thomas Jones (1742–1803), a pupil of Richard WILSON, who was in Rome at the same time as Pars.

EJ

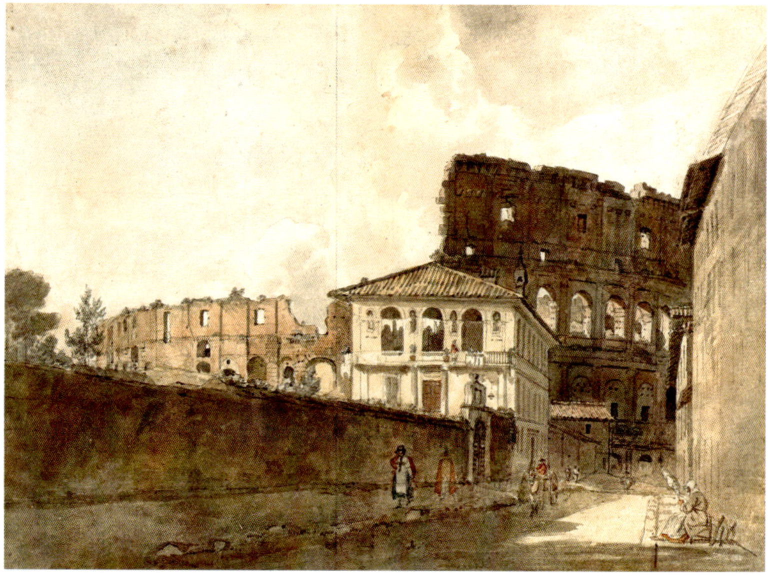

Victor PASMORE, R.A.

[1908–98]

Sea Green, 1960

bodycolour on paper, 75.3 × 48.2 cm
inscribed: *VP 1960*

P.429
PROVENANCE: Marlborough Fine Art as *Abstract Motif in Sea Green and Indigo;* New London Gallery, from whom purchased by Gallery, July 1962.
EXHIBITIONS: *Recent Paintings and Constructions by Victor Pasmore,* London, New London Gallery 1961; *Victor Pasmore–Retrospective Exhibition 1925–65,* London, Tate Gallery, Edinburgh, Scottish National Gallery of Modern Art, Liverpool, Walker Art Gallery, 1965, no.148.

Originally titled *Green and Black* this was altered by Pasmore himself in 1965. When shown a photograph of *Sea Green* at an exhibition of his prints in 1990, Pasmore said it was very similar to the works on display.

Pasmore was only a spare-time painter until 1937; he then taught at the Euston Road School 1938–9 and painted views on the Thames and in London parks in the 1940s. In 1948, under the influence of Paul Klee and theories of harmonious proportion, he converted to abstract paintings and collages. He was architectural designer for the new town of Peterlee, County Durham, from 1956 and a Trustee of the Tate from 1963. In 1966 he moved to Malta, where he lived for the rest of his life.

EJ

Mervyn PEAKE

[1911–68]

The Barking Hounds, c.1946

pen and ink on paper, 35.6 × 25.4 cm
inscribed: *Peake*

P.284
PROVENANCE: Waddington Galleries, from whom purchased by Gallery, April 1959.

Peake was born in China and some of his early work reveals Chinese influence. Here, for example, the right-hand hound's jaw and tongue remind one of those fire-breathing dragons on Chinese porcelain and scrolls. His pen-work is wonderfully assured and crisp and very close stylistically to Peake's illustrations to *In Quest of Sita,* by Maurice Collis, 1946, which suggests a similar date for this drawing. Reviews described these illustrations as 'emphatic calligraphy'.

Peake's best-known books, *The Gormenghast Trilogy*, 1946–59, a Gothic work of immense complexity, was illustrated by Peake himself. He claimed that he usually fixed his characters in his mind by drawing them first.

EJ/JM

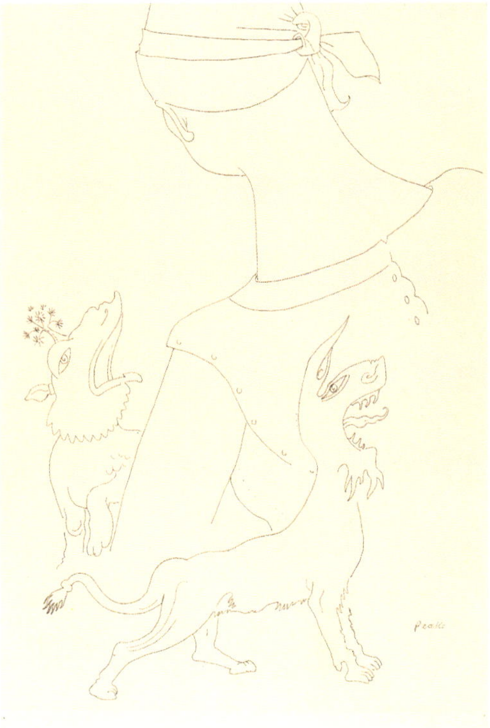

Mervyn PEAKE

[1911–68]

The Gay Monster, 1958

pen and ink on paper, 41 × 43.5 cm
inscribed: *Peake '58*

P.285
PROVENANCE: Waddington Galleries, from whom purchased by Gallery, April 1959.
EXHIBITIONS: *The English Tradition: an exhibition of watercolours from two private collections,* Bedford, Cecil Higgins Art Gallery, 1972, no.66.
NOTES: The drawing has been made on a sheet of chart paper

Peake's extraordinary imagination often produced fantasies of this kind as he drew prolifically. It is a mystery what this drawing means – the monster, half mythological beast, half pantomime horse – appears to be appraising both the front and back views of the nude girl but with what in mind one can only speculate.

Soon after the date of this drawing, Parkinson's disease, from which Peake was already suffering, became much worse and gradually robbed him of his faculties, so that he spent his last four years in a nursing home.

EJ

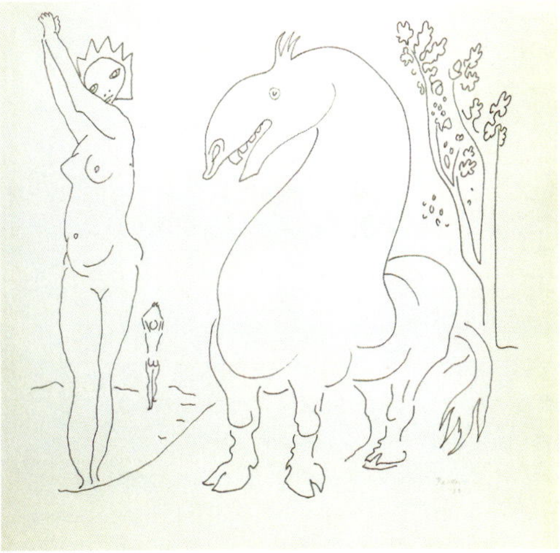

Tom PHILLIPS, R.A.

[b.1937]

Studies for Music, 1968

pencil on paper, 28.5 × 45.4 cm
inscribed on work: *preference:random repeated & random/reversed and repeated.*
one two three
gapmaps:for free use by musicians, poets, dancers etc. To work out interval-seque-
nces of time, space, pitch etc.
Tom Phillips xi.l.mcmlxviii

P.710
PROVENANCE: Angela Flowers; bought by Contemporary Art Society, 1972; given to Gallery by C.A.S., February 1980.
EXHIBITIONS: *Works on Paper,* Arts Council Tour, 1977–8, no.81.

Phillips read Anglo-Saxon at Oxford and then studied at Camberwell School of Art under AUERBACH. He is concerned with chance procedures and the unifying possibilities of musical and literary structures. A great collector of postcards which he used in his picture *Benches* in the Tate, 1970–1, to express the idea of the park bench as an emblem of mortality.

In 1966 he bought a Victorian novel, W.H. Mallock's *A Human Document*, and re-worked the pages isolating various words. This became a new book/art work entitled *A Humument*, 1971 to 1976.

In conversation with Mike von Joel, Phillips said, 'I think of myself as an artist and I think there is one thing that artists do which is teach people to **see**, which sounds rather arrogant. It gives people new things that they didn't see before'. (*Art Line*, vol.3, no.8, summer 1987, pp.24–6.)

EJ

George John PINWELL

[1842–75]

Study for **A Seat in St James's Park, c.1869**

watercolour, graphite, pencil and bodycolour on paper, 19.3 × 23cm
inscribed: *G.J.P*
on reverse: Two pencil sketches; one of a lady's head, the other the top half of a group of three figures.
collector's mark: *H.S. Reitlinger*

P.128
PROVENANCE: H.S. Reitlinger; Leicester Galleries, from whom purchased by Gallery, November 1957.

Pinwell studied at St Martin's Lane School and at Heatherley's. Like Frederick WALKER, he began as a draughtsman on wood, illustrating books and periodicals for the Dalziel brothers. From 1865 he had an opportunity to exhibit watercolours and began by developing these from his black and white drawings.

In 1869 he was made an associate of the O.W.S. and exhibited *A Seat in St James's Park* there, developed from this study and originally based on one of his illustrations. This was so well received – despite the rather gloomy and down-at-heel appearance of the occupants of the bench – that he was elected a full member in 1870.

Martin HARDIE considers Pinwell the equal of Charles KEENE as a draughtsman but admits that the backgrounds of his watercolours 'tend to smack of the studio rather than the open air'. A long and severe illness cut short his promise when aged only thirty-three.

EJ

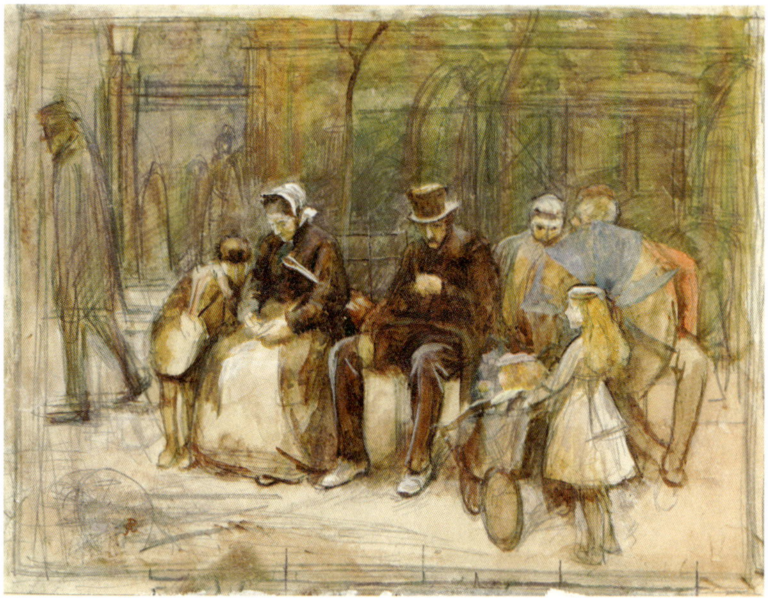

George John PINWELL
[1842–75]
After Work (Harvesters)

watercolour, pencil and bodycolour on paper, 16.2 × 12 cm
inscribed: *G.J. Pinwell*
After work GJP

P.200
PROVENANCE: P&D Colnaghi Ltd, from whom purchased by Gallery, April 1958.

HARDIE recounts a story of a prospective purchaser asking Pinwell if he used Chinese White, to which he replied: 'Chinese White! God forbid. I only use body colour'. But Hardie also notes with approval that Pinwell 'Through his search for textures in clothing, his happy appreciation of the play of light and shadow, he gives dignity and constant charm to rustic subjects'.

EJ

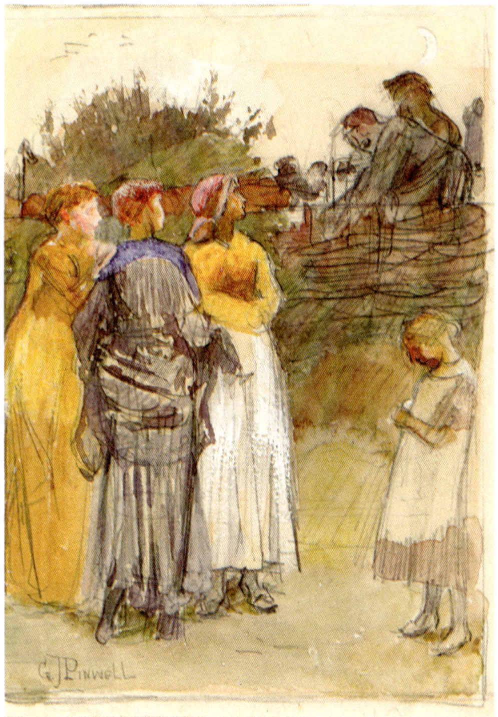

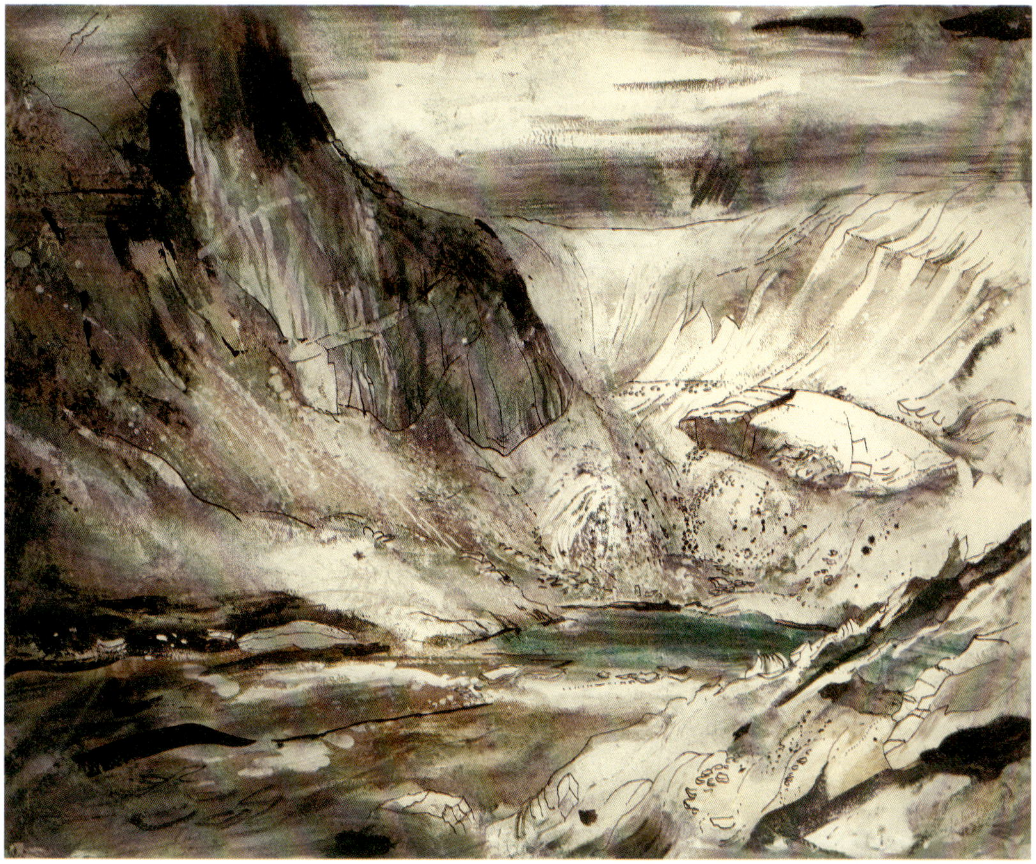

John PIPER
[1903–92]
Fynnon Loer – Frost and Snow, after 1943

watercolour and ink and bodycolour on paper, 55.3 × 69.4 cm
inscribed: *John Piper*
inscribed on reverse: *Fynnon Loer John Piper*

P.266
PROVENANCE: W.R. Jeudwine; Wilton Gallery; purchased by Thos. Agnew & Sons Ltd on behalf of Gallery, October 1958.

According to the artist, Fynnon Loer means something like 'The Well of the Moon'. It is a small lake below Carnedd Dafydd in Snowdonia.

Piper first went there in 1943 but the drawing is more likely to date from the late 1940s or early 1950s as he regularly visited a cottage near there from 1949 (information from David Fraser Jenkins, Tate Gallery, on behalf of John Piper, 1986). It was a part of Wales that clearly inspired Piper, who has captured the loneliness and intense cold of the scene before him with compelling authenticity.

EJ

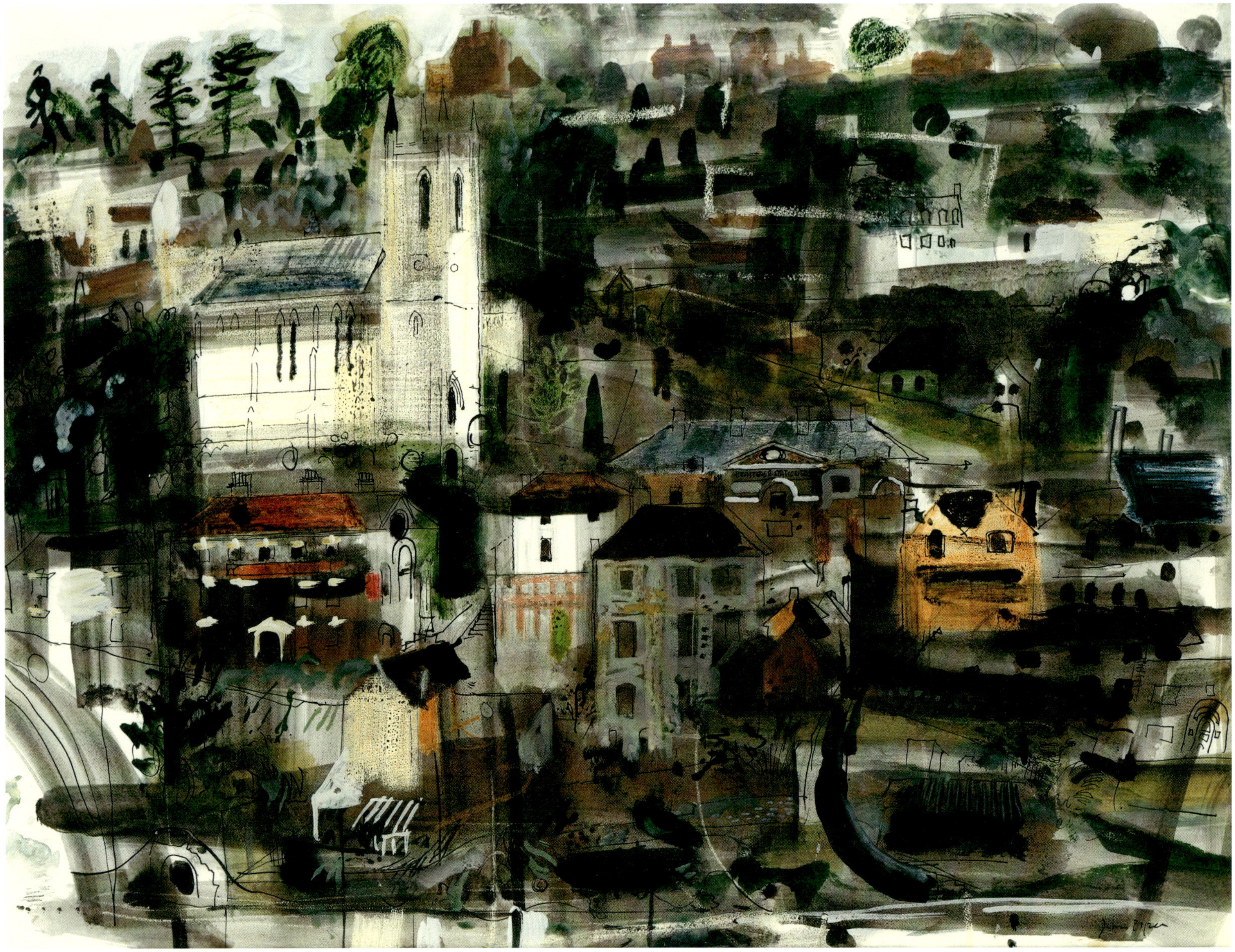

John PIPER
[1903–92]
Ironbridge, c.1957

watercolour and bodycolour on paper, 57.2 × 76.2 cm

P.143
PROVENANCE: The artist; Leicester Galleries, from whom purchased by Gallery, December 1957.
EXHIBITIONS: *New paintings and watercolours by John Piper,* London, Leicester Galleries, November 1957, no.1; *Watercolours from Bedford,* Norwich, Castle Museum, 1965, no.43; *John Piper*, London Tate Gallery, 1983, no.144.

Probably painted in the year that it was acquired. Ironbridge in Shropshire is now part of the Great Telford complex. The bridge (just visible in the bottom left corner) is the oldest cast-iron bridge in the world, built by Abraham Darby III (1750–1789) and opened in 1779.

Piper began working with his father, a solicitor, and did not turn to art until 1928. He assisted his wife, Myfanwy, on *Axis*, 1935–7 and his long association with the Curwen Press as a printmaker also dates from this time. As an Official War Artist his depiction of Britain's bombed cities revealed his great skill as an architectural draughtsman.

His strong colours and bold sense of design led to many commissions to design ballets and operas (six for Benjamin Britten), as well as stained glass including windows for the rebuilt Coventry Cathedral.

EJ

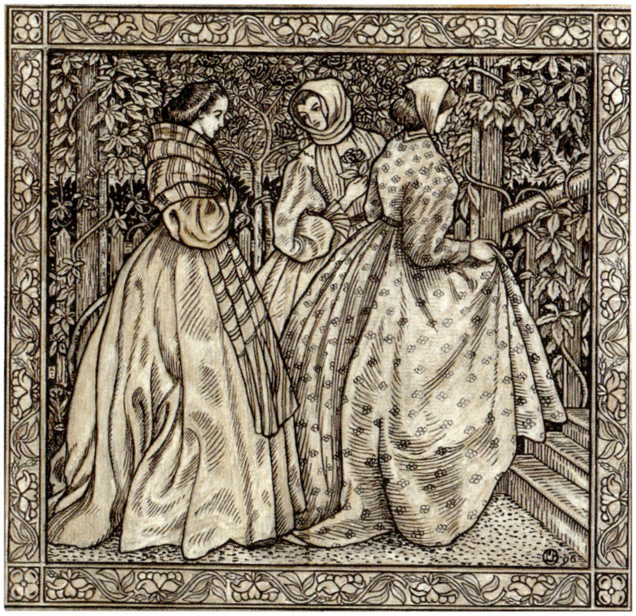

Lucien PISSARRO
[1863–1944]
Roses d'Antan, 1896

pen and ink drawing for an engraving on paper, 15.7 × 16.7 cm
inscribed: monogram, *'96*
ROSES D'ANTAN to reduce to 5½ ins

P.467
PROVENANCE: Mrs Balthazar; Piccadilly Gallery, from whom purchased by Gallery, November 1964.
EXHIBITIONS: *Lucien Pissarro – Eragny Press,* London, Leicester Galleries, 1947, no.7.

The woodcut is referred to in a letter from Camille to Lucien (letter written from Rouen on 6 November 1896), who describes it as 'very beautiful'. Later in the letter he writes: 'There are one or two lines in the dresses that could have been more supple, and there is a buckle that seems somewhat exaggerated. This is perhaps because the shadow was not introduced in the way you desired. The girl about to mount the staircase also has one harshly drawn line but it doesn't amount to much…the ornamentation is beautiful', (Rewald, (ed.), *Camille Pissarro Letters to his son Lucien*, 1943, p.299, woodcut repr. p.301).

JM

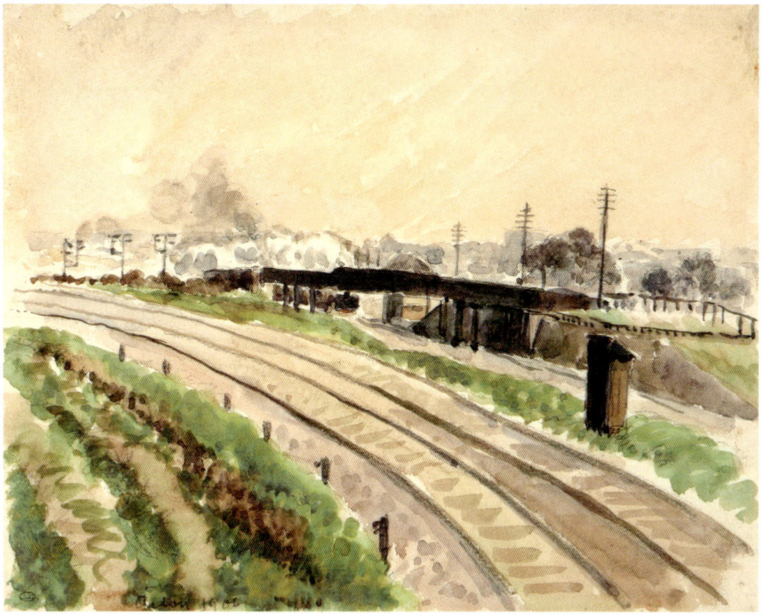

Lucien PISSARRO
[1863–1944]
The Great Western Railway, Acton, 1906

watercolour and pencil on paper, 22.1 × 28.6 cm
inscribed: monogram and *Acton 1906*

P.201
PROVENANCE: Leicester Galleries, from whom purchased by Gallery, April 1958.

Lucien was the eldest son of Camille Pissarro (1831–1903) and father of Orovida, also a painter. He was an important link between the French Impressionists and English art. He studied under his father and was influenced by Seurat.

Lucien settled in London in 1890, moving in 1893 to Epping with his wife, where he ran the Eragny Press (named after his father's final home) between 1894–1914. He exerted great influence on book illustration and printing in this country. Pissarro was naturalized 1916 but called himself a 'Channel Painter'. He was a founder member of the Camden Town group and exhibited at the R.A. from 1934.

The subject here inevitably recalls his father's pictures of railways such as *Lordship Lane Station, Dulwich*, (1871), in the Courtauld Gallery, London, painted whilst Camille was in England due to the Franco-Prussian War.

EJ

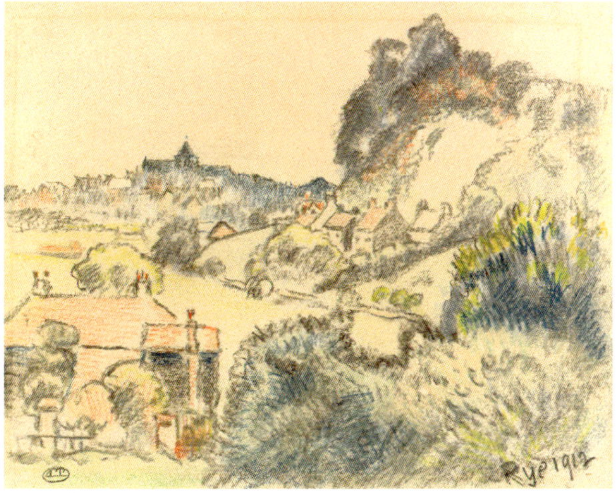

Lucien PISSARRO
[1863–1944]
Rye, 1912

pastel on paper, 12 × 15.8 cm
inscribed: *L.P* in monogram
Rye 1912

P.202
PROVENANCE: Leicester Galleries, from whom purchased by Gallery, April 1958.

Rye, in Sussex, has for long provided landscape artists with a subject to appeal to them; Van Dyck, for example, made some particularly fine drawings of Rye as early as 1630.

EJ

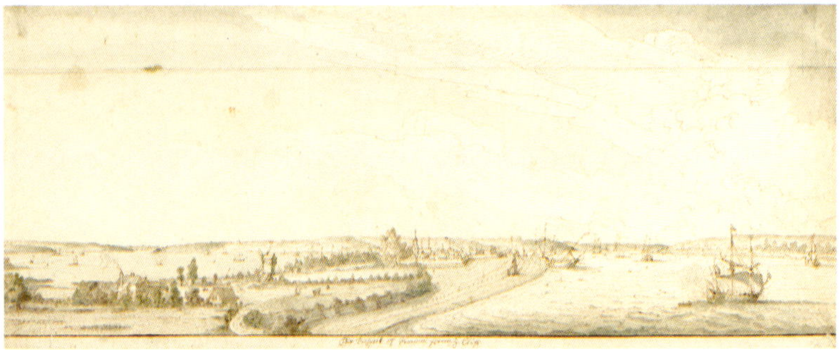

Francis PLACE
[1647–1728]
Prospect of Harwich, c.1683

pen and ink and watercolour on paper, 14.2 × 35.4 cm
inscribed: *The Prospect of Harwich from ye Cliff*

P.230
PROVENANCE: Fraser sale ? (no.141); H.W. Arthurton; R.A. Lee; P&D Colnaghi Ltd, from whom purchased by Gallery, February 1958.
EXHIBITIONS: *Watercolours and Drawings from The Cecil Higgins Art Gallery, Bedford*, London, Thos. Agnew & Sons Ltd, 1962, no.15; *English Watercolours from The Cecil Higgins Art Gallery, Bedford*, Reading, Reading Museum & Art Gallery, 1965, no.38; *Francis Place 1647 – 1728*, York, York City Art Gallery, The Iveagh Bequest, London, Kenwood House, 1971, no.36.
REFERENCES: F. Hussey, *Suffolk Invasion.The Dutch attack on Landguard Fort*, 1983, p.86, repr. p.58, as *Prospect of Harwich from Beacon Hill*.

With no. P.583, this is one of the earliest landscape drawings in the Gallery's collection. A preparatory sketch is in the Prints and Drawings Department of the National Gallery of Scotland (no. D4816).

Place, an amateur artist of private means, was much influenced by the example and work of his friend Wenceslaus Hollar, (1607–77). He was one of the first native artists interested in landscape drawing as an art form and undertook several sketching tours including those to Wales, Ireland and the Low Countries. He also etched, drew portraits in crayons and experimented in making pottery.

The delicacy and crispness of his early work was later replaced with a bolder use of shadow reflecting the influence of Claude and Rembrandt.

EJ/JM

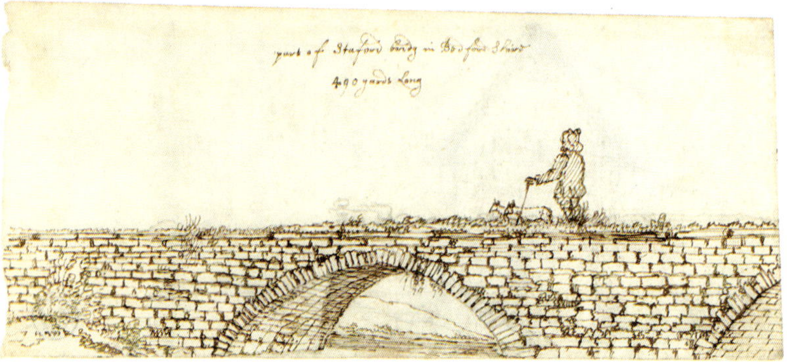

Francis PLACE
[1647–1728]
Stafford Bridge, Odell, Bedfordshire

pen and ink on paper, 9 × 20.5 cm
inscribed: *part of Staford bridg in Bedford Shire* [sic] *490 yards long*

P.583
PROVENANCE: Sir Bruce Ingram; Richard Hodgkin Ltd, from whom purchased by Gallery, May 1968.
EXHIBITIONS: *The English Tradition: an exhibition of watercolours from two private collections*, Bedford, Cecil Higgins Art Gallery, 1972, no.68.

A characteristically rapid sketch by Place and probably an early work as he appears to have begun to use colour more frequently from the 1680s onwards. The figure here adds much to the appeal of the scene.

Mentioned in Pevsner's guide to *Bedfordshire, Huntingdon and Peterborough,* 1982, p.132, 'Stafford Bridge across the Ouse, originally of four arches and 13th century'. In fact the title is misleading as Odell is a good two miles away and the bridge lies between Pavenham and Oakley.

There are two other drawings by Place of bridges in Bedfordshire, one being a large finished drawing in Leeds City Art Gallery. The other is a small sketch pasted onto page 81 of the large Place sketchbook in the V&A (E.1496–1931).

EJ

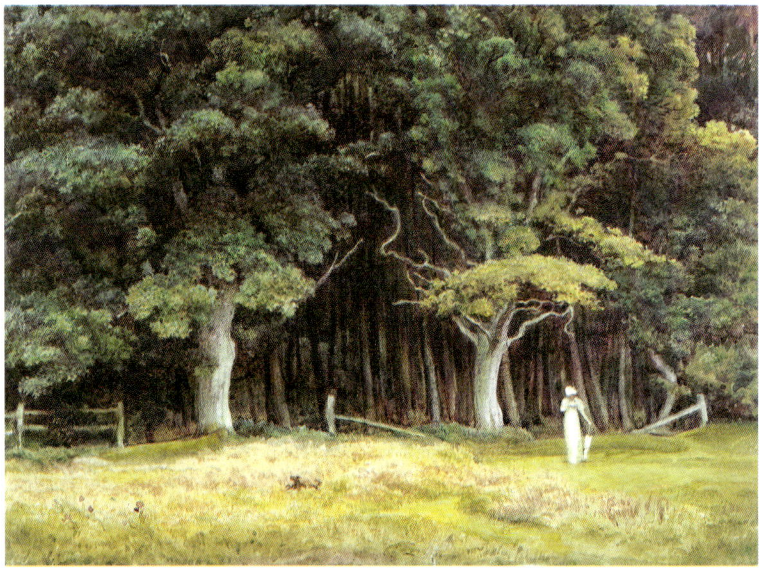

Sir Edward John POYNTER, Bt., P.R.A., R.W.S
[1836–1919]
The Wooded Landscape, c.1900

watercolour on paper, 26.5 × 36 cm

P.291
PROVENANCE: Leicester Galleries, from whom purchased by Gallery, April 1959.

Poynter has been described as 'the consummate late Victorian artist-administrator'. He trained in Rome and showed at the R.A. from 1861, his painting devoted to subjects from ancient history often on a very large scale. He was the first Slade Professor (1871–5) and later both Director of the National Gallery and President of the R.A. In his former role he supervised the opening of the Tate Gallery.

EJ

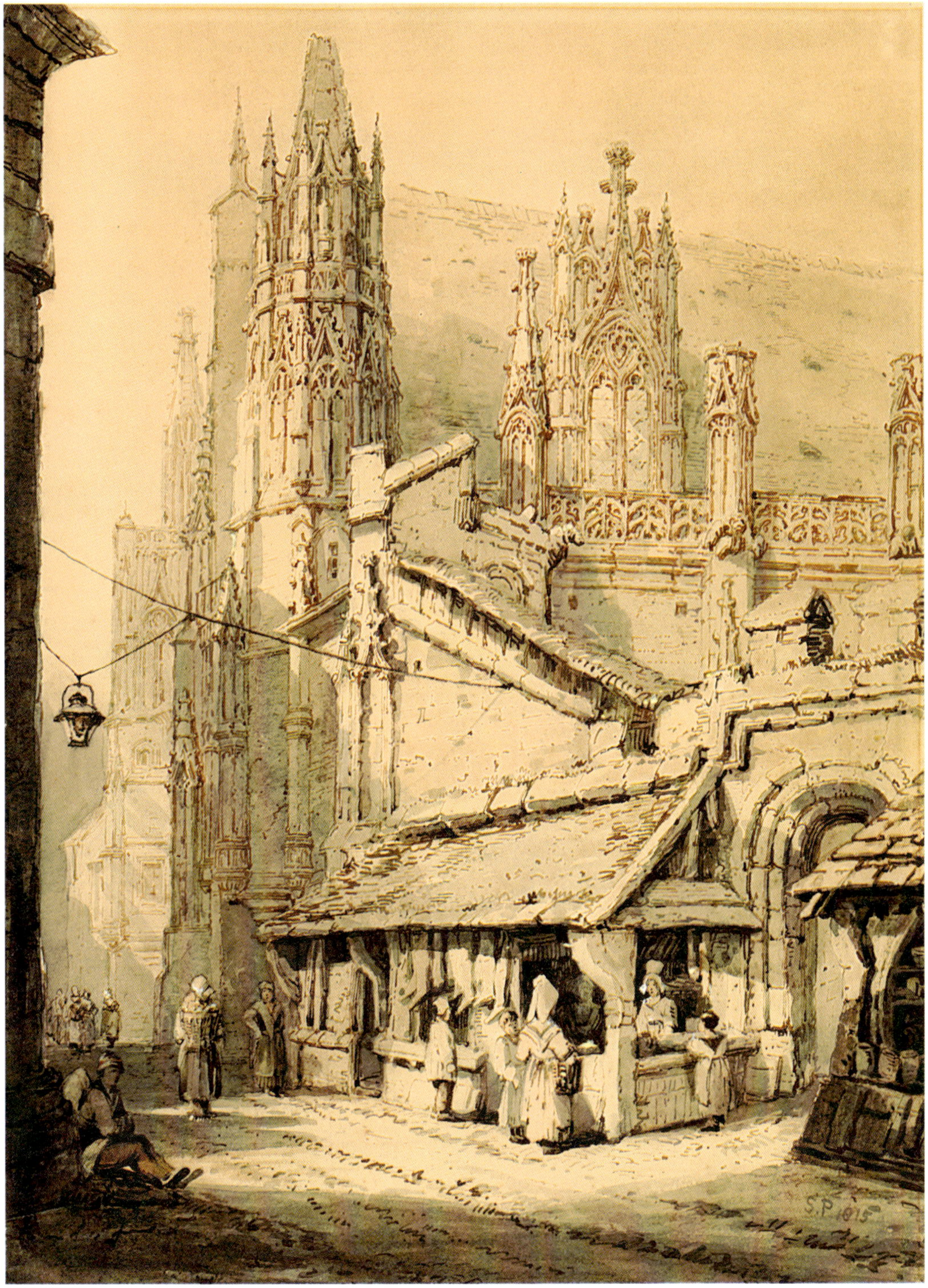

Attributed to **Samuel PROUT**
[1783–1852]
Palais de Justice, Rouen (formerly known as
A Continental Cathedral and Market Scene),
c.1819–21

pen and brown ink with washes of grey, heightened with white on light brown paper, 43 × 31.6 cm
inscribed: *S.P 1815*

P.348
PROVENANCE: C. Kersley ?; P&D Colnaghi Ltd, from whom purchased by Gallery, July 1960.

When bought this was titled *A Continental Cathedral and Market Scene*, but the view was identified by Richard Lockett, author of *Samuel Prout*, 1985. Lockett advises that Prout never signed S.P and did not go to France until 1819. Lockett dates this 1819–21 and compares it to *Street View with St Laurent, Rouen* in the Manchester City Art Gallery. Prout painted several other watercolours of the Palais de Justice but one formerly attributed to him in the Whitworth Art Gallery, Manchester, dated 27 September 1817, is now ascribed to EDRIDGE, whose drawings are closely connected to Prout's at this date.

EJ

James PRYDE

[1866–1941]

Spanish Fantasy, c. 1902

bodycolour on paper, 17.5 × 12 cm
inscribed: *Pryde*

P.203
PROVENANCE: Wilton Gallery, from whom purchased by Gallery, April 1958.
EXHIBITIONS: *The Victorian Romantics,* London, Leicester Galleries, 1949, no.147; *Watercolours and Drawings from The Cecil Higgins Art Gallery, Bedford,* London, Thos. Agnew & Sons Ltd, 1962, no.89; *James Pryde 1866–1941,* Edinburgh, Scottish National Gallery of Modern Art, 1992, no.17 as *Spanish Phantasy.*
REFERENCES: National Galleries of Scotland, *James Pryde,* 1992, p.92, no.17, repr. as *Spanish Phantasy,* c.1899, listed as a tribute to Velázquez. A companion gouache (private collection) exists but is badly water-damaged.

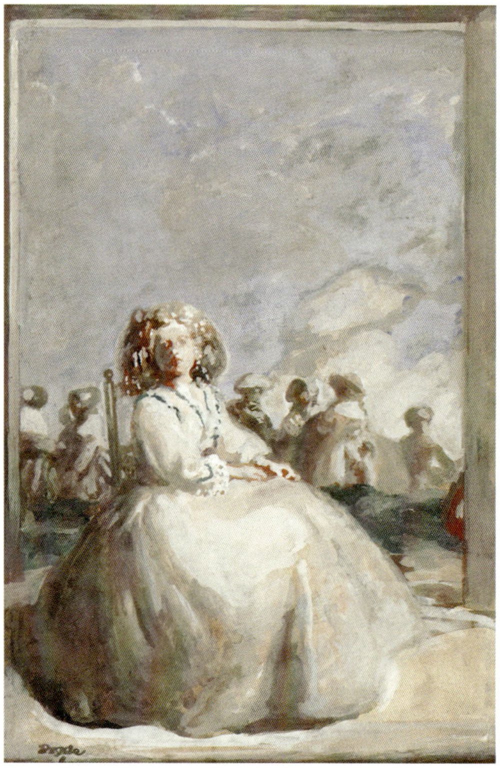

The Gallery's records date this c. 1902 whereas the 1992 exhibition prefers c. 1899 and points out that this was intended as a tribute to Velázquez, the tercentenary of whose birth fell in 1899. Indeed the voluminous skirts of the sitter are somewhat reminiscent of those worn by the Infanta Margarita in her portraits now in the Kuntshistoriches Museum, Vienna.

The catalogue also mentions a companion gouache, *Scene after Velázquez,* but this is now badly water-stained.

EJ

James PRYDE

[1866–1941]

The Unknown Corner, c. 1912

bodycolour on paper, 18.3 × 15.3 cm

P.449
PROVENANCE: Piccadilly Gallery, from whom purchased by Gallery, May 1963.
EXHIBITIONS: *Watercolours from Bedford,* Norwich, Castle Museum, 1965, no.44; *James Pryde 1866–1941,* Edinburgh, Scottish National Gallery of Modern Art, 1992, no.60.
REFERENCES: National Galleries of Scotland, *James Pryde,* 1992, p.100, no.60.
NOTES: There is an oil version of this c.1912, oil on canvas, first exhibited at the Goupil Gallery, 1912, and as *The Balcony* in Pryde's one-man show at the Leicester Galleries, 1933 (dimensions 85.8 x 70.2 cm).

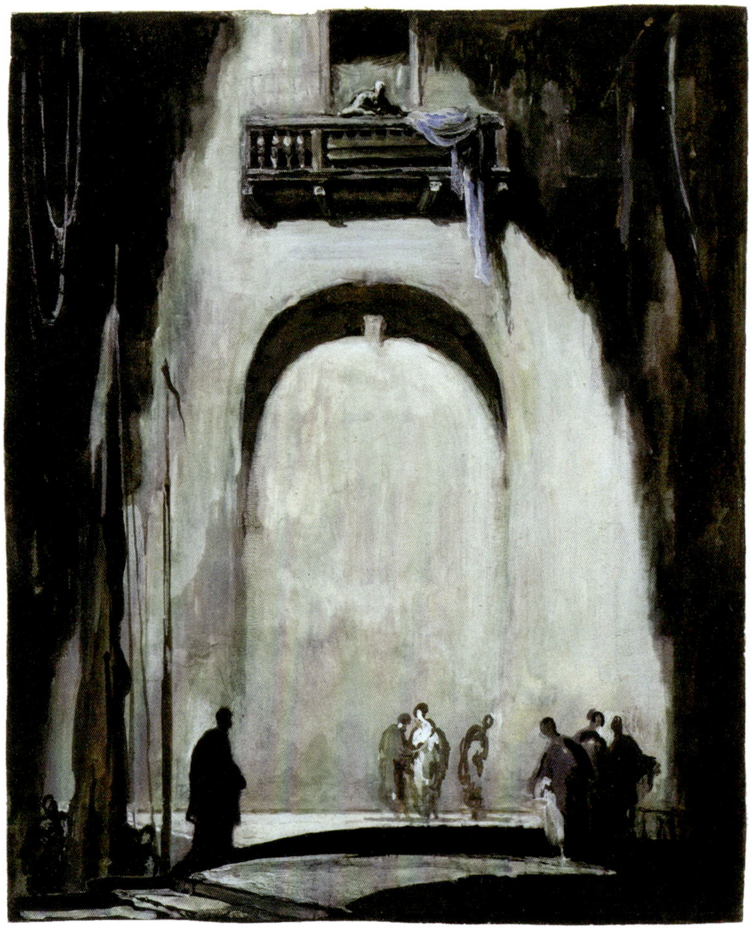

Painted c. 1912, this is a study for an oil (85.8 × 70.2 cm) exhibited at the Goupil Gallery in 1912 and now belonging to Robert Fleming Holdings (no.559 in the 1992 exhibition).

Pryde was born in Edinburgh, the son of the headmaster of Queen Street Ladies College. Through his mother he was descended from two Scottish artists, Robert Scott Lauder and J.E. Lauder. He studied at the Royal Scottish Academy and then in Paris, for three months under Adolphe – William Bouguereau (1825–1905), before settling in London in 1890. There he joined his brother-in-law, William NICHOLSON, designing posters under the name of 'J. & W. Beggarstaff'. He produced little after 1925 although he designed sets for Paul Robeson's *Othello* in 1930.

EJ/JM

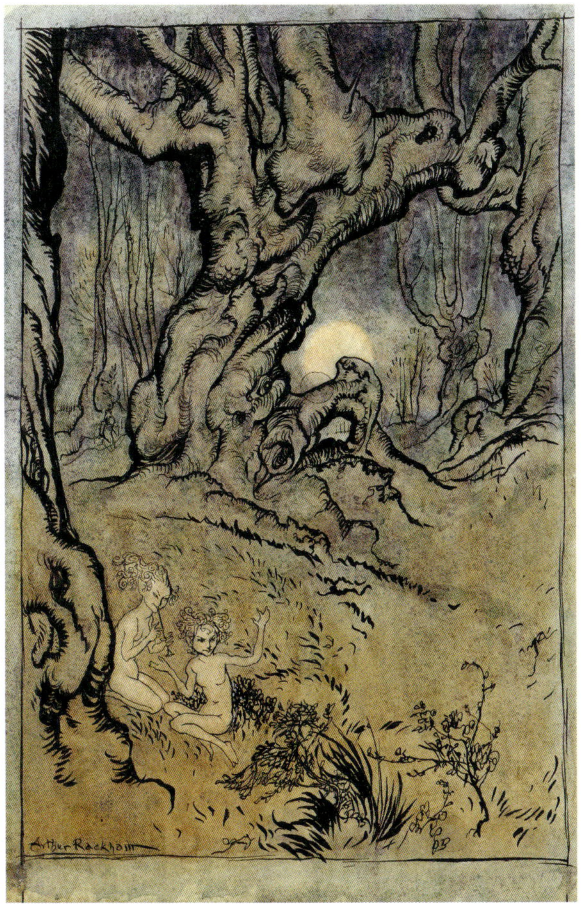

Arthur RACKHAM, R.W.S.
[1867–1939]
Moonlight – Fairies in A Wood, Illustration for a poem by Percy Maskeras

pen and ink with watercolour and bodycolour on buff paper, 25.8 × 16.8 cm
inscribed: *Arthur Rackham*

P.204
PROVENANCE: Leicester Galleries, from whom purchased by Gallery, April 1958.

Rackham studied at the Lambeth School of Art before he began work as an illustrator for magazines and books, among them Grimm's *Fairy Tales*, 1900, *Rip van Winkle*, 1905, and many others.

In these volumes he showed his fertile imagination coupled with a rare quality of line and tone. His fairyland was peopled by elves and sprites, dwarfs and gnomes, while his landscapes were full of gnarled and twisted trees whose branches had a menacing air as in this example. Besides his illustrative work, he exhibited many fine landscape watercolours and was elected R.W.S. in 1908.

EJ

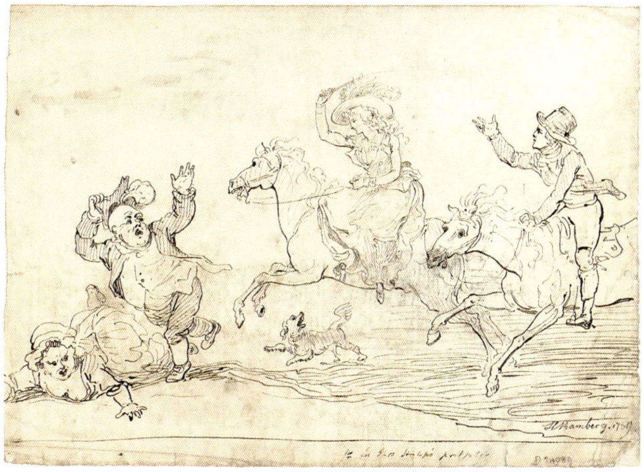

Johann Heinrich RAMBERG
[1763–1840]
The Chase, 1789

pen and dark brown ink on paper, 30.4 × 24.7 cm
inscribed: *H Ramberg 1789*
'ft (?) *Sir Thos Hislop's portfolio, D24089*

P.336
PROVENANCE: C.A. Carnshaw; P&D Colnaghi Ltd, from whom purchased by Gallery, April 1960.

The inscription is puzzling but may mean that this was copied from a Rowlandson drawing *in* Sir Thomas Hislop's portfolio or, possibly, that the copy was made *for* the portfolio.

Ramberg was invited to England in 1781 by George III and trained at the R.A. Schools. He painted rustic genre scenes and subjects such as *The Sailor's Farewell*, as well as a few caricatures. Perhaps a pupil of Benjamin WEST and also BARTOLOZZI, he exhibited at the R.A. 1782–88, but then left England to devote himself to engraving and etching, returning to Hamburg.

EJ

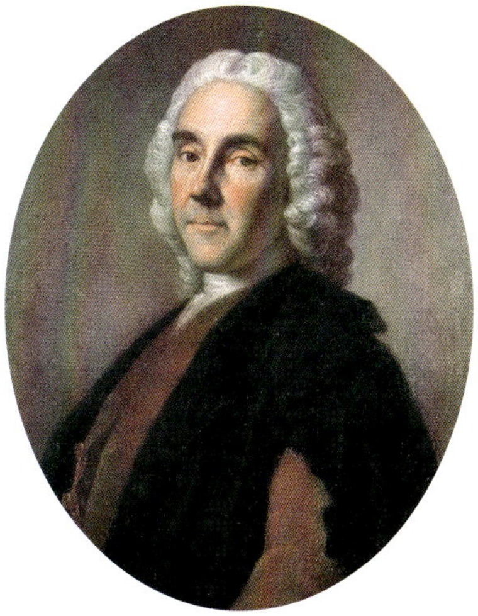

After **Allan RAMSAY**
[1713–84]
Portrait of Alexander Munro, M.D., after 1749

pastel on paper, 25 × 20.3 cm

P.300
PROVENANCE: Gifford Kerr, Edinburgh; his sale Dowell's, Edinburgh 26 July 1957 (no.179); P&D Colnaghi Ltd, from whom purchased by Gallery, October 1959.
EXHIBITIONS: *Watercolours and Drawings from The Cecil Higgins Art Gallery, Bedford*, London, Thos. Agnew & Sons Ltd, 1962, no.24.
REFERENCES: A. Smart, *Allan Ramsay – A Complete Catalogue of his Paintings*, 1999, p.160, no.369ii – where it is listed as a copy perhaps after the engraving by J.Basire 1775 after the 1749 portrait in oil of Munro in a private collection (another oil version was bought by the Scottish National Portrait Gallery in 1990). Other versions are listed by Smart and still more are known to exist. The status of these, as regards authenticity including the Gallery's pastel, needs further research. Ramsay rarely used pastel but the Scottish National Portrait Gallery has a self-portrait in pastel which is reported as being 'rather more freely handled than the Cecil Higgins' portrait'.

Alexander Munro (1697–1767) was the second eminent physician in the family and arguably the greatest. After training in London, Paris and Leyden, he returned to Edinburgh where he was appointed Professor of Anatomy at the age of only twenty-three. He is remembered for his practical teaching, published writings and his important role in medical politics. He was also largely reponsible for the creation of the Royal Infirmary in Edinburgh. When he died, the importance of his work led to Edinburgh replacing Leyden as the world centre of medical teaching.

EJ

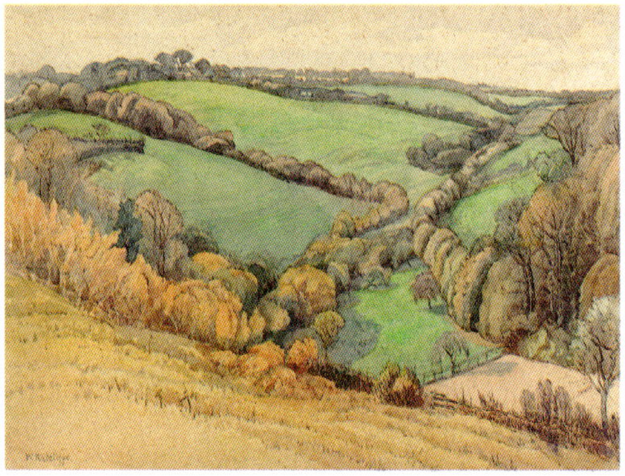

William RATCLIFFE
[1870–1955]
Wilkings Farm, Herts , c.1915–22

watercolour on paper, 38.6 × 51.9 cm
inscribed: *W. Ratcliffe*

P.359
PROVENANCE: Leicester Galleries, from whom purchased by Gallery, July 1960.
EXHIBITIONS: *Drawings of the Camden Town Group*, London, Arts Council Gallery, 1961, no.90; *The Camden Town Group*, Bedford, Cecil Higgins Art Gallery, 1969, no.44.

A painter, wood engraver and designer, Ratcliffe studied at the Manchester School of Art and worked designing wall-papers for almost twenty years. In 1908 he met Harold GILMAN who persuaded him to take up painting. He was a founder member of the Camden Town Group and later of the London Group. Ratcliffe lived latterly in Letchworth, Hertfordshire, and painted in oils infrequently after 1921. This drawing shows traces of the influence of Robert BEVAN.

EJ

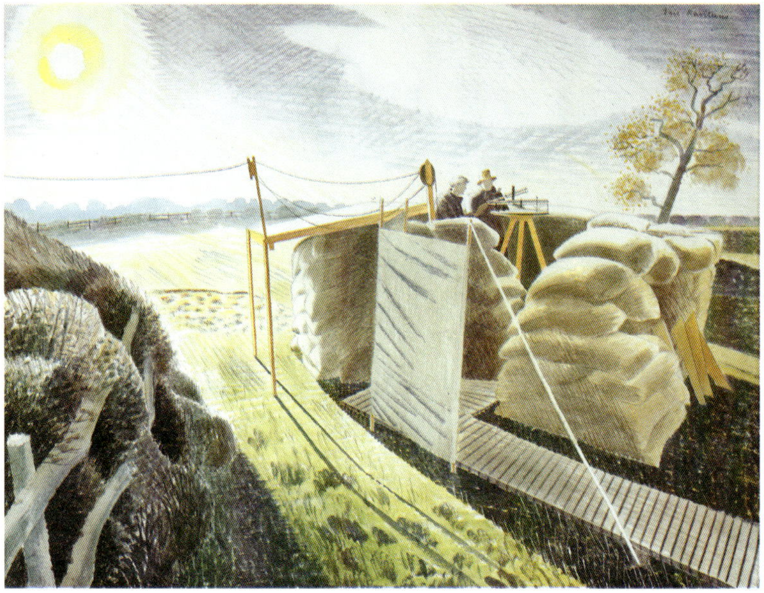

Eric RAVILIOUS
[1903–42]
Observer's Post, c.1939–40

watercolour and graphite on paper, 43.4 × 58.4 cm
inscribed: *Eric Ravilious*

P.223
PROVENANCE: Leicester Galleries; Miss Raymond; Redfern Gallery, from whom purchaed by Gallery, April 1958.
EXHIBITIONS: *Contemporary British Artists*, London, Leicester Galleries, 1941, no.3; *Eric Ravilious*, Sheffield, Graves Art Gallery, 1958, no.79.

Ravilious studied at the Design School of the R.C.A., 1922–5, meeting Edward BAWDEN; whilst there he came under the influence of Paul NASH. He and Bawden painted murals for the Refreshment Room, Morley College, London, 1928 (destroyed in an air-raid, 1940). Bawden credited Ravilious for his 'skill in organising space and in creating in it figures to be sent dancing and swinging in ballet movement across the walls'.

He was a watercolourist mainly of topographical subjects, many of which lack figures, giving them a haunted look. He also worked as an engraver and designer from 1937 designing china for Wedgwood.

At the outbreak of the Second World War, he joined the Royal Observer Corps, but in February 1940 he became an Official War Artist attached to the Royal Marines. He died on active service in September 1942 when he tragically disappeared on a mission over Iceland.

EJ

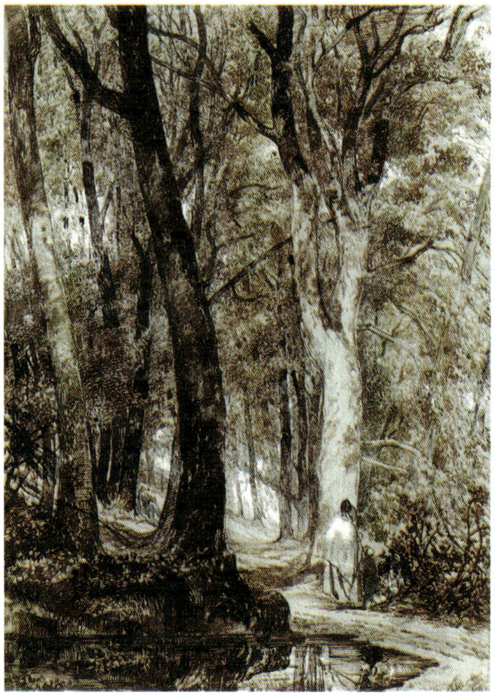

Richard REDGRAVE, R.A
[1804–88]
Interior of a Wood

pencil, pen and ink and chalk on blue paper, 32.8 × 24.7 cm
inscribed: *Rich. Redgrave*

P.333
PROVENANCE: Professor Isaacs, from whom purchased by Gallery, January 1960.

Redgrave entered the R.A. Schools in 1826 and enjoyed a distinguished career as an artist, art historian and administrator. He was the first Keeper of Paintings at the South Kensington Museum (now V&A) and Surveyor of the Queen's Pictures. Also co-author with his brother Samuel of *A Century of Painters of the English School*, 1866. He was elected R.A. in 1851 but wrote in 1856: 'I regret to find that I am so identified with office work that it is almost forgotten that I am a painter'. To judge from similar drawings of woods in the V&A, this example may very well depict the woods at Abinger in Surrey near Redgrave's home.

EJ

Alan REYNOLDS
[b.1926]
Studies for **Coil Composition 1) Old Man's Beard**
2) Teazles 3) Group based on field Poppy and Old Man's Beard, 1954

ink and watercolour on paper, 59 × 33.9 cm
inscribed: *Reynolds '54*
Top left hand*: Old Man's beard. this turns the hedgerow like Old Silver in Autumn and Winter and has an extraordinary effect on Tonal perspective. Centre group are of Teazle. This appears to grow consciously in a comparatively symmetrical fork. The central stem almost invariably bears the finest head. this was taken from the crown of a plant about 14 ft height. The lower right hand is a group based upon the heads of the common field poppy.*

P.216
PROVENANCE: Wilton Gallery, from whom purchased by Gallery, April 1958.
REFERENCES: A. Ambrose, *Discovering English Watercolours,* 1987, p.91, pl.32.

These studies of plants are a feature of Reynolds' preparation for his paintings at this date. Here they include Old Man's Beard, Teazles and Field Poppy accompanied by a detailed inscription.

EJ

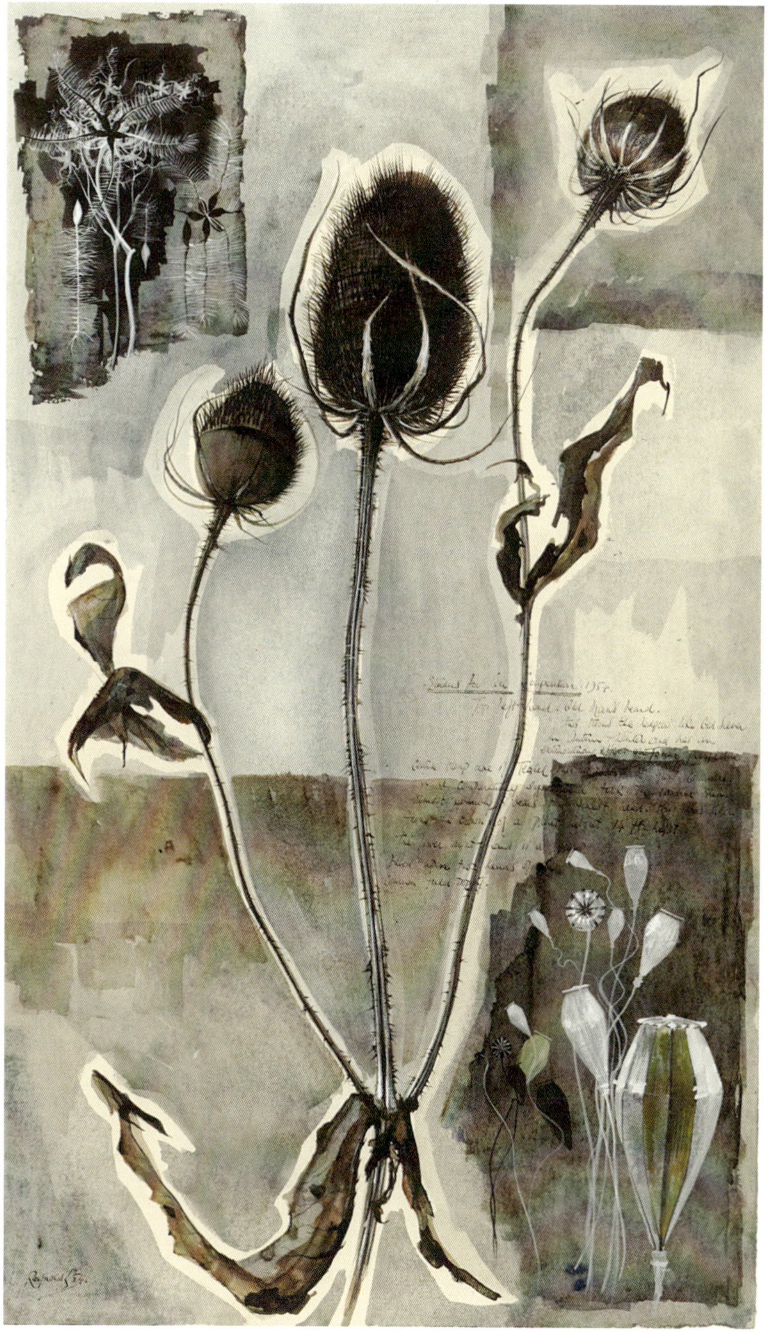

Alan REYNOLDS
[b.1926]
Moonlight, 1957

watercolour on paper, 25 × 31.9 cm
inscribed: *Reynolds 57* and *35*

P.217
PROVENANCE: Leicester Galleries, from whom purchased by Gallery, 1958.
EXHIBITIONS: *Watercolours and Drawings from The Cecil Higgins Art Gallery, Bedford,* London, Thos. Agnew & Sons Ltd, 1962, no.109.

Reynolds made his reputation as a painter of romantic landscapes somewhat in the tradition of Samuel PALMER. His work was eagerly collected and highly praised by, among others, Kenneth Clark. He was trained at Woolwich Art School and at the R.C.A. He exhibited with great success in the 1950s at the Redfern Gallery, London, and at Durlacher Bros., New York. In 1960 he developed a completely abstract style, teaching at St Martin's School of Art from 1962.

EJ

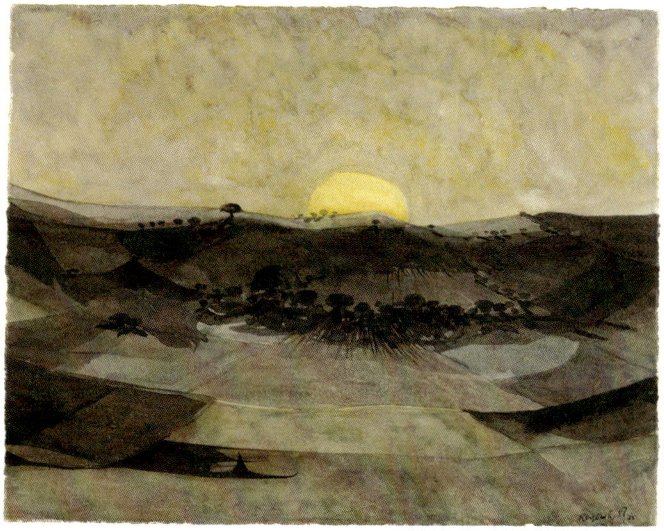

Ceri RICHARDS, C.B.E.
[1903–71]
The Flowering Skull, c.1953

watercolour with scratching out on paper, 32.2 × 40.2 cm

P.249
PROVENANCE: The artist, from whom purchased by Gallery, 1958.
EXHIBITIONS: *Watercolours from Bedford*, Norwich, Castle Museum, 1965, no.45.

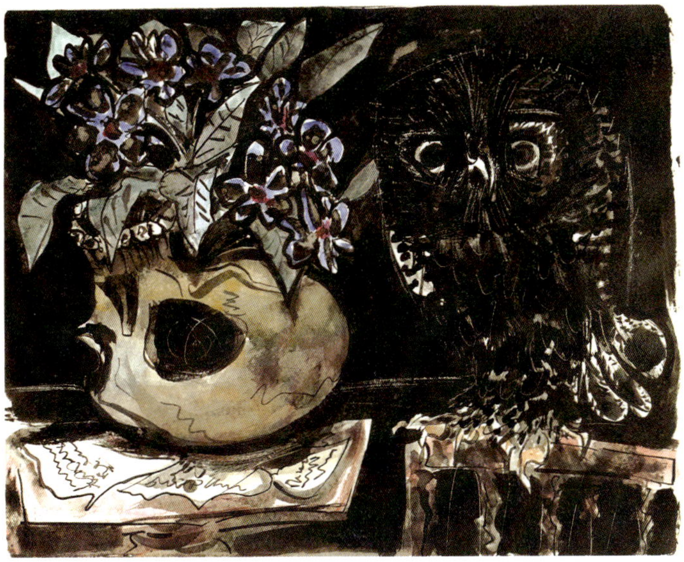

See the entry for *The Flowering Pen* (P.250) for the source of these two watercolours. Born at Duvant near Swansea, Richards studied at the Swansea School of Art 1921–4 and then at the R.C.A. 1924–7. He was influenced by Surrealism in the 1930s but took little part in the movement. Inspired by Picasso's constructions and by Max Ernst, he made reliefs using wood and metal. Much of his most striking work derives from music and poetry as in the examples owned by the Gallery.

EJ

Ceri RICHARDS, C.B.E.
[1903–71]
The Flowering Pen, c.1953

watercolour and pen and ink on paper, 39.5 × 56.7 cm

P.250
PROVENANCE: The artist, from whom purchased by Gallery, 1958.
EXHIBITIONS: *Watercolours and Drawings from The Cecil Higgins Art Gallery Bedford*, London, Thos. Agnew & Sons Ltd, 1962, no.117; *Watercolours from Bedford*, Norwich, Castle Museum, 1965, no.45.

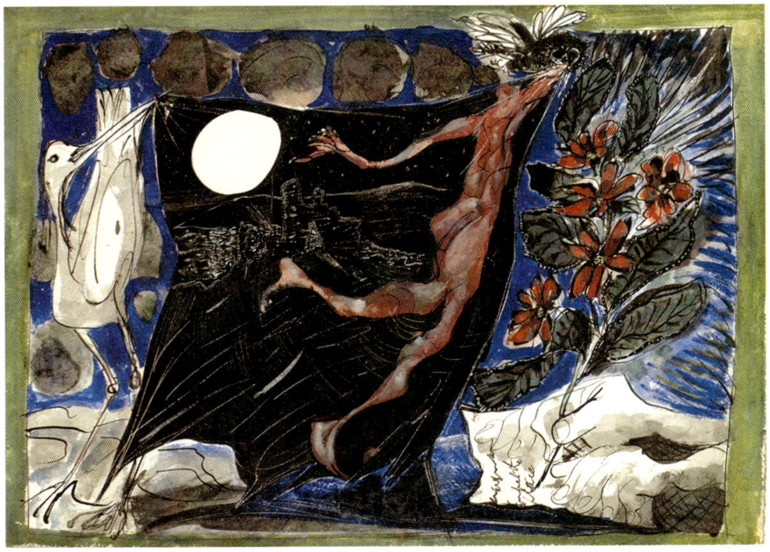

Painted c.1953, this is one of several studies of a dropcloth design for the memorial reading of Dylan Thomas's poems at the Globe Theatre in January 1954 (Thomas having died in America in November 1953). See also *The Flowering Skull*, (P.249).

On both, scraps of writing are visible. The words here are from *The Author's Prologue*, – *Hark I trumpet the place, from fish to jumping hill !* The running figure is set against the landscape of Richards' native Gower in South Wales with the ruins of Pennard Castle on the dunes and, beyond, the moonlit bay with Oxwich Point.

There are recurrent themes and motifs in all Richards' works inspired by Thomas' poetry which, while not directly illustrating images from the poems, indicate the powerful affinity the artist felt with the verse. The owl, the heron, the owl or heron bearing a shroud, the skull sprouting forth life, the blossoming pen of the poet: these reminders of darkness and death, but also fertility and renewal, are images and metaphors that Richards made his own.

EJ

Ceri RICHARDS, C.B.E.
[1903–71]
Claire de Lune, 1964

bodycolour and collage on paper, 32.7 × 27.2 cm
inscribed: *Ceri Richards 1964*

P.531
PROVENANCE: Marlborough Fine Art, from whom purchased by Gallery, May 1966.
EXHIBITIONS: *Nolan, Piper, Richards*, London, Marlborough Fine Art, 1966, no.7.

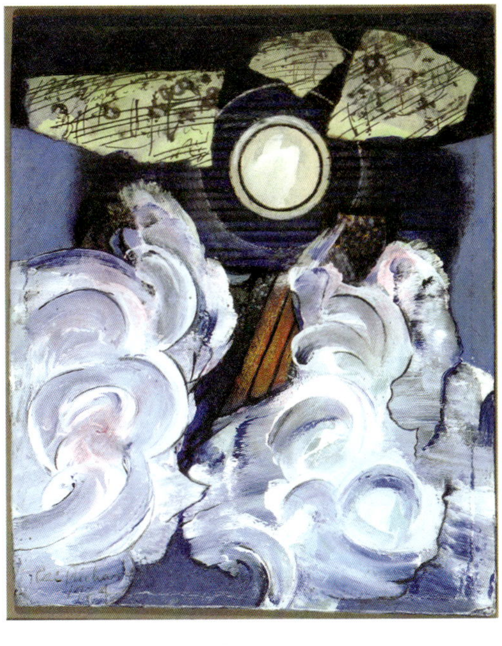

Richards was himself an accomplished pianist, and music frequently provided him with a source for his painting. This gouache is part of an ongoing series of drawings, prints and paintings begun in about 1959 and continued throughout the 1960s. Claude Debussy (1862–1918) was one of his favourite composers and Richards made many works on the themes of his piano preludes; in this case *Claire de Lune*, from the *Suite Bergamasque*, 1886–90, (published 1905). Corresponding to the scraps of poetry in the Dylan Thomas drawings (P.249 & 250), here are fragments of a music manuscript, floating like clouds beside the moon; below are waves and breakers.

EJ

The compiler owes grateful thanks to Rhiannon Gooding, the artist's daughter, for help with the entries for these three drawings.

Sir Albert RICHARDSON, K.C.V.O., P.P.R.A., F.R.I.B.A, F.S.A.
[1880–1964]
Sell and Willshaw's Shop Front, High Street, Bedford, 1930

pen, ink and watercolour on paper, 37.3 × 49.4 cm
inscribed: *High Street Bedford aug 27 1930 a E Richardson*

P.506
PROVENANCE: Bequeathed by the artist to Gallery, July 1964.
EXHIBITIONS: *Exhibition of Water-Colours and Drawings by Sir Albert Richardson,* Bedford, Cecil Higgins Art Gallery, 1963, no.8.

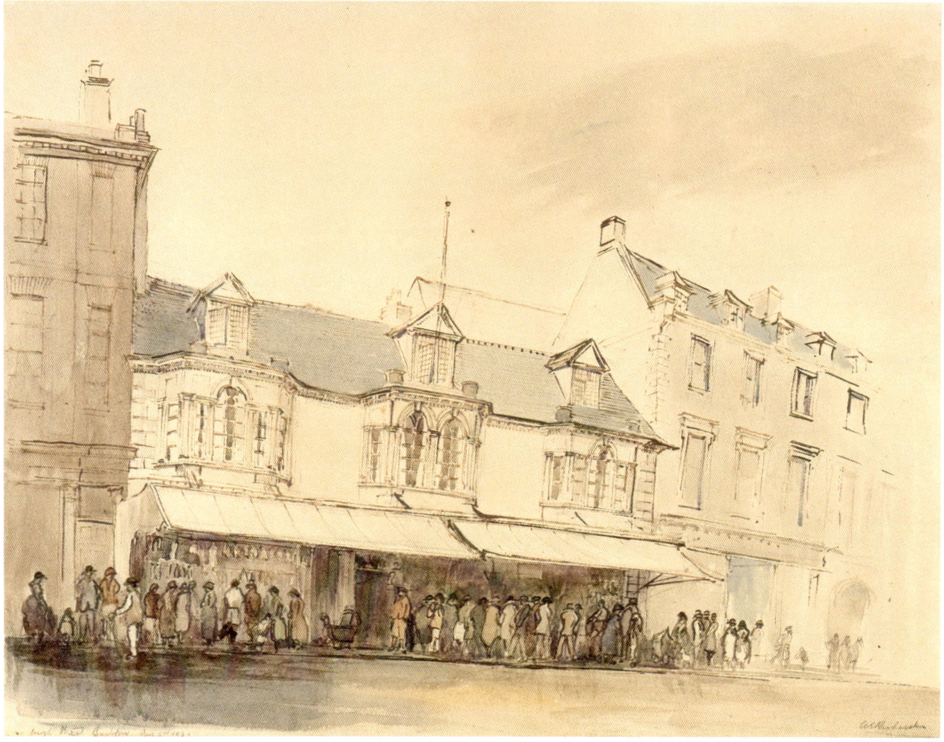

This 17th century building at 42–44 High Street, Bedford, was usually referred to as 'Sell and Willshaw's' (after the fishmonger's business who occupied the ground floor). In the 1860s John Usher, the architect, had his offices there. The building was demolished in 1964.

Albert Richardson was born in London and lived for much of his life in Ampthill near Bedford. He became President of the R.A. in 1954, only the fourth architect to be elected to this position since the R.A.'s foundation. He was unusual in being a prolific painter and exhibitor in watercolours. Famous amongst his designs was Bracken House, the old Financial Times building (near St Paul's Cathedral), completed in 1958. When first built it was largely ignored by the architectural establishment, but thirty years later became the first post-war building to be listed, thus preventing its re-development.

Sir Albert Richardson had strong connections with the Cecil Higgins Art Gallery, sitting on the committee which in November 1944 issued a survey of findings for its future development of the Gallery. Most famously he railed in the press against the acquisition of an Alan DAVIE painting by the Gallery (see P.313), going on to describe non-figurative art as 'entering an age of barbarism'.

JM

Sir Albert RICHARDSON, K.C.V.O., P.P.R.A., F.R.I.B.A, F.S.A.
[1880–1964]
Summer 1851. A Fantasy inspired by Edward German's 'Merrie England', 1934

pen, ink and blue and brown wash on paper, 48.4 × 70.2 cm

P.505
PROVENANCE: Bequeathed by the artist to Gallery, July 1964.
EXHIBITIONS: *The Watercolours of Sir Albert Richardson,* Luton, Luton Museum and Art Gallery, 1963, no.121; *Exhibition of Water-Colours and Drawings by Sir Albert Richardson,* Bedford, Cecil Higgins Art Gallery, 1963, no.74.

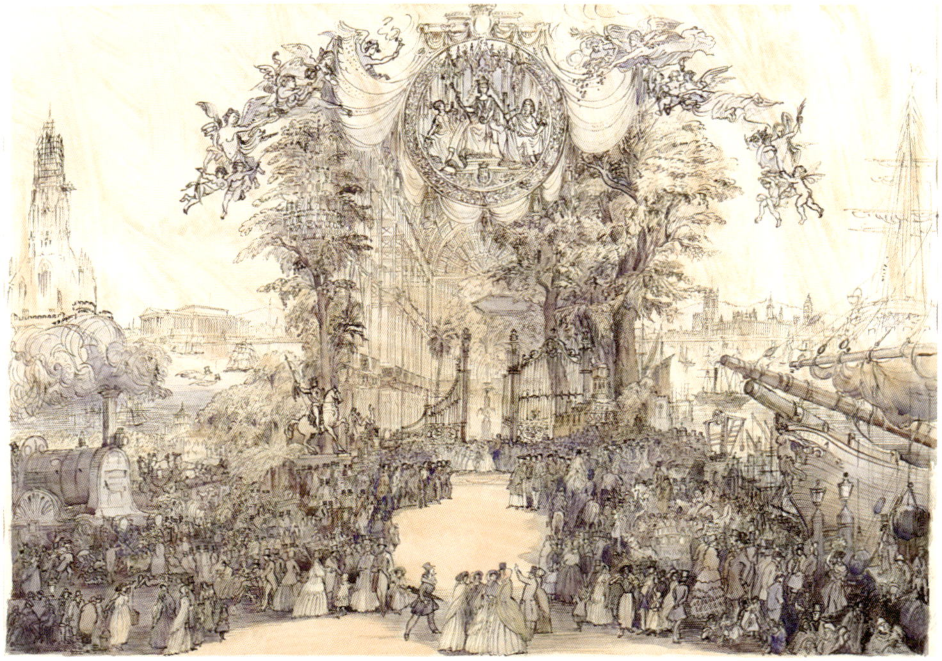

This fantasy, drawn in 1934, was inspired by *Merrie England*, the light opera by Edward German (1862–1936). The medley of buildings include, on the left, Truro Cathedral under construction with, next on the right, St George's Hall, Liverpool. In the centre is the opening of the Crystal Palace with the Houses of Parliament on the right in the distance.

Richardson was an architect who designed many buildings in London. He was Professor of Architecture at the Bartlett School of Architecture, University College, London, 1919–46. After the war he designed new buildings in the City and restored damaged ones including St James's, Piccadilly. He was created P.R.A. in 1954, and knighted, 1956. Richardson was local to the Gallery, living in Ampthill, near Bedford.

EJ

Charles RICKETTS, R.A.
[1866–1931]
Ruined Pylon, an illustration to Oscar Wilde's 'The Sphinx', c.1890

pen and ink on paper, 18.4 × 14.9 cm

P.542
PROVENANCE: Charles Shannon; Mrs Virginia Surtees; Maas Gallery, from whom purchased by Gallery, November 1966.
EXHIBITIONS: *Works by Orpen, McEvoy, Ricketts,* Manchester, Manchester City Art Gallery, 1933, no.193, as *The Ruined Pylon: illustration for "The Sphinx",* 1st Series; *Early English Watercolours,* London, Maas Gallery, 1966, no.82.

The Sphinx, a poem of eighty-seven couplets, occupied Wilde (1854–1900) over many years; he later told Robert Ross that he had begun work on it in Paris in 1874 as a result of reading Edgar Allan Poe and Swinburne, for the poem 'spanned the gnomic message of *The Raven* and the imputation of ageless profligacy in *Dolores*'. Wilde worked on it again in Oxford in 1890 and it was finally published in 1892 in a deluxe edition illustrated by Ricketts and dedicated to Marcel Schwob, Wilde's principal guide in Paris.

Ricketts was born in Geneva, the son of a retired English naval officer, and grew up in Italy and France. In 1882 he entered the Lambeth School of Art where he met his lifelong companion Charles Shannon (1863–1937). Throughout the 1890s he was primarily active in book illustration, design and typography, coming close to rivalling BEARDSLEY. A notable connoisseur, he and Shannon were significant collectors, many of the works they owned now being in the Fitzwilliam Museum, Cambridge.

EJ/JM

Charles RICKETTS, R.A.
[1866–1931]
Theatrical Costume Study, 1919

watercolour and pencil on paper, 46.1 x 29.1 cm
inscribed: *R* and *To a Drinkwater from C Ricketts June 1919*

P.498
PROVENANCE: A.E. Drinkwater; Maas Gallery, from whom purchased by Gallery, June 1965.
EXHIBITIONS: *The Last Romantics: The Romantic Tradition in British Art, Burne-Jones to Stanley Spencer,* London, Barbican Art Gallery, 1989, no.301.

The production for which this sumptuous costume was designed has not yet been identified. The drawing is dedicated to A.E. Drinkwater, father of the poet and playwright John Drinkwater, who was an actor-manager.

EJ/JM

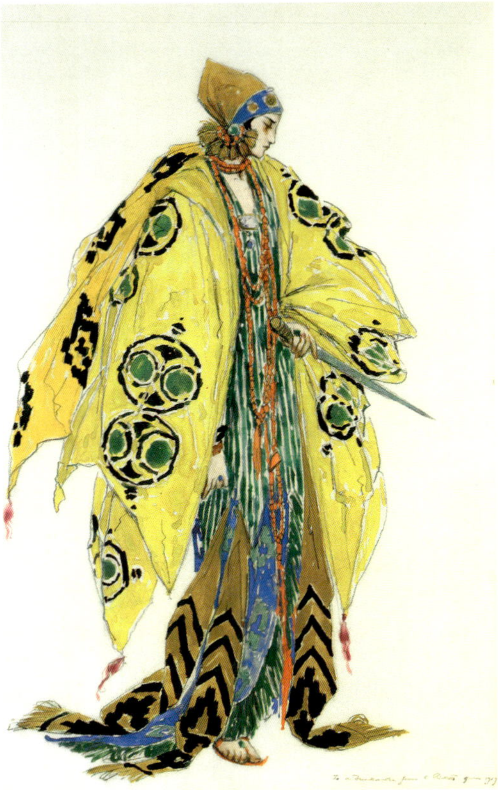

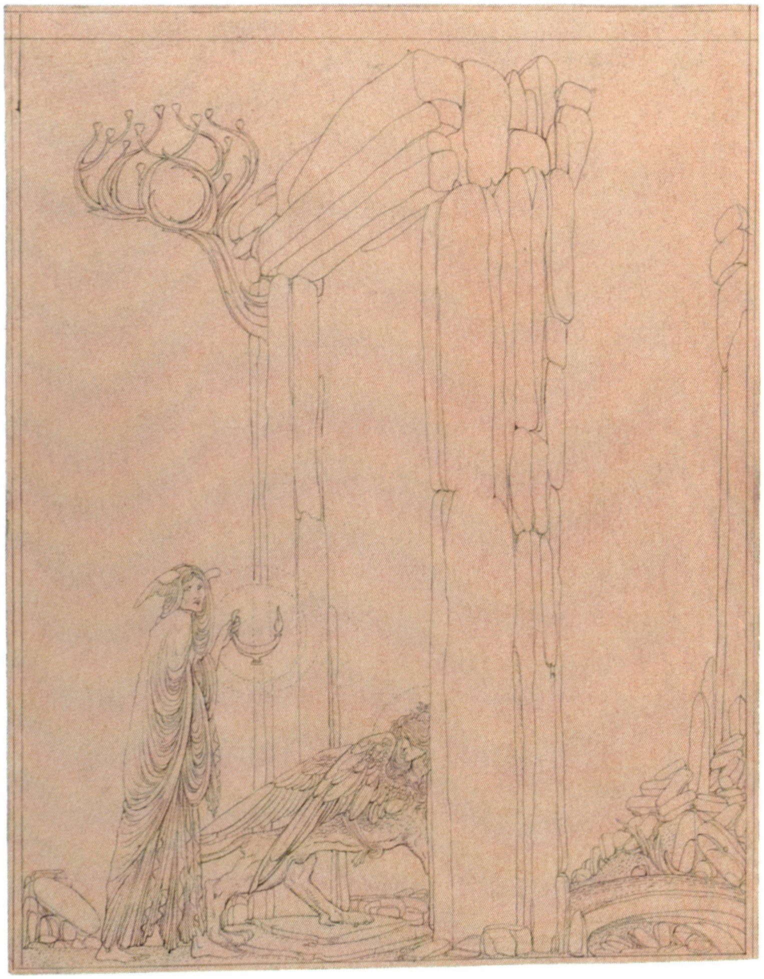

Bridget RILEY, C.B.E.
[b.1931]
Untitled no.10, c.1965

bodycolour and pencil on graph paper, 74.3 × 46.6 cm
inscribed: *Bridget Riley*
Intermediary bands all cold 12 and numbered above bands left to right 12,11,10,9,8,7,6,5,4,3,2,0,2,4,6,8,10,12

P.534
PROVENANCE: Robert Fraser Gallery, from whom purchased by Gallery, July 1966.

Riley was born in London but spent her early years in Cornwall and Lincolnshire. She trained at the Goldsmith's College from 1949–52 and at the R.C.A., 1952–55, followed by work in illustration and design.

Her move into abstraction began in 1960, exploring the possibilities of optical dynamism within her work. Between 1964 and 1967 she worked on a series that explored the possibilities of 'warm' and 'cold' greys, before introducing a more expressive use of colour in the late 1960s.

JM

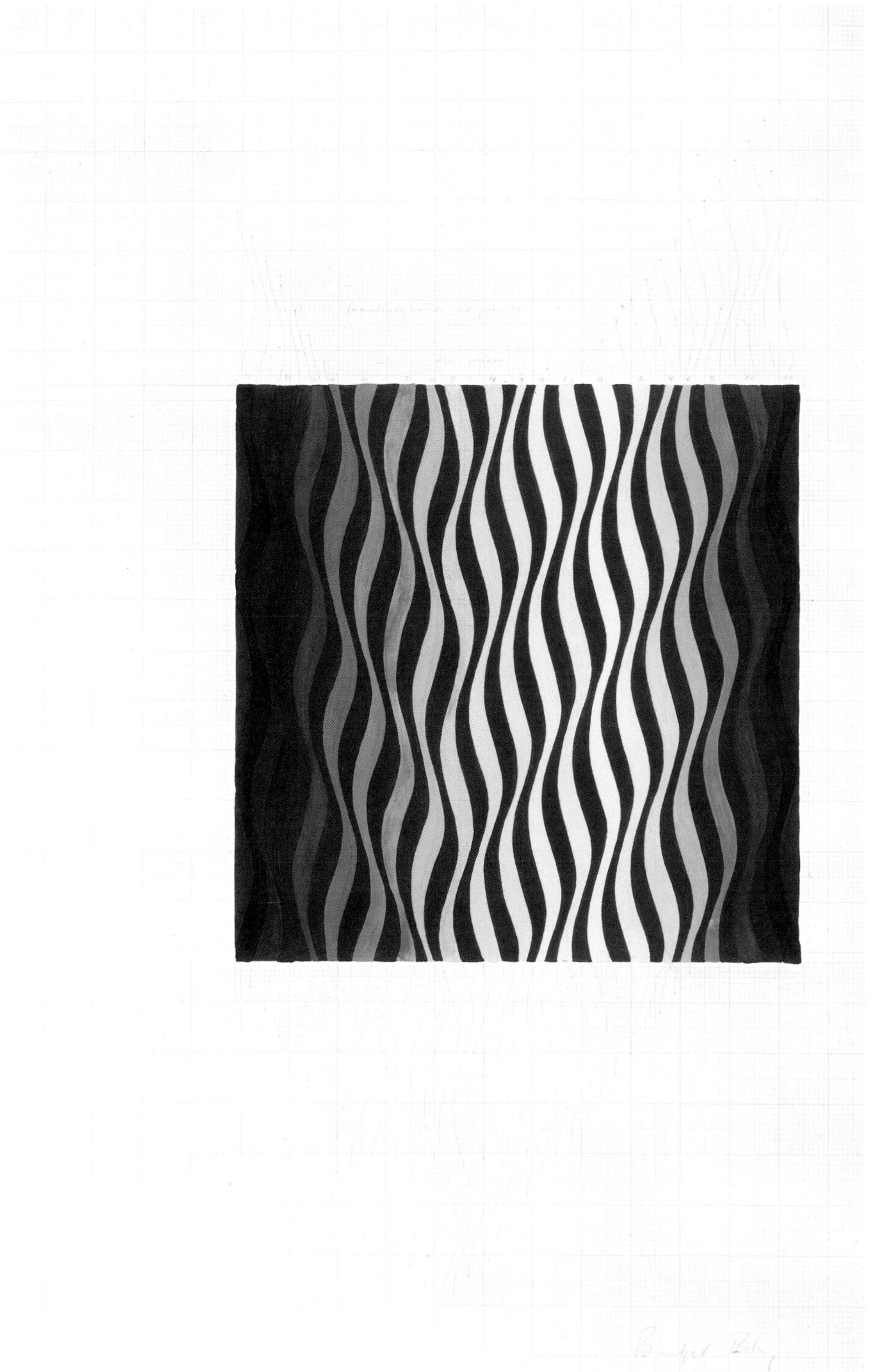

David ROBERTS, R.A.

[1796–1864]

Chapel of the Convent of St Saba, 1839

watercolour and pen and ink heightened with white on grey paper, 34.4 × 24.3 cm
inscribed: *David Roberts 1839*
April 5th 1839 Chapel of the Convent of St Saba

P.154
PROVENANCE: Appleby Brothers; P&D Colnaghi Ltd, from whom purchased by Gallery, January 1958.
EXHIBITIONS: *David Roberts,* London, Barbican Art Gallery, 1986–7, no.155.
REFERENCES: H. Guiterman & B. Llewellyn (eds.), *David Roberts,* 1986, p.117, no.155.

This famous monastery, about eleven miles south-east of Bethlehem, was founded by St Saba, c.478 A.D. This is a study for a finished drawing (untraced) used for a lithograph (vol.II, pl.50) in Roberts' six volume publication covering *The Holy Land, Syria Idumea, Arabia, Egypt and Nubia*, 1842–9.

Roberts' diary, quoted in the Barbican catalogue, describes how the monks allowed him to make this sketch even though a service was about to begin.

EJ

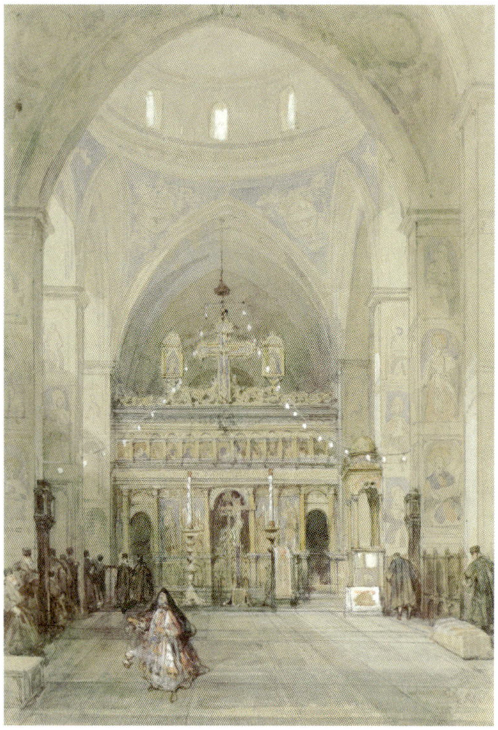

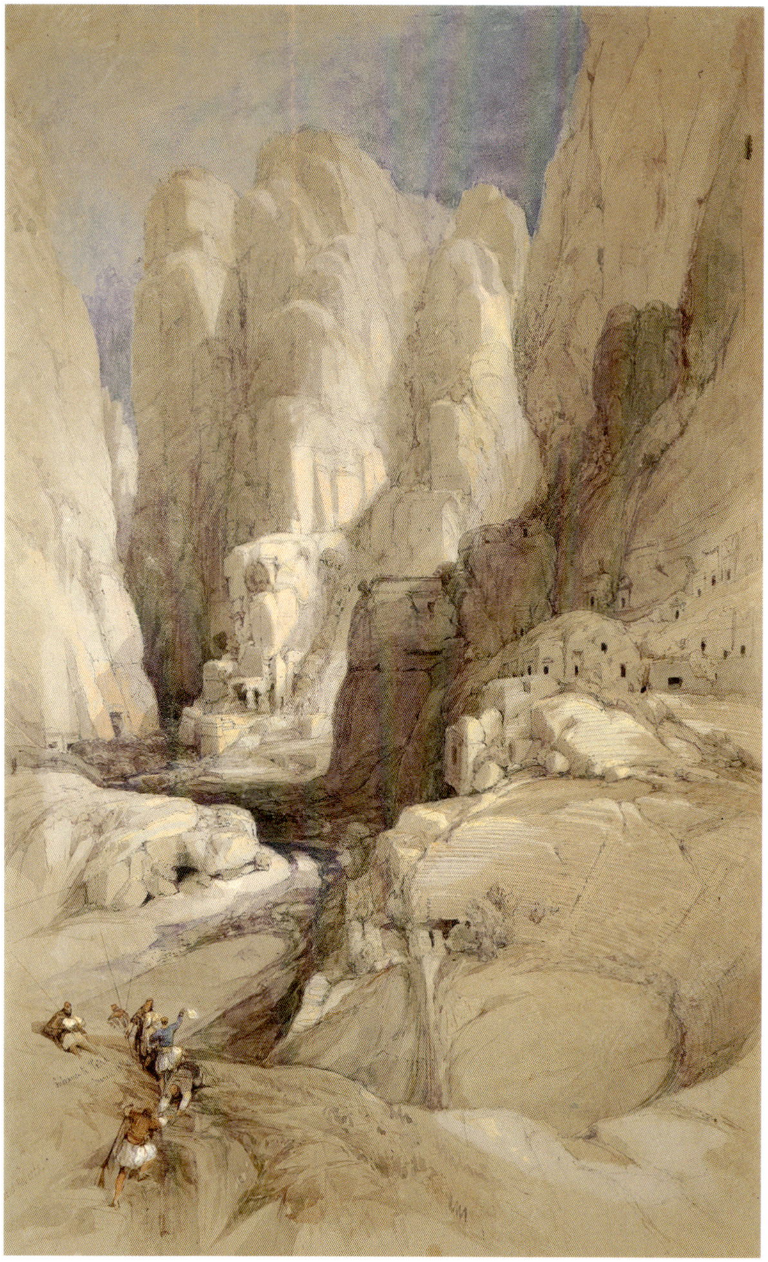

David ROBERTS, R.A.

[1796–1864]

Entrance to Petra, 1839

watercolour with lead heightened with white on light grey paper, 54 × 34 cm
inscribed: *David Roberts 1839*
Entrance to Petra, March 10th 1839

P.337
PROVENANCE: G. Norman; P&D Colnaghi Ltd, from whom purchased by Gallery, April 1960.
EXHIBITIONS: *Primitives to Picasso,* London, R.A., 1962, no.404; *English Watercolours from The Cecil Higgins Art Gallery, Bedford,* Reading, Reading Museum & Art Gallery, 1965, no.41; *British Watercolours: A Golden Age 1750–1850*, Kentucky, J.B. Speed Art Museum, 1977, no.77; *On the banks of the Jordan: British 19th Century Painters,* 1986–7, Amman, Jordan National Gallery, 1986–7, no.38.
REFERENCES: S. Somerville, *British Watercolours: A Golden Age, 1750–1850,* 1977, p.106, repr. p.107, no.77.

Roberts was at Petra from 6–10 March 1839. On the 10th he noted in his Journal: 'Heavy rain today, notwithstanding I have made several sketches of this extraordinary place' (see J. Ballantine, *Roberts*, 1866, p.123). These were later worked up into finished watercolours as the basis for a group of fourteen lithographs. In a modern booklet on the series this watercolour is engraved as *Petra – The Theatre*.

Roberts became a tremendous traveller: from France in 1831, he ventured further afield to Spain and Tangier 1832–3; in 1838 he went to Egypt and the Holy Land. These journeys produced many oils and watercolours (see also P.154) and the basis for several series of engravings of which *Views in the Holy Land, Syria Idumea, Arabia, Egypt and Nubia*, containing about 250 plates and published in six volumes from 1842–9 at a cost of £50,000, is the most celebrated. All these activities contributed to the considerable fortune that Roberts made.

EJ

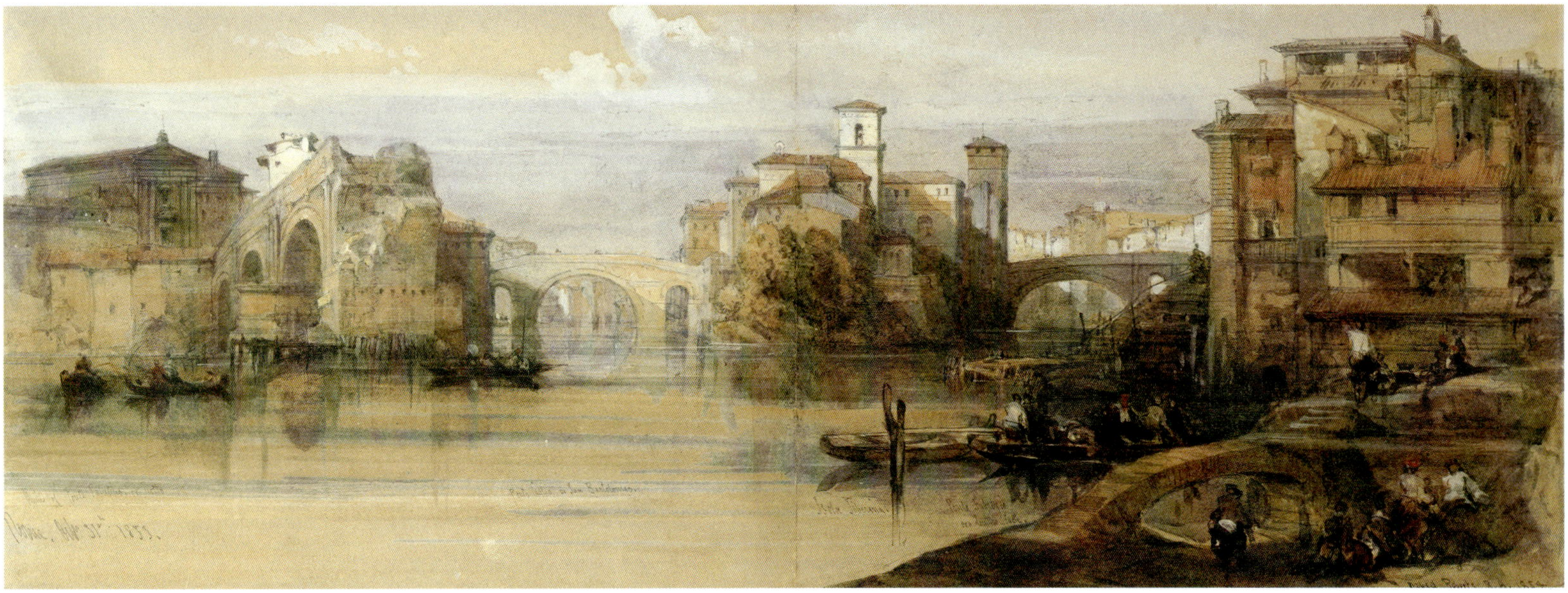

David ROBERTS, R.A.
[1796–1864]
The Ponte Rotto and Isola Tiberina, Rome
(Formerly known as Ruins of Ponte Palatine; Rome 1853/54), c.1853–54

watercolour heightened with white and pencil, on two joined sheets of paper, 24.1 × 65.7 cm
inscribed and redated: *David Roberts. R. A. 1854.*
Rome Oct 31st 1853 Ruins of Ponte Palatino, or Rotto Ponto Cestio. or San Bartolomeo. Isola Tiberina. Ponte Fabrizio or a Quattro Capi.

P.256
PROVENANCE: B.B. MacGeorge by 1901; by descent J.B. MacGeorge, sale Morrison, McChlery & Co, Glasgow 16 May 1958 no.126; bought Thos. Agnew & Sons Ltd, from whom purchased by Gallery, October 1958.
EXHIBITIONS: *International Exhibition*, Glasgow, Glasgow Art Gallery & Museum, 1901, no.873 as *Ruins of Ponte Palatine*, (lent by B.B. MacGeorge); *The Scottish National Exhibition*, Edinburgh, 1908, no.731 as *Rome*, (lent by B.B. MacGeorge); *Scottish Exhibition of National History, Art and Industry*, Glasgow, 1908, no. 655, (lent by B.B. MacGeorge); *Annual Watercolour Exhibition*, London, Thos. Agnew & Sons Ltd, 1959, no.90; *Watercolours and Drawings from The Cecil Higgins Art Gallery, Bedford*, London, Thos. Agnew & Sons Ltd, 1962, no. 34; *English Watercolours from The Cecil Higgins Art Gallery Bedford*, Reading, Reading Art Gallery, 1965, no.39; *David Roberts*, London, Barbican Art Gallery, 1987, no.195; *Imagining Rome*, Bristol, Bristol City Museum and Art Gallery, 1996, no.23.
REFERENCES: H. Guiterman & B.Llewellyn (eds.), *David Roberts*, 1986, p.123, pl.58; M. Liversidge & C. Edwards (eds.), *Imagining Rome; British Artists and Rome in the Nineteenth Century*, 1996, p.102, fig. 23.

On the left are the three arches then surviving of the ancient Pons Aemilius, built 179–142 B.C., the first stone bridge in Rome and one of the great engineering feats in the city's history. It was damaged by a flood in 1598, hence its name Ponte Rotto (broken bridge).

Roberts painted three oils of the bridge from a different viewpoint and a drawing from yet another viewpoint. One oil is now in the Beaverbrook Art Gallery, Frederictown, New Brunswick, Canada.

A watercolour by William CALLOW, taken from a spot nearer to Roberts' showing the Ponte Rotto and the Ponte Cestio, is in the Gallery's collection (P.318).

EJ

David ROBERTS, R.A.
[1796–1864]
Edinburgh Castle from Greyfriars

watercolour heightened with white on paper, 33.2 × 48.5 cm
inscribed: *David Roberts RA*
The Castle from Greyfriars

P.317
PROVENANCE: Sotheby's lot 58; P&D Colnaghi Ltd, from whom purchased by Gallery, January 1960.
EXHIBITIONS: *English Watercolours from The Cecil Higgins Art Gallery, Bedford*, Reading, Reading Museum & Art Gallery, 1965, no.40; *David Roberts*, London, Barbican Art Gallery, 1986–7, no.26.

According to the *Edinburgh Illustrated Guide*, Greyfriars Churchyard 'is of awesome monumental grandeur. The Adam family of architects are buried there'. In 1638, the National Covenant binding the signatories to resist the introduction of Popery and Episcopacy by Charles I was signed there.

Roberts, born near Edinburgh, served a long apprenticeship to a house painter before he obtained a post as scene painter at Drury Lane theatre in London in 1822. He continued working for the theatre until 1830, then turned to topography and architecture in both oil and watercolour achieving immediate success.

This fine drawing must date from after 1841 when Roberts was elected R.A. It combines his gift for accurate observation with spirited handling.

EJ

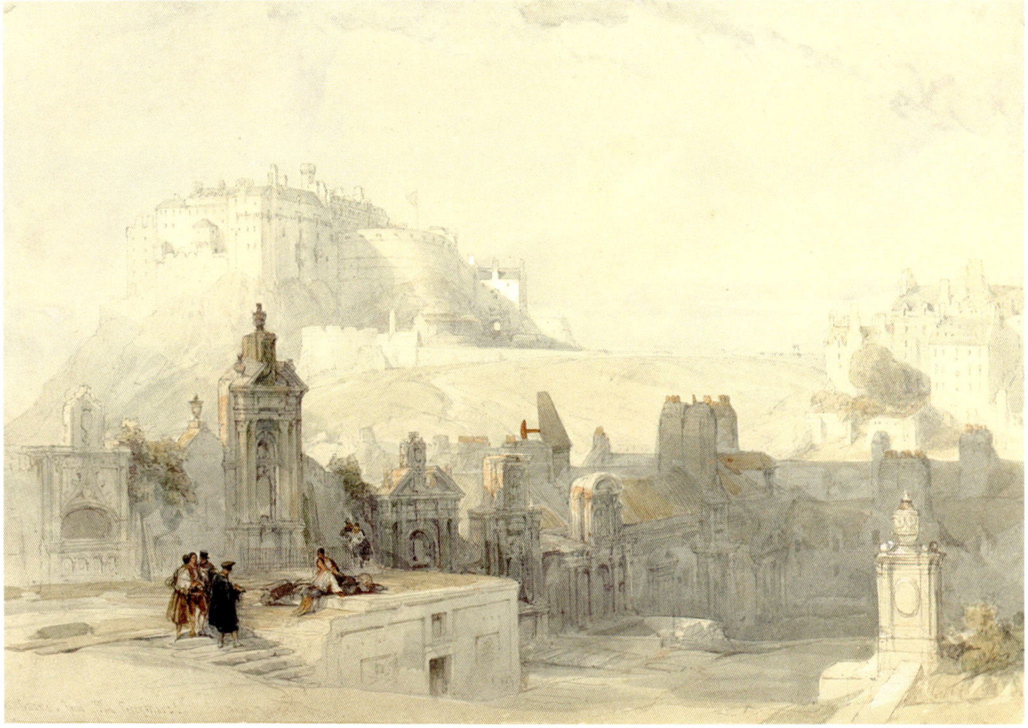

William ROBERTS, R.A.
[1895–1980]
The Battering Ram, c.1919

watercolour and pencil on paper, 36 × 36.1 cm
inscribed: *William Roberts.*

P.251
PROVENANCE: Purchased at Sotheby's sale (various properties), July 1958, no.2.
EXHIBITIONS: *William Roberts A.R.A.: retrospective exhibition,* London, Tate Gallery, (Arts Council), 1965, no.133.

Drawn c.1919 and clearly influenced by Wyndham LEWIS. The 1965 exhibition catalogue notes that the title is that used by Sotheby's but comments that it is 'almost certainly incorrect.'

EJ

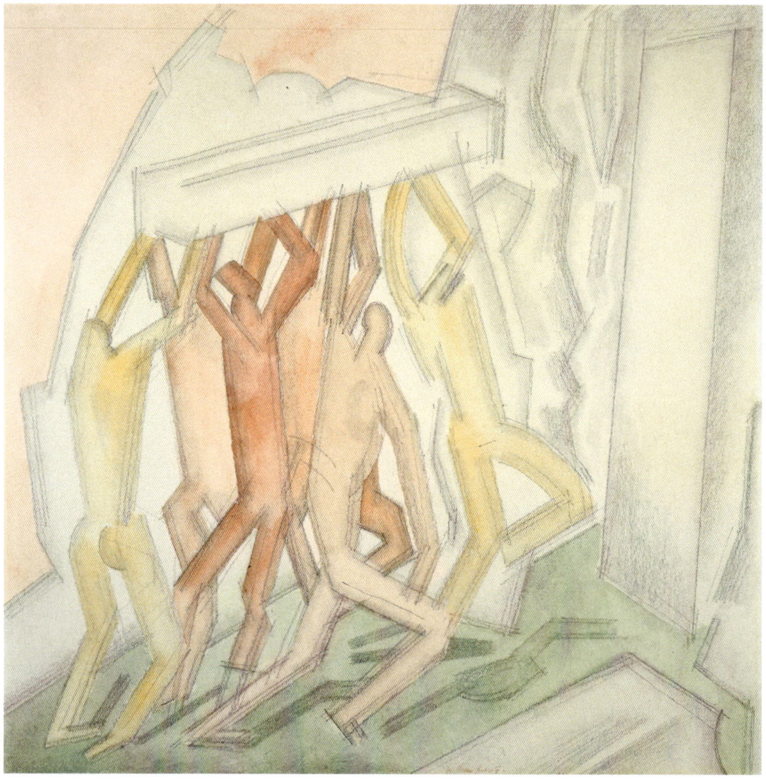

William ROBERTS, R.A.
[1895–1980]
Study for At the Hippodrome, 1921

chalk and wash squared in pencil on paper, 49 × 46.6 cm
inscribed: *William Roberts 1921*

P.547
PROVENANCE: Fine Art Society, from whom purchased by Gallery, January 1967.
EXHIBITIONS: *Decade 1920–30,* Arts Council Touring Exhibition, 1970, no.53; *Cityscape 1910–39,* Bradford, Bradford City Art Gallery, London, R.A., 1977–8, no.119.

Roberts' early work was influenced by Wyndham LEWIS. However, once he had ceased to imitate Lewis closely, Roberts developed into an extremely consistent artist choosing multi-figure compositions illustrating urban, chiefly cockney life. Unmistakable are his animated but stiff figures, drawn with straight, hard outlines as seen here. His figures became more rounded later in the 1920s.

EJ

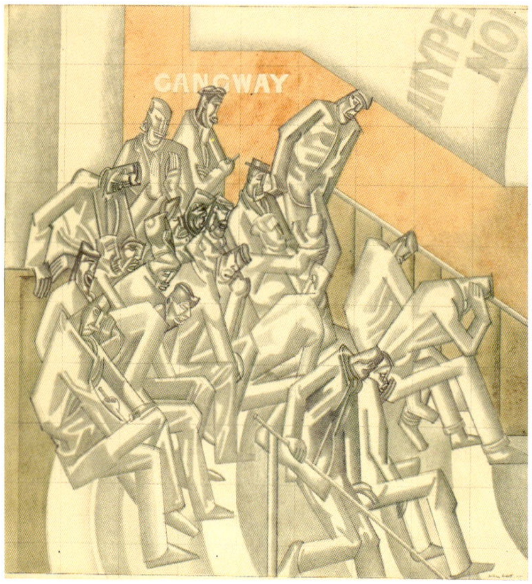

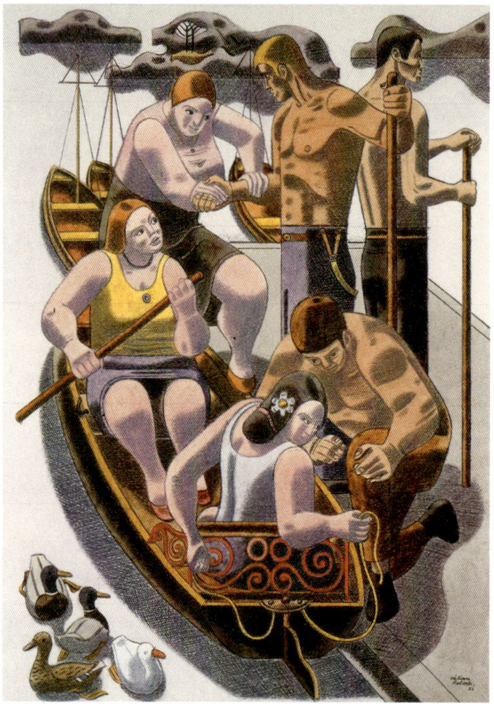

William ROBERTS, R.A.
[1895–1980]
The Boatpond, 1956

chalk and watercolour squared in pencil on paper, 49.4 × 35.6 cm
inscribed: *William Roberts '56*

P.215
PROVENANCE: Leicester Galleries, from whom purchased by Gallery, April 1958.
EXHIBITIONS: *Paintings and Drawings by William Roberts,* London, Leicester Galleries, 1958, no.43; *Watercolours and Drawings from The Cecil Higgins Art Gallery, Bedford,* London, Thos. Agnew & Sons Ltd, 1962, no.84; *Watercolours from Bedford,* Norwich, Castle Museum, 1965, no.46; *William Roberts A.R.A.: retrospective exhibition,* London, Tate Gallery, Arts Council, 1965, no.199.

Roberts was born in London and was apprenticed at the age of fourteen to the advertising firm of Sir Joshua Causton. During this period he also enlisted for evening classes at St Martin's School of Art. He won a scholarship to the Slade 1910–13, meeting David BOMBERG, Edward WADSWORTH and Christopher NEVINSON amongst others.

In 1913 he joined the Omega workshop, decorating table tops and fabrics with Cubist designs. He was invited by Wyndham LEWIS to join the Rebel Art Centre, a breakaway group of Omega artists; although he never officially joined this group he became involved with Lewis's circle, appearing as a signatory to the 'Vorticist Manifesto' in the first volume of *Blast*.

Roberts' figures from the 1950s contain a degree of distortion and even caricature combined with a strong sense of design.

JM

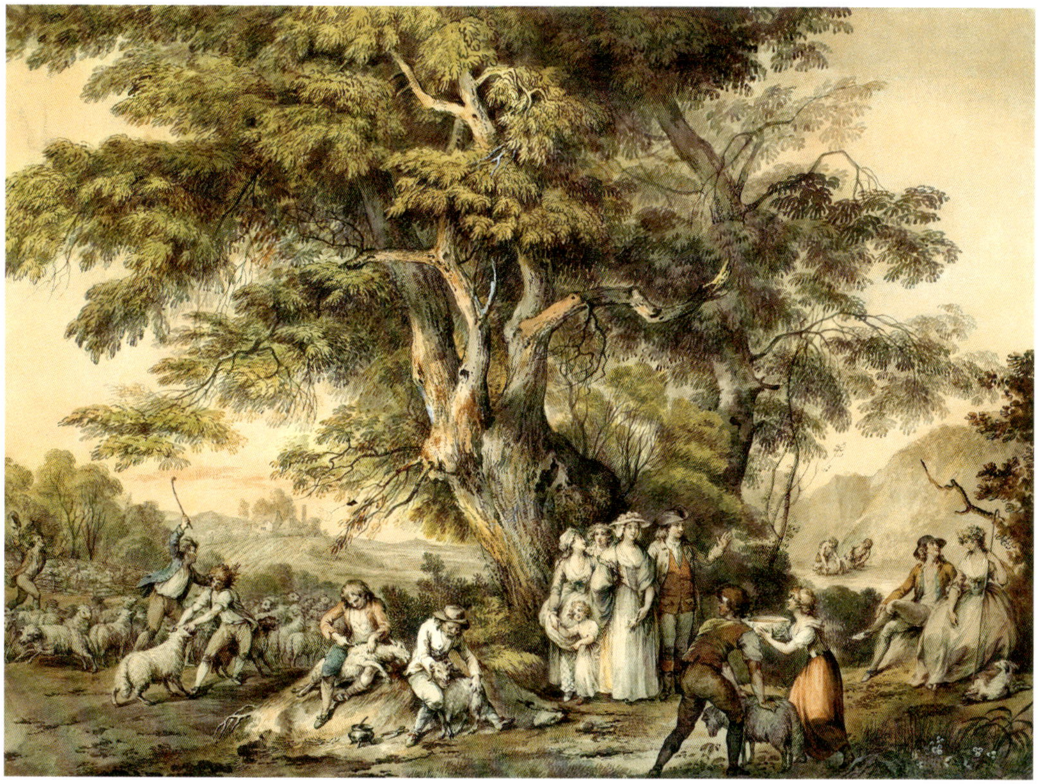

George ROBERTSON

[c.1748–88]

Summer: Sheep Shearing, c.1780

watercolour and bodycolour on paper, 30.3 x 41.7 cm
inscribed on reverse: *Robertson del int.*

P.82
PROVENANCE: Fine Art Society, from whom purchased by Gallery, January 1953.
EXHIBITIONS: *Early English Watercolours*, London, Fine Art Society, 1953; *English Watercolours from The Cecil Higgins Art Gallery, Bedford*, Reading, Reading Museum and Art Gallery, 1965, no.42.
REFERENCES: A. Buck, *Dress in 18th Century England*, 1979, p.202, illus no.89 (detail).

Robertson won a premium at the Society of Arts in 1761. He later went abroad to Rome and Jamaica under the patronage of William Beckford, of Somerley Hall, historian of Jamaica (not the owner of Fonthill), returning about 1770. In London he struggled against ill-health and adverse circumstances, 'his work having, no very brilliant success with the publick (sic)', so he had to fall back on teaching. But his pastoral subjects, peopled with lively human figures, show him to be a draughtsman of great skill with an admirable gift for composition. His work shows the influence of both SANDBY and Salvator Rosa. Iolo Williams notes that, according to C.F. Bell, Robertson appears to have been the originator of the trick of scratching out the highlights.

He died in 1788 after two years suffering as a result of falling from his horse.

EJ

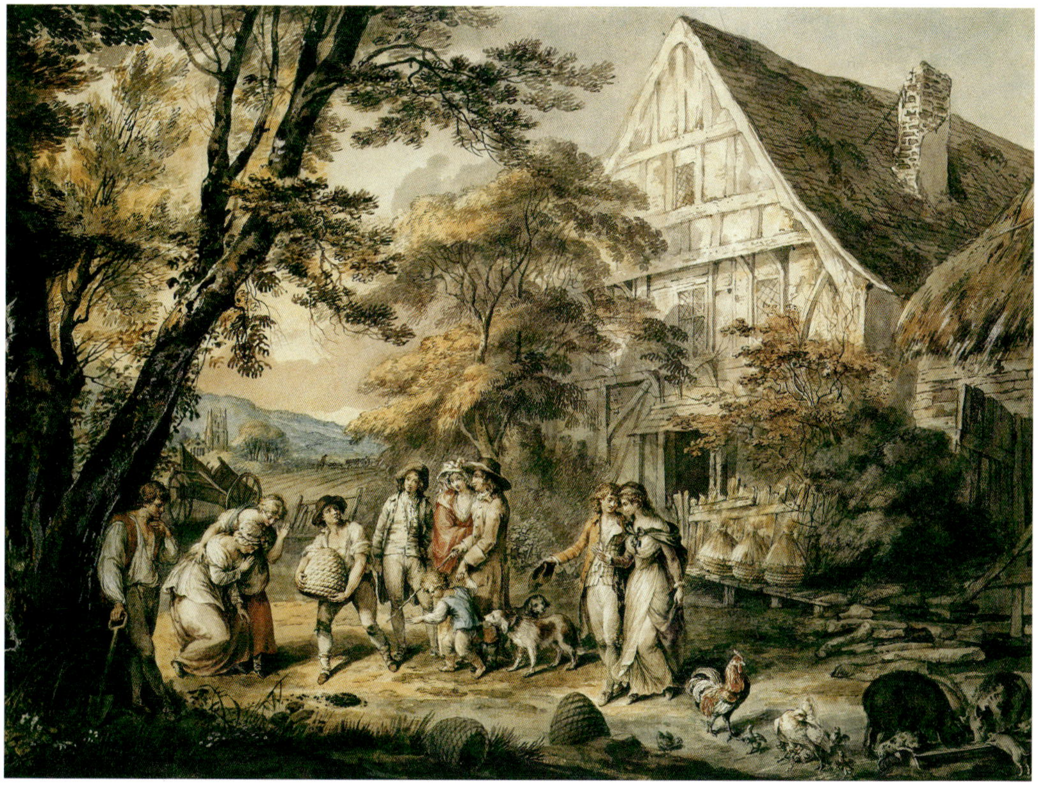

George ROBERTSON

[c.1748–88]

Autumn: Swarm of Bees, c.1780

watercolour and pen and ink on paper, 30.3 × 41.6 cm

P.83
PROVENANCE: Fine Art Society, from whom purchased by Gallery, January 1953.
EXHIBITIONS: *Early English Watercolours*, London, Fine Art Society, 1953; *English Watercolours from The Cecil Higgins Art Gallery, Bedford*, Reading, Reading Museum and Art Gallery, 1965, no.43; *British Watercolours: A Golden Age (1750 – 1850)*, Louisville, J.B. Speed Art Museum, 1977, no.39.
REFERENCES: A. Bury, 'The Cecil Higgins Museum Bedford', *Old Watercolour Society's Club*, 1961, vol.xxxvi, p.33, pl.xi; A.W. Coysh & R.K. Henry Wood, *The Dictionary of Blue and White Printed Pottery 1780–1880*, 1982, p.38, illus. as *Swarm of Bees, Autumn*.

The ceramic pattern known as *The Beemaster* is based on this picture by Robertson depicting a rural scene with a countryman carrying a beehive watched by three men, a woman and a child.

JM

George ROMNEY
[1734–1802]
The Milner Sisters

brush drawing in brown wash and black lead on paper, 39.5 × 25.5 cm

P.234
PROVENANCE: Roland, Browse and Delbanco, from whom purchased by Gallery, 1958.
REFERENCES: Spink & Leger, *Head and Shoulders, Portrait Drawings and some Small Pictures,* 1999, p.40 illus no.16.

Formerly entitled simply *The Sisters*, the correct identification is due to another study of the same sitters appearing in Spink-Leger's portrait exhibition in November 1999 together with a photograph of the oil painting *The Milner Sisters* (private collection) for which both drawings are preliminary studies. The composition of this drawing is so close to that of the oil that it must clearly be the final study, drawn later than the Spink-Leger version.

Known principally as a portrait painter who was considered a serious rival to Reynolds and GAINSBOROUGH, Romney's bold and inventive brush drawings have only recently become highly regarded as works of art in their own right. Here Romney's loose handling and freedom of touch show him at his best.

EJ

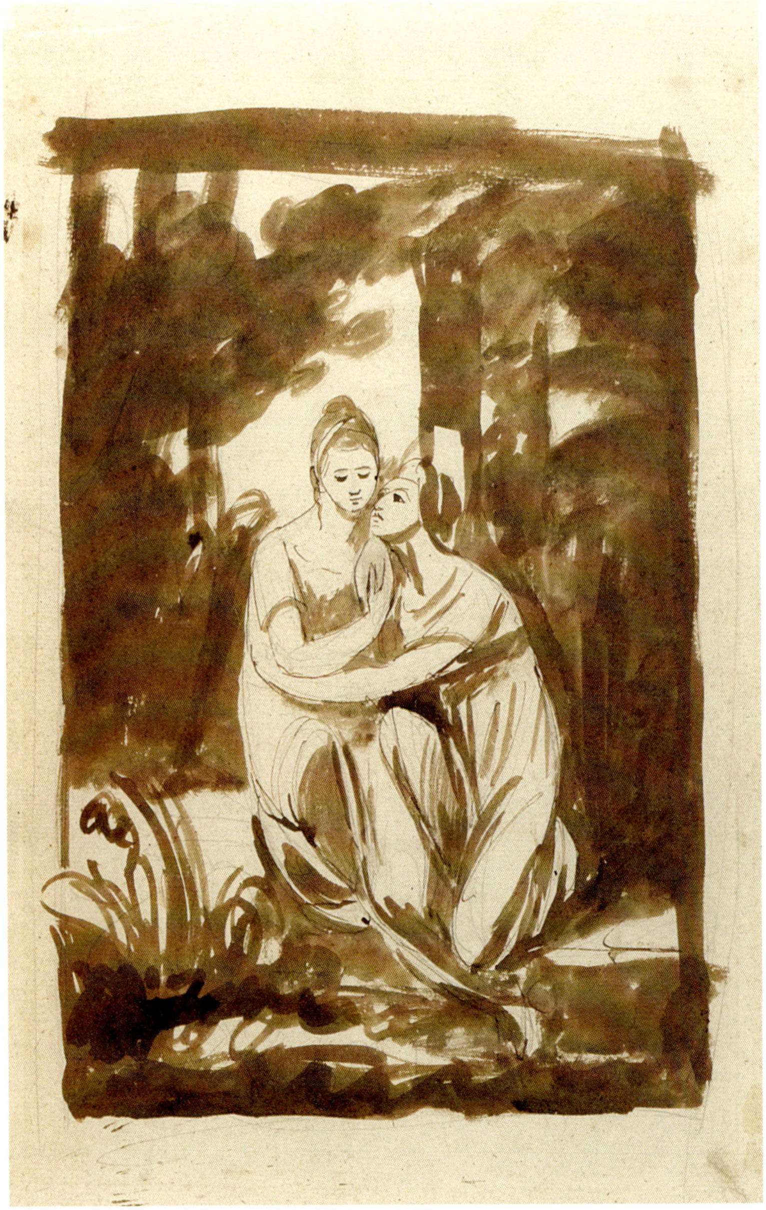

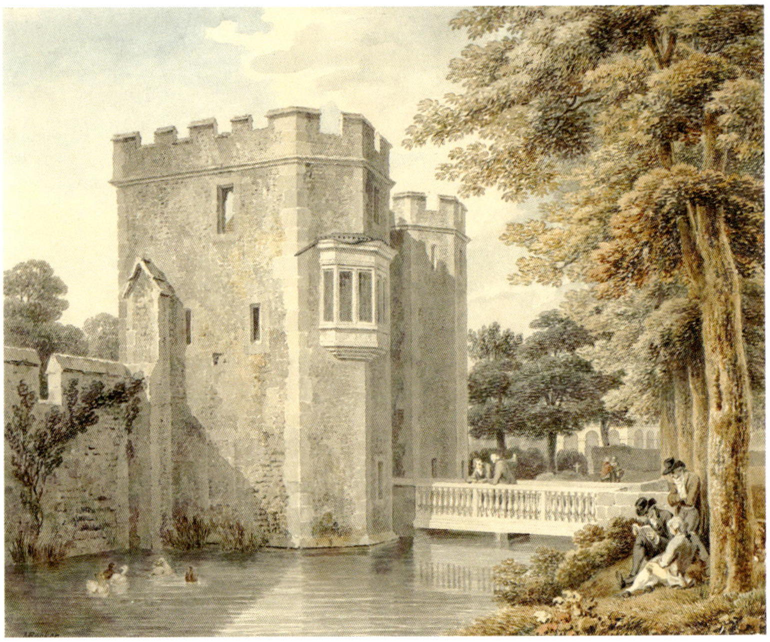

Michael 'Angelo' ROOKER, A.R.A.
[1743–1801]
Entrance to the Bishop's Palace at Wells

watercolour on paper, 22.5 x 28 cm
inscribed: *M. Rooker*

P.235
PROVENANCE: H.W. Rous; P&D Colnaghi Ltd, from whom purchased by Gallery, July 1958.
EXHIBITIONS: *Watercolours and Drawings from The Cecil Higgins Art Gallery, Bedford*, London, Thos. Agnew & Sons Ltd, 1962, no.10.

Rooker was the son of an engraver who placed him for instruction with Paul SANDBY, who gave him the nickname of 'Angelo', which stuck to him. He was elected A.R.A. in 1770. For most of his life he was the principal scene-painter at Colman's Theatre in the Haymarket. From 1788 he began a series of summer sketching tours; his architectural drawings in particular are both lively and scrupulously accurate.

Although his career was not a commercial success, HARDIE considers him underrated, pointing out that both GIRTIN and TURNER learnt much from his example – indeed Turner bought more than a dozen sketches at Rooker's posthumous sale in 1801.

EJ

Dante Gabriel **ROSSETTI**

[1828–82]

Elizabeth Siddal, c.1855–58

pen and sepia, shaded with the finger on paper, 15.6 × 9.4 cm
inscribed on reverse by W.M. Rossetti: *Liz, by G. circa 1855 or perhaps as late as 1858.*

P.433

PROVENANCE: W.M. Rossetti, then by descent, Mary Rossetti; Mrs H. Rossetti Angeli; Mrs Dennis; Maas Gallery, from whom purchased by Gallery, October 1962.

EXHIBITIONS: *Paintings and Drawings of the 1860 Period*, London, Tate Gallery, 1923, no.186; *The Pre-Raphaelites and their Contemporaries*, London, Maas Gallery, 1962, no.72; *Dante Gabriel Rossetti 1828–1882*, Newcastle upon Tyne, Laing Art Gallery, 1971, no.8; *Rossetti's Portraits of Elizabeth Siddal*, Oxford, Ashmolean, Birmingham, Birmingham, City Museum and Art Gallery, 1991, no.18.

REFERENCES: *Arts Review*, vol.xiv, no.21, 1962, p.3, repr. p.2; V. Surtees, *Dante Gabriel Rossetti 1828–1882: The Paintings and Drawings: A Catalogue Raisonné, 1971*, vol.I, p.191, no.469; V. Surtees, *Rossetti's portraits of Elizabeth Siddal*, 1991, pl.18.

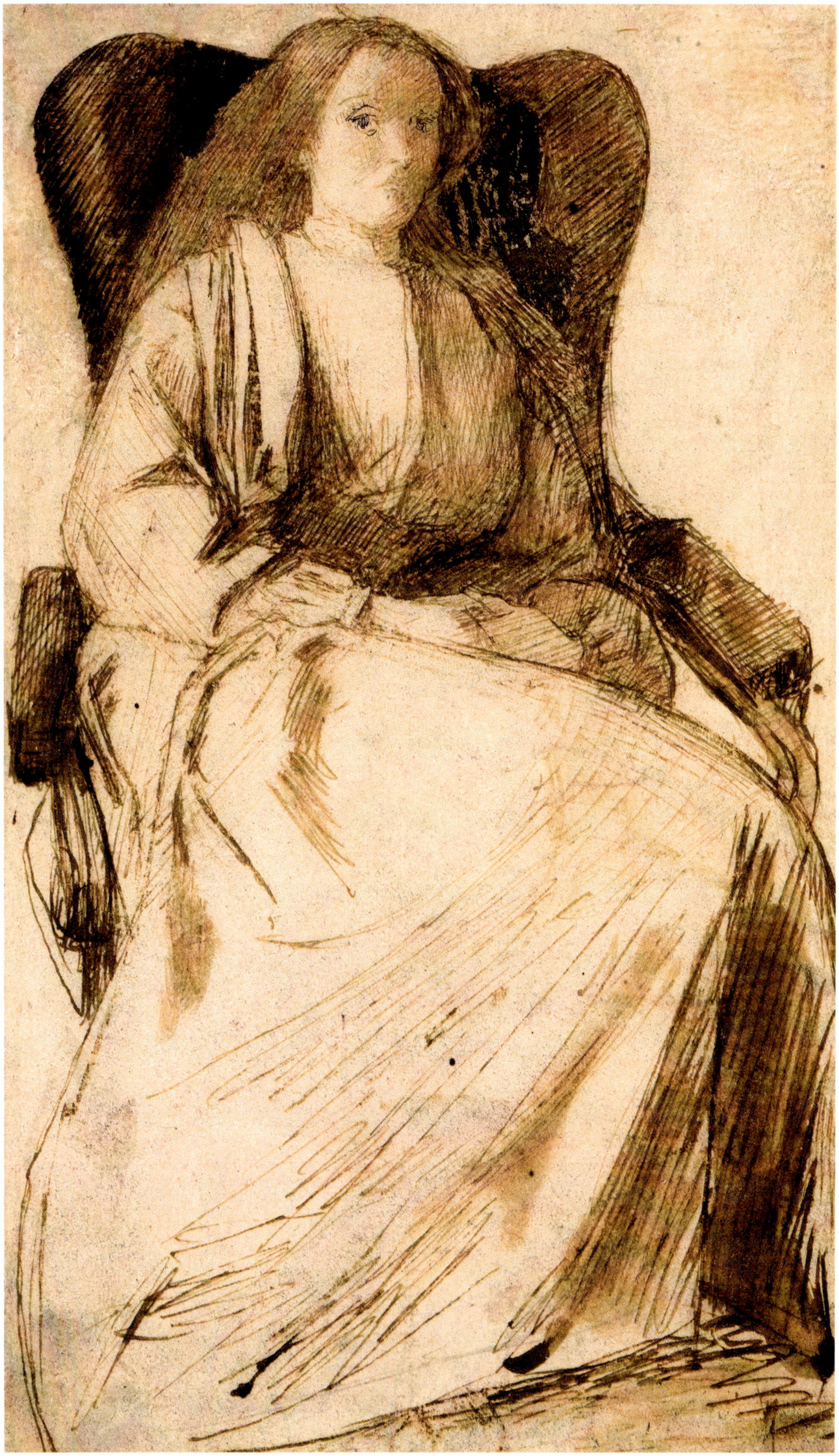

Rossetti met Elizabeth SIDDAL (1829–62) in 1850 when she was twenty or twenty-one. She had bright copper coloured hair and drooping eyelids and was called 'Gug' or 'Guggums' by Rossetti who drew her innumerable times – 'it is like a monomania with him', Madox BROWN wrote. Eventually they married in Hastings (where this had probably been drawn – see inscription) in 1860; Rossetti described her at this time as 'looking lovelier than ever' but the marriage was not a success.

Siddal, who was herself an amateur painter (see P.400), died in February 1862 probably from an overdose of laudanum. Rossetti was so distraught that he buried his manuscript poems in her coffin but gained permission to disinter them in 1869 as he wished to make a complete edition of all his poems. Unwilling to do this himself, the task was undertaken by his friend and agent Charles Augustus Howell.

EJ/JM

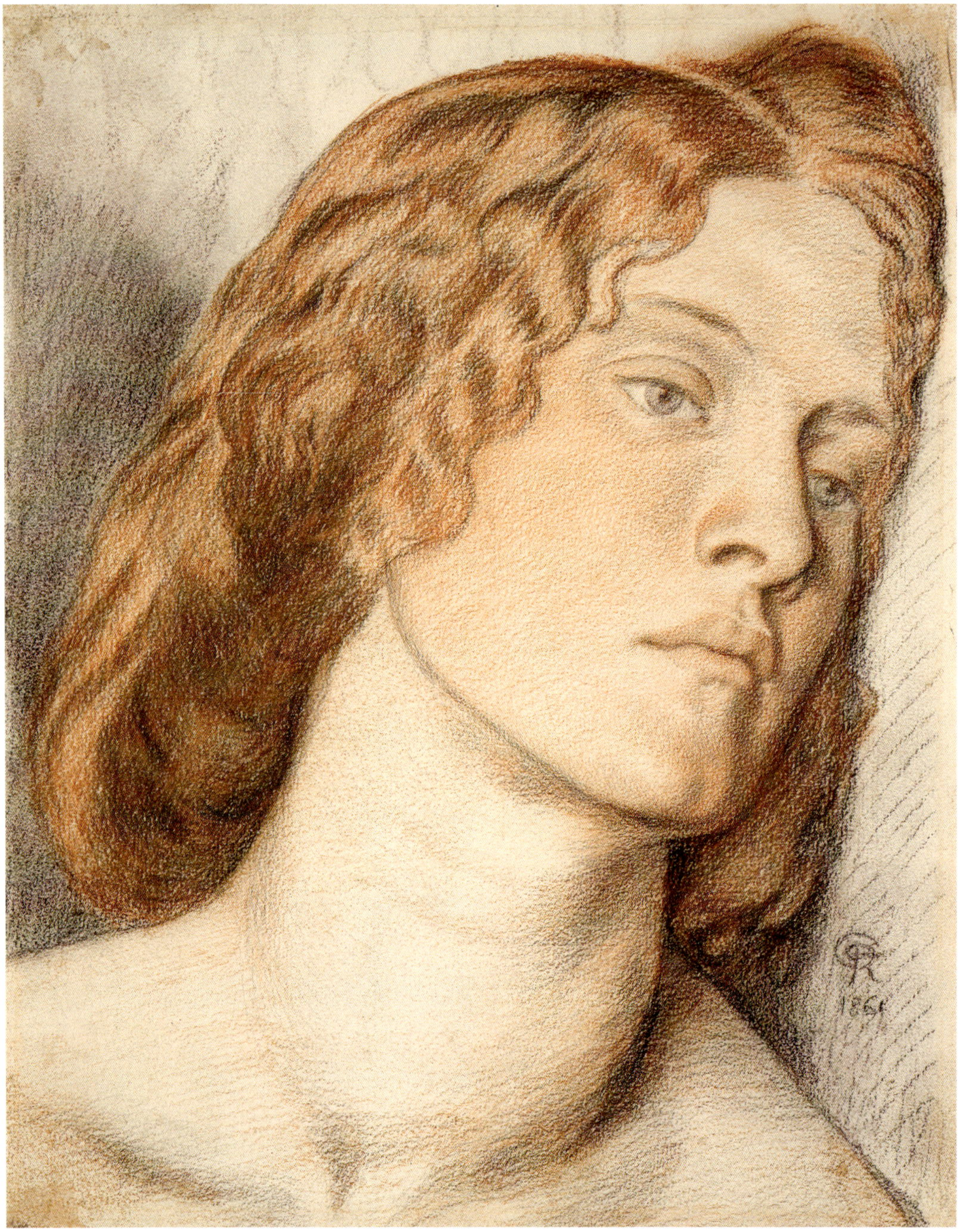

Dante Gabriel ROSSETTI

[1828–82]

Fanny Cornforth (study for **Fair Rosamund**), 1861

coloured chalks on paper, 32.2 × 25.9 cm
signed: monogram, *1861*

P.297

PROVENANCE: Mrs Arthur Clifton; sold on her behalf as 'Miss Ford' to the Gallery by Thos. Agnew & Sons Ltd, July 1959.
EXHIBITIONS: *The English Tradition: an exhibition of watercolours from two private collections,* Bedford, Cecil Higgins Art Gallery, 1972, no.69; *Rossetti,* Tokyo, Bunkamura Museum of Art, Nagoya, Aichi Prefectural Art Gallery, Kurume, Ishibashi Museum of Art, 1990–91, no.24.
REFERENCES: D. Sonstroem, *Dante Gabriel Rossetti and the Fair Lady,* W.U.P, 1970, repr. facing p.63; V. Surtees, *Dante Gabriel Rossetti 1828–1882 The Paintings and Drawings A Catalogue Raisonné,* 1971, vol. I (text), p.81, no.128A, illus. vol. II (plates), no.199; M. Henderson, *Dante Gabriel Rossetti,* 1973, illus. p.12; S. Wildman, *Dante Gabriel Rossetti,* Tokyo, 1990, pp.28 & 71, no.24, illus. no.24; G. Daly, *Pre-Raphaelites in love,* 1989, illus. as *Study for Fair Rosamund;* L. Lambourne, *The Aesthetic Movement,* 1996, repr. p.190.

A study for the oil of the same year, (Surtees no.128) in the National Museum of Wales, Cardiff. Probably based on the ballad *Fair Rosamund* by Thomas Deloney (?1560–1600).

Rosamund Clifford (c.1139–76) awaits the arrival of her lover, Henry II, in 1174. In the story a secret retreat was built for her in the centre of a maze at Woodstock, near Oxford. She was finally discovered by Queen Eleanor, who had her put to death.

Fanny Cornforth (1824–1906) became Rossetti's model in 1858. She also became his mistress before his wife's death, later acting as a sort of housekeeper in Cheyne Walk. She was described by William Rossetti as having 'no charm or breeding, education or intellect'; Swinburne referred to her as a 'bitch'. She is also noted though for having an affectionate nature, married twice and finally grew so stout that William Bell Scott described her as 'that three waisted creature'.

EJ/JM

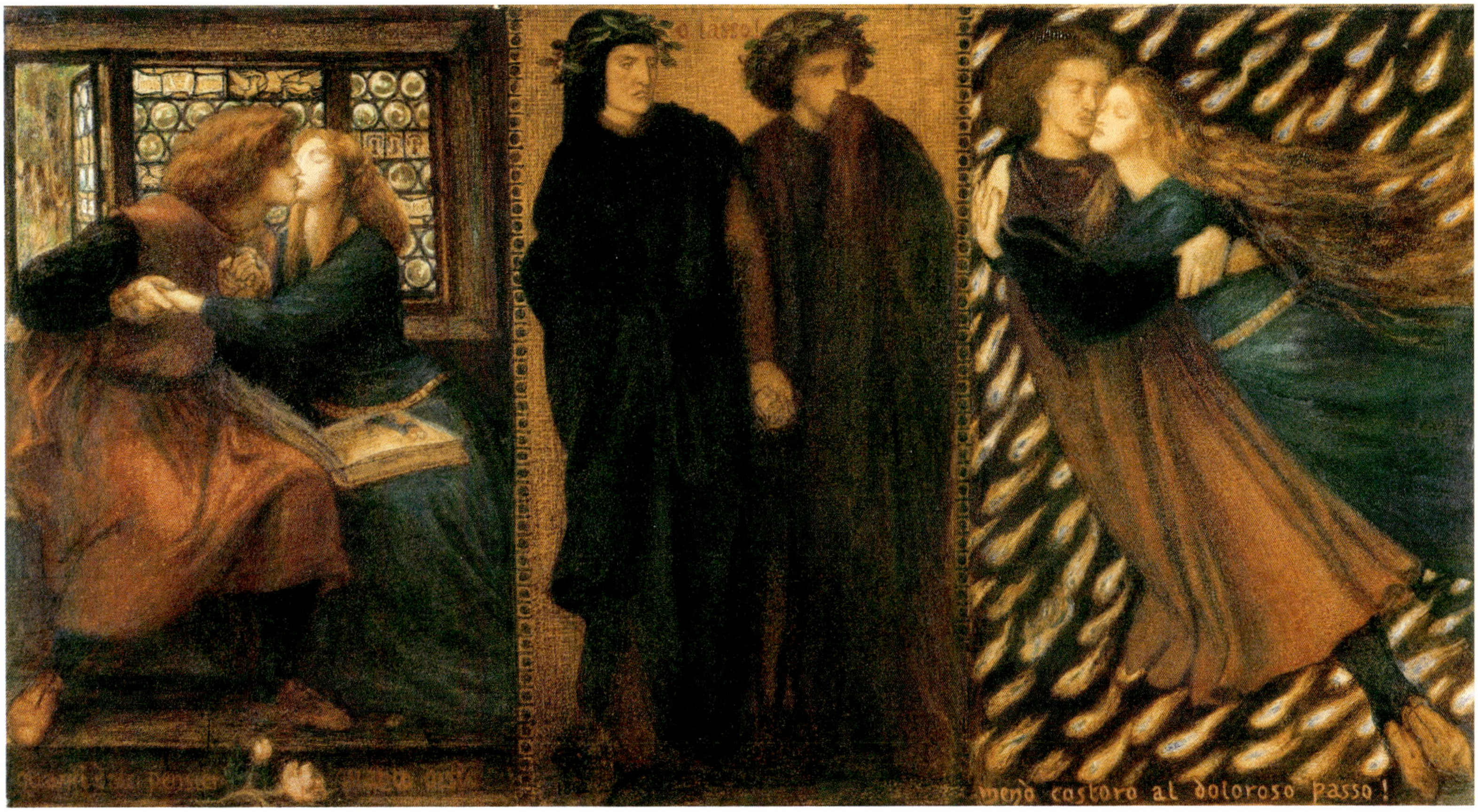

Dante Gabriel ROSSETTI

[1828–82]

Paolo and Francesca, 1862

watercolour on paper, 31.7 × 60.3 cm
inscribed: monogram, *1862*
O lasso, in central panel; inscribed along the foot of the first compartment, *Quanti dolci pensier Quanto disio,* inscribed along the foot of the second compartment, *Meno costor al doloroso passo!*. Originally on the back of the picture Rossetti had transcribed two verses from the Inferno and added *'Francesca da Rimini (watercolour) D.G. Rossetti Sept.1862'*

P.548

PROVENANCE: Commissioned by James Leathart; by descent to his son, T.H. Leathart; Sir Edmund Davies, his sale Christie's 7 July 1939, no.88; bought by Kerrison Preston, who later gave it to Gordon Bottomley, who willed back to Preston, his sale Sotheby's, 15 March 1967, no.34; purchased Thos. Agnew & Son Ltd on behalf of Gallery.

EXHIBITIONS: *Winter Exhibition,* London, R.A., 1883, no.291; *Winter Exhibition*, London, R.A., 1901, no.159; London, Goupil Gallery, 1896, no.11; *Franco-British Exhibition,* Paris, 1908, no.429; *The Pre-Raphaelite Brotherhood (1848–62),* Birmingham, Birmingham City Museum & Art Gallery, 1947, no.123; *Paintings and Drawings by the Pre-Raphaelites and their Followers,* Bournemouth, Russell-Cotes Art Gallery, 1951, no.59; *The Leathart Collection,* Newcastle upon Tyne, Laing Art Gallery, 1968, no.62; *Pre-Raphaelites – Patrons and Painters in the North East,* Newcastle upon Tyne, Laing Art Gallery, 1989–90, no.93; *Dante Gabriel Rossetti 1828–1882* , Japan, Tokyo, Nagoya and Kurume, 1990–91, no.20.

REFERENCES: *The Athenaeum*, Sept. 1873, p.342; H.C. Marillier, *Dante Gabriel Rossetti, Illustrated Memorial of his Art and Life,* 1899, pp.66, 125–6, 244, no.136; W.M. Rossetti, *Dante Gabriel Rossetti: His Family Letters, with a Memoir,* Cassell and Co,1899, vol.I, p.188; *Art Journal,* May 1896, p.132; R.Ironside and J. Gere, *Pre-Raphaelite Painters,* 1948, p.32; K. Preston (ed.), *Letters from Graham Robertson,* 1953, pp.423–6; O. Doughty and J.R. Wahl, *Letters of Dante Gabriel Rossetti,* 1965 & 1967, p.450; V. Surtees, *Dante Gabriel Rossetti 1828–1882; The Paintings and Drawings A Catalogue Raisonné,* 1971, Vol. I (text), p.38, no.75. R1, Vol.II, (plates), no.88; J. Marsh, *Pre-Raphaelite Women,* 1987, p.58, illus. no.46 (detail).

When I made answer, I began: "Alas!
How many sweet thoughts and how much desire
Led these two onward to the dolorous pass!"
Then turned to them, as who would fain inquire,
And sad: "Francesca, these thine agonies
Wring tears for pity and grief which they inspire:
But tell me, in the season of sweet sighs,
When and what way did love instruct you so
That he in your vague longings made you wise ?"
Then she said to me: "There is no greater woe
Than the remembrance of past happy days
In misery: and this thy guide doth know.
But if the first beginnings to retrace
Of our sad love, may yield thee solace here,
So will I be as one that weeps and says:
'One day we read, for pastime and sweet cheer
Of Lancelot how he found Love tyrannous:
We were alone and without any fear.
Our eyes were drawn together reading thus
Full oft, and still our cheeks would pale and glow;
But one sole point it was that conquered us.
For when we read of that great lover, how
He kissed the smile which he had longed to win-
Then he whom nought can sever from me now
For ever, kissed my mouth, all quivering.
A pander was the book and he that writ:
Upon that day we read no more therein'.

This illustrates the story related by Dante in Canto V of his *Inferno* in which Francesca with her lover and brother-in-law, Paolo Malatesta, are murdered by her husband, Sigismondo Malatesta. The left-hand compartment shows the lovers kissing. In the central panel Dante and Virgil stand crowned with laurel and bay-leaf, looking pityingly at the right-hand panel where the lovers, locked in each others arms, float through the flames of Hell, forever united.

Rossetti had this subject in mind from c.1849: a sheet of four sketches on paper show three groups of seated lovers with an open book on their knees whilst the fourth group are standing. The earliest triptych version was acquired by RUSKIN and is now in the Tate Gallery (N03056). This, the slightly enlarged second version, was painted for the collector James Leathart; it is reputed to have been one of his favourite paintings, with Leathart likening its colour to 'jewels'. A third version is in the National Gallery of Victoria, Melbourne (No.3266/4).

EJ/JM

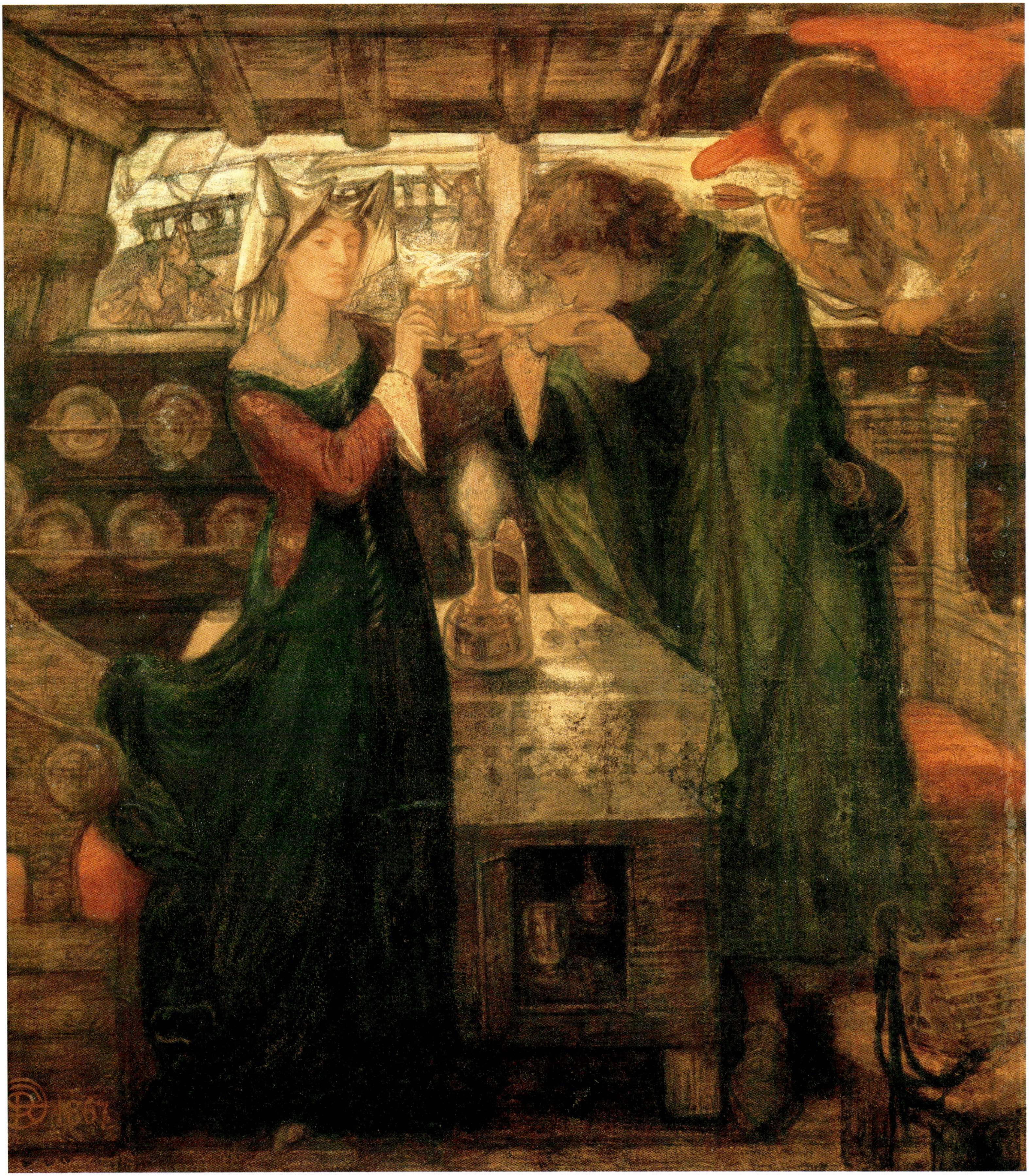

Dante Gabriel ROSSETTI

[1828–82]

Sir Tristram and La Belle Yseult Drinking the Love Potion, 1867

watercolour on paper, 62.3 × 59.1 cm
inscribed: monogram, *1867*

P.401
PROVENANCE: Bought in 1867 from the artist by T.H. McConnell; sold to James Leathart for £200, 1872; sold from the Goupil Gallery in 1896 to M.Sears of Boston; The Hon. Lady Hood; Mr John Flanagan; Terence G.W. Rowe c.1954; E. Holden; Maas Gallery, from whom purchased by Gallery, December 1961.
EXHIBITIONS: London, R.A., 1883, no.355; Leeds, Leeds City Art Gallery, 1889; Birmingham, Birmingham City Museum and Art Gallery, 1891, no.160; London, Goupil Gallery, 1896, no.16; Boston, Museum of Fine Arts, Loan 27 July 1905 – 24 October 1907, returned to Mrs Sears; Loan 17 April 1917–7 November 1917, accession no.338.17; *The Pre-Raphaelite Influence,* London, Leighton House Art Gallery, 1960, no.87; *Pre-Raphaelites and their Influence,* London, Maas Gallery, 1961, no.78; *Watercolours from Bedford,* Norwich, Castle Museum, 1965, no.47; *The Leathart Collection,* Newcastle upon Tyne, Laing Art Gallery, 1968, no.66; *Rossetti: painter and poet,* London, R.A., Birmingham, Birmingham City Museum and Art Gallery, 1973, no.217; *Pre-Raphaelites – Patrons and Painters in the North-east,* Newcastle upon Tyne, Laing Art Gallery, 1989–90, no.96; *Dante Gabriel Rossetti 1828 – 1882,* Japan, Tokyo, Bunkamura Museum of Art, Nagoya, Aichi Prefectural Art Gallery, Kurume, Ishibashi Museum of Art, 1990–91, no.43; *The Quest for Camelot: The Arthurian Legend in Art,* Edinburgh, City Art Centre, 2001–2.
REFERENCES: *Arts Journal* 1884, p.168; H.C. Marillier, *Dante Gabriel Rossetti: an illustrated memorial of his art and life,* 1889, pp.114–5, no.200; W.M. Rossetti, *D.G. Rossetti as a Designer and Writer,* 1889, p.41–2; A.C. Benson, *Rossetti,* 1904, p.184; O. Doughty & J.R. Wahl (eds.), *Letters of Dante Gabriel Rossetti,* 1967, 4 vols. pp.929,1123,1144; D.Sonstroem, *Rossetti and the fair lady,* W.U.P., 1970, p.88; V. Surtees, *Dante Gabriel Rossetti 1828–1882:The Paintings and Drawings, A Catalogue Raisonné,* 1971, vol. I (text), p.114, no.200, illus. vol. II (plates) no.290; D. Mancoff, *The Arthurian Revival in Victorian Art,* 1990, p.66, illus. no.58; N.J. Lacy, *The Arthurian Encylopedia,* 1990, p.463.

This is the watercolour version of an original cartoon (not traced) for a series of stained glass windows made by the Morris firm for the entrance hall of Walter Dunlop's house, Harden Grange, Bingley in Yorkshire, 1862. The stained glass panels, including Rossetti's other design for the series, *The Fight with Sir Marhaus*, are now in Bradford Art Galleries & Museums.

The subject is taken from Malory's *Morte d'Arthur* (c.1450) and was one of the most popular love stories of the Middle Ages. Tristram travels to Cornwall to seek adventure, where, in his first major feat, he kills Sir Morholt, brother-in-law and champion of Anguish, King of Ireland. Tristram, suffering terrible wounds from the struggle goes to Ireland to seek help from Yseult (daughter of Anguish), who has special healing skills. During his convalescence Yseult falls in love with him, although her hand is promised to King Mark of Cornwall. On their return to Cornwall Tristram and Yseult share the love potion intended for her future husband; it bursts into flames as their glasses touch. Above, to the right, the figure of Love with crimson wings draws an arrow from his quiver. The lovers continue the deception until trapped by Mark. Yseult eventually returns to Mark whilst Tristram goes into exile.

Rossetti considered it to be 'one of my very best watercolours particularly full and deep in colour', (letter to James Leathart 8 May 1872). This was not however an opinion shared by Leathart (1820–95), who, having acquired the picture, stated in a letter, 'I am sorry to say the drawing does not come up to my expectations. Its colour is doubtless fine but not equal to that of the 'Paolo and Francesca' (see P.548) whilst in every other quality it is as far behind that noble work' (draft of a letter from James Leathart 25 May 1872). Rossetti does however capture the full emotional intensity of the moment, concentrating the viewer's gaze on the lovers duplicity. Jane Morris is recognizable as the model for Yseult.

EJ/JM

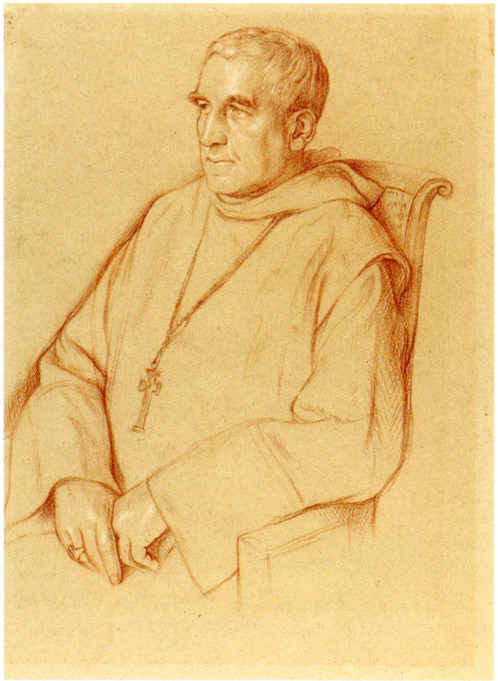

Sir William ROTHENSTEIN

[1872–1945]

The Right Rev. Dom. Wilfrid Upson, O.S.B., Abbott of Prinknash, Glos, 1940

red chalk on paper, 54.3 × 38.9 cm
on reverse: portrait sketch of a man's head in red chalk.

P.187
PROVENANCE: Sir John Rothenstein, from whom purchased by Gallery, April 1958.
EXHIBITIONS: *Watercolours and Drawings from The Cecil Higgins Art Gallery, Bedford*, London, Thos. Agnew & Sons Ltd, 1962, no.81; *Portrait Painting and Drawings*, Rye, Rye Art Gallery, 1967, no cat.

Drawn in 1940; the sitter was Abbott of Prinknash (pronounced 'Prinnish') Abbey in Gloucestershire and head of the Benedictines of Great Britain.

Rothenstein studied at the Slade School and in Paris where he made friends with WHISTLER and Edgar Degas (1834–1917). Back in England he became known for his portrait drawings chiefly of the famous. Head of the R.C.A., 1920–35 and a trustee of the Tate Gallery 1927–33. He was knighted in 1931 and a memorial exhibition was held at the Tate in 1950. His correspondence and memoirs are a rich source of information on his times.

EJ

Thomas ROWLANDSON
[1756–1827]
Two Musicians

watercolour and pen and ink on paper, 18.2 × 17.5 cm

P.801
PROVENANCE: Sydney Kitson; given to the Gallery by Alice Barbara Kitson, October 1992.

One of several versions of this watercolour, others being in the Huntingdon Art Gallery, California and the Olivia Shaler Swann Collection at the Art Institute of Chicago.

The Huntington version is inscribed in Rowlandson's hand: *Concerto Spirituale/Messrs. Boch* [sic] *& Abel*. This refers to Johann Christian Bach (1735-82), the eleventh son of Johann Sebastian, and Karl Friedrich Abel (1725-87). These two musicians gave highly successful concerts together in London from 1765 to the early 1780s.

A probable source for this subject was a print entitled *Concerto Spirituale* engraved by Bretherton after Bunbury and published 23 March 1773. It contains three musicians rather than two and differs in other ways, but could well be the inspiration for Rowlandson's work. It has been suggested that the large gentleman playing the viola da gamba in Bunbury's design is Abel.

A print by another hand, based on Rowlandson's design and entitled *A Duet*, is in the Dyson Perrins collection at the Metropolitan Museum, New York.

JM

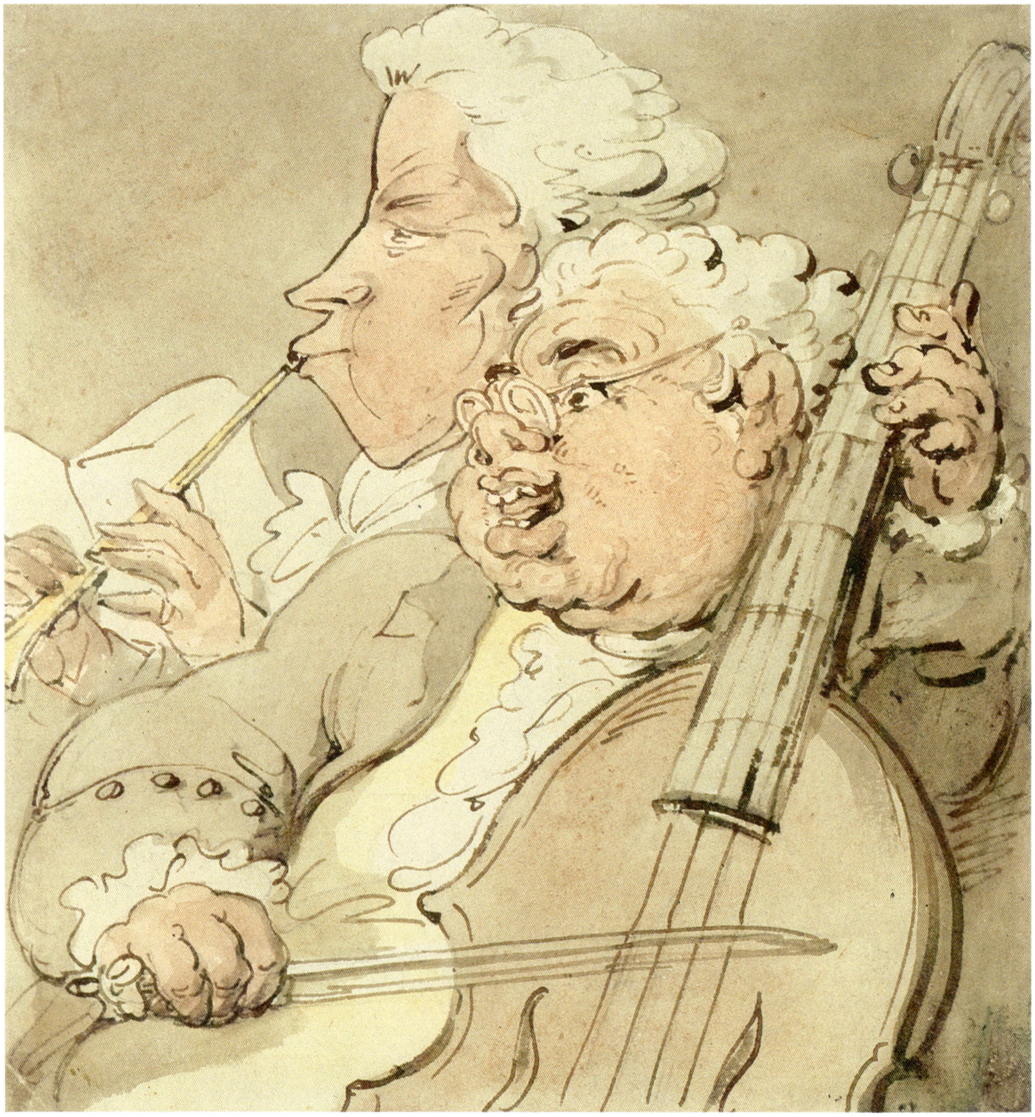

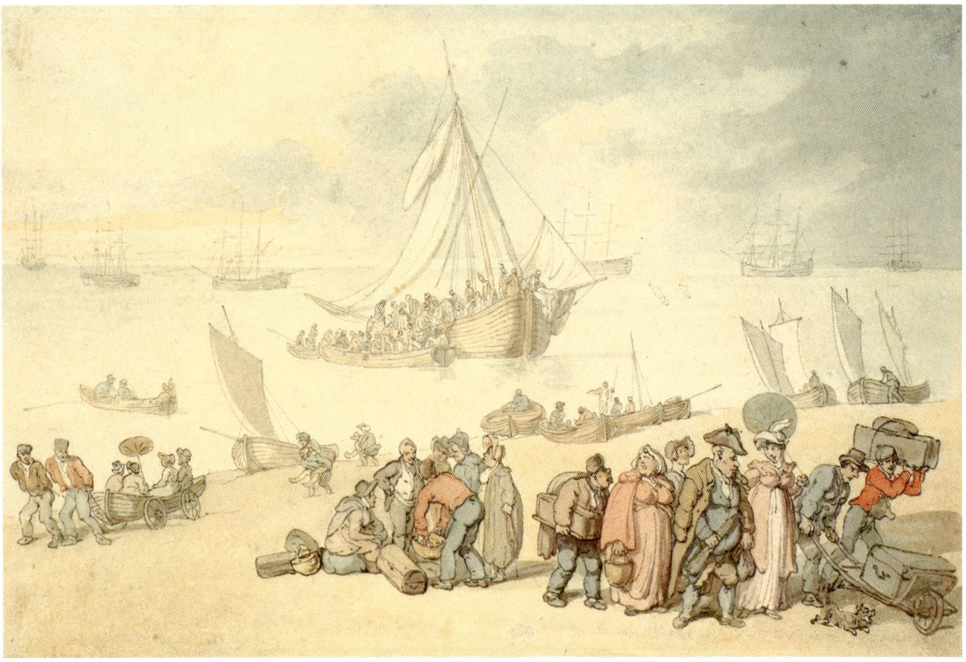

Thomas ROWLANDSON
[1756–1827]
Disembarkation at the Medina River, Isle of Wight

watercolour and pen and ink on paper, 16.5 × 25.5 cm

P.84
PROVENANCE: Thos. Agnew & Sons Ltd, from whom purchased by Gallery, March 1954.
EXHIBITIONS: *Watercolours and Drawings from The Cecil Higgins Art Gallery, Bedford*, London, Thos. Agnew & Sons Ltd, 1962, no.19.

Rowlandson visited the Isle of Wight in 1784, most probably in late September, together with his friend Henry Wigstead. Starting from London the expedition lasted about twelve days including five or six nights at Lymington opposite Yarmouth on the Island and at least one at Cowes. Sixty-eight drawings illustrating the trip are now in the Huntingdon Art Gallery, California and were published as *A Tour in a Post Chaise* by Dr Robert Wark in 1962.

This is a fine example of Rowlandson's early and best period when his colours were applied in a light uniform wash with little gradation of colour within the washes. In addition it demonstrates Rowlandson's infinite variety and inventiveness as a figurative draughtsman.

EJ

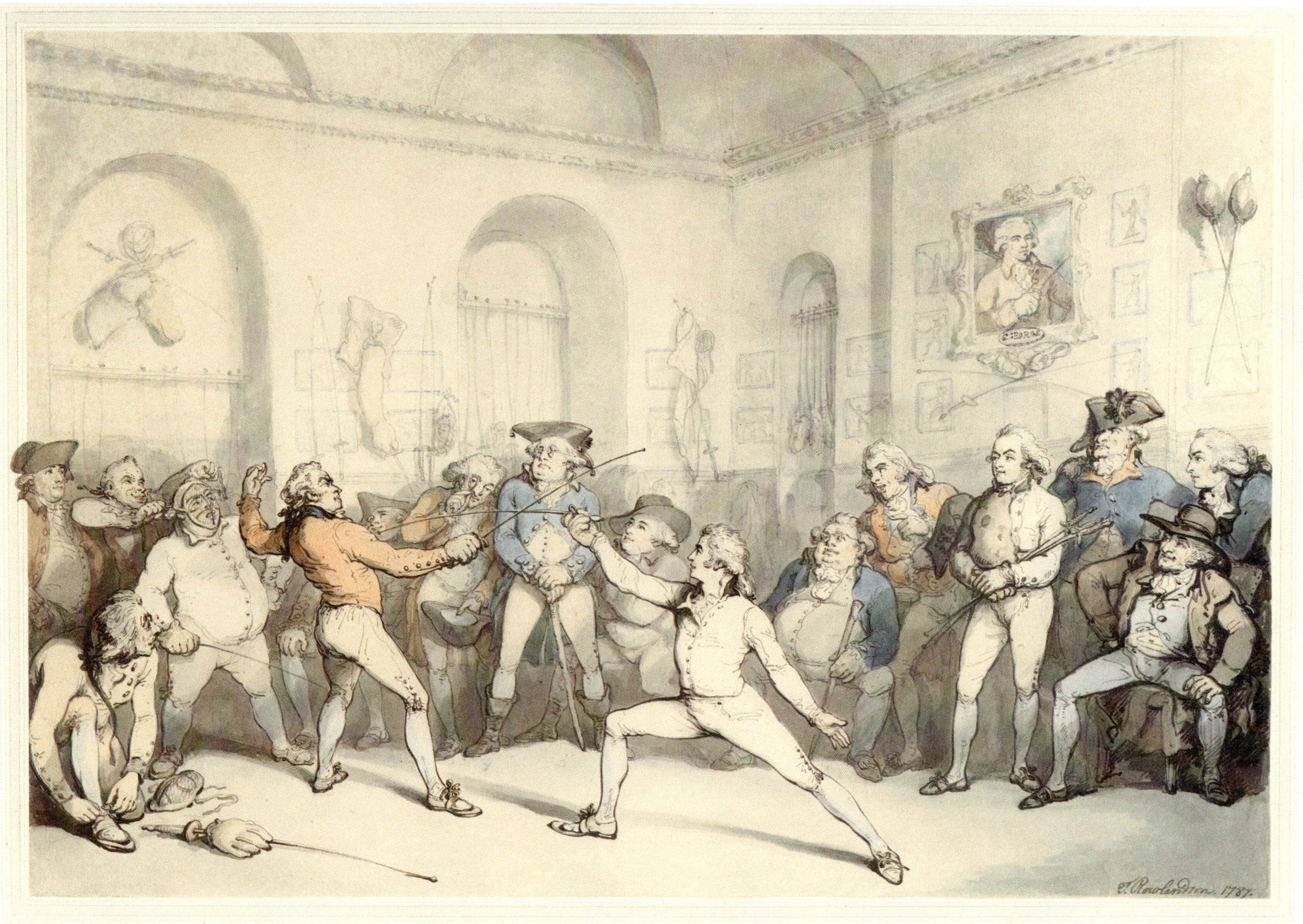

Thomas ROWLANDSON

[1756–1827]

Mr Henry Angelo's Fencing Academy, 1787

pen, grey and grey-black ink and watercolour over pencil on paper, 34.8 × 51.3 cm
inscribed: *T.Rowlandson 1787*

P.115

PROVENANCE: Gooden & Fox; Thos. Agnew & Sons Ltd, from whom purchased by Gallery, March 1957.

EXHIBITIONS: *Primitives to Picasso,* London, R.A., 1962, no.367, as *Mr Angelo's Fencing School; Watercolours and Drawings from The Cecil Higgins Art Gallery, Bedford,* London, Thos. Agnew & Sons Ltd, 1962, no.11; *English Watercolours from The Cecil Higgins Art Gallery, Bedford*, Reading, Reading Museum & Art Gallery, 1965, no.44; *Watercolours from Bedford,* Norwich, Norwich Castle Museum, 1965, no.48; *British Portrait Exhibition,* (Arts Council) Bucharest, Budapest, 1972–3; *British Watercolours: A Golden Age 1750–1850,* Lousiville, J.B. Speed Art Museum, 1977, no.36; *The Art of Thomas Rowlandson,* New York, Frick Art Museum, Pittsburgh, Baltimore Museum of Art, 1990, no.38; *Art Treasures of England,* London, R.A., 1998, no.216.

REFERENCES: M. Salaman, 'A Group of Rowlandson Drawings', *Apollo*, 1929, p.24, repr. p.21; A. Bury (ed.), 'The Cecil Higgins Museum' Bedford, *Old Watercolour Society's Club,* 1961, vol. xxxvi, p.35, pl.XII; S. Somerville, *British Watercolours: A Golden Age 1750 – 1850,* 1977, p.56, no.36, repr. p.57; J. Hayes, *The Art of Thomas Rowlandson,* 1990, p.104, no.38, repr. p.105; *Art Treasures of England: The Regional Collections,* 1998, p.282, no.216 (aquatint reproduced).

NOTES: The Gallery also holds an aquatinit of this picture by P. Rosenberg, dated 1791 (P.121)

Henry Angelo (1760–1839?) was amongst Rowlandson's closest friends. His fencing academy in the Haymarket was visited in 1787 by the greatest swordsman of the day, the Chevalier St George, who presented Angelo with his portrait by Mather Brown (1761–1831), seen here hanging above the mantelpiece. There is another portrait of Henry Angelo by Mather Brown in the N.P.G. (NPG.5310).

In the 1998 exhibition catalogue Lindsay Stainton suggests that the fencer in the red jacket may be the Chevalier himself while his opponent may be the comic actor and friend of Rowlandson, Jack Bannister; the head in profile on the extreme right may be a self-portrait. A later version from 1791, now in the Frick Collection, New York, was aquatinted by P. Rosenberg (see notes). It differs in that the gentleman on the extreme left of the picture has been replaced by a young boy.

Angelo's fencing rooms over the entrance to the pit door of the Opera House in the Haymarket were destroyed by fire in 1789. He published his *Reminiscences* in two volumes 1828–30.

EJ/JM

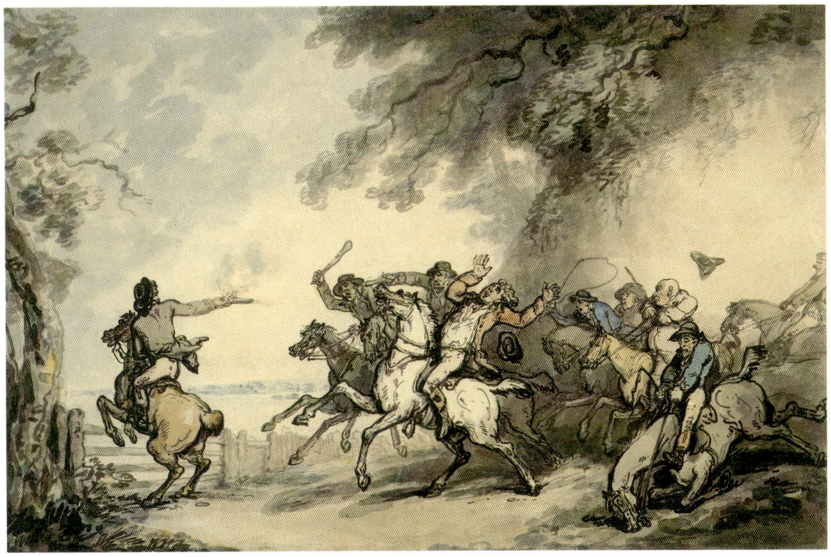

Thomas ROWLANDSON

[1756–1827]

The Chase of a Highwayman, c.1790

pen and grey and grey-black ink and watercolour over traces of pencil on paper, 26.3 × 41.4 cm
inscribed: collector's mark of Gilbert Davis

P.274
PROVENANCE: Gilbert Davis; P&D Colnaghi Ltd, from whom purchased by Gallery, January 1959 .
EXHIBITIONS: *Works by Thomas Rowlandson from the Collection of Gilbert Davis*, Bristol, Bristol City Art Gallery, 1949, no.44; *Watercolours and Drawings by Thomas Rowlandson*, London, (Arts Council), 1950, no.63; *Watercolours and Drawings by Thomas Rowlandson*, London, Whitechapel Art Gallery, 1953, no.47, *Watercolours and Drawings from The Cecil Higgins Art Gallery, Bedford*, London, Thos. Agnew & Sons Ltd, 1962, no.7; *English Watercolours from The Cecil Higgins Art Gallery, Bedford*, Reading, Reading Museum & Art Gallery, 1965, no.46; *The Art of Thomas Rowlandson*, New York, Frick Art Museum, Baltimore, Baltimore Museum of Art, Pittsburgh, Pittsburgh Art Museum, 1990, no.44.
REFERENCES: J. Hayes, *The Art of Thomas Rowlandson*, 1990, no.44, repr. p117.

Rowlandson at his most spirited and brilliant. The pursuers seem to be pressing so closely upon each other's heels that all may end in a heap while the miscreant escapes. Two variants of the composition exist: one, exhibited at Spink's in 1973, was catalogued as an unpublished drawing for the artist's Dr Syntax series; the other, signed and dated 1790, was formerly in the Collection of Sidney L. Phipson.

EJ

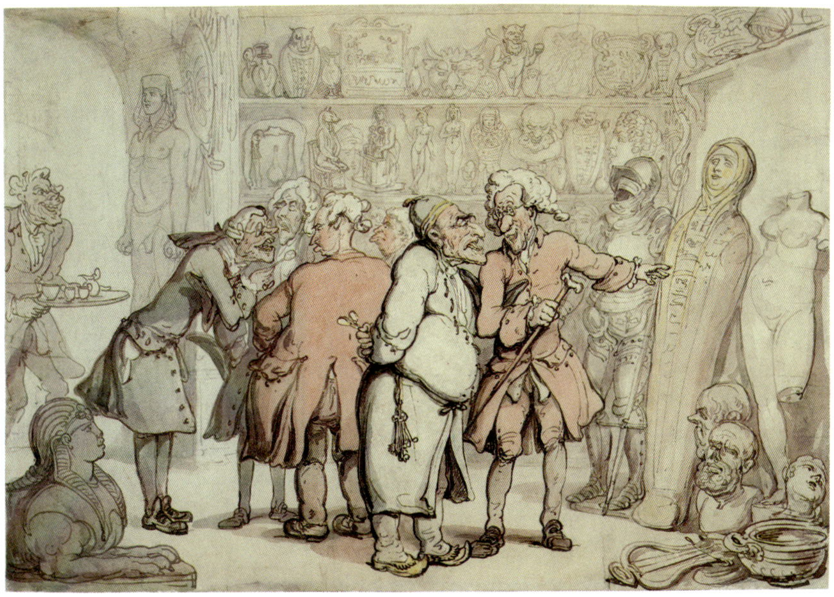

Thomas ROWLANDSON

[1756–1827]

A Group of Antiquaries, c.1805

pen and ink with watercolour on paper, 25.6 × 37.6 cm
on reverse: pencil sketch of a figure and *812/99*

P.222
PROVENANCE: Purchased from Appleby Brothers, April 1958.
EXHIBITIONS: *British Portrait Exhibition*, (Arts Council), Bucharest, Budapest, 1972–3.

The object that the central figure is holding behind his back appears to be a double eye-glass. Another can be seen in an early 19th century picture of people taking the waters at Carlsbad.

Although the two foreground figures are admiring the nude female plaster, the other antiquaries seem to be gossiping together as happens at most *conversazioni* of this kind.

EJ

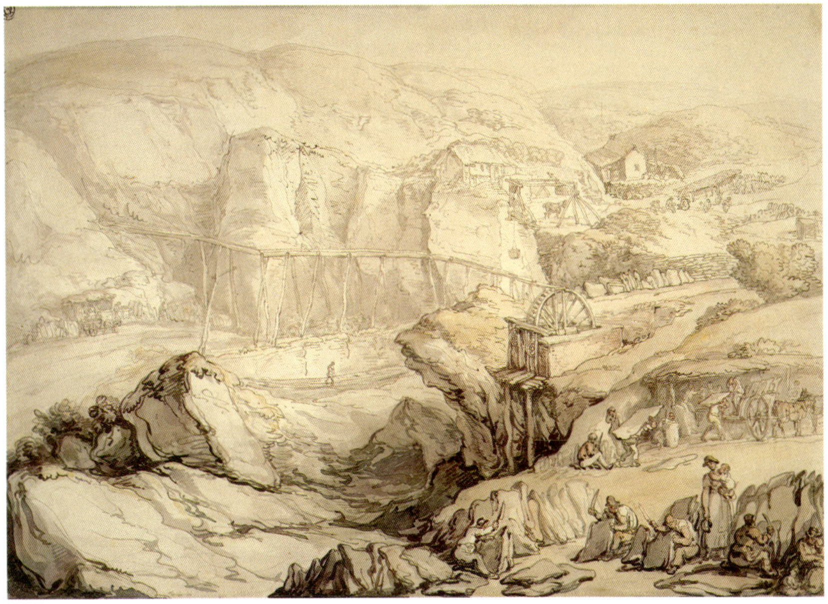

Thomas ROWLANDSON

[1756–1827]

Delabole Slate Quarry, after 1808

pen and grey and vermilion ink and watercolour over pencil on Whatman paper watermarked 1808, 32.8 × 47.1 cm
inscribed: collector's mark of Gilbert Davis

P.231
PROVENANCE: Gilbert Davis; anonymous sale Sotheby's 19 March 1958, no.87; P&D Colnaghi Ltd, from whom purchased by Gallery.
EXHIBITIONS: *English Watercolours from The Cecil Higgins Art Gallery, Bedford*, Reading, Reading Museum & Art Gallery, 1965, no.45; *The Art of Thomas Rowlandson*, New York, Frick Art Museum, Pittsburgh, Baltimore Museum of Art, 1990, no.81.
REFERENCES: A. Bury, 'The Cecil Higgins Museum Bedford', *The Old Watercolour Society Club*, 1959, vol. XXXVI, p.35; J. Hayes, *The Art of Thomas Rowlandson*, 1990, p.190, no.81, repr. p.191; J.E. Ayres, *Building the Georgian City*, 1998, fig.92.

The slate quarry at Delabole, near Camelford, was certainly being worked by 1600. It continued to thrive until recently but it is now disused.

Another more faded version of the subject is in the V&A (P.111–1931), and another drawing of the quarry, taken from a different viewpoint, is in a private collection.

EJ

Thomas ROWLANDSON
[1756–1827]
Savoyards Performing in a Garden, c.1810

pen and brown and red ink and watercolour on paper, 23.6 × 33.5 cm
inscribed: *T Rowlandson*

P.275
PROVENANCE: Gilbert Davis; P&D Colnaghi Ltd, from whom purchased by Gallery, January 1959.

Savoyards are itinerant musicians with a hurdy-gurdy and a monkey (not visible here, though there are acrobats by way of substitutes). They have wisely left themselves a line of retreat in case the dog in the foreground breaks loose.

EJ

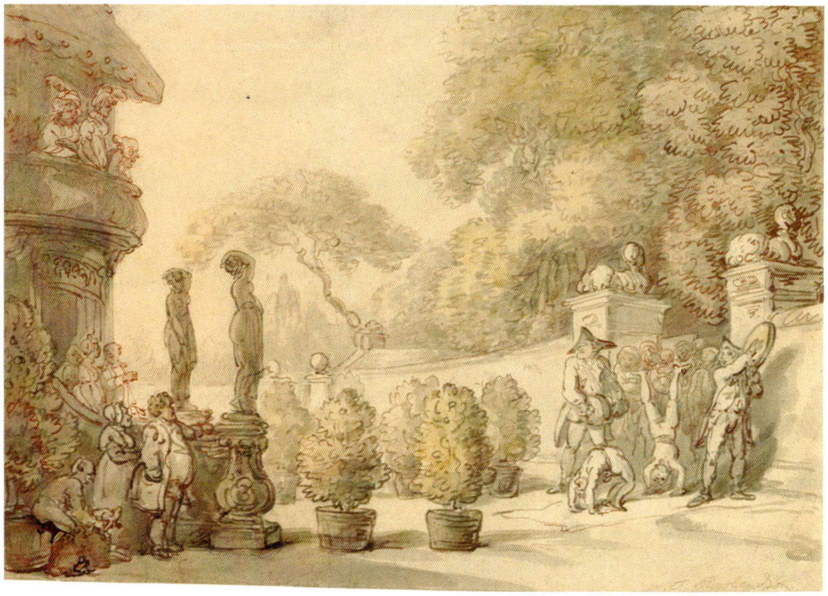

Thomas ROWLANDSON
[1756–1827]
Visitors in Venice, c.1810

pen and brown ink and watercolour on paper, 14.8 × 23.7cm

P.623
PROVENANCE: Miss Ward, from whom purchased by Gallery, January 1973.
EXHIBITIONS: *An Album of 18th Century Venetian Operatic Caricatures formerly in the Collection of Count Algarotti*, Toronto, Art Gallery of Ontario, 1980, no.16; *Visions of Venice*, London, Bankside Gallery, 1990, no.1.
REFERENCES: E. Croft-Murray, *An Album of 18th Century Venetian Operatic Caricatures formerly in the Collection of Count Algarotti*, 1980, p.21, no.16; J.G. Links, T. Wilcox & J. Christian, *Visions of Venice, Watercolours and Drawings from Turner to Procktor*, 1990, repr. p.32, no.1.

Rowlandson went to Italy in 1782 and again c.1820; the first visit may have included Venice, the second certainly did. Dr Riely of Yale dates the drawing c.1810 although the costumes are late 18th century. He suggests that the figures owe something to the caricatures of the Roman artist Pier Leone Ghezzi (1674–1755). There are at least two other versions in existence, both with the composition laterally inverted: one, *Fashions at Venice*, was sold at Sotheby's 13 March 1980, the other, *High Life in Venice*, dated to the 1790s is in the National Gallery of Victoria, Melbourne.

The Piazza San Marco, with the Doge's Palace visible here on the left, was a well-known spot for courtesans to 'cast their amorous glances without reserve upon those whom they think might answer their purposes' (Henry Cox, *A Picture of Italy*, 1815, p.423).

EJ

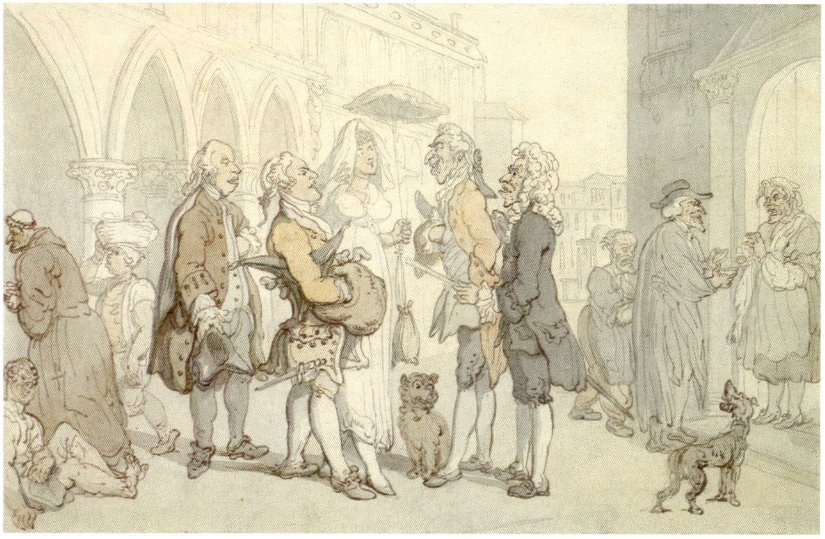

Thomas ROWLANDSON
[1756–1827]
Water Nymphs and River Gods (formerly **Nymphs and Satyrs**), **c.1810–15**

pen and ink and watercolour on paper, 17.7 × 25.6 cm

P.302
PROVENANCE: Desmond Cole; Abbott and Holder, from whom purchased by Gallery, October 1959.
EXHIBITIONS: *The English Tradition: an exhibition of watercolours from two private collections,* Bedford, Cecil Higgins Art Gallery, 1972, no.71, as *Nymphs and Satyrs.*

Rowlandson frequently borrowed scenes from Classical and Renaissance art. The seated group on the right has been taken almost line for line from the engraving *The Judgement of Paris* by Antonio Raimondi which in turn was after *The Judgement of Paris* by Raphael. The same composition appears in both Giorgione's *Concert Champêtre* and Manet's *Le Déjeuner sur l'herbe*. The original source of this composition has been traced back to a classical sarcophagus.

CB/JM

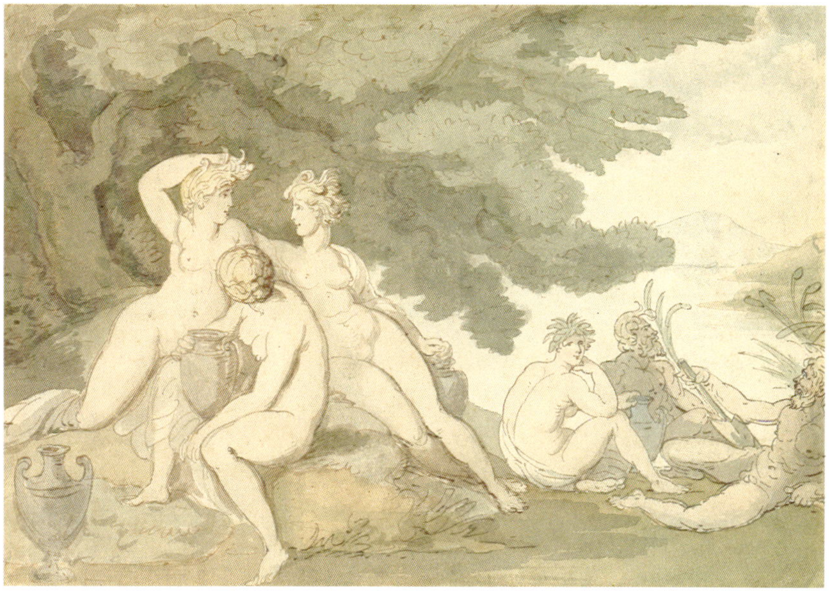

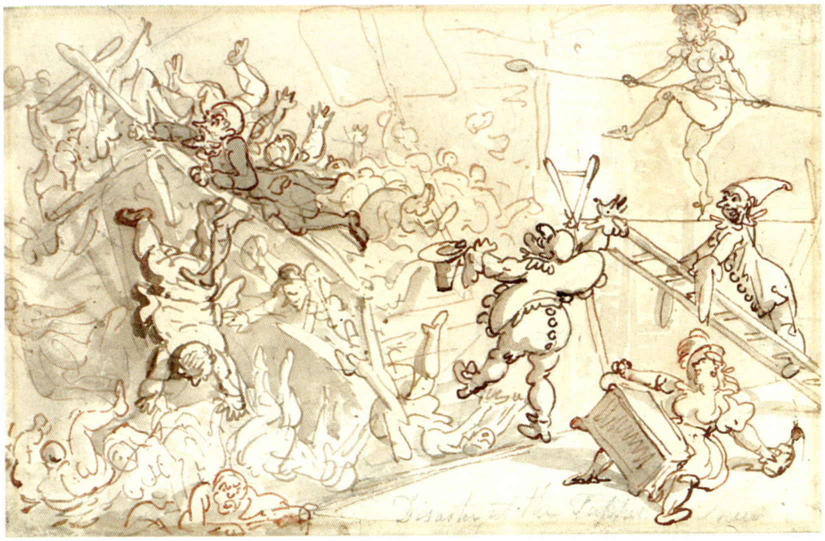

Thomas ROWLANDSON
[1756–1827]
Disaster at the Puppet Show

watercolour on paper, 13 × 20.5 cm
inscribed: *Disaster at the Puppet Show*

P.800
PROVENANCE: Given to Gallery by Alice Barbara Kitson, October 1992.

Rowlandson's sense of humour is well displayed here by the figure of the tightrope walker who is carrying on with her act seemingly quite oblivious to the utter confusion within a few feet of her.

EJ

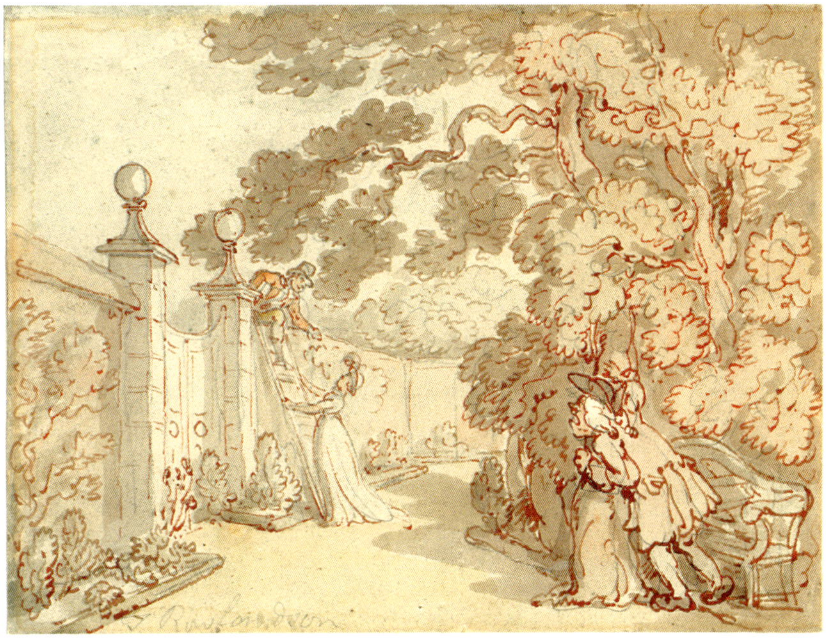

Thomas ROWLANDSON
[1756–1827]
Lovers Surprised by a Jealous Husband

watercolour on paper, 12.8 × 17.2 cm
inscribed: *T Rowlandson*

P.802
PROVENANCE: Given to Gallery by Alice Barbara Kitson, October 1992.

No doubt a very nasty surprise awaits the lovers when the young gentleman has finished descending the ladder.

JM

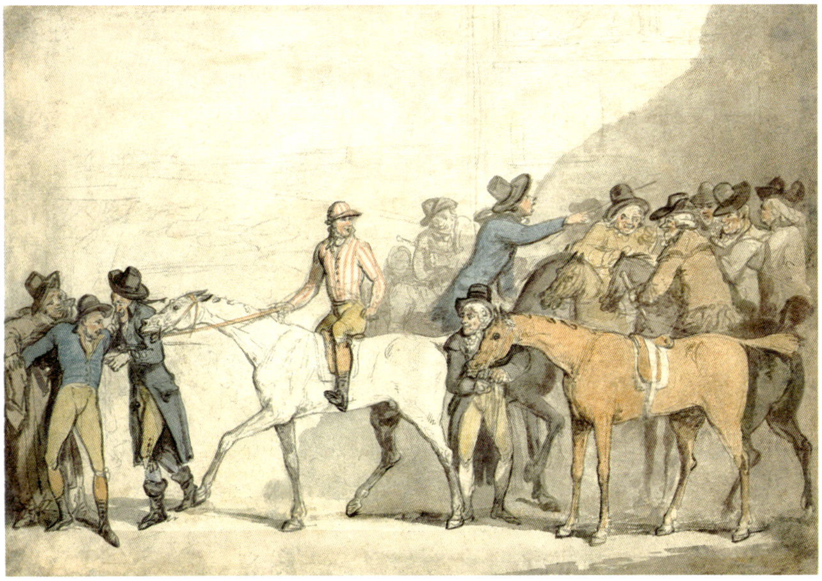

Attributed to **Thomas ROWLANDSON**
[1756–1827]
The Mount

watercolour on paper, 34.1 × 49.8 cm
on reverse in a hand much later than the picture: *The Mount 1789/Thomas Rowlandson/the original drawing for one of the famous racing scenes executed by the artist/for the Prince of Wales (George IV)/from the McCalmount and Mrs Cunliffe collection.*

P.176
PROVENANCE: Mrs McCalmount and Mrs Cunliffe; F. Sabin, from whom purchased by Gallery, December 1957.

Several experts, among them Edward Croft-Murray, Dr Riely of Yale and Dr John Hayes, all concur in rejecting Rowlandson although Croft-Murray thought that a collaboration between Rowlandson and George or Henry Wigstead was a possibility. Riely added that, judging by the costume, the drawing was certainly later than 1789.

EJ

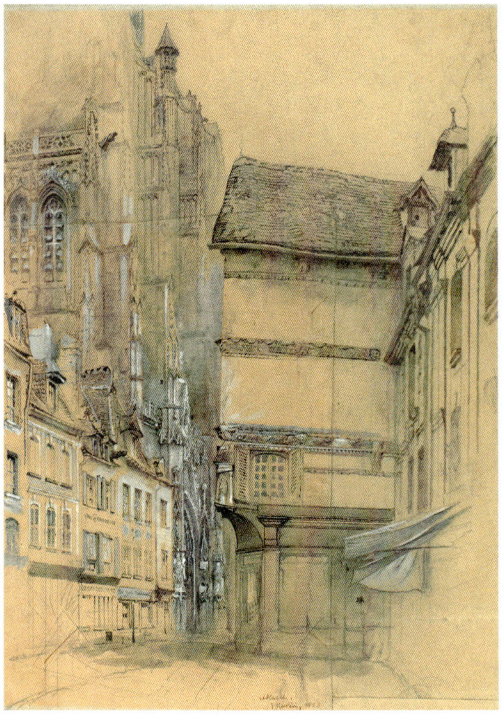

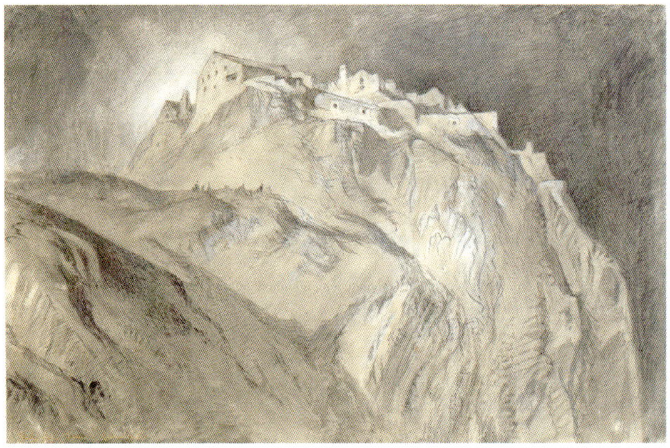

John RUSKIN
[1819–1900]
Abbeville, 1868

ink and wash and pencil heightened with white on buff coloured paper, 49 × 35.4 cm
inscribed: *J. Ruskin 1868 Abbeville*

P.206
PROVENANCE: P&D Colnaghi Ltd, from whom purchased by Gallery, April 1958.
EXHIBITIONS: *Watercolours and Drawings from The Cecil Higgins Art Gallery, Bedford*, London, Thos. Agnew & Sons Ltd, 1962, no.27; *Watercolours from the Cecil Higgins Art Gallery, Bedford*, Norwich, Norwich Castle Museum, 1965, no.49.

In 1868 Ruskin spent seven weeks in Abbeville in Normandy and drew intensively while there, recording old buildings and Gothic churches with the care and attention to detail that recall the work of one of his boyhood heroes, Samuel PROUT.

In his autobiography he wrote, 'My most intense happinesses have of course been among the mountains. But for cheerful, unalloyed, unwearying pleasure, the getting in sight of Abbeville on a fine summer afternoon, jumping out in the courtyard of the Hôtel de l'Europe, and rushing down the street to see St. Wulfran again before the sun was off the towers, are things to cherish the past for – to the end'. (E.T. Cook and A. Wedderburn (eds.), *The Works of John Ruskin*, 39 vols, 1903–12, vol. VI, p.238).

EJ

John RUSKIN
[1819–1900]
Grandeville

pencil and wash heightened with white on paper, 25.4 × 38.8 cm
inscribed: *Study from Turner's Grandeville...failure J.Ruskin*

P.205
PROVENANCE: P&D Colnaghi Ltd, from whom purchased by Gallery, April 1958.

Ruskin was the first owner of TURNER'S watercolour of *Grandeville*, drawn c.1830 (Wilton no.1050), now in a private collection. Ruskin made numerous copies of Turner's watercolours and he also encouraged young artists to follow his example, sometimes even paying them to do so. Several of these copyists came from the drawing classes at the Working Men's College. Notable among them was William Ward (1829– 1908), of whom Ruskin wrote that he was a copyist 'with perfect fidelity in rendering the work of Turner'. This has since resulted in Ward's copies being occasionally passed off as by Turner himself.

EJ

John RUSKIN
[1819–1900]
Talloires, Lake of Annecy

watercolour heightened with bodycolour on buff paper, 14.5 × 23 cm
inscribed on reverse: *JR (?) Herne Hill Lake of Annecy Chateau of Juniet (?) from Talloire* and *(9)*

P.437
PROVENANCE: Given to Sir Sydney Cockerell (1867–1962) by Joan Severn from Brentwood after Ruskin's death; sale Sotheby's (property of the late Sir Sydney Cockerell), 14 November 1962, no.70; purchased by Thos. Agnew & Sons Ltd on behalf of Gallery.
NOTES: compiler's question marks for inscription on reverse.

Sydney Cockerell first met Ruskin in 1887. They soon became friends and Cockerell was invited to stay at Brantwood. He was later director of the Fitzwilliam Museum, Cambridge, 1908–37, and was knighted in 1934. Talloires is on the eastern shore of the Lake of Annecy, dominated by the imposing Rochers de Lanfon. This was a part of France that Ruskin visited several times.

EJ/JM

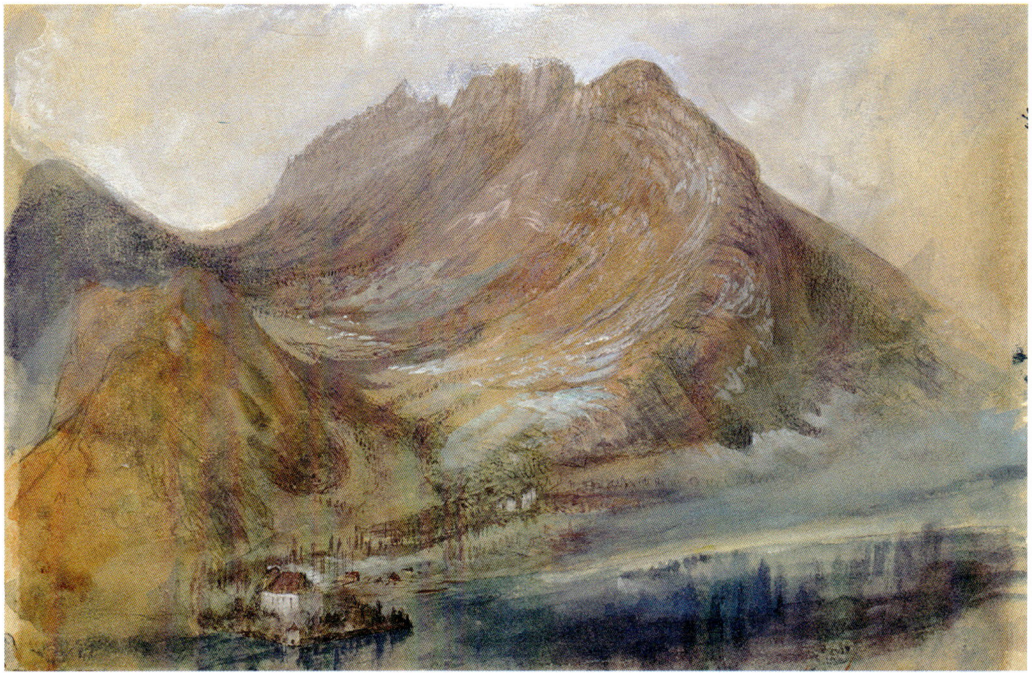

Paul SANDBY, R.A.
[1731–1809]
Rosamond's Pond, St James's Park, 1758

pencil, chalk and watercolour on paper, 37.4 x 52.4 cm
inscribed: *Paul Sandby del*
Rosomond's [sic] *Pond, St James's Park, 1758, P.S*

P.85
PROVENANCE: Spink & Son Ltd, from whom purchased by Gallery, January 1952.
EXHIBITIONS: *English Watercolours from the Hickman Bacon and other Collections*, Bedford, Cecil Higgins Art Gallery, 1952, no.65; *Watercolours and Drawings from the Cecil Higgins Art Gallery, Bedford*, London, Thos. Agnew & Sons Ltd, 1962, no.1; *Paintings and Drawings by Thomas and Paul Sandby*, Reading, Reading Museum & Art Gallery, Bolton, Bolton Museum & Art Gallery, 1972, no.101.
REFERENCES: A. Bury, 'The Cecil Higgins Museum Bedford', *Old Watercolour Society's Club*, 1961, vol.xxxvi, p.33, pl.x.

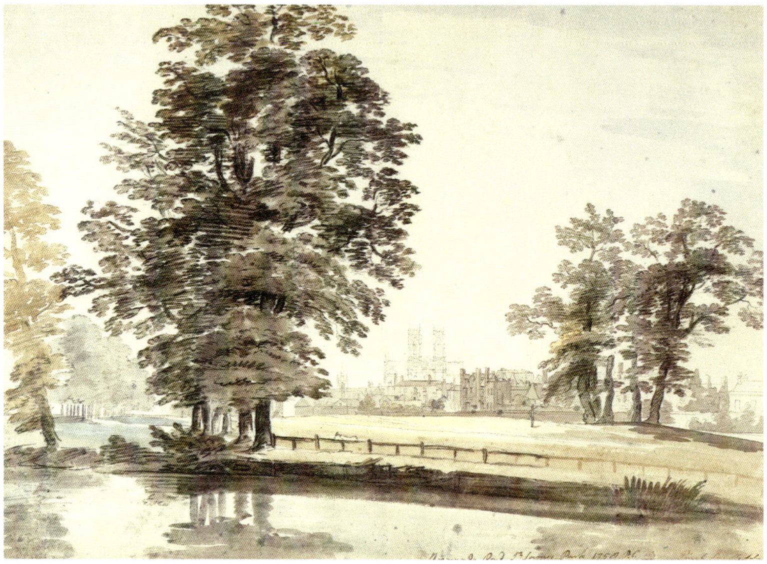

Paul was probably living with his brother Thomas in Great Pulteney Street near Piccadilly Circus in 1753, having returned from Scotland. It was during this period c.1758 that they conceived a group of engravings of *Six London Views*, engraved by Edward Rooker, but not published until 1766.

Rosamond's Pond was situated in the south west corner of St James's Park and according to one source 'afforded great entertainment to the Contemplative eye'. However, it also had a 'melancholy secluded situation', and, due to the number of suicides by drowning, (especially young women), it was filled up in 1770.

JM

Paul SANDBY, R.A.
[1731–1809]
A Swaggering Man, c.1760

watercolour and black chalk on paper, 20 × 14.4 cm

P.504
PROVENANCE: Lord Bruce; P&D Colnaghi Ltd, from whom purchased by Gallery, July 1965.
EXHIBITIONS: *English Drawings and Watercolours*, London, P&D Colnaghi Ltd, 1965, no.9.

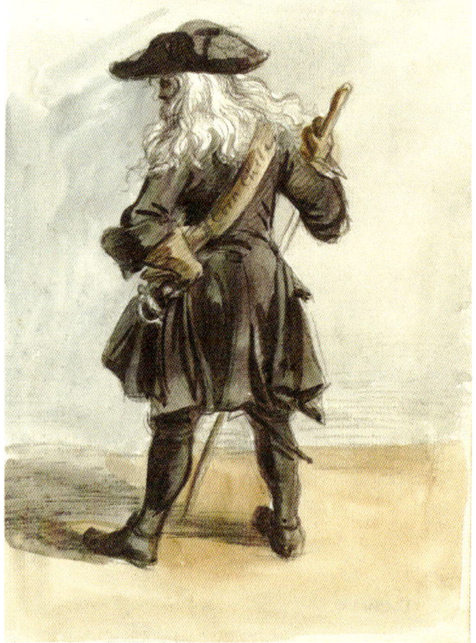

This belongs to a group of seventy-six studies of known and remarkable street wanderers of the day. Among these, twelve closely related subjects were etched and published in 1760 as part one of a book, *London Cries done from ye Life by P.Sandby*. The set also contained a frontal view of the same sitter now in the Yale Center for British Art, New Haven. There the man has a stout stick in his right hand while his left hand is on his hip as though striking an attitude. Unfortunately, the writing on the sashes of both men is quite indecipherable.

EJ

Paul SANDBY, R.A.
[1731–1809]
Landscape with River and a Tower, 1791

watercolour and pencil on paper, 49.4 × 64cm
inscribed: *P. Sandby 1791*

P.87
PROVENANCE: Miss Jessel; by descent to the Hon. Mrs Agnew, for whom sold by Thos. Agnew & Sons Ltd to Gallery, June 1952.
EXHIBITIONS: *English Watercolours from the Hickman Bacon and other Collections*, Bedford, Cecil Higgins Art Gallery, 1952, no.67; *English Watercolours from The Cecil Higgins Art Gallery, Bedford*, Reading, Reading Museum and Art Gallery, 1965, no.48.

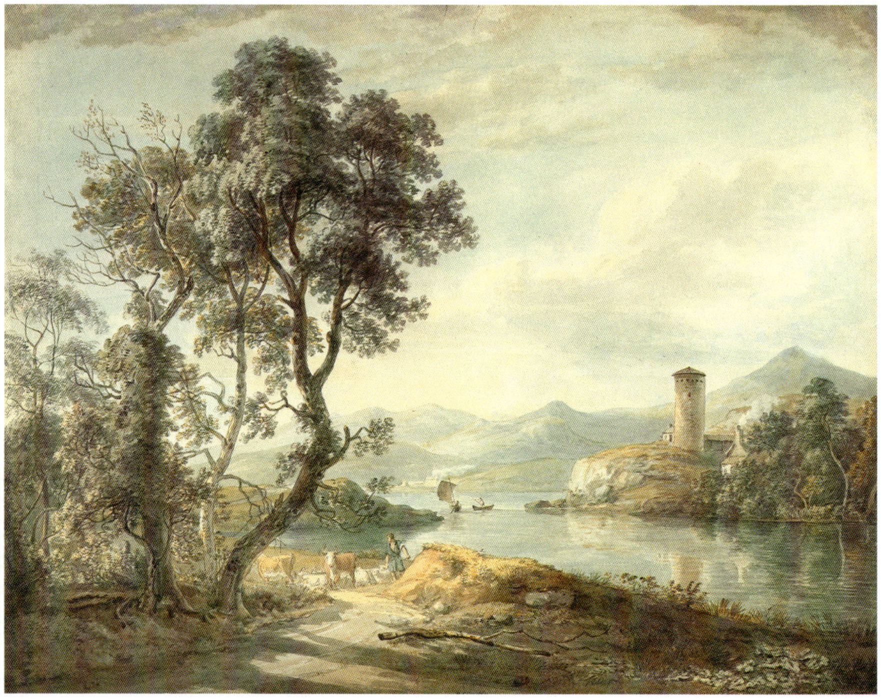

During the 1780s both the Sandbys adopted a much freer manner in their handling of watercolour. Paul also became more concerned with the overall design of the picture as opposed to purely topographical depiction, with a greater consideration shown in the rendering of light and shade for compositional effect.

JM

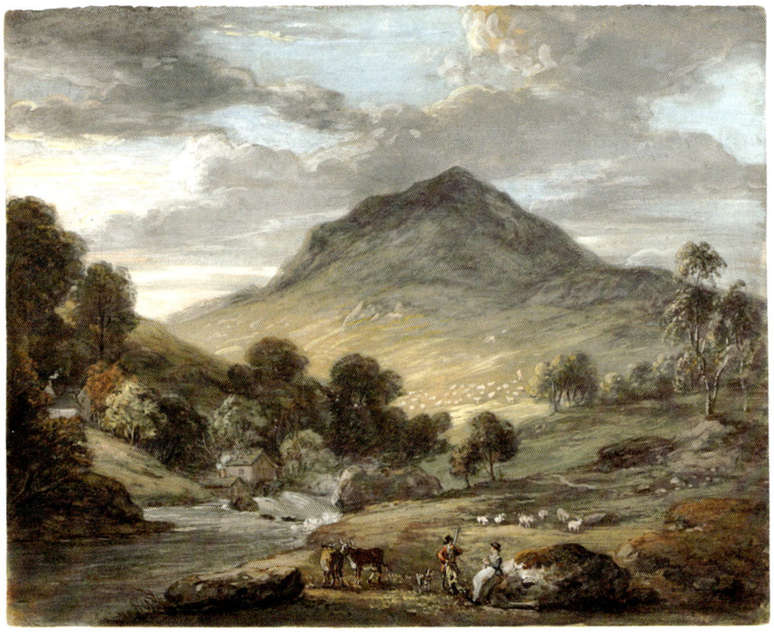

Paul SANDBY, R.A.
[1731–1809]
Pandy Pen Machno , 1796

bodycolour on paper, 26 × 32.5 cm

P.86
PROVENANCE: J. Leger & Sons, from whom purchased by Gallery, 1952.
EXHIBITIONS: *English Watercolours from the Hickman Bacon Collection,* Bedford, Cecil Higgins Art Gallery, 1952, no.66 as *Pandy Pei, Machno; Watercolours and Drawings from The Cecil Higgins Art Gallery, Bedford,* London, Thos. Agnew & Sons Ltd, 1962, no.12; *Paintings and Drawings by Thomas and Paul Sandby,* Reading, Reading Museum & Art Gallery, Bolton, Bolton Museum & Art Gallery, 1972, no.99 as *Pandy Bei Machno, Nr.Llanwrst.*

Llanwrst is in the Conwy Valley about five miles north of Bettws-y-Coed on the A470. Sandby made several sketching tours in Wales and, according to Iolo Williams, it was he who 'broadly speaking opened the eyes of Englishmen to the pictorial interest of Wales'. His first visit was to accompany Sir Watkin Williams Wynn to his seat at Wynnsaty in 1769 or 1770.

According to his son, Sandby later travelled in Wales, probably in the 1770s, with Sir Joseph Banks, Daniel Charles Solander and John Lightfoot, exhibiting his first watercolour of a Welsh subject in 1773.

EJ

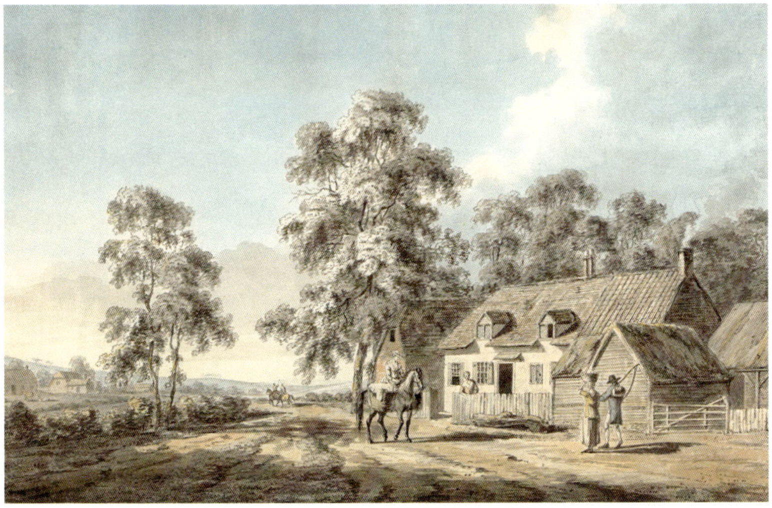

Paul SANDBY, R.A.
[1731–1809]
Landscape with Travellers on a Road

watercolour and pen and ink on paper, 29.7 × 46.8 cm

P.88
PROVENANCE: Squire Gallery, from whom purchased by Gallery, January 1953.
EXHIBITIONS: *English Watercolours from The Cecil Higgins Art Gallery Bedford,* Reading, Reading Museum and Art Gallery, no.47.

Thomas GAINSBOROUGH said of Sandby that he was 'The only man of genius who has painted real views from nature in this country'.

JM

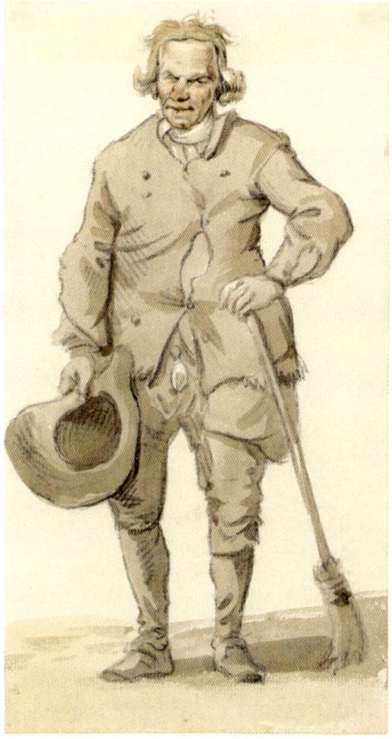

Paul SANDBY, R.A.
[1731–1809]
Figure Study: A Gardener

watercolour over black chalk on paper, 29.2 × 15.8 cm

P.347
PROVENANCE: Sotheby's; P&D Colnaghi Ltd, from whom purchased by Gallery, July 1960.
EXHIBITIONS: *The English Tradition: an exhibition of watercolours from two private collections,* Bedford, Cecil Higgins Art Gallery, 1972, no.72; *Paintings and Drawings by Thomas and Paul Sandby,* Reading, Reading Museum & Art Gallery, Bolton, Bolton Museum and Art Gallery, 1972, no.100.

This probably depicts a Windsor character. In 1751 Paul joined his elder brother, Thomas, who had been appointed Deputy Ranger of Windsor Great Park shortly after 1746. There he helped Thomas with the construction of Virginia Water and began his long series of drawings and engravings of Windsor, both its personalities and topography.

EJ

Paul SANDBY, R.A.
[1731–1809]
Three Figures

watercolour and black lead on paper, 16.4 × 13.8 cm

P.89
PROVENANCE: Thos. Agnew & Sons Ltd, from whom purchased by Gallery, 1954.
EXHIBITIONS: *81st Annual Exhibition of Watercolour Drawings*, London, Thos. Agnew & Sons Ltd, 1954, no.28; *Watercolours and Drawings from The Cecil Higgins Art Gallery, Bedford*, London, Thos. Agnew & Sons Ltd, 1962, no.13.
REFERENCES: A. Buck, *Dress in Eighteenth Century England*, 1979, p.48, fig.22.

Paul Sandby is often referred to – not quite accurately – as 'the father of the British Watercolour School', but he was largely responsible for watercolour (until then merely considered as a useful method of making studies for oils), being raised to an independent status and worthy in itself of serious regard. He was certainly the most versatile and finest of the topographers and worked in bodycolour as well as pure watercolour. He and his brother Thomas (1723–98) were both foundation members of the R.A.

Although primarily a landscape painter, Sandby was also a prolific and accomplished figure draughtsman. In the Royal Library at Windsor there are many fine examples of his figure drawings, while, in 1959 Christie's had two sales amounting to several hundred drawings from the collection of William Sandby, a descendant, including a good number of figure drawings, many of them of named sitters.

EJ

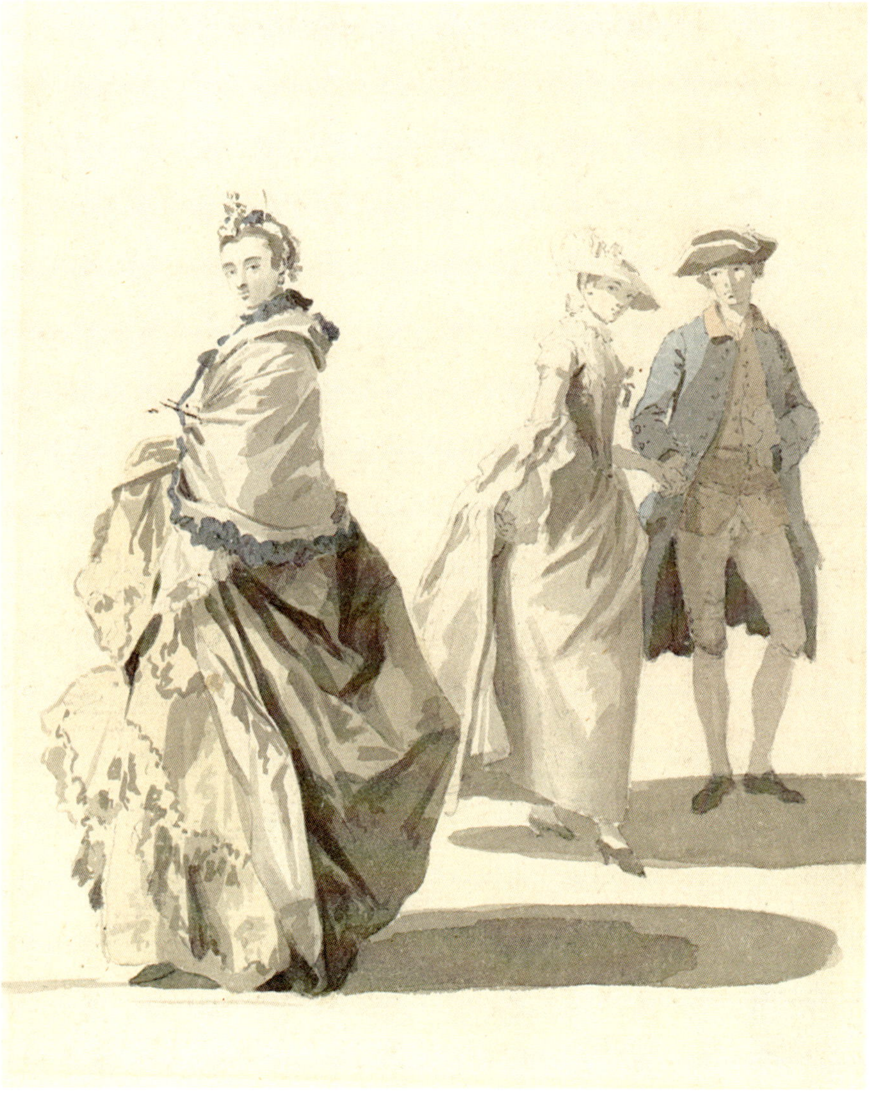

Frederick SANDYS
[1829–1904]
Penelope, 1878

coloured chalks on paper, 52.4 × 43.9 cm
Original label inscribed: *'Penelope' study for an oil painting of Frederick Sandys [l]ent by C.E. Fry Esq, 55 Baker Street W – Price £126.0.0*

P.253
PROVENANCE: Clarence E. Fry; his sale Christie's 18 April 1891, no.57, bought for £39.18.0 by Francis Buxton; given by the Hon. Mrs Francis Buxton to the Red Cross sale at Christie's 15 April 1916, no.1317, bought in for £7.17.6; Christie's 15 June 1925, no.62, bought in; presented by Miss F.M. Buxton to the Red Cross sale at Christie's 19 July 1940, no.1715, purchased for 2 guineas by Wilson; Leicester Galleries, from whom purchased by Gallery, 1958.
EXHIBITIONS: *Watts and Sandys*, London, R.A., Winter Exhibition, 1905, no.272.
REFERENCES: E. Wood, 'A Consideration of the Art of Frederick Sandys', *The Artist*, Special Winter 18 November 1896, p.39, repr. p.42; *Frederick Sandys 1829–1904*, 1974, p.37 no.153, pl.112 (not shown in exhibition); I. Simpson, *Painter's Progress, an art school year in twelve lessons*, p.454; *The World of Interiors*, Nov. 1990, p.211; B. Elzea, *Frederick Sandys 1829–1904, a catalogue raisonné*, Antique Collectors Club, 2001, pp.257–8, repr.p.258 as *Penelope II*.

Pre-Raphaelite painter, portraitist and illustrator, Sandys studied at the R.A. Schools under George Richmond and Samuel Lawrence, who taught him to draw in chalks. He soon became a member of the circle surrounding ROSSETTI and Swinburne, whose poems he illustrated.

This drawing, made in 1878, of a rather Amazonian Penelope, is characteristic of Sandys' more dramatic and highly finished portraits influenced by Rossetti. Comparison with the illustration in *The Artist*, 1896, reveals that they are the same drawing which has been cut down from 76.2 × 53.3 cm (sometime after 1940, the last time it was recorded with the original dimensions), removing the right shoulder and unfinished forearm. Two drawings of the same model were shown at the Fine Art Society in 1972, one of them very similar in pose to that in the Gallery's drawing.

EJ/JM

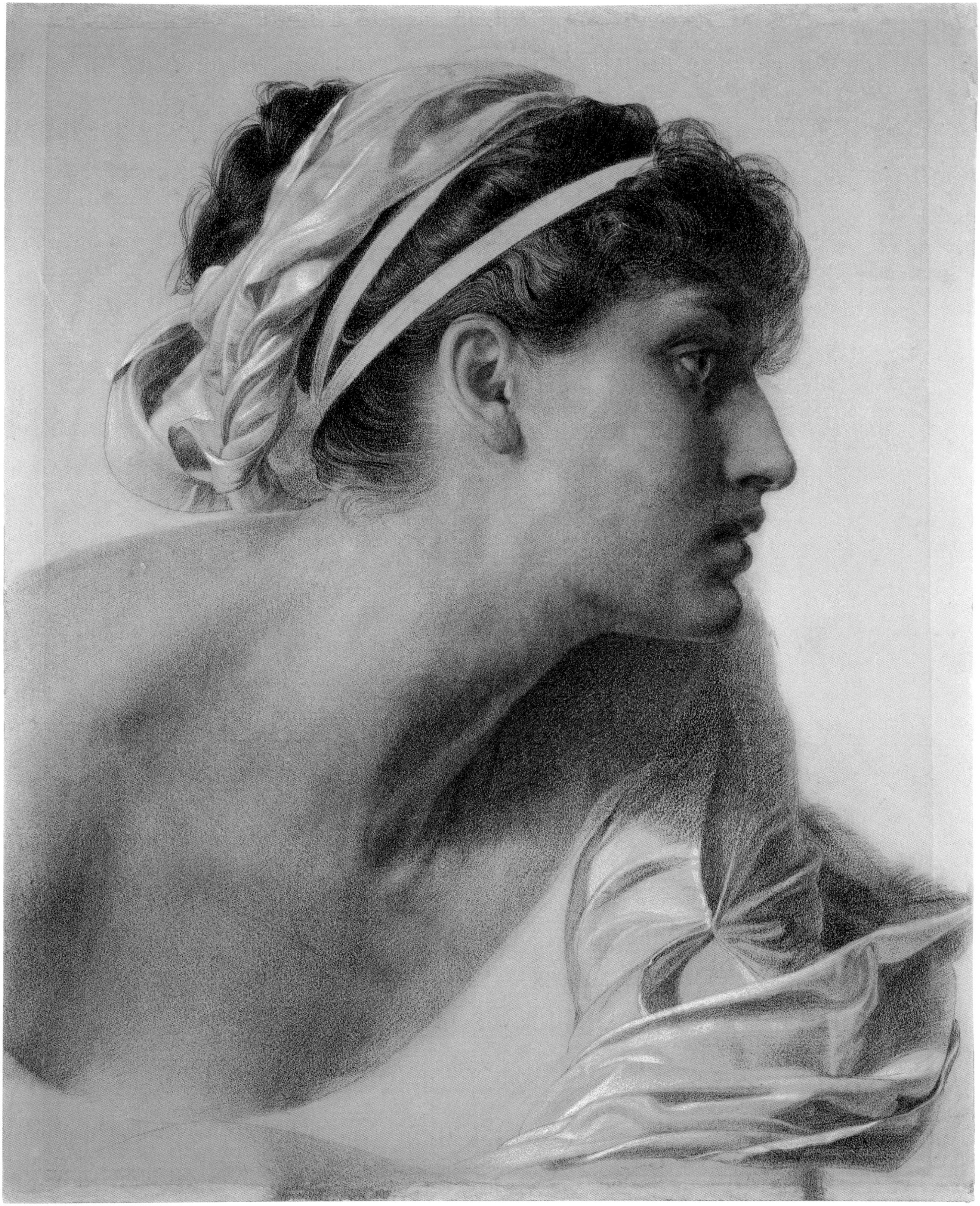

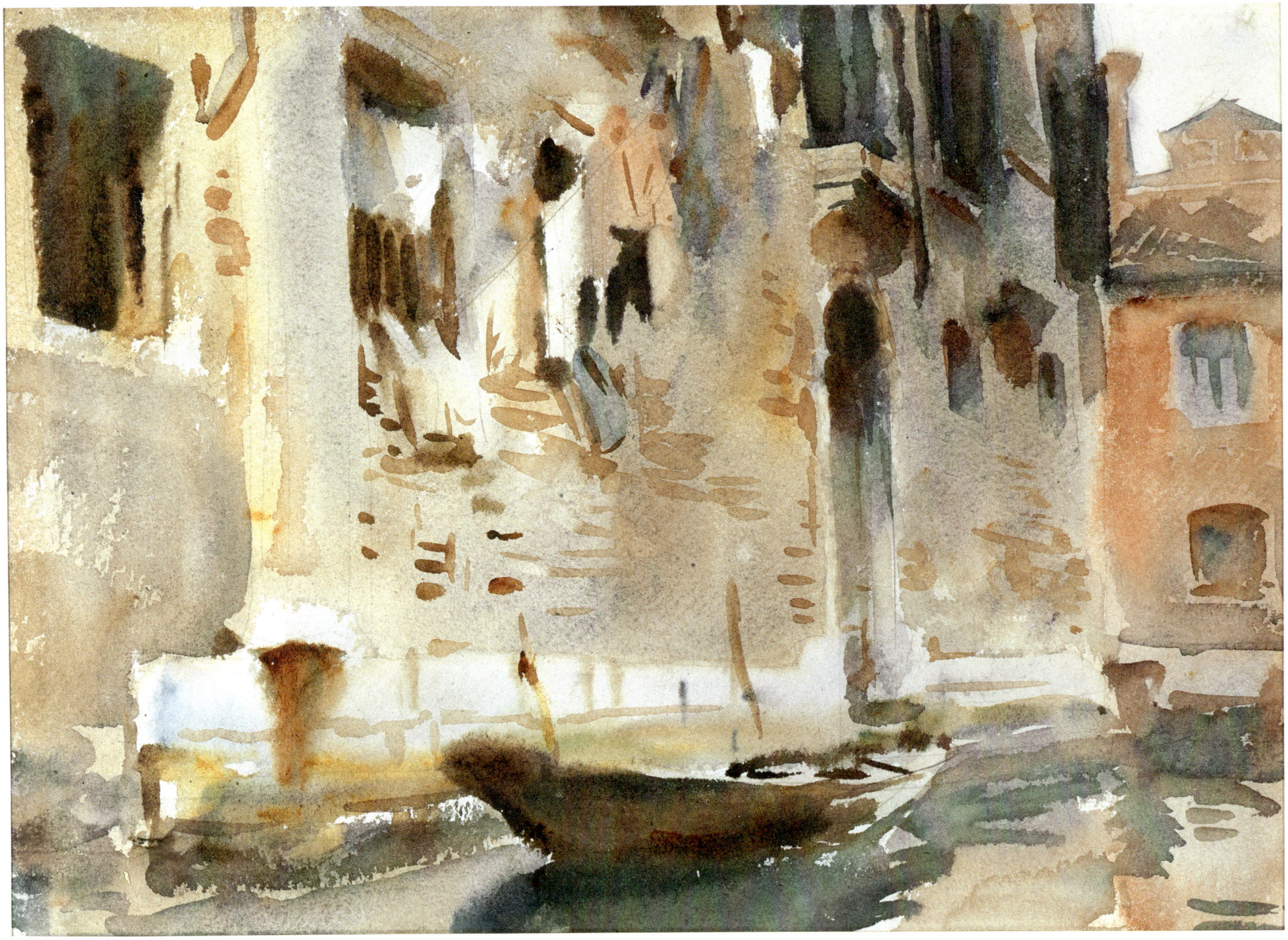

John Singer SARGENT, R.A., R.W.S.
[1856–1925]
A Venetian Canal

watercolour and pencil on paper, 24.3 × 34.5 cm

P.412
PROVENANCE: Mrs F. Ormond; by descent to her daughter Mrs Hugo Pitman (the artist's niece); Thos. Agnew & Sons Ltd, from whom purchased by Gallery, January 1962.
EXHIBITIONS: *Watercolours and Drawings from The Cecil Higgins Art Gallery, Bedford*, London, Thos. Agnew & Sons Ltd, 1962, no.82.

It is not easy to date Sargent's Venetian watercolours which, as here, are very freely painted with a loaded brush. It seems that he began painting them on his second visit to the city in 1880 and on many subsequent visits, which became part of his annual break from portrait painting from the late 1890s onwards. He described his choice of subjects there as 'I can paint objects, I can't paint vedutas'.

Sargent was born in Florence of American parents; studying in Paris under Carolus-Duran (1837–1917), he remained in France until 1884 before coming to England where he became the most fashionable portrait painter since Sir Thomas Lawrence (1769–1830). Superficiality was always his enemy but occurred less in his landscapes to which he turned almost exclusively after 1910. Pissarro summed him up as 'an adroit performer'.

EJ

Randolph SCHWABE
[1885–1948]
Portrait of J.D. Innes, c.1910

watercolour and red crayon on paper, sheet size 28.4 × 18cm
on reverse: four pencil drawings of heads

P.541
PROVENANCE: Roland, Browse and Delbanco, from whom purchased by Gallery, October 1966.

Randolph Schwabe, Slade Professor at University College, London, from 1930 to 1949, published 'Reminiscences of Fellow Students', in *The Burlington Magazine*, January, 1943, a principal source of information about INNES. His portrait has captured the 'prominent nose, glittering black eyes and features of a slightly cadaverous cast', as noted by Augustus JOHN in his autobiography (*Chiaroscuro*, 1952, p.202).

Schwabe was born in Manchester and studied at the R.C.A., the Slade School and in Paris at the Académie Julian. He showed with the London Group and R.W.S. making his name as a painter, printmaker, theatre designer and illustrator. He served as an Official War Artist between 1914 and 1918.

EJ/JM

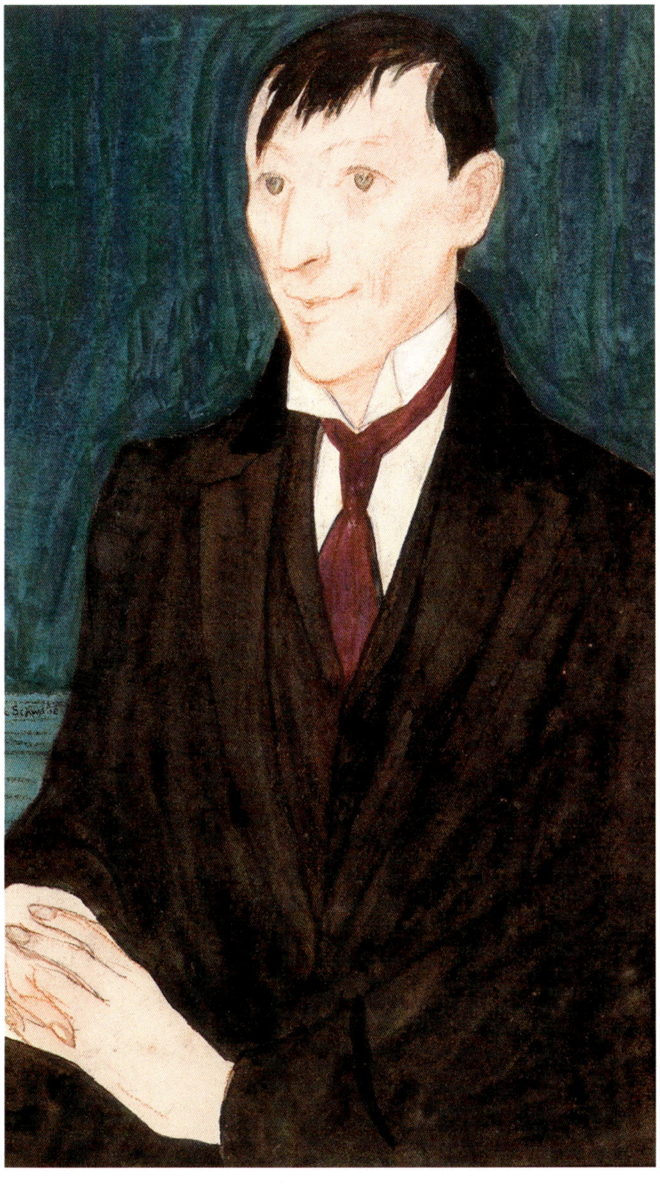

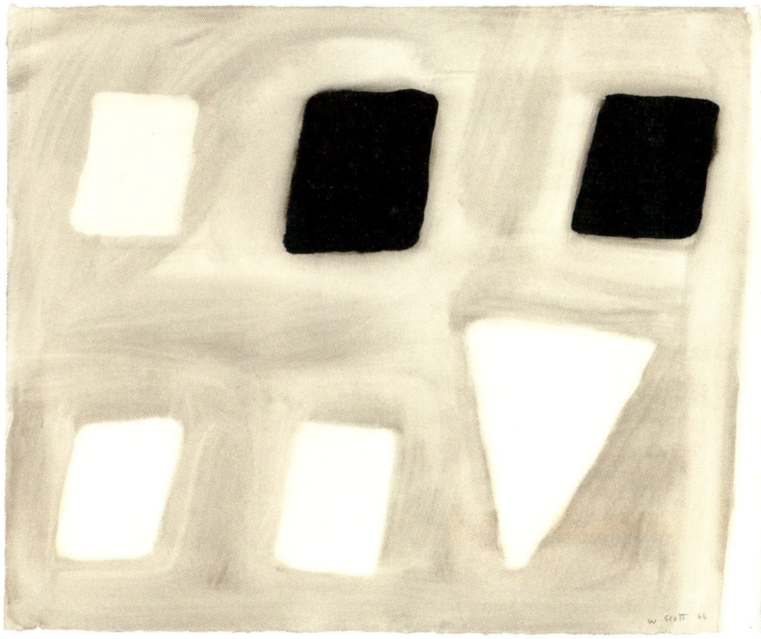

William SCOTT, C.B.E.
[1913–89]
Angle, 1964

bodycolour on paper, 54.6 × 68.5 cm
inscribed: *W. Scott 64*

P.577
PROVENANCE: Hanover Gallery, from whom purchased by Gallery, January 1968.

Scott studied at Belfast College of Art, 1928–31, and the R.A. Schools, 1931–5. After war service he became a member of the London Group in 1949.

His still lifes of the late 1940s and early 1950s led to a brief trial with pure abstraction. In 1963–4 he spent a scholarship year in Berlin discarding his earlier style for a more symmetrical arrangement of shapes on a flat ground.

EJ/JM

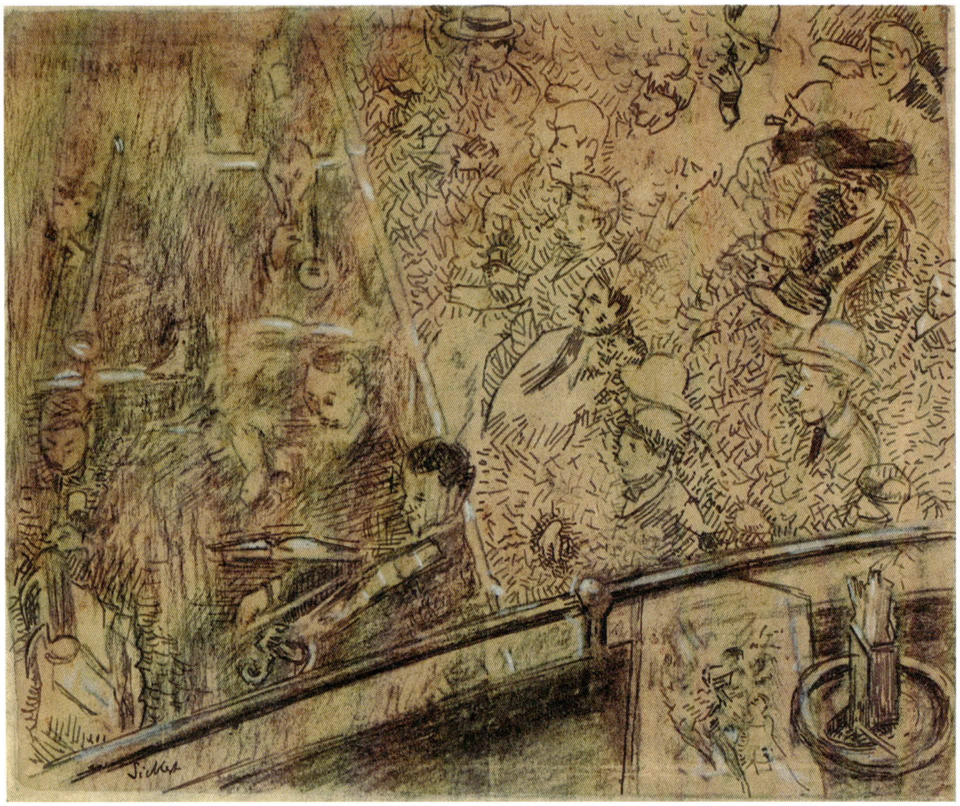

Walter Richard SICKERT
[1860–1942]
The Old Middlesex, c.1906 or c.1910–11

pen and charcoal heightened with white on brown paper, 25 × 31 cm
inscribed: *Sickert*

P.335
PROVENANCE: Roland, Browse and Delbanco, from whom purchased by Gallery, January 1960.
EXHIBITIONS: *Paintings and Drawings by Sickert,* London, Roland, Browse and Delbanco, 1960, no.41; *Sickert*, London, Tate Gallery, 1960, no.29; *The Graphic Art of Walter Sickert,* New Haven, Yale Center for British Art, 1979, no.62, *Walter Sickert,* Amsterdam, Van Gogh Museum, 1993.
REFERENCES: W. Baron, *Sickert*, 1973, p.342, no.232, fig.161; A. Troyen, *Walter Sickert as Printmaker,* 1979, repr. p.46, no.62.

Baron assigns the drawing to c.1906 after a much earlier suggested dating of c.1887, (when Sickert first began to paint Music Halls): 'The extraordinary technique of this drawing is sufficient in itself to preclude an early dating of the painting, (Baron no.231), now in the Beaverbrook Art Gallery, Fredericton, New Brunswick, Canada for which it is a study.' Aimée Troyen in the Yale Catalogue, 1979, points to a similar etching (first state c.1910), made at Rowlandson House, Sickert's School for etching, with the first and third (of five states) dedicated by Sickert to Madeleine Knox. She assisted in the printing of the early states but left at Christmas 1910 due to a breakdown. Troyen also notes the strong similarities in the drawing and etched versions, especially the individual audience figures who correspond exactly. However, it was not uncommon for Sickert to make highly finished drawings into etchings at a slightly later date such as the drawing for *Nude at a Wash Stand*, c.1911 (P.209), made into the etching *Sally*, c.1915.

EJ/JM

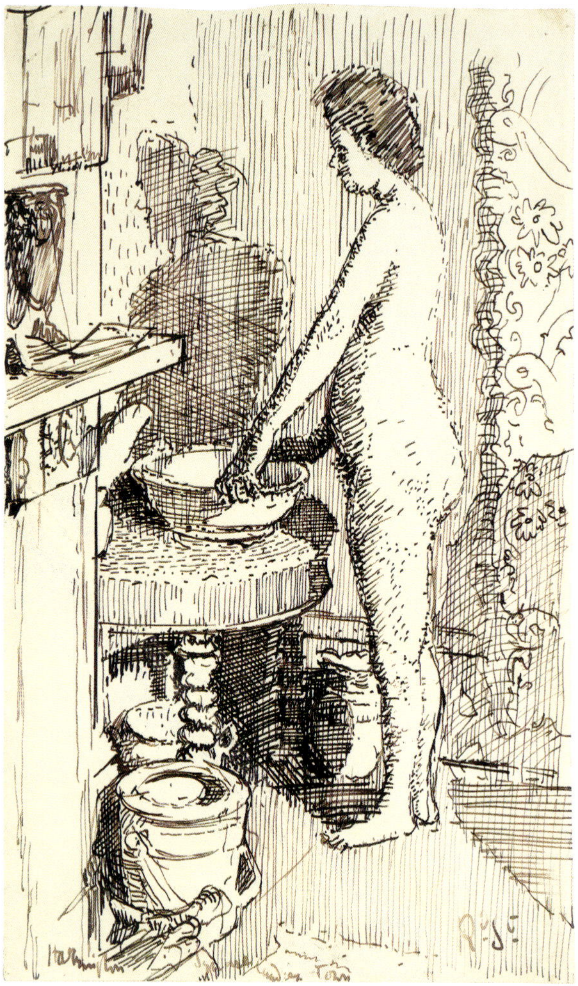

Walter Richard SICKERT
[1860–1942]
Nude at a Washstand (Drawing for the etching Sally), c.1911

pen and ink on paper, 31.1 × 19.1 cm
inscribed: *Rd St*
Harrington Square, Camden Town

P.209
PROVENANCE: Roland, Browse and Delbanco, from whom purchased by Gallery, May 1958.
EXHIBITIONS: *Sickert: Paintings and Drawings,* London, Tate Gallery, 1960, no.130; *Watercolours and Drawings from The Cecil Higgins Art Gallery, Bedford,* London, Thos. Agnew & Sons Ltd, 1962, no.75; *The Graphic Art of Walter Sickert,* New Haven, Yale Center for the study of British Art, 1979, no.74; *Walter Sickert:Paintings, Drawings, Etchings,* Amsterdam, Van Gogh Museum, 1993, shown as *Sally; Exposed: The Victorian Nude,* London, Tate Britain, 2001–2, no.175
REFERENCES: W. Baron, *Sickert,* 1973, pp.122–3,361, no.327, fig.229; A. Troyen, *Walter Sickert as Printmaker,* 1979, p.56, no.74, repr. p.57; A.Smith, (ed.), *Exposed: The Victorian Nude,* London, Tate Britain, 2001–2, no.175, illus.

A drawing for the etching entitled *Sally* of which a version is in the Gallery's collection. Formerly dated to 1909, Baron points out that it cannot date before 1911, the year that Sickert moved, after his marriage, to Harrington Square. She also notes that the technique, involving the combination of a wide variety of forms of hatching, is very close to that in the drawing of *Alice* (Baron, fig.228), which is dated June 1911. Sickert produced a number of ink drawings of figures in 1911–12, several of which became the basis for later prints.

EJ/JM

Walter Richard SICKERT
[1860–1942]
Charwoman in a Plumed Hat
(Study for A Few Words), c.1912

charcoal and blue wash on paper, 30.5 × 24.8 cm

P.334
PROVENANCE: Mrs Grace Wheatley; sale Christie's 11 November 1958, no.12; Roland, Browse and Delbanco, from whom purchased by Gallery, January 1960.
EXHIBITIONS: *Sickert*, London, Tate Gallery, 1960, no.133, *Watercolours and Drawings from The Cecil Higgins Art Gallery, Bedford*, London, Thos. Agnew & Sons Ltd, 1962, no.64.
REFERENCES: W. Baron, *Sickert*, 1973, no.319; W. Baron & R. Shone (eds.), *Sickert*, 1992, p.218, fig.156.

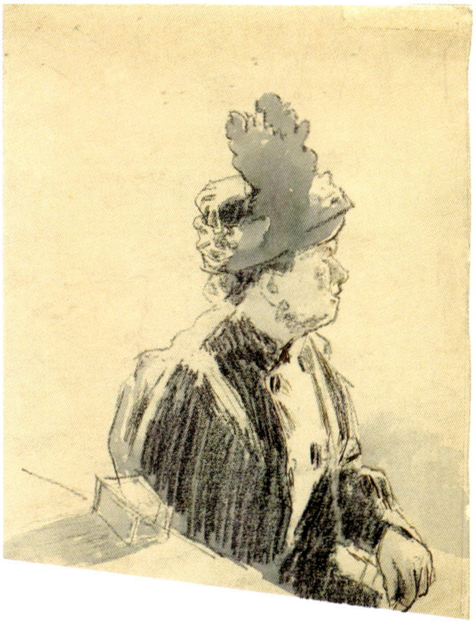

The charwoman appears in the foreground of *A Few Words* (Baron, no.304, fig.213, collection of Mr and Mrs Kenneth Snowman), which uses the composition of *Off to the Pub*, (Baron, no.303, fig.212), with the charwoman added. Baron suggests a date of c.1912 for both pictures adding that the charwoman often modelled for Sickert at this period.

Another drawing of her appears in *That Boy of Mine will Ruin Me* (R. Emmons, *The Life and Opinions of Walter Sickert*, London, 1941, repr. facing p.200).

EJ

Walter Richard SICKERT
[1860–1942]
Jack Ashore, c.1912–13

charcoal with pen and ink on paper, 38 × 28.1 cm

P.367
PROVENANCE: Mrs Grace Wheatley, R.W.S.; her sale Christie's 11 November 1958, no.16 as *A Man Conversing with a Woman;* Thos. Agnew & Sons Ltd from whom purchased by Gallery, October 1960.
EXHIBITIONS: *Centenary Loan Exhibition of 111 Pictures by Sickert from Private Collections*, London, Thos. Agnew & Sons Ltd, 1960, no.243; *The Drawings of Walter Richard Sickert,* Perth, Art Gallery of Western Australia, Brisbane, The Brisbane Civic Art Gallery, Melbourne, The National Gallery of Victoria, 1979, no.54.
REFERENCES: W. Baron, *Sickert*, 1973, p.359, under no.319.

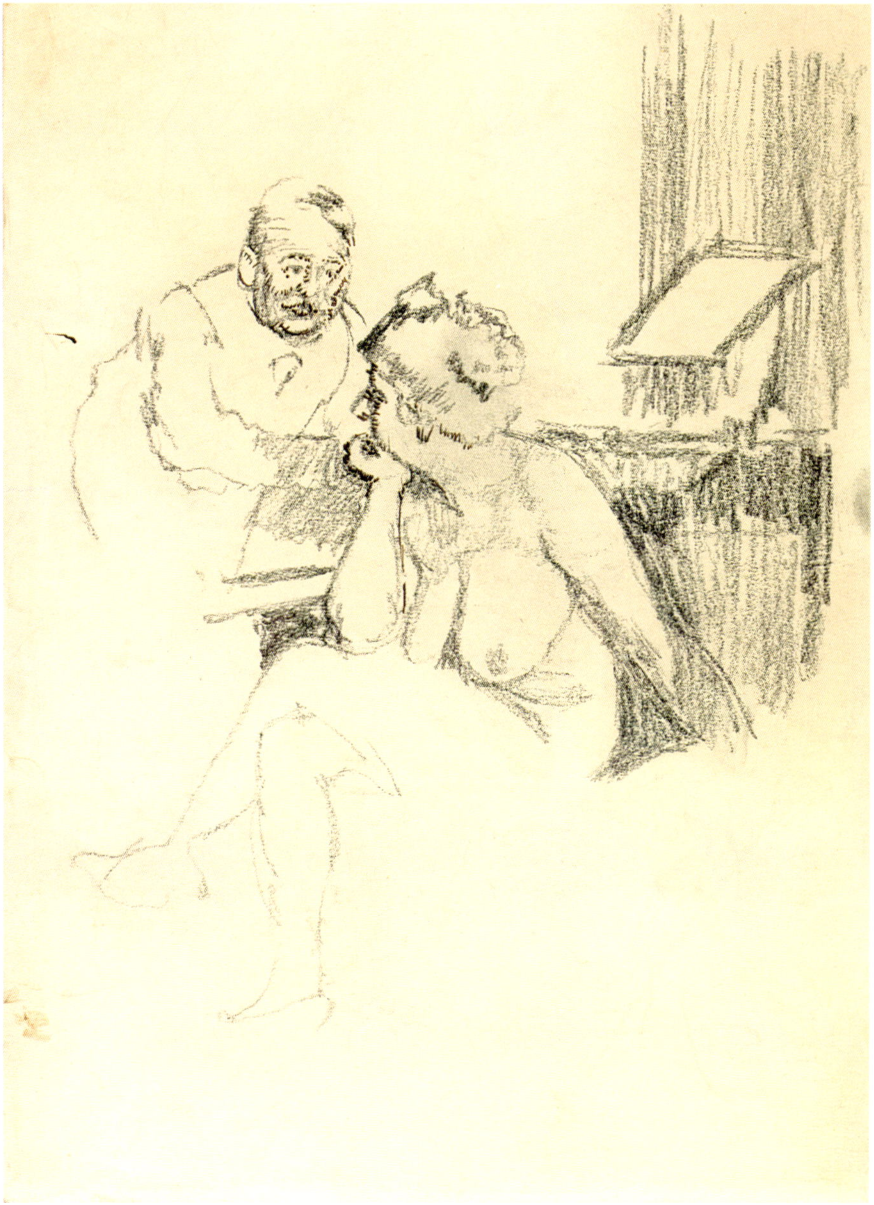

The fact that Hubby was the model in *Jack Ashore* proves that it could not have been executed before the autumn of 1911 when Hubby seems to have joined Sickert's ménage as an odd-job man. He was rumoured to have had a colourful life at sea, which may have prompted the title here. His wife, Marie, appears with him in nearly all Sickert's figure pictures of 1912–14.

EJ

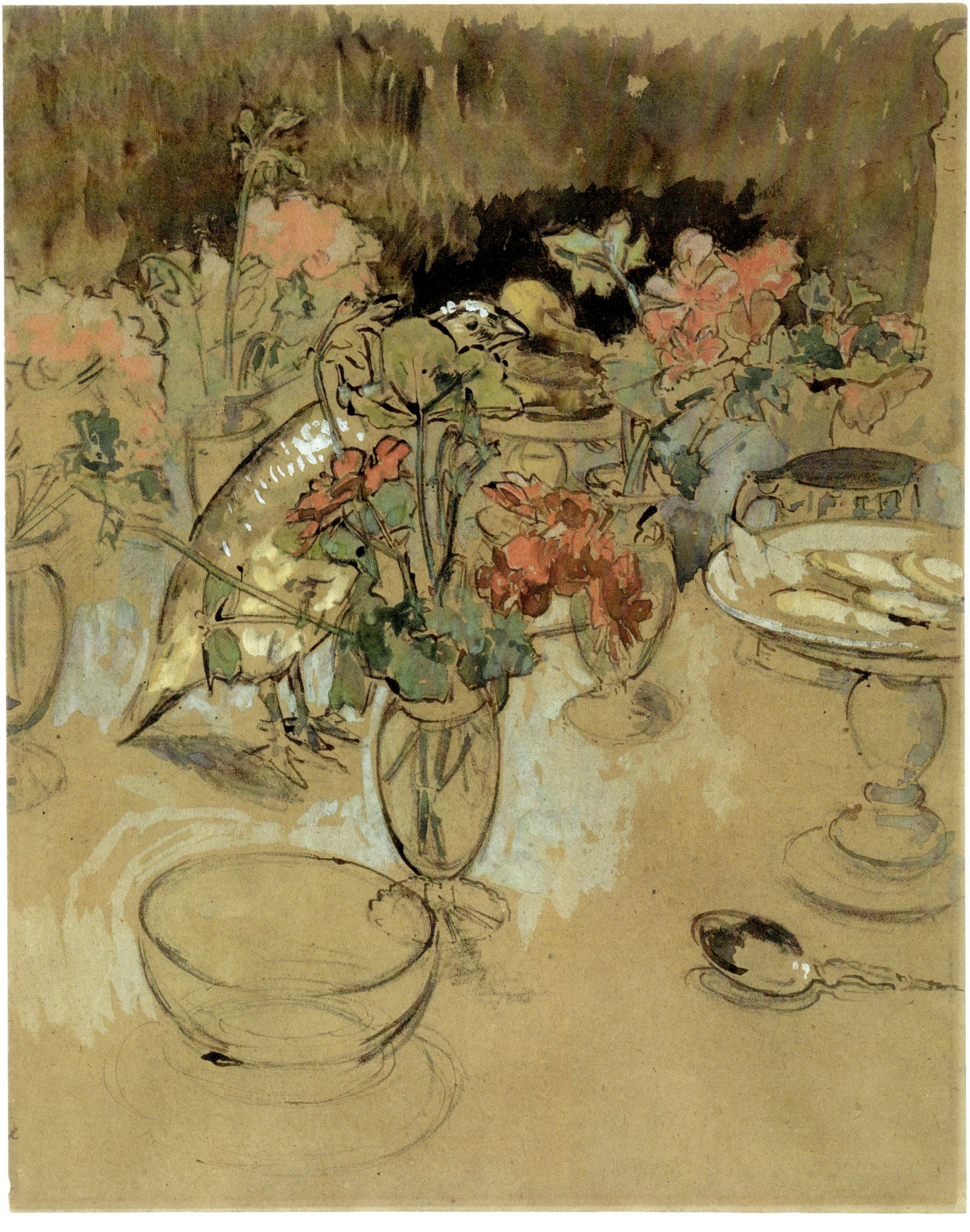

Walter Richard SICKERT
[1860–1942]
Still Life on a Dinner Table, c.1919

pen, charcoal, watercolour and bodycolour on toned board, 37.5 × 31.1 cm

P.208
PROVENANCE: Beaux Arts Gallery; Roland, Browse and Delbanco, from whom purchased by Gallery, May 1958.
EXHIBITIONS: *Watercolours and Drawings from The Cecil Higgins Art Gallery, Bedford*, London, Thos. Agnew & Sons Ltd, 1962, no.77; *Watercolours from Bedford*, Norwich, Castle Museum, 1965, no.50.
REFERENCES: L. Browse, *Sickert*, 1960, p.90.

Sickert was born in Munich, the son of Danish and Anglo-Irish parents. He first came to London at the age of five for an operation. The Sickerts came to England in 1868, initially residing in Bedford, where nearly all the family caught typhoid, before moving to Notting Hill in London.

Sickert's early career, 1879–80, was as an actor under the pseudonym of Mr Nemo. As an artist he trained briefly at the Slade before joining WHISTLER, as a pupil and assistant. Courtesy of a letter of introduction from Whistler, Sickert met Edgar Degas (1834–1917) in Paris in 1883, whose influence saw a change in subject matter with new paintings of horse racing, a circus and a beach crowded with holiday makers; he also began to work from drawings in the studio at this time, allowing a greater control over the development of his paintings.

Sickert's career spanned and determined many of the developments in English art in the late 19th and early 20th century. He exhibited at the N.E.A.C. from 1888 and, more critically for British art, formed the Fitzroy Street Group in 1907 with Spencer GORE, Harold GILMAN and William ROTHENSTEIN amongst others. This was subsumed into the Camden Town Group in 1911: a group containing many of the key figures in early 20th century British art.

Elected an A.R.A. in 1924 and R.A. in 1934. He resigned in 1935 in protest at the President of the R.A.'s refusal to support an appeal for the preservation of Epstein's sculptures on the British Medical Association's building in the Strand.

A flamboyant character and a prolific artist, Sickert's later works based on newspaper photographs (known as 'echoes') demonstrate an artist always willing to explore the boundaries of painting technique, combined with a rich visual intelligence. However, Sickert maintained a belief in the importance of draughtsmanship. In a lecture he stated: 'I would like you to believe me when I say there is nothing particular in painting. Any fool can paint, but drawing is the thing and drawing is the test. If you are a good draughtsman you are ipso facto a good painter' (extract from a series of six lectures given to the Thanet School of Art between 26 October and 29 November 1934).

JM

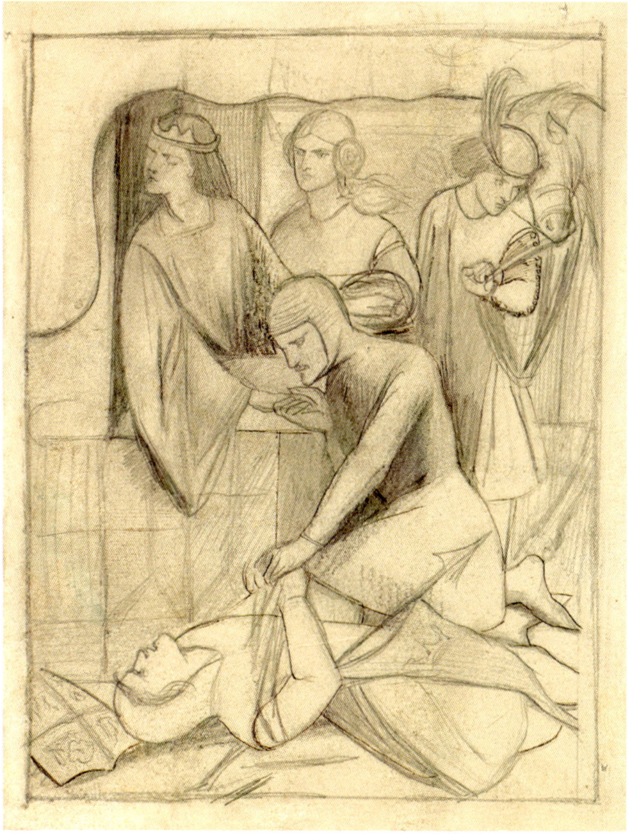

Elizabeth SIDDAL
[1829–62]
The Woeful Victory, 1860

pen and pencil on paper, 17.7 × 14 cm

P.400
PROVENANCE: Charles Fairfax Murray; Sir Geoffrey Mander; Maas Gallery, from whom purchased by Gallery, December 1961.
EXHIBITIONS: *Pre-Raphaelites and Contemporaries*, London, Maas Gallery, 1961, no.102; *Elizabeth Siddal, 1829–1862, Pre-Raphaelite Artist*, Sheffield, Ruskin Art Gallery, 1991, no.54.
REFERENCES: H.C. Marrillier, *Dante Gabriel Rossetti*, London, 1899, pp.57–8; Georgina Burne-Jones, *Memorials of Sir Edward Burne-Jones*, 1904, vol. I, p.219; G. Daly, *Pre-Raphaelites in Love*, 1989, pp.81–2 & 195–6; J.Marsh, *The Legend of Elizabeth Siddal*, 1989, pp.57, 125, 195–6, 204, repr. after p.148, this is incorrect as the version shown is in a private collection; J. Marsh & P. Nunn, *Women Artists and the Pre-Raphaelite Movement*, 1989, p.71; 'The Woeful muse', *The Antique Collector*, April 1990, pp.58–96, fig.3; J. Marsh, *Elizabeth Siddal Pre-Raphaelite Artist 1829–1862*, 1991, pp.28, 74, illus. no.54.

Elizabeth Siddal was working in a milliner's shop when she was 'discovered' by Walter Deverell (1827–54). She was frequently used as a model: for MILLAIS', *Ophelia* for instance, but mainly by ROSSETTI, whose mistress she became although they did not finally marry until 1860. She produced a number of drawings and poems, mainly echoes of Rossetti, as is clear in this drawing, but she was much admired by RUSKIN, who arranged to pay £150 per annum in exchange for work. In 1862 she was found dead from an overdose of laudanum – the verdict was accidental death but suicide has always been suspected.

The Ashmolean Museum owns a book, presented by Fairfax Murray, with photographs of Siddal's work annotated by Rossetti. There are three versions of this composition: A poor photograph of almost certainly this drawing; A highly finished version (collection of Mark Lasner, Washington, reproduced in Jan Marsh, *The Legend of Elizabeth Siddal*, 1989, after p.148.); A more finished version, at present untraced, of no.1 with slight differences but, in both, the lady averts her eyes as she gives the prize of victory to the knight who has slain her lover.

H.C. Marillier, *Dante Gabriel Rossetti*, 1899, reproduces either no.2 or no.3 above (pp.57–8). He states that there is good reason to believe that it was intended as an illustration to Rossetti's poem *The Bride's Prelude*.

EJ/JM

Charles SIMS, R.A.

[1873–1928]

Spiritual Idea (formerly known as Religious Study), 1927

tempera on paper, 35.4 × 50.6 cm
on reverse: *Spiritual Idea* and *Sketch No.14,* also *In Oil* (twice) and *five (?) figures*

P.353
PROVENANCE: Wilton Gallery, from whom purchased by Gallery, July 1960.

Sims was the son of a costume manufacturer and was sent to Paris during 1887–8 to study commerce. However, he began studies at the R.C.A. in 1890, the Académie Julian, Paris, 1891–2, (under Benjamin Constant and Jules Lefebre), and the R.A. Schools, 1892–5, where he was awarded the Landseer Scholarship. His early work was influenced by Orchardson and Bastien-Lepage, whilst his later works reflect his interest in Italian quattrocento painting. He exhibited at the R.A. from 1894, with his first one-man exhibition at the Leicester Galleries in 1906. Sims was elected an A.R.A. 1908, R.W.S. 1911 and a full R.A. 1915, Keeper of the R.A. 1920–6 and Trustee of the Tate Gallery 1920–7.

In the 1920s Sims began to suffer from hallucinations and mental illness. This coincided with his painting some pictures of a mystical nature, of which this is clearly an important example to judge from the number of preliminary sketches. However, no finished work in oil connected with this sketch has yet come to light so the significance of the *Spiritual Idea* at present remains a mystery. The year after he painted it he committed suicide.

EJ

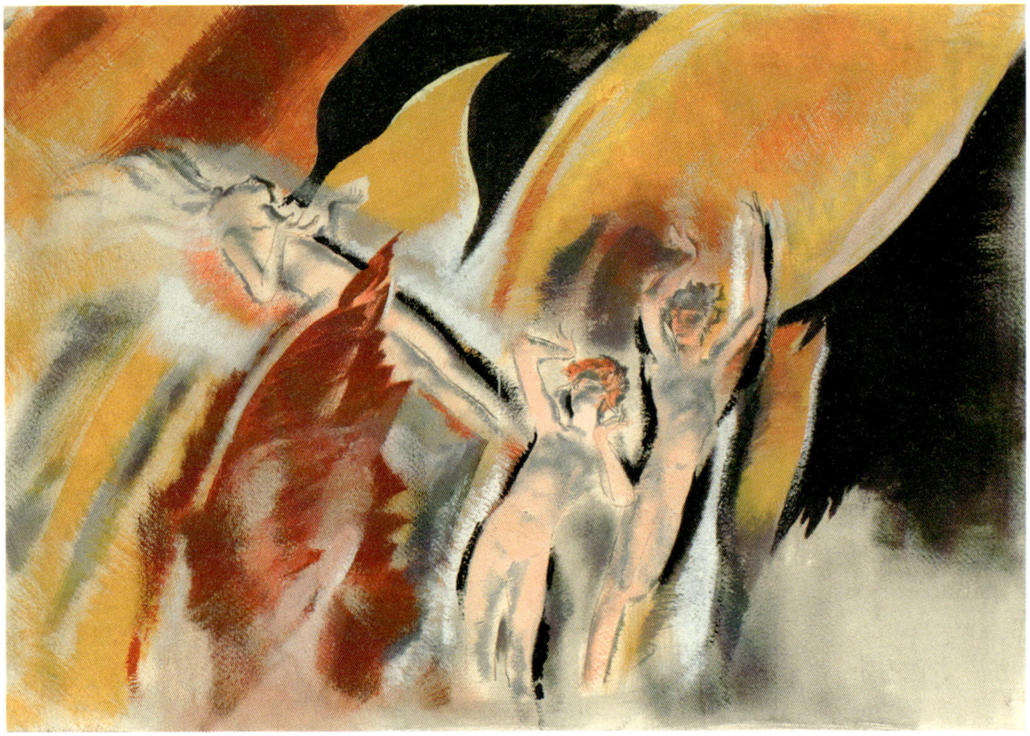

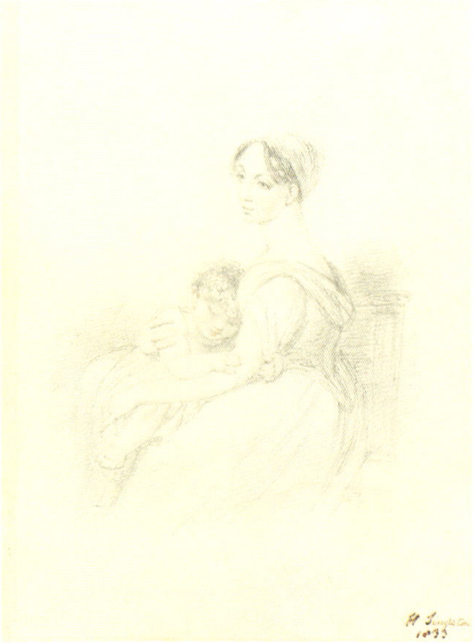

Henry SINGLETON

[1766–1839]

Mother and Child , 1833

pencil on paper, 24.5 × 18.6 cm
inscribed: *H.Singleton 1833*

P.90
PROVENANCE: Cecil Higgins (1856–1941); transferred to Gallery collection, 1949.

Painter of portraits, history and literary subjects as well as an illustrator. He entered the R.A. Schools in 1783 and exhibited there frequently from 1784–1839. Singleton's pictures often show a blend of WHEATLEY and MORLAND. He produced many historical, mythological and allegorical drawings, many of which were engraved, but very few of his large number of drawings are in watercolour. This picture belonged to Cecil Higgins and hung in his London House.

EJ

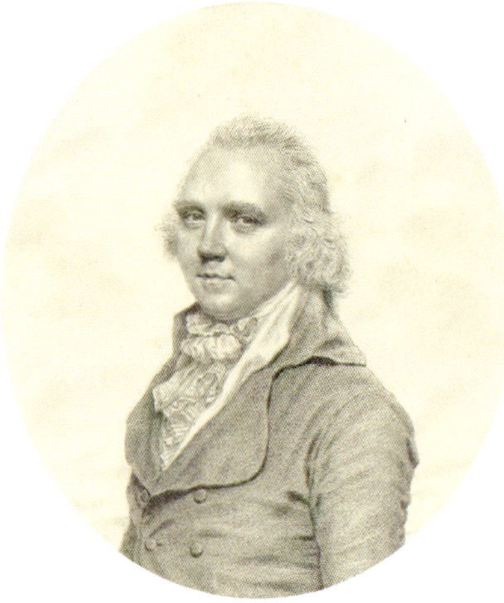

John SMART, R.A.

[1741–1811]

A Gentleman, 1795

pencil on paper, sheet size 23 × 19.2 cm
inscribed: *John Smart del. Sept. 1795*
On board the Melville Castle, E.Indiaman

P.386
PROVENANCE: C.H. Samuelson; his sale Christie's 9 February 1960, no.43, bought by Thos. Agnew & Sons Ltd from whom purchased by Gallery, January 1961.
EXHIBITIONS: *88th Annual Watercolour Exhibition,* London, Thos. Agnew & Sons Ltd, 1961, no.156.

Smart was one of the best miniature painters of the second half of the 18th century. He trained at Shipley's Academy before taking up miniature painting in 1760. He was active in the Society of Artists before a very successful period practising in Madras from 1785–95. It must have been on the return to England that he drew this fellow passenger on board ship. The *Melville* left Madras on the 27 April, and Smart was joined in St Helena by his daughter and her family. His daughter, Anna Maria Woolf, had left Madras on 20 October in the previous year (on board the *Dutton*), but had been obliged to disembark at St Helena to give birth to her sixth child, John William. The ship finally docked in Portsmouth on 19 November 1795.

His meticulous accuracy gave clients an alternative to the more bravura style of Richard COSWAY.

EJ/JM

John 'Warwick' SMITH

[1749–1831]

Mount Splügen, 1781

watercolour on paper, 34.8 × 51.3 cm
inscribed: monogram

P.91
PROVENANCE: Gilbert Davies; P&D Colnaghi Ltd, from whom purchased by Gallery, 1953.
EXHIBITIONS: *English Watercolours from The Cecil Higgins Art Gallery Bedford,* Reading, Reading Museum & Art Gallery, 1965, no.50; *The English Tradition: an exhibition of watercolours from two private collections,* Bedford, Cecil Higgins Art Gallery, 1972, no.73; *Sublime Itineraries,* Lugano, Museo Cantonale D'Arte, 1998, no.247.
REFERENCES: A. Bury, 'The Cecil Higgins Museum Bedford', *Old Watercolour Society's Club,* 1961, vol.xxxvi, pp.33–4, pl.xii; T. Wilcox, *Francis Towne,* 1997, p.95, fig. no.32; F. Ambrosio (ed.), *Itinerari sublimi Viaggi d'artisti tra il 1750 e il 1850*, 1998, p.151, no.247.

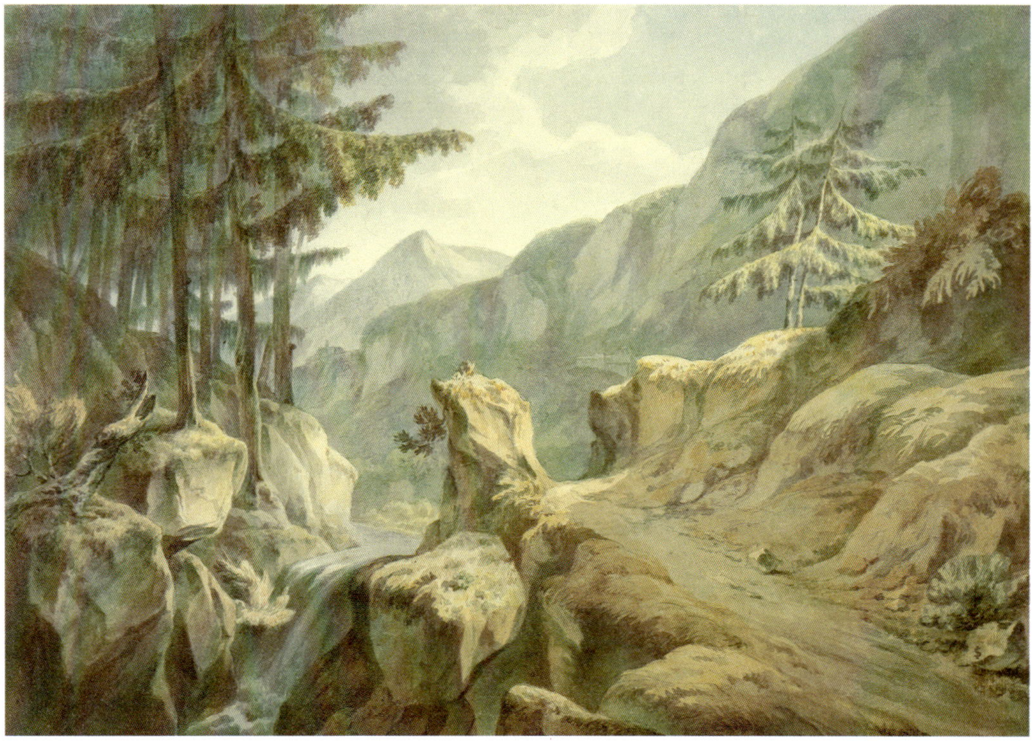

John Smith became known as 'Warwick' either because he was patronised by Lord Warwick who financed Smith's five-year sojourn in Italy from 1776–81, or because, on his return, Smith settled in Warwick, marrying there in 1783.

While in Rome, Smith became friends with both PARS and TOWNE travelling back with the latter to England via Switzerland in the autumn of 1781 when this drawing, which shows Towne's influence, must have been made. In fact Smith and Towne often sketched the same subjects, sharing a liking for strong contrasts of light and shade, though Smith's watercolours are less formal and more naturalistic than Towne's.

Later he made many sketching trips in Britain, visiting Wales frequently between 1784 and 1806.

EJ

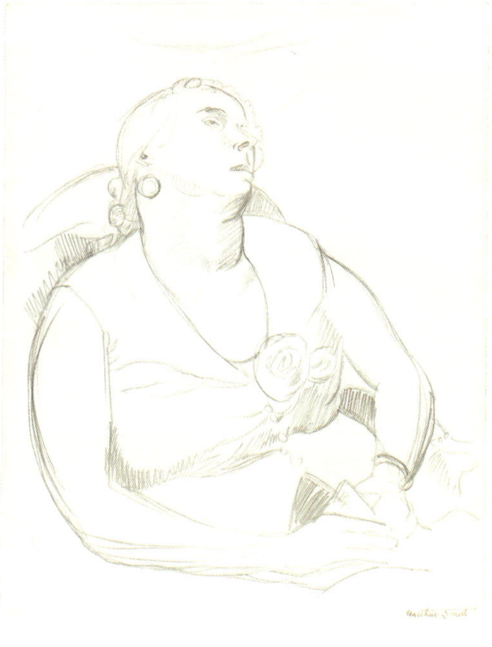

Sir Matthew SMITH, C.B.E., R.A.

[1879–1959]

Seated Woman

pencil on paper, 42.9 × 34.8 cm
inscribed: *Matthew Smith*
on reverse: a pencil drawing of the sitter from a different angle

P.311
PROVENANCE: Mayor Gallery, from whom purchased by Gallery, October 1959.

This unknown sitter has been invested by Smith with something of the voluptuous quality that is characteristic of many of his paintings of nudes.

EJ

Sir Matthew SMITH, C.B.E., R.A.
[1879–1959]
Still Life with Jugs

watercolour on paper, 50.2 × 37.7 cm
inscribed: *Matthew Smith*

P.345
PROVENANCE: Reid Gallery, from whom purchased by Gallery, April 1960.

Matthew Smith was born in Halifax the son of a copper wire manufacturer. He started in the family firm before convincing his father to allow him to study art, initially Applied Design at the Manchester School of Art. Owing to ill health he was allowed to live in London studying at the Slade from 1905–7 under Henry TONKS. Again, because of ill health his doctor recommended a sojourn abroad, and in September 1908 he settled in Pont Aven, finally arriving in Paris in 1910. There he joined Matisse's school just as it was about to close (meeting him only three times).

Smith returned to England in 1912 marrying Gwen Salmond, whom he had known at the Slade, and they journeyed widely through France for their honeymoon. Smith's financial situation improved considerably with the death of his father in 1914, living at 2 Fitzroy St, a close neighbour at this time being Walter SICKERT. Smith finally decided he was 'getting somewhere' as a painter after a visit to Cornwall in 1920, the resulting landscapes revealing the intensity of his feeling for colour and his ability to organise pictorial space. His first one man exhibition at the Mayor Gallery, 1926, was a success with most of the canvases sold. The exhibition attracted the attention of Roger Fry, who wrote that 'he is pushing to the furthest limits the essentially modern view of the functional as opposed to the ornamental rôle played by colour in pictorial design'.

The 1930s were largely spent in the south of France, Smith being evacuated by the R.A.F. at the outbreak of the Second World War, leaving many canvases behind in Aix. Personal tragedy also struck at this time with the death of his sons Mark and Dermot, after which he hardly painted for two years.

His later years were spent largely in London, living in Chelsea Cloisters, Sloane Avenue, and renting studios at various locations around town. He was appointed C.B.E. in 1949 and knighted in 1954.

EJ/JM

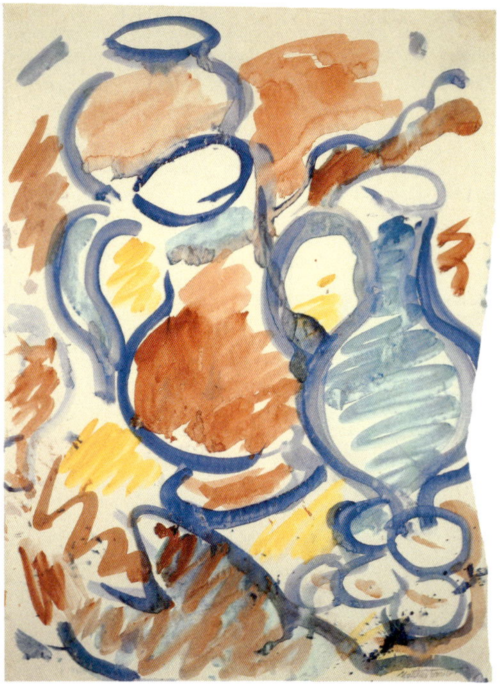

Simeon SOLOMON
[1840–1905]
The First Offering of Aaron, 1864

pen and black carbon ink on paper, 14.5 × 18.4 cm
inscribed: monogram, *9/64*

P.330
PROVENANCE: Professor Isaacs, from whom purchased by Gallery, January 1960.

The drawing illustrates the ninth Chapter (hence the '9' in the inscription) of the Book of Leviticus, in which Moses instructed Aaron to make atonement both for himself and for the golden calf as his 'sin offering' and a goat as the people's. Then he also slew a bullock and a ram as the people's peace offerings.

Finally: 'And there came a fire out from before the Lord, and consumed upon the altar the burnt offering and the fat, which when all the people saw, they shouted and fell on their faces'.

EJ

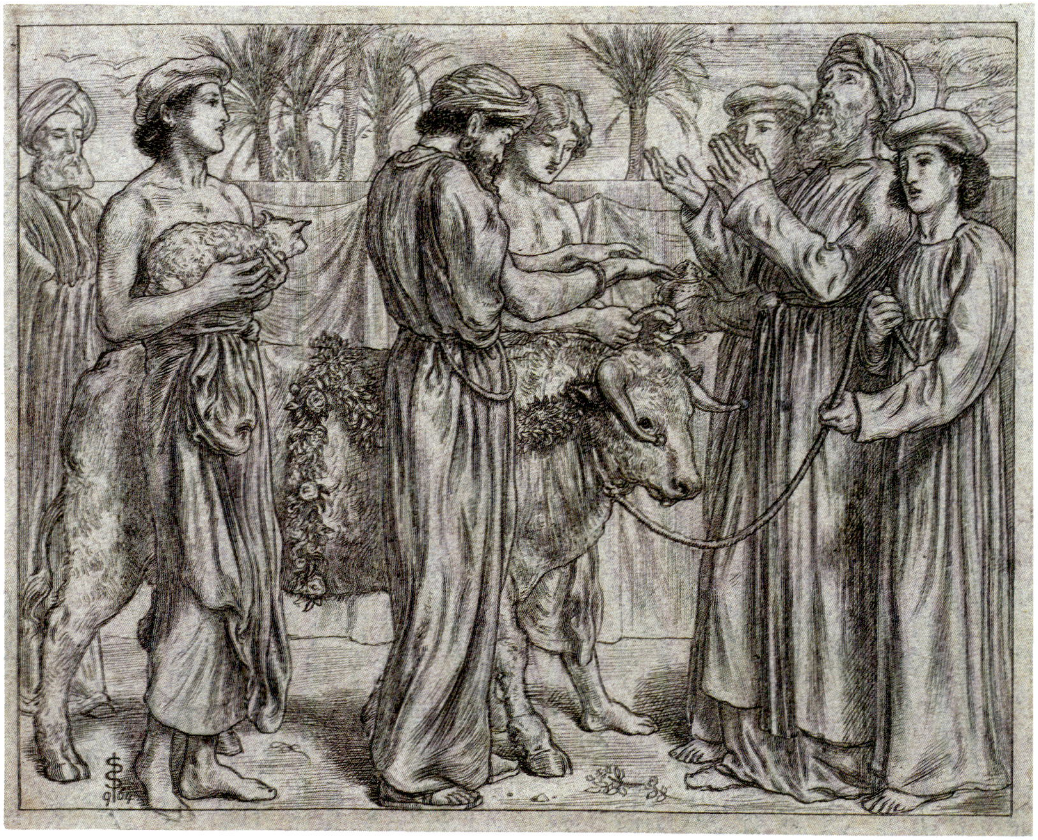

Simeon SOLOMON

[1840–1905]

Coptic Baptismal Procession , 1865

watercolour, bodycolour and gum arabic on paper,
26.5 × 42.4 cm
inscribed: monogram, *'65*

P.430
PROVENANCE: David Gould; Maas Gallery, from whom purchased by Gallery, October 1962.
REFERENCES: R. Burman (ed.), *From Prodigy to Outcast Simeon Solomon – Pre Raphaelite Artist,* 2001, p.19, repr.p.18; See: K. Frank, *Lucie Duff Gordon: A Passage to Egypt,* 1994.

One of several illustrations that Solomon, who never visited Egypt, made for Lady Duff Gordon's *Letters from Egypt*, 1865.

Lady Duff Gordon was born in 1821 but, suffering from tuberculosis, went to Egypt for her health in 1862 and died there seven years later. Copts are descendants of the Egyptian Christians who did not convert to Islam when the Arabs conquered Egypt in the 7th century A.D.

The baptismal procession is described by Lady Duff Gordon in a letter of 21 May 1863 following a visit to a new Coptic church in Cairo. There she witnessed the priest in a black robe leading the procession with:

two young ecclesiastics in yellow satin copes (contrasting queerly with the familiar tarboosh of common life on their heads), these carried little babies and huge wax tapers, each a baby and a taper … A lot of closely veiled women stood on one side in the aisle, and among them the mothers of the babies who received them from the men in yellow copes at the end of the ceremony.
(from a letter to Mrs Austin, 21 May 1863, Cairo).

The painting bears strong compositional similarities to the drawing *Carrying the Scrolls of the Law* from the *Jewish Ceremonies Series*, 1862, published as photographs by Coundall, Downes & Co.

A Pre-Raphaelite painter and illustrator and the younger brother of Abraham and Rebecca, Solomon trained at the R.A. Schools. Brilliantly precocious, he produced most of his best work in the 1860s including illustrations for Dalziel's Bible and many drawings of Jewish life and ritual. He met ROSSETTI, BURNE-JONES, Pater and Swinburne. After being arrested in 1873 for his homosexuality, he became a social outlaw. His death was due to chronic alcoholism.

EJ/JM

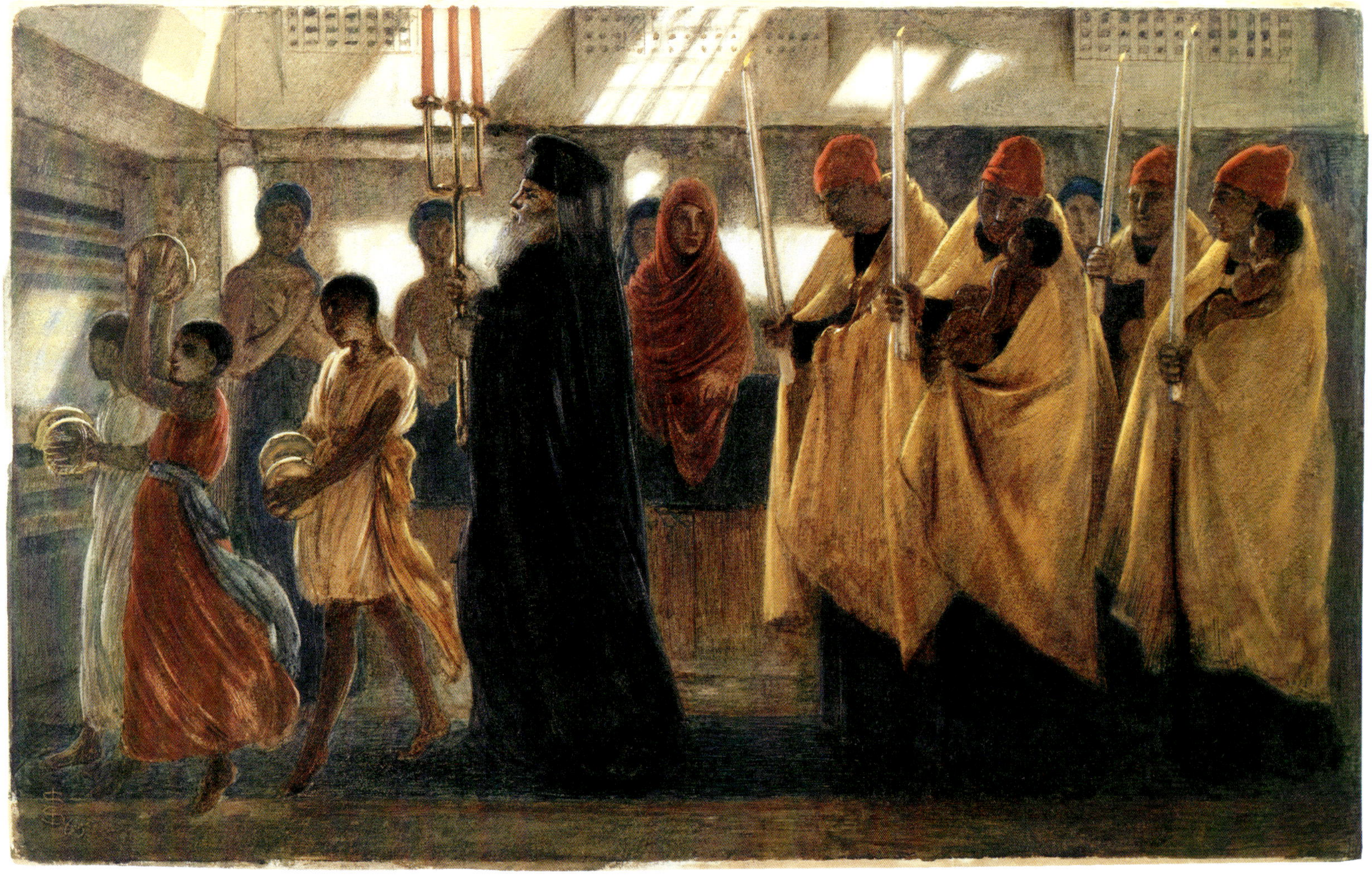

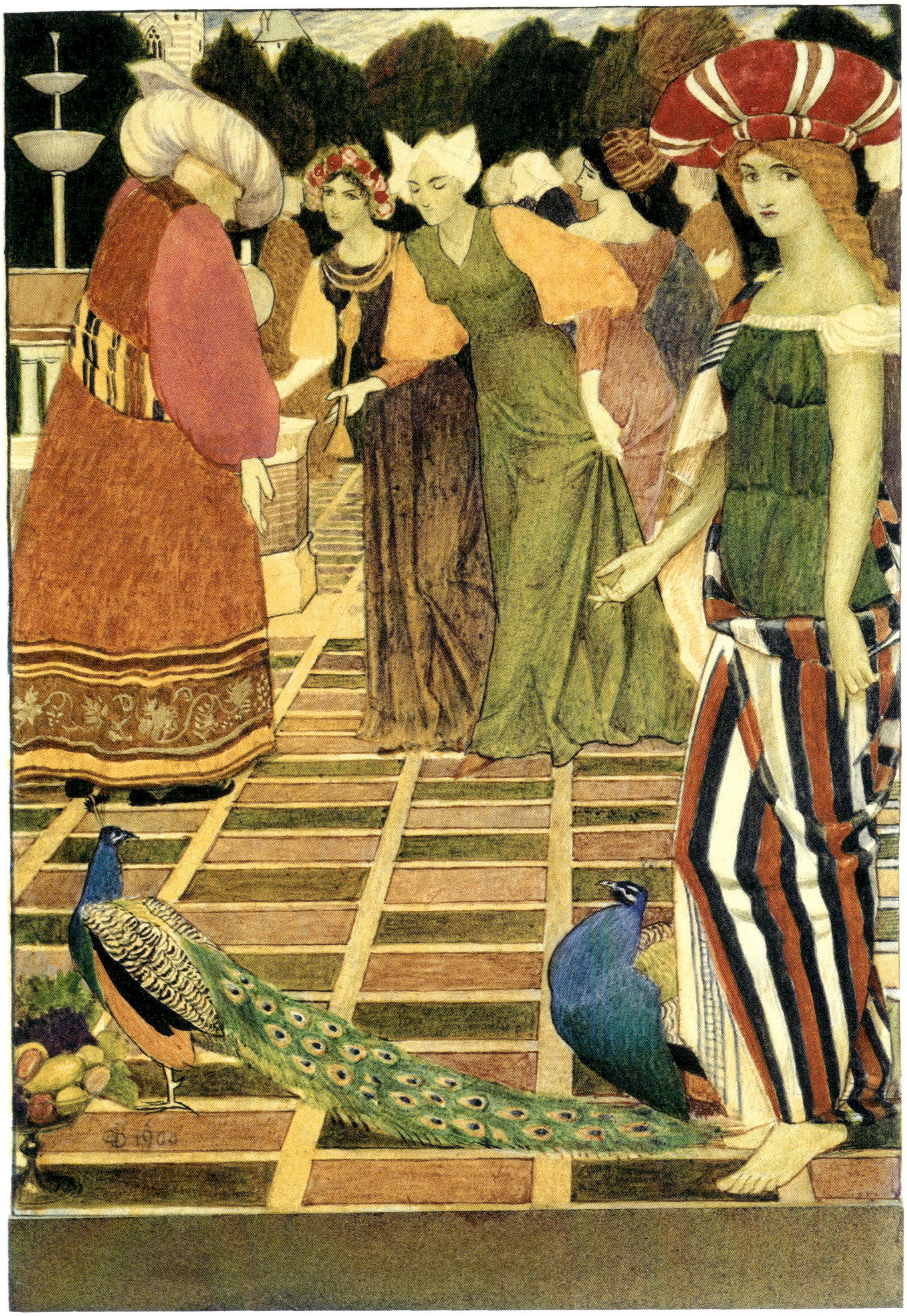

Joseph Edward SOUTHALL

[1861–1945]

New Lamps for Old, 1900

watercolour, ink and gold paint on paper, 17 × 12.3 cm
inscribed: monogram, *1900*

P.806

PROVENANCE: Handley-Read Collection; Fine Art Society; Thomas Stainton; Nigel Stainton, from whom purchased by Gallery, with the assistance of the V&A/M.G.C. Purchase Grant Fund, November 1992.
EXHIBITIONS: *An Exhibition of Drawings by British Book Illustrators 1875–1925*, London, Hartnoll & Eyre Galleries, 1969, no.25, (repr.); *Victorian & Edwardian Decorative Art. The Handley-Read Collection*, London, R.A., 1972, no.E137, (repr.); *The Paintings, Watercolours and Drawings from the Handley-Read Collection*, London, Fine Art Society, 1974, no.80, (repr.); *Joseph Southall 1861–1944 Artist-Craftsman*, Birmingham, Birmingham City Museum & Art Gallery, 1980, no.B5(iii).
REFERENCES: 'Tempera Painting', *The Studio*, vol.XXIII, no.1001, August 1901, pp.155–65, illus.

The story depicted begins with the African magician (the tall figure in the left foreground) who coveted Aladdin's wonderful lamp. He bought some new lamps and, while Aladdin was away hunting, approached his Palace crying out: 'New lamps for Old!' whereupon the Princess, Aladdin's wife, not knowing the magic qualities of the lamp, sent a maid out with it to change it for a new one.

This is a detailed study for the finished picture, also signed with a monogram and dated 1900, in the Birmingham City Art Gallery. All the figures are friends or relations of the artist, some of them prominent Quakers in Birmingham (where Southall lived) and many are identified in the Birmingham catalogue. The artist himself appears on the extreme left in the Birmingham version but not here, although his wife appears as the woman in profile with dark hair below a gold striped turban towards the right of the picture.

The Birmingham catalogue suggests that the picture had a special significance for Southall in that, with the succession of the first year, in 1901, of the new century for the old, he might hope for a new standing among his colleagues now that he had mastered many of the problems of tempera painting. (He had recently founded The Society of Painters in Tempera.)

EJ

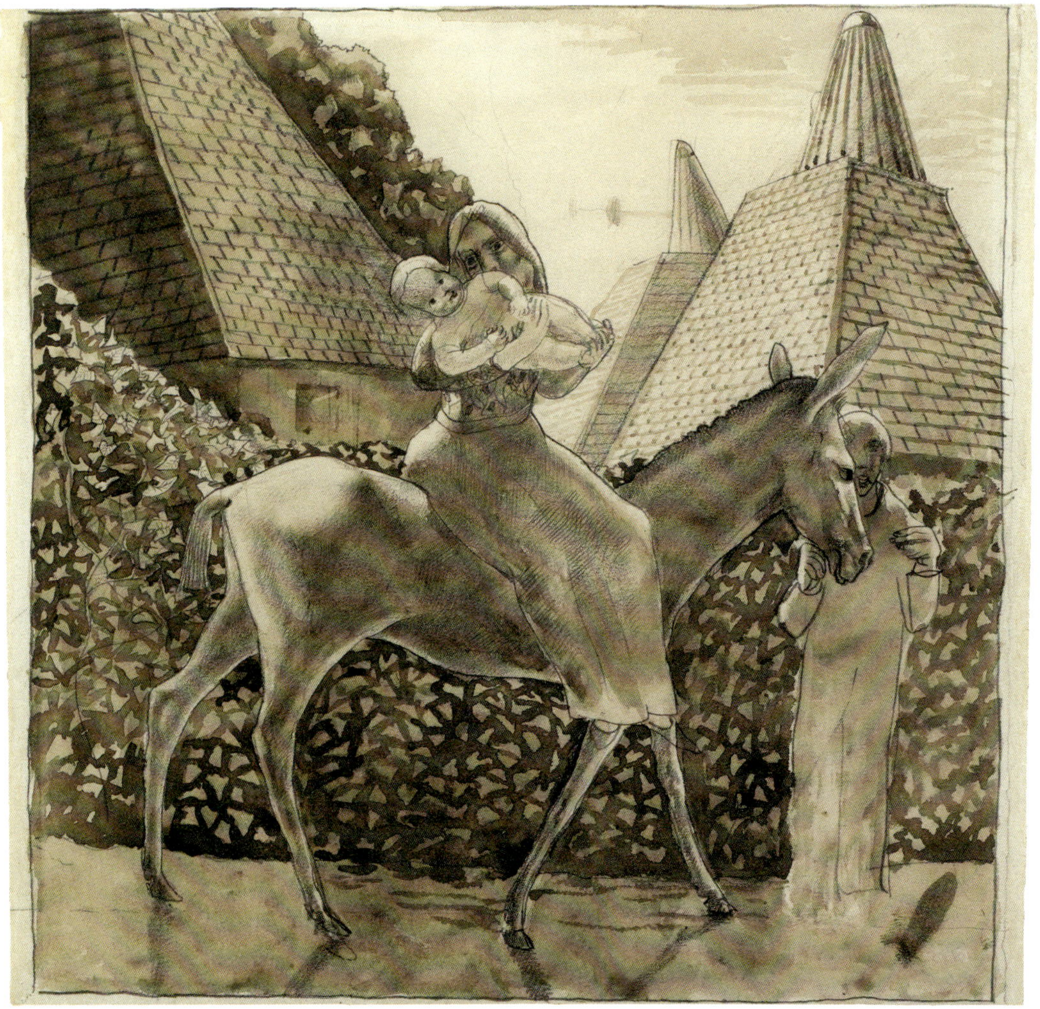

Sir Stanley SPENCER, C.B.E., R.A.
[1891–1959]
The Flight into Egypt, c.1913

pencil and wash with brown ink on paper, 22.8 × 23.6 cm

P.134
PROVENANCE: Leicester Galleries, from whom purchased by Gallery, November 1957.
EXHIBITIONS: *Watercolours and Drawings from The Cecil Higgins Art Gallery, Bedford*, London, Thos. Agnew & Sons Ltd, 1962, no.80.

Spencer, one of the most eccentric figures in all British art, studied at the Slade 1908–12; his early pictures, depicting biblical subjects set in the village of Cookham in Berkshire, were the result of a mystical experience he had had there. After war service (see P.254), his colour in the 1930s became drier and paler, his compositions more claustrophobic. The erotic element and anatomical distortions in his figure subjects alienated the public so that he often turned to landscape for commercial reasons.

Knighted in 1959 and twice married, he continued to write love letters to his first wife, Hilda Carline, even after her death. In 1962 a Stanley Spencer Gallery was opened in Cookham.

EJ

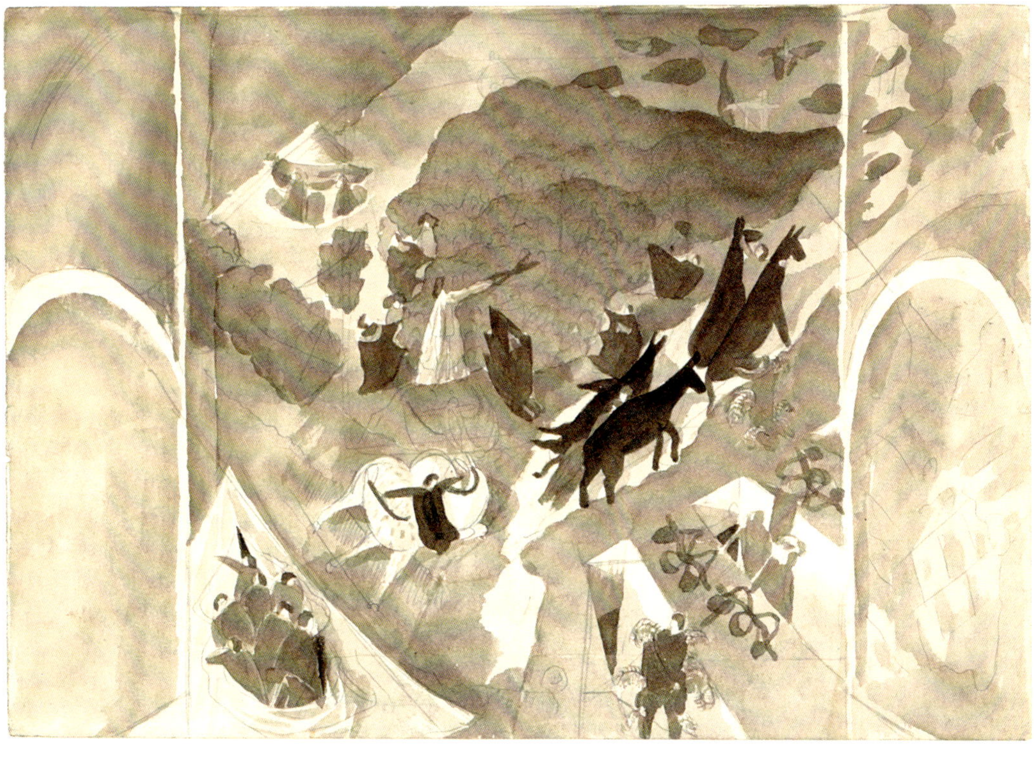

Sir Stanley SPENCER, C.B.E., R.A.
[1891–1959]
Study for Mural (Burghclere Chapel Series), c.1922

sepia and wash and pencil on paper, 24.6 × 35.4 cm
on reverse: two sketches of heads and a figure holding a ball under left arm.

P.254
PROVENANCE: Leicester Galleries, from whom purchased by Gallery, 1958.

In 1915 Spencer enlisted in the Royal Army Medical Corps and was later sent to Macedonia with the ambulance brigade. His experiences there formed the basis for his decoration of the Sandham Chapel at Burghclere in Hampshire. These paintings were commissioned by Spencer's most important patron, J.L. Behrend, and his wife as a memorial to her brother, Lieutenant Henry Willoughby Sandham, who died in 1919 from an illness contracted while on active service during the First World War.

The work occupied Spencer on site from 1926–32 resulting in a most striking ensemble of canvases. His skill in arranging multi-figure compositions in this series can be seen later in his pictures of the Resurrection and those of Lithgow's shipyard at Port Glasgow, which he painted during the Second World War when he was an Official War Artist.

EJ

Sir Stanley SPENCER, C.B.E., R.A.
[1891–1959]
The Harvest Festival (formerly known as Church Pews and People), c.1926

pen and ink on paper, 32.8 × 50 cm
inscribed: *Stanley Spencer October 5/8th*

P.346
PROVENANCE: Reid Gallery, from whom purchased by Gallery, April 1960.
EXHIBITIONS: *Watercolours and Drawings from The Cecil Higgins Art Gallery, Bedford*, London, Thos. Agnew & Sons Ltd, 1962, no.111.
REFERENCES: A page for *A Chatto & Windus Almanack,* 1927, repr.as *Saturday October 1st.*

Drawn c.1926 and presumably commissioned by Chatto & Windus for their Almanack. One wonders if this is an accurate portrayal of the general level of attention among the congregation in Cookham church during the Harvest Festival service.

EJ

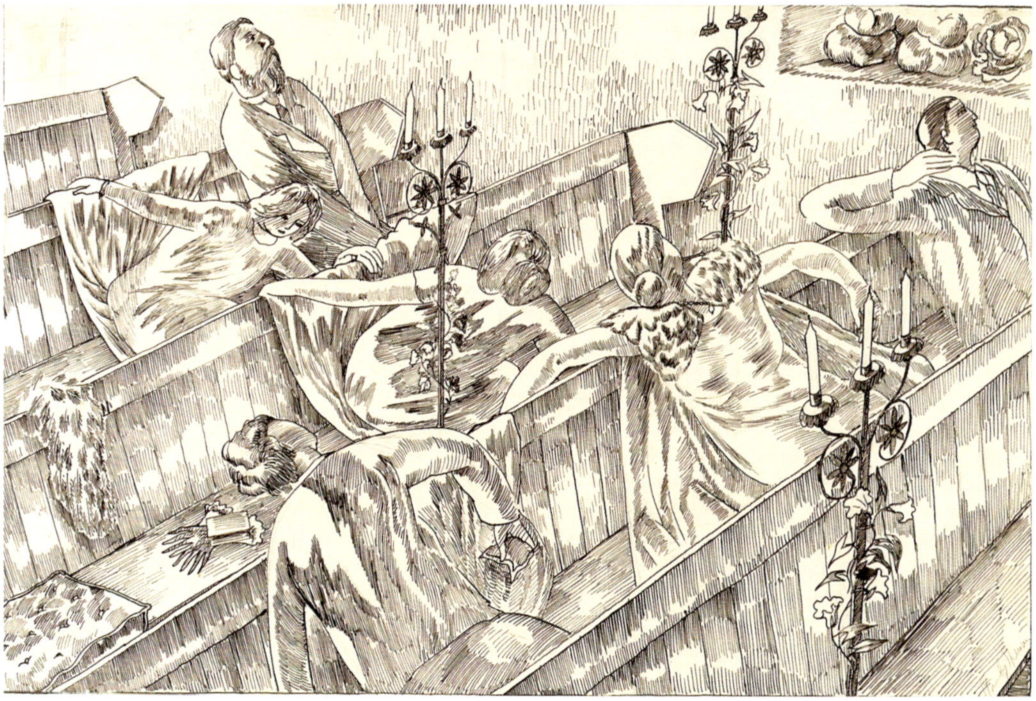

Sir Stanley SPENCER, C.B.E., R.A.
[1891–1959]
Self Portrait, c.1940

pencil on ruled paper, 32.5 × 19.6 cm
on reverse: two small sketches in pencil of figures

P.373
PROVENANCE: Arthur Tooth & Sons Ltd; Reid Gallery, from whom purchased by Gallery, October 1960.

Self portraits were a recurrent theme throughout Spencer's life, ranging from head studies, such as this, to full nudes. During portrait demonstrations for students at the Slade, Spencer began with one eye and then worked across the forehead before completing the second eye.

CB/JM

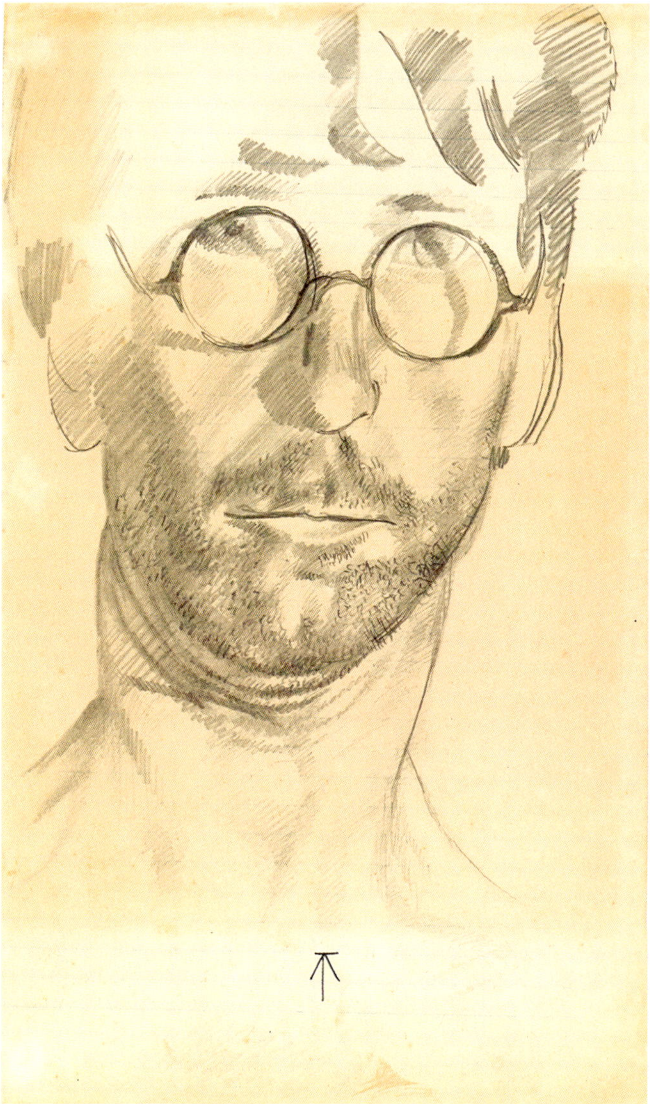

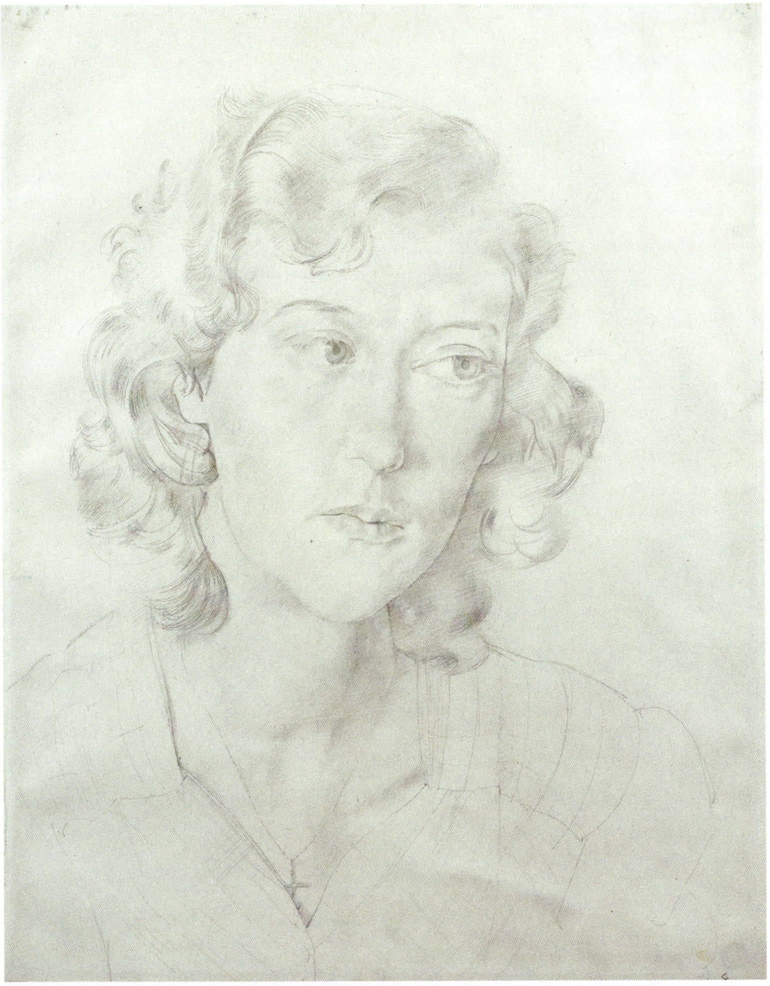

Sir Stanley SPENCER, C.B.E., R.A.
[1891–1959]
Rafaela, c.1947

pencil on paper, 50.4 × 40.5 cm

P.92
PROVENANCE: Arthur Tooth & Sons Ltd, from whom purchased by Gallery, August 1952.
EXHIBITIONS: *Some 20th Century English Paintings and Drawings,* Arts Council, 1950, no.80, lent by Arthur Tooth & Sons Ltd; *Drawings by Stanley Spencer,* London, Arts Council, 1954, no.48; *The English Tradition:an exhibition of watercolours from two private collections,* Bedford, Cecil Higgins Art Gallery, 1972, no.76.

Drawn c.1947 and thus at the same date (and with the dimensions) as the drawing of Pamela Spencer (P.93). Nothing is known about the sitter but perhaps she was a young friend of Pamela Spencer's, so that both were drawn at the same time.

EJ

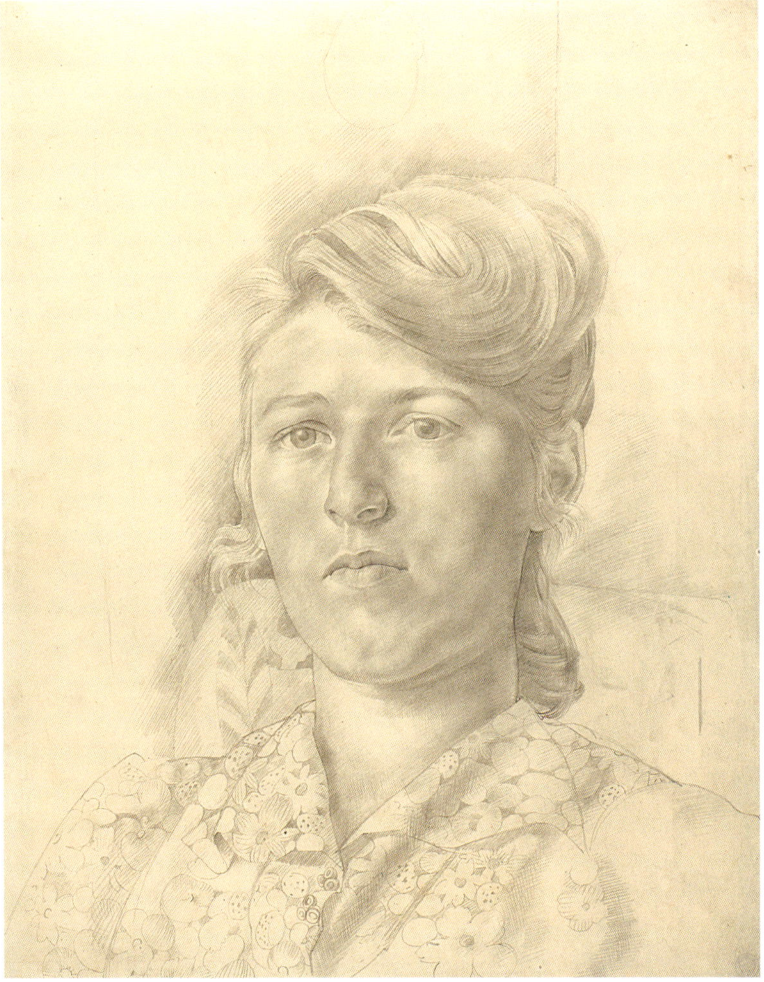

Sir Stanley SPENCER, C.B.E., R.A.
[1891–1959]
Pamela Spencer, c.1947

pencil on paper, 50.4 × 40.2 cm

P.93
PROVENANCE: Arthur Tooth & Sons Ltd, from whom purchased by Gallery, August 1952.
EXHIBITIONS: *Portrait Painting and Drawings,* Rye, Rye Art Gallery, 1967, no cat.

Pamela was the daughter of Stanley's brother Percy. She is first mentioned as a bridesmaid at Gilbert Spencer's wedding in 1930. Later, Stanley refers to her as his 'fair niece' as opposed to Sylvia, his brother Horace's daughter, who was his 'dark niece'.

In Kenneth Pople's biography of Stanley (*Stanley Spencer. A biography*, 1991), Pamela is thanked for her help as the curator of many of the Spencer family diaries and records which had been preserved by Stanley's sister Florence.

EJ

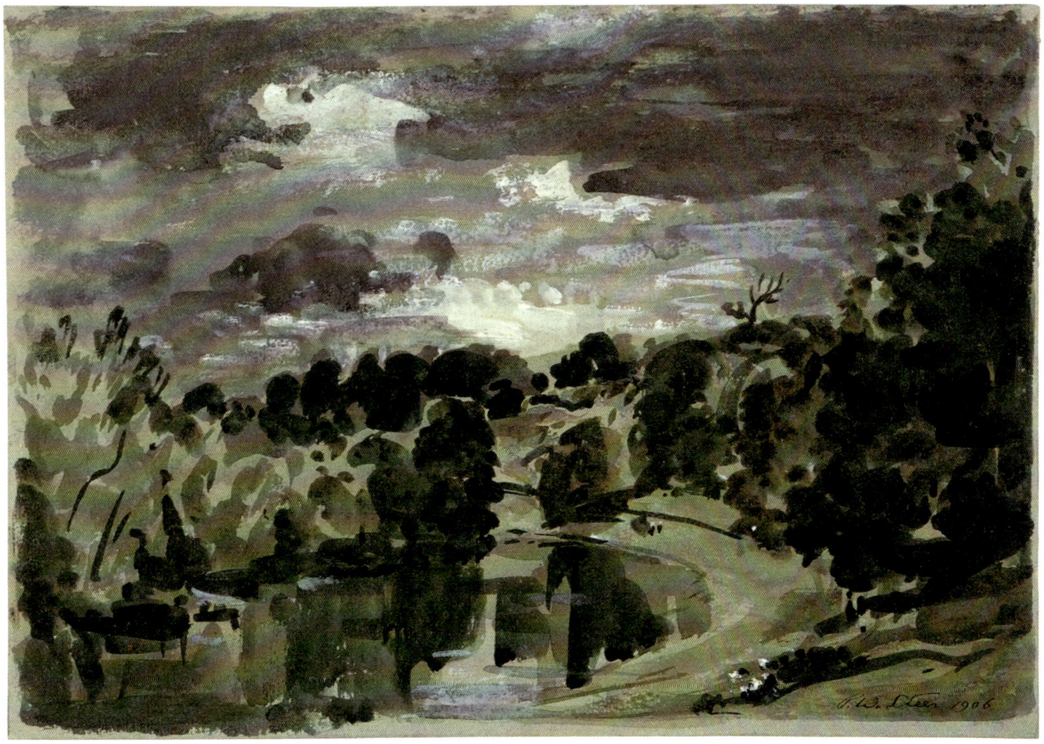

Philip Wilson STEER, O.M.

[1860–1942]

The River Teme at Ludlow, 1906

watercolour and bodycolour on paper, 26.4 × 38.1 cm
inscribed: *P.W. Steer 1906*

P.391
PROVENANCE: H.C. Lawrence; Colonel Nigel Warren, on whose behalf sold to Gallery by Thos. Agnew & Son Ltd, January 1961.
EXHIBITIONS: *88th Annual Watercolour Exhibition*, London, Thos. Agnew & Sons Ltd, 1961, no.170; *Primitives to Picasso*, London, R.A., 1962, no.427; *Watercolours and Drawings from The Cecil Higgins Art Gallery, Bedford*, London, Thos. Agnew & Sons Ltd, 1962, no.73.

One of Steer's finest and most dramatic watercolours with the lowering clouds threatening an imminent downpour. Steer painted a number of pictures in the neighbourhood of Ludlow in 1906; this may be connected with an oil, *The Teme at Ludlow*, in the collection of Mrs Russell (cf. D.S. MacColl, *Steer*, 1945, p.208), and a watercolour of the subject, the same size as P.391 is in the Walker Art Gallery, Liverpool.

Steer studied mainly in Paris where he came under the influence of WHISTLER, to emerge, c.1887–94, as England's best Impressionist landscape painter. Around 1900 his style became more closely linked to the tradition of GAINSBOROUGH, CONSTABLE and TURNER, and from 1920 he turned increasingly to watercolour. He taught at the Slade from 1899 to 1930 and was awarded the O.M. in 1931.

EJ

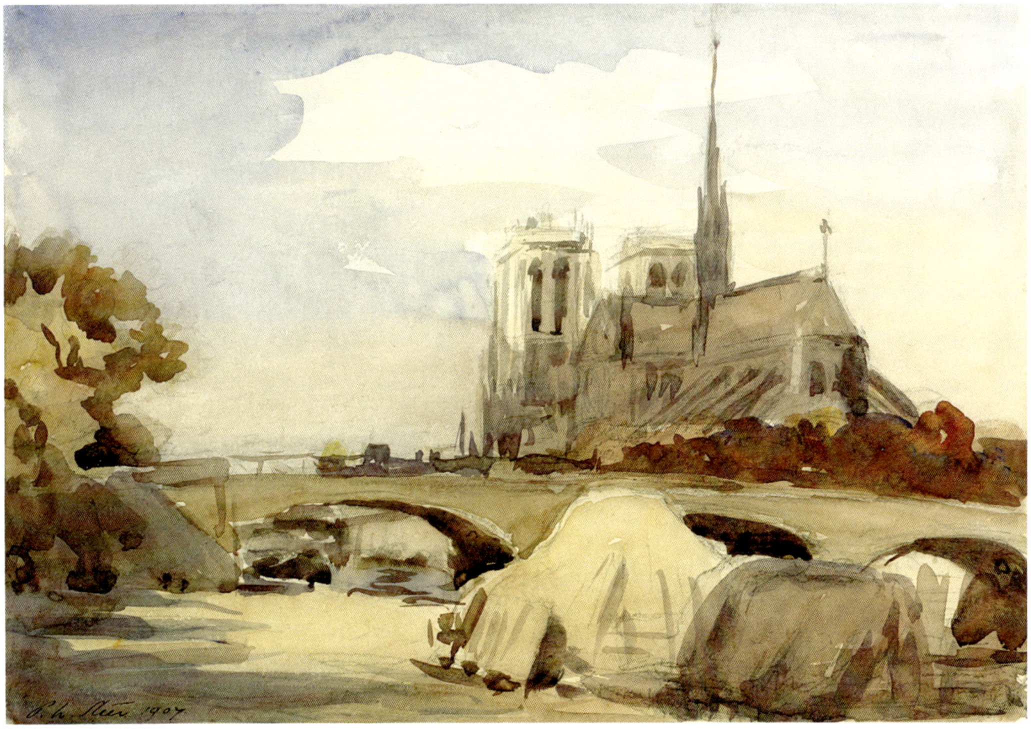

Philip Wilson STEER, O.M.

[1860–1942]

Notre Dame, Paris, 1907

watercolour on paper, sheet size 28.5 × 39.5 cm
inscribed: *P.W. Steer 1907*

P.803
PROVENANCE: Given to Gallery by Alice Barbara Kitson, October 1992.

Obviously painted very rapidly: the bridge and the main bulk of the Cathedral seem solid enough but the spire is so attenuated that it looks as if the first gale will topple it. Steer spent the summer of 1907 at Montreuil (Pas de Calais) with Fred Brown, W.C. Coles and Ronald Gray.

EJ

Philip Wilson STEER, O.M.
[1860–1942]
Rainclouds: Maldon, 1920

watercolour on paper, 24 × 34.2 cm
inscribed: *P.W. Steer 1920*

P.210
PROVENANCE: Mrs W.F. Jackson; C.J. Aaron; Herbert E West ?; bought Christie's 13 May 1955, no.78, J.R.D. Byfield with Christies for Wilton Gallery, from whom purchased by Gallery, April 1958.
EXHIBITIONS: London, Tate Gallery, 1929; *Memorial Exhibition of the works of Philip Wilson Steer O.M 1860–1942,* London, Tate Gallery & National Gallery, 1943, no.107, lent by Herbert West as *Maldon the river;* Festival of Britain, *Wilson Steer Exhibition,* Birkenhead, Williamson Art Gallery, 1951, no.81 as *Rainclouds; The Modern Movement in British Watercolour Painting,* Norwich, Castle Museum, 1957, no.12.

The estuary at Maldon in Essex was a favourite subject of Steer's. Here, although rain is in the offing, Steer's handling is very different from that in *The River Teme at Ludlow*, (P.391): the tonality is far lighter, the colours less strong and the brushwork applied more thinly and rapidly.

EJ/JM

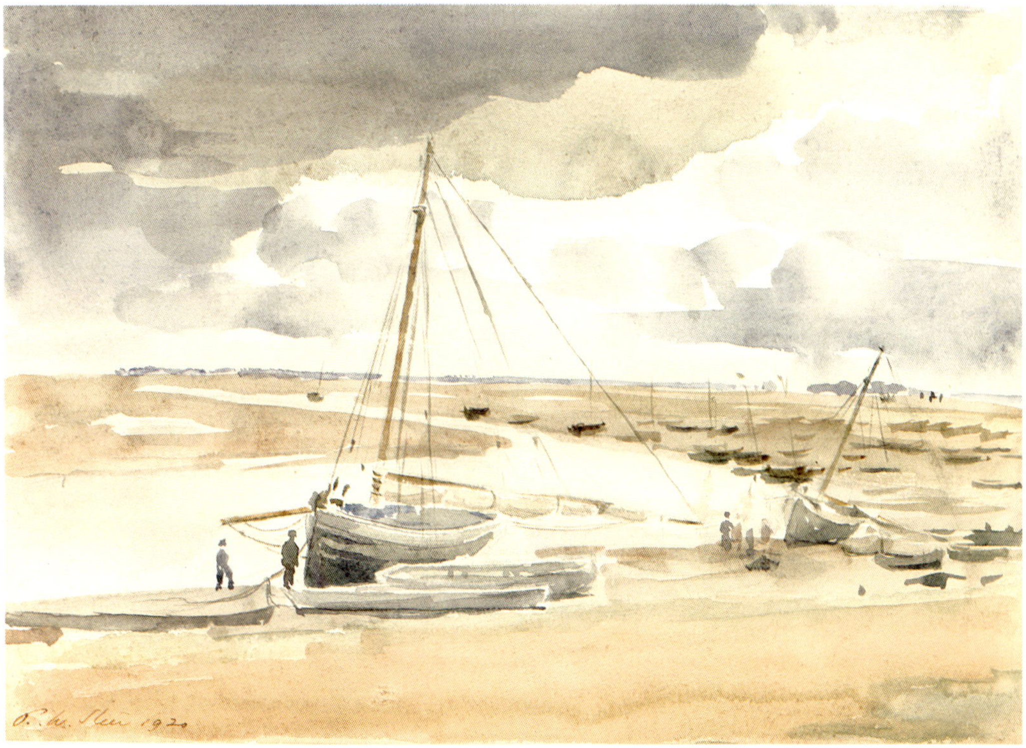

Philip Wilson STEER, O.M.
[1860–1942]
Low Tide, 1926

watercolour on paper, 33.8 × 22.5 cm
inscribed: *P.W. Steer 1926*

P. 180
PROVENANCE: R.H. Kitson; Thos. Agnew & Sons Ltd, from whom purchased by Gallery, January 1958.
EXHIBITIONS: *Philip Wilson Steer O.M.* 1860–1942, Leeds, Temple Newsam, 1944, no.78.

The catalogue for the Temple Newsam exhibition lists this as probably painted at Shoreham. During the six years between this and P.210, Steer's handling has become still looser and the atmosphere more evanescent, a change of style perhaps partly attributable to deteriorating eyesight.

EJ/JM

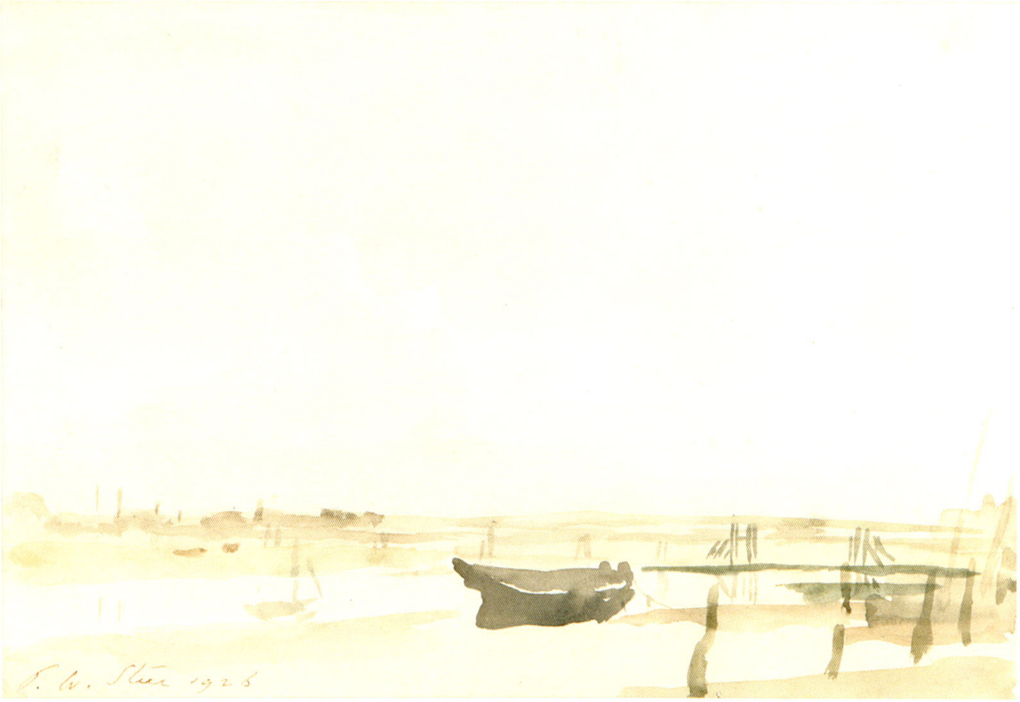

Alfred STEVENS
[1817–75]
Studies for the decoration of Dorchester House, London, c.1855–6

red chalk, squared in pencil on paper, sheet size 32 × 26.4 cm

P.321
PROVENANCE: Mrs Madeleine Clifton; sold on her behalf by Thos. Agnew & Sons Ltd to Gallery, January 1960.
EXHIBITIONS: *Watercolours and Drawings from The Cecil Higgins Art Gallery, Bedford*, London, Thos. Agnew & Sons Ltd, 1962, no.39.

Born in Dorset, Stevens lived in Italy 1833–42, where he studied under Bertel Thorwaldsen (1770–1844) in Rome and made many red chalk drawings in the manner of Raphael, whose influence is clearly apparent in this study. His rare watercolours have an imaginative quality, which shows him to have much in common with the Pre-Raphaelite movement.

Chiefly known for his sculpture, his two greatest achievements were the Wellington monument in St Paul's Cathedral and the decorative ensemble, c.1856, for the dining room at Dorchester House, London, the fireplace of which is now in the V&A.

EJ

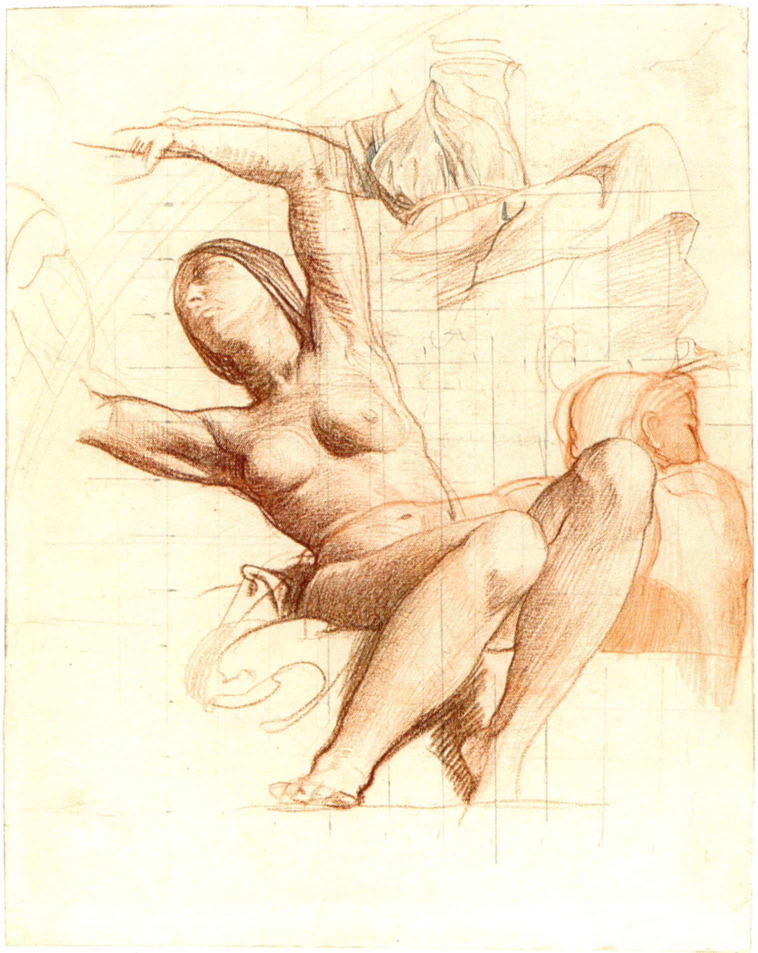

Alfred STEVENS
[1817–75]
Compositional Studies

pen and ink on paper, 17.7 × 11 cm

P.332
PROVENANCE: Professor Isaacs, from whom purchased by Gallery, January 1960.

It is not known whether these vigorous sketches were ever developed by Stevens – or indeed precisely what they represent. Perhaps the two figures in the top study were the first idea for a sculpture or picture of Tarquin and Lucretia. If so, the right-hand lower figure is probably related and a study for Lucretia about to stab herself.

EJ

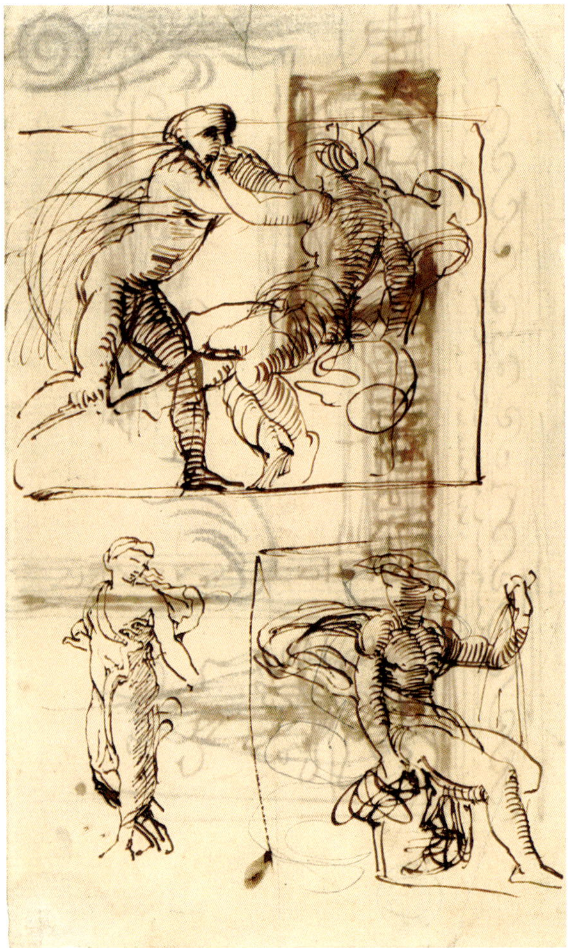

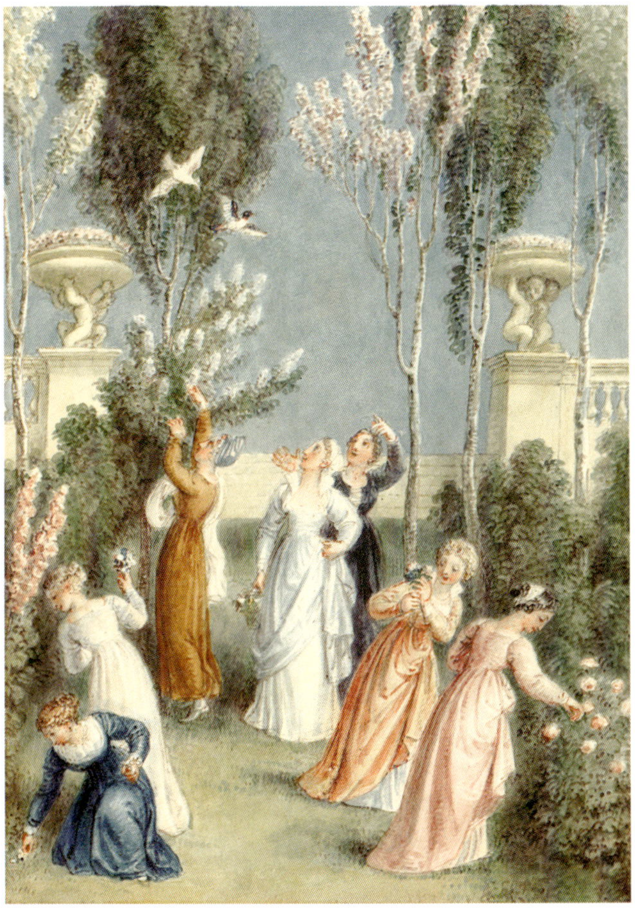

Thomas STOTHARD, R.A.
[1755–1834]
The Eighth Day of the Decameron, c.1825

pen and brown ink and watercolour on paper, 26.4 × 19 cm

P.713
PROVENANCE: Mrs George Haldiman who, according to J.L. Roget, commissioned George Fennel Robson (1788–1833) to assemble for her 'a representative album of drawings by the best watercolour painters of the day'. This he did between 1826–28. Although the Collection in three albums changed hands in 1861, it remained intact until sold, still as the Haldiman Collection, at Christie's, 18 March 1980, no.279, bought by Thos. Agnew & Sons Ltd for the Gallery with assistance of the V&A/M.G.C. Purchase Grant Fund.
EXHIBITIONS: *The Haldiman Collection of English Watercolours formed between 1826 and 1828,* London, Christie's, 1980, no.279.
NOTES: Another version, of identical size but with slight differences in the disposition of the figures, is in the British Museum (1886.6.7.3). It is illustrated in M. Hardie, *Watercolour Painting in Britain,* 1966, vol.1, pl.140. Another illustration to *The Decameron* by Stothard is in the Yale Center for British Art, New Haven, Connecticut.

The Decameron, by Giovanni Bocaccio (1313–75), recounts how, in 1348, a party of young patricians take refuge from the plague that is raging in Florence in a villa outside the City. To pass the time they tell each other stories: ten each day for ten days. This illustration appears on p.376 of an English translation printed in 1872 although the watercolour dates from c.1825.

The passage illustrated occurs at the end of the eighth day's storytelling when Emilia (the 'Queen' for the next day), suggests that they rest and recover their energy. Accordingly 'the company turned to various garlands and otherwise amusing themselves whilst the young men sang songs and played games'.

This is the kind of subject that Stothard excelled at illustrating: seven pretty young girls gathering nosegays in a sunlit garden, although it is not easy to identify the two birds in flight at the top left of the scene.

EJ

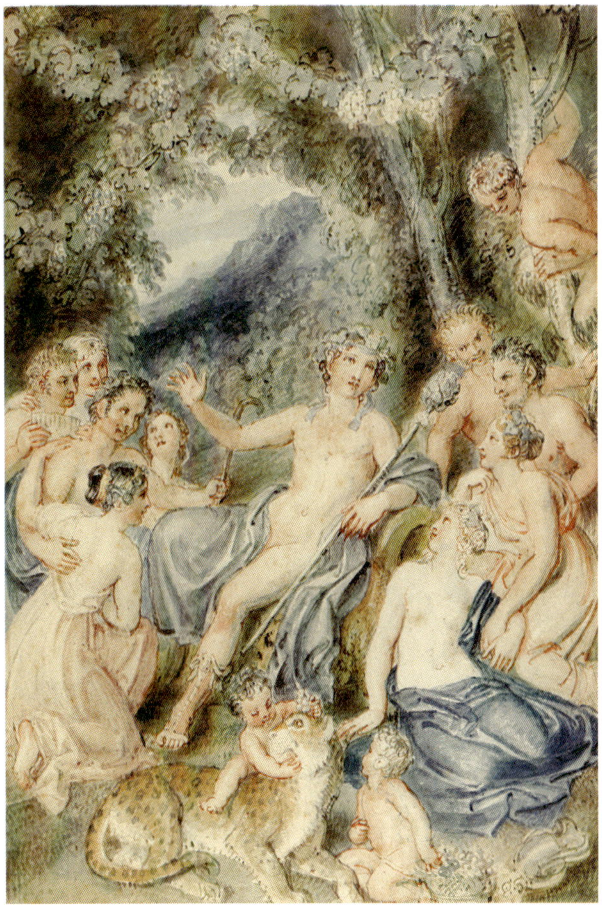

Thomas STOTHARD, R.A.
[1755–1834]
Bacchus and his Attendants

watercolour with pen and ink on paper, 24 × 16.4 cm

P.303
PROVENANCE: J. Fida & Andrade?; P&D Colnaghi Ltd, from whom purchased by Gallery, October 1959.

Bacchus, the god of wine, was the son of Jupiter and Semele. He is said to have married Ariadne after she was deserted by Theseus. He is usually shown crowned with vine and ivy leaves, as here, and holding in his left hand a thyrsus, a kind of wand or staff , with a fir cone for its head. His chariot is often drawn by panthers (as in Titian's famous *Bacchus and Ariadne* in the National Gallery, London), although Stothard's panther here looks as docile as a tabby cat.

Stothard, who entered the R.A. Schools in 1777, became perhaps the most prolific book-illustrator in history, winning great popularity for the charm and refinement of his work. Incidentally, he was regularly shaved in Covent Garden by TURNER'S father and is said to have encouraged the barber to allow his son to become an artist.

Elected R.A. in 1794, Stothard illustrated, among many others, *Joseph Andrews*, (see P.75 illustrated by Thomas HEARNE), *Tristram Shandy*, *Clarissa Harlowe* and *The Pilgrim's Progress*.

EJ

Thomas STOTHARD, R.A.
[1755–1834]
Illustration to the **Heart of Midlothian**

watercolour on paper, 15.6 × 11.8 cm

P.614/1
PROVENANCE: Maldwin Drummond sale, Christie's (with 11 other Stothard drawings 'Property of Maldwin Drummond' 11 June 1970, no.53 bought Tree; Christie's 17 November 1970, no.2, purchased Thos. Agnew & Sons Ltd for Gallery.

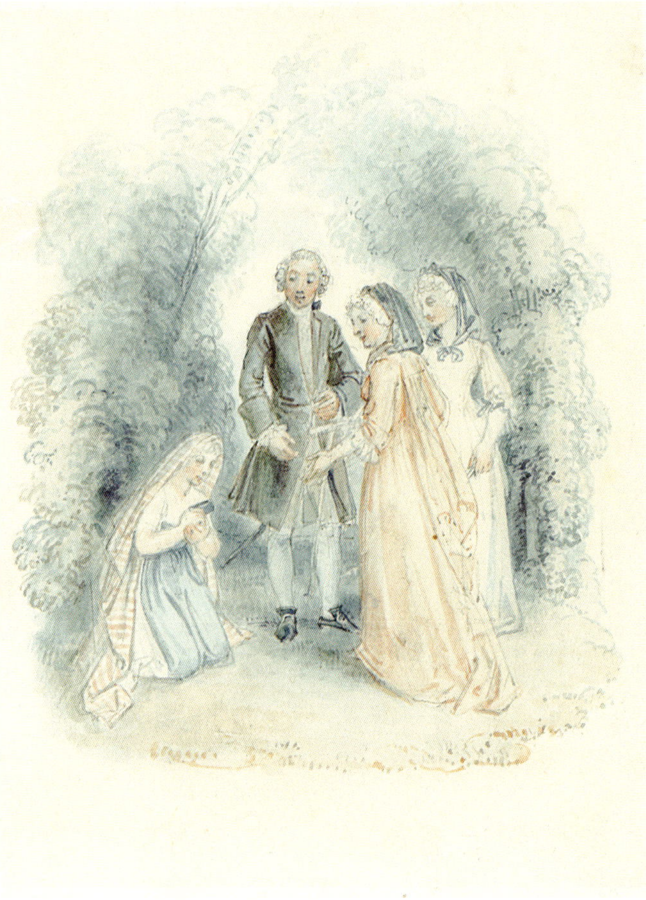

When sold in 1970 this was catalogued as illustrating *The Bride of Lammermoor*, but this watercolour bears no relation to any incident in the novel. Instead, the source has now been correctly identified as *The Heart of Midlothian*, published in 1818 as the second series of Sir Walter Scott's *Tales of My Grandfather*.

The novel centres partly round the Porteous Riots of 1736 and partly on the story of two sisters, Effie and Jeanie Deans. Effie is imprisoned in the Tolbooth-Gate of Edinburgh, accused of child murder (which she did not commit) and, because Jeanie will not perjure herself to save her sister, is condemned to death.

Jeanie then walks to London to plead for Effie's life. There the Duke of Argyle mediates on her behalf and takes her to the grounds of Richmond Palace where he introduces her to Queen Caroline and her attendant Lady Suffolk. These are the four figures shown here.

Jeanie pleaded her cause so eloquently that the Queen promised to intercede on her behalf with the King and, on parting, gave Jeanie a small housewife or pocket-book. It is this that Jeanie is clasping as she kneels before the Queen. It was found to contain, besides the usual needles and scissors, a bank-bill for £50 to help defray Jeanie's expenses on the long journeys to and from Edinburgh. The King did pardon Effie but only on condition of 'her banishing herself forth of Scotland for fourteen years'.

In a sheet of pen and ink sketches illustrating *Rob Roy*, there is a preliminary sketch of Jeanie kneeling in front of the Queen (Oppé Collection, T10013, Tate Gallery, London).

EJ

Thomas STOTHARD, R.A.
[1755–1834]
Come to Daddy Then

watercolour on paper, 11.4 × 8.3 cm

P.614/2

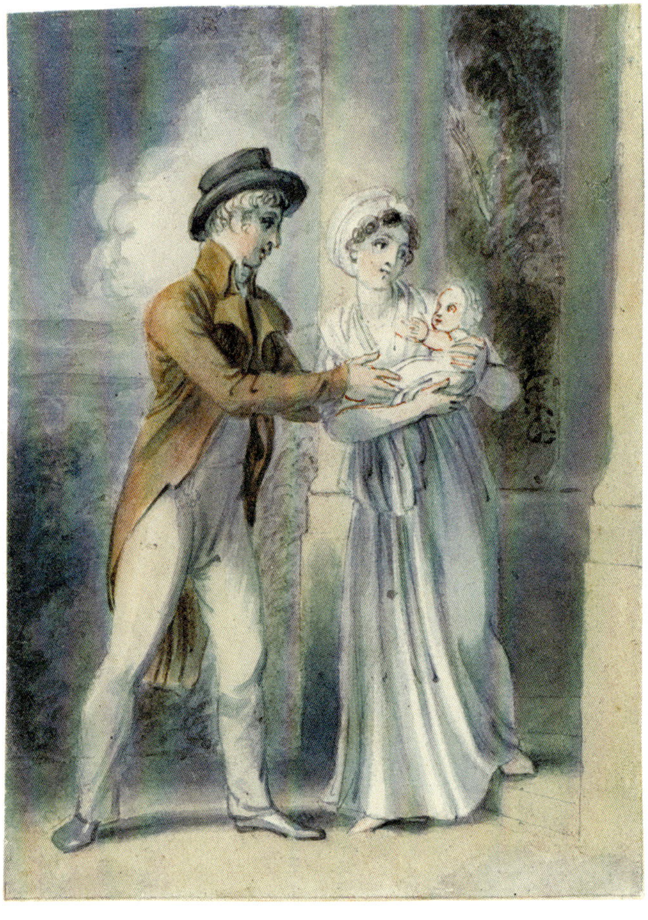

The source for this illustration has yet to be identified.

EJ

Thomas STOTHARD, R.A.
[1755–1834]
Study for two figures from Milton's *Comus*

pen, ink and watercolour on paper, 13.6 × 12 cm

P.614/3

Comus, a masque by John Milton (1608–74), was first performed at Ludlow Castle in 1634 to celebrate the Earl of Bridgewater's entry on the Presidency of Wales and the Marches.

In classical mythology Comus is the god of revelry, the son of Bacchus and Circe, who waylays travellers and transforms their faces into those of wild beasts by giving them a magic liquor. The Lady, played by the Earl's 15 year-old daughter, meets Comus, disguised as a shepherd, who lures her to his cottage, falsely promising protection.

The Lady's two younger brothers (the Earls' sons) appear and are told what has happened by the Attendant Spirit Thyrsis. The scene changes to a palace where Comus with his rabble tempts the Lady to drink his magic potion. She resists and the brothers then burst in and disperse the company but fail to secure Comus' wand and are thus unable to release the Lady from her enchanted chair.

Thyrsis now invokes the aid of Sabrina, goddess of the river Severn, in the song *Sabrina Fair*. She appears from the water, frees the Lady, helping her to rise from her chair as shown in this sketch. The Lady and her brothers are then returned to Ludlow and presented to their parents.

EJ

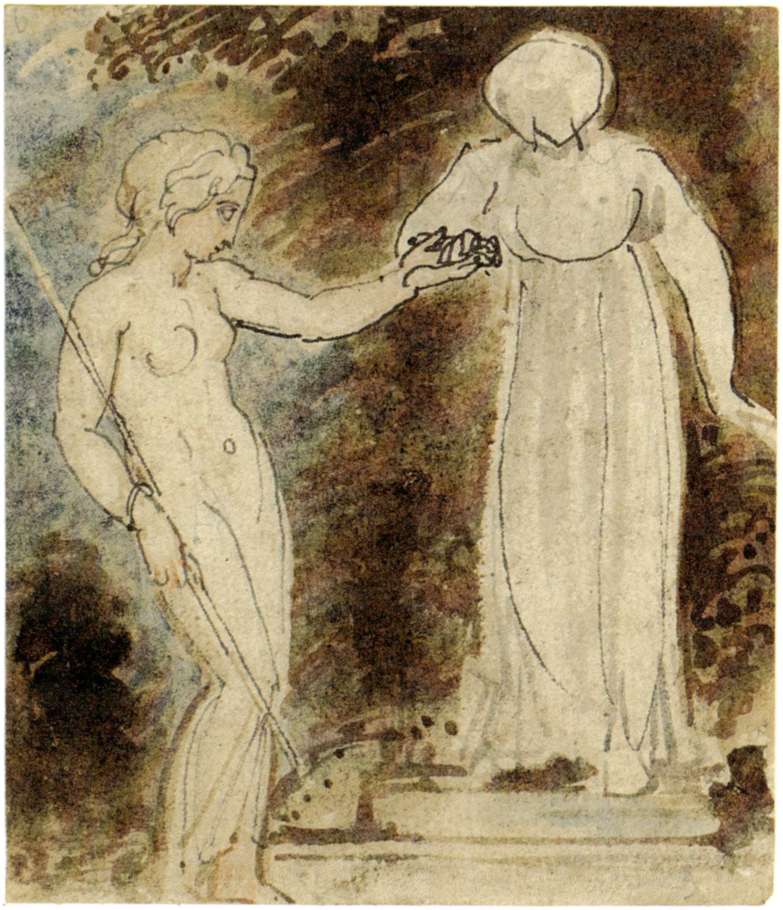

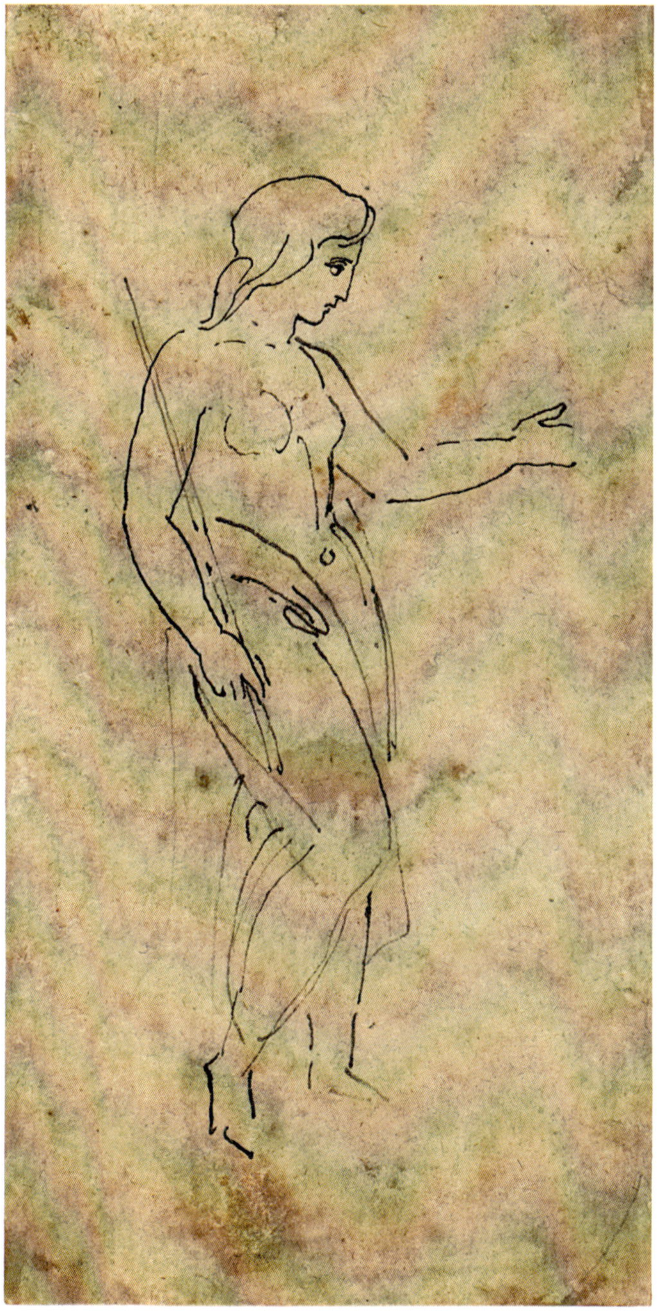

Thomas STOTHARD, R.A.
[1755–1834]
Study for **Sabrina** from Milton's *Comus*

pen and ink on paper, 20.3 × 10.3 cm

P.614/4

Although on a larger scale, Sabrina is here in essentially the same position as when she appears in no. P614/3 with the Lady.

There, Sabrina, having broken the spell which Comus cast on the chair which confined the lady to it, is helping her to rise from it. See the entry for no. P614/3 for the full story.

EJ

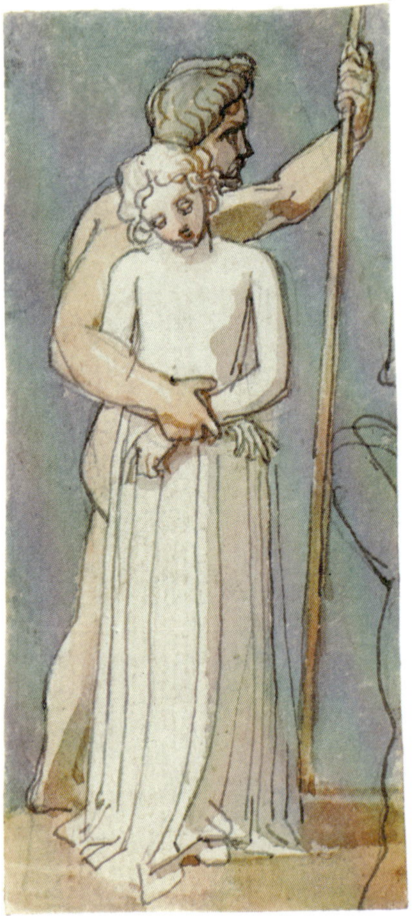

Thomas STOTHARD, R.A.
[1755–1834]
Scene from Milton's *Comus*

pen, ink and watercolour on paper, 10 × 4.6 cm

P.614/5

Originally entitled *Figure of a Woman Embraced by a Man Holding a Staff*, this was among twelve Stothard drawings which included two identified as illustrating scenes from *Comus*. It seems certain that this is a third and shows Comus, disguised as a shepherd, leading the Lady back to his cottage having promised her protection.

EJ

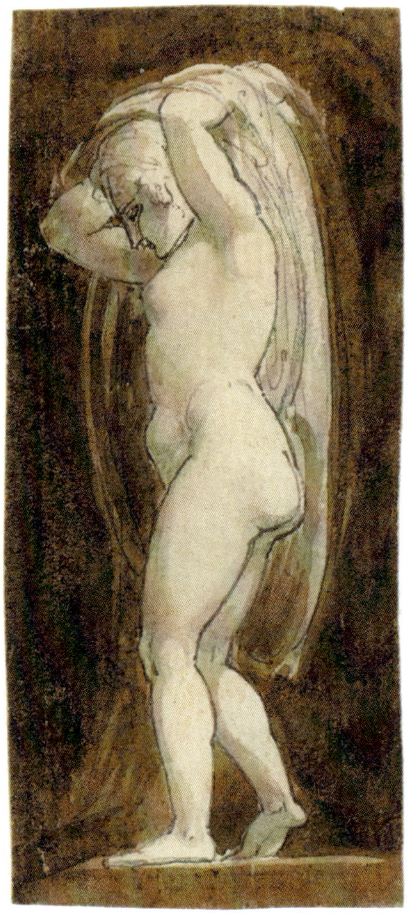

Thomas STOTHARD, R.A.
[1755–1834]
Figure Study

pen, ink and grey wash on paper, 12.7 × 6 cm
on reverse: outline sketch of a bather

P.614/6

A fragment from a larger work.

EJ

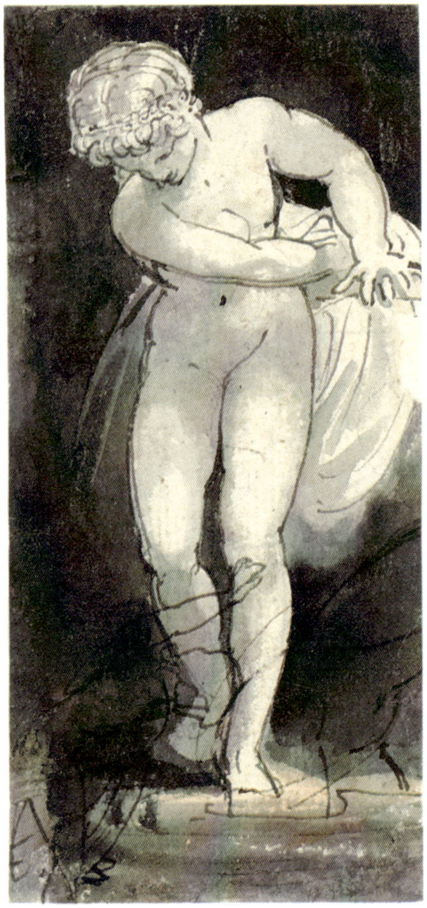

Thomas STOTHARD, R.A.
[1755–1834]
Figure Study

pen, ink and brown wash on paper, 8.9 × 4.1 cm

P.614/7

A fragment from a larger work.

EJ

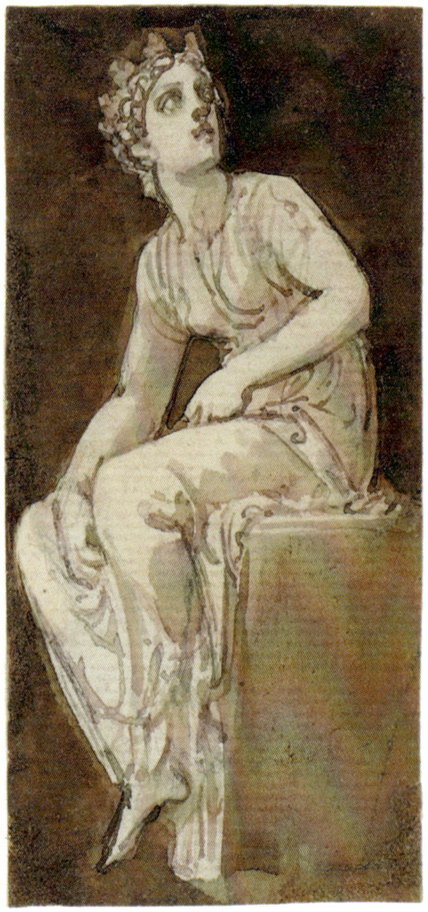

Thomas STOTHARD, R.A.
[1755–1834]
A Seated Classical Figure

brown wash on paper, 9 × 4.5 cm

P.614/8

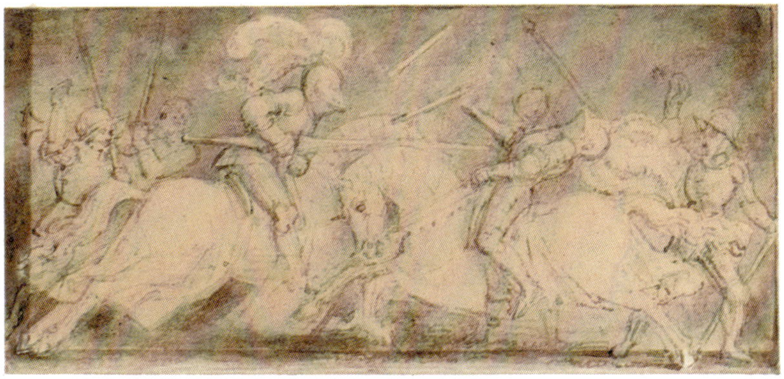

Thomas STOTHARD, R.A.
[1755–1834]
Mounted Knights in Combat

pen and brown wash on paper, 4.2 × 8.8 cm

P.614/9

Thomas STOTHARD, R.A.
[1755–1834]
Pastoral Scene with Sheep and Sheepdog

wash on paper, 4.2 × 8.6 cm

P.614/10

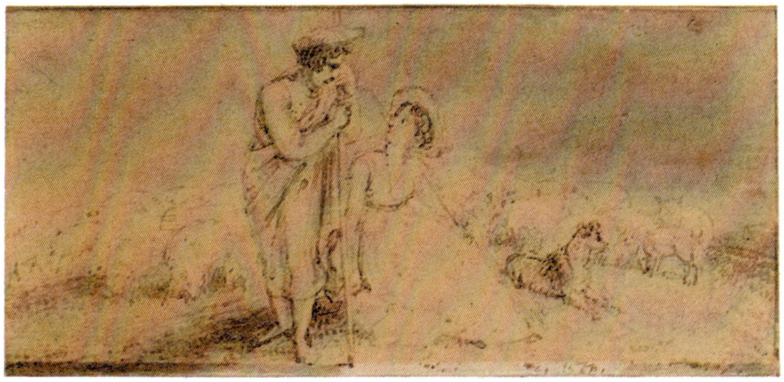

Thomas STOTHARD, R.A.
[1755–1834]
Figures Dancing

watercolour on paper, 6.9 × 8.9 cm

P.614/11

Perhaps this dance was started up spontaneously to celebrate the end of the hay harvest as the onlookers are sitting on top of the rick nearby. Stothard was as prolific an illustrator as any British artist so it may be difficult to identify the scene shown here, a typical example of Stothard's skill in portraying the animation and pleasure of these young people.

EJ

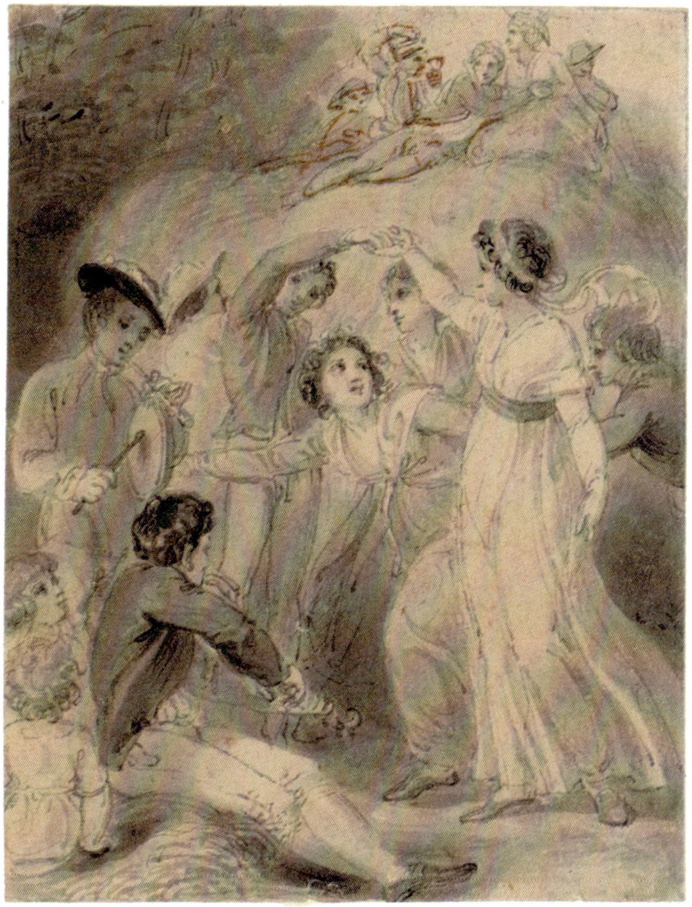

Thomas STOTHARD, R.A.
[1755–1834]
Sketch for a Battle Scene

pen and ink on paper, 11.9 × 14.8 cm
on reverse: watercolour sketch of a pomegranate

P.614/12

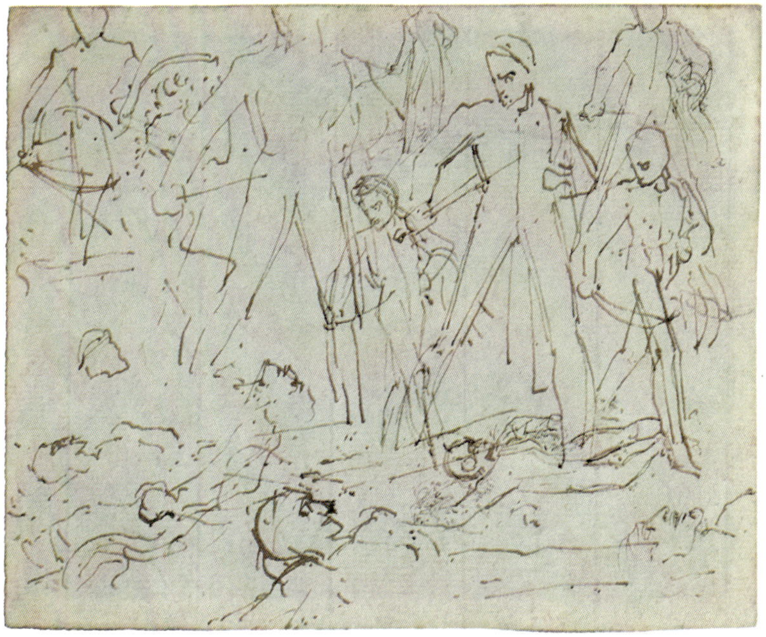

Graham SUTHERLAND, O.M.
[1903–80]
Sheet of four studies: **Trees under Mynedd Pen Cyrm, 1939**

pen and watercolour on paper, 29.8 × 22.4 cm
inscribed: *Sutherland*
top: *Sutherland /39.* left centre: *Sutherland. and ed Trees under Mynedd Pen Cyrm Christmas Day 1939.* centre right: *Sutherland.1939.* bottom: *Sutherland Sept.24/39.*
inscribed on reverse: *G Sutherland Sketchbook page 457*

P.252
PROVENANCE: Sir Kenneth Clark; Redfern Gallery, from whom purchased by Gallery, 1958.
EXHIBITIONS: *Works by Henry Moore, John Piper, Graham Sutherland*, Leeds, Temple Newsam, 1941, no.146 as *Three Studies of Trees* (shown without the study centre right); *Watercolours from The Cecil Higgins Art Gallery*, London, Thos. Agnew & Sons Ltd, 1962, no.100; *Watercolours from Bedford*, Norwich, Castle Museum, 1965, no.51.

The top drawing is a study for *Tree forms in an Estuary*, 1940, and the centre left drawing is for *Association of Oaks,* 1940. No larger version has been traced for the bottom drawing.

These neo-romantic studies clearly influenced the young Keith VAUGHAN.

EJ

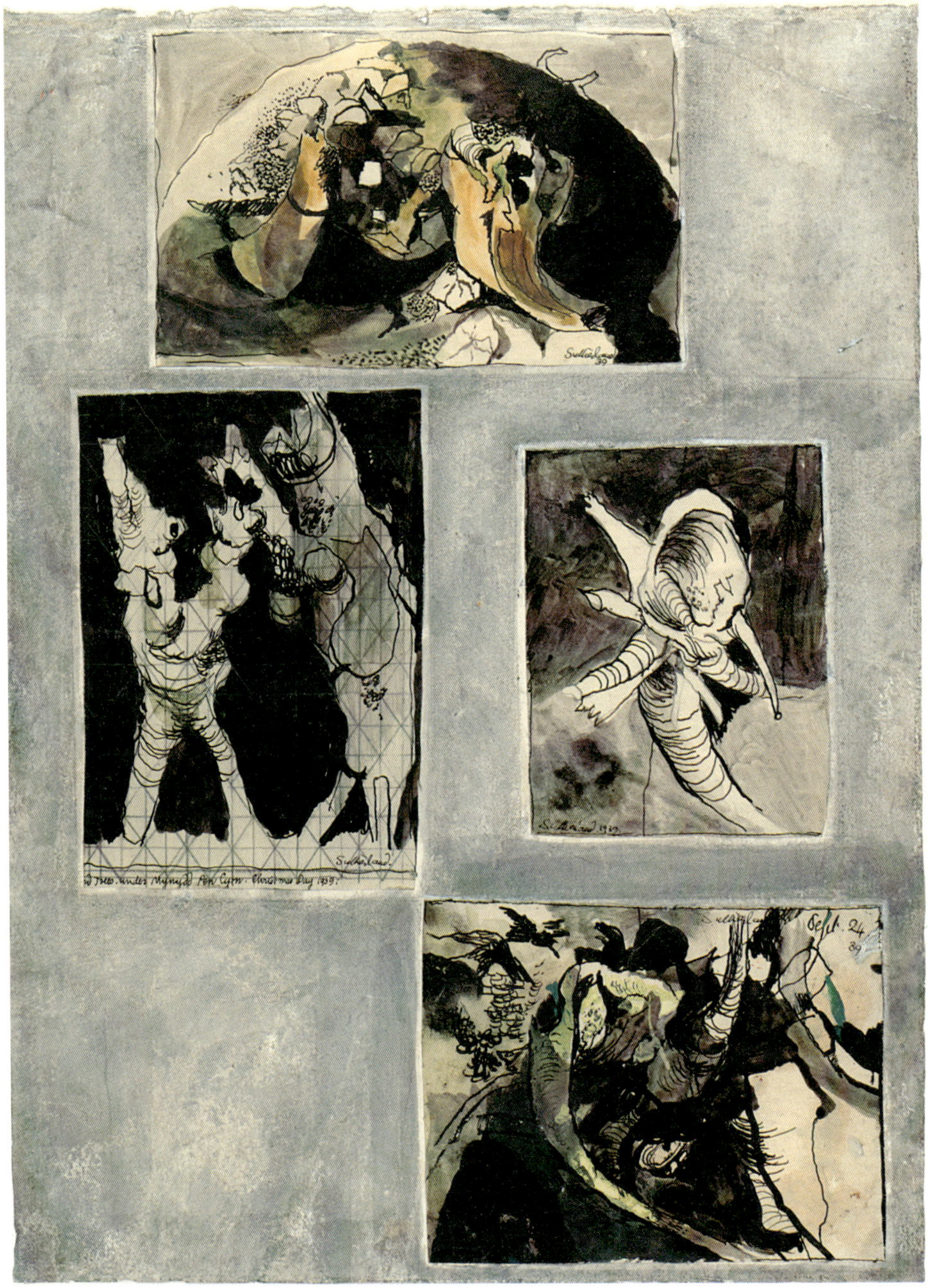

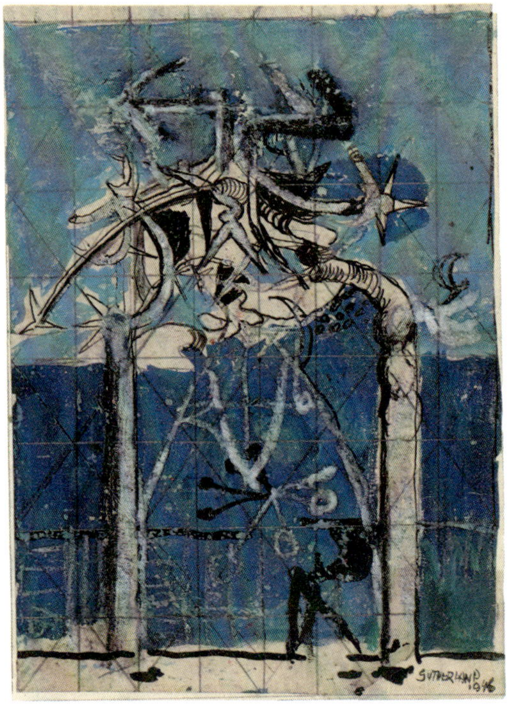

Graham SUTHERLAND, O.M.
[1903–80]
The Thorntree, 1946

bodycolour with ink, pencil and wax crayon on paper, 20.5 × 15.2 cm
inscribed: *Sutherland 1946*

P.141
PROVENANCE: Roland, Browse and Delbanco, from whom purchased by Gallery, November 1957.

In 1945 Canon Walter Hussey commissioned a *Crucifixion* for the Church of St Matthew, Northampton. It was whilst searching for a suitable motif that Sutherland noted 'I made some drawings [of thorn bushes], and as I made them a curious change developed. As the thorns rearranged themselves, they became, whilst still retaining their own pricking, space-encompassing life, something else – a kind of 'stand-in' for a Crucifixion and a crucified head..' (*Thoughts on Painting,* 1951).

JM

Graham SUTHERLAND, O.M.
[1903–80]
Vine Pergola no.2, 1948

bodycolour on paper, 44.9 × 56.7 cm
inscribed: *Sutherland 1948*

P.357
PROVENANCE: Redfern Gallery, from whom purchased by Gallery, July 1960.
EXHIBITIONS: *Watercolours and Drawings from The Cecil Higgins Art Gallery, Bedford*, London, Thos. Agnew & Sons Ltd, 1962, no.99; *Watercolours from Bedford*, Norwich, Norwich Castle Museum, 1965, no.52.

Sutherland spent his early years as an apprentice at the Midland Railway Works in Derby, making drawings in the evenings. After studying at Goldsmith's College of Art, specialising in printmaking, he pursued a career working as an illustrator and designer, including posters for London Underground and designs for 'Foley' china. His painting career began in earnest after his first visit, in 1934 to Pembrokeshire which he revisited each summer until the outbreak of the Second World War.

After the war, spent as an Official War Artist recording scenes of bomb damaged cities, he returned to nature for subject matter, often exploring themes with an underlying religious metaphor.

Sutherland made his first visit to France in 1947 and from then on spent a part of each year there, finally buying a house at Menton in 1955. This led to the use of more vivid colour and an interest in Mediterranean motifs such as vine pergolas and palm palisades.

JM

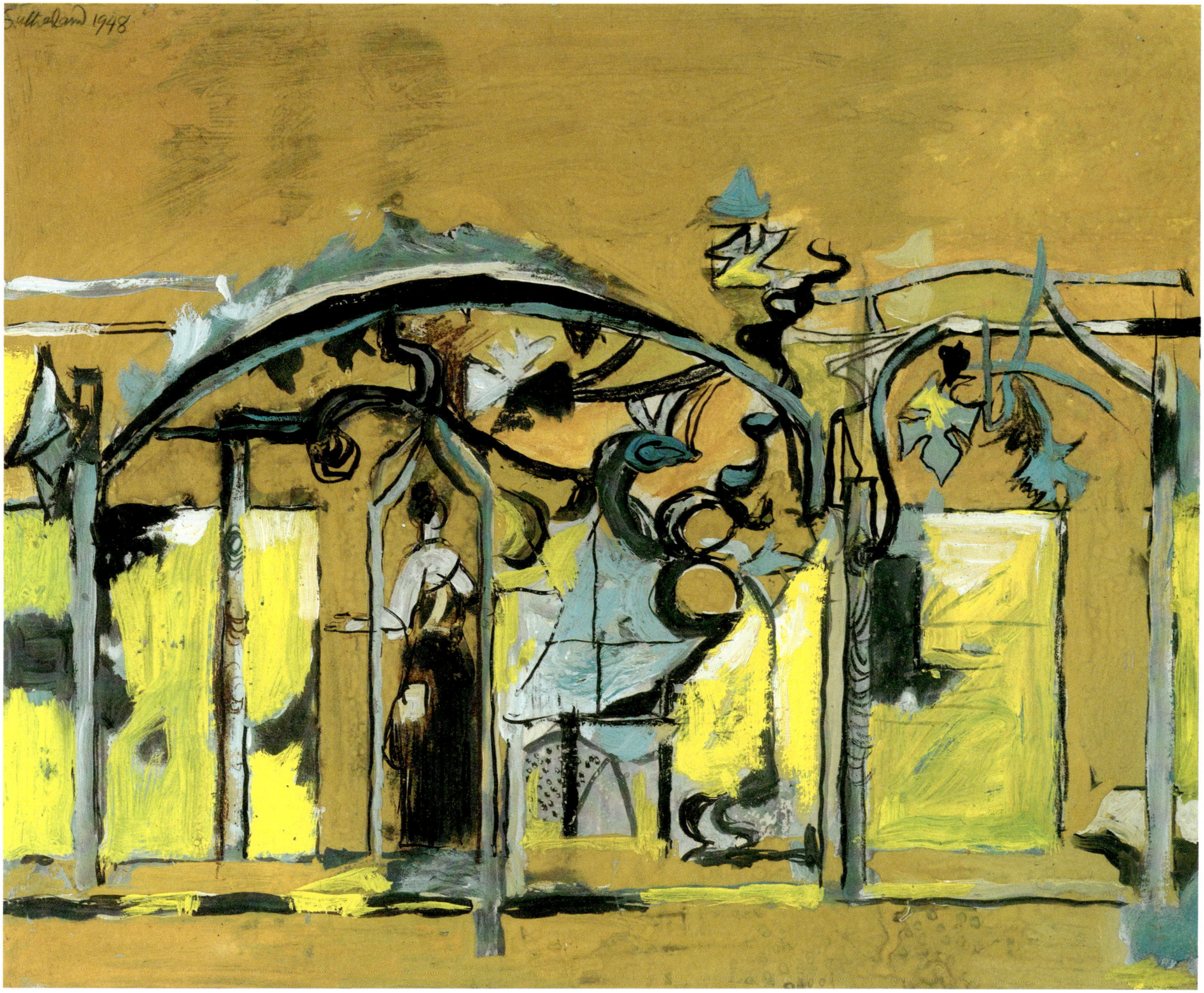

Graham SUTHERLAND, O.M.
[1903–80]
Birds and foliage, design for tapestry, 1949

bodycolour and chalk on paper, 32.1 × 27.8 cm
inscribed: *Sutherland 1949*

P.339
PROVENANCE: Piccadilly Gallery, from whom purchased by Gallery, April 1960.
EXHIBITIONS: *Watercolours and Drawings from The Cecil Higgins Art Gallery, Bedford*, London, Thos. Agnew & Sons Ltd, 1962, no.98.

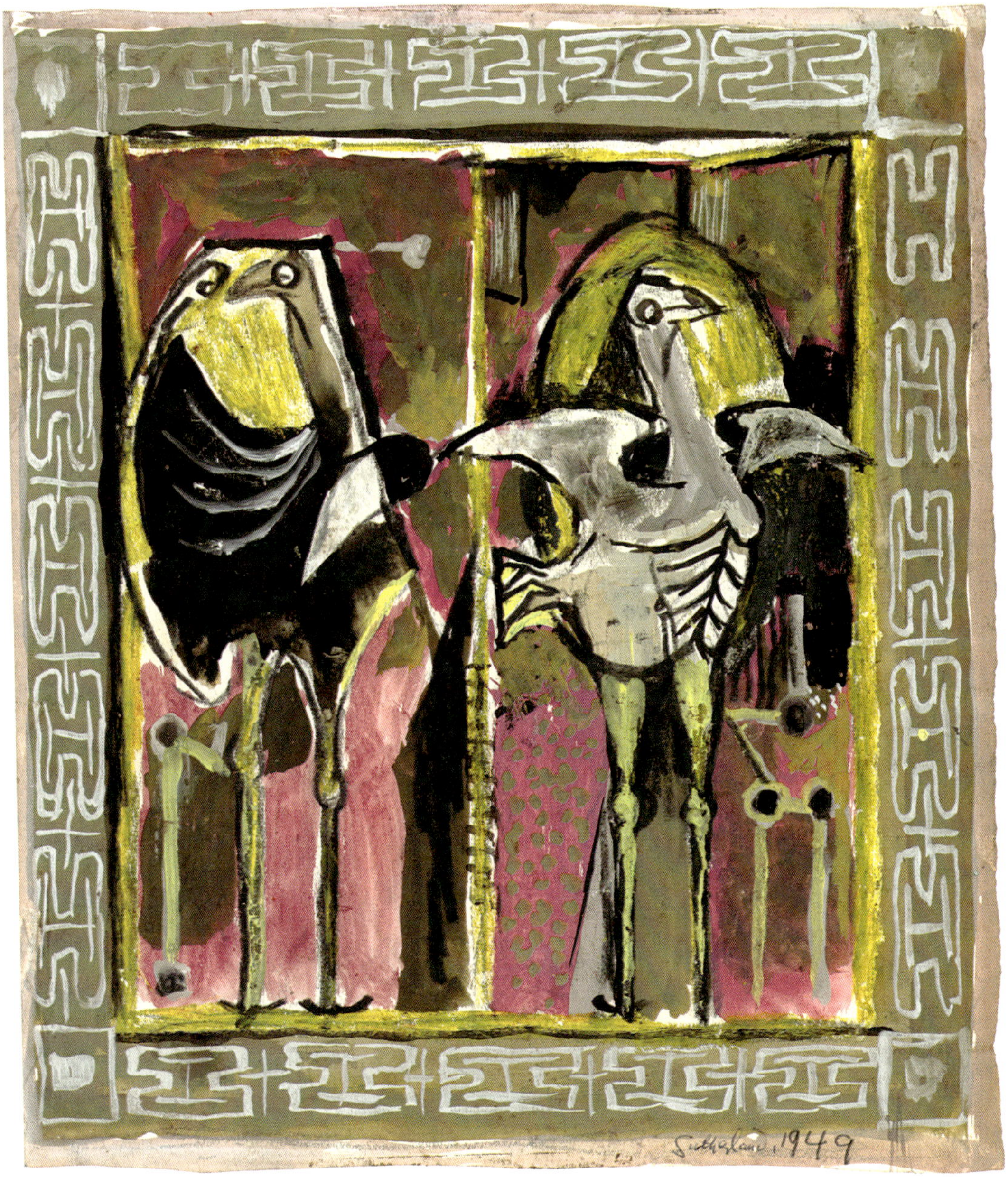

In 1949 the Edinburgh Tapestry Company, under its newly appointed artistic director Sir Francis Rose, decided to ask well-known British artists to contribute designs for a nominal fee. Sutherland contributed several designs in gouache, two of which were made up into finished tapestries by the company.

The principal colours of mustard yellow and purple caused some technical difficulties for the company due to post war austerity measures; the finished tapestries were therefore woven in a mixture of blue and red thread to realize the original design.

JM

Philip SUTTON, R.A.
[born 1928]
River Landscape, 1959

charcoal on paper, 56 × 76.2 cm
inscribed: *P.Sutton 1959*

P.355
PROVENANCE: Roland, Browse and Delbanco, from whom purchased by Gallery, July 1960.
EXHIBITIONS: *Philip Sutton*, Leeds, Temple Newsam, 1960.

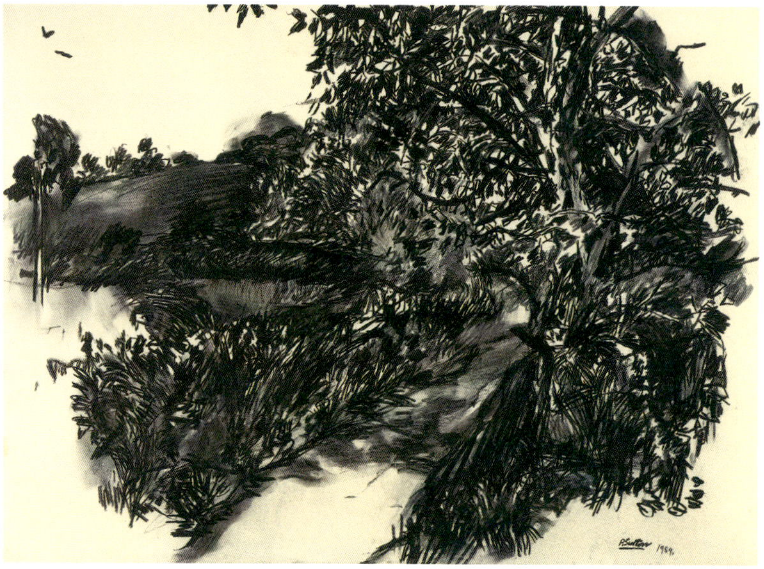

Sutton was born at Poole in Dorset and studied at the Slade, 1949–53, being awarded the Slade School Summer competition prize in 1952 and a French State Scholarship. He taught at the Slade from 1955 to 1963; it was in 1963 that he went to live in the Fiji Islands for eleven months with his wife and children, developing a strong sense of colour harmony within his work. This drawing may have been made at Snape, near Aldeburgh in Suffolk, where the Suttons lived for a period in the 1950s and 1960s. It is characteristic of Sutton's early work executed in his expansive style with a hint of mystery about what awaits the traveller when he reaches the spot where the path enters the dark trees. Sutton was elected to the London Group in 1956, elected A.R.A. and in 1988, R.A.

EJ/JM

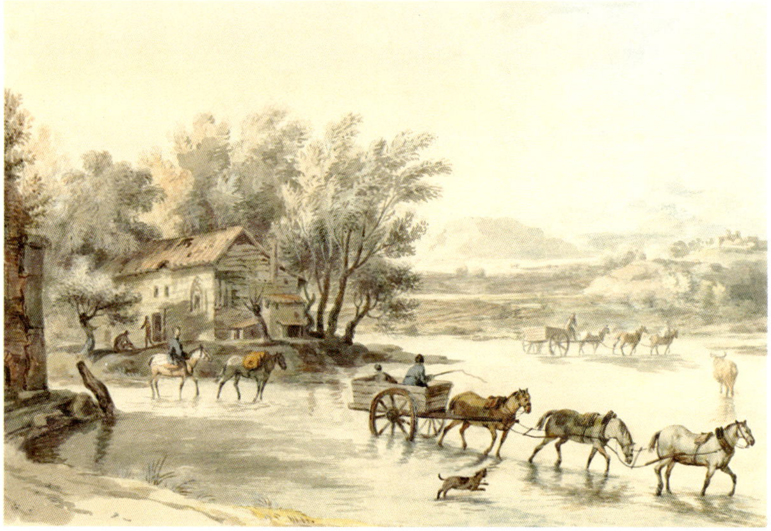

William TAVERNER
[1703–72]
Landscape with Horses and Carts Fording a River

watercolour and pencil with some bodycolour on paper, 28.2 × 41.5cm

P.94
PROVENANCE: Gilbert Davies; P&D Colnaghi Ltd, from whom purchased by Gallery, 1953.
EXHIBITIONS: *Watercolours and Drawings from The Cecil Higgins Art Gallery, Bedford*, London, Thos. Agnew & Sons Ltd, 1962, no.2.

Little is known about Taverner, an amateur who was reluctant to show his work and rarely dated it. Although the claim in his obituary in *The Gentleman's Magazine,* that he was 'One of the best landscape painters England ever produced' is exaggerated, his best work has a poetical feeling that is immensely attractive, though the figures in his more classicizing landscapes, deriving from those by Marco Ricci or the 17th century Italianate Dutch painters, are sometimes rather weak. He was an early exponent of using bodycolour, and there is tribute to him in Smollett's *Humphrey Clinker*, 1771.

EJ

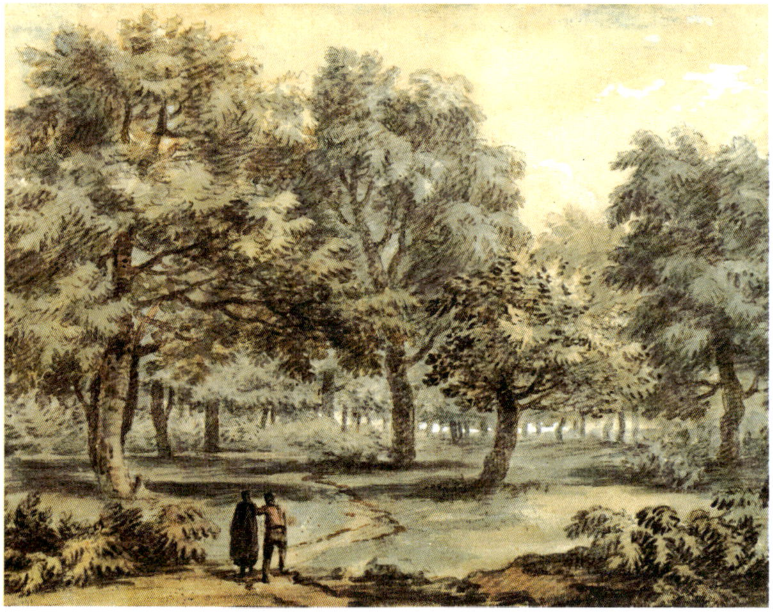

William TAVERNER
[1703–72]
Woodland Landscape

watercolour over black chalk heightened with white on paper, 19.2 × 25.5 cm
on original surround: *Taverner*

P.462
PROVENANCE: John Mills; P&D Colnaghi Ltd, from whom purchased by Gallery, August 1964.
EXHIBITIONS: *English Watercolours from The Cecil Higgins Art Gallery Bedford*, Reading, Reading Museum & Art Gallery, 1965, no.51; *Watercolours from Bedford,* Norwich, Castle Museum, 1965, no.53.

A characteristic subject of Taverner's, reflecting the influence of Claude and Poussin, especially in the interlocking forms of the foliage and trees. Despite this, Taverner infuses the scene with a poetical touch which makes it at once recognizably English.

EJ

Sir John TENNIEL
[1820–1914]
Incident on Dartmoor, 1859

pen and ink on paper, 5.9 × 9.9 cm

P.310
PROVENANCE: Rogers, Chapman & Thomas, lot 494; P&D Colnaghi Ltd, from whom purchased by Gallery, October 1959.

Tenniel was largely a self-taught painter, illustrator and cartoonist who exhibited at the R.A., the N.W.S. and elsewhere between 1835 and 1880. He was on the staff of *Punch*, between 1851 and 1901, drawing nearly all of the principal cartoons; however he is chiefly famous for having illustrated *Alice's Adventures in Wonderland*, (1865), and *Alice through the Looking Glass* (1871).

This drawing was an illustration for *Once a Week*, 24 November, 1859, and powerfully conveys how bleak a prospect it would be to be caught in a snowstorm in one of the loneliest spots in England.

EJ

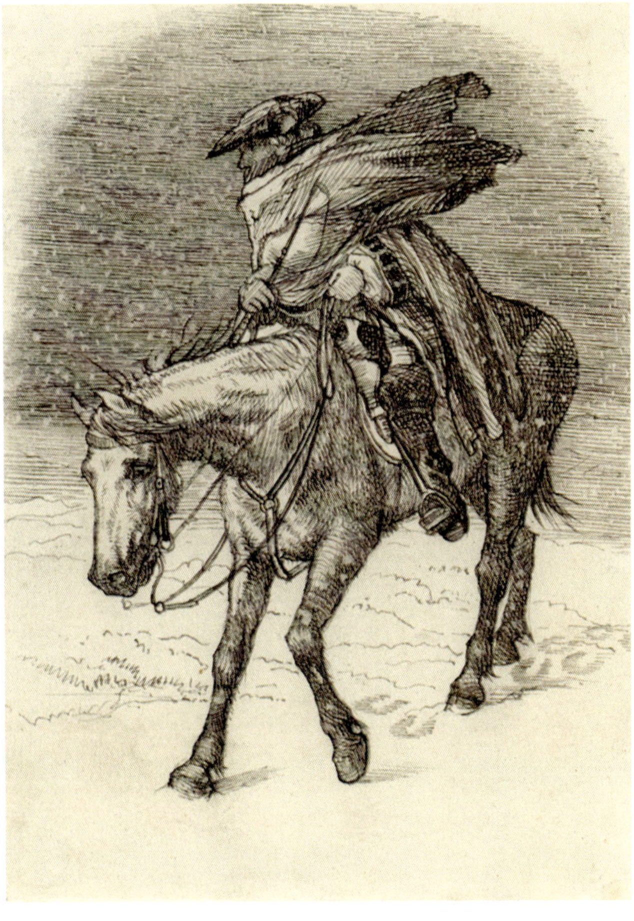

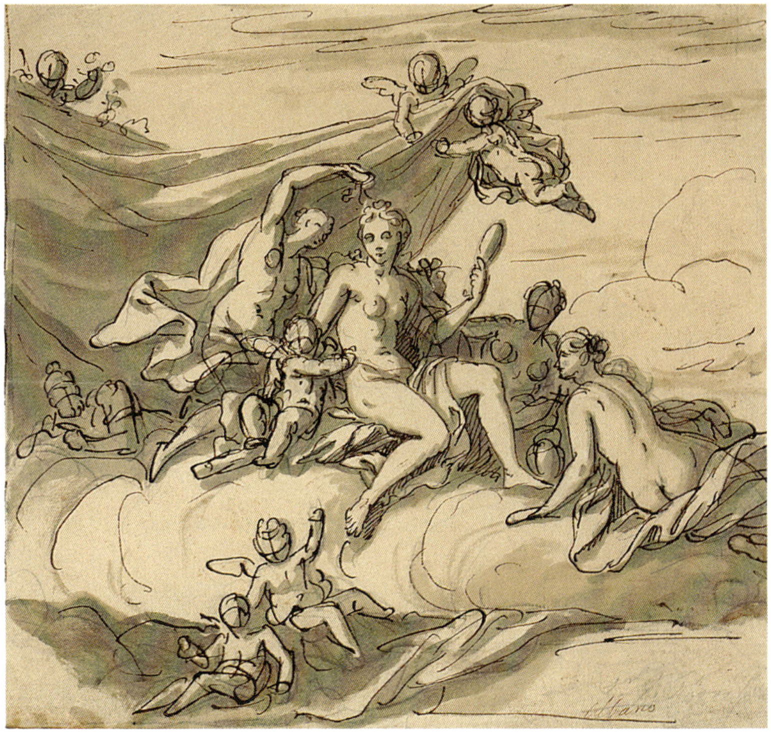

Sir James THORNHILL
[1675–1734]
Study for a painted ceiling: Venus and Cupid

pen and dark brown ink with grey wash on paper,
19.2 × 20.5 cm
inscribed: *Sir J Thornhill Albano*

P.95
PROVENANCE: H.M. Calmann; P&D Colnaghi Ltd, from whom purchased by Gallery, August 1952.
EXHIBITIONS: *English Watercolours from the Hickman Bacon and other Collections,* Bedford, Cecil Higgins Art Gallery, 1952, no.68.

An unidentified design for a painted ceiling. Thornhill was one of Britain's leading ceiling painters. His most famous work was undertaken for the Great Hall at the Royal Naval College, Greenwich, and completed in 1727. It took him nineteen years to complete for which he was paid £6,685 (£3 per square yard for the ceiling and £1 for the walls).

EJ

Sir James THORNHILL
[1675–1734]
The Adoration of the Magi

brown ink and wash on paper, 22.1 × 17.3 cm
inscribed on reverse: *Sr James Thornhill*

P.112
PROVENANCE: P&D Colnaghi Ltd, from whom purchased by Gallery, September 1956.
EXHIBITIONS: *Watercolours and Drawings from The Cecil Higgins Art Gallery, Bedford*, London, Thos. Agnew & Sons Ltd, 1962, no.5; *English Watercolours from The Cecil Higgins Art Gallery Bedford,* Reading, Reading Museum & Art Gallery, 1965, no.52; *Watercolours from Bedford,* Norwich, Castle Museum, 1965, no.54.
REFERENCES: '250 years of English Watercolours', *Country Life*, October 25, 1962, repr. p.1018.

Designs for the east wall of the Chapel at Wimpole, Cambridgeshire, built by James Gibbs (1682–1754) for Edward Harley, second Earl of Oxford (1689–1741).

Thornhill was the first painter born in England to compete with foreign artists such as Louis Laguerre (1663–1721) and Antonio Verrio (c.1630–c.1707) for major wall-painting commissions. These included the Painted Hall at Greenwich Hospital and the cupola of St Paul's Cathedral. His success culminated in a knighthood in 1720. Later, however, through Lord Burlington's intrigues, his protégé, William Kent, won the commission to decorate Kensington Palace and Thornhill received no more work of this kind. Thornhill's daughter Jane married William HOGARTH.

EJ

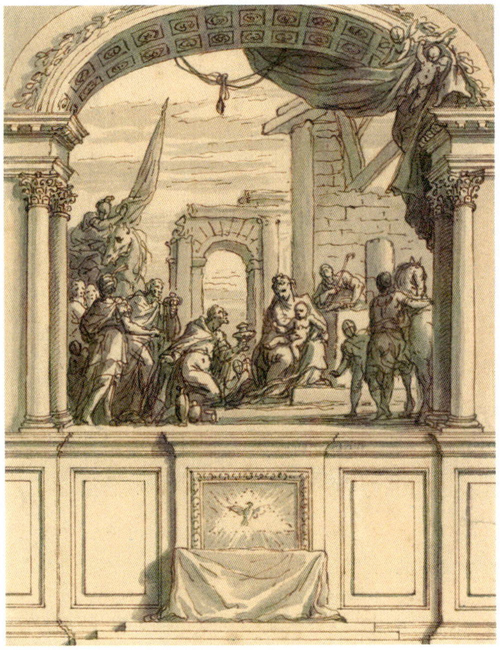

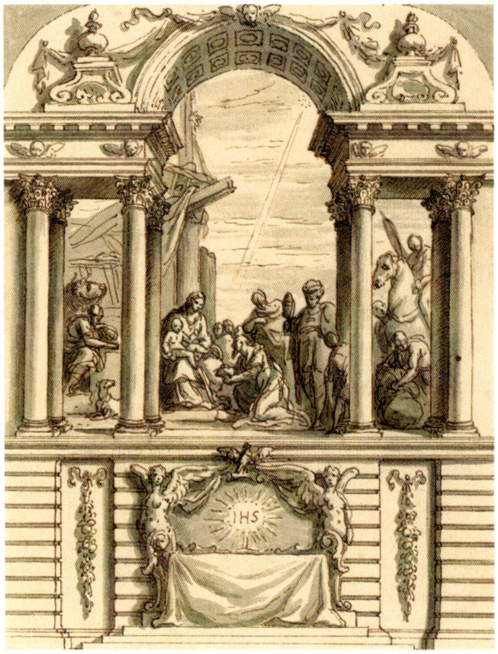

Sir James THORNHILL
[1675–1734]
The Adoration of the Magi

brown ink and wash on paper, 22.1 × 17.3 cm
inscribed on reverse: *Sr James Thornhill*

P.113
PROVENANCE: P&D Colnaghi Ltd, from whom purchased by Gallery, September 1956.
EXHIBITIONS: *Watercolours and Drawings from The Cecil Higgins Art Gallery, Bedford*, London, Thos. Agnew & Sons Ltd, 1962, no.5; *English Watercolours from The Cecil Higgins Art Gallery Bedford,* Reading, Reading Museum & Art Gallery, 1965, no.52; *Watercolours from Bedford,* Norwich, Castle Museum, 1965, no.54.

Design for the the Chapel at Wimpole, (see P.112).

JM

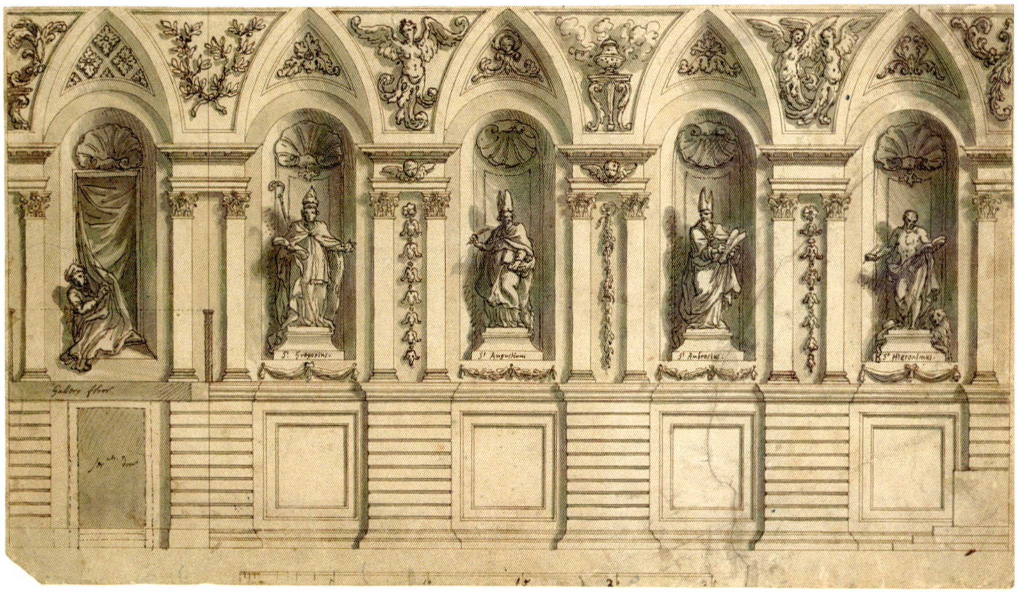

Sir James THORNHILL
[1675–1734]
The Fathers of the Church

brown ink and wash on paper, 26.1 × 46.6 cm
inscribed: *Ground floor, and St Gregorius, St Augustinus, St Ambrosius, St Hieronimus* and *for nh door*

P.120
PROVENANCE: P&D Colnaghi Ltd, from whom purchased by Gallery, September 1956.

Design for the North wall of the Chapel at Wimpole (see P.112).

JM

Henry TONKS
[1862–1937]
The Villa D'Este, Tivoli, 1920

watercolour with pen and ink on paper, 27.5 × 37.5 cm
inscribed: *Tivoli Hry Tonks 1920*

P.288
PROVENANCE: Leicester Galleries, from whom purchased by Gallery, April 1959.

Tivoli has been a favourite subject with artists for centuries. The Villa D'Este, built 1550, was designed by the mannerist architect Pirro Ligorio for the Governor Cardinal Ippolito II d'Este. Before being confiscated as his residence the property had been a Benedictine convent. Today the villa is less noteworthy than the parks and fountains, whose water is supplied by two canals especially dug for the purpose. Tonks seems more intrigued here by the motley groups of sightseers than by the Villa itself.

EJ/JM

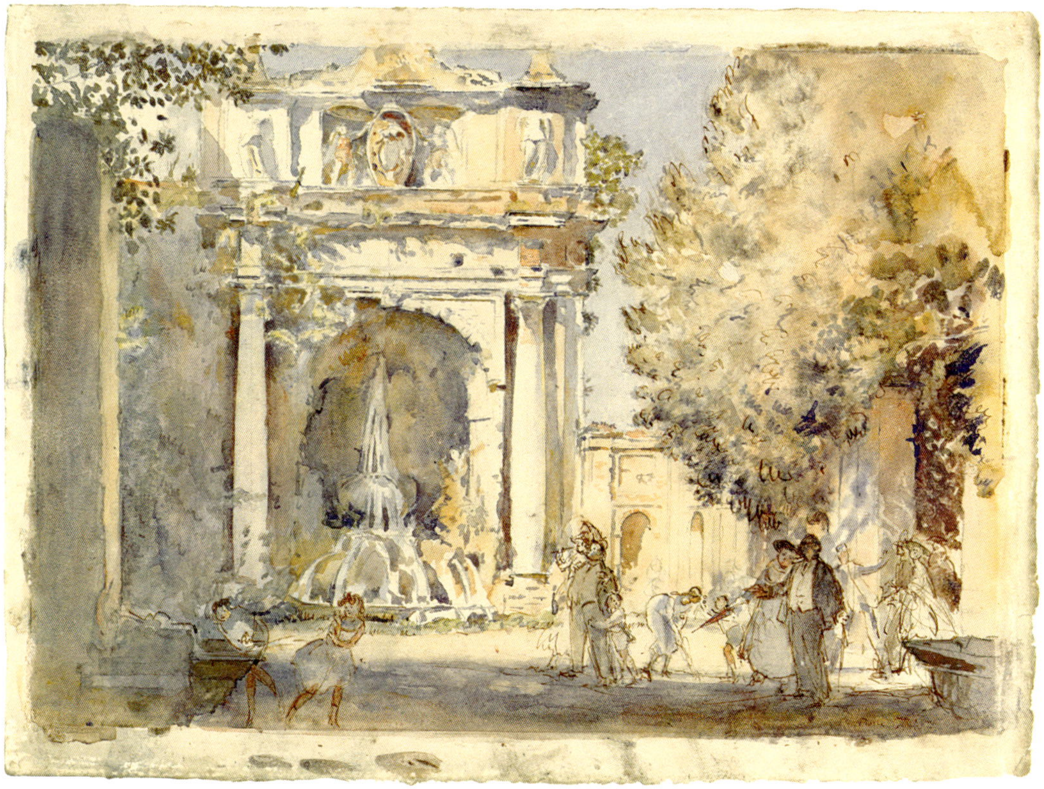

Henry TONKS
[1862–1937]
Woman Walking on the Sand

watercolour and pencil on paper, 23.5 × 34.7 cm
inscribed: *Henry Tonks*

P.323
PROVENANCE: Lady Margaret Montagu-Pollock; Sotheby's, lot 70; Thos. Agnew & Sons Ltd, from whom purchased by Gallery, January 1960.

Alone on this vast stretch of sand, Tonks has placed the figure in the composition so skilfully that she immediately becomes the focus of our attention.

Tonks first qualified as a surgeon before attending Westminster School of Art under Fred Brown. He gave up medicine in 1893 to join the staff of the Slade, becoming Professor there, 1918–30. As a teacher he had a notable influence on English draughtsmanship, teaching, amongst others, Matthew SMITH, Augustus JOHN and Harold GILMAN. As one would expect, his own sensitive figure studies are based on a thorough knowledge of anatomy.

He never accepted Post-Impressionism and opposed the doctrines of Roger Fry, but many artists' memoirs refer to the 'great days of the Slade under Tonks'.

EJ/JM

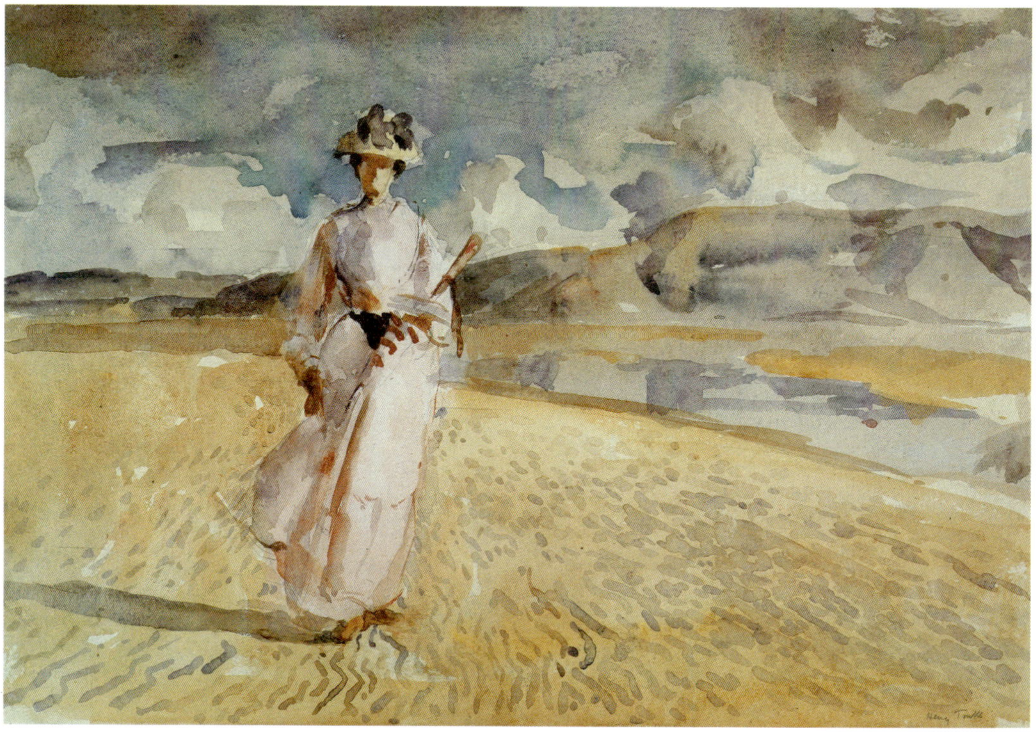

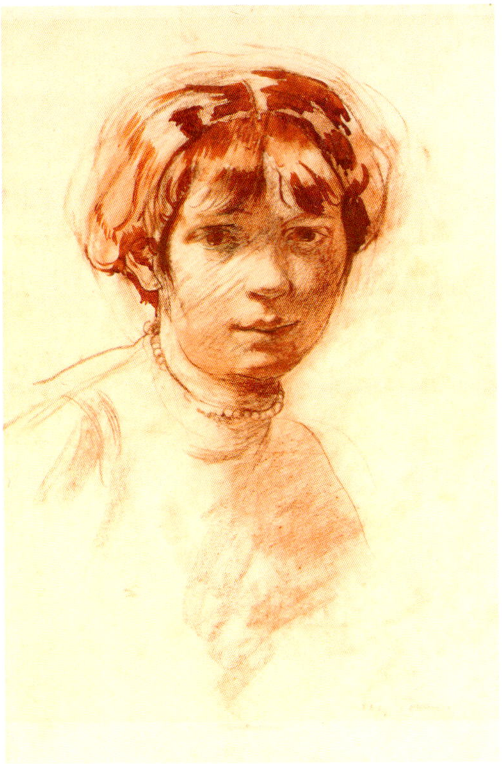

Henry TONKS

[1862–1937]

Head of a Woman Wearing a Necklace

red chalk and wash on paper, 45.7 × 30.6 cm
inscribed: *Henry Tonks*

P.390

PROVENANCE: Sir Michael Sadler; John Brophy; P&D Colnaghi Ltd, from whom purchased by Gallery, January 1961.
EXHIBITIONS: *Watercolours and Drawings from The Cecil Higgins Art Gallery, Bedford*, London, Thos. Agnew & Sons Ltd, 1962, no.110; *Watercolours from Bedford*, Norwich, Castle Museum, 1965, no.55.
REFERENCES: J. Brophy, *The Human Face*, 1945, pl. I, repr. as frontispiece and labelled *Woman with Necklace by Henry Tonks*.

The very direct gaze of the sitter in this strong, but also sympathetic portrait, shows Tonks's skills at their best.

EJ

Francis TOWNE

[1740–1816]

A Scene in Italy, 1780–81

watercolour and pen on paper, 19 × 26 cm
inscribed on reverse: *by Francis Towne bought from (?) Julia Muirvale, (?) 1934, B.P.*

P.804

PROVENANCE: Julia Muirvale; given to Gallery by Alice Barbara Kitson, October 1992.

A Devonian, Towne seems to have worked mainly in Exeter until 1780, having shown his first exhibits in oil at the R.A. in 1775. His visit to Italy in 1780–1 and his return through Switzerland with "Warwick" SMITH (see P.91) marked the highpoint of his watercolour output.

This was founded on a sure sense of structure and bold simplification of form which gave his drawings great authority. His penwork, as shown here, is fine and delicate and his colour clear and enveloped in mellow light.

Although he undertook several sketching tours in Britain on his return from Italy, his reputation today rests very largely on his watercolours of 1780–1, of which this is one.

EJ

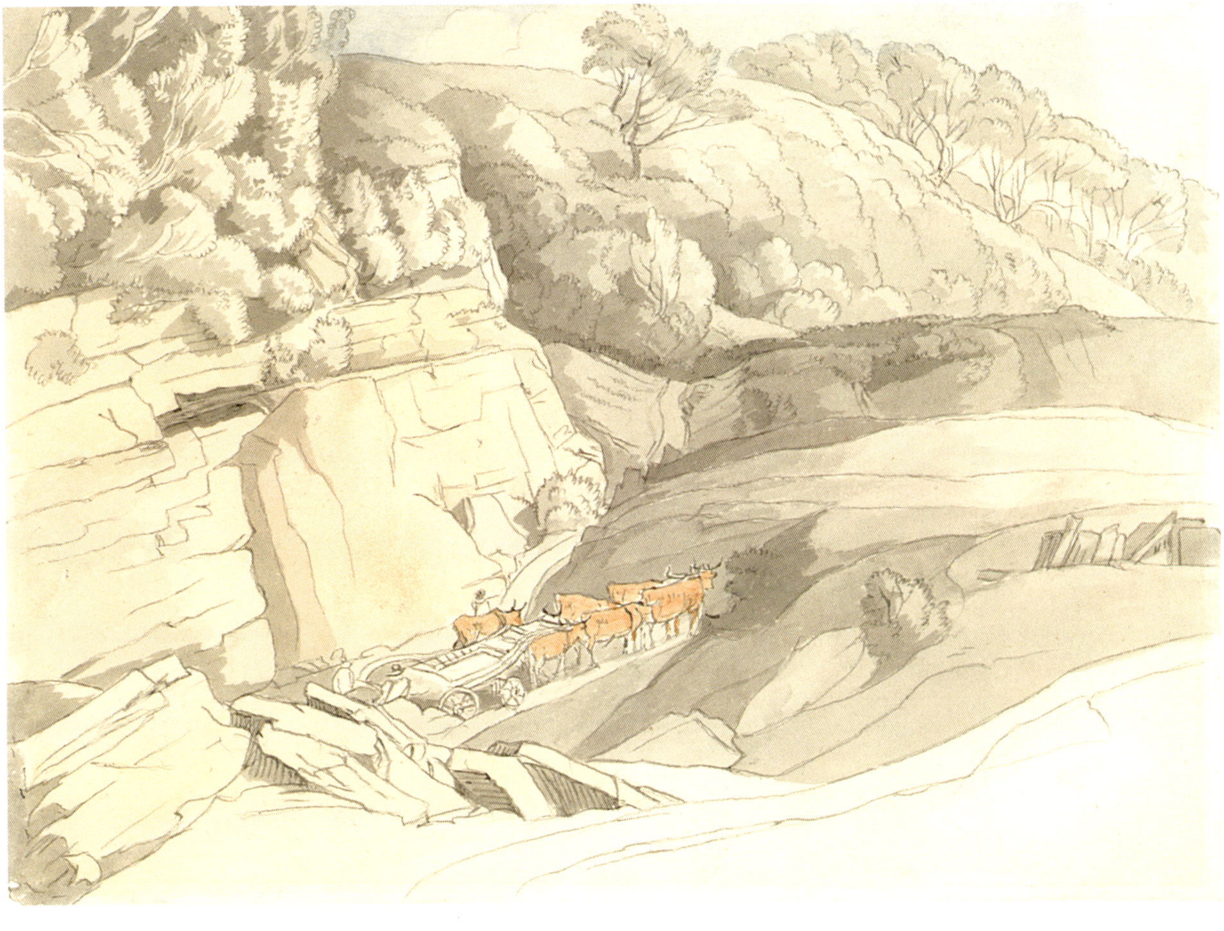

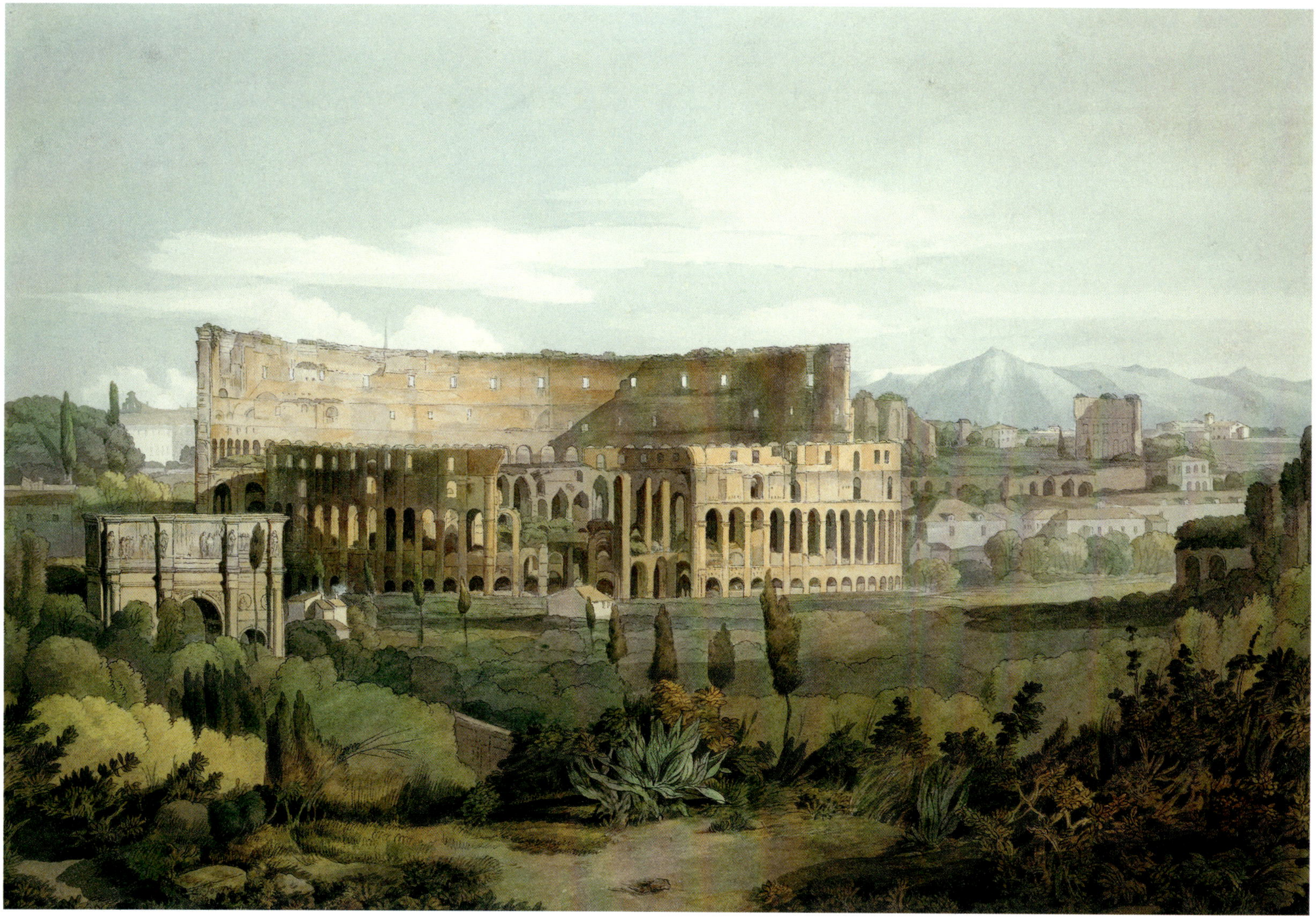

Francis TOWNE

[1740–1816]

The Colosseum from the Caelian Hills, 1799

watercolour with pen and black ink over pencil on paper, image size 31.3 × 46.5 cm
inscribed: *F. Towne 1799*
inscribed on the mount: *Rome The Coloseo, with the Baths of Titus, & Arch of Constantine, taken from the Palatine Mount. Francis Towne del t 1799*

P.96

PROVENANCE: Champernowne family, Devonshire neighbours of Towne's at Dartington Hall; Mrs K.J. Paull, Chichester, sale Sotheby's, bought Thos. Agnew's & Sons Ltd, from whom purchased by Gallery, January 1953.
EXHIBITIONS: *English Watercolours from the Hickman Bacon and other Collections*, Bedford, Cecil Higgins Art Gallery, 1952, no.70, lent by Thos. Agnew & Sons Ltd; *English Watercolours 1750 – 1850,* Norwich, Castle Museum, 1955, no.16; *Primitives to Picasso,* London, R.A., 1962, no.362; *Watercolours and Drawings from The Cecil Higgins Art Gallery, Bedford*, London, Thos. Agnew & Sons Ltd, 1962, no.14; *English Watercolours from The Cecil Higgins Art Gallery,* Reading, Reading Museum & Art Gallery, 1965, no.53; *Watercolours from Bedford,* Norwich, Castle Museum, 1965, no.56, as *The Colosseum from the Caelian Hill with the Arch of Constantine on the left; Art Treasures of England: The Regional Collections,* London, R.A., 1998, no.212.
REFERENCES: A. Bury, 'The Cecil Higgins Museum Bedford', *Old Watercolour Society's Club,* 1961, vol. no.xxxvi, p.35, pl.xv; A. Bury, *Francis Towne: Lone Star of Water-colour Painting,* 1962, p.103, pl.xv.

The arch of Constantine can be seen on the left. Towne visited Italy in 1780–81, arriving in Rome in October 1780. During the next five months he made a number of studies of the Colosseum emphasizing its combination of splendour and decay, sometimes concentrating on architectural details, at others, as here, on its grandeur as seen from a distance. During his stay he would have met PARS who had lived in Rome since 1775 and who was a life-long friend.

Back in England he used his Italian sketchbooks as the basis for finished watercolours and a few oils, but he never received any recognition in his lifetime and was passed over four times for election to the R.A. It was only between the wars, due to the championship of Paul Oppé and other collectors, that Towne began to be recognized as a major watercolourist. Adrian Bury describes this as 'among the memorable drawings done in the 1790s'.

EJ

Francis TOWNE
[1740–1816]
Woodland Scene (previously known as In Devonshire from a note on the back of a former mount), **1803**

watercolour, ink and black lead on paper, 25.5 × 38.5 cm
inscribed: Fr.*Towne. delt 1803*
rock
on reverse: *This outline drawn at Canon-teign Septrm. 1803 from 2 till 4 light from the left hand Frances Towne*

P.705
PROVENANCE: Sydney Kitson; Elisabeth and Alice Barbara Kitson, given to Gallery, May 1973.
EXHIBITIONS: *The English Tradition: an exhibition of watercolours from two private collections*, Bedford, Cecil Higgins Art Gallery, 1972, no.79, as a permanent loan to the Gallery from the Kitson Collection.

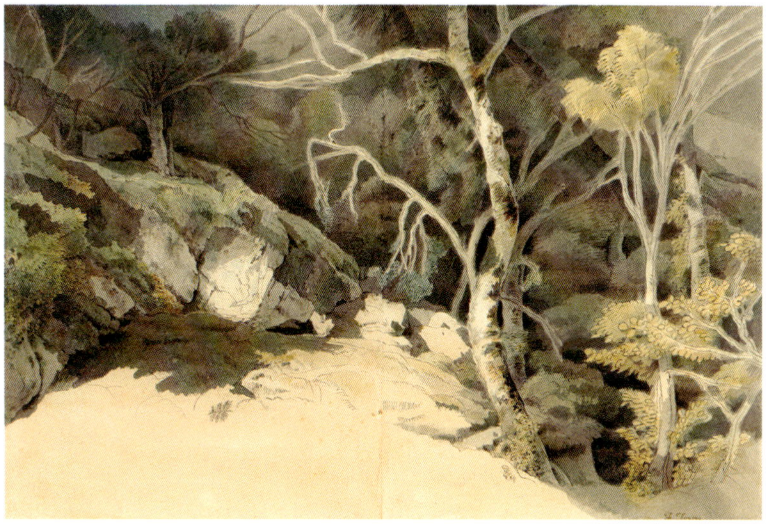

Canonteign House is nine miles south-west of Exeter, situated among steep hills about half a mile west of the river Teign as it flows towards Newton Abbot and Teignmouth. The waterfalls at Canonteign are listed as the highest in England.

EJ/JM

John TUNNARD
[1900–71]
Aerial Appointment, 1944

watercolour, bodycolour and charcoal on paper, 38.5 × 56.5 cm
inscribed: *John Tunnard 44*
inscribed on reverse: *John Tunnard aerial appointment; 20 guins; D142*

P.219
PROVENANCE: Leicester Galleries, from whom purchased by Gallery, April 1958.
EXHIBITIONS: *Watercolours and Drawings from The Cecil Higgins Art Gallery, Bedford*, London, Thos. Agnew & Sons Ltd, 1962, no.115.

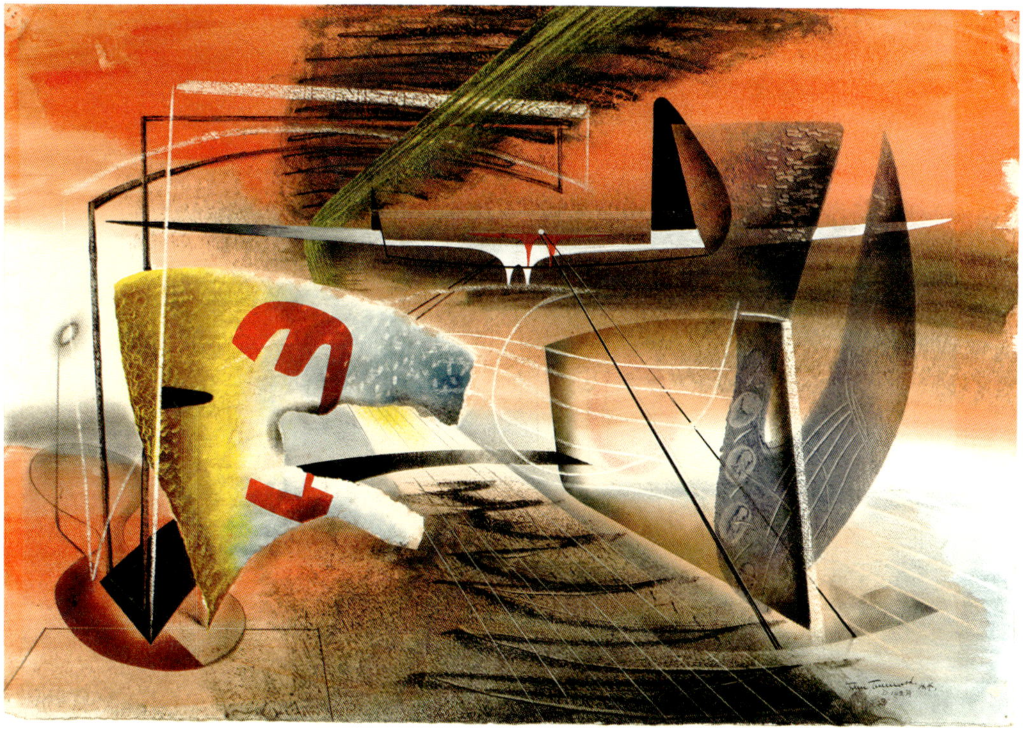

Tunnard was born at Sandy, Bedfordshire, the son of J.C. Tunnard, a sporting painter. He studied at the R.C.A. and began as a textile designer. He took up landscape painting in 1930 but was then decisively influenced by Herbert Read's *Surrealism*, 1936, and the work of Joan Miró and Paul Klee.

His pictures are partly surrealist and partly constructivist, many of them fantastic compositions in deep space with strongly contrasting shapes and colours.

EJ

Joseph Mallord William TURNER, R.A.
[1775–1851]
Cote House near Bristol, c.1791

watercolour and pen on paper, 29.2 × 25.5 cm

P.173
PROVENANCE: T.W.R. Woodman; purchased from him by the Gallery in 1957 through the British Museum whose Keeper of Prints and Drawings, Edward Croft-Murray, had published the watercolour in 1949 and was also advisor to the Gallery.
EXHIBITIONS: *J.M.W. Turner*, London, Whitechapel Art Gallery, 1953, no.111; *Watercolours and Drawings from The Cecil Higgins Art Gallery, Bedford*, London, Thos. Agnew & Sons Ltd, 1962, no.9.
REFERENCES: E. Croft-Murray, 'An unpublished early Watercolour by J.M.W Turner, Cote House, Bristol', *Burlington Magazine*, vol. 90, 1948, pp.107–109, fig.2; A Wilton, *The Life and Work of J.M.W. Turner*, London, 1979, repr. no.21.

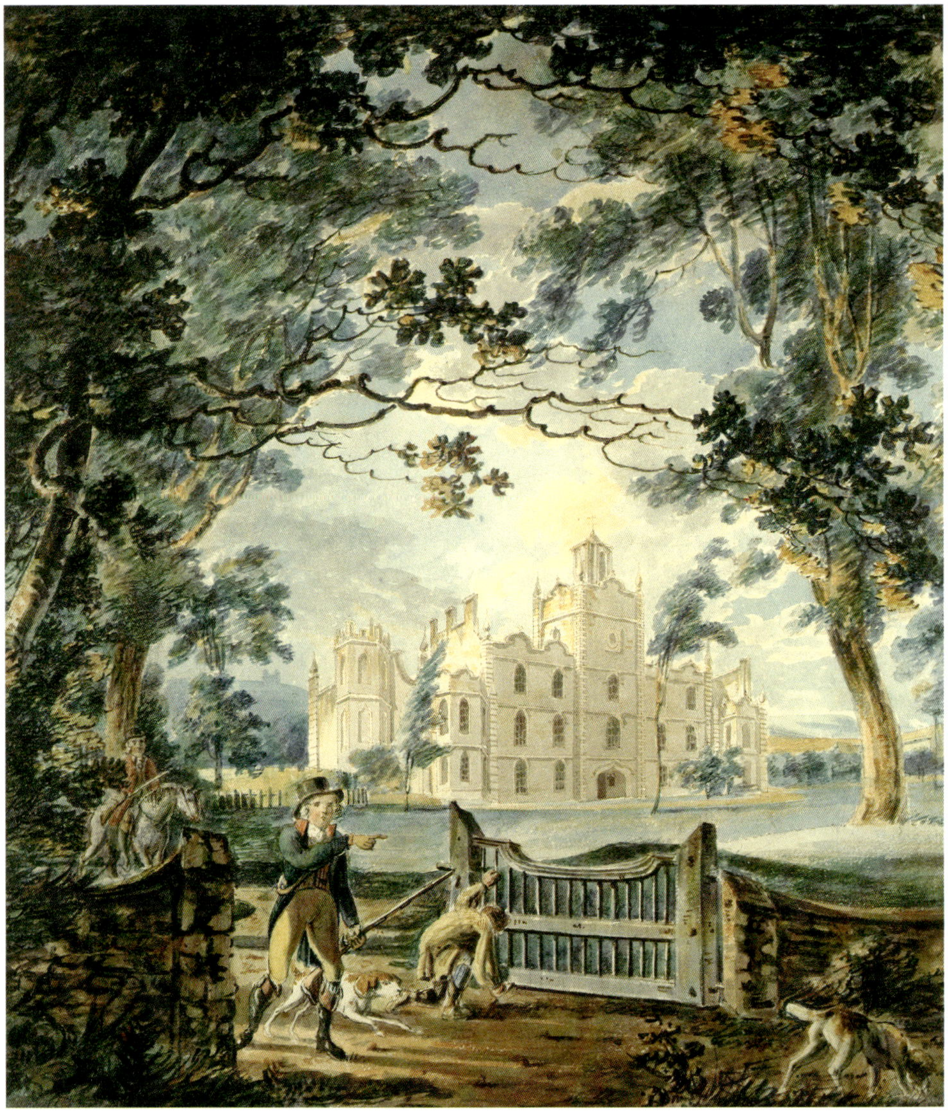

It was probably in the summer of 1791 that Turner, a student at the R.A. Schools, went to stay with his father's friend, John Narraway, a prosperous glue-maker, in Bristol.

Turner's sketches of the surrounding countryside are recorded in the *Bristol and Melmesbury* sketchbook (Turner Bequest inventory VI). On page 17 Turner has written in pencil: 'Mr Fowler's on Durdum Downs near Bristol' and in ink, 'Captain Fowler, seat on Durdum Down near Bristol'. On the reverse is a watercolour outlined in brown ink depicting Cote House which formed the basis of the finished watercolour. Apart from the figures the view is essentially the same but there are minor differences in the central tower of the house and the gate is closed in the sketch. Captain Fowler may have been the drawing's first owner or it may have been among several given by Turner to the Narraways.

Croft-Murray dates the drawing 1792–5 but Wilton more plausibly suggests c.1791; certainly the rather clumsy figures and the painting of the trees with strongly striated foliage are both characteristic of Turner's earliest style.

EJ

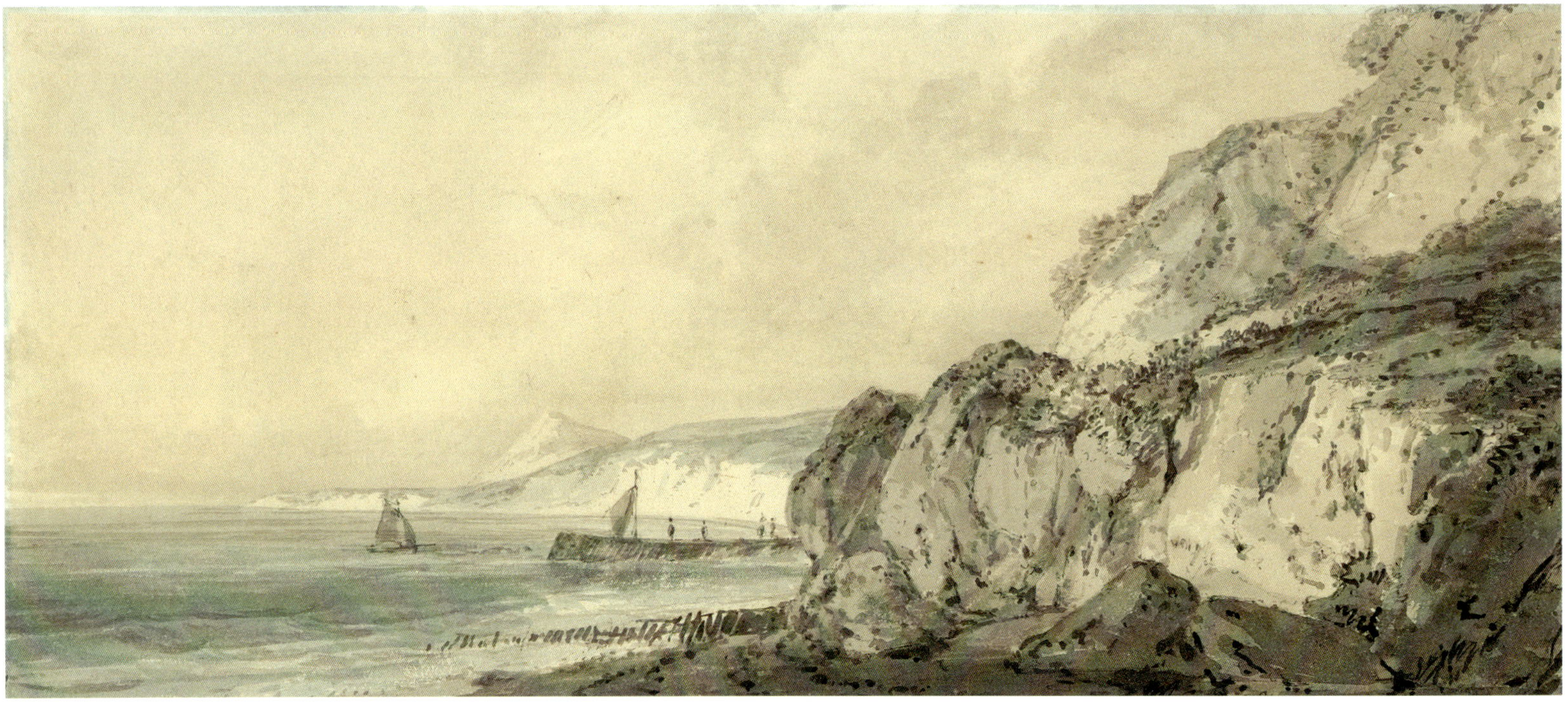

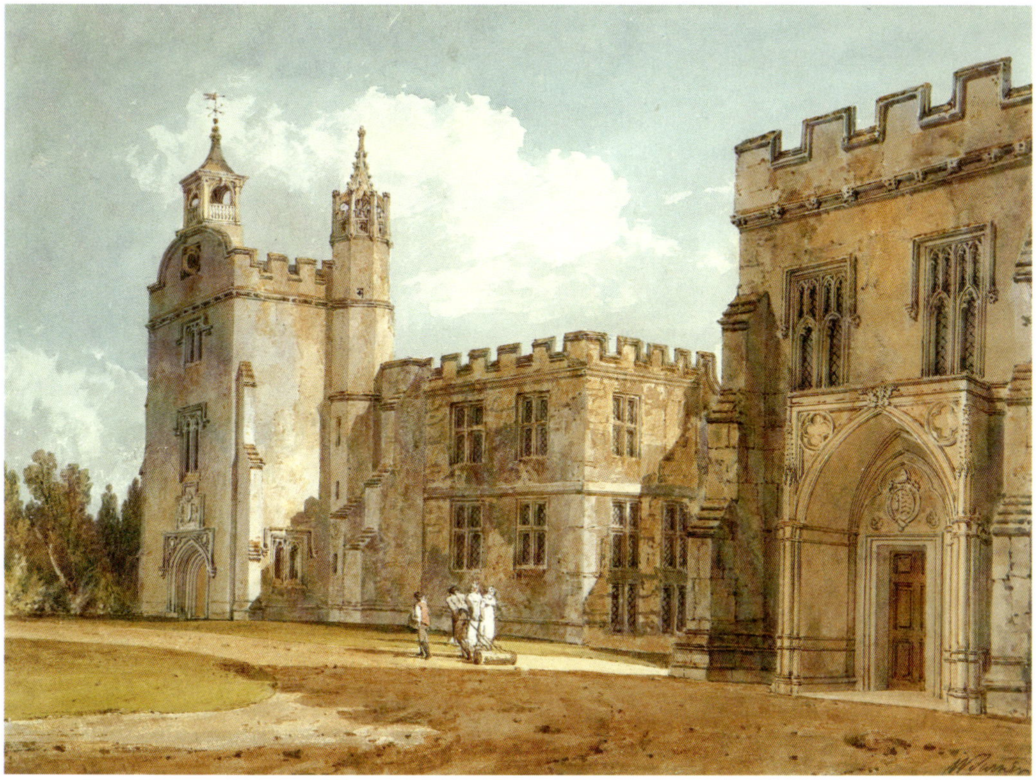

Joseph Mallord William TURNER, R.A.
[1775–1851]
The Bishop's Palace, Salisbury, c.1795

watercolour on paper, 28.4 × 35.9 cm
inscribed: *W.Turner*

P.97
PROVENANCE: Drawn for Sir Richard Colt Hoare of Stourhead (1758–1838), c.1795; Sir Henry Hoare, sale Christie's 30 July, 4 & 7 August 1883 (in a volume), bought by the Rev. J.H. Ellis; by descent to H.A. Steward, sale Christie's 28 July 1927, no.6, bought by Thos. Agnew & Sons Ltd; Dr A.W. Young 1932; bought from the Fine Art Society 30 May 1949 by Thos. Agnew & Sons Ltd, from whom purchased by Gallery, September 1952.
EXHIBITIONS: *77th Annual Exhibition of Watercolour Drawings,* London, Thos. Agnew & Sons Ltd, 1950, no.30; *Paintings by J.M.W. Turner (1775–1851). To Commemorate The Centennial of his Death,* Toronto, Art Gallery of Toronto, Ottawa, National Gallery of Canada, 1951, no.31; *English Watercolours from the Hickman Bacon and other Collections,* Bedford, Cecil Higgins Art Gallery, 1952, no.71; *English Watercolours 1750 – 1820,* Norwich, Castle Museum, 1955, no.42; *Watercolours and Drawings from The Cecil Higgins Art Gallery Bedford*, London, Thos. Agnew & Sons Ltd, 1962, no.35; *English Watercolours from The Cecil Higgins Art Gallery,* Reading, Reading Art Gallery, 1965, no.54.
REFERENCES: Sir W. Armstrong, *Turner*, 1902, p.275; A.J. Finberg, *The Life of J.M.W. Turner R.A.*, 1961, pp.42, 61; A. Wilton, *The Life and Work of J.M.W. Turner*, 1979, repr., p.322, no.204; E. Shanes, *Turner: The Masterworks,* 1990, p.52.

Turner and Sir Richard Colt Hoare were in touch by 1795 as Turner's *Isle of Wight* sketchbook (Turner bequest XXIV), in use that year, has a note in the inside cover of two drawings of Salisbury ordered by 'Sir Richard Hoare'. These were intended for a history of Wiltshire which Hoare never finished. The original commission was extensive and consisted of two sets each of ten drawings, seventeen of which were completed. They occupied Turner from c.1795 to c.1805. The larger-sized set concentrated on the Cathedral itself, the smaller, to which this belongs, on views and buildings in the City.

The Palace was the official residence for much of its time for the Bishops of Salisbury from 1220 to 1947. After the Second World War the Bishop decided that the Palace was far too large for his needs, and it now houses Salisbury Cathedral School.

Turner painted the North Front soon after extensive alterations had been made to the Palace by Bishop Shute Barrington (1782–91). He employed Sir Robert Taylor (1714–88) to carry out 'restoration' work. Within the space of three years Taylor had managed to alter almost every part of the Palace. Amongst these alterations a new porch was cut through the North Front (visible on the right of Turner's picture) to make the north chamber into a grand entrance hall. This porch described as 'Romantic Gothic' has been much criticised for clashing in style and scale with the rest of the Medieval building. Above it are the carved and painted arms of Bishop Barrington.

EJ/JM

Joseph Mallord William TURNER, R.A.
[1775–1851]
Coast near Dover, c.1793–97

blue and grey washes on paper, 16.6 × 38 cm

P.181
PROVENANCE: Mrs E. Mirylees, Aberystwyth, from whom purchased by Gallery, January 1958.

It has been suggested that the cliff in the distance is Shakespeare's Cliff (see *King Lear*, act IV, scene VI), the subject of another Turner drawing in the Fitzwilliam Museum, Cambridge (PD114.1950).

Turner made a tour of Kent and Sussex in the autumn of 1793 (see A.J. Finberg, *Life*, p.23), during which he may have visited Dover. Wilton illustrates a watercolour of *A Barn: The Interior of the ruined refectory of St Martin's Priory, Dover*, (W.35, now in the V&A, P.25–1934), which he dates, c.1793.

The V&A watercolour may have belonged to Dr MONRO which at once raises the problems of the 'Monro School' drawings, a number of which depict Dover and its neighbourhood, and the almost insuperable difficulties, in some cases, of distinguishing the different hands responsible for them.

EJ

Joseph Mallord William TURNER, R.A.
[1775–1851]
Norham Castle on the Tweed, Sunrise
1798

pencil, watercolour and some bodycolour on paper, 50.1 × 70.5 cm

P.724
PROVENANCE: Painted for Edward Lascelles at Harewood in 1798; Harewood sale Christie's 1 May 1858, no.55, bought Colnaghi's; John Dillon, sale Christie's 17 April 1869, no.48 bought Agnew's for W. Moir; bought from Mrs Moir by Agnew's February 1899 and sold to Laundy Walters; by descent to his daughter Mrs Penrose and from her to her daughters the Misses Penrose; lent by Miss Penrose to the Gallery in February 1978 and later bequeathed by her to the National Art Collections Fund, who donated it to the Gallery in 1982.
EXHIBITIONS: *Loan Collection of Pictures and Drawings by J.M.W Turner R.A*, London, Corporation of London Art Gallery, Guildhall, 1899, no.55; *Watercolours by J.M.W. Turner R.A.*, London, Thos. Agnew & Sons Ltd, 1913, no.39; *The First Hundred Years of the Royal Academy 1769–1868*, London, R.A., 1951–2, no.497; *Bicentenary Exhibition 1768–1968*, London, R.A., 1968, no.531; *Turner in the North of England 1797*, London, Tate Gallery and Harewood House, 1997, no.130.
REFERENCES: W. Thornbury, *Life and Correspondence of Turner*, London, 1877, p.139; C.F. Bell, *The Exhibited Works of J.M.W. Turner R.A*, 1901, pp.34–5; Sir W. Armstrong, *Turner*, 1902, p.268; A.J. Finberg, *The Life of J.M.W. Turner*, 1961, pp.49–50; A. Wilton, *The Life and Work of J.M.W. Turner*, 1979, pp.324,325, no.226; D. Hill, *Turner in the North*, 1996, pp.88ff, 180, pl.130.

Another version was exhibited at the R.A. in 1798 (no.353) as *Norham Castle on the Tweed, Summer's morn*, with four lines from James Thomson's poem *Seasons*. It was sold at Christie's in 1987 and is now in a private collection. However, in past exhibitions and literature the Gallery's watercolour was often listed as the R.A. exhibit until Hill clarified the confusion, although a soupçon of doubt may still exist.

Thornbury recounts the story of Turner and Cadell, Scott's publisher, passing Norham in 1831. Turner then took off his hat and made a low bow to the ruins, explaining to the astonished Cadell: 'I made a drawing or painting of Norham several years since. It took; and from that day to this I have had as much to do as my hands could execute'. It seems very possible that this is the watercolour to which Turner was referring.

There are a number of preparatory drawings and studies of Norham in the Turner Bequest and this watercolour was used as the basis for an engraving in the *Liber Studiorum*, 1816, (drawings in the possession of the late Lord Lascelles).

EJ

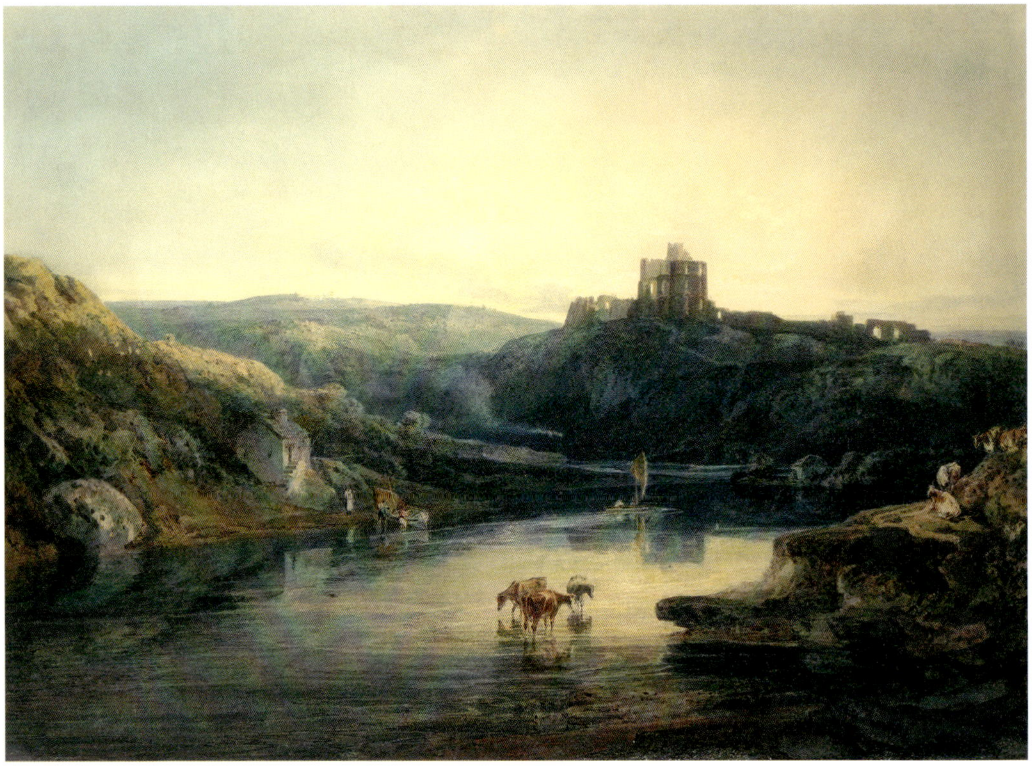

Joseph Mallord William TURNER, R.A.
[1775–1851]
The Great Falls of the Reichenbach, 1804

watercolour on paper, 102.2 × 68.9 cm
inscribed: *J M W Turner R A 1804*

P.98
PROVENANCE: Bought from Turner by Walter Fawkes of Farnley Hall; Fawkes sale Christie's 2 July 1937, no.37, bought in; Mrs F.M.C. Raymond; sale at Christie's 13 October 1954 no.29; bought by Thos. Agnew & Sons Ltd, from whom purchased by Gallery, December 1954.
EXHIBITIONS: Turner's Gallery, 1804; London, R.A., 1815, no.292; London, Grosvenor Place (Fawkes' London House), 1819, no.2; *Watercolours from Farnley Hall*, Leeds, Music Hall, 1839, no.23; *Old Masters of the British School*, London, R.A., 1886, no.34; *Old Masters of the British School*, London, R.A., 1906, no.205; *Exhibition of British Art*, London, R.A., 1934, no.708; *68th Annual Exhibition of Watercolours*, London, Thos. Agnew & Sons Ltd, 1941, no.36; *L'Aquarelle Anglaise*, Geneva, Zurich, 1955–56, no.117; *The Romantic Movement*, London, Tate Gallery, 1959, no.440; *Primitives to Picasso*, London, R.A., 1962, no.380; *Watercolours and Drawings from The Cecil Higgins Art Gallery, Bedford*, London, Thos. Agnew & Sons Ltd, 1962, no. 61; *Royal Academy Bi-centenary Exhibition*, London, 1968–9, no.203; *La Peinture Romantique Anglaise et les Préraphaélites*, Paris, Petit Palais, 1972, no.284; *Turner*, Paris, Le Grand Palais, 1984, no.100, *William Wordsworth and the Age of Romanticism*, Chicago, The Chicago Historical Society, 1988, no.292; *The Great Age of British Watercolours 1750–1880*, London, R.A. and Washington, National Gallery of Art, 1993, no.284; *Le Cattredali della Terra*, Milan, Museo della Permanente, 2000, no.3; *Turner The Great Watercolours*, London, R.A., 2000–1, no.18.
REFERENCES: Farnley Hall catalogue, 1850; F. Wedmore, *Turner and Ruskin*, 1900, vol.I, repr. facing p.100; C.F. Bell, *The Exhibited Works of J.M.W. Turner, R.A.*, 1901, pp.51,170; Sir W. Armstrong, *Turner*, 1902, pp.130 & 272; A.J. Finberg, *Turner's Sketches and Drawings*, 1910, p.39; ibid. *Turner's Watercolours at Farnley Hall*, 1912, pp.1–2,21–2 pl.IX; A.J. Finberg, *The Life of J.M.W. Turner R.A.*, 1939, pp.107, 219, 258, 466,477,479,503; A.P. Oppé, *The Burlington Magazine*, vol.78, April 1941, p.131; I. Williams, *Early English Watercolours*, 1952, pp.111,114; J. Gage, *Turner: A Wonderful Range of Mind*, 1987, p.42, fig.63; B. Dawson, *Turner in the National Gallery of Ireland*, 1988, pp.64–66; E. Shanes, *Turner: The Masterworks*, 1990, p.56, pl.57; D. Hill, *Turner in the Alps*, 1992, pp.119–125, repr. p.120. E. Shanes et al, *Turner The Great Watercolours*, 2000, p.86.

Turner was born on 23 April 1775, the son of William Turner, a barber in Covent Garden. After the death of his sister, and 'in consequence of illness', he was moved to Brentford, living with his uncle, where he attended Brentford Free School as a day boy. His earliest known work is a copy of an engraving of *Friar Bacon's Study and Folly Bridge, Oxford* (Oxford Almanack, 1780), made when he was twelve; it was at this time that he produced many sketches of churches, abbeys and city streets. A friend remembered Turner declaring that 'if he could begin life again, he would rather be an architect than a painter'.

Entering the R.A. Schools in 1789, his training is remembered by Edward DAYES who said 'The way he acquired his professional powers was by borrowing, where he could, a drawing or picture to copy from; or by making a sketch of any one in the Exhibition early in the morning, and finishing it at home. By such practices... the fine taste and colour his drawings possess are scarcely to be found in any other'.

The Great Falls of the Reichenbach was first shown at Turner's own gallery held on the first floor of what was 64 Harley Street. Turner had conceived the idea of his own gallery due to uncertainty over the future of the R.A. in late 1803, with rumours abounding that Turner would not be showing at the the R.A. in 1804. Sir George Beaumont (who saw the Turner exhibition) complained of 'the strong skies and parts not corresponding with them'.

The Great Falls is a superb watercolour, made soon after Turner's first visit to Switzerland in 1802, and is based on a sketch (Wilton no.361) now in the National Gallery of Ireland, Dublin. The view is taken from the valley of Hasli above Meiringen with Great Scheidegg beyond and shows Turner tackling a 'Sublime' subject with enormous confidence. Turner's pride in the work is shown by the fact that it was again exhibited at the R.A. in 1815.

EJ/JM

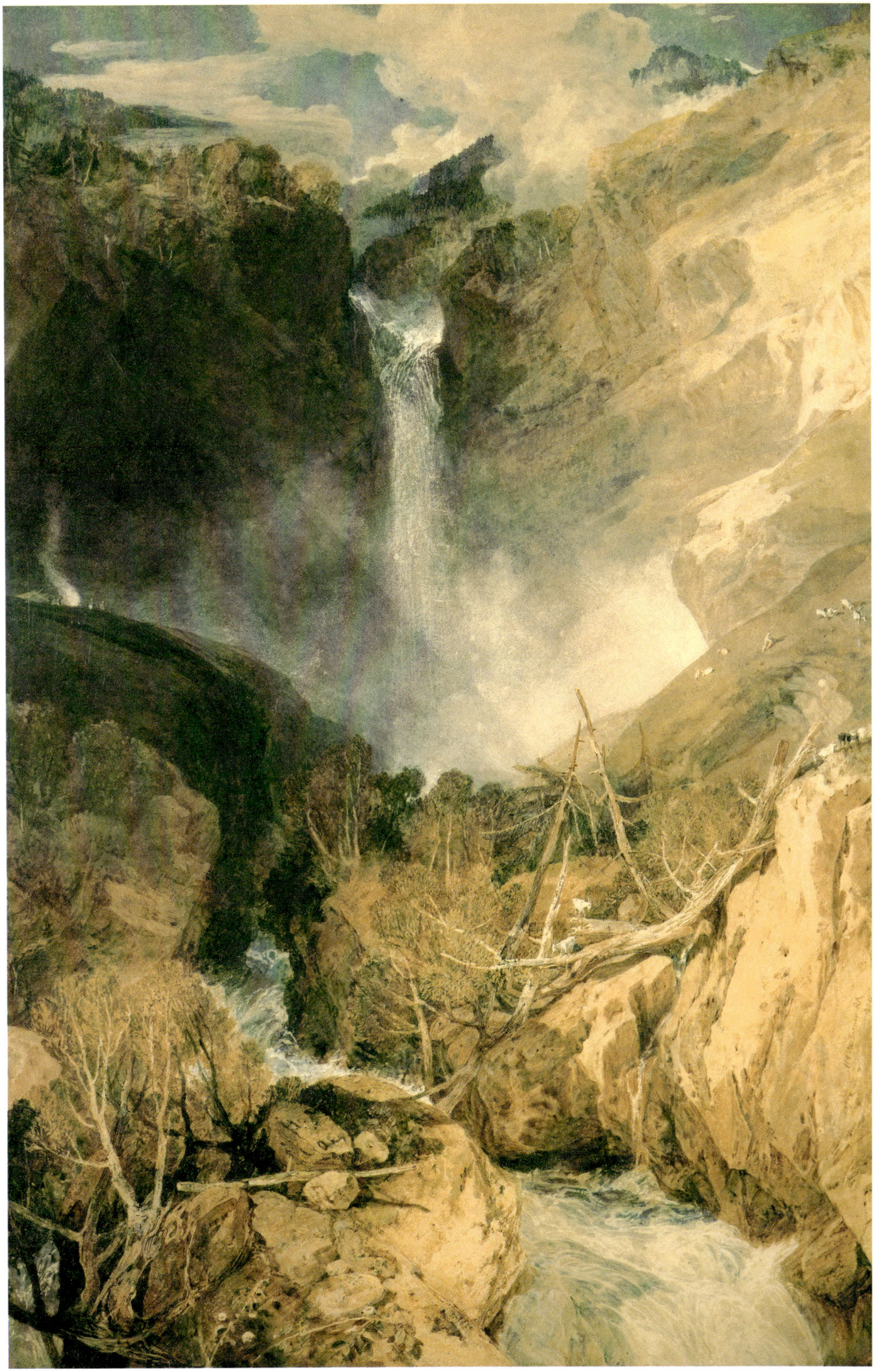

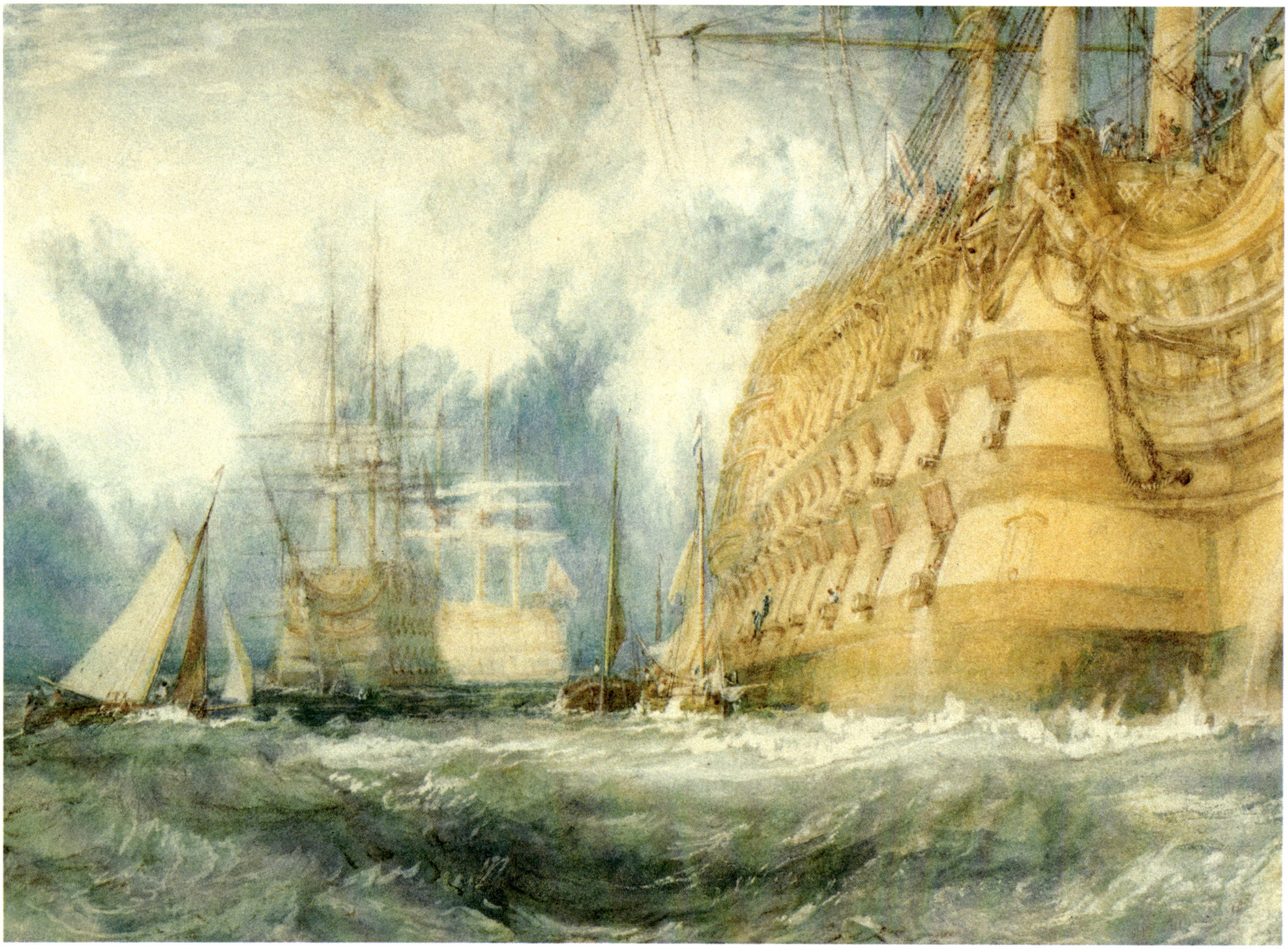

Joseph Mallord William TURNER, R.A.

[1775–1851]

A First Rate Taking in Stores, 1818

pencil and watercolour, heightened with white on paper, 28.6 × 39.7cm
inscribed: *J.M.W. Turner 1818*

P.99

PROVENANCE: Painted for Walter Fawkes (1769–1825); by descent to W.R. Fawkes; his sale Christie's 2 July 1937 no.44 bought Tooth's; sold to David (later Viscount) Eccles, for whom sold by Thos. Agnew & Sons Ltd, to Gallery, January 1953.

EXHIBITIONS: 45 Grosvenor Place (Fawkes's London House), 1819 no.20; Leeds, Music Hall, 1839, no.14; *Old Masters*, London, Grafton Galleries, 1911, no.205; *65th Annual Watercolour Exhibition,* London, Thos. Agnew, 1938, no.148; *70th Annual Watercolour Exhibition,* London, Thos. Agnew, 1943, no.71; *Centenary Loan Exhibition of Watercolour Drawings by J.M.W. Turner, R.A.*, London, Thos. Agnew, 1951, no.46; *80th Annual Watercolour Exhibition*, London, Thos. Agnew, 1953, no.83; Norwich Castle Museum, 1954; *Primitives to Picasso,* London, R.A., 1962 no.382; *Watercolours from Bedford,* Norwich, Castle Museum, 1965, no.57; *150th Anniversary Loan Exhibition of Paintings and Watercolours by J.M.W. Turner, R.A.*, London, Thos. Agnew & Sons Ltd, 1967, no.54; *Bicentenary Exhibition 1768–1968,* London, R.A., 1968–9, no.204; *Turner 1775–1851,* London, R.A., 1974–5, no.194; *J.M.W. Turner,* Paris, Grand Palais, (British Council), 1983–4, no.129; *Masters of the Sea: British Marine Watercolours,* New Haven, Yale Center for British Art, London, National Maritime Museum, 1987, no.77; *The Art of Seeing: John Ruskin & the Victorian Eye,* Phoenix, Phoenix Art Museum, Indianapolis, Indianapolis Museum of Art, 1993; *Watercolours by J.M.W. Turner R.A.,* London, Thos. Agnew & Sons Ltd, 1994, no.2; *Making and Meaning: Turner & 'The Fighting Temeraire',* London, National Gallery, 1995, no.14; *J.M.W. Turner,* Canberra, National Gallery of Australia, Melbourne, National Gallery of Victoria, Melbourne, 1996, no.50; *Turner: The Great Watercolours,* London, R.A., 2000–1, no.47.

REFERENCES: W. Thornbury, *The Life of J.M.W. Turner, R.A.,* 1877, pp.239,589; F. Wedmore, *Turner and Ruskin,* 1900. vol.II, p.290; C.F. Bell, *A list of the works contributed to Public Exhibitions by J.M.W. Turner, R.A.,* 1901, p.169; Sir W. Armstrong, *Turner,* 1902, pp.67–8,253; E.T. Cook & A. Wedderburn (eds.), *The Works of John Ruskin,* 39 vols., 1903–12, v, p.33; xii, p.386, pl.21; xiii, p.48; xxx, p.352; A.J. Finberg, 'Turner's Water-Colours at Farnley Hall', *The Studio,* 1912, part I, pp.10–11,25 & pl.viii; C. Clare, *J.M.W. Turner, his Life and Work,* 1951, p.65; H.P.R. Finberg (ed.), A.J. Finberg, *The Life of J.M.W Turner,* 1961, 2nd edition, pp249–50; M. Butlin, *Turner Watercolours,* 1962, pp.10,28, pl.5; A. Wilton, *The Life and Work of J.M.W. Turner,* 1979, pp.104, 357, no.499; J. Gage, *J.M.W. Turner – A Wonderful Range of Mind,* 1987, pp.159–60; A. Wilton, *Turner in his Time,* 1987, p.114; E. Shanes, *Turner: the Masterworks,* 1990, p.72, pl.73; C. Finch, *19th Century Watercolours,* 1991, pp.47–8; E. Shanes et al, *Turner The Great Watercolours,* 2000, p.135 repr. p.134; E. Shanes, 'Turner and the creation of his First-rate in a Few Hours A Kind of Frenzy ?', *Apollo*, March 2001, pp.13–15, illus no.1.

NOTES: See the entry for *The Loss of an East Indiaman* (P.902), for the suggestion that it and *A First Rate Taking in Stores* were painted as pendants.

Apart from its great beauty, this is one of Turner's most famous watercolours and perhaps the best documented. Turner's dislike of being watched while painting is well known but he made an extraordinary exception in this case.

In November 1818 Turner was staying at Farnley Hall in Yorkshire, the home of his friend and most prolific patron, Walter Fawkes. One morning at breakfast Fawkes said to Turner: 'I want you to make me a drawing of the ordinary dimensions that will give some idea of the size of a man of war'. The idea evidently appealed to Turner, for with a chuckle, he said to Fawkes's eldest son, Hawksworth, a boy of about 15: 'Come along Hawkey, and we will see what we can do for Papa' and so the boy sat by his side the whole morning watching the evolution of *A First Rate Taking in Stores*.

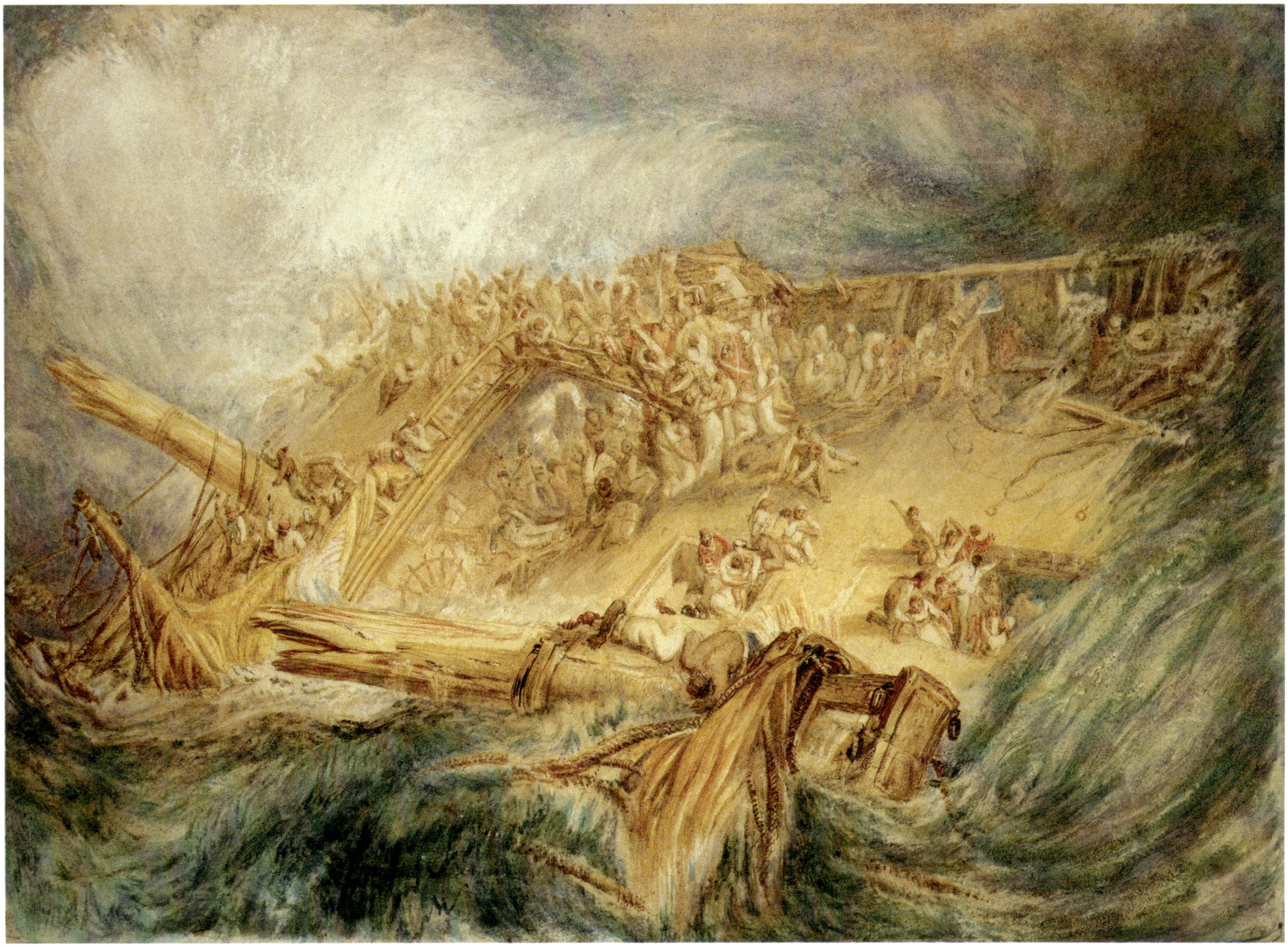

His description of the way Turner went to work was extraordinary:

> He began by pouring wet paint on to the paper until it was saturated, he tore, he scratched, he scrabbled at it in a kind of frenzy and the whole thing was chaos – but gradually and as if by magic the lovely ship, with all its exquisite minutia [*sic*] came into being and by luncheon time the drawing was taken down in triumph.

This manuscript account by Mrs Edith Mary Fawkes (daughter-in-law of Walter Fawkes's third son, the Rev. Ayscough Fawkes) tallies with Thornbury's description (source unknown) of how Turner 'tore up the sea with his eagle-claw of a thumbnail' when painting this watercolour 'between breakfast and lunch'.

EJ

Joseph Mallord William TURNER, R.A.

[1775–1851]

The Loss of an East Indiaman, c.1818

watercolour on paper, 28 × 39.5cm

P.902

PROVENANCE: Painted for Walter Fawkes c.1818; by descent to Major Le G.G.W. Horton Fawkes; Fawkes sale Christie's 2 July 1937, no.43 as *Shipwreck of Man-o'-War'* bought in; sold to Agnew's as *The Shipwreck,* May 1938; bought by G. Mitchell, February 1943; sold for him by Agnew's as *Foundering of a Ship of the Line,* February 1956 to Mrs Christopher; bought back from her by Agnew's June 1973 as *The Wreck of the Transport Ship;* sold to Professor and Mrs Lipton November 1973; their sale Sotheby's 17 November 1997, no.108 bought Thos. Agnew & Sons Ltd for Gallery, purchased with the assistance of The Heritage Lottery Fund, The National Art Collections Fund and the V&A/M.G.C. Purchase Grant Fund.

EXHIBITIONS: 45 Grosvenor Place, Walter Fawkes's London House, 1819 no.22; Music Hall, Leeds, 1839, no.15; *65th Annual Exhibition of Watercolours and Pencil Drawings,* London, Thos. Agnew & Sons, Ltd, 1938, no.148 as *The Foundering of a Ship of the Line; Turner's Watercolour Explorations 1810–1842,* London, Tate Gallery and Southampton, Southampton City Art Gallery, 1997 no.2; *Turner The Great Watercolours,* London, R.A., 2000–1, no.48.

REFERENCES: *Illustrated London News,* 12 March 1938, p.452, fig. 2, as *The Foundering of a ship of the Line;* C.F. Bell, *The Exhibited Work of J.M.W. Turner, R.A.,* 1901, p.169; Sir W. Armstrong, *Turner*, 1902, p.277 as 'a damaged drawing that has been restored'; A.J. Finberg, *The Life of J.M.W. Turner, R.A.*, 1961, pp.480,502, nos.231,488; A. Wilton, *The Life and Work of J.M.W. Turner,* 1979, pp.104,357 no.500, as *Loss of a Man-of-War;* ibid., *Turner and the Sublime,* 1980, p.147 under no.59 the 'Beginning' for this watercolour; E. Shanes, *Turner's Watercolour Explorations 1810–1842,* 1997, pp.33–35, repr. p.35; E. Shanes et al., *Turner The Great Watercolours,* 2000, p.135, repr. p.134; E. Shanes, 'Turner and the creation of his First Rate in a few hours A kind of frenzy ?', *Apollo,* March 2001, pp.13–15, illus. no.3.

Painted c. 1818 and originally exhibited in 1819 as *Loss of a Man of War*. This was corrected when shown at Leeds in 1839 although it underwent several changes of title later (see above).

Eric Shanes has shown convincingly that this disaster was based on the tragedy of the *Halsewell*, a merchantman, which sank on 6 January 1786. Only 74 of the 240 people on board survived, the ship finally breaking up on the rocks off Seacombe between Peverel Point and St Alban's Head on the Isle of Purbeck. There were many accounts of the disaster which continued to appear until at least 1810 so that Turner would certainly have been aware of them. He actually referred to the sinking in an unpublished poem he wrote 1811–13 to accompany the letterpress to *Picturesque Views on the Southern Coast*. It is also likely that Turner knew Robert Smirke's painting *The Halsewell, East Indiaman* or the aquatint after it by Robert Pollard published in 1786, as he and Smirke were well acquainted. But Turner has infused his version with such a sense of terror, danger, catastrophic wreckage and imminent loss of life that it bears little relation to Smirke's despite some similarities – the broken mizzenmast for example.

There is a 'Beginning' for the watercolour in the Turner Bequest (CXCVI N), watermarked 1816 and inscribed: 'Beginning for Dear Fawkes of Farnley'. This surely means that Turner came across it after Fawkes' death in 1825 and inscribed it in a more affectionate manner than he would have done if Fawkes had still been alive and liable to read it.

Eric Shanes, who curated the 1997 exhibition, believes that this was intended as a pendant to *A First Rate Taking in Stores*, (P.99); if so, Turner must have painted it between November 1818 and April 1819 when the Grosvenor Place exhibition opened. Indeed Shanes argues that the *Indiaman* may even have been started while the *First Rate* was drying and cites the predominant yellow-ochre colour in both as support for this. They are the same size and are both 'seapieces' so that it is not surprising that they were hung together both in 1819 and 1839. But despite Shanes's suggestion that they fit in with the 'War' and 'Peace' contrast between pairs of pictures which was much in Turner's mind from 1810–20, the subjects seem too unrelated, if this followed the 'First Rate', to make the pendant theory wholly convincing. However, an alternative explanation seems possible, bearing in mind the 1816 watermark on the 'Beginning' for this watercolour: why should it not have been painted *before* the 'First Rate' and then acquired by Fawkes? As Fawkes then believed it to depict the loss of a Man of War, he may, while looking at it, have found it difficult to grasp the size of the ship because only part of Turner's sinking vessel is visible in the watercolour yet it makes the ship seem as big as an ocean liner. So one can understand his request to Turner to 'make me a drawing of the ordinary dimensions that will give some idea *of the size of a man of war*' (compiler's italics). Indeed, perhaps the word 'ordinary' extended to the dimensions of the ship as well as to the drawing since he found those of the 'Indiaman' far from ordinary.

EJ

Joseph Mallord William TURNER, R.A.
[1775–1851]
Rokeby, 1822

watercolour on paper, 20.2 × 14.6 cm

P.100
PROVENANCE: Commissioned by Walter Fawkes of Farnley Hall in 1822 as one of seven watercolours to illustrate a volume of selected verses by Scott, Byron and Moore; by descent to Major Horton-Fawkes, who sold it to Thos. Agnew & Sons Ltd, 22 May 1952, from whom purchased by Gallery, September 1952.
EXHIBITIONS: *The Farnley Collection of Paintings and Drawings by J.M.W. Turner R.A.*, Lawrie & Co, 1902, no.71; *Turner Watercolours from Farnley Hall,* Leeds, Leeds City Art Gallery, 1948, no.34 (wrongly entitled *Glen Artney – another Fawkes watercolour illustrating Scott's The Lady of the Lake);* *English Watercolours from the Hickman Bacon and other Collections,* Bedford, Cecil Higgins Art Gallery, 1952, no.72, as *Rokeby; Twixt Rock and River;* *Watercolours and Drawings from The Cecil Higgins Art Gallery, Bedford*, London, Thos. Agnew & Sons Ltd, 1962, no.49; *Turner in Yorkshire*, York, York City Art Gallery, 1980, no.77; *Walking the Landscape: Cotman and Turner in Teesdale,* Barnard Castle, Bowes Museum, 1996; *Turner's Watercolour Explorations 1810–1842,* London, Tate Gallery, Southampton, Southampton City Art Gallery, 1997, no.79.
REFERENCES: Sir W. Armstrong, *Turner*, 1902, p.274; A.J. Finberg, 'Turner's Watercolours at Farnley Hall', *The Studio,* 1912, p.27, no.167 as *Glenartney, 'Here twixt rock and river';* A. Wilton, *The Life and Work of J.M.W. Turner*, 1979, p.424, repr. no.1053; G.Finley, *Landscapes of Memory: Turner as Illustrator to Scott,* 1980, p.75, pl.25 as *View on the Greta River;* D. Hill, *In Turner's Footsteps,* 1984, p.69, pl.65; E. Shanes, *Turner's Watercolour Explorations 1810–1842,* 1997, pp.84–86, repr.p.85.

Rokeby, a long poem by Sir Walter Scott, composed at Rokeby in 1809 and published in 1813, describes events after the battle of Marston Moor in 1644. The subject would have been of particular interest to Fawkes as he possessed a number of relics which had belonged to the Cromwellian General Thomas Fairfax (1612–71), who commanded a detachment at Marston Moor.

Turner made a number of sketches of these relics which were bound in an album of 'Fairfaxiana' still at Farnley. The poem is dedicated to John Morritt, owner of Rokeby park, where the 'Rokeby Venus' by Velasquez in the National Gallery came from, about three miles south-east of Barnard Castle in County Durham. Turner passed by Rokeby at the end of July 1816 on his northern tour that summer and pencil sketches inscribed 'Rokeby' occur in the 'Yorkshire 2' and 'Yorkshire 4' sketchbooks (Turner bequest CXLVII).

The watercolour depicts a narrow gorge between Rokeby and Mortham through which the River Greta pours just before it joins the River Tees. On the two large boulders in the foreground Turner has inscribed eight lines, not always accurately, from the poem's second canto.

Here, twixt Rock and River grew
A dismal grove of sable yew
With whose sad tints were mingled seen
The blighted firs sepulchar'l [*sic*] green (Stanza IX,9–12)
He who winds twixt scar and wave
May hear the headlong torrent rave
May view her chase her waves to spray
O'er every rock that bars her way (Stanza VII, 15–16, 19–20)

Eric Shanes, author of the 1997 exhibition catalogue *Turner's Watercolour Explorations 1810–1842*, reproduces four preliminary studies, now in the Tate Gallery, London, for *Rokeby*. These show the trouble Turner took to ensure that his watercolour reflected the images described in the poem, particularly the 'headlong torrent', and the dark tree girt ravine. The shut-in composition is further emphasised by the figure scarcely able to get along the path between the trees on one side and the drop into the Greta on the other.

EJ

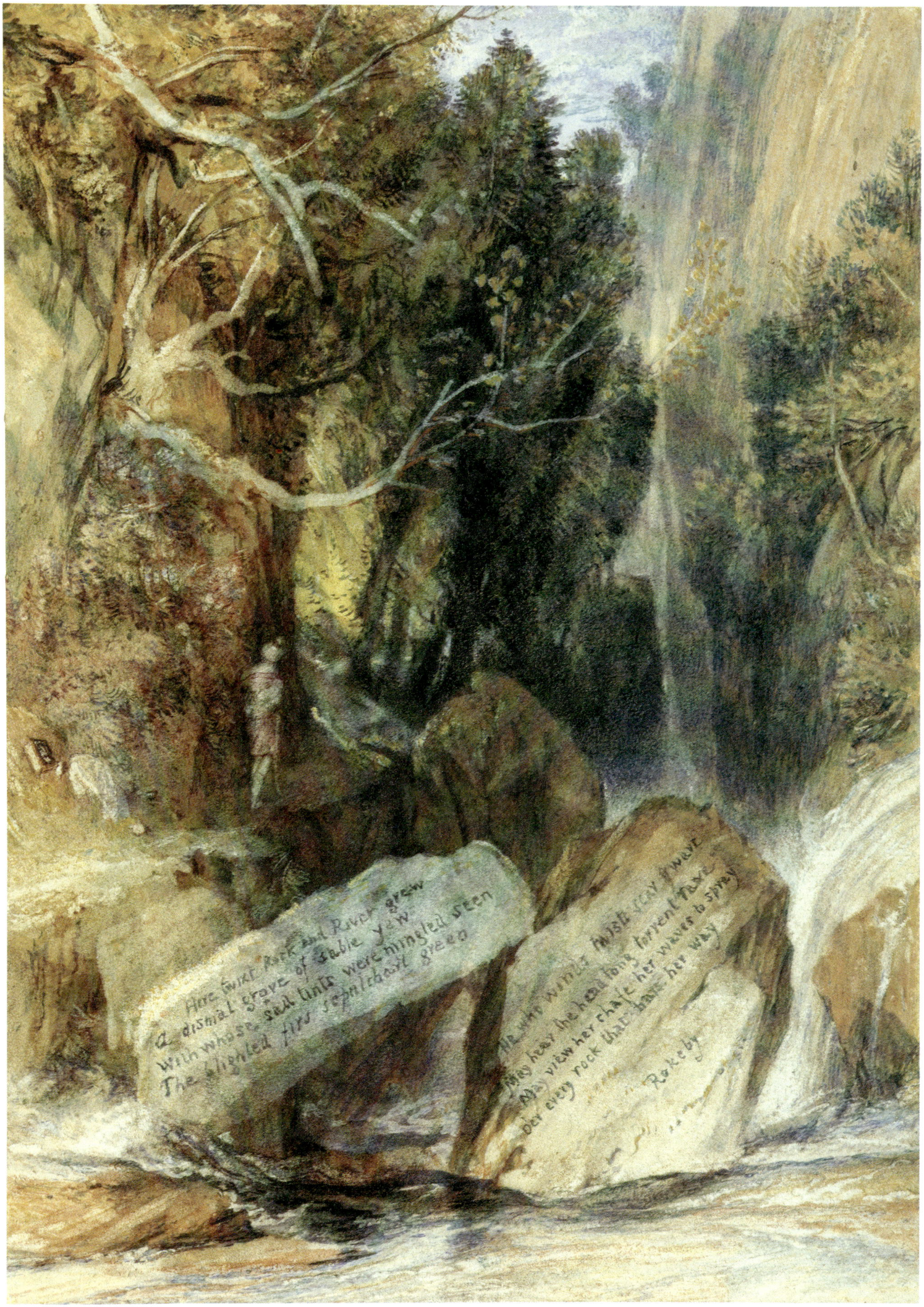
Here twixt Rock and River grew
A dismal grove of sable yew
With whose sad tints were mingled seen
The blighted firs sepulchral green
May hear the headlong torrent rave
May view her chafe her waves to spray
O'er every rock that bars her way
Rokeby

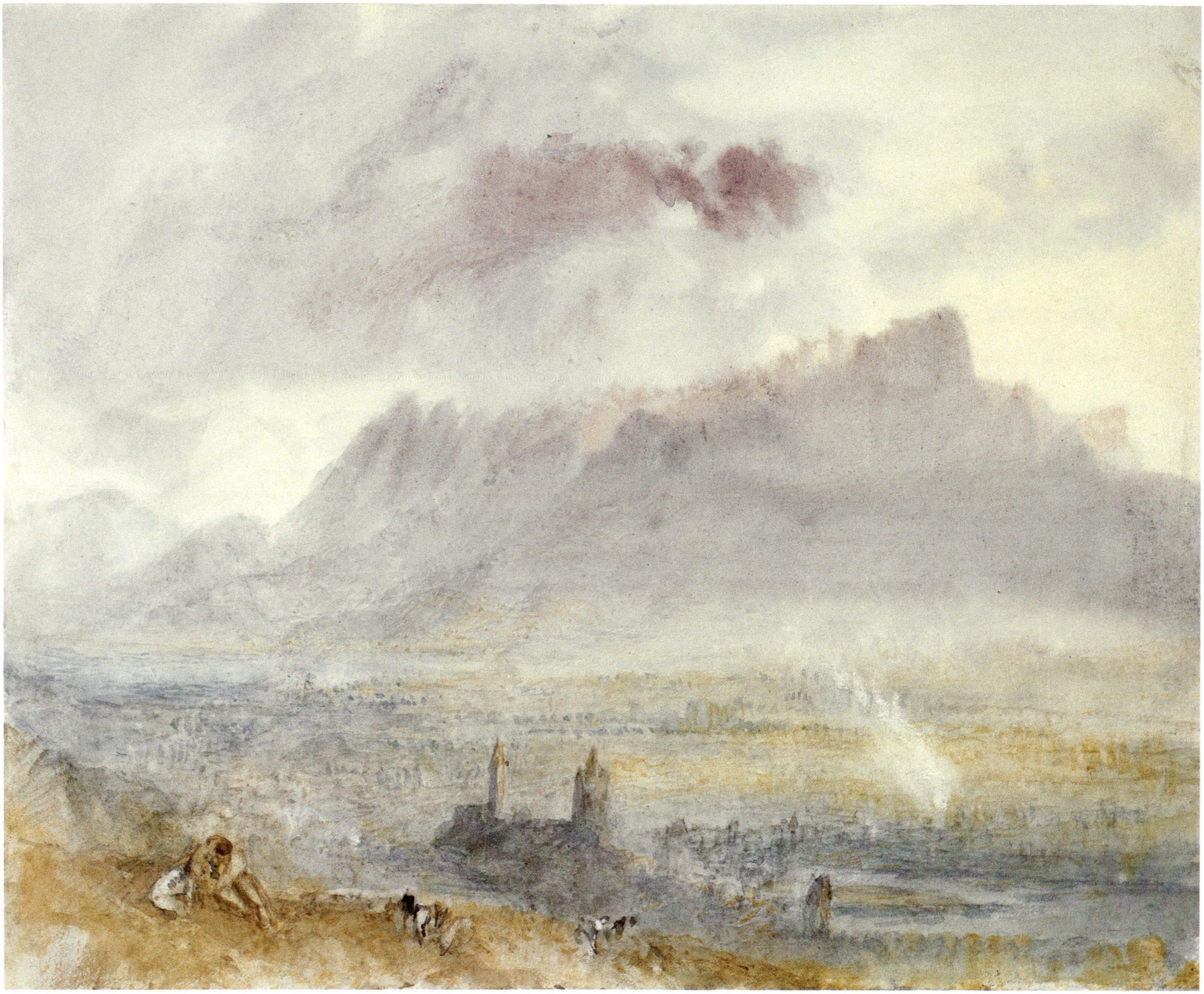

Joseph Mallord William TURNER, R.A.
[1775–1851]
The Town and Lake of Thun
c.1841

watercolour on paper, 22.7 × 28.7 cm

P.122
PROVENANCE: John Edward Taylor (1830–1905) by 1899; his sale Christie's 5 July 1912, no.71; bought Thos. Agnew & Sons Ltd for A.A. Allen; his sale Sotheby's 4 April 1935, no.110 bought in; Mrs Arthur Allen, her sale Sotheby's 15 May 1957, no.64, purchased Thos. Agnew & Sons Ltd for Gallery.
EXHIBITIONS: *Loan Collection of Pictures and Drawings by J.M.W. Turner. R.A., and of a Selection of Pictures by some of his Contemporaries,* London, Corporation of London Art Gallery, Guildhall, 1899, no.139; *Retrospective Exhibition of British Art,* Brussels, Musée Moderne, 1929, no.189; *77th Annual Exhibition Centenary Loan Exhibition of Watercolour Drawings by J.M.W. Turner R.A.,* London, Thos. Agnew & Sons Ltd, 1951, no.92; *Watercolours and drawings from the Cecil Higgins Art Gallery, Bedford,* London, Thos. Agnew & Sons Ltd, 1962, no.62; *Matthew Arnold Centenary Exhibition,* Grasmere, Wordsworth Trust, 1989; *Le Cattedrali della Terra,* Milan, Museo della Permanente, 2000, no.4; *J.M.W. Turner: The Miracle of Light,* Essen, Folkwang Museum and Zurich, Kunsthaus, 2001–2, no.172.
REFERENCES: Sir W. Armstrong, *Turner*, 1902, p.280; *Apollo,* 1962, repr. p.27; A. Wilton, *The Life and Work of J.M.W. Turner,* 1979, p.480, repr. no.1505.

Turner visited Switzerland each summer from 1841–4 but 1841 seems the most likely date for this exquisite drawing which shows Turner's mastery of the medium at its finest. Sureness of touch, delicacy of colour and subtlety of the play of light combine to give the impression that it was painted 'in tinted steam' to borrow CONSTABLE'S marvellous description of Turner's late work.

John Edward Taylor, proprietor of *The Manchester Guardian*, was a major Turner and English watercolour collector. He gave some of his collection to the Whitworth Art Gallery, Manchester but the bulk was dispersed at the sale in 1912 which included 107 Turners. At this sale *The Town and Lake of Thun* fetched 1,350 guineas which was more than it brought in 1957.

The reason that this watercolour was included in the Matthew Arnold exhibition was because Arnold fell in love with the mysterious 'Marguerite', a resident of the Hotel Bellevue at Thun. He travelled to Lake Thun in September 1848 and again in 1849 to meet her. She inspired a whole sequence of love poems but has never been successfully identified.

EJ

After **Joseph Mallord William TURNER, R.A.**
[1775–1851]
Lancaster from the Aqueduct Bridge

watercolour on paper, 32.9 × 48.1 cm

P.101
PROVENANCE: Spink & Sons, from whom purchased by Gallery, January 1952.
EXHIBITIONS: *English Watercolours from The Cecil Higgins Art Gallery Bedford,* Reading, Reading Museum & Art Gallery, 1965, no.55 as being by Turner.
REFERENCES: A. Wilton, *The life and work of J.M.W. Turner,* 1979, p.391.

This is a very good copy of the original Turner now in the Lady Lever Art Gallery, Port Sunlight, Cheshire, that was drawn c.1825 and was engraved in 1827 by R. Wallis for *Picturesque Views in England and Wales*. In fact the Gallery's copy is rather larger, being extended on both sides, whereas the Lady Lever original measures 28 x 39.4 cm.

In Andrew Wilton's 1979 catalogue, the Lady Lever drawing is no.786 and he has this to say about the Gallery's drawing: 'Another version of the subject exists in the Cecil Higgins Art Gallery, Bedford; it is a very close copy and was apparently accepted by Finberg (MS Index), but is perhaps a drawing in the same category as the elaborate copy of the 1843 *Faido* in the Rhode Island School of Design executed by a member of Ruskin's circle'.

Turner's pencil drawing for the original is in the 'Yorkshire 5' sketchbook (Turner Bequest CXLVIII–35 verso).

EJ

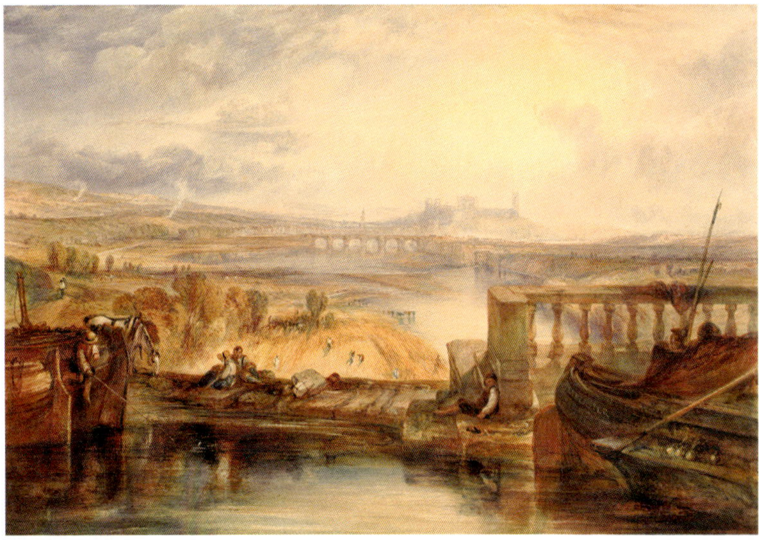

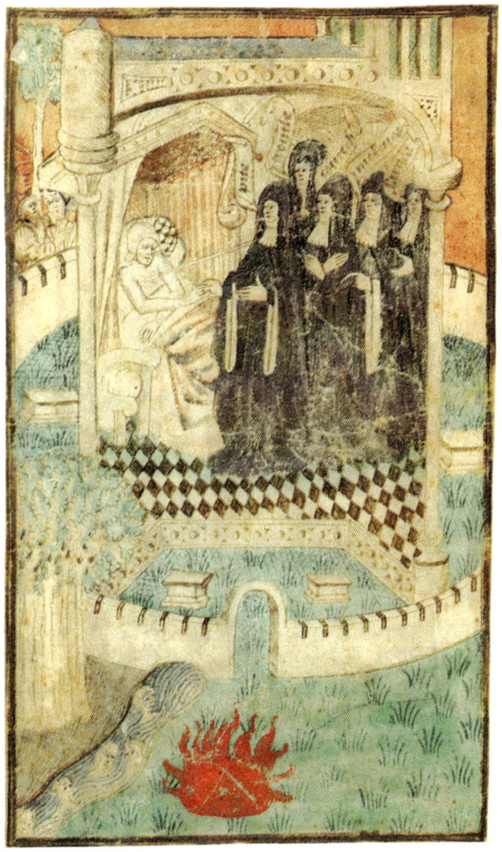

Unknown, ENGLISH

Page from MSS of **Ars Moriendi, mid 15th century**

pen and brown ink with bodycolour and watercolour on vellum, 14.8 × 8.8 cm

P.444
PROVENANCE: Maggs Bros Ltd, from whom purchased by Gallery, January 1963.
EXHIBITIONS: *Watercolours from Bedford*, Norwich, Castle Museum, 1965, no.1.

This miniature seems to come from an Octavo manuscript of an unrecorded English version of the Ars Moriendi. The style recalls the manuscript of Thomas Chaundler's works in the library of Trinity College, Cambridge.

JM

Keith VAUGHAN, C.B.E.

[1912–77]

Canto I and **Untitled Drawing, 1943**

bodycolour and pen and ink on paper, sheet size: 27.8 × 20.2 cm (**P.452A** 6.7 × 5.4 cm)
inscribed: *Keith Vaughan/43*

P.452
PROVENANCE: Lord Gowrie; Piccadilly Gallery, from whom purchased by Gallery, January 1964.
EXHIBITIONS: *Watercolours from Bedford*, Norwich, Castle Museum, 1965, no.58.

During conservation a small drawing (P.452a) was found under the bottom left drawing of *Canto 1*.

Vaughan started his career at Lintas, the advertising agency of Unilever, as a trainee in the Art Department, making figure compositions in his spare time.

Through the writings of Clive Bell and Roger Fry he became aware of Paul Cézanne's work and the idea of 'significant form'. It was this interest that lead to his concern with human subject matter, and he paid little attention to the French tradition of still life.

Vaughan remained apart from other artists until the Second World War where, after registering as a conscientious objector, he served in the Pioneer Corps as an interpreter in a camp for German prisoners of war. At this time he met Graham SUTHERLAND and John MINTON. In Minton especially, he found another artist concerned with the recording of people in their day to day lives.

His later, more abstract works reveal shared concerns with the New York based Abstract Expressionists. Vaughan said in 1961: 'I sometimes think that space is being used as a more respectable word for nothingness, and that what many artists are doing is demonstrating the fact that they have nothing any more to paint'.

For the Festival of Britain, 1951, he painted the *Theseus* mural in the Dome of Discovery. He was awarded an Honorary Fellowship from the R.C.A. and awarded the C.B.E. in 1965.

EJ/JM

John VARLEY

[1778–1842]

River Scene

watercolour, paste and black lead on paper, 26.4 × 45.2 cm

P.707
PROVENANCE: Sydney D. Kitson, Elisabeth and Alice Barbara Kitson; given to the Gallery by Alice Barbara Kitson, May 1973.
EXHIBITIONS: *The English Tradition: an exhibition of watercolours from two private collections*, Bedford, Cecil Higgins Art Gallery, 1972, no.81, as a permanent loan to the Gallery from the Kitson Collection.

Varley is among the best known and most prolific of all watercolourists. He was a hard and rapid worker who exhibited as many as sixty drawings at the Watercolour Society in 1809 alone. His best work was done early in his career and shows the influence of GIRTIN with simpler, stronger compositions and more convincingly realistic colour.

Later, his everlasting debts caused him to produce too many stereotyped and mechanical views, but he was a good teacher and influenced a number of younger artists of distinction, especially David COX. He was also a friend of William BLAKE and had a keen interest in astrology.

EJ

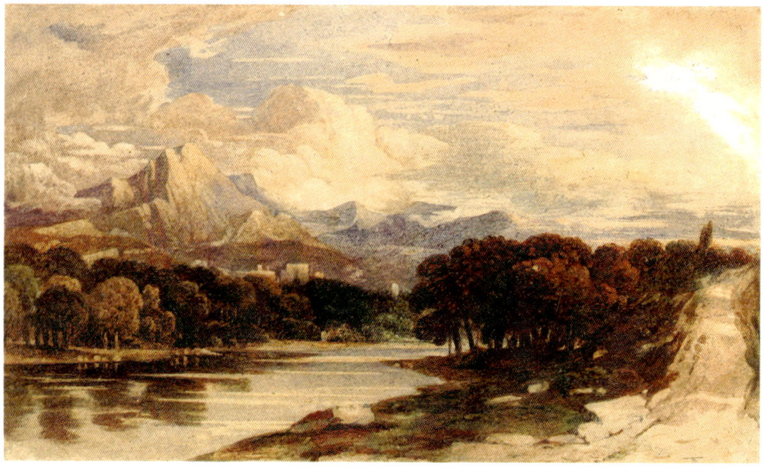

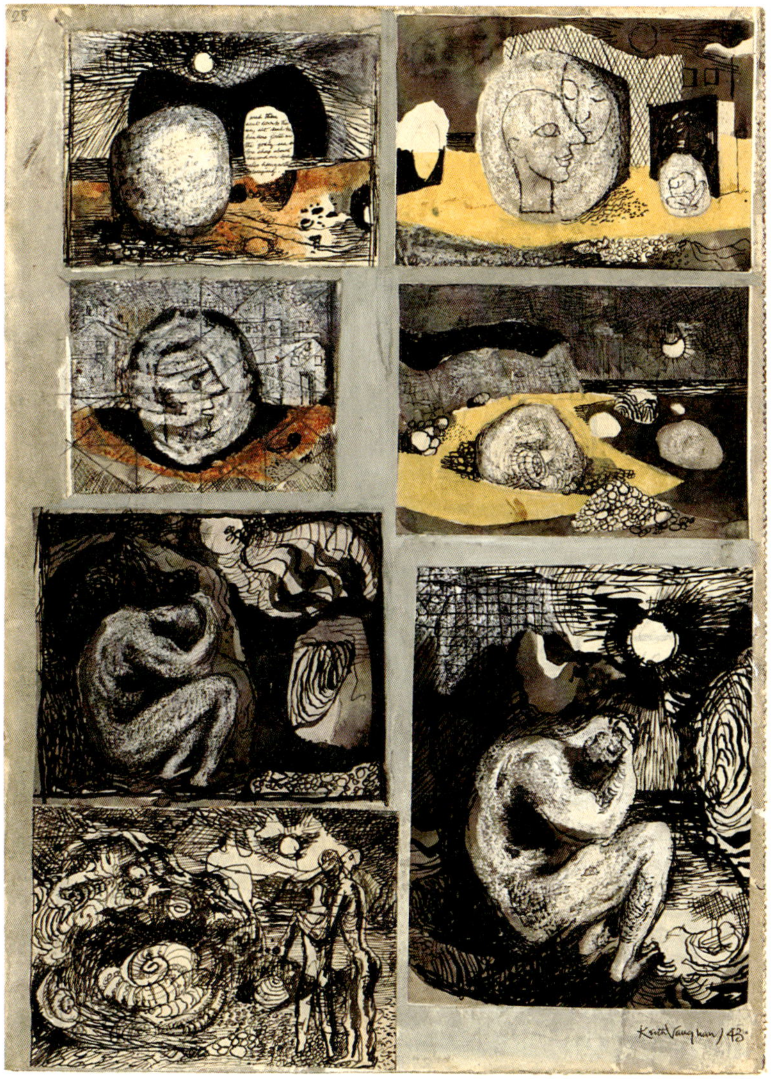

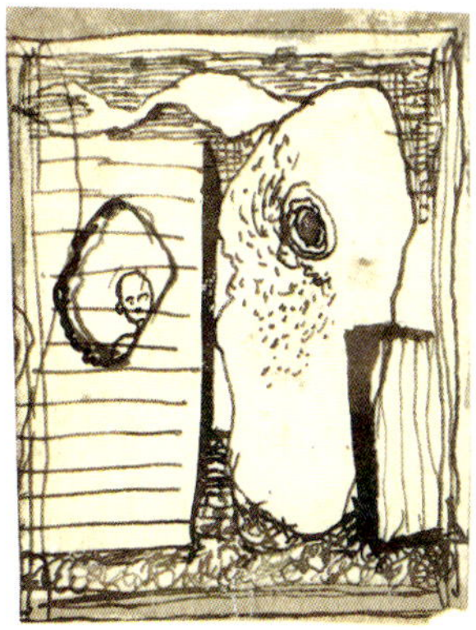

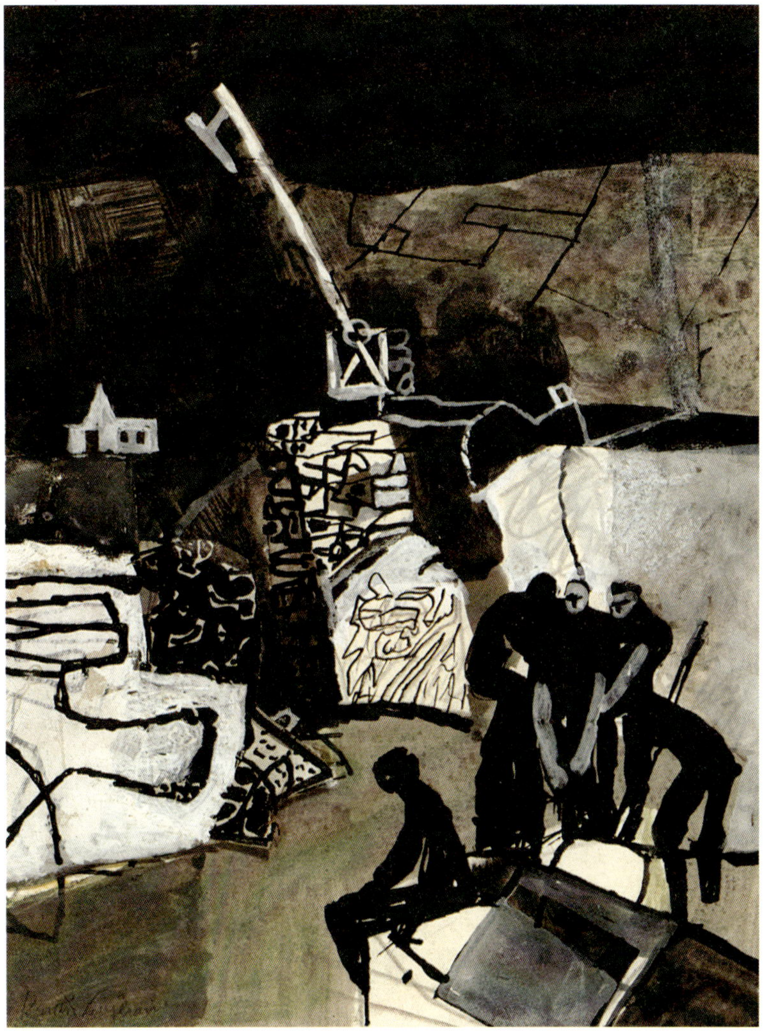

Keith VAUGHAN, C.B.E.

[1912–77]

Finisterre, Seaweed Hoist, c.1951

watercolour and hinged collage on paper, 17 × 13.1 cm
inscribed: *Keith Vaughan*

P.221

PROVENANCE: Leicester Galleries, from whom purchased by Gallery, April 1958.
EXHIBITIONS: *Watercolours and Drawings from The Cecil Higgins Art Gallery, Bedford*, London, Thos. Agnew & Sons Ltd, 1962, no.91; *Watercolours from Bedford*, Norwich, Norwich Castle Museum, 1965, no.59.

Vaughan's sense of design became firmer in the early to mid 1950s, with his thoughtfulness and intelligence reflected in a realisation that the figure was a 'personal, symbolic subject'.

He said of the sea: 'On the whole human beings seem to have behaved best when at sea; apart from the galleys and pirates (and even in the galleys conditions were worse when in port)'.

JM

Attributed to **Jan van der VINNE**
[1663–1721]
Extensive view of Oxford

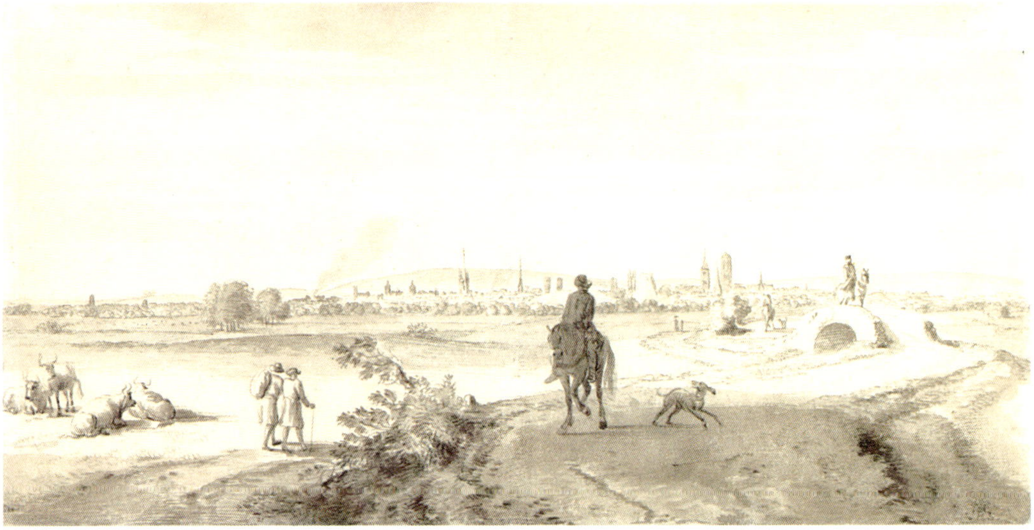

black chalk and grey wash on paper, 18.4 × 36.8 cm
inscribed: *P.S.*

P.447
PROVENANCE: R.E. Alton; Maas Gallery, from whom purchased by Gallery, March 1963.
EXHIBITIONS: *Spring Exhibition,* London, Maas Gallery, 1963, no.81.

The view is taken from the west of the city and just north of the Botley Road. Jan van der Vinne, also known as Jean de Nageoires, was born in Haarlem, the son and pupil of Vincent Laurensz van der Vinne (1629–1702). At some time around 1686 he visited England, where he may have worked with Jan Wyck (1652–1700). He later returned to Haarlem, in the Netherlands, where he is said to have opened a silk-weaving factory with his brother Isaak, also a painter.

The attribution is currnetly under question owing to the inscrpition. Although a similar view exists in the British Museum collection (*Oxford from the South-West)* which is firmly attributed to van der Vinne, the style is also reminiscent of early Paul Sandby drawings.

EJ/CB

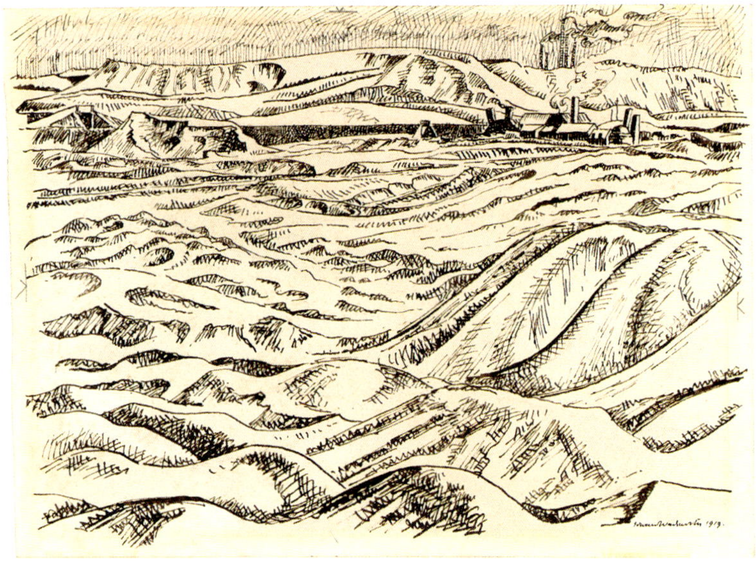

Edward WADSWORTH, A.R.A.
[1889–1949]
View near Tipton, Staffs, 1919

pen and ink on paper, 25.5 × 35.2 cm
inscribed: *Edward Wadsworth, 1919*

P.255
PROVENANCE: The artist's widow; Piccadilly Gallery, from whom purchased by Gallery, 1958.
EXHIBITIONS: *Edward Wadsworth Memorial Exhibition,* London, Tate Gallery, 1951, no.62; *Edward Wadsworth, 1889–1949,* Bradford, Cartwright Hall, 1989–1990, no.65.
REFERENCES: J. Lewison (ed.), *A Genius of Industrial England. Edward Wadsworth 1889–1949,* 1990, repr. p.34, no.65.

Tipton is about six miles south of Wolverhampton and fourteen miles due east of Bridgnorth. Wadsworth made a series of 'Black Country' landscapes just after the First World War chronicling the effects of industrialization on the environment. These proved to be a critical success with reviewers welcoming a return from the abstraction of the pre-war period to a new realism.

Wadsworth had become familiar with this area during train journeys to Liverpool where he had been deployed in camouflaging ships.

EJ/JM

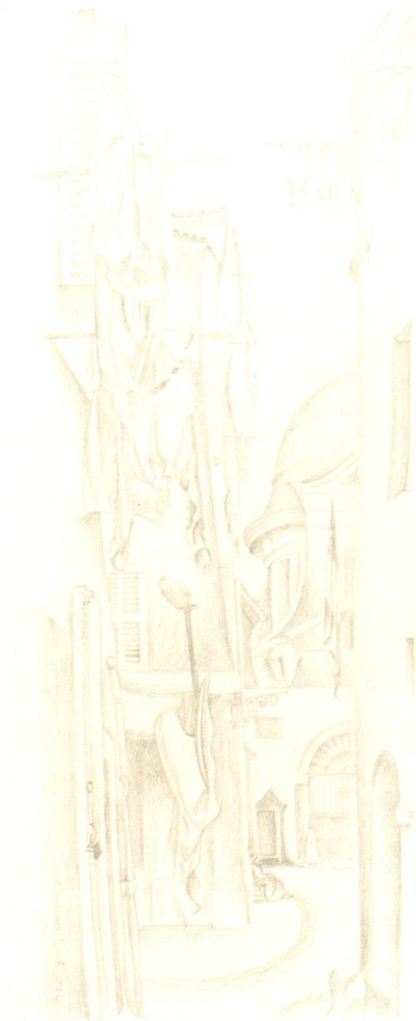

Edward WADSWORTH, A.R.A.
[1889–1949]
Street in Marseilles (also known as **Hospice de la Charité, Marseilles**), **1924**

pencil on paper, 47.9 × 22.8 cm
inscribed: *Edward Wadsworth 1924*

P.329
PROVENANCE: The artist's widow; Mayor Gallery, from whom purchased by Gallery, January 1960.
EXHIBITIONS: *Edward Wadsworth Memorial Exhibition*, London, Tate Gallery, 1951 as no. 75,76, or 77 (all three have the same date and virtually identical measurements); *Edward Wadsworth, 1889–1949*, Bradford, Cartwright Hall, 1989–1990, no.86 as *Hospice de la Charité*.
REFERENCES: J. Lewison (ed.), *A Genius of Industrial England. Edward Wadsworth 1889–1949*, 1990, p.47, no.86, repr. as *Hospice de la Charité, Marseille*.

Marseilles and the nearby naval base at Toulon enjoyed a reputation in the early 1920s as a bohemian centre for artists and writers. Wadsworth was amongst the first English artists to go there, with others such as Edward BURRA, and Paul NASH following soon after. It was during this period that he fell out with Wyndham LEWIS whose novel, *The Apes of God*, railed against 'champagne bohemia' and criticized many from Wadsworth's circle of friends.

JM

Edward WADSWORTH, A.R.A.
[1889–1949]
Composition, 1930

pencil and bodycolour on paper, 35.3 × 50.9 cm
inscribed: *E WADSWORTH 1930*

P.327
PROVENANCE: Mrs Wadsworth the artist's widow, from whom purchased by Gallery, January 1960.

Wadsworth was born at Cleckheaton in 1889, the son of Fred Wadsworth, a well known name in the worsted spinning industry of Yorkshire. He studied at the Knirr Art School, Munich, the Bradford School of Art and the Slade 1910–12. He befriended Wyndham LEWIS and exhibited in London with the Vorticists and various other independent groups.

His war service was as an intelligence officer in the R.N.V.R. based at Mudros, on the Aegean isle of Lemnos. He was invalided home in 1917 and later engaged with dazzle camouflage at various English ports.

In the 1930s Wadsworth was a member with Ben NICHOLSON, Paul NASH and others of Unit One and was also commissioned to make two paintings for the liner *Queen Mary*.

EJ

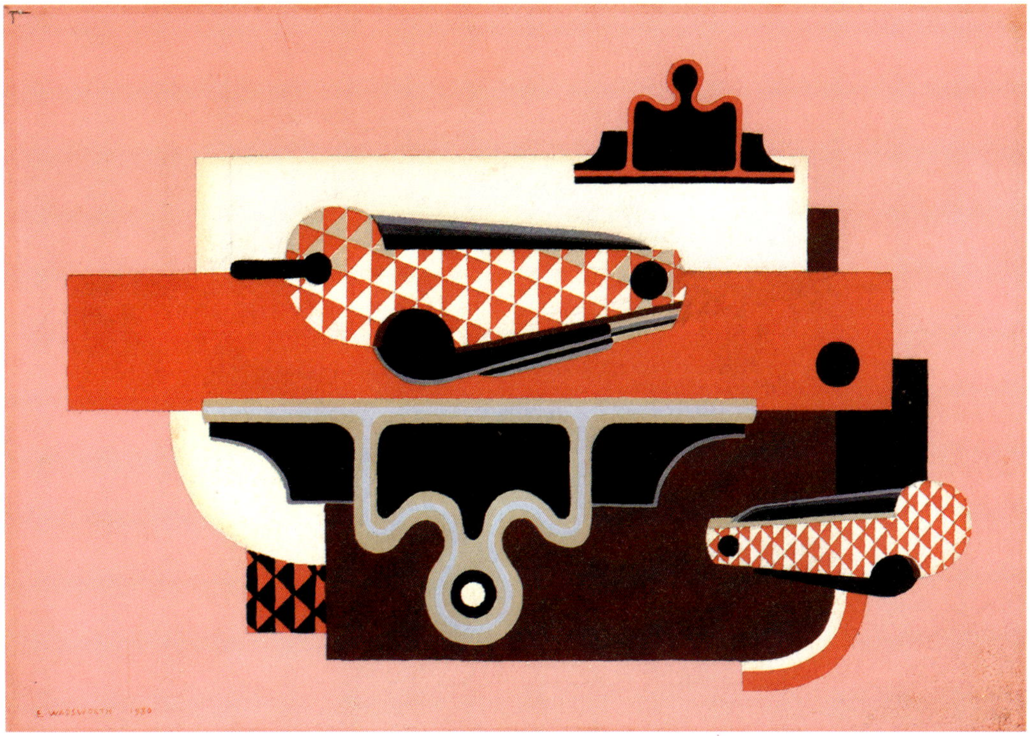

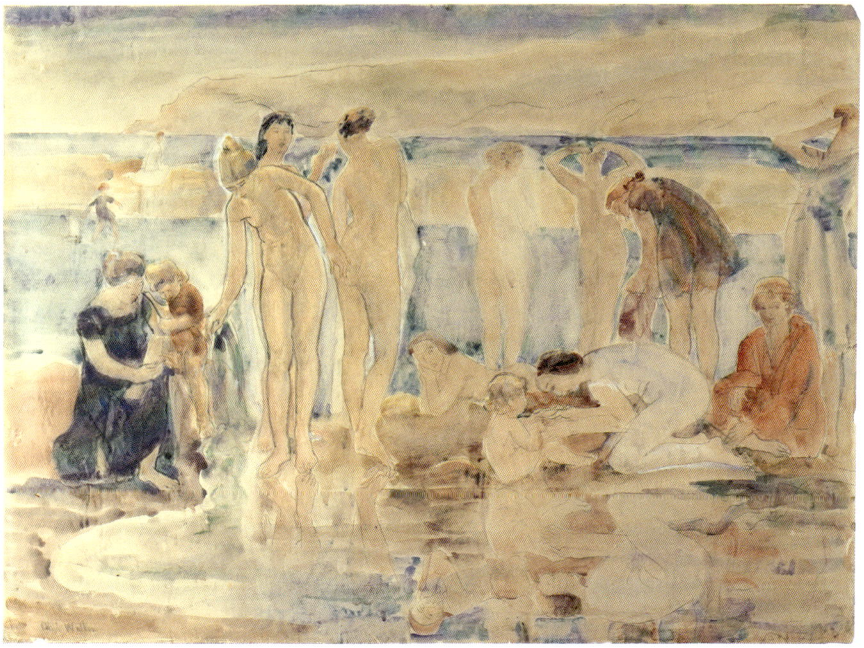

Dame Ethel WALKER, C.B.E., A.R.A.
[1861–1951]
The Bathing Pool, 1923

watercolour and pencil on paper, 65.7 × 88.4 cm
inscribed: *Ethel Walker*

P.232
PROVENANCE: Leicester Galleries, from whom purchased by Gallery, November 1957.

An imaginary composition based on numerous life drawings. There are similar compositions in the Tate Gallery and the Laing Art Gallery, Newcastle upon Tyne. Ethel Walker, one of the foremost women painters of her generation, produced many portraits and landscapes over her long career. However, she is probably best remembered for her large mythical, decorative subjects.

Born in Edinburgh, she studied with Fred Brown at the Westminster School of Art and the Slade. She attended evening classes given by SICKERT, to whom she claimed she 'owed a good deal'. She was awarded a C.B.E. in 1938, created an A.R.A. in 1940 and a Dame in 1943, the first female artist to be knighted for her work. Ethel Walker featured in George Moore's autobiography *Hail and Farewell* as 'Florence', where her relationship with fellow painter, Clare Christian, was discussed at some length. Living into her ninetieth year, she outlived all her contemporaries, and when STEER died in 1942 she said 'Now he and Sickert are gone I'm the only artist left'.

CB

Frederick WALKER, A.R.A.
[1840–75]
A Cosy Couple (Darby and Joan), 1861

watercolour and bodycolour on paper, image size: 26.5 × 32.4 cm
inscribed: *F. Walker 61*

P.142
PROVENANCE: Fine Art Society, from whom purchased by Gallery, January 1958.

Immortalized as Little Billee in DU MAURIER'S *Trilby*, Walker emerged as one of the most brilliant illustrators of the 1860s. His most famous oil *The Harbour Refuge*, 1872, (Tate Gallery), showed that he was being hailed, even before his early death from tuberculosis, as the leader of a school destined to succeed the Pre-Raphaelites. In watercolour the main influences on his development were W.H. HUNT and BIRKET FOSTER, but his colour was not always successful. RUSKIN criticised his skies as 'the colour of buff plaster'.

EJ

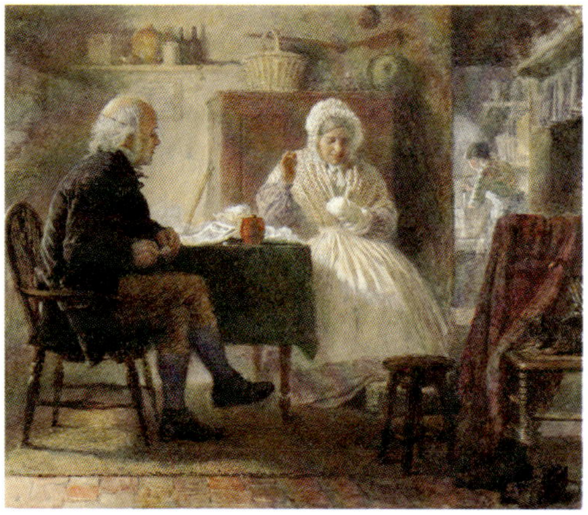

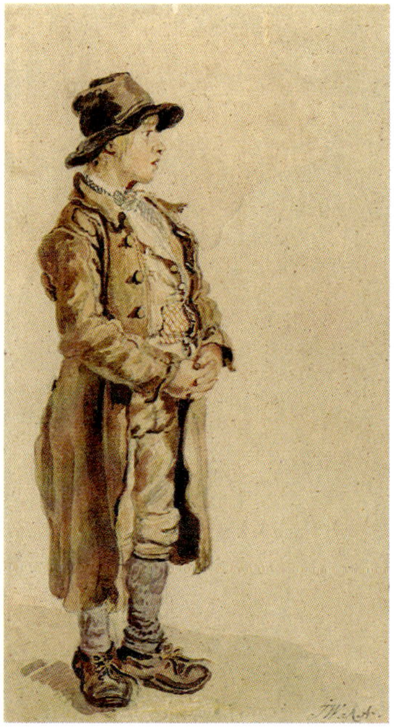

James WARD, R.A.
[1769–1859]
The Young Countryman, after 1811

watercolour and graphite on paper, 31.3 × 17.4 cm
inscribed: *JW. RA.*

P.271
PROVENANCE: By descent to the artist's grandson, Mulgrave Phipps Jackson, who presented it to T.W. Nunn in December 1877; The Nunn Trust; Fairways Ltd, from whom purchased by Gallery, December 1956.
EXHIBITIONS: *Watercolours and Drawings from The Cecil Higgins Art Gallery Bedford*, London, Thos. Agnew & Sons Ltd, 1962, no.56.

The form of signature means a date after 1811 when Ward was elected R.A.

Apprenticed to the engraver J.R. Smith, James won a considerable reputation as an engraver of animal and landscape subjects, being appointed 'painter and mezzotinter' to the Prince of Wales in 1794. He turned to oils, painting genre scenes in the manner of George MORLAND, his brother-in-law. This he also forsook in favour of the Dutch and Flemish Schools and, in particular, Rubens, whose influence on Ward's masterpiece, *Gordale Scar, Yorkshire*, c.1815 (Tate Gallery), is clear. Ward was a superb draughtsman of animals, while this study of a young bumpkin is simply masterly. His watercolours of landscapes are rare but deserve more attention than they have so far received.

Label on the reverse reads: 'An original sketch by my Grandfather the late James Ward R.a. [*sic*] In grateful testimony of W.Nunn's skill and kindness during illness. Mulgrave Phipps Jackson. December 1877'.

EJ/JM

John WEBBER R.A.
[1751–93]
Heights at Dovedale, Derbyshire, 1789

pen and ink with washes of blue and grey on paper, image size: 36.7 × 48 cm
inscribed: *J. Webber del 1789*
inscribed on mount: *Heights at Dovedale, Derbyshire*

P.102
PROVENANCE: Squire Gallery, from whom purchased by Gallery, 1952.

Born in London, the son of a Swiss sculptor named Weber, John studied in Berne and Paris before joining the R.A. Schools in 1775. In 1776 he accompanied Captain Cook on his last voyage; he was present at Cook's death and made a drawing of the event which was engraved by Byrne and BARTOLOZZI. Returning to England he was elected A.R.A. in 1875 and R.A. in 1791.

His group of drawings of rock scenery in Derbyshire, made in 1789, are notable for the delicacy of the colouring. HARDIE considers that Webber, 'takes a high place, higher than has yet been recognized, among the fore-runners of GIRTIN and TURNER'.

EJ

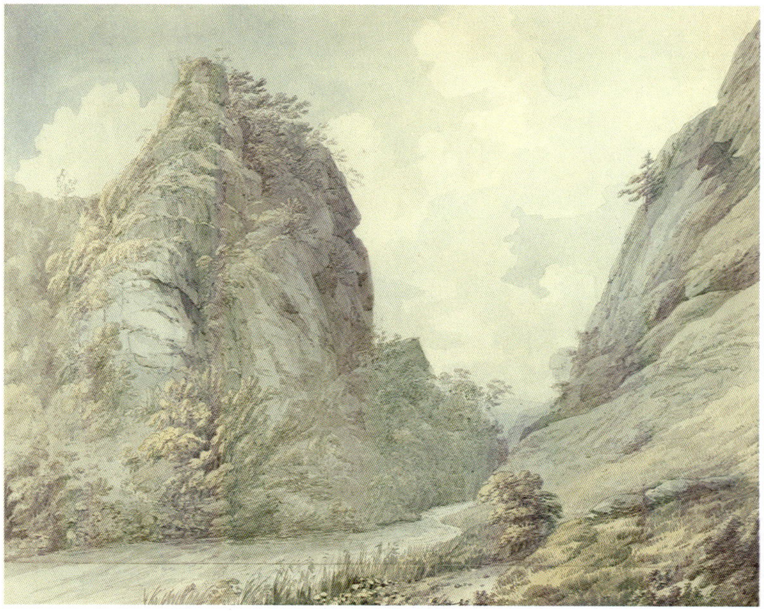

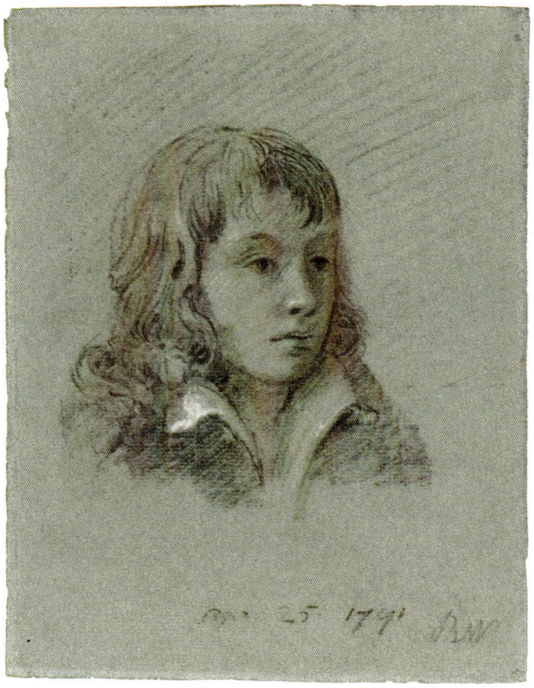

Benjamin WEST, P.R.A.
[1738–1820]
Portrait of a Boy, 1791

black and red chalks, heightened with white on blue paper, 25 x 19.9 cm
inscribed: *BW apr 25 1791*
inscribed on reverse: *Bichere (?)*

P.387
PROVENANCE: Sotheby's sale 9 November 1960, no.7 (various properties); Thos. Agnew & Sons Ltd, from whom purchased by Gallery, January 1961.
EXHIBITIONS: *88th Watercolour Exhibition,* London, Thos. Agnew & Sons Ltd, 1961, no.5.

This sympathetic portrait, although no doubt sketched quite rapidly, shows West's skill as a draughtsman to be very considerable.

EJ

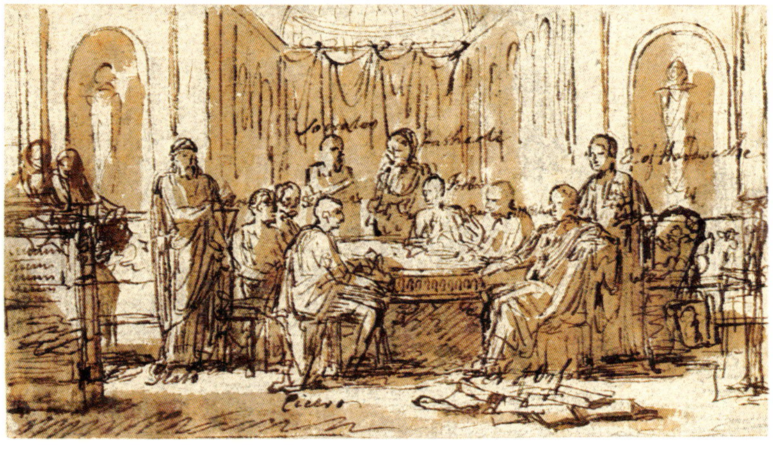

Benjamin WEST, P.R.A.
[1738–1820]
Disputation between Contemporary Cognoscenti and Ancient Philosophers and Poets

pen and brown ink and brown wash on paper, 11.6 × 21.1 cm

P.388
PROVENANCE: P&D Colnaghi Ltd, from whom purchased by Gallery, January 1961.

This appears to be a preliminary drawing for a picture planned but apparently never carried out. Unfortunately some of the identifications in ink are no longer decipherable. Those that are include Plato standing on the left, and Cicero seated at the table facing the Earl of Orford with, standing behind him, the Earl of Hardwicke. Socrates is to the left hand of the two men standing beyond the table.

After studying in Rome, West settled in England in 1763 where he was employed by George III to paint a series of pictures for Windsor Castle and St George's Chapel which occupied him for most of the rest of his life. He succeeded Reynolds as President of the R.A. in 1792. He tried to combine the conventions of history painting with contemporary subjects such as *The Death of General Wolfe*. Although a prolific draughtsman, he only used watercolour occasionally.

EJ

Richard WESTALL, R.A.
[1765–1836]
Macbeth and the Witches, c.1797

pen and ink, with washes of grey and yellow, over black lead on paper, 21.6 × 15.6 cm
inscribed: Collector's mark of the Second Earl of Warwick (1746–1816)

P.236
PROVENANCE: The Second Earl of Warwick; Roland, Browse and Delbanco, from whom purchased by Gallery, 1958.

The subject was a popular one with 18th-century artists, most notably Henri FUSELI. Westall was a prolific illustrator of Milton, Gray, Crabbe and Shakespeare. He also wrote some poems and instructed the future Queen Victoria in drawing.

Iolo Williams observes that much of Westall's work contains an element of the ludicrous, citing 'a rather over-dramatised' sleep-walking scene from *Macbeth* in the V&A (Dyce 912), of similar size to this drawing. His most successful watercolours are those which include a landscape element.

EJ/JM

Francis WHEATLEY, R.A.
[1747–1801]
Country Scene with Washerwoman, 1782

watercolour and carbon based ink on paper, 52 × 45.4 cm
inscribed: *Wheatley/del 1782*

P.421
PROVENANCE: P&D Colnaghi Ltd, from whom purchased by Gallery, July 1962.
EXHIBITIONS: *Watercolours and Drawings from The Cecil Higgins Art Gallery, Bedford*, London, Thos. Agnew & Sons Ltd, 1962, no.22; *English Watercolours from The Cecil Higgins Art Gallery Bedford*, Reading, Reading Museum & Art Gallery, 1965, no.57; *Watercolours from Bedford*, Norwich, Norwich Castle Museum, 1965, no.60.
REFERENCES: M. Webster, *Francis Wheatley*, 1970, p.45, fig.46, Webster identifies this as an Irish subject and therefore drawn c.1779–83.

Wheatley is chiefly known for his charming but quite unrealistic portraits of street vendors in the *Cries of London* prints. His watercolours tend to be elegant rather than vigorous but his drawings of country fairs are very well observed. Some of his watercolours are very large, for example, *Lake Windemere* (V&A, P.1–1948), which is 61 × 94 cm.

His dissipated way of life led to such crippling gout that he painted little towards the end of his life.

EJ

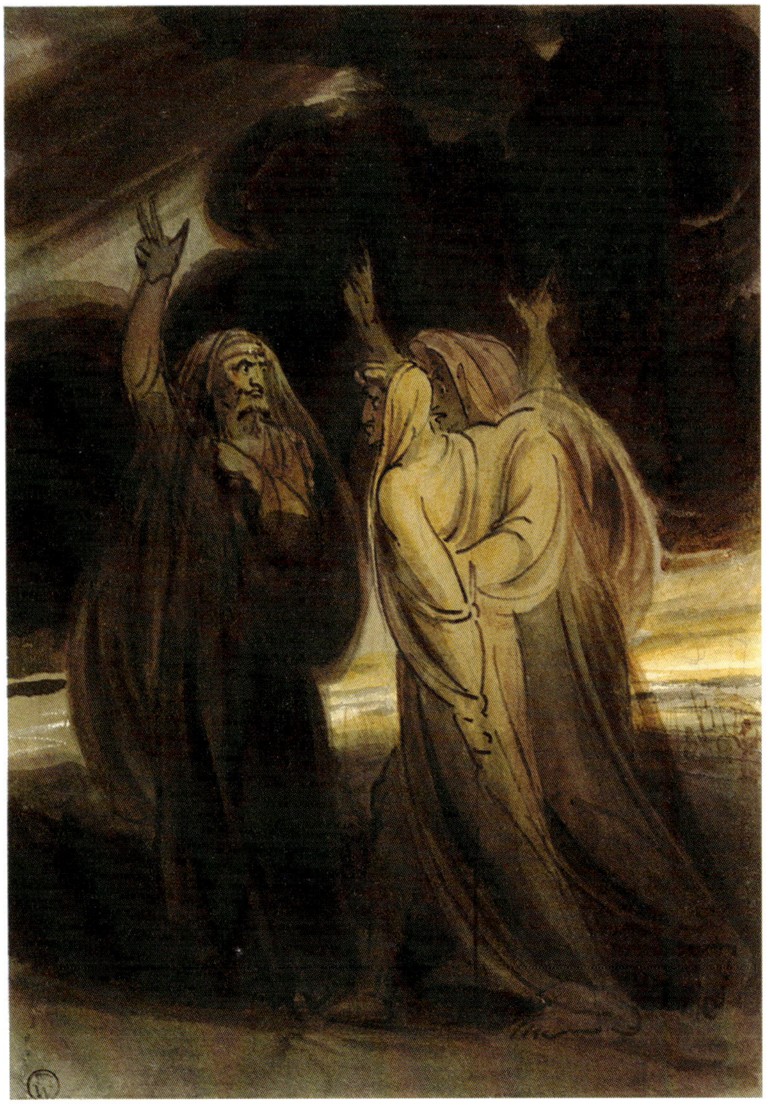

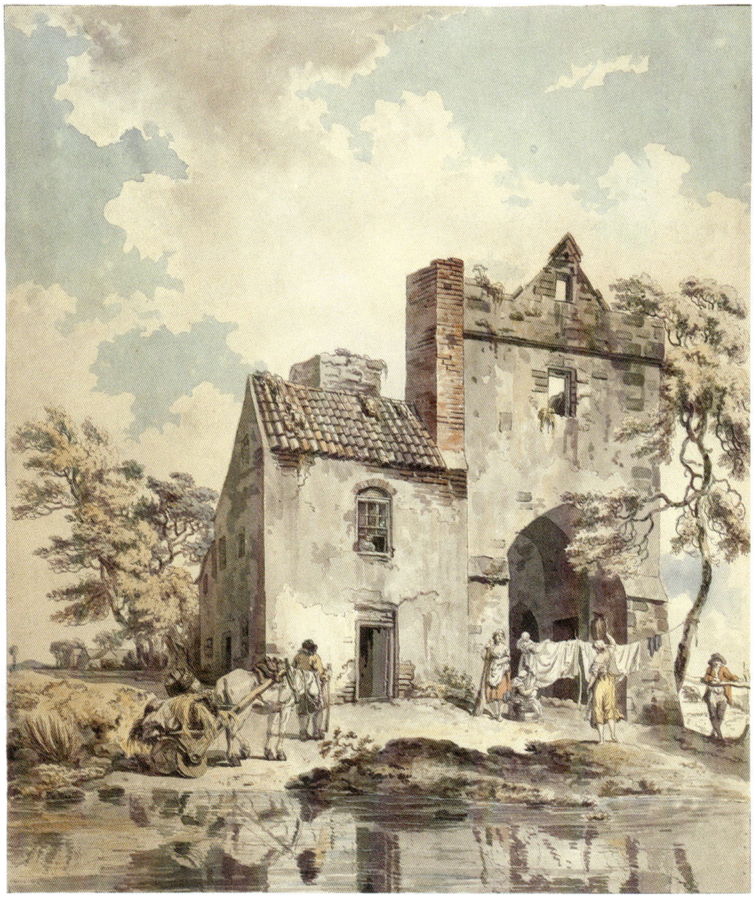

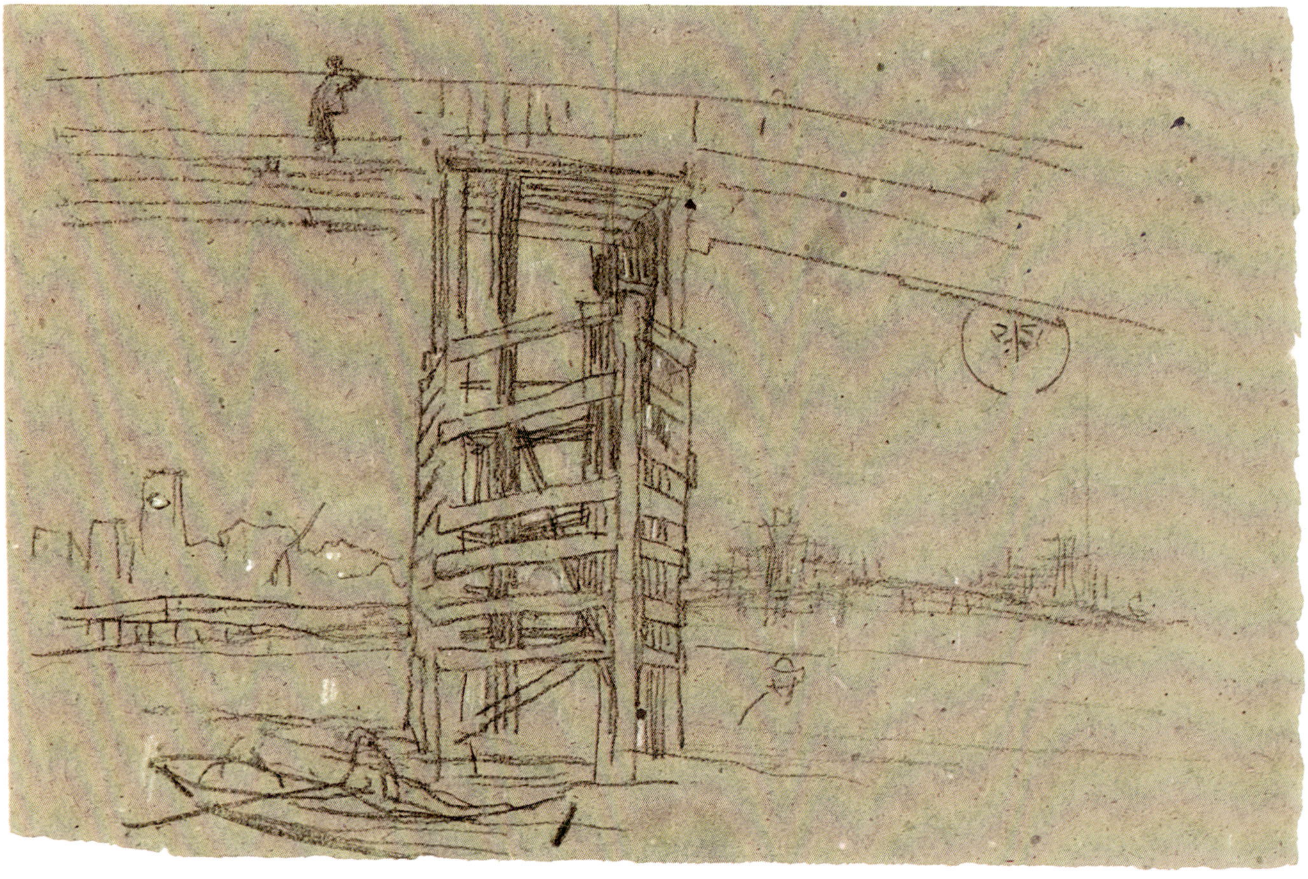

James McNeill WHISTLER
[1834–1903]
A Pier of Old Battersea Bridge, (formerly known as A Pier of Old Putney Bridge), c.1872–3

chalk on paper, 18.4 × 28.3 cm
inscribed: Butterfly monogram
on reverse in the hand of Harold Wright (Colnaghi's Print Director): *Whistler 'Old Putney Bridge' (1878 or 1879) ex Collection of Miss R. Birnie Philip the artists executrix and sister-in-law*

P.150
PROVENANCE: In Whistler's studio at his death in 1903 and bequeathed to his sister-in-law, Miss R. Birnie Philip; sold to P&D Colnaghi Ltd as *A Span of Old Putney Bridge* 22 October 1957, from whom purchased by Gallery, January 1958.
EXHIBITIONS: *Watercolours and Drawings from The Cecil Higgins Art Gallery, Bedford*, London, Thos. Agnew & Sons Ltd, 1962, no.74; *James McNeill Whistler (1834–1903),* Berlin, Nationalgalerie, Staatliche Museen, 1969, no.78 as *Old Putney Bridge*.
REFERENCES: E.G. Kennedy, *The Etched Work of Whistler,* illustrated by reproductions in collotype of the different states of the plates, 1910, no.177/178; M.F. Macdonald, *James McNeill Whistler. Drawings, Pastels and Watercolours. A Catalogue Raisonné,* 1995, repr. p.179, no.481, as *A span of old Battersea Bridge*.

This was entitled *A Pier of Old Putney Bridge* until correctly identified by Margaret Macdonald, who points out that Putney Bridge had triangular embrasures jutting out over the piers and that, furthermore, Albert Bridge, is visible in the distance here. Both old wooden bridges had certain similarities clearly seen in Whistler's etchings. For long dated c.1878–9, Macdonald suggests 1872–3.

Whistler moved to Paris in 1855 studying intermittently under Marc Charles Gabriel Gleyre (1806–74), before moving to London, where he enjoyed instant success with his paintings and etchings. He introduced 'blue and white' Japanese porcelain into London from Paris, and the vogue for *Japonisme* anticipated the Aesthetic Movement, of which Whistler's cosmopolitanism, dandyism and wit made him the natural leader. In the 1870s Whistler painted a number of views on the Thames by night which he described as *Nocturnes*, one of which, exhibited in 1877, led to the famous lawsuit with RUSKIN. Although Whistler won he was only awarded damages of one farthing.

He was also a brilliant portrait painter and a superb printmaker, his etchings of Venice being quite outstanding. In 1888 he married Beatrix Godwin (née Philip) the widow of E.W. Godwin who built Whistler's house in Tite Street.

SICKERT and Mortimer Menpes were among his many pupils. Sickert said of Whistler: 'Whistler's sense of a line was acute. That sense – which is the whole art of drawing – made of him a marvelously gifted, intuitive draughtsman, and master of perspective'.

EJ/JM

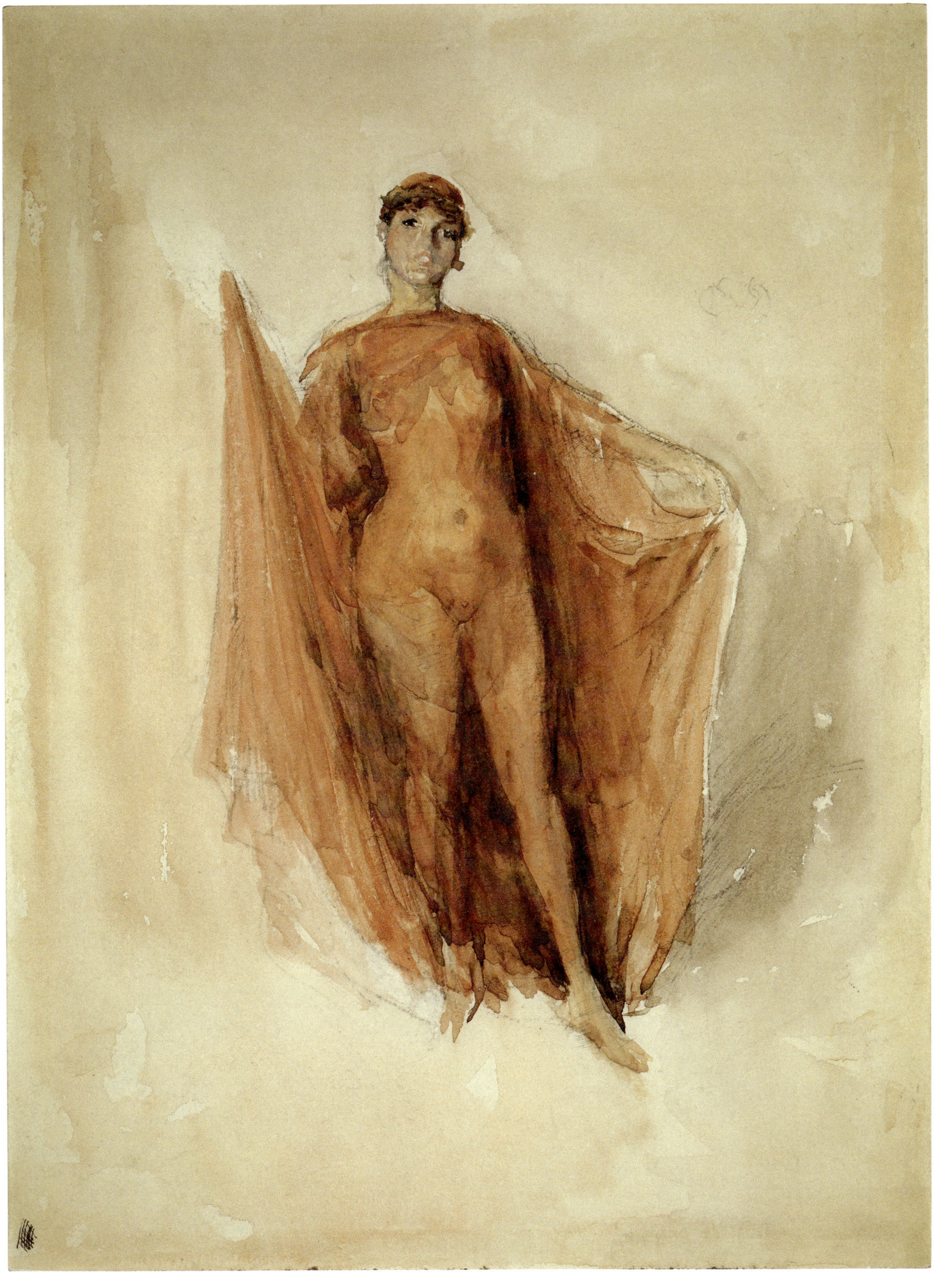

James McNeill WHISTLER

[1834–1903]

The Dancing Girl, c.1885–90

watercolour over pencil on off white wove paper, 29.7 × 22.3 cm
inscribed: Butterfly monogram
inscribed on reverse in the hand of Harold Wright (Colnaghi's Print Director): *J McNeill Whistler / Model draping (The model probably / one of the Pettigrews) / (ex Collection of Miss R. Birnie Philip) / the Artist's Executrix & Sister-in-Law. / (Done during the Cheyne Walk period) 1896 or later.*

P.432

PROVENANCE: In Whistler's studio at his death in 1903 and bequeathed to his sister-in-law, Miss R. Birnie Philip; P&D Colnaghi Ltd, October 1957; from whom purchased by Gallery, May 1958.
EXHIBITIONS: *James McNeill Whistler (1834–1903)*, Berlin, Nationalgalerie, Staatliche Museen, 1969, no104 as *Tanzendes Mädchen; James McNeill Whistler*, London, Tate Gallery, Paris, Musée d'Orsay, 1995, no.174; *Songs on Stone. James McNeill Whistler and the Art of Lithography*, Chicago, The Art Institute of Chicago, Ottawa, National Gallery of Canada, 1998–99, no.95.
REFERENCES: R. Dorment & M.F. Macdonald, *James McNeill Whistler*, 1994, p.252, no.174, illus. no.174; M.F. Macdonald, *James McNeill Whistler. Drawings, Pastels and Watercolours. A Catalogue Raisonné*, 1995, repr. p.397, no.1068; M. Tedeschi, *Songs on Stone: James McNeill Whistler and the Art of Lithography*, 1998, p.59, p.73, illus no.68; L. Lambourne, *Victorian Painting*, 1999, p.297, pl.357.

Originally dated c.1867 this was corrected to 1885–90 in the 1994 Tate catalogue, thus confirming Harold Wright's opinion given above.

Margaret Macdonald suggests that Wright was wrong about the Pettigrews (see above), although his information came from Miss Birnie Philip, as she believes this drawing is earlier than 1890 when the Pettigrews began to model for Whistler. She also believes that the figure was drawn with such care as to suggest that it was originally intended to be a drawing rather than a watercolour. However, she later writes: 'The colour is magnificent, full of rich, glowing shades of russet and brown … The explicit painting of the nude figure, with the transparent drapes enhancing and not in any way concealing the body is unusual in Whistler's work'.

EJ

James McNeill WHISTLER

[1834–1903]

Head and Shoulders of Ronald Philip, c.1900–1901

pencil on paper, 15.2 × 10 cm
inscribed: Butterfly monogram
inscribed on reverse in the hand of Harold Wright (Colnaghi's Print Director): *Ronald Philip (Mrs Whistler's / brother) / by / Whistler / ex Collection of Miss R. Birnie Philip) / the artist's sister-in-law and executrix.*

P.153

PROVENANCE: In Whistler's studio at his death in 1903 and bequeathed to his sister-in-law, Miss R. Birnie Philip; P&D Colnaghi Ltd, from whom purchased by Gallery, January 1958.
REFERENCES: M.F. Macdonald, *James McNeill Whistler. Drawings, Pastels and Watercolours. A Catalogue Raisonné*, 1995, p.588–9, repr. p.589, no.1637.

Ronald Murray Philip (1871–1940) was the son of the sculptor John Birnie Philip and Frances Black. He was the same age as Whistler's son Charles Hanson and was treated by Whistler like a favourite nephew, being portrayed by him on a number of occasions.

JM

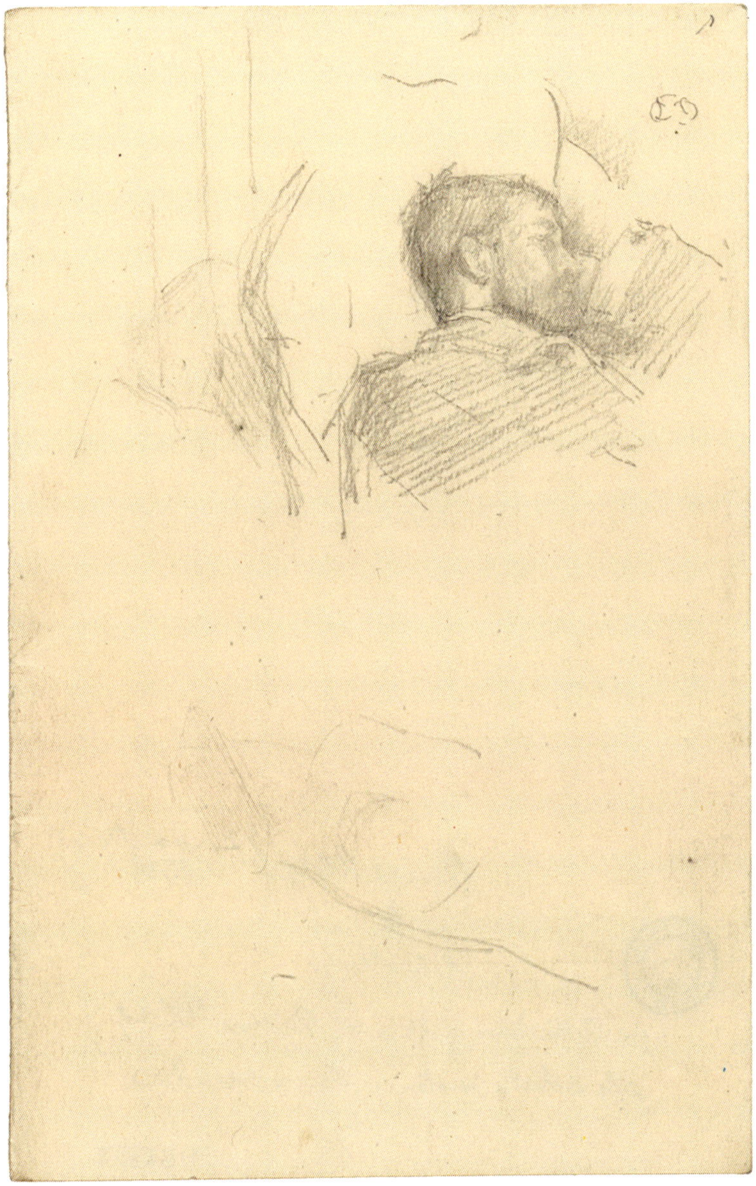

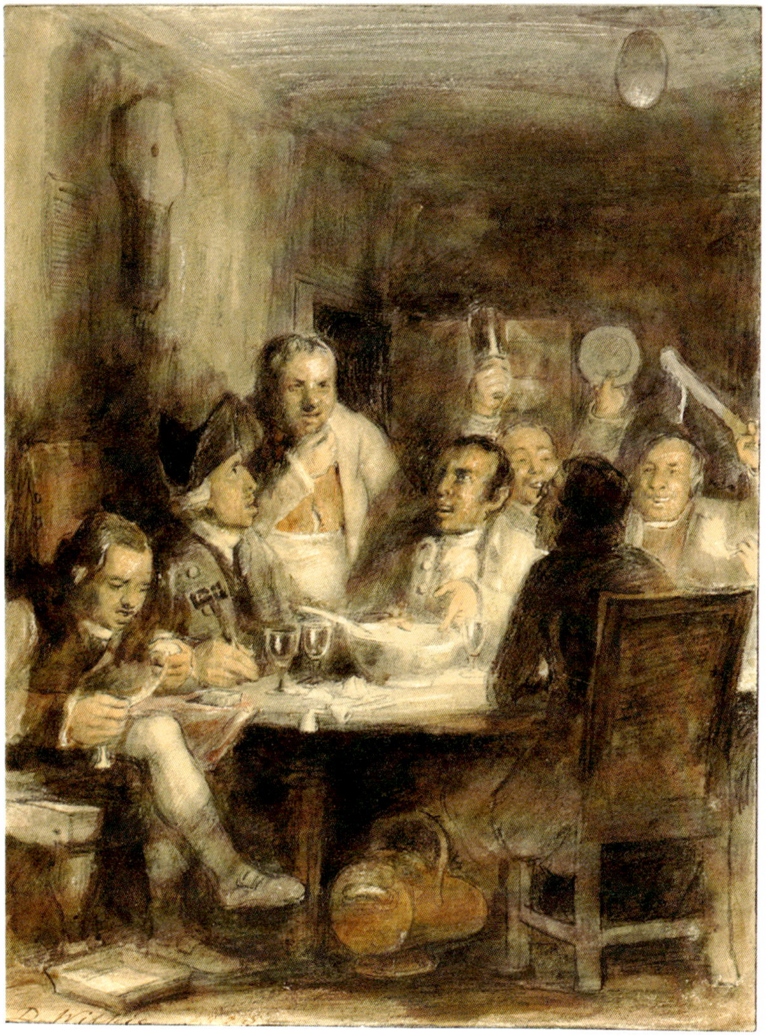

Sir David WILKIE, R.A.
[1785–1841]
The Clubbists, c.1806

watercolour and graphite and ink on board, 22.7 × 17.5 cm
inscribed: *D.Wilkie* and indecipherable date

P.259
PROVENANCE: P&D Colnaghi Ltd, from whom purchased by Gallery, October 1958.

Wilkie's picture of *The Clubbists* was painted as an illustration for the first volume of Leigh Hunt's *Classic Tales*, published from 1806–7. Wilkie probably began his picture late in 1806, certainly before 1 January 1807, because on that date Anker Smith's engraving was published.

This is a characteristic Wilkie subject, deriving from 17th century Dutch and Flemish examples, notably Adriaen van Ostafe (1610–84) and more especially, David Teniers the Younger (1610–90), who had a seminal influence on Wilkie, particularly earlier in his career.

EJ

Sir David WILKIE, R.A.
[1785–1841]
A View of Cults, Fifeshire, 1817

watercolour on paper, 16.1 × 26.8 cm
inscribed: *D.Wilkie f 1817*

P.237
PROVENANCE: David Wilkie, great-nephew of the artist; P&D Colnaghi Ltd, from whom purchased by Gallery, July 1958.
EXHIBITIONS: *Watercolours and Drawings from The Cecil Higgins Art Gallery Bedford*, London, Thos. Agnew & Sons Ltd, 1962, no.50.

Wilkie was born at Cults, a son of the Manse. In 1805 he came to London and entered the R.A. Schools. His *Village Politicians* (R.A. 1806, Earl of Mansfield's collection) was the picture of the year and he soon had many patrons including the Prince Regent. He was elected R.A. in 1811 aged only twenty-six, and knighted in 1836 by William IV. He died at sea on his way back from the Middle East in 1841.

Most of his watercolours are studies for his oil paintings but, although his colour is never very strong, it is both delicate and applied with a fluid touch. Another view of Cults, also painted in 1817, is in a private collection.

EJ

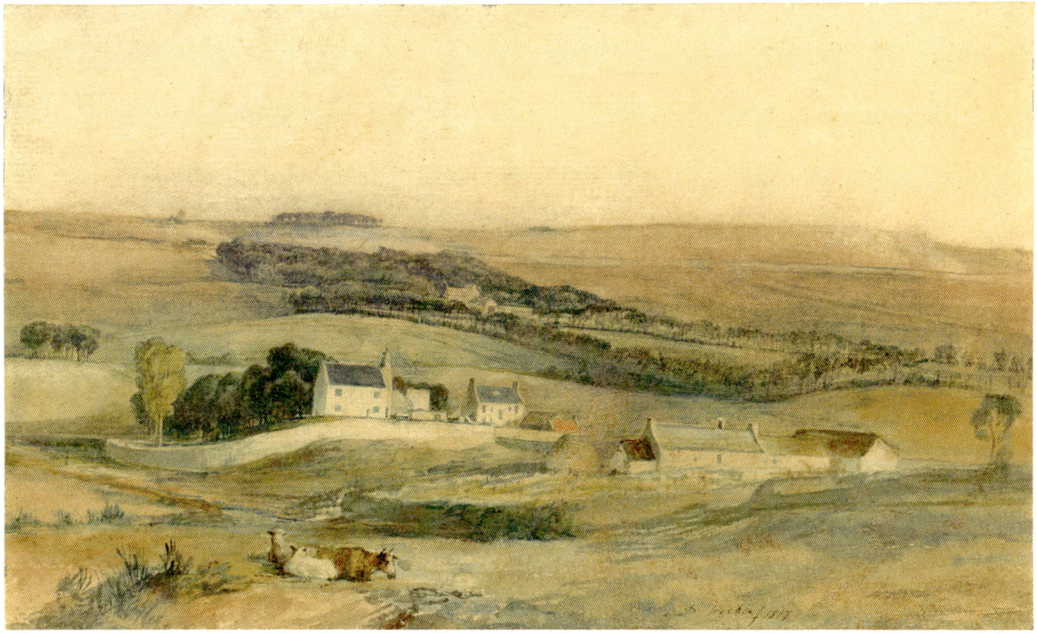

Richard WILSON, R.A.

[c.1713–82]

The Palatine Mount, 1754

black chalk and stump on grey wired paper heightened with white, size including mount
35.8 × 49.8 cm
inscribed: *R.W.f. Roma 1754. Palatine Mount. No.5*
inscribed on reverse: *55*

P.123
PROVENANCE: Bought from the artist in Rome by William Legge, 2nd Earl of Dartmouth (1731–1801); descended in the Dartmouth Collection until discovered in 1948, having been lost to sight completely for almost 150 years in a cupboard in Patshull House, Warwickshire home of the family; Dartmouth sale Christie's 29 January 1954, no.7, Thos. Agnew & Sons Ltd, from whom purchased by Gallery, July 1957.
EXHIBITIONS: *Richard Wilson and his Circle*, Birmingham, Birmingham City Museum & Art Gallery, 1948–9, no.74 and London, Tate Gallery, 1949, no.73; *Italy and the Grand Tour*, Norwich, Castle Museum, 1958, no.63; *Watercolours and Drawings from The Cecil Higgins Art Gallery, Bedford*, London, Thos. Agnew & Sons Ltd, 1962, no.20; *Rome Centenary Exhibition*, Palazzo delle Esposizioni, Rome, 1971; *Richard Wilson*, London, Tate Gallery, Cardiff, National Museum of Wales, New Haven, Yale Center for the Study of British Art, 1982–3, no.44.
REFERENCES: B. Ford, *The Drawings of Richard Wilson*, 1951, pp.23,60, repr. pl.56; D.H. Solkin, *Richard Wilson*, 1982, p.169, illus. no.44; C. Powell, *Turner in the South*, 1987, p.46, pl.54.

The diarist Joseph Farington records having seen sixty-eight Wilson drawings in Lord Dartmouth's Collection, but only twenty-five were found in 1948, twenty being views in Rome or its environs. These are now recognized as his finest highly finished drawings and are mainly in perfect condition. Wilson was in Rome from 1750 to 1757.

The Dartmouth Collection also contained another quite different view of the Palatine Mount (Whitworth Art Gallery, Manchester) and there are also drawings of the Palatine Mount from different angles and in varying degrees of completion in the Tate Gallery (Oppé Collection) and the Iolo Williams Collection.

It is no surprise that Lord Dartmouth ordered two views of the Palatine, for the Mount had a special status for English Grand Tourists due to its historical associations. These included the legend that, even before the founding of the city, the heroes Evander and Faustulus had lived on the hill which later became the seat of dynamic power in the Roman Empire. Furthermore, in Republican times, Catiline, Cicero and Clodius all lived on the Palatine, and Augustus was born on it, later transferring his residence there after the battle of Actium in 31 B.C.

EJ

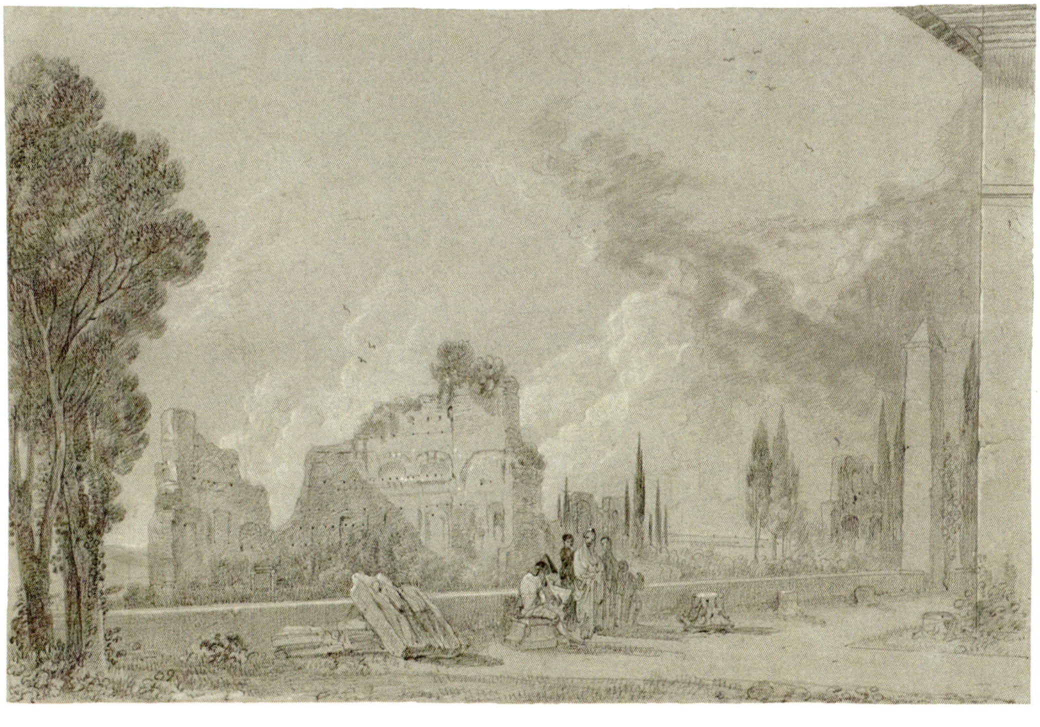

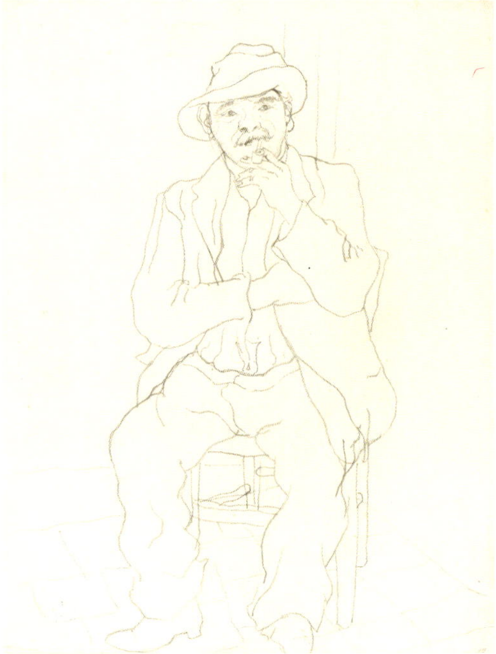

Christopher WOOD

[1901–30]

Breton Man Smoking a Pipe, c.1929–30

pencil on paper, 32.6 × 25.4 cm
inscribed: *10*

P.278
PROVENANCE: Robert. L. Banks; sold from his collection by the Leicester Galleries to Gallery, January 1959.
EXHIBITIONS: *The Complete works of Christopher Wood*, London, New Burlington Galleries, 1938, no.391; *Robert L. Banks Collection*, London, Leicester Galleries, 1959, no.28; *Watercolours and Drawings from The Cecil Higgins Art Gallery, Bedford*, London, Thos. Agnew & Sons Ltd, 1962, no.79.

Wood's initial training was as an architect, studying at Liverpool University (1919–20). In 1920 he met the French collector Alphonse Kahn, who invited him to Paris where he trained at the Académie Julian in 1921. It was during this period that he met Pablo Picasso and Jean Cocteau, amongst others, through an introduction by the Chilean ambassador, Antonio de Gandrillas.

In 1926 Wood joined the London Group and the Seven and Five Society 1926–30, exhibiting with Winifred and Ben NICHOLSON at the Beaux Arts Gallery in 1927. It was with the Nicholsons that Wood travelled to St Ives in 1928 'discovering' the naïve artist Alfred Wallis (1855–1942). St Ives had a tradition of artistic connections; first visited by SICKERT and WHISTLER in the winter of 1884 and subsequently an artistic centre for artists such as Barbara HEPWORTH, Patrick HERON and Terry Frost.

Wood's best work, revealing a strong individual talent, was done in Cornwall and Brittany 1929–30, the date of this drawing. Wood threw himself under a train at Salisbury in August 1930 whilst travelling with paintings for an exhibition. It has been suggested that the emotional instability that cut short his life was due to opium withdrawal.

JM

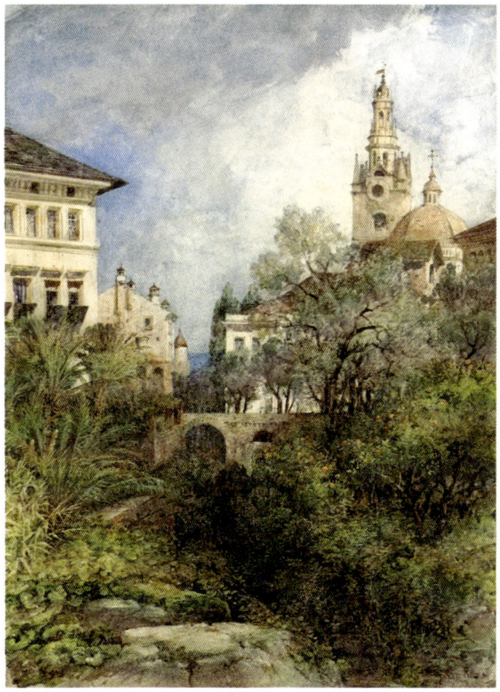

William WYLD
[1806–89]
San Remo, 1883

watercolour, graphite and bodycolour on paper, 33.5 × 25 cm
inscribed: *W.Wyld. San Remo, 8.8.83*

P.316
PROVENANCE: E. Martin; P&D Colnaghi, from whom purchased by Gallery, January 1960.

Wyld was born in London but spent much of his life in Paris. This initially came about through a family connection with the statesman George Canning (1770–1827), on whose account Wyld found a position in the diplomatic service. He was stationed with the British Consulate in Calais, and in this he may have succeeded his teacher Louis FRANCIA, who by his own account was Secretary to the British Consulate.

He exhibited from 1849 to 1882 at the R.A. and the N.W.S., and at the Salon in Paris, where he won two medals. Although HARDIE makes little reference to Wyld he credits him with having played a leading role in the development of watercolour painting in France.

Amongst other works are some fifty lithographs for a book on Algiers (*Voyage Pittoresque dans La Régence d'Alger pendant l'Année 1833*), and twenty lithographs appeared in *Monuments et Rues de Paris*, 1839.

Wyld was awarded the Légion d'Honneur in 1855. He died in Paris.

EJ/JM

Jack Butler YEATS
[1871–1957]
A Cigar for a Kick (formerly known as At a Small Race Meeting)
1897

watercolour on paper, 35.3 × 25.4 cm
inscribed: *Jack B Yeats 97*

P.396
PROVENANCE: Waddington Gallery, from whom purchased by Gallery, January 1961.
EXHIBITIONS: *Jack Butler Yeats Watercolour Sketches*, London, Clifford Gallery, 1897, no.4; *Jack Butler Yeats, Centenary Exhibition*, Dublin, National Gallery of Ireland, 1971, no.10.
REFERENCES: J. Plunkett, *P.J. Carroll & Co Ltd Dublin and Dundalk*, 1974, p.23; H. Pyle, *Jack B. Yeats. His Watercolours, Drawings and Pastels*, 1993, p.66, no.67, pl.3.

One of Yeats's most brilliant and witty early watercolours which was previously known as *At a small Race Meeting*. As the notice states, if you manage to kick the football through the round hole in the wooden fence, you win 'a good cigar'. However the lad who has just done this seems to regard his prize with some misgivings. Note the extraordinary angle of his bowler hat and how wonderfully the light catches its rim.

Yeats, brother of the poet W.B. Yeats, was born in London and studied under Fred Brown at Westminster School of Art, but he exhibited chiefly at the R.H.A. and is best known for his scenes of Dublin and Irish life, as in this outstanding example.

EJ

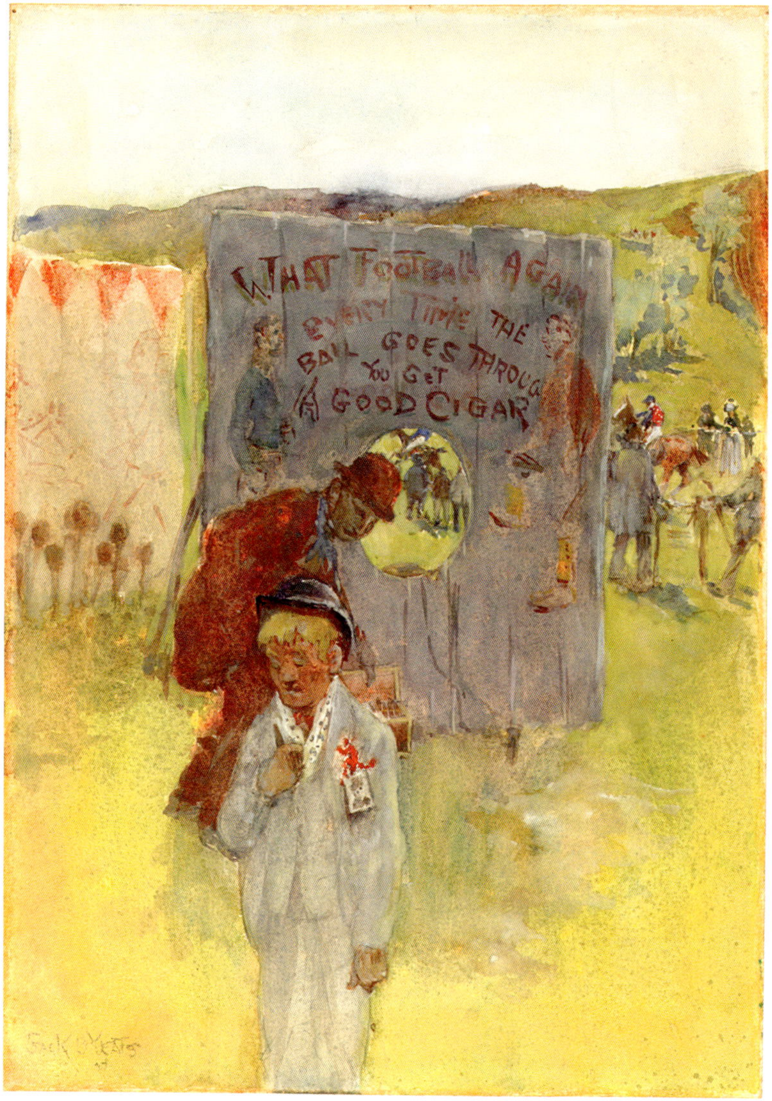

Jack Butler YEATS

[1871–1957]

Below the Valley Wood, Dublin, 1900

watercolour on paper, 25.6 × 36.8 cm
signed: *B*
inscribed on reverse: *April 25 1900*

P.413
PROVENANCE: Waddington Galleries, from whom purchased by Gallery, February 1962.
REFERENCES: H. Pyle, *Jack B. Yeats. His Watercolours, Drawings and Pastels*, 1993, repr. p.87, no.211.

Yeats began his career as a watercolourist and illustrator for the family press (later known as the Cuala Press). He did not begin painting regularly in oil until about 1905. He exhibited at *The Armory Show*, New York, 1913.

This freely painted watercolour anticipates his later landscape style, which approaches Expressionism but with an underlying base of Irish romanticism which has won him many admirers.

EJ

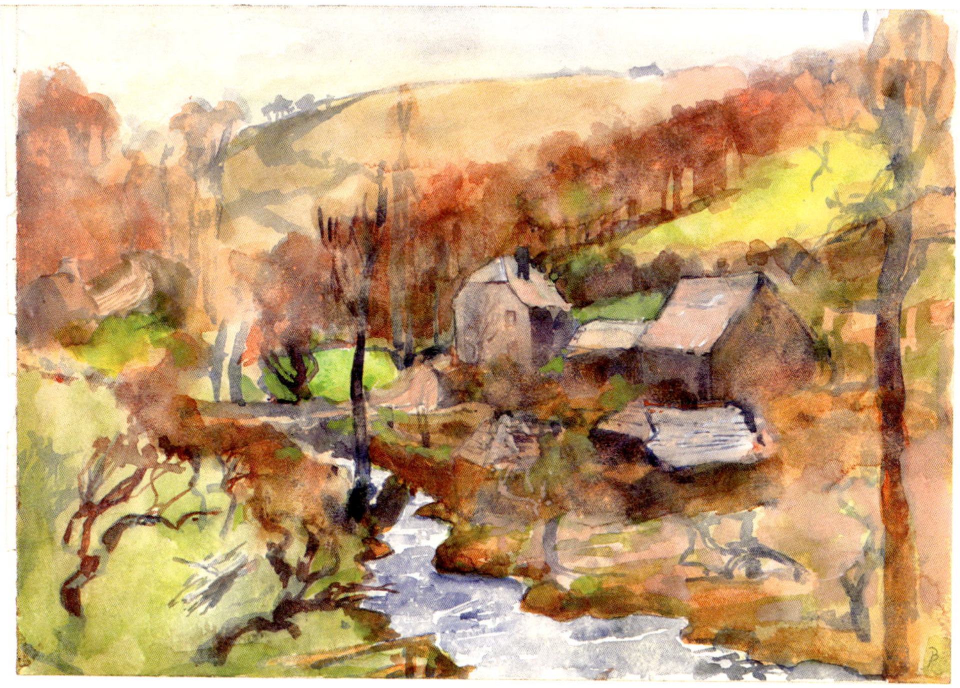

OVERLEAF

Antonio ZUCCHI, R.A.

[1736–95]

Roman Landscape with Ruins and Figures , 1760s

pen, ink and wash heightened with white on paper,
41.4 × 27.6 cm
inscribed: *ant.Zucchi*

P.448
PROVENANCE: Maas Gallery, from whom purchased by the Gallery, March 1963.

A characteristic drawing of Roman scenery with all the ingredients designed to appeal to the visiting tourist. It could also be used to show a potential patron who might be considering commissioning an oil painting of this kind of subject.

Zucchi was born and trained in Venice but left in 1761 for Rome with James Adam, with whom he travelled in Italy in 1762 making drawings for decoration. He returned to Venice but, in 1766, accepted an invitation from Robert Adam to come to London. There he became Robert Adam's chief decorative painter developing an elegant neo-classical style. He was elected A.R.A. in 1770, exhibiting mainly architectural scenes at the Academy 1770–9. In 1781 he married Angelica Kauffmann (1740–1807), a founder member of the R.A.; in the same year they settled together in Italy.

The most likely date for this drawing is the early 1760s during Zucchi's time with Robert Adam.

EJ/JM

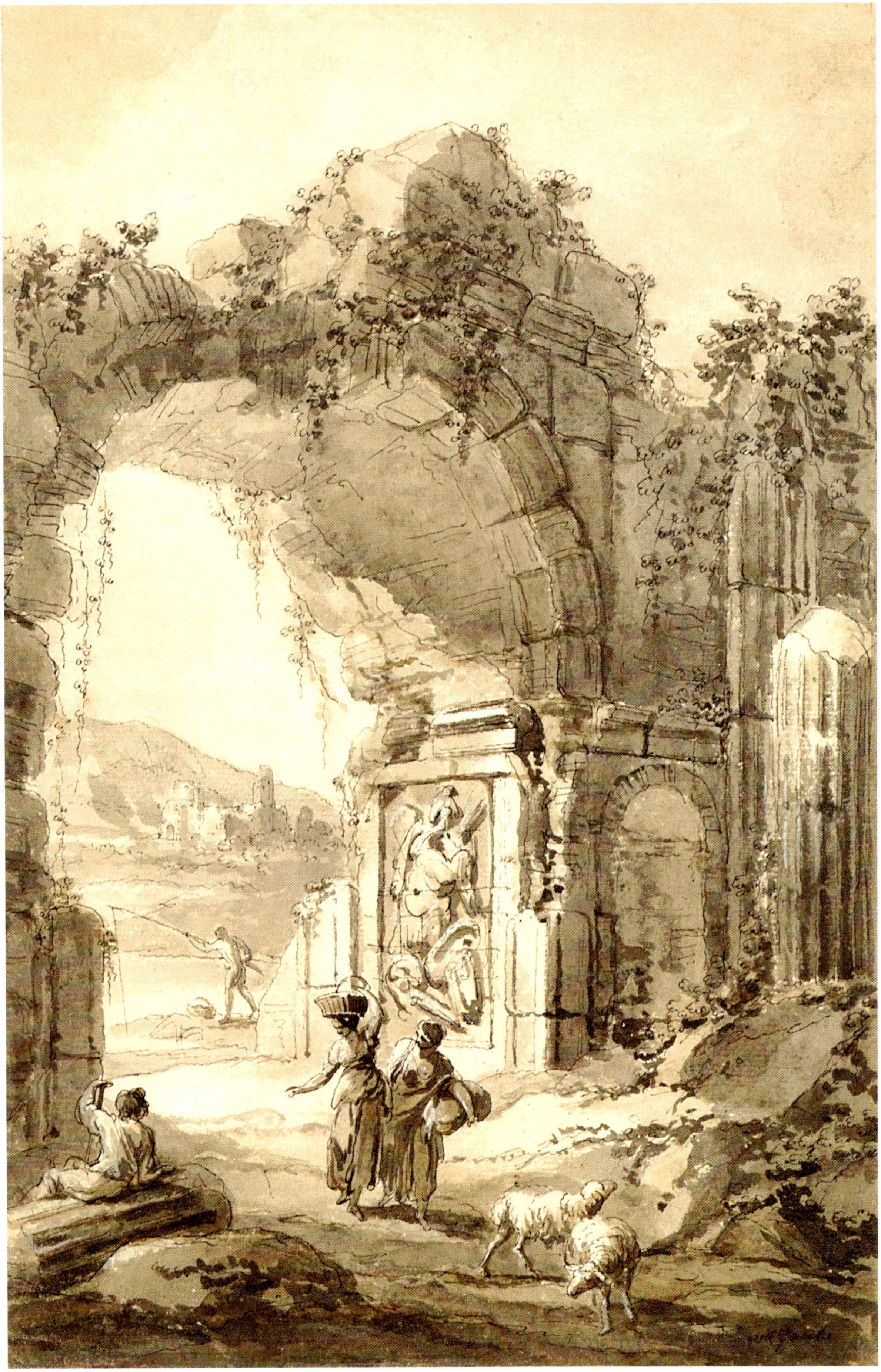

Index

All references are to page numbers; those in **bold** indicate illustrations